THE
ENCYCLOPEDIA
OF
AMERICAN
POLITICAL
HISTORY

EDITORIAL BOARD

THE

ENCYCLOPEDIA

OF

AMERICAN

POLITICAL

HISTORY

Edited by

Paul Finkelman
University of Tulsa College of Law

Peter Wallenstein
Virginia Polytechnic Institute and State University

CQ PRESS

A Division of Congressional Quarterly Inc.
Washington, D.C.

CQ Press
A Division of Congressional Quarterly Inc.
1414 22nd Street, N.W.
Washington, DC 20037
(202) 822-1475; (800) 638-1710
www.cqpress.com

Printed and bound in the United States of America

∞ The paper used in this publication meets the minimum requirements of the American National Standard for Information Sciences—Permanence of Paper for Printed Library Materials, ANSI Z39.48-1992.

05 04 03 02 01   5 4 3 2 1

LIBRARY OF CONGRESS CATALOGING–IN–PUBLICATION DATA
The encyclopedia of American political history / editors-in-chief, Paul Finkelman, Peter Wallenstein.
    p.   cm.
  Includes bibliographical references and index.
  ISBN 1-56802-511-4 (alk. paper)
    1. United States—Politics and government—Encyclopedias.   2. Political science—United
States—History—Encyclopedias.   I. Finkelman, Paul, 1949-   II. Wallenstein, Peter.
  E183.E48 2001
  973'.03–dc21   00-066812

For
Byrgen Finkelman
and
Sookhan Ho

CONTENTS

INTRODUCTION

We prepare this introduction as the outcome of the 2000 presidential contest, a month after the votes were cast, is at last known. The complexity of this election has reaffirmed the importance of understanding our political history. As Americans watched the recounts in Florida, they turned to scholars—particularly historians—for guidance and explanations. The questions asked were fundamentally historical. Was this the worst debacle in presidential election history? Had other presidents been elected under equally confusing circumstances? Had third parties previously changed the outcome of an election? Had there been elections in which one candidate won the popular vote and another the electoral vote? Why did we have an electoral college in the first place?

One goal in the more than 240 articles in this book is to provide speedy access for readers seeking answers to questions such as these. This book is not a substitute for in-depth books and articles about specific aspects of America's political history. Rather, it is a starting place for ready answers to immediate questions about political history. It is designed to serve many audiences. Teachers and scholars will find succinct answers or definitions on many topics and issues. Librarians can use this volume as a ready reference to answer many questions that daily make the reference desk both fun and challenging.

Elementary and secondary school teachers will find a wide variety of entries on topics that dovetail with the *National Standards for United States History,* published by the National Center for History in the Schools. High school and college students seeking detail and analysis beyond that provided by their textbook will find information and ideas to guide them through the complexities of American political history. For example, the standards stress the importance of the Civil War and the surrounding events. This encyclopedia has entries on all of the major statutes and compromises leading up to the secession crisis of 1860–1861 and the Civil War, as well as the impact of slavery on politics and the importance of the Supreme Court in American politics. Other entries focus on Reconstruction and the issues surrounding it. Finally, we have separate entries on each president.

We begin and end with two tools we hope will add to the utility of the encyclopedia. The descriptive time line at the front of this volume helps put American political history in a chronological perspective and offers thumbnail information about crucial events, many of them discussed in more detail in entries elsewhere in the volume. Although history is not about the memorization of dates and names, knowing the sequence of events is vital to understanding history.

At the back of the encyclopedia we have provided what we believe is a unique reference tool for American history: a dictionary of abbreviations in American history. Often, writers and scholars use abbreviations for well-known concepts. Abbreviations known to scholars and professionals, however, may be unfamiliar to students—or even to scholars in other disciplines. Moreover, often the same set of initials applies to more than one institution in our political history. For most younger Americans, NRA stands for the National Rifle Association, but for older Americans and scholars of the New Deal, NRA is the acronym of the National Recovery Act, the centerpiece of President Franklin D. Roosevelt's New Deal. Our list of abbreviations will help scholars, students, and librarians quickly sort out what a set of initials might mean in a given text or context.

Like American history itself, this book is a work in progress. New editions will cover developments of new presidential administrations and will place past administrations in greater historical perspective. Future editions will allow for the updating and rewriting of articles to reflect recent developments, new historical information that has come to light, and changing historical understandings of existing information. We will also fill in holes, and to that end, we seek the recommendations and advice of the users of this book. Please contact us by e-mail (paul-finkelman@utulsa.edu and pwallens@vt.edu), or the publisher by regular mail, as you use this volume. Let us know of anything we have missed, any topics that need greater coverage, and any errors you might notice. Please tell us if there are abbreviations that ought to be added to the appendix.

Encyclopedias are always the work of many individuals, and this one is no exception. We have relied, in the first instance, on the knowledge, wisdom, and guidance of our editorial board: David Bennett of Syracuse University, Lori Bogle of the United States Naval Academy, Peter Onuf of the University of Virginia, and Ray Smock, former historian of the U.S. House of Representatives. In addition, Robert Cottrol of George Washington University gave generously of his time to advise the editorial board during the early planning stages of this project. Without their efforts in planning and later in manuscript reviewing, this volume could not have been completed. We extend our deep appreciation to the many scholars who, taking time away from other writing activities and from academic teaching responsibilities, contributed entries to this book. Many of our authors are dis-

tinguished scholars in their fields, while others are younger and newer to the profession but will in time become leading authorities in their various branches of American history. At CQ Press the encyclopedia, begun under sponsoring editor Patricia Gallagher, was seen through development and completion by David Tarr. Both were assisted ably by Grace Hill, to whom fell the vast logistics of initiating and maintaining author contact and tracking manuscript development from start to finish. The dedication is to our favorite people, our brides.

PAUL FINKELMAN
PETER WALLENSTEIN

ABOUT THE EDITORS

Paul Finkelman is Chapman Distinguished Professor, College of Law, University of Tulsa, Oklahoma. He was the recipient of the 1986 Joseph C. Andrews Award for the best book in legal bibliography from the American Association of Law Libraries. Educated at the University of Chicago and Harvard Law School, Finkelman is the editor of three encyclopedias, including the *Macmillan Encyclopedia of World Slavery* (Macmillan Reference USA, 1998), and the author of more than a dozen books.

Peter Wallenstein, associate professor of history at Virginia Polytechnic Institute and State University, earned his B.A. at Columbia University and Ph.D. at Johns Hopkins University. His two hundred publications include *From Slave South to New South: Public Policy in Nineteenth-Century Georgia* (University of North Carolina Press, 1987) and *Virginia Tech, Land-Grant University, 1872–1997: History of a School, a State, a Nation* (Pocahontas Press, 1997).

CONTRIBUTORS

CAROL JACKSON ADAMS
Salt Lake Community College
Civil Rights Act of 1875
Freedmen's Bureau Acts
Gag Rule
Popular Sovereignty
Treaties: Commercial
Treaties: Peace, Armament, and Defense
Treaty Making
War Powers

GINETTE ALEY
Iowa State University
Populist (People's) Party

MARGO ANDERSON
University of Wisconsin–Milwaukee
Census

DAVID H. BENNETT
Syracuse University
Civil Unrest and Rioting
Clinton, Bill
Iran-Contra Scandal
Know Nothing (American) Party
Nativism
New Deal
Teapot Dome and Other Harding Administration Scandals

MICHAEL BLANCHARD
Western New England School of Law
Affirmative Action (coauthor)

LORI BOGLE
United States Naval Academy
Coxey's Army
McCarthyism
National Woman's Party

APRIL L. BROWN
University of Arkansas
Spanish-American War
Vietnam War

DAVID BURNER
SUNY at Stony Brook
New Frontier

BALLARD C. CAMPBELL
Northeastern University
State Government

CHARLES CAREY
Lynchburg College / Central Virginia Community College
Anti-Masonic Party
Immigration and Naturalization: Society and Politics
New Freedom
New Nationalism
Panic of 1837
Panic of 1857
Panic of 1893
Statehood
Think Tanks and the Academic Policy Community
Vice Presidency

RICHARD J. CARROLL
Independent scholar
Currency and Money Supply
Economic Sanctions
Federal Reserve System
Political Contributions in the Late Nineteenth Century
Private and Public Welfare, Pre-New Deal
Taxation and Twentieth-Century Politics
Welfare State

GABRIEL J. CHIN
University of Cincinnati College of Law
Affirmative Action (coauthor)

Immigration and Naturalization: Twentieth-Century
  Law and Policy

DEBRA CLARK
Virginia Commonwealth University
Reproductive Rights

MARK J. CONNOLLY
DeVry Institute of Technology
Bonus March
Comstock Act
Crédit Mobilier Scandal
Socialist Party

RON DePAOLO
Independent author
American Independent Party
Breckinridge Democrats
Communist Party USA
Liberal Party
Liberty Party
National Debt
Peace and Freedom Party
Progressive Labor Party
Reform Party
Soft Money and Twentieth-Century Politics

ROBERT A. DIVINE
University of Texas at Austin
Great Society

MELVYN DUBOFSKY
Binghamton University, SUNY
Labor Politics and Policies

DANIEL FELLER
University of New Mexico
Jackson, Andrew

ROBERT H. FERRELL
Indiana University
Truman, Harry S.

PAUL FINKELMAN
University of Tulsa College of Law
Adams, John Quincy
Bill of Rights
Black Suffrage (coauthor)
Buchanan, James

Compromise of 1877
Constitution, Ratification (coauthor)
Constitution, U.S.
Constitutional Convention
Democratic Party (coauthor)
Emancipation Proclamation
Fillmore, Millard
Fugitive Slave Laws
Harrison, William Henry
Jeffersonian Democracy
Judiciary Acts
Missouri Compromise
Political Parties (coauthor)
Presidential Elections
Slavery
Taylor, Zachary
Three-Fifths Clause
Tyler, John
Watershed Elections

KRIS FRESONKE
Iowa State University
Grant, Ulysses S.
Manifest Destiny
Mexican-American War

TIM ALAN GARRISON
Portland State University
Indian Policy

VICTOR W. GERACI
Central Connecticut State University
Federal Housing Programs
Gilded Age
Great Depression
Roosevelt, Franklin D.
Tennessee Valley Authority

GREGORY L. GIROUX
Congressional Quarterly
Apportionment
State Apportionment

LEWIS L. GOULD
University of Texas at Austin
Coolidge, Calvin
Harding, Warren G.
Initiative, Referendum, and Recall
McKinley, William

Progressive Era
Progressive Party (H. Wallace)
Progressive Party (La Follette)

HUGH DAVIS GRAHAM
Vanderbilt University
Civil Rights Acts (Modern)

JOHN ROBERT GREENE
Cazenovia College
Bush, George
Ford, Gerald R.
Reagan, Ronald

K. R. CONSTANTINE GUTZMAN
John Jay College, CUNY
American Revolution
Nullification
Secession
Sectionalism
States' Rights/Sovereignty

WALTER HIXSON
University of Akron
National Security Document 68
Red Scare

JOSEPH ISENBERG
Iowa State University, Ames
Shays's Rebellion

RICHARD JENSEN
Rensselaer Polytechnic Institute
Antitrust
Lincoln, Abraham
Nixon, Richard M.
Republican Party
Tariff History
Whig Party

J. WAYNE JONES
University of Arkansas
Persian Gulf War

KENNETH JOST
Congressional Quarterly
Brown v. Board of Education of Topeka
Buckley v. Valeo
Reapportionment Cases
Shaw v. Reno

LINDA KOWALCKY
Northeastern University
Petition Campaigns

DAVID E. KYVIG
Northern Illinois University
Prohibition and Temperance

SABRA BISSETTE LEDENT
Independent author
Adams, John
Carter, Jimmy
Cleveland, Grover
Garfield, James A.
Hayes, Rutherford B.
Johnson, Lyndon B.
Kennedy, John F.
Pierce, Franklin
Roosevelt, Theodore
Taft, William Howard
Van Buren, Martin

JAMES E. LEWIS JR.
Independent scholar
Constitution, Ratification (coauthor)
Embargo
Monroe, James
Territorial Government and New State Formation
War of 1812

JEFFREY LITTLEJOHN
University of Arkansas
Civil War
Korean War
World War II: Domestic Politics
World War II: Foreign and Military Policy

RALPH LUKER
Virginia Foundation for the Humanities
Marches on Washington
Rainbow Coalition

RICHARD MAJOR
Independent scholar
Compromise of 1850
Harrison, Benjamin
Polk, James K.
Watergate
World War I

JOHN F. MARSZALEK
Mississippi State University
Eaton Affair

L. JOHN MARTIN
University of Maryland
Polling and Public Opinion

JOHN MAYFIELD
Samford University
Free Soil Party

ROBERT M. S. McDONALD
United States Military Academy
Sally Hemings Affair

COLLEEN McGUINESS
Independent author
Congressional Budget Office
Electoral College
Office of Management and Budget

MARIAN MOLLIN
Virginia Polytechnic Institute and State University
Woman's Suffrage Movement

JOHN MOORE
Independent author
Campaigning
Democratic Party (coauthor)
Political Parties (coauthor)

KELLY MYLES
American Association of University Affiliated Programs
Interest Groups
Lobbyists

MICHAEL NELSON
Rhodes College
Presidency
Presidential Succession Amendments

PATRICIA ANN O'CONNOR
Independent author
Cabinet
Committee System

KEITH W. OLSON
University of Maryland
G.I. Bill

PATRICK M. O'NEIL
Broome Community College, State University of New York
Civil-Military Relations
Conservative Party
Fair Deal
Logan Act
Social Security
Square Deal
Term Limits
Third Parties
Twelfth Amendment

PETER ONUF
University of Virginia
Declaration of Independence
Jefferson, Thomas

ROBERT V. REMINI
University of Illinois at Chicago
Bank War

DONALD A. RITCHIE
U.S. Senate Historical Office
Senate Leadership: Early Period
Senate Leadership: Modern

MARK H. ROSE
Florida Atlantic University
Interstate Highway System

JUDITH V. ROYSTER
University of Tulsa College of Law
Federalism

JONATHAN D. SALANT
Associated Press
Campaign Finance
Political Action Committees

BRIAN D. SCHOEN
University of Virginia
Articles of Confederation
Calhoun, John C.
Federalists
Northwest Ordinance
Whiskey Rebellion

JACQUELINE SMITH-MASON
State Council of Higher Education for Virginia
Arthur, Chester A.
Sex Discrimination in Higher Education: Title IX

RAYMOND W. SMOCK
Independent historian
Cloture
Congress
Filibuster
Gerrymandering
House Leadership: Speaker
Koreagate

ALVIN D. SOKOLOW
University of California, Davis
Local Government

ROBERT J. SPITZER
State University of New York, Cortland
Gun Control and Policy
Veto Power

DONALD STELLUTO JR.
California State University, Fullerton
Constitutional Union Party
Seminole War

MICHELLE A. STRETCH
Independent author
Equal Rights Amendment
Sex Discrimination in Employment: Title VII

DAVID R. TARR
CQ Press
Scandals and Corruption

KARA MILES TURNER
Virginia State University
Black Panthers

MELVIN I. UROFSKY
Virginia Commonwealth University
Supreme Court

DAUN VAN EE
Johns Hopkins University
Eisenhower, Dwight D.

EMILY FIELD VAN TASSEL
Indiana University School of Law, Bloomington
Impeachment
Independent Counsel

TIMOTHY WALCH
Herbert Hoover Presidential Library
Hoover, Herbert C.

PETER WALLENSTEIN
Virginia Polytechnic Institute and State University
Black Suffrage (coauthor)
Civil Rights Act of 1866
Civil Rights Movement
Constitutional Amendments
Dixiecrats (States' Rights Party)
Hartford Convention Resolutions
Higher Education Act
Jacksonian Democracy
Johnson, Andrew
Kansas-Nebraska Act
Landslide Elections
Madison, James
Morrill Land-Grant College Acts
Poll Tax
Reconstruction
Seneca Falls Convention
Suffrage
Super Majority
Territorial Expansion
Wilson, Woodrow

BRIAN C. WHITE
University of Illinois at Chicago
Newspapers and Political Parties
Talk Radio
Television and American Politics

CARY D. WINTZ
Texas Southern University
African American Politics

ROBERT E. WRIGHT
University of Virginia
Panic of 1819

ROSEMARIE ZAGARRI
George Mason University
Washington, George

DESCRIPTIVE TIME LINE OF POLITICAL EVENTS IN U.S. HISTORY

AMERICAN REVOLUTION AND CONFEDERATION, 1775–1787

Second Continental Congress meets: Delegates from the thirteen colonies meet (1775), establish a continental army (1775), declare independence from Great Britain (1776), authorize colonies to write constitutions as independent states (1776), and frame the Articles of Confederation (1778).

Declaration of Independence is written. (1776)

American Revolution occurs. (1775–1783)

State constitutions are framed: All states but two write constitutions during this period, some writing more than one; Rhode Island and Connecticut continue to govern themselves under their colonial charters, with all references to Britain and the king deleted. (1775–1784)

Articles of Confederation create a framework of government for a "perpetual Union" between the states. The Articles provide for a unicameral legislature but no national executive or judiciary. Agreed to by Congress in 1778, they are ratified in 1781 and remain in effect until superseded by the Constitution in 1788.

French Alliance begins the longest continuous peaceful foreign relationship in U.S. history. (1778)

Articles of Confederation are ratified by the last of the thirteen states in 1781. The Articles require unanimous consent of the states for amendments, so efforts at amendment (such as adding the power to tax) fail. Under the Articles, the new nation gains its independence from Great Britain.

Treaty of Paris ends the American Revolution. (1783)

Land ordinance: A system for the sale and settlement of western lands owned by the United States is established and remains largely in place until the Homestead Act of 1862. (1785)

Virginia bill for religious freedom passes, prohibiting the use of state funds to support any religious group in Virginia,

guaranteeing freedom of religious belief, and prohibiting religious tests for officeholding. (1786)

Shays's Rebellion: Agrarian unrest involving economic difficulties in the aftermath of American independence leads to short-lived armed insurrection in western Massachusetts. (1786–1787)

Northwest Ordinance establishes a system for creating government in the western territories and also prohibits slavery north of the Ohio River. (1787)

CONSTITUTION AND EARLY REPUBLIC, 1787–1801

U.S. Constitution: Convention in Philadelphia drafts a constitution for the new nation. (1787)

Federalist Papers are published to explain the proposed new Constitution and justify adopting it. (1787–1788)

Constitution is ratified by the required nine states and goes into effect. (1788)

George Washington, president, 1789–1797.

Bill of Rights: First amendments to the Constitution are sent to the states for approval. (1789)

Judiciary Act implements the judiciary clause of the Constitution, organizing the federal judiciary; provides for a Supreme Court and lower federal courts. (1789)

John Jay, first chief justice of the United States, 1789–1795.

First U.S. census is taken as provided in the Constitution; the United States becomes the first nation in the world to provide by law for a periodic enumeration of its people. (1790)

Bill of Rights, the first ten amendments to the Constitution. (Ratified 1791)

First Bank of the United States: Congress charters the bank with a capital stock of $10 million. (1791)

Republican and Federalist Parties emerge, marking the beginning of the political party system in the United States. (1791–1793)

First fugitive slave law: Congress empowers owners (or their agents) of fugitive slaves to seize and return them to servitude. (1793)

Whiskey Rebellion: Large-scale resistance movement in back-country areas protesting a federal excise tax on domestically produced whiskey results in a short-lived insurrection. (July–November 1794)

Treaty of Greenville: Signed after Gen. "Mad" Anthony Wayne's victory at the Battle of Fallen Timbers, the treaty signals the end of major Indian resistance to white settlement in the Old Northwest. (1795)

Jay's Treaty provides for British withdrawal from Northwest Territory, addresses U.S. shipping rights, and creates a commission to deal with Americans' pre–Revolutionary War debts to British citizens. (Signed 1794; ratified 1795)

State lawsuit immunity: The Eleventh Amendment to the Constitution removes from the jurisdiction of federal courts those cases in which a state is sued without its consent. (Ratified 1795)

Oliver Ellsworth, chief justice of the United States, 1796–1800.

Pinckney's Treaty: Officially called the "Treaty of San Lorenzo," agreement with Spain settles the nation's southwestern boundary. (1795)

John Adams, president, 1797–1801.

Alien and Sedition Acts: Congress passes a group of laws dealing with citizenship, imprisonment and deportation of aliens, and imprisonment of individuals who criticize the federal government; the acts are used by Federalists against the emerging Democratic-Republican Party led by Thomas Jefferson. (1798; expire in 1801)

Virginia and Kentucky Resolutions: State legislatures pass resolutions—framed by James Madison and Thomas Jefferson—maintaining that the Alien and Sedition Acts are unconstitutional. (1798–1799)

Logan Act prohibits any citizen from dealing with a foreign government involving "any disputes or controversy with the United States." (1799)

VIRGINIA DYNASTY, REPUBLICAN ERA, 1801–1829

Thomas Jefferson, president, 1801–1809.

John Marshall, chief justice of the United States, 1801–1835.

Marbury v. Madison: Supreme Court decision establishes the principle of judicial review and the Court's power to declare an act of Congress unconstitutional; written by John Marshall and often called the single most important ruling in the Court's history. (1803)

Louisiana Purchase: The United States doubles its territory and acquires the west bank of the Mississippi River by purchasing France's claim to an area extending from New Orleans and the Gulf of Mexico to the present-day boundary with western Canada. (1803)

Presidential elections: The Twelfth Amendment to the Constitution requires electors to vote separately for president and vice president. (Ratified 1804)

Cumberland Road Act authorizes a national road from Cumberland, Maryland, to the Ohio River, an important step in federal activity to open the nation's interior. (1806)

Embargo Act prohibits the shipping of U.S. products to other nations, an unsuccessful effort by President Jefferson to prevent provocations on the seas that could lead to war with Britain or France. (1807)

James Madison, president, 1809–1817.

War of 1812 between the United States and Britain is prompted by the British capture of American commercial ships and their crews and British aid to hostile Indians on the frontier. (Declared June 1812; ended with the Treaty of Ghent, signed December 1814)

Battle of New Orleans: Gen. Andrew Jackson and his militia inflict a major defeat on British forces, restoring some U.S. pride, wounded by defeats in the War of 1812; the battle occurs before news of the December 1814 peace treaty reaches the United States. (January 1815)

Hartford Convention: New England Federalists, disgruntled by the War of 1812 and domination of the national government by Southern Republicans, meet to demand constitutional amendments or even consider secession. (December 1814–January 1815)

Martin v. Hunter's Lessee: Supreme Court decision establishes that states must obey the U.S. Constitution. (1816)

Second Bank of the United States chartered for twenty years with the government subscribing to one-fifth of its authorized capital of $35 million and the bank to serve as non–interest paying depository for federal funds. (April 1816)

James Monroe, president, 1817–1825.

First Seminole War. (1818)

Florida is acquired from Spain. (1819)

Panic of 1819: A financial panic results from a large balance of payments deficit, poor central bank leadership, and price inflation. The panic deepens into the nation's first major peacetime recession and lays the groundwork for the second party system and Andrew Jackson's emergence as the leader of the Democratic Party.

McCulloch v. Maryland: Supreme Court decision establishes the supremacy of federal law over state law. (1819)

Missouri Compromise: Intended to settle sectional rivalry over the extension of slavery into the territories, the compromise authorizes the admission of Missouri as a slave state but stipulates that slavery is "forever prohibited" in the remaining areas of the Louisiana Territory north of 36° 30' north latitude; it offends southerners by establishing the principle that Congress can legislate on slavery and northerners by accepting the expansion of slavery; undone in the Kansas-Nebraska Act of 1854 and declared unconstitutional by the Supreme Court in 1857; northern anger over these events in the 1850s leads to Abraham Lincoln's election in 1860. (1820)

Denmark Vesey, a free black living in Charleston, South Carolina, recruits slaves to attack whites in the city; his conspiracy is uncovered and he and others are executed. (1822)

Monroe Doctrine, proclaimed by President James Monroe, declares that the United States will resist European intervention in the affairs of independent nations in the Western Hemisphere. (1823)

Four-way presidential election produces no winner in the electoral college, throwing the race into the House of Representatives, which selects John Quincy Adams, son of former president John Adams. (1824)

John Quincy Adams, president, 1825–1829.

Anti-Masonic Party forms, the first third-party movement in the United States and the first to hold a presidential nominating convention and draft a platform. (Late 1820s)

"Tariff of Abominations" amends tariff laws by raising duties on imported goods to an average of 41 percent. (1828)

THE JACKSON ERA, 1829–1841

Andrew Jackson, president, 1829–1837.

Maysville Road bill authorizes federal money for a road in Kentucky between Maysville and Lexington but is vetoed by President Jackson, reflecting his opposition to federal aid to transportation improvements. (1830)

Indian Removal Act calls for resettlement of all eastern Indians to lands west of the Mississippi River and appropriates funds for compensation and removal costs. (1830)

Radical abolitionist movement begins with publication of the *Liberator* newspaper under William Lloyd Garrison. (1831)

Nat Turner, a slave in Virginia, and more than fifty other participants move through the Virginia countryside, killing about sixty whites, making the Turner rebellion the most noted of American slave revolts; Turner and many colleagues are executed, and other blacks are killed by vigilantes. (1831)

John C. Calhoun resigns as vice president. (1832)

President Jackson vetoes recharter of the Second Bank of the United States. (1832)

Tariff of 1832 lowers the duties on many imported goods to a level significantly below that required by the Tariff Act of 1828. (1832)

Bank War: A political contest erupts between President Andrew Jackson and the president of the Second Bank of the United States, Nicholas Biddle, reflecting Jackson's belief that the bank's financial resources were used to influence national elections and politics in the interests of wealthy citizens; Jackson vetoes rechartering of the bank, contributing to his own reelection in 1832, significant expansion of presidential influence on legislation, and—in response—the rise of the Whig Party. (1832–1833)

Nullification: A South Carolina convention declares the tariff laws of 1828 and 1832 unconstitutional, null and void, and not binding on the state and threatens state secession from the Union; President Jackson rejects these positions and asks Congress to authorize funds and the use of the military to enforce revenue laws and put down rebellion. (1832–1833)

Compromise of 1833 defuses the tariff issue as Congress adds many imported items to the tariff-free list and provides for the gradual reduction of duties to 20 percent by 1842. (1833)

Roger B. Taney, chief justice of the United States, 1836–1864.

Texas declares independence from Mexico. (1836)

Second Seminole War. (1835–1842)

Martin Van Buren, president, 1837–1841.

Panic of 1837: A major nationwide economic depression develops in large part from misguided federal fiscal policy and weaknesses in the American banking system; undercuts the administration of President Martin Van Buren and contributes to the election of the first Whig president in 1840. (1837–1842)

Gag rule: The House of Representatives, hoping to avoid debate on slavery, adopts a rule automatically tabling (rejecting) any of the numerous antislavery petitions sent by opponents of slavery. (March 1836–December 1844)

Liberty Party: Antislavery third party forces the slavery issue to national prominence; in the 1844 election it draws enough support in New York to push that state to Democrat James Polk and deny victory to Whig candidate Henry Clay. (Organized 1839)

PRE–CIVIL WAR ERA, 1841–1860

William Henry Harrison, president, 1841, dies in office.

John Tyler, president, 1841–1845, first president not elected to that office.

United States annexes Texas, an independent nation, in the face of threats of war with Mexico. (1845)

James K. Polk, president, 1845–1849.

Mexican-American War ends by a treaty in which Mexico cedes California and New Mexico to the United States. (War declared May 1846; treaty signed July 1848)

Wilmot Proviso: Efforts in Congress to prohibit slavery in the territory acquired from Mexico as part of the Mexican-American War are successful in the House of Representatives but fail in the Senate. (1846)

Seneca Falls Convention is held at Seneca Falls, New York. It deals with women's rights, is the first such event ever held, and is a landmark in the development of the women's movement for equal rights with men; organized by Lucretia Mott and Elizabeth Cady Stanton. (1848)

Free Soil Party, another antislavery party calling for an end to the expansion of slavery in the West, enters national politics, dividing Democrats and contributing to a Whig victory in the 1848 presidential election. (1848)

Zachary Taylor, president, 1849–1850, dies in office.

Millard Fillmore, president, 1850–1853.

Compromise of 1850: Congress passes a group of bills, including the Fugitive Slave Act of 1850, aimed at reconciling North-South differences over slavery but succeeds only in papering over irreconcilable sectional disagreements.

Franklin Pierce, president, 1853–1857.

Gadsden Purchase of land from Mexico completes U.S. expansion in the southwest. (1853)

Know Nothing Party emerges; largely anti-Catholic and anti-immigrant. (1854)

Kansas-Nebraska Act repeals Missouri Compromise of 1820 and seeks "popular sovereignty" regarding the expansion of slavery into new territories, thereby aggravating the slavery issue. (1854)

Republican Party emerges. (1854)

James Buchanan, president, 1857–1861.

Panic of 1857, an American name for a global depression that followed the Crimean War in Europe; although short-lived in the United States, it further sours relations between North and South.

Dred Scott v. Sandford: Supreme Court decision denies Congress the power to ban slavery in the territories and bars African Americans from citizenship. (1857)

Lincoln-Douglas debates: Abraham Lincoln, running as the candidate of the new Republican Party, debates Sen. Stephen A. Douglas during 1858 senatorial race in Illinois. Lincoln loses the election but gains national prominence for his articulate attack on the *Dred Scott* decision and on the proslavery politics of the Democratic Party. (1858)

Constitutional Union Party, 1860 election: Trying to skirt the great issues of 1860, some former Whigs run a separate ticket in a four-way contest for the presidency.

Breckinridge Democrats, 1860 election: The Democratic Party divides, with the Breckinridge wing insisting on greater guarantees for slavery.

SECESSION, CIVIL WAR, AND RECONSTRUCTION, 1860–1877

Eleven southern states secede from the United States after Lincoln is elected: South Carolina, Mississippi, Florida, Alabama, Georgia, Louisiana, and Texas, followed—after his inauguration—by Virginia, Arkansas, Tennessee, and North Carolina. (1860–1861)

Abraham Lincoln, president, 1861–1865 (assassinated in office).

Civil War is fought between the Confederate States and the rest of the United States over preservation of the Union and abolition of slavery. (1861–1865)

National Banking Act establishes a national banking system, including office of the Comptroller of the Currency; the act requires banks to invest one-third of their capital in U.S. securities and authorizes national bank notes. (1862)

Homestead Act provides a free grant of up to 160 acres of surveyed western public land to any citizen over age twenty-one who can occupy it for five years and improve it, or allows settlers to purchase the land at $1.25 an acre after six months of residence. (1862)

Transcontinental Railroad Act authorizes the Union Pacific and Central Pacific railroads to build a railroad and telegraph line between Omaha, Nebraska, and San Francisco, California, and provides financial support. (1862)

Morrill Land-Grant College Act grants each state thirty thousand acres of public land in the West for each senator and representative in Congress, with the proceeds from the state sale of the lands to finance one or more colleges teaching "agriculture and mechanic arts." (1862)

Emancipation Proclamation by President Lincoln frees slaves in states or parts of states still held by the Confederacy. (January 1, 1863)

Salmon P. Chase, chief justice of the United States, 1864–1873.

Andrew Johnson, president, 1865–1869.

Slavery ended: The Thirteenth Amendment to the Constitution abolishes slavery. (Ratified 1865)

Freedmen's Bureau Acts: Late in the Civil War, Congress creates the Bureau of Refugees, Freedmen, and Abandoned Lands to provide food, shelter, clothing, and fuel for "destitute and suffering refugees and freedmen" in southern states under U.S. army control; a year later it extends the agency's life and enlarges its responsibilities. (1865 and 1866)

Civil Rights Act of 1866 declares former slaves to be citizens and specifies their basic legal rights.

Ku Klux Klan: In various locations white southerners form terrorist groups to maintain economic and political control during Reconstruction. (1866)

Reconstruction Acts: Rejecting President Johnson's policies, Congress takes over the process of Reconstruction and directs that, under the supervision of federal troops, new elections to a state constitutional convention be held in each of ten states of the former Confederacy; black men, as well as whites, may vote in those elections; the new state constitutions must recognize black men's right to vote, and the ten states must ratify the Fourteenth Amendment before their representatives can take their seats in Congress. (First of a series, March 1867)

Alaska is purchased from Russia. (1867)

President Johnson is impeached and tried for his handling of Reconstruction; he is acquitted by one vote. (1868)

Fourteenth Amendment to the Constitution grants citizenship to all persons born in the United States, bans states from denying any person life, liberty, or property without due process of law, and bans states from denying any person equal protection of the laws. (Ratified 1868)

Ulysses S. Grant, president, 1869–1877.

Voting rights guaranteed: The Fifteenth Amendment to the Constitution declares that states cannot use race as the basis of denying the right to vote. (Ratified 1870)

Comstock Law makes it a crime to send any "obscene, lewd, or lascivious" book or printed material through the public mails. (1873)

Crédit Mobilier Scandal: A member of the U.S. House uses stock in this construction company, owned by the Union Pacific Railroad, to bribe members of Congress to continue financial support for transcontinental railroad and not to investigate corruption in connection with it. (1872–1873)

Slaughterhouse Cases: Supreme Court decision narrowly interprets the Fourteenth Amendment. (1873)

Panic of 1873 leads to a serious depression that lasts several years.

Morrison R. Waite, chief justice of the United States, 1874–1888.

Civil Rights Act of 1875: Congress seeks to ban racial discrimination, including segregation, in such public facilities as trains and hotels; Supreme Court overturns these provisions in 1883.

LATE NINETEENTH CENTURY "GILDED AGE," 1877–1901

Compromise of 1877: In the resolution to the disputed presidential election of 1876, Rutherford B. Hayes takes the presidency after promising to withdraw all remaining federal troops from the Deep South states.

Rutherford B. Hayes, president, 1877–1881.

Railway strike: The nation's biggest industry suffers from the depression of the 1870s, and huge numbers of workers go on strike, especially in Pennsylvania, over wage cuts. (1877)

Greenback Labor Party, 1880 election: Hard-pressed farmers want cheaper money that will raise the price of crops they sell and reduce the interest they pay on farm mortgages.

James Garfield, president, 1881, assassinated in office.

Chester A. Arthur, president, 1881–1885.

Pendleton Civil Service Reform Act ends patronage in most federal jobs and creates a professional civil service system for employees hired on merit and protected from pressures to support, and contribute to, political parties and candidates. (1883)

Grover Cleveland, president, 1885–1889, 1893–1897, the only president to serve nonconsecutive terms.

Interstate Commerce Act establishes federal regulation of interstate common carriers and shipping rates, prohibits discriminatory rates, and requires public posting of rates. (1887)

Melville W. Fuller, chief justice of the United States, 1888–1910.

Benjamin Harrison, president, 1889–1893.

Sherman Anti-Trust Act empowers the federal government to prosecute monopolistic practices by corporations. (1890)

Morrill Land-Grant College Act of 1890 adds to funds available under the 1862 Morrill Act; as a condition of receiving benefits under this law, any state with segregated white land-grant schools is required to fund a school for black students.

National American Woman Suffrage Association is formed. (1890)

People's (Populist) Party, 1892 and 1896: Farmers organize an independent political party as they seek policies more favorable to agriculture.

Panic of 1893, the second-worst economic depression in American history, lasting five years, results from the collapse of the stock market and uncertainties concerning the soundness of the nation's monetary standard.

Coxey's Army is one of the groups that, during the depression of the 1890s, make the first protest marches on Washington. (1894)

Pullman strike, a major event in the development of organized labor, results when the Pullman Sleeping Car Company fires a third of its workers, cuts wages for the rest, and refuses to negotiate with the American Railway Union, headed by Eugene V. Debs; imprisoned, Debs emerges as a Socialist and hero of labor. (1894)

Plessy v. Ferguson: The Supreme Court approves the concept of separate but equal, according to which racially segregated trains or schools do not violate the Fourteenth Amendment's equal protection clause if each group's facilities are more or less equal. (1896)

William McKinley, president, 1897–1901, assassinated in office.

Spanish-American War (1898; continued in the Philippines).

Hawaii is annexed. (1898)

Philippine islands: United States takes control from Spain. (1899)

PROGRESSIVE ERA, WORLD WAR I, AND THE TWENTIES, 1901–1929

Theodore Roosevelt, president, 1901–1909.

Socialist Party forms in response to harsh conditions of industrialization and urbanization, reflecting ideologies brought to the United States by European immigrants; however, the party fails to establish itself in the United States, as it does throughout industrialized nations of Europe.

"Muckrakers": journalists investigate and expose the social and political evils of urban and industrial society.

Lochner v. New York: The U.S. Supreme Court strikes down major social welfare laws in the states. (1905)

Pure Food and Drug Act is passed, aimed at assuring safe and effective products for consumers. (1906)

William Howard Taft, president, 1909–1913.

Edward D. White, chief justice of the United States, 1910–1921.

Bull Moose Party forms under former president Theodore Roosevelt. (1912)

Woodrow Wilson, president, 1913–1921.

Federal income tax: The Sixteenth Amendment to the Constitution empowers Congress to levy a tax on incomes, which Congress swiftly approves. (Ratified 1913)

Federal Reserve System is established, creating a central banking system for the United States. (1913)

Direct Senate elections: The Seventeenth Amendment to the Constitution provides for the election of U.S. senators by the voters instead of by state legislatures. (Ratified 1913)

Harrison Narcotic Act implements an international drug treaty and forms the cornerstone of subsequent U.S. drug-control efforts. (1914)

World War I is fought. (1914–1918 in Europe; U.S. is a participant 1917–1918)

National Woman's Party forms. (1917)

Espionage Act (1917) and Sedition Act (1918): Two laws make illegal a wide variety of actions, including criticizing the government, armed forces, Constitution, and flag, thereby raising constitutional tests of the limits of free speech; both laws are upheld by the Supreme Court.

Red Scare: Economic dislocation, political upheaval, and the specter of the Bolshevik Revolution in Russia after World War I give rise in the United States to superpatriotism, xenophobia, and assaults on civil liberties. (1919–1920)

Prohibition: The Eighteenth Amendment to the Constitution prohibits the manufacture, sale, and transportation of liquor. (Ratified 1919)

Women's Suffrage: The Nineteenth Amendment to the Constitution extends the right to vote to women. (Ratified 1920)

Warren G. Harding, president, 1921–1923 (dies in office).

William Howard Taft, chief justice of the United States, 1921–1930.

Budget and Accounting Act creates the first unified budgeting system for the federal government. (1921)

Teapot Dome: This major scandal in President Harding's administration involves the illegal leasing of federal oil reserves in the West. (1923)

Calvin B. Coolidge, president, 1923–1929.

Progressive Party, an important third-party movement led by Robert M. La Follette Sr., receives 17 percent of the popular vote and thirteen electoral votes in the 1924 presidential election.

Herbert Hoover, president, 1929–1933.

GREAT DEPRESSION, NEW DEAL, AND WORLD WAR II, 1929–1945

Great Depression: The decade between the great stock market crash of 1929 and reindustrialization at the beginning of World War II brings soaring unemployment, business bankruptcies, bank failures, and political turmoil. (1929–1941)

Charles Evans Hughes, chief justice of the United States, 1930–1941.

Bonus March: About one thousand World War I veterans march on Washington, demanding immediate payment of promised pensions; the march is harshly put down by police and military forces approved by President Hoover, further tarnishing his reputation in the face of the worsening Great Depression. (1932)

Presidential inauguration: The Twentieth Amendment to the Constitution shortens the time between a presidential election and inauguration by designating January 20 as inauguration day, and it sets January 3 as the date for convening a new Congress. (Ratified 1933)

Prohibition repealed: The Twenty-first Amendment to the Constitution repeals the Eighteenth Amendment. (Ratified 1933)

Franklin D. Roosevelt, president, 1933–1945 (dies in office).

First New Deal

Civilian Conservation Corps Act authorizes the employment of 250,000 jobless men ages eighteen to twenty-five in projects to conserve and improve U.S. natural resources. (1933)

Agricultural Adjustment Act is created to raise farm prices by paying farmers to reduce farm production. (1933)

Tennessee Valley Authority is created as an independent public corporation to construct dams and power plants, develop plans for flood control and rural electrification, and help reforestation on the Tennessee River; given power to produce, distribute, and sell electricity. (1933)

National Industrial Recovery Act seeks to revive industrial and business activity and reduce unemployment through a cooperative system of codes and voluntary agreements but gives the president power to prescribe codes. (1933)

National Housing Act establishes the Federal Housing Administration to stimulate residential construction by creating a new system of home financing. (1934)

Schechter v. United States: The Supreme Court rules on federal powers under the Commerce Clause, crippling New Deal legislation to deal with the Depression. (1935)

Second New Deal

National Labor Relations Act (Wagner Act) creates a National Labor Relations Board empowered to determine appropriate collective bargaining units under trade union control and to investigate and halt unfair employer practices; bitterly opposed by businesses. (1935; upheld by the Supreme Court in 1937)

Social Security Act creates a national self-financing system of pensions for citizens age sixty-five or older, establishes a joint federal-state unemployment insurance program for workers, and provides monetary assistance to states for state-sponsored pensions and relief work for impoverished Americans; a central element in the New Deal program, the law is upheld by the Supreme Court in 1937. (1935)

Rural Electrification Act creates agency to make loans to electric cooperatives and nonprofit organizations to bring power and lights to rural localities. (1936)

Wickard v. Filburn: Supreme Court decision on a federal law concerning agricultural production gives broad approval of congressional use of the commerce power to regulate economic activity. (1942)

Third New Deal

Second Agricultural Adjustment Act revives portions of the 1933 law that had been declared unconstitutional; authorizes marketing quotas and acreage allotments, government loans to farmers, and surplus crop storage. (1938)

Fair Labor Standards Act establishes a minimum wage and maximum work week and bans child labor. (1938)

Smith Act makes it illegal to advocate the overthrow of the government by force or violence. (1940)

Lend Lease Act allows the United States to send armaments to allies in World War II. (1941)

World War II, the first truly global war, involves the United States, Britain, the Soviet Union, and other allies against Germany, Italy, and Japan. (U.S. participation December 1941–September 1945)

March on Washington Movement: A. Philip Randolph, president of the Brotherhood of Sleeping Car Porters, organizes a march to force President Roosevelt to act on racial discrimination but suspends it after Roosevelt by executive order forbids job discrimination by defense contractors and establishes the Fair Employment Practices Committee. (1941)

Fair Employment Practices Committee: President Roosevelt by executive order establishes the FEPC to investigate racial discrimination; expires in 1946. (1941)

Harlan F. Stone, chief justice of the United States, 1941–1946.

G.I. Bill: Congress passes legislation to accommodate the needs of returning soldiers after the war and ease the economy's transition from war to peace; one of its provisions proves a landmark in educational policy. (1944)

United Nations: Victorious allies establish an international organization at the end of World War II to prevent future wars and provide a forum to resolve issues among nations. (1945)

TRUMAN AND EISENHOWER, 1945–1961

Harry S. Truman, president, 1945–1953.

Atomic weapons: The United States drops two atomic bombs on Japan, first on Hiroshima and then on Nagasaki, leading to Japanese surrender and the end of World War II. (August 1945)

Fred M. Vinson, chief justice of the United States, 1946–1953.

Employment Act commits the federal government in principle to work for "maximum employment, production, and purchasing power." (1946)

Legislative Reorganization Act makes substantial changes in the structure and operations of Congress. (1946)

Taft-Hartley Act: Congress approves business-friendly legislation, officially the Labor-Management Relations Act, to offset or neutralize various gains by organized labor under the New Deal. (1947)

Truman Doctrine: President Truman, in an address to Congress, says the United States will support "free peoples who are resisting attempted subjugation by armed minorities or by outside pressures"; coming at the beginning of the cold war and in the face of perceived Soviet Union efforts to expand communism, the doctrine becomes the basic U.S. foreign policy in the subsequent struggle with the USSR. (1947)

Marshall Plan: The United States launches a bold program that eventually provides over $13 billion to rebuild western Europe following World War II; the program is named for Secretary of State George C. Marshall. (1947)

National Security Act lays the foundation for a unified military service headed by a secretary of defense and creates the Central Intelligence Agency and other apparatus of the cold war state. (1947 and 1949)

Military desegregation: President Truman orders the desegregation of the U.S. armed forces. (1948)

Israel created: Backers of a homeland for Jews declare an independent state in Palestine, immediately recognized by President Truman. (May 1948)

Berlin blockade, airlift: The Soviet Union stops all Allied traffic to jointly run Berlin, located inside the Soviet-controlled area of Germany following World War II; the United States and its allies begin a nearly yearlong airlift of food and fuel before Soviets reopen the border in 1949. (1948–1949)

Dixiecrats: Southern Democrats opposed to their national party's stance on race and states' rights form a third-party movement; their presidential candidate wins 2.4 percent of the popular vote and thirty-nine electoral votes, all from the Deep South. (1948 election)

Progressive Party: Henry Wallace leads disaffected liberals from the national Democratic Party in a third-party effort; his presidential candidacy wins 2.4 percent of the popular vote but no electoral votes. (1948 election)

Communist China: Civil war in China ends when the forces of communist leader Mao Zedong defeat those of Nationalist leader Chiang Kai-shek and establish the People's Republic of China; communist victory leads to recriminations in U.S. politics over the "loss of China." (1949)

National Security Document 68: Apocalyptic document sets the tone for the militarization of American foreign policy in the cold war. (1950)

McCarthyism: A period of political repression during the early years of the cold war is named after Sen. Joseph McCarthy, a leading anticommunist; investigations are directed at Americans suspected of activities supporting communism and the Soviet Union. (High point 1950–1954)

Korean War: North Korea and South Korea fight a civil war that involves the United States and its allies on one side and eventually the People's Republic of China on the other. (June 1950–July 1953)

Presidential terms: The Twenty-second Amendment to the Constitution limits presidents to two full terms in office. (Ratified 1951)

Dwight D. Eisenhower, president, 1953–1961.

Earl Warren, chief justice of the United States, 1954–1969.

Brown v. Board of Education of Topeka: The Supreme Court declares segregated schools unconstitutional, overturning *Plessy v. Ferguson.* (1954, 1955)

Interstate Highway Act creates a plan and financing to build a nationwide network of modern, high-speed highways. (1956)

Civil Rights Act of 1957: Congress seeks to overcome racial discrimination in voting rights. (1957)

National Defense Education Act: In reaction to Russian achievements in space technology, Congress makes a major federal commitment to higher education, especially in math and science. (1958)

Sit-ins: Civil rights activists protest racial segregation laws and practices. (1960)

Civil Rights Act of 1960: Congress expands the 1957 law to further promote African Americans' voting rights. (1960)

NEW FRONTIER AND GREAT SOCIETY, 1961–1969

John F. Kennedy, president, 1961–1963 (assassinated in office).

D.C. voting: The Twenty-third Amendment to the Constitution grants voters in the District of Columbia the right to vote for president and vice president. (Ratified 1961)

Engel v. Vitale: The Supreme Court rules that prayer in public schools violates the Constitution. (1962)

Reapportionment Cases: The Supreme Court, adopting the principle of one person, one vote, prohibits legislative districts with vastly differing number of voters. (1962–1964)

Vietnam War: North Vietnam and South Vietnam fight a civil war following the collapse of French colonial rule in 1954; in the context of superpower cold war tension, the conflict becomes an American-backed war, involving U.S. as well as South Vietnamese armed forces, as part of American foreign policy to contain international communism. (1954–1975; U.S involvement principally 1965–1973)

March on Washington for Jobs and Freedom: An estimated 200,000 people gather on the Mall in Washington as a highlight of a year of boycotts and demonstrations by African Americans and supportive whites throughout the country to protest racial discrimination in employment, voting, and other areas; Martin Luther King Jr. delivers his "I Have a Dream" speech. (1963)

United Farm Workers Association formed. (1963)

Lyndon B. Johnson, president, 1963–1969.

Gulf of Tonkin Resolution: At President Johnson's urging, Congress passes a resolution after North Vietnamese ships allegedly attack U.S. warships off the coast of Vietnam. The president later uses the resolution as legal justification for U.S. military escalation in that war. (1964)

Freedom of Information Act: Congress passes a law allowing greater public access to government documents labeled secret or confidential by officials. (1964)

Poll tax: The Twenty-fourth Amendment to the Constitution forbids requiring the payment of a poll tax to vote in a federal election. (Ratified 1964)

Economic Opportunity Act: In a key component of President Johnson's Great Society program, Congress approves legislation to combat poverty in the United States. (1964)

Civil Rights Act of 1964: The most far-reaching civil rights legislation since the Reconstruction era bans racial discrimination in employment, education, and public accommodations and also bans sex discrimination in employment. (1964)

Elementary and Secondary Education Act: Congress approves a major federal commitment to public elementary and secondary education. (1965)

Voting Rights Act: Federal law is significantly expanded by providing for direct federal action to end disfranchisement by enabling black southerners to register and vote. (1965)

Higher Education Act provides assistance to colleges and college students, including loans and scholarships for needy students. (1965)

Medicare-Medicaid: Congress establishes a federal program of medical coverage for the elderly, based on the Social Security model, and a parallel program of medical aid for the indigent of any age. (1965)

Immigration and Nationality Act ends the national origins quota system that had been the basis of immigration to the United States since 1921. (1965)

Griswold v. Connecticut: The Supreme Court decision establishes a right-of-privacy concept and strikes down a state law that prohibits married couples from obtaining contraceptives. (1965)

Black Panther Party formed. (1966)

National Organization for Women founded. (1966)

Presidential disability: The Twenty-fifth Amendment to the Constitution provides for succession to the office of the president in the event of the incumbent's death or incapacity and for filling vacancies in the office of the vice president. (Ratified 1967)

American Indian Movement founded. (1968)

American Independent Party, a third-party movement led by segregationist Alabama governor George Wallace, wins 13.5 percent of the popular vote and forty-six electoral votes in the 1968 election.

NIXON, FORD, AND CARTER, 1969–1981

Richard M. Nixon, president, 1969–1974. Resigns from office.

Warren E. Burger, chief justice of the United States, 1969–1986.

Legislative Reorganization Act of 1970: Congress approves the first substantial reform of its procedures since 1946, including opening Congress to closer public scrutiny and curbing the power of committee chairmen.

Earth Day is held nationwide and becomes widely seen as a seminal event in launching the environmental movement. (April 22, 1970)

Occupational Safety and Health Act: Congress approves landmark legislation requiring the federal government to adopt and enforce safety standards for the workplace. (1970)

Environmental Protection Agency is established as an independent federal agency in which are consolidated all major programs to combat pollution. (1970)

The Twenty-sixth Amendment to the Constitution extends the right to vote to persons who are age eighteen and older. (Ratified 1971)

New Economic Policy: President Nixon's economic program includes a comprehensive system of wage and price controls to curb inflation that had developed from several years of simultaneously pursuing the Great Society and the Vietnam War. (1971)

Federal Election Campaign Act limits certain campaign spending of presidential and congressional candidates and establishes other means to control election costs. (1971)

Educational amendments: In legislation to extend and expand aid to higher education, Congress bars (in Title IX) discrimination on the basis of sex in schools receiving federal aid, a prohibition later to become contentious in colleges and universities. (1972)

Equal Rights Amendment. Congress approves and sends to the states a constitutional amendment barring sex discrimination; the amendment fails to gain ratification. (1972)

Roe v. Wade: Supreme Court ruling provides legal access to abortions and becomes the foundation of subsequent battles over abortion rights. (1973)

War Powers Resolution: Over President Nixon's veto, Congress approves legislation limiting a president's power to commit U.S. forces abroad without congressional approval. (1973)

OPEC oil embargo: As an outgrowth of the Arab-Israeli conflict in the Middle East, oil-producing countries launch a largely successful effort to stop the delivery of oil to the United States and other industrialized nations. (1973)

Vice president resigns: Spiro Agnew resigns as vice president to Richard Nixon after he is implicated in a bribery scheme; he becomes one of only two persons—John C. Calhoun the other—to quit this office. (1973)

Watergate scandal: A series of events beginning in 1972, including criminal actions, involve President Nixon and his administration and lead to Nixon's resignation from office in 1974 in the face of probable impeachment and removal by Congress.

Gerald R. Ford, president, 1974–1977, succeeds Richard Nixon to become the only unelected American president, after having been appointed to the vice presidency under the Twenty-fifth Amendment to replace Spiro Agnew.

Ford pardons Nixon for any crimes he may have committed in connection with Watergate. (1974)

Buckley v. Valeo: Supreme Court ruling significantly weakens regulation of federal election campaigns. (1976)

Congressional Budget and Impoundment Control Act: Congress passes complex legislation to control federal spending and give itself new tools to impose its priorities over those of the president. (1976)

Jimmy Carter, president, 1977–1981.

Independent Counsel Act: In the wake of the Watergate scandal, Congress passes a law to create a mechanism to investigate and prosecute executive misconduct; it is renewed three times before lapsing in 1999. (1978)

Panama Canal Treaty provides for the return of full sovereignty of the waterway to Panama on December 31, 1999. (1977)

Camp David Accords, an agreement in principle engineered by President Carter for peace agreements between Egypt and Israel, concluded at the presidential retreat in Maryland. (1978)

American hostage crisis: In Tehran, Iranian students seize the U.S. embassy and 66 hostages, holding 52 of them for 444 days until the day of inauguration of Ronald Reagan, Carter's successor. (November 4, 1979–January 20, 1981)

REAGAN TO GEORGE W. BUSH, 1981–2001

Ronald Reagan, president, 1981–1989.

Economic Recovery Tax Act: Congress approves major economic legislation early in the Reagan administration, with large tax cuts as its centerpiece. (1981)

National debt quadruples under pressures of reduced taxes, increased defense spending, and an economic downturn. (1981–1992)

Rainbow Coalition: Rev. Jesse Jackson organizes a lobbying group and quasi-political party. (1984)

Iran-contra Affair: A congressional investigation follows the discovery that various actions of the Reagan administration—some in violation of U.S. law—resulted in the proceeds from secret arms deals between the United States and Iran going to finance rebels fighting Nicaragua's Marxist Sandinista government. (1986)

William H. Rehnquist, chief justice of the United States, 1986–.

George Bush, president, 1989–1993.

Persian Gulf War: The United States organizes and leads a multination military campaign to expel Iraq from Kuwait, which had been occupied by the army of Iraqi dictator Saddam Hussein. (1991)

Reform Party: Billionaire Ross Perot organizes a third party and capitalizes on voter discontent to win 19 percent of the popular vote, but no electoral votes, in the 1992 presidential elections. (1992–)

Congressional pay: The Twenty-seventh Amendment to the Constitution bans Congress from increasing its members' salaries until after an election intervenes. (Ratified 1992)

Bill Clinton, president, 1993–2001.

Shaw v. Reno: Supreme Court decision calls into question the validity of often strangely configured congressional districts drawn for the purpose of increasing the chances of African American victories. (1993)

North American Free Trade Agreement: Congress passes legislation to create open trade between Mexico and the United States; bitterly contested by organized labor and many environmentalists. (1993)

Family and Medical Leave Act: Legislation creates new rights to unpaid leave for some employees with newly born or adopted children or with family medical problems; the legislation is opposed by business interests. (1993)

Republicans control Congress: For the first time since 1952 the GOP wins control of both chambers after capturing the House from Democrats. (1994 elections)

Welfare reform: Congress passes the Personal Responsibility and Work Opportunity Reconciliation Act, which ends the federal guarantee of cash welfare to eligible low-income women and children and gives states block grants instead of cash to pass through to recipients. It also gives states control over other assistance programs. (1996)

Clinton impeachment and trial: The Republican-controlled House impeaches President Clinton over allegedly false statements made under oath that grew from a personal relationship he first denied, then admitted, with a young White House female intern; the Senate, however, votes to acquit. (1998–1999)

Bush elected: Republican George W. Bush, son of former president George Bush, is elected president in a disputed national election not settled until more than a month after the voting; Bush loses the popular vote to opponent Albert Gore but narrowly wins the electoral college vote; he becomes the second son of a president to win the office (John Quincy Adams was the other); the GOP controls the White House and both houses of Congress for the first time since 1953–1955, the first two years of Dwight Eisenhower's administration. (2000)

THE

ENCYCLOPEDIA

OF

AMERICAN

POLITICAL

HISTORY

ADAMS, JOHN

The second president of the United States (1797–1801), a renowned political philosopher, and the author of the Massachusetts Constitution of 1780, John Adams as president averted a potentially disastrous war with France.

Adams was born October 30, 1735, into a family of Massachusetts farmers of Puritan ancestry. After graduating from Harvard College in 1755, he first taught school and then practiced law in Braintree (now Quincy).

The young lawyer was quickly swept up in patriot causes and colonial politics, as he fiercely protested the injustice of British rule. In 1774, after a brief stint in the Massachusetts legislature, Adams became one of his state's delegates to the First Continental Congress. There he advocated separation from England and served on the committee to draft a declaration of independence. He retired from Congress in 1777. Adams spent ten of the next eleven years in Europe, serving in various diplomatic posts, including minister to Holland and as America's first envoy to Great Britain. In 1783, while serving in the latter post, Adams signed the armistice ending the war with the British and wrote *Defense of the Constitutions of Government of the United States,* a work cited frequently by delegates to the 1787 Constitutional Convention.

The year 1789 found Adams, frustrated with Britain's unwillingness to improve relations, returning home to fill a seat in Congress to which he had been elected under the new Constitution. He never took his seat, however; that same year he was elected vice president of the United States by virtue of his second-place finish after Gen. George Washington in the electoral college balloting.

After eight years as vice president, a job he found uninteresting, Adams was elected to the presidency in 1796, though not without controversy. Political maneuvering led by fellow Federalist Alexander Hamilton and the vagaries of the electoral college—which at this time did not distinguish between candidates for the presidency and vice presidency—left him with a vice president, Thomas Jefferson, from the Democratic-Republican Party.

RELATIONS WITH FRANCE AND BRITAIN

Immediately upon taking office, Adams faced what became the principal crisis of his presidency—the threat of war with revolutionary France. For four years the United States had remained neutral in the struggle between France and Britain, even though Britain persisted in its policy of seizing neutral

John Adams   *Library of Congress*

ships—including U.S. ships—that traded with France. To stop this practice, the United States negotiated Jay's Treaty in 1794, which appeased Britain but infuriated France. The French began to harass American ships. Facing intense political pressure from both pro-British Hamiltonians, who favored a joint U.S.-British effort to prevent French domination of Europe, and Jefferson's Democratic-Republicans, who defended France and opposed war, Adams chose to strengthen the nation's military while continuing negotiations with the French. In the summer of 1797 he sent John Marshall, Charles Cotesworth Pinckney, and Elbridge Gerry to Paris to seek an agreement that would avoid war and end French attacks on American shipping. Their efforts, however, were short-lived. When they met with agents of French foreign minister Charles Talleyrand, the French demanded a bribe for Talleyrand, a loan for the country, and an official apology for the president's criticism of France.

When Adams released documents about the incident (known as the "XYZ Affair") in April 1798, Americans, insulted by events, called for revenge. In view of the undeclared naval war already under way between the two nations, Congress, responding to the president's call for more defense measures, ordered expansion of the army, establishment of a Navy Department, and construction of new ships. George Washington was even called out of retirement to lead the army. Adams, however, refused to declare war against France, even though it would have been a politically expedient move.

In early 1799 Adams once again made peaceful overtures to France in response to conciliatory signals. The public, faced with higher taxes to support a war, was no longer enthusiastic, and the president asserted he would not declare war unless forced into it by the French. Fortunately, the crisis passed. In November 1800 he learned that the U.S. delegation had successfully concluded the Treaty of Morfontaine (September 30, 1800), ending hostilities in the undeclared war and releasing the United States from its obligations under the 1778 treaties with France.

DOMESTIC POLITICS

At home the Adams administration faced a political crisis stemming from the president's support of the controversial Alien and Sedition Acts of 1798, which were designed to end attacks in the Democratic-Republican press on Federalist members of Congress and cabinet members. The acts, by posing serious limits on the rights of free speech and dissent, constituted one of the greatest incidents of legislated suppression of freedom of expression in the history of the United States. Sporadic enforcement of the bills spurred the revival of Democratic-Republican fortunes.

Adams lost the 1800 election to his vice president and rival, Thomas Jefferson. The disunity of the Federalist Party,

epitomized in the widening rift between Adams and Hamilton, and the unpopularity of the Alien and Sedition Acts were largely to blame. However, the electoral college majority for Jefferson was slim, and without the electoral votes based on counting slaves for representation, Jefferson would have lost the election.

Before leaving office, Adams pushed for judicial reforms and, in a series of "midnight appointments," named more than two hundred men to judicial posts. He also appointed John Marshall chief justice of the United States, a position he would hold for thirty-four years. Rivals Adams and Jefferson, who had long since reconciled, both died on July 4, 1826, the fiftieth anniversary of the Declaration of Independence.

See also *American Revolution; Federalists; Jefferson, Thomas; Political Parties; Sedition Act of 1798.*

SABRA BISSETTE LEDENT, INDEPENDENT AUTHOR

BIBLIOGRAPHY

Brown, Ralph A. *The Presidency of John Adams.* Lawrence: University Press of Kansas, 1975.
Ellis, Joseph J. *Passionate Sage: The Character and Legacy of John Adams.* New York: Simon and Schuster, 1988.
Handler, Edward. *America and Europe in the Political Thought of John Adams.* Cambridge: Harvard University Press, 1964.
Thompson, C. Bradley. *John Adams and the Spirit of Liberty.* Lawrence: University Press of Kansas, 1998.

ADAMS, JOHN QUINCY

The son of a president, John Quincy Adams (1767–1848) was elected under controversial circumstances and served one term (1825–1829).

Adams was probably the most prepared man ever to win the presidency, yet as president he was generally unsuccessful because of his poor political skills. His earliest training for public service came in 1778, when he accompanied his father to France and Holland during the American Revolution. He returned to the United States in 1785, graduated from Harvard, read law, and began to practice in 1790. Starting in 1794, at age twenty-seven, he represented the administrations of George Washington and John Adams in The Hague and Berlin. President Thomas Jefferson removed him from his diplomatic post, and Adams became a Federalist U.S. senator (1803–1809). Adams began to break with his father's party by serving as James Madison's ambassador to Russia in 1809 and later helped negotiate the end of the War of 1812. As President James Monroe's secretary of state (1817–1825), Adams signed the treaty that obtained Florida from Spain and drafted what became known as the Monroe Doctrine.

In 1824 he ran second to Andrew Jackson in the popular vote and electoral vote, but in a four-way race no one had a majority of the electoral college. This sent the election to the House of Representatives, which had to choose among the top three vote-getters—Jackson, Adams, and William Crawford of Georgia—with each state delegation having one vote. The candidate who ran fourth, Henry Clay, used his influence in the House to secure the election for Adams. Jackson claimed Adams was elected through a corrupt bargain with Clay, which seemed to be confirmed when Clay became secretary of state. There was no bargain. Clay disliked Jackson and agreed with Adams on the need for internal improvements and a strong nationalist government in Washington. Adams, who lacked guile or great political skills, appointed Clay because he thought him the best person for the job.

Adams's administration was marked by conflicts with Congress, where supporters of Jackson became increasingly powerful. He tried to avoid partisanship and party politics, would not campaign for reelection, and did little to reward his supporters with patronage. His administration continued the nationalist policies of Monroe while building greater international respect for the nation. Adams was competent as an administrator and brilliant in foreign affairs, but he was a poor politician with little charisma. In 1828 Jackson, the hero of the Battle of New Orleans, won seventeen states to Adams's ten and 647,231 popular votes to Adams's 509,097.

John Quincy Adams *Library of Congress*

In 1831 Adams became the only elected president to later serve in Congress. (Andrew Johnson, who succeeded to the presidency, subsequently represented Tennessee in the U.S. Senate from March 4, 1875, until his death on July 31, 1875.) Without campaigning, he won reelection every two years until his death. With no ambition for higher office, or even a great desire to stay in Congress, he became the conscience of the House of Representatives, sometimes single-handedly battling proslavery congressmen from the South and their "doughface" northern allies—northerners with southern sympathies. For nearly nine years he fought the "gag rule," which prohibited the reading of abolitionist petitions on the floor of the House of Representatives. He vigorously opposed the annexation of Texas and the war with Mexico. Known as "Old Man Eloquent," he embarrassed supporters of slavery with his wit, sarcasm, and encyclopedic knowledge of American history and Anglo-American law. In 1841 he helped argue for the liberty of thirty-nine illegally enslaved Africans in *The United States v. Amistad*. By the time of his death Adams was revered throughout the North as the nation's most important congressional opponent of slavery. Southerners feared his sharp tongue, and many respected him, even as they tried, and failed, to censure him or to still his constant pleas for human liberty and respect for the American institutions his father had helped create.

See also *Gag Rule; Jackson, Andrew; Monroe, James; War of 1812*.

PAUL FINKELMAN, UNIVERSITY OF TULSA COLLEGE OF LAW

BIBLIOGRAPHY

Hargreaves, Mary W. M. *The Presidency of John Quincy Adams.* Lawrence: University Press of Kansas, 1985.

Richards, Leonard L. *The Life and Times of Congressman John Quincy Adams.* New York: Oxford University Press, 1986.

Russell, Greg. *John Quincy Adams and the Public Virtues of Diplomacy.* Columbia: University of Missouri Press, 1995.

AFFIRMATIVE ACTION

Broadly defined, the term *affirmative action* means efforts to include members of minority groups in various institutions of American society.

Affirmative action was developed during the latter half of the 1960s and early 1970s alongside the civil rights movement. President John F. Kennedy first used the term in 1961 in Executive Order 10925, requiring government contractors to "take affirmative action" to ensure that persons are employed and treated during employment "without regard to their race, creed, color, or national origin." President Lyndon B. Johnson's Executive Order 11246 prohibited employment discrimination by contractors and created the Office of Federal Contract Compliance (OFCC) to enforce the prohibition. But it was under the auspices of President Richard M. Nixon's Labor Department that the OFCC first specified the requirements of contractors' written affirmative action plans and required contractors to make "every good faith effort" to achieve their affirmative action goals.

Before affirmative action, the federal government's participation in the advancement of civil rights had concentrated on attempts to eradicate the Jim Crow regime of racial discrimination that flourished before and after the Supreme Court announced the "separate but equal" doctrine in *Plessy v. Ferguson* (1896). Beginning with the Court's 1954 decision in *Brown v. Board of Education,* which outlawed segregation in public schools, and the Civil Rights Act of 1964, which prohibited discrimination in public accommodations, schools, federally assisted programs, and employment, the federal government tried to reverse more than a half-century of state-sanctioned segregation. While these measures combated the discriminatory *exclusion* of minority groups from various institutions, the affirmative action initiatives of the 1960s and 1970s were intended to encourage the *inclusion* of such groups.

Affirmative action is not easily confined to any single uniform definition. It can simply mean outreach programs to expand the pools of minority group applicants for employment or entry into academic institutions. More commonly, affirmative action involves employers or schools explicitly taking race into account when making selection decisions. Where past discrimination by a specific institution—a business, a government agency such as a fire department, or a labor union—has been proven, courts have imposed quotas to remedy prior exclusion of African Americans. In other instances where minorities were underrepresented, employers have voluntarily offered preferences to nonwhites, as a prophylactic against litigation or out of a desire to diversify a job force.

In light of America's centuries-long history of racial discrimination, supporters of affirmative action have viewed such race-conscious programs as critical to assisting individuals in overcoming the effects of past and present-day discrimination. As Justice Harry Blackmun wrote in *Regents of the University of California v. Bakke* (1978), "In order to get beyond racism, we must first take account of race. There is no other way. And in order to treat some persons equally, we must first treat them differently." Supporters also have emphasized the positive effect that racial diversity brings to various institutions as a justification for race-conscious programs.

Opponents of affirmative action, by contrast, argue that taking race into account violates the principle that people should be regarded as individuals rather than as members of a group. Many critics hostile to affirmative action assert that such programs unfairly favor individuals based on their race

and thereby constitute "reverse discrimination." In *Adarand Constructors, Inc. v. Peña* (1995), Justice Antonin Scalia stated, "In the eyes of the government, we are just one race here. It is American." Opponents further argue that granting benefits on the basis of race compromises merit-based achievements.

Neither the federal civil rights statutes nor the Constitution specifically addresses the legality of affirmative action. The core legal questions raised by affirmative action programs focus on what kinds of justifications are required to permit race-conscious decision making. For constitutional purposes, this question is which of the three levels of equal protection review developed by the Supreme Court since its decision in *Brown* would be applied to affirmative action programs. "Strict scrutiny" is the most stringent test and is traditionally applied to racial classifications designed to discriminate against minorities. "Intermediate scrutiny" is often applied to classifications involving sex. The third is "rational basis scrutiny," the most deferential form of judicial review, which is traditionally applied to economic regulation. This inquiry involves important subsidiary questions about whether particular justifications are "compelling," whether the federal government has more power to engage in affirmative action than states and localities, and whether private employers are treated differently from governments.

AFFIRMATIVE ACTION IN THE COURTS

Beginning in 1978 the Supreme Court considered the lawfulness of several important forms of affirmative action. In *Bakke* the Court reviewed a challenge to a set-aside for minority applicants to the medical school at the University of California at Davis. Justice Lewis F. Powell Jr. wrote the controlling decision, which struck down the particular program but upheld affirmative action in admissions in general. Powell held that the Equal Protection Clause of the Fourteenth Amendment applied as much to whites as to racial minorities, and therefore affirmative action programs must be reviewed under the strict scrutiny standard of judicial review, which requires that there be a compelling interest advanced by the government's program.

Powell considered and rejected several possible justifications for affirmative action. Among these possible justifications was remedying past discrimination, increasing the number of nonwhite professionals, and improving medical care to underserved areas. He accepted, however, that "attainment of a diverse student body" was a compelling interest that could satisfy strict scrutiny. Colleges and universities across the country responded to this holding by taking race into account in their admissions policies.

United Steelworkers of America v. Weber (1979) involved a private employer and therefore focused on the antidiscrimination provisions of Title VII of the Civil Rights Act of 1964, rather than the Constitution. *Weber* involved a racial set-aside for a training program that led to skilled craft positions—occupational specializations from which African Americans had traditionally been excluded. The set-aside provided that 50 percent of the training program spots be reserved for blacks until their percentage of craft workers corresponded with their percentage of the local labor force. Upholding the programs, the Court concluded that Title VII permitted "the private sector to adopt affirmative action plans designed to eliminate conspicuous racial imbalance in traditionally segregated job categories."

In *Fullilove v. Klutznick* (1980) the Court analyzed the last major category of affirmative action—set-asides for businesses contracting with the government. *Fullilove* involved a challenge to a large federal public works bill, which required that 10 percent of the federal funds be used to engage minority contractors or suppliers. The Court noted that "any preference based on racial or ethnic criteria must necessarily receive a most searching examination to make sure it does not conflict with constitutional guarantees." As it had in *Bakke* and *Weber*, the Court rejected the idea that the law was completely color-blind; rather, the Court recognized a distinction between programs designed to exclude on account of race and those designed to overcome past discrimination.

In 1989, however, the Supreme Court began to signal the constitutional vulnerability of affirmative action programs. In *City of Richmond v. J. A. Croson Co.* a majority of the justices held that strict scrutiny had to be applied even to remedial affirmative action programs designed to include disadvantaged minorities rather than exclude particular races based on hostility or animus. The Court rejected the idea that "benign" racial classifications were different from Jim Crow discrimination and stated that "unless racial classifications are strictly reserved for remedial settings, they may in fact promote notions of racial inferiority and lead to a politics of racial hostility." Six years later, in *Adarand*, the Supreme Court imposed another major legal constraint on affirmative action, holding that racial classifications created by Congress, like those of the states, were to be evaluated under strict scrutiny as well.

Lower courts and opponents of affirmative action picked up the signal sent by the Supreme Court. In *Hopwood v. Texas* (1996) the U.S. Court of Appeals for the Fifth Circuit revisited the issues raised in *Bakke* and held, in seeming contradiction to *Bakke*, that the University of Texas Law School could never take race into account in admitting students. The Supreme Court declined to review the Fifth Circuit's decision, leaving the *Hopwood* decision intact. Following *Hopwood*, long-standing university programs designed to encourage diversity have been challenged and overturned. For example, the U.S. District Court for the Southern District of Georgia held in *Johnson v. Board of Regents of the University Sys. of Georgia* (2000) that the university's admissions policies, which took race and sex into account, violated Title VI's proscription against racial discrimination because "the promotion of student body diversity in higher education is not a compelling interest."

Other race-neutral strategies have been developed as well. In 1999 Gov. Jeb Bush advanced the controversial One Florida Plan, which is modeled on similar plans in Texas and California. The plan ensures the diversity of state college student bodies by providing for automatic college admission for the top 20 percent of each Florida high school graduating class. Because Florida high schools are effectively segregated, the One Florida Plan would ensure representative diversity in state colleges.

THE FUTURE OF AFFIRMATIVE ACTION

At the same time that the Supreme Court began to take a more conservative stance on affirmative action programs, the efficacy of race-based affirmative action itself came under attack. For instance, some have proposed that affirmative action programs be based on social class, rather than race.

It remains unclear whether the Supreme Court will reaffirm or overrule *Bakke* or allow lower courts to redefine the permissible boundaries of affirmative action. It is equally unclear whether political and social influences will change the fundamental approach of affirmative action to displace race-based and other distinctions with class-based policies or masked race-based programs. What is clear, however, is that the race question—or, as W. E. B. DuBois labeled it, "the problem of the twentieth century"—will continue to occupy center stage in American public policy well into the twenty-first century.

See also *African American Politics;* Brown v. Board of Education; *Civil Rights Movement; Supreme Court.*

MICHAEL BLANCHARD, WESTERN NEW ENGLAND SCHOOL OF LAW, AND GABRIEL J. CHIN, UNIVERSITY OF CINCINNATI COLLEGE OF LAW

BIBLIOGRAPHY

Belz, Herman. *Equality Transformed: A Quarter-Century of Affirmative Action.* New Brunswick: Transaction Publishers, 1991.

Chin, Gabriel J., ed. *Affirmative Action and the Constitution.* New York: Garland, 1998.

Edley, Christopher Jr. *Not All Black and White: Affirmative Action, Race, and American Values.* New York: Hill and Wang, 1996.

Garvey, John H., and T. Alexander Aleinikoff, eds. *Modern Constitutional Theory: A Reader.* 4th ed. St. Paul, Minn.: West Group, 1999, chap. 10.

Swain, Carol M., ed. *Race Versus Class: The New Affirmative Action Debate.* Lanham, Md.: University Press of America, 1996.

Tomasson, Richard F., Faye J. Crosby, and Sharon D. Herzberger. *Affirmative Action: The Pros and Cons of Policy and Practice.* Washington, D.C.: American University Press; Lanham, Md.: Distributed by arrangement with University Publishing, 1996.

AFRICAN AMERICAN POLITICS

African American involvement in U.S. politics, at least in terms of voting rights, began during the era of the Revolutionary War. During the two hundred years that followed, African Americans struggled to retain and expand their basic political rights and then to achieve their share of power through the political process.

Initially, most northern states and several southern states placed no racial restrictions on suffrage. However, beginning in 1810, blacks lost the right to vote in those few southern states that had granted them suffrage. In the rest of the country, the extension of universal suffrage to white men generally coincided with restrictions on black suffrage. After 1820 most northern states either abolished black suffrage or, in the case of New York, retained property qualifications for black voters. In spite of these difficulties, blacks took advantage of every opportunity to pursue their political interests. In New York the black vote sometimes provided the margin in close elections, while during Dorr's Rebellion in Rhode Island blacks helped defeat the reformers' efforts to extend suffrage at the expense of blacks. On the eve of the Civil War only five New England states—Maine, Massachusetts, New Hampshire, Rhode Island, and Vermont—allowed equal suffrage for blacks.

EMANCIPATION AND RECONSTRUCTION

The Civil War and emancipation did not immediately enfranchise African Americans. Few northern states rushed to extend suffrage to blacks. In the former Confederate states black suffrage became connected to efforts to ensure the loyalty of southern governments, as well as to provide the base of the Republican Party in the South. The Fourteenth Amendment, approved by Congress in 1866, contained provisions for reducing a state's representation in Congress if it denied suffrage to a significant number of men. The Reconstruction Act of 1867 went further, demanding that blacks participate in the establishment of new governments in the former Confederate states and extending suffrage to the freedmen. The state constitutional conventions that convened in 1867 and 1868 contained significant black representation; in South Carolina blacks held a majority of the seats, while in Louisiana they held exactly 50 percent. Blacks focused their efforts in these conventions in making sure that they were guaranteed equal rights in the reconstructed southern states and that public school systems were established and accessible to them.

The Loyal Union Leagues that were established across the South in support of the Republican Party mobilized black political participation in the elections that followed. Blacks naturally voted Republican—it was the party of Lincoln and emancipation. In turn the Republicans became dependent on the black vote to maintain power both in the South and in the nation. The importance of the black vote in the presidential election of 1868 led to the enactment of the Fifteenth Amendment, which outlawed denial of the right to vote based on race, color, or previous condition of servitude. Black politicians used suffrage to gain access to political power—political office, influence in the Republican Party, and civil service jobs. In the South Republican power relied on the black vote and the disfranchisement of former Confederates; ultimately, the struggle over the role of blacks in the party split Republicans into two factions—one committed to black power in the party and one opposed to it.

Blacks in the South remained politically active, almost exclusively within the Republican Party, through the rest of the nineteenth century. They held office in state government, gained election on occasion to Congress, and were rewarded with patronage for their vote. By the mid-1870s Democrats had regained control of most state and local governments in the South, and African American political influence began to wane.

At the beginning of the twentieth century the dominant political issue in the black community was disfranchisement. Throughout the South, state after state enacted constitutional or legislative impediments to black suffrage. At the same time internal conflicts within state Republican organizations reduced and then eliminated blacks from significant political power as the white faction took control of the party. The result was that by the early years of the new century African American officeholders disappeared from the governments of the former Confederate states, as the number of enfranchised blacks dwindled. However, African American political influence continued at the national level. Booker T. Washington used his personal connections with Presidents Theodore Roosevelt and William Howard Taft in an effort to maintain the Republican Party's commitment to civil rights. In addition Washington and his political allies continued to dispense patronage from the Republican Party.

AFRICAN AMERICAN POLITICS AND THE GREAT MIGRATION

As African Americans lost their political rights in the South, they intensified their struggle for equal rights and began to emerge as a political force in the North. The former development centered on W. E. B. Du Bois and the organization of the National Association for the Advancement of Colored People (NAACP) in 1910. The NAACP pursued a relatively militant civil rights agenda and launched legal challenges to segregation and disfranchisement. In the 1920s the organization's efforts spread to the antilynching campaign that coalesced around the attempt by Representative L. C. Dyer (R–Mo.) to make lynching a federal crime. African American involvement in northern black politics was a natural outgrowth of the migration of hundreds of thousand of black southerners northward during the 1910s and 1920s. In the industrial cities where black migrants concentrated, their vote became crucial in local elections. Participation in electoral politics soon produced black candidates, first for local and state positions and then for Congress. Winning election to Congress in 1928 from Chicago's south side as a Republican, Oscar DePriest was the first African American elected to Congress from a northern state and the first elected in the twentieth century.

In the 1920s and 1930s African American political activity became more effective, even though the number of elected black officials remained very small. The NAACP took the lead, educating black voters about candidates who deserved their support or their opposition. In 1923 black voters began targeting members of Congress who opposed the Dyer antilynching bill; in 1930 they organized to defeat the confirmation of John J. Parker to the U.S. Supreme Court because of racist statements attributed to him.

Also in the 1920s African American political alignment began to change, as many blacks questioned their support of the Republican Party. In an effort to build on the inroads in the South that they achieved in the 1928 presidential election, Republican leaders courted the support of white southerners, often at the expense of blacks. At the same time Democrats began to seek black political support and reward it with patronage. This was particularly evident during Franklin D. Roosevelt's administration, when he called on prominent African Americans to advise him on race issues as a "black cabinet" and appointed others to positions in his administration. Reflecting these changes, black Democrat Arthur W. Mitchell was elected to the House to replace DePriest in 1934, and Democrat Adam Clayton Powell Jr. of Harlem won a House seat in 1944. In spite of these developments many African Americans remained suspicious of Democrats because of Roosevelt's failure to confront the southern wing of his party on the race issue and remained dissatisfied because of discrimination in New Deal relief programs.

In the 1940s, as the struggle for civil rights intensified, the African American drift toward the Democratic Party accelerated. In 1941 President Roosevelt gave in to political pressure from civil rights activist A. Philip Randolph and signed Executive Order 8802, which outlawed race-based job discrimination in the defense industry. In 1944, in *Smith v. Allwright,* the NAACP won a Supreme Court decision that ruled all-white primaries unconstitutional and created a growing num-

President Dwight D. Eisenhower meets in the Oval Office with Martin Luther King Jr. (left) and A. Philip Randolph (right), June 23, 1958. During Reconstruction, African Americans were firmly in the Republican camp, but by the 1960s their allegiance to the Democratic Party would be largely solidified. *National Archives*

ber of registered black voters in the South. Randolph pressured President Harry S. Truman in 1948 to order the armed forces to desegregate. Truman and the Democratic Party endorsed a strong civil rights platform during the election of 1948, a gamble that almost backfired, as some southern Democrats bolted and formed the segregationist Dixiecrat Party. Truman won the election, with support from the black vote in both the North and the South, signaling the increasing importance of this vote for the Democrats.

In the 1950s these trends continued, although the black vote was not strong enough to offset Republican Dwight D. Eisenhower's popularity. Neither party had a clear hold on the civil rights agenda. The *Brown v. Board of Education* decision, Eisenhower's four-point proposal for civil rights in 1957, his use of troops to desegregate Little Rock's Central High School, and the Civil Rights Acts of 1957 and 1960 strengthened the Republicans' claim on the black vote, while Adlai Stevenson's ambiguous stand on civil rights and the southern Democrats' hard line on segregation temporarily slowed down the political shift away from the Republicans.

THE 1960S AND BEYOND

By 1960 the Civil Rights Acts of 1957 and 1960, the elimination of the white primary, and the registration of black voters in the border states gave blacks a greater political voice than they had enjoyed since Reconstruction. The civil rights movement mobilized this consciousness, as blacks demanded political solutions to discrimination. In the election of 1960 John F. Kennedy courted the black vote by carefully endorsing limited civil rights proposals; the black vote was critical in the key states that provided his narrow victory. The Democrats also benefited from the ratification in 1964 of the Twenty-fourth Amendment, which outlawed the poll tax. The 1964 election consolidated the political realignment and tied the black vote to the Democratic Party for the rest of the century. President Lyndon B. Johnson engineered the passage of the 1964 Civil Rights Act and selected Hubert Humphrey, a long-time advocate of civil rights, as his running mate. Emerging from the controversy over seating black delegates from the Mississippi Freedom Democratic Party at the Democratic Convention, the party outlawed segregated delegations in future conventions. After a landslide victory, the Johnson administration consolidated its efforts to protect black political power with the 1965 Voting Rights Act. The Kennedy/Johnson civil rights legislation, and the voter registration drives that followed, assured political rights for African Americans, altered the face of southern politics, and consolidated the alliance between African American voters and the Democratic Party.

As blacks began exercising their political rights, the number of black officeholders increased rapidly across both the North and the South. The number of black members of Congress increased from two in 1945, to six by 1965, to sixteen—including Republican senator Edward Brooke of Massachusetts—by 1973. In 1956 there were approximately forty blacks serving in state legislatures, all in the North and West; by 1973 more than two hundred African Americans served in thirty-seven state legislatures.

In the years that followed, political inroads were made nationwide. Many major cities, including Los Angeles, Houston, Atlanta, New Orleans, and New York, elected black mayors, and thousands of African Americans served in state, county, and city governments. In 1967 civil rights attorney Thurgood Marshall became the first black to serve on the Supreme Court. Gen. Colin Powell served as the highest-ranking military officer, chair of the Joint Chiefs of Staff, during the 1991 Persian Gulf War. In 1984 Jesse Jackson mounted a serious campaign for the presidential nomination of the Democratic Party.

As blacks moved into the Democratic Party, and as their vote became essential for Democratic success, they demanded a greater role in the party. As early as the 1968 election, African Americans provided 20 percent of the total Democratic vote. Recognizing this political power, Democrats made sure their platform reflected issues of interest to blacks and to some extent shared power, at least by supporting black candidates in black districts (and creating these districts). Meanwhile, conservative whites, especially in the South, fled the party, joining the Republicans. The Dixiecrat revolt in 1948 was an early example of this process, as was George Wallace's American Independent Party in 1968. Republicans welcomed conservative southerners into their party, establishing the political alliance that Herbert Hoover had partly generated in 1928. Barry Goldwater followed this strategy in his unsuccessful bid for the presidency in 1964, and Richard Nixon relied on this "southern strategy" in his victories of 1968 and 1972, as did Ronald Reagan and George Bush in the 1980s.

At the end of the twentieth century African Americans were firmly entrenched in the Democratic Party. In presidential elections Democrats can count on approximately 90 percent of the black vote. In turn Democrats support issues like affirmative action and economic and social programs favored by blacks, and they appoint blacks to visible positions within the party and the government. Republican efforts to attract African American political support have met with only limited success.

See also *Black Suffrage; Civil Rights Acts (Modern); Civil Rights Movement; Democratic Party; Dixiecrats; Eisenhower, Dwight D.; Hoover, Herbert; Johnson, Lyndon B.; Kennedy, John F.; Nixon, Richard M.; Reconstruction; Republican Party; Roosevelt, Franklin D.; Truman, Harry S.*

CARY D. WINTZ, TEXAS SOUTHERN UNIVERSITY

BIBLIOGRAPHY

Franklin, John Hope, and Alfred A. Moss Jr. *From Slavery to Freedom: A History of African Americans.* 8th ed. New York: McGraw-Hill, 2000.

Goings, Kenneth W. *The NAACP Comes of Age: The Defeat of Judge John J. Parker.* Bloomington: Indiana University Press, 1990.

McPherson, James M. *The Struggle for Equality: Abolitionists and the Negro in the Civil War and Reconstruction.* Princeton: Princeton University Press, 1964.

Pfeffer, Paula F. *A Philip Randolph: Pioneer of the Civil Rights Movement.* Baton Rouge: Louisiana State University Press, 1990.

Sitkoff, Harvard. *The Struggle for Black Equality, 1954–1992.* New York: Hill and Wang, 1993.

AMERICAN INDEPENDENT PARTY

The founder of the American Independent Party, Alabama governor George C. Wallace, campaigned for president in 1968 with retired U.S. air force general Curtis LeMay as his running mate. Echoing many of the issues that had galvanized the States' Rights Democratic Party, or "Dixiecrats," in 1948, Wallace ran on a populist, anti–racial integration, anti-Washington platform.

Without an organization, the American Independent Party functioned more as an individual, ideological candidacy for Wallace. His campaign asserted itself in areas where his message of racial separation and economic injustice would be welcome, that is, in the Deep South and among working-class northern whites who had been an important part of the electoral coalition put together decades earlier by President Franklin D. Roosevelt. Although identified with the South because of his gubernatorial position and the continuing fight over segregation, Wallace struck a chord in northern states when he attacked what he called "limousine liberals" who favored integration everywhere except in their own schools. He also routinely attacked persons—college students in particular—who were protesting the Vietnam war.

In the 1968 election, Wallace's goal was to be a controlling factor in the race between Republican Richard Nixon and Democrat Hubert Humphrey, the incumbent vice president. Wallace wanted to win enough electoral votes to deadlock the election and throw it into the House of Representatives, where he expected to hold the balance of power. Among his major demands were the repeal of all civil rights legislation and the ending of all federal antipoverty programs.

Wallace received 9.9 million votes (13.5 percent of the total), won five southern states, and captured forty-six electoral votes, but that was not enough for Wallace to achieve his goal. If Nixon had lost one major state, such as California, he would have been denied an electoral majority.

Wallace returned to the Democratic Party in 1970 and was paralyzed in a 1972 assassination attempt while again campaigning for president; he died in 1998. The American Independent Party fielded a leader of the ultraconservative John Birch Society, Rep. John G. Schmitz (R-Calif.), as its 1972 presidential nominee and took 1.4 percent of the vote. In 1980 the party's presidential slate, its last, got forty-one thousand votes nationwide.

See also *Democratic Party; Dixiecrats; Third Parties.*

RON dePAOLO, INDEPENDENT AUTHOR

AMERICAN REVOLUTION

The American Revolution, which began in 1775 with the battles of Lexington and Concord and ended eight years later with the Treaty of Paris of 1783, established the United States of America as a union of thirteen "free and independent states." The Revolution deprived the United Kingdom of most of the fruits of its victory in the Seven Years' War, effectively bringing the First British Empire to an end. In addition, the American Revolution precipitated the bankruptcy of France and thus laid the groundwork for the French Revolution.

AFTERMATH OF THE SEVEN YEARS' WAR

When the Seven Years' War ended in 1763, Great Britain stood alone at the top of the European state system. With an energetic new monarch, King George III, Europe's strongest economy, and extensive overseas territories augmented by the addition of France's former colony of Québec, England at last seemed to have put its centuries-old rivalry with its cross-channel neighbor to rest, and a promising new age beckoned. The United Kingdom's navy was superior to the combined fleets of its potential enemies, and its many rich possessions in the Caribbean and North America promised to help it maintain its supremacy indefinitely.

Historians generally agree now, though, that England's sweeping victory contained the seeds of almost inevitable upheaval within a short time after 1763. The colonies of New England had been founded, in the main, by English settlers dedicated to establishing communities isolated and insulated from what they regarded as the corruption of the English state and the established Anglican Church. Under their colonial charters, they retained significant powers of self-government, and the tradition of "salutary neglect" established by Sir Robert Walpole under George I and George II grew, to some degree, out of the fact that New England simply did not merit Whitehall's attention. After 1763, though, the situation changed. The expulsion of France from Québec eliminated the New Englanders' felt need for British military protection.

George III intended to rule his empire himself, and the 1760s were marked by a succession of six weak ministries dominated by the backstage maneuvering of the Crown. Decades before the English electoral reforms of the 1830s, the House of Commons remained filled with representatives of "rotten boroughs," military officers, and other de facto agents of the king. Unlike George I and George II, George III saw himself as English first and a Hanoverian prince second; he had grown up in the English court and spoke English as a native. He insisted that the North American colonists help foot the colossal expense of England's recent conquests.

TAXATION AND OTHER ISSUES

Traditionally, the mainland colonies had provided funds to the British government in response to requisitions. Colonial history reinforced the colonists' predilection to see their local assemblies as standing in the same relationship to the Crown as Parliament did in England. In 1763, though, George III's government decided it would be more convenient to tax the colonists directly. The United Kingdom concluded the Treaty of Paris, ending the Seven Years' War, on February 10, 1763, and fifteen days later the ministry told the Commons that the North American colonists would be required to support royal troops in North America. On October 10 of that same year, King George issued a proclamation reserving his western lands in North America for the Indians, whose unhappiness with European encroachment had recently taken the form of a bloody rampage led by the Ottawa leader Pontiac. George III's subjects on the frontier had suffered grievously at the hands of this local chieftain, and the policy of barring westward migration, coupled with the retention of a large army contingent in North America, was meant in part to prevent recurrence of this problem.

The parliamentary act that brought this new disposition to the center of colonists' consciousness was the Stamp Act of 1765. This act, enacted by Parliament at the request of George Grenville's government, required the use of stamped paper for all legal documents, such as wills and deeds. The colonists' response was electric: from Maine to Georgia, they refused to comply. Courts were closed, stamp agents were harassed, and virtually no money was raised. The Stamp Act imbroglio made it clear that the Crown's governors lacked the requisite force to ensure compliance in the face of public opposition. The opposition tactics used in the Stamp Act crisis—intimidation of compliant civilians and royal officials—would be employed with increasing frequency over the following decade.

Continental opposition congealed in the Stamp Act Congress, an intercolonial coordinating body organized by political leaders from Massachusetts. Delegations from nine colonies reiterated a set of resolutions adopted by the Virginia House of Burgesses at the insistence of Patrick Henry. Henry's position was that taxation without representation was unconstitutional. The Congress toned down his rhetoric while adopting his principle. Parliament relented and repealed the Stamp Act. In doing so, however, it insisted on a principle to which the colonists never would consent. In the so-called Declaratory Act, Parliament claimed the right to legislate for the colonies "in all cases whatsoever." Parliament would not concede that Great Britain's colonists retained "the inherited rights of Englishmen." Some opposition members of Parliament, including Edmund Burke and William Pitt, agreed with the most pro-American colonists on this score. Pitt even told the Commons that the colonists would be "slaves" if they could be taxed without representation—as the Declaratory Act said they could be.

In 1767 Chancellor of the Exchequer Charles Townshend secured adoption of measures that exacerbated the tensions between the Crown and the colonies. First, he suspended the New York Assembly because it refused to comply with commands to fund British troops stationed in that colony. Most important, he levied taxes in America on tea, glass, lead, paint, and paper. In addition, Townshend moved to open admiralty courts, in which judges presided without juries, in Boston, Philadelphia, and Charleston. He also persuaded Parliament to empower judges to issue "writs of assistance" that allowed English customs officers to search colonists' homes for contraband. To top it off, Townshend announced that the Crown would assume the colonial assemblies' traditional responsibility for paying the salaries of judges, governors, and other officials appointed by the Crown—who would now be beholden to the British government, rather than the colony, for their income. Edmund Burke warned Townshend in the House of Commons that the Americans would resist this program, but Townshend had a large majority at his disposal, and his proposals won adoption.

In America, John Dickinson responded to Townshend's legislation with his *Letters from a Farmer in Pennsylvania*. Dickinson explored the implications of Townshend's measures and found them all constitutionally suspect. Dickinson insisted that while Parliament could regulate the trade of the whole empire, it had no right to pass measures whose purpose was to raise revenue in the colonies. If colonists could be taxed for revenue at the pleasure of a legislature in which they were unrepresented, they were no better than "slaves."

After meeting substantial resistance and gaining little in the way of revenue, and after suffering an embargo that bankrupted many English merchants, Britain repealed most of Townshend's acts. The new prime minister, Lord North, preferred the idea of full repeal of Townshend's initiatives, but King George—who had sponsored North's rise to power—insisted that "there must always be one tax to keep up the right, and as such I approve of the tea duty." Parliament left the king's preferred duty in effect.

On March 5, 1770, after a few days of rising tension between the army and the local civilians, a hostile crowd in Boston cornered a group of eight British soldiers. Shouting and pelting followed, and finally a soldier slipped; as he arose, his weapon discharged into the crowd. In the next few seconds, five Bostonians were either killed or mortally wounded, and six others suffered less serious injuries. Within no time, Samuel Adams and the radicals around him circulated fliers showing six coffins: five for the dead, a sixth for American liberty. Thus was born the myth of the "Boston Massacre."

Colonial agitators recognized the significance of the tea duty's retention. Despite the fact that Parliament ingeniously manipulated the various duties to which tea was subject in order to make East India Company tea less expensive than the smuggled Dutch tea on which colonials had been reliant, colonists refused to purchase the tea. In Boston local politicians staged the famous "Tea Party." On Thursday, December 16, 1774, a large number of masked men intimidated the guards into abandoning their posts and then, under the watchful eye of a British admiral, dumped the tea stored in three British vessels into Boston Harbor. To this day the ringleaders remain anonymous. Their act precipitated the final confrontation between the colonies and Great Britain.

Even British politicians who had sympathized with the North American colonists' constitutional arguments, such as Burke and Pitt (by then Earl of Chatham), now joined in insisting that at least Boston must be punished. Parliament's response, which colonists up and down the Atlantic coast of North America dubbed the Coercive Acts, was intended at once to extract compensation for the stolen tea from the populace of Boston and to replace the town-meeting system with institutions of colonial government more susceptible to British control. The Boston Port Bill closed the port of Boston until the government decided that the duties could be collected. The second of the Coercive Acts called for a reorganization of the Massachusetts provincial government, a substantial abridgment of the 1691 charter with the aim of reducing "democracy" in Massachusetts.

The third Coercive Act provided for trial in England of anyone accused of crime in Massachusetts in the course of trying to enforce English law. Finally, a Quartering Act was passed with the intention of facilitating the housing of English troops under Gen. Thomas Gage, the new governor of Massachusetts, who was also military commander in North America. The Port Act went into effect on June 1, 1774, and by month's end a series of town meetings had left Bostonians with the firm conviction that they must resist the ministry. Soon the whole province was orga-

In this eighteenth-century satirical drawing by a British artist, Bostonians gleefully pour tea down the throat of a customs official, who has just been tarred and feathered. In the distance, colonists dump tea into Boston Harbor. And, lest one British misdeed go unnoticed, a symbol of the hated Stamp Act, passed in 1765, appears on the "Liberty Tree" at right.   *National Archives*

nized behind a boycott of British goods. When Gage called the provincial legislature into session, it refused his call to compensate the East India Company and began planning a continental congress.

In the summer of 1774, Parliament adopted the Québec Act, an act to provide for the governance of the new-won territory north of New York. This act stirred colonial hostility by extending the former French colony into territory claimed by several of the old English colonies. Perhaps more significantly, it also allowed the French residents of that territory to retain their ancestral religion, Roman Catholicism, which was cordially (when not fanatically) despised south of Québec, particularly by New Englanders. It even provided for ongoing collection of tithes by the Roman Catholic establishment in the province, thus making state support of popery the British policy.

Different factors drove the coming of the revolution in other colonies. In Virginia, for example, political power was concentrated in the hands of the wealthy tobacco and wheat planters east of the Blue Ridge. In the 1760s and 1770s these planters faced especially dreary economic circumstances. Their own conspicuous consumption, coupled with the vagaries of the world tobacco market, left them increasingly indebted to factors in Scotland and England. Their ire came increasingly to be directed at Great Britain, which seemed to be conspiring to reduce them to penury. Furthermore, the king's decision to close off western lands bore hard on Virginia gentlemen whose chief assets were land and slaves. By the end of 1775 Gov. Lord Dunmore's proclamation that slaves who joined his forces would be granted their freedom made royal government as unpopular in the Old Dominion as it was in the Bay State.

LEXINGTON AND CONCORD

With the countryside in ferment against him and Boston essentially blockaded by hostile civilians, Gage decided in April 1775 that he must take action. The president of the informal Provincial Congress, John Hancock, called for the citizenry to prepare for conflict. On hearing that weapons and gunpowder had been gathered at Worcester and Concord, Gage dispatched a detachment of regulars to seize the stores in the latter town. The residents of Boston detected Gage's move, and Paul Revere and others rode out into the Massachusetts countryside to warn the "patriots" that the regulars were coming.

The British detachment encountered mustered Massachusetts militia drawn up in line of battle on the Lexington town square. The results of that April 19 confrontation were the deaths of several locals and the beginning of what would soon be a world war involving Europe's leading naval pow-

ers. Having overcome the men at Lexington, Gage's soldiers continued toward Concord, where they suffered a severe check attempting to enter the town. As they retreated toward Boston, the regulars drew fire from men and boys drawn from the surrounding countryside, and only Gage's decision to send out a second detachment prevented his regulars' annihilation.

News of Lexington and Concord reverberated across English North America. Patriot leaders in other colonies, such as Virginia's Patrick Henry, insisted that the people of Boston were suffering in a common cause, and they demanded immediate deployment of forces from their own colonies. The First Continental Congress responded by naming Virginia's George Washington to lead a Continental Army and sent him to command the forces ringing Boston, where Gage's men were entrenched. The war had begun.

BRITISH MILITARY EFFORT AND DEFEAT

From the British side, the war of 1775–1783 was a desultory affair. It took only two years for most statesmen in Britain to realize their cause was lost. However, the prestige and influence of the Crown in British politics meant that a determined king could wage war long after the commoners' minds had been made up, and that is the story of the political events surrounding the British war effort.

In America, the war was dominated by four major events. First, the "Americans" (as they called themselves) endeavored repeatedly either to persuade the king's subjects in Canada to join in their effort or to conquer the territory. Despite heroics by Benedict Arnold and others, and despite the high hopes of American politicians, the French-Canadians proved too little interested in politics and the English Canadians proved too loyal to the Crown for this to happen. Large contingents of residents of the thirteen colonies who proved loyal to George III migrated to Canada and founded what is now the province of Ontario. Many of the Virginia slaves who flocked to Lord Dunmore's banners eventually were resettled in Nova Scotia, where their descendants remain numerous.

Second, in 1777, miscommunication between the British minister responsible for the war in North America (Lord George Germain) and the commander in chief of the British forces in North America (Gen. Sir William Howe) led to the isolation of a British army in upstate New York. These events, which culminated in Gen. Sir John Burgoyne's surrender of his entire army at Saratoga, served at once to heighten American morale and to destroy the foreign impression that British victory over the Americans was inevitable. In consequence, third, France entered into a military alliance with the United States in 1778. By the war's end, Spain and Holland also joined the anti-British coalition, each for its own reasons, but the de-

Gen. Lord Charles Cornwallis surrenders to Gen. George Washington following the battle of Yorktown. The painting is by the Italian-born artist Constantino Brumidi, who is best known for his frescoes in the U.S. Capitol. *National Archives*

cision by France to back American independence made American success virtually inevitable.

Finally, a joint Franco-American land-sea operation resulted in the surrender of a second British army, commanded by Gen. Lord Charles Cornwallis, at Yorktown, Virginia, in 1781. After years of strategic flailing, the British forces finally had succeeded in establishing control of South Carolina and Georgia, and their prospects for military success seemed to be improving. The story of Washington's triumph over Cornwallis is one characterized, as most military triumphs are, by human error, wise planning, and coincidence. Washington had to be persuaded by his French counterpart, the comte de Rochambeau, to attack Cornwallis instead of besieging the main British stronghold of New York, but the strategy proved completely effective. Even Lord North, who had served as King George's obsequious prime minister since 1770, finally decided the king had to be told there simply was no hope of success.

Despite their agreement in 1778 that they would not conclude a separate peace, and despite their repeated avowals of an intention to negotiate in their and Louis XVI's joint interests, Benjamin Franklin, John Adams, and particularly John Jay played off France against Britain in the name of American interests. The territorial and other elements of the Treaty of Paris suited America's interests far better than those of France or Spain. Great Britain agreed to allow Americans to fish in Canadian waters, to remove its soldiers from posts in what is now the Midwest, and—most important—to recognize the independence of the United States. The Americans' western boundary would be the Mississippi River. The Confederation Congress ratified the treaty unanimously.

See also *Articles of Confederation; Washington, George.*

K. R. CONSTANTINE GUTZMAN, JOHN JAY COLLEGE, CUNY

BIBLIOGRAPHY

Alden, John R. *A History of the American Revolution.* New York: Knopf, 1969.

Bailyn, Bernard. *The Ideological Origins of the American Revolution.* 2d, expanded edition. Cambridge: Harvard University Press, 1992.

Gross, Robert A. *The Minutemen and Their World.* New York: Hill and Wang, 1976.

Holton, Woody. *Forced Founders: Indians, Debtors, Slaves, and the Making of the American Revolution in Virginia.* Chapel Hill: University of North Carolina Press, 1999.

Morris, Richard. *The Peacemakers: The Great Powers and American Independence.* New York: Harper and Row, 1965.

ANTI-MASONIC PARTY

The Anti-Masonic Party was the first third party in U.S. politics to secure any electoral college votes. It also was the first party to hold a nominating convention and to write a platform of political principles.

Formed in 1826 in Batavia, New York, the party opposed Freemasonry, the country's largest secret society. Earlier that year William Morgan, an ex-Mason, had published a book accusing Freemasons of intending to secretly control national politics. Shortly afterward Morgan was believed murdered, but no one was charged with his death. A group of outraged New Yorkers, led by politicians Thurlow Weed and William H. Seward, used the furor over the murder to thwart the political power of Martin Van Buren and the so-called Albany Regency. Weed established several Anti-Masonic newspapers in New York. Believing that Freemasons were behind Morgan's murder, Weed and Seward formed the Anti-Masonic Party.

By 1828 the party was a major political force in New York, Pennsylvania, and Vermont. In 1831 the Anti-Masons met publicly in Baltimore, Maryland, to nominate a candidate for president. In prior campaigns the national parties had chosen their presidential candidates in private caucuses attended only by party leaders, many of whom were Freemasons. Although the Anti-Masons did not draft a party platform in the modern sense, they did write an "address to the people" that primarily condemned Freemasonry for its secrecy and elitism.

In the election of 1832 the Anti-Masons elected twenty-five congressmen from six states. Their presidential candidate, William Wirt, won 8 percent of the popular vote and carried Vermont. In 1836 the major parties held their own national conventions and wrote their own platforms. This killed the Anti-Masonic Party, and most of its members joined the Whig Party. Despite its short life, the Anti-Masonic Party greatly influenced American politics by making it more open.

See also *Third Parties; Van Buren, Martin; Whig Party.*

CHARLES CAREY,
LYNCHBURG COLLEGE/CENTRAL VIRGINIA COMMUNITY COLLEGE

BIBLIOGRAPHY

Ratner, Lorman. *Antimasonry: The Crusade and the Party.* Englewood Cliffs, N.J.: Prentice-Hall, 1969.

Vaughn, William Preston. *The Antimasonic Party in the United States, 1826–1843.* Lexington: University Press of Kentucky, 1983.

ANTITRUST

The antitrust laws constitute what the Supreme Court calls a "charter of freedom," designed to protect the core republican value of free enterprise in America. The word "trust," although it had a technical legal meaning, was commonly used to denote a big business, especially a large, growing manufacturing conglomerate of the sort that suddenly emerged in great numbers in the 1880s and 1890s. At this time, for example, hundreds of small, short-line railroads were being bought up and consolidated into giant systems. Republicanism requires free competition and the opportunity for Americans to build their own businesses without being forced to sell out to an economic colossus. As Sen. John Sherman, R–Ohio, put it, "If we will not endure a king as a political power we should not endure a king over the production, transportation, and sale of any of the necessaries of life." The Sherman Antitrust Act passed Congress almost unanimously in 1890 and remains the core of antitrust policy. The Sherman Act makes it illegal to try to restrain trade or to form a monopoly. It gives the Justice Department the mandate to go to federal court for orders to stop illegal behavior or to impose remedies.

ANTITRUST ENFORCEMENT IN THE PROGRESSIVE ERA

Business consolidation roared along in the 1890s and 1900s. In response the Progressive movement put antitrust measures high on the agenda. President Theodore Roosevelt sued forty-five companies under the Sherman Act, and William Howard Taft sued seventy-five. In 1902 Roosevelt stopped the formation of the Northern Securities Company, which had threatened to monopolize transportation in the Northwest. The most notorious of the trusts was the Standard Oil Company, a monopoly that John D. Rockefeller built in the 1870s and 1880s, using economic threats against competitors and secret rebate deals with railroads. In 1911 the government broke the monopoly

Progressive-era reformers objected to trusts not only for their effect on the economy but also for their corrupting influence in politics. Joseph Keppler, one of the most popular political cartoonists of his day, satirizes the "Bosses of the Senate." By 1889 the Senate was known as the millionaires' club. *Library of Congress*

into separate companies that would compete with one another, including Standard Oil of New Jersey (later known as Exxon), Standard Oil of Indiana (Amoco), Standard Oil of New York (Mobil), and Standard Oil of California (Chevron).

In approving the breakup of Standard Oil the Supreme Court formulated the "rule of reason": the Court would break up, not all big companies and monopolies, but only those that damaged the economic environment of their competitors. Roosevelt, for his part, distinguished between good trusts, which built the world's greatest economy, and bad ones, which preyed on smaller fry. U.S. Steel, which was much larger than Standard Oil, won its antitrust suit in 1920 because it showed the Court that it was well behaved. International Harvester likewise survived its test in court, but trusts in tobacco, meatpacking, and bathtub fixtures were broken up. Over the years hundreds of executives of competing companies who met together illegally to fix prices went to federal prison.

The biggest problem in conducting business under the Sherman Act was that businesses did not always know what specific actions were prohibited. Therefore in 1914 Congress passed the Clayton Act, which prohibited specific business actions (such as price discrimination, tie-in sales, exclusive dealership agreements, mergers, acquisitions, and interlocking corporate directorships) if they substantially lessened competition. Also in 1914 Congress established the Federal Trade Commission (FTC), whose legal and business experts could force business to agree to "consent decrees," which provided an alternative mechanism to police trusts.

POSTPROGRESSIVE ANTITRUST ENFORCEMENT

America adjusted to bigness after 1910. Henry Ford dominated auto manufacturing, but he built millions of cheap cars that put America on wheels, and at the same time he promoted efficiency, lowered prices, and raised wages. Ford became as much of a popular hero as Rockefeller had been a villain. "Welfare capitalism" made large companies an attractive place to work; new career paths opened up in middle management; local suppliers discovered that big corporations were big purchasers. Talk of trust-busting faded away. In the 1920s and 1930s the primary threat to the free-enterprise system seemed to come from unrestricted, cutthroat competition, which drove down prices and profits and caused inefficient production. Under the leadership of Secretary of Commerce Herbert Hoover, the government in the 1920s promoted business cooperation, fostered the creation of self-policing trade associations, and made the FTC an ally of respectable business. The New Deal likewise tried to stop cutthroat competition. The National Recovery Administration

(NRA) was a short-lived program in 1933–1935 designed to strengthen trade associations and raise prices, profits, and wages at the same time. The Robinson-Patman Act of 1936 sought to protect local retailers against the onslaught of the more efficient chain stores, by making it illegal to discount prices. To control big business the New Deal preferred to institute federal and state regulation—controlling the rates and services provided by American Telephone and Telegraph (ATT), for example—and to build up countervailing power in the form of labor unions.

By the 1970s fears of cutthroat competition had been displaced by confidence that a fully competitive marketplace produced fair returns for everyone. Many instead feared that monopolies caused higher prices, less production, inefficiency, and less prosperity for all. As unions faded in strength, the government paid more attention to the damages that unfair competition could cause to consumers, especially in terms of higher prices, poorer service, and restricted choice. In 1982 the administration of Ronald Reagan used the Sherman Act to break up ATT into one long-distance company and six regional "Baby Bells," arguing that competition would benefit consumers and the economy as a whole. The pace of business takeovers quickened in the 1990s, but whenever one large corporation sought to acquire another it first had to obtain the approval of either the FTC or the Justice Department. Often the government demanded that certain subsidiaries be sold, so that the new company would not monopolize a particular geographical market. In 1999 a coalition of nineteen states and the federal Justice Department sued software company Microsoft. A highly publicized trial demonstrated that Chairman Bill Gates—the new Rockefeller—had strong-armed many companies to squelch the competitive threat posed by the Netscape browser. In 2000 the trial court ordered Microsoft split in two, to punish it and prevent future misbehavior. Gates argued that Microsoft always worked on behalf of the consumer, and that splitting the company would diminish efficiency and slow down the torrid pace of software development.

See also *Gilded Age; Hoover, Herbert; Labor Politics and Policy; New Deal; New Freedom; New Nationalism; Progressive Era; Roosevelt, Theodore; Taft, William Howard.*

RICHARD JENSEN, RENSSELAER POLYTECHNIC INSTITUTE

BIBLIOGRAPHY

Freyer, Tony. *Regulating Big Business: Antitrust in Great Britain and America, 1880–1990.* Cambridge: Cambridge University Press, 1992.

Letwin, William. *Law and Economic Policy in America: The Evolution of the Sherman Antitrust Act.* New York: Random House, 1965.

Peritz, Rudolph J. R. "Three Visions of Managed Competition, 1920–1950." *Antitrust Bulletin* 39 (spring 1994): 273–287.

Thorelli, Hans. *The Federal Antitrust Policy: Origination of an American Institution.* Baltimore: Johns Hopkins University Press, 1954.

APPORTIONMENT

Apportionment, the decennial exercise of allocating congressional seats to reflect population shifts, is fundamentally about political power. By distributing the 435 House of Representatives seats among the states, apportionment determines how loud a voice each state will have in Congress and in the electoral college.

THE REAPPORTIONMENT PROCESS

The reapportionment process begins with the U.S. census, which is taken every ten years and strives for an accurate count of the nation's population. Census forms are sent to households in the spring of years ending in "0." Census officials take several months to tabulate the numbers. By December 31 of the census year, the commerce secretary, whose department oversees the Census Bureau, is required by law to deliver to the president the state-by-state population counts as of April 1 of that year. Within a week after the next Congress convenes the following January, the president is required to provide the clerk of the U.S. House of Representatives the number of House representatives to which each state is entitled. Detailed population counts are delivered to the states by April 1 of the year following the census.

Reapportionment is different from redistricting, which is the process by which state legislatures and/or the courts redraw congressional district lines. However, the two go hand in hand: Though congressional lines cannot be redrawn until the official reapportionment is complete, House members and interested parties constantly monitor population trends and assess scenarios by which districts may be reshaped, long before that process is completed.

The population shifts signify a transfer of political power between the states. States gain seats when their populations increase more rapidly than the national average; states lose

In the reapportionment that followed the 1990 census, the Northeast and Midwest continued their decades-long loss of U.S. House seats.
CQ Press

seats when their populations increase less rapidly than the national average. Because the size of the House is fixed at 435 members, any one state's gain is another state's loss.

Reapportionment has far-ranging ramifications on House members, whose political careers could be greatly affected. For example, if a House member represents a slow-growing state, his or her district could be eliminated, or the district could be reshaped to include new constituents with whom the representative is not acquainted, which could undermine his or her political base.

Reapportionment can force incumbents to retire, run in another district, or even challenge other incumbents. For example, Illinois lost two seats after the 1990 reapportionment—one from downstate, one from the Chicago area. That spawned two incumbent-versus-incumbent battles. Downstate, Democratic representative Glenn Poshard defeated Rep. Terry Bruce in the 1992 primary. In a recrafted Chicago district, Democratic representative William Lipinski defeated Rep. Marty Russo in the primary.

Reapportionment also signals the changing contours of political power in the United States. For much of the nation's history, the industrial Midwest and Northeast were the dominant sources of political power. After the 1930 reapportionment, New York had 45 members, Pennsylvania 34, and Illinois 27—a combined total of 106 House seats, or about one-fourth of the total House membership.

Those three states have been hurt by the population explosion in the South and West. In 1998 New York, Pennsylvania, and Illinois together controlled just seventy-two House seats. The 1990 reapportionment left New York with just thirty-one House seats and marked the fifth consecutive decade the Empire State lost seats in reapportionment. Pennsylvania's House delegation has shrunk in every reapportionment since 1930.

California, which with fifty-two seats in 1998 controlled the nation's largest delegation, has gained seats in every reapportionment since 1860. Texas, which has gained seats or held even in every reapportionment since 1860, will control more House seats than New York following the 2000 reapportionment.

EARLY REAPPORTIONMENT METHODS

Although it has been more than two centuries since the first reapportionment, the fight over how to distribute House seats endures. Various methods of allotting congressional seats have been used over the centuries, and the historical debate over how to reapportion the House has involved some of the nation's most prominent political figures. Every method used has been the source of controversy: Rural jurisdictions have argued that some formulas of redistributing seats discriminate against them. In 1920 the process became

so fraught with controversy that no House reapportionment was performed.

Article I, section 2 of the Constitution requires that each state be assigned at least one House seat. Allocating one House seat to each of the fifty states, in a 435-member House, leaves 385 additional House seats to allocate among the states. But determining the fairest way to do so has been a knotty challenge.

The Constitution performed the first apportionment. The membership of the sixty-five-member House of Representatives was resolved as follows: New Hampshire received three seats; Massachusetts, eight; Rhode Island, one; Connecticut, five; New York, six; New Jersey, four; Pennsylvania, eight; Delaware, one; Maryland, six; Virginia, ten; North Carolina, five; South Carolina, five; and Georgia, three.

In the first reapportionment legislation considered after the 1790 census, Congress considered a bill that used the constitutional minimum of thirty thousand people as the size of each congressional district. But dividing a state's population by that number did not produce a whole number, for no state's population is an exact multiple of thirty thousand. Congress decided to resolve the quirk by awarding seats to states that had the largest fractional remainders. For example, a state with 200,000 inhabitants would see its apportionment rounded up from 6.67 representatives (200,000 divided by 30,000) to 7 representatives. But President George Washington vetoed the bill—the first presidential veto in American history. "The bill has allotted to eight of the States more than one for every thirty thousand," Washington said in his March 1792 veto message to Congress. (Today, if each House member had thirty thousand constituents, the House would have more than nine thousand members.)

The following month Congress approved a new bill that provided for a ratio of one House member for every thirty-three thousand citizens and fixed the total House membership at 105. It disregarded any remainders arising from dividing state populations by thirty-three thousand. Devised by then-secretary of state Thomas Jefferson, the formula is known as the method of rejected fractions or the method of greatest divisors.

Jefferson's method appeared to favor larger states over smaller states: A Vermont district would contain 42,766 inhabitants, a New Jersey district 35,911, and a Virginia district just 33,187. Nonetheless, Jefferson's method was used after each of the next four censuses. In the 1800 reapportionment, the thirty-three thousand persons-per-representative ratio was again used, yielding a total House membership of 141. A reapportionment bill enacted in 1811 fixed the ratio at thirty-five thousand, producing a total House membership of 181. Congress finally abandoned Jefferson's method in 1842, when it adopted an approach favored by Sen. Daniel Webster,

Whig-Mass. His plan fixed a ratio of one House member for every 70,680 people. The Webster method rounded the fractional remainders to the nearest whole number. Webster's plan actually reduced the size of the House for the only time in history. Otherwise, under the Jefferson and Webster methods, the House membership swelled as new states joined the Union and the populations of existing states grew. Following the 1850 census, Congress first fixed the size of the House and then distributed the seats. Under a formula proposed by Rep. Samuel F. Vinton, Whig-Ohio, the nation's population was divided by the desired number of representatives. The population of each state was divided by that ratio to determine each state's allotment of representatives. To reach the predetermined size of the House, additional representatives were assigned to states having the largest fractional remainders.

Six reapportionments were carried out using Vinton's method. However, the method also spawned a quirk known as the Alabama Paradox, according to which one state would lose a seat if the size of the House increased, even if there had been no proportional change in the state's population. It was revealed that under Vinton's method the state of Alabama would receive eight seats in a 299-member House but seven seats in a 300-member House.

In 1911 Congress fixed the House membership at 433, while providing for the addition of one representative apiece for Arizona and New Mexico, which became states the following year. The size of the House then reached 435, where it remains to this day. (The admission of Alaska and Hawaii as states in 1959 temporarily raised the House membership to 437.)

Following the censuses in 1910, 1930, and 1940, the House was reapportioned using a formula devised by Walter Willcox, a Cornell University statistician. The formula is known as the method of major fractions.

The 1920 census was the first to demonstrate that a majority of Americans lived in urban areas. Farmers, aware that the pending reapportionment would reduce their political clout, succeeded in postponing reapportionment legislation for nearly a decade. Rural representatives insisted that the farm population was undercounted and that large numbers of noncitizens were concentrated in the cities.

In early 1921 the House Census Committee, adhering to a long-standing principle that no state should lose seats in reapportionment, drafted a bill to increase the House membership from 435 to 483. The House voted to keep its membership at 435, and reapportionment legislation died when Congress adjourned in March. Other efforts to revive a reapportionment bill later in the decade also failed, and the House was not reapportioned until after the 1930 census.

MODERN TIMES: THE METHOD OF EQUAL PROPORTIONS

In 1941 Congress adopted the formula known as the method of equal proportions, which has been used ever since. The formula, which the National Academy of Sciences Committee on Apportionment in 1929 decided was the best reapportionment method, is not easily explainable. After each of the fifty states is allotted one representative as mandated by the Constitution, the formula assigns "priority numbers" for states to receive their next congressional seat. The priority numbers are calculated by dividing the state's population by the square root of $n(n-1)$, where n is the number of House seats for that state.

In 1992 the method of equal proportions came under attack by Montana officials, who alleged in a lawsuit that the method violated Article I, section 2 of the Constitution because it "does not achieve the greatest possible equality in the number of individuals per representative." The 1990 reapportionment reduced Montana's House delegation from two to one; under a different reapportionment formula, the state would have retained its two seats. A federal court agreed with Montana's position, but the Supreme Court reversed the ruling, saying that the method of equal proportions was constitutional and that Congress properly exercised its authority over reapportionment. "The decision to adopt the method of equal proportions was made by Congress after decades of experience, experimentation, and debate about the substance of the constitutional requirement," the Court wrote in *United States Department of Commerce v. Montana*. "Independent scholars supported both the basic decision to adopt a regular procedure to be followed after each census, and the particular decision to use the method of equal proportions. For a half-century the results of that method have been accepted by the States and the Nation. That history supports our conclusion that Congress had ample power to enact the statutory procedure in 1941 and to apply the method of equal proportions after the 1990 census."

Much of the recent reapportionment debate has focused on sampling, a statistical technique that corrects population undercounts of the census. The National Academy of Sciences and many statisticians have endorsed sampling. The concept generally receives praise from Democrats, who would benefit politically from sampling because it would boost population counts of undercounted minority groups who traditionally lean to their party. Most Republicans support the traditional head-count method, arguing that the Constitution mandates an "actual enumeration" of the population.

After the 1990 census, which resulted in an undercount of several million people, some communities—including New York City, which has a large minority population—filed suit, claiming that the unsampled numbers denied them representation. A federal judge in New York refused to overturn the George Bush administration's decision not to adjust the numbers.

In 1999 the Supreme Court ruled that the Census Act, as amended in 1976, prohibits the use of statistical sampling for reapportioning congressional seats *(Department of Commerce et al. v. United States House of Representatives et al.,* No. 98-404; *Clinton v. Glavin,* No. 98-564). It did not rule on the constitutionality of using sampling for redistricting.

See also *Census; Electoral College; Gerrymandering; Reapportionment Cases; Shaw v. Reno; Suffrage.*

GREGORY L. GIROUX, CONGRESSIONAL QUARTERLY

BIBLIOGRAPHY

Chafee, Zechariah, Jr. "Congressional Reapportionment." *Harvard Law Review* (1929): 1015–1047.

Moore, John L., ed. *Congressional Quarterly's Guide to U.S. Elections,* 3d ed. Washington, D.C.: Congressional Quarterly, 1994, 925–939.

Poston, Dudley L. "The U.S. Census and Congressional Reapportionment." *Society,* March 13, 1997.

Schmeckebier, Laurence F. *Congressional Reapportionment.* Washington, D.C.: Brookings Institution, 1941.

Schwab, Larry M. *The Impact of Congressional Reapportionment and Redistricting.* Lanham, Md.: University Press of America, 1988.

ARTHUR, CHESTER A.

President James A. Garfield's assassination in 1881 made Chester A. Arthur, who was born October 5, 1830, the twenty-first president. Before being elected to the vice presidency as a Republican in 1880, Arthur practiced law in New York, was an ardent opponent of slavery within the Republican Party, served on the New York governor's staff assisting with supplying troops during the Civil War, and was appointed by President Ulysses S. Grant as collector of the port of New York in 1871. The greatest achievement of Arthur's administration was enacting the Pendleton Civil Service Act (1883), which established the merit system of appointment to federal employment.

Diagnosed during his presidency with Bright's Disease, an inflammation of the filtering units of the kidneys, Arthur did not seek reelection in 1884. He completed his term and returned to New York, where he died November 18, 1886.

See also *Garfield, James A.*

JACQUELINE SMITH-MASON,
STATE COUNCIL OF HIGHER EDUCATION FOR VIRGINIA

BIBLIOGRAPHY

Poole, Susan D. *Chester A. Arthur: The President Who Reformed.* Reseda, Calif.: M. Bloomfield, 1977.

Reeves, Thomas C. *Gentleman Boss: The Life of Chester Alan Arthur.* Newtown, Conn.: American Political Biography Press, 1991.

ARTICLES OF CONFEDERATION

The Articles of Confederation, the first written constitution of the United States, helped govern the nation during its critical early years. Although often viewed as a failure that had to be replaced by the Constitution, the Articles of Confederation served as an important precedent for the Constitution.

EARLY EFFORTS AND OBSTACLES

Benjamin Franklin and Connecticut representative Silas Deane each proposed a union of the colonies before 1776, but the hope of reconciliation with Great Britain forestalled any serious discussion of their efforts. After the Second Continental Congress voted to declare independence, the delegates addressed the formation of a stronger centralized government, believing this to be necessary for the Revolutionary War effort.

On July 12, 1776, a committee led by John Dickinson of Pennsylvania submitted to the Continental Congress a plan that restricted the authority of states and extended congressional authority over diplomacy, western lands, and disputes between states. The debate that followed revealed the obstacles to union.

Despite a shared belief that Congress needed to have more authority in order to mobilize the war effort and attract foreign allies, delegates strongly disagreed over three major issues: apportionment of representation within Congress; allocation of the burden of paying national expenses, including the costs of the war; and control over the extensive western land claims of many states.

Large states desired that representation—hence, power—be related to wealth and population, but small states demanded one vote per state. As the basis for determining each state's financial obligations to the national government, the committee proposed apportioning the costs on the basis of total population. However, slave-holding states wanted only the white population to be counted for this purpose; and several of the smaller, more populous northern states argued for using territory, not population, as the standard. That consideration, in turn, brought into focus the matter of who would control the interior lands. States with extensive western claims (New York and Virginia, for example) rejected the committee's proposal that these lands should be made part of a larger national domain controlled by Congress.

Unanimous agreement could not be reached. In late 1776, pressing concerns of managing a war—including a series of military defeats that forced Congress to flee Philadelphia—led Congress to postpone further discussion.

AGREEMENT AND PROVISIONS

Inconclusive though the debates were, delegates agreed on many matters. Most delegates believed that Congress should have exclusive control over determining war and foreign policy and that states must retain control over internal policy, including the taxation of their citizens. An amendment to the committee's proposal, approved after Congress returned to Philadelphia in April 1777, suggests the type of dual sovereignty that the Articles of Confederation came to embody (in Article II). Each state would retain "its sovereignty, freedom and independence, and every power, jurisdiction and right" that was not "expressly delegated" to Congress. Although eleven of the thirteen states voted for this amendment, the old obstacles returned and prevented final action during the summer.

When Congress reconsidered and passed the articles in October 1777, the states were in the midst of a severe inflation caused by the dire wartime economic conditions. It was thought that a stronger central government might help gain approval of a more effective economic and financial policy, in part by increasing the public's confidence that the continental currency would retain its value and the nation's debts would be repaid in full. Furthermore, after an important American military victory at Saratoga, delegates had greater reason to hope that France could be drawn into the war, and they believed that a stronger national government might make France and other potential European allies more confident about the American cause.

Driven by these pragmatic factors as well as the consistent belief that Congress must exert more authority, the delegates overcame earlier disagreements. Each state would retain one vote (Article V), and states would keep their claims to western territory, but each state's contribution to a common national treasury would be based on the value of its real estate (Article VIII). On November 15, 1777, a final copy of the Articles of Confederation was signed and sent to the states for ratification.

Under the articles, thirteen in all, "the United States of America" (Article I) was officially recognized as a "firm league of friendship" among the states "for their common defense" (Article III), a "Union" that "shall be perpetual" (Article XIII). Article V governed the recruitment of Congress's membership and the method of voting on any measure. Each state would have between two and seven delegates, appointed by their state legislatures for annual terms of one year. Regardless of the number of delegates a state had at any time, they would vote as a unit (whether for a measure, against it, or divided), and no delegate could serve for more than three years out of any six.

Although the articles established no separate executive or judiciary, Article IX established a judicial method for resolving disputes between the states, and it also authorized legislative committees. In particular, Article IX authorized Congress to establish a "Committee of the States," which would have one delegate for each state, including a president who could serve for no more than a year at a time, to oversee the confederation's business when Congress itself was in recess.

Free trade was established among the states, which were to recognize each other's citizens and laws (Article IV). Article VI established Congress's supremacy over external matters, including the right to make foreign treaties. States were given the authority to raise and maintain militias and protect themselves if attacked (Article VII), but Congress had the exclusive power to declare war and maintain a navy (Article VI). Article XI offered Canada a place in the confederation.

Article IX, the most important, reiterated congressional authority over foreign policy. The articles also gave Congress the power to regulate currency and to borrow and appropriate funds, but these major actions, as well as declaring war, required the assent of a super majority of nine states. A simple majority of the states (seven of thirteen) sufficed to take such routine actions as standardizing weights and measures or establishing a system of post offices.

RATIFICATION AND WEAKNESSES

The final article (Article XIII) required the unanimous consent of all thirteen state legislatures to put the articles into effect or to make any subsequent amendments. Nine states ratified the Articles of Confederation by July 1778. The controversy over some states' western lands, however, kept several states from ratifying. Not until Virginia agreed to cede its extensive interior claims did Maryland's legislature ratify, and the articles went into effect in February 1781.

Even before ratification, the articles revealed weaknesses. Delegates had assumed that states would fulfill their financial and military obligations to the union. When states failed to meet their responsibilities, the national government suffered from lack of funds because Congress had no direct way of raising money or enforcing payment of the states' quotas. It proved impossible to obtain unanimous approval of an amendment that would have authorized Congress to impose a tax on imported goods.

Delegates might have hoped that these problems resulted from the pressures of war. Peacetime conditions, however, proved no solution. During the 1780s, James Madison and others became greatly alarmed over the tumultuous and often irresponsible character of state legislatures, which regularly failed to meet their financial obligations. When Massachusetts attempted fiscally responsible measures, the result was Shays's Rebellion, a revolt by Massachusetts backcountry farmers in 1786.

Nor were the Articles of Confederation effective in the realm of diplomacy. The inability of individual states to achieve "free and open" commerce, a result of British and French restrictions on American trade, inclined many states to grant Congress some regulatory powers over commerce. Well-defined state interests, however, particularly in Rhode Island, again prevented the unanimous approval necessary to amend the articles. In short, the states' diverse interests—particularly over commerce and debt payment—made defining a single national interest difficult and diminished the new nation's ability to command respect overseas. These conditions, along with concern about internal discord, raised the possibility that the confederation would break into either separate nations or clusters of states. The Philadelphia convention of 1787 represented an effort to amend the articles and supply the national government with more power.

LEGACY

The fairly rapid passage of the articles by Congress and the ratification by most of the states helped provide a sense of common principles during the War of Independence. Yet, because the articles were not ratified until so late in the war, they cannot be said to have been instrumental in America's military victory. Under the Articles of Confederation, Congress did ratify the Treaty of Paris of 1783, which confirmed American independence, and enacted the Northwest Ordinance of 1787, which guided early westward expansion. A greater legacy of the articles lies in the precedent they provided for the later founders, particularly regarding the allocation of national and state powers. More than anything else, the articles advanced the political and theoretical possibility of thirteen separate polities coming together to form a single nation.

See also *American Revolution; Constitution, U.S.; Constitutional Convention; Federalism; Northwest Ordinance; Shays's Rebellion; Super Majority.*

BRIAN D. SCHOEN, UNIVERSITY OF VIRGINIA

BIBLIOGRAPHY

Hoffert, Robert W. *A Politics of Tensions: The Articles of Confederation and American Political Ideas.* Niwot: University Press of Colorado, 1992.

Jensen, Merrill. *The Articles of Confederation: An Interpretation of the Social-Constitutional History of the American Revolution, 1774–1781.* Madison: University of Wisconsin Press, 1940.

Matson, Cathy D., and Peter S. Onuf. *A Union of Interests: Political and Economic Thought in Revolutionary America.* Lawrence: University Press of Kansas, 1990.

Rakove, Jack N. *The Beginnings of National Politics: An Interpretive History of the Continental Congress.* New York: Knopf, 1979.

Wood, Gordon S. *The Creation of the American Republic, 1776–1787.* Chapel Hill: University of North Carolina Press, 1969.

B

BANK WAR

The Bank War was a political contest between President Andrew Jackson and the president of the Second National Bank of the United States, Nicholas Biddle. It was a power struggle between two proud, willful, opinionated, and stubborn men. It began because Jackson believed the bank's enormous financial resources were used to control political elections, influence congressional legislation, and serve the interests of wealthy citizens. The bank, according to Jackson, threatened the liberty of the American people.

In his first message to Congress, in December 1829, the president demanded changes in the bank's operation. He charged that it had failed in its purpose of establishing a uniform and sound currency—which was nonsense. The bank had been chartered by the federal government in 1816 as a national financial institution that was to serve as a depository for the government's revenues and act as its agent in the collection of taxes. It was chartered for twenty years, with a capital stock of $35 million, one-fifth of which the government owned and the rest of which was owned by private investors. The stockholders elected the president and twenty members of the board of directors, who ran the institution. The government appointed five members of the board. The bank could issue bank notes redeemable in specie and also had the right to open branches in the major cities throughout the country. Almost immediately eighteen branches were established.

Under Biddle's astute leadership the bank grew in size and power and exercised enormous control over the nation's credit and currency. It also became involved in political elections and subsidized a number of influential statespersons.

Congress paid little heed to Jackson's call for reform of the bank. Instead, in 1832 it renewed the bank's charter for another twenty years, even though the current charter had four more years to run. Jackson promptly vetoed the bill, citing not only constitutional but economic, political, and social objections as well. In addition he criticized those who would use the federal government to advance their own interests. But his critics accused him of using the veto power to intrude into the legislative prerogatives of Congress and claim for the chief executive the power of making laws.

The bank issue was fought out in the presidential election of 1832, when Henry Clay, a Whig senator from Kentucky, ran against Jackson. Clay was decisively defeated, and after the election Jackson removed the government's deposits from the

This 1836 cartoon depicts Andrew Jackson attacking the Bank of the United States with his veto stick. Vice President Martin Van Buren, center, helps kill the monster, whose heads represent Nicholas Biddle, president of the bank, and directors of the state branches. *Library of Congress*

bank and placed them in state banks called "pet" banks. The Senate, under Clay's leadership, censured Jackson and his secretary of the treasury, Roger B. Taney. Biddle in turn retaliated against Jackson by tightening credit and calling in loans, an action that triggered a financial panic. But the action backfired. The House of Representatives concluded, after an investigation, that the bank's charter should not be renewed.

The immediate effect of the Bank War was that it precipitated the rise of the Whig Party; its long-lasting effect deprived the country of a central banking system until the passage of the Federal Reserve Act in 1913.

See also *Federal Reserve System; Jackson, Andrew; Panic of 1837; Whig Party.*

ROBERT V. REMINI, UNIVERSITY OF ILLINOIS AT CHICAGO

BIBLIOGRAPHY

Govan, Thomas P. *Nicholas Biddle, Nationalist and Public Banker.* Chicago: University of Chicago Press, 1959.

McFaul, John M. *The Politics of Jacksonian Finance.* Ithaca: Cornell University Press, 1972.

Remini, Robert V. *Andrew Jackson and the Bank War.* New York: Norton, 1968.

Wilburn, Jean Alexander. *Biddle's Bank: The Crucial Years.* New York: Columbia University Press, 1967.

BILL OF RIGHTS

The Constitution of 1787 did not include a bill of rights, even though most of the state constitutions at the time had one. A majority of Framers at the Philadelphia Convention did not believe a bill of rights was necessary in the national constitution, and some argued it would be dangerous to attempt to list all the rights of the people. If any were left out, men like James Madison and Alexander Hamilton argued, then the national government might trample on these rights. Elbridge Gerry of Massachusetts and George Mason of Virginia refused to sign the final constitution, citing, among other reasons, the lack of a bill of rights. During the ratification struggle many rank-and-file Antifederalists opposed the Constitution solely because of their concern that the national government would encroach on the people's rights without a bill of rights. However, most of the leading opponents of the Constitution, such as Patrick Henry and Richard Henry Lee, opposed a strong central government for more narrow political reasons, especially fears of diminishing state powers, even though they used the lack of a bill of rights to gain support for their cause.

During the ratification struggle James Madison denied the necessity of a bill of rights, but after ratification he agreed during his campaign for Congress to introduce amendments. Following up on this promise, Madison introduced a series of amendments in the First Congress, and in the fall of 1789 they were sent to the states for ratification. Antifederalists, like Henry, now opposed the amendments, because they knew that if the amendments were ratified, most opposition to the Constitution would disappear, as in fact it did after 1791 when ten amendments, the Bill of Rights, were ratified.

BILL OF RIGHTS
IN THE NINETEENTH CENTURY

Until World War I the Bill of Rights was rarely used to protect fundamental liberties. The Sedition Act of 1798 flagrantly violated the rights of freedom of speech and press in the First Amendment, but no federal judge ruled it unconstitutional. In the 1830s and 1840s the House of Representatives passed a series of "gag rules," under which the House refused to allow antislavery petitions to be read or sent to any committee, despite the provision in the First Amendment guaranteeing the right to petition Congress. In *Barron v. Baltimore* (1833) the Supreme Court ruled that the Bill of Rights limited the actions of only the national government and did not restrain the states. The Court reiterated this view in *Permoli v. New Orleans* (1845).

In *Dred Scott v. Sandford* (1857) the Supreme Court used the Fifth Amendment to strike down a federal ban on slavery in the territories. The amendment prohibits the national government from denying anyone "life, liberty, or property, without due process of law." Abolitionists argued this clause could be applied to free any slave within the jurisdiction of the national government, but Chief Justice Roger B. Taney applied the clause not to give freedom to slaves, but to protect the property interest of masters.

After the Civil War, Congress attempted to apply most of the Bill of Rights to the states, by declaring in the Fourteenth Amendment that no state could deprive people of "the privileges or immunities of citizens of the United States." Congress wanted to insure that former slaves in the South would have free speech, fair trials, and even the right to serve in the militia. However, in *The Slaughterhouse Cases* (1873), the Supreme Court ruled that the Fourteenth Amendment was not designed to guarantee these rights. Thus the states remained free to deny fundamental liberties to their citizens until the 1920s and 1930s, when the Supreme Court began to selectively apply the Bill of Rights to the states.

Meanwhile, in the 1870s and 1880s Congress continued to ignore First Amendment rights, by denying religious freedom to Mormons and Native Americans. In such cases as *Reynolds v. United States* (1879) and *Davis v. Beason* (1890) the Supreme Court upheld the prosecutions of Mormons for practicing or even believing in polygamy. In the 1890s Congress revoked the charter of the Mormon Church and seized its property. These actions were reversed after the church changed its theology and renounced polygamy. During this period Congress also passed the Comstock Law (1873), which the government used to suppress literature on birth control and sex education, in what would today be seen as a violation of the First Amendment.

EMERGENCE OF THE MODERN BILL OF RIGHTS

During World War I Congress passed a series of laws designed to suppress antiwar dissent. In *Schenck v. United States* (1919) the Supreme Court, for the first time, offered an interpretation of the meaning of the First Amendment. Justice Oliver Wendell Holmes Jr., speaking for the Court, interpreted free speech narrowly, in upholding a ten-year sentence for an opponent of the draft. Later that year, in *Abrams v. United States,* Holmes and Justice Louis D. Brandeis, this time dissenting, offered a more libertarian view of freedom of expression. Gradually the Court moved toward the view of Holmes and Brandeis that freedom of speech is essential to a flourishing democracy. By the 1960s the courts regularly protected the freedom of expression of radicals and revolutionaries, as well as artists whose work in an earlier period might have been deemed obscene.

Starting in the 1920s the Court, through a process known as selective incorporation, began to apply most, but not all, provisions of the Bill of Rights to the states. This practice reached a crescendo in the 1950s and 1960s as the Court began to require the states to provide fair trials and due process to criminal defendants, denied the power of the states to persecute some religious minorities, struck down state bans on birth control and abortion, and ruled that religiously motivated parents could remove their children from schools. The most controversial of these decisions involved criminal justice and abortion. In *Gideon v. Wainwright* (1963) and *Miranda v. Arizona* (1966) the Court, under Chief Justice Earl Warren, held that an arrested person had a right to an attorney from arrest through trial, as well as a right to remain silent and a right not to be coerced or forced to confess to arresting officers. Conservative politicians harshly criticized *Miranda* and similar cases, although in reality the Warren Court decisions probably led to few guilty persons being released from custody. Eventually, police officials endorsed these decisions for providing a fairer criminal justice system with clear guidelines as to what the police can and cannot do. In *Griswold v. Connecticut* (1966) and *Roe v. Wade* (1971) the Court upheld the right of a women to obtain birth control or even to terminate a pregnancy. Both decisions stemmed from a "right to privacy" that the Court construed from various parts of the Bill of Rights, including those limiting govern-

ment searches and the right to freedom of speech. Although criticized by conservatives and some religious groups, a large majority of Americans, in almost all opinion polls, have supported these opinions.

Tied to these changes in civil liberties was an even more important change in civil rights, as the Court stimulated the dismantling of racial segregation in America. Often the two changes were intertwined. The Court decision in *New York Times v. Sullivan* (1961), which liberated the press from archaic rules that made frank reporting on the actions of politicians difficult, resulted from the southern civil rights struggle. Sullivan, a minor Alabama official, tried to stop northerners from reporting on the mistreatment of blacks in the South by suing the paper for libel, counting on a sympathetic jury of whites in the South to award him a substantial judgment. The jury did find for Sullivan, but the Supreme Court overturned this result. Similarly, in *Loving v. Virginia* (1967) the Supreme Court struck down state bans on interracial marriages, partly on the basis of liberties protected in the Bill of Rights.

Roe v. Wade was symbolic of a "rights revolution" that began under Chief Justice Warren and continued under Chief Justice Warren Burger. In 1968 Richard Nixon had directed much of his successful presidential campaign at the Supreme Court and at the libertarian views of the Warren Court that had expanded the reach of the Bill of Rights. Nixon appointed Chief Justice Burger and Associate Justice Harry Blackmun to roll back the libertarian decisions of the Warren Court. This, however, did not happen: Nixon's own appointee (Blackmun) wrote the decision in *Roe.*

Presidents Ronald Reagan and George Bush continued Nixon's attack on civil liberties and the Bill of Rights by appointing four conservative justices—Sandra Day O'Connor, Anthony Kennedy, Antonin Scalia, and Clarence Thomas—and elevating one Nixon appointee, William Rehnquist, to the chief justiceship. Although they stemmed the "rights revolution," even these conservatives have not fully undermined the Warren Court's accomplishment of placing the Bill of Rights and the Fourteenth Amendment at the center of constitutional law.

CONTEMPORARY BILL OF RIGHTS

At the political level the Bill of Rights remains a potent icon for American liberty. Politicians on the right and the left are vulnerable if they attack the core American values embodied in the Bill of Rights, such as freedom of speech, press, and religion. While demanding law enforcement that protects them from criminals, most Americans have also come to see that the due process protections of the Bill of Rights are necessary to a free state, just as they understand that a free society must tolerate speech that many might find disagreeable or offensive.

In arguing against the need for a Bill of Rights, Madison asserted that "parchment barriers" would never stop a determined majority in Congress from trampling on the liberty of the people. American history offers numerous examples—from the Sedition Act of 1798 to numerous laws passed by southern legislatures to prevent civil rights demonstrations—illustrating Madison's point. But, in a letter to Thomas Jefferson, Madison set out what he thought was the best argument for a Bill of Rights. He argued that "political truths declared" in a "solemn manner" would "acquire by degrees the character of fundamental maxims of free Government, and as they become incorporated with the national sentiment, counteract the impulses of interest and passion." This view dovetailed with Madison's assertion in *Federalist 57* that liberty is ultimately protected, not by parchment barriers, but by the "vigilant . . . spirit which actuates the people of America." This history of the Bill of Rights in American politics shows how correct Madison was, and how, after two hundred years, the rights set out in the first ten amendments to the Constitution have been accepted by most Americans as part of their political birthright, even if they are often unable to articulate where those rights come from, or what part of the Constitution protects them.

See also *Comstock Act; Constitution, U.S.; Constitutional Amendments; Federalism; Gag Rule; Sedition Act of 1798.*

PAUL FINKELMAN, UNIVERSITY OF TULSA COLLEGE OF LAW

BIBLIOGRAPHY

Finkelman, Paul. "James Madison and the Bill of Rights: A Reluctant Paternity." *Supreme Court Review* 1990 (1991): 301–347.

Levy, Leonard W. *Origins of the Bill of Rights.* New Haven: Yale University Press, 1999.

Urofsky, Melvin, and Paul Finkelman. *A March of Liberty: A Constitutional History of the United States.* New York: Oxford University Press, 2001.

BLACK PANTHERS

By the mid-1960s many black Americans had become dissatisfied with the nonviolent tactics and integrationist goals of the civil rights movement. Tired of turning the other cheek while obtaining little substantive relief from their oppression, many young, urban blacks, especially in the North and West, began shifting away from the "We Shall Overcome" approach to civil rights. Instead, they embraced Black Power. With its members clad in uniforms of black leather jackets, black pants, and black berets, spouting their provocative terminology ("Off the pigs!"), and toting their omnipresent shotguns, the Black Panther Party quickly became the most prominent and controversial Black Power organization.

Founded in October 1966 in Oakland, California, by Huey P. Newton and Bobby Seale, the party gained the awe and admiration of Oakland's black community by patrolling the community armed with guns and lawbooks, policing the police force's interaction with black citizens. Inspired by the organization's brash commitment to armed self-defense and self-determination of black communities, thousands of blacks in some forty cities across the country belonged to Panther chapters by 1969. Chapter activities included community "survival programs," such as free health clinics and free breakfast for children.

Initially, the party was a black nationalist organization seeking "land, bread, housing, education, clothing, justice, and peace" for black people. The Panther Party's ideology evolved into an "intercommunal" philosophy advocating revolutionary change for the dispossessed of the world. From 1967 to 1971 the Panthers were at the forefront of a burgeoning radical anti-imperialist, anticapitalist movement in the United States, forming alliances with white leftist organizations and various Third World socialist movements. By the mid-1970s, however, internal dissension and police and FBI repression had caused the organization's membership and influence to decline precipitously.

See also *African American Politics; Civil Rights Movement.*

KARA MILES TURNER, VIRGINIA STATE UNIVERSITY

BIBLIOGRAPHY

Foner, Philip S., ed. *The Black Panthers Speak.* Philadelphia: J. B. Lippincott, 1970.

Jones, Charles E., ed. *The Black Panther Party Reconsidered.* Baltimore: Black Classic Press, 1998.

Van Deburg, William L. *New Day in Babylon: The Black Power Movement and American Culture, 1965–1975.* Chicago: University of Chicago Press, 1992.

BLACK SUFFRAGE

African Americans' voting rights have influenced U.S. elections since the nation's beginning. Black voters have always been political actors, and since the eighteenth century, black suffrage has been a political issue for white Americans.

FROM THE AMERICAN REVOLUTION TO THE CIVIL WAR

When the American Revolution began, most blacks in the new United States were slaves, and the few who were free were almost universally excluded from voting. During the Revolution, however, great changes began. In 1778 the Massachusetts legislature proposed a constitution, but to the surprise of the state's leaders, citizens rejected it in part because it neither ended slavery nor enfranchised nonwhites. A new constitution, drafted by John Adams and ratified in 1780, enfranchised all adult males, without regard to race, and also led to emancipation as a consequence of blacks' appeals to the courts and judicial interpretations in favor of freedom. Slavery ended in Massachusetts in the 1780s and throughout the North by the 1830s, and free black men gained the right to vote in many states.

By the 1790s free blacks could also vote on the same basis as whites in New Hampshire, New Jersey, New York, North Carolina, Pennsylvania, and the fourteenth state, Vermont. Although not a significant factor in most elections, blacks did participate in the political process leading to the creation of the new nation. When Tennessee became a state in 1798 it followed North Carolina's lead, and when Maine became a state in 1820 it echoed Massachusetts, as both new states granted black suffrage. Rhode Island granted black residents voting rights in 1842 when it adopted its first state constitution.

African Americans in the early national period generally voted Federalist, in part because Thomas Jefferson and the other leaders of the Democratic-Republicans were slave-owning southerners, and in part because the party in the North consistently used race-baiting tactics and rhetoric in political campaigns. Jefferson's followers and their successors opposed voting rights for black men.

In 1821, for example, the Jeffersonians in the New York state constitutional convention tried to disfranchise all blacks. At the time New York had a property requirement for voting. The Jeffersonians tried to eliminate the property requirement for whites while prohibiting blacks from voting at all. Federalists, led by the jurist James Kent, defeated the attempt to disfranchise blacks altogether but were unable to win equal suffrage for them. Thus, from 1821 until the Civil War era, black New Yorkers could vote only if they held sufficient property, whereas whites could vote without holding any property.

Continuing their war on black suffrage in the 1830s, the Jacksonian Democrats disfranchised free blacks in New Jersey, Pennsylvania, North Carolina, and Tennessee. Where blacks could vote—in all of New England except Connecticut, and in New York if they held sufficient property—they voted for Whigs, Liberty Party candidates, Free Soilers, and (beginning in 1856) Republicans. In the 1850s Republicans tried but failed to gain equal suffrage for all races in Connecticut, New York, and Wisconsin.

RECONSTRUCTION AND ROLLBACK

The Civil War permanently altered American race relations, including African Americans' right to vote. Shortly before President Abraham Lincoln was assassinated in 1865, he endorsed limited black suffrage, arguing that at a minimum blacks who had served in the U.S. Army should be able to vote. In the aftermath of Union victory, Congress acted in 1866 to foster black suffrage. Section 2 of the Fourteenth Amendment, passed that year and sent to the states for ratification, offered states a choice: grant black men the right to vote, or have their representation decreased in proportion to the number of men not permitted to vote. That formula would not affect states with few black residents, but it would impact many states in the South. Ten of the eleven former states of the Confederacy (all but Tennessee) rejected the amendment, however, so the amendment was in jeopardy of failure.

Congress found another way to address the problem of black voting and representation. In the Reconstruction Acts of March 1867, Congress required ratification of the Fourteenth Amendment, plus enfranchisement of black men, before any of the ten states could be restored to normal political relations. In short, the federal government forced those ten former Confederate states to ratify the Fourteenth Amendment and to accept black suffrage. Congress required the registration of black voters in those states, and the army enforced the new law. Black men voted in elections to a constitutional convention in each of the ten states, and the new constitution that was to be framed had to establish black voting rights. In 1867, therefore, black men voted for the first time in such states as Georgia, Alabama, and Mississippi.

During Reconstruction, Congress also passed other measures supporting black voting rights. The Fifteenth Amendment, ratified in 1870, provided that "The right of citizens of the United States to vote shall not be denied or abridged by the United States or any State on account of race, color, or previous condition of servitude." The Fifteenth Amendment applied to all the states, not just the ten subjected to the Reconstruction Acts. Beginning in the late 1860s, not only did black voters across the nation go to the polls, but many black candidates were elected to state and local office, and black congressmen were elected from eight southern states. Except during a single session of Congress, at least one black southerner was serving in Congress between 1870 and 1901.

Black voting rights came under pressure across the South, however. During Reconstruction, as black men went to the polls and ran for office, the Ku Klux Klan and other white terrorist organizations did much to diminish black political power through violence and intimidation. For a time, Congress took action against such groups. By 1900, however, a variety of state measures cut black voting back to a very low level. Mississippi exemplified the ingenuity and insistence with which white southerners went about the task of disfranchising black citizens. A poll tax would put an economic obstacle in the way of black voting. Residence requirements

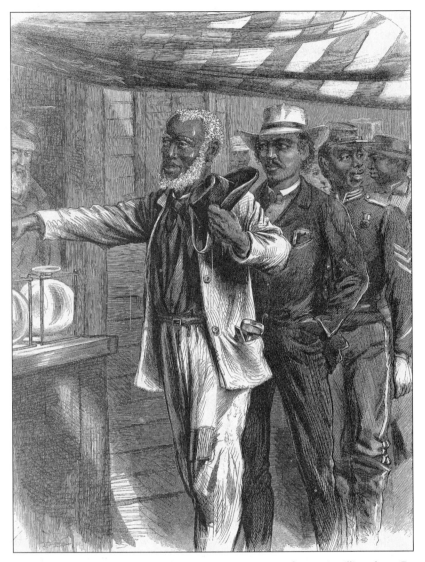

The collapse of the Confederacy led to the emancipation of some 4 million slaves. By 1867, hundreds of thousands of freedmen were voting in southern elections. *Library of Congress*

would impede voting by sharecroppers and tenant farmers who changed location from one year to the next. A literacy test and an "understanding" requirement would force prospective voters to demonstrate an ability to read or explain a section of the state constitution to the satisfaction of white registrars.

BLACK SUFFRAGE: THE NORTH, THE SOUTH, AND THE NATION

After the adoption of the Fifteenth Amendment, black men could vote everywhere in the North and the South. From then on, black northerners voted, and they became a significant factor in northern elections in the twentieth century. By contrast, voting by black southerners—of whom there were

far more until well into the twentieth century—diminished. Black voting rights were so powerful an issue for white voters in the South that black voting was largely eliminated by about 1900 across most of the region.

The South eliminated the black voter, and the nation abandoned him. In *United States v. Reese* (1876) the Supreme Court held that the Fifteenth Amendment did not confer a right to vote on black citizens, but only prevented racial discrimination in voting. Therefore, "nonracial" limitations on voting were permissible. By the 1890s, as in Mississippi, the white "redeemer" governments had begun to use literacy tests, poll taxes, and various voter registration techniques to eliminate the black vote.

In *Williams v. Mississippi* (1898) the Supreme Court followed its reasoning in *United States v. Reese* and approved Mississippi's disfranchisement plan, which had effectively removed blacks from the voter registration rolls. Although Mississippi had established new obstacles to voting primarily in order to eliminate black citizens from the electorate, its legislation did not specify racial considerations and therefore, according to the Court, did not violate the Fifteenth Amendment. Other states took advantage of the Court's interpretation to perfect their own means of black disfranchisement. Moreover, violence accomplished what the law did not. Riots by whites in Wilmington, North Carolina (1898), and Atlanta, Georgia (1906), led to a virtual end to black voting in those two states.

THE TWENTIETH-CENTURY STRUGGLE FOR BLACK VOTING RIGHTS IN THE SOUTH

Twentieth-century efforts by black southerners to regain their voting rights took two forms. *Williams v. Mississippi,* although unsuccessful, displayed black southerners' willingness to go to court in support of their constitutional right to vote, and such efforts persisted into the 1960s. In a second approach, black southerners regained the right to vote by moving to the North.

The black migration out of the South, which grew to great magnitude during World War I and lasted through the 1950s, led to large pockets of black voters in many cities in the North and West, and these growing concentrations of black voters eventually led to the election of black officeholders. For example, Oscar DePriest, an Alabama native elected by black voters who had been born in the South but had moved to Illinois, became Chicago's first black alderman in 1918, and in 1928 he was elected the first black congressman from a northern state. New York City's Harlem district elected Adam Clayton Powell Jr. to Congress in 1944. Black political power was on the rise in northern cities and states.

In the South, black disfranchisement persisted. Only rarely before the 1940s did the Supreme Court interpret the Fourteenth Amendment or the Fifteenth Amendment to support voting rights for African Americans. In *United States v. Guinn* (1915) the Court did strike down Oklahoma's "grandfather clause." That rule had exempted voters from literacy tests if their fathers or grandfathers had been legal voters before 1867, and since the escape hatch let through only whites, the Court struck it down. Similarly, in *Nixon v. Herndon* (1927) the Court struck down Texas's practice of not allowing blacks to vote in primary elections. However, states easily could get around both decisions. When literacy tests were administered, white test givers could make sure that most blacks failed while most whites passed. As for the white Democratic primary, Texas turned the primary election process over to the Democratic Party, which as a private organization was constitutionally able to discriminate, as the Court ruled in *Nixon v. Condon* (1932). In *Smith v. Allwright* (1944), however, the Court finally held that racial discrimination in primary elections violated the Constitution, regardless of who ran the primaries.

Black suffrage in most of the South remained very limited until the mid-1960s. Reflecting in part the presence of black voters in the North, Congress passed laws in 1957 and 1960 designed to reduce the barriers to black voting in the South, but to little effect. Attempts to register black voters in Mississippi and other Deep South states led to riots, police beatings of would-be voters, and even the murder of civil rights workers. Revulsion against the violence in the South helped spur passage of the Voting Rights Act of 1965, a law that eliminated literacy tests and provided federal enforcement to guarantee minority suffrage. By constitutional amendment and Supreme Court decision, moreover, the poll tax was eliminated as an obstacle to voting in federal or state elections. The Supreme Court upheld the 1965 Voting Rights Act in *South Carolina v. Katzenbach* (1966) and *Katzenbach v. Morgan* (1966). With the passage of the 1965 act (and its renewal in 1970, 1975, and 1992), black voting became a significant factor in local, state, and national elections in the South as well as the North.

BLACK VOTING RIGHTS, PARTY IDENTIFICATION, AND REPRESENTATION

From the 1850s until the 1930s black voters in the North and in the South generally supported the Republican Party, the party of Lincoln and emancipation. Especially in the South, however, the Republican Party purged blacks from positions of power by the 1920s. In the 1930s and 1940s, by contrast, the Democratic Party began to encourage and welcome black voters. The shift did not happen everywhere or all at once, and as late as the 1960s many blacks were Republicans, especially in New York and Massachusetts. In 1964, however, the Republican Party's nominee for the presidency was Barry Goldwater, who had voted against the 1964 Civil Rights Act. After that, virtually all African Americans supported the Democratic Party.

In the 1870s and again by the 1970s, black voters demonstrated their political power by influencing the political positions of white candidates and officeholders and by electing black candidates to public office. By the 1970s blacks represented several congressional districts in the North, and by the 1990s black mayors had been elected in many major cities, including cities with white majorities, such as Los Angeles, New York, Chicago, Minneapolis, and Denver. Black candidates proved that they could win statewide elections, too. In 1966 Massachusetts elected an African American, Edward W. Brooke, to the U.S. Senate, where he served two full terms, and in 1992 Carol Moseley-Braun of Illinois became the first black woman elected to the Senate. In the South, L. Douglas Wilder was elected governor of Virginia in 1989.

After 1965, African Americans finally secured the right to vote everywhere, yet black representation remained in doubt. Whites continued to be generally unwilling to vote in large numbers for black candidates. Starting in the 1970s, some states, in their congressional redistricting, deliberately created "majority-minority districts" that would ensure the election of blacks to Congress. In *Shaw v. Reno* (1993) and subsequent cases, however, the Supreme Court found such districts unconstitutional. Thus, at the beginning of the twenty-first century the major issue surrounding black suffrage was not the right to vote but the meaning of that vote.

See also *African American Politics; Civil Rights Acts (Modern); Civil Rights Movement; Constitutional Amendments; Democratic Party; Gerrymandering; Jacksonian Democracy; Political Parties; Poll Tax; Reconstruction; Republican Party;* Shaw v. Reno; *Suffrage; Supreme Court.*

PAUL FINKELMAN, UNIVERSITY OF TULSA COLLEGE OF LAW, AND PETER WALLENSTEIN, VIRGINIA POLYTECHNIC INSTITUTE AND STATE UNIVERSITY

BIBLIOGRAPHY

Gillette, William. *The Right to Vote: Politics and the Passage of the Fifteenth Amendment.* Baltimore: Johns Hopkins University Press, 1965.

Kousser, J. Morgan. *The Shaping of Southern Politics: Suffrage Restriction and the Establishment of the One-Party South, 1880–1910.* New Haven: Yale University Press, 1974.

————. *Colorblind Injustice: Minority Voting Rights and the Undoing of the Second Reconstruction.* Chapel Hill: University of North Carolina Press, 1999.

Lawson, Steven F. *Black Ballots: Voting Rights in the South, 1944–1969.* New York: Columbia University Press, 1976.

Nieman, Donald G. *Promises to Keep: African-Americans and the Constitutional Order, 1776 to the Present.* New York: Oxford University Press, 1991.

BONUS MARCH

In late May 1932, approximately 330 unemployed World War I veterans arrived in Washington, D.C., to demand enactment of a bill pending in Congress that would authorize immediate distribution of their military pensions, or bonuses. Earlier, in February, President Herbert Hoover, desperately trying to balance the budget during the early period of the Great Depression, had vetoed a bill authorizing a loan of 50 percent on these military pensions. Democrats then proposed that the entire bonus be paid in cash.

To increase pressure for legislative approval, more than fifteen thousand unemployed veterans from across the United States converged on the capital to urge immediate and full payment of their pensions. This so-called Bonus Expeditionary Force remained in Washington for more than a month, living in rough and unsanitary conditions, determined to stay until Congress authorized a cash payment. When that legislation failed, Congress provided funds for the veterans to return home. All except two thousand dispersed. When Washington, D.C., police tried to remove the remaining bonus marchers, two officers and two veterans were killed. On July 28, Hoover ordered federal troops—with fixed bayonets, cavalry, and tanks—under the command of Gen. Douglas MacArthur to complete the removal of the protesters.

Hoover's use of troops against unarmed, disciplined, impoverished veterans was met with a nationwide wave of angry criticism and offered additional proof to the president's growing number of critics that his administration had little compassion for, or understanding of, the nation's poor. Although public sentiment was not sympathetic to the marchers, Americans generally disagreed with the government's actions.

See also Great Depression; Hoover, Herbert C.; Marches on Washington; World War I.

MARK J. CONNOLLY, DEVRY INSTITUTE OF TECHNOLOGY

BIBLIOGRAPHY

Daniels, Roger. *Bonus March: An Episode of the Great Depression.* Westport, Conn.: Greenwood Press, 1971.

BRECKINRIDGE DEMOCRATS

In 1860 the Democratic Party divided over slavery. Its northern wing nominated Sen. Stephen A. Douglas of Illinois as its presidential candidate. John C. Breckinridge (1821–1875) of Kentucky, the incumbent vice president under President James Buchanan, accepted the proslavery southern wing's nomination. The platforms of the Douglas and Breckinridge Democrats agreed that the Fugitive Slave Law must be enforced, but the Breckinridge Democrats also insisted on a federal slave code for the territories and on the right of slaveholders to take their slave property into the western territories, decisions that the Douglas platform said it would leave to the Supreme Court and that the Republican Party and its candidate, Abraham Lincoln, absolutely opposed. The four-way election also included John Bell of the Constitutional Union Party.

The Breckinridge Democrats placed third in popular votes behind Lincoln and Douglas and, by winning eleven of the fifteen slave states, second in electoral votes with seventy-two. Lincoln took only 40 percent of the popular vote, but

John C. Breckinridge   *Library of Congress*

his victory in the electoral college did not depend on a divided opposition, for he took an absolute majority in enough northern states to win regardless. Breckinridge's support came mostly from the South, although it did not necessarily reflect the degree of proslavery sentiment in the region, since some voters who later supported secession voted for Douglas or Bell, and many of Beckinridge's supporters were traditional Democrats who did not see themselves as voting on secession. Indeed, Breckinridge saw himself as the only candidate who could prevent secession, since if he won, the South would happily remain in the Union.

Lincoln's election led to secession by seven Deep South states, and four more joined the Confederacy soon after his inauguration. Before Lincoln's inauguration, Vice President Breckinridge worked with other Democrats in Washington to fashion a compromise that might prevent a civil war. On the main point of contention, however, slavery in the territories, Lincoln would not budge, so no settlement could be reached. Breckinridge, while still vice president, had been elected to the U.S. Senate, his term to begin when his vice presidency ended. As a senator in 1861 he defended the right of southern states to secede and opposed Lincoln's efforts to raise an army.

By late 1861 Union and Confederate forces alike had entered Kentucky, and Breckinridge offered his services to the Confederacy. He resigned from the Senate before it expelled him for his pro–Confederate behavior. He served as a major general in the Confederate army and then as Confederate secretary of war. When the war ended with the Confederacy's defeat and slavery's abolition, the particular issues that had animated Breckinridge's presidential bid in 1860 no longer mattered. Yet more general issues regarding race and power long persisted.

See also *Democratic Party; Slavery; Third Parties.*

RON dePAOLO, INDEPENDENT AUTHOR

BIBLIOGRAPHY

Davis, William C. *Breckinridge: Statesman, Soldier, Symbol.* Baton Rouge: Louisiana State University Press, 1974.

BROWN V. BOARD OF EDUCATION OF TOPEKA

In *Brown v. Board of Education* (1954) the Supreme Court prohibited public schools from segregating pupils by race. The unanimous decision marked a defining moment in the effort by African Americans to attain legal equality. It also engendered determined resistance, first in the

South and later in other parts of the country. Five decades later, racial separation remained widespread in public schools because of residential segregation, and many African Americans viewed other educational reforms as more important than school desegregation.

RULING AGAINST SEGREGATION

While racial segregation existed before the Civil War, the practice spread after Reconstruction ended. The Supreme Court sanctioned segregation in an 1896 decision, *Plessy v. Ferguson,* upholding a Louisiana law requiring racial segregation in railroad cars. Segregation, the Court said, did not "necessarily imply the inferiority of one race to the other."

By the late 1930s the National Association for the Advancement of Colored People (NAACP) and its chief legal strategist, Charles Hamilton Houston, had begun laying the groundwork for challenging the "separate but equal" doctrine in public schools. By 1950 the NAACP had successfully challenged segregation in public graduate and law schools in a number of states. Building upon those victories, Thurgood Marshall, who had become head of the NAACP's legal team, worked to develop cases challenging segregation in secondary and elementary schools.

The Supreme Court agreed to rule on the issue in four cases involving local school systems in southern and border states—Topeka, Kansas; Clarendon County, South Carolina; Prince Edward County, Virginia; and New Castle County, Delaware—and a fifth case from Washington, D.C. The Topeka case was brought in the name of Linda Carol Brown, who attended an all-black elementary school a mile from her home even though an all-white school was closer. A federal district court found that segregation was detrimental to black children but ruled that there was no constitutional violation because the black and white primary schools were substantially equal.

After hearing the appeals in the five cases in December 1952, the justices were divided and scheduled a second round of arguments. By the time of the reargument in December 1953, Chief Justice Fred Vinson had died and been succeeded by Earl Warren, the popular, three-term Republican governor of California.

Warren strove to produce a unanimous decision striking down racial segregation. He secured the agreement of the other justices both by writing an opinion free of recrimination against the South and by promising gradual enforcement of desegregation. The decision, announced May 17, 1954, declared that racial segregation in schools violated the Equal Protection Clause of the Fourteenth Amendment. "Separate educational facilities are inherently unequal," Warren wrote. A year later the Court issued a follow-up ruling. It required

Under the rule of separate but equal established in *Plessy v. Ferguson* (1896), states could require racial separation if facilities for blacks and whites were of equal quality. In public education black schools were rarely equal to those reserved for whites. The *Brown* decision reversed *Plessy*.   *Library of Congress*

school officials to comply with the ruling not immediately but instead "with all deliberate speed."

IMPLEMENTATION AND COURT SUPERVISION

Despite Warren's efforts, the ruling provoked a firestorm of criticism in the South. Southern leaders promised "massive resistance" to the decision and developed various strategies of defiance or evasion. More than one hundred members of Congress signed the so-called Southern Manifesto in 1956 declaring the decision illegitimate. President Dwight D. Eisenhower lent no support to the ruling beyond promising to enforce the law.

The Supreme Court initially left implementation of the ruling largely to the lower federal courts, which took on the role of fashioning desegregation decrees and superintending compliance. By the 1960s the Supreme Court stepped in to bar "freedom of choice" pupil assignment plans and, in 1968, to insist on no further delays in developing desegregation plans.

Also in 1968 Republican Richard Nixon campaigned for the presidency with a so-called southern strategy aimed at exploiting regional discontent with the Democratic Party's pro–civil rights stance. As president, Nixon reshaped the Court by appointing a conservative federal judge, Warren Burger, as chief justice in 1969 and naming three other conservative-to-moderate justices.

At first, the Burger Court backed continued desegregation. Burger himself wrote a unanimous opinion in a North Carolina case, *Swann v. Charlotte-Mecklenburg County Board of Education* (1971), that upheld the use of busing as a desegregation tool. Court-ordered plans requiring busing of students to achieve racial balance provoked fierce opposition not just in the South but in such northern cities and western cities as Boston, Detroit, and Denver. By 1974 the Court began to retreat. By a 5–4 vote, it ruled in the Detroit case that federal judges had no authority to combine inner city schools with suburban districts in order to achieve desegregation. Two years later the Court said school districts were not required to maintain a specific racial balance if shifting residential patterns resulted in "resegregation."

Gradually, the goal of school integration faded. By the 1990s the Supreme Court was signaling to federal courts that they should withdraw from continued supervision of desegregation decrees. Racial isolation, which had been declining since the 1960s, began to increase. As the 1990s began, nearly two-thirds of black students were attending schools with predominantly minority enrollment.

See also *Civil Rights Acts (Modern); Civil Rights Movement; Eisenhower, Dwight D.; Supreme Court.*

KENNETH JOST, CONGRESSIONAL QUARTERLY

BIBLIOGRAPHY

Armor, David J. *Forced Justice: School Desegregation.* New York: Oxford University Press, 1995.

Bartley, Numan V. *The Rise of Massive Resistance: Race and Politics in the South during the 1950s.* Baton Rouge: Louisiana State University Press, 1969.

Kluger, Richard. *Simple Justice: The History of* Brown v. Board of Education *and Black America's Struggle for Equality.* New York: Knopf, 1976.

Orfield, Gary, Susan E. Eaton, and the Harvard Project on School Desegregation. *Dismantling Desegregation: The Quiet Reversal of* Brown v. Board of Education. New York: New Press, 1996.

Patterson, James T. *Brown v. Board of Education: A Civil Rights Milestone and Its Troubled Legacy.* New York: Oxford University Press, 2001.

Sarat, Austin, ed. *Race, Law, and Culture: Reflections on* Brown v. Board of Education. New York: Oxford University Press, 1997.

Wilkinson, J. Harvie, III. *From* Brown *to* Bakke: *The Supreme Court and School Integration.* New York: Oxford University Press, 1979.

BUCHANAN, JAMES

Born in Pennsylvania on April 23, 1781, James Buchanan grew up in moderate circumstances, graduated from Dickinson College, began law practice, and quickly became relatively wealthy. He entered local politics in 1813 and served in the state legislature and Congress (1821–1831). Initially a Federalist, he became a Jacksonian Democrat in 1828 and served as Andrew Jackson's ambassador to Russia (1831–1834), as U.S. senator (1834–1845), as secretary of state under James Polk (1845–1849), and, after a brief retirement, as ambassador to Great Britain (1853–1856). In 1844, 1848, and 1852 he sought the Democratic presidential nomination, which he finally won in 1856. Buchanan swept the South, losing only eight electoral votes to the Know Nothing candidate, Millard Fillmore, but won only five northern states, losing the rest of the North to the Republican candidate, John C. Frémont. With 45 percent of the popular vote, Buchanan was not only a minority president, but a clearly sectional one. Although a northerner, Buchanan already had the reputation of a classic doughface—a northern man with southern principles.

James Buchanan *Library of Congress*

Buchanan's administration fully reflected this reputation. In his inaugural address he declared that the Supreme Court should be allowed to settle the issue of slavery in the territories, fully aware, because of private communication with some of the justices, that the Court would take a proslavery position on the issue. He supported southerners in Kansas, attempting to make that territory into a slave state over the opposition of the majority of the settlers. In 1858 he tried to achieve Kansas statehood under the proslavery Lecompton Constitution that had been written by a fraudulently elected convention and ratified in a thoroughly corrupt election, in which opponents of slavery were not allowed to vote against Kansas coming in as a slave state. He then retaliated against northern Democrats, like the popular Sen. Stephen A. Douglas of Illinois, who did not necessarily oppose slavery in Kansas but would not support it against the will of the people in the territory. In trying to force this issue Buchanan destroyed his own party. He vigorously enforced the Fugitive Slave Law of 1850, ordered the American navy to protect all ships flying the U.S. flag, even when they were clearly involved in the illegal slave trade, and asked Congress for $30 million to buy Cuba from Spain, not only to provide more territory for slavery, but to acquire the vast slave population of the island. Buchanan openly supported William Walker's filibustering attempts to seize part of Central America for the United States, again, to provide more land for slavery and territory for slave states.

Buchanan's administration set the stage for Democratic defeat in 1860, as his party collapsed along sectional lines. Buchanan was adamantly opposed to the candidacy of Stephen A. Douglas, the only Democrat who could have won. Buchanan's southern allies walked out of the party convention and later nominated his vice president, John C. Breckinridge, who carried most of the South in the national election. The Republican, Abraham Lincoln, carried all of the North and the election. By the end of December 1860 South Carolina had seceded from the Union, and before Buchanan left office six other states had done the same, forming the Confederate States of America. Buchanan denied the legality of secession but also denied that he had any power to maintain the Union. Thus, Buchanan became the only president to see the size of the United States shrink during his term in office.

Proslavery and prosouthern to the end, Buchanan remained surrounded by southern sympathizers, and even after secession was in progress his secretary of war attempted to ship recently manufactured heavy cannon to southern states for use by their militia.

Leaving his office with the nation in chaos, Buchanan was accused, unfairly, of treason during the Civil War. Nevertheless, he opposed all of Lincoln's policies and in 1866 wrote a memoir blaming the entire war on abolitionists, free blacks, and Republicans. He died in 1868, largely disgraced. Ironically, generally judged the nation's worst president, he was succeeded by the man whom many historians judge to be the nation's greatest president. Lincoln understood, as Buchanan never did, that the root of the nation's problem was slavery, and using his war powers, Lincoln was able to face the problem and eliminate it.

See also *Fugitive Slave Laws; Kansas-Nebraska Act; Sectionalism.*

PAUL FINKELMAN, UNIVERSITY OF TULSA COLLEGE OF LAW

BIBLIOGRAPHY

Finkelman, Paul. *Dred Scott v. Sandford: A Brief History.* Boston: Bedford Books, 1997.
Smith, Elbert B. *The Presidency of James Buchanan.* Lawrence: University Press of Kansas, 1975.

BUCKLEY V. VALEO

The Supreme Court in *Buckley v. Valeo* (1976) upheld the constitutionality of limiting individual contributions to political candidates but barred on First Amendment grounds total limits on campaign spending. The ruling invalidated a major part of a federal campaign finance law enacted in the wake of the Watergate scandal and blocked future attempts by Congress and state and local legislative bodies to control the rising costs of political campaigns.

Federal law had limited campaign spending for federal office since 1925, but the limits were unrealistically low and were universally violated with impunity. Congress in 1971 passed a new law limiting media spending by candidates for federal office and requiring disclosure of contributions and expenditures. Three years later Congress returned to the subject because of disclosures of questionable or illegal campaign finance practices by President Richard M. Nixon's 1972 re-election campaign.

The Federal Election Campaign Act amendments of 1974 set new limits on spending by candidates for Congress and limited to $1,000 the amount an individual could donate to a political candidate. The act also tightened reporting requirements, established a system of public financing for presidential elections, and created a new enforcement body, the Federal Election Commission (FEC).

The law was challenged on constitutional grounds by an ideologically diverse group of plaintiffs that included James L. Buckley, a conservative New York senator; Eugene J. McCarthy, a former liberal Democratic senator; and the American Civil Liberties Union. They contended that spending and contribution limits violated the First Amendment rights of candidates and campaign donors. Francis Valeo, secretary of the Senate and one of two congressional officials who served as ex officio members of the FEC, was listed as the first of the defendants.

The Court, in a long and complex decision, upheld most of the law but not the campaign spending limits. The contribution limits, the Court said, were justified on grounds of preventing corruption or the appearance of corruption in campaigns. But the limits on overall spending unconstitutionally abridged candidates' freedom of speech, the Court ruled. "Virtually every means of communicating ideas in today's mass society requires the expenditure of money," the Court explained.

The ruling upheld the public financing of presidential campaigns—including the provision that candidates accepting public funds must abide by overall spending limits. On one other issue, the Court invalidated on separation-of-power grounds the provision for congressional appointment of some members of the FEC. Congress quickly repaired the defect in the FEC's membership but had little room under the Court's decision to control spending on House or Senate races.

Unrestrained by federal limits, spending in congressional races steadily increased. Spending on House and Senate races in 1996 totaled around $650 million—more than triple the total in 1980. By the mid-1990s the average House candidate was spending about $440,000, the average Senate candidate $4.4 million. Candidates complained that the $1,000 contribution limit forced them to spend an ever-increasing amount of time on fund raising. Proposals to raise the contribution limit, however, did not advance in Congress. Meanwhile, wealthy candidates were free under the *Buckley* decision to spend unlimited amounts of their own money.

Public financing of presidential campaigns, however, did serve to control spending in those races. Nixon spent $60 million in his 1972 campaign. Twenty years later President George Bush and his Democratic challenger, Bill Clinton, spent about $90 million each. The effect of the public financing system was undermined, however, by a gap in the law for so-called soft money—money raised and spent by party committees for party-building and general election-related activities.

The FEC in 1978 held that these general party expenditures were not subject to the federal contribution limits or disclosure provisions. Quickly, "soft money"—not subject to the "hard" limits of federal law—became an important element of campaign spending. The two parties spent $19 million in soft money during the 1978 election cycle. By 1996 the figure swelled to $260 million.

Congress through the 1990s considered a host of campaign finance reform proposals, including efforts to ban soft money, limit spending by political action committees, or provide public financing for congressional races. None was enacted. Meanwhile, the Supreme Court reaffirmed the central features of the *Buckley* decision. The Court in *Colorado Republican Federal Campaign Committee v. Federal Election Commission* (1996) struck down federal limits on "independent expenditures" by political parties on behalf of congressional candidates. But in 2000 the Court in *Nixon v. Shrink Missouri, Government PAC* upheld a Missouri law setting *Buckley*-type limits on contributions to candidates for state offices. Contribution limits, Justice David H. Souter wrote, "aim to democratize the influence that money itself may bring to bear upon the electoral process."

See also *Campaign Finance; Political Action Committees; Political Contributions in the Late Nineteenth Century; Soft Money and Twentieth-Century Politics.*

KENNETH JOST, CONGRESSIONAL QUARTERLY

BIBLIOGRAPHY

Alexander, Herbert E. *Financing Politics: Money, Elections, and Political Reform,* 4th ed. Washington, D.C.: CQ Press, 1992.

Mutch, Robert E. *Campaigns, Congress and the Courts: The Making of Federal Campaign Finance Laws.* New York: Praeger, 1988.

Sorauf, Frank. *Inside Campaign Finance: Myths and Realities.* New Haven: Yale University Press, 1992.

BUSH, GEORGE

George Herbert Walker Bush, the forty-first president of the United States (1989–1993), was born June 12, 1924, in Milton, Massachusetts. He was raised in Greenwich, Connecticut, by wealthy parents, and his was a genteel yet disciplined upbringing. His father, Prescott Bush, was a U.S. senator from Connecticut.

Bush attended an elite day school and later preparatory school at Philips Academy in Andover, Massachusetts. He learned about the Japanese attack on Pearl Harbor while a senior, and he enlisted in the U.S. Navy immediately upon his graduation, on his eighteenth birthday. Bush became the youngest pilot in the U.S. Navy and saw action in the Pacific before his plane was shot down on September 25, 1944, just south of the island of Chichi Jima. Bush's crew was lost, but he was picked up by a submarine.

In the fall of 1945 Bush enrolled at Yale University, graduating Phi Beta Kappa in June 1948. He then chose to leave the Northeast and enter the oil business in Texas. From 1950 to 1966 Bush built his independent oil business—Zapata Oil—into a multimillion dollar concern.

EARLY POLITICAL CAREER

In 1964 Bush made a failed attempt for the U.S. Senate. Two years later he was more fortunate, being elected to Congress from Houston's Seventh District. Bush served two terms before he failed in a second bid for the Senate, being defeated in 1970 by Democrat Lloyd Bentsen.

His defeat, however, began the second phase of Bush's political career, as he served in a number of positions in the federal bureaucracy in the administrations of Richard M. Nixon and Gerald R. Ford. In December 1970 he was appointed ambassador to the United Nations, where he served until his June 1972 appointment as chairman of the Republican National Committee. On the short list for Ford's vice president in August 1974, Bush was passed over for Nelson Rockefeller and instead accepted the position of envoy to the People's Republic of China. Ford called him home in December 1975 to head the struggling Central Intelligence Agency, where he served until his dismissal by President Jimmy Carter in 1977.

Bush ran unsuccessfully for the presidency in 1980, a campaign distinguished by his characterization of opponent Ronald Reagan's policies as "voodoo economics." Nevertheless, Bush was chosen as Reagan's running mate and served in the vice presidency for the entirety of Reagan's two terms in office.

PRESIDENTIAL ADMINISTRATION

Despite questions about his personal style (dubbed in the press as the "wimp factor") and nagging questions about possible involvement in the Iran-contra affair, Bush won the Republican nomination for the presidency in 1988. That fall his campaign was constantly on the offensive, attacking his opponent, Massachusetts governor Michael Dukakis, for opposing the recitation of the pledge of allegiance in schools and originally supporting a controversial parole program for incarcerated criminals in Massachusetts (a position Dukakis reversed before the campaign). In an election that sported the lowest voter turnout since 1924, Bush captured 54 percent of the popular vote and 426 electoral votes, to Dukakis's 112.

Bush inherited a $2.7 trillion federal budget deficit (in 1988) and a Congress controlled by the Democrats. Both factors conspired to severely limit Bush's performance in domestic policy. Attempts to initiate an education plan ("Education 2000") and a new plan for the enforcement of drug laws were gutted by budget concerns. Other domestic programs went down to defeat. Two notable exceptions, however, were the Americans with Disabilities Act and the Clean Air Act amendments of 1990, both of which were passed with White House support.

Bush's attempt to strengthen his economic hand cost him any hope of dealing with Congress in his second two years. In 1990, faced with a widening deficit, he reneged on his campaign promise to the Republican convention in 1988: "Read My Lips—No New Taxes." The Omnibus Budget Reconciliation Act of 1990 contained an income tax hike of 31.5 percent for the nation's wealthiest Americans; one month after its passage, Republicans lost ten Senate seats, twenty-five House seats, and two governorships in the off-year elections.

Between 1989 and 1991 the Bush administration's foreign policy met with substantial criticism, largely for being overcautious toward continuing the rapprochement with the Soviets that had begun in the final year of the Reagan administration. Nevertheless, Bush refused to plunge headlong into talks with Soviet premier Mikhail Gorbachev until he could properly gauge both Gorbachev's intentions and his chances for political survival. The Soviets were infuriated about the one-year delay, but Bush did not meet with Gorbachev until December 1989 at Malta, where the two leaders strengthened a personal bond that would serve Bush well one year later.

President George Bush confers with King Fahd of Saudi Arabia in the Royal Pavilion in Riyadh, November 21, 1990. *George Bush Presidential Library and Museum*

Bush was also criticized for his measured response to the June 4, 1989, massacre in China's Tiananmen Square and for his cautious reaction to the fall of communism in eastern Europe at the end of the year. However, Bush received some credit in the press for, in the words of one reporter, "refusing to dance on the remains of the Berlin Wall," thus contributing to a sense of stability in the midst of European revolution.

Bush was also denounced for his administration's support of an unsuccessful attempt in October 1989 to overthrow the government of Manuel Noriega. This precipitated the American invasion of Panama (Operation Just Cause) in December 1989 in response to the killing of one American soldier in Panama City and the detainment and beating of another and his wife. This military action ended in the overthrow and capture of Noriega.

The fall of the Berlin Wall and the Panamanian invasion strengthened Bush's hand in foreign policy and allowed him to enjoy moderately high approval ratings, despite his domestic travails with Congress. Bush's approval rating would soar—despite the budget talks that were concurrently under way—with his reaction to the August 2, 1990, invasion of Kuwait by Iraqi forces under the command of that nation's president, Saddam Hussein. Quickly mobilizing the forces of

public opinion and gaining the support of the United Nations (in its strongest show of support for a violated nation since its creation in 1945), Bush was able to forge a worldwide coalition of political might against Iraq—highlighted by the unexpected support of the Soviet Union. Before the end of August eighty thousand coalition troops had been committed to Saudi Arabia to prevent Iraq from steaming ahead into that nation. After four months of diplomatic wrangling, on January 17, 1991, Operation Desert Shield became Operation Desert Storm. For five and one-half weeks Iraq was besieged with near constant air bombardment. When the ground war began on February 24, it took but one hundred hours to decimate the Iraqi offensive capability.

A LOST BID FOR REELECTION

Two years after what can be argued as America's greatest military achievement since World War II, Bush was defeated for reelection by a wide margin. One factor in his defeat was that Saddam remained in power. However, the overthrow of Saddam was never a military priority, as Bush feared entering the quagmire of another Vietnam. Saddam's survival mixed with a sharp downturn in the economy in 1991. By June 1991 the national unemployment rate had risen to 7.8 percent, the highest in eight years—and Bush's approval ratings plummeted. Bush also lost the support of his party's conservatives for repudiating his no-tax pledge and refusing to abandon

Gorbachev to the Russian revolutionary movement of Boris Yeltsin, even after many of his advisers had argued that Gorbachev's fall was inevitable. (Gorbachev would be ousted from power in December 1991; with him went the Soviet Union.) The administration was further weakened by the contentious nomination of Clarence Thomas to the Supreme Court in fall 1991.

By 1992 Bush's reelection bid carried significant baggage. The Bush candidacy was ultimately doomed by the astute challenge of Gov. Bill Clinton of Arkansas, a third-party candidacy launched by Texas billionaire Ross Perot, an acrimonious bid by television commentator Pat Buchanan to wrest the nomination from Bush, and a campaign staff that did not seem to have the positive-reaction time of the 1988 team (for many reasons, the two campaign teams were almost completely different). In November 1992 Clinton wrested the presidency by winning 43 percent of the popular vote to Bush's 38 percent and Perot's 19 percent; Clinton won 370 electoral votes to Bush's 168.

In retirement Bush moved back to Houston and centered his energies on the building of his presidential library at Texas A & M University, lecturing, and traveling. He also saw two of his sons enter national politics; John Ellis ("Jeb") was elected governor of Florida, while George W. was twice elected governor of Texas and then won the presidency in the election of 2000.

See also *Clinton, Bill; Persian Gulf War; Ronald Reagan.*

JOHN ROBERT GREENE, CAZENOVIA COLLEGE

BIBLIOGRAPHY

Bush, George, and Brent Scowcroft. *A World Transformed.* New York: Alfred A. Knopf, 1998.

Greene, John Robert. *The Presidency of George Bush.* Lawrence: University Press of Kansas, 2000.

Parmet, Herbert S. *George Bush: The Life of a Lone Star Yankee.* New York: Scribner, 1997.

CABINET

The president's cabinet is a body of the top officials of the executive branch. It is composed of the president, the vice president, the heads of the executive departments, and others the president chooses to include.

The popular image of the cabinet is of a high-level advisory board that meets regularly to debate and make national policy. In practice, however, it rarely does that. The cabinet serves important political functions, but policy making usually is not among them.

Most presidents enter the White House pledging to give their cabinets a meaningful policy role. Cabinet officials are carefully selected and introduced to the public with great fanfare. But once in office, presidents find themselves reluctant to delegate decision-making power to a group that could become strong enough to challenge their power and curtail their control of resources and information. Many presidents prefer to deal with their department heads (who are known as secretaries, with the exception of the attorney general) individually or in small groups that are focused on specific policy issues. Cabinet officials themselves often prefer to deal with presidents one-on-one instead of competing in an open forum for a president's attention and resources. Moreover, presidents are mindful of the fact that many cabinet members are chosen for political reasons, or for their expertise in a particular area, and may be more loyal to their departments' interests than to the president.

Presidents tend to rely instead on their own staff and on what presidential scholar Thomas E. Cronin has labeled the "inner cabinet"—the secretaries of state, defense, Treasury, and the attorney general. Both groups usually are chosen on the basis of personal friendships, loyalty, and views similar to the president's.

The cabinet, however, has valuable roles to play. Its principal purpose is to give the president informal advice on matters brought before it. Since its members represent diverse groups, the cabinet is able to provide a broad spectrum of views.

The cabinet also plays an important symbolic role. It serves as a reminder of a president's commitment to listen to and consult with representatives of the major social, economic, and political groups in American society. President Bill Clinton highlighted the cabinet's symbolic importance when he appointed more women and minorities to cabinet posts than any president had before because he wanted a cabinet that "looks like America." Elevation of a government agency to the cabinet level indicates the nation's commitment to certain goals, such as when the cabinet departments of Energy and Education were created during President Jimmy Carter's administration and the Veterans Affairs Department was created during the Ronald Reagan presidency.

The cabinet has political usefulness as well. Cabinet appointments can be used to settle electoral debts, to rally support for administration policies, and to show unity behind a president.

CABINET ORIGIN

The cabinet is an unusual institution in many ways, not the least of which its origin. The cabinet has no constitutional or statutory mandate. Its membership, its functions, and its very existence were a matter of presidential discretion.

The idea of some kind of advisory council for the president was discussed at the Constitutional Convention, but the concept failed to win adoption. The majority of Framers apparently feared that the presidency might become overburdened with unnecessary advisory councils. Consequently, all that remained of the idea when the Constitution was drafted was the authorization in Article II, section 2, that the president "may require the Opinion, in writing, of the principal Officer in each of the executive Departments, upon any Subject relating to the duties of their respective Offices."

When George Washington was inaugurated in 1789, he laid the foundation for the cabinet. Seeking both administrative and advisory help in his new administration, Washington asked Congress to create three executive departments to oversee foreign affairs, military affairs, and fiscal concerns. Similar departments had existed under the Articles of Confederation. Congress debated his request for several months

Gentlemen of the Senate.

I nominate for the Department of the Treasury of the United States —

Alexander Hamilton (of New York) Secretary.

Nicholas Eveleigh (of S° Carolina) Comptroller.

Samuel Meridith (of Pensylvania) Treasurer.

Oliver Wolcott Jun.r (of Connecticut) Auditor.

Joseph Nourse (in office) Register.

For the Department of war —

Henry Knox.

For Judge in the Western Territory, in place of William Barton who declines the appointment

George Turner.

President George Washington notified the Senate of his cabinet appointments in this note, which is preserved at the National Archives. *National Archives*

before establishing the Foreign Affairs and War Departments under the executive branch and the Treasury Department under the control of Congress. The latter, however, in the hands of the first secretary of the Treasury, Alexander Hamilton, became a stronghold of executive power.

Washington initially had hoped the Senate would serve as an advisory council, but that chamber shunned the role when Washington sought its advice on a treaty in 1790. Conse-

quently, he turned to members of his administration for counsel. At first he met with his department heads individually, but by 1792 he was holding frequent meetings with his secretaries of Treasury, state, and war, and his attorney general (the Justice Department was not established until 1870). In 1793 James Madison, then a member of the House of Representatives, applied the word *cabinet* to those conferences, and the term has been used ever since.

Washington's hopes for cabinet advisers who would consult with one another and work together harmoniously were soon dashed by a rift between Hamilton and Secretary of State Thomas Jefferson. The two detested each other and disagreed on important policy issues. After his experience with this cabinet and its successor, which was composed of men of cooler heads but lesser talents, Washington apparently abandoned his hopes of the cabinet serving as an advisory board.

This disillusionment and uncertainty over the role of the cabinet have troubled almost every administration since Washington's.

HISTORICAL DEVELOPMENT

President John Adams, who succeeded Washington, was even more disillusioned with his cabinet than Washington had been with his. He had significant differences of opinion with his department heads, and he found them to be more loyal to Hamilton, who had left government during Washington's presidency, than to him. Yet the formal cabinet remained Adams's principal official advisory body.

The cabinet declined in importance during the first part of the nineteenth century. As the selection of cabinet members came to be dictated by political and geographic considerations, presidents often appointed cabinet members whom they did not know personally and did not necessarily trust. Indeed, presidents frequently had to struggle to maintain control over their cabinets.

Andrew Jackson was the first president to largely ignore his cabinet. In fact, during his first two years in office he never even met with his cabinet; during the remaining six years he convened it only sixteen times. Jackson preferred to consult with his so-called Kitchen Cabinet, an informal group of advisers consisting largely of newspapermen who could keep him apprised of public opinion.

Abraham Lincoln appointed a strong cabinet that included political antagonists, but the president maintained the upper hand. According to one story, when Lincoln was outvoted on a critical decision—seven nays to his one aye—he declared, "the ayes have it!"

There was some movement in the latter part of the nineteenth century to make the cabinet answerable to Congress instead of the White House, thereby giving Congress greater access to information on the executive branch. But proposals to allow department secretaries to occupy seats on the House floor never were enacted.

Early in the twentieth century the cabinet expanded in size but continued to play a modest role as an advisory body. Woodrow Wilson rarely met with his full cabinet, relying instead during World War I on the advice of his Council of National Defense, composed of the secretaries of war, navy, interior, agriculture, commerce, and labor. Franklin D. Roosevelt used his cabinet for discussion rather than decision making, but he did make one significant change when he began the practice of including the vice president in the cabinet. Harry S. Truman at the outset attempted to use his cabinet as a board of directors, asking them to vote on issues, but toward the end of his presidency he turned to others for advice.

Dwight D. Eisenhower took his cabinet more seriously than most twentieth-century presidents. He established a cabinet secretariat, expanded the cabinet to include important aides in his administration, and gave the vice president more cabinet responsibilities. He asked his cabinet to advise him on major issues and to see that decisions were carried out, but his cabinet still took no part in making final policy decisions.

John F. Kennedy met with his department heads individually but seldom held formal cabinet meetings. His successor, Lyndon B. Johnson, made far greater use of his cabinet, but it was mostly to create the impression of consensus within his administration and not to hold substantive discussions. Richard M. Nixon, who had enjoyed an expanded cabinet role as Eisenhower's vice president, held few cabinet meetings during his own presidency, relying instead on his White House staff.

Nixon's reliance on his staff inspired Gerald R. Ford's efforts to make his cabinet a meaningful advisory group. Ford was convinced that the Watergate affair was the result of Nixon's carelessness in allowing his personal aides to gain too much power at the expense of his cabinet. Ford reestablished the cabinet secretariat, which had been abandoned after Eisenhower, and met with his cabinet regularly.

Ford's successor, Jimmy Carter, also came into office pledging to use his cabinet as a decision-making body but, like most presidents, ended up turning to his senior White House staff instead. Carter went from weekly cabinet sessions in his first year to sporadic meetings in his final year.

Similarly, Ronald Reagan did not meet often with his cabinet during his two terms, but he was successful in using the members as an advisory group. Reagan divided the cabinet into councils that focused on specific policy areas. George Bush gave his cabinet an even greater policy role than Reagan had given his, but major decisions still were made by the president and a few close advisers. Bill Clinton, Bush's successor, also relied on a handful of advisers when it came time for major policy decisions.

CABINET MEMBERS

The evolution of cabinet-level departments from George Washington's initial three reflects the emergence of new issues and responsibilities facing the national government. Over the years cabinet departments have been created, downgraded, consolidated, divided, and renamed.

By 2000 there were fourteen cabinet departments: agriculture, commerce, defense, education, energy, health and human services, housing and urban development, interior, justice, labor, state, transportation, Treasury, and veterans affairs.

In addition to the vice president, other officials have been included in the cabinet at a president's discretion. Bush, for example, bestowed cabinet rank on his director of the Office of Management and Budget and the U.S. Trade Representative. Clinton named those and others as well to his cabinet, including his chief of staff, the chairman of the Council of Economic Advisers, the administrator of the Environmental Protection Agency, the U.S. ambassador to the United Nations, and the director of the Federal Emergency Management Agency. Presidents also may invite others to particular cabinet discussions.

Selection of the department secretaries is an indication of the policy direction of a new administration and provides presidents with their best early opportunity to show their leadership. In making their selections, presidents must weigh a variety of factors besides administrative skills. They must take into account factors such as loyalty, politics, and expertise, as well as ethnic, gender, geographic, and constituent-group representation.

Another important factor is acceptability to Congress, because cabinet appointments must be submitted to the Senate for majority confirmation. For some nominees, approval comes easily, but for others it can be a long, grueling process. Nominees must prove to the Senate and the American people that they have the managerial skills necessary to administer a large public bureaucracy, as well as knowledge of the subject area of their departments. Their personal lives also are subject to scrutiny. The nomination of former Texas senator John Tower to be Bush's secretary of defense was defeated on the Senate floor in 1989 in part because of allegations of alcohol abuse and womanizing. Clinton in 1993 had to drop his first two choices for attorney general after questions arose over their use of undocumented immigrants as domestic workers. The first nominee had illegally hired two workers and failed to pay Social Security or unemployment taxes for them at the time. Clinton's second choice had done nothing illegal but got caught up in the controversy anyway and asked that her name be withdrawn.

See also *Presidency; Washington, George.*

PATRICIA ANN O'CONNOR, INDEPENDENT AUTHOR

BIBLIOGRAPHY

Bledsoe, W. Craig, and Leslie Rigby. "The Cabinet and Executive Departments." In *Congressional Quarterly's Guide to the Presidency.* 2d ed. Edited by Michael Nelson. Washington, D.C.: CQ Press, 1996.
Cronin, Thomas E. *The State of the Presidency.* 2d ed. Boston: Little, Brown, 1980.
Fenno, Richard F., Jr. *The President's Cabinet.* New York: Vintage, 1959.

CALHOUN, JOHN C.

John C. Calhoun (1782–1850), planter, politician, and political theorist from South Carolina, played a prominent role in most of the important political and economic debates of the first half of the nineteenth century. As a state and national legislator, cabinet member, and vice president, Calhoun served as the preeminent spokesman for southern—particularly South Carolinian—interests, defending states' rights and the economically, socially, and legally sanctioned system of slavery.

The son of a wealthy backcountry planter, Calhoun chose to pursue an education instead of farming. In 1802, following his studies at a new frontier academy run by his brother-in-law, he traveled north where he graduated from Yale. After a brief clerkship in Charleston, he studied law at Tapping Reeve's renowned Connecticut school. Calhoun returned to South Carolina and in 1810 was elected to the South Carolina House of Representatives. His debating skills won him immediate acclaim among the planter elite, who helped elect him to the Twelfth Congress, which convened in 1811.

RISE TO PROMINENCE

Calhoun made an immediate impact on national politics, joining an emerging group of young nationalist-minded members of Congress to argue for war as the only redress for Great Britain's violations of American neutrality. The decisions of Calhoun's early congressional career reflect his desire to strengthen a young nation. As a powerful member of the House Committee on Foreign Relations and later as secretary of war during James Monroe's administration (1817–1825), Calhoun sought to fortify national defenses and create a more efficient army. In the midst of the economic decline resulting from the War of 1812, Calhoun was instrumental in reviving a national bank. He voted for the protective tariff of 1816 and pushed for the "bonus bill," a federally funded program for internal improvements that President James Madison ultimately vetoed for constitutional reasons.

Having established himself as a national figure, Calhoun made a bid for the presidency in 1824, but, as was the case in his successive attempts for the highest office (the last in 1844), he was unable to muster the widespread party support necessary to become the Democratic Party's candidate. Instead, he settled for the vice presidency, an office he held uncomfortably under both John Quincy Adams and Andrew Jackson.

The rise of a national abolitionist movement and a strong South Carolinian anti–tariff movement in the late 1820s and early 1830s caused a turning in Calhoun's political thought. He continued to support policies he thought would bridge sectionalism by economically and politically tying different regions together, but he became increasingly sectionalist in his outlook, encouraging the South to remain unified in support of states' rights and slavery.

The nullification crisis culminating in 1832 and 1833 marked a crucial moment in Calhoun's political and ideological thought, leading to his concept of concurrent majorities, for which he is known. In a move to protect northern manufacturers, Congress had raised the tariff in 1828, which increased the price southern planters would pay for European finished goods. Calhoun had initially expressed tempered support for such a measure, but, when constituents in South Carolina (suffering from depressed cotton prices) sharply criticized the measure for favoring manufacturing interests over agriculture, he provided a constitutional basis for challenging it. In *Expositions and Protest,* written for the South Carolina legislature in 1828, Calhoun argued that, although Congress had been given the constitutional authority to regulate trade and internally tax for the general welfare, a tariff must be for revenue only and could not be enforced to benefit one interest at the expense of another. Calhoun felt that the Framers' belief that an extended republic with diverse counterbalancing interests would protect minority groups had not been farsighted enough. Revolutions in transportation and the development of a complicated party system (a process Calhoun often lamented) had made it possible for an "absolute majority"—the numeric majority—to neglect "concurring majorities"—the separate interest groups and communities making up the whole. Additional safeguards were necessary to protect these interests against "tyranny by the majority."

Calhoun's complex solution, later elaborated in his *Disquisitions on Government* and *The Constitution* (essays written during the 1840s and published posthumously in 1851), drew from a selective but close reading of constitutional documents, including Thomas Jefferson's and James Madison's *Kentucky and Virginia Resolutions,* and American political and economic history. Ratification of the Constitution had, according to Calhoun, enacted a compact whereby sovereign states, themselves concurrent majorities, yielded enumerated powers to a federal government. The states had not, however, relinquished their sovereignty to a national government controlled by an absolute majority. In rare cases when federal legislation, such as the tariff, unduly oppressed a concurrent majority, states could invoke their original sovereignty and nullify the act through a state convention.

Although Calhoun was a moderate within the state, his arguments provided legitimacy to South Carolina's extreme forces, who in a state convention nullified the tariffs of 1828 and 1832. These actions and Calhoun's role in them angered President Jackson, further alienating Calhoun from the president and cabinet. Protesting Jackson's threat to use troops to enforce the tariff and feeling that his impact would be greater in Congress, Calhoun resigned his position as vice president and accepted a Senate seat. There he joined with Kentuckian Henry Clay to pass a compromise tariff, effectively ending the controversy.

CALHOUN AND SLAVERY

Calhoun's fear of increased consolidation of federal power continued to drive his stances on major political issues, particularly his desire to protect slavery. Calhoun, a slaveholder, believed blacks to be inherently inferior and argued that racial slavery was a system socially, economically, and politically superior to the unfettered capitalism he perceived in the North and Britain. Sharing the Senate stage with Clay and Daniel Webster of Massachusetts, Calhoun assumed the leadership of an extreme bloc of southern congressmen who fought for a gag order on abolitionist petitions and proposed secession as a last resort if antislavery forces emerged victorious.

As westward expansion fueled questions over slavery in the territories, Calhoun tenaciously sought to protect southern slave interests. While serving as John Tyler's secretary of state (1844–1845), Calhoun pushed for the annexation of Texas, believing it would add to the power of the slaveholding South; and he sought a peaceful settlement of the Oregon boundary with Britain. Not an expansionist in principle, Calhoun opposed the Mexican-American War, rightfully

fearing that it would create a heated debate over the slavery issue and thus endanger the Union. Calhoun led those opposing the Wilmot Proviso, an attempt to ban slavery in all of the territory won from Mexico, and argued against admitting California as a free state. In early 1850 Calhoun was suffering from severe pneumonia, which eventually took his life. His final speech to the Senate, read aloud by James Mason of Virginia, predicted that secession was inevitable unless southern slaveholders were assured that their property and interests would be permanently protected.

Though not always successful, and often contradictory or opportunistic in his positions, Calhoun resolutely negotiated volatile party politics in order to preserve his own understanding of union while protecting isolated (though powerful) interests within it. Not able to muster the widespread popular support of Jackson, the compromising skill of Clay, or the legal astuteness of Webster, Calhoun nonetheless proved to be one of the most powerful and forceful political minds of his time.

See also *Compromise of 1850; Gag Rule; Jackson, Andrew; Mexican-American War; Nullification; Slavery; Tariff History; Territorial Expansion; War of 1812.*

BRIAN D. SCHOEN, UNIVERSITY OF VIRGINIA

BIBLIOGRAPHY

Bartlett, Irving. *John C. Calhoun: A Biography.* New York: W. W. Norton, 1993.

Niven, John. *John C. Calhoun and the Price of Union: A Biography.* Baton Rouge: Louisiana State University Press, 1988.

Peterson, Merrill D. *The Great Triumvirate: Webster, Clay, and Calhoun.* New York: Oxford University Press, 1987.

Wilson, Clyde. *The Essential Calhoun: Selections from Writings, Speeches, and Letters.* New Brunswick: Transaction Publishers, 1992.

Wiltse, Charles M. *John C. Calhoun.* 3 vols. Indianapolis: Bobbs-Merrill, 1944–1951.

CAMPAIGN FINANCE

The issue of campaign finance has been fodder for critics who charge that American politicians are overly influenced by special interest groups, but reform efforts have failed to stem the tide of money from groups and individuals with a major stake in the outcome of legislation or an executive decision.

Congress passed the first campaign finance overhaul measure in 1867, when the naval appropriations bill that year contained a provision preventing federal employees from soliciting contributions from Navy Yard workers. The issue first made headlines at the beginning of the twentieth century, when President Theodore Roosevelt was found to have benefited by large corporate contributions to his 1904 campaign. In response, Roosevelt called for campaign finance reform in both his 1905 and 1906 State of the Union addresses.

The resulting legislation, passed in 1907, was known as the Tillman Act and banned corporations and national banks from contributing to federal campaigns. Four decades later, Congress applied the same ban to contributions from labor unions; the prohibition was part of the Taft-Hartley Act of 1947. (During World War II, southern Democrats had teamed with Republicans to outlaw labor donations, but the 1943 bill, adopted over President Franklin D. Roosevelt's veto, expired at the end of the war.)

At the close of the twentieth century, campaign finance again became a major issue. The Democratic National Committee returned millions of dollars in questionable contributions in 1996, much of it from foreign sources, and both parties were accused of getting around federal spending limits by running advertisements in support of their presidential nominees. The Republican-controlled Congress held hearings into alleged Democratic abuses, but lawmakers failed to pass any new campaign finance legislation.

Despite Congress's inaction—or perhaps because of it—campaign finance is an issue that will not go away. In 2000, both Republican John McCain and Democrat Bill Bradley made overhauling the campaign finance laws a key element of their presidential campaigns. Although neither gained his party's nomination, the candidates who defeated them—Texas governor George W. Bush on the Republican side and Vice President Al Gore on the Democratic side—called for changes in the way campaigns are financed.

Today's campaign finance system is largely a product of the post-Watergate reforms enacted in 1974. The Watergate scandal, which brought down President Richard M. Nixon, included six-figure donations to the presidential campaign from individuals and corporations with issues pending before the White House. Congress since then has rebuffed almost yearly efforts to impose new rules on fund raising and spending. The laws are enforced by a six-member Federal Election Commission (FEC), which was created in 1974. Three of the six members are Republicans and three are Democrats, with four votes needed to approve a course of action. Critics say this bipartisan split makes the FEC a weak and ineffective watchdog. And the FEC is so understaffed that it often does not investigate potential violations of laws until years later, too late to prevent candidates from abusing the regulations during a campaign.

Candidates raise most of their money from three sources: their own pockets, individual contributors, and political action committees (PACs). Corporations and unions cannot give directly to federal campaigns. Individuals can give no more than $1,000 per election or $2,000 per election cycle (primary and general election) to one candidate. Political action committees can give $5,000 per election or $10,000 per cycle.

Presidential candidates can get money from a fourth source: the U.S. taxpayer. The account is funded through a $3 checkoff on income tax returns. If a presidential candidate agrees to limit his or her spending while seeking the nomination and raises at least $100,000 in contributions of no more than $250 each, the federal government will match the first $250 of each individual contribution. Since the system went into effect for the first post-Watergate presidential election in 1976, only three candidates—Republicans John Connally in 1980, Steve Forbes in 1996 and 2000, and George W. Bush in 2000—have refused the federal funds and therefore were not bound by spending limits for the primary campaigns.

Once the Democrats and Republicans choose their nominees, the entire cost of the full campaign is covered by taxpayers. The nominees agree to spend only what the federal government provides and to refrain from raising any more money for their campaigns. No major-party candidate yet has refused federal funding for the general election.

No federal funds are provided for congressional campaigns, and efforts to provide taxpayer funding of House and Senate races have failed in the face of Republican opposition. Nor are there any limits on how much a congressional candidate can spend; the Supreme Court struck down restrictions on spending in *Buckley v. Valeo* (1976). In that landmark case the Court upheld contribution limits but struck down restrictions on spending, calling them a violation of the First Amendment. That Court decision also struck down limits on how much money candidates could pour into their own races. Some proponents of campaign finance reform have proposed amending the U.S. Constitution to overturn the decision and allow Congress to limit campaign spending and thus the need to raise so much money from special interests.

POLITICAL ACTION COMMITTEES

Political action committees, or PACs, are the giving arms of special interests. The first PAC was formed in the 1940s by the Congress of Industrial Organizations, the labor federation that later merged with the American Federation of Labor to become the AFL-CIO.

But PACs did not come into their own as a major financing force until the 1970s. In 1972, President Nixon signed legislation allowing unions and corporations, otherwise banned from giving directly to campaigns, to pay the expenses of PACs that would be funded with voluntary contributions from employees, officers, union workers, or members of organizations. The number of PACs skyrocketed as a result, from 608 at the end of 1974 to 3,954 at the end of 1984. The growth of PACs—and the perception of a growing influence on the political process—led to unsuccessful efforts to ban them.

Besides corporations and unions, ideological organizations also have formed their own PACs, such as the National Rifle Association, which backs gun owners' rights, or the pro-Israel National PAC.

Corporate PACs traditionally favor incumbents, most of whom win reelection time after time. The extent to which these PACs favor current officeholders was illustrated starkly when the Republicans took control of the House in 1995. During the 1993–1994 election cycle, Democrats, who had a majority of the House, took in 54 percent of the corporate PAC money. But after the GOP gained control, corporate PACs gave the Republicans 70 percent of their contributions in 1995–1996.

In recent years, members of Congress and other public officials have founded their own PACs, known as leadership PACs. These organizations offer special interests another way to contribute to powerful lawmakers; after giving $10,000 to a candidate's reelection campaign, a special interest PAC can give another $5,000 to that candidate's leadership PAC.

Protesters from the National Campaign Finance Reform Coalition shout at people entering a Republican fundraising event at the Washington Convention Center, in Washington, D.C.   *R. Michael Jenkins, Congressional Quarterly*

Most lawmakers use these PACs to make donations to candidates of their own political party. This financial assistance helps them earn the gratitude of incumbents and newly minted lawmakers, who may be asked at a later date to support their patron's attempt to win a leadership role in the party conference.

SOFT MONEY

Although corporations have been banned from contributing to federal campaigns since 1907 and unions have been blocked since 1947, both groups still contribute millions of dollars each year to help elect favored candidates. They do so thanks to a loophole known as "soft money," which is not regulated by federal election laws and therefore cannot go directly to the candidates; rather, it goes to the political parties. The parties cannot spend the money on activities that urge a vote for or against a particular candidate, which is known as "express advocacy."

Soft money is a relatively recent phenomenon. In 1979, Congress voted to allow the political parties to raise these unregulated contributions for party-building activities such as voter registration and get-out-the-vote drives. However, the

political parties began using the money to air what are known as "issue advertisements." This practice came to a head during the 1996 presidential elections, when both parties ran advertisements in support of their nominees. Indeed, FEC auditors said that the political party advertisements were nothing more than campaign commercials and recommended that both campaigns repay millions of dollars in federal funds for exceeding spending limits. The six-member commission rejected its auditors' recommendations.

Both political parties continue to raise record amounts of soft money, despite efforts in Congress to ban it. In both 1998 and 1999, the House passed a ban on soft money, but Senate Republicans successfully blocked the legislation. Even members of Congress have begun to raise soft money for their leadership PACs. Some have set up PACs in the state of Virginia, which does not limit the size of campaign contributions to candidates or PACs. Others do not even disclose their donors, and because the money is not used to directly elect a federal candidate, the FEC does not regulate those committees. Besides the candidates and the parties, a host of interest groups—including antiabortion forces, term limits supporters, gun rights advocates, unions, and environmental groups—have run their own advertisements for or against candidates.

If their advertisements urge viewers to vote for or against a particular candidate (express advocacy), the organizations must disclose their spending with the FEC. More frequently, however, the organizations run advertisements that mention a particular candidate but do not urge a vote for or against that person. This is called "issue advocacy," and the courts have ruled that the FEC cannot regulate this First Amendment exercise of free speech. As a result, millions of dollars worth of commercials are being broadcast, often times without anyone knowing who is funding the effort. Because they are not considered campaign advertisements, the commercials can be funded out of union dues or corporate treasuries. Efforts to curb such advertisements, or at least require that their source be disclosed, have run into opposition from some lawmakers who claim that the proposals violate the First Amendment.

MODERN REFORM EFFORTS

Modern efforts to overhaul the campaign finance system have their roots in the election of President John F. Kennedy in 1960. Stung by allegations that his family's wealth bought his narrow victory, Kennedy formed a campaign finance commission in 1961. The panel recommended placing limits on the size of contributions and disclosing campaign contributors. In 1964, Kennedy's successor, Lyndon B. Johnson, hosted $1,000-a-plate "President's Club" dinners, but the Democratic National Committee declined to release the names of the donors. To avoid the appearance of anonymous big donors buying a candidate, Congress passed legislation providing for public financing of presidential campaigns through an income tax checkoff, but the program was suspended until rules could be developed to govern the distribution of the money.

Congress did vote in 1970 to impose limits on how much candidates for president, vice president, senator, representative, governor, and lieutenant governor could spend on broadcast advertisements, but President Nixon vetoed the measure. Two years later, however, Nixon signed legislation that limited how much money candidates could contribute to their own campaigns and how much money they could spend on advertising. The bill also authorized the establishment of political action committees.

In 1974, in the wake of Watergate, President Gerald Ford signed legislation imposing new restrictions on campaign fund raising. The bill limited campaign contributions to $1,000 per individual per election, set spending limits for federal campaigns while repealing the restrictions on media expenditures, imposed restrictions on how much money candidates could give to their own campaigns, set up the current system of public financing for presidential elections, imposed new reporting requirements for contributions and expenditures, and established the FEC. The Supreme Court two years later declared unconstitutional the spending limits as well as the restrictions on how much candidates could spend on their own campaigns.

In the wake of the Supreme Court decision, congressional Democrats tried to draft legislation that would provide public financing of campaigns if candidates voluntarily agreed to limit their spending, but the proposals repeatedly ran into opposition from Republicans. The only time Congress managed to pass a bill, offering Senate candidates taxpayer-financed vouchers to buy television time and House candidates federal matching funds, President George Bush vetoed it.

During the second half of the 1990s, McCain and Democratic senator Russell D. Feingold of Wisconsin and Reps. Christopher Shays, R-Conn., and Martin Meehan, D-Mass., proposed bipartisan campaign finance overhaul legislation. Their initial legislation would have banned PACs and offered financial incentives to candidates to voluntarily limit their spending. The latest version of the legislation simply would have banned soft money. But a majority of Senate Republicans, claiming that further restrictions of campaign contributions would violate the First Amendment right to free speech, but also wishing to preserve their party's traditional edge in raising money, were able to block the legislation from reaching the Senate floor for a vote.

See also Buckley v. Valeo; *Political Action Committees; Political Contributions in the Late Nineteenth Century; Progressive Era; Roosevelt, Theodore; Soft Money and Twentieth-Century Political Campaigns; Watergate.*

JONATHAN D. SALANT, ASSOCIATED PRESS

BIBLIOGRAPHY

Corrado, Anthony. "Money and Politics: A History of Federal Campaign Finance Law." In *Campaign Finance Reform: A Source Book,* ed. Anthony Corrado, Thomas E. Mann, Daniel R. Ortiz, Trevor Potter, and Frank J. Sorauf, 27–35. Washington, D.C.: Brookings Institution Press, 1997.

Mann, Thomas E. "The U.S. Campaign Finance System under Strain." In *Setting National Priorities: The 2000 Election and Beyond,* ed. Henry J. Aaron and Robert D. Reischauer. Washington, D.C.: Brookings Institution Press, 1999.

Rosenkranz, E. Joshua. *Buckley Stops Here: Loosening the Judicial Stranglehold on Campaign Finance.* New York: Century Foundation, 1998.

Salant, Jonathan D. "Despite Attempts, Loopholes in Law Remain Unplugged." *Congressional Quarterly Weekly Report,* November 16, 1996.

———. "Introduction." *Congressional Quarterly's Federal PACs Directory.* Washington, D.C.: Congressional Quarterly, 1998.

CAMPAIGNING

A political candidate's success in winning election depends largely on his or her effectiveness in campaigning—the process of seeking votes through a wide variety of means. These may range from door-to-door neighborhood visits to gigantic outdoor rallies; from simple lawn signs to elaborate and costly television barrages.

STAGES OF CAMPAIGNING

Whether for local office, such as the city council, or national office, such as Congress or even the presidency, all political campaigns go through the same stages. First is the exploratory stage, in which the candidate sizes up the competition and assesses the chances of winning. Sometimes the candidate will form an exploratory committee or hire a polling organization to help make the decision.

If the decision is to run, the candidate must file with the appropriate elections authority and perhaps pay a filing fee. To get on the ballot, many jurisdictions require the submission of petitions signed by a specified number of qualified voters. Candidates for the presidency and Congress must file with the Federal Election Commission (FEC) and report regularly on receipts and spending.

Another campaign stage is the formation of an organization, usually made up mostly of volunteers. For all but the least competitive races, a candidate needs help—to raise money, devise strategy, gain media attention, operate phone banks, and do all manner of things to try to win the nomination and the election. Today, most nominations are made in primary elections or caucuses. Candidates who clear that first hurdle are likely to keep and augment the same organization for the general election campaign.

Modern elections are expensive, particularly for television advertising. In the 1996 election, television spots were the largest single expense for President Bill Clinton and challenger Robert J. Dole. Between them they spent $113 million on television ads, dwarfing their next-highest combined expense, $32 million for nonmedia campaigning. For most other candidates, local and state, television advertising is also the largest expense. It is the medium by which most candidates reach the voters in the early twenty-first century.

To raise sometimes massive funds in conformance with federal or state campaign finance laws, the candidate may form a separate organization called a political action committee (PAC). Under the Federal Election Campaign Acts (FECA) of 1972 and 1976, political parties may also accept money for party-building activities. The use of this so-called soft money to skirt FECA spending limits for presidential candidates exposed a significant and controversial loophole in existing campaign reform laws. Presidential candidates who accept public funding must abide by spending limits. Congressional campaigns are not publicly funded and therefore are not subject to spending limits under the Supreme Court's *Buckley v. Valeo* decision (1976), which in effect said that such limits inhibit free speech.

EVOLUTION OF CAMPAIGNING

The use (or misuse) of money has been a hallmark of campaigns since the earliest days of the Republic. Some candidates, including George Washington, reportedly rewarded their supporters with free whiskey. With the growth of government and the "spoils system," politicians held out the promise of jobs as an enticement for votes. Later reforms in campaign finance and the civil service system outlawed some of the more blatant vote-inducing practices, but one of the most prevalent—negative campaigning—remains a characteristic of many U.S. political contests. Some nineteenth-century campaign rhetoric—focusing on an opponent's physical appearance, for example—makes today's "attack ads" seem mild.

Supporters of President John Quincy Adams in 1828 dredged up thirty-five-year-old allegations that challenger Andrew Jackson and Rachel Robards had married before her divorce became final (they had remarried in 1794). Jackson won, but Rachel died of a heart attack before his inauguration, a death Jackson attributed partly to her distress over the attacks on her morality. In their famed 1858 debates over the national issue of slavery, Senate candidates Stephen Douglas and Abraham Lincoln pandered to racial fears and assailed each other with insults. But instead of being "turned off" by the slurs, the large crowds cheered and jeered in delight.

Sometimes a derogatory political taunt can backfire, as happened to opponents of Grover Cleveland's presidential candidacy in 1884. They chanted, "Ma! Ma! Where's my Pa?" because Cleveland had fathered an illegitimate son, whom he continued to support. After Cleveland won, his supporters gloated, "Gone to the White House, ha, ha, ha!"

The use of the term *campaign* in U.S. politics dates to the early nineteenth century. John Quincy Adams used it in 1816, referring to one of his political efforts. But early presidential candidates, including Adams in his 1824 and 1828 campaigns, considered it unseemly to solicit votes directly from the people. Believing the office should seek the candidate, they left it largely to their supporters to publicize their qualifications and positions on issues, in hopes of obtaining the electoral vote majority needed for election.

The popular vote was less important in early U.S. elections than it is today. State legislatures chose electors in many cases, and the right to vote was extended only gradually to all adult citizens. South Carolina in 1868 was the last state to choose presidential electors by popular vote. Black males did not gain the vote in all states until ratification of the Fifteenth Amendment in 1870, and by 1900 the South had disfranchised most of them. They did not regain the vote in substantial numbers until passage of the Voting Rights Act of 1965. Women did not gain voting rights in all states until ratification of the Nineteenth Amendment in 1920. Popular election of U.S. senators became mandatory with the Seventeenth Amendment in 1913.

As the nation inched closer to universal suffrage (at least for males), it became essential for candidates to gain exposure to

Grover Cleveland is lampooned for fathering a child out of wedlock in a cartoon that appeared in *Judge* on September 27, 1884, just over a month prior to the election. *Library of Congress*

large numbers of voters. To that end, supporters held parades and rallies to whip up enthusiasm for their causes and leaders. Among the most colorful paraders were cape-wearing young men belonging to the Wide Awake Society, a Republican marching club. The "Wide Awakes" carried lanterns, sang songs, and performed intricate maneuvers as they marched for Abraham Lincoln in 1860. Almost half a million "Wide Awakes" helped make Lincoln the first Republican president.

In the late nineteenth century, large barbecues or picnics became common as events where politicians could mingle with the voters, "pressing the flesh" (shaking hands), and perhaps addressing the crowd from the bandstand. In the twenty-first century, such gatherings remain popular at the local level.

The practice of presidential aspirants traveling extensively to appeal for votes began in 1896 when William Jennings Bryan covered eighteen thousand miles by train to make six hundred speeches. Nevertheless, Republican William McKinley defeated Bryan with a front-porch campaign in Canton, Ohio. The term *whistle stop,* however, did not come into popular usage until President Harry S. Truman popularized it with his cross-country train treks in 1948. Truman scored an

upset victory over New York governor Thomas E. Dewey.

Truman's fiery speeches also gave rise to a slogan—"Give 'em hell, Harry!"—that became permanently identified with his campaign. Other candidates have tried to find catchy phrases to use on campaign buttons, which first appeared in 1896, and on more recent inventions such as bumper stickers and television spot ads. The first buttons featured McKinley's likeness and his "full dinner pail" slogan.

Most slogans are positive, such as "I Like Ike" for Dwight D. Eisenhower, or "Tippecanoe and Tyler, Too," for the 1840 ticket of William Henry Harrison, hero of the 1811 Battle of Tippecanoe, and John Tyler. But others are negative, such as "Dump the Hump," used against presidential nominee Hubert H. Humphrey in 1968, and "If Tydings Wins, You Lose," used by gun owners to defeat Sen. Joseph Tydings of Maryland in 1970.

Although President Herbert Hoover denied that he ever promised Americans "a chicken in every pot, a car in every garage," food has long been associated with appeals for votes, especially from ethnic groups. In New York City, with its large Jewish population, candidates pose for pictures while eating kosher Coney Island hot dogs. In a Polish community, the favored sausage may be kielbasa. In Chinatown, candidates may opt for chopsticks and egg rolls. As African Americans and Hispanics have grown in number, so have the pictures of politicians devouring stereotypical ribs or tortillas.

But ethnic campaigning is not confined to food. To court the Irish vote, candidates don green and strut in St. Patrick's Day parades on March 17. In October they try to be seen at Columbus Day festivities in Italian areas. The wise candidate tailors his or her campaign to the characteristics of the constituency at stake.

The high cost of political advertising on television leaves candidates little money to spend on campaign buttons, billboards, and other traditional artifacts of campaigning. Modern campaigns often hand out buttons only in return for donations, and the buttons' scarcity adds to their value as collectors' items. Nevertheless, candidates and their supporters

President Gerald R. Ford, campaigning in San Antonio for reelection in 1976, bites into a tamale with the husk on and seems to convey to his bemused Hispanic audience that he does not know what he has done wrong.   *Gerald R. Ford Library*

buted as a ditty. During the Great Depression, "Happy Days Are Here Again!" became the theme song of Democrats and their 1932 presidential candidate, Franklin D. Roosevelt. Republicans happily sang Irving Berlin's "I Like Ike" for their war hero nominee, Eisenhower, in the 1950s. And after the nomination of Clinton in 1992, the Democratic convention hall rocked to Fleetwood Mac's "Don't Stop Thinking About Tomorrow."

Campaigning takes many other forms of electioneering. There is no one sure way to campaign. What works for one candidate may do nothing for another; or it might do the candidate more harm than good. Most candidates make promises to the voters, sometimes effectively. Eisenhower kept his 1952 pledge to go to Korea to seek an end to the war there. But Walter Mondale's admission that he or Ronald Reagan would have to raise taxes if elected in 1984 proved detrimental to Mondale's already weak campaign against the popular Reagan.

After losing the Republican presidential nomination to George W. Bush in 2000, Arizona senator John McCain recanted his campaign pledge to let the people of South Carolina decide whether to let the Confederate flag continue flying over the statehouse in defiance of African Americans offended by the flag. Calling for the flag's removal, McCain admitted he had compromised his principles for fear of losing the South Carolina primary. He lost anyway to Bush, who had taken the same leave-it-to-the people stand.

usually manage to buy relatively inexpensive printed material such as bumper stickers, posters, and lawn signs on stakes. When several competitive races are being fought, suburban lawns may sprout a forest of cardboard messages vying for the voters' eyes and attention. The objective is to build support for the candidates through name recognition that may translate into votes on election day.

Music, too, may be important to a campaign. The anti-Cleveland chant in 1884 was set to music and widely distri-

The first face-to-face debate between presidential nominees took place in 1960 between John F. Kennedy and Richard Nixon. Since then, televised candidate debates have become commonplace in state and local races, as well as those for president and vice president. In 1998 C-SPAN (Cable-Satellite Public Affairs Network) broadcast 103 congressional and gubernatorial candidate debates, many of which were also covered by the commercial and public networks.

Televised debates at all levels also figured prominently in the 2000 primary elections. Both major party front-runners, Republican Bush and Democrat Al Gore, debated their presidential primary opponents. By May 13 each had secured his party's nomination—the earliest ever for candidates who faced significant opposition for the White House nomination.

Besides debates, standard forms of modern electioneering include stump speeches, greeting voters at factory gates, direct mail, obtaining endorsements from newspapers and community leaders, operating phone banks, and appearing on radio and television talk shows. Use of the Internet also has become a standard campaign procedure. In the 2000 elections, most major candidates had their own Web sites.

CANDIDATE-CENTERED CAMPAIGNS

Most political campaigns today are candidate-centered as opposed to party-centered. Far-reaching changes in election procedures and communications technology since the early twentieth century have freed candidates from much of their former dependency on political party organizations for money and other necessities of an effective campaign. Through telephones, radio, television, and the Internet, candidates may now pitch their appeals directly to the electorate. They gain nomination by winning party primaries and caucuses, rather than by being hand-picked by the Democratic or Republican Parties, which have dominated the American two-party system since the mid–nineteenth century. In a primary or caucus the candidates compete, in effect, for the party's endorsement. Only a few states permit a formal preprimary endorsement, which indicates on the ballot the candidate favored by the party leadership.

Although the primary system has empowered rank-and-file voters, it has also contributed to the long duration and skyrocketing cost of political campaigns. The successful candidate must campaign extensively to win the nomination, then campaign again to defeat the opposing party's nominee in the general election. Both campaigns can be expensive. In early 2000 Bush raised a record $70 million for his campaign and reportedly spent most of it just in winning the Republican nomination to oppose Gore.

A decline in party identification among voters also has contributed to the trend toward candidate-centered campaigns. Since the 1970s, when the major parties (especially the Democrats) changed their rules to strengthen the primary system and give more representation to women and racial minorities, more voters began to think of themselves as independents rather than as Democrats, Republicans, or third-party members. A 1995 Gallup poll showed 36 percent of voters identified themselves as independents, compared with about 32 percent for each of the two major parties. Similarly, studies detect a rise in ticket splitting and a decline in voting the straight party ticket.

Faced with this situation, candidates try to focus the campaign on their own positive attributes, including personality, physical appearance, education, experience, and views on issues of concern to the constituencies they want to represent. In most cases the candidate will not run away from the party but will merely say little about it in campaign speeches or advertising. Where the party or its philosophy is deemed a liability, the candidate may try to disassociate the campaign from the national party or some of its most prominent members. In the 1980s, for example, when the term *liberal* was widely shunned as "the L-word," Democratic candidates in some states preferred not to be linked with Sen. Edward M. Kennedy of Massachusetts or others closely associated with liberal causes.

For offices where candidates run as a pair, as for president and vice president, or governor and lieutenant governor in some states, the top candidate may try to find a running mate who balances the ticket geographically, philosophically, or in some other way. In 2000, for example, Bush chose veteran public servant Richard Cheney to compensate for Bush's own lack of experience in foreign affairs. And although most nominees strive for a geographic balance, Clinton of Arkansas chose Gore of Tennessee as vice president in 1992, making it the first successful all-southern ticket since Andrew Jackson of Tennessee and John C. Calhoun of South Carolina won in 1828. With Gore, Clinton won with a largely candidate-centered campaign.

Candidate-centered campaigns rely more on the news and advertising media than on the party to get their messages to the voters. And with the rise of the Internet they are even becoming less dependent on the print and broadcast media. Campaign Web sites, besides disseminating the candidate's position on issues, help collect the e-mail addresses of swing voters as well as likely supporters. These addresses may be used in turn for candidate appeals for money or volunteers to make phone calls or do other work for the campaign. The collected names and addresses can be stored for future campaigns as well as the one at hand. In this way, said political scientist Michael Cornfield, a specialist in political Internet usage, the candidates are "building digital political machines" with a potential for continuous two-way correspondence between the politician and the voters.

Candidate-centered campaigning is more personal than party-centered campaigning and therefore is more likely to be negative, attacking the opponent's character and qualifications instead of emphasizing the attacker's own fitness for the office being sought. Consequently, it is not surprising that recent elections have seen a rise in negative campaigning, despite the public's distaste for it as shown in numerous polls. A classic example of negative political advertising was the use of the "Willie Horton" ad in 1988 by supporters of presidential candidate George Bush. The controversial television spot sought to portray Bush's opponent, Massachusetts governor Michael S. Dukakis, as soft on crime because he had signed a prisoner furlough law. William R. Horton Jr., a convicted murderer, had raped a woman while on furlough from a Massachusetts prison. In the 1990s a new type of attack ad became prevalent, partly through the use of "soft money" given to parties supposedly for party-building activities. Such ads circumvented federal and state contribution limits because they did not use the candidate's name even though clearly targeted at a particular candidate.

See also Buckley v. Valeo; *Campaign Finance; Polling and Public Opinion; Soft Money and Twentieth-Century Political Campaigns; Suffrage; Talk Radio; Television and American Politics.*

JOHN MOORE, INDEPENDENT AUTHOR

BIBLIOGRAPHY

Boller, Paul F., Jr. *Presidential Campaigns.* Rev. ed. New York: Oxford University Press, 1996.

Guber, Susan. *How to Win Your First Election.* Boca Raton, Fla.: St. Lucie Press, 1997.

Milbank, Dana. "Is Negativity Good for Politics? Positively." *Washington Post,* April 2, 2000, B1.

Mitchell, Jack. *How to Get Elected: An Anecdotal History of Mudslinging, Red-Baiting, Vote-Stealing and Dirty Tricks in American Politics.* New York: St. Martin's Press, 1992.

White, Ben. "The Campaign on the Web: Electrons as Electors? Probably Not Yet." *Washington Post,* April 16, 2000, A10.

CARTER, JIMMY

The thirty-ninth president of the United States (1977–1981) and avowed champion of human rights, James Earl Carter Jr. battled economic woes on the domestic front and chalked up a mixed record in the foreign policy arena.

Carter was born October 1, 1924, in Plains, Georgia. After high school, he accepted an appointment to the U.S. Naval Academy, where in 1946 he graduated fifty-ninth in his class of 820. Over the next six years he served on submarine duty and took classes in nuclear physics at Union College in Schenectady, New York. When his father—a farmer, storekeeper, and insurance broker—died in 1953, Jimmy retired from the navy and went back home to Plains to take over the family peanut farm.

Carter's career in public service began with an appointment to the Sumter County School Board in 1955 and in-

cluded two terms in the Georgia State Senate. He ran for governor in 1966 but lost in the primary election. He was successful in 1970, when he defeated former governor Carl E. Sanders in the Democratic primary and went on to win the general election.

As governor, Carter openly called for both an end to racial segregation and the removal of racial barriers; in doing so, he became a symbol of the "New South." He also reorganized the state government, supported measures to protect the environment, and opened government meetings to the public.

Carter served his one term as governor—Georgia law prohibits two terms—and decided to seek an even higher office, the presidency. One month after leaving the governor's mansion in 1974 he announced he would seek the 1976 Democratic presidential nomination.

Following a two-year quest for the nomination against several better-known Democrats, Carter won the nomination. He left the June 1976 Democratic National Convention in New York with a solid lead in public opinion polls over Republican incumbent Gerald R. Ford, who was reeling from his pardon of former president Richard M. Nixon following the Watergate scandal and from the high unemployment and ongoing inflation battering the economy. This gap narrowed as the election approached, but Carter won 297–241 in the electoral college.

DOMESTIC POLITICS

Although the American public liked Carter's small-town informality and admired his efforts to "depomp" the presidency by making it more open and responsive to citizen appeals, his administration was plagued from its earliest days by the nation's continuing economic woes. Moreover, Carter's relationship with Congress, controlled by his own party, was strained. Members found the president aloof and his administration clearly inexperienced at the art of political deal making. Overall, he was viewed as a Washington outsider who failed to adopt an effective inside strategy in dealing with Congress.

A minor scandal erupted in the late summer of 1977 over revelations that Carter's budget director and close personal friend, Bert Lance, had engaged in questionable financial practices during his previous banking career. Lance, who resigned, was later exonerated, but the Lance affair—and other controversies involving U.S. ambassador to the United Nations Andrew Young, Attorney General Benjamin R. Civiletti, and Carter chief of staff Hamilton Jordan—seemed to contradict Carter's claim that he was holding members of his administration to a higher ethical standard than had previous presidents.

The already shaky economy bedeviled the Carter presidency, and efforts to rectify the situation led to a short recession. Carter did manage to claim an increase of nearly 8 million new jobs and a decrease in the budget deficit, but inflation and interest rates were at record levels. Prices, which had risen 6.5 percent during Carter's first year in office, rose 11.3 percent in 1979 and 13.5 percent in 1980. Unemployment was also high—at about 7.7 percent in 1980.

An energy crisis added to the president's troubles. Carter tried to reduce U.S. dependence on imported oil by encouraging alternative sources of energy and deregulating the price of American-produced oil and natural gas. The latter, however, caused a rise in inflation, which worsened an already ailing economy. Carter refused to impose price or wage controls and pleaded with big business to hold down prices and with labor unions to avoid new wage demands. His pleas, however, seemed to fall on deaf

President Jimmy Carter (center), with Anwar Sadat of Egypt (left) and Menachem Begin of Israel (right), at the signing of the peace treaty between the two countries. *Jimmy Carter Library*

ears. The president also called on the public to adopt energy conservation measures, and he proposed mandatory energy efficiency standards for home appliances and tax credits for home insulation, among other things. The public, though, already skeptical about the oil companies and their operations, could not bring itself to support such measures. In fact, most citizens did not really believe there had been an energy crisis.

In other areas of domestic policy, Carter was more successful. He prodded the government toward high efficiency through civil service reform, and he launched deregulation of the trucking and airline industries. He sought environmental protection measures, including expansion of the national park system, and proposed establishment of a Department of Education. Also under his administration, record numbers of women, African Americans, and Latinos were appointed to government jobs, including in the judiciary.

FOREIGN AFFAIRS

In foreign policy, Carter also had mixed results, but some of his successes were notable. In 1978 he tackled the impasse in the Middle East by inviting Prime Minister Menachem Begin of Israel and President Anwar Sadat of Egypt to Camp David, the Maryland presidential retreat. The Camp David Accords that emerged from their talks established peace between those two countries. Closer to home, he secured Senate approval in 1978 of treaties transferring control of the Panama Canal to Panama on December 31, 1999. Then turn-

ing to the Far East, he formalized relations with the People's Republic of China on January 1, 1979.

During the last two years of his term, however, Carter's luck on the foreign policy front ran out. On June 18, 1979, Carter and Soviet leader Leonid Brezhnev signed a treaty in Vienna to limit strategic nuclear weapons, but Senate approval of the agreement, known as SALT II, was not forthcoming. In December 1979 the Soviets invaded Afghanistan to prop up a procommunist government there, prompting Carter to withdraw the SALT II treaty in 1980. He also imposed a grain embargo on the Soviet Union and refused to allow U.S. participation in the 1980 Olympic games in Moscow.

On November 4, 1979, Iranian militants stormed the U.S. embassy in Tehran, taking fifty-two American diplomats and embassy personnel hostage. Carter made several attempts to free the hostages, including an abortive helicopter raid in April 1980 in which eight soldiers died, but all his efforts failed, and the crisis dominated the last year of his presidency. The Iranians released the hostages on January 20, 1981, minutes after Carter left office.

In 1980 Carter was defeated in his reelection attempt by another former governor—Ronald Reagan of California. Carter won only six states and the District of Columbia.

After leaving the presidency, Carter returned home to Plains. He founded the nonprofit Carter Center in Atlanta to promote peace and human rights worldwide and ventured out regularly to lecture and embark on diplomatic missions.

In 1994 the former president carried out a series of high-profile missions to North Korea, Bosnia, and Haiti. But even in retirement the former president still had his critics. They argued that in undertaking diplomatic missions, Carter was too willing to accommodate despotic leaders and that his activities undermined standard diplomacy.

See also *Treaties: Peace, Armament, and Defense; Treaty Making.*

SABRA BISSETTE LEDENT, INDEPENDENT AUTHOR

BIBLIOGRAPHY

Abernathy, M. Glenn, ed. *The Carter Years: The President and Policy Making.* New York: St. Martin's Press, 1984.

Brzezinski, Zbigniew. *Power and Principle.* New York: Farrar, Straus, Giroux, 1983.

Glad, Betty. *Jimmy Carter: In Search of the Great White House.* New York: Norton, 1980.

Hargrove, Erwin C. *Jimmy Carter as President: Leadership and the Politics of the Public Good.* Baton Rouge: LSU Press, 1988.

Jones, Charles O. *The Trusteeship Presidency: Jimmy Carter and the United States Congress.* Baton Rouge: LSU Press, 1988.

Smith, Gaddis. *Mortality, Reason and Power: American Diplomacy in the Carter Years.* New York: Hill and Wang, 1986.

CENSUS

The U.S. Constitution requires the federal government to take a population census every ten years and use the results to apportion seats among the states in the House of Representatives. Since 1790 the government has conducted twenty-two censuses. The U.S. population has grown from 3.9 million people in the thirteen original states to today's estimated 275 million in fifty states.

ORIGINS

In 1787 delegates from twelve states—every state but Rhode Island—met in Philadelphia to amend the Articles of Confederation and ended up framing a new national government. The result of their labors, the U.S. Constitution, created a system of government with executive, legislative, and judicial branches. The document mandated a bicameral legislature, with seats in the lower house apportioned among the states by population and elected by the voters. Seats in the upper house were apportioned equally among the states and elected by the state legislatures. The head of the executive branch, the president, would be elected by the voters through the electoral college. The new system increased the power of the national government considerably, yet it also included checks and balances to guarantee the powers of citizens and the states.

The Constitution allocated seats in the House by state population and in the Senate by fixed number, two for each state. Since direct taxes also were allocated by state population, the large states received the most House seats but bore the heaviest potential tax burden. The Constitution calculated

states' strength in the electoral college by adding the Senate and House members of each state.

In creating the census system, the Framers drew on their experience and their understanding of the various methods of allocating political power and assessing taxes. During the Philadelphia Convention they discussed methods based on population, land assessments, and other measures of wealth. They agreed in theory that political power should be based on population and tax assessments on wealth. They also agreed that population was easier to measure than wealth and that wealth and population were highly correlated. They therefore favored population as the measure of apportionment. The methods they devised for taking the census and apportioning House seats laid the foundation for the Great Compromise, which resolved differences between the large and small states over how representation in Congress would be determined and made a national government possible. The Framers decided that the periodic adjustments required to account for population growth would be made automatically every ten years. The automatic decennial schedule differed from the more frequent cycles of elections for the House, the Senate, and the presidency.

Besides determining how the census would be conducted, the Framers debated who would be counted as taxpaying members of society. Most delegates to the Constitutional Convention favored an expansive approach, one that counted women, children, and the poor, though members of these groups neither voted nor were necessarily responsible for paying taxes. The problem came when the Framers considered how to count slaves and Indians. Should the southern states, for example, be granted political representation for their slaves? At the time, southerners considered slaves property for purposes of tax assessments but did not count slaves when apportioning the state legislatures. The double rule established by the Framers—that of using state population size to calculate both representation and taxation—broke down for slaves. The Framers also discussed whether tribal Indians, who generally were considered members of foreign nations, should be counted to determine representation and taxation.

Convention delegates answered these questions by hedging their double rule in the Constitution's "census clause." The clause in Article I, section 2, paragraph 3, states that the "respective Numbers [of the population] . . . shall be determined by adding to the whole Number of free Persons, including those bound to Service for a Term of Years, and excluding Indians not taxed, three fifths of all other Persons." This so-called three-fifths compromise required the census to count slaves separately for the apportionment, as three-fifths of the "Number of free Persons." Moreover, the compromise eliminated "Indians not taxed" from the census altogether. Only "taxed" or "civilized" Indians—those Indians who had

DISTICTS	Free white Males of 16 years and upwards, including heads of families.	Free white Males under sixteen years.	Free white Females, including heads of families.	All other free persons.	Slaves.	Total.
Vermont	22435	22328	40505	255	16	85539
N. Hampshire	36086	34851	70160	630	158	141885
Maine	24384	24748	46870	538	NONE	96540
Maſſachuſetts	95453	87289	190582	5463	NONE	378787
Rhode Iſland	16019	15799	32652	3407	948	68825
Connecticut	60523	54403	117448	2808	2764	237946
New York	83700	78122	152320	4654	21324	340120
New Jerſey	45251	41416	83287	2762	11423	184139
Pennſylvania	110788	106948	206363	6537	3737	434373
Delaware	11783	12143	22384	3899	8887	59094
Maryland	55915	51339	101395	8043	103036	319728
Virginia	110936	116135	215046	12866	292627	747610
Kentucky	15154	17057	28922	114	12430	73677
N. Carolina	69988	77506	140710	4975	100572	393751
S. Carolina	35576	37722	66880	1801	107094	249073
Georgia	13103	14044	25739	398	29264	82548
	807094	791850	1541263	59150	694280	3893635

Total number of Inhabitants of the United States exclusive of S. Weſtern and N. Territory.	Free white Males of 21 years and upwards.	Free Males under 21 years of age.	Free white Females.	All other Perſons.	Slaves.	Total
S. W. territory	6271	10277	15365	361	3417	35691
N. Ditto	—	—	—	—	—	—

Above is a printed summary of results for the 1790 census. *National Archives*

renounced their tribal allegiance—were to be included in the decennial count and therefore in the apportionment totals.

In defining the populations to be included in the census and the method by which they were to be counted (in whole or in part), the Constitution established four classifications based on civil status—free, slave, Indians not taxed, and unfree indentured servants. To avoid ambiguity, the Constitution specified that unfree indentured servants, that is, "those bound to Service for a term of Years," were to be counted as "free Persons." Nowhere did the Constitution mention a racial classification, and in fact the Framers used the ambiguous "other Persons" to define "slave." Yet, seeking to clarify the civil statuses, census officials by 1790 had begun using the racial classifications "white," "black," "colored," and "Indian" in popular discourse and on the census form. Whites were considered free even if indentured. Blacks or coloreds were counted as slaves unless clearly specified as free blacks or free coloreds.

DEMOGRAPHIC HISTORY

In 1790 the United States became the first nation in the world to institute a regular population count to apportion political power. The principles that political power was a function of population and that population could be measured were innovative in the eighteenth century and proved

to be lasting only as they were implemented in the nineteenth and twentieth centuries.

The census might have been a minor constitutional innovation were it not for the extraordinary demographic character of the American population, one of the most heterogeneous and demographically dynamic populations in world history. Since 1776 the United States has seen rapid population growth, major migrations, and sharp demographic transitions—including the change from a population with high mortality and high fertility to one with low mortality and low fertility—all while remaining a racially and ethnically heterogeneous population. In 1775 the population exceeded 2 million, which grew to 3.9 million by 1790 and a quarter billion by 2000. The current land area of the country is four times what it was in 1790, and the population is almost sixty times larger. In 1850 the country was 85 percent rural; in 2000 it was 74 percent urban. From 1700 to the Civil War years, the American population grew 30–35 percent every decade. From 1860 to 1910, it grew about 24 percent a decade, and since 1910 it has grown about 13 percent a decade. The median age of the population has increased greatly. In the early nineteenth century it was around sixteen, reflecting the era's high birth rates and short life expectancy. By 2000 it had more than doubled, to around thirty-four. In the early nineteenth century the life expectancy was about forty years; in 2000 it was about seventy-five.

ROLE OF THE CENSUS

Because of the dramatic patterns they reveal in the population, the decennial census and its apportionments are major social, political, and intellectual events. Census-based apportionments are supposed to take difficult questions about the distribution of political power and economic resources off the immediate legislative agenda and address them through predetermined allocations. Yet because so much is at stake, the census runs the risk of being politicized. Each decade the census numbers are subject to close scrutiny and analysis, as Congress, state legislatures, and other government bodies use the population-based apportionment formulas to redistribute legislative seats, tax revenue, and grants-in-aid. Politically delicate and painful, the apportionment process is a zero-sum game—for every gainer, there must be a loser. Legislators can soften the pain for the losers by shifting relative, but not absolute, power or revenue. That is, they can enlarge the House and allocate additional seats to growing states—without taking seats from other states. Accordingly, the development of the census itself as a progressively more elaborate and more scientific count each decade is intimately bound up with the political and social history of the nation.

DEVELOPMENT OF THE CENSUS: 1790–1840

By authority of the first census law, the secretary of state directed the U.S. marshals to count the population in six categories: free white males under sixteen, free white males sixteen and over, free white females, free coloreds, and slaves. Enumerators, or officials authorized to collect census data, tallied the results for their local jurisdictions, then sent the totals to the marshal in charge of their district. The marshal compiled the district totals and forwarded them to the secretary of state. The count took eighteen months to complete. In late 1791 Congress began the second phase of the decennial census: reapportionment. The Constitution was silent on the method of apportionment. Treasury Secretary Alexander Hamilton and Secretary of State Thomas Jefferson, leaders of the new government's emerging political factions, advocated two different methods of apportionment. Each method had a different impact on the distribution of seats in the House. A long debate ensued, and Congress passed Jefferson's bill. President George Washington sought advice from Hamilton and vetoed the bill, using the presidential veto for the first time. Weeks later, Congress passed a second bill, which favored Hamilton's method. Washington signed the measure, and all parties put the issue behind them.

Over time, the strengths and weaknesses of the census captured the attention of the early Republic's politicians and mathematical tinkerers. With a few decades of census results, one could calculate growth rates for the nation, states, and local areas. Almanacs reprinted the latest figures. The data informed the political discourse of the nation and inspired curiosity about the character of the population. Each decade Congress refined the count's age and sex breakdowns and added to the survey a few new questions. By 1840 the six questions of 1790 had grown to seventy or more. The widening sectional split between North and South echoed ominously through the decennial census and apportionment process as free states grew faster than slave states. Free-state representatives increasingly dominated the House, and votes in the electoral college similarly tilted toward the North. Southerners watched these trends with apprehension.

REFORMING THE CENSUS: 1850–1902

After a controversy over the accuracy of the 1840 census, and in the midst of contentious debates over the future of slavery in the territories, Congress initiated a major overhaul of the census law. Before 1850 the census focused on the family unit and reported few data on persons. To add detail to published results, the 1850 census collected data on each individual. The burden of tallying the results was shifted to Washington. Besides instituting an individual-level census, the United States created a large but temporary census office to tabulate the data and expanded the publications derived from the census. Housed in the new Department of the Interior, the office grew rapidly. In the mid-nineteenth century the Census Office employed about 10 percent of the federal employees in Washington when census processing was under way. Congress called on the Census Office to collect and publish more data than before on the demographic, social, and economic character of the population. The 1850 census reform law created specialized schedules, or census forms, for collecting data on mortality, agriculture, manufacturing, and the population, as well as "social statistics" (data on such topics as schooling, the disabled, or religious bodies). The data in these schedules were tabulated and published as separate census volumes and summarized in an abstract or compendium.

During the Civil War and Reconstruction, the government continued to take the census and publish the results. The Thirteenth Amendment made former slaves whole members of the "representative population," enlarging the representation of southern states and leading Congress to pass section 2 of the Fourteenth Amendment. The section reduced the number of seats apportioned to states that denied freedmen the right to vote. The Fifteenth Amendment mandated that the right to vote "shall not be denied or abridged . . . on account of race, color, or previous condition of servitude." The Fourteenth and Fifteenth Amendments required that census officials continue to collect data on the racial composition of the population.

By 1880 Congress had streamlined the census machinery to permit the census superintendent to appoint the field staff, speed up the enumeration process, and hire technical experts in Washington. In 1902 the Census Office became a permanent government agency in the Department of the Interior. The office was made a bureau in the Department of Commerce and Labor in 1903. When the department split along functional lines in 1913, the bureau joined the newly created Department of Commerce.

THE TWENTIETH CENTURY

As it had done before the Civil War, Congress "solved" the problem of differential population growth after the war by increasing the size of the House with each census. In the 1860s Congress had 243 members; by 1910 it had 435. As the science of statistical data collection developed, census officials improved their capacity to collect, process, and publish data.

During the 1920s the chief controversy surrounding the census concerned the failure of Congress to reapportion itself. For the only time in the nation's history, Congress for several reasons could not muster a majority to pass a reapportionment bill. Congress had decided in 1910 to stop the growth of the House. The 1920 reapportionment therefore was a zero-sum game. Several mathematicians produced competing apportionment methods, which produced different allocations for key states. The demographic trends evident in the 1920 census results rankled the Republican majority in Congress. The results showed major shifts in population to the cities, to the Far West, and to places populated by immigrants. Charging that the census had to be wrong, critics of the count proposed and failed to pass a reapportionment bill. In the late 1920s they proposed another measure—an automatic reapportionment law that would take effect after the 1930 census. Congress passed the bill, along with a provision that removed the mandate—included in every apportionment bill since 1840—that congressional districts be compact and as equal in size as possible within states. Congress reapportioned power among the states but acquiesced to

The Bureau of the Census, owing to the massive amounts of census data to be processed, was the first civilian federal agency to computerize its operations. The bureau acquired its first computer, above, in March 1951. *National Archives*

rural malapportionment within states. States with growing urban populations gained seats, but those seats were not necessarily allocated to urban districts. This practice led in the 1960s to the "reapportionment revolution," a series of Supreme Court decisions that required state legislatures to create equal-size congressional and legislative districts.

The 1920s reapportionment stalemate affected the census in several ways. Since state legislatures did not need to create legislative districts of equal size, the accuracy of local area data was not a top priority. Freed from having to answer the political questions posed by reapportionment, the Census Bureau was called on to address the demographic issues raised by the Great Depression and the Second World War. Officials from President Franklin D. Roosevelt's alphabet agencies called on the bureau to provide data on unemployment and socioeconomic status. Congress built the grants-in-aid system to allocate tax money from the federal government to state and local governments, and lawmakers sought population data on poverty, income distribution, and migration. The bureau introduced sample surveys to measure unemployment, reorganized the agency's bureaucratic structure, intensified employees' statistical training, built a research unit, and analyzed and revamped classification systems. Many of these innovations were incorporated into the 1940 census. That census, the sixteenth, included sample questions for the first time,

a housing census, and evaluation studies to measure systematically the coding bias, sampling error, and accuracy of the enumeration, as well as the reliability of tabulation and coding procedures.

As part of the general trend toward statistical innovation, statisticians calculated the first systematic estimates of census undercount. The selective service registration of October 1940 yielded data that allowed demographers to compare the total number of men who had registered for the draft with the total number of men of draft age (twenty-one to thirty-five years), as determined by the April 1940 census. Statisticians found that the registration had recorded about 453,000 more draft-age men than had been counted by the census. In other words, the census had missed about 3 percent of draft-age men. The level of the undercount varied by region and race: about 13 percent of draft-age black men, for example, were missed in the census.

After an undercount in 1950 of 2.5 percent nationally and 11 percent for "nonwhites," the accuracy of the census became a prominent political issue. In the 1960s the issue attracted attention because of three developments. First, Congress since the early 1900s had used the grants-in-aid system to allocate federal funds to state and local governments for vocational education, highway construction, agricultural extension, and public health programs. The extensive programs of the post–World War II era—for example, urban renewal initiatives, the interstate highway system, and hospital construction subsidies—were funded using the grants-in-aid system. Census data underpinned many of the formulas Congress used in the 1960s to allocate the grants-in-aid funds to particular jurisdictions. Second, the Supreme Court in 1962 ruled that malapportioned state legislatures were unconstitutional, inviting the decade of lawsuits that sparked the reapportionment revolution. By 1964 the phrase "one person, one vote" had entered the nation's political vocabulary to define the new principle of legislative apportionment. Finally, the civil rights movement of the 1950s and 1960s framed many of its arguments about discrimination in terms of the underrepresentation of minorities in major areas of American society: in the labor force, in the public life of the community, and in the housing market, where minorities fought for equal access. Civil rights attorneys and activists used census data to make their case. They argued that if 30 percent of a local labor market was black, then blacks should hold roughly 30 percent of the jobs in every occupation. Congress responded in the late 1950s and early 1960s by passing several major civil rights laws. To administer and implement the laws, officials required quality census data. In passing the Voting Rights Act of 1965, which enforced the Fifteenth Amendment to the Constitution, Congress created clear, census-based numerical tests of compliance with the constitutional guarantee of universal voting rights. Again, census data had a direct impact on a highly charged political issue.

Statisticians and politicians realized in the 1970s that the census undercount had denied political representation to the uncounted, and for the next two decades they worked on a two-pronged strategy to remedy the problem. The bureau resolved to do a better job of counting the population during the April enumeration. It also conceded that it was impossible to count everyone in a nation as diverse and mobile as the United States. This latter argument prompted discussion of whether it was possible or prudent to "adjust" or "correct" the traditional enumeration to reflect the known undercount. The adjusted counts would be useful for apportioning House seats and setting national policy. By the late 1980s the bureau had developed a new sample survey, the post-enumeration survey, which was to be included in the design for the 1990 census. The bureau proposed to count three hundred thousand households a second time and then to match the results of the survey with those of the census to determine who had been missed, counted twice, or counted at the wrong location. The bureau also recommended using these estimates of error or underenumeration to correct the counts of different demographic and regional groups, or "post strata," and to adjust the counts for the rest of the country. The administra-

tions of Ronald Reagan and George Bush canceled the survey, though it was restored to the 1990 census design after New York City and a coalition of jurisdictions and civil rights organizations sued the Commerce Department.

The 1929 census statute gave the authority for technical decisions about the census to the secretary of commerce. President George Bush's commerce secretary, Robert Mosbacher, declined to adjust the 1990 census results. Party changes in the White House and Congress in the 1990s led to renewed debate about adjusting the 2000 census. Although the administration of Bill Clinton supported census adjustment, Republican congressional leaders did not. Unable to resolve the issue by political means, they resorted to litigation in 1998 and 1999. The Supreme Court ruled in *Department of Commerce v. United States House of Representatives* (1999) that Title 13, the federal statute governing the census, required Congress to apportion House seats among the states using the *unadjusted* population counts from the April enumeration. The Court further construed the law to mandate sampling, if "feasible," for purposes other than apportionment. The bureau interpreted this finding to require *adjusted* data for other census uses, including redistricting and the allocation of funds, if such data were found to be more accurate than the unadjusted counts. These rulings were expected to result in the publication of two sets of census data for the nation's local jurisdictions.

See also *Apportionment; Civil Rights Movement; Congress; Constitution, U.S.; Electoral College; Reapportionment Cases; Reconstruction; Slavery; Suffrage; Three-Fifths Clause.*

MARGO ANDERSON, UNIVERSITY OF WISCONSIN—MILWAUKEE

BIBLIOGRAPHY

Anderson, Margo J. *The American Census: A Social History.* New Haven: Yale University Press, 1988.

———. *Encyclopedia of the U.S. Census.* Washington, D.C.: CQ Press, 2000.

Anderson, Margo J., and Stephen E. Fienberg. *Who Counts? The Politics of Census-Taking in Contemporary America.* New York: Russell Sage, 1999.

Bryant, Barbara Everitt, and William C. Dunn. *Moving Power and Money: The Politics of Census Taking.* Ithaca: New Strategist Publications, 1995.

Choldin, Harvey. *Looking for the Last Percent: The Controversy over Census Undercounts.* New Brunswick, N.J.: Rutgers University Press, 1994.

Skerry, Peter. *Counting on the Census? Race, Group Identity, and the Evasion of Politics.* Washington, D.C.: Brookings Institution Press, 2000.

CIVIL-MILITARY RELATIONS

The subordination of the military to civilian authority in the United States grew out of English tradition and eighteenth-century experience, but various issues have shaped the development of those relations over the past two centuries.

AMERICAN REVOLUTION

During the period leading up to the American Revolution, the British military carried on policies that many colonists saw as serious abuses of proper civil-military relations. Trials of civilians accused of smuggling were moved to vice admiralty courts, which did not employ juries. In the Boston Massacre (1770), Redcoats fired on an unarmed mob. Civilians were compelled to accept British troops as lodgers in their houses under the Quartering Act (1765) and subsequent British laws. Soldiers were often employed to enforce warrantless searches or search with general warrants—although in such instances the use of military or civilian officers of the Crown would have been equally unacceptable.

As Thomas Jefferson charged in the Declaration of Independence, British troops were removed from civilian judicial authorities to be tried abroad for alleged crimes against American civilians. Finally, sections of the colonies were placed under martial law, with the writ of habeas corpus suspended. After independence, the Continental Army came close to mutiny at one point in the so-called Newburgh Mutiny, when officers of the unpaid and underprovisioned Continental Army contemplated marching on Congress in New York City. Only the appearance of the retired general George Washington dissuaded them.

THE U.S. CONSTITUTION

When the Framers drew up the Constitution, they were acutely aware of the major problems of civil-military relations under law. Under that basic document, Congress was given the power to declare war and to raise and support armies, although appropriations for that purpose could not exceed a term of two years. Congress was also empowered to create and maintain a navy, establish a code of military law, control the calling up of the militia into federal service, and regulate the militias in general. States were forbidden to keep troops and ships of war in times of peace or to issue letters of marque and reprisal, while the president was made commander in chief of the armed forces and of the militias called into the service of the Union. Finally, the government of the United States was obliged to protect states from invasion and from domestic violence.

When the Bill of Rights was added to the U.S. Constitution in 1791, two of its amendments spoke directly to civil-military relations, and almost every one of them had potential implications for such interaction. The Second Amendment protected the right of the citizenry to keep and bear arms in order that the states could maintain their militias effectively, while the Third Amendment denied to the military the compulsory power to quarter troops in civilian dwellings in time of peace.

MILITARY CONSCRIPTION

The first crisis of civil-military relations may be seen in the controversies that surrounded the draft. The Constitution is silent about the draft specifically, but scholars have recognized that the call-up of militia envisioned by the Constitution constituted a draft, given that participation was required for all free, white, male citizens not specifically exempted. During the Civil War this simple procedure for raising armies through the call-up of militias proved inadequate, and President Abraham Lincoln persuaded Congress to pass the Enrollment Act (1863), which instituted the first federal draft. Resistance to the draft proved so severe that Lincoln suspended habeas corpus for those accused of encouraging draft resistance. Throughout the North, riots erupted from attempts to enforce the draft, with the worst violence occurring in New York City from July 13 through 16, 1863.

The draft also arose as a serious point of contention at other periods in U.S. history. In the *Selective Draft Law Cases* (1918), the Supreme Court upheld the constitutionality of the World War I draft. Enforcement of the draft during that war involved severe restrictions on speech and political agitation and led to other Supreme Court cases, including *Schenck v. United States* (1919), in which the Court upheld the imprisonment of war protesters who had distributed an antidraft pamphlet.

A draft was reimposed on the eve of the nation's entry into World War II and was resumed in 1948, in response to the emergence of the cold war. The most troubling issues arose during the Vietnam War (1965–1973), when opposition to the war and to the draft that supported it became inseparable. In *United States v. Seeger* (1965) the Supreme Court voided the requirement that application for conscientious objection to military service be based on deeply held religious convictions, ruling instead that any philosophical belief that holds a position in a person's life similar to religion would suffice. The draft was terminated in 1973.

MILITARY JUSTICE

The issue of military justice has proven to be another difficult arena for civil-military relations. In *Ex parte Milligan* (1866) the Supreme Court ruled that the military cannot try civilians under ordinary circumstances unless a conflict has actually closed the ordinary federal courts. In *Reid v. Covert* (1957) the Supreme Court further restricted the extent to which civilians accompanying U.S. forces abroad could be subject to military justice.

The system of military justice for enlisted personnel has also been a point of contention at various times in U.S. history. During the American Revolution, Congress enacted Articles of War (to govern the army) and Articles for the Government of the Navy. Congress later revised these several times under the Constitution's grant of authority to "make Rules for the Government and Regulation of the land and naval forces."

Military justice tended to be strict and without the refinements of civilian justice, but in the crisis of World War I, with its millions of conscripts, an incident occurred that led to the revision of the Articles of War in 1920. In 1917 a race riot took place in Houston between black troops and white civilians, leading to the deaths of fifteen civilians and four soldiers. In the aftermath, thirteen soldiers were hanged after procedures that many compared to judicial lynching. The 1920 revisions provided for the right to counsel in general courts-martial, required that acquittals be announced in open court, prescribed unanimity for the imposition of the death sentence and a two-thirds vote for lesser penalties, and reduced the sentencing power of summary courts-martial.

In reaction to the severity of punishment meted out by military tribunals during World War II, Congress in 1950 created the Uniform Code of Military Justice (UCMJ), applicable to all the armed services. In general courts-martial a defendant enjoys the right to counsel at the government's expense, and he or she may elect to be tried by a military judge directly. In special cases, appeals to the Court of Military Appeals, with its three civilian judges appointed by the president, are allowed.

Despite the UCMJ's guarantee of certain rights, the courts have never held that the Bill of Rights applies to the military justice system. Lesser offenses may be dealt with in a nonjudicial manner by a summary court-martial, and the Supreme Court ruled in *Middendorf v. Henry* (1976) that the right to government-financed counsel does not apply in cases of summary court-martial.

PRESIDENTIAL AUTHORITY

Another area of civil-military relations is the subordination of the military to civilian authority, and, in particular, to the president as commander in chief. In the two greatest instances of military-presidential rivalry—President Abraham Lincoln versus Gen. George McClellan and President Harry S. Truman versus Gen. Douglas MacArthur—the contests

Commander in Chief George Bush greets Marine general Norman Schwarzkopf, leader of all U.S. military forces in the Persian Gulf War, at the victory parade in Washington, D.C.   *R. Michael Jenkins, Congressional Quarterly*

ended when the commander in chief summoned the political will to dismiss the offending officer. Both McClellan, who ran for president against Lincoln in 1864, and MacArthur, who spoke against Truman upon his removal in 1951, attempted to undo the practical effect of their dismissal, but they were unsuccessful.

Civil-military relations may also include certain aspects of the presidential uses of military force or of presidential authority as commander in chief. The president's use of martial law powers is normally limited by the constitutional requirement that the legislature of a state petition for intervention in cases of domestic violence or, when the legislature is not in session, that the executive of the state request such intervention. However, in any rebellion or attempted secession by a state that requirement must be presumed to be waived.

In the Civil War, Lincoln suspended habeas corpus on his own authority. The Constitution clearly envisioned its being accomplished by act of Congress in time of rebellion or invasion, but Lincoln maintained that when Congress is not in session, the power to suspend habeas corpus devolves upon the president, although such actions could later be confirmed or revoked by Congress. In the aftermath of the war, Congress undertook the "reconstruction" of the states of the former Confederacy with the Military Reconstruction Acts of 1867. Those states (except Tennessee) were divided into five military districts, each under a brigadier general who was responsible for keeping the peace. Military commissions were set up with the power to overrule state governments and were empowered to call for elections to constitutional conventions. In keeping the peace in the reconstruction districts, the military could ignore constitutional requirements for trial by jury, warrants, due process, and habeas corpus.

WAR POWERS

Presidential authority has often been supplemented through the invocation of the chief executive's war powers. In the Japanese internment cases, the Court upheld the right of the president to remove Americans of Japanese ancestry from Washington State, Oregon, and California and to intern them in camps for the duration of World War II. In the most famous of those cases, *Korematsu v. United States* (1944), Justice Robert Jackson claimed in his dissent that these decisions are "a loaded weapon ready for the hand of any authority that can bring forward a plausible claim of an urgent need." In some cases the Court has placed limits on the president's war powers, as in the case of *Youngstown Sheet & Tube Co. v. Sawyer* (1952), in which the Court ruled that President Truman did not have "inherent powers" to seize steel mills as part of a move toward a strike settlement during the Korean War, when Congress had already declined to approve that action.

On account of the dual role of the president as chief executive of the civilian government and commander in chief of the nation's military forces, the power of presidents to utilize armed force without congressional approval and without a formal declaration of war has sometimes been seen as a civil-military issue. Alexander Hamilton wrote the *Pacificus* papers in response to the crisis over President George Washington's issuance of the Proclamation of Neutrality in the Anglo-French struggles in 1793, in seeming contravention of the Franco-American Treaty of Alliance. As Hamilton appraised it, presidential powers in foreign policy and war are precisely those of the British monarch, restrained only by the limitations specifically imposed by the Constitution.

Presidents enjoy the inherent authority to employ military force short of general war. There are many reasons why a president might not seek a declaration of war even when Congress would be likely to accede to the request. Declarations of war are appropriate only against sovereign nations, so they are never used against riots, rebellions, secessions, Indian tribes, or Barbary pirates. Sometimes, fear of widening a conflict has precluded formal declarations of war, as in the Quasi-War with France in the administration of John Adams or in the Vietnam War. Since World War II, military action has sometimes been conducted as peacekeeping or police action under United Nations (UN) auspices, as in the Korean War, or to enforce a UN resolution, as in the Persian Gulf War, or in conjunction with NATO in Kosovo.

Throughout the cold war era, presidents were committed to launching massive nuclear retaliation without a congressional declaration of war, but the issue in those circumstances was the need for instantaneous reaction. Since the Constitution recognizes the right of states—which are ordinarily barred from engaging in war or foreign policy—to employ armed force in self-defense when the situation will allow no delay, then *a fortiori* the president, who conducts military and foreign policy, enjoys that inherent power.

During the long and bitter controversies surrounding the Vietnam War, Congress passed the War Powers Resolution of 1973, requiring that a president consult with Congress (where practical) before committing troops to foreign conflict and limiting to sixty days the time he can keep troops in the field without specific congressional authorization. Because Congress and the presidents since 1973 have studiously avoided a court test of the constitutionality of the resolution, the boundaries of presidential war powers have remained vague and subject to the give-and-take of political compromise.

MILITARY SPENDING AND CIVILIAN POLITICS

Particularly since World War II, major issues in U.S. politics have revolved around military spending and military bases. Civilians demand military bases to energize local economies, but they also seek federal financial support to offset lost tax revenues from military establishments and to supply schools for military dependents. Regardless of the priorities of the military establishment, every House member wants to enhance military spending in his or her district, and therefore every state in the Union has at least one significant military facility. In much the same way, the military obtains vast federal financing for weapons development and other military contracts, but civilian politicians have tremendous influence in shaping and directing those expenditures. Military considerations also foster and shape other civilian policies, as in the National Defense Education Act of 1958, which provided federal money for public education to assist in the training of students in the sciences.

See also *American Revolution; Civil War; Cold War; Lincoln, Abraham; Persian Gulf War; Presidency; Truman, Harry S.; Vietnam War; War Powers; World War I.*

PATRICK M. O'NEIL,
BROOME COMMUNITY COLLEGE, STATE UNIVERSITY OF NEW YORK

BIBLIOGRAPHY

Bishop, Joseph W., Jr. *Justice under Fire.* New York: Charterhouse, 1974.
Everett, Robinson O. *Military Justice in the Armed Forces.* 2d ed. Westport, Conn.: Greenwood Press, 1976.

Levy, Leonard W., Kenneth L. Karst, and Dennis J. Mahoney, eds. *Encyclopedia of the American Constitution.* New York: Macmillan, 1986.

Lindley, John M. *"A Soldier Is Also a Citizen": The Controversy over Military Justice, 1917–1920.* New York: Garland, 1990.

O'Sullivan, John, and Alan M. Meckler, eds. *The Draft and Its Enemies: A Documentary History.* Urbana: University of Illinois Press, 1974.

CIVIL RIGHTS ACT OF 1866

The abolition of slavery, through the Emancipation Proclamation in 1863, separate state action as in Maryland in 1864, and the Thirteenth Amendment in 1865, left uncertain what rights and opportunities freed people—indeed, all African Americans—would have. President Andrew Johnson viewed the Thirteenth Amendment and the former Confederate states' repudiation of secession as sufficient bases on which normal political relations might be restored between those states and the federal government. Republicans rejected Johnson's view. The nature of the unfinished business came into focus in late 1865, as the former Confederate states began legislating a new status for black southerners.

In December 1865 the Thirteenth Amendment achieved ratification and the Thirty-ninth Congress convened. Proposed in January 1866, the Civil Rights Act was a response by congressional Republicans to the Black Codes enacted by the legislatures of former Confederate states to recognize but limit the rights of former slaves. Mississippi's new law, for example, stipulated that black residents could not own land outside the towns. If black Mississippians could not own agricultural land, most would have to work white Mississippians' land, and one of the salient characteristics of slavery would persist. Lyman Trumbull, chairman of the Senate Judiciary Committee, had the Black Codes in mind when he promised "to destroy all these discriminations."

The Civil Rights Act represented congressional Republicans' first attempt to modify public policy in the South to accommodate emancipation. Going beyond declaring an end to slavery, Congress drew upon its authority under section 2 of the Thirteenth Amendment to enforce emancipation by offering a working definition of freedom for black southerners. Rebutting the U.S. Supreme Court's decision in *Dred Scott v. Sandford* (1857), which had denied black citizenship, section 2 declared African Americans to be citizens and outlined their core rights.

The act focused on what were understood to be "civil rights," among them the right to make contracts, own land, and testify in court, as well as blacks' right to be free of criminal penalties that applied only to them. It also provided for the "full and equal benefit of all laws and proceedings for the security of person and property, as is enjoyed by white citizens." The act did not establish political rights—the right to vote or the right to run for and hold public office. Neither did it promise land distribution, except in the sense that black southerners would have the same legal right as any white purchaser to buy land from a willing seller. Nor, finally, did it encompass social rights that might challenge racial segregation.

Republicans viewed the Civil Rights Act as an imperative modification of President Johnson's program of restoring the South to normal political relations with the federal government. It did not go as far as some Republicans wanted, but it was a starting place on which Republicans could agree. The president vetoed the bill, however, and couched his veto message in strident terms that objected not only to specific provisions but to the entire rationale for federal authority over race relations in the South. By votes of 33 to 15 in the Senate and 122 to 41 in the House, the Civil Rights Act of 1866 became the first major U.S. law to be enacted over a presidential veto.

Republicans fretted that the Civil Rights Act might not survive future legislative or judicial assault. A subsequent Congress might repeal it, and a Democratic president would sign such a bill. Even if that did not happen, the Supreme Court might agree with Johnson that the act was unconstitutional. Congressional Republicans therefore moved to incorporate the act in section 1 of what became the Fourteenth Amendment, so as to place it beyond the reach of either congressional repeal or judicial invalidation. To obtain ratification of the Fourteenth Amendment, they found that they had to establish voting rights for freedmen.

As the instrument of choice for addressing the denial of civil rights, the 1866 act was replaced by section one of the Fourteenth Amendment, especially its Equal Protection Clause, which the U.S. Supreme Court invoked in *Brown v. Board of Education* (1954). The Court relied on the 1866 act in some cases, however, among them *Jones v. Alfred H. Mayer Co.* (1968), which dealt with segregated housing.

See also *Civil Rights Act of 1875; Johnson, Andrew; Reconstruction.*

PETER WALLENSTEIN,
VIRGINIA POLYTECHNIC INSTITUTE AND STATE UNIVERSITY

BIBLIOGRAPHY

Benedict, Michael Les. *A Compromise of Principle: Congressional Republicans and Reconstruction, 1863–1869.* New York: Norton, 1974.

Foner, Eric. *Reconstruction: America's Unfinished Revolution, 1863–1877.* New York: Harper and Row, 1988.

Maltz, Earl M. *Civil Rights, the Constitution, and Congress, 1863–1869.* Lawrence: University Press of Kansas, 1990.

CIVIL RIGHTS ACT OF 1875

By 1875 the civil rights legislation that Congress had passed in 1866 over President Andrew Johnson's veto had done little to eliminate segregation. Many Republicans argued that supplementary civil rights legislation was necessary. Most white Americans had not accepted that egalitarianism included social equality as well as political and legal equality. Sen. Charles Sumner of Massachusetts, an advocate of equal rights for African Americans throughout the Civil War and the early period of Reconstruction, died in March 1874. Other Republicans feared that his death signaled the end of postwar fervor for racial equality.

Sen. Frederick T. Frelinghuysen of New Jersey proposed a new civil rights bill. Supporters argued that the Fourteenth Amendment, which defined citizenship for African Americans, required legislation to ensure its implementation. The bill demanded equal access to accommodations in private railroads, steamboats, stagecoaches, streetcars, restaurants, hotels, and theaters; outlined equality in schools, land-grant colleges, and cemeteries; and ensured the right to serve on juries. The prohibition of racial segregation in schools posed the largest obstacle to passing the bill. Individuals who opposed this legislation did not think that legal rights and social privileges were related. They also questioned the constitutionality of the bill, because the control of public institutions established under state laws and supported by state and local taxes were the prerogative of states alone. Moreover, if a state's people did not support the legislation, it would be unworkable.

Although earlier versions of the bill had faced defeat, this draft had a better chance of passing. A new bill would honor Sumner's memory and possibly reunite a divided Republican Party during the coming fall congressional campaign. African Americans pressured the party to pass the legislation as a price for continued support. On May 22, 1874, the Senate passed the bill with an exclusion only of churches. Perhaps the body anticipated that the House of Representatives would kill the bill, thus allowing the Senate to escape blame. The upper house had passed similar bills in 1872 and 1873, only to see them defeated in the House. All representatives faced reelection in 1874 and possibly contemplated their constituents' reaction to additional civil rights legislation. The Senate bill did not reach the floor of the House.

The House's inaction actually guaranteed that civil rights would be a crucial issue in the campaign and a target for the Democratic Party. During the campaign, the population in southern and border states viewed the election as a referendum on Reconstruction and on civil rights. Republican defeats were numerous and, in reality, gave the bill a final chance. The violence in southern states during the campaign convinced many congressional Republicans that an additional bill was the only way to protect African Americans. Republicans further interpreted their losses as a sign that Reconstruction zeal was coming to an end as the rest of the country tired of the issues.

The Forty-third Congress reassembled in December 1874 with the lame-duck Republicans in control. They proposed a new civil rights bill as well as a new enforcement act that expanded the president's power to stop intimidation of voters and included the right to suspend the writ of habeas corpus. Earlier, the Enforcement Acts of 1870 and 1871 had defined any interference with qualified African Americans' right to vote as a federal crime and granted federal courts jurisdiction over such cases. Other bills provided a two-year army appropriation to prevent the incoming House from limiting the military role in the South. Over the opposition of Democrats and twelve Republicans, the House of Representatives passed a diluted version of the earlier Senate Civil Rights Bill, omitting the provisions relating to schools and cemeteries. The Republicans' support for the bill in the House is misleading, however. They argued that it would give the illusion of achievement without provoking lasting resentment among the white population or desertion by African Americans from the party. The new enforcement act and the two-year army appropriations bill died when the Forty-third Congress adjourned.

The House version of the Civil Rights Act faced a doubtful future in the Senate, because Republicans there considered the bill too weak. But because time was running out on the session, Republicans had to choose between a weak bill or no bill at all. Time was insufficient to revise it and send it back to the House for another vote, and there was no guarantee of passing a changed bill there. Democrats in the Senate believed that the Supreme Court would declare the law unconstitutional within two years. To ensure success of some form of the bill, Republican senators accepted it without any amendments.

Republican president Ulysses S. Grant signed the bill on March 1, 1875, but issued no statement supporting it. Southern Democrats condemned it as granting legal claims to social status, and many southern Republicans left the party. Even supporters of the concept of equality criticized the bill as coercive and not conciliatory and worried that southern whites would take out their anger on African Americans, endangering black citizens even more. Some northerners opposed the legislation, believing that it was inadequate because it excluded education. It was worthless to grant equal access to accommodations while barring entrance to schools or colleges, they argued.

The Civil Rights Act of 1875 made little significant difference. It lacked any provision for enforcement, and prejudice was difficult to punish. The responsibility for initiating complaints fell on African Americans, most of whom could not afford a lawsuit to gain equal access. The federal government did not have the money, staff, or desire to enforce the law. The Department of Justice hesitated in distributing copies of the act to local federal officials. Republicans did not think that the act would apply to private businesses. Federal judges ruled inconsistently on the act's constitutionality and its scope, and the Supreme Court postponed a decision until 1883.

The Civil Rights Act of 1875 marked the end of Reconstruction as the last major federal legal reform in the interest of civil rights in the aftermath of the Civil War. The debate over the bill brought into office the enemies of Reconstruction. More important, northern support for civil rights decreased as the issue became politically unpopular and as former Confederates continued to regain control of southern state governments. Losing political control of the South forced the Republican Party to change its focus to keep voters in the North.

CIVIL RIGHTS CASES

In 1883 the Supreme Court struck down the work of the Civil Rights Act of 1875 as unconstitutional. Defendants in five cases from California, Kansas, Missouri, New York, and Tennessee allegedly had denied black citizens access to hotels, theaters, and railroad cars. The Supreme Court ruled that portions of the law securing equal accommodations were unconstitutional. Justice Joseph P. Bradley's opinion for the majority held that the Fourteenth Amendment restricted action by states and not by private individuals. Discrimination in hotels, trains, and theaters was not a result of slavery and, therefore, the Fourteenth Amendment was not applicable. Indeed, according to Bradley, African Americans had to stop believing that legislation would automatically favor them.

Justice John Marshall Harlan, a former slaveholder from Kentucky, was the lone dissenter on the Court. He argued that the Thirteenth and Fourteenth Amendments should be interpreted more broadly to abolish inequity by legislation. Discrimination in public facilities did constitute discrimination by states, in his view, and the federal government did have jurisdiction. He further warned that the United States had ceased protecting the rights of African Americans.

The public supported decisions by the Supreme Court that hampered enforcement of civil rights. The Court had retreated from intervention in civil rights and southern politics during the 1870s and 1880s. Rulings in the *Slaughterhouse Cases* (1873), *United States v. Cruikshank* (1876), and *United*

States v. Reese (1876) had weakened the federal government's authority and responsibility to African Americans. In the *Slaughterhouse Cases* the Supreme Court ruled that the Fourteenth Amendment protected the rights of citizens and states, and thus state governments—not the federal government—had the responsibility to protect those rights. *Cruikshank* overturned the conviction of three white citizens charged in the massacre of African Americans in Louisiana on the grounds that the indictments had been too vague and without reference to race as the motive for the violence. The Court further argued that the Reconstruction amendments had prohibited violations of civil rights only by states and not by private individuals, who must be punished by local and state authorities. In *Reese* the Court ruled sections of the Enforcement Act of 1870 unconstitutional because the Fifteenth Amendment forbade state and federal governments only from excluding citizens from voting on the basis of race or previous condition of servitude. According to this decision, the amendment did not guarantee the right to vote. These decisions contributed by judicial means to the end of the Reconstruction-era civil rights movement.

The failure of civil rights legislation in 1875 meant that segregation in public accommodations continued until 1964. Almost a hundred years after Reconstruction had begun, President Lyndon B. Johnson, a southern Democrat, pushed new legislation through Congress that banned discrimination in places such as theaters, hotels, restaurants, and gasoline stations. The Civil Rights Act of 1964 empowered the U.S. attorney general to end segregation in public schools, hospitals, libraries, and playgrounds. In addition, the bill prohibited discrimination in businesses or labor unions that employed or counted as members a hundred or more individuals. This legislation did not meet the same fate as the Civil Rights Act of 1875; the Supreme Court upheld the 1964 law.

In theory, the Civil Rights Act of 1866 guaranteed citizens the right to purchase, lease, or sell property without regard to race. In reality, African Americans had continually confronted discrimination in housing for more than a hundred years, which prompted Congress to pass the Civil Rights Act of 1968. The act immediately provided open housing in federally owned and multiunit dwellings with mortgages guaranteed by the Federal Housing Administration or the Veterans Administration. At the end of that year, the ban on discrimination would apply to other multiunit dwellings and to real estate developments. As of January 1, 1970, it would extend to single-family houses sold or rented through brokers. When cases of discrimination in housing based on race reached the U.S. Supreme Court, it ruled on the basis of the Civil Rights Act of 1866. For example, in *Jones v. Alfred H. Mayer* (1968), the Court decided that if an African American could not buy or rent a home solely because of race, he or she did not enjoy the same rights as white citizens, a clear violation of the law. The Court reversed the decision of the court of appeals that the earlier law had applied only to state action and not to that of private individuals. The Supreme Court further ruled that the Thirteenth Amendment had authorized Congress to eliminate restrictions on civil rights to fulfill the abolition of slavery.

The civil rights legislation of the Reconstruction period did not end the discrimination that it addressed. However, it did provide the basis for new laws during what has been called the second Reconstruction era. The civil rights movement of the 1960s forced government action, and the new legislation gave teeth to the laws by providing federal enforcement and the withholding of federal funding to ensure compliance.

See also *Civil Rights Act of 1866; Civil Rights Acts (Modern); Civil Rights Movement; Freedmen's Bureau Acts; Reconstruction.*

CAROL JACKSON ADAMS, SALT LAKE COMMUNITY COLLEGE

BIBLIOGRAPHY

Benedict, Michael Les. *A Compromise of Principle: Congressional Republicans and Reconstruction 1863–1869.* New York: W. W. Norton, 1974.

Foner, Eric. *Reconstruction: America's Unfinished Revolution 1863–1877.* New York: Harper and Row, 1988.

Gillette, William. *Retreat from Reconstruction, 1869–1879.* Baton Rouge: Louisiana State University, 1979.

Hyman, Harold M. *A More Perfect Union: The Impact of the Civil War and Reconstruction on the Constitution.* New York: Alfred A. Knopf, 1973.

Nieman, Donald G. *To Set the Law in Motion: The Freedmen's Bureau and the Legal Rights of Blacks, 1865–1868.* Millwood, N.Y.: KTO Press, 1979.

Simpson, Brooks D. *The Reconstruction Presidents.* Lawrence: University Press of Kansas, 1998.

CIVIL RIGHTS ACTS (MODERN)

The Civil Rights Act of 1964 and the Voting Rights Act of 1965 are the legislative foundation of modern American civil rights law. Before the 1960s, Congress had passed no legislation seriously threatening the system of racial segregation in the South since the Reconstruction statutes of the 1870s. Political pressure to end southern race discrimination increased after World War II, quickened by the Allied victory over fascism, United Nations commitments to universal human rights, embarrassment to American leadership in the cold war (for example, segregated restaurants in Washington, D.C., refusing service to dark-skinned diplomats), and the Supreme Court's school desegregation decision (*Brown v. Board of Education*) in 1954.

The system of white supremacy in the South, however, was formidably defended in Congress. Over the years the re-

gion's one-party system had accumulated seniority for safe-seat Democrats, who as a consequence came to dominate congressional committee chairmanships. By 1960 southerners chaired nine of thirteen standing committees in the Senate and twelve of eighteen in the House, including the House Rules Committee, with gatekeeper authority to prevent bills from reaching the House floor.

In the Senate, rules of procedure required a super majority vote (three-fifths of senators voting) to shut off debate and force a floor vote on legislation. Filibusters led by southern Democrats, often supported by conservative Republicans from midwestern and Rocky Mountain states, had always been a successful last line of defense. In 1957 a filibuster was avoided because the civil rights bill passed that year was a symbolic law about voting rights that powerful southern members of Congress assumed, correctly, would not produce significant change.

To overcome these defenses, reformers needed to build a bipartisan coalition capable of winning a national mandate and capturing the elected branches of government in Washington. The liberal Democratic coalition that had passed Franklin D. Roosevelt's New Deal—an uneasy alliance of organized labor, southern white Democrats, northern blue-collar ethnic voters, black Americans, and intellectuals—was too divided by the racial issue during the immediate postwar years to overcome conservative defenses.

This was changed, however, by the black civil rights movement in the South, led by grassroots activists and inspired by the leadership of Rev. Martin Luther King Jr., who won worldwide attention in 1955 leading the Montgomery, Alabama, boycott against segregated buses. "The Movement" rallied the liberal coalition to a great moral crusade against racial oppression in the South, in the process mobilizing national church organizations in solidarity with southern black church leaders. Meanwhile, protest leaders learned to use television to great advantage, staging desegregation rallies in towns and cities known for their segregationist police chiefs, whose vicious attacks on nonviolent demonstrators—most notably in Eugene "Bull" Connor's Birmingham, Alabama, in the spring of 1963—intensified public pressure on Congress to act.

THE CIVIL RIGHTS ACT OF 1964

In June 1963, in the wake of the Birmingham violence, President John F. Kennedy, who previously had sponsored no significant civil rights legislation, sent Congress a strong civil rights bill. By the fall of 1963 the bill had been shaped in the House Judiciary Committee to reflect four assumptions crucial to its passage and effectiveness. First, the nation's civil rights problem was a regional problem, confined essentially to the South. Second, fixing this problem required national enforcement of a nondiscrimination standard barring any role for race in public policy. The bill repeatedly prohibited any use of racial classifications, ratios, quotas, or preferences. Third, to be effective the new law would enforce nondiscrimination in the private as well as the public sector. Fourth, to overcome southern defenses, the bill would have to win bipartisan support, especially in the Senate, where Republican votes would be needed to break the southern filibuster.

When Kennedy was assassinated in November 1963, his vice president, former Texas senator Lyndon Johnson, pledged as president to pass the civil rights bill as a tribute to the martyred Kennedy. Early in 1964 the House leadership forced the civil rights bill out of the Rules Committee, where conservative opponents, in an attempt to defeat the bill by overburdening it, added a ban on sex discrimination in employment.

As passed by the House and sent to the Senate in February 1964, the bill had three main provisions. The most controversial of the provisions was Title II, banning discrimination on account of race, color, religion, or national origin in places of "public accommodation," meaning privately owned hotels, restaurants, department stores, theaters, and so forth. Also controversial was Title VII, prohibiting discrimination in employment (including sex discrimination). Title VII established a new federal agency, the Equal Employment Opportunity Commission (EEOC), to receive complaints of job discrimination. Senate Republicans, as the price of voting to end the southern filibuster, stripped the EEOC of enforcement power, leaving it a fact-finding, complaint-processing mediating agency. Titles II and VII, like all parts of the bill, applied to the entire nation but were aimed at the South. This was because by the 1960s segregation in private businesses was found mostly in the southern states and because job discrimination outside the South was thought to be modest and sufficiently policed by antidiscrimination agencies already operating.

The bill's third main provision, Title VI, was little debated at the time. It prohibited race discrimination by any enterprise, public or private, that received federal financial assistance (grants, loans, or contracts). The target was discrimination in the South's segregated defense plants in the private sector and segregated school districts in the public sector. The federal government intended to enforce the provisions by cutting off funding and denying contracts. Businesses and state and local governments outside the South, operating for

President Lyndon B. Johnson signs the Civil Rights Act, July 2, 1964, before an audience of distinguished guests. *Lyndon Baines Johnson Library*

years under their own antidiscrimination agencies, expected little federal intrusion into their affairs through Title VI.

Throughout the debate over the civil rights bill, President Johnson refused to yield to the southern opposition and rejected charges that the bill, especially Title II, was unconstitutional. The Justice Department under Presidents Kennedy and Johnson avoided basing the bill's unprecedented expansion of federal authority over private businesses on the Fourteenth Amendment's Equal Protection Clause. Although equal protection was the chief instrument used by the Warren Court to strike down southern segregation laws, its application to private businesses had been ruled impermissible by the Supreme Court in the Civil Rights Cases of 1883. Because the Fourteenth Amendment was directed against state action, Titles II and VII of the Civil Rights Act, which covered private businesses and employers, were based constitutionally on the Commerce Clause, which the Supreme Court since the late 1930s had broadly interpreted to permit congressional regulation of interstate commerce.

On June 10, 1964, the Senate voted to shut off the southern filibuster; on June 19 it passed the bill; and on July 2 the House passed it and sent it to the White House, where President Johnson signed it the same day. Before the year was out, the Supreme Court unanimously upheld the law's broad ban on discrimination in public accommodations. In *Heart of*

Atlanta Motel v. United States (1964) the Court declared that Congress had ample authority to regulate hotels and motels serving interstate travelers. In *Katzenbach v. McKlung* (1964) the Court ruled that, even though local restaurants such as Ollie's Barbecue in Birmingham did not serve out-of-state customers, some of the food served came from out of state.

THE VOTING RIGHTS ACT OF 1965

For several reasons, the Civil Rights Act of 1964 contained no significant provisions for voting rights. Because changes in voting law might have affected the career survival of elected officials, the bill's sponsors in 1963 and 1964 regarded an expanded federal role in policing local elections as too burdensome for the already controversial bill. By 1965, however, circumstances had changed significantly. Although Johnson crushed Barry Goldwater in the election of 1964, he lost the Deep South states of Alabama, Georgia, Louisiana, Mississippi, and South Carolina, and a majority of white voters in Arkansas, North Carolina, Tennessee, and perhaps Virginia also rejected the president. With the civil rights reform issue alienating southern white voters, the Democratic Party needed a crash program to enfranchise southern black people. Prospects for effective voting rights legislation were bright in 1965 because Johnson's landslide over Goldwater brought enormous Democratic majorities into the Eighty-ninth Congress—295 to 140 seats in the House and 68 to 32 in the Senate.

Immediately after the November 1964 election Johnson directed Attorney General Nicholas Katzenbach to draw up a strong voting rights bill, and in his January 4 State of the Union address Johnson announced his intention to eliminate "every obstacle" to the right to vote. In Alabama, King led voting rights protests in Selma that culminated on March 7, "Bloody Sunday," when state police and Dallas County Sheriff Jim Clark's horsemen charged civil rights marchers on the Edmund Pettis Bridge, clubbing demonstrators and sending seventy people to the hospital. As in 1964 the nation once again was angered by televised racial brutality in Alabama, and on March 15 Johnson asked a joint session of Congress to pass his voting rights bill.

Like the Civil Rights Act, the Voting Rights Act was framed in national terms but targeted the South. It was couched in race-neutral language yet was designed to halt discrimination against black Americans. Offending electoral jurisdictions were identified through a two-part formula in section 4 of the bill. The attorney general would determine whether a literacy test or similar device had been used as a voter qualification in the presidential election of 1964, and the director of the census would determine whether less than 50 percent of the voting-age population of that jurisdiction

was registered or had voted in the 1964 election. If a voting jurisdiction (usually a county) failed both tests, all literacy tests or devices were suspended and the attorney general was authorized to dispatch federal examiners to register voters.

In addition, a "preclearance" provision, section 5, required jurisdictions that had failed the tests to obtain prior approval from the attorney general or a three-judge federal court in the District of Columbia before making changes in election laws or procedures. This provision was added to prevent covered jurisdictions from sabotaging the Voting Rights Act by constantly changing their election laws, procedures, and district maps.

Given the Democrats' overwhelming majorities in the Eighty-ninth Congress, there was never much doubt that Congress would pass the Voting Rights Act. On May 25 the Senate broke a desultory southern filibuster and the next day approved the bill by a vote of 77 to 19. On July 9 the House passed its version by an even larger margin of 333 to 85, and on August 6 Johnson went to the Capitol building to sign the bill into law. The following year, the Supreme Court in *South Carolina v. Katzenbach* (1966) ruled by a vote of eight to one that the Voting Rights Act fell within the broad authority of Congress to enforce the Fifteenth Amendment.

THE EFFECTIVENESS OF THE CIVIL RIGHTS LAWS OF THE 1960s

The civil rights laws of 1964 and 1965 worked swiftly to destroy the biracial caste system in the South. Segregated public accommodations disappeared almost immediately, surprising the Johnson White House and demonstrating the readiness of southern business leaders to abandon segregation. Private employers and labor unions in the South moved promptly, under the command of Title VII and the EEOC, to dismantle racial job classifications and segregated union locals. Leading this effort were large defense contractors such as Lockheed-Marietta in Georgia and Newport News Shipbuilding in Virginia. National firms, such as Lockheed, were quick to comply; others were persuaded by contract-compliance officials in the Labor Department and Pentagon, acting under Title VI. Southern state and local governments, exempted from EEOC coverage in the 1964 bill to ease its passage, were brought under EEOC jurisdiction in 1972 by Congress.

Similarly, most southern electoral districts complied with the new voting rights law. In a few defiant, majority-black counties, federal examiners registered voters, and Justice Department officials used preclearance to block attempts to evade the law. By 1970 almost a million new black American voters were registered. White politicians shifted to court the new voters—including even Alabama governor George C. Wallace, champion of segregation in the 1960s. By the mid-

1970s racial demagoguery had largely disappeared from southern politics. The region produced a wave of racially liberal "New South" governors, including future presidents Jimmy Carter of Georgia and Bill Clinton of Arkansas. Growing Republican success, especially in congressional and state legislative elections, invigorated two-party competition. Rising prosperity in the Sunbelt South, strengthened by the demise of segregation, solidified these gains, and black immigration in the 1970s reversed a century of flight from the region.

Outside the South, the effectiveness of the civil rights acts of the 1960s is more difficult to assess, in part because the color-blind, antidiscrimination command at the heart of the 1960s laws (including the Open Housing Act of 1968, which banned racial discrimination nationwide in the sale and rental of housing) was displaced in the 1970s by the race-conscious policies of affirmative action. Based on a compensatory model of equal results rather than equal treatment, affirmative action programs were justified as remedies for past discrimination and "institutional racism." They were developed by federal officials who were alarmed by the "long, hot summers" of racial rioting from 1965 to 1968 and who were eager to speed job redistribution to minorities. The new programs were shaped not by Congress but by the new civil rights enforcement agencies, such as the EEOC, the Office of Federal Contract Compliance in the Labor Department, and the Office of Civil Rights in the Department of Health, Education and Welfare. They were approved by the federal courts, despite opponents' claims that minority preferences violated the Civil Rights Act itself.

The new, post-1960s civil rights enforcement strategies included, under Title VII, the "disparate impact" standard requiring rough proportional representation in employment for minorities and women, developed by the EEOC and upheld by the Supreme Court in *Griggs v. Duke Power Company* (1971). In a parallel development, the Labor Department under the administration of Richard M. Nixon required government contractors under Title VI to eliminate underrepresentation for protected minorities in their workforce. Similarly, in voting rights, a new results-oriented model of political representation seeking to maximize the election of minority officials was developed in the 1970s by the Justice Department, upheld by the federal courts, and affirmed by Congress in 1982.

Assessing the effectiveness of the 1960s civil rights laws is complicated by economic and cultural factors. The onset of affirmative action in the 1970s coincided with a weakening national economy and a surge of immigration that brought more than 25 million newcomers to America—three-fourths of them from Latin America and Asia and hence eligible for affirmative action programs. Socioeconomic indicators showed marked gains since the 1960s for women, Asian Americans, and married African Americans. Unmarried black men and women in the inner city, however, statistically remained mired in social pathology.

The rapid expansion of the "rights revolution" after the 1960s, extending protected class coverage beyond black Americans to include newly mobilizing constituencies—women, language minorities, and elderly and disabled individuals—built on foundations laid in the 1960s. Although federal affirmative action policies have remained controversial into the twenty-first century, and although the Supreme Court sharply narrowed their reach in the 1990s, the legislative achievements of the 1960s are widely venerated in American society. They constitute the heart of a rare, radical change in American life that transformed the old order.

See also *Affirmative Action; African American Politics; Black Suffrage; Civil Rights Movement; Filibuster; Kennedy, John F.; Johnson, Lyndon B.; Sex Discrimination in Employment; Sex Discrimination in Higher Education; Suffrage; Super Majority.*

HUGH DAVIS GRAHAM, VANDERBILT UNIVERSITY

BIBLIOGRAPHY

Graham, Hugh Davis. *Civil Rights and the Presidency.* New York: Oxford University Press, 1992.

Lawson, Steven F. *Running for Freedom: Civil Rights and Black Politics since 1941.* New York: McGraw-Hill, 1990.

Whalen, Charles W., and Barbara Whalen. *The Longest Debate: A Legislative History of the 1964 Civil Rights Act.* New York: New American Library, 1985.

CIVIL RIGHTS MOVEMENT

In courtrooms, legislative halls, and protest demonstrations, proponents of racial integration, equal opportunity, and voting rights in the United States struggled to create a world in which opportunity no longer depended on racial identity. This was the civil rights movement.

The political struggle for civil rights reached its high point of litigation, legislation, and direct action in the years from 1941 through 1965, as African Americans stepped up their resistance to segregation, exclusion, and disfranchisement. Eventually, all three branches of the federal government acted to curtail the power of "Jim Crow" laws, which had long been used to repress black America to the advantage of white America. The civil rights movement was not only about race, power, and policy, but also about jobs, schools, respect, and fair play.

Before 1941 the National Association for the Advancement of Colored People (NAACP) had chalked up victories in federal court in various areas—voting rights, housing, higher education, and criminal justice—but the 1940s, 1950s, and 1960s brought the litigation campaign to fruition. Moreover, executive orders in the 1940s reflected black pressure and generated racial change, and congressional action beginning in 1957 produced the first civil rights legislation since 1875. The civil rights movement is often dated from the mid-1950s—from *Brown v. Board of Education* (1954) and the Montgomery bus boycott of 1955–1956—to the mid-1960s, culminating in the Civil Rights Act of 1964 and the Voting Rights Act of 1965. But the movement's history properly begins in 1941 with plans for a march on Washington.

THE 1940s: A REVOLUTION BEGINS

In the spring and summer of 1941 the United States was inaugurating a military draft and supplying material to bolster Great Britain's efforts in World War II, but the nation had not yet entered the war. Black workers were excluded from new jobs that were opening in defense plants. Labor leader A. Philip Randolph planned a march on Washington to demand equal employment opportunities for African Americans in defense plants and in federal bureaucracies, and he also demanded an end to segregation in the U.S. military. Randolph suspended plans for the march when President Franklin D. Roosevelt agreed to issue Executive Order 8802, which established a Fair Employment Practices Committee (FEPC). The FEPC was charged with curtailing job discrimination at defense plants. After that, "Rosie the Riveter"—the nickname given to women working in defense plants—could be African American.

World War II was won, but the cold war soon followed, and Congress enacted a peacetime draft. African Americans continued to serve in segregated units with white officers. Gearing up for the latest challenge and opportunity, Randolph threatened to foster opposition to the draft unless the military was desegregated. In response, President Harry S. Truman in 1948 issued Executive Order 9981, which began the desegregation of the military, a process accelerated by the Korean War (1950–1953). In both 1941 and 1948 international affairs created conditions for a leading African American to nudge a segregated society toward more equal opportunity.

Across the 1940s, mostly in cases argued by Thurgood Marshall, the NAACP brought lawsuits that chipped away at segregation in areas other than jobs or the military. In *Mitchell v. U.S.* (1941) and *Morgan v. Virginia* (1946), the U.S. Supreme Court banned segregated transportation on interstate trains and buses. In *Smith v. Allwright* (1944), it ruled against black exclusion from Democratic primary elections in southern states. In *Shelley v. Kraemer* (1948), the Court banned the judicial enforcement of restrictive covenants, the preferred tool at the time for segregating suburban housing, and the Federal

Housing Administration (FHA) and the Veterans Administration (VA) stopped requiring such covenants in real estate documents as a condition of obtaining mortgage loans. In several cases between 1948 and 1950 the Court ruled against segregation in graduate programs and law schools at state universities. Thus the civil rights revolution was under way in voting, housing, transportation, and education.

THE 1950s: POLITICS WITH THE VOTE— AND WITHOUT IT

The NAACP successfully attacked the separate-but-equal formula asserted in *Plessy v. Ferguson* (1896). The victories in the higher education cases established the basis for desegregation decisions regarding elementary and secondary schools in *Brown v. Board of Education* (1954 and 1955). The Supreme Court soon extended the integrationist thrust of *Brown* to cases involving such public facilities as parks and playgrounds. In 1956 the Court applied *Brown* to all public institutions of higher education in a law school case from Florida brought by Virgil D. Hawkins and in an undergraduate admissions case from North Carolina involving Leroy Benjamin Frasier. The *Brown* decision gave fresh energy and enthusiasm to untold numbers of people who struggled against segregation.

In Congress, Adam Clayton Powell Jr., who represented the Harlem area of New York City beginning in 1945, pushed for a permanent FEPC. Time and again he proposed the "Powell Amendment," a restriction on spending bills that would prevent federal spending on programs that discriminated against African Americans. Such efforts, although unsuccessful, revealed the importance of even one black member of Congress; in addition to representing the constituency that had elected him, Powell was viewed as congressman-at-large for disfranchised black southerners. Powell also embodied the crucial significance for American national politics of the people of the Great Migration—the black southerners who had left Virginia for New York or Alabama for Chicago and had, when they crossed the Mason-Dixon line or the Ohio River, picked up the right to vote.

The political mobilization of black northerners led to the election of an occasional black member of Congress and forced increasing numbers of white politicians, whether members of Congress or candidates for the presidency, to be receptive to the political needs of African Americans. In the late 1950s Congress entered the fray as a proponent of change rather than an obstruction to it. The Civil Rights Acts of 1957 and 1960, the first civil rights statutes enacted since Reconstruction, created a Civil Rights Section in the Justice Department, established a Civil Rights Commission to investigate race relations, and encouraged action against restrictions on black voting in the South.

Although protests and marches made headlines, much of the work of the civil rights movement was related to organization and public relations. Above, staff members work in the NAACP headquarters in Manhattan in the 1950s. *Library of Congress*

Black southerners played a central role in the movement during the 1950s. In Alabama, black citizens sustained the Montgomery bus boycott in 1955 and 1956 to protest segregated city buses. Other black communities—including Baton Rouge, Louisiana, and Tallahassee, Florida—had carried out similar protests, but the Montgomery boycott thrust a new leader, Martin Luther King Jr., into the national spotlight. King embodied the nonviolent direct-action approach, which he fused with the rhetoric and style of a black Baptist preacher. By contrast, white citizens in places like Little Rock, Arkansas, engaged in a violent version of direct action as they resisted school desegregation, demonstrating that court rulings alone might not end traditional practices.

THE 1960s: HEAVY SURF, HIGH TIDE

In February 1960 four black students at North Carolina Agricultural and Technical College sat in at a lunch counter in Greensboro. Other sit-ins against segregated facilities had occasionally occurred in the past—at a library in Alexandria, Virginia, in 1939; at lunch counters in Chicago and Washington, D.C., during World War II; in Oklahoma City in 1959. The Greensboro sit-in, however, gained national attention. Student sit-ins in 1960 in dozens of other cities, among them Nashville, Tallahassee, Atlanta, and Richmond, kicked off the direct-action protests of the early 1960s. Segregation was under siege nearly everywhere.

Various national or regional groups participated in the civil rights movement during the early 1960s. The Southern Christian Leadership Conference, which had emerged from the Montgomery bus boycott, and the Student Nonviolent Coordinating Committee, which emerged from the sit-ins, joined with such older groups as the Congress of Racial Equality, the American Civil Liberties Union, and the NAACP.

A host of people in a host of communities worked for civil rights in the early 1960s, but developments were particularly conspicuous in Birmingham and Selma, two cities in Alabama. In 1963 no city in the nation was more segregated or more committed to staying that way than Birmingham, and Martin Luther King viewed it as the right place to force the question of desegregation across the South. Public Safety Commissioner T. Eugene "Bull" Connor readied his forces for a confrontation, and television broadcast into homes across the nation searing images of men in police uniforms waging war against peaceful protesters, even children, by means of billy clubs, cattle prods, fire hoses, and police dogs. President John F. Kennedy decided that he had to lend his support to a civil rights bill. After Kennedy died, President Lyndon B. Johnson led the effort to obtain congressional passage of what became the Civil Rights Act of 1964. The new law, far more ambitious and thoroughgoing than its 1957 or 1960 predecessors, attacked continuing segregation in education and public accommodations together with racial discrimination in employment.

The 1964 act did not focus on voting. Between 1962 and 1964 the Voter Education Project—funded by northern foundations through the Southern Regional Council to local groups of activists—worked to increase the number of black voters, although whites' resistance proved enormous. In the meantime, Congress in 1962 approved the Twenty-fourth Amendment, which banned the use of poll taxes as a requirement for voting in federal elections. That amendment secured ratification in time for the 1964 elections (and two years later, in *Harper v. Virginia Board of Elections,* the Supreme Court applied the ban to state elections as well). Yet nothing had cracked the procedural obstacles or curtailed the violence that prevented black electoral activity in the Deep South. During the "Freedom Summer" of 1964, activists concentrated on registering blacks in Mississippi to vote—or on demonstrating the danger of doing so, as the bodies of one black southerner and two white northerners were pulled from an earth dam where they had been left after opponents of black voting murdered them. In early 1965 Martin Luther King Jr. helped lead an effort in Selma to push black political empowerment, and the local white reaction resembled that in Birmingham in 1963 and Mississippi in 1964. As in 1964, Congress responded. The Voting Rights Act of 1965 curtailed literacy tests and various other measures that had prevented black voter registration, and it authorized the use of federal registrars to register voters.

Segregationists challenged the constitutionality of the 1964 and 1965 legislation, but the U.S. Supreme Court turned back such challenges in *Heart of Atlanta v. United States* (1964) and *South Carolina v. Katzenbach* (1966). Congress, the White House, and the Supreme Court were all on more or less the same page in the mid-1960s, and it was a far cry from where they had been at the beginning of the century or even in 1941.

POLITICS IN MANY STRIPES AND COLORS

As international relations influenced domestic politics in the United States, the cold war shaped the civil rights movement in contradictory ways. On the one hand, domestic opponents of desegregation routinely branded the proponents of change as "communists" and "enemies of the nation"; advocates of racial equality, black and white alike, were portrayed as "reds." On the other hand, the cold war fostered efforts at domestic change when segregation's intractable practices and ugly incidents impeded the nation's effectiveness in pursuing international support, particularly among nonwhite nations, in its cold war rivalry with the Soviet Union. Moreover, inauguration of a peacetime draft for the cold war had occasioned Randolph's protest and Truman's executive order in 1948 to desegregate the military.

In addition, direct action and conventional politics were interrelated throughout the civil rights movement. Without Randolph's actions in 1941 and again in 1948, Presidents Roosevelt and Truman would never have issued their executive orders regarding defense plants and military segregation. The year-long Montgomery bus boycott finally achieved victory when the Supreme Court ruled against local bus segre-

gation in *Browder v. Gayle* (1956). To highlight court victories and test compliance with them, biracial groups known as Freedom Riders responded in 1947 to *Morgan v. Virginia,* and again in 1961 to *Boynton v. Virginia* (1960), by traveling South. Massive civil disobedience, together with the extraordinary violence that was visited upon the protesters, propelled action in Congress. Events in Birmingham led to the Civil Rights Act of 1964; Selma led to the Voting Rights Act of 1965. The politics of the civil rights movement, played out on street corners and in courtrooms as well as in Congress and the White House, shaped the struggle against the power of Jim Crow policies.

CHANGE AND ITS LIMITS

The civil rights movement generated extraordinary change. Almost no school in the South, even at the graduate level, enrolled both black and white students before 1941 or even before 1948. By 1965, however, most institutions of higher education, even such recalcitrant ones as the University of Mississippi and the University of Alabama, had admitted at least a few black students. Every state had also begun to desegregate its elementary and secondary schools. The 1964 Civil Rights Act spurred the beginnings of desegregation at both public and private institutions. In the summer of 1964, black and white customers could seat themselves in salt-and-pepper fashion at a Howard Johnson's lunch counter in Florida, something impossible according to law and custom a few months earlier.

Notwithstanding the transformed policy environment, the limits of change were also evident, as the 1960s hardly brought an end to traditional racial restrictions. Invalidation of state-level massive resistance in Virginia in 1959 led to limited desegregation of elementary and secondary schools, but Prince Edward County adopted a local version of the same policy that year and closed its public schools rather than desegregate them. In the summer of 1964, after the Civil Rights Act banned official segregation in public facilities, towns from Lynchburg, Virginia, to Monroe, Louisiana, adopted a drain-and-chain policy regarding what had previously been all-white municipal swimming pools, choosing to close the facilities rather than open them to all; equal opportunity was now required but was defined as exclusion, rather than inclusion, of everyone regardless of race. At most universities that historically had been closed to black students, from Virginia Tech to Texas A & M, black enrollment reached no higher than single or double digits when fall classes began in 1965. Housing patterns across the nation continued to reflect the former Jim Crow policies of the FHA and VA, as well as the private discrimination of white realtors, bankers, and homeowners. In sixteen states—a third of the nation—state laws continued to ban interracial marriage until the Supreme Court overturned them in *Loving v. Virginia* in 1967.

Protesters had demonstrated, presidents had ordered, courts had ruled, and Congress had legislated. As a consequence, Jim Crow policies had lost their absolute power to govern, but their tracks were still all over the landscape.

See also *Black Suffrage;* Brown v. Board of Education; *Civil Rights Acts (Modern); Cold War; Eisenhower, Dwight D.; Federal Housing Administration; Kennedy, John F.; Johnson, Lyndon B.; Marches on Washington; Truman, Harry S.*

PETER WALLENSTEIN,
VIRGINIA POLYTECHNIC INSTITUTE AND STATE UNIVERSITY

BIBLIOGRAPHY

Branch, Taylor. *Parting the Waters: America in the King Years, 1954–63.* New York: Simon and Schuster, 1988.

Graham, Hugh Davis. *The Civil Rights Era: Origins and Development of National Policy, 1960–1972.* New York: Oxford University Press, 1990.

Halberstam, David. *The Children.* New York: Random House, 1998.

Lawson, Steven F. *Black Ballots: Voting Rights in the South, 1944–1969.* New York: Columbia University Press, 1976.

Williams, Juan. *Thurgood Marshall, American Revolutionary.* New York: Random House, 1998.

CIVIL UNREST AND RIOTING

Civil unrest and rioting have been parts of American political history since before the nation's independence. Sometimes citizens took action against other groups of private individuals, and sometimes they challenged government authority. Many significant examples of civil unrest were the result of opposition to wars or the draft, racial and ethnic tensions, labor strife or anger at economic conditions, or the perception of unfair treatment by officials and tax collectors.

Protest was sometimes peaceful, sometimes violent. Unrest led sometimes to violent repression, sometimes to redress of grievances, sometimes to both. The varied episodes revealed social, cultural, economic, and political tensions that took the form of political action other than electoral behavior (voting to change the party or groups in power) or major wars (such as the American Revolution and the Civil War).

ERA OF THE AMERICAN REVOLUTION

In the period before the outbreak of the Revolutionary War, resistance to colonial taxation and the costs of military occupation stimulated unrest and created the setting for the war of independence. In 1765 secret organizations known as the Sons of Liberty were formed in many towns; in Boston the citizens turned to violence—with rioters looting the home of the chief justice—in opposition to enforcement of the Stamp Act. In 1770 anger at the Quartering Act, which required authorities in the colonies to provide supplies and barracks to British troops, led to riots in New York City that came to be known as the "Battle of Golden Hill." That same year, in western North Carolina, the Regulators Revolt involved two thousand men clashing with the militia in a sectional protest against lack of representation in colonial government. Mass meetings in 1773 to protest the colonial tea tax led to the Boston Tea Party, during which hundreds of chests of tea were dumped into Boston Harbor.

After the American Revolution, political and economic concerns continued to spark confrontations. In 1786 Shays's Rebellion erupted in Massachusetts when a group of debt-ridden farmers under the leadership of a destitute agrarian named Daniel Shays organized to demand cheap (paper) money and an end to farm foreclosures. Shays led a force of twelve hundred in a failed effort to seize an arsenal before a large government force crushed his rebellion, but in the following months the legislature addressed some of the debtors' concerns. Fury at the enforcement of a federal excise tax on liquor led in 1794 to the Whiskey Rebellion in western Pennsylvania, in which fifteen thousand militia were called out to put down this armed resistance by back-country farmers.

PRE–CIVIL WAR AMERICA

Political and economic concerns fueled civil unrest in pre–Civil War America as well. In 1839 agrarian anger at perpetual land leases dating to the colonial period led to anti-rent protests in upstate New York; not until Gov. Silas Wright called for legislation restricting the duration of farm leases in 1846 did the unrest come to an end. In 1842 the Dorr Rebellion in Rhode Island—a movement that called for abolishing the restriction on the voting rights of those who did not own land—led Rhode Island to adopt a state constitution to replace the antiquated colonial charter. This constitution granted the vote to virtually all men in the state.

Ethnicity and race emerged as major causes of unrest in the middle years of the nineteenth century. Intense nativist hostility against Catholics during a period of rapid growth in Catholic immigration was at the heart of a great ethnic confrontation that ravaged large parts of Philadelphia in 1844. Supporters of the American Republican Party, an organization that called for restricting the immigration of people they characterized as un-American and inassimilable newcomers, played the key role in armed confrontations with Irish Catholic groups defending their neighborhoods and churches.

From the 1830s through the 1850s the issue of slavery stimulated civil unrest and rioting. Antiabolitionist riots rocked various northern communities. In the 1830s mobs led by "gentlemen of property and standing" attacked abolitionists in many places, including Utica, New York; Boston; and New York City. In Philadelphia the abolitionists' recently constructed building, Pennsylvania Hall, was burned to the ground. In 1837 a mob in Alton, Illinois, set fire to the building housing the press of antislavery printer Elijah Lovejoy, who was then killed.

Resistance to the return of fugitive slaves led to riots and rescues in Boston; Syracuse, New York; Wellington, Ohio; and other cities and towns. Fugitive slaves in Christiana, Pennsylvania, successfully resisted capture after killing a slaveowner and wounding a number of men with him. In 1831 the slave Nat Turner led a brief but bloody rebellion against slavery, before his makeshift army was destroyed.

The passage of the Kansas-Nebraska Act in 1854, which called for popular sovereignty in those territories, led to violent assaults in 1856 in Lawrence, Kansas, by proslavery men who burned and pillaged in an effort to intimidate abolitionists. John Brown led a retaliatory raid at Pottawatomie, killing five proslavery settlers. In 1859 Brown led an assault at Harpers Ferry, Virginia, where he seized a federal arsenal and armory, hoping to instigate a slave insurrection. Brown was hanged, and abolitionists mourned him as a martyr.

CIVIL WAR AND RACIAL TENSIONS

The Civil War stimulated unrest in both the Confederacy and the Union. A bread riot in 1863 in Richmond, Virginia, revealed the desperation many white women felt when they could not feed their families. The New York City draft riots in 1863 involved thousands of blue-collar protesters, many of them Irish immigrants and their sons, who smashed storefronts and lynched African Americans in reaction to the notion that they should fight to abolish slavery. The draft resisters were particularly enraged by the provisions of the conscription act that mandated military service for all men age twenty to forty-five except those who could afford to procure a substitute or pay $300 to avoid service.

The most significant instance of civil unrest in U.S. history was the Civil War itself, in which eleven slave states made war on the national government, starting with the military assault on Fort Sumter, in Charleston Harbor.

Racial tension remained a source of unrest after the war and through the first years of the twentieth century. Race riots erupted throughout the defeated South. In 1866 white mobs attacked black neighborhoods in Memphis, Tennessee, killing forty-six people; in New Orleans white mobs and police assailed black delegates en route to a political meeting,

killing forty. The Ku Klux Klan emerged as a secret society to intimidate black citizens through violence in an effort to preserve white supremacy. In 1871 Congress passed the Third Enforcement, or Ku Klux Klan Act, which strengthened sanctions against those who engaged in intimidation or prevented blacks from voting. Thousands were arrested. While many escaped conviction, the Klan was suppressed.

Violence against blacks recurred in later years. In 1898 an antiblack riot rocked Wilmington, North Carolina. In 1906 white rioters in Atlanta murdered twenty-six black citizens and burned black homes. During this era, many black southerners were lynched, with some lynchings involving massive crowds and the burning or mutilation of the bodies of the victims. Rioting and other violence were not limited to the South in this period, however. In Abraham Lincoln's hometown of Springfield, Illinois, blacks were attacked in 1908.

Racial and ethnic hatred was also directed at other minorities. In the 1870s mobs attacked Chinatowns up and down the West Coast. Neighborhoods were burned and entire communities were expelled from some cities and towns. In Los Angeles in 1871 approximately twenty Chinese were killed by a mob, many being lynched from the city's new gas lampposts. During this period Italian immigrants were also attacked and killed in New Orleans.

World War I and its aftermath brought increased racial tension, as black migration north to jobs created by the war led to white working-class anger and anxiety. Attacks on black residents were widespread, and blacks sometimes inflicted casualties on their white attackers. In 1921 in Tulsa, Oklahoma, white mobs burned entire black neighborhoods while local public officials orchestrated the violence. The National Guard, outnumbering the African Americans (many of them World War I veterans) defending their communities by a ratio of ten to one, crushed the resistance. The death toll included twenty-six black and ten white Tulsans.

LABOR UNREST

While racial and ethnic themes played a central role in civil unrest in the nineteenth and early twentieth centuries, labor strife stimulated other confrontations. In these cases, state and federal officials often intervened on the side of the owners to break strikes.

Large wage cuts made by managers of eastern railroads in 1877 led to a railroad strike. Riots convulsed Pittsburgh, rail service was disrupted to St. Louis, and rail equipment was destroyed. State militias were mobilized in Maryland and Pennsylvania; President Rutherford B. Hayes ordered federal troops to suppress disorders in West Virginia.

In 1892, at the gigantic Homestead Works of the Carnegie Steel Corporation near Pittsburgh, a strike of epic proportions followed wage cuts mandated by Andrew Carnegie and his associate, Henry Clay Frick, who had decided to crush the steel workers union. Strikebreakers were brought in, protected by an army of private detectives. Pitched battles with guns and dynamite ensued, resulting in death and injury to many strikers and guards. The governor of Pennsylvania called out eight thousand troops to suppress the strikers, and the strike was broken.

The Pullman railroad sleeping car works near Chicago was the site in 1894 of another huge strike—again stimulated by large wage cuts, this time in the midst of the economic depression following the crash of 1893. Federal troops were mobilized to break the strike, and a federal court issued an injunction forbidding the union from continuing the strike. Rail union leader Eugene V. Debs was arrested and imprisoned for defying the court order, and the strike collapsed.

Such confrontations continued into the twentieth century. In 1914, for example, the "Ludlow Massacre" in Colorado involved state militia attacks on workers' tent colonies during a strike that followed the eviction of striking coal mine workers and their families from company housing. There were thirty-nine deaths.

In the post–World War I period, widespread labor unrest involved 4 million workers and thousands of strikes as wartime government controls on industry were removed and employers canceled recognition of unions, laid off workers, and cut back benefits. The biggest strike, involving 350,000 steelworkers, led to violent repression at the U.S. Steel plant in Gary, Indiana, where nativist vigilantes attacked workers they characterized as "these foreigners." Boston had a police strike, with the National Guard called in to maintain order, and Seattle had a general strike (involving 60,000 workers), in which red-baiting mayor Ole Hanson, crying "revolutionaries," brought in federal troops to occupy the city.

THE GREAT DEPRESSION

The economic prosperity of the "roaring twenties" reduced labor strife, but the Great Depression created enormous hardship. Mass unemployment, hunger, and homelessness led to unrest. Some cities experienced mass break-ins of grocery stores or mass refusal to pay street car fares. Desperate members of the Farm Holiday Association blockaded roads into midwestern communities, hoping to cut the supplies of agricultural commodities and bid up prices in order to save their land, which was menaced by foreclosure.

The New Deal and its reforms eased the crisis, as federal relief efforts and the National Labor Relations Act—a "declaration of independence" for organized labor—reduced the need for confrontations. Before the act had its impact, however, violent repression of strikes took place in the auto and

steel industries, as the Ford Motor Company and the Republic Steel Corporation sought to disrupt union organizing drives in the "Little Steel Strike" of 1937.

WORLD WAR II

World War II brought renewed racial tensions. Discrimination in public accommodations was met with pioneering sit-ins organized by the Congress of Racial Equality (CORE) at restaurants in Chicago and elsewhere. Discrimination in the workplace led to mass meetings organized by African American labor leader A. Philip Randolph. The pressure led President Franklin D. Roosevelt to issue Executive Order 8802, creating the Fair Employment Practices Committee. The committee was empowered to hear complaints and take "appropriate steps to redress grievances"; this resulted in enhanced access for African Americans to the expanding job market.

As in World War I, vast numbers of African Americans from southern farms traveled north to the abundant factory jobs available in wartime. In 1943, with thousands of black newcomers moving into older neighborhoods, more than 250 conflicts erupted in 50 cities. The largest confrontation took place in Detroit, where twenty-three blacks and nine whites were killed; seven hundred were injured.

Wartime tensions led to riotous activities involving other groups as well. In 1943 sailors in uniform who were preparing for combat took umbrage at what they saw as the "unpatriotic garb"—baggy trousers and long, draped, broad-lapel jackets—worn by some young Mexican Americans in southern California and attacked those wearing it. Riots broke out, and these "zoot suit" riots, as they would be called, continued for five days.

THE 1950s AND 1960s

The social upheavals of the tumultuous 1960s were the setting for historic racial confrontations, student activism, and protest against an unpopular war. Even in the 1950s the civil rights movement had emerged with the Montgomery, Alabama, bus boycott (1955) and the creation of the Southern Christian Leadership Conference (SCLC), headed by Rev. Martin Luther King Jr. In Little Rock, Arkansas, whites took to the streets in 1957 to thwart school desegregation, and ultimately the U.S. Army was needed to enforce a court order to integrate the schools. Beginning in 1960 sit-ins at segregated lunch counters and other facilities also stimulated violent responses from angry whites in southern communities. Other explosions of racial hostility occurred in 1961 when CORE Freedom Riders rode on integrated buses into the heart of the segregated South. In Anniston, Alabama, a mob incinerated a Greyhound bus, and although the FBI took no

Soldiers of the U.S. Army enforce the desegregation of Central High School in Little Rock, Arkansas, in 1957 on order of President Dwight D. Eisenhower. *Library of Congress*

deprivation in an increasingly affluent America, had stimulated these explosions. The first was the vast inner-city disturbance in Los Angeles in 1965. The Watts riot left thirty-four dead, four thousand arrested, and property damage of $35 million. It was followed by episodes of black unrest in Chicago, Philadelphia, Atlanta, and other cities the next year and then two great riots in Newark and Detroit in 1967. The National Guard and elite units of the army were mobilized. In Newark twenty-six people were killed and twelve hundred wounded; in Detroit, a booming auto center where almost half the black families owned their homes, forty-three were killed and two thousand injured, and four thousand fires burned out a large part of the city. Despite fears that racial riots would continue to erupt in every "long, hot summer," these episodes of civil unrest did not continue past the brief eruption of violence—particularly in Washington, D.C.—following the assassination of Martin Luther King in 1968.

While racial concerns were stimulating unrest and riots—as well as major legislative achievements—in the tumultuous 1960s, an emerging student movement was also having a major impact in many parts of America. In 1964 the Berkeley student rebellion at the University of California captured national attention. This first great student upheaval began with a protest against minor restrictions on campus organizing, but the free speech movement at Berkeley became an instrument for protest against the policies of university educators everywhere, even against the very nature of modern American culture. When school administrators called local law enforcement to deal with thousands of demonstrators, many were injured and eight hundred arrested.

The Berkeley rebellion was followed by student movements at colleges and universities across America. Dozens of campuses large and small featured confrontations over social regulations, educational policies, and racial issues. The Vietnam War and its draft notices created new reasons for protest. On many campuses, buildings were occupied, police were called, and presidents were dismissed for failing to keep things under control. A number of universities—notably Chicago

action, the Justice Department finally moved to ban segregation in carriers and terminals.

The civil rights movement was gaining momentum. Federal officials intervened to guarantee the enrollment of one African American, James Meredith, at the University of Mississippi in 1962, as thirty thousand troops had to be mobilized in the face of an enormous mob of white protesters. The next year, in Birmingham, Alabama, SCLC-led peaceful demonstrations against segregation resulted in violent repression by local law enforcement, seen across the land on television. In the courtroom of national opinion, support was building for the passage of the Civil Rights Act in 1964. Another famous confrontation with repressive local police, in Selma, Alabama, in 1965, mobilized support for passage of the Voting Rights Act.

Yet even as this landmark legislation empowering black Americans in the South was being signed into law, the end of official segregation was having no impact on African Americans elsewhere. Racial upheavals began in the North and West. Analysts speculated that feelings of anger at continuing racial wrongs in the North, as well as the sense of economic

and Columbia—experienced major confrontations involving charges that the institution was "complicit" in the war effort.

In the late 1960s the student movement increasingly became linked with protest against U.S. involvement in the Vietnam War. This form of civil unrest was not restricted to college campuses and involved protests in many American cities. In 1967 more than 10,000 people gathered to block war materials loaded at the Oakland Army Terminal in California, and more than 100,000 gathered in Washington to demand an end to American involvement in the war. In 1968, in one of the most significant examples of civil unrest in the twentieth century, an enormous protest movement in Chicago at the time of the Democratic National Convention led to a bloody confrontation between thousands of police and a huge mass of antiwar demonstrators. "The whole world is watching," the protesters cried toward the television cameras, as Chicago police brutally attacked crowds heading for the convention hall after the rejection of an antiwar plank in the Democratic Party's platform.

The "Vietnamization" policy that followed President Richard M. Nixon's election in 1968 promised to end the draft and slowly extricate the nation from the war. But when Nixon ordered American troops into Cambodia in 1970, student activists responded with passionate protests at this seeming re-escalation of the war, and more than two hundred college campuses were rocked by unrest. When National Guardsmen shot and killed four students protesting at Kent State University, the demonstrations grew in intensity both on campus and in Washington, where thousands of young Americans gathered to protest wartime policies. As "Vietnamization" resumed and American combat troops in South-east Asia were withdrawn over the next two years, the student protests became a thing of the past.

UNREST SINCE THE 1960s

The social upheavals of the 1960s had also involved themes other than racial activism, student protest, and war resistance. The women's movement, gay liberationists, and growing groups of Chicano, Native American, and Asian American activists all were involved in demonstrations in support of their causes. Only on occasion were there violent confrontations. The great exception came at Wounded Knee, South Dakota, in 1972, when FBI agents moved against insurgent members of the American Indian movement who had occupied the site of an 1890 massacre of Indians and had sworn to hold their position by force.

In later years, unemployment in the inner city, urban poverty, and perceptions of racial discrimination could still ignite rage. The televised beating of a black Los Angeles motorist, Rodney King, by a group of police officers led to a convulsion in Los Angeles in 1991. Stores were looted, fifty people were killed, and more than five hundred buildings were burned as riots swept through large parts of the city. But unlike the 1960s, this upheaval did not spread across the land.

The late 1990s offered another kind of civil unrest, as a new movement, harking in some respects back to the student movement of the 1960s, sought to capture public attention by confronting representatives of institutions considered destructive or repressive. In Seattle, Washington, in November 1999, a massive demonstration involving more than fifty thousand people erupted in response to a meeting of the World Trade Organization. In April 2000 the streets in Washington, D.C., were blocked by ten thousand protesters attempting to disrupt the meetings of the World Bank and International Monetary Fund. These protesters were concerned with environmental protection and with the well-being of millions of workers around world. In their view, the new global economy managed by these international agencies was conducting a war on the poor, and world leaders of finance recognized that some changes would have to be considered. The passions of the idealists of the 1960s were once again at work in the actions of these demonstrators, who added yet another important chapter to the history of civil unrest in America.

See also *American Revolution; Civil Rights Movement; Civil War; Great Depression; Kansas-Nebraska Act; Labor Politics and Policy; Marches*

An anti-Vietnam War protester offers a flower as a symbol of peace to a military police officer, October 21, 1967, in Arlington, Virginia. *National Archives*

on Washington; New Deal; Reconstruction; Shays's Rebellion; Suffrage; Vietnam War; Whiskey Rebellion; World War I; World War II: Domestic Politics.

DAVID H. BENNETT, SYRACUSE UNIVERSITY

BIBLIOGRAPHY

Feldberg, Michael. *The Turbulent Era: Riot and Disorder in Jacksonian America.* New York: Oxford University Press, 1980.

Hollon, W. Eugene. *Frontier Violence: Another Look.* New York: Oxford University Press, 1974.

Miller, James. *"Democracy Is in the Streets": From Port Huron to the Siege of Chicago.* New York: Simon and Schuster, 1987.

Waskow, Arthur I. *From Race Riot to Sit-In: 1919 and the 1960s.* New York: Doubleday, 1966.

CIVIL WAR

The Civil War (1861–1865) was a political and military conflict between the United States of America and eleven southern states that attempted to form their own nation, which they called the Confederate States of America. A result of long-developing tensions between the North and South, many of which involved slavery, the war was provoked by the 1860 election of Abraham Lincoln, the first Republican president, and the resulting secession of seven southern states by February 1861. Combat began on April 12, 1861, at Fort Sumter in Charleston, South Carolina, and soon four additional states joined the Confederacy. Although many Confederate and U.S. leaders believed the war would be short, it dragged on until May 26, 1865, when the last Confederate troops surrendered. More than 620,000 people died as a result of the conflict, and property damage was estimated at $5 billion. The victory of the United States meant the preservation of the Union and the abolition of slavery.

COMPROMISES OVER SLAVERY

The most obvious cause of the Civil War was the dispute over slavery and the extension of slavery into U.S. territories. Politicians had struggled with these issues during the first seventy-five years of the Republic (1776–1850), and most pursued a pragmatic course of compromise, which resulted in three great settlements. First, delegates from northern states that were emancipating their slaves compromised at the Constitutional Convention (1787) with representatives of the southern states who sought to maintain their slave systems. Although the words "slave" and "slavery" do not appear in the Constitution, the institution was ensconced in the document by the three-fifths clause (Article I, section 2) and the fugitive slave clause (Article IV, section 2) and the twenty-year prohibition on congressional action outlawing the international slave trade (Article I, section 9).

Between 1818 and 1820, northerners and southerners bargained over slavery's extension west of the Mississippi River. With the Missouri Compromise (1820), Congress granted Missouri admission to the Union as a slave state but forbade the further extension of slavery north of the 36°30′ line drawn across the Louisiana Territory.

Thirty years later came the third and final compromise. As a result of the Mexican-American War (1846–1848), the United States acquired more than 500,000 square miles of new territory. The Democratic and Whig Parties handled the ensuing debate over slavery in the new lands by cobbling together the Compromise of 1850, which provided that California would be admitted as a free state, while the rest of the Mexican cession would be divided into two territories— Utah and New Mexico—where the legality of slavery would be decided by popular sovereignty. In return for California's admission as a free state, enough northerners of both parties joined all southerners in Congress to pass a stronger fugitive slave law as a concession to the South.

The 1850s brought an end to sectional settlement. The decade began with Harriet Beecher Stowe's serial publication of *Uncle Tom's Cabin* (1851), an abolitionist novel that leveled a blistering attack on slave owners in the South. Three years later, Stephen Douglas, the Democratic senator from Illinois, introduced the Kansas-Nebraska Act, which brought the idea of popular sovereignty from Utah and New Mexico to the newly organized territories of Kansas and Nebraska. This act was controversial because both Kansas and Nebraska were above the 36°30′ line in the Louisiana Territory and had been declared free by the Missouri Compromise of 1820.

After it was passed with southern and western support, the Kansas-Nebraska Act had three dramatic results. First, it led to Bleeding Kansas (1854–1860), a local civil war in which slaveholders from Kansas and Missouri fought antislavery groups for control of the Kansas statehood process. Second, it heralded the disintegration of the Whig Party because southerners increasingly voted by section, not by party. Third, and most significant, the act led to the creation of the Republican Party in the North.

The Republican Party formed in 1854 as northerners of both major parties joined in opposition to the expansion of slavery into the territories. First at Ripon, Wisconsin, and later at Jackson, Michigan, disaffected Whigs, antislavery Democrats, and members of the smaller Free Soil Party formed the coalition of an incipient party.

This Republican coalition solidified after the Supreme Court in 1857 handed down its decision in *Dred Scott v. Sandford.* The case had been brought to court by a slave, Dred Scott, who argued that after his master took him into free territory, he was no longer a slave. The Court's majority found that Scott was not free and that he did not have the right to file suit in state or federal court because no African American could be a citizen of the United States. The Court also stated that Congress had no power to exclude slavery from the territories, and thus the Missouri Compromise and any other legislation limiting slavery's expansion was unconstitutional. The *Dred Scott* decision boosted the Republican Party's appeal as many northerners decried the southern "slave power" that they felt was undermining the Constitution to protect the South's "peculiar institution."

THE ELECTION OF 1860 AND THE OUTBREAK OF WAR

By the presidential election of 1860, the slavery issue overshadowed all others. The Republicans nominated Abraham Lincoln, a lesser-known but influential moderate who insisted that the *Dred Scott* decision was wrong and that slavery must not expand into the territories. As the Democrats searched for a nominee and a platform, they divided along sectional lines, much as the Whigs had done. Northern Democrats nominated Stephen Douglas, while southern Democrats supported a proslavery platform led by John C. Breckinridge of Kentucky. The Constitutional Union Party, which condemned the sectional nature of the emerging political scene, nominated a Tennessee politician, John Bell, who argued that the Union was more important than the slavery issue.

Lincoln won the election with 180 electoral votes and 1,866,452 popular votes. Although Douglas had 1,376,957 popular votes, he received only 12 electoral votes because Breckinridge secured 72 electoral votes from the southern states. Bell received support in the Upper South—Virginia, Tennessee, and Kentucky—where he won 39 electoral votes and most of his 588,879 popular votes.

Throughout the 1860 campaign, radical southern leaders threatened to secede from the Union if Lincoln were elected. When the election result was clear, the South Carolina legislature led by summoning a special convention to consider secession. In December the convention unanimously passed an ordinance dissolving "the union now subsisting between South Carolina and other States." Other southern states—Alabama, Florida, Georgia, Louisiana, Mississippi, and Texas—soon held similar conventions, and all left the Union by February 1, 1861.

After secession, delegates from six southern states met in Montgomery, Alabama, on February 4, 1861, to set up a provisional government for the Confederate States of America. On February 8 they adopted a constitution, and the next day the provisional Confederate Congress elected Jefferson Davis of Mississippi as president and Alexander Stephens of Georgia as vice president. When Lincoln assumed the presidency on March 4, 1861, he said the federal government would not "assail" the states of the South, but that he meant to "hold, occupy, and possess the property and places belonging to the government."

Within a month, however, Confederates had pushed Union military forces out of the South, with one exception: soldiers at Fort Sumter, in Charleston Harbor, South Carolina. There the war began when Confederate general Pierre Beauregard ordered his troops to flush Union forces out on April 12, 1861. The next day, Sumter fell to the Confederates, leading Lincoln to call up 75,000 militia from the states on April 15, 1861. Facing this show of federal force, Arkansas, North Carolina, Tennessee, and Virginia seceded, adding significant population, power, and wealth to the new southern nation.

ACTION IN THE U.S. CONGRESS

With most southern delegates out of the U.S. Congress, many northerners—mostly Republicans and former Whigs—set out to bring their progressive economic ideals to fruition. First, they acted to finance the war and provide a stable economic order. In 1861 Congress passed the Morrill Tariff, which raised import duties to approximately twice what they were before the war and protected industry in the North. Congress then passed the National Banking Act, which was meant to replace the old national banks (of 1791 and 1816) by creating a uniform financial order and a fluid system of paper notes that would foster trade and help finance the war. As expenses rose during the conflict, Congress in 1862 passed the Internal Revenue Act, which levied the first tax on income in U.S. history to help defray the cost of blockading and invading the South. Congress also began giving Morrill Land Grants to support higher education in loyal states.

The U.S. Congress also made great leaps in western development. In 1862 it passed the transcontinental railway plan, which assigned grants of land to railroad companies that would seek to unite by rail the East and the West. The first transcontinental line was completed in 1869, when the Union Pacific met the Central Pacific at Promontory, Utah. Also, Congress, through the Homestead Act of 1862, granted 160 acres of western land to settlers who pledged to homestead for at least five years on the frontier.

PROGRESS OF THE FIGHTING

Although Congress made great strides in national development, Union forces in 1861 and 1862 did not fare well in the most important theater of the war, the East. After losses in Virginia at First Bull Run (July 1861), in the Peninsular Campaign (summer–fall 1862), and at Second Bull Run (August 1862), many northern critics of Lincoln were demanding a victory in the East. Radical Republicans in Congress demanded a more forceful prosecution of the war through the abolition of slavery and the introduction of African American troops. Lincoln opposed these measures because he believed he lacked the constitutional power to end slavery and sufficient northern political support to enlist African American troops.

Nevertheless, the president decided and secretly declared that he would soon emancipate Confederate slaves, which he did after Robert E. Lee's Confederate army was halted at the battle of Antietam, near Sharpsburg, Maryland, on September 17, 1862—the bloodiest day in U.S. military history with twenty-three thousand dead, missing, and wounded. Five days after this "victory," Lincoln issued a preliminary Emancipation Proclamation, made final on January 1, 1863, freeing all the slaves in the Confederacy. By emancipating Confederate slaves and freeing all the slaves in areas held by Confederates and emphasizing the enlistment of African American soldiers in the Union army, Lincoln sought to rally support in the North, undermine the solidarity of the Confederacy, and make it impossible for foreign powers to recognize the legitimacy of the Confederate government because, in doing so, European powers would help prop up a slave-holding regime. In addition to making this a moral war, the U.S. Congress followed the Confederate lead by instituting a draft in July 1863 under the Enrollment Act.

Gen. Robert E. Lee and his Confederate soldiers won two more great victories in Virginia—at Fredericksburg in December 1862 and at Chancellorsville in May 1863. But by the summer of 1863 Union troops were turning the tide of the war. At Gettysburg, Pennsylvania (July 1–3, 1863), Lee was pushed from the North again; and at Vicksburg, Mississippi, on the same day Lee retreated (July 4, 1863), Union general Ulysses S. Grant captured the last Confederate stronghold on the Mississippi River and its army of twenty-seven thousand Confederates. In November 1863 Grant was given command of all U.S. forces; and by May 1864, under his command, the United States launched a coordinated campaign of invasion. Grant commanded the Army of the Potomac, and William T. Sherman commanded Union forces in the West.

In the fall of 1864, as Grant and Sherman led Union troops in Confederate territory, President Lincoln faced another election year. Moderate and conservative Republicans and "War Democrats" supported Lincoln. Radical Republicans, who felt he was too lenient on the Confederacy, and Copperheads, Democrats who wanted peace without victory and an end to Lincoln's "tyranny" in the North, opposed him. The Democrats nominated Gen. George McClellan to face Lincoln. But, after Sherman's capture of Atlanta, Georgia, in September 1864 and Philip Sheridan's successful Shenandoah Valley campaign in the fall of 1864, Union sentiment supported Lincoln. He won 212 of 233 electoral votes and 55 percent of the popular vote.

With Lincoln's reelection, the Confederacy's cause was lost. It was only a matter of time before Grant's and Sherman's armies wore down Confederate forces. Sherman led his "March to the Sea" from Atlanta to Savannah, Georgia, in late 1864, destroying vast stores of food and military supplies. In early 1865 Grant's long siege of Petersburg, Virginia, proved successful when Lee abandoned his position there. Grant captured Petersburg and then the Confederate capital at Richmond. By the spring of 1865 the Confederate losses had mounted to such an extent that

Confederate saboteurs destroyed railroad tracks in Virginia that the Union army had been using. The track was taken up, the wooden ties set afire, and the heated rails bent. Much of the Confederacy's infrastructure was damaged or destroyed during the war. *Library of Congress*

Lee surrendered his army to Grant at Appomattox Court House on April 9, 1865. The war ended shortly thereafter, when the last Confederate forces surrendered.

THE SIGNIFICANCE OF THE CIVIL WAR

Union victory in the Civil War meant first and foremost the preservation of the Union, although the United States had yet to experience the painful realignments of Reconstruction. President Lincoln was assassinated on April 14, 1865, at Ford's Theater, but the Republican Party continued to dominate U.S. political life until 1912, when Woodrow Wilson was elected (only one Democratic president, Grover Cleveland, was elected between 1860 and 1912).

The Civil War also caused significant changes in the Constitution. The Thirteenth Amendment (1865) carried Lincoln's Emancipation Proclamation to its logical conclusion by outlawing slavery in the United States. The Fourteenth Amendment (1868) was the most far reaching of the Reconstruction amendments: it granted U.S. citizenship to all persons born in the United States, overturning the *Dred Scott* decision that had denied African Americans citizenship; it provided for due process rights at the state level; and, finally, it declared that states must not deny any person equal protection of the laws. In the future, it would provide the Supreme Court the tool for incorporating provisions of the Bill of Rights—applying them to the states. The Fifteenth Amendment (1870) denied states the ability to limit voting rights based on "race, color, or previous condition of servitude." White, Democratic southerners worked their way around the Fourteenth and Fifteenth Amendments, but the Thirteenth Amendment survived. Slavery was not reestablished.

See also *Compromise of 1850; Constitution, U.S.; Constitutional Amendments; Constitutional Convention; Emancipation Proclamation; Kansas-Nebraska Act; Missouri Compromise; Morrill Land-Grant College Acts; Popular Sovereignty; Secession; Sectionalism; Slavery; Territorial Expansion.*

JEFFREY LITTLEJOHN, UNIVERSITY OF ARKANSAS

BIBLIOGRAPHY

Finkelman, Paul. *Dred Scott v. Sandford: A Brief History.* Boston: Bedford Books, 1997.
Fredrickson, George. *The Inner Civil War: Northern Intellectuals and the Crisis of the Union.* New York: Harper and Row, 1965.
Gallagher, Gary. *The Confederate War.* Cambridge: Harvard University Press, 1997.
McPherson, James. *Battle Cry of Freedom: The Civil War Era.* New York: Oxford University Press, 1988.
Potter, David. *The Impending Crisis, 1848–1861.* New York: Harper and Row, 1976.

CLEVELAND, GROVER

The twenty-second (1885–1889) and twenty-fourth (1893–1897) president of the United States and the only president to serve two nonsequential terms, Grover Cleveland was a dedicated reformer who was bent on transforming the spoils and tariff systems.

Born March 18, 1837, he was the fifth of nine children of a Presbyterian minister and his wife. Cleveland began his climb in politics in his home state of New York. His early political career, which was interspersed with his Buffalo law practice, saw his rise from sheriff of Erie County, to mayor of Buffalo, to state governor. In all these positions he was known as an uncompromising reformer, committed to rooting out corruption, fiscal abuse, and the spoils system.

In 1884 his success with reforms at the state level brought Governor Cleveland to the attention of the national Democratic Party. He mounted a successful bid against Republican James G. Blaine, although the election was marred by well-founded accusations that he had fathered a child out of wedlock. Instructing his campaign workers to "tell the truth," Cleveland overcame the scandal and went on to victory, thanks largely to reform-hungry Republicans, known as the Mugwumps, who joined Democrats in supporting the reform-minded candidate.

During his first term, Cleveland focused on invoking the reformist principles he had applied so successfully as governor of New York. He implemented the Pendleton Civil Service Act, signed into law by his predecessor, Chester A. Arthur, which shifted the source of thousands of government jobs from patronage to a merit system of hiring. He also vetoed numerous private pension bills for individual Civil War veterans. But in tariff reform, one of his favorite issues, and in dealing with the huge federal budget surplus caused by high tariffs, he failed, incurring the wrath of not only many members of his own party but also the powerful business interests.

In 1888 Cleveland ran for reelection against Indiana Republican Benjamin Harrison. Although he defeated Harrison by 100,000 popular votes, Cleveland lost to him in the electoral college 233–168. Dispirited, Cleveland moved to New York City to resume his law practice.

Four years later, however, he found himself back in the running for the presidency against his old rival, the incumbent president Benjamin Harrison. After four years of Harrison's reckless spending, the country was sliding into a crisis. Tariffs by then were so high that imports had almost stopped, and the Sherman Silver Purchase Act of 1890 had caused a steady outflow of gold from the Treasury. Cleveland defeated

Harrison in the electoral college by a 277–145 vote but received only 46.3 percent of the popular vote because of the third-party candidacy of James B. Weaver of the Populist (or People's) Party.

Two months after Cleveland's inauguration, the panic of 1893 swept the country, sparking a deep economic depression. Hundreds of banks failed, unemployment skyrocketed, and many businesses went bankrupt. Moreover, because citizens began to hoard gold, Treasury reserves sank to dangerous levels.

To address the currency crisis, as well as to tackle inflation and the erosion of business confidence he believed responsible for the depression, Cleveland called a special session of Congress. Young orator and U.S. representative William Jennings Bryan (D-Neb.) spoke for three hours, urging the free and unlimited coinage of silver. Supported by many congressional Republicans, Cleveland convinced legislators to repeal the somewhat inflationary Sherman Silver Purchase Act. He also dealt with the government's shrinking gold reserves by authorizing the purchase of several million ounces of gold from private holders. The depression, however, continued.

Meanwhile, strikes across the country in mines, railroads, and textile mills worsened the situation. In 1894 a local strike at the Pullman Palace Car Company near Chicago led to a debilitating railroad strike throughout the Midwest and eventually to riots by strikers in Chicago. When the president sent federal troops to quell the violence, he gained the support of the business community but the enmity of labor organizations. Cleveland was blamed for the nation's economic crisis, even though it was not of his making.

In foreign affairs, Cleveland steadfastly opposed any attempt to expand the country. In March 1893 he withdrew from the Senate a treaty calling for the annexation of Hawaii. He also refused to bow to public pressure to declare war on Spain over its suppression of a rebellion in Cuba that began in 1895.

After Republicans gained congressional seats in the 1894 midterm elections, Cleveland had difficulty exerting much control over Congress or even his own party. In fact, as his second term came to an end, his party rejected the gold standard and nominated William Jennings Bryan for president, thereby also repudiating Cleveland's conservative policies, as his critics saw it, at a time of growing progressive sentiment. Republican William McKinley won the election.

Upon leaving office for the second time, Cleveland settled in Princeton, New Jersey, where in 1901 he was appointed to the board of trustees of Princeton University. In 1904 he became president of the board; future president Woodrow Wilson was at the time president of the university. Cleveland died of a heart attack in Princeton in 1908.

See also *Panic of 1893; Populist (People's) Party; Tariff History.*

SABRA BISSETTE LEDENT, INDEPENDENT AUTHOR

BIBLIOGRAPHY

Cleveland, Grover. *Presidential Problems.* Freeport, N.Y.: Books for Libraries Press, 1971.

McElroy, Robert. *Grover Cleveland: The Man and the Statesman: An Authorized Biography.* 2 vols. New York: Harper and Brothers, 1923.

Tugwell, Rexford G. *Grover Cleveland.* New York: Macmillan, 1968.

Welsh, Richard E., Jr. *The Presidencies of Grover Cleveland.* Lawrence: University Press of Kansas, 1988.

CLINTON, BILL

Bill Clinton was elected president of the United States in 1992 and was reelected in 1996. The third-youngest person to serve as president, he presided over a remarkable resurgence in the American economy. When he left office in 2001, he had fulfilled the promise made in his first campaign: to help "build a bridge to the twenty-first century."

EARLY YEARS

Clinton was born August 19, 1946, in Hope, Arkansas. His given name was William Jefferson Blythe III, after his father, William Jefferson Blythe II, who was killed in an auto accident months before his son's birth. His mother married Roger Clinton in 1950, and the future president changed his name to William Jefferson Clinton when he was fifteen.

His stepfather was an alcoholic and an abusive husband during Bill Clinton's youth; his mother was the powerful early influence in his life. After two years in a Roman Catholic elementary school, he attended public schools in Hot Springs, Arkansas, where he earned high grades and became a student leader. In a famous photographed incident, he visited Washington, D.C., in 1962 as a delegate to Boys Nation, an American Legion leadership training program, and was first in line to shake the hand of President John F. Kennedy at the White House. Clinton would point to Kennedy and Dr. Martin Luther King Jr., whose "I Have a Dream" speech he watched, as heroes.

After high school he attended Georgetown University and served as class president. His strong record at Georgetown helped him win a coveted Rhodes scholarship at Oxford University. After two years as Rhodes scholar, he entered Yale Law School in 1970, holding part-time jobs to supplement scholarship funds. It was at Yale that he met another law student, Hillary Rodham, of Park Ridge, Illinois. They were married on October 11, 1975, and later had one child, daughter Chelsea.

A LIFE IN POLITICS

After receiving his doctor of law degree in 1973, Bill Clinton returned to his home state and joined the faculty of the University of Arkansas School of Law in Fayetteville. He made an unsuccessful race for a seat in the House of Representatives in 1974 but won the Democratic primary for Arkansas attorney general and ran unopposed in the general election in 1976. Two years later, he was elected governor of Arkansas with a campaign that focused on economic development and education.

His first term as governor was less than successful, and he was defeated in his reelection effort by Frank D.White, a conservative Republican savings and loan executive. A chastened Clinton joined a law firm in Little Rock and made plans for the gubernatorial race in 1982. During the campaign he persuaded voters that he had learned from the problems in his first term, and he decisively defeated White. Elected three more times (a constitutional amendment changed the term of office to four years in 1986), he served as governor until he won his race for the White House.

As governor, he promoted reforms in education, including certification examinations for new teachers and college scholarships for poor and middle-class students. He worked to attract high-technology companies to his state and shaped other plans to reduce unemployment and increase business interest in Arkansas.

While governor he sought a greater role on the national stage. He chaired both the National Governors Association and the Democratic Leadership Council, an organization of moderate Democrats. He advocated national welfare reform and gave the nominating speech for Gov. Michael S. Dukakis, the unsuccessful Democratic candidate for president in 1988.

In 1991 Clinton announced his own candidacy for the White House. He emerged from a crowded field of aspirants for the Democratic nomination and won a series of primary contests. He was named his party's candidate at its New York convention, where he picked Tennessee senator Al Gore as his running mate.

During the primaries, he dealt with personal issues that menaced his nomination. Stories of his marital infidelity in Arkansas were headline news, forcing Bill and Hillary Clinton to respond with a televised discussion in which they acknowledged problems but called their marriage a strong one. Stories that Clinton had tried to evade the draft during the Vietnam War were answered by denials that he had acted improperly.

The campaign featured a Clinton assault on the economic policies of his opponent, President George Bush. With the nation mired in a wrenching recession, Bill Clinton declared he would stimulate growth and raise taxes on wealthy Amer-

President-elect Bill Clinton chats with business owners along Georgia Avenue in Washington, D.C. *R. Michael Jenkins, Congressional Quarterly*

icans to help reduce the escalating federal budget deficit, which was approximately $290 billion in 1992, the largest in history. "It's the economy, stupid," was the banner in Clinton campaign headquarters.

With the candidate proving to be a brilliantly effective campaigner—a warm and personable presence in town meetings and televised debates, an articulate and persuasive speaker in larger settings—Bill Clinton was elected the forty-second president of the United States. He received 43 percent of the vote and decisively defeated not only incumbent George Bush (who achieved 38 percent) but also a third-party challenger, the wealthy, populist Texas businessman Ross Perot, the choice of almost 19 percent of voters.

DOMESTIC INITIATIVES

Clinton's first months in the White House were a troubled time. His efforts to end the ban on homosexual men and women in the armed services failed when met with angry resistance from conservatives and key figures in the military establishment. He had difficulty filling some key offices, particularly attorney general, when two of his nominees proved to have legal problems. He became the subject of an investigation into a failed real estate venture in Arkansas—the Whitewater Development Company—in which he had invested while attorney general; congressional committees pursued the matter, and an independent counsel was appointed to probe the case.

More important, the major legislative initiative of his first term—reform of the nation's health care system—ended in failure. His health care task force, chaired by his wife, rejected a simple but dramatic, Canadian-style, national single-payer plan in favor of a complex scheme involving private insurance companies. Because powerful private interests and influential Republicans fiercely opposed the plan and it elicited only lukewarm support from some key members of Clinton's own party, it came to naught.

These difficulties had a direct impact on elections in 1994, when the Republican Party won a stunning victory, taking control of both houses of Congress. The GOP leadership, with its "Contract with America" and strong social agenda, called for a decisive turn to the right. The contract proposed slashing federal spending, cutting taxes, and reducing the federal regulatory role. The newly resurgent Christian Coalition mobilized voters who opposed abortion and favored programs protecting traditional family values.

Bill Clinton responded to the 1994 election results by moving closer to the political center. Earlier he had achieved some significant gains for his activist agenda, in particular by pushing through a major expansion of tax credits for low-income families that would help raise many out of poverty in coming years. After the 1994 elections, however, he pointed to the need to balance the budget. His larger economic program already was having an impact on a lagging economy, and the improving economy allowed Clinton to achieve a series of legislative triumphs in 1996 that included requiring insurance companies to allow workers to retain health coverage after leaving their jobs and raising the minimum wage.

When Clinton ran for reelection in 1996, the nation's economy was on an upswing and his Republican opponent, former senator Robert Dole, proved an uninspiring candidate. Clinton was able to focus attention on the increasingly unpopular Speaker of the House, Newt Gingrich, who had been the chief spokesperson for the failed Contract with America. Stories concerning illegal campaign contributions troubled the Democrats just before the election, but Bill Clinton easily won a second term, although Republicans retained control of Congress.

Clinton's second term featured an aggressive attack on the perils of tobacco, with Clinton calling for tougher federal regulation. He increased funding for child care and for children's health care. He pushed through the Family and Medical Leave Act and increased spending for education. After an early legislative success in banning some assault weapons, he continued to call for gun control.

But these were not large-scale initiatives. Liberal critics who rejected his cautious budget-balancing posture and called for major new social programs criticized him for being poll-driven and unimaginative, for not doing more. They were particularly hostile to the welfare reform measure he had championed, fearing that it did not contain sufficient protections for the vulnerable in less-prosperous economic times.

But Clinton was a New Democrat and had argued for many years that welfare dependency must be addressed; following passage of the reform measure, he could point to a 50 percent reduction in welfare roles as millions moved from welfare to work. As for the larger question of why this president did not propose a dramatic New Deal or Great Society reform agenda in the 1990s, supporters would answer that there simply was no political setting for success of such an ambitious effort in that decade. Bill Clinton had to work with a hostile Republican congressional majority whose leadership reviled activist government and could strangle any large-scale initiatives.

A SUCCESSFUL ECONOMY

Few would criticize economic developments in the Clinton years. With a shrewd and able economic management team led by Secretary of the Treasury Robert Rubin, Clinton and his administration raised revenue and encouraged trade expansion, which helped stimulate growth and provide the impetus to economic expansion.

In a critical vote early in his first term, the president won a massive tax increase on the wealthiest Americans. It was a rejection of the policy of the Reagan-Bush years, and every member of the opposition Republicans—many predicting economic disaster—voted against the plan in a deadlocked Senate; the vice president cast the deciding vote.

Clinton also took on powerful forces in his own party and in organized labor to promote policies that advanced global trade and interdependence. These included approval of the North American Free Trade Agreement (NAFTA), which eliminated most trade barriers with Mexico and Canada, and permanent normal trade relations with China, which eliminated yearly congressional debates and votes and based the U.S.-China relationship on a more predictable framework.

The administration also responded rapidly and successfully to dangerous economic crises in Mexico and Asia that threatened to have an impact on the United States. Because the Federal Reserve Board believed that inflation was under control, interest rates remained stable and did not impede the coming stock market boom or the vast increases in productivity.

The result would be the greatest achievement of the Clinton years. By the end of his second term, the huge budget deficit he had inherited had been eliminated. The budget surplus in 2000 was more than $200 billion, and the immense national debt—which had multiplied by four during the Reagan-Bush years—was being repaid. More than 22 million new jobs were created (more than in the twelve years of his two predecessors), and real wages increased by 6.5 percent in his eight years in office (compared with a real-wage decline of 4.3 percent in the preceding twelve years). Unemployment was down from 7.5 percent in 1993 to 4 percent in 2000, and African American unemployment decreased from 14 percent to 7 percent. For the first time since 1968, the child poverty rate fell for five consecutive years. All this was accomplished with the smallest federal civilian workforce in forty years as the National Partnership for Reinventing Government, under Vice President Gore, helped account for a 20 percent reduction in the number of federal workers.

Many reasons can be cited for the economic achievements of the 1990s. The rise of the "new economy," with computer and Internet companies leading the way, played a central role. And main-line U.S. corporations from the "old economy," recovering from the economic defeats of previous decades, also became more competitive and took advantage of new global trade opportunities. But it was the administration's policies that not only helped create the boom but also sustained it.

FOREIGN POLICY

Throughout both terms, Clinton had to focus attention on complex foreign policy issues in a post–cold war environment. He suffered an early setback in 1993 when he was forced to withdraw from Somalia the U.S. forces that had been sent by the previous administration as a humanitarian response to famine there. The effort had lost its focus, and the press and public reacted adversely to U.S. casualties suffered in a clash with one of the warlords in that small, chaotic East African nation. But in 1994 Clinton had a diplomatic success when he used armed force to intimidate a military junta that had overthrown the president of Haiti; the United States forced the usurpers into exile and reinstated the elected president, Jean-Bertrand Aristide.

More significant was Clinton's use of U.S. air power and the U.S. commitment to North Atlantic Treaty Organization (NATO) peacekeeping to help bring an end to the murderous ethnic cleansing in Bosnia in 1995, after Serbian forces devastated Muslim communities and humiliated United Nations representatives in that Balkan state. In 1999, in Kosovo, U.S. air power also played the critical role in NATO's defeat of Serbia, whose troops had terrorized that small province. Bill Clinton was shaping a policy to respond to regional threats to peace in areas where U.S. power could be usefully projected.

Clinton used his diplomatic skills to advance peace in other ways. He played a role in efforts to end the enduring conflict in Northern Ireland. He also helped shape—with Israeli prime minister Yitzhak Rabin and Palestinian chairman Yasir Arafat—a Mideast peace accord in 1993. In 2000, during a lengthy Camp David meeting with Arafat and Prime Minister Ehud Barak of Israel, he for a time brought the two parties even closer to a comprehensive Middle East settlement.

FROM WHITEWATER TO IMPEACHMENT

Bill Clinton as president faced strong ideological opposition from the very beginning. In the private sector, the right-wing Christian proselytizers and cable channels, national talk radio shows, and right-wing Washington think tanks strove to demean, disgrace, and paralyze him. In Congress, throughout his two terms, many of his most fervent ideological opponents sought to weaken him by calling for investigations of scandal. And Bill Clinton gave his enemies the means with which to damage him.

The lengthy investigation of the Whitewater affair cost more than $50 million. The first independent counsel to investigate Whitewater, the Republican Robert B. Fiske Jr., found no presidential wrongdoing. The GOP leadership fired Fiske after their 1994 election victory. Kenneth Starr, Fiske's replacement and a well-known conservative, vigorously renewed the Whitewater inquiry but also failed to find any illegal activity by the president. In fact, Starr's successor as independent counsel, Robert W. Ray, ultimately conceded that there was no scandal in other incidents—"Filegate" (inappropriate movement of White House files) and "Travelgate" (replacement of White House travel staff)—that had created such political heat and press coverage in the Clinton years. In September 2000, Ray—like Robert Fiske before him—reported that evidence was not sufficient to show criminal wrongdoing in the Whitewater case by either President Clinton or his wife.

A sex scandal was something different, however; and it would become the focus of an effort to impeach Clinton. In 1998 Clinton was forced to admit that he had had "inappropriate" sexual contact with a young White House intern, Monica Lewinsky. After the first news reports about this affair, Clinton made a notorious finger-wagging denial on national television. Although mounting evidence led to his admission of the relationship (a politically damaging act that haunted him during his remaining months in office), his earlier untruthful denial of this private (and consensual) sexual affair was not an impeachable offense.

The Republicans instead sought to impeach him for a related incident. To an Arkansas grand jury, the president had denied allegations by a former state employee in Arkansas, Paula Jones, that he had made unwanted sexual advances toward her on one occasion when he was governor. When confronted with a surprise question about Monica Lewinsky by Jones's attorneys, who were passionate ideological opponents of Clinton, Clinton denied any sexual relationship with the intern. The Jones case in Arkansas was later dismissed by the judge who earlier had thrown out even the questions about the Lewinsky matter, but the president's denial under oath about Lewinsky to Jones's attorneys became a central issue in the 1998 impeachment effort in the House of Representatives.

Other serious charges—that Bill Clinton obstructed justice and suborned perjury—were alleged by his enemies but never proved. And the convoluted report to the House by the independent counsel (the Starr report) was so filled with graphic sexual material that the report itself became a matter of controversy, more damaging to the reputation of the counsel than the president. But Clinton's denial about Lewinsky loomed large during the angry and partisan debate leading to a House vote (along party lines) to impeach the president. An impeachment trial followed in the Senate, but few believed that Clinton could be removed from office. There was little drama, because the Senate vote, again largely along party lines, fell far short of conviction.

CONFOUNDING HIS OPPONENTS

Throughout Clinton's presidency the national news media attacked him ferociously. During the Lewinsky matter, television comedians nightly made him the object of scornful, salacious humor. Polls showed, however, that the public strongly approved of Clinton's performance in office, and the Democratic Party's surprisingly powerful showing in the midterm congressional races in the fall of 1998, which hastened the resignation of Clinton's foe, Speaker Newt Gingrich, indicated public rejection of any effort to force this leader from the White House.

In 1999 and 2000, Bill Clinton retained strong support for his leadership and proposed an ambitious domestic and foreign policy agenda. The impeachment issue—which had proved to be dangerous for his opponents—quickly faded from view. But "Clinton fatigue," that popular unhappiness with his personal behavior, lingered on in some circles to damage the presidential prospects of his vice president, Al Gore, in the 2000 election.

See also *Campaign Finance; Clinton-Era Scandals; Impeachment; Independent Counsel; Soft Money and Twentieth-Century Political Campaigns; Talk Radio; Watershed Elections.*

DAVID H. BENNETT, SYRACUSE UNIVERSITY

BIBLIOGRAPHY

Drew, Elizabeth. *Showdown: The Struggle Between the Gingrich Congress and the Clinton White House.* New York: Touchstone Books, 1997.

Maraniss, David. *First in His Class: The Biography of Bill Clinton.* New York: Touchstone Books, 1996.

Toobin, Jeffrey. *A Vast Conspiracy: The Real Story of the Sex Scandal That Nearly Brought Down a President.* New York: Random House, 2000.

CLINTON-ERA SCANDALS

The administration of Bill Clinton, especially after the election of a Republican Congress in 1994, was troubled by a series of scandals, judicial probes, and congressional investigations, culminating in the president's impeachment in the House in December 1998 and trial before the Senate in January 1999. From all of these difficulties, Clinton emerged remarkably unscathed.

When Bill Clinton was sworn in as president in January 1993, after terms as Arkansas attorney general and governor, he became the first Democratic president in twelve years, since Jimmy Carter left the White House in 1981. Moreover, he defeated an incumbent Republican president, George Bush. Clinton and his influential wife Hillary Rodham Clinton were never fully accepted as legitimate by many Republicans, particularly in the conservative wing of the party that had dominated national politics since 1980, when Ronald Reagan defeated Carter. His most conservative opponents, both in Congress and in the newspapers and journals affiliated with the right wing of the Republican Party, came to concentrate increasingly on Clinton's personal integrity in addition to his political programs, the traditional fulcrum of contention between political parties.

Some actions by Clinton and his associates lent credence in conservative minds to questions of integrity and misuse of political power. These included a significant reordering of the White House Travel Office and firing of personnel, allegations about the misuse of FBI files on outgoing Republican administration officials, and questionable campaign financing practices. But two events—the affair known as Whitewater and Clinton's sexual relationship with a young female intern in the White House named Monica Lewinsky—were more serious than other charges and plagued Clinton throughout much of his eight years in office. The Lewinsky matter eventually produced a presidential impeachment, only the second in the Republic's history.

The complicated matter of Whitewater, a failed Arkansas real estate venture in the 1980s managed by old friends of the Clintons, would dog the administration for almost two full terms. The Clintons had invested in the scheme, managed by James and Susan McDougal, and lost money; the McDougals' real estate business sank into bankruptcy. The McDougals eventually were indicted; Jim died and Susan was impris-

Senators take an oath of impartiality at the start of the impeachment trial of President Bill Clinton.   *U.S. Senate*

oned, refusing to implicate the Clintons in any illegalities. It was not clear whether the Clintons themselves broke financial regulations or misused government influence to protect their friends. In any case, the affair was so intricate and complicated that it had limited political weight until the unexplained suicide in July 1993 of Vincent Foster, the Clintons' deputy counsel, and the swift removal of files on Whitewater from Foster's office. These developments gave the affair an air of drama and caused the appointment in January 1994 of a special prosecutor under Watergate-era legislation, while the Senate (in Republican hands once more) convened hearings.

The first independent counsel to investigate Whitewater, the Republican Robert B. Fiske Jr., found no presidential wrongdoing. The GOP leadership fired Fiske after 1994 elections gave them control of both the House and Senate. Kenneth Starr, Fiske's replacement and a well-known conservative, vigorously renewed the Whitewater inquiry but also failed to find any illegal activity by the president. In fact, Starr's successor as independent counsel, Robert W. Ray, ultimately conceded that there was no scandal in the other inci-

dents that had created such political heat and press coverage in the Clinton years. In September 2000, Ray—like Robert Fiske before him—reported that there was insufficient evidence to show criminal wrongdoing in the Whitewater case by either President Clinton or his wife.

Although Whitewater fizzled as an issue, Starr had moved in another direction: toward sexual scandal. Rumors had long existed about inappropriate sexual conduct by Clinton, even as governor of Arkansas. In 1996 a former state employee named Paula Jones sued him for having made unwanted sexual advances in the 1980s. Clinton denied her allegation under affidavit, and a judge dismissed the case. But Starr had added this matter to his Arkansas investigations and began looking into rumors concerning Lewinsky, which surfaced publicly early in 1996. Clinton at first denied this charge but later, as more evidence emerged, confessed to "inappropriate" sexual contact with Lewinsky. These developments hardened conservative criticism of Clinton, but the actual impeachment arose from a different, if related, incident in which he denied to an Arkansas grand jury looking into the Jones case that he had had a sexual relationship with Lewinsky. This potential perjury under oath became the grounding for the impeachment and subsequent failed Senate trial to convict.

Some scholars have viewed the Clinton-era scandals as part of an ongoing tension between Congress and the executive to establish paramount political power and define the national policy agenda, in this case overlaid with a veneer of supermarket tabloid salaciousness. With Clinton the struggle was exacerbated by important social and economic differences that divided the conservative Republican Party that controlled Congress and the generally liberal to moderate Democratic position of the president and his closest allies.

The public's view was reflected in the voting booth. The House impeachment action came in December 1998, just a month after the GOP had suffered a stinging defeat at the polls in off-year congressional elections, when it just barely retained control of Congress. Clinton's popularity suffered little. It appeared that many people drew a distinction between Clinton's official, public duties and his personal life, and while disapproving of his personal conduct, they did not believe it warranted removal from office. Furthermore, most Americans overwhelmingly approved of the job he was doing as president.

See also *Clinton, Bill; Scandals and Corruption.*

BIBLIOGRAPHY

Campbell, Colin, and Bert A. Rockman, eds. *The Clinton Legacy.* New York: Chatham House, 2000.

Dershowitz, Alan M. *Sexual McCarthyism: Clinton, Starr, and the Emerging Constitutional Crisis.* New York: Free Press, 1998.

Thomas, Evans, ed. *Back from the Dead: How Clinton Survived the Republican Revolution.* New York: Atlantic Monthly, 1997.

CLOTURE

Cloture is a parliamentary process for ending (closing) debate. In the U.S. Senate, where rules generally permit unlimited debate, there are two methods to limit debate. The simplest is for the Senate to agree by unanimous consent. If, however, even one senator objects, then unanimous consent does not work and cloture must be employed.

The first Senate rule providing for cloture was adopted in 1917 as a method of limiting filibusters. To invoke cloture a senator needed to gather the signatures of sixteen senators on a petition calling for cloture. The senator then filed the petition with the presiding officer, and on the second calendar day after the petition was presented, the Senate voted to end debate. Under the 1917 cloture rule, a vote of two-thirds of the senators present and voting was necessary to end debate.

In 1975 Senate rules were changed to deal with the rising use of the filibuster, which often seriously delayed Senate business. Given the increasing workload in the Senate, a compromise was needed to curtail the Senate tradition of unlimited debate. Cloture was made easier by reducing the majority vote needed from two-thirds to three-fifths of those senators present and voting. Invoking cloture does not mean that debate ceases immediately, but it does give the Senate the right to move forward with its business. In 1979 a further refinement of cloture put a time limit of one hundred hours on all debate on amendments to a bill to avoid new filibusters that originated after a cloture vote.

See also *Filibuster.*

RAYMOND W. SMOCK, INDEPENDENT HISTORIAN

BIBLIOGRAPHY

Binder, Sarah, and Steven S. Smith. *Politics or Principle? Filibustering in the United States Senate.* Washington, D.C.: Brookings Institution Press, 1997.

Burdette, Franklin L. *Filibustering in the Senate.* Princeton: Princeton University Press, 1940.

Byrd, Robert C. *The Senate, 1789–1989: Addresses on the History of the United States Senate.* Vol. 2, ch. 5. S. Doc. 100–120, 100th Cong., 1st Sess. Washington, D.C.: Government Printing Office, 1991.

COLD WAR

Cold war, a term apparently coined by journalist Walter Lippmann, is the name given to the global confrontation between the United States and the Soviet Union, and their respective allies, over the years 1947–1991. On an ideological level, the war was waged between communism and capitalist democracy. The struggle also had military, economic, cultural, and diplomatic dimensions.

If, as nineteenth-century Prussian army officer Carl von Clausewitz asserted, war is the continuation of politics by other means, the long duel between America and the Soviet Union is best seen as the continuation of war by other means. The cold war had many of the characteristics of the century's two world wars: it occupied almost as much of the national attention and the federal budget, and it ended with a victory as significant, as total, and (it would seem) at least as permanent as the Allied victory over Germany, Italy, and Japan in 1945. Yet the cold war also was remarkably different; it was fought as much for ideological as for geopolitical reasons, and, militarily, it was not waged directly between the "superpowers," which after 1945 towered over the rest of the world.

Because of its ideological quality, historians have found it difficult to describe the cold war. With the opening of the Soviet archives since 1989, the "revisionist" view of the cold war as a contest between two equally aggressive world empires has been largely discounted, with some scholars contending that Soviet leader Joseph Stalin, who ruled from the mid-1920s until his death in 1953, was clearly the instigator of the conflict. Others have asserted, however, that American leaders dominated the discourse of foreign policy during the cold war, routinely vilifying the communist countries, exaggerating threats abroad in order to preserve American dominance, and persistently glorifying Western values of free enterprise, limited government, and democracy.

ORIGINS OF THE COLD WAR

After the Russian Revolution of 1917, dread and detestation of Bolshevism were widespread in America. That perception was disrupted in 1941 when Germany—already at war with Britain and France—suddenly assaulted the Soviet Union and later declared war on the United States after the Japanese attack on Pearl Harbor. The Soviet Union and United States thus found themselves improbable allies. Officially, the United States was enthusiastic about its hard-pressed Soviet partner and optimistic about a new world order of peace once Germany and Japan were crushed.

The war aims of the Allies, however, were partially incompatible, and these differences became apparent at the Yalta conference in February 1945, when President Franklin D. Roosevelt met for the last time with Stalin and British prime minister Winston Churchill. The Soviets had made it clear that they would not agree to restore the prewar, fiercely anticommunist Polish government, and since the Red Army was in the process of conquering eastern Europe, Stalin's views prevailed. At Yalta, the "Big Three" papered over the Polish question with a deliberately ambiguous agreement. Stalin then imposed a communist puppet regime on the Poles, and as Poland went so went all the nations of eastern Europe, one by one. In the spring of 1946 Churchill would proclaim, in a speech at Fulton, Missouri, that an "iron curtain" had descended across Europe, separating the area of Soviet domination from that of Anglo-American domination.

THE TRUMAN DOCTRINE
AND ITS CONSEQUENCES

This new confrontation would not remain a strictly European matter, as had many others in the past. America would have a role in it. The U.S. impulse in 1945, as in 1919, was for rapid disengagement, and it took some time for the warm wartime sympathy for the Soviets to cool.

The first spasms of the new conflict—for example, a brief war in 1944 in Athens between Greek communists and the British—were resented in Washington. A turning point in American foreign policy came in February 1947, when Britain informed the U.S. State Department that, exhausted and bankrupt, it could no longer continue its showdown with the Soviets, particularly in Greece, where a resurgent

communist rebellion was on the verge of victory. In March President Harry S. Truman, summoning a joint session of Congress, declared that if Greece were lost, Turkey and the other eastern Mediterranean nations would fall like dominoes. Thus America had to abandon its isolationist tradition, reverse its military withdrawal from Europe, promise immediate aid to Greece and Turkey, and commit itself to supporting friendly regimes against communism whenever they were threatened. This so-called Truman Doctrine was followed by the Marshall Plan (named after Secretary of State George Marshall), which extended massive American aid to the shattered nations of Europe. The United States included the Soviet Union and the countries of eastern Europe in the offer because to do otherwise would invite blame for the division of Europe and the intensification of the cold war. Predictably, Stalin and his satellites rejected the plan, with the result that the division of Europe deepened, between a rapidly recovering western Europe, ideologically and economically oriented toward America, and a poor, isolated eastern Europe, dependent on and occupied by the Soviets. By this time, George Kennan, one of the State Department's experts on the Soviet Union, had already advanced his "containment theory," calling for the Soviet empire to be hemmed in everywhere at all costs because Soviet hostility would continue until the capitalist world had been completely destroyed. The North Atlantic Treaty Organization (NATO) was established in 1949 to promote the containment goal; the Soviet Union organized an alliance with its east European satellite states, known as the Warsaw Pact, in 1955 to defy it.

In June 1948 Stalin attempted to force the Allies out of Berlin. In 1945 Germany had been divided into zones of occupation by the victors in the war; the German capital was deep inside the Soviet zone but was itself divided among the four powers. When the Soviets tried to starve the Allies out by instituting a blockade of the city, Truman resorted to a massive airlift of supplies to save the American, British, and French zones in West Berlin; to relieve the city by ground convoy would risk armed conflict between the superpowers. The airlift was a tremendous success, and in the face of Western resolve, Stalin lifted the blockade. Stalin then established a puppet regime in his zone of Germany, which was countered by the liberal-capitalist regime supported by the Allies in West Germany. Elections about the same time in France and Italy saw the victory of anticommunists, and the ideological alignment of 1948 proved permanent.

THE GLOBAL CONFLICT

The division of Europe was now thorough, and the pattern was set for a potential third world war. But two developments derailed this apparent inevitability: a nuclear balance of terror, which froze the confrontation in Europe, and the globalization of the conflict, which opened the possibility for proxy wars or limited wars outside of Europe.

In July 1949 the Soviets exploded an atom bomb, and the nuclear monopoly that the United States had enjoyed since 1945 was over. In October that year, after decades of civil war, Chinese communist insurgents under Mao Zedong overthrew the Nationalist government, led by Chiang Kai-shek, and signed a friendship treaty with the Soviet Union. Chiang and the remnants of the Nationalists fled to Taiwan (then called Formosa), where they were effectively sheltered by the American navy.

Mounting concerns within the Truman administration led to the release in April 1950 of a report known as NSC-68, a dire warning by the National Security Council about communist expansion beyond Europe. The report was intended to gain congressional support for a major increase in U.S. defense spending and to alarm the general public so that it would support the escalation of the cold war.

Events only a few months later confirmed the report's warnings. In June 1950 the communist regime in North Korea (the Korean Peninsula, previously Japanese territory, had, like Germany, been divided) attacked the pro-Western government of the south. This invasion was launched with Soviet concurrence, although not on Stalin's initiative. Truman, perceiving the beginning of a general communist assault, led America and its allies—with the support of the United Nations—into a major war of containment, but UN forces changed their objectives and sought to go far beyond containment. By October 1950 the UN forces had broken the North Koreans and almost reached the Chinese frontier. At this point, Mao intervened, and 300,000 Chinese troops thrust the Americans and their allies back into South Korea. Military stalemate followed, and in 1953 President Dwight D. Eisenhower achieved an armistice, leaving the peninsula divided into two hostile nations. (In June 2000, however, a thawing of relations was evident, when the first-ever summit was held between North and South Korean leaders, Kim Jong Il and South Korean president Kim Dae-jung.)

Within America, the cold war had a profound effect on politics and society. Building on the "red scare" that had emerged at the end of World War I and the Smith Act of 1940, which contained the first peacetime antisedition measures since 1798, many political and social leaders began to perceive communists, conspiracies, and communist influences in many areas, from Hollywood, to the community of atomic scientists, to the State Department and universities, to labor organizations. The movement to identify and root out communist influences in the United States began shortly after World War II ended in 1945, and it gained momentum in 1949, after the Soviet Union exploded an atom bomb, aided

to some degree by its spy network. Republican senator Joseph McCarthy of Wisconsin took the crusade to a new level with his aggressive and highly controversial congressional probe into communist influence and espionage, which quickly degenerated into a witch hunt. Meanwhile, the American economy boomed on a permanent wartime footing.

In Europe, the East German government erected the Berlin Wall in late 1961 to close East Germans' escape route to the West. The wall became the most visible symbol of the protracted cold war. The struggle for power, influence, and advantage would move from Europe to the developing world.

THE CONTEST FOR THE DEVELOPING WORLD

After 1945 the colonial powers of Europe were too weak to hold onto their empires, which broke up into new nations. The superpowers were lavish in offering arms and other aid to these new states, in an effort to curry allies in the global ideological competition. The Chinese communist regime also participated in the competition for influence, particularly in Asia and especially after 1960, when Chinese relations with the Soviet Union soured.

The superpower competition was played out across dozens of nations, in nearly every region of the world, from the 1950s through the 1980s. The most significant of these clashes took place in Cuba and Indochina. In 1959 Cuba had fallen into the hands of a young revolutionary, Fidel Castro. After taking power, Castro aligned himself with communism and the Soviet Union. In April 1961 the newly installed administration of John F. Kennedy endorsed a plan devised by the Central Intelligence Agency during the Eisenhower administration to stage an invasion by Cuban exiles at Cuba's Bay of Pigs. The invasion failed. Khrushchev, in a gesture of support for his Caribbean ally and an effort to even the strategic nuclear balance, began to deploy Soviet nuclear weapons in Cuba. The missile sites were spotted by American spy planes while still under construction. Kennedy—rejecting proposals for a full-scale invasion of Cuba or even a preemptive nuclear attack on the Soviet Union—put in place in October 1962 a naval quarantine of the island to prevent the entry of Soviet ships.

The Cuban missile crisis was the climax of the cold war and the closest the world came to catastrophic nuclear war. Khrushchev, after a harrowing few days, agreed to remove the missiles from Cuba. The crisis itself was a sobering display of "brinkmanship." In the end, the crisis led to arms control, beginning with the Test Ban Treaty of 1963 and the Non-Proliferation Treaty of 1968, which tried to keep the bomb out of the hands of non-nuclear states. A new, settled caution grew between the two superpowers. Nuclear weapons, it seemed, were not actually weapons; they were a deterrent

A U.S. Navy reconnaissance photo of Cuba's Mariel Naval Port, taken November 2, 1962, confirms that Soviet nuclear weapons are being removed from Cuba in the aftermath of the Cuban missile crisis. *U.S. Navy*

munist Party and its nationalist supporters waged a guerrilla war to prevent the British from reestablishing control. The British, however, won the military battle, in large part because they won the struggle for popular support. By the time Malaya declared its independence in 1957, the communists had been marginalized, and they ceased the guerrilla war in 1960.

The guerrilla warfare in Indochina followed a very different pattern. Indochina was French until 1954, when France abandoned its attempt to crush the rebellion of Vietnamese nationalists and communists, led by Ho Chi Minh. In the agreement that extricated France from Vietnam, the country was "temporarily" divided, like Germany and Korea, with Ho Chi Minh ruling the north and a pro-Western nationalist, Ngo Dinh Diem, the south. Beginning in 1960, guerrilla warfare escalated dramatically throughout the south. The pro-Soviet forces in the south, the Viet Cong, were supported by the north. Diem, and then a military junta after 1963, were supported with increasing intensity by the United States. President Eisenhower had sent American advisers to support the South Vietnamese

against major war. "Mutual assured destruction" (MAD), or the certainty that neither side could escape massive retaliatory damage, guaranteed peace.

Following his consolidation of power in Cuba, Castro set about to foment revolution elsewhere. His willingness to send combat troops and advisers overseas in support of socialist regimes and guerrilla movements made him a valuable Soviet ally. Castro caused the United States great discomfit from 1959 through the mid-1980s in such places as Angola, Mozambique, Bolivia, El Salvador, Nicaragua, and Grenada. In the short run, Cuban influence contributed to a few communist successes—notably in Grenada and Nicaragua—where leftist governments came to power for a time. In the end, however, Cuba's efforts in support of communist expansion either came to naught or were subsequently reversed.

Communist-backed guerrilla warfare also failed in Malaya. The British colonial administration in Malaya was overrun by Japan during World War II. After the war, the Malayan Com-

army, and President Kennedy had continued that policy. President Lyndon B. Johnson escalated the war in response to strategic fears about losing this "domino," and with it Southeast Asia. By 1968 half a million American troops were fighting in South Vietnam against the Viet Cong and the North Vietnamese, but the American escalation was widely unpopular in the United States. Johnson was so embattled that he announced he would neither seek nor accept the 1968 Democratic nomination. The Democratic Party, split into factions over the war effort, lost the election. The incoming administration of Richard M. Nixon turned the war's military conduct over to a strengthened South Vietnamese army and expanded its scope into Laos and Cambodia. In January 1973 the administration concluded a peace treaty with North Vietnam that allowed final disengagement and the exchange of prisoners, but South Vietnam was not viable without U.S. forces, and in spring 1975 the whole of Indochina fell into the hands of pro-communist regimes.

The Soviet Union never considered sub-Saharan Africa to be a vital interest but was opportunistic in exploiting power vacuums. The sudden and ill-planned demise in the mid-1970s of the Portuguese empire in Africa—of which Angola and Mozambique were the largest components—was one example where a power vacuum led to Soviet influence. An earlier opportunity had arisen over Congo's sudden and chaotic separation from Belgium in 1960. Shortly after pulling its troops out of Congo, Belgium sent them back to protect Europeans living there, who were under widespread attack. The troops also effectively shielded Katanga province—site of lucrative copper and cobalt mining operations important to Belgian interests—which announced its secession from Congo. Congolese prime minister Patrice Lumumba, at odds with the pro-Western president of Congo, Joseph Kasavubu, appealed to Moscow for support. Lumumba was later assassinated, and pro-Western Mobutu Sese Seko established an authoritarian regime.

Overall, Soviet influence in sub-Saharan Africa was limited by a number of factors: many states retained ties to their colonial rulers; many African leaders skillfully played the Soviet Union against the West to maximize the aid they received; the Soviet Union was never able to provide as much economic aid as the West; Marxism-Leninism was not widely popular in a continent beset by ethnic, rather than class, cleavages; and the Soviet Union was not highly motivated to invest resources in the struggle for influence in the continent.

North Africa and the Middle East were another matter. Owing to the region's vast oil resources and the opportunities created by the Arab-Israeli conflict, the Soviet Union sought influence there. However, a number of factors limited its success.

In 1955 Egypt became the first Soviet client state in the region and the first Arab country to purchase Soviet-made arms. Arab armies, equipped by the Soviet Union, lost devastating wars to Israel in 1956 and 1967; Israel's territorial gains in 1967 redrew the map of the region and remain to this day a source of conflict. The Soviet Union's prestige among the Arabs plummeted when it provided little aid during the fighting in 1967 and backed a cease-fire while Israel occupied Arab territories. Despite reequipping the Egyptian, Syrian, and Jordanian militaries after the 1967 war, the Soviet Union refused to sell them some offensive weapons that they sought and also tried to restrain them from going to war with Israel to regain lost territory; détente with the West was more important to the Soviet Union than was influence in the Arab world. After the October 1973 Arab-Israeli war, the Soviet Union worked with the United States to end the conflict, further eroding its influence in Arab capitals. With no influence over Israel and waning influence over Egypt, Syria, and

Jordan, the Soviet Union was frozen out of subsequent developments in the peace process.

The Soviet Union then began to court other allies in the Middle East but ran into difficulties. Conservative absolute monarchs in the Persian Gulf region were suspicious of the communist Soviet Union. Improved relations with Ethiopia in 1977 cost the Soviet Union its good relations with Ethiopia's nemesis, Somalia. Iran, after its 1979 Islamic revolution, was as distrustful of the Soviet Union as of the United States. Cordial relations with Saddam Hussein's Iraq and Libya's Muammar al-Qadhafi never netted substantial benefits. And the Soviet invasion of Afghanistan in 1979 destroyed the last vestige of Soviet influence in the Islamic world.

ARMS CONTROL AND DÉTENTE

The defeat in Indochina in 1975 brought America's global prestige to its lowest level since 1941, and many observers concluded that the Soviets, now patrons of large blocs of the developing world and Eurasia, were winning or had won the cold war. In the 1970s, wars in Angola, Ethiopia, Somalia, Cambodia, and Vietnam were actually between Marxist factions; the West had no anticommunist forces to support.

By the late 1960s the Soviet Union and United States had nuclear arsenals so large that neither could use the weapons without inviting a devastating retort. The Soviet Union, however, enjoyed a superiority of conventional forces in Europe. According to some views, Europe was therefore indefensible, because the U.S. government might not risk provoking a Soviet nuclear strike on the continental United States by defending Europe against a conventional attack. (The British and French had their own, independent, nuclear strike capacity, but it was more for prestige than deterrence.)

The 1970s saw East and West Germany partly reconciled and President Nixon's sudden announcement of American rapprochement with China (both in 1971), and in August 1975, at Helsinki, the Soviet Union and other European combatants from World War II recognized the postwar division of the continent in return for insincere guarantees of "human rights" within the Soviet bloc.

The nuclear balance was threatened in the early 1970s not only by continuing Soviet strategic growth but also by technological innovations that were widely believed in the United States to be undermining the stability of nuclear deterrence. For one thing, the Soviet Union had deployed an antiballistic missile system around Moscow. Observers feared that if the ABM system were able to shoot down enough American nuclear missiles to reduce their destruction to "acceptable" levels, the U.S. deterrent would be undercut. The United States improved its offensive technology by developing the multiple interdependently targetable reentry vehicle

President Richard M. Nixon and Secretary General Leonid Brezhnev shake hands after signing the SALT I agreement at the 1972 summit in Moscow.   *National Archives*

(MIRV)—a device to accommodate multiple warheads that separate in flight, change trajectory, and fly to assigned and dispersed targets. The advantage of MIRVs was that the large numbers of warheads would overwhelm any missile defense system, allowing the United States to destroy Soviet society in a retaliatory blow. Under the second strategic arms limitation treaty, SALT II, which President Jimmy Carter and Soviet leader Leonid Brezhnev signed in neutral Vienna in June 1979, each side would have an equal number of strategic weapons: 2,400 missiles and bombers, of which 1,320 could have MIRVs. Proponents of the treaty pointed out that it provided for real reductions in strategic launchers, but critics responded that the ceilings set were still too high; they rendered the term *arms control* meaningless. Moreover, the treaty would give the Soviet Union strategic superiority because Soviet missiles were much larger and could carry bigger warheads.

ENDGAME

The year 1979 was one of the turning points of cold war history. In late 1979 the Soviet Union invaded Afghanistan, fearful that the Islamic fundamentalism then sweeping Iran and Pakistan might engulf Afghanistan and then spread to the 50 million Soviet Muslims on the Soviet Union's southern border. In response, President Carter stepped up military spending, took other measures to express U.S. displeasure, and

announced the Carter Doctrine: the United States would consider any threat to the oil-rich Persian Gulf a direct threat to its own vital interests. With these Soviet steps and U.S. responses, détente vanished. Moreover, Carter withdrew the SALT II treaty from Senate consideration, and in 1979 and 1981 two ardently right-wing leaders, British prime minister Margaret Thatcher and President Ronald Reagan, took office and assumed tough stances on the international stage. Cold war tensions rose again, and for the first time since 1950 its epicenter was in Europe. Strategic missile strength was in a sense meaningless after both sides had passed the point of mutual destruction. But intermediate-range nuclear forces (INFs, warheads delivered by accurate rockets with a range of up to about three thousand miles), which might be tactically decisive in a European war, took on immense military and psychological value. In the late 1970s the Soviet Union had begun deploying a sophisticated new generation of INFs, the SS-20, throughout the Warsaw Pact countries, thus gaining a potential advantage in any purely European conflict. In the 1980s the Reagan administration countered by deploying newly developed cruise missiles and a new generation of INFs, over widespread public opposition in Europe.

The Soviet Union began to buckle in the early 1980s, in part because of the intense economic pressures of the renewed arms race and in part because of the economic failure of communism. Brezhnev and his immediate successors sullenly presided over stagnation. By the time a vigorous leader, Mikhail Gorbachev, came to power in 1985, very thorough rethinking was necessary if the Soviet system were to survive. The economic, and later political, reforms that he instituted in the Soviet Union did not save the system; they undermined it. And they also undermined the legitimacy of unreformed regimes in the Soviet satellite states in eastern Europe. Gorbachev's "peace offensive"—rapid, bold, unilateral proposals and even acts of disarmament—further weakened the rationale behind his allies. Only military terror had given the Soviet bloc any coherence. In May 1988 the Soviet leader offered to withdraw all INFs from Europe if NATO would do the same. By the end of 1988, Gorbachev had unilaterally begun to reduce the Red Army's presence in Europe, and within a year even the Pentagon was sure the Soviet Union no longer had the power to invade the West. It also had lost its power and will to maintain its hegemony behind the iron curtain, and the shallow basis of Soviet influence in the region was suddenly apparent. In the fall of 1989, with the Soviet army withdrawing from eastern Europe, the client regimes that the Soviet Union had installed and propped up since 1944 simply dissolved, almost bloodlessly.

Throughout the world, the fading of Soviet power triggered the evaporation of communist ideology. Even the Chinese communists, after suppressing a wave of protest in June 1989 (the Tiananmen Square massacre), began a cautious experiment with capitalism while maintaining their monopoly on political power. Having freed his satellites from the communist system, Gorbachev was compelled to begin freeing Soviet citizens too. First the Baltic republics of the Soviet Union—Estonia, Latvia, and Lithuania—began agitating for independence, then others followed. On February 7, 1990, the Communist Party of the Soviet Union renounced its constitutional monopoly on power, and thus the cold war struggle between the superpowers lost its ideological point.

In July 1991 the United States and Soviet Union signed the START (Strategic Arms Reduction Talks) treaty, reversing rather than limiting the growth of the arms race. One month later, a final attempt to restore communism by putsch misfired, and the Soviet Union itself dissolved effective December 25, 1991, when Gorbachev resigned as president.

Capitalist and democratic Russia remained truculently outside the new and unchallenged American world hegemony, but its military strength and economy were feeble. NATO then began its expansion into former Warsaw Pact territory; the victory was rounded out in the developing world, where by century's end only North Korea and Cuba remained America's beleaguered cold war opponents.

See also *Korean War; McCarthyism; National Security Document 68; Red Scare; Truman, Harry S.; Vietnam War.*

BIBLIOGRAPHY

Gaddis, John Lewis. *We Now Know: Rethinking Cold War History.* Oxford: Clarendon, 1997.

Hook, Steven W., and John Spanier. *American Foreign Policy since World War II.* 15th ed. Washington, D.C.: CQ Press, 2000.

Inglis, Fred. *The Cruel Pace: Everyday Life in the Cold War.* New York: Basic Books, 1991.

McCullough, David. *Truman.* New York: Simon and Schuster, 1992.

McWilliams, Wayne C., and Harry Piotrowski. *The World Since 1945: A History of International Relations.* 4th ed. Boulder: Lynne Rienner, 1997.

COMMITTEE SYSTEM

Committees are where the bulk of Congress's legislative work is done—where most bills are written or refined, where compromises are worked out, where the public and interest groups express their views, and where House and Senate members build expertise and reputations. Committees also conduct investigations that highlight national problems or disclose wrongdoing, and they are responsible for overseeing government programs and agencies.

Members' influence in Congress, particularly in the House, often is closely related to the committees on which

they serve. Moreover, assignment to a powerful committee guarantees plentiful campaign contributions.

Committees vary greatly in how much power they have. Among the enduring centers of power are the House Ways and Means and Senate Finance Committees, which write tax bills, and the House and Senate Appropriations Committees, which have jurisdiction over federal spending. The House Rules Committee works with the majority leadership to control the flow of legislation to the floor and to set the ground rules for floor debate on most major bills.

The clout of other committees often depends on their leaders or on public interest. For example, in the 1960s Arkansas Democrat J. William Fulbright held Senate Foreign Relations Committee hearings that helped organize widespread opposition to Vietnam War policies. The Senate Energy and Natural Resources Committee was at the forefront in the 1970s, when energy policy was a major economic issue. Michigan Democrat John D. Dingell turned the House Energy and Commerce Committee into a major power center in the 1980s. In the 1990s representatives sought assignments on the House Transportation and Infrastructure Committee because of its jurisdiction over vast numbers of transportation projects.

COMMITTEE DEVELOPMENT

The congressional committee system had its roots in the British Parliament and the colonial legislatures. Its development, however, reflected changes and influences peculiar to American life.

In its earliest days, Congress had little need for the division of labor that today's committee system provides. Congress was small and its workload light. Legislative proposals were considered first on the Senate or House floor and then sent to a temporary committee appointed to work out the details. Once the committee submitted its report on the bill, it was dissolved. This arrangement allowed each chamber to maintain effective control over all legislation.

But as the nation grew and took on more complex responsibilities and problems, Congress had to develop expertise and mechanisms to deal with the changing world. From the somewhat haphazard arrangement of ad hoc committees evolved a highly specialized system of permanent committees that would in time wield substantial power.

The House led the way in the creation of standing (permanent) committees. Faced with an expanding membership and workload, the House began to delegate responsibility for initiating legislation to a handful of standing committees. Four committees had been established by 1795 and six more by 1810.

The Senate was slower in establishing standing committees, creating only four in its first twenty-five years of existence, and those were more administrative than legislative. But eventually the burden of appointing so many ad hoc legislative committees (nearly one hundred in the 1815–1817 session) exhausted the patience of the Senate, and in 1816 it added eleven more standing committees. Most of the new committees were parallel in function to previously created committees of the House.

The standing committee system became firmly established in the first half of the nineteenth century. As the permanent committees replaced temporary panels, legislation came to be referred directly to the committees. This practice gave the committees initial authority over legislation within their specialized jurisdictions, subject to subsequent review by the full chamber.

Among the most powerful committees to emerge in the nineteenth century were those that dealt with revenue and spending. The House Ways and Means Committee, first established as an ad hoc committee in 1789 and made permanent in 1802, had been ensured a position of influence by the Constitution's requirement that all revenue measures originate in the House. The Ways and Means Committee and the Senate Finance Committee, created in 1816, handled all aspects of federal finances until the mid-1860s, when the Appropriations panels were set up to oversee spending. The clout of these four panels continues today.

By the end of the nineteenth century, the committee system had gained such great power that Congress was said to have abdicated its lawmaking function to its committees. Although created by and responsible to their parent bodies, committees by this time functioned with almost total independence. The panels tended to be dominated by their chairs, who were majority party members with the longest continuous service on their committees. The chairs often did not share the prevailing views of Congress as a whole or even of their own party. Yet their powers were so great that Woodrow Wilson in 1885 described the system as "a government by the chairmen of the standing committees of Congress."

The number of committees reached a peak in 1913, when there were sixty-one in the House and seventy-four in the Senate. Those numbers dropped in the next decade, as some long-defunct bodies—such as the Senate Committee on Revolutionary Claims—were abolished and other panels with similar responsibilities were merged.

By 1922 a committee system had emerged that resembled in most important respects the one in existence today, according to political scientists Christopher J. Deering and Steven S. Smith. Characteristics they cite include an internal structure with subcommittees, set committee jurisdictions, legislative authority, procedures for appointing members, established leadership positions and methods of recruitment,

and the logistical support and resources needed to do their jobs.

A major overhaul of the committee structure took place in 1946, when the number of House committees was reduced from forty-eight to nineteen and Senate committees from thirty-three to fifteen. The Legislative Reorganization Act of 1946 also defined in detail the jurisdictions of committees and attempted to set ground rules for their operations.

These efforts in the twentieth century to consolidate the burgeoning committee system served to strengthen the streamlined committees and their leaders. Congress did not take major steps to curb committee powers until the 1970s, when junior House members demanded and won fundamental changes in the way Congress, particularly the committees, operated. The changes diluted the authority of committee chairs and other senior members and redistributed power among their younger and less experienced colleagues. Many of these junior members became chairs of newly created subcommittees.

The most significant of the 1970s reforms was a decision by the House and Senate Democrats to allow their party members, then a majority in each chamber, to elect committee chairs. Although most chairs continued to be chosen on the basis of seniority, the election requirement made them accountable to their colleagues for their conduct. Several House chairs ultimately were deposed.

When the number of subcommittees skyrocketed in the wake of the 1970s reforms, critics charged that they were fragmenting responsibility, increasing members' workloads, and slowing the legislative process. Both chambers subsequently took action that limited the number of subcommittees, among other changes.

TYPES OF COMMITTEES

Standing committees are at the center of the legislative process. Legislation usually must be considered and approved in some form at the committee level before it can be sent, or "reported," to the House or Senate floor for further action. Standing committees are permanent bodies with responsibility for broad areas of legislation, such as agriculture or transportation.

Most standing committees have *subcommittees* that provide the ultimate division of labor within the committee system. They help Congress handle its huge workload, and they permit members to develop specialized knowledge in a particular field. Subcommittees are especially important in the House, where they usually are responsible for conducting hearings and for considering the provisions of a bill in detail and making revisions—"marking up" a bill—before sending it on to the full committee. In the Senate, subcommittees may hold hearings, but the full committee generally does the writing of legislation.

Both chambers from time to time create *select committees* and *special committees* to study particular problems, such as aging or hunger, or to conduct investigations, such as the Senate panel that investigated the Watergate scandal in 1973 and 1974 and the House and Senate panels that jointly investigated the Iran-contra affair in 1987. Select and special committees may make recommendations, but they usually are not permitted to report legislation. In most cases they remain in existence for a short time. Exceptions are the Select Intelligence Committees in both chambers, which are permanent panels that consider and report legislation.

Joint committees are usually permanent panels composed of both House and Senate members. None of the four joint panels in existence in 2000 had authority to report legislation. Instead, they conducted studies, performed staff work, or dealt with administrative matters.

Conference committees, a special kind of joint committee, are temporary bodies with important powers. Their job is to settle differences between bills that have passed the House and Senate. They go out of business when the job is done.

At the beginning of the 106th Congress (1999–2001) the House had nineteen standing committees and one permanent select committee; the Senate had seventeen standing committees, two permanent select committees, and two special committees. There were also the four joint committees.

See also *Congress; Taxation and Twentieth-Century Politics.*

PATRICIA ANN O'CONNOR, INDEPENDENT AUTHOR

BIBLIOGRAPHY

"The Committee System." In *Congressional Quarterly's Guide to Congress.* 5th ed. Washington, D.C.: CQ Press, 1999.

Deering, Christopher J., and Steven S. Smith. *Committees in Congress.* 3d ed. Washington, D.C.: CQ Press, 1997.

Fenno, Richard F., Jr. *Congressmen in Committees.* Boston: Little, Brown, 1973.

Goodwin, George, Jr. *The Little Legislatures: Committees of Congress.* Amherst: University of Massachusetts Press, 1970.

Unekis, Joseph K., and Leroy N. Rieselbach. *Congressional Committee Politics: Continuity and Change.* New York: Praeger, 1984.

COMMUNIST PARTY USA

The Communist Party arose in the United States in 1919 as part of the social and economic turmoil that followed World War I and the Bolshevik Revolution in Russia. Two organizations emerged from the left wing of the American Socialist Party: the larger Communist Party of America and the Communist Labor Party. The U.S. government aggressively prosecuted the parties during the period around 1920, causing a drop in their already small membership and forcing the organizations to go underground.

Further attempts to organize party groups led in the mid-1920s to the founding of the Communist Party of the USA (CPUSA) to implant the revolutionary aims of the Soviet Union in America. The CPUSA received Soviet money and utilized the Bolshevik tactics of division and subversion as it attempted to spread its influence among what it considered the country's discontented minorities, including African Americans, workers, intellectuals, and new immigrants. Its efforts largely failed.

Even during the Great Depression of the 1930s, when U.S. unemployment was at record levels, membership never amounted to more than thirty thousand. Perhaps 10 percent were African Americans; most were European immigrants living in large cities.

In 1935 Soviet dictator Joseph Stalin, acting through the Seventh World Congress of the Comintern (a worldwide association of communist parties) created the so-called Popular Front movement to build coalitions in response to the growing fascist political movement in Europe and in hope of winning U.S. support to resist fascism's advances. After this abrupt change in the party line, American communists ended their opposition to any person and any program that was not pro-communist, including the New Deal. Communists began to cooperate with liberal antifascist groups and individuals, leading to a blurring of distinctions in the left wing of the American political movement that was, when the Soviet Union became a U.S. adversary after World War II, to haunt many individuals who were charged with subversion and spying for the Soviets.

Americans' fear of communism increased after World War II. Fanned by conservative politicians and government officials in Washington and elsewhere, it led to federal prosecution of the party's leaders and inflated the CPUSA into a perceived deadly threat to American society. This widely held view was instrumental in the government's aggressive use of the Smith Act, passed in 1940 to outlaw membership in the Communist Party and the advocacy of the violent overthrow of the established government. Under this law, the U.S. government in 1948 prosecuted and obtained convictions of eleven leaders of the national board of the Communist Party. In 1951 the Supreme Court, in *Dennis v. United States,* upheld the convictions and the law. The decision emboldened the government to prosecute other individuals and was important in upholding other loyalty programs in the 1950s.

The upshot of this period was that many left-wing intellectuals who had flirted idealistically with communist doctrine in the Great Depression years of the 1930s encountered black-listings and jail sentences in the late 1940s and early

Members of the Washington Communist Society plan a demonstration to take place in front of the White House, circa 1930. *Library of Congress*

1950s because of the anticommunism that then permeated American politics.

The CPUSA did participate in electoral politics. In 1932 the CPUSA's presidential candidate, William Z. Foster, took fourth place in the general election with 102,000 votes. It was the party's electoral high point. By 1984 the party's presidential slate won only 36,000 votes and came in eighth overall. It disappeared entirely from presidential ballots after that year.

See also *McCarthyism; Political Parties; Progressive Labor Party; Red Scare; Third Parties.*

RON dePAOLO, INDEPENDENT AUTHOR

COMPROMISE OF 1850

The Compromise of 1850 was a raft of measures passed by Congress in the session of 1850 aimed at settling the bitter sectional controversy touched off by the conquests of the Mexican-American War. It was the last peaceful compromise between North and South and lasted only four years.

ORIGINS OF THE COMPROMISE

The Missouri Compromise of 1820 had partitioned the Louisiana Purchase into a zone from which free states would eventually enter the Union and a zone from which slave states would be formed. This worked well enough until 1845, when America began expanding again, into Mexican lands, annexing the rebellious province of Texas (February 28, 1845) and then, after the Mexican-American War (1846–1848), vast territory stretching to the Pacific Ocean. Texas had entered the Union in December 1845 as a slave state, and the debate arose over whether the other new lands would evolve to be free or slave.

The annexation of Texas had been a rushed affair of doubtful constitutionality and was bitterly opposed by many northerners. The Mexican-American War was an essentially partisan and sectional war: a war promoted by the South and West, Democrats and expansionists. It tore the United States apart. Three months into the war, shortly before the mid-term election of 1846, an undistinguished northern Democrat, Rep. David Wilmot of Pennsylvania, proposed the principle that no territories of Mexico (which had itself abolished slavery) should be opened to slavery by American conquest. This was the Wilmot Proviso, and although it did not pass the Senate, it threw American politics into angry turmoil for four years.

President James Polk was in favor of extending the Missouri Compromise line to the ocean: southern California and New Mexico (including Arizona) would hence be open to settlement by slaveholders. But neither faction was in the mood for such compromise. Northerners insisted that Congress had a duty to prohibit slavery wherever it could. Sen. John C. Calhoun of South Carolina in response advanced a new doctrine—that Congress had no right to interfere with property allowed by one state in territory held in partnership by all; the Missouri Compromise itself, therefore, was unconstitutional and void.

The result was deadlock. No administrative provision was made for the newly acquired territory. In the presidential election of 1848 the Democrats split over the Wilmot Proviso, and Zachary Taylor, a slaveholding Whig, was elected, as was a greatly factional Congress. By the time Taylor took office in March 1849, legislation on the status of the West had been preempted by westerners themselves. A gold rush had suddenly populated California with almost 100,000 free white individuals. California was thus lost to the South and was clamoring to enter the Union as a free state. Taylor recommended to the new, rancorous Congress that California be admitted—briskly, as Texas had been. The crisis reached its apogee: South Carolina was trying to lead the South into secession; Calhoun, dying, was defiant; Sen. William H. Seward, a New York Whig, was equally defiant for the North. Taylor threatened to crush any secession by arms. It seemed war was inevitable.

On January 27, 1850, Sen. Henry Clay of Kentucky, magnificent and compelling, proposed a settlement of five points. (1) California would indeed be admitted. (2) The other newly acquired territory from the Mexican-American War would be organized without mention of the slave question, which would eventually be decided (almost certainly in favor of freedom, given the geography) by the inhabitants; thus, the Wilmot Proviso would be granted, but implicitly. (3) Congress would assume the debts of the Republic of Texas but would trim its territory. (The vast western lands claimed by Texas were renounced and were later to form part of New Mexico, Utah, and Colorado.) (4) The slave trade in the District of Columbia, long detested by the North, would be abolished. (5) The flight of slaves over the Mason-Dixon line, long resented by the South, would be stanched with a stern Fugitive Slave Law, making any citizen subject to being conscripted into a posse.

Clay's package was denounced from both sides, by Seward and Calhoun, and even from above, because Taylor, a Jacksonian nationalist, was constitutionally dismayed: If California wished to enter the Union, why need the South be bribed to agree? The measures failed to pass as a single, coherent package, as the Compromise of 1820 had passed. Clay, sick and old, departed from the national political scene. Calhoun was unmoved in his rejection of such terms: Better disunity than inequality for the South within the Union. Daniel Webster of Massachusetts threw behind the compromise the weight of his massive authority and oratory (his "Seventh of May" speech became a classic), but the North remained revolted at what it was expected to accept.

In the end, all of Clay's provisions went through, propelled by the brilliant and unscrupulous parliamentary management of the young Illinois Democrat, Stephen Douglas, and by

Henry Clay presents his compromise in the Senate. Millard Fillmore is presiding, and John C. Calhoun is to Fillmore's right. Daniel Webster sits, with his head in his hand. *Library of Congress*

happenstance, when Calhoun died in March 1850 and Taylor in July. Millard Fillmore, Seward's bland rival within New York Whiggery, was the new president, and he would accept what Seward would not. Webster, abandoning the Senate, became Fillmore's secretary of state, to harry the Whigs into line behind the compromise with the power and patronage of federal government. The "Little Magician," Douglas, engineered shaky and shifting majorities for each of the compromise's measures. In September Fillmore signed them all.

RESULTS

With the compromise passed, the struggle then went to the people—and seemed at first entirely vindicated. In the midterm elections of 1850, Whigs and conservative Democrats who supported the compromise won in the North; in the South, where a single issue had for the moment replaced party labels, Union men defeated immediate secessionists (except in South Carolina), and, after an ominous pause, it became clear that the South would not break away—yet.

The effort of passing this last sectional compromise was immense; however, the settlement was flimsy and its results ironic. It was a Whig compromise, and it doomed the Whig Party. From 1852 the South, aggrieved over what it had been forced to accept, turned overwhelmingly to the Democratic Party, which thus became predominantly the party of southern truculence. Meanwhile the northern Whigs, no longer held together by Webster (who died, like Clay, in 1852), began to break into "conscience," or antislavery, and "cotton," or compromising, factions. They won no more national elections.

In the South the legacy of 1850 was Calhounite bitterness and an obsession with the (often impractical) claims of slavery in all the territories. Thus, in 1854, when Douglas proposed the organization of the Great Plains in his Kansas–Nebraska bill, the South turned intransigent and the spirit of give-and-take of 1850 died.

In the North the most important, counterproductive, and ominous aspect of the compromise was the Fugitive Slave Law. This legislation compelled all public officials to aid in hunting escaped slaves; threatened draconian fines and imprisonment for those who aided the runaways or impeded the hunters; and prescribed such low standards of proof of ownership that even legally free northern blacks were at risk. Only the tremendous authority of Webster had made the North accept such an extension of the "peculiar institution" into the free states, and each exercise of the law enraged even moderate northern opinion. An "underground railroad" was established to smuggle slaves escaping from the South toward Canada and safety; the fugitive legislation therefore worked only fitfully.

Citizens of the North considered the passage of the Kansas–Nebraska Act of 1854, which repealed the Compromise of 1820 and opened the Great Plains to settlement by slaves, to be a betrayal of the 1850 settlement. The day after the act passed, a captured runaway named Anthony Burns could be led to the wharf at Boston and back to servitude only by two dozen militia companies, so furious were the citizens. He was the last fugitive returned from Massachusetts, which then explicitly nullified the Fugitive Slave Law—at this point moot, anyway, throughout the North.

The Compromise of 1850, in return for implicitly keeping slavery out of the Southwest, overtly injected one of its most obnoxious features into the Northeast; the Fugitive Slave Law of 1850 had radicalized the free states on the slavery issue, from which followed the sectional victory of the Republicans in 1860, and then the Civil War.

See also *Calhoun, John C.; Civil War; Free Soil Party; Fugitive Slave Laws; Kansas-Nebraska Act; Mexican-American War; Missouri Compromise; Popular Sovereignty; Secession; Sectionalism; Territorial Expansion; Whig Party.*

RICHARD MAJOR, INDEPENDENT SCHOLAR

BIBLIOGRAPHY

Hamilton, Holman. *Prologue to Conflict: The Crisis and Compromise of 1850.* Lexington: University of Kentucky Press, 1964.

Holt, Michael F. *The Political Crisis of the 1850s.* New York: Wiley, 1978.

Rozwenc, Edwin Charles. *The Compromise of 1850.* Boston: Heath, 1957.

Stegmaier, Mark J. *Texas, New Mexico, and the Compromise of 1850: Boundary Debates and the Sectional Crisis.* Kent, Ohio: Kent State University Press, 1996.

COMPROMISE OF 1877

The presidential election of 1876 was one of the most complicated and corrupted in American history. The Republicans had gained the White House with the election of Abraham Lincoln in 1860. The assassination of Lincoln in 1865 put Andrew Johnson, a southerner and former slaveowner, in the presidency. Johnson's deep opposition to black equality, together with his stubborn refusal to recognize the revolution in both race relations and state-federal relations brought about by the Civil War, put him at odds with the Republican Party that had made him Lincoln's running mate in 1864. The huge Republican majority in Congress overrode many of his vetoes involving civil rights and protections for former slaves.

When Johnson left office, the Republicans turned to the war hero, Ulysses S. Grant, who won huge victories in 1868 and 1872. Grant's presidency was marred by corruption within his cabinet and violence perpetrated by white southern terrorists against blacks and white unionists.

In 1876 the Republicans nominated Rutherford B. Hayes, a major general in the Civil War, member of Congress, and three-term governor of Ohio. Neither Hayes's stellar career nor Grant's personal honesty and heroic stature could fully overcome the taint of corruption that permeated the entire party during the campaign. The Democrats, capitalizing on Republican corruption, nominated Gov. Samuel J. Tilden of New York, a reformer who had gained national attention by attacking corruption in both parties in the Empire State.

CONTESTED VOTE COUNTS

The election was relatively honest in the North, although vote fraud by both parties was common in large cities like New York and Chicago. In the South, by contrast, armed whites terrorized blacks, tampered with ballot boxes, and did whatever they could to prevent former slaves from voting because they would have voted Republican. Nationwide, Tilden had a clear majority of the popular vote—based on actual ballots cast—although had blacks been able to vote in much of the South the result would have been less certain.

Despite his popular majority, Tilden missed an electoral majority by a single vote. Both sides claimed to have received a majority of the popular vote in three states—South Carolina, Florida, and Louisiana. It is likely, although not certain, that the white intimidation prevented so many blacks from voting for Hayes in those three states that Tilden did in fact obtain a popular majority of the ballots cast in at least one of them. However, if there had been no intimidation, violence, and fraud to prevent blacks from voting, most historians agree, Hayes would have carried all three states. Meanwhile, in Louisiana and South Carolina both Republicans and Democrats claimed victory in state elections, and both prepared to claim their state's governorship.

The counting of the electoral votes produced a sharp conflict. Both the Democratic and the Republican electors sent in ballots from the disputed states. Meanwhile, a new conflict emerged in Oregon. Hayes had clearly carried Oregon, but when a Republican elector died before the electoral votes were counted, the Democratic governor of Oregon appointed a Democrat to replace him, in an attempt to steal the election for Tilden. The governor's action led to yet one more disputed electoral vote. Eventually this issue was settled in favor of the Republicans, who had clearly won the state.

In the South, partisans on both sides threatened to enforce their rights with violence, and in a nation filled with Civil War veterans, such threats had to be taken seriously. Leaders of the nation's business communities, as well as Hayes, Tilden, and President Grant, all sought compromise, but neither Tilden nor Hayes was ready to concede the election.

RESOLVING THE DILEMMA

On January 29, 1877, Congress created an Electoral Commission, consisting of seven Democrats and seven Republicans. The act creating the commission named four Supreme Court justices to choose a single justice to be the "independent" tie breaker on the commission. Everyone assumed that the Court would choose Justice David Davis. Davis had been a close friend of Lincoln, who appointed him to the Court, but he had been hostile to emancipation and had shown little support for black rights. He often voted with the Democrats on the Court, had been critical of the Republicans during Reconstruction, and had been openly hostile to Grant's renomination in 1872. But he had also been critical of Democrats. Through this "independent" commissioner, believed to favor Tilden, the Democrats in the House of Representatives expected to gain the presidency.

However, Davis never liked his work on the Court, wanted to be president, and in 1877, before the commission could meet, resigned from the Court when the Illinois legislature elected him to the U.S. Senate. The justices then chose Justice Joseph P. Bradley, who sided with the Republicans on the commission. On March 2, 1877, by a vote of 8–7, the commission certified the Republican electors in all of the disputed elections, and two days later Hayes was sworn in as president.

The result was more of a compromise than an exercise of political muscle. Before taking office, Hayes agreed to recog-

nize the Democrats as the victors in the disputed state elections in Louisiana and South Carolina, and he also promised to remove the last of the U.S. troops from the South. Moreover, Hayes appointed Democrats and Republican reformers to his cabinet. The result was a peaceful, although hardly smooth, transition from one presidency to the next.

The biggest losers in this compromise were not the disappointed candidates but the Deep South's African Americans, who could no longer count on the national government to protect their liberty or their right to vote, serve on juries, hold elective office, or have access to public services. Shortly after Hayes became president, the South began to expand racial segregation and disfranchisement on a massive scale. Some southern blacks would hold office as late as the end of the century, but the Compromise of 1877 signaled not merely the end of Reconstruction, but the end of any chance the nation had to create a measure of racial fairness and equality in the nineteenth-century South.

See also *Hayes, Rutherford B.; Presidential Elections; Reconstruction.*

PAUL FINKELMAN, UNIVERSITY OF TULSA COLLEGE OF LAW

BIBLIOGRAPHY

Hoogenboom, Ari. *The Presidency of Rutherford B. Hayes.* Lawrence: University Press of Kansas, 1988.

Polakoff, Keith Ian. *The Politics of Inertia: The Election of 1876 and the End of Reconstruction.* Baton Rouge: Louisiana State University Press, 1973.

Woodward, C. Vann. *Reunion and Reaction: The Compromise of 1877 and the End of Reconstruction.* Boston: Little, Brown, 1951.

COMSTOCK ACT

The Comstock Act of 1873 banned obscene materials from the U.S. postal system. Specifically included on the list of banned goods was every article, instrument, substance, drug, medicine, or thing adapted, designed, or intended "for preventing conception or producing abortion, or for indecent immoral use." Although state statutes prohibiting various forms of abortion had been on the books since the 1820s, few explicit restrictions on contraception existed before the 1870s.

In 1872 New Yorkers created the first purity society, the New York Society for the Suppression of Vice. Firebrand for the society's cause was a dry goods salesperson named Anthony Comstock, who went to Washington in 1872 to lobby on behalf of a rigorous national antivice statute. Comstock successfully enlisted the aid of Vice President Henry Wilson and a justice of the Supreme Court, William Strong, in drafting a new obscenity law, which passed with little debate on March 1, 1873.

Quickly dubbed the Comstock Law, the act made it a crime to send through the public mails any "obscene, lewd, or lascivious" book or printed material "designed to incite lust." Harsh penalties accompanied the act: a $5,000 fine, one-to-ten years at hard labor, or both. In addition, at the vice president's urging, Comstock was appointed a special postal agent charged with enforcing the law. Comstock was responsible for the arrest of more than three thousand persons and the destruction of 160 tons of allegedly objectionable books and pictures.

The number of antivice societies continued to grow. By 1885 the Social Purity Alliance had convinced twenty-two state legislatures to enact general antiobscenity laws, and other states to ban birth control and abortion. Birth control proponents and sexual reformers, however, continued to confront issues emerging from the new sexual relationships in the changing U.S. society.

See also *Reproductive Rights.*

MARK J. CONNOLLY, DEVRY INSTITUTE OF TECHNOLOGY

BIBLIOGRAPHY

Beisel, Nicola. *Imperiled Innocents: Anthony Comstock and Family Reproduction in Victorian America.* Princeton: Princeton University Press, 1997.

Rabban, David M. *Free Speech in Its Forgotten Years, 1870–1920.* New York: Cambridge University Press, 1997.

CONGRESS

The Congress of the United States, the lawmaking branch of the federal government, derived its historical roots from the British parliamentary system that had evolved over the previous five centuries. Its more immediate origins stemmed from the central debate of the American revolutionary era: how to guarantee a political system in which the people would remain the highest sovereign power. Beginning with the American colonial challenges to parliamentary power in the 1760s, and continuing in the debates that led to the creation of state governments following the declaration of independence from Great Britain, the leaders of the new nation became convinced that a representative assembly that was responsible to its constituents was the best way to preserve political liberty.

When delegates from the original thirteen states met in Philadelphia in 1787 to revise the nation's first constitution, the Articles of Confederation, they spent considerable time debating the nature of the legislative branch of government. Article I of the Constitution of the United States grants all legislative powers to a Congress, "which shall consist of a Senate and House of Representatives." One of the most important decisions in the convention of 1787 was made on July 16, when the delegates agreed on the creation of a two-house legislature. This became known as the "Connecticut Compromise" or the "Great Compromise." It provided for a Senate consisting of two senators from each state, regardless of population, and a House of Representatives whose members would be apportioned among the states based on population.

Congress met for the first time on March 4, 1789, in New York City in an unfinished building called Federal Hall, at the corner of Broad and Wall Streets. However, neither the House nor the Senate conducted any business until quorums were achieved in the House on April 1 and in the Senate on April 6, 1789. The first order of business was to count the electoral ballots and declare George Washington and John Adams to be elected president and vice president of the United States.

In 1790, after two sessions in New York, Congress moved to Philadelphia. It remained there for ten years, meeting in Congress Hall, a brick building adjacent to Independence Hall, where the Constitutional Convention had met. In 1800 the entire federal government moved to Washington, D.C.

CONGRESSIONAL STRUCTURE

To understand how Congress works it is important to know its rules of procedure. Both the House and Senate established parliamentary rules in the early days of the First Congress. As Sen. Robert C. Byrd has said about the importance of rules, "the only difference between a lynching and a fair trial is procedure."

Members of Congress may disagree sharply on issues, but all must play by the same rules. House and Senate rules have been modified many times since 1789, sometimes in dramatic fashion that substantially reformed institutional practice and procedure. The House of Representatives must approve and adopt a rules package at the beginning of each new Congress every two years. The Senate, which elects only one-third of its members every two years, is not required to approve its rules at the beginning of each Congress.

During the first 124 years of Congress the House of Representatives was the only house of Congress elected directly by the voters in their respective states and districts. Members of the Senate were elected by the state legislatures. Direct election of senators by the people of their state did not occur until after the ratification of the Seventeenth Amendment in 1913. The original practice of indirect election of senators had been a concession to some of the delegates at the Constitutional Convention who feared too much democracy would lead to mob rule. By 1913 the argument that carried the day was that direct election of senators would be reform in favor of more democracy.

DIFFERENCES BETWEEN THE HOUSE AND SENATE

The House and Senate are two separate bodies with similar, but distinct, legislative roles. Both bodies must concur before legislation can be sent to the president for approval. The House has the constitutional authority to initiate all revenue bills, which can then be modified in the Senate. The Senate has the power to ratify treaties and to approve the president's nominees for high office, such as ambassadors, consuls, and members of the Supreme Court. The House can initiate an impeachment proceeding against the president or a high government official, but the impeachment trial is conducted by the Senate.

The difference in size between the House and Senate has grown over the years. As the nation grew, so did Congress. The House had 65 representatives in the First Congress and the Senate had 26 members. By 1883 the House had grown to 332 members and the Senate to 76. In 1911 Congress passed a law that froze the size of the House at 433 members, with a stipulation that when Arizona and New Mexico attained statehood the final size would be 435. This has remained the maximum limit of the House since then, with the exception of a brief period when it jumped to 437 when Hawaii and Alaska were admitted as states; it returned to 435 after the 1960 census. The seats are divided among the states based on current population, with each state having at least one representative. The Senate, with two senators per state, has grown to 100 members.

Size differences between the House and Senate have accounted for differences in their rules. In the House the time allowed for debate by individual members is strictly limited. The Senate allows for unlimited debate. While both the House and Senate work their will by majority vote, raw numbers needed for a majority vote are more important in the daily operation of the House. The Senate conducts much of its business by unanimous consent of the members. One senator could hold up or block Senate action by objecting to the proceedings, whereas in the House one member does not wield that kind of power.

With a limit of 435 seats in the House, the workload of each member has increased as the number of constituents of each House member has increased. In 1790 each member of the First Congress represented approximately 30,000 people. Following the 1910 census, each member represented ap-

When the House and Senate versions of a bill differ significantly, each house appoints conferees, who meet in a conference committee to try to reach consensus. *Congressional Quarterly*

proximately 210,000 people. Following the 1990 census each House member represented about 570,000 people; the 2000 census estimates place approximately 632,000 people in each congressional district. However, states with smaller populations, such as Wyoming and Vermont, may have districts with fewer people in them.

LEADERSHIP

The Constitution provides a different leadership structure for the House and Senate. The chief parliamentary leader of the House is the Speaker, derived from the Speaker of the British House of Commons. In the Senate the vice president of the United States is the presiding officer and when serving in this capacity is called the president of the Senate. Leadership in the House and Senate has evolved over time. The speakership, at first considered primarily a neutral parliamentary position, soon developed into an office of political leadership and power. The Speaker has become the chief administrative officer in managing the House and a key player in selecting the committees of Congress. Henry Clay, beginning in 1811, was the first Speaker to substantially extend the political power of the office. He was not only a parliamentarian but a leader of his party who often engaged in floor debates and used his office to further his own party's political goals. Since the Constitution is silent on the actual duties of a Speaker, the office has evolved through rules and through the personalities of individual Speakers. In 1911 the House dramatically changed its rules to limit the control Speakers had over selection of House committees and committee chairmen in reaction to the concentration of power in the hands of late nineteenth- and early twentieth-century Speakers, especially Thomas B. Reed and Joseph G. Cannon, who ran the House in an autocratic manner.

Senate leadership followed a different path. Although the vice president of the United States is still the constitutional presiding officer of the Senate, the vice president seldom performs this function except to cast a tie-breaking vote. The Constitution provides for the office of president pro tempore (president for the day), a title usually given to the senior senator of the majority party, who presides over the sessions of the Senate. In the twentieth century the Senate formalized the office of majority leader, who became the chief administrative officer of the Senate and had control of the legislative agenda of the Senate. This office is not mentioned in the Constitution, but it has evolved as an important office through the rules and traditions of the Senate.

CONSTITUTIONAL POWERS

The powers of Congress derive from its lawmaking function and the enumerated powers listed in Article I, section 8, of the Constitution, which gives Congress the power to tax citizens for the purpose of "common defence and general Welfare." Congress can borrow money on the credit of the United States, regulate commerce, coin money, establish post offices, promote the arts and sciences, determine maritime laws, raise armies and navies, declare war, have jurisdiction over the District of Columbia, and "make all laws which shall be necessary and proper for the carrying into Execution of the foregoing Powers, and all other Powers vested by this Constitution in the Government of the United States." This statement is commonly referred to as the "Necessary and Proper" or the "Elastic" Clause. It gives Congress broad authority not specifically mentioned in the Constitution.

The Constitution provides a system of checks and balances, or shared powers, between the executive, judicial, and legislative branches of government. The tensions between these shared powers have often led to dramatic clashes, especially between Congress and the executive branch. The power to declare war illustrates these clashes. When the Constitution was drafted, wars moved only as fast as horses, troops, and equipment. Congress had time to meet and deliberate before war was declared. Modern war has changed the tensions between Congress and the executive. With the advent of nuclear weapons and intercontinental ballistic missiles, when wars could be launched in minutes and be over in days, how much power does the president have to act without the approval of Congress? This fundamental question remains unresolved, although the War Powers Act, passed in 1973 in the aftermath of President Richard M. Nixon's order to bomb Cambodia during the Vietnam War, sets guidelines that spell out a timetable for the president and Congress regarding decisions about the use of military power.

GROWTH OF CONGRESSIONAL STAFF

The size of the congressional staff has increased dramatically in the twentieth century, especially since World War II. This increase is due, in part, to congressional desire to maintain oversight of the executive branch and not lose the power to set the national agenda, and in part to congressional desire to accommodate the needs of members of Congress and its committees. Although Congress has always had the power of the purse, the executive branch has gained dominance in determining the details of the annual budget. In the nineteenth century Congress functioned with little staff beyond a handful of doorkeepers and clerks. Members of the House and Senate did not have separate offices, unless they were elected leaders or chairmen of important committees.

The first office buildings for members of the House and Senate were occupied in 1908 (House) and 1909 (Senate). At first called simply the House Office Building and the Senate

Office Building, they were later renamed in honor of prominent members of the House and Senate. New office buildings were added to the House and Senate sides of the Capitol in 1933 and 1965 (House) and 1958 and 1982 (Senate).

Just as the Capitol itself has grown in size along with the country, so has the size and complexity of Congress. In 1891 there were 103 committee staff members in the House and Senate combined and probably less than 100 personal staff members in both bodies, although the personal staff figures for the House are not available. By 1957 personal and committee staffs in Congress had increased to more than 4,500. The numbers leveled off and even declined in the 1980s and 1990s, but staff size in 1999 stood at 7,216 personal staff and 1,267 committee staff in the House and 4,272 personal staff and 910 committee staff in the Senate, for a total of 13,665 in these two major categories. Other staff categories, such as congressional support agencies (including the Congressional Budget Office and the Library of Congress, leadership staff, and joint committee staff), accounted for an additional 9,983 positions, bringing the total to 23,648 in 1999.

The Legislative Reorganization Act of 1946 provided a major overhaul of Congress to address the loss of functional power over the national agenda that had shifted because of economic depression and war to the executive branch. This act cut the number of congressional committees from forty-eight to nineteen in the House and from thirty-three to fifteen in the Senate. While the number of committees was reduced, the size of congressional staff continued to increase. One of the effects of the act was a concentration of power in the hands of a small number of committee chairmen. This concentration became a serious problem in the 1960s when a handful of southern Democrats who were committee chairmen were able to thwart the will of a majority in Congress on the passage of civil rights legislation. This spurred another reform movement that passed as the Legislative Reorganization Act of 1970. The 1970 act addressed a broad range of issues, including the use of electronic vote counting in the House. The act also opened the proceedings of Congress to more public scrutiny and made marked improvements in the professional qualities of congressional staff to meet the needs of an increasingly complex technological society.

CONGRESS AND THE SUPREME COURT

Congress is subject to judicial review by the Supreme Court, which has the power to declare laws passed by Congress to be unconstitutional. The Constitution does not mention this power specifically, but it was discussed by the delegates to the Constitutional Convention of 1787 and defended by Alexander Hamilton in the *Federalist Papers*. Chief Justice John Mar-

shall established the principle of judicial review in 1803 in the landmark case of *Marbury v. Madison*. Marshall said it was "the province of the judicial department to say what the law is." Although the high court has struck down numerous laws, it tends to avoid judgments that impinge on the internal rules and conduct of the House and Senate. In the twentieth century the Supreme Court has evolved to become the chief arbiter of the constitutionality of a law or an action of the legislative and judicial branches. The Court's 1976 decision in *Buckley v. Valeo* addressed campaign finance abuses growing out of the Watergate investigations and upheld parts of the Federal Election Act of 1971. The decision in the *Buckley* case, however, has complicated attempts at campaign finance reform by declaring that a restriction on the amount of money a person or group may contribute to a campaign is a restriction on free speech.

As Howard Nemerov, poet laureate of the United States, proclaimed in the poem he wrote for the bicentennial of Congress in 1989 and delivered before a joint session of Congress, Congress is "the fulcrum of us all." It is the place where political wills representing diverse constituencies clash to make laws that affect all citizens. Despite the many changes and reforms that have swept Congress over more than two centuries, it still performs its fundamental mission under the Constitution very much the way it did two centuries ago. In this regard, although Congress sometimes changes its rules and procedures and the nation itself has changed dramatically in two centuries, if the founders of the U.S. Constitution were to return to Congress today, they would find a familiar place in a world that would be beyond their imagining.

See also *Apportionment; Articles of Confederation;* Buckley v. Valeo; *Campaign Finance; Census; Cloture; Committee System; Congressional Budget Office; Constitution, U.S.; Filibuster; House Leadership: Speaker; Senate Leadership: Early Period; Senate Leadership: Modern; War Powers.*

RAYMOND W. SMOCK, INDEPENDENT HISTORIAN

BIBLIOGRAPHY

Congressional Quarterly's Guide to Congress. 5th ed. Washington, D.C.: CQ Press, 2000.

Baker, Richard Allan. *The Senate of the United States: A Bicentennial History.* Malabar, Fla.: Robert E. Krieger Publishing Company, 1988.

Byrd, Robert C. *The Senate, 1789–1989: Addresses on the History of the United States Senate.* Vol. 2. S. Doc. 100–120, 100th Cong., 1st Sess. Washington, D.C.: Government Printing Office, 1991.

Currie, James T. *The United States House of Representatives.* Malabar, Fla.: Robert E. Krieger Publishing Company, 1988.

Davidson, Roger H., and Walter J. Oleszek. *Congress and Its Members.* 7th ed. Washington, D.C.: CQ Press, 2000.

Smock, Raymond W., ed. *Landmark Documents on the U.S. Congress.* Washington, D.C.: CQ Press, 1999.

CONGRESSIONAL BUDGET OFFICE

The Congressional Budget Office (CBO) supports Congress by conducting objective, nonpartisan, and timely analyses of public policy issues needed to make economic and budget decisions and by providing information and estimates required as part of the budget process.

The CBO was established by the Congressional Budget and Impoundment Control Act of 1974 and officially opened its doors on February 24, 1975. The impetus for passage of the budget act in part was President Richard M. Nixon's challenge of Congress's power of the purse. Nixon, faced with budget deficits and rising inflation, sought to reduce federal spending. Congress largely resisted, so the president obtained his cuts by vetoing legislation and impounding appropriations. The 1974 law provided needed structure to the congressional budget process and reclaimed some congressional control over federal budget decisions that had been ceded to the executive branch over the years.

The budget act stipulated that CBO serve, first and foremost, the House and Senate Budget Committees, which also were created by the new law. Next in line were the House and Senate Appropriations Committees, the House Ways and Means Committee, and the Senate Finance Committee. CBO then must respond to all other committee requests. Although the statute said that CBO need compile information and conduct analyses only for congressional committees, it would respond to individual members' inquiries.

The CBO's duties and functions include assisting Congress in preparing the annual federal budget plan, helping ensure that legislators adhere to the plan, determining the impact of unfunded federal mandates, and providing analyses and information on budget issues and economic policy–related issues.

Congress is required to pass a concurrent resolution, which is not signed by the president and does not have the force of law, laying out a budget blueprint for the upcoming fiscal year. In support of this task, CBO provides Congress with economic forecasts and projections regarding gross domestic product, unemployment, inflation, and interest rates. CBO uses major econometric models, commercial economic forecasting services, and a distinguished panel of advisers to draw up its projections. The projections serve as a baseline against which Congress can judge the effects of different tax and spending proposals and thus decide what policies to include in the budget resolution. CBO also analyzes the president's budget plan, using its own forecasts and projections.

After adoption of the budget resolution, Congress begins work on implementing its goals. CBO prepares a cost estimate for almost every bill reported from committee. It sometimes is asked to analyze draft bills, floor amendments, and conference legislation as well. CBO keeps tabs on all congressional action that affects the spending or revenue-raising aspects of pending legislation—a concept known as scorekeeping. It also issues three sequestration reports per year, advising if statutory limits on spending had been exceeded and if enacted legislation increased the federal budget deficit.

Congress in 1995 passed the Unfunded Mandates Reform Act, in response to the growing frustration of state, local, and tribal governments and private businesses that are subject to directives from the federal government but are not provided the necessary funding to comply with them. According to the law, CBO was to identify provisions of committee-reported bills that mandated spending above certain thresholds and, if possible, estimate the costs.

CBO is responsible for studying programs and policies that affect the federal budget and the economy. It reports its nonpartisan findings to Congress without making any recommendations. Its studies cover budget analysis, economic and fiscal policy, federal taxes, natural resources and commerce, health and human resources, national security, and budget concepts and processes and general government.

CBO is headed by a director, who is chosen by the Speaker of the House and president pro tempore of the Senate upon recommendation of the congressional budget committees. The director is appointed for a four-year term but is not limited in the number of terms he or she may serve. CBO has had five directors: Alice M. Rivlin, Rudolph G. Penner, Robert D. Reischauer, June E. O'Neill, and Dan L. Crippen.

All CBO staff are appointed by the director, and political affiliation is not a factor in hiring. As of 1999 CBO's full-time-equivalent staff numbered 232, most of whom were economists. About 85 percent of CBO's fiscal 1999 appropriation of $25.7 million was dedicated to personnel. The second largest expenditure—about 8 percent—went for the cost of computers.

See also *Congress; Nixon, Richard M.; Office of Management and Budget.*

COLLEEN MCGUINESS, INDEPENDENT AUTHOR

BIBLIOGRAPHY

Congressional Budget Office Web site at *http://www.cbo.gov.*

Congressional Quarterly's Guide to Congress. 5th ed. Washington, D.C.: CQ Press, 2000, 757–759.

CONSERVATIVE PARTY

In 1962 the New York State Conservative Party began to take shape under the direction of J. Daniel Mahoney, a New York attorney, and his brother-in-law, Kieran O'Doherty. They were motivated primarily by the belief that real political alternatives were no longer being offered to the state electorate. They saw the three dominant parties in the state—the Liberal Party, the Democratic Party, and the Republican Party under Gov. Nelson A. Rockefeller and Sen. Jacob K. Javits—as offering a generally liberal agenda.

Although political commentators predicted the early demise of the party—particularly in the aftermath of Barry Goldwater's overwhelming defeat in the 1964 presidential elections—the party continued to grow both in membership and in candidate endorsements. In 1965 the nationally known columnist and intellectual William F. Buckley ran for mayor of New York City, generating national publicity for the party. One year later, the Conservative candidate for governor, Professor Paul Adams, outpolled Liberal Party candidate Franklin D. Roosevelt Jr., obtaining Row C of the ballot for the party. (A party's position on the ballot is determined by the number of votes cast for its candidate for governor. Appearing in Row C is significant because the higher the row, the more notice voters are likely to take of the party's candidates.) In 1970 James Buckley was elected to the U.S. Senate on Row C alone, and from the mid-1970s onward no statewide Republican candidate gained office without Conservative Party cross-endorsement.

Although the Conservative Party suffered some setbacks, such as the loss of Row C to the Independence (Reform) Party in 1996 and the siphoning off of some supporters to the Right-to-Life Party, it remains a major force in New York State politics. The Conservative Party has opposed abortion since it became a political issue; nonetheless, the party has occasionally backed prochoice candidates whose conservative credentials were otherwise satisfactory. The Right-to-Life Party never backs prochoice candidates.

Even though some members of the Conservative Party are Protestant fundamentalists, the plurality of its membership and much of its leadership are traditionalist Roman Catholics. In a very real sense, the rise of the party has mirrored the rise of the conservative movement in America—from Goldwater's capture of the 1964 Republican nomination to Ronald Reagan's electoral triumphs in 1980 and 1984. In addition, the party has successfully fought the image of extremism while generally remaining true to its core principles—tax limitation, education reform, and tough anti-crime policies.

See also *Political Parties; Third Parties.*

PATRICK M. O'NEIL, BROOME COMMUNITY COLLEGE,
STATE UNIVERSITY OF NEW YORK

BIBLIOGRAPHY

Mahoney, J. Daniel. *Actions Speak Louder.* New Rochelle, N.Y.: Arlington House, 1968.

CONSTITUTION, RATIFICATION

On September 17, 1787, after nearly four months of work, thirty-nine of the fifty-five delegates who attended the Philadelphia convention signed the Constitution. Charged with proposing revisions to the Articles of Confederation, the delegates exceeded their original mandate by framing an entirely new system of government. The choices that the convention made about the process by which the Constitution would be ratified fueled subsequent debates about the nature of the Constitution and even about its legitimacy.

The convention had a number of options for the ratification process. It could have returned the new Constitution to the Confederation Congress for adoption by the unanimous approval of the states, which is how the Articles of Confederation were ratified. This method would have been consistent with the convention's assigned task, which was to propose amendments to the Articles of Confederation. But such a process was doomed to failure, since the Confederation Congress could adopt amendments only unanimously. Rhode Island had refused even to send delegates to the convention, and thus its approval of the result seemed unlikely. A quorum of the New York delegation had left the convention in disgust over the nationalizing tendencies of the proposed Constitution, and so there was little chance that New York would give its consent if unanimity were necessary for adoption of the Constitution. The convention delegates could also have sent the proposed Constitution to the state governments for their approval. But this too would probably have doomed the document to failure, since many of the state legislatures were made up of men hostile to a stronger national government. The delegates might also have asked for a national referendum, but this was equally unlikely to succeed because the weakness of the Articles of Confederation undermined any national activities.

Instead of these options, the delegates decided, with little debate, to send it to specially elected conventions in each state. Furthermore, to avoid the impossible task of getting unanimous consent, the delegates put in the Constitution a provision that it would take effect as soon as nine states had approved it. It was clear, however, that the Constitution would serve its purposes best if all of the states ratified it and that it might not work at all without most or all of the largest states: Virginia, Pennsylvania, Massachusetts, New York, and North Carolina.

Beginning in the fall of 1787, the politically active portion of the nation divided into two camps: the Federalists, who supported the Constitution, and the Antifederalists, who opposed it.

THE FEDERALISTS' ADVANTAGES

The Federalists had a number of advantages. Most important, perhaps, they generally advocated the Constitution for the same reasons. Also, they tended to be better educated, wealthier, and more concentrated in urban areas. Thus, they had better access to the press, which allowed them to put their views before the voters in hundreds of newspapers, pamphlets, and broadsides. The Federalists also had strong arguments on their side. The nation's finances were a disaster, and trade with foreign nations was constantly undermined by the actions of individual states. The nation lacked the military power to defend itself or even to compel Great Britain to vacate forts in American territory along the Canadian border. Federalists pointed to Shays's Rebellion, which occurred in 1786, as an example of the potential for anarchy and civil war if a stronger national government were not created. The Federalists capitalized on the weakness of the Antifederalist arguments, which were often inconsistent, to make the point that the nation needed a government with purpose, with direction, and with vigor.

The Antifederalists frequently disagreed among themselves in their opposition to the Constitution and what should be done if it were rejected. Some wanted drastic changes in the Constitution prior to ratification, others a new convention, while others asked for libertarian amendments that would form a bill of rights. The hardcore Antifederalists, such as Patrick Henry of Virginia, did not want any changes in the Articles of Confederation and deeply feared and vigorously opposed a stronger national government. However, many more moderate Antifederalists recognized the need for some structural changes at the national level. On substantive issues they disagreed as well. Some southern Antifederalists, like Patrick Henry and Rawlins Lowndes of South Carolina, thought the Constitution threatened slavery, while some northern Antifederalists condemned the Constitution because of its compromises that protected slavery.

Analyzing the votes for convention delegates shows a relatively even split between Federalists and Antifederalists and suggests some of the key divisions in late eighteenth century society. The Federalists were typically stronger in commercially oriented and cosmopolitan regions. The Antifederalists were usually stronger in agrarian and localistic regions. Still, enough variation existed—Federalist voters in backcountry Georgia and Virginia, or the Antifederalist stronghold in Rhode Island, for instance—to require caution when generalizing.

ANTIFEDERALIST STRATEGY

From the beginning of the debate over ratification the Antifederalists made a major strategic blunder. Rather than facing and defeating the Constitution where they were strong, the Antifederalists adopted a tactic of delay and obstruction. The better organized Federalists, meanwhile, won early victories by wide margins in Delaware, Pennsylvania, New Jersey, Georgia, and Connecticut in December 1787 and January 1788. Thus, by the time Antifederalist strongholds such as Massachusetts and Virginia held their conventions, the momentum had turned in favor of the Federalists. The Antifederalists nearly won in Massachusetts, where they seemed to have a majority when the state convention opened. But, rather than calling for a quick vote, the Antifederalists used delaying tactics, which gave the Federalists a chance to persuade a number of people to change their position, and in February 1788 the Massachusetts convention ratified by a close vote (187 to 168). Had Massachusetts voted earlier, before the Federalist victories in other states, the outcome might have been different.

Relatively easy ratification in South Carolina and Maryland in the spring of 1788 gave the Federalists eight states—one short of the nine necessary for ratification. The only defeat had been in Rhode Island, where the legislature voted overwhelmingly against even summoning a ratification convention. But Rhode Island was a "rogue" state, and no one had expected it to participate in the ratification process. Conventions had yet to meet in the Antifederalist strongholds of Virginia, New York, and North Carolina, or in New Hampshire, where the vote was close. Had Virginia and New York met early in the process and defeated the Constitution, the outcome might have been very different. But Patrick Henry, the most powerful politician in Virginia, and George Clinton in New York foolishly delayed calling a convention in their states. When their conventions met, the momentum for ratification was extremely strong.

In Virginia Henry continued to delay even after the convention was in session, demanding long debate on each clause of the Constitution. This strategy ultimately backfired. In these debates, Federalists like James Madison and Edmund Randolph were able to convince wavering delegates that the Constitution was not nearly as dangerous as Henry had claimed. Ultimately, Virginia ratified by an 89–79 vote. Even before that vote was taken, New Hampshire had ratified by a

57–46 vote. New York had elected the most strongly Antifederal convention of any state, but there too the Antifederalist delegates insisted on protracted debate, to the delight of Federalist leaders like John Jay and Alexander Hamilton. In July New Yorkers heard that the ninth state, New Hampshire, had ratified, and then that Virginia had as well. The New York Convention voted 30–27 to ratify, even though the overwhelming majority of the New York delegates had been elected as Antifederalists. Their leader, Melancton Smith, understood that New York could not "go it alone." North Carolina and Rhode Island still refused to ratify, but their opposition could not last, and by 1790 both had joined the new government.

ARTICULATING THEIR DIFFERENCES

The battle over the Constitution in the key states of Virginia and New York led to some of the clearest statements of what each side thought. For the Federalists, this took the form of eighty-five essays written under the pseudonym of "Publius" by Alexander Hamilton, James Madison, and John Jay. These essays were later collected as *The Federalist*. The "Publius" essays began by explaining the necessity and logic of the "more perfect union" that would result from adopting the Constitution and continued with defenses of each of the new government's branches and its respective powers.

With more diverse views, the Antifederalists never assembled a single document comparable to *The Federalist*. But, in scattered essays and speeches, key Antifederalists developed a critique of the Constitution based on their belief that it was unnecessary, dangerous, and even counterrevolutionary. They rejected the idea that there was a crisis in the country too severe for the Confederation government to handle. They also revived some traditional arguments about republican governments, particularly the belief that they could not be large without falling under the control of a designing few. According to many Antifederalists, the Federalists had manipulated a nonexistent crisis to create a government that would reverse the democratic momentum of the Revolution. The Constitution would protect the wealth and power of a small elite far better than the rights and liberties of the common people. It would transfer power from state governments that were relatively close to the people to a small and distant federal government (which was initially to include only 129 men, including representatives, senators, the vice president, and the president).

Many Antifederalists and some Federalists were especially disturbed by the failure to include in the Constitution a bill of rights that would place unequivocal limits on the power of the federal government over citizens and states. In the Massachusetts and Virginia conventions, the promise of support for a bill of rights was essential in winning ratification. Only

after the Bill of Rights, which was composed of elements of the more than two hundred amendments proposed by the state conventions, passed Congress and was sent to the states for ratification did North Carolina (in November 1789) and Rhode Island (in May 1790) vote to enter the Union.

"ORIGINAL INTENT"

The ratification debates, and the ratification process generally, have been returned to repeatedly over the course of American history to understand the nature, powers, and limits of the federal government. In attempting to answer questions about the "original intent" of the Constitution, scholars, lawyers, and judges have repeatedly referred to the *Records of the Federal Convention of 1787*, as well as to the essays in *The Federalist*. Madison argued that such questions should really be answered by reviewing the debates in the state conventions. However, only a few state conventions kept careful records of their debates, none kept complete records, and some kept no records at all. The hybrid ratification process left open an even more critical question about whether the United States was a union of states or of citizens; it would take the Civil War to resolve finally the long debates over this question.

See also *Constitution, U.S.; Constitutional Amendments; Federalists; Madison, James.*

PAUL FINKELMAN, UNIVERSITY OF TULSA COLLEGE OF LAW,
AND JAMES E. LEWIS JR., INDEPENDENT SCHOLAR

BIBLIOGRAPHY

Cornell, Saul. *The Other Founders: Anti-Federalism and the Dissenting Tradition in America, 1788–1828*. Chapel Hill: University of North Carolina Press, 1999.

Jensen, Merrill, et al., eds. *The Documentary History of the Ratification of the Constitution*. 15 vols. to date. Madison: State Historical Society of Wisconsin, 1976–.

Rutland, Robert A. *The Ordeal of the Constitution: The Antifederalists and the Ratification Struggle of 1787–1788*. Norman: University of Oklahoma Press, 1966.

Storing, Herbert J. *What the Anti-Federalists Were For*. Chicago: University of Chicago Press, 1981.

CONSTITUTION, U.S.

The Constitution affected American political history in three important ways. First, the Constitution created a political structure for American government. Second, the Constitution has been at the center of many of the most important policy and political debates in U.S. history, sometimes limiting Congress and the executive branch, and sometimes providing a solution to difficult policy problems. Finally, throughout history Americans, especially those who have been in the minority, have appealed to the Constitution for protection and vindication of their rights.

GOVERNMENTAL STRUCTURE

At one level, all American politics begins with the Constitution, because that document sets out the structure of national politics. The American constitution-makers copied much from Great Britain's unwritten constitution. Like Britain, the United States has a bicameral legislature, an executive, and a judiciary. But, unlike its British forebear, the U.S. Constitution provides for an entirely different political jurisdiction as well: the states. Again, unlike Britain, the United States has not only a written constitution but one that spells out the powers and responsibilities of each branch of government and sets specific limitations on what each branch may do.

The legislature is composed of a lower house, which represents "the people," much like Britain's House of Commons, and a more elite branch, the Senate, which represents "the states," somewhat like the House of Lords. As befits a democracy where titles of nobility are prohibited, senators serve for a specific number of years (six), rather than for life. Under the original wording of the Constitution the state legislatures chose persons to serve in the Senate, but since the ratification of the Seventeenth Amendment in 1913, senators have been elected by the people of each state. From the beginning the Constitution apportioned representation in the House of Representatives on the basis of population and required a reapportionment every ten years, after a national census. This requirement prevented the development of congressional seats that had few or no people, like England's "rotten boroughs"—parliamentary districts that had been created in the medieval period but had almost no population by the eighteenth century.

The U.S. Constitution sets out various powers of Congress that are national in scope, but it reserves to the states legislative power over local issues. The boundaries of these jurisdictions are not always clear, and they have been shaped by Congress, the president, and the Supreme Court. The relationship between the national government and the states, known as federalism, is complex. Over the years the powers of Congress have expanded in reaction to events such as the Civil War and the Great Depression, through Constitutional amendments, and through Supreme Court decisions. All of these powers are, to a greater or lesser extent, shaped by the language of the Constitution itself.

The president, unlike members of Congress, is the only national leader who represents all the people of the United States. Ironically, the president is not actually elected by the people. For a variety of reasons the Framers created a device called the "electoral college" that would choose the president. Each state would get as many electors as it had members in the House of Representatives and the Senate combined. The Constitution gave the president few specific, but many potential, powers.

With a few exceptions, among them Andrew Jackson, Abraham Lincoln, and William McKinley, most nineteenth-century presidents were weak leaders. Combining his personal charisma and status as a military hero, Andrew Jackson vetoed important legislation passed by Congress, and he suffered little for it. Events strengthened Jackson's hand. When South Carolina nullified the federal tariff, Jackson threatened to personally lead an army into the state to suppress this treason. Similarly, when Chief Justice John Marshall challenged Jackson's policies toward Native Americans, Jackson ignored him. Most nineteenth-century presidents, lacking Jackson's nerve and charisma, were unwilling to challenge the other branches of government. Lincoln, facing the nation's greatest crisis, stretched the Constitution to save the Union and end slavery, but he worked closely with Congress in doing so. Using his constitutional power as commander in chief, Lincoln was perhaps the most powerful president before the 1930s. In the twentieth century the most successful presidents used the office—in Theodore Roosevelt's words—as a "bully pulpit" to strengthen the office and expand the meaning of its constitutional powers.

In the twentieth century the larger federal bureaucracy and huge federal expenditures led to stronger presidents and expanded presidential powers. Wars throughout the century also expanded presidential power, at least until the controversial Vietnam War undermined the power of the president and forced the incumbent, Lyndon B. Johnson, out of office and led to the War Powers Act, limiting a president's war-making authority. The increasing importance of foreign policy also shifted power to the White House, because the Constitution places almost all diplomatic initiatives in the executive branch. However, the Senate's power to defeat treaties, such as the one ending World War I, illustrates the balancing of constitutional power even in this area. For example, when that war ended, President Woodrow Wilson was unable to bring the United States into the League of Nations because Congress would not support the initiative.

Despite the growth of presidential power in the twentieth century, congressional control of the budget and the power of the Senate to confirm appointees and ratify treaties limit the constitutional powers of the president. Even in the modern era some presidents have been weak and ineffective, while others have used the office to the fullest, dominating Congress and pushing their agendas.

The third branch, the judiciary, is the weakest in the constitutional structure. The lower courts are created by Congress, which has the power to strengthen or reduce their role. In *Marbury v. Madison* (1803), Chief Justice John Marshall, who served from 1801 until 1835, asserted the power of the Court to declare an act of Congress unconstitutional, but he never used that power again. Marshall's successor, Roger B. Taney (served 1836–1864), used the power once as well, in *Dred Scott v. Sandford* (1857), but with disastrous results that contributed to the onset of the Civil War. From the 1870s to the 1930s the Supreme Court constantly thwarted the will of Congress and the state legislatures by gutting civil rights legislation, limiting the powers of the government to control the effects of industrialization, and striking down numerous pieces of reform legislation, such as minimum wage laws and restrictions on child labor. Yet, the courts were always reactive, and could only respond to "cases and controversies," as the Constitution provided. The courts did not give advisory opinions, initiate investigations on their own, or comment on the political process.

In the second half of the twentieth century the Supreme Court developed into a far more powerful institution. It became the political body of last resort, asked to decide great social issues and settle seemingly impossible political questions. As a result, the Court became controversial and often an issue in presidential campaigns. In 1968, for example, Richard Nixon ran *against* the Supreme Court, promising to appoint conservative jurists if elected. In the end, however, only one of the justices he appointed, William Rehnquist, turned out to be as conservative as he wanted. The courts must constantly balance their need to interpret and enforce the Constitution with the inherently undemocratic concept of nine unelected life-time appointees overturning laws passed by democratically elected legislatures.

THE CONSTITUTION AND POLICY DEBATES

Beginning with the administration of George Washington, debates within Congress and presidential cabinets have often focused on the constitutional limitations on policy initiatives. The most famous example was also the first example. It concerns the bank of the United States and illustrates the complexity of constitutional considerations in political debate.

At the Philadelphia convention James Madison proposed that Congress be given the power "to grant charters of incorporation in cases where the Public good may require them." However, the convention rejected this proposal. In 1790 Secretary of the Treasury Alexander Hamilton asked Congress to charter the Bank of the United States. Supporters of the bank argued that it was necessary for a smoothly functioning economy and that Congress had implied powers to carry out the functions of government specifically stated in the Constitution. Rep. James Madison of Virginia vigorously opposed the bank, arguing that while "convenient" for the economy, establishing a bank was not a "necessary and proper" function of the government.

In Washington's cabinet, Attorney General Edmund Randolph argued against the bank, asserting that the meaning of the Constitution should "be decided on by the import of its own expressions." Secretary of State Thomas Jefferson took a similar position, reminding the president "that the very power now proposed as a means, was rejected as an end, by the Convention which formed the constitution." In support of the bank Hamilton argued that the government possessed "implied as well as express powers," and that the power to create a bank was implied by Congress's power to collect taxes and regulate trade. He similarly argued for a broad interpretation of the word "necessary" in the "necessary and proper" clause. President Washington, persuaded by Hamilton, signed the bank bill into law.

Twenty years later the bank's charter expired, and Congress refused to renew it. But in the wake of the War of 1812 Madison, by then the president, concluded a bank was necessary and proper. He asked Congress for a new bank, "waiving the question of the Constitutional authority of the Legislature to establish an incorporated bank as being precluded in my judgment by repeated recognitions under varied circumstances of the validity of such an institution in acts of the legislative, executive, and judicial branches of the Government, accompanied by indications, in different modes, of a concurrence of the general will of the nation." In 1819 the Supreme Court upheld the bank bill in *McCulloch v. Maryland*. Speaking for the Court, Chief Justice John Marshall asserted:

> It must have been the intention of those who gave these powers, to insure, as far as human prudence could insure, their beneficial execution. This could not be done by confiding the choice of means to such narrow limits as not to leave it in the power of Congress to adopt any which might be appropriate, and which were conducive to the end. This provision is made in a constitution intended to endure for ages to come, and consequently, to be adapted to the various crises of human affairs. To have prescribed the means by which government should, in all future time, execute its powers, would have been to change, entirely, the character of the instrument, and give it the properties of a legal code. It would have been an unwise attempt to provide, by immutable rules, for exigencies which, if foreseen at all, must have been seen dimly, and which can be best provided for as they occur.

The final chapter of the bank story came in 1832, when President Andrew Jackson vetoed a bill to extend the bank's charter. Despite Marshall's opinion upholding the constitutionality of the bank, Jackson declared that the bank was "unauthorized by the Constitution, subversive of the rights of the States, and dangerous to the liberties of the people."

The Constitution also restrained and shaped Lincoln's policy toward emancipation. On entering the office he attempted to reassure the seceding states, reminding them that he had no constitutional power to touch slavery where it already existed. However, as the war progressed Lincoln discovered such a power in his role as commander in chief of the army. This role was of course constitutionally limited. Lincoln's Emancipation Proclamation could only be applied to those states in rebellion and those areas not yet under control of the United States. The partial nature of the proclamation is explained by the way in which the Constitution constrained presidential action.

Since the Civil War, members of Congress and presidents have often been less constitutionally scrupulous about passing and signing politically popular legislation. Nevertheless, on some important matters Congress has tried to pay great attention to the Constitution. For example, after passing the Civil Rights Act of 1866, some members of Congress worried about its constitutionality and proposed the Fourteenth Amendment, which required the states to give people equal protection of the laws. The amendment did not, however, prohibit private discrimination, and thus in the Civil Rights Act of 1964 Congress used the Commerce Clause to assert its jurisdiction over private discrimination in hotels, motels, and restaurants.

THE APPEAL TO RIGHTS

Throughout our history, people, especially those in the minority, have appealed to the Constitution to protect their rights, liberties, and special interests. These appeals were political in nature and directed not at courts, but at the court of public opinion. In 1798 the legislatures in Virginia and Kentucky passed resolutions denouncing the Alien and Sedition Acts, not merely as bad policy, but as violations of the Constitution. In the 1830s abolitionists flooded Congress with petitions to end slavery. When Congress refused even to accept these petitions, the abolitionists appealed to the northern public, arguing that slavery threatened the rights of all free people in the nation. After the Civil War, women's rights advocates argued that the Constitution's newest amendment gave them the vote and other political rights. These were constitutional arguments brought to the public for debate and consideration. Trade unionists and labor radicals made similar arguments. The Industrial Workers of the World exploited notions of freedom of speech not only to express their views but also as a form of protest in itself.

Similarly, in the 1950s and 1960s civil rights activists used two different kinds of constitutional concepts in their struggles against segregation. First they argued that segregation violated constitutional norms of equality and fairness. Segregation was morally wrong in part because it was constitutionally wrong. Second, they used constitutional rights, especially those of speech and assembly, to protest segregation.

When these protests led to violent responses by southern officials, the civil rights movement, like the abolitionists before them, successfully made the political point that racial oppression threatens all liberty.

Many of the groups mentioned here took their appeals to the courts, as well as the streets. But, the legal claims they made on the Constitution were often secondary to their political claims. The modern civil rights movement, for example, depended at least as much on legislation and the force of public opinion to energize the executive branch as on court decisions.

THE CONSTITUTION AS POLITICAL ICON

Unlike most nation-states, the United States began without a national church or a royal or noble class. But, as the revolutionary pamphleteer Tom Paine noted, in America the "constitution is king." Similarly, Alexis de Tocqueville observed that in America lawyers were the only aristocrats. His observation made sense because lawyers and judges were the keepers of the Constitution, and thus the "priests" and "high priests" of America's civil religion. At the center of that civil religion is the Constitution. The most important form of worship has been politics, and the highest form of that has been constitutional politics.

See also *Civil Rights Act of 1866; Civil Rights Movement; Congress; Constitution, Ratification; Constitutional Amendments; Constitutional Convention; Federalism; Gag Rule; Jackson, Andrew; Lincoln, Abraham; Presidency; Presidential Succession Amendments; Supreme Court; War Powers; Wilson, Woodrow.*

PAUL FINKELMAN, UNIVERSITY OF TULSA COLLEGE OF LAW

BIBLIOGRAPHY

Kammen, Michael. *A Machine That Would Go by Itself: The Constitution in American Culture.* New York: Alfred A. Knopf, 1986.

CONSTITUTIONAL AMENDMENTS

The Framers of the Constitution at the Philadelphia convention in 1787 hoped they had done their work well, but they knew that they must leave later generations with a means to amend it to meet changing conditions.

WHETHER AND HOW TO AMEND THE CONSTITUTION

The Framers believed that the fundamental law ought to be far more difficult to change than simply passing legislation with simple majorities. Yet they also recognized—from their experience with the Articles of Confederation, which had resulted in the Philadelphia convention in the first place—that the amending process had to require less than unanimous consent. In Article V, therefore, they proposed several means, each of which required super majorities but not unanimous consent of the states.

According to the method that has always been followed, an amendment is proposed in Congress, where a two-thirds majority in each house is required for it to gain congressional approval, and then three-fourths of the states must approve it before it can be declared ratified and go into effect. From time to time, proposals surface to follow another mode that the Constitution provides, according to which two-thirds of the state legislatures can call for a constitutional convention. (Whether such a convention could have a restricted agenda or might reconsider anything, including the Bill of Rights, remains an open question.)

Article V also specified, however, that not everything was subject to amendment. As part of the Compromise of 1787 over slavery, the Constitution stipulated that no majority could change the provision that postponed until at least 1808 any congressional action to inhibit the importation of additional slaves into the nation.

In 1789, at the time Congress proposed the Bill of Rights, it was determined that amendments would be placed at the end of the document, rather than integrated into it. The amendments themselves appear, each with a number to indicate the sequence of adoption, as an appendix to the original document.

SUBSTANCE AND TIMING

The twenty-seven amendments ratified through the year 2000 can be arranged into various subgroups, including the Bill of Rights, amendments to redefine the electorate, and amendments to redefine the selection and tenure of presidents. The Bill of Rights, ratified in 1791, was designed to reassure citizens that the new federal government had limited power over such matters as freedom of religion and the security of property. The Eleventh Amendment (1795) sought to ban suits against states by citizens of other states. At the close of the Civil War, the Thirteenth Amendment (1865) abolished slavery, and the Fourteenth (1868) updated the Three-fifths Clause and recognized black citizenship. Some later amendments addressed individuals' voting rights according to race (Fifteenth, 1870), gender (Nineteenth, 1920), age (Twenty-sixth, 1971), or whether prospective voters in federal elections had paid a poll tax (Twenty-fourth, 1964). Two amendments addressed alcoholic beverages: the Eighteenth (1919) imposing prohibition and the Twenty-first (1933) repealing the Eighteenth.

Several amendments modified the process of recruiting federal officeholders or redefined their terms of office. The Twelfth Amendment (1804), responding to an impasse in the presidential election of 1800, separated the elections of president and vice president. The Seventeenth (1913) shifted to the voters the responsibility for electing U.S. senators, who had previously been appointed by state legislatures. The Twentieth (1933) provided that presidents' terms (which had previously ended in March) would end on January 20. That amendment also dealt with presidential succession (in the event of a president's death) and the selection of a new vice president, as did the Twenty-fifth (1967). The Twenty-second Amendment (1951), responding to Franklin D. Roosevelt's four elections to the presidency, limited future presidents to two terms (although someone who became president, like Lyndon B. Johnson, with less than half a term to serve, could still be elected to two full terms). The Twenty-third Amendment (1961) treats the District of Columbia as a state for purposes of choosing members of the electoral college in presidential elections.

In every decade, hundreds of amendments are introduced in Congress, but in no decade after the 1790s (through 2000) have more than four been approved or ratified. Some proposed amendments gained approval and ratification very quickly, others more slowly, and most not at all. Not until the Eighteenth Amendment did a proposed amendment carry a seven-year limit for ratification. The Nineteenth Amendment, proposed in 1878, was passed by Congress in 1919 and ratified in 1920. The Equal Rights Amendment, originally proposed in 1923, finally gained approval in Congress in 1972 but failed to gain ratification, even after its seven-year deadline was extended for another three years to 1982. An amendment passed in 1978, which would have replaced the Twenty-third and made the District of Columbia a state for purposes of voting in presidential elections and electing members of Congress, did not obtain ratification within its allotted seven years.

The fastest to gain ratification has been the Twenty-sixth (1971), which lowered the voting age to eighteen. It became part of the Constitution within months of being proposed. The slowest has been the Twenty-seventh, originally proposed as part of the Bill of Rights. It was declared ratified in 1992, a full two centuries after ten of its companions.

CONSTITUTIONAL AMENDMENTS IN THE EARLY REPUBLIC

The proponents of ratifying the proposed Constitution in 1787 and 1788 encountered massive opposition, and approval in a number of states was by small margins. To gain the support of enough delegates at the ratifying conventions, supporters promised that amendments would be offered. Among a great many considered, twelve were approved in September 1789. Ten gained ratification by December 1791 as the Bill of Rights, and one more, the Twenty-seventh (prohibiting Congress from giving itself a pay raise effective before another election had taken place), gained ratification two centuries later. Some people who had originally argued for amendments, among them Virginia's George Mason, had in mind more substantive restrictions on the powers of the federal government (regarding taxation, commerce, slavery, and the power of the federal judiciary), but the guarantees of individual rights went far to satisfy many citizens in the Republic's early years.

From early on, partisan and sectional agendas led to proposals for additional constitutional amendments. Late in the War of 1812, the Hartford Convention Resolutions called for amendments terminating the Three-fifths Clause (according to which slaves were fractionally counted in the formula for determining representation in Congress) and requiring a two-thirds vote in each house (rather than a simple majority) to declare war or admit new states. Beginning in the 1830s, northerners sought a host of amendments that would have curtailed the protections enjoyed by slavery under the Constitution.

SLAVERY, RACE, POWER, AND THE UNION

The secession crisis of 1860–1861 arose when Abraham Lincoln was elected president and many southerners perceived him as a threat to slavery. To resolve the crisis, various proposals for constitutional amendments emerged in Congress or southern conventions. Most of those proposals were designed to safeguard slavery against congressional interference. Some called for unanimous approval by all the states as a condition of further amendment (thus reviving the Articles of Confederation formula) or even stipulated that a proposed amendment, if ratified, could not itself be amended to authorize action (thus echoing the provision that had originally guaranteed the international slave trade against congressional termination for at least twenty years).

The Corwin Amendment, which actually gained approval in both houses of Congress and went to the states for ratification, would have prevented Congress from ever acting against slavery in any state. Other proposals, none of which got even that far toward adoption, would have prevented any tampering with the Three-fifths Clause or the Fugitive Slave Clause; prohibited African Americans from voting in federal elections; and extended the Missouri Compromise line, separating western territories open or closed to the expansion of slavery, west to the Pacific Ocean.

Such proposals failed to gain ratification or prevent the Civil War, and the Union victory in the war led to very different constitutional amendments between 1865 and 1870 than had been proposed in 1860 and 1861. The Thirteenth Amendment (1865) abolished slavery throughout the nation. The Fourteenth Amendment (1868), which overturned the 1857 *Dred Scott* decision and addressed the meaning of the Three-fifths Clause in a world without slaves, declared all persons born in the United States to be citizens and provided that, for any state that refused black men the right to vote, its representation in the House of Representatives and the electoral college would be reduced accordingly. The Fifteenth Amendment (1870) went farther by declaring that no state can deny voting rights on account of a person's race.

COURT, CONGRESS, AND THE CONSTITUTION

The Constitution is in constant change, or at least is subject to constant amendment, in ways subtle or great. Formal amendment is not the only way to change the Constitution. The Supreme Court interprets the language of the Constitution when applying it to state or federal legislation, and in the process the Constitution can change. For many years, for example, federal courts interpreted the Fourteenth Amendment as permitting state laws that mandated racial segregation in such matters as education, transportation, and marriage. The language of the Fourteenth Amendment's Equal Protection Clause has remained unchanged, but the meaning of those words underwent great change from *Plessy v. Ferguson* (1896), in which the Supreme Court approved the formula "separate but equal," to *Brown v. Board of Education* (1954), in which the Court repudiated that formula. In addition, the Court gradually interpreted the Fourteenth Amendment's Due Process Clause as "incorporating" most of the Bill of Rights so as to limit the powers of state governments as well as the federal government.

If large numbers of Americans object to an interpretation by the Court, Congress can propose formal amendments to reverse the Court's decision by changing the language of the Constitution. Indeed, two amendments overturned decisions by the U.S. Supreme Court. The Fourteenth Amendment (1868) overruled *Dred Scott v. Sandford* (1857), which held that the Founders had not considered African Americans to be U.S. citizens. The Sixteenth Amendment (1913) overruled *Pollock v. Farmers' Loan and Trust* (1895), a decision in which the Supreme Court had invalidated federal income taxes. In addition, the Nineteenth Amendment (1920) can be understood as a belated response to *Minor v. Happersett* (1875), in which the Court had ruled that the Privileges and Immunities Clause of the Fourteenth Amendment was not meant to grant women the right to vote.

The Supreme Court has itself ruled on the amending process. In two decisions named *Hawke v. Smith* (both in

1920), the Court ruled that Ohio could not require that ratification of an amendment be accomplished by popular referendum. In *Dillon v. Glose* (1921), one of the matters the Court considered was the length of time between congressional approval and state ratification. In that case, which arose regarding the Eighteenth Amendment and prohibition, the court ruled that Congress could, if it wished, specify a seven-year deadline for ratification, and that such was in fact consistent with the implied need to obtain a more or less contemporary ratification, rather than stringing the process out over a century and more.

Coleman v. Miller (1939) dealt with the Child Labor Amendment, proposed by Congress in 1924 (in response to a Supreme Court decision) but never ratified. The Kansas legislature, having rejected the amendment

U.S. senators rally in support of a constitutional amendment—never achieved—to ban desecration of the American flag, June 14, 1990. *R. Michael Jenkins, Congressional Quarterly*

in 1925, later changed its mind and voted to ratify in 1937. Stepping away from the decision in *Dillon,* a divided Court ruled that the matters of both the previous rejection and the thirteen-year delay were "political questions" for Congress to decide.

Consistent with the ruling in *Coleman,* Congress accepted the very belated ratification of the Twenty-seventh Amendment, something *Dillon* had specifically said seemed inappropriate. Whether a state can change its mind on ratification remained an issue into the twenty-first century (this question came up regarding the proposed Equal Rights Amendment), as did the legitimacy of a lengthy delay between when an amendment is proposed by Congress and when a vote on ratification is taken.

AN AMENDABLE CONSTITUTION

In modern American political history, formal amendments have been proposed to address a wide variety of policy matters. Some would have denied federal courts jurisdiction over legislative districting or established a single presidential term of six years. A centerpiece of Ronald Reagan's election campaign in 1980 called for constitutional amendments to require a balanced federal budget, permit prayer in the public schools, ban abortion, and prohibit the use of busing to achieve public school desegregation. Though none of those proposals gained adoption, they revealed the salience of the issues, the attractiveness of the procedure, and thus the continued likelihood that Americans would resort to the amend-

ing process to adjust the conduct of the nation's politics and the content of its policies.

See also *Articles of Confederation; Bill of Rights; Congress; Constitution, U.S.; Equal Rights Amendment; Hartford Convention Resolutions; Presidency; Presidential Succession Amendments; Reconstruction; Suffrage; Super Majority; Three-fifths Clause; Twelfth Amendment.*

PETER WALLENSTEIN,
VIRGINIA POLYTECHNIC INSTITUTE AND STATE UNIVERSITY

BIBLIOGRAPHY

Bernstein, Richard B., with Jerome Agel. *Amending America: If We Love the Constitution So Much, Why Do We Keep Trying to Change It?* New York: Times Books, 1993.

Grimes, Alan P. *Democracy and the Amendments to the Constitution.* Lexington, Mass.: Lexington Books, 1978.

Kyvig, David E. *Explicit and Authentic Acts: Amending the U.S. Constitution, 1776–1995.* Lawrence: University Press of Kansas, 1996.

Levinson, Sanford, ed. *Responding to Imperfection: The Theory and Practice of Constitutional Amendment.* Princeton: Princeton University Press, 1995.

Vile, John R. *Encyclopedia of Constitutional Amendments, Proposed Amendments, and Amending Issues, 1789–1995.* Santa Barbara: ABC-CLIO, 1996.

CONSTITUTIONAL CONVENTION

From May 14 to September 17, 1787, thirty-nine delegates, representing twelve states, met in Philadelphia to write what became the United States Constitution. The convention was called to amend the existing Articles of Confederation, but almost immediately the delegates set about to create an entirely new framework of government. Amendments to the Articles of Confederation required the unanimous ratification of all the states, but when submitting their framework of government to the states, the delegates provided that the new Constitution would go into effect after the ratification of only nine states. In this way the Constitution can be seen as "revolutionary." However, its initial adoption by eleven states in 1787–1788, and the subsequent ratification by the remaining two (North Carolina in 1789 and Rhode Island in 1790), preempted arguments that the writing of the Constitution was unconstitutional.

A delegate to the Constitutional Convention signs the document while George Washington looks on. *Library of Congress*

From the beginning of the Philadelphia convention almost all the delegates agreed on the urgency of creating a stronger, more effective national government. Delegates differed, however, on structural details of how to remake the new national government and on substantive issues of the powers to grant it. So salient were some of those issues that the convention was in danger of dissolving. Little wonder that many people, both then and later, considered it a miracle that the delegates were able to agree on anything, let alone on the Constitution that they proposed for ratification.

Three major issues complicated the debates. First, there was a split between the large and small states over representation. The small states wanted equal representation in the new national legislature, as had been the case under the Articles of Confederation. The larger states wanted representation based on population. A second major issue concerned the powers of Congress. Northerners, especially New Englanders, wanted Congress to have power to regulate commerce and foreign policy. Southerners feared commercial regulation. And third, complicating both issues, was the place of slavery in the new constitutional order. In addition to these three major issues, the delegates disagreed over how to elect the president, how to control the military, and numerous other details of government.

At the beginning of the convention Edmund Randolph, the governor of Virginia, introduced what is known as the Virginia Plan. Sometimes called the Randolph Plan, the proposal was in fact drafted by James Madison. The plan called for a bicameral national legislature in which the states would have been represented on the basis of population. The strong national government outlined by Madison would have had the power to overturn state legislation, take jurisdiction, and pass laws "wherever . . . the separate States are incompetent" or to preserve the "harmony of the United States." Furthermore, the national government would have been able to use the military to enforce its laws and decrees. Delegates from the most populous states, such as Virginia, Pennsylvania, and Massachusetts, wanted representation in the national legislature to be based on population and generally favored Madison's plans.

However, delegates from the smaller states, especially New Jersey, Delaware, and Connecticut, feared such a strong national government, especially one in which the largest states would seemingly be able to control the entire government. These states did not advocate a continuation of the Articles of Confederation, and many of their delegates were strongly nationalist. But, they believed Madison's proposal went too far. On June 15 William Paterson offered a counter-proposal, known as the New Jersey Plan, or Paterson Plan. It would have given each state equal representation in the national Congress. However, in other ways it was nationalistic. Paterson favored a national judiciary backed up by a "supremacy clause," declaring that the national constitution and laws were superior to state laws.

Even as most delegates watched the debate between the small and large states, some delegates argued it was a false issue. The small states feared that the large states would vote as a bloc and that three or four of the largest states could dominate the national legislature. But, as James Madison correctly noted, these fears were unrealistic, because the large states would have more in common with their small state neighbors than with larger states in other parts of the country. Thus, James Madison argued,

> the States were divided into different interests not by their difference of size, but by other circumstances; the most material of which resulted partly from climate, but principally from their having or not having slaves. These two causes concurred in forming the great division of interests in the U. States. It did not lie between the large and small States: it lay between the Northern and Southern, and if any defensive power were necessary, it ought to be mutually given to these two interests.

Madison's analysis eventually proved correct. The convention rejected part of the New Jersey Plan and accepted a stronger national government with representation based on population in the House of Representatives. However, the delegates also endorsed what is known as the Connecticut Compromise, or Great Compromise, which gave the states equal representation in the Senate, but—unlike the Articles—allowed each senator to vote as an individual. Under the compromise, the states gained equality in the Senate, with each state having two senators, while representation in the House of Representatives was based on population. Once this compromise was reached, the small states ceased to vote as a bloc and voted on sectional or economic interests.

The Great Compromise satisfied the small states by giving them equal representation in one house of Congress. However, it reopened an equally difficult problem: who to count for purposes of representation in the other house. The southern states, led by Virginia and South Carolina, wanted to count slaves when apportioning representation; the northern states argued that slaves should not be counted when determining the size of a legislature to represent a free nation. As William Paterson asked, "Has a man in Virga. a number of votes in proportion to the number of his slaves?"

Slavery also affected how the national executive would be chosen. Most delegates understood the need for a national executive, which was lacking under the Articles of Confederation, but they spent a great deal of energy trying to determine how to choose the officeholder, how long the term of office should be, and what powers the executive would have. Political advantage figured in this debate as well. Virginians wanted population, including slaves, to figure in choosing the president, but they did not want the president to be chosen by a popular vote, because, as James Madison noted, the "right of suffrage was much more diffusive in the Northern than the Southern States; and the latter could have no influence in the election on the score of the Negroes."

Eventually the convention reached compromises over slavery that mostly favored the South. Under the three-fifths clause, five slaves were counted as three "full persons" for representation. These slaves, who of course could not vote, provided a substantial number of congressional seats in the House of Representatives. Equally important, the three-fifths clause applied to the election of the president, providing electoral votes based on slaves. In 1800 the electoral votes created by counting slaves would provide the margin for the election of Thomas Jefferson.

Slavery also figured in the commerce clause debates. Northerners, especially New Englanders, wanted the new Congress to regulate interstate and international commerce by a simple majority, while most southerners agreed with South Carolina's Gen. Charles Cotesworth Pinckney that "it was the true interest of the S. States to have no regulation of commerce." Southerners feared that commercial regulations would favor the maritime states at the expense of the commodity producing slave economies of the South. Most important, South Carolina and Georgia did not want Congress to be able to regulate or ban the African slave trade. In the end another compromise was reached. The Deep South supported allowing Congress to regulate commerce by a simple majority in return for a guarantee that no laws would be passed to prohibit the African slave trade for *at least* twenty years.

Most delegates were pleased with the outcome of their efforts. A few, however, thought the summer a failure. Two New York delegates left the convention in early July because they opposed the direction of the convention toward a stronger national government. At the end of the convention, George Mason of Virginia and Elbridge Gerry of Massachusetts refused to sign the document for the same reason. In addition, Mason and Gerry feared the lack of a bill of rights they thought necessary to protect the liberties of the people. But the majority of the convention dismissed such fears. These delegates saw a government of limited powers, able to govern a nation of diverse interests, but not able to directly affect the lives and liberties of the people.

See also *Articles of Confederation; Constitution, Ratification; Constitution, U.S.; Federalists; Madison, James; Slavery; Three-fifths Clause.*

PAUL FINKELMAN, UNIVERSITY OF TULSA COLLEGE OF LAW

BIBLIOGRAPHY

Beard, Charles A. *An Economic Interpretation of the Constitution of the United States.* New Brunswick, N.J.: Transaction Publishers, 1998. Originally published New York: Macmillan, 1913.

Bowen, Catherine Drinker. *Miracle at Philadelphia.* Boston: Little, Brown, 1986. Originally published 1966.

Farrand, Max. *The Records of the Federal Convention of 1787.* New Haven: Yale University Press, 1966.

Finkelman, Paul. *Slavery and the Founders: Race and Liberty in the Age of Jefferson.* Armonk, N.Y.: M. E. Sharpe, 1996.

Levy, Leonard W. *Original Intent and the Framers' Constitution.* New York: Macmillan, 1988.

Rakove, Jack. *Original Meanings: Politics and Ideas in the Making of the Constitution.* New York: Alfred A. Knopf, 1996.

CONSTITUTIONAL UNION PARTY

The Constitutional Union Party ran a presidential ticket in the election of 1860, seeking to provide a third alternative to addressing the national issues of slavery and disunion.

With the disintegration of the Whig Party in the 1850s, northern and southern conservatives joined either the Democratic Party or the Know Nothing (American) Party. Growing sectional strife, evident in the increasing political strength of the Republicans and the Democratic split in 1860, convinced American conservatives that they needed to create an alternative party to mitigate growing sectional strife over slavery and unite northern and southern Democrats, conservative Republicans, and former Know Nothings and Whigs.

The Constitutional Union Party lacked a strong, dynamic candidate; offered a vague party platform; failed to create a national coalition of anti-Republican opposition; and refused to address the problem of slavery in the territories. Founders of the party included former Whigs Edward Everett of Massachusetts and John J. Crittenden of Kentucky. Led by Crittenden, fifty conservative members of Congress met in December 1859. The party's simple political platform consisted of supporting the Union and the Constitution, enforcing the law, and avoiding the slavery issue. At its Baltimore convention in May 1860, Crittenden declined to be its presidential candidate. John Bell, a Tennessean and former Whig, was nominated as the presidential candidate, with Everett as the vice presidential candidate. Republicans won decisive northern elections, Breckinridge proslavery Democrats gained southern support, and northern unionists had to support either John C. Breckinridge or the Republicans. Bell and Everett won only 39 of the 303 electoral college votes, winning the three border states of Virginia, Kentucky, and Tennessee. With the election of Lincoln and the secession of South Carolina, the party's reason for existence vanished.

See also *Breckinridge Democrats; Know Nothing (American) Party; Political Parties; Third Parties; Whig Party.*

DONALD STELLUTO JR., CALIFORNIA STATE UNIVERSITY, FULLERTON

BIBLIOGRAPHY

Brown, Thomas. "Edward Everett and the Constitutional Union Party of 1860." *Historical Journal of Massachusetts* 11, no. 2 (1983): 69–81.

Crouch, Barry A. "Amos A. Lawrence and the Formation of the Constitutional Union Party: The Conservative Failure in 1860." *Historical Journal of Massachusetts* 8, no. 2 (1980): 46–58.

Curl, Donald Walter. "The Baltimore Convention of the Constitutional Union Party." *Maryland Historical Magazine* 67, no. 3 (1972): 254–277.

Kelly, Jack. "John J. Crittenden and the Constitutional Union Party." *The Filson Club History Quarterly* 48, no. 3 (1974): 265–276.

Mering, John V. "Allies or Opponents? The Douglas Democrats and the Constitutional Unionists." *Southern Studies* 23, no. 4 (1984): 376–385.

Stabler, John Burgess. "A History of the Constitutional Union Party: A Tragic Failure." Unpublished doctoral dissertation, Columbia University, 1954.

COOLIDGE, CALVIN

The thirtieth president, Calvin Coolidge (1872–1933) provided political stability and conservative policies during the prosperous 1920s.

Born in Plymouth Notch, Vermont, Coolidge pursued a political career in Massachusetts. He was elected governor in 1918, and he handled the Boston police strike in a manner that gained him a place as the Republican vice presidential candidate in 1920. President Warren G. Harding's death in August 1923 elevated Coolidge to the White House.

In office the new president cut taxes and followed pro-business policies that pleased most middle-class, white Americans. He won a landslide election victory in 1924 in his own right. During the good economic times of the decade, Coolidge enjoyed great popularity. "Silent Cal" was known for his reticence and New England manner. In 1927 he announced that he would not seek another term in 1928. His wife's health and the tragic death of his son Calvin Jr. in 1924 diminished his interest in the presidency. The Great Depression of the 1930s cast a shadow over Coolidge's record, and he was faulted for failing to take steps to reduce risks to the overheated economy. Despite persuasive attempts to rehabilitate his presidency, presidential scholars continue to rank him as one of the least effective chief executives of the twentieth century.

LEWIS L. GOULD, UNIVERSITY OF TEXAS AT AUSTIN

BIBLIOGRAPHY

Ferrell, Robert H. The Presidency of Calvin Coolidge. Lawrence: University Press of Kansas, 1998.

McCoy, Donald R. *Calvin Coolidge: The Quiet President.* New York: Macmillan, 1967.

Murray, Robert K. *The Politics of Normalcy: Governmental Theory and Practice in the Harding-Coolidge Era.* New York: W. W. Norton, 1973.

COXEY'S ARMY

Coxey's Army, as it came to be called by the press, was one of a number of groups that during the depression year of 1894 made the first protest march on

Washington. During the panic of 1893 (1893–1895), Jacob Coxey launched a mass march, or "petition in boots," in the hopes of convincing Congress to adopt a "Good Roads Bill." According to Coxey and his supporters, the depression would end if legislators appropriated $500 million in inflationary paper money for the construction of national highways and mandated a minimum wage on that project of $1.50 for an eight-hour day.

To publicize his ideas, Coxey joined forces with cartoonist and promoter Carl Browne. Together, they organized unemployed workers into a mass march on Washington known as the Commonweal of Christ. Browne, a believer in theosophy, claimed that 100,000 individuals who shared large measures of Jesus Christ's soul would be drawn together during the march. When they arrived at the nation's capital on Easter Sunday, Coxey (the cerebrum of Christ) and Browne (the cerebellum of Christ) would have effectively brought the kingdom of heaven to earth and Congress would not be able to resist their will. Banners for the march proclaimed "Peace on Earth. Good will to men. He hath risen but death to interest on bonds."

Probably few marchers agreed with Browne's peculiar religious beliefs, but many of the protestors did agree with the movement's demand that the national government should take immediate and even drastic steps to end the suffering of the nearly 4 million unemployed. Some groups came from as far away as San Francisco, but instead of the 100,000 marchers that Browne and Coxey had hoped for, all the industrial armies marching on Washington that spring totaled about 10,000 men. Most of them organized along military lines, enlisting recruits in various towns along the march route and relying on local communities to donate food and water. The first group of 500 marchers arrived in Washington in May 1894, where they were disbanded by troops called out to defend the Capitol. The rest arrived over the following months and lived in shanty towns until it became clear that Congress would not hear their demands and they returned home.

Although Coxeyism failed in its immediate goals, it played a significant role in politics at the end of the nineteenth century. Aware of the public support that Coxey and his followers received throughout the march and the fact that the Commonweal of Christ had been able to do what other organizations had not—attract both industrial workers and farmers into its fold—the Populist Party incorporated several of the movement's demands, such as the eight-hour workday and currency inflation, into its platform.

See also *Civil Unrest and Rioting; Cleveland, Grover; Marches on Washington; Panic of 1893; Populist (People's) Party.*

LORI BOGLE, UNITED STATES NAVAL ACADEMY

BIBLIOGRAPHY

McMurry, Donald L. *Coxey's Army: A Study of the Industrial Army Movement of 1894.* Seattle: University of Washington Press, 1968.

Schwantes, Carlos A. *Coxey's Army: An American Odyssey.* Lincoln: University of Nebraska Press, 1985.

Vincent, Henry. *The Story of the Commonweal.* New York: Arno Press, 1969.

CRÉDIT MOBILIER SCANDAL

The Crédit Mobilier scandal, which broke in 1872, was one of many in post–Civil War America that proved immensely embarrassing to the Republican Party. The Democratic Party, however, was dirtied by its own scandals: Tammany Hall and the Tweed Ring. In an era of scandal, both parties were soiled.

Crédit Mobilier was a construction company organized in 1864 by promoters of the Union Pacific Railroad to divert to themselves huge sums of construction money, some of which was supplied by the federal government, during the building of the eastern part of the transcontinental railroad. Crédit Mobilier charged the Union Pacific $94 million for construction expenses that totaled no more than $44 million.

Late in the 1872 presidential campaign, the *New York Sun* exposed this as one of the largest political-financial scandals in U.S. history. The newspaper charged the sitting vice president, Schuyler Colfax; the vice presidential nominee, Henry Wilson; a future president, Rep. James A. Garfield (R-Ohio); and ten other prominent politicians of accepting Crédit Mobilier stock.

After the exposé in the *Sun,* House and Senate investigators found that managers had skimmed as much as $23 million during construction of the transcontinental railroad. Investigators also learned that in November 1867, while Congress was leaning toward investigating the Union Pacific–Crédit Mobilier combination, Rep. Oakes Ames (R-Mass.), who also headed Crédit Mobilier, distributed at least 160 shares of Crédit Mobilier stock among senators and representatives. The 1867 investigation never occurred.

The 1872 investigations resulted in the censure of Ames and Rep. James Brooks (D-N.Y.) and an expulsion recommendation for Sen. James W. Patterson (R-N.H.), who retired instead when his term expired on March 3, 1873. Although Colfax escaped impeachment because his alleged misconduct had occurred before he became vice president, the scandal ruined him politically. Others, like Garfield, who was elected president in 1880, would overcome any temporary tarnish.

See also *Grant, Ulysses S.; Scandals and Corruption.*

MARK J. CONNOLLY, DEVRY INSTITUTE OF TECHNOLOGY

BIBLIOGRAPHY

Crawford, Jay B. *Crédit Mobilier of America.* 1880. Reprint, New York: AMS Press, 1971.

CURRENCY AND MONEY SUPPLY

Currency includes notes and coins that are the current medium of exchange in a country and backed by the national government. For much of its history, the United States did not have a uniform national currency; instead, currencies were issued in individual states by state-chartered banks. This currency regime proved inadequate to accommodate the rapidly growing American economy. Currency management was not possible without a national banking system with uniform banking practices. Andrew Jackson's veto of a bill passed by Congress to renew the charter of the second Bank of the United States in 1832 left the country with essentially no central bank and ushered in troubled times for U.S. banking in which unsound banking practices flourished. It was not until passage of the National Currency Act of 1863, which was later amended and renamed the National Banking Act, that the United States had a uniform national currency and a national banking system.

DEMISE OF THE GOLD STANDARD

In order to finance the Civil War (1861–1865), the United States issued "greenbacks," so called because of the green coloring on one side of the bills. Greenbacks were different from the standard currency used at that time in that they were not redeemable for gold. Because so many greenbacks were needed to finance the war, they steadily lost value, dropping to half the value of standard money and gold coin of the same face value. After the war, greenbacks gained new life in the agriculture movement as farmers lobbied the government to increase the supply of greenbacks as a remedy for depressed prices for agricultural commodities.

The system created by the National Banking Act proved too inflexible to accommodate periods of growth and contraction. Efforts to reform the banking system led to the establishment in 1914 of the Federal Reserve System (the Fed). The Fed immediately fixed two major problems of the financial sector by regulating the volume of money and credit in the economy and by establishing a single paper currency, known as federal reserve notes, to replace the various currencies that had been issued by national banks.

Gold and some national currencies, such as the U.S. dollar, are also considered international reserve currencies because they are acceptable for the settlement of international debts. In the United States, paper currency was backed by gold until the Great Depression. Because of large outflows of gold, the United States could not remain on the gold standard, and in 1933 President Franklin D. Roosevelt removed the dollar from the gold standard. In 1971 President Richard M. Nixon further uncoupled the dollar from gold, and the United States no longer settled deficits in balance of payments in gold. Neither action spurred much political controversy because the moves were dictated by the powerful pressures of economic forces.

THE MONEY SUPPLY AND CONTROLLING INFLATION

The money supply is the total amount of currency and financial assets in the economy that can be quickly converted to goods and services. The Fed tracks the money supply by several measures, from the cash and coin in circulation and in checking deposits (which is called M1), to everything up to large, interest-bearing time deposits and money market mutual funds and euro dollars. The Fed has three policy instruments to regulate the money supply: open market operations (OMO), changing the discount rate, and changing the required reserve rate. Raising either of the two rates shrinks the money supply, because after a rate hike less borrowing generally takes place. OMO refers to the buying and selling of government securities. If the Fed wants to stimulate the economy by expanding the money supply, the Fed buys government securities, thus increasing the amount of cash in circulation. If

The manufacturing of U.S. currency   *Bureau of Engraving and Printing*

the Fed wants to reduce the money supply, it sells government securities, which takes cash out of circulation.

When an economy is in recession, the Fed increases the money supply to stimulate economic growth. When the economy is inflationary, the prescription is to slow the growth in the money supply, which will, in turn, reduce inflation. During the early 1980s, the Fed under the direction of Chairman Paul Volcker placed top priority on defeating inflation, which had been very high by U.S. standards since the 1970s. In fighting inflation, the Fed pursued a tight monetary policy that indeed drastically reduced inflation from 13.5 percent in 1980 to 3.2 percent by 1983. The cost, however, was high: a deep recession in which the gross domestic product shrank 1.9 percent from 1981 to 1982—the deepest recession since the Great Depression. Although its battle against inflation contributed to this recession, the Fed drew little criticism from the executive branch of government.

During the remainder of the 1980s and the 1990s, the U.S. economy experienced two long-term expansions, separated by a mild recession in 1990. Economists attributed much of the credit for the economic success to the Fed, by virtue of its careful management of the U.S. money supply. The removal of Federal Reserve policies from political pressures has allowed the Fed to pursue its best professional judgment in the management of one of the most important aspects of the economy.

See also *Bank War; Federal Reserve System; Jackson, Andrew; Panic of 1893.*

RICHARD J. CARROLL, INDEPENDENT SCHOLAR

BIBLIOGRAPHY

Bannock, Graham, R. E. Baxter, and Evans Davis. *The Penguin Dictionary of Economics.* New York: Penguin Books, 1992.

The Economist Guide to Global Economic Indicators. New York: John Wiley and Sons, 1994.

Governors of Federal Reserve System Board. *Federal Reserve System: Its Purposes and Functions.* New York: AMS Press, 1984.

Meulendyke, Ann-Marie. *U.S. Monetary Policy and Financial Markets.* New York: Federal Reserve Bank of New York, 1998.

Stein, Herbert, and Murray Foss. *An Illustrated Guide to the American Economy.* Washington, D.C.: American Enterprise Institute, 1995.

DECLARATION OF INDEPENDENCE

Adopted by a vote of the colony delegations in the Second Continental Congress on July 4, 1776, the Declaration of Independence inaugurated the existence of the United States of America as an independent nation. Congressional representatives had been exercising sovereign powers since the beginning of the Revolutionary War, fifteen months earlier, but had resisted mounting pressure from radicals to formalize the break with Great Britain because they feared alienating moderates who were particularly numerous in the middle colonies.

Popular sentiment for independence spread rapidly in the wake of pamphleteer Thomas Paine's attacks on royal authority and Britain's mixed constitution in his enormously successful *Common Sense* (1776); meanwhile, revolutionary leaders in the colonies sought leadership and legitimacy from Congress, which finally responded by calling for the formal constitution of new state governments (May 10). Some representatives urged the formation of a confederation, formalizing the ad hoc delegation of authority from the rebellious states and cementing their union, before declaring independence. But the critical need for a wartime alliance with France and other European powers dictated swift action that could not wait for protracted negotiations over Articles of Confederation (finally ratified in March 1781). Addressed to a "candid world," the Declaration of Independence was primarily a diplomatic document that reflected the revolutionaries' recognition that victory ultimately depended on manipulating the European balance of power. Beyond announcing the end of royal authority, it had no direct constitutional effect on the status of Congress itself.

ORIGINS AND PURPOSE

The move for independence was initiated on June 7 by delegate Richard Henry Lee, who submitted instructions from Virginia's revolutionary Convention resolving "that these United Colonies are, and of right ought to be, free and independent States." On June 11 Congress named a drafting committee, including Benjamin Franklin, John Adams, Roger Sherman, Robert R. Livingston, and Thomas Jefferson. Because of his reputation as a writer and because his colleagues were nearly overwhelmed by other assignments, Jefferson took on the role of chief author. His draft, with editorial changes suggested by the committee, was reported to Congress on June 28; the Virginia resolutions for independence were adopted on July 2, and the declaration itself was debated and amended from July 2 to 4.

The Declaration of Independence is now most famous for the eloquent discussion on social contract theory in its second paragraph:

> We hold these truths to be self-evident: that all men are created equal; that they are endowed by their creator with certain inalienable rights; that among these are life, liberty, and the pursuit of happiness: that to secure these rights, governments are instituted among men, deriving their just powers from the consent of the governed.

By the end of the paragraph, Jefferson had moved from the general premise of consent to its specific application as a "right" of revolution that Americans could justly invoke in the current circumstances. The burden of the rest of the document was therefore not to argue for its "self-evident" truths but rather to elaborate the "long train of abuses and usurpations" that revealed King George III's intention to establish "an absolute tyranny over these states." The resulting indictment constitutes a radical Whig history of the imperial crisis that focused obsessively on the supposedly illegitimate exercise of royal authority and virtually ignored the British Parliament's controversial claims to legislative authority over the colonies. By 1776 the crucial question was whether the Americans and their "British brethren" constituted a single people: Allegiance to a common sovereign was the only remaining bond of union. What was now clear was that George III had "abdicated" his authority in America "by declaring us out of his protection and waging war on us."

Thomas Jefferson's original four-page draft of what would become the Declaration of Independence is still preserved at the Library of Congress. *Library of Congress*

parently self-serving argument seriously. But Jefferson's diatribe illuminates the larger thrust of the declaration: to exorcise monarchical authority by revealing its malign designs against the liberty of Africans as well as Americans, while demonstrating to the world—and to Americans themselves—that they *were* a people, entitled by "the laws of nature and of nature's God" to determine their own national destiny.

CONCEPTION OF AMERICAN NATIONHOOD

The importance of the Declaration of Independence to emerging conceptions of American nationhood became apparent only as the ultimately successful prosecution of the war effort secured the new nation's independence. Jefferson's authorship became widely known only in the 1790s, when Republican opponents of Federalists in power sought to exalt their own and their leader's political pretensions. In 1776 Jefferson and his colleagues thought that the constitution of new republican governments in Virginia and throughout the Union would be the crucial and lasting achievement of the Revolution. The declaration's tedious recitation of George III's abuses against his American subjects was very much a tract for its own times, not for the ages. As the revolutionaries embraced the logic of Jefferson's indictment and became conscious of themselves as a people, the specific charges against the king ceased to be significant. They could then celebrate the declaration, and particularly its opening paragraphs, as "sacred scripture," the foundational document of their new regime.

Reformers who have sought more inclusive definitions of citizenship and nationhood have invoked the egalitarian language of the declaration throughout American history. Prominent early examples, pushing far beyond Jefferson's original intentions, included the "declarations" of the American Anti-Slavery Society (1833) and the Seneca Falls Convention (1848) advocating women's rights. The Declaration of Independence also became a touchstone for patriots who sought to sustain the nation in times of crisis. For Abraham Lincoln, its "definitions and axioms" constituted the basis of enduring union. Jefferson deserved "all honor," Lincoln asserted, for linking "a struggle for independence by a single people" with universal principles that appealed to peoples everywhere. The American founding had thus initiated a "new order for the ages." When, in the midst

Jefferson later insisted that Congress had mangled the logic and language of his draft. The most significant excision was a polemic against the "*Christian* king of Great Britain" for enslaving Africans and inflicting the institution of slavery on his America colonies. By fomenting slave revolts, George now sought to pay "off former crimes committed against the *liberties* of one people, with crimes which he urges them to commit against the *lives* of another." Jefferson's colleagues rightly doubted whether a "candid world" would take such a transof the Civil War, Lincoln called for a "new birth of freedom" in his famous Gettysburg Address (November 19, 1863), he returned yet again to the declaration: "Four score and seven years ago our fathers brought forth on this continent, a new nation, conceived in Liberty, and dedicated to the proposition that all men are created equal."

See also *American Revolution; Jefferson, Thomas; Lincoln, Abraham.*

PETER ONUF, UNIVERSITY OF VIRGINIA

BIBLIOGRAPHY

Fliegelman, Jay. *Declaring Independence: Jefferson, Natural Language, and the Culture of Performance.* Stanford: Stanford University Press, 1993.

Maier, Pauline. *American Scripture: Making the Declaration of Independence.* New York: Alfred A. Knopf, 1997.

McDonald, Robert M. S. *Jefferson & America: Episodes in Image Formation.* Ph.D. dissertation, University of North Carolina, 1998.

DEMOCRATIC PARTY

The Democratic Party is the oldest political organization in the United States. Indeed, a history of the party is in some ways a political history of the nation. In the first few years of the republic, political parties did not exist, although factions tied to issues and the personal ambitions of political leaders influenced elections and policies. The Democratic Party traces its roots to this factionalism, beginning with opposition to the Federalist policies of Alexander Hamilton in the first administration of George Washington.

ORIGINS OF THE DEMOCRATIC PARTY

Opposition to Federalist policies, organized by U.S. Rep. James Madison and Secretary of State Thomas Jefferson, first coalesced around Hamilton's proposal for a national bank, which Congress passed and Washington signed, over the strenuous objections of Jefferson and Madison. The two Virginians were more successful in preventing the adoption of Hamilton's larger plan for federal support for the development of American industry. The Federalists, led by Hamilton and John Adams, favored a strong central government and a flexible interpretation of the Constitution. Key to their program was a national bank, which would facilitate economic growth and strengthen national and international commerce.

Jefferson's Democratic-Republicans advocated "strict construction" of the Constitution and opposed a national bank. Moreover, they favored friendly relations with France, while the Federalists sought to forge friendly diplomatic and commercial relations with England. Both parties had supporters throughout the country, but the Democratic-Republicans were strongest in the South and among slaveowners, and the Federalists were strongest in New England and among men with commercial and manufacturing interests. From the 1790s until the late 1820s various terms—Democratic-Republicans, Jeffersonian Republicans, Jeffersonian Democrats, and National Republicans—were applied to the people and leaders who, opposed to the Federalists, gradually became known as Democrats.

The Democratic-Republicans grew stronger as the Federalists began to fade during the presidency of John Adams. A new alliance of agrarian southerners and urban northerners helped Jefferson defeat Adams in 1800 and win reelection in 1804. After Jefferson the presidency went to his friends and allies, James Madison (1809–1817) and James Monroe (1817–1825). By 1820 the Federalist Party had all but disappeared, and James Monroe won reelection with no opposition.

Indicative of the change in the party of Jefferson was its attitude toward the Bank of the United States. In 1791 Jefferson and Madison had vigorously opposed the creation of this bank, arguing that establishment of such a bank was unconstitutional. We might date the development of the Democratic Party from that debate over the bank. In 1811 the bank's twenty-year charter expired, and the Democrats who controlled Congress and the presidency did not renew it. By 1816, however, Madison supported the creation of a new bank and renounced his former public policy and constitutional opposition to it. Congress, controlled by Democrats, passed the bill.

The inherent instability of one-party politics became clear in 1824, as four candidates—Andrew Jackson, John Quincy Adams, William Crawford, and Henry Clay, all claiming to represent the Jeffersonian tradition—ran for president. No candidate received a majority of popular or electoral votes, and the House of Representatives chose John Quincy Adams, although Andrew Jackson had received more popular votes and more electoral votes. After 1824 the old Jeffersonian party unraveled. Adams had broken with the Federalist Party during the War of 1812 and had served as Monroe's secretary of state, but he was never a true "Jeffersonian." By the end of his administration in 1829 he and supporters like Henry Clay emerged as members of a faction that eventually became the Whig Party.

THE JACKSON LEGACY

War of 1812 hero Andrew Jackson defeated John Quincy Adams in 1828 and became the first president to represent the "Democratic Party." The party has maintained that name ever since, although it was often divided over issues such as slavery, economic policy, and national unity in the nineteenth century and foreign policy, civil rights, and economic policy in the twentieth.

Jackson, nominated in 1828 by the Tennessee legislature, led the Democrats into adopting a nominating convention as the method for choosing the party's future standard-bearers. The Democrats held their first national convention at Baltimore, Maryland, in 1832, eight months after the Anti-Masons held the first such convention, also in Baltimore. The 1832 Democratic convention adopted two rules that lasted more than a century. The two-thirds rule, requiring a two-thirds majority for nomination, led to numerous floor fights over the choosing of a Democratic presidential candidate. The unit rule allowed convention delegations to override minority objections within the delegation and to vote as a whole for one candidate or position.

From Jackson's election in 1828 through the end of James Buchanan's term in 1861, the Democrats dominated national politics. In this period the Democrats opposed any national bank, high tariffs, internal improvements, and even a uniform bankruptcy law. High points of Jackson's presidency included his veto of bills to support internal improvements and to extend the charter of the Second Bank of the United States. Jackson and other Democrats in this period vigorously supported territorial expansion through Indian removal, the annexation of Texas, and ultimately the Mexican-American War. Their support for territorial gains followed Jefferson's expansionist policies that led to the peaceful acquisition of Louisiana from France in 1803. Most Democrats, and almost all party leaders, supported the demands of the South between 1828 and 1861 on issues involving slavery. Meanwhile, Jackson's opponents—led by Henry Clay, Daniel Webster, and William Henry Harrison—formed the Whig Party. The Whigs—who favored higher tariffs, a national bank, federally funded internal improvements, and a weak presidency—provided the main opposition to the Democrats until the emergence of the Republican Party in 1854.

Jackson's election ushered in an era known as "Jacksonian Democracy," which stressed political equality—for white men. Jacksonians throughout the country made war on black voters, taking away their voting rights in Pennsylvania, New Jersey, Tennessee, and North Carolina and opposing their voting rights elsewhere. Jackson himself led the movement to force Native Americans out of the states east of the Mississippi River.

Jefferson, already considered the "father" of the Democratic Party, had been the first president to remove officeholders, to replace them with his supporters. Jackson renewed this policy through the "spoils system," a term that stemmed from the phrase "to the victors go the spoils." As the party in power during most of the period 1829–1861, the Democrats controlled the growing bureaucracy and rewarded many supporters with patronage jobs.

Jackson's legacy was a Democratic Party that endured into the twenty-first century. Dominating national politics during the first half of the nineteenth century, the Democrats lost the presidential election only twice (in 1840 and 1848) between 1800 and 1856. From Jackson's inauguration in 1829 until the year 2001, the Democrats controlled the House of Representatives for fifty-five two-year sessions and the Senate for forty-six sessions; the Whigs or Republicans controlled the House for thirty-two sessions and the Senate for forty-one sessions.

Despite their long-term success, the Democrats barely survived their severest test, over slavery and secession. In 1846 northern Democrats supported the Wilmot Proviso, introduced in the House by Pennsylvania Democrat David Wilmot. The proviso would have prohibited slavery in any territory acquired during the Mexican-American War. Southern Democrats uniformly opposed the proviso. In 1848 many antislavery Democrats from New York, Pennsylvania, and New England voted for former president Martin Van Buren, who was running on the Free Soil Party ticket. These defections led to the election of the Whig candidate, Zachary Taylor. The Democrats regained the presidency in 1852, but slavery soon splintered the party. In 1856 Democrat Franklin Pierce became the first elected president denied renomination by his own party. He had alienated fellow northerners by signing legislation that allowed slavery into Kansas Territory, which in turn led it to become a battleground between pro- and antislavery forces. Another northerner, James Buchanan, won the nomination but also became a one-term president. By 1860 many northern Democrats, among them Sens. Salmon P. Chase of Ohio and Hannibal Hamlin of Maine, had joined the new Republican Party.

At the 1860 convention in Charleston, South Carolina, northern and southern Democrats were divided over how much support to give slavery in the territories. Northerners, backing Stephen A. Douglas of Illinois, favored opening all territories to slavery under a system of popular sovereignty, in which settlers would decide for themselves whether to permit slavery. Most of the southerners bolted after the defeat of platform planks endorsing a federal slave code for the territories and guaranteeing the right of slaveowners to carry their human property into all federal territories. The northern delegates nominated Douglas for president. The southern Democrats nominated John C. Breckinridge of Kentucky for president. Even had the Democrats remained united, it is doubtful they could have prevented the Republican candidate, Abraham Lincoln, from winning an electoral majority, as he swept every free state but New Jersey, which he split with

Douglas. The split in the Democratic Party presaged the more important split in the nation, which occurred with the secession of eleven southern states in 1860–1861.

DECLINE AND RESURGENCE

During the Civil War, northern Democrats remained divided. War Democrats generally supported the war effort and Lincoln's initial goal of bringing the South back into the Union, although they objected to Lincoln's emancipation policies and after 1863 were far less enthusiastic about the war or its goals. Throughout the war, by contrast, the Copperhead faction opposed the war effort and sought peace negotiations with the Confederacy.

Democrats came back together after the Civil War, but their commitment to white supremacy and their image of disloyalty both continued. During Reconstruction, Democrats opposed civil rights laws and the Fourteenth and Fifteenth Amendments, which were designed to establish black citizenship, recognize blacks' civil rights, and guarantee black voting rights. As late as the 1880s, the Democrats were termed the party of "rum, romanism, and rebellion," because of the party's opposition to temperance laws, its support among Irish Catholics, and the fact that much of its support came from former Confederates.

In 1876 the Democratic governor of New York, Samuel J. Tilden, won the popular vote against Republican Rutherford B. Hayes, but Tilden lost the election when a congressional compromise awarded Hayes all the disputed electoral votes of three southern states. Election fraud, intimidation, and outright violence by white southern Democrats prevented thousands of blacks from voting. Had the election been run fairly, it is likely that Hayes would have won outright. As part of the compromise that brought Hayes to the White House, the new president promised to remove federal troops from the South, effectively ending Reconstruction. Their removal led to a gradual disfranchisement of blacks in the South, which soon became solidly Democratic and would remain largely so until the presidential election of 1964. Despite a virtual lock on all southern electoral votes, the Democrats captured the presidency only twice between 1860 and 1912; Grover Cleveland won in 1884 and 1892.

By the late nineteenth century the Democratic Party's policies had changed somewhat from the antebellum period. Still a "white man's party," it was hostile to African Americans' civil rights and to Chinese immigration. With slavery ended, however, the party had dropped its aggressive expansionism of the earlier period. Cleveland refused to annex Hawaii, and some Democrats opposed the Spanish-American War in 1898. Democrats remained hostile to high tariffs, but they split on the issue of an expansive monetary policy; western Democrats favored the free coinage of silver, and eastern Democrats, among them Cleveland, opposed it. Most southern whites gave their allegiance to the Democrats, but in the North by the 1890s, and especially following the 1893 depression, economic and cultural issues outweighed memories of Civil War enmity in voter choices between the two major parties.

The GOP continued to dominate presidential politics for twelve years into the twentieth century. In 1912 the Republicans split when former president Theodore Roosevelt failed in his attempt to gain his party's nomination over the incumbent, William Howard Taft. Roosevelt ran anyway, on the Progressive—or Bull Moose—ticket, winning six states and 4.1 million votes. Roosevelt came in second, and Taft a dis-

By 1874 the donkey and the elephant had emerged as symbols of the Democratic and Republican Parties, respectively, based on these editorial cartoons by Thomas Nast. *Library of Congress*

tant third, but Taft and Roosevelt combined for 1.3 million more popular votes than the Democrat, Woodrow Wilson. Had the Republicans been united, their candidate—either Roosevelt or Taft—would have won. But divided they enabled Wilson to carry forty states and the election, ending the Democrats' long presidential drought. Wilson demonstrated the Democrats' hostility to civil rights and racial equality, as he ordered the segregation of all federal facilities in Washington, D.C. He was a progressive reformer on many issues, however, and brought such innovations as the Federal Reserve System, in contrast to historic Democratic hostility to federal government intervention in the economy.

Wilson also led the Democrats away from their historic position on foreign policy. Before the Civil War, the Democrats, in part spurred by the demands of the South for more territory for slavery, had pursued an aggressive policy of land acquisition, ultimately leading to war with Mexico. Pre–Civil War Democrats had had little interest in international affairs beyond the Western Hemisphere, however. In 1917, by contrast, Wilson successfully asked Congress for a declaration of war, and he continued his internationalist policies after the end of World War I, as he vainly attempted to bring the United States into the League of Nations. For the next half-century the Democratic Party stood for intervention and international responsibility, while the Republicans retreated into a large measure of diplomatic isolationism.

After World War I the Republicans took back the White House in 1920, kept it in 1924, and won again with Herbert Hoover's 1928 victory over Democrat Alfred E. Smith, the first Roman Catholic presidential nominee. After the stock market crashed in 1929, however, the Great Depression paved the way for a new Democratic dominance in the White House and an even longer one in Congress.

NEW DEAL TO GREAT SOCIETY

The election of Franklin D. Roosevelt in 1932 made a dramatic and lasting change in American politics. Democrats sang "happy days are here again" as they became the majority party and rallied behind FDR's bold New Deal programs. Democrats, long the party of states' rights and localism, became identified with national initiatives on economic and social issues. During the New Deal, rural electrification brought light and heat to much of the nation; a range of programs helped the poor and the unemployed; the nation's labor policy went through a sea change with the Wagner Labor Relations Act; and massive public works programs, such as the Tennessee Valley Authority, not only created jobs but constructed public buildings, roads, and dams. Once a party opposed to regulation, the Democrats helped create the regulatory state. Social programs, most notably Social Security, set

the stage for the modern industrial state that provides a social safety net for citizens.

At Roosevelt's urging, the 1936 Democratic convention abolished the controversial two-thirds rule, which in effect had long given the South a veto in choosing the national party ticket. Southern delegates agreed to a compromise, basing the size of future delegations on a state's Democratic voting strength instead of population size.

During the Roosevelt years and after, for the first time in its history, the Democratic Party welcomed black support and even supported some civil rights legislation, and President Roosevelt and his successor, Harry S. Truman, issued executive orders to combat some types of racial segregation and other discrimination. The "New Deal coalition"—northern blacks, southern whites, farmers, labor unionists, intellectuals, and ethnic urban voters—kept Roosevelt and Truman in office for twenty consecutive years, ending in 1953.

As Europe moved toward war in the 1930s and then fought in World War II, Roosevelt pushed an international agenda, building on Wilson's legacy. Here Roosevelt had the support of southern Democrats, who opposed some of his domestic agenda. Opposition came from Republican isolationists, but, unlike Wilson, FDR was able to bring the nation along with him, and thus the United States took the lead in establishing the United Nations. Truman continued this internationalist policy, first with the Marshall Plan to help Europe recover from World War II and then with the development of NATO and other international defense pacts. In 1950 Truman pushed for UN intervention when North Korea attacked South Korea, and soon the United States was heavily involved in another war in Asia.

In domestic politics, Truman pushed an activist agenda that he called the "Fair Deal" and called for expanded enforcement of African Americans' civil rights. Running for another term in 1948, he confronted schisms within his party from two quarters: the South and the left. Displeased with Truman's civil rights plank, conservative southerners bolted the Democratic Party in 1948 and ran J. Strom Thurmond of South Carolina as the States' Rights Democratic (Dixiecrats) nominee. Under the Progressive Party banner, Henry A. Wallace also challenged Truman. Thurmond won four states; Wallace took none. Despite the split, Truman defeated Republican Thomas E. Dewey.

After Truman left office in 1953, a Republican, Dwight D. Eisenhower, served the next two terms, but then the Democrats took back the White House in 1960, as John F. Kennedy, the first Roman Catholic president, narrowly defeated Eisenhower's vice president, Richard Nixon. Kennedy's slogan, "A New Frontier," mirrored traditional Democratic slogans, such as Wilson's "New Freedom," FDR's

"New Deal," and Truman's "Fair Deal." Kennedy continued the Democratic agenda of internationalism, with the Peace Corps and aid to the pro-Western regime in South Vietnam, and of federal support for domestic improvements, with a massive tax cut and federal programs in housing. Kennedy made tentative moves toward an expanded role for the national government in civil rights, but he moved cautiously because of the power of southern whites within his party.

After Kennedy's assassination in 1963, President Lyndon B. Johnson completed much of Kennedy's "New Frontier" agenda and called for additional programs in pursuit of the "Great Society," including a civil rights program that was termed by some a "Second Reconstruction." Applying all the skills he had learned as Senate majority leader, Johnson pushed through the Civil Rights Act of 1964. Johnson's support for civil rights ended the "solid South" as a Democratic stronghold. In 1964 Johnson won in a landslide. Carrying all but five states, he took 61.1 percent of the popular vote, the largest popular victory in any presidential election in U.S. history. The Deep South, however, supported Republican Barry Goldwater, who had opposed the Civil Rights Act of 1964 and had flirted with the ultra-right John Birch Society and segregationist White Citizens' Councils. Johnson's mandate enabled him to win passage of the Voting Rights Act of 1965, further solidifying Democratic support among African Americans while further undermining Democratic power among white southerners.

Johnson expanded U.S. involvement in an increasingly unpopular war in Vietnam, thereby splitting the party and prompting his decision against running for reelection in 1968. Two antiwar candidates, Sen. Robert F. Kennedy of New York, brother of the slain president, and Sen. Eugene McCarthy of Minnesota, dueled for the nomination in primaries across the nation. But Kennedy was assassinated the night he won the California primary, and McCarthy was outmaneuvered by party insiders. The Democratic convention that year, held in Chicago, was marred by police violence against antiwar demonstrators. Hubert H. Humphrey, nominated without entering any primaries, also faced competition in November from the American Independent candidacy of George C. Wallace, former Democratic governor of Alabama. All these divisive factors contributed to Humphrey's narrow defeat by Republican Richard Nixon.

THE DEMOCRATIC PARTY SINCE 1968

Still chafing from the dissension and bossism at the 1968 convention and the subsequent loss to Nixon, the Democrats in the 1970s drastically reformed their delegate-selection and nominating rules, encouraging minority representation, dividing delegations equally between men and women, and awarding delegates to candidates in proportion to their primary votes. The party's 1972 candidate, George S. McGovern, led many of the reforms, most of which took effect in 1980. The changes enhanced the role of primaries in the nominating process, leading to more primaries and fewer state caucuses.

The 1972 election was the last privately financed presidential election. Nixon raised $61.4 million versus McGovern's $21.2 million. McGovern, running as a peace candidate with a commitment to massive domestic spending, lost to Nixon in a landslide. The election-related Watergate scandal, however, drove Nixon from office two years later and brought Vice President Gerald R. Ford to the presidency. Evidence from the Watergate investigation showed that Nixon's operatives had used "dirty tricks" in the Democratic primaries to sabotage the candidacy of Edmund S. Muskie, who might have been a more formidable candidate than McGovern.

Skillful use of the primaries, as well as Ford's unpopular full pardon of President Nixon for his criminal activities in the Watergate cover-up, helped the relatively unknown Jimmy Carter of Georgia defeat incumbent Ford in 1976. Carter's primary strategy also served him in 1980, staving off a renomination challenge from Sen. Edward M. Kennedy, brother of the late president. But Carter's inability to curb inflation or obtain the release of American hostages held in Iran for 444 days doomed him to a one-term presidency and to defeat at the hands of Republican Ronald Reagan.

Although the popular Reagan handily won reelection in 1984, his vice president and successor, George Bush, fell victim in 1992 to Bill Clinton of Arkansas, as Democrats returned to the White House after twelve Republican years. As a presidential candidate Clinton addressed economic worries. His advisers reminded campaign workers, "It's the economy, stupid," and the strategy worked. He was the first Democrat to win without taking Texas and, with Al Gore of Tennessee as his running mate, the first president elected on an all-South ticket since 1828.

Clinton won as a moderate, declaring that "the era of big government is over." Behind him was a modified New Deal coalition that included "Reagan Democrats," union members, women, African Americans, Hispanics, Jews, a majority of Roman Catholics, public sector employees, and intellectuals. In one of his first acts he instituted a "don't ask, don't tell" policy toward homosexuals in the military. Although Clinton's convention call for a "New Covenant with the American People" never caught on as a slogan, and although he and Hillary Rodham Clinton failed in an abortive attempt to reform the nation's health system, peace and an improved economy soon had the Democratic administration basking in high approval ratings in public opinion polls. Nevertheless, the voters in 1994 broke the Democratic lock on Congress, turning both chambers over to Republican control.

Two years later the electorate opted to continue a divided government, giving Clinton another four-year term in 1996 while leaving Congress in GOP hands. Although he was the first Democrat elected to a second full term since Franklin Roosevelt, Clinton again won with less than a majority of the popular vote. Clinton's victories erased any doubts that the Democrats' once-solid South had become a Republican bastion. Of the eleven states of the Old Confederacy, the Clinton-Gore ticket won four in 1992 and four in 1996.

Democrats made history on various fronts from 1960 through the end of the century. In 1960 the party ran the nation's first successful Catholic presidential candidate, John F. Kennedy. In 1968 New York voters elected Democrat Shirley Chisholm as the first black woman member of the U.S. House, and in 1992 another Democrat, Carol Moseley-Braun of Illinois, became the first black woman U.S. senator. When former vice president Walter F. Mondale chose Geraldine A. Ferraro as his running mate against Reagan in 1984, she became the first woman in U.S. history to run on a major-party ticket. In 1989 L. Douglas Wilder of Virginia became the first African American to be elected state governor. In 2000 the Democratic nominee for president, Vice President Albert Gore, chose Sen. Joseph Lieberman as his running mate. This was the first time a Jew was on a national ticket. Also in 2000, Hillary Rodham Clinton became the first presidential wife to seek a major elective office, a U.S. Senate seat from New York, which she won.

See also *African American Politics; Breckinridge Democrats; Civil Rights Movement; Civil War; Clinton, Bill; Compromise of 1877; Dixiecrats (States' Rights Party); Great Society; Indian Policy; Jacksonian Democracy; Jefferson, Thomas; Kansas-Nebraska Act; Labor Politics and Policy; Madison, James; New Deal; New Frontier; Political Parties; Republican Party; Slavery; Tariff History; Wilson, Woodrow.*

PAUL FINKELMAN, UNIVERSITY OF TULSA COLLEGE OF LAW,

AND JOHN MOORE, INDEPENDENT AUTHOR

BIBLIOGRAPHY

Flanigan, William H., and Nancy H. Zingale. *Political Behavior of the American Electorate.* 9th ed. Washington, D.C.: CQ Press, 1998.

Havel, James T. *U.S. Presidential Candidates and the Elections: A Biographical and Historical Guide.* 2 vols. New York: Macmillan Library Reference USA, 1996.

Israel, Fred L. *Student's Atlas of American Presidential Elections, 1789 to 1996.* Washington, D.C.: Congressional Quarterly, 1997.

Maisel, L. Sandy, ed. *Political Parties and Elections in the United States: An Encyclopedia.* 2 vols. New York: Garland Publishing, 1991.

Rutland, Robert A. *The Democrats, from Jefferson to Carter.* Baton Rouge: Louisiana State University Press, 1979.

DIXIECRATS (STATES' RIGHTS PARTY)

The Dixiecrats (derived from Democrats from Dixie), a third party that originated in the Deep South in reaction to civil rights initiatives at the national level, ran its own candidates in opposition to incumbent President Harry S. Truman in the 1948 election.

The Democratic Party shielded from federal interference traditional southern ways on racial matters from the 1870s into the 1930s, but by the 1940s it no longer provided a reliable defense against federal initiatives on segregation and disfranchisement. Many southern Democrats grew restive as the national Democratic Party adopted positions and enacted programs that threatened to undermine their traditional political control and policy agenda. President Truman's initiatives on civil rights and the proposals that his Committee on Civil Rights made in 1947 threatened white supremacy across the South, particularly the Deep South. Moreover, President Franklin D. Roosevelt's New Deal, especially the 1935 Wagner Labor Relations Act, augured greater power for industrial workers in labor relations.

Prominent Democrats from the Deep South—among them Frank M. Dixon of Alabama, James O. Eastland of Mississippi, and Leander Perez of Louisiana—led a growing protest against the national party, culminating in a Dixiecrat convention in Birmingham, Alabama, in July 1948. The catalyst was the adoption by the Democrats, in their convention in Philadelphia earlier that month, of a stronger civil rights plank than the 1944 platform had contained. Many delegates from Mississippi and Alabama withdrew from the Philadelphia convention; others supported the candidacy of Richard B. Russell of Georgia.

For the presidency, the Birmingham convention nominated Gov. Strom Thurmond of South Carolina, the state with the largest percentage of blacks in its population; as his running mate it selected Gov. Fielding Wright of Mississippi, the state with the second highest percentage of blacks. The Dixiecrats, or States' Rights Party, hoped to prevent Truman's victory in the 1948 balloting. Either Truman would lose, and national Democrats would learn that they could not take the Deep South for granted, or the Dixiecrats would throw a close election into the U.S. House of Representatives, where they could negotiate a settlement favorable to the continuance of segregation. Truman, however, won without Dixiecrat support. The Dixiecrats took only four states, each with a large black population but an overwhelmingly white electorate: Mississippi, South Carolina, Alabama, and Louisiana.

In all four, the state Democratic Party had presented the Thurmond–Wright ticket as the party's official nominees.

Not all Democrats from the Deep South supported the Dixiecrats. Sen. John Sparkman of Alabama, for example, campaigned for the national ticket in 1948; four years later, he gained the Democratic nomination for the vice presidency. Many defectors moved back into the Democratic Party in 1952, but many others used the Dixiecrat interlude as a way station on the road to the Republican Party, at least in presidential campaigns. Thurmond himself later became a Republican.

Like many third parties, the Dixiecrats arose because of a locally salient issue and lasted only a short time. More than most, the party foreshadowed an electoral realignment, as southern whites, in very large numbers over the next quarter-century, abandoned the Democratic Party.

See also *Civil Rights Movement; Democratic Party; Labor Politics and Policy; New Deal; Republican Party; Truman, Harry S.*

PETER WALLENSTEIN,
VIRGINIA POLYTECHNIC INSTITUTE AND STATE UNIVERSITY

BIBLIOGRAPHY

Bartley, Numan V. *The New South, 1945–1980.* Baton Rouge: Louisiana State University Press, 1995.

Cohodas, Nadine. *Strom Thurmond and the Politics of Southern Change.* New York: Simon and Schuster, 1993.

Garson, Robert A. *The Democratic Party and the Politics of Sectionalism, 1941–1948.* Baton Rouge: Louisiana State University Press, 1974.

Key, V. O. Jr. *Southern Politics in State and Nation.* New York: Knopf, 1949.

EATON AFFAIR

The Eaton affair, a controversy during the first two years of Andrew Jackson's presidency (1829–1837), had a profound effect on politics and gender relations at the time. Margaret Eaton, known as Peggy among her detractors, was the daughter of Washington innkeepers. She was a beautiful young woman and very outspoken, and rumors began that she was sexually promiscuous. Her marriage to John B. Timberlake, a navy purser, did not end the gossip, and when Timberlake committed suicide at sea in April 1828, stories circulated that it was the result of her illicit relationship with Democratic-Republican senator John Henry Eaton from Tennessee.

With the blessing of his good friend Jackson, John Eaton married the widow Timberlake in January 1829. After Jackson's inauguration in March 1829, Jackson named John Eaton secretary of war, making his bride a cabinet wife and shocking "proper" Washington society. Women at the time were expected to be the arbiters of morality, and the women of Washington society shunned Margaret Eaton as a result of her reputation.

Jackson was outraged by the treatment Margaret Eaton suffered. His own wife Rachel had died on Christmas Eve 1828, the result, he believed, of the personal attacks of his political opponents. Jackson became convinced that such name-calling about Eaton was another attempt to destroy him and his presidency.

The dispute escalated into a major political battle. Jackson and Secretary of State Martin Van Buren, a widower, and John Barry, postmaster general and head of a family Eaton had befriended, were on one side. Vice President John C. Calhoun and the rest of the cabinet were on the other. The controversy came to represent all the differences between the supporters of Jackson and Van Buren and those of Calhoun, including Calhoun's castigation of Jackson's aggressive activities during the Seminole War and the nullification controversy. In the spring of 1831, Van Buren and John Eaton resigned in an effort to force the other cabinet members out and allow Jackson to find a new set of advisers. This cabinet dissolution established the precedent that the president, not the Senate, controlled the cabinet. When Jackson tried to reward Van Buren for his loyalty, Calhoun cast the deciding Senate vote that kept Van Buren from the office of minister to Great Britain. The pettiness actually aided Van Buren's political advancement.

The Eaton Affair was a major reason why Van Buren replaced Calhoun as vice president for Jackson's second term in office. Calhoun and Jackson never made up their differences, and Van Buren was elected president in 1836. Van Buren later recalled John Eaton from his diplomatic post in Spain, and in response Eaton changed parties and became a Whig. On return from Europe, Margaret Eaton was eventually accepted into Washington society, but when she was an old woman—years after John Eaton died—a young Italian dance instructor married her, stole her money, and ran away with one of her granddaughters. By then few knew of her, and she died penniless and alone. She is buried next to John Eaton in an unmarked grave in Washington, D.C.

See also *Calhoun, John C.; Jackson, Andrew; Seminole War; Van Buren, Martin.*

JOHN F. MARSZALEK, MISSISSIPPI STATE UNIVERSITY

BIBLIOGRAPHY

Latner, Richard B. "The Eaton Affair Reconsidered." *Tennessee Historical Quarterly* 36 (winter 1977): 330–351.

Marszalek, John F. *The Petticoat Affair: Manners, Mutiny and Sex in Andrew Jackson's White House.* New York: Free Press, 1997.

———. "The Eaton Affair: Society and Politics." *Tennessee Historical Quarterly* 55 (spring 1996): 6–19.

Wood, Kristene. " 'One Woman So Dangerous to Public Morals': Gender and Power in the Eaton Affair." *Journal of the Early Republic* 17 (summer 1997): 237–275.

ECONOMIC SANCTIONS

Economic sanctions are financial or trade penalties that a nation or nations impose against another. Sanctions can include increasing tariffs against or banning all imports from the sanctioned country, prohibiting exports or supplies to the sanctioned country, decreasing aid, freezing assets, denying most-favored-nation trading status, and prohibiting investment or credit either to or from the country. Sanctions are applied either unilaterally, that is, only one nation imposing the sanction, or multilaterally, that is, many nations imposing the sanction.

Sanctions are usually triggered by offenses such as human rights violations (South Africa in the 1980s, Serbia in the 1990s), aggression (Iraq against Kuwait in 1990), noncompliance with an armistice agreement (Iraq in the mid-1990s), environmental transgressions (such as not adhering to the ivory ban or ban on imports of products from any endangered species). Sanctions are also applied to force compliance with treaty provisions. Trade agreements, such as the North American Free Trade Agreement (NAFTA), which came into effect in 1994, and the General Agreement on Tariffs and Trade (GATT), which came into effect in 1995, require that sanctions be imposed against countries that break the rules.

Sanctions are often applied as much as a political response to express outrage with actions by an offending country as they are to accomplish the goal of behavior modification. Leaders are often under political pressure to respond when a country misbehaves, and economic sanctions provide a vehicle. The major stakeholders in sanctions policies are businesses and labor. Although it depends on the sanction, businesses usually oppose sanctions for fear of losing markets in the sanctioned country or of retaliation against American goods. Labor might oppose sanctions on the same grounds or support sanctions when they prohibit imports from competing firms in the sanctioned country. Economists who advocate free trade are quick to point out the costs of sanctions, whereas human rights advocates emphasize the need to use sanctions as a way to take a moral stand against violations of human rights.

Sanctions have a mixed record of success. Historically, sanctions have often been imposed under conditions that undermine their effectiveness. Sanctions largely failed when they were levied in the 1970s and 1980s against the Soviet Union, Cuba, Iran, Vietnam, and China. Sanctions had mixed success in South Africa (during apartheid), Iraq after the Persian Gulf War, and Haiti in the early 1990s.

Unilateral sanctions tend to be weak because the sanctioned country can circumvent the sanctions by doing business with another country. Sanctions also tend to lose their

U.S. Navy personnel peer into one of the scuttles of an Iranian cargo ship. Crew members of the USS *John S. McCain* boarded the ship in the Persian Gulf on March 6, 1998, to inspect for possible contraband. *Department of Defense photo by Petty Officer 2nd Class Gloria J. Barry, U.S. Navy*

power over time when the sanctioned country can adapt to the sanctions. Still, sanctions are difficult to remove if the objective has not been accomplished, as in the case of Cuba, which by 2000 had been under U.S. sanctions for nearly forty years. Sanctions may also have long-term negative consequences for the sanctioning country. For example, when the Organization of Petroleum Exporting Countries (OPEC) imposed its oil embargo against the United States in 1973, the United States was damaged in the short run and even suffered a serious recession (though there were additional causes). Over time, the United States developed greater fuel efficiency and OPEC lost most of its power.

Sanctions may also invite retaliation, especially when two parties have equal power. In 1980 President Jimmy Carter forced a boycott of the Summer Olympics in Moscow against the Soviet Union (for its invasion of Afghanistan). Four years later the Soviet Union retaliated by boycotting the 1984 Summer Olympics in Los Angeles.

Sanctions are more effective when the sanctioned country has just suffered a military defeat, the sanctions are multilateral, the target country is weak, the target country has a lot to lose (such as an export market), the costs to the sanctioning country are minor, or the goal is minor (such as the release of hostages or political prisoners). Economic sanctions are effective when the benefits outweigh the costs and when sanctions and their effects are evaluated on a continuing basis, in both the sanctioned and sanctioning countries, to determine whether benefits still exceed costs.

See also *Embargo; Iran-Contra Scandal; Persian Gulf War; Tariff History; Treaties, Commercial.*

RICHARD J. CARROLL, INDEPENDENT SCHOLAR

BIBLIOGRAPHY

Buchholz, Todd G. *From Here to Economy.* New York: Plume, 1995.
Haass, Richard N. *Economic Sanctions: Too Much of a Bad Thing.* Brookings Policy Brief 34. Washington, D.C.: Brookings Institution, June 1998.
Smolowe, Jill. "Haiti: Shadow Play." *Time,* May 23, 1994.

EISENHOWER, DWIGHT D.

As soldier, political leader, and international statesperson, Dwight David Eisenhower (1890–1969) helped shape the world of the mid-twentieth century. The thirty-fourth president of the United States (1953–1961) was born in Denison, Texas. Soon after, his parents settled in Abilene, Kansas, a small agricultural community. Originally named David Dwight after his father—and called "Dwight" to avoid confusion—Eisenhower had a relatively unremarkable childhood. A 1915 graduate of West Point (where he inadvertently but permanently reversed his first and middle names), Eisenhower spent most of his adult life in the U.S. Army, and as a soldier he acquired most of his professional experiences and ideas about organization, planning, and priorities.

During World War I Eisenhower learned to work with citizen soldiers at his first command, a post near Gettysburg, Pennsylvania. He became known in the Army for his skills at writing speeches and reports as well as for his abilities as a leader. Eisenhower spent a number of years learning about federal-level politics in Washington, D.C., as a subordinate in various capacities under the brilliant Gen. Douglas MacArthur.

THE WARRIOR

In the 1920s and 1930s the possibility of another global conflict concerned thoughtful military people who, like Eisenhower, had witnessed the tremendous advances in military technology during World War I. Together with fellow junior officer George S. Patton, Eisenhower helped develop techniques of using tanks and waging armored warfare. He also worked to keep up with the rapid changes taking place in military aviation. At the age of forty-eight he became a licensed pilot. As war approached, he quickly rose within the Army hierarchy. Following the Japanese attack on Pearl Harbor on December 7, 1941, Army Chief of Staff George C. Marshall called him to Washington to direct the course of

Gen. Dwight D. Eisenhower confers with British prime minister Winston Churchill. *Library of Congress*

strategic planning. Within a year Eisenhower was in command of the major American effort in Europe.

Eisenhower's first overseas posting was to London, where he quickly gained the respect and affection of the British. They realized that Eisenhower was sincere in his determination to transcend nationalistic considerations and that he would respect their interests. Throughout the war he was able to deal effectively with such strong-minded leaders as Field Marshal Bernard Montgomery and Prime Minister Winston Churchill. The leaders of the United Kingdom willingly placed their forces under Eisenhower's command, and their confidence in his ability was rewarded with coalition victories over the Italians and Germans in North Africa, the Mediterranean, and finally in northwest Europe. His greatest triumph came when he successfully oversaw the Allied landings at Normandy on D-Day, June 6, 1944.

Eisenhower's World War II service demonstrated that his skills were more than purely military; his critics charged that he was not really a combat leader. He was, according to some, merely a "chairman of the board," chatting with foreign dignitaries, presiding over conferences, handling the press, allocating resources, and dealing with civilian officials in Washington and London. Much of this criticism derived from his leadership style, which was characterized by a willingness to give credit to subordinates and a reluctance to criticize them publicly. He did not possess the icy reserve of MacArthur or the swaggering bluster of Patton. He did, however, gain a reputation for openness and fair dealing with the media, and these attributes paid off in favorable press coverage.

THE RELUCTANT CANDIDATE

Extolled as a "soldier of democracy," Eisenhower grew uncomfortable as speculation arose concerning his political future. In July 1945 President Harry Truman even offered to help him win the presidency. Startled, Eisenhower brushed off the proposal, but support for his candidacy continued to grow throughout his service as commander of occupation troops in Germany and, after December 1945, as Army chief of staff. National opinion polls indicated that he would be a formidable political candidate, and volunteers began organizing to draft him. In 1948 groups of Democrats and Republicans, liberals as well as conservatives, all urged him to try for the White House. Eisenhower declared that he was not available—and that he would not accept either party's nomination.

In 1948 Eisenhower became president of Columbia University, where his tenure had political implications. Freed from the Army's prohibitions on political activity, he began to speak out on the fundamental principles that he felt should guide the university's course. He praised the American system of values, by which he meant individualism, self-reliance, free enterprise, federalism, and strict limitations on the powers of government—especially the federal government. He began to travel throughout the country in search of wealthy individuals—potential supporters and donors who could help fulfill Eisenhower's goal of making Columbia a truly national institution. These individuals—mostly Republicans and southern Democrats—liked his ideas and would come to form a core group of political supporters.

In December 1950 President Truman appointed Eisenhower to command the North Atlantic Treaty Organization's (NATO) forces in Europe. The seventeen months that he spent at the Supreme Headquarters, Allied Powers Europe, served several purposes. Eisenhower added to his favorable reputation by successfully establishing a coordinated fighting force and a workable command system. Moreover, he was able to convince Congress, the American people, and the Europeans themselves of the feasibility of defending Western Europe from a threatened Soviet attack. He also succeeded in removing himself from the political thicket at a time when speculation about his role in the 1952 election was becoming intense and opportunities for a fatal misstep abounded.

Although reluctant to risk his reputation by entering the unfamiliar arena of electoral politics, Eisenhower eventually acquiesced to the impassioned entreaties of friends and politicians. By 1952 he had allowed himself to be persuaded that

he had a duty to answer the call of the people to serve in the nation's highest office. Even with his immense personal popularity, however, Eisenhower's run for the White House was not easy. The Democrats, in power since 1933, were accustomed to winning presidential elections by using their powerful urban and labor machines. The most likely Republican nominee was "Mr. Republican," Ohio senator Robert A. Taft. Although tainted by isolationism, Taft had the support of the party professionals bent on wresting control from the moderates, whose leader, New York governor Thomas E. Dewey, had lost the last two elections. But Dewey, Massachusetts senator Henry Cabot Lodge, and New Hampshire governor Sherman Adams skillfully used the media to mobilize enough popular support to secure Eisenhower's nomination. In November Eisenhower won a victory even more decisive than his convention triumph when he defeated his Democratic opponent, Illinois governor Adlai E. Stevenson. Eisenhower's triumph was ensured when he pledged to settle the Korean War by making a personal trip to the war-torn peninsula.

THE PRESIDENT

In January 1953 Eisenhower took office as president, determined to reverse what he felt was a trend toward greater government intervention in the lives of private citizens, a process that had characterized Franklin D. Roosevelt's New Deal and Truman's Fair Deal. He also wanted to place the nation on a sound, inflation-free economic footing; to do so, he thought, would require an end to excessively large federal deficits. With these two objectives in mind, Eisenhower focused on the most important of his goals—maintaining the American system of democracy and free enterprise. This task would involve a foreign policy and national security strategies that would provide for eventual victory in the cold war against communism without national bankruptcy or the creation of a regimented garrison state in which individual liberties and economic freedoms would be lost.

Temperamentally as well as philosophically, Eisenhower was inclined toward moderation. He firmly believed that going to extremes in politics was counterproductive and that a middle course between left and right was almost always the safest and most preferable. He also realized that such social-welfare innovations as Social Security, unemployment insurance, laws protecting labor, and farm subsidies had become firmly embedded in the American political landscape. Any elected official or political party that attempted to abolish these programs would quickly be swept away by popular outrage.

In matters involving domestic policy, he usually proceeded with caution. His concern for fiscal integrity was tempered by his knowledge that Congress was influenced by interest groups whose concerns, he felt, were not for the good of the whole country. Given the constant pressures to spend money on social programs or on local or regional projects, Eisenhower resigned himself to reducing the rate of growth in the federal budget. He made modest progress in reducing agricultural subsidies, and with some difficulty he forced the Tennessee Valley Authority, which provided state-subsidized electrical power to a wide area and was seen as a threat to private enterprise, to cut back on its plans for expansion. His massive interstate highway program was financed on a pay-as-you-go basis by new gasoline taxes.

The president's greatest fiscal successes came as a result of his cutbacks in military spending. The administration's New Look defense policies, predicated on increased efficiency, smaller conventional forces, and greater reliance on air-delivered atomic weapons, were designed to achieve the necessary amount of security at a cost that would not hurt the economy too much. Eisenhower was effective at holding down the cost of new weapons systems, a task made more difficult by the October 1957 missile launch of the Soviet earth satellite, *Sputnik 1.* These measures were largely responsible for bringing the budget into structural balance, with actual surpluses in the 1956, 1957, and 1960 fiscal years. Economic downturns during the Eisenhower years, except for the recession of 1957–1958, were relatively mild and brief in duration.

The president's budgetary successes were not matched in the political realm. He lost a valuable ally when Senate Majority Leader Taft died in 1953. Taft's successor, California Republican senator William Knowland, often proved to be a thorn in Eisenhower's side. Even more troublesome were challenges from another Republican, Wisconsin's Joseph R. McCarthy. Refusing to confront the communist-hunting senator directly, Eisenhower carefully orchestrated a behind-the-scenes effort that contributed to McCarthy's personal downfall. This accomplishment, however, neither gained credit for the president nor ended the excesses of anticommunism, which included his own administration's drive to purge "security risks" from federal service.

Eisenhower had hoped to replace the conservatives within his party with moderates and progressives, but in the end he was unable to manage this feat. Although in 1956 he again decisively defeated Stevenson—in the midst of foreign policy crises in Hungary and the Middle East—he blamed the persistence of stubborn conservatism for the loss of Republican control of Congress after 1954. In 1960 the presidency itself was lost, in an election that he found hard to understand. In reality, however, his Democratic successor, John F. Kennedy, entered the White House in part because Eisenhower had difficulty in making a wholehearted commitment to a viable successor, whether it was to be his vice president, Richard M. Nixon, or New York's dynamic governor, Nelson A. Rockefeller.

Eisenhower also had difficulty in dealing with the growing civil rights crisis. His preference for gradual, middle-of-the-road approaches did not serve him well in this instance. He had close personal connections with white southerners and thought that states, localities, and individuals should solve most problems, including civil rights, for themselves without interference from the federal government. Although he brought a few African Americans into his administration, his belief in the limitation of federal authority and in the separation of governmental powers made him reluctant to intervene in the school segregation cases. Those beliefs also prevented him from endorsing the Supreme Court's unanimous ruling in 1954 in *Brown v. Board of Education,* the landmark case that held it unconstitutional to segregate schools based on race. Although reluctant to mobilize public opinion by forthrightly condemning racial prejudice, Eisenhower was determined to secure voting rights for black Americans, and he sponsored the first federal civil rights act since Reconstruction. In 1957 he used his presidential powers to enforce lower court rulings after obstructionist local authorities and segregationist mobs created a school segregation crisis in Little Rock, Arkansas. Eisenhower's greatest contributions to advances in civil rights may have been his legal and judicial appointments, which included such progressive leaders as attorneys general Herbert Brownell and William Rogers, as well as jurists Earl Warren, William Brennan, Frank Johnson, John Minor Wisdom, and Elbert Tuttle.

The cold war was the president's primary concern. Having made the promised first-hand inspection of the battlefield, Eisenhower brought an end to the Korean War in July 1953. Eisenhower covertly intervened to meet perceived communist threats in Iran and Guatemala, but he decided that domestic political support and international support was lacking for any large-scale military ventures in Southeast Asia. In 1958 he was, with some difficulty, able to defuse tense situations in Lebanon and the Formosa Strait. After his secretary of state, John Foster Dulles, became ill and resigned, Eisenhower embarked on a course of personal diplomacy highlighted by numerous trips to meet with foreign leaders. The hopes engendered by Nikita Khrushchev's 1959 visit to the United States were ruined, however, by the Soviet downing of an American U-2 spy plane and the subsequent collapse of the 1960 Paris summit meeting. Eisenhower bitterly regretted his failure to find a satisfactory formula for disarmament and the reduction of international tension, but he was successful in his struggle to maintain peace without losing the geopolitical conflict.

In 1961, as he left office, he warned against the military–industrial complex, an inadvertent cold war alliance between defense contractors and members of the armed services who sometimes disregarded the overall health of the economy in their quest for complete security and costly weapons systems. The absence of firm presidential control of the military,

Eisenhower cautioned, might threaten the American political process. After a politically active retirement, Eisenhower died in 1969. He had made it his life's work to facilitate the painful transition from a sedate society, oriented toward agriculture and traditional values, to a faster paced modern world, dominated by large organizations and interdependence. Both in and out of uniform, he had attempted to preserve those things that were essential and beneficial to American life, even while prodding reluctant constituencies and institutions to accept the inevitability of change. His personal style—warm, generous, and unpretentious—had suited him for these tasks. He was a master at the art of leadership by persuasion, an ability that helped him reconcile divergent interests and get difficult personalities working toward common goals.

See also Brown v. Board of Education; *Cold War; Kennedy, John F.; McCarthyism; World War II: Foreign and Military Policy.*

DAUN VAN EE, JOHNS HOPKINS UNIVERSITY

BIBLIOGRAPHY

Ambrose, Stephen E. *Eisenhower.* 2 vols. New York: Simon and Schuster, 1983–1984.

Eisenhower, Dwight David. *The Papers of Dwight David Eisenhower,* ed. Alfred D. Chandler, Jr., Louis Galambos, and Daun van Ee. 17 vols. to date. Baltimore: Johns Hopkins University Press, 1970–2000.

Perret, Geoffrey. *Eisenhower.* New York: Random House, 1999.

ELECTORAL COLLEGE

The Constitution provides that electors—collectively known as the electoral college—select the president and the vice president of the United States.

Each state legislature decides the manner in which electors are chosen. The number of electors assigned to each state is equal to the number of its U.S. House members plus its two U.S. senators. The current electoral college has 538 members, corresponding to the 435 representatives and 100 senators plus 3 electors for the District of Columbia, as provided in the Twenty-third Amendment. The Founders expected electors to be distinguished citizens, but the Constitution stipulates only that an elector cannot be a member of Congress or a "Person holding an Office of Trust or Profit under the United States."

The electoral college does not gather as a single body. The electors meet to cast their votes in their own states, per 1934 law on the first Monday after the second Wednesday in December. The vice president, acting in his constitutional role as the president of the Senate, counts the ballots before a joint session of Congress on January 6, or as otherwise specified by Congress. Electors are not required by the Constitution to vote for any specific candidates. This has raised the specter of faithless electors—electors who vote for candidates to whom they are not pledged. At least nine instances of faithless electors have occurred, but none altered the electoral outcome.

As the electoral college was fashioned in the original Constitution, the electors voted for two candidates, with no distinction made between the ballot for president and for vice president. The candidate who received a majority of the electoral votes became president; the candidate who received the second most votes, vice president. This system quickly ran into trouble. Newly formed political parties lined up all their electors to vote for a complete national ticket—that is, their presidential and vice presidential candidates. The highest vote-getters in the 1800 election were the Democratic-Republican nominees for president and vice president, who received an equal number of votes. The Constitution at the time stipulated that, in the event of a tie, the House would choose the president from the two candidates.

The Twelfth Amendment, which separated the elections for president and vice president, was ratified in time for the 1804 election. The House continued to serve as tie-breaker in the presidential race. If no one received a majority (currently 270 electors), the House would choose from the top three candidates, instead of from the top five, as provided for originally. In the House, each state had one vote, two-thirds of the states made a quorum, and the winning candidate had to receive a majority of the votes. If no one won a majority in the vice presidential race, the Senate would choose between the top two candidates. Since the ratification of the Twelfth Amendment, the presidential contest has been thrown into the House once (1824 election) and the vice presidential race into the Senate once (1836 election).

Hundreds of proposals have been introduced in Congress to change the electoral college system. Only the Twelfth Amendment succeeded. However, over time the system became something different from what the Founders envisioned. As national political parties rose, the idea of the elector as a well-known, independent-minded statesman was supplanted by the idea of the elector as an anonymous, loyal party member backing the designated nominees. Today most ballots list the names of the candidates to whom the electors are pledged, not the names of the electors. The Founders thought that the electoral college would serve, in effect, as a nominating body and that the House would decide most presidential elections. The rise of political parties meant that in most instances the electoral college, not the House, chose the president. As the electorate expanded, democratic ideals took hold, and questions regarding state legislative politics arose, almost all electors came to be chosen in statewide, winner-take-all popular elections, on the first Tuesday after the first Monday in November every four years. In the early history of the republic, other methods also were used, such as districtwide popular votes and appointment by state legislatures.

Critics cite numerous problems with the electoral college system: a candidate could win the popular vote but lose the electoral college vote and thus the election (as Democrat Grover Cleveland did against Republican Benjamin Harrison in 1888); electors could be faithless; state legislatures could decide to choose the electors, taking the popular vote away from the electorate; a state could perpetrate a fraud, thus denying the rightful winner of his or her electoral votes and changing the national election result; political considerations could affect an election decided by the House; and the winner-take-all system encourages candidates to concentrate on the large states and discourages the participation of third parties.

See also *Cleveland, Grover; Harrison, Benjamin; Twelfth Amendment.*

COLLEEN MCGUINESS, INDEPENDENT AUTHOR

BIBLIOGRAPHY

Bickel, Alexander M. *Reform and Continuity: The Electoral College, the Convention, and the Party System.* New York: Harper and Row, 1971.
Congressional Quarterly's Guide to Congress, 5th ed. Washington, D.C.: CQ Press, 2000, 377–391.
Congressional Quarterly's Guide to the Presidency, 2d ed. Washington, D.C.: Congressional Quarterly, 1996, 44–48, 185–189, 307–313.
Glennon, Michael J. *When No Majority Rules: The Electoral College and Presidential Succession.* Washington, D.C.: Congressional Quarterly, 1992.
Longley, Lawrence D., and Neal R. Peirce. *The Electoral College Primer.* New Haven: Yale University Press, 1996.
Peirce, Neal R. *The People's President: The Electoral College in American History and the Direct-Vote Alternative.* New York: Simon and Schuster, 1968.

EMANCIPATION PROCLAMATION

In his first inaugural address Abraham Lincoln acknowledged that the national government had no power to interfere with slavery in the states where it existed. Although he understood that slavery was at the root of both secession and the Civil War, Lincoln did not believe he had

President Abraham Lincoln reads a draft of the Emancipation Proclamation to his cabinet. *Library of Congress*

the constitutional power to end slavery. Despite pressure from abolitionists, the Republican Party rank and file, and some military leaders like Gen. John C. Frémont, Lincoln refused to move against slavery early in the war. But he soon changed course. On March 6, 1862, Lincoln proposed compensated emancipation, and in May and again in July he urged the border states to end slavery, warning politicians in those states, "The incidents of war can not be avoided." Privately, Lincoln was now prepared to free any slaves he could. The humanitarian goal he had always favored could now be justified as a military measure. On July 22 he told his cabinet he planned to issue an emancipation proclamation. All but one cabinet officer supported the decision, but Secretary of State William H. Seward wisely convinced Lincoln to wait until the Union's fortunes on the battlefield had improved.

On September 22, 1862, following the U.S. victory at Antietam, Lincoln issued the Preliminary Emancipation Proclamation, declaring that in one hundred days he would free all slaves held by rebel masters. On January 1, 1863 he issued the Emancipation Proclamation.

Lincoln wrote the proclamation as a narrowly focused legal document. The historian Richard Hofstadter criticized Lincoln as a cynical politician, "among the world's great political propagandists," and likewise criticized the proclamation as having all the "moral grandeur of a bill of lading." Yet, this is what Lincoln intended. He knew there would be a backlash against the emancipation among some northerners, and he was uncertain about the legality of freeing slaves. Thus, he issued the proclamation as a war measure, in his capacity as commander in chief of the army and navy. He limited its reach to those parts of the South that were still in rebellion, because he had no power, as commander in chief, to move against slavery in the loyal slave states or in those parts of the Confederacy that had been brought back under the control of the United States. Nevertheless, following the proclamation, every mile the U.S. Army moved deeper into the South brought freedom to more and more slaves. Gen. William Tecumseh Sherman, marching through Georgia and South Carolina, became in fact the great emancipator, freeing hundreds of thousands of slaves at the head of a great army of liberation. The proclamation also called for the enlistment of "suitable" slaves, and by the end of the war more than two hundred thousand blacks, a majority of them exslaves, had served as soldiers and sailors, and countless others had aided the military effort in civilian jobs.

Despite the proclamation's great success, Lincoln and other Republicans retained some doubts about the constitutionality of converting slave property into free people by military proclamation. Moreover, the proclamation did not affect slaves in Missouri, Maryland, Delaware, Kentucky, and substantial portions of Virginia and Louisiana. The Thirteenth Amendment, proposed in early 1865 and ratified on December 6, 1865, completed what the Emancipation Proclamation had started, preempting any further controversy about the legality of slavery in the United States.

See also *Lincoln, Abraham; Reconstruction; Slavery.*

PAUL FINKELMAN, UNIVERSITY OF TULSA COLLEGE OF LAW

BIBLIOGRAPHY

Cox, LaWanda. *Lincoln and Black Freedom: A Study in Presidential Leadership.* Columbia: University of South Carolina Press, 1981.
Franklin, John Hope. *The Emancipation Proclamation.* Chicago: University of Chicago Press, 1963.
McPherson, James. *Ordeal by Fire: The Civil War and Reconstruction.* New York: Alfred A. Knopf, 1982.

EMBARGO

An embargo is a form of economic coercion used as a diplomatic tool by the United States and other nations. Derived from the Spanish verb *embargar* (to impede), "embargo" has always meant an officially imposed prohibition on trade. But the specific form has varied greatly.

Embargoes have been enacted by both individual nations and multinational organizations, such as the United Nations and the Organization of Petroleum Exporting Countries (OPEC). Modern embargoes have generally been imposed upon a nation or group of nations. Following Italy's invasion of Ethiopia in 1935, for example, the League of Nations urged its members to join in a partial embargo against the aggressor. Similarly, from October 1973 to March 1974, OPEC stopped oil shipments to western Europe, Japan, and the United States as punishment for supporting Israel in the Yom Kippur War.

The most famous embargo in American history was imposed by the federal government, not upon a foreign nation, but upon its own citizens. In December 1807 President Thomas Jefferson requested, and a Republican-dominated Congress enacted, an embargo that banned all exports of American goods and all sailings of American ships except in the coastal trade. Initially, the Embargo Act was only to be enforced in ports, but it was soon extended to riverine and overland exports as well. The effects of the embargo on American commerce were dramatic: exports plummeted from $108.5 million in 1807 to $22.5 million in 1808, reexports of foreign products dropped from $59.5 million to $13.0 million, and shipping earnings fell from $42.1 million to $23.0 million.

The thinking behind this drastic policy has been much debated by historians. The Embargo Act needs to be understood in the context of the escalating conflict between Great Britain and Napoleonic France. Following the renewal of European warfare in 1803, both powers had attempted to restrict the trade of neutral nations with their enemy. The British had also resumed the practice of impressing seamen that they viewed as British subjects from American ships. This practice had generated a war scare in the summer of 1807. Shortly after Congress convened in the fall, Jefferson learned that the British were about to tighten even further their restrictions on neutral commerce. As a diplomatic tool, the Embargo Act was apparently meant to serve a dual purpose. Keeping American ships in port would reduce the likelihood of a new collision over either impressment or seizure and would protect them from capture in case of war. Banning exports of American produce in either American or foreign ships would put pressure on the British and French economies that might force a relaxation of their restrictions.

Jefferson apparently also viewed the embargo as a way of testing and demonstrating American resolve. Virtuous American citizens, he believed, could withstand the suffering inherent in the embargo better than British or French subjects. In this assumption, he was quickly and severely disappointed. Widespread smuggling evinced a general disdain for the embargo. Popular antipathy to the embargo appeared in newspapers, petitions, and orations and led to a Federalist resurgence in state and congressional elections in 1808. By the winter of 1808–1809, reports of separatist activities in New York and New England were commonplace.

War was avoided, but the embargo's failure as either a method of "peaceable coercion," as Jefferson described it, or a demonstration of American resolve was obvious. During the final months of his presidency, Congress sought a substitute that would continue the pressure on the British and French, while removing the danger of a domestic explosion. In March 1809 Jefferson reluctantly accepted the replacement of the embargo with the milder Non-Intercourse Act.

Since the repeal of the Embargo Act, the United States has avoided forms of economic coercion with such broad coverage and sweeping effects, at least at home. On its own and through the United Nations the United States has implemented punitive embargoes that have had devastating effects on the targeted nations (Iraq in the 1990s, for example). The 1935 Neutrality Act was limited to arms sales and was activated only against Italy and Ethiopia, who were relatively minor trading partners.

See also *Economic Sanctions; Jefferson, Thomas.*

JAMES E. LEWIS JR., INDEPENDENT SCHOLAR

BIBLIOGRAPHY

Doxey, Margaret P. *Economic Sanctions and International Enforcement.* New York: Oxford University Press, 1971.

Jonas, Manfred. *Isolationism in America, 1935–1941.* Ithaca: Cornell University Press, 1966.

Sears, Louis Martin. *Jefferson and the Embargo.* Durham: Duke University Press, 1927.

Spivak, Burton. *Jefferson's English Crisis: Commerce, Embargo, and the Republican Revolution.* Charlottesville: University Press of Virginia, 1979.

Tucker, Robert W., and David C. Hendrickson. *Empire of Liberty: The Statecraft of Thomas Jefferson.* New York: Oxford University Press, 1990.

EQUAL RIGHTS AMENDMENT

The Equal Rights Amendment, which was first proposed in 1923 and fell just short of ratification in 1982, stated that women should have the same rights under the law as men.

In the early 1920s, after the passage of the Nineteenth Amendment, granting women the vote, the goals of women's rights activists split into two factions: the League of Women Voters (LWV) and the National Woman's Party (NWP). The LWV decided to focus on issues that they believed were more important to women than to men. Such reform issues included protection of children and working women, education, and public health. The NWP adopted as its primary goal women's full equality and introduced a constitutional amendment in 1923 that would guarantee men and women the same protection and opportunities. No longer, according to the Equal Rights Amendment, would sex be considered a legal classification.

The majority of women activists, however, felt that the NWP was not acting in the best interests of all women, especially the lower classes. Previously, suffragists had been successful at passing protective laws to gain for women higher wages, better working conditions, and shorter hours. These reformers felt that protective laws were necessary and should not be revoked because, they claimed, women were physically weaker than men, became pregnant, and needed to care for small children. The NWP argued that these laws ultimately protected men from having to compete with women for jobs as employers were unwilling to hire women with such restrictions. For most of the decade, women's groups remained split over protective laws. With a fractured support base, the ERA faltered. Congress, realizing that women would not vote as a bloc, turned away from the ERA and other women's issues.

By 1944 both the Republican and Democratic Parties as well as the General Federation of Women's Clubs gave their support for the ERA. The needs of the home front during World War II increased the status of women. Many women hoped that gains made during these times of emergency would not be lost. However, opponents of the ERA, such as the LWV and influential trade unions, reacted to these gains by asserting that the ERA would hurt women, by repealing protection laws within the workforce. In 1946 the ERA reached the floor of the Senate, but it did not obtain a two-thirds majority.

In 1961, partly in payment of a political debt owed to his feminist supporters, John F. Kennedy formed a President's Commission on the Status of Women. This commission was the first national committee mandated to investigate women's rights and roles and to develop a plan regarding how men and women would achieve an equal partnership. Many leaders hoped this commission would serve as a political substitute for the ERA. The commission's first report rejected the ERA on the grounds that the Constitution already guaranteed equal rights to women under the Fifth and Fourteenth Amendments, although "definitive court pronouncements are needed to invalidate laws that discriminate against women." The commission's decision was ambiguous in that it supported equality but did not create a legal means of securing it.

In the late 1960s the National Organization for Women (NOW) made the ERA, along with abortion rights, part of its platform. Since protective laws now applied to both genders, many feminists believed that passage of the ERA would be successful. This latest surge of interest in the ERA, however, resulted in a backlash against feminism, led by Phyllis Schlafly, called "Stop ERA." Schlafly and her followers claimed that the amendment attacked American womanhood and would ultimately destroy family life. Despite passage by

Despite the support of first ladies Rosalynn Carter (second from left) and Betty Ford (third from left), the Equal Rights Amendment failed to pass. *Jimmy Carter Library*

Congress in 1972, the amendment died in 1982 after a ten-year journey through the fifty states for ratification and a congressional extension. ERA fell just three states short of ratification. In 1983 Congress again considered the amendment, but it failed.

See also *Constitutional Amendments; Labor Politics and Policy; National Woman's Party; Woman's Suffrage Movement.*

MICHELLE A. STRETCH, INDEPENDENT AUTHOR

BIBLIOGRAPHY

Babcock, Barbara Allen, Ann E. Freedman, Eleanor Holmes Norton, and Susan C. Ross. *Sex Discrimination and the Law: Causes and Remedies.* Boston: Little, Brown, 1975.

Brown, Barbara A., Ann E. Freedman, Harriet N. Katz, and Alice M. Price. *Women's Rights and the Law: The Impact of the ERA on State Laws.* New York: Praeger Special Studies, 1977.

Fox-Genovese, Elizabeth. *Feminism without Illusions: A Critique of Individualism.* Chapel Hill: University of North Carolina Press, 1991.

Kerber, Linda K., and Jane Sherron De Hart. *Women's America: Refocusing the Past.* 3d ed. New York: Oxford University Press, 1991.

Woloch, Nancy. *Women and the American Experience.* 2d ed. New York: McGraw-Hill, 1994.

FAIR DEAL

In his 1949 State of the Union address, President Harry S. Truman announced his "Fair Deal" legislative program, clearly modeled upon and echoing Franklin D. Roosevelt's New Deal. Fresh from his unexpected victory over Republican presidential candidate Thomas E. Dewey, Truman proposed to Congress that it enact a battery of social welfare programs, including better housing, a higher minimum wage, better price supports for farmers, special construction projects, full-employment legislation, civil rights laws, and the extension of social security.

Although the expression "Fair Deal" was not used officially until 1949, many historians employ the term to cover Truman's first term as well, when he succeeded to the presidency upon the death of President Franklin D. Roosevelt. In September 1945 President Truman proposed a twenty-one point program that was designed to fulfill the promises made in the Democratic Party platform of 1944, which had aimed at expanding the New Deal. In the bitterly fought campaign of 1948 Truman promised an array of liberal reforms, reminding voters of the legacy of FDR's New Deal, but also implying going beyond the reforms implemented by the Roosevelt administration.

Among other things, Truman proposed the construction of a St. Lawrence Seaway, the development of peaceful uses of atomic energy, greater spending on public housing, federal aid to education, a federal program of health insurance, a full employment act, which provided the president with authority and means to stimulate the economy when recession threatened, and the establishment of the war-time Fair Employment Practices Committee as a permanent agency. A notable legislative success during his first term was the Employment Act of 1946, which created the Council of Economic Advisors to advise the president about basic economic policy.

In his second term, Truman was able to get some of his Fair Deal proposals passed by Congress. The Housing Act of 1949 established a nationwide program of slum clearance. An amendment to the Fair Labor Standards Act of 1938 raised the minimum wage from 40 cents to 75 cents per hour. The Social Security Act of 1950 extended Social Security coverage to over ten million more individuals. Failures were notable, too. Congressional filibusters prevented the passage of an anti–poll tax bill and a fair employment practices bill.

Interest in the pursuit of Fair Deal goals waned as public and official interest was diverted by developments in the cold war, and especially by the outbreak of the Korean War in June 1950. The increasing prosperity in the United States also seemed to make governmental programs less important in the public mind.

The Fair Deal had little success in civil rights, although mounting pressures began to move the issue of racial discrimination onto the national agenda. However, Congress during this period was dominated by southern Democrats who blocked civil rights legislation. On this issue, Truman was fighting his own party. Truman's support of a civil rights plank in the 1948 Democratic Party platform was instrumental in splitting the party, leading to a walkout by south-

President Harry S. Truman's Fair Deal initiatives, including those in the area of civil rights, largely foundered in the face of a southern-dominated Democratic Party and Congress. However, by Executive Order 9981 of 1948, he ordered the integration of the armed forces. Above, an integrated unit fights in Korea, a war that would distract the American public from the Fair Deal. *National Archives*

erners who united in the States' Rights Party (better known as Dixiecrats), which ran South Carolina governor J. Strom Thurmond for president.

Some civil rights advances were made in the private sector, as when Jackie Robinson's successes led to the integration of major league baseball. The U.S. Supreme Court also made a significant contribution to civil rights by its decision in *Shelley v. Kraemer* (1948), in which the Court found the judicial enforcement of a discriminatory restrictive covenant in housing to be contrary to the Fourteenth Amendment.

See also *Civil Rights Movement; Dixiecrats (States' Rights Party); New Deal; Truman, Harry S.*

PATRICK M. O'NEIL, BROOME COMMUNITY COLLEGE, STATE UNIVERSITY OF NEW YORK

BIBLIOGRAPHY

Ferrell, Robert H. *Harry S. Truman and the Modern American Presidency.* New York: Harper Collins, 1983.

Hamby, Alonzo L. *Beyond the New Deal: Harry S. Truman and American Liberalism.* New York: Columbia University Press, 1982.

McCoy, Donald R. *The Presidency of Harry S. Truman.* Lawrence: University Press of Kansas, 1984.

FEDERAL HOUSING PROGRAMS

During the Great Depression President Franklin D. Roosevelt proposed, as part of his New Deal programs for economic recovery, that Americans inherently had the right to affordable housing. Behind these policies lay the New Deal's search for government activity—construction in this case—that would boost economic activity and create jobs. But the notion of community planning and building also started a new era as the U.S. federal government assumed a leadership role in securing homes for all Americans. Part of this plan was the National Housing Act of June 28, 1934, which created the Federal Housing Administration (FHA) for the purpose of insuring loans made by banks, trust companies, and building and loan associations.

The FHA was part of a complex reform plan to institute federal policies capable of offsetting the destructive effects on the American family of poverty and inadequate housing. Roosevelt's idea of public-sector community building produced four experimental New Deal housing programs.

The first was subsidized housing for urban slums under Title II of the National Industrial Recovery Act (June 16, 1933). The act eventually induced thirty-one states to pass low-income housing legislation.

A second plan, also funded by the National Industrial Recovery Act, built eight thousand homes in ninety-six rural communities between 1933 and 1941 under the administration of the Subsistence Homesteads Division of the Interior Department, then the Resettlement Administration in 1935, and finally the Farm Security Administration.

A third community experiment produced the suburban greenbelt-town program modeled on the British garden city tradition and the town of Radburn, New Jersey. The resulting three cutting-edge planned communities (Greenbelt, Maryland; Greenhills, Ohio; and Greendale, Wisconsin) drew wide criticism for their high cost and socialistic features. Sale of the communities, to private investors and developers in the 1950s, ended government involvement with ownership of planned communities.

A fourth, and eventually permanent, attempt to provide affordable housing emanated from a mix of public support and private enterprise. In 1933 the New Deal Congress passed the emergency Home Owners Loan Corporation Act and followed it up with the 1934 National Housing Act. The Housing Act expanded home ownership by allowing private enterprise to build quality, affordable homes with loans guaranteed by the federal government. By reducing down payments from 30 percent to 10 percent and extending mortgage payments from twenty to thirty years, the act enabled more Americans to afford housing. The Wagner Housing Act of 1937 gave the federal government responsibility to provide "safe and sanitary dwellings for families of low income." However, the laws of that time included provisions that effectively blocked assistance for racial minorities and even contained definitions that discriminated against women and ethnic and religious groups. These restrictions perpetuated discriminatory housing policies for many additional years until overturned by civil rights laws beginning in the late 1950s.

The permanence of the commitment to affordable housing is evident by such follow-up legislation as the G.I. Bill of Rights (1944), the 1954 Housing Act, the 1965 creation of the Department of Housing and Urban Development, and the Urban Development Act of 1970. Together the legislation allowed for an increase of home ownership from 46 percent in 1936 to 65 percent in 1980. By 1996 the number of FHA-insured mortgages passed the 24 million mark with a value of more than $900 million in insured loans. The idea of a cooperative enterprise between public and private interests became the model for community development and continued into the twenty-first century.

See also *Fair Deal; G.I. Bill; Great Depression; Great Society; New Deal; Roosevelt, Franklin D.*

VICTOR W. GERACI, CENTRAL CONNECTICUT STATE UNIVERSITY

BIBLIOGRAPHY

Baxandall, Rosalyn, and Elizabeth Ewen. *Picture Windows: How the Suburbs Happened.* New York: Basic Books, 2000.

Jackson, Kenneth T. *Crabgrass Frontier: The Suburbanization of the United States.* New York: Oxford University Press, 1985.

FEDERAL RESERVE SYSTEM

The Federal Reserve (the Fed) is the central bank of the United States. The main function of the Fed is to conduct the nation's monetary policy to ensure that there is sufficient credit for a growing economy while also maintaining stable prices. The currency of the United States is technically called "Federal Reserve Notes," which constitute the majority of liabilities for the Federal Reserve Banks.

The Federal Reserve System has three main components: the Board of Governors (the Board), the Federal Reserve Banks, and the Federal Open Market Committee (FOMC). The Board sets reserve requirements and approves discount rates as part of monetary policy, supervises and regulates member banks, establishes and administers protective regulations in consumer finance, and oversees Federal Reserve Banks. The Federal Reserve Banks are located in twelve cities throughout the country. These banks propose discount rates; hold reserve balances for depository institutions and lend to them at the discount window; provide currency; collect and clear checks and transfer funds for depository institutions; and handle U.S. government debt and cash balances. Although the Federal Reserve Banks are privately owned and have their own boards of directors, they are supervised and regulated closely by the Board, which oversees the discount and required reserve rates, the banks' budgets, and the selection of one-third of the banks' directors. The FOMC directs open market operations—the buying and selling of U.S. government securities—which is the main instrument of monetary policy.

The Federal Reserve System was established by Congress in 1913 through the Federal Reserve Act, the same year that the Sixteenth Amendment to the Constitution established the federal income tax. This act was precipitated by the severe financial panic of 1907. Congress in 1908 established the National Monetary Commission, which made several proposals to counter such financial disruptions. Policy makers sought a way to control the money supply, provide facilities for discounting commercial credits, and improve supervision of the banking system.

The Fed is widely regarded as independent of the other branches of government. However, the president, with the consent of the Senate, appoints all members of the Board and designates the chairman and the vice chairman. Although the Fed acts without approval from any other branch of government, the Fed must report to Congress on its policies, and, in that sense, is accountable to the broader public. The Fed occasionally comes under political attack, particularly if the monetary policy is contractionary (pursued to combat inflation), because such a policy tends to slow economic growth.

The broad objectives of the Fed have evolved with several major pieces of legislation, including the Banking Act of 1935, the Employment Act of 1946, the 1970 amendments to the Bank Holding Company Act, the International Banking Act of 1978, the Full Employment and Balanced Growth Act of 1978, the Depository Institutions Deregulation and Monetary Control Act of 1980, and the 1999 repeal of the Glass-Steagall Act.

Monetary policy under the Fed matured substantially after the Great Depression and World War II. During the Depression, the Fed followed a tight monetary policy that restricted credit, deepened the financial crisis, and impeded recovery. The Fed became more adroit in later decades, as open market operations became an increasingly important policy instrument. In the late 1970s the Fed had difficulty in targeting the money supply and, for a period, experimented with targeting interest rates. Many believe that this policy led to the high inflation of the late 1970s and early 1980s. The Fed soon changed its policy back to pursuing money supply targets and was viewed as a key to radically reducing inflation and contributing to the back-to-back expansions of the 1980s and 1990s.

Because of the long terms of its governors (fourteen years) and, once appointed, the relative safety of its chairman and vice chairman, the Fed is often said to be removed from politics. Still, because of the effects of Fed actions on the economy, it does generate political controversy. Often disagreement arises between high-growth and managed-growth advocates. In the 1990s Chairman Alan Greenspan was frequently pressured to loosen the reins of monetary growth by those from the outside who believed that faster growth could be sustained without producing much inflation. During far more difficult times, such as those faced by Chairman Paul Volcker in the early 1980s, the popular pressure on the Fed can be enormous. Confronted with double-digit inflation carrying over from the administration of President Jimmy Carter, Chairman Volcker had the unpleasant task of tightening the growth rate of the money supply in order to eliminate inflation. Although he was successful in that objective, the resulting recession of 1981–1982, with unemployment exceeding 10 percent, made it very difficult in the face of heavy public criticism to stick to the anti-inflation policy. President Ronald Reagan, however, never publicly criticized Volcker, and the Volcker policy was successful in ushering in a new era of lower inflation.

See also *Currency and Money Supply.*

RICHARD J. CARROLL, INDEPENDENT SCHOLAR

BIBLIOGRAPHY

Bryant, Ralph C. *Controlling Money: The Federal Reserve and Its Critics*. Washington, D.C.: Brookings Institution, 1983.

Governors of Federal Reserve System Board. *Federal Reserve System: Its Purposes and Functions*. New York: AMS Press, 1984.

Meulendyke, Ann-Marie. *U.S. Monetary Policy & Financial Markets*. New York: Federal Reserve Bank of New York, 1998.

Morris, Irwin, L. *Congress, the President, and the Federal Reserve: The Politics of American Monetary Policy*. Ann Arbor: University of Michigan Press, 2000.

FEDERALISM

Federalism describes the constitutional relationship between the federal government and the states, as well as the states' relationship with one another.

Under the concept of federalism, authority to govern is divided between the federal and the state governments. The fundamental relationship is best explained by the Tenth Amendment: "The powers not delegated to the United States by the Constitution, nor prohibited by it to the States, are reserved to the States respectively, or to the people." In general, the federal government exercises those powers granted to it in the U.S. Constitution. In areas where Congress is authorized to legislate, such as its power to "regulate Commerce . . . among the several states" under the Commerce Clause, it has the discretion to determine the means necessary to carry out its powers. Moreover, in those cases the Supremacy Clause of the Constitution provides that federal laws are supreme over, or "preempt," state law.

The power to enforce the federalism lines laid out in the Constitution is vested in the federal courts. Over time, the U.S. Supreme Court's view of federalism—of the appropriate and desirable allocation of power between the federal and state governments—has gone through several distinct phases.

PHASES IN THE SUPREME COURT'S VIEW OF FEDERALISM

Chief Justice John Marshall, in *Gibbons v. Ogden* (1824), ruled that congressional authority over commerce "among the several states" encompassed the power to regulate commercial interactions not only between but also within states if the activities impacted interstate commerce. So long as Congress was acting within its powers, Marshall did not view the Tenth Amendment as imposing any additional limitations on what Congress could do.

In this period the Court also developed four interrelated concepts of power within the federal system. Under the "preemption doctrine" the states were prohibited from passing legislation to regulate areas of national interest, if Congress had already acted. In *Prigg v. Pennsylvania* (1842), for example,

the Court struck down a Pennsylvania law regulating the return of fugitive slaves because the Fugitive Slave Law of 1793 preempted legislation in this area. The Court also developed a notion of the "dormant" powers of Congress that prohibited the states from passing laws in the absence of federal law. Thus in *Prigg* the Court asserted that even if Congress had not passed a law on this subject, dormant powers of Congress stopped the states from legislating on the matter. The third concept was that of dual jurisdiction. Thus the states could pass their own inspection or tax laws even though Congress had passed laws on these subjects. Finally, the Court developed the doctrine of state police powers, which allowed the states to regulate aspects of commerce that were local in nature. For example, in *Cooley v. Port Wardens of Philadelphia* (1852) the Court upheld a state law requiring the use of local pilots when ships engaged in interstate or international commerce docked in Philadelphia.

In this period the Court also gave great deference to the states in regulating personal status, race, and slavery. However, when pushed, the Court generally supported southern claims, upholding the right of the southern states to deny liberty to slaves who had lived in the North, in *Strader v. Graham* (1851) and *Dred Scott v. Sandford* (1857), while denying northern states the power to protect the liberty of fugitive slaves and free blacks in *Prigg*. Ultimately, the Civil War and the adoption of the Thirteenth and Fourteenth Amendments settled these issues.

In the second phase, from 1887 to 1937, the Court took a very restrictive view of congressional power under the Commerce Clause. The Court ruled that interstate commerce included only such activities as buying, selling, and transporting goods; it did not include such activities as producing goods or mining. Moreover, even if Congress was otherwise acting within its commerce power, it could not invade the province of the states reserved by the Tenth Amendment. Under this view of federalism, for example, the Court held unconstitutional a federal statute that prohibited the interstate shipment of goods manufactured using child labor. In the child labor case *(Hammer v. Dagenhart,* 1918), the Court determined that Congress was attempting to regulate production and interfere with the state's prerogative to regulate.

The third phase of the Court's approach to federalism was ushered in by *United States v. Darby* (1941), which overruled *Hammer v. Dagenhart*. In this era, lasting into the 1990s, the Court abandoned the distinction between "commerce" and production, holding instead that Congress could regulate matters that had substantial effects on interstate commerce. The Court further found that the Tenth Amendment was merely a "truism" and did not impose any independent limits on congressional authority. Under this new approach, for example, the Court held constitutional the prohibition against discrimination in places of public accommodation in the Civil Rights Act of 1964. In *Heart of Atlanta Motel v. United States* (1964), the Court found that racial discrimination by a motel in Atlanta had substantial effects on interstate commerce and thus was within Congress's commerce power.

In the 1990s the Supreme Court entered a fourth phase that may mark a partial return to its pre-1937 approach. In this new era the Court invalidated federal statutes under the Commerce Clause for the first time since 1937. Thus the Court held in *United States v. Lopez* (1995) that Congress could not criminalize the mere possession of a gun within one thousand feet of a school zone, because no economic activity was involved and nothing in the federal statute required a link between the particular gun and interstate commerce. Similarly, in *United States v. Morrison* (2000) the Court ruled that the civil remedy for gender-based violence in the federal Violence Against Women Act was beyond the federal commerce power because it did not involve economic activity. The Court further refused to defer to congressional findings of sufficient effects on interstate commerce. "The Constitution," the Court stated, "requires a distinction between what is truly national and truly local." Under this distinction, the Court determined that intrastate violence is a local concern.

In addition to the Commerce Clause cases, the Court has used the Tenth Amendment to place new limits on congressional authority, ruling in cases such as *New York v. United States* (1992) and *Printz v. United States* (1997) that Congress may not coerce state legislatures into enacting a federal regulatory scheme or commandeer state officials into carrying out federal programs. Under the Supremacy Clause, Congress can preempt state law so long as Congress is acting pursuant to its constitutional powers. Thus, if Congress is acting under the commerce power, for example, it can create a federal program and implement that program in the states through federal officials. It can also offer the states financial or other incentives to encourage the states to enact and implement the federal programs, but it may not require the states to do so.

Finally, the Court has looked at the federal-state relationship under Congress's constitutional power to tax and spend. Prior to 1937, in keeping with its approach to the commerce power and the Tenth Amendment, the Court ruled that Congress could not use its taxing and spending power as a way around the Commerce Clause limitations. After 1937, however, the Court abandoned that approach, permitting Congress to enact taxing and spending laws with regulatory effects and finding it constitutional for Congress to offer monetary incentives to the states to encourage particular state action. In *South Dakota v. Dole* (1987), for example, the Court upheld a federal law withholding 5 percent of federal high-

way funds from any state that did not adopt a drinking age of twenty-one years. The Court found that the condition on federal funding was reasonably related to the purpose of the federal highway program and that Congress had not coerced the states because the states were free to ignore the condition and forgo federal highway moneys.

RELATIONS AMONG THE STATES

In addition to the federal-state relationship, federalism also describes the relationship among the states. All states were admitted into the Union on an equal footing with the original thirteen, so that all states have the same powers, rights, and duties.

Article IV of the Constitution requires the states to respect each other's laws and judicial rulings and to treat the citizens of other states more or less the way they treat their own citizens. Before the Civil War the state-to-state federalism often broke down over the rights of northern free blacks and even some whites to enter the slave states. Later, states dueled in the courts over issues of marriage, divorce, and child custody, with some states adamantly refusing to recognize the law and decisions of other states. Many states long prohibited their own citizens from entering into interracial marriages and even refused to recognize interracial marriages that had been validly performed in other states, until the Supreme Court's decision in *Loving v. Virginia* (1967) banned all such laws against interracial marriage. In the 1990s some states passed laws declaring they would not recognize same-sex marriages performed in other states. In the Defense of Marriage Act (1996), Congress authorized states to take this position if they wished. When this issue reaches the courts, it will likely lead to new jurisprudence in interstate federalism.

To ensure that the interests of larger states do not dominate those of small states, the U.S. Senate has equal representation from each state. To ensure that the interests of smaller states do not dominate those of large states, the U.S. House of Representatives has representation apportioned by population. Moreover, although states may exercise those powers reserved to them by the U.S. Constitution, they may not interfere with the rights of other states. Thus, under the so-called dormant aspects of the Commerce Clause, individual states may regulate commerce within their borders but only up to the point where the state regulations interfere with or unduly burden interstate commerce.

See also *Constitution, U.S.; Labor Politics and Policy; Slavery; Supreme Court.*

JUDITH V. ROYSTER, UNIVERSITY OF TULSA

BIBLIOGRAPHY

Bennett, Walter Hartwell. *American Theories of Federalism*. Tuscaloosa: University of Alabama Press, 1964.

Berger, Raoul. *Federalism: The Founders' Design*. Norman: University of Oklahoma Press, 1987.

Chemerinsky, Erwin. *Constitutional Law: Principles and Policies.* New York: Aspen Press, 1997.

Ostrom, Vincent. *The Meaning of American Federalism: Constituting a Self-Governing Society.* San Francisco: ICS Press, 1991.

Tribe, Laurence H. *American Constitutional Law.* 3d ed. New York: Foundation Press, 2000.

FEDERALISTS

Two related groups in late eighteenth-century American politics called themselves *Federalists.* First were the proponents of ratifying the Constitution as framed in 1787, chief among them Alexander Hamilton and James Madison. They won. Next was the group that dominated national politics in the 1790s, as Americans began to form political parties.

The two groups were not identical. Madison, successful in promoting adoption of the new Constitution, led a political opposition that emerged in 1792. He, along with fellow Virginian Thomas Jefferson, argued for strict construction, or a narrow interpretation, of the powers of the new national

Alexander Hamilton was a Federalist in both senses of the term: he supported ratification of the Constitution and subsequently became a leader of the faction advocating strong central government and a broad interpretation of the Constitution. *Library of Congress*

government and organized a rival political party, the Democratic (or Jeffersonian) Republicans, which came to power with Jefferson's election in 1800.

The Federalist Party, led by Hamilton as President George Washington's secretary of the Treasury, dominated national politics during the administrations of Washington and John Adams. The Federalists wanted to make the national government stronger by assuming state debts, chartering a national bank, and supporting manufacturing interests. In foreign affairs, they pursued policies that would protect commercial and political harmony with Britain, goals that led to ratification of Jay's Treaty in 1795. Under the treaty, Britain withdrew the last of its troops from American outposts and the United States agreed to honor debts owed to British merchants.

Though committed to a republican form of government, Federalists believed society to be properly hierarchical. Federalists such as William Cooper of New York and Henry Knox of Massachusetts professed that politics was an arena best left to the "natural aristocracy" of wealthy and talented men. Consequently, Federalists generally sought to limit suffrage, tighten naturalization policy, and silence antiadministration opinions. Recent examinations of the Federalists have disclosed a softer side to their conservatism, showing that, as self-proclaimed protectors of society, they sometimes sought to protect the basic rights of minorities. They tended to be more sympathetic than their Jeffersonian opponents to the plight of Native Americans and African Americans and less resistant to the inclusion of women into political processes.

Federalists drew their support primarily from the Northeast, where their procommercial and promanufacturing policies attracted merchants and businessmen. Although they had some southern strongholds in parts of Virginia and the Carolinas (especially Charleston), Federalists had considerably less success in attracting the support of western farmers and southern planters who opposed their elitism, antislavery bias, and promanufacturing economic policies.

Several factors contributed to the demise of the Federalist Party. Its passage of the highly unpopular Alien and Sedition Acts of 1798 served as a rallying cry for Jeffersonian Republicans. A more important factor may have been the Federalists' sharp division in the 1800 elections over Adams's foreign policies. Second-generation Federalists continued to mobilize regional support, mainly in New England, and, after Jefferson's unpopular embargo forbidding exports (1807–1809), they made something of a national comeback in the 1808 and 1812 elections. Many Federalists opposed the War of 1812, however, and in 1814 the Hartford Convention, a meeting of arch-Federalists, considered secession from the union, thereby permanently tainting the Federalist name and ending the party's legitimacy at the national level. Federalists continued to play a limited, though sometimes important, role in state and local politics into the 1820s, challenging for key offices in several states.

Federalist leadership during the nation's critical early years contributed greatly to preserving the American experiment. In large part Federalists were responsible for laying the foundation for a national economy (later carried forward by National Republicans and then the Whigs), setting a national foreign policy agenda, and creating a strong national judicial system. The last of these was perhaps the Federalists' most enduring legacy as John Marshall used his position as chief justice (1801–1835) to incorporate Federalist principles into constitutional law.

See also *Adams, John; Embargo; Hartford Convention Resolutions; Madison, James; Political Parties; Sedition Act of 1798; War of 1812; Whig Party.*

BRIAN D. SCHOEN, UNIVERSITY OF VIRGINIA

BIBLIOGRAPHY

Banner, James M. *To the Hartford Convention: The Federalists and the Origins of Party Politics in Massachusetts, 1789–1815.* New York: Knopf, 1970.

Ben-Atar, Doron, and Barbara B. Oberg. *Federalists Reconsidered.* Charlottesville: University Press of Virginia, 1998.

Elkins, Stanley, and Eric McKitrick. *The Age of Federalism: The Early American Republic, 1788–1800.* New York: Oxford University Press, 1993.

Fischer, David Hackett. *The Revolution of American Conservatism: The Federalist Party in the Era of Jeffersonian Democracy.* New York: Harper and Row, 1965.

Kerber, Linda. *Federalists in Dissent: Imagery and Ideology in Jeffersonian America.* Ithaca: Cornell University Press, 1970.

Sen. Strom Thurmond of South Carolina in the midst of his record-setting filibuster of August 28–29, 1957. *Library of Congress*

FILIBUSTER

Filibuster is a term that has been used since the mid-nineteenth century to describe parliamentary tactics designed to delay legislative action and prevent the passage of a bill. The word has both Dutch and Spanish origins meaning *freebooter* or *pirate*.

In the early history of Congress there are examples of filibusters in both the House and the Senate, but the term has come to have special meaning in relation to the Senate. Since Senate rules allow for unlimited debate once a senator is recognized, the filibuster is still used. Senate rules also favor the use of unanimous consent to move legislative business along, which means that one senator can hold up Senate business by objecting to a unanimous consent request. Because the House is a much larger body, its rules greatly limit the amount of time each member may speak, thus effectively eliminating the filibuster as a delaying device in that body.

In 1917 the Senate changed its rules and adopted its first cloture rule, which constrains discussion and is designed to limit the use of the filibuster. Under the cloture rule a vote of two-thirds of the Senate was necessary to limit the remaining debate to one hour on each side, thus killing the filibuster. The cloture rule was changed in 1975, and currently a vote of three-fifths of the members is necessary to invoke cloture, except in cases of changes in Senate rules, which still require a two-thirds vote.

Filibusters have had varying degrees of success over the history of the Senate. Even when a filibuster fails to achieve its purpose of killing a bill, the filibuster itself—or even the threat of a filibuster—can lead to compromise or concessions.

Sometimes the purpose of a filibuster is to call attention to an issue and not to stop a bill from passing. In the 1950s and 1960s the filibuster was used by southern senators opposed to civil rights legislation. The longest filibuster on record was against the Civil Rights Act of 1957, conducted August 28–29, 1957, by Sen. Strom Thurmond of South Carolina (a Democrat at the time; he switched to the Republican Party in 1964). Thurmond held the floor for twenty-four hours and eighteen minutes by lecturing on the law and reading from newspaper columns and court decisions. He hoped his filibuster would spark a rally against the Civil Rights Act, but even members opposing the bill failed to join in the debate. Two weeks after this filibuster the Senate passed the Civil Rights Act of 1957.

See also *Cloture.*

RAYMOND W. SMOCK, INDEPENDENT HISTORIAN

BIBLIOGRAPHY

Binder, Sarah, and Steven S. Smith. *Politics or Principle? Filibustering in the United States Senate.* Washington, D.C.: Brookings Institution Press, 1997.

Burdette, Franklin L. *Filibustering in the Senate.* Princeton: Princeton University Press, 1940.

Byrd, Robert C. *The Senate, 1789–1989: Addresses on the History of the United States Senate.* S. Doc. 100-20, 100th Congress, 1st session. Vol. II, ch. 5. Washington, D.C.: Government Printing Office, 1991.

FILLMORE, MILLARD

Born on January 7, 1800, in Cayuga County, New York, Millard Fillmore had an impoverished childhood and was barely literate until his teens. By 1823 he had gained an education and admission to the bar. He practiced law from 1828 to 1848, was honorary chancellor of the University of Buffalo, served in Congress, and held various state offices.

Elected vice president as Zachary Taylor's running mate, Fillmore became America's second "accidental president" on July 9, 1850, when Taylor died. He immediately asked for the resignation of all cabinet officers, thus alienating him from important factions in the Whig Party. Fillmore supported the Compromise of 1850 and throughout his presidency sought to placate the South on all issues involving slavery and sectional conflict. He supported an aggressive enforcement of the Fugitive Slave Law of 1850 and urged that northerners who resisted it be prosecuted to the fullest. His policy led to an absurd—and failed—treason prosecution of forty-one men in Pennsylvania. Fillmore embodied the idea of a "doughface politician," a northern man with southern principles.

His proslavery principles and hostility to members of his own party cost him the nomination in 1852. Four years later he ran on the nativist Know Nothing ticket, coming in a distant third. With the Whig Party no longer fielding a national candidate, he won 43 percent of the popular vote in the South in 1856, but only 13 percent in the North. Unlike most Whigs, he refused to join the Republican Party and, although opposed to secession, refused to support emancipation. In 1864 Fillmore campaigned for the Democratic presidential candidate, George B. McClellan, arguing for peace with the Confederacy. He died on March 8, 1874, a forgotten president with no constituency, who had failed to appreciate the immorality of slavery or its fundamental threat to the American political system.

See also *Whig Party.*

PAUL FINKELMAN, UNIVERSITY OF TULSA COLLEGE OF LAW

BIBLIOGRAPHY

Rayback, Robert J. *Millard Fillmore: Biography of a President.* Buffalo: Buffalo Historical Society, 1959.

Smith, Elbert B. *The Presidencies of Zachary Taylor and Millard Fillmore.* Lawrence: University Press of Kansas, 1988.

FORD, GERALD R.

Gerald R. Ford, the thirty-eighth president of the United States (1974–1977), was born in Omaha, Nebraska, on July 14, 1913, with the birth name Leslie Lynch King. After his mother escaped an abusive relationship by moving to Grand Rapids, Michigan, and remarrying, the child adopted the name of his stepfather— Gerald Rudolph Ford. After graduating from the University of Michigan in 1935 and Yale University Law School in 1941, Ford returned to Grand Rapids to practice law. During World War II, Ford served on the USS *Monterey,* which saw action in the South Pacific theater of war.

EARLY POLITICAL CAREER

Ford was one of the many returning veterans who parlayed their youth, internationalism, and vigor into an immediately successful political career. In 1948 he upset a four-term incumbent representative in the Republican primary and was elected to represent Grand Rapids's Fifth District. From that first victory, Ford would never poll less than 60 percent of the vote in his district; he would be reelected to his House seat for twelve terms. In January 1963 Ford was elected chairman of the House Republican Conference; two years later he was elected House minority leader. Respected on both sides of the aisle, Ford was chosen by President Lyndon Johnson to serve on the bipartisan committee (known as the Warren Commission) that investigated the assassination of John F. Kennedy.

Richard M. Nixon seriously considered Ford as his running mate in 1968, but Ford declined; the offer went instead to Maryland governor Spiro T. Agnew. Five years later Nixon chose Ford to replace Agnew, who had resigned the vice presidency as a result of charges of bribery.

ASCENDING TO THE PRESIDENCY

The first man to be confirmed under the auspices of the Twenty-fifth Amendment, which stipulated that upon a vice-presidential vacancy the president would nominate a successor

Gerald R. Ford consciously sought to change the image of the presidency, following the administration of Richard Nixon. Above, Ford invites reporters into his kitchen.   *The White House*

who would take office upon confirmation by a majority vote of both houses of Congress, Ford served as vice president from December 6, 1973, to August 9, 1974, when he was sworn in as president after Nixon's Watergate-related resignation.

Ford initially basked in the glow of a high approval rating. His candor, down-home charm (he was once photographed swimming in his pool with an inflatable rubber duck; another time photographers caught his teenage daughter pushing him, fully clothed, into the pool), and promise of honesty contrasted sharply with the many indictments and broken promises of the Nixon administration. Ford's honeymoon ended, however, exactly one month after it began. On September 8, 1974, Ford announced that he was granting Nixon a full pardon for all federal crimes he "committed or may have committed or taken part in" while in office. Cries went out that a clandestine deal had been made between Ford and Nixon (a claim that subsequent research has shown to be false). Nevertheless, in less than a week Ford's approval rating plummeted from 71 percent to 50 percent; his administration never fully recovered.

The Ford presidency was doomed in large part by the legacy of the Lyndon Johnson and Nixon years. Forced to deal with the contraction of a post-Vietnam and Great Society economy—which featured both high inflation and unemployment, as well as a significant gap in the nation's energy supply—the Ford administration chose tax cuts as a solution. However, the results of that choice did not manifest themselves until after his successor was in office. It was on Ford's

watch in April 1975 that the North Vietnamese violated the 1973 peace accord and completed their overrunning of South Vietnam; for many, the film of the last American troops being airlifted from Saigon was the most enduring image of the Ford presidency, despite the administration's attempt to reassert its strength by moving quickly to free the crew of the USS *Mayaguez,* which was taken prisoner by Cambodian troops one month later.

Charging that the nation had become internationally weak, former California governor Ronald Reagan challenged Ford for the Republican nomination in 1976. Ford won the nomination with a majority of only 117 delegates; the brutal primary battle left him financially wounded and open to the attacks of former Georgia governor Jimmy Carter, who concentrated on his criticisms of the "Nixon and Ford administrations." In a narrow victory, Carter beat Ford (49.9 percent of the vote to Ford's 47.9, and 297 to 241 electoral votes).

Ford retired to a life of teaching and lecturing. In 1980 he agreed to become Ronald Reagan's running mate, only to have the deal fall through after Ford prematurely announced it on national television.

See also *Carter, Jimmy; Nixon, Richard M.; Political Parties; Vietnam War; Watergate.*

JOHN ROBERT GREENE, CAZENOVIA COLLEGE

BIBLIOGRAPHY

Cannon, James. *Time and Chance: Gerald Ford's Appointment with Destiny.* New York: Harper Collins, 1994.

Greene, John Robert. *The Limits of Power: The Nixon and Ford Presidencies.* Bloomington: Indiana University Press, 1992.

———. *The Presidency of Gerald R. Ford.* Lawrence: University Press of Kansas, 1995.

FREE SOIL PARTY

Free Soil was an American third-party movement active in state and national elections between 1848 and 1854 on a platform that would have restricted the expansion of slavery into western territories. The movement was strongest in New England, upstate New York, and the counties around the Great Lakes. Its supporters included radical northern Democrats (or "Barnburners"), "Conscience" Whigs, and political abolitionists from the short-lived Liberty Party.

These disparate factions had for various reasons become disaffected with their parent parties over issues raised by the annexation of Texas as a slave state in 1845. Barnburners felt that their favorite son, former president Martin Van Buren, had been denied the Democratic nomination in 1844 by a conspiracy of southerners. Conscience Whigs found their party's cooperation with proslavery southerners equally intolerable. Certain members of the Liberty Party wanted to broaden their tiny party's base.

The ensuing war with Mexico and the introduction in 1846 of the Wilmot Proviso—a proposal that would have ex-

Charles Sumner of Massachusetts, elected to the U.S. Senate in 1850 on the Free Soil ticket, was a vocal opponent of slavery. In 1856, two days after Sumner delivered a scathing attack on slavery from the Senate floor, U.S. Rep. Preston S. Brooks of South Carolina bludgeoned him as he sat at his desk. Sumner became a Republican a year later and a leader of the Radical Republicans during Reconstruction. *Library of Congress*

cluded slavery from any territories carved out of Mexican cessions—brought them together in 1848. Meeting in Buffalo, the groups joined under a party platform almost wholly devoted to the question of blocking slavery in the territories. Given the serious divisions among them over economic policies, the factions could agree on little else. Delegates nominated Van Buren for president, and the party polled about 14 percent of the votes in the general election.

For the next four years Free Soilers attempted to build a power base in the states, with a few successes—notably in Massachusetts and Ohio. The discovery of gold in California, however, forced the major parties to hammer out a compromise over slavery in 1850—a compromise that most Americans accepted for the time. This temporary resolution of the problem and the Free Soilers' own inability to overcome their past party affiliations undermined the movement. Barnburners left, and in 1852 the party nominated John P. Hale of New Hampshire under a more radical, almost abolitionist, platform. He polled only half of Van Buren's total, and the party collapsed. Still, Free Soil was significant in that it introduced the slavery issue irrevocably into the national political discourse, helped break up the Whig Party, and thus became an important forerunner of the Republican Party. In addition, it provided several of the most prominent early Republican leaders, including Salmon P. Chase of Ohio and Charles Sumner of Massachusetts.

See also *Compromise of 1850; Mexican-American War; Slavery.*

JOHN MAYFIELD, SAMFORD UNIVERSITY

BIBLIOGRAPHY

Blue, Frederick J. *The Free Soilers: Third Party Politics, 1848–1854.* Urbana: University of Illinois Press, 1973.

Foner, Eric. *Free Soil, Free Labor, Free Men: The Ideology of the Republican Party before the Civil War.* New York: Oxford University Press, 1970.

Mayfield, John. *Rehearsal for Republicanism: Free Soil and the Politics of Antislavery.* Port Washington, N.Y.: Kennikat Press, 1980.

Rayback, Joseph G. *Free Soil: The Election of 1848.* Lexington: University Press of Kentucky, 1971.

Sewell, Richard H. *Ballots for Freedom: Antislavery Politics in the United States, 1837–1860.* New York: Oxford University Press, 1976.

FREEDMEN'S BUREAU ACTS

The first Freedmen's Bureau Act, passed in March 1865, created the Bureau of Refugees, Freedmen, and Abandoned Lands to facilitate self-reliance in the aftermath of emancipation. The bill limited the bureau's life span to one year after the end of the Civil War. The bureau lacked direct funding for staff and existed under the military authority of the War Department. Its duties included dividing abandoned and confiscated land into forty-acre plots for rent to freed persons and loyal white refugees and distributing clothing, fuel, and food.

THE ACT OF 1865

A month after the Freedmen's Bureau Act became law, the assassination of President Abraham Lincoln put Andrew Johnson into the White House as the nineteenth president. The new president adopted a lenient policy toward former Confederates while opposing the expansion of black Americans' rights. Former slaves had thought that the federal government would redistribute Confederates' land, but Johnson immediately demanded the return of abandoned and seized property to the original owners. Only confiscated land that had already been sold to third parties should not be returned, in his opinion. It was perhaps incongruous that one of the bureau's primary functions was to administer the restoration of seized and abandoned property to pardoned Confederates. Republicans were unwilling to confiscate land for freedmen because the issue repudiated the constitutional protection of property.

President Johnson became increasingly hostile toward the Freedmen's Bureau and challenged the protection of freed persons by the bureau's courts and the military. In April 1866 he proclaimed the official end to the rebellion by the southern states and stated that civil courts should settle disputes involving civilians. This view contradicted the Republican belief that military authority continued despite the end of the war.

The chairman of the Senate Judiciary Committee, Lyman Trumbull, proposed a bill in 1866 funding the Freedmen's Bureau for an indefinite time period. He tried, nonetheless, to convince the bill's opponents that the bureau would not be a permanent institution. The bill authorized bureau agents to assume jurisdiction of cases involving African Americans and to punish by fines up to $1,000 and by imprisonment up to one year any state officials who denied freed persons the civil rights belonging to white citizens or who continued to tolerate discrimination. African Americans in former Confederate states had the right to make and enforce contracts, testify in courts of law, begin lawsuits, and own and convey real and personal property. In addition, the legislation allotted 3 million acres of public land in Florida, Mississippi, and Arkansas for homesteading and authorized the bureau to purchase land for resale. Congress later passed the Southern Homestead Act, stipulating that 46 million acres of southern public lands could be acquired only by homesteading and not purchasing. The ban on Confederates' obtaining land lasted for six more months; both African

Americans and all white citizens could homestead after January 1, 1867. The Freedmen's Bureau took an active role in assisting freedpeople to acquire homesteads but confronted problems ranging from fraud to racism among the southern white population.

Trumbull proposed both the Civil Rights Act of 1866 and the Freedmen's Bureau Bill in response to the 1865 Black Codes of Mississippi and South Carolina, which openly targeted African Americans. Under these codes, freedmen could not rent or lease land in rural areas. Freedmen were forced to sign annual labor contracts that included work from sunup until sundown. South Carolina even barred African Americans from any occupation except that of farmer or servant. The codes established specific courts to try cases involving freedmen, whereas existing state courts heard cases concerning white defendants. Trumbull's bills failed to protect freed persons from the Black Codes of 1866 that seemed to be nondiscriminatory by omitting reference to race, such as vagrancy laws that appeared to apply to whites and African Americans alike. Judges and juries had discretion in punishing criminals, however, so most of the time African Americans received harsher penalties than white citizens who had committed the same crimes.

Johnson vetoed the new Freedmen's Bureau Bill, which ensured a political struggle between the president and Congress over control of the process of Reconstruction. He believed the agency was unconstitutional and unaffordable. Congress did not provide economic relief and schools or purchase land for whites, he said, and it should not do so for former slaves. Johnson asserted that the bureau hurt the self-reliance of freed persons because it implied they did not have to work. The president knew that the bureau was unpopular with southern white citizens and northern Democrats and hoped that he could provoke the Radical Republicans into opposing him and hurt them politically. The House of Representatives voted to override the veto, but the Senate fell one vote short of the necessary two-thirds.

THE ACT OF 1866

Congress enacted the second Freedmen's Bureau Act in July 1866, guaranteeing freed persons the same rights possessed by white citizens that the vetoed bill had ensured. It did not authorize the bureau to punish state officials who denied African Americans those equal rights. The bill further lacked earlier provisions concerning land redistribution and concentrated instead on providing protection and educational opportunities. Johnson vetoed this bill as well; Congress overrode his veto. The Freedmen's Bureau never had the ability to provide freedmen with land, leaving them to work as agricultural laborers under primarily white control. Therefore, its policies maintained the class system and planter dominance in the South.

Congressional Republicans extended the bureau in July 1868 because they wanted agents present in the South during the November presidential election to ensure the right to vote. As of January 1, 1869, the commissioner would discontinue all of the bureau's activities except for educational work and the collection and payment of bounties to African American veterans. Agents left the South, thus signaling the end of the limited protection the bureau had provided.

See also *Civil Rights Act of 1866; Johnson, Andrew; Reconstruction.*

CAROL JACKSON ADAMS, SALT LAKE COMMUNITY COLLEGE

BIBLIOGRAPHY

Benedict, Michael Les. *A Compromise of Principle: Congressional Republicans and Reconstruction, 1863–1869.* New York: W. W. Norton, 1974.

Cimbala, Paul A., and Randall M. Miller, eds. *The Freedmen's Bureau and Reconstruction: Reconsiderations.* New York: Fordham University Press, 1999.

Foner, Eric. *Reconstruction: America's Unfinished Revolution, 1863–1877.* New York: Harper and Row, 1988.

Nieman, Donald G. *To Set the Law in Motion: The Freedmen's Bureau and the Legal Rights of Blacks, 1865–1868.* Millwood, N.Y.: KTO Press, 1979.

Nieman, Donald G., ed. *The Freedmen's Bureau and Black Freedom.* New York: Garland Publishing, 1994.

FUGITIVE SLAVE LAWS

Congress passed a fugitive slave law in 1793 and an "amendment" to that law in 1850, which in reality was an entirely new statute. Congress repealed both laws in 1864. The 1793 law passed with little debate and overwhelming support in both houses of Congress. The 1850 act stimulated rancorous debate and passed by a thin margin as part of a series of laws known as the Compromise of 1850. Both laws stimulated opposition in the North, and sometimes resistance led to violence.

FIRST FUGITIVE SLAVE LAW—1793

Article IV, section 2 of the U.S. Constitution provided that "fugitives from labour" could not be emancipated by escaping to other states, but instead had to be returned "on demand" of the person to whom they owed "service or labour." The clause did not contain any provision for enforcement. In 1790 the governor of Virginia refused to allow the extradition of three white Virginians accused of kidnapping a free black in Pennsylvania. This controversy landed in Congress, which in 1793 passed an act to regulate the return of both fugitives from justice and fugitive slaves.

Under the 1793 act an alleged fugitive slave was to be brought before any state or federal judge or magistrate for a summary hearing to determine if the person seized was the runaway slave of a claimant. If the judge ruled for the claimant, he would issue a certificate of removal, allowing the claimant to take the slave back to his home state. The law provided a $500 fine for anyone interfering with the return of a fugitive slave. In addition, a master could sue anyone helping his slave for his costs plus the value of any slaves actually lost.

Lax evidentiary rules, as well blatant acts of kidnapping by some southerners, led the free states to pass personal liberty acts, to provide extra procedures to protect free blacks from kidnapping. In *Jack v. Martin* (1835), New York's chancellor, Reuben Walworth, declared that Congress had no power to pass the 1793 law, a position affirmed by judges in New Jersey and Pennsylvania.

In *Prigg v. Pennsylvania* (1842), Justice Joseph Story of Massachusetts, speaking for an 8–1 majority, upheld the 1793 law and struck down all state laws that interfered with the return of a fugitive slave. Story also held that slaveowners had a common-law right of recaption to seize and remove slaves without any judicial hearing, if this seizure could be accomplished without any breach of the peace. Finally, although he believed state courts had a moral obligation to take jurisdiction in fugitive slave cases, he asserted Congress could not constitutionally obligate them to do so.

FUGITIVE SLAVE LAW OF 1850

After *Prigg* the free states passed new personal liberty laws, withdrawing state support for enforcement of the 1793 law. Southerners now demanded a new, stronger law with federal enforcement, which led to the Fugitive Slave Law of 1850. Under the 1850 law federal commissioners, appointed throughout the nation, were empowered to hear fugitive slave cases and to call out federal marshals, posses, or the military to aid masters. Penalties for violating the law included $1,000 fines and six-month jail sentences. In addition, anyone helping fugitive slaves could be sued for $1,000 by the master to compensate for the loss of each slave. Any marshal who allowed a slave to escape from his custody could be sued for the slave's value.

The law outraged the North because of its lack of due process. The law prohibited the use of a writ of habeas corpus to interfere with the process; the status of the alleged slave was determined without a jury; the alleged slave could not testify; and a U.S. commissioner hearing such a case would get five dollars if he decided in favor of the alleged slave, but would get ten dollars if he held for the master. This disparity was in theory designed to compensate commissioners for the extra work of filling out certificates of removal, but to most northerners it seemed a blatant attempt to bribe commissioners to help slaveowners.

CAUTION!!
COLORED PEOPLE
OF BOSTON, ONE & ALL,
You are hereby respectfully CAUTIONED and advised, to avoid conversing with the
Watchmen and Police Officers of Boston,
For since the recent ORDER OF THE MAYOR & ALDERMEN, they are empowered to act as
KIDNAPPERS
AND
Slave Catchers,
And they have already been actually employed in KIDNAPPING, CATCHING, AND KEEPING SLAVES. Therefore, if you value your LIBERTY, and the *Welfare of the Fugitives* among you, *Shun* them in every possible manner, as so many *HOUNDS* on the track of the most unfortunate of your race.
Keep a Sharp Look Out for KIDNAPPERS, and have TOP EYE open.
APRIL 24, 1851.

This handbill began to circulate in Boston after a runaway slave had been forcibly returned from Boston to Georgia following enactment of the Fugitive Slave Law of 1850. *Library of Congress*

The law led to riots, rescues, and resistance in a number of places. In 1851 a mob in Boston stormed a courtroom to free the slave Shadrach; a mob in Syracuse rescued the slave Jerry from jail; and a fugitive slave killed his master in Christiana, Pennsylvania. In 1854 a recently appointed federal deputy marshal in Boston was killed, and the abolitionist editor Sherman Booth led a mob which freed the fugitive slave Joshua Glover. Two years later, in Ohio, the slave Margaret Garner killed her child rather than allow the child to be returned to bondage, and in 1858 students and faculty of Oberlin College rescued a fugitive slave from a courthouse in Wellington, Ohio. All of these cases led to prosecutions, but most were unsuccessful. The trials in Ohio and Wisconsin led to confrontations between the national government and the states. In *Ableman v. Booth* (1859) the Supreme Court firmly upheld the 1850 law and asserted that states could not interfere with the federal courts.

The 1793 and 1850 slave laws did little to help masters recover runaway slaves but did much to undermine the Union. Outrage in the North over the 1850 law helped create the constituency for the Republican Party and helped Abraham Lincoln's election. In 1860–1861 a number of southern states cited failure to enforce the fugitive slave laws as one of their reasons for secession. In 1864 Congress, dominated by Republicans, repealed both fugitive slave laws. President Lincoln happily signed the bill into law.

See also *Compromise of 1850; Slavery*.

PAUL FINKELMAN, UNIVERSITY OF TULSA COLLEGE OF LAW

BIBLIOGRAPHY

Campbell, Stanley. *The Slave Catchers.* Chapel Hill: University of North Carolina Press, 1968.

Finkelman, Paul. *Slavery in the Courtroom.* Washington, D.C.: Library of Congress, 1984.

———. "Story Telling on the Supreme Court: *Prigg v. Pennsylvania* and Justice Joseph Story's Judicial Nationalism," *Supreme Court Review* 1994 (1995): 247–294.

Morris, Thomas D. *Free Men All: The Personal Liberty Laws of the North, 1780–1861.* Baltimore: Johns Hopkins University Press, 1974.

GAG RULE

As the abolitionist movement gathered steam in the 1830s, a surge of petitions against slavery reached Congress, and southern members of the House of Representatives (in December 1835) and the Senate (in January 1836) proposed a way to dispose of them. Some southerners urged that Congress not even receive such petitions, while some northerners opposed any such rule as violating the First Amendment and the principles of republican government. In what masqueraded as a compromise, the House in May 1836 adopted a rule that "all petitions . . . relating in any way . . . to the . . . abolition of slavery" would be received but then immediately rejected. Two months earlier, the Senate had adopted a similar rule.

Although the "gag rule" was used in the House for eight years, it did not silence the movement against slavery. Arguing that the gag rule denied the right to petition the federal government, abolitionists were able to dramatize the rule as compelling evidence that slavery threatened the liberties of white northerners as well as black southerners. Former president John Quincy Adams, serving in the House, led the charge against the rule. Every year, when it came up for readoption, Adams opposed it.

In 1840 the House adopted a permanent gag rule, one that did not need to be passed again at each session. The new version went beyond the original to declare that petitions regarding slavery "shall not be received by this House." Adams attempted at each session thereafter to convince the House to rescind the rule, just as he had previously worked to have it rejected. Over the next few years the majority supporting the gag shrank as increasing numbers of northern Democrats saw the gag rule as a political liability, resisted the South's domination of their party, and aligned with Adams on this issue. In December 1844 the House voted 108–80 to rescind the rule.

See also *Adams, John Quincy; Slavery.*

CAROL JACKSON ADAMS, SALT LAKE COMMUNITY COLLEGE

BIBLIOGRAPHY

Freehling, William W. *The Road to Disunion.* Vol. 1: *Secessionists at Bay, 1776–1854.* New York: Oxford University Press, 1990.

Miller, William Lee. *Arguing About Slavery: The Great Battle in the United States Congress.* New York: Knopf, 1996.

Richard, Leonard L. *The Life and Times of Congressman John Quincy Adams.* New York: Oxford University Press, 1986.

GARFIELD, JAMES A.

The last of the "log cabin" presidents, James A. Garfield (1831–1881) attempted to impose political reform in an era of patronage abuse and scandal, but he was cut down by an assassin's bullet only months after his inauguration in 1881. After gaining election to the Ohio legisla-

James A. Garfield   *Library of Congress*

ture as a Republican in 1859 and being admitted to the practice of law in 1860, Garfield joined the Union Army when the Civil War began in 1861. In 1862, while in the army, Garfield was elected to the U.S. House of Representatives, where he served from 1863 to 1880. During his tenure in the House, he worked his way up to Republican minority leader.

At the 1880 Republican presidential convention, in which nomination was hotly contested by the Stalwart and Half-Breed factions, Garfield found himself the successful "dark-horse" nominee. In the general election he defeated Democrat Winfield Scott Hancock, who, like Garfield, had been a U.S. Army general during the Civil War. On taking office as the twentieth president of the United States, Garfield angered Stalwarts, led by New York senator Roscoe Conkling, with his support of anticorruption measures, and he appointed a Conkling political rival, William Robertson, to the coveted post of collector of the port of New York. An embittered office seeker, Charles J. Guiteau, shot the president on July 2, 1881, in the Pennsylvania Railroad Station in Washington, D.C. Garfield died on September 19 of the same year.

SABRA BISSETTE LEDENT, INDEPENDENT AUTHOR

BIBLIOGRAPHY

Booraem, Hendrik. *The Road to Respectability: James A. Garfield and His World, 1844–1852.* Lewisburg, Penn.: Bucknell University Press, 1988.

Leech, Margaret, and Harry J. Brown. *The Garfield Orbit.* New York: Harper and Row, 1978.

Peskin, Allan. *Garfield: A Biography.* Kent: Kent State University Press, 1978.

GERRYMANDERING

Gerrymander is a term that describes the process of drawing the boundaries of an electoral district in a manner that favors one political party or a particular racial or ethnic group. The word *gerrymander* is derived from an 1812 explanation of the political boundaries of Essex County, Massachusetts. Elkanah Tisdale, an artist for the *Boston Gazette,* drew a cartoon showing a winged dragon with a long neck and sharp claws that was composed of districts drawn to favor the Republican Party. The word is a combination of the name of Massachusetts governor Elbridge Gerry and the second half of *salamander,* the "monster" depicted in the cartoon.

While the original use of the term related to the drawing of state senatorial districts, it has come to define favoritism in the drawing of any electoral district at the local, state, or federal levels of government. In 1812 the Federalist Party used the word *gerrymander* to criticize Governor Gerry for overseeing the creation of political districts that were unfair to the

Federalists and undermined their chances to win state and national offices. It has been an important part of the political lexicon of the United States ever since.

REAPPORTIONMENT AND THE GERRYMANDER

Gerrymandering is closely linked to the entire constitutional process of determining representation. Sometimes it is difficult to tell where legal processes end and conscious manipulation of voting strength begins. There are numerous ways besides gerrymandering in which congressional representation may be considered unfair to states or to certain political parties and groups within a state. The constitutional process of a census and reapportionment of House seats has been the subject of much political debate since the census of 1790. The U.S. Constitution requires that congressional districts be reviewed following a national census every ten years to determine the number of representatives each state should receive.

The process of determining representation has always been a thorny problem fraught with the potential for political intrigue and partisan pressure. A number of plans for determining reapportionment of the House have been tried over the years, with varying degrees of success. Plans developed by Thomas Jefferson, Daniel Webster, and Ohio representative Samuel Vinton grappled in different ways with determining how many citizens should compose each congressional district and how many districts each state should have. Finally, in 1911 the size of the House was fixed by law at 433, with provisions for expansion after the admission of Arizona and New Mexico, which would bring the total to 435. A new method of apportionment, referred to as major fractions, was devised by W. F. Willcox of Cornell University and used to reapportion the House following the censuses of 1910, 1930, and 1940. The current system, known as equal proportions, relies on complex mathematical formulas to derive the number of districts in each state.

Gerrymandering is a political tool that can be used to affect the outcome of a reapportionment of Congress. There are several varieties of the gerrymander. In a partisan gerrymander, state officials from one party draw the lines of congressional districts to benefit their own party. Another kind of gerrymander favors incumbent members of the House, who get favorable treatment to ensure that their district remains largely in the hands of the incumbent's party. In states where there is a close balance in political power between two parties, both parties may attempt to control political competition by drawing some districts to favor Democrats and others to favor Republicans.

Attempts to deal with the problems related to reapportionment have found their way into the U.S. court system, which at first refused to address the issue. As U.S. population increased, the problem eventually became so serious at the state and federal levels that the courts became involved in the assaults on malapportioned municipalities, states, and congressional districts. In 1932 the Supreme Court, in *Wood v. Brown* (287 U.S. 1), upheld a Mississippi redistricting law that failed to provide for equal representation. Thirty years later, in 1962, the Court reversed itself in a landmark case, *Baker v. Carr* (369 U.S. 186), which challenged the state of Tennessee for failing to reapportion its legislature for more than sixty years, during which time the state's population shifted dramatically from rural areas to cities. The Supreme Court declared that it had jurisdiction in this state matter under the Equal Protection Clause of the Fourteenth Amendment. A year later, in *Gray v. Sanders* (372 U.S. 368), the Court found that Georgia had a system that heavily favored rural districts in statewide primaries. This case established the one-person, one-vote rule and overturned the Georgia system, which gave rural voters ten times the voting strength of their city counterparts. In 1964 the Court applied the standard of one person, one vote to congressional redistricting in *Wesberry v. Sanders* (376 U.S. 1). Other cases followed in the 1960s that forced most states to redraw their congressional district lines.

RACIAL GERRYMANDERING

Gerrymandering for the purpose of disenfranchising persons on the basis of race has been illegal since the Voting Rights Act of 1965. Before this law was passed it was common in many states and localities to draw boundaries in ways that seriously weakened the votes of African Americans. Some of the contortions on district maps, designed to bypass African American communities or to force some of them into predominantly white districts, clearly violated the generally approved concept that congressional districts should be compact, contiguous, and geographically symmetrical whenever possible. Yet some congressional districts zigzagged and meandered unnaturally in an attempt to dilute the voting strength of minorities. Subsequently the Voting Rights Act extended its protection to other minorities, including Hispanics, American Indians, Native Alaskans, and Asian Americans.

To address the many injustices of racial gerrymandering in the past, several states took aggressive new directions in the 1990s that increased the number of African Americans in Congress. In 1991 there were twenty-five African Americans in the House of Representatives. In the 103d Congress, which began in 1993, the number of African Americans in the House jumped to thirty-eight, with thirteen of the newly elected members of Congress coming from districts especially created to concentrate black voters and increase their representation in Congress. In 1993 the Supreme Court, in *Shaw v. Reno,* questioned the validity of predominantly black districts in North Carolina that were created specifically to increase African American representation in Congress. The

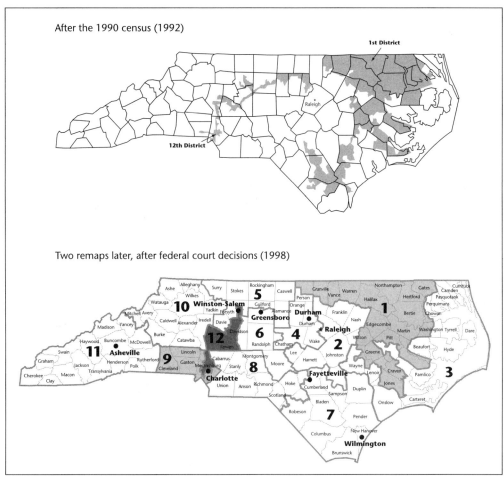

Gerrymandering in the 1990s: North Carolina's First and Twelfth Districts   *CQ Press*

Court said: "Racial gerrymanders, even for remedial purposes, may balkanize us into competing racial factions; it threatens to carry us further from the goal of a political system in which race no longer matters—a goal that the Fourteenth and Fifteenth Amendments embody, and to which the Nation continues to aspire."

North Carolina's Twelfth Congressional District stretched along a narrow section of Interstate 85 for 160 miles. The configuration of the district resembled a serpent and harkened back to the original gerrymander cartoon from 1812. The creation of predominantly black districts for the purpose of redressing past racial discrimination held an additional partisan dimension, since the new black districts benefited the Democratic Party.

The new black districts, created for the purpose of increasing African American representation in Congress and redressing a long legacy of racial discrimination, were challenged in a 1995 court ruling, *Miller v. Johnson* (515 U.S. 900). This case involved three predominantly black districts in the state of Georgia, which the Supreme Court declared to be in violation of the Equal Protection Clause of the Fourteenth Amendment. The Court said: "While redistricting usually implicates a political calculus in which various interests compete for recognition, it does not follow that individuals of the same race share a single political interest." Although *Miller v. Johnson* did not overturn the constitutionality of all predominantly black districts drawn to increase African American representation, it and *Shaw v. Reno* still raise the question of whether drawing districts along racial lines, for whatever purpose, is a legitimate means of dealing with minority representation.

See also *Apportionment; Black Suffrage; Census; Congress; Shaw v. Reno; Suffrage.*

RAYMOND W. SMOCK, INDEPENDENT HISTORIAN

BIBLIOGRAPHY

Benenson, Robert, Peter Bragdon, Rhodes Cook, Phil Duncan, and Kenneth E. Jaques. *Jigsaw Politics: Shaping the House after the 1990 Census.* Washington, D.C.: Congressional Quarterly, 1990.

Canon, David T. *Race, Redistricting, and Representation: The Unintended Consequences of Black Majority Districts.* Chicago: University of Chicago Press, 1999.

Hacker, Andrew. *Congressional Redistricting: The Issue of Equal Representation.* Rev. ed. Washington, D.C.: Brookings Institution, 1964.

Swain, Carol M. *Black Faces, Black Interests: The Representation of African Americans in Congress.* Cambridge: Harvard University Press, 1993.

G.I. BILL

The G.I. Bill for World War II veterans sought to help returning soldiers and the U.S. economy adjust to the end of the war. It was a great success and made a positive difference in the lives of veterans.

ORIGINS

On June 22, 1944, sixteen days after the Allied invasion of western Europe, President Franklin D. Roosevelt signed into law the Servicemen's Readjustment Act of 1944, the title of which was quickly shortened to G.I. Bill. Comprehensive and far-reaching, the G.I. Bill became immensely popular and left a legacy as perhaps the most admired and least criticized federal program of the remainder of the twentieth century.

Since the Colonial period Americans have awarded benefits to able-bodied veterans following the end of hostilities. These benefits—land grants, pensions, or cash bonuses—varied according to the conditions during and after the fighting. U.S. involvement in World War II brought new demands for veterans' benefits. Initial concern arose in the summer of 1940, when congressional leaders wrote the nation's first peacetime conscription law at a time when the unemployment rate stood close to 15 percent. The law included a provision that guaranteed reemployment rights to individuals who left a regular job when their draft notices arrived. This provision for protecting veterans following their discharge foreshadowed the central theme of the G.I. Bill.

Once the United States entered the war in December 1941, Roosevelt, both houses of Congress, and the American Legion (the country's major World War I veterans' organization) recognized that the demobilization period would require a major program to aid veterans because of their large numbers and fear of the return of the Depression. The awareness that prompted this belief stemmed from three historical experiences: the World War I veterans' bonus controversy, which endured for fifteen years as a major political issue (in 1924, Congress approved a delayed bonus for World War I veterans, who wanted to be paid immediately); the role disgruntled veterans played in undermining democracy across Europe during the 1920s and 1930s (Adolf Hitler in Germany and Benito Mussolini in Italy sought support from disgruntled veterans); and the great weight of the memory of the Great Depression of the 1930s.

Legislative proposals originated first in Roosevelt's executive agency, the National Resources Planning Board (NRPB), which borrowed ideas from the 1919 plan Wisconsin implemented for its World War I veterans and from the plan Canada already had enacted for its World War II veterans. The Wisconsin plan, for disabled veterans, was based in principle on rehabilitative aid for a limited period. The American Legion wanted a plan for able-bodied veterans, and it wanted a comprehensive plan, including education and unemployment insurance. Roosevelt appointed an armed forces committee, which in most ways reiterated the NRPB report. The American Legion, meanwhile, worked with leaders of both the House and the Senate to achieve its goal. During hearings, supporters of legislation warned of inevitable trouble if legislation were *not* passed, of revolutionary conditions if unemployed veterans returned home to bread lines and soup kitchens and to selling apples on street corners. Eventually an omnibus bill reached Roosevelt's desk with the sponsorship of eighty-one of the ninety-six senators and with unanimous passage in the House. At the time of its passage the G.I. Bill represented an anti-Depression measure—more a fear of millions of unemployed veterans than an expression of gratitude toward veterans.

PROVISIONS

The Servicemen's Readjustment Act of 1944 contained six titles. Titles I and VI involved administration. Title II covered all types of training and education at all levels. Under Title III came farm, home, and business mortgages. Title IV dealt with employment, and V with unemployment. Almost sixteen million veterans qualified for benefits, of whom approximately one million were black and 350,000 were women. Nearly 80 percent of all veterans took advantage of at least one of the G.I. Bill's benefits; about 33 percent used two benefits; and 10 percent used three benefits.

The most popular benefit was the readjustment allowance of $20 a week for fifty-two weeks, in which 58 percent of veterans participated, most for periods of less than a year. Under Title III, 28 percent of veterans purchased a home, farm, or business. Under Title II, 9.1 percent of all veterans received on-the-job training; 4.5 percent trained on-the-farm; 22.7 percent attended schools below the college level; and 14.3 percent enrolled in higher education. These Title II programs were used by almost 51 percent of veterans.

Of the several provisions of Title II, the higher education component easily captured the imagination and attention of the public and the media. Soon the G.I. Bill became synonymous with veterans on college campuses. For half a dozen years following World War II, veterans dominated colleges; no other provision of the G.I. Bill had such a visible impact.

The 2,232,000 veterans (2.9 percent of whom were women) who enrolled in college surprised almost everyone by their numbers and their academic performance. They especially surprised administrators such as James B. Conant, president of Harvard, and Robert M. Hutchins, president of the University of Chicago, who feared veterans (from all socioeconomic backgrounds) would be detrimental to higher education. Instead, veterans won universal praise as the best college and university students in history. At peak enrollment they made up more than 70 percent of male students and almost 50 percent of all students. Thanks in large part to the G.I. Bill, black college enrollment tripled between 1940 and 1950. College faculty and administrators as well as other students adjusted with ease to veterans despite shortages of classrooms, laboratories, and housing.

The G.I. Bill surpassed the intentions of those responsible for its passage and for the amendments of December 1945. The amendments liberalized the higher education provisions by removing the restriction that limited veterans over twenty-five to one year of college unless they could prove the war interrupted their education. In addition, the amendments lengthened the time period within which veterans could initiate and complete their education, and they raised the monthly subsistence allowance. The G.I. Bill poured $14.5 billion into the American economy in 1948, when the projected fiscal-year budget was $37.7 billion. Better trained workers paid indirect economic and personal dividends. Veteran's Administration mortgages, meanwhile, spurred the suburbanization that has characterized housing patterns since. The success of the G.I. Bill, moreover, led to later G.I. bills for Korean, post-Korean, and Vietnam-era veterans, as well as for peacetime veterans.

See also *Roosevelt, Franklin D.; World War II: Domestic Politics.*

KEITH W. OLSON, UNIVERSITY OF MARYLAND

BIBLIOGRAPHY

Bennett, Michael J. *When Dreams Came True: The GI Bill and the Making of Modern America.* Washington, D.C.: Brassey's, 1996.
Montgomery, G. V. "Sonny." "The Montgomery GI Bill: Development, Implementation, and Impact." *Educational Record* 75 (fall 1994): 49–55.
Olson, Keith W. *The G.I. Bill, the Veterans, and the Colleges.* Lexington: University Press of Kentucky, 1974.
Ross, David R. B. *Preparing for Ulysses: Politics and Veterans during World War II.* New York: Columbia University Press, 1969.
Wilson, Reginald. "GI Bill Expands Access for African Americans." *Educational Record* 75 (fall 1994): 32–39.

GILDED AGE

The *Gilded Age* refers to the historical period between the Civil War and the Progressive era, approximately 1865 to 1900. During this time America prospered unevenly as the nation's economic base shifted from rural agriculture to urban industry. In the process, a few businessmen became captains of industry at the expense of the vast majority of working-class citizens. Mark Twain and Charles Dudley Warner first used the term in their 1873 novel *The Gilded Age: A Tale of Today*. Later, historians adopted the term as an apt characterization of the era's economic realities. Like the gilding that covers a baser metal, a thin layer of speculative wealth covered up a deteriorating infrastructure laden with poverty and human suffering.

Despite its negative image, the era provides a simple lesson of how national periods of transition with unbridled speculative prosperity create a disproportional distribution of wealth that in turn leads to philanthropy and social, political, and economic reform. More important, Gilded Age politicians, businesspeople, and working-class citizens planted the seeds for the twentieth century, what *Time-Life* editor Henry Luce in the 1950s labeled the American Century.

Many Americans of the time understood the pervasive greed of the era. Responding to a dare from their wives, Twain and Warner wrote *The Gilded Age* to satirize the American political and economic landscape, which they perceived as being dominated by greed and insidious corruption. Yet for a long time many history books benignly focused on the domination of Robber Barons like Andrew Carnegie and John D. Rockefeller, who built monopolistic empires like U.S. Steel and Standard Oil. The Robber Barons succeeded by using unbridled capitalist mechanisms like vertical and horizontal integration, holding companies, and trusts. Politicians demonstrated similar greed as, with no regulations on politicians or elections, local leaders became "bosses" and laid the groundwork for the party machines of the 1920s and 1930s. The bosses learned how to manipulate the rapidly growing immigrant populations and the working class to gain personal wealth and power. Historian Alfred Steinberg, in the introduction to his 1972 book *The Bosses*, describes this climb to power as a process whereby "some they beat; some they bought; all they swindled."

The new industrialists of the Gilded Age crisscrossed the nation with railroads and factories while creating employment opportunities for almost 12 million immigrants. Flooding unprepared cities like New York, Boston, Chicago, and San Francisco, job seekers overwhelmed public services such as police, fire, water, trash, sewer, and health. As a result, many immigrants and poor workers lived in crowded, unsafe tenements, in subhuman conditions. Deepening the problem were unresponsive local, state, and federal governments. *Laissez-faire* policies promoted unregulated business growth. At the same time, many wealthy citizens saw no need for the government to alleviate urban poverty and unhealthy conditions because they thought that rugged individualism, Social Darwinism, and the private philanthropy of Christian Capitalism would resolve urban problems.

Adding to the burgeoning cities were migrants from a dwindling agricultural service sector. America was changing from a rural agricultural economy to an industrial economy. Between 1870 and 1920 farm workers dropped from 52 percent to 27 percent of the workforce. Agriculture itself was changing. Small, family-run farms were supplanted by agribusiness that used new science and technology to grow wheat, cattle, corn, and cotton on large, cheap tracts of western land tied by the railroads to urban centers.

At first all farms successfully stepped up production to meet the needs of growing urban populations. However, overproduction lowered prices to a point where many small farmers could no longer afford to farm. To survive, farmers began to act more like corporations, integrating businesses to enlarge their operations and marketing their products on a broader scale. Worst hit were southern farmers, who never recuperated after the Civil War and the depressions that occurred in the middle of each decade during the Gilded Age.

In a last-ditch effort to stall the movement from family farms to agribusiness, small farmers established the Populist Party. The Populists sought to suppress monopolistic railroads and other big business, democratize politics (via initiatives, referendums, and direct election of senators), and protect small farms. The Populist movement laid the groundwork for the Progressive movement of the early twentieth century.

Despite these grim growth figures, the nation also experienced a new, rapidly expanding middle-class and quest for highbrow culture in large urban centers. Shopkeepers, mid- and lower-level business managers, and skilled laborers earned higher wages than ever and consumed vast amounts of industrial goods and services. Thus, the Gilded Age gave birth to the department stores and catalog sales of Montgomery Ward, J. C. Penney, and Sears Roebuck.

Magazine and book publishing also grew, and improved transportation allowed Americans to travel to museums, libraries, parks, and expositions, leading to a greater democratization of American culture. Wealthy philanthropists built museums, concert halls, art galleries, and parks, while citizens enjoyed the writing of Mark Twain and Stephen Crane and the art of Mary Cassatt, Winslow Homer, and Thomas Eakins. The era also produced great strides in public health services, the development of modern police and fire departments, public transportation systems, land-grant universities, expanded education opportunities, and new labor laws.

During the Gilded Age America seemed to transform itself overnight into a modern industrial urban-based nation, all without public or private planning and regulation. The national economy provided growth and wealth for a few businesspersons and politicians, and it opened the way for the twentieth-century middle-class consumer. All of this came, however, at the expense of marginal groups—recent immigrants, African Americans, women, and indigenous peoples. From the era grew a national concern for environmental, regional, resource, and city planning and the need for social reform to ensure access for more Americans to goods and services.

See also *Civil War; Populist Party; Progressive Era.*

VICTOR W. GERACI, CENTRAL CONNECTICUT STATE UNIVERSITY

BIBLIOGRAPHY

Steinberg, Alfred. *The Bosses.* New York: Macmillan, 1972.

Twain, Mark, and Charles Dudley Warner. *The Gilded Age: A Tale of Today.* New York: Meridian Press, 1994.

Zunz, Olivier. *Why the American Century.* Chicago: University of Chicago Press, 1998.

GRANT, ULYSSES S.

Ulysses Simpson Grant (1822–1885), the eighteenth president of the United States, served two terms (1869–1877). He was the commander of the Union Army and led the North to victory over the Confederacy.

EARLY YEARS AND CIVIL WAR

Grant was born in Point Pleasant, Ohio, the son of a tanner. He reluctantly attended West Point in 1839 and graduated near the bottom of his class. At West Point he was given, through a clerical error, the middle initial "S"; he was actually born Hiram Ulysses Grant, but he accepted the renaming with equanimity. In 1845 he fought in the Mexican-American War under the command of Gen. Zachary Taylor, who would be elected the twelfth president in 1848. Grant objected to the Mexican-American War even as he fought in it. He believed it to be corrupt, waged by a clearly superior power on a weaker one, and helpful mainly to individuals who wanted to be president. During the Mexican-American War Grant met a number of people whom he would face fifteen years later as opponents in the Civil War—including Robert E. Lee, who was senior to Grant and a captain in Mexico.

After resigning from the army in 1854, Grant failed as a farmer and then as a storekeeper. He was a poor businessperson, by his own admission. He claimed he did not like being good at soldiering, but he knew he was gifted at it. When Fort Sumter fell and the Civil War broke out in 1861, Grant applied to serve as a Union officer. "I never went into our leather store after that meeting," he wrote, exhilarated to leave the profession he so disliked. Grant, a veteran and a West Point graduate, was made a colonel and was eventually promoted to brigadier general.

Grant's early victories were in Tennessee, on the western front of the war, at Fort Donelson and at Shiloh. Fort Donelson showed off Grant's style of command, displayed impressively in his demand to the southern general Simon Bolivar Buckner: "No other terms than immediate and unconditional surrender. I propose to move immediately on your works." Later in 1862, at Shiloh, a bloody battle with massive casualties on both sides, Grant's direct and forceful leadership put him at odds with Gen. Henry Halleck, as it often would with Union generals. Grant had been trained in military tactics, but it was not his best subject. His field tactics, though, were usually bold and original, and they were disliked by Halleck, who had been trained formally and who was unsettled by Grant's strategic audacity. Shiloh, an equivocal victory for the Union, is probably the result of this conflict of leadership.

In early 1863, Grant attacked the Mississippi River town of Vicksburg—control of river traffic had been a goal of the Union forces for some time—not by invading from the north, as might be expected, but from the south. By doing so, Grant's troops were dangerously isolated from supply lines, a risk no other general in the Union Army would dare to take. But Grant chose consciously—and, it turns out, ingeniously—to cut his own supply lines and have his troops live off the land. The strategy had never been tried before, but it worked. Vicksburg was won after a six-week siege against the occupying Confederate army. Grant later admitted, "I do not believe the officers [at Vicksburg] ever discovered that I had not studied the tactics I used."

It is said that Vicksburg made Grant a hero, and the Battle of Chattanooga made him a military genius. Despite the trapped position of Gen. William Rosecrans's Union troops, surrounded by Confederates in southeastern Tennessee and beaten badly at Chickamauga, Grant managed to turn what seemed like a certain defeat into a victory. Chattanooga opened the passage for a Union invasion of the South through Georgia, which became part of Grant's eventual plan for defeating the Confederates.

The Union leadership pressured President Abraham Lincoln, during 1863, to remove Grant from command. Lincoln, who liked Grant's bold style, instead promoted him to supreme commander of the Union armies. "I need this man," Lincoln wrote of Grant, "He fights."

SUPREME COMMAND

Grant devised in 1864 what no Union general had thought of during three years of war: a central plan for the Union war effort. It would take place on two fronts: Gen. William Tecumseh Sherman would lead the campaigns in Georgia (the effort eventually dubbed "Sherman's March"), and Grant would lead an offensive against Gen. Robert E. Lee in Virginia. Grant decided to go after the two prominent southern armies, using the tactics of cutting supply and transportation lines, isolating the troops, and wearing them down.

As part of his Virginia operations, Grant's army fought in two of the least successful campaigns of the war. In May 1864, Grant led the Army of the Potomac against the Confederate forces of Lee in a heavily wooded part of Virginia known as the Wilderness, near Chancellorsville and the Rapidan River. His losses were outrageously high, and no military historian since then has regarded the battle as anything but a slaughter. Later that year, the battle of Cold Harbor was also inconclusive for the Union and was one of the two days of the war that Grant later said he regretted.

Lee entrenched Richmond, Virginia, and Grant attacked neighboring Petersburg, the link between Richmond and the Deep South. He besieged Petersburg from June 1864 to April 1865. At the same time, he cut Lee's transportation lines.

The surrender of the South is described in Grant's memoirs in characteristic understatement and humility. He was afflicted with a migraine in his tent when Lee's note of surrender reached him by messenger on April 19: "The pain in my head seemed to leave me the moment I got Lee's letter." Grant was caught by surprise and went immediately, wearing his mud-splattered uniform, to the Appomattox Court House, where he met General Lee. The two men exchanged pleasantries of their memories of war in Mexico, and Grant claims he nearly forgot the object of their meeting. In the next few minutes, Grant outlined the terms of surrender by writing them himself on a piece of paper, which Lee signed. The war ended shortly thereafter.

TWO TERMS AS PRESIDENT

A war hero and greatly admired throughout America, Grant was the Republican Party's presidential candidate in 1868. (Grant, as it happens, had never voted for this party before in his life.) The radical or abolitionist wing of the Republican Party had doubts about Grant's political views on liberated slaves, but by 1868 even this faction realized that Grant's acclaim would unite a party bitterly divided by President Andrew Johnson's fights with Congress about Reconstruction. Grant proved, at least at first, to be just this sort of unifying figure. His famous words on accepting the unanimous nomination for the presidency from the Republicans were, "Let us have peace." Privately, Grant confessed to his wife Julia, "I'm afraid I am elected."

Grant was not matched to the office of president, and he had no inclination for the intrigues of politics. His cabinet was poorly selected and consisted mainly of cronies and political contributors, who advised him poorly and corrupted his administration.

Ulysses S. Grant *Library of Congress*

By 1870 it was clear that, having won the war, the nation's peace—in the plan of Reconstruction—was failing. The Ku Klux Klan, a vigilante group of white supremacists, terrorized African Americans in the South to prevent them from voting. Many southern states essentially enacted a counterrevolution to Reconstruction. Grant did not deal forcibly with this problem, although he approved the Force Acts of 1870 and 1871, criminalizing any interference with voting and authorizing the declaration of martial law. Aimed at punishing the crimes and terrorism of the Ku Klux Klan, the Force Acts attempted to supply federal remedies to civil rights violations when states in the South could not—or would not—do it themselves. In South Carolina, particularly, Grant found "a condition of lawlessness," and he declared martial law. But federal intervention was needed on a far greater scale to bring southern states into line with the terms of the Civil Rights Acts of 1866 and 1875, and Grant did not authorize this, out of concern for excessive military force being used against civilians. By 1876 most black Americans had been driven from the polls, and the de facto plantation system was restored in the South.

The 1870s were not prosperous for most Americans, and economic policies under Grant were somewhat inconsistent, focusing on the issue of "hard money," or currency based on gold reserves. The Civil War had been financed by "soft money," or greenbacks, a paper currency not backed by reserves of gold in the U.S. Treasury. Many of these greenbacks were still in circulation, and workers and farmers (who often owed money) wanted soft money to stay. The Republicans urged a return to hard money. The economic depression of the 1870s seemed to justify the hard-money theory, because conservative economists blamed the crash on inflation or the oversupply of soft money. Grant wavered on this question, sympathizing with the small businessperson and farmer, but finally he gave in to Republican pressure and vetoed a major bill, the Inflation Act, that would have extended the life of greenbacks.

During his second term, after an overwhelming victory over Democrat Horace Greeley, Grant saw his administration discredited by the Crédit Mobilier and the Whiskey Ring scandals and by the corrupt dealings of his secretary of war, William Belknap. Crédit Mobilier was a conspiracy of a few U.S. representatives who awarded railroad contracts to themselves and reaped enormous profits in the process; the representatives temporarily provided against investigations by paying off various members of Congress with shares in their companies. Belknap, whose first and second wives both profited from an illegal monopoly on sales of goods at western army posts, resigned in 1876 under Grant's demand, thereby avoiding impeachment when an investigation began a few months later. A far greater scandal was the Whiskey Ring, a plot by various government officials, some in Grant's cabinet, to avoid paying federal taxes on whiskey. Although Grant was never involved in these affairs or indicted for any wrongdoing, the disgrace of the corruption marked his presidency.

After his presidency, Grant and his wife traveled the world, meeting foreign leaders and adoring crowds wherever they went. On return to the United States, Grant had money trouble—he had been advised badly about investments and was nearly broke. At the same time, a doctor diagnosed him with fatal cancer in the throat. Grant spent the last year of his life writing *Personal Memoirs of U.S. Grant,* which his great friend Mark Twain had arranged to publish. Grant completed the book a week before he died on July 23, 1885. The memoirs were so successful that their publication saved his family from financial ruin.

Grant's public funeral and the erection of Grant's Tomb in New York City were a lavish business, with thousands of mourners on the streets. The stately Grant's Tomb stands in Manhattan, overlooking the Hudson River, with the simple words of his nomination acceptance speech inscribed on the entrance: "Let Us Have Peace."

See also *Civil War; Crédit Mobilier Scandal; Reconstruction.*

KRIS FRESONKE, IOWA STATE UNIVERSITY

BIBLIOGRAPHY

Grant, U. S. *Personal Memoirs.* New York: Modern Library, 1999.
Keegan, John. *The Mask of Command.* New York: Viking Penguin, 1987.
McFeely, William S. *Grant: A Biography.* New York: W. W. Norton, 1981.
Simpson, Brooks D. *Let Us Have Peace: Ulysses S. Grant and the Politics of the Reconstruction, 1861–1868.* Chapel Hill: University of North Carolina Press, 1991.
———. *The Reconstruction Presidents.* Lawrence: University Press of Kansas, 1998.

GREAT DEPRESSION

Between 1929 and 1941 the American economy faltered as the nation's banking system collapsed, prices for goods fell, and 25 percent of the nation's labor force faced unemployment in an era that would euphemistically be called the "Great Depression." Adding to this crisis was a worldwide depression that crippled the international economy as bankrupt financial markets and destabilized world currencies fostered trade conflicts between nations. In the end, the lasting legacy of the crisis was that many of the nation's citizens and business, political, and social leaders came to accept federal government responsibility for overseeing the nation's economy and providing a safety net for its citizens.

At first, Americans dismissed the economic downturn as part of the normal capitalist pattern of growth and market adjustment. After all, throughout the post–Civil War decades, as the nation shifted from an agricultural to industrial society, short depressions were common. Private enterprise and a laissez-faire government allowed depressions to weed out marginal businesses. This process seemed to work well and catapulted the American economy into a strong international role after World War I.

As the nation entered the 1920s many Americans had good reason to rejoice. Wages increased, consumption of goods (cars, radios, refrigerators, and other electric appliances) grew more than 20 percent, the recessions of 1924 and 1927 were short-lived, and by 1929 the unemployment rate had dropped to only 3 percent. Experts assured citizens that the nation was on an authentic economic upswing, and many labeled the era the "Roaring Twenties." Paradoxically, just as the nation prospered and developed a burgeoning upper and middle class, in June 1929 it plunged into the worst economic downturn in its history.

CAUSES OF THE DEPRESSION

On October 28, 1929—known as Black Tuesday—the stock market collapsed and the economy began a lethal spiral into depression. Despite a strong decade of growth in the 1920s, an unbridled expansion of the American economy permitted unscrupulous banking practices, created a maldistribution of wealth, failed to deal with "sick industries," permitted margin purchases on the stock market, and became vulnerable to an ailing international economy. John Maynard Keynes, a British economist, in his 1936 book *General Theory of Employment, Interest and Money* described the depression as a failure of spending (demand) to keep pace with the nation's productive capacity (supply). Most agreed with Keynes and the downwardly spiraling theory of less consumption, whereby less production meant fewer jobs, which in turn meant less money in circulation and therefore continuously lowered production and raised unemployment. On the other hand, Wesley C. Mitchell, an American economist, blamed businesses for poor planning practices that allowed the normal cycle—peak–recession–trough–recovery–peak—to spin out of control. Another argument was that monopolistic business structures that greedily sought profits upset the supply-and-demand flow and created a maldistribution of wealth. Also implicated were sick industries, such as agriculture, that had failed to adapt to a restricted market after World War I. Today most agree that the cause rested in a combination of factors and a process whereby causes also became effects.

Once the chain of events was set in motion the recession took on a life of its own, culminating in an international depression. Many feared for the survival of the American capitalist system as numerous nations moved toward socialism and communism in an effort to resolve the international crisis. The American stock market boom (1927) and crash (1929) had hurt foreign investors and curtailed American foreign loans, setting off a series of international retaliatory trade restrictions (like the Smoot-Hawley protective tariff), the 1931 collapse of World War I reparation and debt payments, and abandonment of the gold standard by Britain and others.

In response to the worldwide monetary crisis the American Federal Reserve lowered its discount rate, from a 1929 fee of 6 percent to 1.5 percent in 1931, hoping that cheap money would encourage growth. This tactic failed as the money supply shrank by 25 percent due to banking failures and the breakdown of the international gold market. Foreign nations, with deflated currencies, could no longer afford to purchase American exports, forcing America to deflate its dollar by 41 percent. Deepening the American economic crisis was the refusal of the Federal Reserve to expand the money supply (the Fed feared easy money would result in further 1929-like speculation) while simultaneously lessening

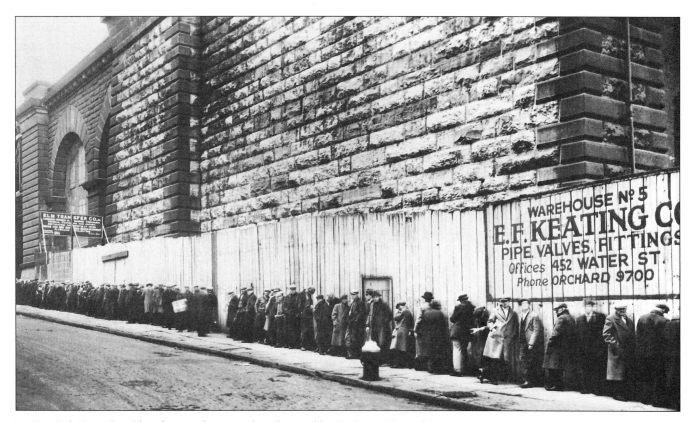

In New York City, a bread line forms at the approach to the Brooklyn Bridge. *Library of Congress*

the amount of money in circulation by raising reserve requirements for banks.

SOLUTIONS

Most politicians and economists quickly realized that the challenge was to get more money in circulation or pump-prime the economy. Yet, no one could agree on how much money the federal government should spend. In 1929 President Herbert Hoover recommended small budgetary expenditures that would be coupled with a 1 percent decrease in income taxes and $200 million in public works spending to ease the recession. Most of Hoover's attempts with federal spending (that is, the Agricultural Marketing Act and Reconstruction Finance Corporation) proved to be too little, too late. In 1932 Hoover attempted to balance the federal budget with the Revenue Act, which raised income taxes, reduced public spending, and cut the salaries of federal employees. Without an adequate pump-prime effect, matters worsened and the depression deepened for farmers, youth, minorities, elderly, and blue-collar workers. Unemployment reached more than 40 percent in some areas by 1932. Dissatisfaction over the Hoover approach promoted the 1932 election of Democrat Franklin D. Roosevelt.

As Roosevelt took office more than thirteen hundred local governments had defaulted on their debts, and public and private charities could not handle requests. Roosevelt responded by creating his New Deal programs, which set in motion a new national era of government intervention and planning in the economy and the personal lives of all Americans. The New Deal programs included a three-pronged attack designed to help the nation provide relief to those worst hit, bring about economic recovery and thus save American capitalism, and, most important, institute a reform of the economic system so as to end the conditions that caused the depression.

Ultimately, government intervention in agriculture, manufacturing, financial markets, and social reform only slowed the Great Depression. Many New Deal programs suffered from underfunding or constitutional challenges and therefore failed to resolve the causes of the depression. Relief from hard times came after 1938, when a return to war-related exports and the nation's entrance into World War II in 1941 created full employment and maximized the country's production capabilities.

The long-lasting legacy of the Great Depression was the paradigm shift in economic and political thought that allowed the federal government to become far more involved in the planning and coordinating of the American capitalist system.

See also *Hoover, Herbert; New Deal; Roosevelt, Franklin D.*

VICTOR W. GERACI, CENTRAL CONNECTICUT STATE UNIVERSITY

BIBLIOGRAPHY

McElvaine, Robert S. *The Great Depression: America, 1929–1941.* New York: Times Books, 1984.

Romasco, Albert U. *The Poverty of Abundance: Hoover, the Nation, the Depression.* New York: Oxford University Press, 1965.

Watkins, T. H. *The Great Depression: America in the 1930s.* Boston: Little, Brown, 1993.

GREAT SOCIETY

The Great Society was the broad reform program Congress enacted in the mid-1960s under President Lyndon B. Johnson.

On May 22, 1964, six months after taking office, President Johnson presented his view of the future in a commencement address at the University of Michigan in Ann Arbor. The Great Society he envisioned had two distinct goals. First, he hoped to achieve a level of national affluence that would permit all Americans to enjoy material well-being. Second, he hoped to move beyond economic abundance "to enrich and elevate our national life and to advance the quality of our American civilization." Thus Johnson sought to realize what many characterized as the American dream—economic opportunity and cultural enrichment for everyone.

The roots of the Great Society go back to 1949 when President Harry S. Truman, fresh from his dramatic reelection, presented Congress with his Fair Deal program. Truman wanted to go beyond the basic economic achievements of Franklin D. Roosevelt's New Deal; he proposed bold initiatives for the federal government in three areas: health care, aid to the nation's schools, and civil rights. In Congress, however, a conservative coalition of southern Democrats and northern Republicans blocked all action. The members of the coalition refused to consider Truman's plan for a comprehensive health care program, they stalled on federal aid to education, and, with threats of a filibuster, southern Democrats stymied the administration's call for ending discrimination against black Americans in employment and in access to public facilities.

In the 1950s Republican president Dwight D. Eisenhower cooperated with the conservative coalition in Congress in opposing any reform initiatives, although he did help preserve and extend New Deal programs such as Social Security. John F. Kennedy promised to revive the Democratic reform agenda in the 1960 presidential campaign, calling for health care, aid to education, and civil rights measures as part of his New Frontier program. The conservative majority in Congress, however, had succeeded in blocking action in all three areas before Kennedy's assassination in November 1963.

In his first appearance before Congress as president, Johnson, far more experienced and adept at congressional maneuvering than Kennedy had been, made an appeal on behalf of the fallen leader: "Let us continue." In 1964 Johnson was able to achieve two important legislative victories. The first was the passage of Kennedy's stalled civil rights bill, which was designed to give African Americans equal access to public facilities in the South. The second built on an embryonic Kennedy program meant to alleviate poverty. Johnson succeeded in persuading Congress to create a new Office of Economic Opportunity to wage what he called "a war on poverty." With the enactment of these measures, along with a tax cut designed to stimulate the economy, Johnson had launched the Great Society.

CONGRESS AND THE GREAT SOCIETY

Johnson's landslide victory in the 1964 election enabled him to secure an avalanche of legislation from the new Eighty-seventh Congress that dwarfed the initial Great Society measures. The Republican choice of Sen. Barry Goldwater, an outspoken conservative, helped Johnson win more than 60 percent of the popular vote and devastated the Republican ranks in Congress. The Democrats gained nearly 100 seats in the House, for their largest majority since 1937; many of the newly elected representatives knew they owed their seats to Johnson and were eager to follow his leadership. Thus the

For years Georgia senator Richard Russell and other southerners had blocked civil rights legislation with the threat of a filibuster. In a photo dated December 7, 1963, two weeks after John F. Kennedy's assassination, President Lyndon B. Johnson warns Russell to stand aside or be run down. *Yoichi R. Okamoto, LBJ Library Collection*

conservative coalition that had blocked all reform proposals for a quarter-century had suddenly been replaced with a liberal majority loyal to the president.

Johnson wasted no time in demanding action on the three major items on the Democratic reform agenda. By August 1965 Congress acted on all three, addressing health care by creating Medicare for elderly citizens, financed by payroll taxes, and Medicaid for indigent individuals, funded from general revenue sources; tackling education by approving measures for federal aid to the nation's public schools, with special focus on poorer school districts, and to colleges and universities as well; and addressing civil rights by passing the Voting Rights Act, which used the power of the federal government to ensure that black Americans would be able to exercise their constitutional right to vote.

The Great Society was more than these major steps toward providing opportunities for disadvantaged citizens, however. President Johnson insisted that Congress improve the quality of American life for all citizens. Measures aimed at achieving clean water and clean air marked the beginning of significant federal efforts to protect the environment. Congress created two national endowments—one for the arts (the National Endowment for the Arts; NEA) and one for the humanities (the National Endowment for the Humanities; NEH)—to use modest government grants to encourage cultural development. Johnson also tried to improve the quality of urban life: through antipoverty agencies such as the Community Action Program, an effort to allow poor individuals to help plan measures to alleviate poverty, and VISTA (Volunteers in Service to America), a domestic version of the Peace Corps in which young idealists helped poor individuals to help themselves; and through anticrime efforts such as the Safe Streets Act.

The Great Society legislation was largely completed during the first session of the Eighty-seventh Congress in 1965. The Democrats had exhausted their reform agenda, and the GOP gains in the 1966 congressional elections made it difficult to pass liberal measures. The only significant addition came in the spring of 1968, when the shock of civil rights leader Martin Luther King Jr.'s assassination and the riots that followed it led Congress to pass the long-stalled Fair Housing Act. That act, which completed Johnson's civil rights program, banned racial discrimination in the rental and sale of dwellings but failed to provide an effective enforcement mechanism.

Many factors contributed to the waning of the legislative phase of the Great Society. Even more influential than Republican gains in Congress and the exhaustion of the liberal reform agenda was the country's deepening involvement in the Vietnam war. Despite Johnson's efforts to hide the enormous sums required by the escalation in Vietnam by using supplemental appropriations rather than increasing the annual budget and by postponing a badly needed tax increase, military spending began to cut deeply into the Great Society programs, many of which were inadequately funded from the outset. Johnson proved to be far better at securing legislation than at administering the resulting federal agencies. A disillusioned Congress was no longer willing to engage in additional experiments when the members found fault with those already under way.

A GREAT SOCIETY BALANCE SHEET

The Great Society was neither a complete success nor a total failure. Most of the measures were flawed from the outset as a result of the compromises necessary to pass legislation in a democratic society. Truman's call for a comprehensive health care program to cover the entire population had led to partial measures such as Medicare and Medicaid that helped those in greatest need—elderly and indigent individuals. Yet by generously funding hospitals and doctors to encourage their participation, these federal programs ignored the issue of cost containment and helped make American medical care the most expensive in the world.

The war on poverty also had mixed results. Supporters of the Great Society could claim that the poverty rate fell dramatically in the 1960s, from 17.3 percent in 1965 to 12.1 percent in 1969. Yet critics argued that generous federal welfare and other transfer programs created most of this apparent decline. Johnson's efforts to undermine the structure of poverty by providing poor individuals with opportunities to achieve a better life through their own efforts were not completely successful, in part because Congress never adequately funded many programs and cut back or eliminated others after 1967. Thus some scholars argue that the war on poverty failed because Congress abandoned it before it could even get off the ground. Welfare would remain a highly contested political issue and a seemingly intractable problem for the next three decades. Federal aid to education clearly helped local schools that had suffered from the influx of children born after World War II (the baby boom) by supplementing inadequate state and local funding. Yet despite this financial assistance, student achievement scores failed to improve and urban schools deteriorated. The flight of middle-class families to the suburbs also hurt, cutting into the revenue base from property taxes and removing highly motivated parents and students from urban schools. The abolition of segregation throughout the South and the increased employment of black Americans in all sectors of the economy were among the most obvious achievements of the Johnson programs.

Ensuring the rights of black Americans to vote proved to be another enduring achievement. Although in the short run, as Johnson predicted, it created a backlash from white voters that hurt the Democratic Party, by the 1980s black mayors had become the norm rather than the exception in large cities, and African American voters often held the balance of power in southern states such as Georgia and Alabama. Black office holding in general increased dramatically, especially in the South. But despite the eradication of legal barriers, de facto segregation in the schools and in most aspects of private life remained the rule, not just in the South but throughout the nation, for the rest of the century and beyond.

Perhaps the most lasting achievements of the Great Society were not the landmark reform laws passed in 1965 but the less noticed efforts to improve the quality of life for all Americans. The NEA and NEH weathered conservative assaults in the 1980s and 1990s and today remain vital to the nation's cultural life. The environmental efforts begun in the 1960s led to major efforts to curb pollution and protect endangered species in the next decade that helped preserve the beleaguered American landscape. The promise that Johnson made at Ann Arbor in 1964 to "enrich and elevate our national life and to advance the quality of our American civilization" was the one he came closest to fulfilling.

See also *Affirmative Action; Civil Rights Acts (Modern); Civil Rights Movement; Higher Education Act; Johnson, Lyndon B.*

ROBERT A. DIVINE, UNIVERSITY OF TEXAS AT AUSTIN

BIBLIOGRAPHY

Andrew, John A., III. *Lyndon Johnson and the Great Society.* Chicago: Ivan R. Dee, 1998.

Bernstein, Irving. *Guns or Butter: The Presidency of Lyndon Johnson.* New York: Oxford University Press, 1995.

Dallek, Robert. *Flawed Giant: Lyndon Johnson and His Times.* New York: Oxford University Press, 1998.

Matusow, Allen J. *The Unraveling of America: A History of Liberalism in the 1960s.* New York: Harper and Row, 1984.

Unger, Irwin. *The Best of Intentions: The Triumphs and Failures of the Great Society.* New York: Doubleday, 1996.

GUN CONTROL AND POLICY

Gun control policy in the United States has deep historical roots. Since 1900, however, measures for limited gun control have caused a high degree of political conflict. Gun control policy extends back to the colonial era, when colonial laws based on race often barred gun ownership by African Americans and Native Americans. Some laws also required loyalty oaths as a prerequisite for gun ownership. From colonial times through the early Federalist era of the 1790s, militia-eligible males were often required by law to own guns, but these laws were almost never enforced.

GUN CONTROL IN THE NINETEENTH AND EARLY TWENTIETH CENTURIES

In the nineteenth century strict gun control laws were enacted in frontier towns, where civic leaders were quick to push for town incorporation in order to establish police forces to enforce local laws that barred the carrying or discharge of guns in their towns. Western-style shoot-outs so often portrayed in books and movies were, in fact, virtually unheard of thanks to these strict measures.

In the twentieth century the fear of gun-related crime and the assassinations of political leaders and celebrities spurred calls for tougher gun laws. Despite enduring popular support for tougher laws, stricter federal gun regulations have been infrequent and limited in scope.

The first modern gun control law arose from the Progressive era, when New York State, suffering from increasing urban violence and the attempted assassination of the New York City mayor, enacted the Sullivan Law (named after the state senator who championed the bill). That law subjected the sale, possession, and carrying of deadly weapons to strict regulation. In particular, pistol-carrying was strictly licensed and violators were charged with a felony.

At the federal level, early efforts to enact gun policy included a 10 percent excise tax on guns enacted in 1919 and a law that prohibited the sale of handguns to private individuals through the mail enacted in 1927. Threats by gangsters in the 1920s and the election of Franklin D. Roosevelt in 1932 boosted support for new gun laws. The National Firearms Act of 1934 strictly regulated gangster-type weapons, including sawed-off shotguns and submachine guns (then known as tommy guns). The Federal Firearms Act of 1938 established a licensing system for gun dealers, manufacturers, and importers.

NEW RESTRICTIONS, 1960s–1990s

After 1938 no new federal gun control laws reached the president's desk until 1968, when a five-year push for tougher laws culminated in the enactment of the Gun Control Act. Pushed over the top by the 1968 assassinations of Martin Luther King Jr. and Sen. Robert Kennedy, the law banned interstate shipment of firearms and ammunition to private individuals; prohibited gun sales to minors; strengthened licensing and record-keeping requirements for dealers and collectors; extended regulations to destructive devices, including land mines, bombs, and hand grenades; increased penalties for gun crimes; and regulated the importation of foreign-made firearms. Cut from the original bill was the proposal, backed by President Lyndon Johnson, to enact blanket registration and licensing.

The next major federal gun law, the Firearms Owners' Protection Act of 1986 (also called the McClure-Volkmer bill), rolled back many of the provisions of the 1968 law at a time when anticontrol forces, led by the National Rifle Association, exerted great influence over Congress and the Ronald Reagan presidency. The 1986 act allowed the interstate sale of long guns (rifles and shotguns), reduced record-keeping for dealers, limited government regulatory powers over dealers and gun shows (in particular, gun dealers could not be inspected more than once a year), and barred firearms registration.

Well-publicized incidents of mass shootings in the late 1980s and 1990s, combined with the election of gun control supporter Bill Clinton to the presidency, resulted in enactment of the Brady Law in 1993 and the assault weapons ban in 1994. Both laws were passed after several years of pressure in Congress. Named after President Ronald Reagan's press secretary, James Brady, who was seriously wounded in the 1981 assassination attempt against Reagan, the Brady Law required a five-business-day waiting period for the purchase of a handgun (local law enforcement authorities were to conduct background checks on purchasers during the waiting period), increased federal firearms license fees, financed improved record-keeping, and called for implementation of an instant, computerized background check to be instituted in 1998. In the first six years after passage, the Brady Law stopped approximately 500,000 handgun purchases. A challenge to the law by gun control foes led to *Printz v. United States,* a 1997 Supreme Court decision that struck down the provision of the law that required local law enforcement to conduct background checks; the court called it a violation of states' rights under the Tenth Amendment of the Constitution. Despite numerous challenges to gun laws as a violation of the Second Amendment's "right to bear arms," no law has ever been struck down as a violation of this provision.

In the 1994 law, Congress enacted a ban on nineteen specified assault weapons, plus several dozen copycat models, that were distinguished from other semiautomatic weapons by their military features, including a more compact design, short barrels, large ammunition clips, lighter weight, pistol grips or thumbhole stocks, flash suppressors, or telescoping stocks (features that facilitate concealability and "spray fire"). The law also exempted from the ban 661 specific weapons.

In 1999, following the shooting of fourteen students and a teacher at Columbine High School in Colorado, the U.S. Senate passed a bill that would have required background checks for all gun-show and pawnshop handgun sales, revoked gun ownership for people convicted of felonies as juveniles, required safety locks for all handgun sales, and banned the import of ammunition clips capable of holding more then ten bullets. The measure stalled in the House of Representatives.

National gun policy is implemented by the Bureau of Alcohol, Tobacco, and Firearms, which has been hampered in its enforcement efforts by legislative restrictions on its authority; budget cutbacks; a tarnished reputation caused by the confrontation at the Branch Davidian compound in Waco, Texas, in 1993; and political opposition and criticism from the National Rifle Association.

See also *Interest Groups.*

ROBERT J. SPITZER, STATE UNIVERSITY OF NEW YORK, CORTLAND

BIBLIOGRAPHY

Bellesiles, Michael A. *Arming America: The Origins of a National Gun Culture.* New York: Knopf, 2000.

Bruce, John M., and Clyde Wilcox, eds. *The Changing Politics of Gun Control.* Lanham, Md.: Rowman and Littlefield, 1998.

Dizard, Jan E., Robert Merrill Muth, and Stephen P. Andrews Jr., eds. *Guns in America: A Reader.* New York: New York University Press, 1999.

Kennett, Lee, and James LaVerne Anderson. *The Gun in America: The Origins of a National Dilemma.* Westport, Conn.: Greenwood Press, 1975.

Spitzer, Robert J. *The Politics of Gun Control.* New York: Chatham House, 1998.

HARDING, WARREN G.

Warren Gamaliel Harding (1865–1923) is regarded by many presidential scholars as the worst president of the twentieth century. A more accurate assessment rates him as a successful candidate for the office and a mediocre performer during his brief term.

Born in Blooming Grove, Ohio, Harding was publisher of the Marion (Ohio) *Star* and *Republican Regular* before winning election to the U.S. Senate in 1914. A deadlocked Republican convention in 1920 chose him as a compromise candidate for president. The handsome and persuasive Harding swamped his Democratic rival, James M. Cox, in the voting.

Warren G. Harding *Library of Congress*

In office he and his wife Florence made the White House more accessible by resuming public receptions that Woodrow Wilson had stopped, allowing tourists more freedom, and reinstating the annual Easter egg roll for children.

The Budget Act of 1921 and the Washington Naval Conference of 1921 were notable achievements. The Budget Act enabled the government to keep better track of its finances, and the Washington Conference looked toward a reduction of naval armaments after World War I. Harding made some wise cabinet appointments in Charles Evans Hughes (State) and Herbert Hoover (Commerce), but many of his other nominees proved to be incompetent or corrupt.

By 1923 rumors of scandal dogged the White House. The most notorious of these involved oil reserves in Wyoming underneath a geological formation that resembled a teapot. Critics charged that Harding's secretary of the interior, Albert B. Fall, had leased these reserves to oil companies in exchange for bribes. Though the president was not implicated in the affair, the case, which eventually led to Fall's conviction on bribery charges, came to stand for the corruption many political opponents said had pervaded the administration. As a result, the Teapot Dome episode became the most enduring symbol of the ethical lapses of the Harding presidency.

On a tour of the West, Harding, long ill with heart disease, succumbed to a fatal circulatory attack in California. The nation mourned a president whose good looks and affable manner had made him personally popular even as his administration ran into trouble. Within a few years after Harding's death, his reputation sagged under the weight of scandals. Popular biographers in the 1930s and scholars in the 1950s and 1960s blamed Harding for many of the ills of the 1920s. Sympathetic historians have tried on occasion to rehabilitate Harding, but these efforts to reappraise his record have not changed the negative historical verdict on his presidency.

See also *Teapot Dome.*

LEWIS L. GOULD, UNIVERSITY OF TEXAS AT AUSTIN

BIBLIOGRAPHY

Ferrell, Robert H. *The Strange Deaths of President Harding.* Columbia: University of Missouri Press, 1996.

Murray, Robert K. *The Harding Era: Warren G. Harding and His Administration.* Minneapolis: University of Minnesota Press, 1969.

Trani, Eugene P., and David L. Wilson. *The Presidency of Warren G. Harding.* Lawrence: University Press of Kansas, 1977.

HARRISON, BENJAMIN

Benjamin Harrison, the twenty-third president (1889–1893), was a reserved, honest, moderate Republican from a politically prominent family. His great grandfather had been a signer of the Declaration of Independence; his grandfather, William Henry, was the ninth president of the United States and built the family estate at North Bend, Ohio. His father, John Scott Harrison, was a Whig member of Congress from 1853 to 1857.

Benjamin was born at North Bend on August 20, 1833, educated at Miami University, and called to the bar in 1853. The next year he moved to Indianapolis, where, with political and military interludes (he was a brigadier general in the Civil War at the age of thirty-one), Harrison lived and practiced law until his death on March 13, 1901.

Republican politics came to him naturally as scion of a dynasty. He entered the Senate in 1881 and was nominated for president in 1888. The Democratic incumbent, Grover Cleveland, won 90,000 more popular votes than Harrison, but the Republicans carried the electoral college, 233 to 168.

It was the age of the spoils system: "I found that the party managers had taken it all to themselves," Harrison lamented, "they had sold out every [cabinet] place to pay the election expenses." Nonetheless, his administration had solid achievements: the Pan-American Union was established; disputes with Germany, Britain, and Chile were resolved; and a high tariff, the McKinley Act, was passed. Harrison was renominated, but agrarian and labor unrest damaged his standing, the bimetalist Sherman Act had caused inflation, and Cleveland returned to the White House.

In retirement, Harrison, who deplored America's acquisition of colonial empire from Spain following the Spanish-American War, represented Venezuela at the international arbitration in Paris of its boundary dispute with Britain over British Guiana (1899).

See also *Tariff History.*

RICHARD MAJOR, INDEPENDENT SCHOLAR

BIBLIOGRAPHY

Harrison, Benjamin. *This Country of Ours.* New York: Scribner's, 1897.

Sievers, Harry J. *Benjamin Harrison.* 3 vols. New York: University Publishers, 1959–1968.

Socolofsky, Homer E., and Allan B. Spetter. *The Presidency of Benjamin Harrison.* Lawrence: University Press of Kansas, 1987.

Benjamin Harrison   *Library of Congress*

HARRISON, WILLIAM HENRY

William Henry Harrison was born in Virginia on February 9, 1773. His father, Benjamin, a signer of the Declaration of Independence, died when William Henry was eighteen. William Henry then entered the army, but in 1798 he resigned his commission to serve in the government of the Northwest Territory. In 1800 he became governor of the newly established Indiana Territory, where he unsuccessfully pushed for a repeal of the ban on slavery in the Northwest Ordinance. In 1811, while still territorial governor, Harrison led a victorious army at the Battle of Tippecanoe, defeating the Shawnee. He accepted a commission in the regular army the following year and defeated the British and their Indian allies in a number of battles. Harrison won election to the U.S. Senate in 1825, then became American ambassador to Colombia. In 1836 Harrison was one of many Whig candidates for the presidency, but the election went to Andrew Jackson's vice president, Martin Van Buren.

Harrison won the presidency in 1840, campaigning as the symbol of the West and the frontier. Although from a wealthy slaveholding background, Harrison was portrayed as a man of the people. On the *Harrison Almanac* the candidate was push-

William Henry Harrison is portrayed as the "Washington of the West" in this 1840 campaign lithograph. *Library of Congress*

ing a plow, while the *Hard Cider and Log Cabin Almanac* portrayed him filling cups of cider, proclaiming his hospitality to all. With a strong popular vote, Harrison won the White House and helped Whigs capture both houses of Congress, but his tenure was short. A month after his inauguration Harrison became the first president to die in office. He was succeeded by John Tyler, a states' rights Democrat who had broken with Jackson but had little sympathy for Whig programs.

PAUL FINKELMAN, UNIVERSITY OF TULSA COLLEGE OF LAW

BIBLIOGRAPHY

Gunderson, Robert G. *The Log Cabin Campaign*. Lexington: University of Kentucky Press, 1957.

Peterson, Norma Lois. *The Presidencies of William Henry Harrison and John Tyler.* Lawrence: University of Kansas Press, 1989.

HARTFORD CONVENTION RESOLUTIONS

As the War of 1812 dragged on, the Massachusetts legislature called in October 1814 for a regional convention to fix the new nation's broken politics. Twenty-three delegates appointed by the legislatures of Massachusetts, Connecticut, and Rhode Island met in the capital of Connecticut from December 15, 1814, to January 5, 1815. So did three delegates chosen by county conventions in Vermont and New Hampshire. In the face of grave challenges in national and international politics, New Englanders would save, if they could, the Federalist Party, the New England region, and the American nation. New western states had already been admitted to the Union, states whose votes supported the Virginia Republicans in national politics against New England Federalists, and any number of additional states seemed on the way. Desperate over the loss of political power in the nation, military costs incurred during the War of 1812, and economic losses suffered because of a trade embargo, the Hartford Convention delegates resolved to address these unhappy developments.

Urging adoption of several constitutional amendments, the convention proposed that henceforth a two-thirds majority rather than a simple majority in each house should be required to pass a measure admitting a new state, declaring war, or placing an embargo on foreign trade. The Three-Fifths Clause (Article I, section 2) should be amended so that slaves would no longer count in determining power in the U.S. House of Representatives or the electoral college. Given that Thomas Jefferson had served two terms as president and fellow Virginian James Madison was in his second term, another proposed amendment took two additional thrusts at Virginia's dominance: No president should serve more than a single term, and successive presidents should not come from the same state.

The convention did not call for secession but left that option open, so its actions might appear moderate even though its demeanor was threatening. If the war persisted and the proposed amendments were not adopted, the delegates vowed to meet again. In short, Hartford Convention delegates acted in a way similar to the First Continental Congress of 1774, which urged adoption of various measures by Great Britain and, when rebuffed, led to the Second Continental Congress, which ended by declaring independence.

As the convention wrapped up its deliberations in January 1815, however, news was on the way that the war had ended, and the proposals went nowhere. By 1861 New England had long since forsaken secession and would not brook it among southerners.

See also *American Revolution; Constitutional Amendments; Embargo; Federalists; Madison, James; Secession; Sectionalism; Slavery; States' Rights; Super Majority; Three-fifths Clause; War of 1812.*

PETER WALLENSTEIN, VIRGINIA POLYTECHNIC INSTITUTE AND STATE UNIVERSITY

BIBLIOGRAPHY

Banner, James M., Jr. *To the Hartford Convention: The Federalists and the Origins of Party Politics in Massachusetts, 1789–1815.* New York: Knopf, 1970.

Dwight, Theodore. *History of the Hartford Convention.* New York: White, 1833.

Robinson, Donald L. *Slavery in the Structure of American Politics, 1765–1820.* New York: Harcourt Brace Jovanovich, 1971.

HAYES, RUTHERFORD B.

President Rutherford B. Hayes (1877–1881) is best remembered as formally ending Reconstruction. His administration was plagued with major economic troubles associated with the depression of 1877.

Born in Ohio in 1822, Hayes became a lawyer, joined the Republican Party, and fought in the Civil War. After the war he served in the U.S. House of Representatives and as governor of Ohio. As the Republican presidential nominee in 1876, he promised to serve only a single term and won an extremely close and disputed election.

After securing promises from white southerners that they would safeguard the civil and political rights of black southerners, Hayes withdrew the last federal troops from Louisiana and South Carolina, where the last Republican state governments then fell to local Democrats. In 1877 he dispatched federal troops to contain a huge strike by railway workers. Stormy relations with Congress, even with such members of his own party as Roscoe Conkling of New York and James G. Blaine

Rutherford B. Hayes *Library of Congress*

of Maine, limited Hayes's effectiveness as president. For example, although he was an advocate of sound money policies, Congress passed over his veto an inflationary measure calling for coinage of overvalued silver coins. Hayes tried to address the ever-popular spoils system by initiating civil service reform, but Congress refused to act on his proposals. He did, however, seek highly qualified citizens to fill government jobs.

SABRA BISSETTE LEDENT, INDEPENDENT AUTHOR

BIBLIOGRAPHY

Davison, Kenneth E. *The Presidency of Rutherford B. Hayes.* Westport, Conn.: Greenwood Press, 1972.

Hoogenboom, Ari. *Rutherford B. Hayes: Warrior and President.* Lawrence: University Press of Kansas, 1995.

Williams, T. Harry. *Hayes of the Twenty-Third: The Civil War Volunteer Officer.* New York: Knopf, 1965.

HIGHER EDUCATION ACT

The Higher Education Act of 1965, a significant component of Great Society legislation, signaled a widened role for the federal government in American higher education.

In various ways before the 1960s, Congress promoted and shaped higher education in the United States. The Morrill Land-Grant College Acts of 1862 and 1890 fostered a system of land-grant institutions, at least one in every state, and subsequent legislation such as the Hatch Act in 1887 and the Smith-Lever Act of 1914 promoted agricultural research and agricultural extension services centered at the land-grant schools.

The New Deal, Second World War, and cold war brought further enhancement of a federal role in fostering higher education. Public works programs during the Great Depression of the 1930s put many thousands of Americans to work constructing libraries and other buildings on college campuses across the nation. The Servicemen's Readjustment Act of 1944 (G.I. Bill) facilitated access to higher education for millions of veterans of World War II, the Korean War, and later service. The National Defense Education Act of 1958, which spurred the advanced training of scientists and engineers, embodied the nation's response to the Soviet Union's successful launch of the *Sputnik I* satellite in 1957.

During the administrations of John F. Kennedy and Lyndon B. Johnson, Congress went further than ever before to promote higher education and Americans' access to it. For example, the Higher Education Facilities Act of 1963 provided financial support for colleges, graduate schools, and technical institutes to construct academic facilities. The Economic Opportunity Act of 1964 established a work-study program for college students, a provision added by the House Committee on Education and Labor, chaired by Adam Clayton Powell Jr. (D-N.Y.). In 1964 Congress also broadened the scope of the National Defense Education Act to include advanced training of students in disciplines such as history and political science.

The Higher Education Act of 1965 was a companion to the Elementary and Secondary Education Act, passed earlier the same year. Both laws reflected the Republican debacle in the 1964 elections, in which Johnson had been elected in a landslide over Barry Goldwater and the Republican ranks in Congress had been decimated. The Democrats were free to pass measures that had met opposition in the past. In part, Congress sought to redirect the land-grant approach of the past to the needs of an urban society. The new legislation was aimed at benefiting urban and private universities as well as land-grant schools and at addressing urban problems.

The 1965 act was designed to help institutions and college students alike. Cold war legislation had focused on faculty and graduate students, but the 1965 act emphasized undergraduate students. In addition, much of the federal funding for science research had been going to a small number of research institutions, but the 1965 act targeted even marginal schools.

In the mid-1960s, as the baby boomers began to graduate from high school, a pressing need for additional spaces in higher education became apparent. Moreover, an ever-higher percentage of teenagers considered attending an institution of higher education, but many families could not afford the cost. In an increasingly technical job market, more training would be required than ever before; nor could the nation afford to ignore the potential benefits to the entire society of enhanced education for far more of its citizens and workers. What emerged in 1965 was legislation that addressed the financial needs of prospective college students from poor and middle-class families alike.

Central to the Higher Education Act of 1965 was Title IV, which offered various types of financial assistance to academically qualified undergraduate students. Approximately half the money appropriated under Title IV went to Educational Opportunity Grants for low-income students who would be unable to attend college without such aid. The other half went to expanded programs that offered part-time employment or low-interest loans to students who did not meet the more stringent needs test.

One provision sought to enlist the nation's stronger institutions to assist traditionally black schools to upgrade their teaching, curricula, and facilities, not only because these schools continued to educate a majority of black undergrad-

uates but also so that they could more effectively seek to attract nonblack students and thereby desegregate their student populations. Other provisions sought to facilitate schools' acquisition of laboratory equipment and to build up school library holdings and prepare professionals for work as librarians and in information sciences.

The Higher Education Act of 1965 also addressed various wider social needs by means of higher education. One provision was designed to recruit institutions of higher education to help solve community problems in areas such as housing, poverty, and health. Yet another established a National Teachers Corps to target instruction in public elementary and secondary schools located in low-income communities.

When Congress passed the bill in late October, President Johnson wanted to make its enactment a memorable occasion. He returned to Southwest Texas State College, where as a young man he had struggled to find the means to stay in school and where, he observed, "the seeds were planted" for his conviction that access to education was critical to the well-being of the individual, the nation, and the world. After celebrating the "key" that would unlock "the door to education" for hundreds of thousands of the nation's young people, he signed the bill into law. Although amended in the years ahead, the Higher Education Act of 1965 proved to be a major marker of federal policy shaping and promoting higher education across the nation.

See also *G.I. Bill; Great Society; Johnson, Lyndon B.; Morrill Land-Grant College Acts; New Deal; Sex Discrimination in Higher Education.*

PETER WALLENSTEIN, VIRGINIA POLYTECHNIC INSTITUTE AND STATE UNIVERSITY

BIBLIOGRAPHY

Chavez, José. "Presidential Influence on the Politics of Higher Education: The Higher Education Act of 1965." Ph. D. dissertation, University of Texas at Austin, 1975.

Graham, Hugh Davis. *The Uncertain Triumph: Federal Education Policy in the Kennedy and Johnson Years.* Chapel Hill: University of North Carolina Press, 1984.

Sundquist, James L. *Politics and Policy: The Eisenhower, Kennedy, and Johnson Years.* Washington, D.C.: Brookings Institution, 1968.

HOOVER, HERBERT C.

Herbert Clark Hoover was born on August 10, 1874, in the Quaker community of West Branch, Iowa. Orphaned at the age of ten, Hoover began an odyssey that would make him a multimillionaire, international humanitarian, secretary of commerce, and thirty-first president of the United States. It was as president that Hoover had the

Herbert C. Hoover *Library of Congress*

misfortune of coming to office as the Great Depression engulfed the United States and the world and—fairly or not—forever colored his reputation in American political history.

In September 1891 Hoover was admitted to the first class at Stanford University, where he studied geology. He devoted the two decades following his graduation in 1895 to making his fortune as an international mining engineer. By 1914, however, he yearned for more than wealth, and World War I provided him with an opportunity for public service. Initially, he aided Americans stranded in Europe. Later, he established the Commission for Relief in Belgium to feed the civilian population of war-torn Europe.

Hoover's compassionate humanitarianism led, in 1917, to an invitation from President Woodrow Wilson to become U.S. food administrator. In this position, Hoover rationed domestic food supplies during World War I to feed the allied armies as well as the American people. In the years after the war, Hoover was director general of the American Relief Administration, an agency established to address the widespread famine in Europe. As a result of his relief work, he was widely admired in the United States and was sought by both political parties as a candidate for president in 1920.

Although at that time Hoover did not exhibit strong leanings toward either party and did not actively seek a place on a national ticket, he eventually declared himself a Republican and accepted President Warren Harding's invitation to serve as secretary of commerce. Through both the Harding and Calvin Coolidge administrations he remained at the Department of Commerce, where he established a wide range of industrial standards for consumer products, developed new theories on the control of the national economy, and encouraged the growth of new industries such as radio and aviation.

PRESIDENTIAL ADMINISTRATION

When Coolidge declined to run for reelection in 1928, Hoover was a logical candidate for the Republican nomination. His defeat of Alfred E. Smith, the Democratic governor of New York, reflected the nation's contentment with the prosperity of the 1920s. Hoover hoped to govern in the progressive tradition of Theodore Roosevelt. True to his ambition, Hoover devoted the first eight months of his presidency to a variety of social, economic, and environmental reforms. In subsequent years he promoted social action through a series of conferences and commissions on topics such as prohibition, child welfare, and unemployment.

Following the stock market crash of October 1929, Hoover focused on the collapse of the U.S. economy. He established new agencies such as the Federal Farm Board, the Federal Drought Relief Committee, the President's Emergency Committee for Employment, the President's Organization for Unemployment Relief, and the Reconstruction Finance Corporation. The single purpose of these programs was to stimulate the economy and get the nation back to work.

Hoover also attempted to use the bully pulpit of the presidency to stimulate confidence in the American people that economic conditions would improve. On May 1, 1930, for example, he told the U.S. Chamber of Commerce that the worst was over and that recovery would be rapid. For a time Hoover proved correct, and by the spring of 1931 the economy had improved. But by the end of that year and throughout 1932 the economy was in a free fall, and Hoover got the blame. By the summer of 1932 the American people had lost faith in Hoover's leadership.

In spite of the worsening crisis, the president would not provide direct federal relief to the unemployed. For Hoover, direct relief—even in hard times—undermined the principles of American liberty. As an alternative, he promoted indirect relief through public works projects, eventually spending more than $3.5 billion on these projects between 1930 and 1933. It was to little avail, however, as the percentage of unemployed workers increased from 3.2 percent in 1929 to 23.6 percent by 1932.

The president's political reputation as the master of emergencies plummeted in the face of rising unemployment. Hoover himself exacerbated the problem by refusing all advice to tell the American people what he was doing to help them. Adding to his declining fortunes was the July 1932 debacle of the Bonus March, in which thousands of jobless veterans were driven from Washington, D.C. U.S. Army troops, led by Gen. Douglas MacArthur and Major Dwight D. Eisenhower, who later would be World War II heroes, attacked unarmed and unemployed veterans. Hoover had not given the order to disperse the veterans, but as president and commander in chief he got the blame nonetheless.

It came as no surprise when Hoover lost a bid for reelection to Franklin D. Roosevelt in 1932. During the months between the election and the inauguration, however, Hoover attempted to enlist Roosevelt in common cause. Roosevelt would have none of it, although later, particularly during the first three months after he took office, he adopted many of Hoover's programs to fight the Great Depression.

PUBLIC PERCEPTION AND POSTPRESIDENTIAL YEARS

Hoover had been frustrated by a political system that failed to respond to his calls for volunteerism and community action. But the American people were also frustrated by Hoover's policies, which seemed ineffective in responding to the realities of the Great Depression. Displaced farmers and workers found themselves living like hoboes in camps and makeshift shantytowns that came to be known as "Hoovervilles" and eating groundhogs and other rodents that were nicknamed "Hoover hogs."

These and other manifestations of the Great Depression left Hoover tarred as an uncaring, distant leader in spite of the actions he attempted to take during his term in office. His critics portrayed him as unable or unwilling to accept responsibility for misreading the economic crisis that continued to roll on and as failing to find adequate remedies. Hoover saw it differently: he viewed Roosevelt as a demagogue who would corrupt the U.S. political system with excessive government programs. Hoover devoted the remainder of the 1930s and the first half of the 1940s to the Republican fight against the New Deal.

In May 1945, six weeks after Roosevelt's death, Hoover met with President Harry S. Truman, and the two men planned for the recovery of postwar Europe. At Truman's request, Hoover traveled the world to provide the president with a personal assessment of international food needs. More important, Hoover also lobbied his fellow Republicans to support Truman's food relief programs. Hoover and Truman also joined forces from 1947 to 1949 on a commission to reorganize the executive branch of the federal government. The commission's recommendations led to a streamlined, more efficient postwar government.

In 1953, pleased to see the Republican Party back in the White House after a twenty-year absence, Hoover agreed to President Dwight D. Eisenhower's request to chair a second Hoover commission, but Hoover was later frustrated by the president's apparent lack of support for the commission's recommendations.

In addition to public service, Hoover devoted his postpresidential years to social causes such as the Boys Clubs of America and the Hoover Institution, a research center he had established on the Stanford University campus in 1919. He also wrote more than forty books of political philosophy and memoir during those years. He died on October 20, 1964, after serving the longest tenure as a former president of the United States.

See also *Bonus March; Great Depression*.

TIMOTHY WALCH, HERBERT HOOVER PRESIDENTIAL LIBRARY

BIBLIOGRAPHY

Clements, Kendrick A. *Hoover, Conservation, and Consumerism: Engineering the Good Life.* Lawrence: University Press of Kansas, 2000.

Fausold, Martin. *The Presidency of Herbert C. Hoover.* Lawrence: University Press of Kansas, 1985.

Walch, Timothy, and Dwight M. Miller, eds. *Herbert Hoover and Franklin D. Roosevelt: A Documentary History.* Westport, Conn.: Greenwood, 1998.

HOUSE LEADERSHIP: SPEAKER

The Speaker of the U.S. House of Representatives is the chief political leader and the top administrative officer of the House of Representatives. The Speaker presides over the House while it is in session, has the power to recognize members who desire to speak, and makes rulings regarding parliamentary proceedings. The Speaker is elected by majority vote of the members of the House at the beginning of each new Congress. While the Constitution does not state that the Speaker has to be a member of Congress, all Speakers have been members of the House and have represented the majority party.

ORIGINS AND EARLY HISTORY

The office of Speaker has its origins in the thirteenth-century English Parliament, where the Speaker was the chief spokesman for the monarchy. Over the centuries the office changed, and by the seventeenth century the Speaker was the presiding officer of the House of Commons, more independent of the crown and sometimes representing political opposition to the crown.

The framers of the Constitution were familiar with the role of the Speaker in Parliament, and adopted the title along with the assumption that the duties would be similar. During the debates at the Federal Convention in Philadelphia in 1787, the framers spent very little time discussing the duties and functions of the Speaker. In fact, the Constitution is silent on any specific definition of the Speaker's duties. It simply states in Article I, section 2, "The House of Representatives shall chuse their Speaker and other Officers. . . ." The word "Speaker" appears only five times in the Constitution.

During the late eighteenth and early nineteenth centuries, the main duty of the Speaker was to be the chief parliamentarian and presiding officer of the sessions of the House. The Speaker sat in a raised seat in the House chamber and kept order and proper decorum during debate. Some early Speakers, such as the first, Frederick A. Muhlenberg of Pennsylvania, did not extend their role as Speaker to include political leadership. Since parties themselves were not clearly defined in the early congresses, Speakers exercised little more political power than any other member. By 1810, however, the Speaker took on greater political authority and administrative responsibilities. This change is evident in the career of Henry Clay of Kentucky, who served as Speaker on and off for twelve years beginning in 1811. Clay played a major role in transforming the office by the strength of his personality and by his energy and desire to be in charge of the House. Clay presided over the House but also regularly voted and engaged in debate. His manipulation of the selection of committee chairmen gave him greater power within the House, which he used to further the interests of the western part of the country and to mount opposition to the agenda of President James Madison.

The power of the Speaker reached its peak with Thomas Brackett Reed, R-Maine, Speaker from 1889 to 1891 and again from 1895 to 1899, and with Joseph Gurney Cannon, R-Ill., who held the position from 1903 to 1911. These men transformed House rules to strengthen the authority of the Speaker over committee assignments; they also increased the ability of the majority party to run the House with less opposition from the minority. Cannon, affectionately called Uncle Joe, was a virtual autocrat in the way he ran the House. Democrats, and some members of Cannon's own party finally revolted against his leadership in 1910 and rewrote House rules to strip the Speaker of some of the power to control committees.

POST–WORLD WAR II

Since World War II the office of Speaker has regained much of the authority it had at the end of the nineteenth century, although several waves of reform in the 1940s and in the 1970s prevented the office from exerting the raw power seen in the days of Joe Cannon. Sam Rayburn, D-Texas, who served longer than any other Speaker, held the office from 1940 to 1961; his long tenure represented a bridge from the war years to the cold war and the age of television. During the long period from 1954 to 1995 when Democrats controlled the House chamber, Democratic Speakers had to share power with long-term, powerful committee chairmen. The modern Speaker presides over a complex institution with thousands of employees, more than two centuries of tradition, and a complex set of rules. Since the Presidential Succession Act of 1947, the Speaker is next in line after the vice president to succeed the president of the United States.

In 1995, for the first time in four decades, the Republican Party gained control of the House and elected Newt Gingrich, R-Ga., as Speaker. Gingrich vowed to change the House and the role of the Speaker in revolutionary ways. He used television to gain public attention and to affect the national agenda. In a sense he was in the tradition of Henry Clay, who changed the office primarily through his own personality and energy. Gingrich concentrated power within the Speaker's office, undermined the power of committee chairmen and other officers, and directly challenged President Bill Clinton on setting the national agenda. Eventually Gingrich's brash style led to a backlash in the country and within his own party. House elections in 1998 resulted in Democratic gains even though Gingrich had predicted a large increase in Republican seats. Gingrich announced that he would not be a candidate for Speaker in the 106th Congress, even though he was reelected as a representative from Georgia. He resigned his seat in Congress shortly thereafter.

See also *Congress; Senate Leadership, Early Period; Senate Leadership, Modern.*

RAYMOND W. SMOCK, INDEPENDENT HISTORIAN

BIBLIOGRAPHY

Davidson, Roger M., and Walter Oleszek. *Congress and Its Members.* 7th ed. Washington, D.C.: CQ Press, 2000.

Peters, Ronald M., Jr. *The American Speakership: The Office in Historical Perspective.* Baltimore: Johns Hopkins University Press, 1990.

U.S. House of Representatives. *Rules of the House of Representatives.* 105th Cong. 2d Sess. Washington, D.C.: U.S. Government Printing Office, 1999.

I

IMMIGRATION AND NATURALIZATION: SOCIETY AND POLITICS

Although the United States was built by immigrants and their descendents, newcomers have not always been welcome. The degree to which an immigrant received a cordial welcome to America has depended in large part on the economic and political conditions of the day and on the ethnicity and skills of the immigrants.

IMMIGRATION IN THE SEVENTEENTH AND EIGHTEENTH CENTURIES

During the colonial era, immigrants were sought after for their labor. Advertisements touting America as the greatest place on earth for a working person were placed throughout Europe in an effort to attract immigrants. Some colonies had so few workers that the colonial governments granted residents unimproved land—usually between fifty and one hundred acres—as an inducement to recruit laborers from Europe. For individuals who wished to come to America but could not afford passage, indentured servitude provided the necessary traveling funds in return for several years' labor. While some black Africans originally traveled to the colonies as indentured servants, in time millions of black Africans were brought to the New World as slaves.

Although most European immigrants during the seventeenth century were English, in the eighteenth century significant numbers of Scots-Irish and Germans also emigrated to the colonies. Because these people resembled the English both culturally and physically, Anglo-Americans accepted them as more or less equals. With the exception of black Africans, who were despised for their status as slaves as much as for their non–Western European customs, colonial America made little distinction between American-born colonists and immigrants because most Anglo-Americans were themselves but a few generations removed from their European ancestry.

Although immigrants were still welcomed in America after the American Revolution, some citizens of longer standing began to feel a need to impose political restrictions on the newcomers. Because most immigrants were attracted to the Democratic-Republican Party, the Federalists used their control of Congress to pass the Alien Acts of 1798, which required immigrants to live in the United States for fourteen years before they could become citizens. Earlier in the national era, the requirement had been five years (and during the colonial period it was assumed that all residents, regardless of how long they had lived in America, were subjects of the Crown). The Alien Acts also empowered the president to detain or deport noncitizens as he saw fit. Bitterly debated in Congress and in taverns and coffeehouses, the acts led directly to the Virginia and Kentucky Resolutions, which declared that the states could invalidate an act of Congress.

IMMIGRATION IN THE NINETEENTH CENTURY

Between 1789 and 1815 the French Revolution and the Napoleonic wars caused so much turmoil in Europe that few immigrants were able to come to America. After 1820 the flow of immigrants resumed at an unprecedented and increasing rate. Between 1820 and 1840 almost 750,000 immigrants made their way to the United States. The number increased to 1.5 million between 1840 and 1850, and to 2.5 million between 1850 and 1860. Many immigrants had sufficient capital to purchase farms in the Northwest Territory. However, many more were destitute and traveled no farther than the cities along the eastern seaboard. Immigrant settlement thus contributed to the rise of American urbanization and industrialization, as large numbers of jobseekers willing to work at low wages provided manufacturers with the workforce necessary to expand operations. Large numbers of unskilled immigrant laborers also were recruited to construct turnpikes, canals, and railroads, contributing significantly to the expansion of the growing country's transportation infrastructure.

Seventeenth-century immigrants were predominantly English, followed by Scots-Irish, German, and African immigrants in the eighteenth century. Early nineteenth-century immigrants were predominantly German and Irish Roman Catholics, many of whom were poor. Protestant Americans distrusted and disliked the Irish and German Catholics, partly because they feared that, in a war with a Catholic country such as France or Spain, the pope would threaten to excommunicate any Catholic who fought on the side of the United States. However, most Americans were not bothered by the great influx of non–English, non–Protestant immigrants. Manufacturers continued to welcome potential laborers, land speculators welcomed potential customers, big-city politicians welcomed potential supporters, and western states welcomed potential residents who would increase the size of their congressional delegations.

Those Americans who perceived the foreign-born as unskilled, uncouth, unpatriotic, and papist, however, were troubled that 10 percent of the free population in the 1850s was foreign-born. These Americans became vocal proponents of *nativism*. Nativists claimed that immigrants were inferior to American-born citizens because they lacked the tools necessary for advancing or even living in American civilization. Many nativists simply were racists who disliked all people who were not white, Anglo-Saxon, and Protestant. Others were temperance crusaders who were disgusted by Irish and German immigrants' apparent fondness for alcohol. Still others resented the competition for jobs that kept factory workers' wages low, given the large number of unskilled immigrants who were willing to work for next to nothing. Finally, members of the Whig Party were upset because most immigrants joined the Democratic Party.

Nativism gained a political voice in 1837 when the Native American Association called for restrictions on immigration. In 1850 the Supreme Order of the Star-Spangled Banner espoused banning Catholics from public office, lengthening the residency requirement for naturalization, and requiring prospective voters to pass a literacy test. The order reorganized itself in 1852 as the American Party, also called the Know Nothings for their secret password, "I know nothing." Although the party did surprisingly well in the election of 1854, it—and nativism—quickly faded from the political scene with the coming of the Civil War. During the Civil War, U.S. officials actually encouraged further immigration as a means of filling the vacancies created by factory workers who were now serving in the Union Army.

While Irish and German immigrants were entering the eastern United States, Chinese immigrants were arriving in the West, drawn mostly by the promise of striking it rich during the California Gold Rush that began in 1849. At first, the established settlers welcomed the Chinese immigrants because they provided much-needed labor. Nevertheless, in 1852 California began passing laws to prevent Chinese and other foreigners from mining gold.

By 1865 large numbers of Chinese immigrants were working as construction workers with the transcontinental railroad. Railroad agents recruited *coolie* laborers because they worked hard for low wages. Almost 90 percent of the Central Pacific's workforce was Chinese, and these immigrants built most of the western portion of the first transcontinental railroad. After the completion of the railroad in 1869, many Chinese immigrants found work in central California as laborers on various irrigation projects. Others worked picking fruits and vegetables for low wages, and a few acquired land and became independent farmers. Eventually, the majority migrated to the cities, where they occupied the lowest rungs of the employment ladder.

Like its eastern counterpart, western nativism also resulted in discrimination against immigrants. Discriminatory acts varied from boycotts of Chinese-made goods and services to anti-coolie riots in which Chinese residents were beaten or killed and their homes and businesses vandalized and destroyed. In 1882 Congress passed the Chinese Exclusion Act. The act banned Chinese immigration for ten years and prevented Chinese residents from becoming naturalized citizens. Renewed for ten more years in 1892 and made permanent in 1902, the ban on Chinese immigration was not lifted until 1943.

While Chinese immigrants were being excluded from citizenship in western states, European immigrants were being encouraged to settle in the West and Midwest. Between 1870 and 1900 more than 2 million Scandinavians, Germans, Irish, Russians, and Czechs took advantage of the Homestead Act of 1862 and subsequent, similar acts to acquire productive farmland on the Great Plains. Russian immigrants' introduction of Ukrainian varieties of wheat in Kansas and neighboring states contributed greatly to the creation of the "wheat belt" in the Midwest.

Meanwhile, European immigration continued in the eastern United States. Between 1860 and 1900 more than 14 million Europeans came to the United States. Before 1890 these immigrants came mostly from England, Ireland, and Germany. After 1890, however, "new immigrants" began arriving in large numbers. Polish and Italian Catholics, eastern European Jews, Orthodox Catholics from Greece and Armenia, Muslims from the Ottoman Empire, French Canadians, Russians, Scandinavians, and Japanese dramatically changed the cultural and social landscape of America. By the late 1880s the presence of unprecedented numbers of new immigrants would stimulate a new wave of nativism.

Many immigrants were lured to America under the provisions of the Labor Contract Law. Employers were authorized by Congress to advance immigrants the money they needed for transportation and then deduct this amount from their wages. In a sense, the Labor Contract Law was a throwback to the indentured servitude system of colonial days. Most immigrants who arrived as contract laborers settled in the industrial cities of the Northeast, and their additions to the factory labor pool contributed to the further expansion of the U.S. economy after the Civil War.

By 1890 immigrants predominated in a number of American cities. For example, foreign-born immigrants and their children made up more than 80 percent of the populations of New York City and Chicago, the two largest U.S. cities. More Irish people lived in New York than in Dublin, more Germans lived in New York than in Hamburg, and more Poles lived in Chicago than in Warsaw. This situation profoundly affected municipal politics. Through ethnically based political machines, the Irish came to dominate city government in New York and Boston, while the Germans dominated city government in Milwaukee and Cincinnati.

In a sense, the political machines acted like powerful fraternities. An immigrant who spoke little or no English or who was out of a job and down on his luck could go to the machine for help. In return, the immigrant was expected to vote for the machine's candidates at the next election. Machines almost always were corrupt; the bosses who ran them often provided services or sold contracts to their supporters in return for graft money or kickbacks. However, most machines also provided extremely well for the vast majority of their immigrant constituents. Their efficiency helped the political machines retain power until the mid-twentieth century.

Not surprisingly, the more aggressive political presence of some immigrant groups and the overall massive influx of new immigrants aroused a new wave of nativism among many Americans. In 1882 Congress banned convicts, paupers, and the mentally incompetent from immigrating and imposed a 50-cent immigration tax on anyone granted entry. In 1887 the American Protective Association, which made little secret of its hatred for Catholics and foreigners, formed to stop the flood of immigration. Seven years later the association had 500,000 members across the Northeast and Midwest. In 1894 the Immigration Restriction League formed, not to stop immigration altogether but to control it. The league advocated the admission of *desirable* immigrants and the screening out of undesirable immigrants via literacy tests and other methods. Congress responded to the league's relatively moderate approach by expanding the list of banned immigrants, increasing the immigration tax, and establishing a literacy requirement for immigrants.

This new wave of nativism had its limits, however: President Grover Cleveland vetoed the literacy requirement, largely because many Americans—including wealthy industrialists—welcomed continued immigration. Immigrants continued to supply a large pool of cheap labor that industrialists relied on to remain competitive. Also, more voters were themselves first- or second-generation Americans and believed that more people, not fewer, deserved the opportunity to live in America.

IMMIGRATION IN THE TWENTIETH CENTURY

Between 1900 and 1920 more than 14 million Europeans emigrated to the United States. This seemingly endless tide of immigrants revived nativistic feelings, which—among other things—resuscitated the Ku Klux Klan. Formed in the South during Reconstruction to keep blacks in their place, the Klan of the 1920s claimed it would protect America from a potential takeover by immigrants who brought with them dangerous ideologies. Public sentiment in the wake of World War I regarded all backgrounds other than Anglo-Saxon as potentially subversive, and widespread public fear of socialist infiltration in the wake of the Russian Revolution had marked anyone from central or eastern Europe as a potential bomb-throwing radical. By 1924 the Klan boasted 4 million mem-

Immigrants en route to the United States stand shoulder to shoulder on the deck of the S.S. *Patricia*, December 10, 1906. *Library of Congress*

bers, had established large chapters in most industrial northern cities, and regularly harassed immigrants across the country.

Several restrictionists rode the rising tide of nativism to gain election to Congress in 1920. The following year the restrictionists succeeded in passing the Emergency Immigration Act, which prohibited the immigration of more than 300,000 people in one year. The act also limited the number of immigrants from any given country in any given year to 3 percent of the number of people from that country in the United States in 1910. The National Origins Act of 1924 banned immigrants from East Asia and lowered the quotas for European nations to 2 percent of the number of people from each country in the United States in 1890. The few immigrants who would be allowed into the country would be primarily from England, Ireland, and Germany—the nationalities considered by restrictionists to be most desirable. In 1929 the total yearly quota was reduced to 150,000. And in 1952 growing fear of communist subversion led to passage of the McCarran-Walter Act, which further restricted immigration from everywhere other than northern and western Europe while granting immigration officials the power to deny entry to anyone deemed a threat to national security. As a result of these measures, only 8 million immigrants were granted entry between 1920 and 1960.

This situation changed somewhat with the passage of the Immigration Reform Act of 1965. This measure eliminated the total yearly quota but set all national yearly quotas at 20,000, thus opening the door to immigrants from any country in the world. The result was that large numbers of Asians and Latin Americans began to immigrate. Between 1960 and 1990 almost 14 million people immigrated to the United States. Of these immigrants, one-third came from Asia, and another one-third came from Latin America. Less than 10 percent came from western Europe.

Changing global political and economic patterns also contributed to shifts in immigration patterns in the twentieth century. The turbulence of World War I and World War II prompted many Europeans to emigrate, not only to the United States but also across borders within Europe and to other non–European countries. After the erection of the Iron Curtain, mass emigration from some east European countries was not an option for many years. And after World War II, many Asian nations began unprecedented political, cultural, and market relationships with the United States. As a global superpower (and a nation experiencing a postwar economic boom) in the 1960s, the United States became a magnet for immigrants from developing and war-torn nations who sought escape from poverty, political oppression, or cultural oppression.

The Immigration Reform Act was slowly changing the basic ethnic composition of the American population. An-

other factor that was contributing to this change was illegal immigration from Mexico, Central America, South America, Africa, Asia, and the Caribbean islands. The rising influx of illegals prompted Congress to consider several immigration bills during the 1980s. By adjusting immigration laws to acknowledge some of the political and economic forces driving illegal immigration, Congress hoped that the flow of illegals could be somewhat contained. The Refugee Act of 1980 restricted entry to those refugees who were fleeing political oppression while denying it to those who simply wished to improve their standard of living. Thus, the act opened America's doors to Cuban refugees escaping from communist domination but closed them to Haitians escaping from joblessness and starvation. The act also denied entry to refugees from Guatemala and El Salvador who were fleeing political oppression at the hands of U.S.-backed regimes. The Immigration Reform and Control Act of 1987 granted residency to illegal aliens who could prove they had entered the country before 1982, but it also imposed stiff fines on employers who knowingly hired illegals.

Despite these acts, illegal immigrants continued to cross U.S. borders at an unprecedented rate. The problems associated with illegal immigration during the last two decades of the twentieth century gave rise to yet another nativist movement. Governor Pete Wilson of California gained considerable political mileage from speaking out against illegal immigration, which had reached epidemic proportions in that state. Meanwhile, presidential contender Pat Buchanan made the issue a central one in his appeals to voters. Other manifestations of nativism included movements to have English made the official language of the United States, ban bilingual education in public schools, and deny welfare and other public assistance to undocumented aliens. Rightly or wrongly, many Americans feared that massive illegal immigration was draining government resources and straining social services. Given the greater disparity of immigrants in the late twentieth century and the promotion of diversity as a cultural norm, the desirability and meaning of assimilation and the melting pot had themselves become hotly debated topics. As had been true since the founding of the nation, however, labor shortages also continued to influence immigration policy at the close of the twentieth century, as America sought to attract high-tech workers from overseas to fill a growing gap in the American labor force.

See also *Know Nothing (American) Party; Labor Politics and Policy; Nativism; Prohibition and Temperance; Sedition Act of 1798; Slavery; Welfare State; Whig Party.*

CHARLES CAREY,
LYNCHBURG COLLEGE/CENTRAL VIRGINIA COMMUNITY COLLEGE

BIBLIOGRAPHY

Barkan, Elliott R. *And Still They Come: Immigrants and American Society, 1920 to the 1990s.* Wheeling, Ill.: Harlan Davidson, 1996.

Daniels, Roger. *Not Like Us: Immigrants and Minorities in America, 1890–1924.* Chicago: Ivan Dee, 1997.

Ferrie, Joseph P. *Yankeys Now: Immigrants in the Antebellum United States, 1840–1860.* New York: Oxford University Press, 1999.

Pedraza, Silvia, and Ruben G. Rumbaut, eds. *Origins and Destinies: Immigration, Race, and Ethnicity in America.* Belmont, Calif.: Wadsworth, 1996.

Portes, Alejandro, and Ruben G. Rumbaut. *Immigrant America: A Portrait.* Berkeley: University of California Press, 1996.

IMMIGRATION AND NATURALIZATION: TWENTIETH-CENTURY LAW AND POLICY

In the twentieth century, as in the nineteenth, U.S. immigration law faced fundamental questions of who would be permitted to live in the United States and, of those here, who would enjoy the full rights of citizenship. The resolution of these questions has had a curiously dual nature, sometimes extremely generous and sometimes astonishingly harsh. For example, the U.S. Congress firmly refused to bend the immigration laws to admit most Jewish refugees from Adolf Hitler's Europe. But the United States also has been the world's most common destination for immigrants and the dispossessed. Immigration policy played out in two main areas: citizenship law and laws governing selection of immigrants.

CITIZENSHIP LAW

U.S. citizens have rights that aliens do not, and aliens are subject to certain government-imposed disadvantages, such as ineligibility for certain government employment and the possibility of deportation. Until the Supreme Court limited state discrimination against aliens in the second half of the twentieth century, citizenship was even more consequential.

At common law, under the principle of *jus soli* (right of land), an individual became a citizen by being born in the nation's territory. A person born to parents who were already citizens became a citizen under the principle of *jus sanguinis* (right of blood). A central legal question faced by nationality law for centuries was whether non–Caucasians were eligible for citizenship by naturalization or birth.

In *Dred Scott v. Sandford* (1857) the Supreme Court held that those of African descent, even if born in the United States, were not citizens. Section 1 of the Fourteenth Amendment (1868) reversed this rule by providing in part that "[a]ll persons born or naturalized in the United States, and subject to the jurisdiction thereof, are citizens of the United States and of the State wherein they reside." In *United States v. Wong Kim Ark* (1898) the Supreme Court held that the Constitution's grant of *jus soli* citizenship was not limited by race, but applied to those of Chinese racial ancestry born in the United States. American Indians affiliated with tribes were not treated as citizens by virtue of the Fourteenth Amendment because they were not "subject to the jurisdiction" of the United States. However, in 1924 Congress granted citizenship to all Native Americans who did not already enjoy it by treaty.

During the late nineteenth century the United States acquired several overseas territories, and the Court had to decide whether children born there were automatically citizens under the *jus soli* principle. The Court found that Alaska, acquired in 1867, and Hawaii, annexed in 1898, were "incorporated" into the United States even before they became states. Persons born in the territories after incorporation were *jus soli* citizens; those already resident were given the right to citizenship by treaty or statute.

Other territories, deemed "unincorporated," had second-class status as mere possessions that were not part of the

Citizens of foreign nations become naturalized U.S. citizens at a ceremony in the U.S. courthouse in Washington, D.C., December 12, 1989. *R. Michael Jenkins, Congressional Quarterly*

United States for constitutional purposes, including *jus soli* citizenship. Unincorporated territories included American Samoa, Guam, the Philippines, Puerto Rico, and the Virgin Islands. Residents at the time of acquisition as well as children born there subsequently were noncitizen "nationals" who had limited political rights, unless and until Congress decided to offer them citizenship. The Philippines became independent in 1946. Through a series of statutes, Congress granted or offered citizenship to virtually all who were residents of Guam, the Northern Mariana Islands, Puerto Rico, and the Virgin Islands at the time of acquisition or born there subsequently. Currently, the only U.S. possessions not subject to the *jus soli* citizenship rule are American Samoa and Swains Island; those born there are noncitizen nationals.

Article I of the Constitution gave Congress the power to grant citizenship through naturalization to those born citizens of other countries. The naturalization law passed by the First Congress in 1790 authorized naturalization only of free whites. Congress amended the naturalization statute in 1870 to extend benefits to aliens of African nativity or descent. Through treaties or statutes, the United States granted citizenship to certain groups that might not have been eligible for naturalization, including Mexicans and Native Americans. Those of Asian racial background were the primary group ineligible to naturalize. Finally, in 1943 Chinese immigrants were made eligible for naturalization; in 1946, Indians and Filipinos. In 1952, after 160 years of discrimination, the naturalization law was made completely race- and color-blind.

IMMIGRATION POLICY

Traditionally, immigration and aliens were regulated by the states, not the federal government. A notable exception was a group of laws called the Alien and Sedition Acts, passed by Congress in 1798. The laws reflected a deep suspicion of aliens; one of the acts gave the president the arbitrary authority to deport them. The Sedition Act, it was hoped, would control subversive newspapers, some of which, Federalists argued, were edited by foreigners. The acts expired in 1800 and 1801 without a test in the Supreme Court, but the nativism and suspicion of aliens they reflected proved to be a persistent feature of immigration law.

By the late nineteenth century the Supreme Court had established that the federal government had the primary responsibility for regulating immigration. Congress prohibited the immigration of prostitutes and convicts in 1875, and in 1882 it passed the Chinese Exclusion Act, severely limiting all Chinese immigration. This racial exclusion policy was extended over time to other Asian immigrants and remained in effect in one form or another until 1965. In 1882 Congress also excluded the mentally ill and those deemed likely to be-

come public charges. After a decades-long struggle, Congress added a literacy test in 1917.

Until this point, federal regulation consisted of exclusionary rules, meaning that everyone could come in except members of prohibited groups or those possessed of specified characteristics. By 1921 the open-borders era was over. Congress added a principle of selectivity: in addition to not being a member of a prohibited class, would-be immigrants also had to satisfy particular qualifications established by law.

In 1921 Congress established a quota system, limiting the number of immigrants and establishing how the lucky few would be chosen from the many who wanted to come to the United States. The National Origins Quota System, in effect in one way or another from 1921 to 1965, allocated visas to countries based on the number of U.S. citizens who traced their origins to that nation. The formulas favored northern and western Europeans, disadvantaged eastern and southern Europeans, almost completely excluded Africans, and continued the policy of Asian exclusion. Within each foreign nation's quota, visas were allocated based on a "preference system," classifying immigrants based on their skills and education or on their family relationships to persons already in the United States.

Modern immigration law traces its origins to the Immigration and Nationality Act Amendments of 1965, which, by abolishing the National Origins Quota System, reflected the philosophy behind the Civil Rights Act of 1964 and the Voting Rights Act of 1965. The law ended immigration discrimination based on race, religion, and national origin, although no single country could take more than a specified share of the available visas. Since immigration was put on a color-blind basis in 1965, most immigrants have come from Asia, Africa, South America, and Central America.

The law continued the policy of recognizing numerous categories of people who, because of criminal convictions, ideological or security problems, health concerns, or other disfavored characteristics, were prohibited from entering as immigrants or as temporary nonimmigrants. It also continued to impose a numerical limit on most categories of immigration.

The 1965 law continued to admit aliens on the principles of family relationships and employment qualifications. Recent law has added a so-called diversity program, awarding visas by lottery to aliens from low immigration areas. Another way in which aliens can come to the United States is through a refugee program, in which displaced persons overseas are brought to the country for resettlement.

See also *Immigration and Naturalization: Society and Politics; Know Nothing (American) Party; Nativism.*

GABRIEL J. CHIN, UNIVERSITY OF CINCINNATI COLLEGE OF LAW

BIBLIOGRAPHY

Chin, Gabriel J. "The Civil Rights Revolution Comes to Immigration Law: A New Look at the Immigration and Nationality Act of 1965." *North Carolina Law Review* 75 (1996): 273–345.

Chin, Gabriel J., Victor C. Romero, and Michael A. Scaperlanda. *Immigration and the Constitution.* New York: Garland, 2000.

Gordon, Charles, Stanley Mailman, and Stephen Yale-Loehr. *Immigration Law and Procedure.* New York: Lexis, 2000.

Hutchinson, Edward P. *Legislative History of American Immigration Policy 1798–1965.* Philadelphia: University of Pennsylvania Press, 1981.

Neuman, Gerald. *Strangers to the Constitution: Immigrants, Borders and Fundamental Law.* Princeton: Princeton University Press, 1996.

Schuck, Peter H., and Rogers M. Smith, *Citizenship without Consent: Illegal Aliens in the American Polity.* New Haven: Yale University Press, 1985.

The mechanics of impeachment and trial are set by the Constitution. Chief Justice William Rehnquist is sworn in by Senate president pro tempore Strom Thurmond at the beginning of the impeachment trial of President Bill Clinton.   *Senate Photo Gallery*

IMPEACHMENT

Impeachment is the mechanism provided by the U.S. Constitution for the accusation, trial, and removal of officers of the United States who misbehave while in office. Impeachment is also a process found in state constitutions and has been used to remove state judges and executives from office. State constitutions are similar to the U.S. Constitution, which states:

> The President, Vice President and all civil officers of the United States, shall be removed from Office on Impeachment for, and Conviction of, Treason, Bribery, or other high Crimes and Misdemeanors.

THE PROCESS OF IMPEACHMENT

Impeachment is a political, not criminal, procedure. All proceedings take place within the legislative branch; the judiciary has no involvement in the process except in presidential impeachment, in which case the chief justice of the Supreme Court presides over the trial. The House of Representatives is given the sole responsibility for impeachment, which takes the form of an indictment, an accusation of wrongdoing. The Senate has the sole power to try the impeached official. The House of Representatives needs a simple majority to approve articles of impeachment, whereas the Senate, in the subsequent trial, must have a two-thirds majority of those senators voting to convict. If the Senate votes to convict, the official must be removed from office. The Senate may also vote to bar the convicted official from ever holding an office of the United States in the future, but the Constitution does not require this outcome. The Constitution bars the Senate from imposing any other punishment, but it also states that "the Party convicted shall nevertheless be liable and subject to Indictment, Trial, Judgment and Punishment, according to Law."

Impeachment as a means for removing public officials from office dates back to fourteenth-century England and was familiar to American colonists, who incorporated impeachment procedures into their state constitutions after independence. Benjamin Franklin observed that the precursor to impeachment had been assassination; the drafters of the federal Constitution sought to incorporate a mechanism that would prevent recourse to such an extreme solution to official misbehavior. The Constitutional Convention debates on impeachment were not extensive, but the focus was decidedly on impeachment as it related to the president and particularly on impeachment as a checking power on the executive. Some delegates opposed inclusion of impeachment provisions in the proposed Constitution, believing that the president would be dependent on whichever branch had the power of removal. These delegates believed that removal of unpopular presidents would be better achieved through the electoral process. The majority favored some sort of nonelectoral removal process, however, to prevent the possibility that corrupt or scheming officials might subvert the government.

The two issues that dominated the convention discussions were (1) who would be subject to impeachment and (2) where the impeachment power would be lodged. There were scattered efforts to define impeachable offenses. Proposed characterizations of impeachable conduct included: "misfeasance, misconduct, malpractice or neglect of duty, mal- and corrupt conduct, incapacity, negligence or perfidy, treachery, and bribery." The list was tentatively narrowed down to "treason or bribery" until George Mason, toward the end of the convention, proposed to add "maladministration." James Madison objected that so vague a term would be "equivalent to a tenure during pleasure of the Senate." According to Madison's notes, the convention responded to these concerns by voting to change "maladministration" to "other high crimes & misdemeanors (agst. the state)."

Although convention participants were most concerned with a method to deal with presidential misbehavior, impeachment has been seriously contemplated against only three presidents, and only two have actually been impeached. Impeachment more commonly has been used against other government officials, particularly life-tenured judges. Presidents may be voted out of office every four years, whereas the only accepted means for removing judges is impeachment.

EARLY IMPEACHMENT EFFORTS

The House of Representatives first exercised its impeachment power when the country was less than a decade old. The subject of this first impeachment was neither president nor judge, but a senator, William Blount of Tennessee. The Senate voted for Blount's expulsion simultaneously with the House impeachment vote, but his Senate trial did not occur until a year and a half later. Although this first impeachment ended with a dismissal for lack of jurisdiction, it established an important early precedent that members of the legislative branch are not "officers of the United States" subject to the Constitution's impeachment clause.

The next set of impeachments played a pivotal role in limiting and defining the function of this device in the American political system. After the first transfer of political power, from the Federalist Party, which had dominated the government for the first decade, to the Democratic-Republicans in 1801, impeachment was seen as a potential means for removing members of the political opposition ensconced in the judiciary; those judges would then be replaced with people more sympathetic to the new president's policies. As Virginia senator William Branch Giles, a Jefferson supporter, put it: "Removal by impeachment was nothing more than a declaration by congress to this effect: you hold dangerous opinions, and if you are suffered to carry them into effect you will work the

destruction of the nation. We want your offices, for the purposes of giving them to men who will fill them better."

The first successful impeachment, leading to the removal of U.S. District Judge John Pickering of New Hampshire in 1804, proved to be an uncertain precedent. Pickering, who was believed to be insane and was clearly an alcoholic, was accused, among other things, of wrongly refusing an appeal and of drunkenness on the bench. As a judge with lifetime tenure, the only way at the time to remove the incompetent Pickering was by impeachment and conviction. The Senate, apparently uncomfortable about convicting an insane man of "high Crimes and Misdemeanors," chose to find him only "guilty as charged."

The Jeffersonian interpretation of the impeachment power was put to its first real test with the impeachment and Senate trial of Supreme Court justice Samuel Chase in 1804–1805. Chase's acquittal, which caused Jefferson to label impeachment "a mere scarecrow," marked the end of Jeffersonian attempts to purge political opponents from the judiciary. Although subsequent impeachments may at times have been politically inspired, no one has successfully urged the interpretation of impeachment as a legitimate partisan tool.

IMPEACHMENT OF JUSTICES

The impeachment of Justice Chase raised a question that has recurred through virtually every impeachment in U.S. history: What constitutes an impeachable offense? The Jeffersonians accused Chase of improperly conducting trials (at that time Supreme Court justices also sat as trial court judges). Chase argued that unless conduct was subject to criminal indictment, it could not rise to the level of impeachable offense. This view has not always prevailed. In 1913, for example, Judge Robert W. Archbald was convicted and removed from office, although none of the charges against him were criminally indictable. Archbald had abused his office by taking gifts from litigants and using his office to gain access to business opportunities. These acts were not criminal—they did not rise to the level of bribery—but the House charged, and the Senate agreed, that Archbald's "sense of moral responsibility had become deadened" and that he had "degraded his high office and has destroyed the confidence of the public in his judicial integrity."

The noncriminal nature of many of the accusations against judges has led some to argue that the standard for impeaching judges is different from the standard for impeaching other government officials. Gerald R. Ford, while a member of the House of Representatives seeking the impeachment of Supreme Court justice William O. Douglas, averred that while elected officials could only be removed for high crimes and misdemeanors, federal judges could be removed for violation of the Constitution's "good behavior" clause. On the question of what might constitute an impeachable violation of the good behavior clause, Ford said: "An impeachable offense is whatever a majority of the House of Representatives considers it to be at any given moment in history."

Because impeachment is a political rather than judicial process, precedents carry a different level of significance than they do in the justice system. While courts are bound to follow precedents laid down in earlier cases, with the threat of having their decisions overturned if they disregard precedent, in impeachment cases Congress is bound to follow precedent only to the extent that the majority votes to do so. The Supreme Court has determined that Congress has the final say in both the conduct and outcome of the impeachment process, which means any failure to follow precedents can be rectified only at the ballot box.

During the nineteenth century and into the twentieth century, Congress regularly, if not frequently, used the impeachment process as a disciplinary tool against life-tenured federal judges. After the successful impeachment and removal of Judge Halsted Ritter in 1936 for bringing discredit to the judiciary, Congress tacitly adopted a different approach to impeachment, leaving judicial discipline to the criminal justice system and the judiciary itself. The apparent reason for this abdication was the enormous expenditure of legislative time and resources required to carry out an impeachment. The shortcomings of this approach surfaced in the 1980s and 1990s, when five federal judges were indicted and tried by the Justice Department for crimes ranging from tax evasion to bribery. When none of the judges resigned, Congress was forced to resort to the impeachment mechanism anyway. Particularly embarrassing was the case of Judge Harry Claiborne, who not only continued to hold his office and draw his salary from his prison cell but also vowed to return to the bench after his two-year conviction for tax evasion. He was removed in 1986.

Congress has tried a variety of ways to streamline the impeachment process for federal officers below the level of the president. The most significant change was the Senate's adoption of a rule allowing impeachment trials to be conducted by a committee of twelve. The committee then reports to the entire Senate, which then votes on conviction or acquittal. This rule has been challenged in court, but the Supreme Court has held that the Senate has sole power to try all impeachments, which includes the power to determine what constitutes a trial.

IMPEACHMENT OF PRESIDENTS

Notwithstanding the Framers' primary concern with executive misbehavior, the first presidential impeachment did not occur until after the Civil War. Andrew Johnson, a former slaveholder from Tennessee, had become president following

President Abraham Lincoln's assassination at the Civil War's end. Congress was sharply at odds with Johnson over the reinstatement of the rebellious southern states and over the ultimate meaning of the Union victory in the war. By early 1868 congressional patience was at an end, and the House of Representatives in February voted to impeach Johnson. The eleven charges against Johnson fell into two categories. Articles 1–9 and Article 11 charged Johnson with violating the Tenure of Office Act and the Army Appropriations Act, and with urging and ordering civilians and military personnel to do the same. Article 10 catalogued Johnson's impetuous, undignified "utterances, declarations, threats, and harangues" against Congress and against specific members of Congress.

At the trial in March, thirty-nine senators—all Republicans—voted to convict Johnson, while nineteen senators—twelve Democrats and seven Republicans—voted for acquittal. This was one vote short of the two-thirds majority necessary for conviction. By the time of his trial Johnson had less than a year to go in his term and was hamstrung by a veto-proof Republican majority.

Another century passed before impeachment was again seriously contemplated against a president. On October 30, 1973, the House Judiciary Committee began a preliminary inquiry into President Richard M. Nixon's involvement in a burglary and its cover-up at the Democratic National Headquarters in the Watergate Hotel in Washington, D.C. Within six months the committee began impeachment hearings, and by July 1974 the committee approved three articles of impeachment. All three charges dealt with Nixon's public behavior as president for his involvement in events that came to be known as "Watergate." The charges were obstruction of justice, abuse of power, and contempt of Congress. By August incontrovertible evidence of Nixon's involvement in the cover-up of the Watergate burglary had emerged. On August 9, 1974, Richard Nixon became the first president in American history to resign. The full House of Representatives never considered or voted on the articles of impeachment. Nevertheless, the existence of the removal mechanism and its threatened use were probably responsible for effectively achieving the Framers' purpose of denying presidential power to one who has abused it.

In 1998 and 1999 President Bill Clinton became only the third president subjected to an impeachment investigation, and the second president to be impeached and brought to trial in the Senate. The impeachment investigation of Clinton may pass into history as a blight on the administration of a single president, or may turn out to be a landmark event in the evolution of the American presidency and the impeachment power. Unlike the impeachment of Johnson, Clinton's impeachment was not about high politics and clashes between branches over issues of great national importance. Unlike the impeachment proceedings against Nixon, it was not about a threat to the constitutional underpinnings of the nation. From one perspective, Clinton's impeachment was about public integrity and whether the president committed perjury and obstructed justice. From another perspective, it was not about the president's public conduct of his office or anything directly connected to his official duties. It began as an investigation about financial transactions that took place more than a decade before Clinton was elected president, and it was transformed into an investigation about a sexual relationship with a White House intern, Monica Lewinsky.

The significance of the Clinton impeachment for the history of the constitutional removal power may lie less in the nature of the charges against Clinton than in how those charges were arrived at by Congress. Unlike the impeachments of Johnson and Nixon, the House did not conduct its own investigation of Clinton, but relied entirely on the report and later the testimony of Independent Counsel Kenneth Starr. Although Starr had been charged with investigating Clinton's financial dealings while he was governor of Arkansas, the impeachment report Starr delivered to Congress, with eleven enumerated charges, contained no material connected to that investigation but dealt solely with the president's sexual behavior with Lewinsky and with accusations that he had obstructed justice in trying to keep his behavior secret.

The American people made it clear that while they did not approve of Clinton's behavior, they likewise did not approve of what appeared to be the use of the impeachment mechanism to overturn the democratic election of the president. The evidence for this was found in both public opinion polling and in the concrete results of the 1998 off-year elections in which House Republicans suffered embarrassing losses. The failure to remove Clinton from office, like the failure to remove Supreme Court justice Samuel Chase nearly two centuries before, may have a similarly limiting impact on the use of the impeachment power for purposes that appear motivated more by partisanship than by actual "high crimes and misdemeanors."

See also *Clinton, Bill; Clinton-Era Scandals; Congress; Independent Counsel; Johnson, Andrew; Nixon, Richard M.; Presidency; Super Majority; Supreme Court.*

EMILY FIELD VAN TASSEL,
INDIANA UNIVERSITY SCHOOL OF LAW, BLOOMINGTON

BIBLIOGRAPHY

Baker, Peter. *The Breach: Inside the Impeachment and Trial of William Jefferson Clinton.* New York: Simon and Schuster, 2000.

Benedict, Michael Les. *The Impeachment and Trial of Andrew Johnson.* New York: W. W. Norton, 2000.

Van Tassel, Emily Field. "Resignations and Removals: A History of Federal Judicial Service, and Disservice, 1789–1992." *University of Pennsylvania Law Review* 333, 142 (1993).

Van Tassel, Emily Field, and Paul Finkelman. *Impeachable Offenses.* Washington, D.C.: CQ Press, 1999.

INDEPENDENT COUNSEL

The events surrounding the Watergate scandal and the various investigations it sparked in the early 1970s convinced the nation's legislators that investigations of high government officials should be insulated from improper influence. But Congress's attempts to find a solution became bogged down in five years of often-testy debates and more than thirty-five different proposals. In 1978 lawmakers finally settled on an independent counsel, and President Jimmy Carter signed the Independent Counsel Law (formally known as the Ethics in Government Act) on October 26, 1978. Some twenty years later, this act, born out of the Watergate scandal that brought down Richard M. Nixon's White House, took a presidential imbroglio known as Whitewater and transformed it into the impeachment of President Bill Clinton.

The Ethics in Government Act required the U.S. attorney general to request a special panel of federal judges to appoint an independent counsel whenever the attorney general determined there was credible evidence of wrongdoing by a high government official. Once appointed, the independent counsel operated under congressional appropriation and could be removed only for cause. Through this act, Congress intended that those investigating alleged wrongdoing by high government officials be insulated from pressure or influence by the targeted officials or their allies.

Before passage of this act, government wrongdoing had been investigated by the Justice Department unless a conflict of interest appeared. In such cases, the attorney general or the president appointed an outside counsel, or special prosecutor. Up to 1978, six presidents had appointed ten special prosecutors. President Ulysses S. Grant appointed the first special prosecutor, John Henderson, to investigate the bribery and extortion enterprise of the collector of internal revenue in St. Louis, Gen. John A. McDonald. The scheme became known as the Whiskey Ring scandal. Before he was fired by President Grant, Henderson obtained indictments against more than 200 distillers and government officials. Of those, 120 pled guilty or were convicted, and another dozen fled the country.

Between the Whiskey Ring scandal and Watergate, the only notable appointment occurred in 1923 when President Calvin Coolidge appointed a little-known Philadelphia lawyer named Owen Roberts to investigate the Teapot Dome scandal of Warren Harding's administration. The investigation of the secret leases of government property to private oil com-

Independent Counsel Kenneth Starr takes an oath prior to testifying before the House Judiciary Committee. *Scott J. Ferrell, Congressional Quarterly*

panies yielded the indictment and conviction of Secretary of the Interior Albert B. Fall and Attorney General Harry M. Daugherty. The special prosecutor in this case would later become a justice of the Supreme Court.

The impetus for passage of the Independent Counsel Law was the need to restore the American public's faith in government in the wake of the Watergate scandal and the "Saturday Night Massacre." In the Saturday Night Massacre, President Nixon moved down through the ranks of the Justice Department seeking an official willing to fire special prosecutor Archibald Cox, who was investigating Nixon's role in the Watergate break-in. Almost from its inception, however, the law attracted criticism and amendment. Over its twenty-one-year life, spanning the presidencies of Jimmy Carter, Ronald Reagan, George Bush, and Bill Clinton, twenty independent counsels were appointed, and they spent more than $167 million pursuing their cases. Opponents of the law claimed it allowed too many politically inspired investigations. Critics also noted that twice as many prosecutors were appointed in twenty years under the law than had been appointed in the previous one hundred years.

The two most expensive, long-lasting, and wide-ranging investigations under the law unleashed the most criticism and agitation for its demise. Independent Counsel Lawrence Walsh's six-year, $48 million investigation of the Reagan ad-

ministration's Iran-contra scandal and Independent Counsel Kenneth Starr's similarly costly five-year investigation of President Clinton's financial dealings and sex life each raised issues of political motivations and unfairness underlying the investigations. Congressional Republicans succeeded in blocking the law's reauthorization in 1992, based largely on the Walsh investigation. The Clinton administration succeeded in reenacting the statute in 1994, only to be confronted with the investigation, led by Starr, that resulted in President Clinton's impeachment. Rather than launch its own investigation into allegations of a presidential affair with a White House intern, the House Judiciary Committee, in recommending impeachment to the entire House, chose to rely almost entirely on Starr's report of his investigation. The committee's decision raised serious constitutional concerns about Congress's apparent ability under the Independent Counsel Law to delegate a portion of its constitutional impeachment duty to a virtually unaccountable prosecutor.

Although the Supreme Court found the Ethics in Government Act constitutional in *Morrison v. Olson* (1988), Justice Antonin Scalia's dissenting opinion that the law gave politically unaccountable prosecutors far too much power may have won the day. Even some special prosecutors, including Kenneth Starr, testified against renewing the act when congressional hearings were held on the act's continued viability. When the Ethics in Government Act finally expired in June 1999, Congress refused to renew it.

See also *Clinton-Era Scandals; Iran-Contra Scandal; Scandals and Corruption; Teapot Dome Scandal; Watergate.*

EMILY FIELD VAN TASSEL,
INDIANA UNIVERSITY SCHOOL OF LAW, BLOOMINGTON

BIBLIOGRAPHY

Johnson, Charles A., and Danette Brickman. *Independent Counsel: The Law and the Investigations.* Washington, D.C.: CQ Press, 2000.

Van Tassel, Emily Field, and Paul Finkelman. *Impeachable Offenses: A Documentary History from 1787 to the Present.* Washington, D.C.: CQ Press, 1999.

INDIAN POLICY

The relations between the United States and the American Indian tribes have been an important concern for U.S. political leaders since the founding of the nation. While the federal government has historically treated the Indian tribes as political entities separate and distinct from the United States, it has, at the same time, claimed to hold dominion and a special trust relationship over them.

FOUNDATIONS, 1776–1815

In 1778, in an agreement with the Delaware Indians, the United States adopted Great Britain's practice of using diplomatic treaties to conduct relations with, and acquire territory from, the Indian tribes. After the American Revolution U.S. treaty commissioners argued that by defeating Britain the United States had acquired sovereignty over the lands of the empire's Indian allies. The United States dictated treaties under this theory to the Iroquois at Fort Stanwix (1784); the Delawares, Wyandots, Chippewas, and Ottawas at Fort McIntosh (1785); and the Shawnees at Fort Finney (1786). Subsequent treaties were both more conciliatory and somewhat ambiguous. In the treaties at Hopewell, South Carolina (1785–1786), for example, the Cherokees, Chickasaws, and Choctaws agreed to live under the protection of the United States, surrendered the power to conduct diplomatic relations, and accorded Congress the right to regulate their trade and manage "all their affairs in such manner" as it thought "proper." In the same agreements, U.S. commissioners negotiated borders with the tribes and recognized the right of tribal councils to determine who could enter their territory, provisions that implied that the U.S. government recognized that the Indian tribes were sovereign peoples possessing rights to their land.

In 1787 the framers of the Constitution endowed Congress with the power to regulate commerce with the Indian tribes and gave the president the authority to make treaties with the consent of the Senate. In 1789 President George Washington originated the precedent of sending U.S.-Indian treaties to the Senate for ratification, another indication that the United States recognized the tribes as distinct political entities. The first Congress reenacted the Northwest Ordinance of 1787, which promised that the United States would always observe "utmost good faith" toward the Indian tribes and never take their land without their consent. Between 1790 and 1834 Congress adopted a series of trade and intercourse acts to govern U.S.-Indian relations. The first act, in 1790, prohibited non–Indians from entering Indian territory without tribal permission, provided punishments for crimes committed by whites on Native American soil, required that those who wanted to trade with Indians obtain a license from the federal government, and prohibited individuals from acquiring Indian land without federal permission.

U.S. leaders like Henry Knox, Washington's secretary of war, believed that their nation had a duty to educate, acculturate, and assimilate Native Americans. Knox proposed that Indians adopt an Anglo-American lifestyle, abandon hunting and communal land ownership, become yeoman farmers on individual tracts of land, and cede their excess land to the United States. In the Trade and Intercourse Act of 1793 Congress appropriated funds to implement this "civilization program" and began supplying Indians with plows, spinning wheels, and other tools and implements. Although the federal government posted agents among the tribes to assist Indians in their transition to yeoman farming, it did not allocate money for Indian education until 1819 and instead entrusted that responsibility to Christian missionary societies.

Congress also used the trade and intercourse acts to foster fair trade with the Indians. Between 1796 and 1822 the federal government operated trading factories, which held a legal monopoly over the fur trade and sold trade goods to Indian customers at cost, in an effort to remedy the predatory tactics of private traders. When negotiations and statutory efforts like the trade and intercourse acts failed to improve Indian-white relations, the United States turned to military force to pacify Indian resistance and obtain Native American land. In 1794, for example, the U.S. Army put down a major uprising of tribes in the old Northwest at the Battle of Fallen Timbers and forced them to cede much of Ohio in the Treaty of Greenville.

ISOLATION: REMOVAL AND RESERVATIONS, 1815–1887

Rapid growth of the American population, the inability of the government to control the westward migration of settlers, and the desire of Native Americans to maintain their own cultural practices doomed the civilization and assimilation efforts. In 1803 Thomas Jefferson concluded the Louisiana Purchase and proposed moving the eastern tribes beyond the Mississippi River. However, he was able to persuade only a small group of Cherokees to migrate, to the Arkansas River valley in 1808.

In the War of 1812 the United States defeated Tecumseh's northwestern confederation at the Battle of the Thames (1813) and a Creek revolt at Horseshoe Bend (1814). These victories, and the British military retreat from the old Northwest, gave the United States military supremacy over the tribes east of the Mississippi. After the war Gen. Andrew Jackson and Secretary of War John C. Calhoun urged President

James Monroe to remove the Indians in the East beyond the reach of American settlement. After his election as president in 1828, Jackson advised several eastern tribes to remove to the West or fall under state jurisdiction. In 1830 Congress passed the Indian Removal Act, which gave the president the authority to negotiate removal treaties with the eastern tribes. That same year the Cherokees filed suit to enjoin the state of Georgia's attempts to annex their territory and abolish their government. In *Cherokee Nation v. Georgia* (1831), John Marshall, the chief justice of the U.S. Supreme Court, declared that the Cherokees were a "domestic, dependent nation" retaining significant powers of sovereignty. He also wrote that the relationship between the United States and the Cherokees was similar to that between a guardian and its ward. In *Worcester v. Georgia* (1832), Marshall went further and chastised Georgia for encroaching upon the rights of a sovereign nation. These two cases provided principles that guided subsequent U.S. policy makers: the tribes were sovereign nations, the states were to be excluded from exercising power over Indian affairs, and the United States possessed a special fiduciary responsibility over Native Americans.

Jackson chose not to enforce *Worcester* against Georgia, and between 1832 and 1843 almost all the eastern tribes were persuaded or coerced into signing removal treaties. The Creeks, Choctaws, and Chickasaws surrendered their lands and relocated to the Indian Territory that Congress had established west of Arkansas. When the Cherokees refused to remove, the U.S. Army rounded them up and marched them to the Indian Territory. The Seminoles successfully resisted the army for several years before surrendering and removing in 1842. Small groups of both tribes escaped removal and became the foundation of renascent populations in the East. The federal government removed most of the northern tribes to present-day Missouri, Kansas, Iowa, Nebraska, and Wisconsin or isolated them on small reserves carved out of their former territory.

The relocated tribes retained their political autonomy, continued their cultural practices, and resurrected their social institutions while the federal government and Christian churches continued to provide educational, vocational, and religious supervision. Between 1830 and 1870 Congress rejected several proposals to integrate the tribes into an Indian state that would be admitted into the Union.

After the removal, the United States annexed Texas (1845), settled the Oregon territory dispute with Great Britain (1846), and acquired California and the Mexican cession (1848). Land, mineral, timber, cattle, and railroad interests quickly moved in to exploit the resources of the West, which was populated by diverse native peoples. In the treaties at Fort Laramie (1851) and Fort Atkinson (1853), several Plains tribes

granted the United States rights of way for roads and railroads through their territory. As settlers moved into the West via the Oregon, California, and Santa Fe trails, they came into conflict with Indians; and the period between 1850 and 1880 was marked by constant conflict between whites and Indians. In the 1850s the federal government began a concerted effort to force the western tribes to cede their territory and relocate to reservations. In 1864 the Colorado state militia massacred more than 150 Cheyennes and Arapahos at Sand Creek. The atrocities at Sand Creek and the continuing Indian-white hostilities in the West prompted Congress in 1867 to create the Peace Commission, which was charged with settling the remaining recalcitrant Plains tribes on reservations.

The Indian people on many of the reservations became impoverished, demoralized, and dependent on federal provisions. When Ulysses S. Grant became president in 1869, he initiated a "peace" policy of reforms to remedy these conditions. For example, he ordered contractors to provide quality supplies to reservation Indians at equitable prices, and he asked the Bureau of Indian Affairs to appoint honest and competent agents. In 1869 Congress created the Board of Indian Commissioners and provided it with joint authority, with the secretary of the interior, over disbursements of Indian appropriations. All of the members of the board belonged to evangelical churches. The government parceled out each reservation to a particular denomination and gave the church the power to appoint Indian agents to the tribes under its jurisdiction. In 1871 Congress abrogated the treaty system and ended the policy of recognizing the tribes as sovereign nations. Up to that point the United States had negotiated almost four hundred treaties with the various Indian tribes.

During this period white hunters, encouraged by the army and the Bureau of Indian Affairs, hunted the buffalo almost into extinction. As a result, some tribes felt compelled to fight the United States to preserve their game, their land, and their way of life. In the 1860s and 1870s the U.S. Army fought major campaigns against the Sioux, the Apaches, the Navajos, the Cheyennes, the Arapahos, the Kiowas, the Comanches, and the Nez Perces. Although its army suffered an occasional whipping, as it did at the hands of the Sioux at Little Big Horn (1876), by 1890 the United States had forced the resisting tribes to submit and relocate to reservations.

ALLOTMENT AND ASSIMILATION, 1887–1932

In 1887 Congress passed the Dawes Severalty Act, which authorized the president to break up the reservations into 80- and 160-acre parcels and allot them to individual Indians. The federal government was to hold the allotment in trust for twenty-five years and then convey it to the allottee in fee simple. Upon allotment, the individual Indian was to become a U.S. citizen and fall under state jurisdiction. (A subsequent amendment delayed the point upon which citizenship would be granted until the end of the trust period. In 1924 Congress granted U.S. citizenship to all Native Americans born in the United States.) The federal government's objectives were to destroy the tribal structure, force Native Americans to abandon communal land ownership, and require individual Indians to assimilate into the majority society. In 1891 Congress amended the Dawes Act to allow Indians who were incapable of occupying or improving their lands to lease them out to white farmers for a share of the land's produce. Congress further liberalized restrictions on the alienation of allotments in the Burke Act of 1906 by allowing some allottees to sell their lands before the end of the 25-year trust period. Between 1887 and the 1934, when the government abandoned allotment, perhaps as much as 90 million acres of Native American land passed out of Indian hands.

Congress temporarily excluded the Pueblos and the Indian Territory tribes from allotment. However, in 1889 the federal government allotted the western portion of the Indian Territory and opened it up for white homesteaders. In 1897 Congress claimed legal jurisdiction over the eastern portion of the territory. The Curtis Act of 1898 abolished the tribal governments in the Indian Territory and brought all persons residing there under the jurisdiction of the federal government. Between 1897 and 1902 the Dawes Commission allotted the remainder of the Indian Territory; and in 1907 Congress admitted Oklahoma, the former Indian Territory, into the Union as a state.

The U.S. Supreme Court abetted Congress's attack on Native American rights during this period. In *U.S. v. Kagama* (1886), the Court upheld the constitutionality of the Major Crimes Act, which provided Congress with criminal jurisdiction over serious offenses committed on the reservations. In *Lone Wolf v. Hitchcock* (1903), the Court held that Congress could abrogate treaty provisions and dispose of Indian lands without the consent of the affected tribe. With that decision, Congress and the Supreme Court had practically annihilated the sovereign rights of the tribes.

THE INDIAN NEW DEAL, 1933–1953

In the 1920s John Collier, a New York social worker, and his organization, the American Indian Rights Association, called for a massive overhaul of U.S. Indian policy. Collier and his associates, many of whom were anthropologists, espoused the principle of cultural relativism, meaning that every culture should be respected for its own merits. Collier condemned the government's allotment and assimilation policies and the general societal tendencies toward industrialism, individual-

ism, and materialism. Collier argued that the government should allow Indians to revive communal land ownership and respect their traditional culture. In 1928 the Merriam Commission, under the auspices of the Brookings Institution, issued a report that described in detail how federal policies had forced many Indians into destitution.

In 1933 President Franklin D. Roosevelt appointed Collier as commissioner of Indian affairs and directed him to implement his suggested reforms. The centerpiece of Collier's administration was the Indian Reorganization Act of 1934 (IRA), which authorized tribes to incorporate, reestablish their governments, and draft tribal constitutions. Collier ended allotment and authorized the Bureau of Indian Affairs to buy back tribal lands and annex unclaimed allotments. He also established a number of programs to encourage economic development on the reservations. He created a fund for student loans, required yield-management programs for forests on Indian land, and promoted stock reduction and soil conservation programs. He also procured an executive order requiring federal employees to respect Indian cultural and spiritual practices. In 1935 Collier convinced Congress to create the Indian Arts and Crafts Board, which established cooperatives for the marketing and sale of Native American products.

From 1937 to 1945 Collier's Indian Office was primarily in a defensive posture against his critics. The American Indian Federation, a proponent of allotment, charged Collier with promoting communism. Christian groups accused Collier of promoting pagan religious beliefs. Others complained that Collier's policies encouraged Indians to segregate themselves from other Americans. Republicans in Congress delayed passing Collier's claims commission legislation, investigated his management of the Indian Office, and limited funding for many of his programs. This resistance caused Collier to resign in 1945. A year later Congress finally established the Indian Claims Commission, which was charged with investigating and compensating violations of federal-Indian treaty rights and misappropriations of tribal annuity funds. Between 1950 and 1969 the Indian Claims Commission awarded over $333 million to 154 claimants.

TERMINATION, 1953–1968

In 1953 Congress again dramatically reversed course on Indian affairs, repudiated the IRA, and adopted a policy of tribal termination. The termination program, which was first proposed in 1947 by Commissioner of Indian Affairs William Zimmerman Jr., was designed to end federal benefits and services to the tribes at the earliest possible date. The termination statute required Congress to classify each tribe into one of three categories based on its capacity to exist without federal assistance, the degree of its acculturation into American society, its economic status, and the willingness of the state in which it was located to take on former federal responsibilities. The first class of tribes, which were deemed acculturated enough to exist without federal assistance, were to be terminated immediately. The second group included tribes that required continued federal support and supervision for a period of up to ten years. The third group included tribes that needed more than ten years to become self-sufficient. After a tribe was deemed ready for termination, a tribal roll was taken and tribal assets and property rights were divided among the enrolled members. Upon final termination, the federal government's trust period ended and the individual members of the former tribe came under state jurisdiction. For some tribes, however, such as the Klamath and the Menominee, the termination experiments were dramatic failures. The individuals in these tribes were not ready for life without federal support, and many of them fell into abject poverty. At the same time, they lost the social network and protection offered by their tribal governments and found it difficult to integrate into the surrounding white communities and economies. These failures emboldened Indian and liberal critics of termination to call for its repeal. In 1956 Secretary of the Interior Fred A. Seaton retreated from the government's original goal of comprehensive termination and promised that a tribe would not be terminated without its consent. During this era Congress also created a relocation program that provided placement offices and vocational training to move young reservation Indians to jobs in urban areas.

SELF-DETERMINATION 1968–

In the 1960s Indian protests forced U.S. policy makers to abandon termination and address the civil rights, financial needs, and political status of Native Americans. The administrations of John F. Kennedy and Lyndon B. Johnson attempted to promote economic enterprise on the reservations; increased funding for Indian education, health care, and occupational training programs; and integrated Native Americans into policy making and administration at the federal and tribal levels.

Between 1968 and 1999 Congress passed a series of laws to remedy particular Indian concerns. The Civil Rights Act of 1968 guaranteed individual Indian civil liberties, protected native religious and cultural practices, and prohibited the states from extending jurisdiction over a reservation without the tribe's consent. The Indian Self-Determination and Education Assistance Act of 1975 provided protection for tribal powers and allowed eligible Indian governments to administer federal programs on the reservations. The American Indian

Religious Freedom Act of 1978 offered legal protection for Indian spiritual and religious practices, while the Indian Child Welfare Act of the same year recognized tribal jurisdiction over abandoned and neglected Indian children. In 1982 the Indian Mineral Development Act allowed tribes to enter joint-venture agreements with mineral developers, while the Indian Tribal Government Tax Status Act provided the tribes with some of the same tax advantages possessed by the states, including the authority to issue tax-exempt bonds. The Indian Gaming Regulatory Act of 1988 allowed tribal governments to operate casinos and other games to support tribal activities. In 1990 Congress passed the Native American Graves Protection and Repatriation Act, which prohibits the sale of Indian remains and certain cultural items and requires federal agencies and private museums receiving federal funds to inventory their collections of human remains and sacred objects, notify the tribes from which they originated, and return them if the tribe requests.

By the year 2000 the Bureau of Indian Affairs (BIA), an under-agency of the Department of the Interior, possessed primary responsibility for the oversight of U.S.-Indian relations. The BIA and several other federal agencies provided funding and assistance for schools and educational programs, hospitals and health care, housing and social services, employment and job training, and local economic development. These programs were designed with the ultimate objective of allowing American Indians and their governments to become self-supporting. Although federal decisions and legislation still occasionally threatened the breadth of tribal autonomy, by the end of the twentieth century the federal government was, generally speaking, attempting to reforge nation-to-nation relationships that reaffirmed and protected tribal sovereign rights.

See also *Jackson, Andrew; Territorial Expansion.*

TIM ALAN GARRISON, PORTLAND STATE UNIVERSITY

BIBLIOGRAPHY

Cohen, Felix S. *Handbook of Federal Indian Law.* Charlottesville: Michie Bobbs-Merrill, 1982 (originally published in 1942).

Fixico, Donald L. *Termination and Relocation: Federal Indian Policy, 1945–1960.* Albuquerque: University of New Mexico Press, 1986.

Hoxie, Frederick E. *A Final Promise: The Campaign to Assimilate the Indians, 1880–1920.* Lincoln: University of Nebraska Press, 1984.

Philp, Kenneth R. *John Collier's Crusade for Indian Reform, 1920–1954.* Tucson: University of Arizona Press, 1977.

Prucha, Francis Paul. *The Great Father: The United States Government and the American Indians.* 2 vols. Lincoln: University of Nebraska Press, 1984.

Satz, Ronald N. *American Indian Policy in the Jacksonian Era.* Lincoln: University of Nebraska Press, 1975.

Trennert, Robert A., Jr. *Alternative to Extinction: Federal Indian Policy and the Beginnings of the Reservation System, 1846–1851.* Philadelphia: Temple University Press, 1975.

Wallace, Anthony F. C. *Jefferson and the Indians: The Tragic Fate of the First Americans.* Cambridge: Harvard University Press, 1999.

INITIATIVE, REFERENDUM, AND RECALL

Initiative, referendum, and recall are procedural reforms in the elective and governing process that became popular during the Progressive era and have endured as elements in the political systems of many states.

During the Progressive era, from 1890 to 1920, unhappiness with the dominance of political parties in government led to campaigns for procedural changes to make it easier for citizens to shape public policy and choose their leaders. Power would be transferred from party bosses and their caucuses to the people themselves. Three popular reforms that embodied this approach were the initiative, the referendum, and the recall. They were grouped under the heading of "direct democracy" and sought to have citizens take over decisions that had been reserved for the political parties.

The initiative allowed a specified percentage of registered voters to require that an issue or proposed law be submitted to the electorate for its approval. The first state to adopt it was South Dakota in 1898 as part of its state constitution; it was implemented by twenty other states in the years that followed. In recent times, Proposition 13 in 1978 lowered property taxes in California, and Proposition 187 in 1994 addressed the question of immigrants and their status, also in California.

The referendum was also first used in South Dakota in 1898 and then spread to other states. William S. U'Ren, a legislator from Oregon, became a leading proponent of the referendum. The device has remained popular in local government and sometimes on the state level in California and Oregon, where it was originally devised.

The most controversial of these three proposals during the early years of the twentieth century was the recall. At that time the recall took two forms. The first had to do with ousting a corrupt public official by means of citizen petitions and an election that turned on the person's fitness to continue in the position to which he or she had been elected. The electorate in Los Angeles used the recall to remove a member of the city council in 1904. Two years later a similar campaign was launched against the city's mayor, and he subsequently resigned. When the recall was applied to sitting judges, it became a source of concern to conservatives, who saw the practice as threatening the independence of judges. Even more controversial was the second form of recall, which gave voters the right to recall an unpopular judicial decision. Providing that power to the electorate at large seemed even more of a threat to the autonomy of judges.

These abstract concepts became matters of national debate in 1911 and 1912. In 1911 President William Howard Taft vetoed the bill authorizing statehood for Arizona because it contained a provision for recalling judges. The following year Theodore Roosevelt made the idea of recalling judicial decisions one of the main elements in his race for the Republican nomination against Taft. Long suspicious of the role of judges in thwarting legislation to achieve social justice, Roosevelt became convinced that some form of popular action against these rulings was in order. In a speech to the Ohio Constitutional Convention in February 1912, Roosevelt endorsed the concept as a way of reducing the power of special interests and large corporations over the judiciary. The people, he contended, needed to have a means of overturning court rulings that blocked regulation of corporations or that struck down laws designed to protect poor and helpless citizens.

The speech attracted progressive Republicans but repelled wavering party members who were suspicious of Roosevelt's critical attitude toward judges and the law. Outraged conservatives rallied to Taft's candidacy. Once he embarked on his third-party candidacy with the Progressive ("Bull Moose") Party in 1912, Roosevelt returned to the idea of recalling judicial decisions. Roosevelt's endorsement of the reform was one of the reasons that many Republicans preferred to see the Democratic candidate, Woodrow Wilson, elected in 1912 rather than give Roosevelt any chance to win.

After Roosevelt's defeat, the impetus behind the recall of judicial decisions receded. The recall remains a device for disciplining officials in many localities and some states. In the hands of well-financed interest groups, the initiative and referendum have proven to be ideologically neutral devices that can support conservative as well as liberal causes. Like so many procedural changes of the turn of the last century, direct democracy turned out to have unintended consequences. At the time of their adoption, they reflected discontent toward the political parties.

See also *Progressive Era; Third Parties.*

LEWIS L. GOULD, UNIVERSITY OF TEXAS AT AUSTIN

BIBLIOGRAPHY

Buenker, John D., and Edward R. Kantowicz, eds. *Historical Dictionary of the Progressive Era, 1890–1920.* New York: Greenwood Press, 1988.

Gould, Lewis L. *Reform and Regulation: American Politics from Roosevelt to Wilson.* Prospect Heights, Ill.: Waveland Press, 1996.

Link, Arthur S., and Richard L. McCormick. *Progressivism.* Arlington Heights, Ill.: Harlan Davidson, 1983.

INTEREST GROUPS

An interest group is, simply stated, an organized group of people who are seeking to influence public policy in order to promote their particular ideals or derive material benefits through the legislative process. Business-oriented interests, called trade associations, dominate the universe of interest groups. Other nonprofit organizations represent the interests of people not as wage earners, stockholders, or farmers, but as citizens, consumers, and taxpayers, and represent populations such as the elderly or those with disabilities. Many of these organizations are called "public interest" groups. Even state and local governments are represented by interest groups in Washington, because the federal government is a critical source of their funds as well as their major regulator.

It is not known exactly how many interest groups are currently operating in the United States, but *The Encyclopedia of Associations* lists more than 22,000 national nonprofit organizations. Almost nine Americans in ten contribute to or are members of some kind of voluntary association, including professional groups and organizations concerned with social issues. The 1995 edition of *Washington Representatives,* a directory of interest groups and lobbyists, had some 14,000 listings, or more than twice the number listed in the 1980 edition. Of those, some 1,500 were representing corporations; 2,100 were representing labor unions and trade and professional associations; 2,200 were advocacy groups (the fastest-growing category); and 2,800 were lawyers registered as lobbyists.

HISTORY OF INTEREST GROUPS

Although the proliferation of interest groups is a recent phenomenon, the influence of such groups in shaping public policy can be traced as far back as the founding of the Republic. James Madison expressed concern about interest groups—or "factions," as he called them—in *The Federalist Papers.* He ultimately conceded, however, that factions were "sown in the nature of man" and, consequently, were impossible and even undesirable to eliminate. Frenchman Alexis de Tocqueville, in describing his firsthand impressions of the United States in 1831–1832, took a more sanguine view of the American tendency to organize into specialized interests, viewing this inclination as emanating out of a desire to participate in democratic politics.

Interest groups have a long history in the United States, but at the turn of the twentieth century several factors led to their rapid proliferation, which in turn spawned heightened awareness of their role in the political system. One factor was the evolution of partisan politics. Political parties assumed their modern form in the mid-nineteenth century, with the golden age of political parties commencing soon after the Civil War. With the growth of regionalism and the increased regulation of political parties, voter turnout began to decline in the 1890s. By the 1970s partisan-centered elector politics had been supplanted by candidate-centered campaigns. In sharp contrast to the decline in partisan politics, interest group politics has steadily flourished since the turn of the century and, most notably, during the past several decades of party de-

cline. Like the party system, the interest group system's niche is mobilizing political action.

Another factor contributing to interest group growth in the twentieth century was the industrialization of the early 1900s, which in turn spawned trade and professional societies to represent the competing interests of commercial and scientific specialties. After President Franklin D. Roosevelt's New Deal in the 1930s, the expanding scope and size of government fostered the creation of professional organizations representing the providers of new public services. This development had the political value of linking constituents to government officials.

Yet another factor in interest group proliferation was the growth of government regulation of certain industries, leading to the birth of new interest groups intent on protecting those industries' interests. The growing popularity of the United States to immigrants also has been a factor; the nation's population has become much more diverse since War World II. This diversification, in turn, has amplified a pluralistic environment of heterogeneous political interests and, in effect, created a political system that can be more effectively maneuvered via mobilized efforts.

The ideology of the 1960s led to interest group growth, with citizens mobilizing based on ideology and the quest for a more democratic society. The broad social movement groups that have developed over the past forty years have often done so to plead the causes of those who face formidable obstacles in organizing for collective action themselves, such as children and the unemployed.

Finally, the communications revolution has been instrumental in the explosion of national organizations, as has the growth of an educated middle class, which is the population that tends to drive the interest group movement. Having proliferated remarkably during the twentieth century, interest groups will likely continue to grow in the twenty-first century, as they seem to have carved out a tenable place for themselves in the political system.

FORMATION OF INTEREST GROUPS

In explaining this remarkable proliferation, the literature on interest groups covers several major theories of interest group formation. In the 1950s political scientist David Truman put forward the disturbance theory of interest group formation, in which significant departures from accustomed behavior in a particular arena (in his studies, farming) give rise to the establishment of special organized interests. According to Truman, groups form spontaneously whenever shared interested are threatened by or could be helped by political action. More than a decade later, economist Mancur Olson's by-product and special-interest theories of group formation emerged. Olson maintained that organized interests sprout

out of a unique niche for political activity that needs to be filled and out of the ability of an organization to offer members particularly appealing, exclusive benefits. In 1970 political scientist Robert H. Salisbury presented his exchange theory of why interest groups form: special interests coalesce when a reciprocal flow of benefits exists between the group's leader and the group's members. A short time later, interest groups scholar Jack L. Walker Jr. came up with the patron theory, which postulates that financial backing gives rise to the organization of special interests. Other theories have contended that interest groups come together because aggressive, independent entrepreneurs form them, many of whom are acting in response to specific events, and that internal resource dimensions (such as exclusive access to members and finances) are critical to the formation of special interests.

Once interest groups are formed, various reasons exist for people to join. Some may have "material incentives" in the form of tangible rewards—such as higher wages or better prices for soybeans—that would result from the group's efforts. Others may have "solidary incentives," such as associating with people with whom they have common bonds, or "expressive incentives," such as receiving the intangible rewards of working for a good cause—for example, preserving a coastal wetland or urging people to vote.

Some groups simply would not exist without the leadership of men and women willing to invest much of their own time and personal resources in the group. For example, Ralph Nader was the driving force behind many consumer organizations. A group may owe its viability to its sponsor, whether a private industry, foundation, the government in the form of grants, or an individual. For example, the National Foundation on Aging, founded to champion the expansion of senior citizens centers across the country, relied in its early years primarily on private foundation grants.

Why is it that some groups form because of shared and specialized interests, yet other groups that have a common concern, such as those who are indigent, do not? The formation and activities of interest groups require a minimum amount of resources, such as funding, political clout, time, staff support, facilities, and equipment. These requisite resources pose a barrier to coalescing around shared concerns for many populations, such as the indigent, children, and people with certain disabilities, who are largely denied access to influencing public policy except by representation by those who have the requisite resources. Some people do not join or form groups that serve their interests, not because they lack the ability, but because they are "free riders"—that is, they recognize that the "collective benefits" of group membership (such as clean air and higher Social Security benefits) are available to them whether or not they join a group. To overcome this problem, many groups offer their members "selective" benefits such as special health insurance rates and discount travel fares.

DETERMINANTS OF INFLUENCE

Some interests groups are better able to influence public policy than others—something they do largely through providing public officials with public support, election campaign as-

Senior citizens' clout stems largely from their high voter turnout. Social Security has earned the moniker, "the third rail of politics," a reference to the high-voltage rail of an electric train system. Politicians who touch it are in danger of being voted out of office. *Scott J. Ferrell, Congressional Quarterly*

sistance, and information. Factors affecting group influence include the characteristics of a group's membership, its leadership and financial resources, how the government itself is organized, and the nature of a group's goals or the conflicts in which it is engaged.

Groups with large memberships (such as the National Rifle Association, or NRA, with more than three million members) have distinct advantages because of the opportunities for influence their large membership base, and therefore large financial base, affords them. Groups like the NRA, compared with smaller public interest groups, often have the financial resources to pay for expensive television ad campaigns, for example, in behalf of their causes. Well-financed groups also are better able to support the information gathering, offices, staffs, and communications equipment needed to exercise political clout. Groups that have highly influential members (such as professional associations of doctors and lawyers) or that are concentrated in one geographic area (such as dairy farmers) also tend to be particularly effective in their efforts to influence public policy.

INTEREST GROUP DYNAMICS AND TACTICS

The post–New Deal expansion of the power and responsibility of the federal government, which contributed to the proliferation of interest groups, also led to the creation of subgovernments or "iron triangles." Iron triangles are a triumvirate configuration of interest groups, legislative decision makers, and executive agency bureaus. In this configuration, a few select interest groups organize around broadly shared policy concerns, working with executive agencies and congressional committees to hammer out policies of mutual benefit to the exclusion of any "outside" input.

Many interest groups, however, are not exclusionary. In fact, some, by breaking the barriers of bureaucracy and mitigating other detrimental aspects of oppressive social institutions, generate communicative processes from which social purposes and shared realities emerge. Today, "issue networks," or loosely connected interest groups, have begun to compete with iron triangles, making it much more difficult for any set of established actors to control and lead in certain areas of policy making. Thus interest groups are beginning to play a role in facilitating a more inclusive and participatory approach to shaping the public policy infrastructure of society.

The primary activity of interest groups is lobbying. The host of methods they have at their disposal for influencing public policy can be broadly categorized into two types—direct, such as creating access to legislators and providing them with information, and indirect, such as mass mailings and telephone appeals.

Interest groups also interact with policy makers through a flourishing phenomenon known as political action committees (PACs), which form around specific issues within broad areas of concern. PACs are organizations authorized by law to collect money and make campaign contributions to congressional and presidential candidates. In return, members of PACs hope to enjoy productive working relationships with Congress, the president, and the president's appointees in the administration and the White House. Corporations, unions, and nonprofit groups often supplement their lobbying and PAC activities with media advertising.

Another avenue for providing information to government officials is through the judicial system. In filing *amicus curiae* (friend of the court) briefs, interest groups are able to supply members of the Supreme Court with valuable information on the cases being heard. This approach to lobbying has become much more prevalent, not only because lobbying activity has exploded in general, but also because the Supreme Court has taken few steps to discourage groups from participating as *amicus curiae* even though its rules allow it to do so. In fact, *amicus curiae* briefs were filed in 80.1 percent of cases heard by the Supreme Court in 1988, as opposed to only 1.6 percent of cases heard in 1928.

Looking into the twenty-first century, the role of interest groups will most likely continue to be one of marshalling and applying political power, but for a larger and more diverse spectrum of special concerns. Yet the influence of interest groups continues to worry members of the American public, who fear that their interests are taking a backseat to those of the special interest groups and PACs.

See also *Lobbyists; Political Action Committees.*

KELLY MYLES,
AMERICAN ASSOCIATION OF UNIVERSITY AFFILIATED PROGRAMS

BIBLIOGRAPHY

Aldrich, John H. *Why Parties? The Origin and Transformation of Political Parties in America.* Chicago: University of Chicago Press, 1995.

Cigler, Allan J., and Burdett A. Loomis. *Interest Group Politics.* 5th ed. Washington, D.C.: CQ Press, 1998.

Clemens, Elisabeth S. *The People's Lobby: Organizational Innovation and the Rise of Interest Group Politics in the United States, 1890–1925.* Chicago: University of Chicago Press, 1997.

Holtzman, Abraham. *Interest Groups and Lobbying.* New York: Macmillan, 1966.

Hrebenar, Ronald J. *Interest Group Politics in America.* 3d ed. Armonk, N.Y.: M. E. Sharpe, 1997.

Salisbury, Robert H., ed. *Interest Group Politics in America.* New York: Harper and Row, 1970.

Truman, David B. *The Government Process.* New York: Knopf, 1951.

Walker, Jack L., Jr. *Mobilizing Interest Groups in America.* Ann Arbor: University of Michigan Press, 1991.

INTERSTATE HIGHWAY SYSTEM

In 1916 Congress and President Woodrow Wilson approved the Federal-Aid Highway Act. During the next five years, the federal government would spend $75 million to construct rural roads. To participate in the program, state officials had to create a state highway department headed by a professional engineer. By 1921 officials in most states had created highway departments.

Early on, the program was cooperative, with engineers such as Thomas H. MacDonald (who headed the U.S. Bureau of Public Roads) emphasizing partnership with his state-level counterparts in designating highway coordinates and getting highways constructed. As a practical matter, federal law put highway construction and maintenance squarely in the hands of state engineers. Nonetheless, federal-level public policy determined how the main highway routes in the United States were constructed.

Between 1921 and 1940 engineers constructed 418,000 miles of roadway, boosting the total to 3.0 million. During the late 1930s, moreover, road builders opened new, limited-access roads in several cities, including Chicago, New York City, and Los Angeles. The fabulous Pennsylvania Turnpike opened to traffic in 1940.

Thomas MacDonald had brought both technical expertise and political savvy to his job. In 1939 MacDonald announced an audacious plan for building a national expressway system. Members of Congress were trying to secure construction of a national system of toll superhighways. Relying on his growing corpus of traffic-flow studies, MacDonald contended that only a small portion of the proposed tollway mileage would ever become self-financing. Instead, MacDonald urged construction of a nationwide system of expressways extending nearly 27,000 miles. Most important, MacDonald asserted, was extension of those rural expressways into cities, where most of the traffic and traffic delays took place.

In 1944 Congress and President Franklin D. Roosevelt approved another Federal-Aid Highway Act. Because no group could assert a paramount claim to federal highway funds, Congress voted simply to spend $500 million a year to build roads. That whopping sum guaranteed plenty of jobs for returning veterans.

Given the fierce competition for road building in city and countryside, however, advocates of direct federal spending on the costly interstate highway system lost out. Congress approved construction of 40,000 miles and even gave the system a formal name, the National System of Interstate Highways. Congress authorized state officials to reallocate a portion of funds from their primary, secondary, and urban systems to build the interstate system. As a practical matter in state politics, however, the interstate system remained largely unfunded and unconstructed until 1952.

Beginning in 1946, federal and state road engineers launched a gigantic program of highway building. Between 1946 and 1950, as truck and auto registrations soared, engineers added 209,000 surfaced miles to the nation's stock of highways. In the face of ever more autos and trucks, however, no amount of additional mileage and improvements brought relief from congestion, delays, and accidents. In 1951 authors of the annual report of the Bureau of Public Roads observed that the nation was "being overwhelmed by a flood of traffic."

THE SEARCH FOR A NEW FINANCE MECHANISM

In 1954 President Dwight D. Eisenhower asked retired general Lucius D. Clay to head a committee that would prepare a report on funding construction of the interstate system. General Clay held public hearings, at which he learned what everyone in the highway field already knew: Neither truckers and farm leaders nor highway engineers could agree about who should pay for highway building, or who ought to benefit from it. At one point, nearly five hundred truck operators lobbied in person for a reduction in tax increases on fuel and trucks that Clay had proposed.

Members of Congress proved as incapable of reaching accord as their active and vocal constituents. By July 1955 the net result of these disagreements was that the U.S. Senate voted for a bill of its own design, and the U.S. House of Representatives rejected every bill that came before it.

By the spring of 1956 everyone was ready for a deal. Leaders of the American Trucking Associations agreed to a modest increase in fuel and equipment taxes. All taxes collected would go into a trust fund for use only to build highways. The federal government no longer would divert gasoline tax revenues to nonhighway purposes. In turn, federal officials would finance 90 percent of the cost of building the interstate system. Farm leaders also gained a legal promise of annual increases in federal spending to build rural roads. Federal officials would continue to disburse gasoline tax revenues to construct less-used roads in the American countryside. Congress also changed the name of the interstate system to the National System of Interstate and Defense Highways. Even President Eisenhower injected the prospect of improved defense as partial justification for building the interstate system. Although he was a supporter of the interstate system on grounds of traffic relief and economic development, Eisenhower also asserted that expressways would make evacuation of cities easier in case of nuclear attack.

Highway construction and reconstruction, both interstate and urban, are joint federal-state undertakings. The federal share of construction costs is paid from a trust fund that is replenished through a tax on gasoline. Photo taken December 15, 1992. *R. Michael Jenkins, Congressional Quarterly*

critics objected to construction of interstate highways through densely populated portions of cities. Leaders of African American communities particularly objected to construction of roads that served mostly white motorists but displaced mostly black householders and neighborhoods. With book titles such as *Superhighway-Superhoax* and *The Pavers and the Paved,* popular writers captured portions of this growing hostility toward highways and the engineer-experts who constructed them. Other critics blamed highways—and again, especially express highways—for having fostered what was described as a bleak, suburban landscape of sprawl, malls, and more traffic jams. Money spent on highways, they argued, could have been spent more productively on public transit, particularly on public transit for lower-income persons residing near downtown and who were seeking jobs that were increasingly located in distant suburbs.

Political and business leaders representing downtown merchants and property owners gained the largest advantage from this new highway spending. The federal government would pay to construct costly urban expressways that most people believed would bring shoppers back downtown, boosting sales, property values, and tax revenues. Motorists and truckers would thus finance not only construction of additional highways, but also the economic resuscitation of the American city. That the tax burden would be dribbled out in the form of a modest increase in gasoline taxes made the burden less painful for truckers and nearly invisible to motorists. Such were the politics of those who sought to merge the tools of economic growth with a technical fix for traffic and urban problems. At last, many believed, engineers could begin to get the traffic through.

FULL-SCALE CONSTRUCTION COMMENCES AND CRITICISM ARISES

Beginning in 1957 state and federal engineers launched full-scale construction of the interstate system. State road engineers surveyed land, fixed route coordinates, directed gigantic earth-moving equipment, and met deadlines. By 1965 engineers had opened nearly 16,000 interstate miles to traffic. Years later, senior engineers would describe road building up to the mid-1960s as an exciting, almost romantic activity.

Beginning in the early 1960s, however, a new and large generation of policy activists assaulted the ideas and practices of those who had led the highway-building regime. Many

Members of a growing environmental movement joined in the assault on highway builders, adding automobile and gasoline manufacturers to the list of culprits. Environmentalists blamed road building for destruction of parks, rivers, and deserts and for an accompanying increase in dirty water and air pollution. Often, leaders of environmental and other groups filed lawsuits that led to cancellation of projects in cities such as Denver, New Orleans, San Francisco, and New York City, and to delayed highway construction in the Rocky Mountains of Colorado. During the 1960s, however, engineers enjoyed the clout and prestige that were prerequisite to seeing most of these large and complex projects through to completion. According to historian Samuel P. Hays, moreover, engineers found the idea of preserving a pristine environment such as a desert or the Rocky Mountains "preposterous . . . if not impossible to accept."

Protesters and litigants lost many of their early contests with engineers. Neither litigation nor protest canceled or even delayed most road projects. In fact, by 1974 federal and state engineers had completed and opened more than 36,000 miles of interstate highways and placed another 2,800 miles under construction. These early opponents of the highway-building regime did, however, establish a counter-tradition to that of the authority of engineers as apolitical experts. By the late 1960s, claims for the environment, mass transit, or local control of transportation enjoyed a political legitimacy that had been unavailable only a few years earlier. Opponents of interstate construction had nudged politicians into the early stages of a broad reconsideration of American transportation policy.

Beginning in 1974 Congress and President Richard M. Nixon approved a program of diverting a portion of the gasoline taxes collected from motorists and truckers. As a practical matter in American politics, by the mid-1970s the program of building vast freeways through the nation's cities and through pristine environments was finished.

See also *Eisenhower, Dwight D.; Interest Groups; Taxation and Twentieth-Century Politics.*

MARK H. ROSE, FLORIDA ATLANTIC UNIVERSITY

BIBLIOGRAPHY

Hays, Samuel P. *Beauty, Health, and Permanence: Environmental Politics in the United States, 1955–1985.* New York: Cambridge University Press, 1987.

Rose, Mark H. *Interstate: Express Highway Politics, 1939–1989.* Knoxville: University of Tennessee Press, 1990.

Seely, Bruce E. *Building the American Highway System: Engineers as Policy Makers.* Philadelphia: Temple University Press, 1987.

IRAN-CONTRA SCANDAL

The Iran-contra scandal erupted in 1986 and blighted the last years of Ronald Reagan's presidential administration. Unlike the smaller scandals that had emerged in the Reagan years, Iran-contra represented—like the Watergate scandal in the previous decade—the corruption of power. Money was not at issue here; at issue was the belief that the White House could (and should) violate the law in service of its own agenda.

A SCANDAL OF FOREIGN POLICY ORIGINS

The earlier scandals—at the Environmental Protection Agency and the Department of Housing and Urban Development—had involved friends of the Reagan team making money while government bureaus were being downsized by administrators ideologically opposed to such federal efforts. In the massive defense buildup, opportunities were taken for kickbacks and illegal payments in return for lucrative contracts.

Iran-contra, however, was different, for two foreign policy fixations led this president and his aides into the abyss of the great scandal of his administration. One was the fear of communist penetration in what they saw as our hemisphere. The other was the fear of appearing weak, of not protecting Americans from hostage takers in the Middle East. The man who had promised to make the United States "stand tall" once more in the world could not afford to fail on these issues.

In the first year of his administration, 1981, President Reagan signed an executive order, a "presidential finding," authorizing a covert operation by the Central Intelligence Agency (CIA) to support the rebel army, known as the contras, in Nicaragua. While presented to Congress as an arms interdiction campaign (cutting off the alleged supply of weapons to guerrillas in El Salvador), in fact this was a plan to overthrow the Sandinista government of Nicaragua. But in 1982 and 1984, in two amendments introduced by Edward P. Boland (D-Mass.), the chair of the House Permanent Select Committee on Intelligence, and enacted by Congress, the White House first was specifically prohibited from attempting to overthrow the Sandinistas and then was told to terminate all assistance to the contras. The first amendment imposed a ceiling on further aid to the contras. The second stated that "no funds available to the CIA, Department of Defense or any other agency or entity of the United States involved in intelligence activities may be obligated or expended for the purpose of supporting military or paramilitary operations in Nicaragua by any nation, group, organization, movement or individual."

The Reagan White House, committed to the secret war, decided to get the money some other way. And although there were fears that this could be "an impeachable offense" (in the words of future chief of staff James Baker), the decision was made to secretly solicit aid from friendly nations (particularly ones dependent on special ties to America) and very affluent leaders. This effort provided almost $30 million for the contras. Also on the agenda: the use of American aid to neighboring Central American states that served as bases to train the contras. (Vice President George Bush delivered $100 million in aid to Honduras. He would state: "There is no quid pro quo.")

THE NATIONAL SECURITY COUNCIL ASSUMES CONTROL

The operation was centered inside the White House in the National Security Council (NSC), replacing the CIA as the planning agency. The NSC directors were important players, but it was their aide, Lt. Col. Oliver North, who became the key coordinator of the war, setting up the arms procurement and distribution system.

Meanwhile, in Lebanon, a small land torn by civil and religious strife, a few American hostages (mostly academics and journalists) were being held by Shi'ite militias seemingly under the influence of the Iranian mullahs, the Shi'ite religious figures in effective control of Iran. The scheme to secretly trade arms to Iran (locked in its bitter war with Iraq) to free the hostages was born despite daily Iranian excoriation of "the American Satan" and Iran's branding by Ronald

Reagan as a "terrorist state." None of this seemed to matter, as long as the outcome might be not only freedom for the hostages but a special bonus from the arms sales to Iran: more money for the contras in Central America.

INVESTIGATING THE AFFAIR

The scandal began to unravel in 1986, and not because of vigilant congressional oversight or heroic investigative reporters. In August North lied to the House Select Committee on Intelligence, denying raising money for the contras or offering any military aid. In October an American mercenary, Eugene Hasenfus, captured by the Nicaraguan army after his plane was shot down, appeared in front of television cameras telling a tale of a U.S.-sponsored covert and illegal arms resupply operation for the contras. One month later, a Lebanese weekly magazine, *Al-Shiraa,* published the story of a secret deal between America and Iran to exchange arms for hostages. President Reagan would soon be forced to admit that the two operations were interrelated.

The resignation of NSC director Robert McFarlane and the dismissal of Oliver North would be followed by the creation of a presidential commission, headed by Sen. John G. Tower (R-Texas), to investigate what now was being called the "Iran-contra affair." Special committees of the Senate and the House were created to conduct their own investigations, and an independent counsel, Lawrence Walsh, was appointed to lead an inquiry into the matter.

But all those seeking answers would be inhibited in their work by Attorney General Edwin Meese, who prevented professional investigators from gaining access to North's NSC offices while political appointees shredded messages, destroyed thousands of documents, and cleared computer tapes. When asked why he had not sealed the office and sent in the FBI, Meese responded: "You don't open fire if you hear rustling in the bushes." Critics would argue that, unlike in Watergate, in Iran-contra the cover-up worked.

After less than three months, the Tower commission filed its "comprehensive review," censoring the president's negligence and "hands-off management style" but presenting a "rogue staff" theory, arguing that NSC operatives were act-

ing on their own initiative, without presidential knowledge or approval.

The president, who had retreated from public view after the scandal broke, was encouraged by this report. And when the House and Senate investigations captured the national spotlight, some Republicans defended a contra initiative they had unsuccessfully backed in congressional battles, whereas others saw the inquiry as a partisan challenge to the conservative ideology of the Reagan White House. More important was the attitude of the Democratic leadership. The House Speaker and the Senate majority leader agreed that "the last thing we needed was an impeachment outcry, a frontal assault on the President's integrity . . . the country didn't need another Watergate."

Thus, Ronald Reagan emerged from the scandal to the warm support of the public in his last year in office. He was protected by the widespread assumption that this president could not be expected to know what his administration's policies were or what his key aides were doing. As the disgraced NSC director McFarlane observed, "President Reagan does not retain much of what comes his way in a day." Even Independent Counsel Walsh, in his scathing final report issued in 1994, concluded that Reagan "knowingly participated or at least acquiesced" in a cover-up, but "such a conclusion runs against his seeming blindness to reality when it came to the rationalization of some of his policies."

Some of the president's men did not emerge unscathed from Iran-contra. However, several aides—including Oliver North—who were prosecuted and convicted had their convictions overturned in appellate court; others received pardons by President George Bush in the next administration.

See also *Reagan, Ronald; Scandals and Corruption.*

DAVID H. BENNETT, SYRACUSE UNIVERSITY

BIBLIOGRAPHY

Draper, Theodore. *A Very Thin Line: The Iran-Contra Affair.* New York: Hill and Wang, 1991.

Kornbluh, Peter, and Malcolm Byrne, eds. *The Iran-Contra Scandal: The Declassified History.* New York: New Press, 1993.

Walsh, Lawrence E. *Firewall: The Iran-Contra Conspiracy and Cover-Up.* New York: W. W. Norton, 1998.

JACKSON, ANDREW

Andrew Jackson, seventh president of the United States (1829–1837) and founder of the Democratic Party, was born in the Carolina backcountry in 1767 to Scotch-Irish immigrants. Fatherless from birth, Jackson lost the rest of his family in the Revolution, in which he fought with patriot irregulars. After the war he studied law and in 1788 moved west to Nashville as public prosecutor. There he rose rapidly, engaging in merchandising and over the years acquiring land, slaves, and racehorses. He cemented his status by marrying Rachel Donelson Robards, member of a prominent local clan and estranged, though not yet formally divorced, from a previous husband. The circumstances of the marriage prompted charges of adultery and wife-stealing in Jackson's later presidential campaigns. But they were happy and adopted a son. Rachel died just after Jackson's election as president in 1828.

RISE TO NATIONAL PROMINENCE

Between 1796 and 1812 Jackson served in Tennessee's state constitutional convention, briefly in both houses of Congress (1796–1798), and as a state judge and militia general. His successful campaign against the Creek Indians in Alabama during the War of 1812 brought him national attention and a major generalship in the regular army. In the final battle of the war, at New Orleans (fought unbeknownst to both sides two weeks after the peace treaty), he inflicted a stunning defeat on a British invading force, causing two thousand casualties while suffering less than two dozen. This legendary triumph made him the greatest American military hero and patriotic symbol since George Washington.

Commanding on the southern frontier, Jackson raided into Florida in pursuit of marauding Seminole Indians in 1818. His action aroused criticism but helped prompt Spanish cession of the province to the United States. Jackson resigned from the army in 1821, served briefly as governor of Florida Territory, and then returned to the Senate in 1823 as an announced candidate for the next presidency.

The Virginia presidential dynasty was about to run out with the expiration of James Monroe's second term. Jackson's immense popularity made him a strong contender in 1824 despite his meager formal education, his lack of experience in statecraft or diplomacy, and a violent past checkered with duels and frontier brawls. In a confused, four-candidate race, Jackson led in both the popular and electoral vote, carrying eleven of twenty-four states. However, he failed to win an electoral majority, throwing the choice of president for the second (and thus far last) time into the House of Representatives. There the runner-up in the popular and electoral vote, Secretary of State John Quincy Adams of Massachusetts, prevailed on the first ballot. House Speaker Henry Clay, himself a defeated candidate and a rival of Jackson's for western favor, was instrumental in Adams's victory, warning congressmen of the dangers of a mere "military chieftain" in the White House. The new president then in turn appointed Clay secretary of state, prompting Jackson to charge that the people's will had been thwarted by a "corrupt bargain."

The cry to clean out the corruptionists and restore purity in government formed the touchstone of Jackson's campaign to unseat Adams in 1828. Skirting issues and playing on their candidate's heroic persona, Jackson's managers devised new techniques of arousing public excitement. Their skill and Adams's political ineptitude turned the contest into a rout. In 1828 Jackson was elected president, carrying New York and Pennsylvania along with the solid West and South for 178 electoral votes to Adams's 83. Jackson was the first president elected from west of the Appalachians and, at sixty-two, the oldest man yet to assume the office.

FIRST ADMINISTRATION

Aside from a vague craving for "reform" (or revenge), Jackson entered the White House with unsettled policy views, at the head of a large but diffuse electoral coalition. He began by instituting sweeping removals among high-ranking government officials, justifying them on the republican principle of "rotation in office." This was the origin of the notorious "spoils system" of bestowing jobs as a reward for party service. Procuring authority from Congress in 1830, Jackson used threats

Andrew Jackson *Library of Congress*

and blandishments to drive most of the remaining eastern Indian tribes to new homelands west of the Mississippi.

The chief issues of Jackson's first term concerned the nationalistic "American System" of economic policy propounded by Henry Clay and furthered by the previous Adams administration. As a fervent patriot and a champion of the developing West, Jackson had hitherto backed the American System's two central measures: a protective tariff to foster domestic manufacturing, and federal subsidies for transportation projects (known as "internal improvements"). But as president, Jackson turned against the system, interpreting its components as vehicles for corruption and for the advancement of special privilege. Beginning with the Maysville Road in 1830, he vetoed a series of internal improvement bills, and in 1831 he renounced protection and endorsed a tariff for revenue only. Harking back to Jeffersonian precepts, Jackson demanded a return to simple, frugal, minimal government. At the same time he reproved the increasingly strident southern sectional opposition to the tariff headed by his own vice president, John C. Calhoun of South Carolina.

Matters reached a head in the winter of 1832 to 1833, when South Carolina, through a state convention, declared the existing tariff law to be unconstitutional and hence null and void. Jackson issued a ringing proclamation that declared the Union indivisible and branded South Carolina's defiance of federal authority as incipient "treason." Jackson prepared coercive measures to uphold the law, but he instead readily accepted a congressional tariff compromise in March 1833 that resolved the crisis.

Meanwhile a new issue had come to the fore. In 1832 the Bank of the United States sought a renewal of its twenty-year congressional charter, due to expire in 1836. Jackson had long been suspicious of the bank's enormous financial and political power, and the conjunction of its application with the presidential candidacy of bank advocate Henry Clay sealed his hostility. Jackson vetoed the recharter bill. Citing constitutional and economic objections, his message also condemned legislation that granted special privileges to the bank's wealthy and well-connected stockholders as denying "equal justice to the high and the low, the rich and the poor."

SECOND ADMINISTRATION AND ORIGINS OF THE DEMOCRATIC PARTY

Jackson handily won reelection in 1832 with 219 electoral votes to Clay's 49. Promptly he renewed his campaign against the bank, ordering the removal of the federal government's own deposits from the Bank of the United States to selected state-chartered banks. This action triggered a brief financial panic and induced the Senate in 1834, for the only time in its history, to formally censure the president for usurping authority "in derogation" of the Constitution and the laws. Jackson protested the censure as itself unconstitutional, lacking either the formal charge or the two-thirds majority requisite for an impeachment conviction. In 1837 a pro-Jackson Senate majority voted to "expunge" the censure.

The federal charter of the Bank of the United States expired in 1836. (It continued as a state-chartered Pennsylvania institution.) Meanwhile Jackson and his followers broadened his war against it into an attack on all bank and other corporate charters, both state and federal, as instruments of special privilege. Jackson denounced banknote currency as the tool of a conspiratorial "money power" and called for its replacement by gold and silver "hard money." To further this end and to arrest a budding inflationary spiral, his treasury secretary in 1836 ordered payment in coin for all purchases of federal western lands.

Carrying the banner of equal rights and minimal government, and claiming direct descent from Thomas Jefferson and his party, Jackson's followers in the states organized themselves into a new political party which they called the Democracy. In this they received essential coordination and direction from Jackson's own White House. Democrats first met in national convention in 1832 to ratify Jackson's choice of Martin van Buren (previously secretary of state) as his vice president and heir apparent. In 1835 they convened again to nominate Van Buren as Jackson's successor.

The constituency of this new party was too diverse for easy characterization. In this it reflected Jackson's own multiple identities as frontiersman, slave-owning planter, wealthy man of humble origins, and a successful entrepreneur and politician who nonetheless viewed himself as an outsider to the established circles of prestige and power. Jackson and his party denounced "aristocracy" at every turn and championed both republican simplicity and spreadeagle expansion. From Jackson the Democracy's rhetoric drew a tone that was populist, egalitarian, and also anticlerical. Though he was a pious Presbyterian in private life, Jackson led Democrats in strenuous resistance to the mingling of church and state, thereby attracting many religious dissenters to the party.

By the time of Jackson's retirement in 1837, the amorphous personal coalition that elected him in 1828 had been transformed into a political machine whose organization and discipline would serve as a model for the gathering Whig opposition and for all future American parties. The demand for party regularity was spurred by Jackson's own difficulties with Congress, which had forced him to use vetoes as his main instruments of policy. In eight years Congress passed only one major piece of legislation, the Indian removal bill of 1830, at Jackson's direct behest. During this time he vetoed twelve bills, more than his six predecessors combined.

POLITICAL VISION

Jackson strengthened himself against Congress by forging direct links between the president and the electorate. His official messages, though directed ostensibly to Congress, were artfully drafted to rally public opinion at large. In these, Jackson cast himself as the people's tribune against special interests and their minions in Washington. In other ways also he expanded the scope of presidential authority. He dominated his cabinet, forcing out members who would not execute his commands. In two terms he went through four secretaries of state and five of the treasury. Holding his official subordinates at arm's length, Jackson devised and implemented his policies through a private coterie of advisers and publicists known as the "Kitchen Cabinet." His bold initiatives and domineering style caused opponents to call him King Andrew and to take the name of Whigs to signify their opposition to executive tyranny.

Jackson was no deep thinker, but his matured policy positions did bespeak a coherent political philosophy. Like Jefferson, he believed republican government should be simple and restrained. He cherished as a personal triumph the extinction of the national debt during his administration (already much reduced under previous presidents from its high in the War of 1812). Regarding cleavages and inequities in society as fostered rather than ameliorated by governmental intervention, he embraced laissez faire as the policy most conducive to economic equality and political liberty. With seven Supreme Court appointments, including Chief Justice Roger Taney (previously a key lieutenant in the Bank War), Jackson turned federal jurisprudence toward restraining privilege while encouraging enterprise. Reversing the Marshall Court's thrust, Jackson and the Court led by Taney sought to devolve political power toward the states, where it was closer to the people.

Jackson's political vision was thus decentralizing but still strongly nationalist. Regarding the Union as indivisible and perpetual, Jackson upheld the paramountcy of federal authority and denied a state's right to nullify acts of Congress or to secede, even as he reproved policies like the tariff which fostered sectional divisiveness. His aggressive Indian removal policy and his espousal of cheaper land prices reflected his nationalism's frontier roots. Jackson owned slaves and never thought seriously about slavery as a moral problem. He saw abolitionism as disruptive of both sectional harmony and Democratic unity, and he condemned it on that ground. He supported southerners and his own postmaster general, Amos Kendall, in suppressing the abolitionist mail and petition campaigns of the 1830s.

In foreign affairs Jackson's presidency was generally uneventful. In 1834–1835 he raised the risk of war by threatening reprisals for France's refusal to pay acknowledged damage claims to American merchants, but the crisis passed when the French relented. Jackson's efforts to purchase Texas from Mexico helped sow seeds of distrust that would later bear fruit in war, though he refrained from officially backing the Texas insurrection that began in 1835.

Jackson's powerful personality played an instrumental role in his political success. He indulged in violent hatreds, and the extent to which his political positions reflected mere personal animus is still debated. He first broke with Calhoun in a bitter feud over the character of Margaret Eaton, the wife of Jackson's old friend and secretary of war John Henry Eaton. Jackson charged Calhoun with persecuting Margaret in order to drive Eaton out of the cabinet. Jackson demonized many of those who crossed him politically, including Henry Clay, Bank of the United States president Nicholas Biddle, and Cherokee Indian chief John Ross.

After his presidency, Jackson retired to the Hermitage, his plantation home outside Nashville, where he continued an active political correspondence. His last important act was to intervene in favor of Texas annexation and the candidacy of

James K. Polk for the Democratic nomination in 1844. Jackson died in 1845.

See also *Adams, John Quincy; Bank War; Calhoun, John C.; Democratic Party; Eaton Affair; Indian Policy; Jacksonian Democracy; Political Parties; Seminole War; Slavery; Tariff History; Van Buren, Martin; War of 1812; Whig Party.*

DANIEL FELLER, UNIVERSITY OF NEW MEXICO

BIBLIOGRAPHY

Cole, Donald B. *The Presidency of Andrew Jackson.* Lawrence: University Press of Kansas, 1993.

Remini, Robert V. *Andrew Jackson.* 3 vols. New York: Harper and Row, 1977–1984.

Schlesinger, Arthur M., Jr. *The Age of Jackson.* Boston: Little, Brown, 1945.

Ward, John William. *Andrew Jackson: Symbol for an Age.* New York: Oxford University Press, 1955.

Watson, Harry L. *Liberty and Power: The Politics of Jacksonian America.* New York: Farrar, Straus and Giroux, 1990.

JACKSONIAN DEMOCRACY

Andrew Jackson's presidency (1829–1837) has long been associated with the "rise of the common man," in particular the extension of voting rights to men without property. Historians have sometimes also associated the various reform efforts of the first half of the nineteenth century with the period of his presidency, even though Jackson had little or nothing to do with such movements as prison reform, temperance, abolition, or the democratization of access to elementary education.

The celebration by "common people" who converged on the nation's capital in 1829 for Jackson's first inauguration and stomped merrily through the White House—the "people's house"—accentuated the connection between democracy and the Age of Jackson. So did Jackson's egalitarian rhetoric in the Bank Bill veto in 1832, when he declared that government ought to "shower its favors alike on the high and the low, the rich and the poor." But Jackson's democratic leanings were hardly evident to all Americans at the time, nor have they been to all historians. Jackson owned slaves and warred against Indians. Aside from the Bank Bill veto, the major policy accomplishments of his presidency can be said to have been the Indian Removal Act of 1830 (democratization of white access to frontier land came at the cost of Indian lands and furthered the expansion of black slavery) and his forceful response to South Carolina's rumblings of nullifying the tariff in 1832 and 1833 (political democracy was not necessarily consistent with states' rights and limited powers of the central government). Jackson's actions as president led to a strange combination of

In this 1832 cartoon, Andrew Jackson—"King Andrew the First"—is depicted as a tyrant trampling the Constitution, a ledger of Supreme Court decisions, and the watchwords *Virtue, Liberty,* and *Independence.* Library of Congress

political enemies, including the emerging Whig Party with its opposition to "King Andrew."

Changes in voting rights during the Age of Jackson—whatever the timing, causes, or consequences of expanding the electorate to include most white men—did nothing to include women and in some states actually removed or at least restricted African American men's voting rights. One historian, moreover, redirecting attention away from political affairs and toward social change and economic inequality (especially in the burgeoning cities) wrote a book entitled *Jacksonian Aristocracy.*

Thus, compared with a generation or two ago, there is little agreement as to the utility, definition, or significance of the term *Jacksonian Democracy.* Yet, viewed more broadly as an elastic ideology of expanding rights, it can arguably encompass such efforts across the nineteenth century—even if only partially accomplished at the time—as promoting the rights and interests of farmers and workers, ending racial proscriptions, and extending voting rights to people without regard to their race, ethnicity, class, or gender.

See also *Black Suffrage; Indian Policy; Jackson, Andrew; Labor Politics and Policy; Nullification; Suffrage; Whig Party.*

PETER WALLENSTEIN,
VIRGINIA POLYTECHNIC INSTITUTE AND STATE UNIVERSITY

BIBLIOGRAPHY

Miller, Douglas T. *Jacksonian Aristocracy: Class and Democracy in New York, 1830–1860.* New York: Oxford University Press, 1967.

Remini, Robert V. *The Legacy of Andrew Jackson: Essays on Democracy, Indian Removal, and Slavery.* Baton Rouge: Louisiana State University Press, 1988.

Schlesinger, Arthur M. Jr. *The Age of Jackson.* Boston: Little, Brown, 1945.

Wallenstein, Peter. *From Slave South to New South: Public Policy in Nineteenth-Century Georgia.* Chapel Hill: University of North Carolina Press, 1987.

Watson, Harry L. *Liberty and Power: The Politics of Jacksonian America.* New York: Hill and Wang, 1990.

JEFFERSON, THOMAS

Thomas Jefferson (1743–1826), author of the Declaration of Independence and third president (1801–1809) of the United States, was born at Shadwell, Albemarle County, Virginia. Jefferson's father Peter was a prominent planter, surveyor, and local official; through his mother, Jane Randolph Jefferson, young Jefferson was connected to the Randolphs and the "first families" of Virginia. After receiving the rudiments of a classical education, Jefferson studied at the College of William and Mary, where a mathematics professor introduced him to the latest in Enlightenment thought. Jefferson became a legal apprentice to George Wythe, leader of the Virginia bar, which prepared Jefferson for a career as a lawyer (interrupted by the imperial crisis and outbreak of the American Revolution) and public servant.

Jefferson's rise in Virginia politics, initiated by election to the House of Burgesses (1769), was facilitated by the extensive holdings in land and slaves he inherited from his father and augmented through marriage to the young widow Martha Wayles Skelton in 1772. In the Burgesses Jefferson quickly established himself as an able committee member and legislative draftsman. When his authorship of the anonymously published *Summary View of the Rights of British America* (1774) became known, Jefferson's fame as a revolutionary writer spread through the colonies. Drafted but not officially adopted as instructions to Virginia's delegation to the First Continental Congress, Jefferson's inflammatory pamphlet challenged George III to save the empire by reversing the disastrous course of British imperial policy. The *Summary View* thus set the stage for the savage indictment of the king in the Declaration of Independence, drafted by Jefferson and significantly edited by his fellow congressional representatives in June and July 1776.

Neither Jefferson nor his colleagues recognized the importance the declaration would subsequently attain as a statement of fundamental American principles, and Jefferson's authorship would not be widely known until he became a standard bearer for the Republican opposition in the 1790s. He was convinced that the truly important political work of the Revolution was taking place in the states, where patriot leaders were effecting the transition from monarchical to republican rule. Stuck in Philadelphia with Congress, Jefferson was prevented from taking part in drafting Virginia's first constitution; what he supposed to be defects of the revolutionary charter would preoccupy him into his retirement years. But Jefferson nonetheless seized the role of republican reformer during his tenure in the new House of Delegates (1776–1779), particularly in spearheading the revisal of the laws, an ambitious revamping of Virginia's legal code in 126 separate bills. The legislature adopted Jefferson's bills to abolish primogeniture (the right of inheritance belonging to eldest sons) and entail (another inheritance restriction), legal props of an aristocratic land system, and subsequently enacted his Bill for Establishing Religious Freedom (in 1786, thanks to the efforts of his ally James Madison). Other provisions dear to the reformer's heart, including legislation to set up a comprehensive system of public education, were never adopted; Jefferson suppressed a proposal for the gradual emancipation of Virginia's slaves until divulging it in his *Notes on the State of Virginia* (English ed., 1787).

Jefferson's first experience in public administration, as Virginia's wartime governor (1779–1781), was not a happy one. Political opponents blamed Jefferson for the state's dismal failure to repel Benedict Arnold's invasion in 1780; the state government was forced to beat an inglorious retreat from its home in Richmond, and Jefferson himself was forced to flee precipitously from his Monticello estate near Charlottesville. Subsequently exonerated of any personal responsibility for this debacle, Jefferson retired from public life. It was at this time that he drafted the *Notes on Virginia,* his only full-length book. Jefferson did not attribute Virginia's weakness to the unwillingness of citizen–taxpayers in popular governments to provide for their own security. Instead, Virginia's problems, he argued, were rooted in its failure to perfect its republican institutions, most notably by having a duly authorized convention draft a state constitution that would be ratified by the people in a special vote. Jefferson's conviction that good government was based on proper constitutional forms and their strict construction would be a defining motif of his subsequent career.

The traumatic loss of wife Martha, who died in October 1782 as the result of complications from a sixth pregnancy, prepared the grieving widower for a return to public service. Jefferson accepted a call to join Congress's delegation at the peace talks in Paris, but his departure was postponed when news arrived that negotiations had been successfully concluded. While awaiting his new assignment as American minister to France, Jefferson served as a member of Virginia's congressional delegation. His brief tenure was marked by Virginia's cession of its vast claims north of the Ohio River to Congress in March 1784 and the enactment of an ordinance for territorial government drafted by Jefferson the next month. Guaranteeing the equality of new states, Jefferson's ordinance established the foundational principle of an expanding federal system, subsequently incorporated in the Northwest Ordinance of 1787. Jefferson also served on the committee that drafted Congress's first ordinance for selling national lands; its provision for imposing a rectangular grid on the landscape was incorporated in Congress's May 1785 land ordinance.

Jefferson's service in Congress made him acutely conscious of the weakness of the national government under the Articles of Confederation as well as of the deepening sectional divisions over major policy issues that threatened the viability of the union. His subsequent diplomatic frustrations in France (1784–1789) reinforced the lesson. Because the European states doubted that the United States would survive in its present form, they were unwilling to enter into serious negotiations with the new nation.

Jefferson took advantage of underemployment leisure to expand his intellectual horizons, forming friendships with like-minded reformers and savants. The onset of the French Revolution in 1789 put Jefferson, spokesperson for its American prototype, at the center of the action. This heady experience crystallized Jefferson's vision of the epochal importance of the worldwide republican revolution. Jefferson's enthusiasm for revolutionary movements did not extend across the color line, however: With his fellow slaveholders, he feared that the example of the Haitian Revolution (1794–1804) would spread to the southern slave states.

SECRETARY OF STATE AND VICE PRESIDENT

Jefferson returned to Virginia in 1789, expecting to return to his post in Paris after attending to private business. Though convinced that federal constitutional reform was long overdue, he had misgivings about the constitution that Madison and his colleagues had drafted at Philadelphia, under which the new federal government was now being organized in

Thomas Jefferson *Library of Congress*

New York. These concerns focused on the constitutional provision for a strong executive and on the absence of a Bill of Rights to secure individual liberties and states' rights. When President George Washington asked Jefferson to join his cabinet as secretary of state, the reluctant Jefferson finally concluded that his presence would counteract the Federalists' bias toward an overly energetic central federal government. Jefferson also recognized the need for a strong and unified foreign and commercial policy that would minimize British influence over the American economy and open up new markets for the new nation's merchants. At the same time, Jefferson thought, the United States could promote the cause of republican revolution in France and throughout the world.

Jefferson's hopes for the new government were soon thwarted. Jefferson's cabinet colleague, Treasury Secretary Alexander Hamilton, set the tone for the administration by launching a bold financial program, predicated on servicing state as well as federal Revolutionary War debts. To secure the government's creditworthiness Hamilton depended on a steady flow of revenue from duties on the English imports that still dominated American markets. Treasury policy thus dictated foreign policy: Regardless of Jefferson's preferences, the United States would adopt a conciliatory—if not submissive—stance toward Britain. While Jefferson's hands were tied at State, Hamilton sought to implement his financial program through a new national bank, leading the emerging opposition party in Congress to fear a dangerous concentration of power under the aegis of a broad or loose interpretation of the federal government's powers under the Constitution. Thus even as the United States showed a weak face to the world, effectively aligning itself with Britain against revolutionary France, the administration threatened to transform itself into a new American version of the old imperial government.

As the pro-British policy orientation of the administration and Hamilton's intention to remodel the federal state along British lines became conspicuous, Jefferson found himself assuming the role of party leader. The uncertain course of the European war kept the ultimate direction of American policy in suspense. British plunder of American shipping pushed the two nations to the brink of war. When Jefferson finally resigned as secretary of state at the end of 1793, he could still hope for a reorientation of administration policy. But the ratification of John Jay's controversial treaty with Britain in 1795 dashed those hopes, climaxing the process of party polarization that gave rise to the first party system.

Jefferson's retirement from office was again brief. As runner-up to John Adams in the presidential election of 1796, he ascended to the vice presidency (1797–1801), finding himself once more in the position of partisan opponent of the administration he ostensibly served. During these years, the Republicans' tilt toward France proved embarrassing, particularly after the French, angered by the Jay Treaty, turned against their erstwhile allies in the Quasi-War (1798–1800). The administration prepared for full-scale war with France, seeking to hobble the Republican opposition through the Alien and Sedition Acts (1798). Though counseling patience during this "reign of witches," Jefferson prepared for the possible collapse of the union; his Kentucky Resolutions (1798) articulated a states-rights interpretation of the Constitution that justified resistance to the federal government. But belligerent Federalists saved the day for Jefferson by overplaying their hand. When the administration party split into bitter divisions in the wake of Adams's successful negotiation for an end to the Quasi-War, the way was clear for a dramatic Republican recovery in the 1800 elections.

PRESIDENTIAL ADMINISTRATIONS

Jefferson hailed his election as a return to the revolutionary principles of 1776. Federalist diehards sought to exploit the tie vote between Jefferson and Aaron Burr in the electoral college (votes for president and vice president were not distinguished until ratification of the Twelfth Amendment in 1804), either by elevating a pliant Burr to the top office or by extracting concessions from Jefferson. But Jefferson felt secure enough in his popular mandate to rebuff these overtures and then to extend the olive branch to moderate Federalists in his inaugural address ("We are all federalists, we are all republicans"). Under the able administration of Treasury Secretary Albert Gallatin, Hamilton's financial system remained intact but would no longer serve as the engine of consolidation; internal taxes were repealed and import revenues were used to pay down the national debt (from $83,000,000 to $57,000,000 by 1809).

Federalists were not purged from appointive offices in the federal bureaucracy, though Jefferson was attentive to the needs of Republican loyalists in making new appointments and though he could not resist removing John Quincy Adams, perhaps the most able diplomat in government service. Republican animosity toward the Federalist judges led to repeal of the Judiciary Act of 1801, expanding the federal court system, and to controversial efforts to impeach particularly obnoxious incumbents such as John Pickering of New Hampshire (convicted and removed in March 1804) and Samuel Chase of Maryland (acquitted in March 1805). But Jefferson was generally much less dangerous to the established order than Federalists had feared.

The success of the Republicans' "revolution of 1800" was reflected in growing majorities in both houses of Congress and by Jefferson's landslide reelection in 1804.

As the nation grew more Republican, it expanded in size: The administration's greatest coup, the Louisiana Purchase of 1803, doubled the extent of American territory and removed the danger of a destabilizing French presence in the Mississippi Valley. Yet the new nation's continuing vulnerability soon became apparent again. The European war opened up extraordinary new market opportunities to American producers and shippers, but it also put them at grave risk: The belligerent powers showed little respect for "neutral rights" when their own vital interests were at stake. Jefferson found that threats of commercial sanctions against the belligerents, culminating in the ill-fated embargo of 1807 to 1809, were ineffective and counterproductive. By the end of Jefferson's presidency, war with either Britain or France—or with both— seemed increasingly likely.

American foreign policy had always been inextricably linked to sectional tensions and centrifugal tendencies in the American federal union. Burr's western "conspiracy of 1806," an alleged plot to separate the western states from the union, illuminated these connections. Jefferson's relentless pursuit of Burr, whose actual intentions remain unclear, culminated in the adventurer's treason trial and eventual acquittal. As opposition to his foreign and domestic policies grew, Jefferson's old enemies gained a new lease on life and Republicans divided into factions, with "Old Republican" purists aligning against moderates who tilted too much toward Federalist heresies. These divisions, originating late in Jefferson's first term, became more pronounced as Republicans looked toward the presidential succession. Insurgent Old Republicans rallied around James Monroe, moderates around James Madison, Jefferson's secretary of state and heir apparent. Some Republicans thought that the only hope for the survival of the party and the union was that Jefferson agree to serve a third term. By 1809, however, the sixty-five-year-old Jefferson, suffering through one of the worst phases of his political career, longed to return to private life.

RETURN TO PRIVATE LIFE

Jefferson never left Virginia after retiring to Monticello in March 1809, now focusing his energies on his home, his family, and his agricultural enterprises. With the vindication of American independence in the War of 1812, Jefferson's reputation quickly rebounded from the political and diplomatic setbacks of his second term. Swarms of admiring visitors came to pay homage, driving the Sage of Monticello into periodic exile at his Poplar Forest plantation in Bedford County, seventy miles away. Despite recurrent physical complaints, these were among Jefferson's happiest years. His reflections on political and constitutional theory led him to reaffirm his commitment to the fundamental principles that had guided him throughout his career. Jefferson's prophetic vision of his country's rise to glory transformed him into an American icon in his own lifetime.

Yet all was not well in Jefferson's world. His dire financial situation, exacerbated by an economic depression in 1819 that was devastating to overextended staple producers, made him acutely sensitive to threats to the economic interests and political power of his class and region. Controversial Supreme Court decisions revived Jefferson's anxieties about the consolidation of power in the federal government. Efforts to check the spread of slavery in Missouri were even more alarming. Jefferson became convinced of a massive conspiracy to tie the slave states to an all-powerful central government. He continued to advocate privately the compensated emancipation and deportation of slaves, but his hopes for this great panacea were undercut by doubts about the good faith of his fellow Americans and by his refusal to support such programs in any public way. Nor could Jefferson extricate himself personally from the institution, though he did secure the freedom of the four mixed-race children born to Sally Hemings, a slave believed to have been his mistress.

Yet there was always consolation in the long historical perspective: The sons of Virginia educated at Jefferson's new university would redeem the revolutionary legacy; the rising generation would, somehow, deal with the problem of slavery; American independence would be an inspiration to oppressed peoples everywhere, "arousing men to burst the chains under which monkish ignorance and superstition had persuaded them to bind themselves." Jefferson was eighty-three years old when he died on July 4, 1826, on the fiftieth anniversary of American independence.

See also *Declaration of Independence; Embargo; Judiciary Acts; Madison, James; Panic of 1819; Political Parties; Sally Hemings Affair; Sedition Act of 1798; Territorial Expansion; Washington, George.*

PETER ONUF, UNIVERSITY OF VIRGINIA

BIBLIOGRAPHY

Burstein, Andrew. *The Inner Jefferson: Portrait of a Grieving Optimist.* Charlottesville: University Press of Virginia, 1995.
Ellis, Joseph J. *American Sphinx: The Character of Thomas Jefferson.* New York: Knopf, 1997.
Finkelman, Paul. *Slavery and the Founders: Race and Liberty in the Age of Jefferson.* Armonk, N.Y.: M. E. Sharpe, 1995.
Malone, Dumas. *Jefferson and His Time.* 6 vols. Boston: Little, Brown, 1948–1981.
Onuf, Peter S. *Jefferson's Empire: The Language of American Nationhood.* Charlottesville: University Press of Virginia, 2000.

JEFFERSONIAN DEMOCRACY

The idea of Jeffersonian Democracy arose during the 1790s, as political parties emerged during the administration of George Washington. The most avid supporters of Washington formed the Federalist Party, which was led by Alexander Hamilton and John Adams. The Federalists believed in representative government but also in the politics of deference. The elite should rule, and the voters should choose among members of the elite. Most Federalists believed the franchise should be limited to those with property or some other stake in society. Although class conscious, Federalists tended to be racial egalitarians; free blacks, where they could vote in this period, supported Federalists.

The opponents of the Federalists, led by Thomas Jefferson and James Madison, were known as Democratic-Republicans and supporters of Jeffersonian Democracy. Jefferson had more faith in the average voter and small property owner than most Federalists did. He was not in favor of universal adult male suffrage, and he opposed black suffrage (as did most of his followers), but he favored a more liberal access to the ballot than did most Federalists. Jefferson had a strong appeal to small farmers—the yeomen farmers of the South—and white working-class urbanites.

The philosophy of Jeffersonian Democracy was tied to Jefferson's own political philosophy. Jefferson favored a small national government, with low taxes and little federal involvement in the economy. He had an almost mystical belief in the importance of the yeoman farmer and feared the creation of a permanent lower class similar to the peasants in France. However, he was deeply hostile to the rights of free blacks and Native Americans. At the bottom of his "democracy" were hundreds of thousands of African American slaves.

Jeffersonian Democracy, with its emphasis on the majority of the population, proved to be enormously successful. Jefferson set the stage for more than a half-century of political dominance by his party. Under Andrew Jackson the party would push for universal adult male suffrage and use the votes of these men to continue to control politics until the 1850s. However, the failure of the proponents of Jeffersonian Democracy was their inability to face the problems of slavery and race in a realistic manner. Ultimately, the defense of slavery would drive many Jeffersonians to extreme positions on states' rights and then to secession and civil war. Ironically, Abraham Lincoln would win the vast majority of northern votes by advocating a return to Jeffersonian principles, but with a distinctly non-Jeffersonian view of slavery.

See also *Adams, John; Jacksonian Democracy; Jefferson, Thomas; Madison, James; Washington, George.*

PAUL FINKELMAN, UNIVERSITY OF TULSA COLLEGE OF LAW

BIBLIOGRAPHY

Onuf, Peter, ed. *Jeffersonian Legacies.* Charlottesville: University Press of Virginia, 1993.

JOHNSON, ANDREW

The seventeenth president of the United States, Andrew Johnson (1808–1875) became president when Abraham Lincoln was assassinated in April 1865. Johnson locked horns with Congress throughout his term in office over policy toward the defeated Confederacy.

A Democrat from Tennessee, Johnson served five terms in the U.S. House of Representatives and more than half a term in the U.S. Senate before his state seceded and joined the Confederacy in 1861. Johnson bitterly opposed Tennessee's secession, refused to acknowledge it when it occurred, and retained his seat in the Senate. In 1862 he resigned from the Senate to accept an appointment from President Lincoln as military governor of Tennessee, when Lincoln was seeking to establish a loyal state government in one of the Confederate states. Then, as a pro-Union Democrat from the South, in 1864 he was tapped as Lincoln's running mate for reelection, when Republicans and War Democrats—Democrats who supported the administration's war against secession—joined forces under the Union Party label. Weeks after Lincoln's sec-

ond inaugural, on April 15, 1865, an assassin made Johnson president, with nearly a full term to complete before the next presidential election.

Johnson had an extraordinarily difficult term in office, and he gave as good as he got. Echoing the experience of President John Tyler a quarter-century earlier, Johnson ascended to the presidency from the vice presidency only weeks into the term, lost the support of the party that had nominated him for the vice presidency, and could find no constituency that might support a subsequent bid for election in his own right. Yet far more was at stake during Johnson's presidency than during Tyler's, and Congress eventually sought to remove Johnson from office.

Congressional Republicans understood Johnson no better than he understood them, and when they *did* understand each other it was to comprehend the huge differences that separated them. The two forces collided irreparably in 1866, when Johnson vetoed two important Reconstruction measures. Congress overrode both vetoes, and the Freedmen's Bureau Act of 1866 and the Civil Rights Act of 1866 became law. Johnson continued thereafter to obstruct congressional efforts to reconstruct the South.

Three very different explanations, quite aside from his pugnacious personality, can account for Johnson's behavior. His constitutional scruples, as expressed in the veto messages, were a legitimate expression of long-held political beliefs about the limits of federal authority. His racial prejudice, similarly powerful, drove him to choose former slaveowners over former slaves in the postemancipation political environment, whereas in previous years he had despised both slaves and their owners. Finally, Johnson's political aspirations shaped his behavior. Lincoln would have been in his second term had he lived, and thus not a viable candidate for reelection. Besides completing Lincoln's second term, Johnson hoped to secure a term of his own. As a lifelong Democrat, however, he could not count on the Republicans to nominate him, so he sought a return to his political home in the Democratic Party.

Congressional Republicans saw far too much at stake to put up with Johnson's obstructionist approach to the enforcement of Reconstruction legislation. After earlier efforts secured insufficient support, the House impeached him on February 24, 1868—the first of only two presidents to be impeached (Bill Clinton suffered the same fate more than one hundred years later)—but he escaped removal by the Senate on May 26, 1868, when seven Republicans joined all the Democrats in voting against conviction. The removal effort failed when it fell short by a single vote of securing the required two-thirds majority. Johnson served out the remaining months of his term and, having failed to obtain the Democratic nomination, returned to Tennessee. After unsuccessful efforts to gain reelection to the Senate in 1869 and the House in 1872, he was returned to the Senate in 1875. He died a few months later, defiant to the end.

See also *Civil Rights Act of 1866; Clinton, Bill; Freedmen's Bureau Acts; Impeachment; Reconstruction.*

PETER WALLENSTEIN,
VIRGINIA POLYTECHNIC INSTITUTE AND STATE UNIVERSITY

BIBLIOGRAPHY

Bowen, David Warren. *Andrew Johnson and the Negro.* Knoxville: University of Tennessee Press, 1989.

Castel, Albert. *The Presidency of Andrew Johnson.* Lawrence: University Press of Kansas, 1979.

McKitrick, Eric L. *Andrew Johnson and Reconstruction.* Chicago: University of Chicago Press, 1960.

Simpson, Brooks D. *The Reconstruction Presidents.* Lawrence: University Press of Kansas, 1998.

Trefousse, Hans L. *Impeachment of a President: Andrew Johnson, the Blacks, and Reconstruction.* Knoxville: University of Tennessee Press, 1975.

JOHNSON, LYNDON B.

Lyndon Baines Johnson, the thirty-sixth president of the United States (1963–1969), was a highly skilled politician who saw his remarkably productive presidency slide into the quagmire called the Vietnam War.

Johnson was born on August 27, 1908, in Stonewall, Texas. After he graduated from a small, unaccredited high school, he spent a year in California and then attended Southwest Texas State Teachers College. Before pursuing a life in politics, he became the only president since Herbert Hoover to teach in a public secondary school.

After a stint in local politics, Johnson, who was also known as LBJ, got his start in national politics by gaining a congressional staff position. In 1931 Democrat Richard Kleberg, a newly elected member of the House of Representatives from Texas, asked Johnson to come to Washington as an aide. During the four years LBJ worked for Kleberg, he not only established an organization of Capitol Hill staffers, an indication of his personal power and acumen, but also learned firsthand about the legislative process and became an ardent supporter of President Franklin D. Roosevelt's New Deal policies. While on Capitol Hill, Johnson studied law briefly at Georgetown University, but he gave up both the studies and his job in 1935 when Roosevelt appointed him Texas director of the National Youth Administration, a program aimed at helping the nation's unemployed youth find jobs and go to school.

In 1937 James P. Buchanan, the House member from Johnson's Texas district, died, presenting Johnson with an opportunity to run for Congress. Campaigning on a pro-Roosevelt platform, LBJ won the special election. He gained

Lyndon B. Johnson takes the oath of office aboard Air Force One, with Jacqueline Kennedy at his side. *Lyndon Baines Johnson Library*

reelection to the House in 1938 and 1940 but was narrowly defeated when he ran for a Senate seat in 1941. After the Japanese attacked Pearl Harbor December 7, 1941, Johnson was the first House member to volunteer for active duty in the armed forces. With the exception of brief military service in the South Pacific, Johnson served in the House until January 1949, when he took the Senate seat he had won the previous November. During the campaign, in which charges of voter fraud and injunctions abounded, Johnson worked both sides of the political fence to get into the Senate. After just four years in that body he was elected minority leader, and in January 1955, when the Democrats took control of the Senate, he was elected majority leader.

Johnson suffered a severe heart attack in July 1955 but recovered fully. During his six years as majority leader, Johnson became known as one of the most skilled legislative leaders in congressional history. His own special brand of flattery and coercion—the "Treatment"—to get his way on legislative matters was a valuable asset that he took with him to the White House.

In 1960 Johnson lost the Democratic presidential nomination to Sen. John F. Kennedy of Massachusetts. When Kennedy offered Johnson the second place on the ticket, the majority leader accepted despite contrary advice from many—including former vice president John Nance Garner, also a Texan. In the general election Kennedy and Johnson narrowly defeated Republicans Richard Nixon and Henry Cabot Lodge. In fact, speculation was high that Kennedy might not have won at all without Johnson on the ticket to help carry several southern states, including Texas.

On November 22, 1963, Kennedy was fatally shot while riding in a motorcade through Dallas; Johnson was riding in a car behind the president. After Kennedy was pronounced dead at a Dallas hospital, Johnson proceeded to the airport and boarded *Air Force One,* where he took the oath of office immediately.

TWO YEARS OF LANDMARK LEGISLATION

In the days following the assassination, Johnson declared his intention to carry out Kennedy's programs and asked Kennedy's cabinet to remain. Then he went to work. During Johnson's five years in the White House the nation witnessed the largest outpouring of domestic legislation since Franklin Roosevelt's first term. Three landmark bills were enacted in 1964 and three more in 1965.

The most historic legislation was the Civil Rights Act of 1964, which expanded voting rights protections for blacks; established the Equal Employment Opportunity Commission; and forbade discrimination on account of race or sex by employers, places of public accommodation, and labor unions. It was the most far-reaching civil rights legislation passed since Reconstruction. President Johnson contributed to passage of the act by refusing to bargain with congressional southerners and by encouraging the legislative strategies that ultimately produced the necessary Republican votes.

Recognizing that public sentiment for the slain president improved his chances of enacting Kennedy's legislative program, LBJ vigorously lobbied Congress in 1964 to enact his "War on Poverty," which largely took the form of the Economic Opportunity Act. Broadly, it called for creating job opportunities and services in poor areas rather than supporting incomes. Passage of this legislation was a testament to Johnson's political skills. In an intensive effort, the president highlighted the measure repeatedly—in his State of the Union address and in his daily remarks. When the bill passed the House by larger-than-expected margins, House majority leader Carl Albert of Oklahoma reportedly told the president, "I can't figure out . . . how in the world we ever got this through."

The landmark tax cut legislation passed in Johnson's first year succeeded in stimulating the economy. Kennedy had called for reductions in every tax bracket, with total reductions of $11 million for individuals and $2.6 billion for corporations. The legislation passed in the House during the Kennedy administration; Johnson had to ensure that it passed in the Senate. After striking a deal with Senate majority leader Harry Byrd, juggling the budget numbers, and sending assurances to conservatives that he would watch deficits closely, Johnson saw his bill pass.

In 1964 Johnson ran for a presidential term of his own against Republican senator Barry Goldwater of Arizona. Because many Americans found Goldwater's conservative positions too extreme, Johnson outpolled Goldwater by more than 15 million votes and defeated him 486–52 in the electoral college. A colleague from his Senate days, Hubert Humphrey of Minnesota, was LBJ's running mate.

Johnson regarded his landslide victory as a mandate to enact the "Great Society" social programs that he had outlined in his campaign. No less helpful, however, was the Democratic legislative sweep of Congress. Democrats held the House by a 155-member margin, the Senate by a 36-member margin. Johnson's Great Society was a comprehensive plan designed to fight poverty, ignorance, disease, and other social problems. Over 1965–1966, LBJ guided numerous bills through Congress providing greater aid for poverty-stricken Appalachia, an increase in the minimum wage, medical care for the elderly (Medicare), federal aid for education, and urban renewal in the form of Model Cities legislation. Conservation also was a concern. On Johnson's watch Congress passed the Water Quality Act, which established pollution standards for the nation's waterways. Finally, enactment of the Voting Rights Act of 1965 suspended the use of literacy tests and authorized the appointment of federal examiners to facilitate black voter registration.

Civil rights demonstrations continued into Johnson's second term. On March 7, 1965, some 200 Alabama state troopers attacked 525 civil rights demonstrators in Selma as they prepared to march to Montgomery to protest voting rights discrimination. After LBJ sent in federal troops to protect the demonstrators, the march began on March 21. Several months later, the president signed the Voting Rights Act, empowering the federal government to suspend all literacy, knowledge, or character tests for voting in areas where less than 50 percent of the voting-age population was registered. The key provision of the legislation was a trigger mechanism that would use low minority voter registration as a basis for appointing federal voting registrars. Despite this legislation, civil rights demonstrations that led to violent police reactions continued to break out across the nation throughout 1966.

Other domestic policy achievements during LBJ's second term included a 1965 law creating the Department of Housing and Urban Development, to be headed by Robert C. Weaver, the first black cabinet member; the 1966 G.I. Bill of Rights, extending education, housing, health, and job benefits to the nation's veterans (hundreds of thousands of Vietnam veterans benefited); and a 1966 bill creating the Department of Transportation. In August 1967 the president also made a noteworthy appointment to the Supreme Court—

Thurgood Marshall, the first African American ever to serve on the Court.

THE GREAT BURDEN: VIETNAM

Although Johnson had run as the peace candidate in 1964 and had hoped that his administration would be able to concentrate on his Great Society programs, he was dogged relentlessly by the country's ongoing involvement in Southeast Asia. Eventually, it dominated and then overwhelmed his presidency.

The communist government in North Vietnam and the communist guerrillas scattered throughout South Vietnam were attempting to unify the country under communist rule by defeating the South Vietnamese regime militarily. Since 1954, when Vietnam had been split into North and South Vietnam, the United States had supported the south with weapons, U.S. military advisers, and economic aid. In 1965 Johnson increased the U.S. commitment by sending American combat troops to South Vietnam, despite his pledge in the 1964 presidential campaign: "We are not going north, nor going south; Asian boys will fight Asia's war."

Over the next few years, Johnson continued to escalate U.S. involvement in the war, even though it was diverting attention and dollars away from his domestic programs. Many citizens supported the U.S. role, but by 1966 college campuses were erupting in protest against it. Johnson hoped that each increase in U.S. troop strength and expansion of bombing targets would produce a breakthrough on the battlefield that would lead to a negotiated settlement preserving the independence and security of South Vietnam. The communists, however, refused to give up their goal of reunification.

By early 1968 public opinion had swung decisively against the war and Johnson. The conflict was costing more than $2 billion a month, young men were burning their draft cards, and the antiwar protests were escalating. Although Johnson was long able to maintain the support of most Americans by repeatedly assuring them that the enemy was being steadily driven back, a huge offensive by the communists in January 1968 forced a major reevaluation of the war effort.

On the political front, Johnson recognized there was a good chance he might not be renominated for president by his party in 1968. Sen. Eugene J. McCarthy of Minnesota and Sen. Robert F. Kennedy of New York, the late president's brother, were running for the Democratic presidential nomination on antiwar platforms and were receiving substantial support. On March 31, 1968, Johnson delivered a television address in which he announced a partial halt to U.S. air attacks on North Vietnam to emphasize the U.S. desire for peace. He then stunned the nation by announcing that he would not seek or accept the Democratic nomination for president.

After leaving Washington in 1969, Johnson retired to his ranch near Johnson City, Texas, where he wrote a book about his presidential years, *The Vantage Point,* published in 1971. On January 22, 1973, while at his ranch, Johnson suffered a heart attack. He was pronounced dead at Brooke Army Medical Center in San Antonio.

See also *Civil Rights Acts (Modern); Civil Rights Movement; Great Society; Landslide Elections; Senate Leadership (Modern Period); Vietnam War.*

SABRA BISSETTE LEDENT, INDEPENDENT AUTHOR

BIBLIOGRAPHY

Bernstein, Irving. *Guns or Butter: The Presidency of Lyndon Johnson.* New York: Oxford University Press, 1996.

Dallek, Robert. *Flawed Giant: Lyndon B. Johnson, 1960–1973.* New York: Oxford University Press, 1998.

———. *Lone Star Rising: Lyndon Johnson and His Times, 1908–1960.* New York: Oxford University Press, 1991.

Firestone, Bernard J., and Robert C. Vogt. *Lyndon Baines Johnson and the Uses of Power.* Westport, Conn.: Greenwood Press, 1988.

Goodwin, Doris Kearns. *Lyndon Johnson and the American Dream.* New York: St. Martin's Press, 1991.

JUDICIARY ACTS

Because the lack of a national court system was one of the major failings of the Articles of Confederation, the Constitution provided for "one supreme Court" and "such inferior courts" as Congress should choose to establish. Various judiciary acts passed between 1789 and 1925 created the federal court system, the third branch of government, while regulating access to the courts and the jurisdiction of the courts. Legislation surrounding the judiciary has been complicated by debates over the proper role of the courts in American politics.

THE JUDICIARY ACT OF 1789

The Judiciary Act of 1789 was one of the first statutes passed by Congress after the Constitution was ratified. The act created the Supreme Court, as mandated by the Constitution, and a series of federal courts for the states. The first Supreme Court consisted of five associate justices and one chief justice. The members of Congress apparently saw no need to create a court with an odd number of justices to avoid tie votes on the bench. The law also created two levels of lower courts with a complex overlapping of both personnel and jurisdiction. The law provided that some suits, such as those involving citizens of different states, could be heard in either state or federal court, but that in many of these cases a defendant would have the option of removing the case from a state to a federal court.

Under the act every state had at least one district judge. Virginia and Massachusetts each received a second judge to sit in the distant parts of those states that later became the separate states of Kentucky and Maine. The district courts had jurisdiction for suits valued at less than $500 and all admiralty cases.

The act also created federal circuit courts to sit in every state. The circuit courts had jurisdiction over cases worth more than $500 and all federal criminal prosecutions, and they had appellate jurisdiction in civil suits worth more than $50 and admiralty cases worth more than $300. The makeup of the circuit courts was enormously complex. The act did not create separate judges to preside over the circuit courts. Instead, each circuit court was staffed by a district judge and two Supreme Court justices who "rode circuit." The act divided the nation into three circuits and assigned two Supreme Court justices to each circuit. The act provided that twice a year the Supreme Court justices would ride from state to state to sit with district court judges to hear cases on circuit.

In addition to its original jurisdiction, the Supreme Court could hear appeals from the lower federal courts, but only if the amount in controversy was more than $2,000. There was no appellate jurisdiction for criminal cases, except that a prosecution involving a constitutional issue might be taken to the Supreme Court.

Under this system a district judge could decide a case in admiralty, then the same judge would sit as a "circuit judge," alongside one or two Supreme Court justices, to review the case in the circuit. The case could then go to the Supreme Court, where the justices who heard the case on circuit would participate in reviewing the case again.

Section 25 of the 1789 act gave the Supreme Court the power to review decisions from the highest state courts and to issue final judgments in such cases, but only where a federal question or a federal law was at stake. In *Martin v. Hunter's Lessee* (1816) the Supreme Court forcefully upheld its authority to review certain state supreme court decisions.

THE JUDICIARY ACTS OF 1801 AND 1802

The Supreme Court justices bitterly complained about having to perform their circuit court duties. Given the difficulty of transportation at this time, it was indeed an onerous task. The Judiciary Act of 1801 eliminated the circuit duties by providing for the appointment of sixteen circuit judges, one for each state. It created two terms for the U.S. Supreme Court, one in June and the other in December. It removed Supreme Court justices from hearing circuit court cases that they might later have to review on the Supreme Court. And it gave the federal courts jurisdiction over all questions involving national law or the Constitution—what is called general federal jurisdiction. All of these provisions strength-

ened the judiciary while removing some of the more onerous and problematic aspects of the first judiciary act.

Unfortunately, these important accomplishments were overshadowed by the blatantly political and partisan aspects of the law. Passed after the election of 1800 by a lame-duck Congress and signed by John Adams, a lame-duck president, this admirable law became a victim of partisan politics. The Federalists in Congress, fearful of president-elect Thomas Jefferson, included in the law a provision to reduce the size of the Supreme Court to five justices by eliminating the next vacancy on the Court. This stipulation prevented Thomas Jefferson, who had defeated John Adams in the recent presidential election, from putting someone on the Court until at least two members left the Court. Furthermore, in his last days in office President Adams filled all sixteen circuit court positions with Federalist Party loyalists. Jefferson correctly saw Adams's actions as an attempt to stack the judiciary with Federalists.

In March 1802 Jefferson's supporters in Congress repealed the 1801 act and passed the Judiciary Act of 1802. Democratic-Republicans argued that, since Congress could create lower federal courts, it could also constitutionally abolish them. The 1802 legislation abolished the new circuit courts, raised the number of justices back to six, and created one Supreme Court term, to be held in February. The new Court calendar meant that the Supreme Court would never meet in the year 1802, because the June and December terms had been abolished, and the law, passed in March, came too late for the new February term. This calculated action prevented the Supreme Court from quickly ruling on the constitutionality of depriving the circuit judges of their lifetime positions. By the time the Court finally met in 1803, the elimination of the judgeships was a fait accompli. In *Stuart v. Laird* (1803) the Court upheld the abolition of the circuit courts.

The Judiciary Act of 1802 also increased the number of circuits from three to six and assigned only one Supreme Court justice to each circuit. This change reduced the travel of the justices by reducing the size of the circuits, but it also led to the potential for tie votes in circuit cases because only two jurists would hear a case.

THE JUDICIARY ACTS OF 1837, 1866, 1869, 1875, AND 1891

Subsequent judiciary acts changed the size of the Supreme Court and also changed the nature of the circuit courts and their jurisdiction. The number of Supreme Court justices fluctuated between six and ten before finally settling at nine. In 1807 Congress raised the number, originally six, to seven. Responding to demands from new western states for representation on the Court, the Judiciary Act of 1837 increased the number to nine, a figure raised to ten in 1863. The Judiciary Act of 1866 cut the number to seven, in part so that President Andrew Johnson would not be able to make appointments. The Judiciary Act of 1869 raised the number to nine, where it has stayed ever since.

The Judiciary Act of 1875 made a fundamental change in federal law by giving the courts general "federal question" jurisdiction, which allowed for the removal to federal court of any case that raised an issue of federal law or the U.S. Constitution and also met the monetary jurisdictional minimums. This law was particularly helpful to railroads and other large companies operating in interstate commerce, because it allowed them to challenge state regulations in federal courts as well as to litigate personal injury cases in those courts, which tended to be more sympathetic than the state courts to big business.

The Judiciary Act of 1891 was of even greater significance. This law created the modern system of intermediate appellate courts—the circuit courts of appeals—and eliminated forever the requirement that Supreme Court justices ride circuit. The act created nine federal circuits, which have since been expanded to eleven, plus a special one for the District of Columbia. In 1948 these courts were renamed simply courts of appeals. The new courts of appeals reduced the workload of the Supreme Court by about a third.

THE JUDICIARY ACT OF 1925

The Judiciary Act of 1925 was largely the handiwork of the justices themselves. The act eliminated most of the Supreme Court's mandatory jurisdiction, and it required that almost all cases coming to the Court first be heard by one of the courts of appeals or by a state supreme court. The 1925 act left the justices themselves in control of their docket. It left to the appeals courts the business of undoing trial court errors, and that meant that few cases would ever reach the Supreme Court. The 1925 act allowed the Supreme Court to evolve into more of a "constitutional court," a tribunal that decided cases of national import involving the Constitution, treaties, or the proper interpretation and implementation of significant federal law.

See also *Supreme Court*.

PAUL FINKELMAN, UNIVERSITY OF TULSA COLLEGE OF LAW

BIBLIOGRAPHY

Ellis, Richard E. *The Jeffersonian Crisis: Courts and Politics in the Young Republic.* New York: Oxford University Press, 1971.

Frankfurter, Felix, and James M. Landis. *The Business of the Supreme Court: A Study in the Federal Judicial System.* New York: Macmillan, 1927.

Provine, Doris Marie. *Case Selection in the United States Supreme Court.* Chicago: University of Illinois Press, 1980.

Surrency, Edwin. *History of the Federal Courts.* New York: Oceana, 1987.

KANSAS-NEBRASKA ACT

Intended as the basis for organizing the territories of Kansas and Nebraska, the Kansas-Nebraska Act (1854) led to warfare in the West over slavery and to the organization of the Republican Party.

Throughout the pre–Civil War years, the future of the West was a perennial issue in American national politics, constantly connected to slavery. The South wanted more territory into which the slave system might expand; the North wanted more land for free labor; and each side wanted to safeguard its power in national politics.

The Missouri Compromise of 1820, although it gave the South an additional slave state, also provided that the remaining area in the Louisiana Purchase north of Missouri's southern boundary would be closed to the expansion of slavery. The compromise held until 1854, when Sen. Stephen A. Douglas, Democrat of Illinois, sponsored a bill to supply territorial government for the area that, according to the Missouri Compromise, was closed to slavery. He was seeking to create conditions that would facilitate the construction of a railroad from Chicago to San Francisco. Other considerations no doubt included his presidential ambitions, his indifference to slavery, and his attraction to "popular sovereignty," according to which the question of slavery in each territory would be determined by the voters there.

In 1854 southerners controlled the Democratic Party; Democrats controlled the national government; and antislavery northerners viewed the future with anxiety. To obtain sufficient congressional support from southerners, Douglas in his bill divided the area in two and provided that each of the proposed territories would be open or closed to slavery depending on "popular sovereignty." Almost surely the northern territory, Nebraska, would remain free, but the southern territory, Kansas, adjacent to the slave state of Missouri, could go either way.

The bill secured the support of southerners of both parties and of enough northern Democrats to gain passage. Signed into law on May 30, 1854, by Democratic president Franklin Pierce, it proved a prescription for disaster. Each side, North and South, was intent on winning in Kansas. Settlers from both sides moved to the territory; weapons flowed in as well; and an economic, political, and military struggle ensued. By 1856 each side had killed opponents, destroyed property, and organized a competing territorial government. In effect, the Civil War broke out in what became known as "Bleeding Kansas."

The immediate political consequence of the Kansas-Nebraska Act was to provoke northerners' anger and fear at what they saw as an increasingly aggressive slave power controlling national politics. They had long viewed as inviolable the Missouri Compromise's ban on slavery in the area, and yet the Kansas-Nebraska Act expressly repealed that ban, declaring it "inoperative and void." In 1854 northerners who were opposed to the act organized a new political party, the Republican Party, often called at first the "Anti-Nebraska Party." It won most northern congressional seats in the 1856 elections; ran a candidate in the presidential election that year; and won the presidency with Abraham Lincoln in 1860. Within weeks of Lincoln's victory, South Carolina seceded. Other slave states soon followed, and the Civil War began. Meantime, in January 1861, Kansas entered the Union as a free state.

See also *Missouri Compromise; Pierce, Franklin; Republican Party; Sectionalism; Slavery; Territorial Expansion.*

PETER WALLENSTEIN, VIRGINIA POLYTECHNIC INSTITUTE
AND STATE UNIVERSITY

BIBLIOGRAPHY

Fehrenbacher, Don E. *The Dred Scott Case: Its Significance in American Law and Politics.* New York: Oxford University Press, 1978.

Morrison, Michael A. *Slavery and the American West: The Eclipse of Manifest Destiny and the Coming of the Civil War.* Chapel Hill: University of North Carolina Press, 1997.

SenGupta, Gunja. *For God and Mammon: Evangelicals and Entrepreneurs, Masters and Slaves in Territorial Kansas, 1854–1860.* Athens: University of Georgia Press, 1996.

Potter, David M. *The Impending Crisis, 1848–1861.* Completed and edited by Don E. Fehrenbacher. New York: Harper and Row, 1976.

KENNEDY, JOHN F.

John Fitzgerald Kennedy, the thirty-fifth president of the United States (1961–1963), was the youngest elected president in American history and one of the most popular presidents of the twentieth century. Kennedy was born on May 29, 1917, in Brookline, Massachusetts, into a wealthy Irish Catholic family. His father, Joseph P. Kennedy, was a millionaire who had built his fortune in the stock market, among other things, and served in the administration of Franklin D. Roosevelt as chairman of the Securities and Exchange Commission and ambassador to Great Britain. His maternal grandfather, John F. "Honey Fitz" Fitzgerald, was a major political figure in Boston, where he served as mayor. From this background arose the so-called Kennedy dynasty. John's brother Robert F. Kennedy served as his attorney general, and another brother, Edward M. Kennedy, served in the U.S. Senate for many years. Today, many of the younger Kennedys are occupying prominent positions in public service.

After attending one of the country's most elite preparatory schools, Choate, and, briefly, the London School of Economics and Princeton University, John entered Harvard University in 1936, where he studied economics and political science. He graduated with honors in 1940. His senior thesis, *Why England Slept*—later published in book form—examined British appeasement of fascism before World War II.

MILITARY SERVICE AND EARLY POLITICAL CAREER

In October 1941 Kennedy received a commission as an ensign in the U.S. Navy. After the United States declared war on Japan in December, he shipped off to fight in the Pacific. On August 2, 1943, the PT boat he commanded was rammed and sunk by a Japanese destroyer. The young commander helped rescue the eleven crew members who survived the attack. After the ordeal Kennedy was sent back to the United States, where he was hospitalized for malaria. In 1944 he underwent back surgery. Back problems, sometimes serious, and Addison's disease would afflict him for the rest of his life.

After a brief stint as a reporter for the International News Service in 1945, JFK decided to run for Congress from his Massachusetts district. He was elected in 1946 and served three terms before being elected to the Senate in 1952. In 1954 and 1955 he underwent two more operations for his chronic back condition, but he put his convalescence to good use by writing *Profiles in Courage,* a book about senators who had demonstrated courage during their careers. The bestseller earned Kennedy the 1957 Pulitzer Prize for biography.

JFK's older brother, Joseph Jr., had been primed by his family to seek the presidency, but when he was killed in World War II the family fell in behind John, using all of its financial resources and political connections to push him toward the White House. In 1956 Kennedy sought the Democratic vice-presidential nomination on the ticket with former Illinois governor Adlai Stevenson, but he lost the nomination to Sen. Estes Kefauver of Tennessee. Yet Kennedy's political reputation continued to grow. In 1957 he was assigned to the Senate Foreign Relations Committee, where he gained foreign policy experience, and in 1958 he won reelection to the Senate by a record margin in Massachusetts.

While in the Senate, Kennedy successfully withstood the pressure from Democratic liberals to denounce McCarthyism. This political attitude, named after Sen. Joseph McCarthy of Wisconsin, was manifested through the use of personal attacks and publicized allegations, largely unsubstantiated, of subversive communist activity. Through congressional hearings, McCarthy achieved almost nationwide hysteria about the threat of communist expansion. The pressure on Kennedy to relent was severe, even extending to former first lady Eleanor Roosevelt.

By 1960 Kennedy was leading the pack for the Democratic presidential nomination. Not far behind were Senate Majority Leader Lyndon Johnson of Texas, Sen. Stuart Symington of Missouri, Sen. Hubert H. Humphrey of Minnesota, and Stevenson. At the July 1960 Democratic National Convention in Los Angeles, Kennedy captured the nomination on the first ballot. Johnson, who had finished second, agreed to be his running mate. Johnson would prove invaluable in garnering southern votes.

Kennedy's opponent in the general election was Vice President Richard Nixon. Over the course of the campaign, Kennedy and Nixon appeared in four televised debates, the first in presidential election history. On election day Kennedy won the contest, but narrowly. Out of almost 69 million votes cast, Kennedy received only 120,000 more than Nixon. Kennedy won in the electoral college 303–219.

THE KENNEDY ADMINISTRATION

With his inauguration, JFK, as the first president born in the twentieth century, ushered in a new era of vitality, style, and exploration. His warmth and humor—refreshing after the stodgier Eisenhower years—were displayed prominently at his press conferences, the first ever held live on television by a president. His young, elegant wife, Jacqueline, had a remarkable influence on American taste. A painter, art collector, and linguist, she undertook a restoration of the White House and featured some of the world's most prominent fig-

President John F. Kennedy with Soviet premier Nikita Khrushchev in Vienna   *Library of Congress*

ures in the arts and culture at White House events. She even served as a fashion trendsetter. Women everywhere emulated her distinctive dress and hairstyle.

Soon after entering office, the young president had his mettle tested in a longtime trouble spot, Cuba. During the Eisenhower presidency the Central Intelligence Agency had devised a plan to arm, train, and land fourteen hundred Cuban exiles in Cuba in an attempt to overthrow the communist regime of Fidel Castro. Upon taking office, Kennedy endorsed the plan. Carried out on April 17, 1961, the operation, later known as the Bay of Pigs invasion, was a complete failure; twelve hundred of the Cuban exiles were captured. The red-faced president accepted full responsibility for the fiasco.

In June 1961 JFK met in Vienna with Soviet premier Nikita Khrushchev. If the president had hoped for a thaw in the cold war, he was quickly disappointed. Khrushchev threatened to negotiate a peace treaty with East Germany and cut off Western access to West Berlin. In the tense months that followed, the United States built up its military strength; the East Germans built the Berlin Wall.

Despite the Bay of Pigs incident, Cuba was the site of the president's most memorable foreign policy success. In October 1962 he learned, much to his alarm, that the Soviets were building offensive missile bases on Cuban soil—a development almost certain to threaten U.S. national security and lead to Soviet attempts to blackmail the United States into con-cessions in other parts of the world.

Demanding that the bases be dismantled, the president proceeded to organize a naval "quarantine" of the island. The Soviets denounced the U.S. action, and Khrushchev warned that the Soviet Union would not cave in to the blockade. The confrontation brought the United States and Soviet Union to the brink of nuclear war. In the end, however, the Soviets backed down and agreed to remove the missiles in exchange for a promise that the United States would not invade Cuba.

On June 28, 1963, JFK delivered an emotional, but controversial, speech in the divided city of Berlin. With the words "Ich bin ein Berliner," Kennedy reaffirmed the cold war alliance between the United States and West Germany. With that, the cold war became even colder.

The Soviet Union, however, was only one of the issues occupying the busy Kennedy White House. Acting on his eloquent inauguration address in which he posed the challenge to Americans, "Ask not what your country can do for you—ask what you can do for your country," Kennedy put in motion many new initiatives both abroad and at home. Abroad, he increased U.S. involvement in the developing world by establishing in 1961 the Peace Corps, an agency that sent skilled volunteers to underdeveloped countries overseas. He also initiated the Alliance for Progress, an aid program aimed at developing the resources of Latin America.

Domestically, Kennedy tackled the cause of civil rights by advocating school desegregation, establishing a program to encourage registration of African American voters, issuing rules against discrimination in public housing built with federal funds, and appointing an unprecedented number of African Americans to public office. Several times Kennedy dispatched federal troops to the South to maintain order and enforce the law during civil rights demonstrations. For example, federal troops and officials oversaw the integration of the University of Mississippi in 1962 and the University of Alabama in 1963. Also in 1963 the president proposed sweeping civil rights legislation, but events that year prevented it from coming to a vote.

On the economic front, although the president's advisers convinced him that a tax cut would stimulate the economy and bring growth without large budget deficits or inflation, Congress, despite the president's best efforts, remained unconvinced. After Kennedy's death, President Lyndon Johnson was able to secure passage of the Kennedy tax cut and civil rights legislation.

ASSASSINATION

In late November 1963 Kennedy scheduled a trip to Texas, one of several he took that year to build political support for his reelection bid in 1964. While riding through Dallas in an open car on November 22, Kennedy was shot in the head and in the neck. He never regained consciousness, and a shocked nation soon learned of his death. Vice President Johnson was sworn in as president the same day.

The alleged assassin, Lee Harvey Oswald, a former marine who had once renounced his U.S. citizenship and lived in the Soviet Union, was quickly arrested. Three days after the shooting, Oswald was murdered in front of millions of television viewers by Jack Ruby, owner of a Dallas nightclub. The seven-member Warren Commission appointed by President Johnson to investigate the assassination ruled that Oswald had acted alone. Many members of the American public, however, believed Oswald may have been part of a conspiracy.

Upon his death, Kennedy became a national idol. Although his presidency was characterized by vigor and panache, Kennedy achieved only moderate successes in his dealings with Congress. In the foreign policy arena, where he spent so much time, he fared better in the cold war sparring but suffered a major stumble with the Bay of Pigs fiasco. Perhaps the adulation that has persisted since his untimely death is best summed up by his own words, uttered on July 11, 1962, at Yale University: "For the greatest enemy of the truth is very often not the lie dcliberate, contrived and dishonest—but the myth—persistent, persuasive and unrealistic."

See also *Cold War; Johnson, Lyndon B.*

SABRA BISSETTE LEDENT, INDEPENDENT AUTHOR

BIBLIOGRAPHY

Beschloss, Michael R. *The Crisis Years: Kennedy and Khrushchev, 1960–1963.* New York: Burlingame, 1991.
Reeves, Richard. *President Kennedy: Profile of Power.* New York: Simon and Schuster, 1993.
Salinger, Pierre. *With Kennedy.* Garden City, N.Y.: Doubleday, 1966.
Schlesinger, Arthur M., Jr. *A Thousand Days: John F. Kennedy in the White House.* Boston: Houghton Mifflin, 1965.
Sorensen, Theodore C. *Kennedy.* New York: Harper and Row, 1965.

KNOW NOTHING (AMERICAN) PARTY

The Know Nothing Party of the 1850s was the most formidable nativist political organization in American history; for two years in mid-decade it was the nation's second-largest party. Nativism involved the fear of aliens and opposition to an internal minority believed to be un-American. Members of the American Party were called Know Nothings because when asked about their organization they were instructed to say, "I know nothing." For them, fear and hatred of Catholics, particularly "papist conspirators," created this need for secrecy.

The Know Nothings emerged from one of the many nativist secret societies proliferating in the pre–Civil War period. The migration of millions of Catholics from Ireland and Germany stimulated an intense anti-alien activism in the United States. Key leaders of the Order of the Star Spangled Banner saw their group as a useful instrument for shaping a new political party in 1853. Like nativists of earlier decades, leaders of the Know Nothing Party accused Catholics of undermining the public school system and of being responsible for a host of social problems accompanying the influx of so many poverty-stricken newcomers in the great port cities.

The party emerged at a critical moment in American political history. The slavery controversy was ripping apart the Whig Party, and the Democratic Party was suffering fissures in different states and sections. Out of this turmoil came a flood of members to the new nativist movement. For many people, a party organized around nativist themes—one that advanced "American" interests and stood for stability and union—offered a way out of the conflict between northerner and southerner, abolitionist and slaveholder. A common crusade against foreigners, they thought, could cement broken institutions and warring people.

The political divisions of the day meant that Know Nothing membership varied from section to section. In New York, where the party was born and had its strongest support, the leadership was composed of conservative Whig refugees, men who opposed free soil and antislavery elements in their former party. These included James Barker and Daniel Ullmann, the party candidate in the New York gubernatorial race in 1855. In New England the antislavery wing of the former Whig Party, "Conscience Whigs," played the key role. Leaders in Massachusetts included Henry Wilson, who was elected a U.S. senator in 1855, and Henry J. Gardner, elected state governor in the Know Nothing landslide that year. Also swelling the party rolls in New England were abolitionists from the other major party, Democrats who opposed the Kansas-Nebraska Act.

In the West, where Know Nothings struggled to find support, nativists sought fusion with free-soil activists in Indiana and Illinois, but in Wisconsin two factions (the Sams and the Jonathans) shared antialien attitudes yet split over slavery.

In the South, which contained a small immigrant population, nativism appealed to those who viewed "aliens" in the Northeast and West as threatening to the southern way of life because it was assumed that newcomers would be opposed to slavery. The nativist party in the South represented an escape from the divisive struggle that threatened civil strife, but it had only limited impact.

Despite its political success in 1854 and 1855, the national Know Nothing Party could not survive the antislavery controversy. At the party gathering in Philadelphia in June 1855, a proslavery resolution led to wild debate and a massive defection led by Massachusetts nativists but including representatives from many states. Further divisions in the party, including personal rivalries between New York leaders Barker and Ullmann, created more problems. In 1856 the party nominated former president Millard Fillmore as presidential candidate. But Fillmore—who had joined a Know Nothing lodge as a political maneuver and had never been a real nativist—failed at the polls, trailing in a three-way race with only 22 percent of the popular vote and taking only Maryland's eight electoral college votes. The Know Nothings did not recover, losing members rapidly in subsequent months. In 1857 the party held its last national council.

See also *Fillmore, Millard; Immigration and Naturalization; Nativism.*

DAVID H. BENNETT, SYRACUSE UNIVERSITY

BIBLIOGRAPHY

Anbinder, Tyler G. *Nativism and Slavery: The Know Nothings and the Politics of the 1850s.* New York: Oxford University Press, 1994.

Bennett, David H. *The Party of Fear: The American Far Right from Nativism to the Militia Movement.* 2d ed. New York: Vintage Books, 1995.

Billington, Ray Allen. *The Protestant Crusade, 1800–1860.* 2d ed. New York: Atheneum, 1963.

KOREAGATE

Koreagate is a shorthand word for a sweeping corruption investigation begun by the Justice Department in 1975, made public by the *Washington Post* in 1976, and investigated by both the House and Senate beginning in 1977. The word is a variant of "Watergate" (the press began to add "gate" to the names of government scandals after the Watergate scandal of 1972–1974). The congressional investigation, formally known as the Investigation of Korean-American Relations, involved about 115 members of Congress who allegedly took illegal gifts from agents of South Korea, led by Tongsun Park, who fled the United States in 1976 but returned two years later to testify in congressional hearings.

The investigations revealed a broad pattern of carefully planned influence peddling, begun as early as 1970, that focused on members of Congress but that also included bribes and gifts to other U.S. government officials as well as journalists and businesspeople. The Republic of Korea supposedly spent upwards of a million dollars a year on the effort, sometimes handing members of Congress and other politicians, or their spouses, envelopes containing cash.

The president of South Korea, Park Chung Hee, received blame for conceiving and promoting the scheme, which was designed to bolster U.S. interests in South Korea, to offset U.S. concern about South Korean human rights violations, and to lobby for retention of U.S. troops to protect the 38th parallel, the border between North and South Korea. Jimmy Carter, campaigning for president in 1976, issued statements condemning human rights violations in South Korea and called for a phased withdrawal of U.S. troops.

During its investigation, the House Committee on Standards of Official Conduct (the House Ethics Committee) kept secret the names of House members allegedly involved in the scandal. Tongsun Park, in his public testimony, named three House members who supposedly had received the largest amounts of cash, totaling hundreds of thousands of dollars: Otto E. Passman, D-La.; Richard Hanna, D-Calif.; and Cornelius Gallagher, D-N.J. Another twenty-five sitting and former House members may have received cash gifts ranging from a few hundred to a few thousand dollars. The Senate Ethics Committee concluded its investigation without recommending any disciplinary action for the senators allegedly involved in the scandal. The House later dropped all charges against the House members named in the investigation.

The House Subcommittee on International Organizations of the Committee on International Relations also investigated the matter, concluding that the Korean Central Intelligence Agency had "annual written plans or operations in the United States" that "envisaged the recruitment of Americans—including Government officials, Members of Congress, journalists, scholars, religious leaders, businessmen, and leaders of citizen's organizations—for the purpose of swaying American public opinion and official policy in favor of the Park government." The subcommittee report stated that "the Koreans have done some bad things; of that there is no doubt. They have misunderstood our mores . . . they have misunderstood our institutions." The report concluded, however, that the government of the Republic of Korea was attempting not to overthrow the U.S. government, but only to influence it, using crude methods, to be sure.

See also *Scandals and Corruption.*

RAYMOND W. SMOCK, INDEPENDENT HISTORIAN

BIBLIOGRAPHY

House of Representatives [Committee Print], Subcommittee on International Organizations of the Committee on International Relations. "Investigation of Korean American Relations," 95th Congress, 2d session, Oct. 31, 1978.

KOREAN WAR

The Korean War (1950–1953) had its origins in the closing days of World War II as Japan was defeated and its colony of Korea became a center of early cold war conflict. Soviet forces moved into the northern half of the Korean Peninsula, and U.S. troops occupied the South—bisecting the country at the 38th parallel. Although the divide was to be temporary, it became permanent in 1948 as the United States and the Union of Soviet Socialist Republics (USSR) cultivated friendly governments in their territories: the Western-style Republic of Korea in the South and the communist Democratic People's Republic of Korea in the North. A full-scale war broke out on June 25, 1950, when Soviet-equipped North Korean forces drove into the South across the 38th parallel. The United States sent troops under the auspices of the United Nations (UN) to defend the Republic of Korea. In October 1950, Chinese communist troops joined the North Koreans on the battlefield. The war ended with a cease-fire on July 27, 1953, and the peninsula was left divided near the 38th parallel. The Korean War made a lasting impact in Asia and left bitter feelings in South Korea for Russia and in North Korea for the United States.

THE DIVISION OF KOREA
AFTER WORLD WAR II

In the closing days of World War II, the Japanese colony of Korea became a point of conflict between the war allies, the United States and the USSR. When the fifty-nation alliance led by the United States, the Soviet Union, and Great Britain splintered, the United States and the USSR emerged as the leading powers in the world, although they had very different postwar visions. Joseph Stalin, the general secretary of the Communist Party of the Soviet Union and the USSR's dictatorial leader, wanted friendly governments in Europe and in East Asia in order to expand the communist world and protect the USSR from future foreign aggression. President

Harry S. Truman and Secretary of State Dean Acheson sought to expand U.S. power in Europe and East Asia by containing communism, opening markets, attracting allies, and improving strategic military capabilities. Ideological conflict between the two emerging superpowers led to a cold war (1945–1989) in which the countries faced off against each other but never fought directly. Korea was one of the earliest cold-war battlegrounds.

When Soviet forces entered the war against Japan in the closing days of World War II, they occupied northern Korea in the first week of August 1945. At the same time, the United States dropped two atomic bombs on Japan—one at Hiroshima (August 6) and one at Nagasaki (August 9)—that ended World War II in the Pacific. On August 10 the United States sent troops into southern Korea to keep the USSR from gaining control of the entire peninsula. Although Korea was ostensibly divided at the 38th parallel to aid in the acceptance of surrendering Japanese troops, this temporary division was soon ensconced on the peninsula as the United States and the USSR each fostered friendly governments in their territories.

The Soviet Union's occupying force supported Kim Il Sung, a young leftist who had fought with the Chinese communists against the Japanese in Manchuria during the 1930s. Kim gained an early political following in the North when he began redistributing land to the poor in early 1946. In fact, the new communist government, the Democratic People's Republic of Korea, was so successful that the USSR was able to pull its troops out of Korea at the end of 1948.

In the South, U.S. forces opposed land seizures, redistribution of wealth, and other radical proposals and backed the leadership of Syngman Rhee, an anticommunist Korean leader who had lived in the United States for many years. Rhee's conservative position was not as popular in the South as Kim's radical position was in the North; and the new southern government, the Republic of Korea, faced guerrilla movements to topple it. U.S. troops were not withdrawn until June 1949.

NORTHERN INVASION AND REPULSION

By the summer of 1949 the North Korean and South Korean armies anxiously faced each other across the 38th parallel. Border fighting had already begun and would continue throughout the year. War did not break out until the morning of June 25, 1950, however, when the northern Korean People's Army (KPA) crossed the 38th parallel and engaged the Republic of Korea Army (ROKA). The Soviet Union had armed the KPA and approved a war plan for the unification of Korea that called for the capture of Seoul in three days and of the entire South in seven. The first part of this plan was fulfilled when Seoul was captured three days later by a KPA force of 37,000 troops.

The United States had originally not wanted to become involved in the fighting. As the KPA pushed deep into the South, however, President Truman and his staff argued that the Truman Doctrine, which called for the containment of communism, should be applied to Korea. China, the most populous nation in the world, had been taken over by a communist government in 1949; also in 1949, the USSR had successfully detonated an atomic device, ending the U.S. monopoly on nuclear weapons. U.S. strategic advisers believed further communist expansion and development must be halted and that a free South Korea must be maintained.

Although the United States never made a formal declaration of war, President Truman and Secretary of State Acheson committed troops to the Korean conflict, which was overseen by the UN. Representatives of the Soviet Union had walked out of the Security Council in January 1950 over the issue of which Chinese government would take the Security Council's China seat; their absence enabled the remaining Security Council members to commit UN troops in Korea. U.S. soldiers entered the war on June 30, 1950, and Gen. Douglas MacArthur was placed in charge of all UN forces in July. The first vital fighting occurred in August and September 1950 on the Pusan front, where 140,000 U.S., South Korean, and British troops began to repel the KPA. Then, in mid-September, MacArthur led 80,000 marines at their landing at Inch'on, from which they fought their way into Seoul. After one month of fierce fighting, the capital of the South was retaken; and by early October 1950 the KPA had been pushed out of the South.

INVASION OF THE NORTH AND STALEMATE

The UN war against North Korea did not end with the repulsion of the KPA from the South. Instead, with President Truman's backing, MacArthur sent troops across the 38th parallel in early October 1950. The objective was to roll back communism in North Korea and reunify the country under democratic leadership friendly to the West.

Although many U.S. intelligence officials believed China would not become involved in the war, the Chinese joined the war in defense of the North (October 16, 1950) as southern forces pushed toward Pyongyang, the North Korean capital. China signaled that it could not accept UN forces, dominated by the United States, north of the 38th parallel. The heaviest fighting between the two sides occurred between November 1950 and March 1951. When forces from the North recaptured Seoul in early 1951, U.S. leaders—including Truman, Acheson, and MacArthur—considered using atomic bombs to defeat both China and North Korea. But after Seoul was retaken in early 1951, cooler heads prevailed. In fact, when MacArthur flouted the president's offer of negotiations with the North and instead demanded that China make peace or be attacked, Truman asked for MacArthur's resignation and then removed him on April 11, 1951.

By the summer of 1951 the war had reached a stalemate roughly along the 38th parallel. Fighting continued while peace negotiations repeatedly began and stalled as the UN and South Korea told the North and its allies that their troops who were held as prisoners of war did not want to return to the North. The ideological and military conflict continued in Korea until a peace was reached in 1953.

U.S. POLITICS AND POLICY

Although bipartisan anticommunism drove the U.S. war effort in Korea, key Republicans used the concept of the communist threat to build their careers. For example, in 1950 when the war in Korea began, Republican senator Joseph McCarthy of Wisconsin declared that communism was not simply a foreign threat but that communist agents had infiltrated the U.S. State Department. The hysteria that followed led to the passage, in 1950, of the McCarran Internal Security Act over President Truman's veto. This legislation called for the registration of all communist organizations in the United States and barred aliens who had belonged to totalitarian parties from immigrating to the United States. These Republican anticommunist moves were supported by Richard Nixon, who used the anticommunism issue to catapult himself to the vice presidency in 1952 under the new Republican president, Dwight Eisenhower. President Truman had earlier announced that he would not be a candidate for reelection in 1952.

During the Korean War the United States carried out the military buildup foreseen by the members of the National Security Council who supported NSC 68 (April 14, 1950), a long memorandum that called for a dramatic increase in the size and strength of U.S. military forces—both nuclear and strategic. Defense spending rose from $17 billion in 1950 to more than $50 billion in 1953 as U.S. political and military leaders sought to strengthen the nation's ability to go beyond containment and roll back communism.

THE ARMISTICE AND THE WAR'S LEGACY

The fighting ended not with a U.S. or a UN victory but with a stalemate. A cease-fire with terms that essentially reestablished the prewar status quo was signed by the UN, North Korea, and China—South Korea did not sign—on July 27, 1953. Korean casualties have been estimated at 4 million, China lost up to 1 million, and the United States suffered 36,934 dead and 103,284 wounded.

Relations between Gen. Douglas MacArthur and President Harry S. Truman strained to the breaking point during the course of the Korean War, leading Truman to fire MacArthur. *Library of Congress*

The Korean War was the first time the cold war went hot, but it would not be the last. Through the lens of the Vietnam conflict, some U.S. leaders saw Korea as a lost chance to push back communism. After U.S. failure in Vietnam and the end of the cold war, many historians argued that the Korean conflict was a local civil war that the United States should have avoided. Other scholars have claimed that U.S. containment in places like Korea won the cold war because Soviet militarism was halted.

JEFFREY LITTLEJOHN, UNIVERSITY OF ARKANSAS

BIBLIOGRAPHY

Cumings, Bruce. *The Origins of the Korean War.* 2 vols. Princeton: Princeton University Press, 1981–1990.

Foot, Rosemary. *The Wrong War.* Ithaca: Cornell University Press, 1985.

Knox, Donald. *The Korean War: Pusan to Chosin: An Oral History.* San Diego: Harcourt Brace, 1985.

Spanier, John W. *The Truman-MacArthur Controversy of the Korean War.* Cambridge, Mass.: Belknap Press, 1959.

Stueck, William. *The Korean War: An International History.* Princeton: Princeton University Press, 1995.

West, Philip. "Confronting the West." *Journal of American-East Asia Relations* 2 (1993): 5–28.

LABOR POLITICS AND POLICIES

Since the founding of the federal republic in 1789, working people have participated in politics and have been affected by public policies. In the nineteenth century, however, the U.S. Constitution left the national government without a role in labor affairs. Federal officials could make labor policy only in areas that touched directly on interstate and foreign commerce or for employees of the national government. All other labor matters belonged to state and local authorities.

The economy also confined most labor matters to the state and local levels. Few large interstate enterprises existed; most businesses produced for local or regional markets. Such enterprises, moreover, were chartered or licensed by state or local authorities.

Workers, most of whom had the right to vote, participated actively in the politics of constitutional ratification and in the battles between Federalists and Jeffersonians. During the era of Jacksonian Democracy, in the late 1820s and 1830s, workers in New England and the mid-Atlantic states created worker parties to achieve their goals. Almost all of these parties sought to promote free public education; relieve workers from imprisonment for debt and from compulsory militia service; obtain mechanics' lien laws that gave workers first claim on the assets of bankrupted employers; and create laws to regulate unscrupulous businesspeople and bankers. The leaders of the Whig and Democratic Parties endorsed many of the workers' proposed public policies. By the late 1830s most northern states had enacted the laws sought by labor. Their achievement and an ensuing deep economic depression between 1837 and 1843 ended independent labor politics temporarily. Workers, however, did not withdraw from the political arena. Instead, throughout the 1840s and 1850s, they pressured local and state governments to pass laws regulating the hours of labor and requiring the national government to provide public lands to workers. Several states limited the working day for factory operatives to ten hours, as did the federal government for its employees, but such laws allowed workers individually to contract for a longer day, in effect rendering them nugatory. During the Civil War the national government enacted a homestead law that allowed settlers to obtain land ownership without payment.

Far more important in the lives of most working people was the impact of the law. Judges regulated almost every aspect of work relations. Under contract law, they determined the obligations employees owed their masters, the responsibilities employers had to their servants, and under what circumstances workers might quit. Judges also limited collective action by workers. Between 1800 and the 1830s, judges in Pennsylvania, New York, and Massachusetts found unions to be common law criminal conspiracies in restraint of trade. Even after Chief Justice Lemuel Shaw of Massachusetts in an 1842 case *(Commonwealth v. Hunt)* declared trade unions to be legal and a strike for the closed shop just, his decision reserved to the judiciary the right to determine the legality of collective action by workers.

THE ERA OF THE "LABOR PROBLEM," 1870–1945

From the end of the Civil War and Reconstruction to the end of World War II, no domestic issue appeared more insoluble than "the labor problem." As a revolution in transportation and communications nationalized the economy, the number of workers dependent on wage labor multiplied geometrically. Wage earners also found themselves recurrently subject to the business cycle. Almost every twenty years, between 1873 and the 1930s, depressions scarred the economy, leaving millions of workers without jobs and wages. A new word entered the vocabulary, "unemployment." Instability of employment, economic dependence in place of independence, and a general sense of material deprivation led working people to organize, to strike, and to act politically.

The depression of 1873–1877 established the "labor problem" as a national issue. In the depression years, workers engaged in strikes, some violent, and they also allied with farmers and other nonworkers to form Greenback Labor political parties. In 1876 workers and their allies created a national Greenback-Labor Party. Unsuccessful nationally, labor parties did succeed in capturing power at the county and municipal levels. Simultaneously, unemployed workers demanded from public officials jobs on public works or food and lodging for the homeless and starving, demands that culminated in several mass protests. In 1877 a nationwide strike of railroad workers shocked the country. It caused enormous property damage in Pittsburgh; street fighting, deaths, and injuries in Baltimore; and nearly an insurrection in St. Louis. It also led several governors to dispatch their state militias to suppress the strikers. When state militias failed to end the violence, President Rutherford B. Hayes sent federal troops to restore the peace.

In the aftermath of the upheaval of the 1870s, the labor question remained at the center of political debate. Prevailing constitutional understandings still required that the separate states deal with the demands of workers for better working conditions. Massachusetts became the first state to establish a bureau of labor statistics charged with compiling information about employment, wages, and working conditions, data that would enable legislators to deal more effectively with the "labor problem." Other states followed the example of Massachusetts. By the end of the nineteenth century, many northern and western states regulated the hours of male workers in dangerous occupations; sought to protect female workers from excessive hours; limited the occupations in which children might be gainfully employed and curtailed their hours of work; and appointed factory inspectors in an effort to ensure safer working conditions. Most of those states also created bureaus of mediation and arbitration to help resolve disputes between labor and management.

Even the federal government acted where the constitution granted it clear authority. In 1885 Congress authorized the creation of a federal bureau of labor statistics. Congress, moreover, used its authority to regulate immigration to limit the ability of employers to recruit contract labor from abroad. Under its power to regulate interstate commerce, the federal government repeatedly intervened in labor disputes on the nation's railroads. Sometimes, federal authorities dispatched marshals and troops to end strikes, as happened most spectacularly during the Pullman boycott and strike of 1894. At other times, Congress used its investigating authority to probe conflicts between railroad managements and unions. Finally, in 1898 Congress passed the Erdman Act, to restore industrial peace on the nation's railroads. The act recognized the right of railroad workers to form independent unions; it banned attempts by management to require employees to sign individual antiunion contracts; and it established federal mediation machinery to resolve labor disputes on the railroads. These more tolerant approaches to trade unionism were partly an effort to turn workers away from radical alternatives. Whenever workers seemed to move in more militant directions, such as in the anarchist-influenced Haymarket incident of 1886, the Pullman strike and boycott of 1894, and the anarcho-syndicalism of the Industrial Workers of the World (IWW) in the early twentieth century, policy makers turned to repression and legal punishment.

This provided even more reason for less radical labor organizations and leaders to continue to play an active political role. The dominant organization of the 1880s, the Knights of Labor, promoted political education and participated in numerous labor and farmer-labor political campaigns. The successor to the Knights, the American Federation of Labor, proved equally committed to political action, lobbying at the state and national levels for protective labor legislation. During the Populist insurgency of the 1890s, coal miners, south-

Following the Pullman railroad strike, U.S. cavalry escorts a train laden with meat as it leaves the Chicago stockyards on July 10, 1894. Reproduced from *Harper's Weekly* of July 28, 1894. *Library of Congress*

ern wage workers, and working people in the far West participated in third-party politics.

Yet the judiciary remained a barrier against public policies that protected working people. State and federal courts found legislation that regulated hours and working conditions to violate constitutional protections of private property and the right to contract freely. Although jurists tolerated limited regulation of the labor of women and children or of men employed in dangerous occupations, they declared as unconstitutional those laws that regulated the working conditions of adult men or the wages of women. Judges continued to condemn collective action. They found most forms of trade union activity to violate the law, and they criticized sympathetic strikes, boycotts, and closed shops. Federal judges found many forms of trade-union action to violate the Sherman Antitrust Act. Between the 1890s and the 1920s, state and federal judges issued thousands of injunctions to forestall strikes and other forms of worker protest, making anti-injunction legislation organized labor's dearest objective.

Indeed, the AFL and its affiliated unions grew far more active politically. Politicians responded to labor's protests, Democrats usually more readily than Republicans. President Theodore Roosevelt allayed labor's concerns in two ways. First, in 1902, during a strike by anthracite coal miners, he compelled mine owners to bargain with the union that represented their workers. Second, he supported legislation to limit the judiciary's power to issue injunctions during labor disputes, a reform that the Republican majority refused to buy. As a consequence, the AFL firmed its alliance with the Democratic Party, a coalition that blossomed after the election of Woodrow Wilson in 1912. Wilson appointed a Democratic congressman and former union official, William B. Wilson, as the first secretary of labor; met regularly with the labor leader Samuel Gompers; and signed legislation that partly reformed injunction law, protected merchant seamen against exploitation, and granted operating railroad workers an eight-hour day. During World War I the Wilson administration provided more benefits to labor. Union officials served on nearly all of the war-production and labor committees, and wartime administrators favored the eight-hour day for all workers, equal wages for women, safer working conditions, the right of workers to form independent trade unions, and good-faith collective bargaining between management and labor. Organized labor came out of the war stronger than ever and with more than 20 percent of the labor force represented by a union.

Although labor's wartime gains dissipated during the 1920s, the Republicans, especially Herbert Hoover, continued the labor policies initiated by Theodore Roosevelt and Woodrow Wilson. In 1926 Congress passed the Railway Labor Act, which recognized the right of railroad workers to form independent unions with which railway managers were required to bargain collectively. The law declared trade unionism and collective bargaining to be in the national interest, leading some scholars to see it as a forerunner of the great New Deal labor reforms. Yet, a few exceptions notwithstanding, the state and federal judiciary continued to block labor reforms. Judges still declared state regulation of hours and wages to be in violation of the Constitution; they also persisted in issuing injunctions that curtailed strikes, picketing, and boycotts.

The Great Depression (1929–1939) and the New Deal transformed politics and public policy affecting labor. Franklin D. Roosevelt brought working people more completely into the Democratic Party coalition. The New Deal provided millions of unemployed workers jobs on public work projects; it promoted minimum wages, maximum hours, and improved working conditions; and it endorsed trade unionism and collective bargaining. In 1935 Congress passed perhaps the most radical single piece of legislation in U.S. history, the National Labor Relations Act, or Wagner Act. The Wagner Act placed the power of the federal government behind the right of workers to form unions and to bargain collectively with employers. It also created an independent agency, the National Labor Relations Board (NLRB), to implement and enforce the law's goals. The same Congress passed the Social Security Act of 1935, which provided old-age pensions, unemployment insurance, disability insurance, and public aid to dependent families and children. In 1938 Congress enacted the first national law regulating hours and wages for workers engaged in interstate commerce, the Fair Labor Standards Act. Simultaneously, many northern and western states created their own "little New Deals." A resurgent and more politically involved sector of the labor movement led by John L. Lewis, who was the founder and president of the Congress of Industrial Organizations (CIO), generously supported Roosevelt's 1936 campaign with money, speakers, and an effective get-out-the-vote drive.

A judicial revolution occurred alongside the New Deal. Beginning in 1935 the Supreme Court declared New Deal policies regulating working conditions and industrial relations constitutional. A majority declared manufacturing a part of interstate commerce, thus enabling the federal government to regulate the conditions of millions of workers. Federal judges declared most forms of union action to be constitutionally protected exercises of First Amendment rights to free speech, free press, and free assembly. By the eve of World War II a veritable political and judicial revolution had made public policy far more beneficial to labor and had tied workers and their unions firmly to the New Deal Democratic coalition.

World War II anchored the New Deal industrial-relations order while tightening the links between organized labor and

Woolworth workers strike for a forty-hour work week in 1937, two years after passage of the National Labor Relations Act. *Library of Congress*

THE POSTWAR ORDER, A PRECARIOUS BALANCE

Despite organized labor's strength in 1945, its power remained precarious. By 1948 labor had linked its future to the Democratic Party and President Harry S. Truman. The CIO made support of Truman in the election of 1948 a litmus test of loyalty. Those leftist unions, mostly communist-controlled or influenced, that supported the third-party candidacy of Henry Wallace instead of Truman were expelled from the

the Democratic Party. During the war the National War Labor Board promoted trade unionism and collective bargaining. It secured the CIO's new mass-production unions in formerly recalcitrant antiunion enterprises and protected them against management hostility. Old-line AFL unions gained equally, spreading the closed shop and unionizing substantial numbers of less skilled workers. At war's end in 1945, organized labor had reached its peak membership, representing more than one-third of the nation's nonagricultural labor force.

CIO. Thereafter, the CIO as well as the AFL served the government faithfully in waging the cold war abroad and combating communist influence in foreign labor movements.

Organized labor had good reason to favor the Democratic Party. The Republicans quickly evinced their antipathy toward organized labor. In 1947 a Republican majority in Congress passed the Taft-Hartley Act over the veto of Truman. While the Republican sponsors of Taft-Hartley claimed to have made the Wagner Act more equitable, their rhetoric told a different story. Congressional Republicans indicted "big labor" as an extortionate monopoly; condemned tyrannical labor "bosses"; and referred to unions as corrupt, crime-ridden exploiters of their innocent members. If Taft-Hartley accepted unions where management already recognized them, it made it more difficult for the labor movement to grow. The new law restructured the NLRB to assist management in repelling unions. It allowed states to enact their own industrial-relations rules that forbade closed shops, union shops, and other forms of union security. This option was used by many southern and western states that enacted so-called right-to-work laws. Although the labor movement continued to grow after 1947, it declined relatively as the size of the labor force grew more rapidly than the number of unionized workers.

If the political balance of power turned against labor, the federal courts continued to defend trade-union rights. Staffed largely by judges appointed by Roosevelt and Truman, the courts favored the New Deal's order of industrial relations. Appellate and Supreme Court decisions endorsed collective bargaining; extended union contract protections even to non–union members, who could be required to pay part of the cost of collective bargaining and contract administration; and continued to defend many aspects of collective action as constitutionally protected civil liberties.

Consequently, throughout the 1950s and 1960s organized labor maintained its political influence, especially after the AFL and CIO reunited in 1955. Although organized labor failed to advance its own special interests—especially repeal of Taft-Hartley—it did provide the political muscle to create the U.S. version of a welfare state. The AFL-CIO acted as the primary lobby to obtain increases in the federal minimum wage; more generous benefits for social security recipients; health protection, especially Medicare; and a wide array of public employment programs to combat joblessness. Lyndon B. Johnson's "Great Society" relied on the support of the AFL-CIO. Labor lobbyists also rounded up the decisive congressional votes needed to pass the Civil Rights and Voting Rights Acts of 1964 and 1965. The AFL-CIO also endorsed the cold war foreign policies of the Dwight D. Eisenhower, John F. Kennedy, and Johnson administrations. Its American Institute for Free Labor Development (AIFLD), funded in part by the CIA and other government sources, actively fought communist influences in trade unions throughout the developing world. And, a few exceptions notwithstanding, most union leaders rallied support for the war in Vietnam.

THE COLLAPSE OF THE POSTWAR ORDER

If the presidency of Lyndon Johnson represented an acme in labor's political influence, it was followed by a period of decline. As economic growth gave way to stagnation in the 1970s and foreign competitors cut into the U.S. share of global markets and penetrated the domestic market, U.S. enterprises took a harder line against unions. By the 1970s unions in the private sector began to lose substantial numbers of members, especially in the mass-production industries. Had not federal and state authorities legalized unionization and collective bargaining among public employees, the labor movement might have suffered more irreparable losses. Almost all of the growth in trade unions after the mid-1960s occurred among public employees.

The primary interests of many white union members began to shift. As the beneficiaries of union-negotiated contract benefits and the largesse of a middle-class welfare state, many white trade unionists identified themselves more as homeowners and consumers than as workers. Increasingly concerned with taxes, interest rates, and prices, such workers enlisted in a Republican-led drive against inflation and the demands of unions. The politics of inflation and deflation undercut the political influence of organized labor. Many white male workers also saw themselves as the victims of affirmative action policies that favored nonwhite and women competitors in the job market. The Nixon administration's "Philadelphia Plan," which sought to open the unions of the more skilled building trades to African American workers, served as a wedge to divide workers racially and to weaken union support for Democrats, who were more closely linked than Republicans to civil rights and affirmative action policies.

This was seen clearly after the election of Jimmy Carter in 1976. The AFL-CIO had supported Carter and in return expected revisions in industrial relations law that would make unionization easier. No such legislation ever passed Congress, but the Carter administration waged war against inflation and union monopoly power. The advocates of deflation and the dismantling of union power spoke more loudly than the defenders of trade unionism. The Carter administration deregulated the trucking and airline industries, much to the disadvantage of the Teamsters' union and the airline employees' unions. Carter served as a bridge to the Reagan Republicans.

The administration of Ronald Reagan sought to undo the New Deal revolution in industrial relations. It appointed a chair of the NLRB (Donald Dotson) who interpreted the law favorably toward management and who perceived trade unionism and collective bargaining as illegitimate. It appointed jurists who shared such views. President Reagan himself in 1981 broke a strike by the union of federal air traffic controllers (Professional Air Traffic Controllers' Organization, PATCO) in a manner reminiscent of Grover Cleveland's repression of the 1894 Pullman strike. Reagan's actions induced employers in the private sector to do the same; increasingly, private enterprises responded to strikes by hiring strikebreakers. In the 1980s unions seemed on the defensive, losing contracts and members, and by the decade's end they represented a smaller proportion of workers than at any time since 1929–1932.

The AFL-CIO determined to return Democrats to national political power, a goal that it achieved in 1992 and again in 1996 with the election and reelection of Bill Clinton. Clinton spoke the words that labor wanted to hear. He endorsed reforms in industrial-relations law and promised legislation to ban the use of replacement workers during strikes. He appointed a chair of the NLRB sympathetic to trade unionism and chose federal judges of a similar temperament. Yet, like Carter before him, Clinton failed to reform labor law or to outlaw the employment of replacement workers. He did, however, achieve passage of the North American Free Trade Agreement (NAFTA), other forms of free trade promotion, and continued deregulation of business. So feeble had labor's political influence become by 1996 that the AFL-CIO endorsed Clinton's bid for reelection.

The future of labor hangs in the balance. Unions continue to lose members and influence. Any major reform in national labor relations law seems unlikely. Yet, as was the case in 1996, the AFL-CIO supported Al Gore in the 2000 election, even though Gore endorsed free trade, economic deregulation, and balanced budgets. An augury perhaps of a different future could be found in events that occurred in Seattle in November 1999. An alliance representing trade unions, environmental groups, and diverse new social movements disrupted a meeting of the World Trade Organization (WTO) intended to promote free trade. Instead, the protesters succeeded in restoring to the public agenda the issue of workers' human rights.

See also *Civil Unrest and Rioting; Panic of 1893; Populist Party; Progressive Era; Progressive Labor Party; Social Security; Socialist Party.*

MELVYN DUBOFSKY, BINGHAMTON UNIVERSITY, SUNY

BIBLIOGRAPHY

Dubofsky, Melvyn. *The State and Labor in Modern America.* Chapel Hill: University of North Carolina Press, 1994.

Greene, Julie. *Pure and Simple Politics: The American Federation of Labor and Political Activism, 1881–1917.* New York: Cambridge University Press, 1998.

Plotke, David. *Building a Democratic Political Order: Reshaping American Liberalism in the 1930s and 1940s.* New York: Cambridge University Press, 1996.

Tomlins, Christopher L. *Law, Labor, and Ideology in the Early American Republic.* New York: Cambridge University Press, 1993.

Tomlins, Christopher L. *The State and the Unions: Labor Relations, Law, and the Organized Labor Movement in America, 1880–1960.* New York: Cambridge University Press, 1985.

LANDSLIDE ELECTIONS

Presidential elections are often close, and many presidents have won with less than 50 percent of the popular vote. On occasion, however, the winner takes 55 or even 60 percent of the popular vote and 80 or even 90 percent of the electoral college vote. Because the winner of a state's popular vote—no matter how small the margin—takes that state's entire electoral vote, the two counts do not necessarily track closely. Rather, a candidate who wins a great many states by narrow margins might win with a large majority in the electoral college.

Through 1820, electors were chosen through other means than popular election. In those nine campaigns, four candidates took more than 90 percent of the electoral college vote: George Washington in both of his elections, Thomas Jefferson when he won reelection in 1804, and James Monroe when he was reelected in 1820. Washington, the only president ever to receive a unanimous vote in the electoral college, accomplished the feat both times. Monroe won every state in 1820, but his final tally was 231 to 1; one elector refused to vote for him, so that Washington would remain the only president to have the honor of being unanimously elected.

Between 1824 and 1996 the nation had forty-four presidential elections. In six elections (14 percent) after 1820, the winner took 90 percent of the electoral college vote. Only four times (9 percent of the time), all in the twentieth century, did the winner get as much as 60 percent of the popular vote.

Those four popular landslide victories are instructive. Rather than signaling a long-term transformation in Americans' voting behavior, they were likely to be soon reversed. The Republican candidate, Warren G. Harding, won in a popular landslide in 1920, yet in 1936 a Democrat, Franklin D.

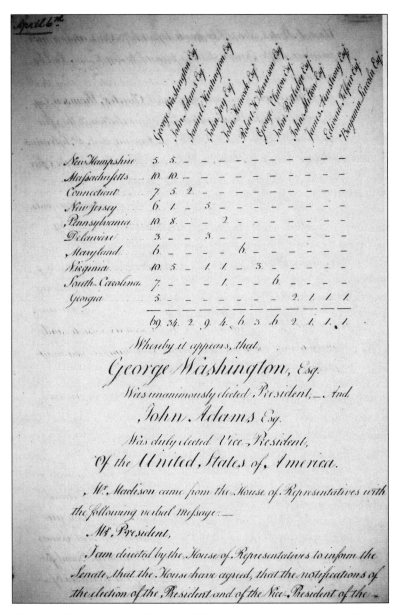

The *Senate Journal,* page 7, of April 6, 1789, records the electoral vote in the first presidential election. George Washington won unanimously, with sixty-nine electoral votes, followed by John Adams with thirty-four. *National Archives*

Roosevelt, won reelection with a similar majority. In 1964 Lyndon B. Johnson, a Democrat, won by the largest popular percentage ever recorded in a U.S. presidential election, but, challenged within his own party four years later, he withdrew from the race rather than seek reelection. Republican Richard M. Nixon won the presidency that year, and in 1972 he won his bid for reelection in a landslide, but he resigned from office in disgrace less than two years later.

Landslide victories in the popular count are not necessarily reflected in the electoral count, and vice versa. Three of the twentieth century's four winners of landslide victories in the popular election also won 90 percent of the electoral college count. Harding's margin in the electoral college was well under 80 percent, however. More notable are Ronald Reagan's two victories. In 1980 he took a bare majority, 50.7 percent, of the popular vote, yet he won by narrow majorities in so many states that commentators have often spoken of his landslide victory, which he did in fact win in the electoral college. Four years later, his winning percentage of the popular vote, though in the high fifties, did not meet the 60 percent threshold, yet he won in the electoral college by an even wider margin than four years earlier, 525 to 13, the fifth widest margin ever, after those of Washington, Monroe, and Franklin Roosevelt.

By definition, a candidate who takes 60 percent of the popular vote beats his nearest competitor by at least 20 percentage points. In the history of American presidential sweepstakes, the widest margin ever recorded came in 1920, when Harding won by 26 points. In addition to the four landslide victors, Theodore Roosevelt won by more than 20 points in 1904.

If one relaxes the requirements and sets the threshold for a landslide victory at 55 percent in the popular vote or 80 percent of the electoral college, far more candidates have won by landslide victories—so many as to dilute the meaning of the term. Fourteen of the forty-four winners from 1824 to 1996 (32 percent) took at least 55 percent of the popular vote, and nineteen (43 percent) took at least 80 percent in the electoral college.

Andrew Jackson, the only president to meet the 55 percent standard before the Civil War, won both of his terms with at least that amount, and he took 80 percent of the electoral college vote in his reelection victory in 1832. Franklin Pierce won in 1852 with only 50.9 percent of the popular vote, but his electoral college count exceeded 80 percent. In 1864, with eleven states out of the Union, Abraham Lincoln met the 55 percent popular standard as well as the higher 90 percent electoral college figure. In 1872 Ulysses S. Grant won with at least 55 percent of the popular vote and 80 percent of the electoral count. No other president of the nineteenth century reached either the 55 percent or the 80 percent threshold figures.

During the twentieth century, winners almost routinely met the lower 55 percent or 80 percent thresholds, if not both. In fact, a majority of winners from 1904 through 1984 accomplished the feat. During those twenty-one campaigns, only seven winning candidates failed to meet at least one of the two easier standards—William Howard Taft in 1908, Woodrow Wilson in 1916, Calvin Coolidge in 1924, Harry S. Truman in 1948, John F. Kennedy in 1960, Nixon in 1968, and Jimmy Carter in 1976. Every winner from 1928 through 1956 won in a landslide according to one of the looser definitions. Franklin Roosevelt won all four times with at least 80 percent of the electoral college count. Dwight D. Eisenhower met both the 55 percent and 80 percent figures in 1952 and again in 1956. After the Reagan years the dominant twentieth-century pattern receded, but it will likely return.

In the history of the republic—or at least since 1820—four presidents have won with 60 percent of the popular vote: two Democrats and two Republicans. Franklin Roosevelt did it once in his four campaigns, and Nixon did it once in his three. What are considered watershed elections, however, were not typically won by landslides. Jefferson narrowly won the "Revolution of 1800," though his victory four years later came by a landslide. Jackson won the election of 1828 by a hefty popular majority, but not 60 percent. Lincoln attracted the support of far less than half the voters in his victory in the four-way campaign of 1860. Franklin Roosevelt's win in 1936 met the 60 percent and 90 percent figures, but his victory four years earlier is better characterized as a watershed election.

See also *Presidency; Presidential Elections; Watershed Elections.*

PETER WALLENSTEIN, VIRGINIA POLYTECHNIC INSTITUTE
AND STATE UNIVERSITY

LIBERAL PARTY

New York State's Liberal Party was founded in 1944 by anticommunist trade unionists and other politically liberal individuals who left communist-dominated political parties. The party in 2000 described itself as providing an "alternative to a state Democratic Party dominated by local party machines rife with corruption and a Republican Party controlled by special interests." Many of the state's labor and educational leaders were instrumental in creating the party, which calls itself the nation's "longest existing third party."

The Liberal Party has played a major role in several elections. It provided crucial support for Franklin D. Roosevelt in 1944 and John F. Kennedy in 1960. Some political historians believe Roosevelt and Kennedy owed their national victories to the Liberal Party vote that carried New York State for them. John Lindsay, nominally a Republican, won reelection in New York City's 1969 mayoral race as the Liberal Party candidate. In 2000 Democrat Hillary Rodham Clinton won the Liberal line in her campaign for the U.S. Senate.

The party proclaims to nominate candidates on the basis of "merit, independence, and progressive viewpoints." Many of the state's most prominent liberal politicians have sought and won the party's nomination for New York City mayor, governor, and U.S. senator, regardless of their major party affiliation. When the party has not run candidates of its own, it has usually been supportive of Democrats. Sometimes, however, the party's role has been that of a spoiler, particularly in close races, where its support represents the balance of power. In modern Senate races, for example, political analysts say Liberal Party endorsement of moderate or liberal candidates has sometimes drawn enough votes from Democratic candidates to throw the election to conservative Republicans.

The party is active in pushing its political agenda, which is pro choice, pro universal health care, and pro public education (it has aggressively opposed school voucher programs, for example). Its successful Supreme Court suit for congressional reapportionment contributed to the 1968 election of Shirley Chisholm of New York, the first African American congresswoman.

Through the latter part of the twentieth century, the Liberal Party served as a counterweight in Empire State politics to New York's Conservative Party. In 1966, for instance, each party's gubernatorial candidate drew over a half million votes. The Liberal nominee was Franklin D. Roosevelt Jr.

Both parties have lost ground at the polls since then, the Liberals a bit more than the Conservatives. In 1998, for instance, the Liberal Party's gubernatorial nominee drew fewer than 80,000 votes, while the Conservative Party line provided Republican incumbent George E. Pataki with nearly 350,000 votes.

RON dePAOLO, INDEPENDENT AUTHOR

LIBERTY PARTY

Founded in 1840 in New York, the Liberty Party focused its attention on the evils of slavery in the United States. As its presidential nominee in the 1840 election, the Liberty Party nominated James G. Birney, a former slaveholder, former Whig, and organizer of the American Anti-Slavery Society in 1834. In the election, Birney obtained only 7,000 votes. In 1844 Birney was once again the nominee, and the party, which was strongest in New York and New England, received 62,000 votes, or 2.3 percent of the total cast. Some scholars argue that its strength in New York prevented Henry Clay, the Whig candidate, from winning that state's thirty-six electoral votes, which went instead to Democrat James K. Polk and assured Polk's victory. However, this theory is based on the dubious presumption that the uncompromising abolitionists who supported Birney would have voted for the slaveholding Clay.

The Liberty Party was subsumed in the antislavery Free Soil Party in 1848 and the new Republican Party in the mid-1850s. Unlike the programs of most third parties, that of the Liberty Party became the law of the land, when the Thirteenth Amendment was ratified in 1865.

RON dePAOLO, INDEPENDENT AUTHOR

BIBLIOGRAPHY

Sewell, Richard H. *Ballots for Freedom: Antislavery Politics in the United States, 1837–1860.* New York: Oxford University Press, 1976.

LINCOLN, ABRAHAM

President Abraham Lincoln (1861–1865) skillfully guided a young nation through its greatest crisis, the Civil War. In doing so, he significantly expanded the powers of the presidency and made permanent a more powerful nation-state.

Born in Kentucky, Lincoln grew up in southern Indiana and Illinois in a hard-luck, hard-scrabble environment. Unusually ambitious and hungry for knowledge, he seemed to his neighbors too tall, too ugly, too clumsy, too lazy, and too disrespectful of his father. But Lincoln told great stories and bawdy jokes, socialized well, and soon tested his remarkable leadership skills with four brilliant terms (1835–1843) as a Whig leader in the Illinois legislature and one as an unimportant backbencher in the U.S. Congress (1847–1849). Lincoln's easy rapport with juries, buttressed by meticulous research and attention to detail, facilitated a successful legal career. He rode circuit half the year through central Illinois, then returned to his home in Springfield to handle all sorts of cases, including high-paying ones for the new railroad corporations.

As an admirer of fellow Whig Henry Clay, Lincoln enthusiastically promoted economic modernization, including banks, railroads, and tariffs. His political problem was that Whigs rarely carried the state of Illinois. Frustrated by the slow collapse of the Whig Party, Lincoln withdrew from politics after 1849, only to return to the fray in 1854 and play a major role in building a powerful new Republican Party in the West. Like many of his "free state" neighbors, Lincoln was shocked and angered by the Kansas-Nebraska Act (1854), which allowed slavery in western territories that had been made "free soil" by the Missouri Compromise (1820). "No man is good enough to govern another man without that other's consent," he insisted in a speech in Peoria in October 1854. "I say this is the leading principle, the sheet-anchor of American republicanism." Slavery, he continued, was incompatible with the "consent of the governed" clause of the Declaration of Independence.

Abraham Lincoln *Library of Congress*

Cultivating the growing German vote, Lincoln avoided nativism and the Know Nothings as he sought political office. In 1855 the Republicans controlled the state legislature, and Lincoln was in line for a seat in the U.S. Senate. He was outmaneuvered, however, and forced to deliver the seat to Lyman Trumbull. Challenging the reelection of Illinois senator Stephen A. Douglas in 1858, Lincoln found himself in the national spotlight. He attacked Douglas (falsely) for being in league with southern slaveholders and warned that Douglas's efforts to compromise between freedom and slavery were doomed:

"A house divided against itself cannot stand." I believe this government cannot endure permanently half slave and half free. I do not expect the Union to be dissolved—I do not expect the house to fall—but I do expect it will cease to be divided. It will become all one thing, or all the other. Either the opponents of slavery will arrest the further spread of it, and place it where the public mind shall rest in the belief that it is in the course of ultimate extinction; or its advocates will push it forward till it shall become alike lawful in all the States, old as well as new—North as well as South.

Intense study of history and the Constitution convinced Lincoln that the nation was founded on equal rights, which meant that slavery had to be stopped from expansion and eventually replaced everywhere by free labor. The debates with Douglas established Lincoln's reputation as the most prominent party leader in the West, even though Douglas won reelection to the Senate.

GAINING THE PRESIDENCY

In 1860 the Republicans expected to win the presidency because they dominated enough northern states to control a majority of electoral votes. The party sought the candidate most likely to carry the closely contested states of Illinois and Indiana. Lincoln's reputation as a "moderate"—antislavery regarding the western territories, but not abolitionist or hostile toward the South—made him acceptable to all factions of the party.

Once nominated, Lincoln gave no speeches. Rather than repeat the fervent crusading campaign of 1856, the confident young Republican Party spent its energy on getting out its votes. Four parties contested the presidency in 1860 because Americans were committed to four radically different interpretations of "republicanism." Lincoln and the Republicans demanded equal rights and freedom for all men, arguing that federal sponsorship of slavery was incompatible with the Declaration of Independence that created the nation in the first place. Douglas and the northern Democrats fervently believed in democracy: the people were always right, and what they wanted—be it slavery or no—was always best. The southern Democrats said the Constitution of 1787 had guaranteed rights protected by the states—namely, the right to own slaves. To the extent the Yankees were repudiating that compact, it was the Yankees who were threatening the Union; the southerners were merely defending their historic rights. Finally, the Constitutional Union Party said equal rights, democracy, and property were all secondary to American nationalism.

No two parties could agree on a coalition. Even if Lincoln's three opponents had formed an alliance, he still would have won the electoral college because of narrow majorities in nearly all the northern states. Eventually Lincoln would try to synthesize the various viewpoints, guaranteeing a permanent Union at the cost of slavery.

To the seven most southern states, Lincoln's election signaled the declaration of permanent Yankee hostility and the inexorable destruction of states' rights. Calling upon the right of rebellion, they seceded, one by one, from the Union, and by February 1861 they had formed a new country, the Confederate States of America, and elected Jefferson Davis as their president. Meanwhile, the border states tried to remain neutral, elder statesmen met to fashion some sort of compromise, and the administration of James Buchanan stood paralyzed as the new Confederacy peacefully took over federal properties in its territory.

Aware that a crisis in mankind's history was at hand, Lincoln pledged in a speech in February 1861 never to surrender "that sentiment in the Declaration of Independence which gave liberty, not alone to the people of this country, but I hope to the world for all future time." Yet for the most part Lincoln stood silent, focusing his attention on the patronage compromises necessary to fashion the first Republican administration. Incorrectly believing that most white southerners were Unionists at heart, Lincoln refused to compromise or even negotiate with Confederate delegations. He also resolved to keep the one bit of property still in U.S. hands, Fort Sumter in Charleston, South Carolina. The Confederates, knowing they could never be recognized as a legitimate nation if some other country had a fort in its major harbor, insisted on surrender of the fort, and finally fired the first shot of the war.

A DIVIDED NATION AT WAR

Lincoln consistently underestimated the scope and strength of the rebellion. After Fort Sumter was attacked, he asked state governors for seventy-five thousand soldiers for ninety days—not appreciating that over twenty times more men would be needed, for nearly twenty times as long. In terms of military policy, Lincoln demanded that his generals march "on to Richmond" in the conviction that the capture of the rebel capital would delegitimize the very existence of a rival nation and lead to the speedy downfall of the Confederacy. Richmond, though, proved impossible to capture until the very end—only when Gen. Robert E. Lee's army had practically melted away and the Union had an overwhelming numerical advantage. By contrast, the president's naval blockade shut down virtually all commercial shipping from southern ports and played a major role in defeating "King Cotton" by strangling the southern economy. The Confederacy soon became a prison, with only fast, small blockade-running ships able to sneak in and out. Cooperation between the army and navy, under Lincoln's close supervision, soon led to landings at key points along the southern coast and to the enormously important capture of New Orleans in April 1862.

Lincoln's success as president stemmed from his single-minded devotion to the Union. His fixed policy was to never compromise with secession. Everything else was on the table, including civil liberties and slavery. He suspended habeas corpus, which allowed his army to arrest outspoken supporters of the rebellion and hold them in military prison without trial. And there were some summary executions by federal forces, especially in Kentucky. Because he needed support from the Unionist slave owners early in the war, Lincoln reversed an August 1861 proclamation by Gen. John C. Frémont freeing slaves in Missouri. Throughout 1862 he worked up plans for Unionist elections in the South, including stillborn schemes for compensated emancipation and deportation of the freed slaves out of the country. His preliminary proclamation in September 1862 threatened emancipation of slaves in areas that did not return to the Union. The proclamation mollified radical elements in his party, but it drove the majority of northern Democrats into opposition to the war. As a result, recruiting white northerners became much more difficult, and the effort to impose a draft produced more resentment than soldiers. At Lincoln's insistence, over 150,000 freed slaves were recruited into military service, and thousands of free blacks volunteered.

Throughout the war, Lincoln felt his role as commander in chief of the military was paramount, and he worked closely with his secretaries of war and navy. He was keenly interested in the development of new rifles, guns, and ships and in recruitment and conscription. His personal involvement even ran to selecting all the generals and promoting or removing them according to a complex calculus of party politics, public opinion, and—most of all—victory on the battlefield. He ran through a series of inept or underconfident generals who kept failing to defeat Lee or capture Richmond. Gen. George McClellan was brilliant at training and organizing an army, but he proved reluctant to actually fight a battle. Frustrated, Lincoln demoted McClellan, but Lincoln then had to reinstate him when the replacements failed. The western theatre provided bigger victories and better generals. Lincoln brought Gen. Henry Halleck east in 1862 to act as chief of staff, and Ulysses S. Grant in 1864 to assume overall command of all the armies. Grant shrewdly accepted all of Lincoln's suggestions on military strategy, and in turn Lincoln gave him complete political support. This proved especially critical in the hot summer of 1864, when agonizingly high casualty totals from Grant's relentless attrition campaign against Lee threatened Lincoln's reelection chances.

In Washington, Lincoln put strong men in his cabinet and let them run their domains. He did monitor the distribution of major patronage appointments, but otherwise largely rubber-stamped Secretary of State William H. Seward's conduct of foreign affairs and Treasury Secretary Salmon P. Chase's finan-

President Abraham Lincoln confers with Gen. George McClellan and his staff following the battle of Antietam. Lincoln closely monitored the progress of Union armies. *Library of Congress*

cial legerdemain. Meanwhile, the Republican Congress was passing momentous legislation, including that calling for heavy new income taxes, excises, high tariffs and massive spending bills, a national banking system, new homesteads out west, transcontinental railroads, and land grants to education. Indeed, the Republicans were enacting their program for rapid modernization of the economy, and although Lincoln had little to do with this legislation, he approved it enthusiastically and repeatedly boasted of the economic growth and prosperity during his term. Lincoln and his generals, with the support of Congress, brought freedom to millions of southern slaves.

Toward the end of the war, in 1864, Congress passed the harsh Wade-Davis plan for Reconstruction, but Lincoln vetoed it. He planned to control Reconstruction himself, following a policy of "malice toward none, with charity for all," and the fastest possible return to full citizenship of the erring southern brethren. Lincoln took the lead in signing up black soldiers, in the knowledge that a record of fighting for the country was the surest test of republican citizenship. Because the 1863 Emancipation Proclamation, freeing the slaves, would expire at the end of the war, Lincoln worked hard to replace it with the permanent Thirteenth Amendment, which passed Congress in February 1865.

Lincoln easily overcame the opposition of Radical Republicans to win renomination in 1864. Although for a few weeks in August his supporters had the jitters, his reelection was certain because the war was triumphantly successful in 1864, the economy was prosperous, the Democratic opposition was deeply split between peace and war factions, and the South was not allowed to vote. Lincoln was assassinated on April 14, 1865.

With a profound sense of American history, unswerving commitment to republican ideals, and an almost Shakespearean command of the language, Abraham Lincoln articulated a vision of a new birth of freedom for the American nation. The destruction of the Confederacy, and of the slave power that menaced republican ideals, affirmed Lincoln's vision and guaranteed that "government of the people, by the people, for the people, shall not perish from the earth."

See also *Civil War; Emancipation Proclamation; Grant, Ulysses S.; Kansas-Nebraska Act; Morrill Land-Grant College Acts; Reconstruction; Republican Party; Secession; Slavery.*

RICHARD JENSEN, RENSSELAER POLYTECHNIC INSTITUTE

BIBLIOGRAPHY

Donald, David Herbert. *Abraham Lincoln*. New York: Simon and Schuster, 1995.
Neely, Mark E. *The Lincoln Encyclopedia*. New York: Da Capo Press, 1984.

Oates, Stephen B. *With Malice toward None: A Life of Abraham Lincoln*. New York: HarperPerennial, 1994.

Paludan, Phillip Shaw. *The Presidency of Abraham Lincoln*. 1945–1955. Reprint, Lawrence: University Press of Kansas, 1994.

Randall, James G. *Lincoln the President*. 4 vols. New York: Dodd, Mead, 1945–1953.

LOBBYISTS

A lobbyist is someone operating outside of government who communicates information or opinions to a public official in an effort to influence a specific public policy outcome. The origin of the term *lobbyist* is uncertain. One theory postulates that it originally referred to the journalists or citizens who waited in the lobbies of England's House of Commons. In the United States the term first appeared in 1808 in the annals of the Tenth Congress. By 1829 the term *lobby-agents* was being applied to favor-seekers at the New York capitol in Albany.

Although lobbying is generally an honorable profession, certain abuses—sometimes known as "influence peddling," involving bribes, kickbacks, or other illegal means—have sullied its reputation in specific cases. The Crédit Mobilier scandal in the 1860s and the "Koreagate" scandal in the 1970s are two examples. Legitimate lobbying, however, is protected by the Constitution as free speech and the right to petition government.

Not everyone who attempts to influence public policy is a lobbyist. Government workers, legislators, political officials, and members of the general public often communicate information for the sole purpose of influencing public policy, but they are not lobbyists. One distinguishing characteristic of lobbyists is that they are employed outside of the three branches of government and interact with government workers, legislators, and political officials in an attempt to influence the legislative process. Also, unlike members of the general public who try to influence public policy as advocates for themselves or those they care about, lobbyists are not operating out of their own personal interests. This does not imply that they cannot or do not personally share some of the same interests that they are representing, but it does mean that lobbying is distinct from advocating. Personal interests and political interests *may* coincide in lobbying; in advocating, they *necessarily* coincide. For example, a professional lobbyist with a disability may be hired by an organization to lobby for a particular disability policy. As a *lobbyist,* she focuses on the group's political goals. Should she also spend her own time and resources in support of the same disability policy, she would be doing so as an *advocate.*

Regulatory compliance offers another means of distinguishing between lobbyists and all others who try to influence public policy. Although individuals from various sectors attempt to influence the legislative process and receive compensation for their efforts as part of their overall job responsibilities, only those whose activities are of a certain scope are required to register with the secretary of the U.S. Senate or the clerk of the House of Representatives under current lobbying disclosure regulations. Supplanting the 1946 Federal Regulation of Lobbying Act, the Lobbying Disclosure Act of 1995 significantly expanded the registration and reporting requirements for those seeking to affect U.S. government policies or the implementation of federal programs. The 1995 act's broad definition of lobbying brings within its scope many individuals and firms whose activities did not require

Lobbyists mix with reporters in the hallway while members of the House banking subcommittee mark up a bill. *Congressional Quarterly*

them to register as lobbyists under the 1946 legislation. Under the 1995 act, a lobbyist is defined as anyone who is paid more than $20,000 and who spends 20 percent or more of his or her compensated time for a particular client over a six-month period in an effort to influence legislation, policy making, or program implementation on behalf of that client.

Lobbying methods can be divided into two categories: direct/inside lobbying strategies and indirect/outside lobbying strategies. Lobbyists prefer direct tactics, which include strategies that create access, relay critical information, involve face-to-face contact, and facilitate active participation in the policy-making process. Direct lobbying strategies represent a more frontal assault on the decision-making process, whereas indirect strategies entail a more circuitous communication process. Examples of indirect lobbying strategies are mass mail and telephone appeals, media campaigns, and picketing.

One of the primary values of lobbyists to politicians and bureaucrats is their service as sources of statistical, political, and opinion information. Lobbyists also can be pivotal in the drafting of legislation. A 1991 report on a survey of Washington, D.C.-based lobbying organizations indicated that 85 percent of respondents helped draft legislation. Thus lobbyists often serve as active partners—if not, leaders—in the critical sharing of information that occurs in the policy-making process.

See also *Crédit Mobilier Scandal; Interest Groups; Koreagate; Political Action Committees.*

KELLY MYLES, AMERICAN ASSOCIATION OF
UNIVERSITY AFFILIATED PROGRAMS

BIBLIOGRAPHY

Gates, John B., and Charles A. Johnson. *The American Courts: A Critical Assessment.* Washington, D.C.: CQ Press, 1991.

Hrebenar, Ronald J. *Interest Group Politics in America.* 3d ed. Armonk, N.Y.: M. E. Sharpe, 1997.

Walker, Jack L., Jr. *Mobilizing Interest Groups in America.* Ann Arbor: University of Michigan Press, 1991.

LOCAL GOVERNMENT

L ocal governments are the geographical building blocks of American politics. They administer the basic election and voter registration machinery for the nation, provide the boundaries for congressional and state legislative districts and for political party organization, and serve as the training ground for many politicians who ascend to state and federal offices.

The 85,000 units of local governments—cities, counties, towns, townships, school districts, and special districts—that operate in the fifty states are important political and govern-

ing arenas in their own right. They are the locations of electoral contests, conflict and deliberation over public policies, and the mobilization of competing interests.

THE ENGLISH TRADITION

Local governments have been a central fixture of community life in the United States since shortly after Europeans began settling the eastern seaboard almost four centuries ago. The first English colonists brought with them familiar community-level institutions. Even today, English antecedents are apparent in many of the common terms used for particular forms and offices, such as county, township, city, mayor, alderman, sheriff, and coroner. Essentially cloned from the institutions of seventeenth-century England, the first local government arrangements in the colonies were imposed by proprietors and royal governors, with colonial assemblies playing a smaller part. The major purpose was to prepare for larger settler populations by establishing social order, creating the conditions for economic prosperity, and defending against the natives. The key functions included courts and constables, economic regulation, and a military capacity. New England settlements were largely the exception to this top-down mode of organization, with town governments created through local initiative but with ultimate approval by higher colonial authorities.

After the Revolutionary War, the new state governments through their legislatures and governors took over the legal responsibility for creating and overseeing local governments. The basic colonial forms were continued and exist today, but many changes in organization and powers have been added in the last two centuries. For governance, especially of rural areas, three different local government systems came to prevail in different parts of the country. One was the New England pattern of town government, focused on the democratic institution of the annual town meeting. The second system, especially dominant in the southern colonies and later states, was an emphasis on county government. The third pattern, taking hold in the middle colonies, was an overlapping combination of counties and towns or townships.

As the country grew to the west, new states adopted one or another of the basic rural forms. Thus the midwestern states, populated mostly by migrants from the mid-Atlantic and northeastern areas, established the hybrid county/township system, with township governments considerably weaker than those in New England. States established later essentially ignored the town/township option, and county governments became the dominant rural institutions throughout the South and West. Laid on top or alongside the basic rural pattern in every state is another form of local government—cities or other municipal units incorporated primarily to serve the greater demands of concentrated, urban populations.

ONGOING TRENDS

Several major trends have characterized the evolution of American local government since the formation of the nation more than two hundred years ago.

The degree of local control—the discretion of communities to govern themselves—has varied according to the actions of state governments. In the nineteenth century the states generally exercised strong control over individual localities through special legislation and other devices. The trend in the twentieth century was in the opposite direction, as general laws replaced special acts, and communities and their governments were given more control over organization, powers, and revenues. A partial reversal of this trend in the last two decades of the twentieth century was the elimination in some states of local control over the property tax, traditionally the most important revenue source for local governments.

In expenditures, programs, and political visibility, cities had become the most important local governments in the United States by the second half of the nineteenth century. This development was the result of both foreign and domestic immigration and the overall urbanization of the nation.

A more recent trend has been the proliferation of single-purpose local governments. The administration of K–12 education was shifted to independent school boards and districts starting in the late nineteenth century (although the number of separate districts was sharply reduced after the 1940s). The comparable trend in the twentieth century was the formation of many special districts for varied functions, such as water supply, parks, waste disposal, and recreation. In both cases the major motivation was to remove these functions from city and county politics and the necessity of competing with other local public services for attention and funds.

As delivery systems for public services, local governments are more competent and professional today than fifty, one hundred, or two hundred years ago. A key feature of this trend has been the emergence of city managers, school superintendents, and other chief executives with strong administrative powers.

The opportunities for citizen participation in American local government have steadily increased over the past two centuries. The expansion in the nineteenth century, especially during the era of Jacksonian Democracy, of the number and variety of local officials subject to election initially fueled this trend. More recent developments include the greater use of citizen boards and commissions, the adoption of open-meeting and public-records requirements, and increases in local ballot-box measures. Citizen interest and participation in local government affairs, however, appear not to have kept up with the expanded opportunities, as suggested by the general decline of voter turnout in local elections.

The one period in American history that contributed the most to originating or accelerating the trends described above was the reform era of the late nineteenth and early twentieth centuries. Much of the energy of the progressive tendency in American politics during this period was directed to reforming local institutions, largely in the interest of cleaning up the corruption of big-city politics and making local governments more efficient and accountable. Between 1890 and 1920 many communities changed from nonpartisan to partisan elections, substituted at-large for district arrangements for electing officials, adopted merit employment and civil service systems for local government personnel, established executive budgets, and separated policy making or legislative functions from administrative routines.

REFORM IN THE TWENTIETH CENTURY

Although the efforts of Progressive reformers were largely spent by World War I, organizational changes in local government have continued to the present time. Indeed, Americans since the colonial years have steadily tinkered with the forms and processes of their local governing institutions, either through the top-down impositions of state legislatures or through the direct initiative of communities.

Throughout the twentieth century many cities substituted other arrangements for the weak-mayor plan for municipal government that had been dominant in the previous century. Reformers had long been critical of the fragmented executive power implicit in the weak-mayor form, which was characterized by large city councils and the election of many officials and boards for separate administrative functions. The commission form, in which members of a small elected governing board individually also served as heads of particular administrative functions, was popular for a short while after its successful application in 1900 by Galveston, Texas, to cope with the municipal problems created by a devastating flood.

The two most popular options for city government have become the strong-mayor and council-manager forms that are found today in more than 90 percent of the cities in the United States. The strong-mayor form is prevalent in larger cities, whereas the council-manager form is more common in small and medium-sized municipalities. Both feature small city councils and no or very few elected officials other than the mayor and council. In the former, the mayor is an independent political figure with considerable executive powers that may include the appointment and control of department heads, budget preparation, and veto over council acts. The council-manager form follows a corporate business model, in which a professional administrator is hired and delegated the responsibility for administering the city, subject to varying degrees of oversight and potential dismissal by the elected council, whose members include a largely ceremonial mayor. County governments increasingly have adopted appointed executive arrangements, although their hired professionals typically have less administrative control than city managers, in large part because counties continue to elect separate administrative officers. However, a form of commission government—in which governing board members share administrative tasks—is still prevalent for most county governments serving rural areas.

Another reform thrust that emerged in the twentieth century, especially in the several decades after World War II, promoted comprehensive regional government. With metropolitan areas as the principal target, leaders of this movement argued a compelling need to overcome the presumed duplication, inefficiency, lack of coordination, and provincialism that arise from a public sector in an area with numerous overlapping and relatively small local governments. Consolidation of county and city governments was the most common suggested approach. But voters and local political leaders were largely unsympathetic to the metropolitan government concept, rejecting more than 75 percent of the consolidation and similar proposals that were put forth in the two decades after the mid-1950s. In fact, organizational change in many big cities starting in the 1960s was in the opposite direction, toward the partial decentralization of municipal bureaucracies and the creation of neighborhood "governments" with limited service delivery functions.

Other, less comprehensive regional institutions have prospered on the local government landscape. Single-purpose authorities or districts are found in many metropolitan areas and other regions. Some are large organizations with extensive budgets, such as the bistate Port Authority of New York and New Jersey (bridges, tunnel, airports, bus terminals, office buildings, and freight terminals) and southern California's Metropolitan Water District (water supply).

Few of these regional governments are led by separately elected boards, but instead are governed by ex officio boards that represent other local governments. This structure leads critics to attack regional governments for their lack of popular accountability as well as their contribution to organizational overlap and proliferation in the areas served.

A CHANGING STATE
AND FEDERAL POLITICAL ROLE

Many of the reforms associated with the Progressives and appearing later in the twentieth century served over time to diminish the political role of American local governments in state and national affairs. Most particularly, the movement to nonpartisan local elections, the adoption of merit in place of patronage systems for local government personnel, and the

centralization of administrative power in the hands of appointed professionals undercut the organizational foundations of the two major political parties. In the long run these reforms helped weaken local campaign structures and bring about the shift from personal to media-orientated campaigns in state and national elections. A similar but less significant disruption in the connections between local and state/national politics was the adoption of equal-population apportionment of state legislative and congressional districts in the 1960s, a change that reduced the importance of county and town boundaries in the design of these districts.

In other respects, local governments today retain their importance as the building blocks of state and national politics. The 85,000 local governments elect almost 500,000 officials, most of them members of city councils, county and school boards, and other governing bodies. Getting elected at this level is still a major route to state and national elective office, particularly for seats in state legislatures and Congress.

See also *Gerrymandering; Immigration and Naturalization; Initiative, Referendum, and Recall; Progressive Era; State Government.*

ALVIN D. SOKOLOW, UNIVERSITY OF CALIFORNIA, DAVIS

BIBLIOGRAPHY

Adrian, Charles. "Forms of City Government in American History." In *The Municipal Year Book, 1991.* Washington: International City/County Management Association, 1991, 3–11.

Griffith, Ernest S. *A History of American City Government: The Colonial Period.* New York: Oxford University Press, 1938.

Griffith, Ernest S. *A History of American City Government: The Progressive Years and Their Aftermath, 1900–1920.* Washington, D.C.: University Press of America, 1983.

Ostrom, Vincent, Robert Bish, and Elinor Ostrom. *Local Government in the United States.* San Francisco: Institute for Contemporary Studies, 1988.

Snider, Clyde F. *Local Government in Rural America.* New York: Appleton-Century-Crofts, 1957.

LOGAN ACT

The Logan Act forbids unauthorized private citizens of the United States from negotiating with foreign governments over pending disputes. The law was inspired by Federalist outrage against the actions of Dr. George Logan, a Philadelphia Quaker and Republican who had entered into negotiations with the French government during his stay in that country in 1798. The act was signed into law January 30, 1799, by President John Adams.

In 1797 Franco-American diplomatic relations had been suspended because of the XYZ Affair, in which French officials demanded a bribe and a loan of $10 million to France in exchange for France's negotiating an end to interference with American trade. By the time of Logan's negotiations, the

United States and France were fighting the Quasi-War, an undeclared naval war. The pro-British Federalist Party, which held the White House and majorities in both houses of Congress, opposed the pro-French Republican Party, which viewed the Federalists as seeking to destroy the Republican Party.

Republicans also suspected that the Federalists desired the abrogation of the treaty of alliance with France, the operation of which had been indefinitely suspended by President George Washington's declaration of neutrality. Logan's personal negotiations with France were seen as treacherous by the Federalists, having the effect of undermining support for President Adams's foreign policy goals. As a result of Logan's interventions, he was given dispatches from Gen. Napoleon Bonaparte, the first consul of France, addressed to President Adams and U.S. secretary of state Timothy Pickering, that promised the freeing of American prisoners of war and an end to the embargo on U.S. ships entering French ports.

At the time of the passage of the act, Congress censured Logan. The law remains on the books, but its practical usefulness may be questionable. If the provisions against negotiations are interpreted as forbidding the mere exchange of ideas with the representatives of a foreign power concerning some ongoing disputes, then the act may be viewed as an unconstitutional abridgment of freedom of speech. If, on the other hand, "negotiating" involves misrepresenting oneself as an official representative of the U.S. government and being negotiated with as such by a foreign power, it is difficult to imagine that the act ever has been, or ever will be, violated.

In the late twentieth century, Americans were sometimes seen as acting in ways that called George Logan to mind. During the Vietnam War, there was considerable demand for the prosecution of Jane Fonda and some members of the American Friends Service Committee of the Quaker Church who had seemed to negotiate with the communist government of North Vietnam while the United States was engaged in an undeclared war in Indochina from 1965 to 1974. The Reverend Jesse Jackson and former president Jimmy Carter have both acted as unofficial ambassadors of the United States, but their actions have generated less criticism, perhaps because they have seemed more successful. Jackson's discussions with the Syrian regime secured the release of a U.S. airman, and Carter's talks with North Korea helped achieve a compromise concerning that nation's drive for nuclear weapons and long-range missile technology.

PATRICK M. O'NEIL, BROOME COMMUNITY COLLEGE,
STATE UNIVERSITY OF NEW YORK

BIBLIOGRAPHY

Bowman, Albert Hall. *The Struggle for Neutrality: Franco American Diplomacy during the Federalist Era.* Knoxville: University of Tennessee Press, 1974.

DeConde, Alexander. *The Quasi-War: The Politics and Diplomacy of the Undeclared War with France, 1797–1801.* New York: Scribner's, 1966.

Tolles, Frederick B. *George Logan of Philadelphia.* New York: Oxford University Press, 1953.

MADISON, JAMES

A key figure in the origins of the U.S. Constitution and the Bill of Rights, James Madison (1751–1836) served as the fourth president of the United States (1809–1817).

MADISON AND THE AMERICAN REVOLUTION

Madison grew to adulthood in the age of the American Revolution. In 1776, at the age of twenty-five, he served in the Virginia convention that declared independence from Great Britain, framed a state constitution, and crafted the Virginia Declaration of Rights. In his most notable initiative there, he promoted a provision in the Declaration of Rights guaranteeing freedom of religion.

Later in the Revolution, he served as a Virginia delegate to the Confederation Congress. During his tenure, between 1780 and 1783, he pushed successfully for Virginia to give up its claims to vast territory in the Old Northwest, an action that facilitated ratification of the Articles of Confederation in 1781. He was instrumental, too, in the call by Congress in 1783 for an amendment to the articles that would authorize a national tariff to supply the new nation with an independent means of revenue. Then, having served as long in Congress as the term limits under the Articles of Confederation permitted, he was elected to the Virginia House of Delegates, where he secured passage in 1786 of Thomas Jefferson's Statute for Religious Freedom.

FATHER OF THE CONSTITUTION

Based on his extensive experience in state and national politics, Madison saw an urgent need for the national government to obtain greater power than the Articles of Confederation granted it. Yet efforts to amend the articles failed to obtain the unanimous consent of the states, despite Madison's 1783 "Address to the States" and a companion call by George Washington, "Circular to the Governors," urging ratification.

In 1786 Madison attended the Annapolis Convention in Maryland, a meeting of delegates from several states that called

James Madison *Library of Congress*

for a general convention of delegates from all thirteen states to meet in Philadelphia the next year. There, he hoped, a stronger framework of national government might be hammered out, one that would give the nation a greater chance of surviving in a dangerous world as an independent republic.

Returning from Annapolis to the Virginia legislature, Madison worked to secure his state's agreement to participate in such a convention. He was selected as one of Virginia's delegates. Seeking to enhance the convention's chance of success, he helped persuade George Washington to participate as another Virginia delegate. If a man of Washington's political stature led Virginia's delegation, he thought, perhaps other states would also send their leading men. Before the convention met in May, Madison was also reelected to the Confederation Congress (which was meeting in New York), so he was able to work there to lay the groundwork for a successful convention in Philadelphia.

The Philadelphia convention met in 1787 from May to September. Madison was the chief author of a collection of resolutions introduced early on by Virginia delegate Edmund Randolph. The "Virginia Plan," as those resolutions came to be called, provided the basis for discussion that led to the proposed Constitution of the United States to which the convention agreed.

The Virginia Plan proposed a complete renovation of the national government that had been struggling along under the Articles of Confederation. Instead of having only a unicameral legislature, the new government would have two legislative houses, and it would also have independent executive and judicial branches. Instead of representation in Congress being identical for every state, it would be apportioned on the basis of state population, although the original plan was changed in convention so that the House of Representatives would be apportioned by population but each state would have equal representation in the Senate.

The new government, as proposed by the Philadelphia convention, would have powers that had been denied the Articles of Confederation government. Whereas the Articles of Confederation government had depended on the states to supply requisitions, the new government would have the power to tax citizens directly to secure revenue. Moreover, it would be authorized to regulate trade among the states and between the United States and other countries, so states could not put up their own tariff barriers. In these and other ways, the new national government would be far more than a committee of the states to deal with little more than war and diplomacy.

Achieving agreement in Philadelphia among most of the delegates was a vitally important start, but it would avail little if the states did not ratify the proposed Constitution. To this effort, Madison next turned his vast ability to frame compelling political arguments and to write. Together mostly with Alexander Hamilton, he wrote *The Federalist Papers,* a series of essays in political theory and history that laid out the arguments for granting the national government greatly enhanced power. A republic was as suited to a large territory as to a single state, Madison insisted, and the Constitution promised a successful conclusion to the Revolution, not a reversal of it. In state after state, those arguments made the difference in convincing majorities, often by only narrow margins, to permit the new government to go into operation. As

a member of the Virginia ratifying convention in 1788, Madison in person helped persuade enough delegates to secure Virginia's ratification.

POLICY, PROTOCOL, AND A BILL OF RIGHTS

Madison and Washington were elected in 1789 to help launch the new national government—Washington as the first president and Madison to the First Congress. President Washington consulted with U.S. Rep. Madison on a wide range of matters. Madison drafted not only Washington's inaugural address but also the House's response to the president. Madison also did much to shape protocol in the new regime. Calling for a democratic etiquette, for example, Madison helped defeat a proposal according to which the president would have been addressed as his "Highness" rather than "Mr. President." Madison also led the way on policy matters. Consistent with his experience throughout the 1780s, he fostered passage of the first federal tariff law.

Central to the actions of the First Congress under the new Constitution were the framing and approval of the Bill of Rights, and Madison was the key player in those efforts. Madison had understood that the new Constitution must be subject to amendment, but he had at first resisted calls for amendments that would serve as a bill of rights. To overcome enough resistance to ratification, however, Federalists had promised to seek guarantees of various rights, and Madison had repeated the promise in his campaign for election to Congress. Moreover, although Madison had pushed throughout the 1780s for a stronger national government, he understood that too strong a national government was also a danger.

Prodded by Madison, Congress considered a large number of proposals for amending the Constitution. Eventually, Congress approved twelve and sent them to the states, and by 1791 ten of them had been ratified by the requisite three-fourths of the states. They came to be known as the Bill of Rights, and Madison came to be known not only as "father of the Constitution" but also "father of the Bill of Rights."

THE DEMOCRATIC-REPUBLICANS

During George Washington's first term as president, Secretary of the Treasury Alexander Hamilton proposed a series of measures to bolster the economy and the federal government. In particular, Hamilton proposed that the U.S. Congress charter a Bank of the United States, but Thomas Jefferson and James Madison were among the leading politicians who opposed that charter. The new Constitution, they argued, nowhere granted the federal government the power to charter corporations. Hamilton held that unless the Constitution prohibited an action, the action was constitutional. Madison argued that, to the contrary, unless the Constitution expressly authorized the action, it was unconstitutional. Thus arose the controversy over whether it was better to follow a "strict" or a "loose" construction, or interpretation, of the Constitution.

The Founders did not anticipate the emergence of a two-party system in American national politics. Yet during the first few years after the Constitution was ratified, a two-party system began to emerge. The two national parties came to be known, for a time, as the Federalists and the Democratic-Republicans.

Madison's political biography demonstrates that the "Federalists" of the struggle over whether to ratify the Constitution were by no means identical to the "Federalists" of the two-party system that emerged in the 1790s under the Constitution. Hamilton and Madison had served as the leading proponents of ratification. For a time, they worked together to achieve a goal they both shared. Soon, however, they became political opponents. Their views of just what the Constitution permitted grew very different, so they clashed. Those who resisted ratification in 1788 are known as Antifederalists. Those who opposed Hamilton's economic policies a few years later were known as Democratic-Republicans or Jeffersonians.

Not only did the two parties oppose each other's interpretation of the Constitution, they contested each other's power in national politics. Thomas Jefferson ran against John Adams in both 1796 and 1800. Jefferson lost in the first contest, over who would succeed Washington and become the nation's second president, but he won the rematch. Meanwhile, Madison declined to run for reelection to Congress in 1796 and instead retired to Montpelier, his plantation home in Virginia.

Between the elections of 1796 and 1800, the nation found itself caught up in European politics and in an undeclared war with France. Democratic-Republicans opposed administration policies in international affairs as well as domestic matters, and Federalists responded by passing the Alien and Sedition Acts in 1798 to muzzle the opposition party's leading politicians and journalists. In what became the Kentucky and Virginia Resolutions, Jefferson and Madison denied that Congress had the authority to pass such measures, which were therefore illegitimate.

Madison wrote in the Virginia Resolutions that the Alien and Sedition Acts were "unconstitutional." They trampled, he said, on "the authorities, rights, and liberties reserved to the states, respectively, or to the people" (in violation of the Tenth Amendment). The Sedition Act, in particular, exercised "a power not delegated by the Constitution, but, on the contrary, expressly and positively forbidden by one of the amendments thereto" (the First). Madison urged that "necessary and proper measures" be taken to prevent the enforcement of the offending laws. The crisis passed, however, when Jefferson defeated John Adams's bid in 1800 for reelection. The Federalists relinquished the presidency and allowed the political opposition to take power.

For all eight years of Thomas Jefferson's presidency, James Madison served as secretary of state. During that time, the Louisiana Purchase doubled the nation's territory, as both Jefferson and Madison determined that, though such an action was nowhere expressly sanctioned in the Constitution, it was nonetheless a permissible act of a sovereign nation.

The international context that gave rise to the Louisiana Purchase from France supplied a tremendous opportunity, but it also caused the nation grave danger and brought enormous challenges to leaders of the national government. For most of the quarter-century after the beginning of the French Revolution in 1789, the two superpowers of their time, France and England, were at war. The United States was constantly caught up in their titanic struggle, mostly because U.S. farmers and merchants wanted to engage in international trade, but neither France nor England wanted to see its enemy benefit from trade with the United States. Each side seized U.S. vessels, and the United States responded with trade embargoes and other measures to discourage such activities.

JAMES MADISON, PRESIDENT

That the new nation was hostage to the good behavior of the great powers was true during Jefferson's second term in office, and it remained true when Madison succeeded Jefferson as president in 1809. Moreover, Great Britain continued, from its Canadian colony, to provide Indians in the Old Northwest with arms and supplies and to encourage their resistance to U.S. expansion into that area. The combination of actions by the British in the West and on the high seas led Madison finally to ask Congress to declare war in June 1812. Later in 1812, Madison was elected to a second term in the White House, with the new nation once again at war with England, just as it had been when Madison entered public life back in the 1770s.

During the war, British forces invaded Washington, D.C., in August 1814 and forced President Madison to flee the nation's capital. New England Federalists, meeting at a convention in Hartford, Connecticut, muttered secession. Times were difficult and dangerous. England finally defeated France, however, and therefore no longer had so great a need to interfere with U.S. shipping. A peace treaty in December 1814 brought a conclusion to the war though no express resolution of the many issues that had led to the war in the first place. The nation had survived, and, with the war over, President Madison and Congress could turn to peacetime policies.

As in the 1780s, during the era of the War of 1812 Madison had seen the dangers of a weak national government. Despite his reservations about the constitutionality of the first Bank of the United States in the 1790s, he came to see that the nation had accepted the chartering of the bank as a legitimate function of the federal government. Seeing the necessity as well as the constitutionality of federal measures to promote economic growth and development, he now called for a new Bank of the United States, a tariff law that provided protection for U.S. manufacturing in addition to federal revenue, and a bill to promote road construction and other internal improvements. Thus did a leading strict constructionist of the 1790s call in late 1815 for a combination of federal policies that would later be hailed as the "American System."

As with Madison's reversal on a bill of rights, his reversal on a national bank reflected a changing political environment. Seeking to navigate his way down a middle way, he continued to display concern about too strong a national government and too weak a one, too broad an interpretation of the Constitution and too narrow a one. Congress enacted all three of his proposals in 1816, but he vetoed the internal improvements bill in the absence of a constitutional amendment that would authorize such a measure.

MADISON'S LEGACY

At the end of his second term as president in 1817, Madison retired from public life once again. In the years to come, he continued the struggle to find a middle way for ordered liberty to thrive between an overgrown national power and an exaggerated states' rights orientation. In addition, he had occasion to reconsider his conservative republican stance in the face of the democratic tendencies that, as in the Virginia constitutional convention of 1829–1830 (which he attended, the only delegate left from the 1776 Virginia convention), increasingly called for an extension of voting rights to all white men.

Madison died in June 1836, days before the sixtieth anniversary of the Declaration of Independence. During his long public life, Virginia and the United States had undergone various transformations. He had played central roles in political developments across the era of the American Revolution, during the framing and ratification of the Constitution and the Bill of Rights, through the War of 1812, and even beyond.

Madison left another legacy. At the Philadelphia convention in 1787, he had kept extensive notes regarding the proceedings. He would not permit those notes to be published until after his death, but they finally appeared in print in 1840. Scholars and citizens since then have been able to know much of what went on during the convention.

See also *American Revolution; Articles of Confederation; Bill of Rights; Constitution, Ratification; Constitution, U.S.; Constitutional Convention; Democratic Party; Federalists; Hartford Convention Resolutions; Jefferson, Thomas; Nullification; Political Parties; Presidency; Sedition Act of 1798; States' Rights/Sovereignty; Tariff History; War of 1812; Washington, George.*

PETER WALLENSTEIN,
VIRGINIA POLYTECHNIC INSTITUTE AND STATE UNIVERSITY

BIBLIOGRAPHY

Banning, Lance. *Sacred Fire of Liberty: James Madison and the Founding of the Federal Republic.* Ithaca: Cornell University Press, 1995.

Leibiger, Stuart. *Founding Friendship: George Washington, James Madison, and the Creation of the American Republic.* Charlottesville: University Press of Virginia, 1999.

McCoy, Drew R. *The Last of the Fathers: James Madison and the Republican Legacy.* Cambridge: Cambridge University Press, 1989.

Rutland, Robert Allen. *The Presidency of James Madison.* Lawrence: University Press of Kansas, 1990.

MANIFEST DESTINY

In 1845 American journalist John O'Sullivan coined the phrase "manifest destiny" in *The Democratic Review* to describe the supposedly providential right of the United States to "overspread the continent allotted by Providence for the free development of our yearly developing millions."

Since the early seventeenth century, with the colonization of New England in 1620, a strong tone of destiny had appeared in writings about America. It was to be the "New Jerusalem" or promised land for the Puritans. Such rhetoric survived into the eighteenth century. Tom Paine suggested (and he was not the first) that America was created by God to provide a haven for Protestant religious refugees. Even the Constitution expresses such views in its suggestion that the new republic would be "a more perfect Union," a nation with enlightened and democratic principles of government.

In the mid–nineteenth century, the United States was in the throes of the Jacksonian era's westward expansion. Manifest destiny was the justification for declaring war against Mexico in 1846 to acquire Texas, California, New Mexico, and Arizona; the United States also struggled through tense negotiations with the British to settle the northern boundary of Oregon Territory. Much of this expansion into the West was described in terms of destiny. By 1860 the *New York Times* editorialized from the obvious fact of America's geographical ecstasy—"there is no nation in the world . . . so thoroughly pervaded with the spirit of conquest—so filled with dreams of enlarged dominions." Such rhetoric had powerful effects. It is worth noting that in 1824 Mexico and the

United States were approximately the same size; in 1848 Mexico lost 40 percent of its territory to the United States in the Mexican-American War.

Oregon and Texas raised similar political debates—mixed Democratic enthusiasm and notable Whig reluctance toward expansion. In the so-called Oregon Dispute with England, Democratic president James K. Polk sought the western state as part of his inaugural promises. Democrats in the South, led by John C. Calhoun, would eventually favor the annexation of Texas, but seizing Oregon and going to war with England seemed to them to jeopardize cotton exports, and so they refused to back Polk's plans. Democrats in the North and Northwest, who had agreed to the annexation of Texas, were vexed that their southern counterparts would not also support territorial expansion in the West. Whigs, led by Daniel Webster, opposed Polk's visions of expansion, predicting increased sectional antagonism and slavery debates over new territories.

The American claims to Oregon were far more definite and defensible than were those to Texas, but Polk chose to back down from aggressive war over Oregon in favor of a southwestern battle. Texas presented southern Democrats with a more appealing prospect of expanding their "peculiar institution." Some northern Democrats opposed war over Texas, fearing that slavery would be permitted in the new territories.

The manifest destiny to expand played a role in the 1898 Spanish-American War. Unlike its earlier manifestation, however, American expansion at the end of the nineteenth century took place *outside* the limits of the American continent—in Hawaii, the Philippines, Cuba, Guam, Puerto Rico, and Panama—and the U.S. public for the most part was unwilling to consider the new territory for statehood because it was believed that "racially inferior" native populations would weaken American national character. Manifest destiny became U.S. foreign policy, authorized less by religious notions of providence than by a need for expanded markets and strategic bases.

Some historians question whether the notion of manifest destiny had an actual effect on American politics and policies in the nineteenth century, but the fact of American expansionism and its sympathetic descriptions make clear that the notion was at least the justification for those policies, if not their occasion.

In the twentieth century, manifest destiny was no longer invoked specifically to justify American policy, but some scholars have seen its imperializing remains in such events as the establishment of the League of Nations and the cold war.

See also *Cold War; Jackson, Andrew; McKinley, William; Mexican-American War; Sectionalism; Spanish-American War; Territorial Expansion; Territorial Government and New State Formation.*

KRIS FRESONKE, IOWA STATE UNIVERSITY

BIBLIOGRAPHY

Hietala, Thomas R. *Manifest Destiny: Anxious Aggrandizement in Late Jacksonian America.* Ithaca: Cornell University Press, 1985.

LaFeber, Walter. *The New Empire: An Interpretation of American Expansion, 1860–1898.* Ithaca: Cornell University Press, 1963.

Stephanson, Anders. *Manifest Destiny: American Expansion and the Empire of Right.* New York: Hill and Wang, 1995.

Weinberg, Albert K. *Manifest Destiny: A Study of Nationalist Expansionism in American History.* Baltimore: Johns Hopkins University Press, 1935.

MARCHES ON WASHINGTON

The idea of assembling in the nation's capital in order to redress grievances rests on a constitutionally guaranteed right of petition. But the first marches on Washington did not come until late in the nineteenth century, when western frontiers no longer offered the informal relief of a safety valve and reformers argued that the national government must play a larger role in an increasingly complex society.

EARLY MARCHES

Jacob S. Coxey, a quiet, middle-aged quarry owner, led the largest of several marches on Washington to promote economic relief from the recession of 1893. On Easter Sunday in 1894, one hundred unemployed workmen followed him from Massillon, Ohio, toward Washington in support of the Populist Party's program and the free coinage of silver. Coxey wanted to create employment and relax tight monetary policies by having the national government issue $500 million in legal tender notes, not backed by specie (that is, gold and silver), for a national road-building program. The marchers hoped to win 100,000 recruits on a six-week trek, but their numbers never exceeded five hundred. When they entered Washington peacefully on May 1, Coxey sought to read a petition from the Capitol steps. He and others were arrested for trespassing on public property. Other so-called industrial armies that planned to join him were disbanded, and the movement waned. Coxey celebrated the twentieth anniversary of his march with a repeat performance in 1914, and he lived to see his basic idea adopted by President Franklin D. Roosevelt in the New Deal. On the fiftieth anniversary of his march, in 1944, Coxey was allowed to ascend the Capitol steps and deliver the speech he had sought to give a half-century earlier.

To promote a national initiative for women's suffrage, Harriet Stanton Blatch led her Equality League on a march from New York City to Albany in December 1912. Three months later she led another march, over the 250 miles from New York City to Washington, D.C. There her followers joined eight thousand others, organized by Alice Paul of the National American Woman Suffrage Association (NAWSA), in the nation's first large parade of women. The police failed to protect them from assault by inebriated male bystanders, and part of the parade route turned into a mob scene. That event earned public sympathy for the suffragists, and, after a Senate inquiry, the police chief lost his job. Paul later turned the Washington office of NAWSA into an effective lobby for the enfranchisement of women in the adoption of the Nineteenth Amendment.

As the campaign for women's suffrage reached its climax, the Ku Klux Klan was reborn on Stone Mountain, Georgia. By 1924 the Klan claimed to hold authority over the nomination of presidents and to control some members of Congress and many state and local officials. Despite internal struggles and rumors of its decline, the Klan massed its largest demonstration on August 8, 1925. Imperial Wizard Hiram W. Evans led between forty thousand and sixty thousand robed Klan members down Pennsylvania Avenue to the Washington Monument in opposition to the United States's adherence to the World Court. A cloudburst ended the Klan's program for the day, but it reconvened the next day to lay wreaths at the tombs of the Unknown Soldier and William Jennings Bryan and to burn an enormous cross in Arlington, Virginia. In 1926 the Klan's decline was evident when its march attracted only half the previous year's numbers.

In the depths of the Great Depression, in May 1932, between twelve thousand and fifteen thousand mostly unemployed veterans of World War I marched on Washington to ask Congress to authorize early payment of their World War I bonus certificates, which were not scheduled to mature until 1945. The government allowed the veterans to encamp in temporary shacks near the Capitol. After Congress rejected proposals for prepayment of the bonuses in late June, most of the veterans left. By late July about two thousand unemployed veterans, having no other place to go, still lived in the shacks they had erected. Fearing communist-inspired demonstrations and possible violence, President Herbert Hoover ordered the U.S. Army to disperse the remaining bonus seekers. On July 28, 1932, federal troops commanded by Chief of Staff Gen. Douglas MacArthur used tear gas and riot weapons to scatter the remaining veterans and set fire to their shacks. Hoover's use of troops against their former comrades-in-arms was widely criticized and contributed to his defeat by Roosevelt later that year.

CIVIL RIGHTS MARCHES

In 1941, at the outset of World War II, employment discrimination against African Americans in government and industry was common. A. Philip Randolph, president of the Brotherhood of Sleeping Car Porters and Maids, summoned 50,000 to 100,000 people to march on Washington in protest in early July. President Roosevelt wanted to avoid signs of domestic unrest during the mobilization for war. On June 25, a week before the march was to occur, he issued Executive Order 8802, which banned racial discrimination in defense plants, where black workers had been widely excluded from employment. Only then did Randolph cancel plans for the march.

Five civil rights marches on Washington occurred between 1957 and 1968. The first three marches protested the Eisenhower administration's failure to address civil rights issues between 1957 and 1959. They were led by Randolph and Martin Luther King Jr. and were coordinated by Randolph's assistant, Bayard Rustin. Roy Wilkins of the National Association for the Advancement of Colored People (NAACP) joined them in a Prayer Pilgrimage to Washington on May 17, 1957. Rustin had hoped that fifty thousand people would attend, but only fifteen thousand to twenty-seven thousand appeared. King spoke at the end of the program. His cry, "Give us the ballot," won media attention as the message of the Prayer Pilgrimage. A year later Randolph announced that a coalition of organizations would hold a Youth March for Integrated Schools on October 11, 1958, with King as honorary chairman. Wilkins and the NAACP did not participate. When an assailant wounded King in September, the march was delayed until October 25. Only eleven thousand people, mostly college students, appeared for the first Youth March. Six months later, Randolph announced a second Youth March for Integrated Schools. About twenty-six thousand people appeared for the second march on April 18, 1959. Attendance at these marches for desegregation and voting rights was disappointing, never rising to the size of the Klan marches over thirty years earlier, but they were among the few events in the late 1950s that anticipated the burst of civil rights activity to follow in the early 1960s.

Early in 1963, Randolph, King, and Rustin agreed that it was time for a massive march on Washington. By June, Wilkins of the NAACP, Whitney Young of the National Urban League, James Farmer of the Congress of Racial Equality (CORE), John Lewis of the Student Nonviolent Coordinating Committee (SNCC), and King agreed to cochair the March on Washington, with Randolph as its national director and Rustin as deputy director. Subsequently, four prominent white leaders joined as cochairs. Between 200,000 and 300,000 people gathered on August 28, 1963, at the Lincoln Memorial in Washington. Lewis resolved a last-minute conflict by agreeing to modify the tone of his speech in deference to objections by Washington's Patrick Cardinal O'Boyle, who gave the invocation. At the end of a long program, ABC, CBS, and NBC broadcast live television coverage of the move-

economic policy, a guaranteed annual income, and funds for the construction of 500,000 units of low-cost housing per year. King sensed the campaign's success was a long shot. CORE, the NAACP, SNCC, and the National Urban League gave it no support, and Rustin was publicly critical of it. A King-led demonstration on March 28 in support of Memphis's sanitation workers ended in violence. The media predicted a similar end to the Poor People's March, and, a week later, King was assassinated. His death prompted greater support, and his successor, Ralph D. Abernathy, pursued plans for the Poor People's March on Washington. Buses of poor people began arriving in Washington on May 11. Resurrection City, the demonstrators' camp of canvas, plywood, and tarpaper near the Washington Monument, was meant to dramatize the plight of poor people. Rain turned it into a muddy, squalid center of petty crime. Sterling

The National Mall, from the Washington Monument to the Lincoln Memorial, is packed with people during the August 28, 1963, March on Washington. *Library of Congress*

ment's largest mass meeting, and Randolph introduced King as "the moral leader of our nation." King began a prepared text before abandoning it for an extemporaneous rendering of his "I Have a Dream" speech. King had given the speech, a patchwork of ideas and themes he had been using for years, in Birmingham and Detroit in the previous six months. Yet, fed by an enthusiastic response from this vast audience, the speech took on fresh power and vitality. King's "I Have a Dream" speech outlived all the other speeches given that day. When King stepped aside, Rustin asked the audience to endorse the march's goals: passage of the Kennedy administration's civil rights bill, a $2 per hour minimum wage, school desegregation, a federal public works program, and federal action to bar racial discrimination in employment. Far larger than any prior march on Washington, the 1963 demonstration would be surpassed in numbers by subsequent gatherings, yet it was the benchmark against which they were measured, and it alone is called simply the March on Washington. A crowd of similar size marked its twentieth anniversary in 1983.

The last of the civil rights movement's five marches, the Poor People's March on Washington, began in King's belief after 1965 that the movement had to address the problem of poverty. In January 1968 he announced that the minimal demands of a Poor People's March would be a full-employment

Tucker of the National Urban League coordinated plans for a Solidarity Day on June 19, which attracted fifty thousand people. Five days later, when the march's camping permit expired, District of Columbia police moved in to raze Resurrection City. Abernathy and three hundred others were arrested as they marched on the Capitol to protest the police action. Shortly thereafter, the SCLC evacuated Washington, D.C., with minor concessions from several federal agencies.

ANTIWAR MARCHES

The first march on Washington to protest the war in Vietnam, on April 17, 1965, was organized by the Students for a Democratic Society. With twenty thousand people, it was the largest peace demonstration the nation's capital had seen. The numbers grew as the war escalated. The Committee for a Sane Nuclear Policy brought thirty thousand people to Washington in November 1966. President Richard Nixon's announcement of plans to de-escalate the war early in 1969 only convinced its opponents that he would pursue it indefinitely. In the next two years, shifting alliances of political radicals, conscientious liberals, pacifists, religious leaders, and antiwar veterans coordinated dramatically larger demonstrations in Washington. On November 15, 1969, the Vietnam Moratorium Committee and the New Mobilization Committee brought 500,000 to 600,000 people to Washington for the largest demonstration in the nation's history. It included lobbying, rallies, concerts, speeches, and an unscheduled attack on the South Vietnamese embassy. The March Against Death, beginning on November 13, was more dramatic. For thirty-eight hours, a candle-lit procession bearing placards with the names of each American killed in the war wound through high winds and rain from Arlington National Cemetery past the White House to the Capitol, where the placards were placed in wooden coffins. Another 350,000 people demonstrated against the war on the same weekend in San Francisco.

Even so, the Nixon administration continued to pursue the increasingly unpopular war, attempting to assuage American public opinion by measured withdrawals of American troops. Vietnam Veterans Against the War became increasingly visible in subsequent months. In the spring of 1971, after a memorial service for fallen comrades at Arlington, organization members limped, marched, and rode their wheelchairs toward the Capitol, where they threw away their war medals in a display of anger at Congress's failure to end the war. On April 24, 1971, between 300,000 and 500,000 others joined the veterans to demand an immediate end to America's role in the war. In San Francisco, 150,000 demonstrators made the same demand. On May 3, 1971, radical activists tried to shut down Washington by blocking bridges and major highways with stalled automobiles, debris, and their bodies. Invoking authority near martial law, Nixon's Justice Department broke the blockade by ordering the indiscriminate arrest of twelve thousand people in the largest mass jailing in the nation's history.

MARCHES SINCE THE 1960s

Another movement borne of the 1960s, women's liberation or second-wave feminism, was responsible for most of the marches on Washington after 1970. In 1972 the movement won major victories in congressional passage of the Equal Employment Opportunity Act and the Equal Rights Amendment (ERA). Written by Alice Paul in 1921, the ERA had been introduced in every session of Congress since 1923. The requirement that thirty-eight state legislatures ratify the amendment shifted the campaign's focus to the state level, but the National Organization for Women (NOW) rallied 40,000 to 100,000 supporters in Washington on July 9, 1978, to hear former representative Bella Abzug, D-N.Y.; feminist authors Betty Friedan and Gloria Steinem; Equal Employment Opportunities Commission director Eleanor Holmes Norton; and NOW president Eleanor Smeal demand an extension of the seven-year limit on state ratification. An extension was in fact granted, but when the new ten-year limit expired, the ERA had been ratified by only thirty-five state legislatures, several of which subsequently sought to revoke their action.

The Supreme Court's controversial January 22, 1973, decision in *Roe v. Wade,* which protected a woman's right to have an abortion, led to more marches on Washington. Antiabortion forces have subsequently gathered annually on January 22 for a vigil against the Court's decision. Their estimated numbers reached as high as sixty-seven thousand in 1989. On April 9 of that year, NOW recruited Abzug, Friedan, Smeal, Steinem, actress Jane Fonda, and NOW president Molly Yard to lead some 300,000 prochoice marchers. Three years later, about 500,000 prochoice demonstrators marched on Washington. These marchers were 90 percent white, 75 percent female, and 50 percent under age thirty, and they tended to be more affluent, liberal residents of the Northeast.

Advocates of gay and lesbian rights mounted significant marches in this period as well. Their 1987 march on Washington attracted about 200,000 people. Police estimated that some 300,000 persons heard Rep. Barney Frank, D-Mass.; the Reverend Jesse Jackson; and tennis star Martina Navratilova demand rights for gay and lesbian people on April 25, 1993.

By mid-decade there were quantitative changes in the analysis of the marches, qualitative changes in their character, and gender shifts in their composition. Disparity was growing between sponsors' claims for attendance at the marches and official estimates of the crowd size given by the National Park Service police. Sponsors' estimates were sometimes three times that of the police. In response to these disparities, organizations on both sides of disputed issues sought other approaches to the numbers game. In 1992 the National Women's Coalition for Life claimed to speak for 1.5 million women, compared with NOW's 280,000. In 1993 a NOW-sponsored march for breast cancer research attracted only one thousand people, but NOW bore petitions with 2.8 million signatures.

Beyond the quantitative change, a qualitative transition and a gender shift occurred between the gay rights march of 1993 and the Million Man March of October 16, 1995. The consciousness raising of women's liberation might lead to advocacy of a social agenda, but it was intensified in gay liberation, where the process of publicly defining or "outing" oneself was for its partisans more intense, making public policy advocacy a more certain consequence.

With little reason to doubt who they were, the African American men who marched on Washington in 1995 nonetheless confirmed the "interiorization" of the decade's marches on Washington by having no explicit public policy agenda. Officially called a Day of Atonement, the march emphasized black male responsibility and solidarity. Its controversial leadership by the Nation of Islam's Louis Farrakhan and its lack of a policy agenda kept longtime civil rights stalwarts Judge A. Leon Higginbotham and Rep. John Lewis, D-Ga., on the sidelines that day. Black women were not invited to participate in the march, but poet Maya Angelou; Malcolm X's widow, Betty Shabazz; and civil rights pioneer Rosa Parks were added to the program to avoid giving offense. Washington mayor Marion Berry, former NAACP executive director Benjamin Chavis, the Reverend Jesse Jackson, NAACP president Kweisi Mfiume, and the Reverend Al Sharpton preceded Farrakhan's two-hour stint at the podium. The official estimate of the crowd's size at 400,000 was so controversial and so far from the sponsors' claim of 1.5 million marchers that Congress subsequently banned the National Park Police from estimating crowd size.

The Promise Keepers' march of October 4, 1997, was officially called Standing in the Gap: A Sacred Assembly of Men. Led by Colorado football coach William McCartney, Promise Keepers began holding regional rallies in 1990. By 1995 more than a million men had attended its rallies at twenty-two stadiums around the country. The national climax two years later seemed to confirm tendencies in the decade's marches on Washington. Lacking official estimates of the crowd size, its sponsors offered assurances that it was tens or hundreds of thousands. Informally they might claim 500,000. No women appeared on the program. One-seventh of the marchers were African Americans, but on average the crowd was more affluent, conservative, and Republican than the nation at large. These men were grappling in a variety of ways with shifting gender roles and family structures, but they came for a day of personal repentance and prayer, not to espouse an explicit public policy agenda. Within a year, Promise Keepers disbanded most of its staff, and attendance at its regional rallies was in decline.

In April 2000, marches on Washington reverted to type as women marched and large crowds promoted specific public policies: environmentalists and labor unions marched against the policies of the International Monetary Fund and the World Bank, environmentalists celebrated Earth Day, gays and lesbians held a Millennium March on Washington, and television talk show host Rosie O'Donnell led a Million Mom March for gun control.

CONCLUSION

Marches on Washington have never guaranteed participants' accomplishment of their goals. Often they have confronted formal or informal hostility. More often, however, they have been harbingers of significant change in national social policy. On balance, they seem to have functioned well as a safety valve, allowing citizens to put the nation's lawmakers, administrators, and judges on notice regarding points of public policy that need careful scrutiny.

See also *Bonus March; Civil Rights Acts (Modern); Civil Rights Movement; Civil Unrest and Rioting; Coxey's Army; Equal Rights Amendment; Reproductive Rights; Suffrage; Vietnam War; Woman's Suffrage Movement.*

RALPH LUKER, VIRGINIA FOUNDATION FOR THE HUMANITIES

BIBLIOGRAPHY

Chalmers, David M. *Hooded Americanism*. Durham: Duke University Press, 1987.

Chatfield, Charles. *The American Peace Movement: Ideals and Activism*. New York: Twayne Publishers, 1992.

Luker, Ralph E. *Historical Dictionary of the Civil Rights Movement*. Lanham, Md.: Scarecrow Press, 1997.

Weatherford, Doris. *A History of the American Suffragist Movement*. Santa Barbara: ABC-CLIO, 1998.

McCARTHYISM

McCarthyism is the name given to political repression in the late 1940s and into the 1950s, at the beginning of the cold war. It was directed at American citizens charged with activities supporting communism and the Soviet Union. Coming in the aftermath of World War II, it resembled in broad outline the Red Scare that followed World War I.

Anticommunist crusaders, especially Republican senator Joseph McCarthy, but others before and after him as well, adopted tactics of suspicion, false information, character assassination, and blatant intimidation in their search for domestic subversion. Whether for personal political gain or out of real concern for national security, the junior senator from Wisconsin (1947–1957) and his supporters were able to operate with relative impunity after a series of foreign policy setbacks occurred in 1949 and 1950. The fall of China to communism in 1949, Soviet development of atomic weapons, which broke the U.S. monopoly on the bomb, and a U.S. policy in the Korean War that was less than a full commitment to victory convinced many Americans that liberals, and Democrats in particular, within the State Department had betrayed their country by leaking top secret materials to the Soviet Union. Recent revelations from newly open Soviet archives lend credence to some of McCarthy's charges and have convinced an increasing number of scholars that the Soviet Union ran a far larger espionage operation in the United States than his opponents were willing to admit. Most of those investigated by McCarthy, however, turned out to be innocent of the charges, but their careers—and sometimes their lives—were ruined in the process. The term *McCarthyism* has continued to be used to describe political attacks that display little respect for the truth or civil liberties.

COLD WAR SUSPICION

McCarthy appropriated tactics initiated earlier in 1947 by conservative Republicans controlling the House Un-American Activities Committee (HUAC) in their investigation of communist influences in the government and other areas of national life, including higher education and the movie and entertainment industries. Critics generally deplored the committee's methods from the start, but two celebrated spy cases added to its political powers.

The first involved Julius and Ethel Rosenberg, a seemingly ordinary couple with two young sons. The Rosenbergs were convicted of passing sensitive atomic secrets to the Soviets as accomplices of Klaus Fuchs. Although historians have been divided over the extent of Julius's guilt, the evidence indicates that at the most Ethel was only peripherally involved in espionage and that her arrest, conviction, and pending execution were ploys to force her husband to name names. The couple was told that both their lives would be spared if they confessed, but they adamantly refused to admit to any guilt and were executed in June 1953.

The second case was an investigation involving Whittaker Chambers, the editor of *Time* magazine and a former communist, and Alger Hiss, a former assistant secretary of state and an icon of the liberal elite of the time. Hiss was serving as president of the Carnegie Endowment for International Peace when Chambers accused him of having been a member of the Communist Party during the 1930s. Hiss denied the charge and sued Chambers for libel; Chambers then accused Hiss of being a Soviet spy. The matter received little attention from the public until a young Republican member of Congress, Richard Nixon, got Hiss to admit under oath that he had once known Chambers. Hiss was indicted for perjury, and the public became convinced of the existence of an internal communist threat. In the wake of these two sensational cases, few could oppose the committee's powers without appearing disloyal themselves.

The administration of Harry S. Truman, in an attempt to deflect criticism that it had been soft on communism, initiated its own Federal Loyalty Program in 1947, purging from government employment all those considered security risks. In addition, the FBI under the direction of J. Edgar Hoover provided clandestine operations and bureaucratic backing for the climate of suspicion and fear necessary for McCarthyism to flourish.

McCARTHY'S CAREER

McCarthy began his meteoric rise to power on February 9, 1950, when he gave an electrifying speech at Wheeling, West Virginia, holding a piece of paper in the air and claiming that it listed the names of 205 communists or communist sympathizers currently operating within the State Department. Although he never actually produced the list and the number of suspects dropped dramatically over the following weeks, McCarthy, with the help of future president Richard Nixon, then a junior House member, and others, was made chairman of a Senate investigating subcommittee that flatly accused the Democratic administrations of the past twenty years of treason.

McCarthy defined communism so broadly that any American who had supported a liberal cause was suspect. He accused Owen Lattimore, a State Department expert on Asia, of being the head of an espionage ring. A special investigation proved this charge groundless, but McCarthy deflected criticism by naming more suspects. Democrats

U.S. Rep. Richard M. Nixon of California (left), a member of the House Un-American Activities Subcommittee, aggressively investigated the loyalty of many people, including Dr. Edward U. Condon (right). Condon was director of the National Bureau of Standards and a noted atomic scientist. Subcommittee chairman John McDowell of Pennsylvania stands between them in this March 1948 photograph. *Library of Congress*

who opposed McCarthy found themselves labeled as soft on communism, a charge, no matter how far-fetched, that could put their political future in jeopardy. Most remained silent, leading to the impression that the senator from Wisconsin was invincible.

Gen. Dwight D. Eisenhower, the Republican candidate for president in 1952, was among those reluctant to offend him. Eisenhower allowed McCarthy to help him campaign in Wisconsin, even though in 1951 the senator had accused Secretary of Defense George C. Marshall, one of the nation's most distinguished military and civilian leaders, of "a conspiracy of infamy so black, that when it is finally exposed, its principles shall be forever deserving of the maledictions of all honest men." After Eisenhower was elected president, the senator continued for a year to operate unhampered.

McCarthy's dominance ended shortly after he questioned the loyalty of the new president and that of Secretary of the Army Robert Stevens. Overworked, drinking heavily, and no longer realistic about his objectives, McCarthy turned his attention toward the epitome of American patriotism, the U.S. Army. Eisenhower retaliated by calling for a special investigation, which became known as the Army-McCarthy hearings. Ostensibly, the hearings were called to determine if McCarthy had acted improperly in seeking privileges for his former assistant, G. David Schine, an army private. In reality, the president and a growing number of congressional supporters used the televised hearings to give the public the opportunity to see McCarthy in action. For two months, McCarthy bullied witnesses, doctored evidence, and told lies clearly discernible by Americans in their living rooms. His public support evaporated. Matters came to a head June 9, 1954, when McCarthy accused Frederick G. Fisher Jr., a law associate associated with the army defense team, of belonging to a subversive organization. The army's chief counsel, Joseph N. Welch, asked McCarthy, "Have you no sense of decency, sir, at long last? Have you left no sense of decency?"

In December 1954 the Senate voted, 67–22, to censure McCarthy for contempt of the Senate. McCarthy continued in office, but he was excluded from Washington society and died in 1957 from complications associated with alcoholism. His die-hard supporters claimed that he had been murdered by liberal forces fearful of future revelations. The phenomenon of McCarthyism continued for a number of years until the 1962 missile crisis, in which Soviet missiles were found in Cuba, and the Vietnam War in the middle years of the decade. With more immediate military problems to solve, the government and public directed considerably less effort toward searching for domestic subversion.

McCarthyism's legacy was considerable. Not only had it brought democracy into grave disrepute overseas at the very time the nation was attempting to offer a moral alternative to communism, it also purged the State Department and other vital government agencies of some of their brightest and most dedicated employees. In light of how their colleagues had been treated, few of those who remained were willing to offer views supportive of peaceful coexistence with the Soviets out of fear that they too would be charged with treason.

See also *Cold War; Eisenhower, Dwight D.; Korean War; Red Scare; Truman, Harry S.; Vietnam War.*

LORI BOGLE, UNITED STATES NAVAL ACADEMY

BIBLIOGRAPHY

Fariello, Griffin, ed. *Red Scare: Memories of the American Inquisition—An Oral History.* New York: W. W. Norton, 1995.

Goldston, Robert C. *The American Nightmare: Senator Joseph R. McCarthy and the Politics of Hate.* Indianapolis: Bobbs-Merrill, 1973.

Oshinsky, David M. *A Conspiracy So Immense: The World of Joe McCarthy.* New York: Free Press, 1983.

Powers, Richard Gid. *Not Without Honor: The History of American Anticommunism.* New York: Free Press, 1995.

Schrecker, Ellen. *Many Are the Crimes: McCarthyism in America.* Boston: Little, Brown, 1998.

McKINLEY, WILLIAM

As the twenty-fifth president (1897–1901), William McKinley (1843–1901) laid the foundation for the modern form of the presidency, especially through his use of the war powers during and after the Spanish-American War (1898).

Born in Niles, Ohio, William McKinley served in the Civil War with the Twenty-Third Ohio Volunteers and attained the rank of major. He then practiced law in Canton, Ohio. He was elected to the House of Representatives in 1876 and served there until he was defeated in 1890. He rose to become chairman of the House Ways and Means Committee and was responsible for the drafting and enactment of the McKinley Tariff of 1890, a measure that raised customs duties on American products. He was elected governor of Ohio in 1891 and reelected in 1893. McKinley was by now identified as a primary advocate of the protective tariff, a key doctrinal element of the Republican electoral appeal. He had developed into one of the most popular speakers among Midwestern Republicans in the 1890s. In 1896 he received the Republican nomination for president and defeated the Democratic candidate, William Jennings Bryan. McKinley campaigned from the front porch of his home in Canton and attracted three-quarters of a million people to his daily appearances. Combined with his advocacy of the gold standard, his effective canvass brought him the most decisive victory since Ulysses S. Grant had defeated Horace Greeley in 1872.

William McKinley *Library of Congress*

McKinley took office at a time when the presidency was at a low ebb. Grover Cleveland had been repudiated because of the panic of 1893 and such controversies as Coxey's Army and the Pullman strike that occurred as a result of the economic downturn. A generation of congressional supremacy had shifted the balance of power in Washington against the White House. Accordingly, McKinley sought to revive the powers of his office. He devoted constant attention to improving relations with the press. It was he, not Theodore Roosevelt, who established a designated area in the White House for the reporters who covered him. The president's personal secretary, George B. Cortelyou, took the lead in evolving procedures to improve relations with the White House journalists. He instituted a system of advance texts for speeches, facilities for reporters who traveled with the president on his frequent trips, and a process of tracking press coverage for the White House staff and McKinley.

McKinley's major foreign policy crisis during his first two years in office was the dispute with Spain over Cuba. The president endeavored to work out a peaceful resolution of the problem that would see Spain leave the Caribbean island. The crisis came to a head during the winter of 1898, especially after the battleship USS *Maine* exploded in Havana harbor on February 15, 1898. That sensational incident inflamed American public opinion and reduced the time in which Spain and the United States could find a peaceful resolution of their differences. After difficult and unproductive negotiations in the spring of 1898 Madrid and Washington chose war when neither side would back down from its position. The United States wanted Spanish withdrawal from Cuba; that Spain would not accept.

In the war that followed, McKinley directed the conflict from the war room at the White House, where telegraph lines kept him in touch with the commander in the field in Cuba. To secure supply lines to the western Pacific, the president used his influence with key lawmakers on Capitol Hill to obtain the votes needed to annex Hawaii.

Other foreign policy problems emerged in the Pacific in the wake of American military successes. After the victory of Commodore George Dewey at Manila Bay on May 1, 1898, McKinley shaped diplomacy to give the United States the option of acquiring the Philippine Islands in the peace settlement.

The fighting between Spain and the United States ended in an armistice brokered by France in August 1898. The United States now had control of Cuba, Puerto Rico, Guam, and the Philippines. Knowing that he would have to win Senate approval for any treaty that ended the war, McKinley sent lawmakers who would later vote on the treaty on the American peace commission to participate in the talks with Spain. Meanwhile, McKinley laid the groundwork at home for gaining legislative endorsement of the treaty. During the autumn of 1898 he made a speaking tour of the Midwest that roused support for acquiring the Philippines.

As the negotiations went on in Paris, McKinley determined that the United States could not return the Philippines to Spain or relinquish them to a foreign power such as Japan or Germany. Believing that no viable Filipino Republic was possible, in late October he decided that the United States must take all of the archipelago in the negotiations over the end of the war. The Treaty of Paris, signed in December 1898, gave the United States the Philippines as McKinley had specified.

During the struggle to ratify the pact in late 1898 and early 1899, McKinley again made a speaking tour of the southern states to win over wavering Democratic senators from that region. He also pressured other lawmakers through the use of patronage and other presidential favors. These efforts culminated in the approval of the treaty on February 6, 1899.

In the Philippines, inhabitants of the island resisted militarily the American occupation that had begun in May 1898. American troops and Filipinos had coexisted uneasily until fighting broke out in February 1899. To curb the insurrection against American authority, McKinley relied on the war power of the president. He directed the military effort to subdue the Filipino resistance and also established a framework of civilian government prior to any formal congressional action. He used a similar rationale to establish a government in the conquered islands of Cuba and Puerto Rico. McKinley's expansive use of the war power to govern the new empire became one of his most important contributions to the modern presidency.

In 1900 the Boxer Uprising occurred in China against the presence of foreigners in the country. The upheaval threatened the lives of westerners in the country's capital, and European nations dispatched troops to relieve the embattled garrison. McKinley sent American troops as part of the international relief expedition into a nation with which the United States was not at war. The president did so at a time when Congress was not in session. An important precedent for executive action in foreign affairs had been established. By the end of McKinley's first term, his political opponents were complaining about the expansion of presidential power that had taken place during his administration.

McKinley was nominated for a second term in 1900 with Theodore Roosevelt of New York as his running mate. The president defeated William Jennings Bryan and the Democrats by an even larger margin than four years earlier. By early 1901 the president pushed through Congress legislation to establish officially a civil government for the Philippines that confirmed what the president had been doing for several years. McKinley also secured adoption of the Platt Amendment, which gave the United States a veto over the foreign policy of the new Cuban republic.

In his second term, McKinley planned to break a precedent and travel outside the United States. He also contemplated actions to enforce the Sherman Antitrust Act against the growing power of large corporations. Now convinced that lower trade barriers were in the national interest, he also endorsed reciprocal trade treaties to reduce protective tariff rates. McKinley was pursuing the second of these policies in Buffalo, New York, at the Pan-American Exposition in September 1901. His speech calling for reciprocity in international trade won applause as an enlightened change in Republican doctrine. The next day, September 6, 1901, he was shot as he stood in a receiving line, and he died eight days later.

McKinley was a major political figure of the late nineteenth century and the architect of Republican electoral success in 1896. Though his innovations as a chief executive have been overshadowed by Theodore Roosevelt, McKinley was a pioneer in creating the modern form of the presidential office.

See also *Coxey's Army; Panic of 1893; Spanish-American War; Tariff History.*

LEWIS L. GOULD, UNIVERSITY OF TEXAS AT AUSTIN

BIBLIOGRAPHY

Gould, Lewis L. *The Presidency of William McKinley.* Lawrence: University Press of Kansas, 1980.
Leech, Margaret. *In the Days of McKinley.* New York: Harper and Row, 1959.
Morgan, H. Wayne. *William McKinley and His America.* Syracuse: Syracuse University Press, 1963.

MEXICAN-AMERICAN WAR

After the United States annexed the Republic of Texas in 1845, tension between Mexico and the United States led to the Mexican-American War (1846–1848), which resulted in Mexico ceding 40 percent of its territory to the United States—land that is now Texas, California, New Mexico, and Arizona.

HISTORY

Mexico gained independence from Spain in 1821. The Northwest Province of Texas was inhabited in the early nineteenth century chiefly by American citizens, whom Mexico welcomed as its new citizens. They were received warmly by Mexico as a vitalizing economic presence. However, the Anglo population in Texas formed a separate enclave within Mexican territory, revolted against the Mexican government in the so-called Texas Revolution, and created an independent Texas republic in 1836. Mexico did not recognize the republic and hoped to reclaim the territory someday.

In the 1830s in the United States, the Democratic Party ushered in a period of expansionist struggles and wars. The rationale for taking over Mexican territory to allow Americans to sweep westward, an expansionist mission known as "manifest destiny," was that Mexico had made nothing of its lands. Yankee ingenuity, reasoned Jacksonian Democrats throughout the 1840s, would turn barren deserts into blooming oases. It was only fitting, so the argument went, that the lands belong to those whose supposed Anglo-Saxon racial superiority would help them properly manage the territory. Jacksonian views of Mexico—part racism and part delusions of grandeur—were fairly typical of the American mindset in the nineteenth century. When the Anglo settlers of the Texas republic sought annexation to the United States in 1845, half of Congress (the Democratic half) reasoned that, given the choice between a Mexican Texas and an American Texas, it was morally suitable for Texas to be joined to a white, not a "racially inferior," nation.

The annexation of Texas was a divisive political issue because it raised again the major crisis of the nineteenth century: slavery. Would Texas be a free or slave state? The Whig Party denounced the Texas annexation as a "slaveocracy conspiracy" by southerners, and Whigs, no particular friends of Mexico, found themselves having to defend Mexican territorial claims to Texas from the 1830s, rather than accept the expansion of U.S. territory and thus slavery.

The Democrats were not united behind James Polk's ambitions to expand into the southwest, but after Polk won the presidential election in 1844 despite all the disagreements about his expansionist policies, there seemed to be a clear mandate for the annexation of Texas. Polk sent diplomat Joseph Slidell to Mexico in 1845 to purchase California and New Mexico, but this mission, never expected to succeed, fell far short of its goal. Congress had seriously debated a policy of "all Mexico," or the conquest of the whole territory, and eventually compromised to get in line with Polk's less ambitious seizure of almost half of the country.

Gen. Zachary Taylor had his troops on the Rio Grande violate the borderline and provoke Mexican troops to move north across the river and attack American soldiers. Thereafter, both the Mexicans and the Americans maintained that they were fighting a defensive war.

AN ACT OF AGGRESSION

President Polk declared that the advance of Mexican troops north of the Rio Grande was an act of aggression on American territory, and on May 13, 1846, the United States declared war. General Taylor won major victories early in the war, such as Buena Vista, and press coverage of the battles in the United States was largely favorable. The war, depending on one's point of view in the nineteenth century, became either a confirmation of American territorial promise or a disaster of foreign policy and of the crisis over slavery. Taylor and his troops took Mexico City in 1847, and the war ended in 1848.

AFTERMATH

Mexicans still call the war "la guerra de la Independencia Mexicana," but it was chiefly portrayed in the United States as an assertion of territorial prerogative. The Treaty of Guadalupe-Hidalgo gave the United States most of its present southwestern territories, and Mexico received an indemnity of $15 million. Gleeful expansionists murmured that Europe, with vague, lingering claims to American territories, would now find it difficult to defend them; others found in the victory the decisiveness that many felt Americans needed.

Historians still debate whether the Mexican-American War led to the Civil War by extending the slavery debate into vast new geographical areas. Many of the officers who served

in Mexico under General Taylor later met one another across the battle lines in the Civil War. Ulysses S. Grant, for instance, first saw action at the battle of Resaca de Palma, and along the way met his future opponent, Robert E. Lee. The war was an early prototype of U.S. imperialism, a political and military undertaking that dominated the nineteenth century.

See also *Free Soil Party; Manifest Destiny; Polk, James K.; Sectionalism; Taylor, Zachary; Territorial Expansion.*

KRIS FRESONKE, IOWA STATE UNIVERSITY

BIBLIOGRAPHY

Hietala, Thomas R. *Manifest Design: Anxious Aggrandizement in the Late Jacksonian Era.* Ithaca: Cornell University Press, 1985.
Horsman, Reginald. *Race and Manifest Destiny: The Origins of American Racial Anglo-Saxonism.* Cambridge: Harvard University Press, 1981.
Johannsen, Robert W. *To the Halls of the Montezumas: The Mexican War in the American Imagination.* New York: Oxford University Press, 1985.
Limerick, Patricia Nelson. *The Legacy of Conquest: The Unbroken Past of the American West.* New York: Norton, 1987.

MISSOURI COMPROMISE

The Missouri Compromise, a series of measures passed by Congress in 1820, was intended to settle sectional rivalry over the extension of slavery into the territories. It was a fundamental part of the national compromise until it was partially undone by the Kansas-Nebraska Act of 1854 and then declared unconstitutional by the Supreme Court in *Dred Scott v. Sandford* (1857). The Missouri Compromise remained a political issue for the rest of the 1850s, and support for it in the North, as well as northern anger at the statute and decision undermining it, helped elect Abraham Lincoln president.

A DELICATE BALANCE

While operating under the Articles of Confederation, the national Congress passed the Northwest Ordinance of 1787, which stated: "there shall be neither slavery nor involuntary servitude" in the territory north and west of the Ohio River. This language did not lead to an immediate end to slavery in the region, and some blacks were held in bondage in Illinois as late as the 1840s, but the law created a political and cultural expectation that new states created in the Old Northwest (as the region was called) would be free states.

At the time Congress adopted the Northwest Ordinance the national territory did not extend west of the Mississippi River, but the Louisiana Purchase of 1803 altered the nation's political geography. When Missouri sought admission to the Union in 1819, northerners, led by Rep. James Tallmadge Jr.

of New York, proposed that no new slaves could be brought into the state and that the institution of slavery be ended through a gradual emancipation process. Tallmadge and his allies argued that Missouri should be a free state because it lay almost wholly north of the line set by the Northwest Ordinance to separate slave states from nonslave states. The Senate defeated this amended bill when a few northern senators joined a solid bloc of southern senators. Congress adjourned, and agitation about Missouri swept North and South, with threats of secession on both sides.

Congress reassembled in early 1820, with the Jeffersonians in a chastened mood. The crisis over Missouri statehood threatened to break up the monopoly on power they had enjoyed since the demise of the Federalist Party in the wake of the War of 1812. Thomas Jefferson, founder of the Democratic-Republicans, was fearful of what the controversy meant for the Union: "[T]his momentous question, like a fire bell in the night, awakened and filled me with terror. I considered it at once as the knell of the Union." Jefferson was not concerned with the status of slavery in the nation, and he opposed any action on emancipation. Rather, he feared that the angry debate over slavery in Congress would unleash passions that would undermine not only national harmony, but the power of his political party, by then called the National Republicans. Jefferson believed that the attack on slavery in Missouri was part of a conspiracy of former Federalists aimed at taking control of the national government.

Despite Jefferson's dire prediction, Sen. Henry Clay of Kentucky steered a compromise through Congress, admitting Missouri as the twelfth slave state, while Maine (until then part of Massachusetts) entered as the twelfth free state. The compromise established Tallmadge's principle: henceforth slavery was prohibited in the territories north of latitude 36°30′, the southern boundary of Missouri. With this compromise, the question of slavery in territories was theoretically settled.

RETURN OF CONTROVERSY

In fact, however, the compromise was unsatisfactory to much of the South. Under the compromise only three new slave states—Arkansas, Florida, and present-day Oklahoma—might enter the Union. With slavery banned in the rest of the Louisiana Purchase, which included the future states of Iowa, Kansas, Montana, Minnesota, Nebraska, North Dakota, and South Dakota—the South could look to the day when most new states would be free states. Thus, most Deep South senators and representatives voted against the compromise, and many considered it unconstitutional.

The issue of slavery in the territories was reignited when Texas became independent in 1836 and sought admission to the Union. Texas annexation in 1845 led to a war with Mexico (1846–1848), the acquisition of new territory, and new debates over slavery. The war produced the most serious sectional crisis since 1820, paralyzing Congress for more than three years over the question of slavery in the new territories. This crisis led to another settlement, the Compromise of 1850, which opened some new territories to slavery but also brought California into the Union as a free state. In this new, bitter sectional debate, Sen. John C. Calhoun of South Carolina theorized that territories are held in partnership of the sovereign states, and Congress has no constitutional right to abolish property rights acknowledged by any state in these common holdings.

Calhoun's theoretical objection became practical when Sen. Stephen Douglas of Illinois introduced his Kansas-Nebraska bill, to organize the Great Plains. To gain the support of southern Democrats for his bill, Douglas produced a new doctrine, "popular sovereignty." The people of a territory, not Congress, would decide whether their future state was to be slave or free, whether north of 36°30′—as Kansas and Nebraska were—or not. Northern opinion was outraged that the Kansas-Nebraska bill would open that territory to the possibility of slavery, but the Democratic Party remained disciplined and passed the bill. The Missouri Compromise was thus partially repealed, as some of the Louisiana Purchase territories were opened to slavery, depending on the decision of their settlers. In Kansas, the freedom to decide the issue led to civil war between proslavery and antislavery settlers.

The Kansas-Nebraska Act led to the formation of a new political organization, the Republican Party, which carried eleven free states in the 1856 election. The Republicans were pledged to prohibit slavery in all the territories and prevent the admission of any new slave states. The Democrat, James Buchanan of Pennsylvania, won only by sweeping the South. At his inauguration, he wistfully appealed to "all good citizens" to accept the final ruling on slavery in the territories, which the Supreme Court was within days of handing down. The judgment concerned Dred Scott, a Missouri slave belonging to an army officer who had once been stationed at a fort in Louisiana Purchase territory north of 36°30′. The southern-dominated Court ruled on March 6, 1857, that Calhoun's theory had been right: Congress had no authority to make territories free.

By 1857 the ban on slavery in the Missouri Compromise was already largely defunct, but the Supreme Court decision ended the ban in the remainder of the region (Minnesota) as well as in the far northwest, which included present-day Oregon and Washington. Politically, the *Dred Scott* decision was an attack on the entire North. Chief Justice Roger B. Taney's decision denied Douglas's theory of popular sovereignty and proved to the North that lasting compromise with the slave states on the issue of expansion was impossible. At the same time it essentially declared that the major program of the Republicans—a ban on slavery in the territories—was unconstitutional.

Despite Taney's ruling, the Republicans continued to campaign against not only Kansas-Nebraska, but the *Dred Scott* decision itself, which had declared the Missouri Compromise unconstitutional. An obscure lawyer in Illinois, Abraham Lincoln, offered a critique of Taney's opinion, as well as of the politics of the Democrats, that resonated throughout the North. Significantly, Lincoln argued that the *Dred Scott* decision was illegitimate because it had struck down a statute—the Missouri Compromise—that Lincoln and other northerners had elevated to a level just below the Declaration of Independence and the Constitution in the pantheon of America's civil religion. This critique of Taney and the Democrats led to Lincoln's presidential victory in 1860, and ultimately to the implementation of the Missouri Compromise on a fully national level, by ending slavery itself.

See also *Calhoun, John C.; Compromise of 1850; Constitution, U.S.; Kansas-Nebraska Act; Northwest Ordinance; Slavery.*

PAUL FINKELMAN, UNIVERSITY OF TULSA COLLEGE OF LAW

BIBLIOGRAPHY

Dangerfield, George. *The Awakening of American Nationalism, 1815–1828.* New York: Harper and Row, 1965.

Moore, Glover. *The Missouri Controversy, 1819–1821.* Lexington: University of Kentucky Press, 1953.

James Monroe   *Library of Congress*

MONROE, JAMES

James Monroe (1758–1831) devoted his life to his country. Between the ages of eighteen, when he left the College of William and Mary to fight in the Revolution, and sixty-six, when he ended his second term as president, he enjoyed only a few periods of private life. His public service was divided between state and nation. He represented Virginia in the Confederation Congress in the mid-1780s and in the U.S. Senate in the early 1790s; he also served as governor on two occasions, from 1800 to 1802 and briefly in 1811. But Monroe's state service was repeatedly interrupted by national posts. He left the Senate to serve as American minister to France in 1794. Within weeks of ending his first service as governor in December 1802, he began a four-year stint as Thomas Jefferson's roving diplomat in Europe—signing the Louisiana Purchase with France, trying to purchase Florida from Spain, and negotiating on neutral rights with Great Britain. He resigned as governor in early 1811, as the nation moved toward war with Great Britain, to become James Madison's secretary of state. Later, he served as acting secretary of war.

A consistent Republican, though some dissident Republicans ran him against Madison in the election of 1808, Monroe was named the party's candidate by a caucus in early 1816 and was elected president by a wide margin that fall. His inauguration began what was quickly, and inaptly, named the "Era of Good Feelings." Although Monroe was reelected in 1820 almost unopposed and almost unanimously, the period of political harmony promised by the death of the Federalist Party after the War of 1812 never materialized. Instead, his presidency witnessed the continuing fragmentation of the national Republican party into ideological camps and personal factions and the emerging development of conflicting political organizations within a number of states. Fueling these new divisions were the intense sectionalism of the Missouri crisis and the devastating economic depression of the panic of 1819. Four candidates contested the election of 1824, but each claimed the Republican mantle.

The greatest accomplishments of Monroe's presidency were in foreign policy. Monroe chose as his secretary of state

John Quincy Adams, perhaps the only man in the country with more diplomatic experience than himself. Though they differed at times about specific measures and broad goals, Monroe and Adams crafted a significant foreign policy legacy. Perhaps most significant from their own perspective, they preserved peace at a time when events in Europe and the New World seemed certain to engulf the weak government and tenuous union of the United States in war. In February 1819 Monroe and Adams signed the Transcontinental Treaty with Spain, ending a long-simmering dispute, acquiring Florida, and strengthening American claims on the Pacific Coast. In early 1822 they effectively validated the independence of the former Spanish colonies in the New World by extending formal diplomatic recognition. And in the fall of 1823 they crafted what would eventually be called the Monroe Doctrine, insisting upon the noninterference of Europe in the Western Hemisphere.

Often dismissed as a mediocrity, particularly in comparison with his Republican predecessors, Monroe might better be viewed as someone whose long commitment to republican government, federal union, and territorial expansion furthered each.

See also *Landslide Elections; Missouri Compromise; Panic of 1819; Territorial Expansion.*

JAMES E. LEWIS JR., INDEPENDENT SCHOLAR

BIBLIOGRAPHY

Ammon, Harry. *James Monroe: A Bibliography.* Westport, Conn.: Meckler, 1991.
———. *James Monroe: The Quest for National Identity.* New York: McGraw-Hill, 1971.
Cunningham, Noble E., Jr. *The Presidency of James Monroe.* Lawrence: University Press of Kansas, 1996.

MORRILL LAND-GRANT COLLEGE ACTS

Significant federal support for higher education began with the Morrill Land-Grant College Act of 1862, and subsequent acts enlarged that aid and further democratized access to higher education in the United States. Justin S. Morrill (1810–1898), a congressman and then a senator from Vermont, championed such assistance from the 1850s until the 1890s. The 1862 act allocated public land in western territories, the sale of which would generate the funds; later acts drew directly from the federal treasury. Although the original law emphasized training in agriculture and engineering, in practice it also promoted teacher training and liberal arts education, and later legislation promoted research and agricultural extension services. Schools varied widely in how they interpreted the requirement that the curriculum include military training.

Congress had passed a land-grant bill in 1859, but Democratic president James Buchanan vetoed it. Three years later, during the Civil War, Congress passed another version, the Morrill-Wade bill, which Republican president Abraham Lincoln signed. Each state was apportioned thirty thousand acres of western land per member of Congress, to be converted to cash and invested in a fund for the annual support of one or more land-grant schools. Such institutions as the University of Maine, Cornell University, and Purdue University were soon established. After the eleven Confederate states were readmitted to the Union, they too benefited from the act, and schools such as today's Auburn University and Texas A & M University were launched (under other names).

The new programs and the money to support them were sometimes attached to established schools, among them Dartmouth College, Brown University, and the state universities of Wisconsin, North Carolina, Georgia, and Mississippi. In some cases, including Georgia and Wisconsin, those arrangements persist to this day. Other states eventually detached the new programs from the older institutions and established new schools, among them the University of New Hampshire, the University of Rhode Island, North Carolina State University, and Mississippi State University. Many land-grant institutions admitted only male students at first, but northern schools typically admitted female students early on, and by the 1960s all land-grant schools did so.

In 1890 the Second Morrill Land-Grant Act, the Morrill-McComas Act, substantially increased the amount of federal support for land-grant colleges. The new law neither required nor prohibited segregation but stipulated that, if black citizens were excluded from one land-grant school in a state, another school receiving land-grant money in that state had to admit black students. The increment of money was thus made contingent on southern states' allocating a share of the money to black education as well as white. Although Mississippi and Virginia had each supported a black college since the 1870s, the new act increased their funds and also led to the establishment or designation of black land-grant schools in fifteen other states. Well into the twentieth century, each of the seventeen southern states maintained a segregated black land-grant institution, among them Oklahoma's Langston University, Missouri's Lincoln University, and Florida A & M University.

Shortly before the Second Morrill Act, Congress inaugurated funding for research at the land-grant schools. An 1887 measure, the Hatch Act, supplied research money for every state, and land-grant schools began to maintain experiment stations and conduct research that led to far greater productivity on the nation's farms. In 1914 Congress passed the

Early students plow the campus of Pennsylvania State University, one of the new land-grant colleges. *U.S. Department of Agriculture*

Smith-Lever Act, dedicated to the proposition that citizens other than students should also benefit directly from the schools. Extension services began to take agricultural and home demonstration projects to farms across every state, as the U.S. Department of Agriculture took on an enhanced role in rural life.

By the 1920s, although the original funds from the 1862 act persisted, the 1890 act supplied greater sums to every state in the nation, and more federal money went to extension activities than to teaching. Also by the 1920s, schools that had begun as undergraduate institutions for in-state students were expanding their graduate programs and admitting students from other states and even foreign countries.

In February 1960 four students at one of the "colleges of 1890," North Carolina A & T, began what became a series of sit-ins, in which students, many of them from black land-grant colleges, propelled the nation away from the segregation policies and practices that had led to the establishment of those schools. Later in the 1960s the federal and state gov-

ernments began to offer far greater aid to higher education than ever before. Having changed course since 1890 on segregation, federal policy required every state to end its policy of racial exclusion. Traditional patterns persisted in the South, however, with most land-grant schools remaining largely—rather than all—either white or black.

See also *Civil Rights Movement; Civil War; Higher Education Act; Lincoln, Abraham; Reconstruction; Territorial Expansion.*

PETER WALLENSTEIN,
VIRGINIA POLYTECHNIC INSTITUTE AND STATE UNIVERSITY

BIBLIOGRAPHY

Cross, Coy F., II. *Justin Smith Morrill: Father of the Land-Grant Colleges.* East Lansing: Michigan State University Press, 1999.

Rainsford, George N. *Congress and Higher Education in the Nineteenth Century.* Knoxville: University of Tennessee Press, 1972.

Rudolph, Frederick. *The American College and University: A History.* New York: Knopf, 1962.

Wallenstein, Peter. *Virginia Tech, Land-Grant University, 1872–1997: History of a School, a State, a Nation.* Blacksburg, Va.: Pocahontas Press, 1997.

NATIONAL DEBT

The national debt represents the total indebtedness of the national government. By the end of fiscal 2000, total federal debt was expected to be approximately $5.6 trillion, of which about $3.5 trillion was owned by the public, with the rest in government accounts (such as retirement funds and Social Security trust funds) that hold federal securities.

The national debt has been a matter of concern to politicians since a fledgling America won its independence from England in 1781. Then the debt amounted to some $10 million, owed to foreign countries, veterans of the Continental Army, and merchants who had supplied it, among others. By 1789 the unpaid interest alone came to nearly $2 million. Secretary of the Treasury Alexander Hamilton, adopting the model set by the Bank of England, argued that debt was a good thing; the bonds that a government issued could be traded in an open market, which while raising money also imposed discipline on the borrower. If the government acted prudently and honestly on debt (that is, paid it off faithfully), Hamilton argued, it could raise needed funds on a stable and consistent basis. Today's lively market in U.S. government securities, financial instruments viewed as safe havens by foreign and domestic investors alike, is testimony to this policy. Debt became a potent way to manage the nation's economy.

The national debt increased dramatically in the twentieth century as a result of war, economic crisis, and political developments in the 1980s. Both World War I and the New Deal policies pursued by President Franklin D. Roosevelt to combat the Great Depression in the 1930s added considerably to the national debt. However, even by 1940—on the eve of U.S. entry into World War II—the total publicly held debt stood at just $43 billion. By 1950, with the expense of financing World War II and the rebuilding of Europe, the public debt had risen to over $219 billion. The debt continued to rise in the following three decades due to the costs of the Korean and Vietnam wars and rapidly increasing domestic programs and payments to individuals—the poor, sick, and elderly as well as retired government workers. The budget deficits required for these outlays pushed the public debt to $710 billion by 1980, on the threshold of Ronald Reagan's election as president.

The decade that followed Reagan's election has become one of the most controversial in the continuing debate about budget deficits and national debt. The Reagan administration pushed through Congress a huge tax cut that reduced revenues by more than $35 billion in early years and by significantly more in later years. At the same time, government spending continued to spiral upward, in part because of the administration's multi-billion-dollar increases in defense spending. The result was huge budget deficits and a public debt of about $2.7 trillion by the time Reagan left office in 1989.

The budget deficits and debt continued to increase under both Republican and Democratic successors in the White House, but by the end of the 1990s, largely as a result of a booming economy and rapidly rising tax collections, the debate shifted fundamentally. Government and private projections indicated that revenues would grow so robustly the debt could be paid off in as little as a decade, if public officials decided that was the appropriate public policy. By the 2000 presidential election campaign, the political arguments focused on whether to use the expanding revenues to pay off the debt or to enact significant tax cuts, or some of each.

Advocates of the pay-down policy said reducing the debt would ensure that future generations would be free of it, thus enabling them to borrow at lower interest rates. And if the government owed less, their argument went, it could do more. An economic downturn and resulting lower tax revenues would have less impact if the debt were lowered, economists said. Moreover, lower debt-service payments would free up monies for discretionary spending programs. Persons in this camp also noted that the future revenue surpluses were only projections and might not materialize. If taxes were cut and surpluses did not materialize, the government would still be left with a huge debt as well as lower revenues to meet public needs.

Fiscal conservatives said the surplus indicated that the federal government was taking in too much money and therefore should lower taxes and put more money in citizens' hands. They argued that additional discretionary income would lead to more consumer spending and thus stimulate the economy. Additionally, these persons, preferring smaller and less activist government in principle, wanted to drain the revenue that they believed public officials would use for new programs.

Some economists and financial analysts doubted that it mattered either way. They argued that the important point was the relation of national debt to economic activity. They contended that if gross domestic product, the sum of all economic activity, grew in step with national debt—or faster than debt—the existence of the debt was not a significant factor affecting the economic health of the nation.

RON dePAOLO, INDEPENDENT AUTHOR

NATIONAL SECURITY DOCUMENT 68

An apocalyptic document set the tone for the militarization of American foreign policy in the cold war. National Security Council Paper 68 (1950) is among the most important policy documents in the history of U.S. cold war diplomacy. Drafted by State Department planner Paul Nitze and approved by Harry S. Truman and his top foreign policy advisers, NSC 68 embodied the American cold war ethos. Two tumultuous international events, both occurring in 1949, provided the backdrop for the drafting and approval of NSC 68: the successful Soviet test of an atomic bomb and the triumph of Mao Zedong and the Chinese Communist Party. With the cold war now firmly cemented and global in scope, NSC 68 called on the United States to lead the "free world" in a massive campaign of economic, political, and military rearmament. Drafted in January 1950 and approved by Truman after the outbreak of the Korean War in June of that year, NSC 68 became the guidepost of U.S. cold war diplomacy for years to come. The document, seventy pages long in its original typescript, remained classified until 1975, but today it can be accessed in the Foreign Relations Series of the United States and myriad secondary sources.

The most significant feature of NSC 68 was its apocalyptic tone. The policy paper argued that "the issues that face us are momentous, involving the fulfillment or destruction not only of the Republic but of civilization itself." NSC 68 depicted a fight to the finish between the "free world"—the United States and its allies—and the international communist movement led by the Soviet Union. Such a struggle would

bring victory or death. Accordingly, NSC 68 advocated dramatic increases in defense spending—allowing whatever officials deemed necessary—to win the battle. The Truman administration interpreted the outbreak of the Korean War as confirmation of the worldview embodied in the NSC paper. Following Truman's approval of NSC 68 on September 30, 1950, the U.S. defense budget soared from $13 billion in 1950 to $49 billion in 1953. After NSC 68 and Korea, U.S. foreign policy reflected a marked tendency toward the militarization of American foreign policy.

See also *Cold War; Korean War; Truman, Harry S.*

WALTER HIXSON, UNIVERSITY OF AKRON

BIBLIOGRAPHY

May, Ernest R., ed. *American Cold War Strategy: Interpreting NSC 68.* Boston: Bedford Books, 1993.

Nitze, Paul H., with Ann M. Smith and Steven L. Rearden. *From Hiroshima to Glasnost: At the Center of Decision, a Memoir.* New York: Grove Weidenfeld. 1989.

Rearden, Steven L. *The Evolution of American Strategic Doctrine: Paul H. Nitze and the Soviet Challenge.* Boulder: Westview Press, 1984.

NATIONAL WOMAN'S PARTY

In 1916 suffragists Alice Paul and Lucy Burns, schooled in British militant feminism, formed the National Woman's Party by merging the Congressional Union (a subcommittee of the National American Woman Suffrage Association) and the Woman's Party (also headed by Paul and Burns). Paul, who had been jailed six times for her activism and had undergone rough treatment including forced feeding at the Occoquan Workhouse in Virginia, adopted the strategy of holding the political party in power responsible for the fate of federal woman's suffrage. Her aggressive tactics, which included picketing, heckling speakers, and hunger strikes, were considered unsavory by the more conservative suffrage associations and had the effect of convincing President Woodrow Wilson to negotiate with moderates such as Susan B. Anthony and Lucy Stone on the issue. With the president's support, the Nineteenth Amendment guaranteeing women the vote was approved in June 1919 and ratified in 1920.

In the aftermath of the suffrage victory, the National Woman's Party became the first and longest operating political organization convinced of the importance of an equal rights amendment to the Constitution. Drafting the legislation herself in 1923, Paul fought many years but was unable to convince other feminist organizations of the importance of further agitation. Fearing that protective legislation for women and children would be dismantled by the amendment, the League of Women Voters and other organizations within the women's movement resisted Paul's arguments until after World War II, when support was more forthcoming. Paul died in 1977, after passage of the Equal Rights Amendment in 1972 and before the amendment failed ratification.

See also *Equal Rights Amendment; Woman's Suffrage Movement.*

LORI BOGLE, UNITED STATES NAVAL ACADEMY

BIBLIOGRAPHY

Becker, Susan. *The Origins of the Equal Rights Amendment: American Feminism Between the Wars.* Westport, Conn.: Greenwood Press, 1981.

Flexner, Eleanor, and Ellen Fitzpatrick. *Century of Struggle: The Woman's Rights Movement in the United States.* Cambridge: Belknap Press of Harvard University Press, 1996.

Lunardini, Christine A. *From Suffrage to Equal Rights: Alice Paul and the National Woman's Party, 1910–1928.* New York: New York University Press, 1986.

NATIVISM

Nativism, the fear and hatred of aliens, particularly religious or ethnic minorities and political radicals, is as old as America. It was present at the birth of the colonies and played a particularly important role in national political history in the mid–nineteenth century and in the 1920s.

Anti–Catholicism, rampant in England before the era of American colonization and rooted in the imperial rivalries with Catholic Spain and France, gained new life in the colonies and became the most enduring part of the nativist tradition in America. Even though there were very few Catholics in the thirteen colonies (only thirty-five thousand as late as the Revolution), New England Puritans insisted that their church be "purged of Romish corruptions." They instructed children in school primers to "abhor that arrant Whore of Rome and all her blasphemies."

NINETEENTH-CENTURY NATIVISM

In the 1830s, as immigration from Ireland and Germany swelled the Catholic population, nativists launched violent attacks on Catholic institutions and published numerous anti–Catholic tracts. By 1843 nativist fears shaped a new political party, the American Republicans. Political nativists played a key role in the brutal street battles between Catholics and Protestants in Philadelphia on Independence Day 1844; thirty died and hundreds were wounded.

Although the American Republican Party briefly prospered, electing the mayors of New York and Philadelphia and six members of the Twenty-ninth Congress in 1844, the party was dead by 1847. Over the next five years, however, the catastrophic potato famine in Ireland stimulated a vast Catholic migration to America, and a new and much more formidable nativist political organization emerged.

Out of one of the numerous nativist secret societies created at this time came the American Party. Because its members were told to respond "I know nothing" when asked about the party (because "Jesuitical conspirators" allegedly menaced the movement), the new organization was called the Know Nothings.

The Know Nothings attacked Catholics for undermining the public school system, for being incapable of democratic citizenship because of papal and priestly manipulation, and for the numerous social problems accompanying the influx of so many poor newcomers in the port cities. The antialiens considered themselves the only real Americans; for them, Catholics were a horde of inassimilable outsiders. With the Whig Party fractured by the abolitionist and free-soil issues, the Know Nothings became the second largest political party in America by 1854. However, their success was of short duration. Like the Whigs and the Democrats, the Know Nothing Party split apart over slavery after 1856 and disappeared in the crisis leading to the Civil War. Nativism, however, did not disappear with it.

In the late nineteenth century, as "new immigration" from southern and eastern Europe brought millions of Italian Catholics, Jews, and Russians and other Slavs, nativism gained strength, particularly during the depression of the 1890s. New antialien groups proliferated, calling for restrictions on immigration and assailing Irish-Catholic political control in the big cities. The largest group was the American Protective Association, whose membership reached 500,000.

TWENTIETH-CENTURY REBIRTH

Nativism declined in the Progressive era, but World War I and the postwar Red Scare briefly revived it. German-Americans were harassed during the war, and raids organized in 1919 by Attorney General A. Mitchell Palmer made the federal government the instrument for protecting America from communist aliens and other proponents of "un-American" ideas.

In the 1920s a new organization with an old name, the Ku Klux Klan, recruited at least 2.5 million members to an anti–Catholic, anti–Semitic, antialien, antiblack crusade. The organization was founded by William J. Simmons, a former circuit-riding minister whose father had been an officer in the post–Civil War Ku Klux Klan, when those hooded vigilantes emerged to repress black freedmen and restore "order" and native white supremacy in the South of Reconstruction. This entirely new and much larger Klan, eventually weakened by scandals involving its leaders, did not survive the decade. However, it made a political impact, attacking the

A resurgent Ku Klux Klan parades along Pennsylvania Avenue from the Capitol in 1926.   *Library of Congress*

and his targets were often members of the native-born elite.

Despite efforts in the 1980s and 1990s to limit immigration and bar illegal aliens, old-style nativism did not return. Only fragmentary extremist cells—Aryan Nations, the tiny Klan chapters, and skinhead gangs—perpetuate the nativist rhetoric of the past. Although a few members of these tiny sects, the purveyors of racial hate and religious intolerance, have attacked Hispanic and Asian immigrants in recent years, there has been no significant antialien movement calling for repression of foreign-born Americans in the name of the old nativism. Instead, political activists of different ideological persuasions have advocated measures to restrict illegal immigration, but with provision for the humane treatment of those undocumented entrants and refugees already in the country and with concern for protection of the civil liberties and rights of citizens and immigrants alike.

See also *Immigration and Naturalization: Society and Politics; Know Nothing Party; Sedition Act of 1798; Suffrage.*

DAVID H. BENNETT, SYRACUSE UNIVERSITY

BIBLIOGRAPHY

Bennett, David H. *The Party of Fear: The American Far Right from Nativism to the Militia Movement.* 2d ed. New York: Vintage Books, 1995.

Billington, Ray Allen. *The Protestant Crusade, 1800–1860.* Chicago: Quadrangle Books, 1964.

Higham, John. *Strangers in the Land: Patterns of American Nativism, 1860–1925.* 2d ed. New York: Atheneum, 1963.

presidential candidacy of the Catholic Al Smith and strongly supporting passage of the Immigration Act of 1924, which restricted immigration and established national quotas directed against southern and eastern Europe. The Klan was moribund in the 1930s and was officially disbanded in 1944. Small state and local organizations, calling themselves Ku Klux Klan and using terminology of the earlier movement as well as dressing members in similar regalia, would reemerge in the late 1940s. They would play occasional roles in antiblack and anti–civil rights violence in the next decades.

Nativism faded from the American scene after the 1920s. After the New Deal of the 1930s championed diversity, and after military recruits of all ethnic groups fought World War II in the early 1940s, it was harder to assail any group as "un-American." With leading social scientists now repudiating racist theories (which had been embraced by many prominent social and political leaders in the past) and with post–World War II prosperity removing the economic anxieties on which nativism had fed, nativism became unacceptable in academia, commerce, and the professions. The climate of repression pervading the early cold war era targeted not religious or ethnic groups but political radicals; indeed, it was an Irish-American Catholic senator, Joseph R. McCarthy Jr., who became the chief hunter of communists in the 1950s,

NEW DEAL

The New Deal was the name given to President Franklin D. Roosevelt's domestic agenda, shaped to address America's worst crisis since the Civil War: the Great Depression. When the Roosevelt administration took office in March 1933, depression had ravaged the nation's economy, produced unprecedented social distress in urban and agricultural regions, and raised questions about the future of a stable democracy. New Deal programs blunted the cutting edge of social and political crisis, producing lasting changes in the role of the federal government and in the power of the presidency. Widely supported by the electorate, the programs influenced political developments long after the end of Roosevelt's presidency.

FROM GREAT DEPRESSION TO NEW DEAL

In 1932, the year of FDR's election, the gross national product was less than half of what it had been in 1928, and unemployment swelled to almost one-quarter of the labor force. A social activist in Philadelphia characterized conditions in that city as "slow starvation and the progressive disintegration of family life." Bankrupt farmers in the West, menaced by foreclosure, burned their wheat in a desperate effort to raise prices. There was a mass refusal to pay streetcar fares in one city, mass break-ins of grocery stores in another. One magazine, despairing of democracy, announced: "Appoint a dictator." This was the situation when Roosevelt took the oath of office.

His "New Deal" was designed to address the crisis; it was not a radical scheme to restructure the American economic or social system. Frances Perkins, Roosevelt's secretary of labor and the first woman appointed to cabinet rank, observed: "the New Deal was not a plan with form and content" but "a happy phrase he had coined during the campaign . . . the idea that the New Deal had a preconceived theoretical position is ridiculous." The New Deal was multifaceted; it involved, as the president once said, "relief, recovery, and reform." Surely relief was a critical part of the program.

Herbert Hoover, Roosevelt's predecessor, had an international reputation as a humanitarian—the man who had mobilized resources to feed and house desperate European victims of the Great War. But by 1932 he had earned the contempt of millions of Americans because he refused to sanction direct relief in the depths of the depression. Hoover believed that such government action would undermine the American dream of individual responsibility. FDR, however, responded to the crisis with a series of bold initiatives.

THE "FIRST NEW DEAL"

With an overwhelming "working majority" in Congress after his landslide victory in 1932, FDR pushed through the Federal Emergency Relief Administration (FERA), the Civilian Conservation Corps (CCC), the Civil Works Administration (CWA), the Public Works Administration (PWA) and, in 1935, the Works Progress Administration (WPA). These "alphabet agencies" addressed the despair of the unemployed. The agencies played a role in Roosevelt's subsequent election triumphs and in the way the New Deal—offering the government as employer of last resort—would impact American politics in decades to come.

The FERA came first, funded at $500 million to provide direct support to states to help the bankrupt relief agencies. Because New Dealers felt that the unemployed wanted jobs and not just "the dole," the CWA (under Harry Hopkins) put more than 4 million people to work on 180,000 temporary projects. But Interior Secretary Harold Ickes argued that if the government was going to supply resources for employment, the work should have lasting value. The PWA, under Ickes, spent more than $4 billion on roads, schools, post offices, and other public structures.

The Civilian Conservation Corps (CCC), designed to provide relief for jobless and desperate young men, not only provided employment for more than 2.75 million in 1,500 camps but also helped protect and conserve the nation's natural resources. Later, the WPA, the largest relief agency, employed more than 8 million Americans and poured $11 billion into the economy, building roads, bridges, schools, and hospitals as well as assisting writers, performers, and artists in such efforts as the Federal Writers' Project.

Relief for the millions of unemployed was a pressing issue in 1933, but so too were the problems confronting the banking and securities industries. A federal "bank holiday" began on March 6, 1933, and continued until March 15, at which time 70 percent of the nation's banks—those with adequate capital and sufficient liquid assets—reopened for business. The Roosevelt team supported banking reform legislation (the Glass-Steagall Act of 1933) to give government the authority to curb stock speculation by banks and to protect small depositors faced with losses due to bank failures through the Federal Deposit Insurance Corporation. The Securities and Exchange Commission (SEC) was established to police the stock market. Thus the New Deal built on Progressive era precedents to enlarge the federal regulatory role following the collapse of the private sector in the depression.

The administration worked on many other fronts to address the crisis, especially during its dramatic first three months in office, the "hundred days" of extraordinary legislative productivity. Later, it created the Home Owners Loan Corporation to help people finance home mortgages, and the Federal Housing Administration (FHA) to insure mortgages for new housing. (The FHA would be criticized for refusing mortgages to blacks moving into white neighborhoods, a "red-line" effort that helped promote segregated city and suburban areas.) It established the Farm Credit Administration for rural Americans who were in danger of losing their

The New Deal was less a planned, cohesive program than a series of responses to problems in the economy and society, as this cartoon of January 5, 1934, notes. *Library of Congress*

land. The Tennessee Valley Authority (TVA) built dams to supply cheap power and provide flood control for a vast and poor region in the southeastern mountains. Some critics called the TVA "creeping socialism," but it provided electrical power for those who had not had access to it in the past, and it provided jobs for thousands of workers in an area with a disastrous level of unemployment.

While all these initiatives were being taken, FDR and his "brains trust" (lawyers, economists, and other academics he had brought to Washington) shaped plans to reform the entire economy. The Agricultural Adjustment Act focused on the problems confronting America's farmers. Another bold but strikingly unsuccessful product of this effort was the National Industrial Recovery Act of 1933. This law established a powerful new agency, the National Recovery Administration (NRA), to oversee codes of "fair competition" for different industries; these codes regulated prices, wages, production, and trade practices. The Roosevelt administration suspended enforcement of antitrust laws to facilitate this effort, under the

leadership of Gen. Hugh Johnson. For a brief time, almost 90 percent of American industry, with 22 million employees, was involved; and 2.5 million firms flew the NRA's "Blue Eagle" flag.

But the flamboyant Johnson proved an ineffective administrator. Critics insisted the NRA was encouraging monopoly. Big businesses complained about regulations; small businesses found wage and hour requirements oppressive. Some NRA supporters joined labor leaders—who had warmly endorsed Section 7A of the law with its guarantee of collective bargaining—in calling the agency the "National Run Around."

Even before the Supreme Court struck down the law in 1935 (in *Schecter Poultry Corporation v. United States),* Roosevelt was moving in other directions. One bitter "brains trust" member, Raymond Moley, attacked the president for failing to fully support the concept behind the NRA. But Roosevelt was no ideologue and had compared himself to a quarterback on a football team, believing that if one play does not work, try another. Working with big business had not worked.

THE "SECOND" NEW DEAL

More significant were the attacks on FDR from the political right. Once the crisis had been ameliorated by relief efforts and the danger of political upheaval had passed, wealthy opponents created the American Liberty League, assailing the president's "dictatorial polices" and "assaults" on the free enterprise system. An angry Roosevelt, now convinced that there was no point in cooperating with these "economic royalists," responded with an attack on their conservative interests. Some historians have characterized the Second New Deal, beginning in 1935, as a turn to the left.

Also pushing the president in this direction were three popular political movements that offered radical alternatives to New Deal reforms. Father Charles E. Coughlin, the "radio priest" who had built a huge national audience for his Sunday sermons and led the National Union for Social Justice, was a former supporter of FDR who turned hostile when Roosevelt rejected his hyperinflationary schemes to end the depression. Dr. Francis Townsend, inventor of the Old Age Revolving Pension Plan (calling for everyone over sixty to receive—and spend—$200 every month), convinced several million followers that he had a panacea to save them and end the depression. Huey Long, the famed senator from Louisiana and founder of the Share-Our-Wealth movement, a scheme to seize all fortunes in the United States over $1.7 million and provide a house, car, and annual income of $2,500 to each family, was assassinated in 1935, but the Rev. Gerald L. K. Smith claimed leadership of a continued national effort. In 1936 Smith and Townsend briefly supported Coughlin's Union Party, which sought to unseat FDR in the presidential election.

Responding to many political pressures and seeking to confront the continuing economic crisis, the New Deal moved in a new direction with a series of important legislative initiatives.

The National Labor Relations Act, the "Magna Carta for organized labor," according to its champions, was passed in 1935. It had strong support in Congress and bore the name of Sen. Robert Wagner of New York. It provided the guarantees for collective bargaining lost when the NRA had been declared unconstitutional; the National Labor Relations Board (NLRB) supervised shop elections and dealt with labor-law violations. The United Auto Workers, United Steel Workers, and other Congress of Industrial Organizations (CIO) industrial unions flourished in a new environment free of coercion.

The Social Security Act was another enduring monument shaped by the renewed reform efforts of 1935. It was a system of insurance, not welfare, that provided coverage to the aged, infirm, widows, and dependent children. Employers and employees shared in providing resources, and by 1940, 28 million Americans were covered by Social Security. Critics noted gaps in initial coverage, and certainly increases in the payroll tax would be needed in future years. But this was the most important piece of social welfare legislation in American history. It provided an "entitlement" that even critics shrank from challenging in subsequent decades, as it became the famous "third rail" of American politics: touch it and you die.

Other parts of the Second New Deal agenda were less historically significant but still important. The Revenue Act of 1935 provided for "wealth taxes"—increased tax rates for wealthy individuals and corporations. The Public Utilities Holding Company Act of 1935 was the "death sentence" for the utilities empires that had proliferated in the 1920s and proven vulnerable after the 1929 market crash. The Tempo-

rary National Economic Committee was organized in 1938 to study concentration of economic and financial power in America. A number of actions addressed the plight of American farmers.

Early in the New Deal, the first Agricultural Adjustment Act (AAA) had been passed, seeking to reduce crop production in order to cut agricultural surpluses, thus ending the fall of farm prices. But the Supreme Court declared the AAA unconstitutional in 1936. Responding, the Roosevelt administration secured passage of the Soil Conservation and Domestic Allotment Act, permitting government to pay farmers to reduce crops in order to conserve soil. Other efforts, aimed at the poorest farmers, included the Resettlement Administration and the Farm Security Administration, which provided loans to farmers to relocate to better lands, as well as the Rural Electrification Administration, establishing utility cooperatives to give some farm families first-time access to electrical power. A second AAA was passed in 1938.

The Supreme Court's actions in striking down first the AAA and then the NRA were the impetus for one of Franklin D. Roosevelt's greatest failures. The president, incensed at the actions of what he saw as obstructionist judges acting on their own conservative ideology to block the program of reform, offered a bill to increase the size of the Supreme Court. He used the excuse that the Court was "overworked" and needed new blood. The Court responded with a series of 5–4 decisions (the "switch in time that saved nine," some called it) that upheld New Deal legislation, including the Wagner Act in 1937. And with conservative southern Democrats joining Republicans in denouncing the "Court packing" scheme—while getting support in the press and public opinion to "protect the Constitution"—FDR lost this fight.

The New Deal now was on the defensive. In 1937 the president failed to gain congressional approval for a plan to reorganize the executive branch of government, which would have increased presidential authority over the federal bureaucracy. He failed in the primary races of 1938 in an effort to purge several southern Democratic conservative leaders from the Senate.

Worst of all, the economy suffered a dramatic setback; the gross national product, which had been less than $40 billion in 1932 and had risen to almost $72 billion in mid-1937, declined rapidly in the next few months. The administration responded with new public works and relief spending to stimulate growth. Critics argued that the recession of 1937 was in part the result of cutbacks in spending that resulted from FDR's failure to fully grasp the basis of the New Deal's antidepression efforts: Keynesian economics. The president, it was argued, continued to be so fearful of deficit financing (called for in the fiscal policies advocated by the famous British economist John Maynard Keynes), that he could not persevere with adequate spending to defeat the depression.

A BALANCE SHEET AND A LEGACY

The New Deal did not completely conquer the depression. By 1939, when the looming World War II crisis marked an end to this era of domestic reform, the statistics of economic strength—gross national product, employment, physical volume of industrial production—all indicated that the nation had come just over halfway back from the depths of the crisis in early 1933. But there were many reasons—beyond inconsistencies in the New Deal itself—why the problems had not been solved in six years.

There was the failure of business to invest once the economy started moving forward, perhaps a result of the psychological effect of the new interventionist state on private enterprise, where many feared government investment and were concerned that deficit financing was at odds with the conventional wisdom for curing recessions. There was the continuing recession abroad and thus no real revival in foreign trade, despite the New Deal's far-sighted rejection of tariff barriers and its creation of reciprocal trade agreements. There was the decline in the birth rate. There was the lack of a new "flagship industry," such as automobiles in the 1920s, and aircraft and electronics in the 1950s. Finally, there were the political obstacles to government investment on the scale needed to do the job. It would take World War II, a crisis in which all would agree that the "dollar sign must be eliminated" to defeat the Axis enemies (leading to over $300 billion being poured into the economy), to finally bring full prosperity.

Although the New Deal did not quickly solve all economic problems, it was an enormous political, social, and psychological success. The vast majority of Americans believed it had brought hope back to a dispirited nation. The confident and eloquent Franklin D. Roosevelt, effective in public addresses and in radio broadcasts, offered charismatic leadership in a desperate hour. A brilliant politician, FDR won a spectacular reelection victory in 1936 and went on to unprecedented triumphs in two more presidential races. Indeed, the so-called Roosevelt coalition, which included labor voters and many Americans from ethnic, racial, and religious constituencies that had been in desperate need in 1933 (and who credited the New Deal with coming to their aid), remained a force in national politics long after FDR's death in 1945.

The New Deal was replaced by a massive effort to prepare for conflict and then win the world war in the last years of Roosevelt's presidency. In shaping his domestic program, however, this leader put his signature on American history.

The "hidden agenda" left over from the New Deal provided the goals for reform administrations in the postwar period: civil rights, national health care, aid to education, women's concerns, and more. But the New Deal operated in the midst of crisis and had a remarkable record of accomplishment. Modern presidential government, the enhanced role of federal power in many new areas, and the concept of a social "safety net" all became accepted parts of national life as a result of the New Deal. The grim prospect of a nation facing political upheaval in 1933 was replaced by a new, a more optimistic vision of the future.

See also *Federal Housing Administration; Hoover, Herbert; Labor Politics and Policies; Roosevelt, Franklin D.; Social Security; Tennessee Valley Authority; World War II: Domestic Politics.*

DAVID H. BENNETT, SYRACUSE UNIVERSITY

BIBLIOGRAPHY

Badger, Anthony J. *The New Deal: The Depression Years, 1933–1940.* New York: Hill and Wang, 1989.

Brinkley, Allen. *The End of Reform: New Deal Liberalism in Recession and War.* New York: Vintage Books, 1996.

Leuchtenburg, William E. *Franklin D. Roosevelt and the New Deal.* New York: Harper Collins, 1963.

Schlesinger, Arthur M., Jr. *The Coming of the New Deal.* New York: American Heritage Library, 1988.

NEW FREEDOM

New Freedom was the progressive political agenda of President Woodrow Wilson. Wilson crafted his campaign platform in 1912 as a response to Theodore Roosevelt's New Nationalism, which had been unveiled two years earlier. The successful implementation of New Freedom resulted in major changes in American business and society.

The New Freedom agenda, like that of New Nationalism, espoused significant government involvement in making American society more egalitarian. Both views agreed that the president should heavily influence public opinion and act as the principal architect of domestic as well as foreign policy. Both believed in the necessity of tax reform and tariff reduction. And both agreed that the federal government must play a major role in regulating American business.

One of the major differences between New Freedom and New Nationalism was the degree to which each thought business should be regulated. Although New Nationalism regarded trusts and cartels as potentially dangerous because of their ability to inflate prices, it considered large corporations to be efficient and therefore worth preserving; consequently, New Nationalism sought only to regulate "Big Business."

New Freedom, by contrast, believed that all large business concerns were inefficient as well as unfair to consumers and would-be competitors, so it sought to destroy "Big Business." Another difference was that New Nationalism also advocated the passage of social legislation, such as workmen's compensation and wage-and-hour regulations for child labor, to ease the plight of the working class. New Freedom, on the other hand, largely ignored the lower class.

When Wilson defeated Roosevelt in the presidential election of 1912, New Freedom triumphed over New Nationalism. Almost immediately Wilson, with the full support of a Congress controlled by fellow Democrats, began implementing the various aspects of his agenda. In 1913 the Underwood-Simmons Tariff cut import duties by an average of over 35 percent and greatly expanded the list of tariff-free items, thus forcing American manufacturers to lower prices in order to compete with foreign factories. Later that year the Federal Reserve Act reorganized the nation's banking system and placed it under the control of presidential appointees. In 1914 the Federal Trade Commission Act created a federal agency with the power to prohibit businesses from engaging in monopolistic practices.

In 1916 Wilson broadened the scope of New Freedom by responding to the demands of Roosevelt progressives for social legislation. Congress subsequently passed legislation that offered long-term, low-interest credit to farmers, prohibited interstate railroads from working their employees more than eight hours a day, regulated child labor via the Keating-Owen Act (1916), established workmen's compensation, and provided federal funds for building schools and highways.

New Freedom's promise ensured Wilson's election in 1912, and its success secured his reelection in 1916. Some of the programs advanced by New Freedom, however, never lived up to their promise; for example, the Supreme Court declared the Keating-Owen Act unconstitutional in 1918. Despite such setbacks, New Freedom established the precedent for active federal involvement in domestic affairs that would become so important during the New Deal.

See also *Labor Politics and Policies; New Nationalism; Roosevelt, Theodore; Tariff History; Wilson, Woodrow.*

CHARLES CAREY, LYNCHBURG COLLEGE/
CENTRAL VIRGINIA COMMUNITY COLLEGE

BIBLIOGRAPHY

Clements, Kendrick A. *The Presidency of Woodrow Wilson.* Lawrence: University Press of Kansas, 1992.

Heckscher, August. *Woodrow Wilson.* New York: Scribner, 1991.

Steigerwald, David. *Wilsonian Idealism in America.* Ithaca: Cornell University Press, 1994.

NEW FRONTIER

"We stand today at the edge of a New Frontier. . .," announced Democratic presidential nominee John F. Kennedy in 1960 when he accepted the party's nomination, "a frontier of unknown opportunities and perils. . ." Following JFK's inauguration in January 1961, the label adhered to the new administration's policies, particularly, but not exclusively, to its domestic policies.

New Frontier—with its suggestion of daring and wide-open possibility—suited the Democrats, who had presented themselves as the party of vigorous activity after the relatively placid eight-year administration of Republican Dwight D. Eisenhower. It suited as well an age of swift advances in missile and communications technology. Outer space—specifically travel to the moon, a voyage Kennedy proposed—offered an actual physical frontier of distance to be traversed; in fact, during Kennedy's administration the first American was launched in a satellite that circled the Earth.

Kennedy's narrow popular-vote victory over Richard M. Nixon in November 1960 brought to the White House a

Although not achieved until 1969, the U.S. goal of placing an astronaut on the moon owed much to John F. Kennedy's vision. *National Aeronautics and Space Administration*

group of advisers notable for the number of certified intellectuals. At the Department of Defense, JFK placed a former Harvard Business School professor and automobile executive, the liberal Republican Robert McNamara. Secretary of State Dean Rusk was also a liberal; he was a longtime member of the National Association for the Advancement of Colored People and at an early date lunched publicly with the African American Nobel laureate Ralph Bunche, who was under secretary of the United Nations. The historian Arthur M. Schlesinger Jr. became an adviser to JFK. Kennedy himself managed to acquire the look of an intellectual. He appeared as the author of a couple of books somewhat more scholarly than most that bear the name of a politician.

That Kennedy's wife was beautiful, witty, and accomplished and that he appeared in exuberant health—although he had suffered a lifetime of illness—added to the sense that the executive branch was on the go. Even Kennedy's womanizing, in this age just preceding the feminist movement, could suggest to his close associates—the public was ignorant of his infidelities—that he was a sophisticated man of the world.

DOMESTIC ISSUES

The administration initially had little to do with the social frontier of racism, at a time when black and a handful of white Americans were pressing beyond the boundaries of white supremacy. The president responded timidly, his caution reinforced by his brother, Attorney General Robert F. Kennedy, who was later to become a champion of civil rights. JFK appointed a number of African Americans to federal government positions. He sent troops to the University of Mississippi to subdue mobs opposing the enrollment of James Meredith, an African American. In the midst of violence in Birmingham, Alabama, he called for a law prohibiting discrimination in private institutions serving the public. And he became friendly to the great March on Washington in the summer of 1963 at which Martin Luther King Jr. made his "I have a dream" speech. These gestures were genuine, although circumstances coerced them.

On other domestic matters Kennedy's administration did map out a fairly venturesome course. Kennedy's interest in the legislative process was slim, and a Congress narrowly Democratic yet essentially conservative severely limited his options. But Kennedy, genuinely disturbed by the wretchedness he had seen in West Virginia during his presidential campaign and situations presented in Michael Harrington's book on poverty, *The Other America,* approached poverty in a more innovative way than Franklin D. Roosevelt did during the New Deal.

Roosevelt had addressed the fact of poverty; Kennedy wanted to eliminate its causes, which meant training workers for jobs that a high-technology economy was creating even as it destroyed other jobs. It also meant creating programs for renovating communities in which poverty had become impacted, materially and psychologically. Such enterprises were appropriate to a president who, during his campaign, had promised to awaken the languishing energies of his country. The poor—like the advocates of civil rights—were not merely to be aided: they would be coworkers on the scientific and technological frontier of Kennedy's time, a time that was not of his making but that benefited from his increasing support.

Early in his administration, Kennedy signed the Area Redevelopment Act, which provided businesses with loans for relocating to underfulfilled areas and grants for improving roads and bridges in such areas. A year later came the Manpower Development and Training Act, which taught workers new skills and paid them during training. The administration achieved a raise in the minimum wage. A tax cut, which Kennedy at the time of his assassination had not yet moved all the way through Congress, was intended to spur economic activity and tax receipts, allowing more spending to stimulate the economy. A measure more directly aimed at aiding the needy was a medical plan for the elderly, fixed to Social Security so that it would represent not welfare but earnings. It failed to pass in Congress during Kennedy's lifetime but did become law fewer than two years later.

DEFENSE AND FOREIGN POLICIES

On defense policy, Kennedy's administration did some of its freshest thinking. Reaching beyond Eisenhower's strategy of reliance on massive retaliation, which meant that in a military crisis the United States would have to choose between doing nothing and exterminating the world, Kennedy settled on plans for more flexible encounters with the communist world. Twin weapons in Kennedy's challenge to communism were the Peace Corps and the U.S. Army Special Forces. Members of the Peace Corps labored at small-scale economic and educational projects in impoverished foreign communities. The Green Berets of the Special Forces were trained to work with foreign anticommunist insurgent and counterinsurgent groups in a way that would aid the foreigners in combat techniques and encourage democratic community development.

All this was in the spirit of the Alliance for Progress for Latin America. Coming after the disastrous U.S.-supported Bay of Pigs invasion against Cuba in an attempt to overthrow Fidel Castro, the alliance was initially a plan for economic aid to stimulate progressive political change. Very soon, however, its idealism vanished amid the intense fear of communism. The concept of the Alliance for Progress, the Green Berets, and the Peace Corps emanated from the halls of the Central Intelligence Agency, which was briefly influenced by the vision of some liberal academics who believed that the way to fight communism abroad was to nourish social-democratic alternatives.

That liberal vision did not embed itself in future U.S. policy. Better remembered were the moments of tension and confrontation between Kennedy and the leader of the Soviet Union, Nikita Khrushchev: over the divided city of Berlin in 1961 and over Russian missiles in Cuba the following year. Kennedy, using a mixture of prudence and firmness, handled both creditably. After the 1962 missile crisis came the treaty banning nuclear testing, ratified by the Senate after Kennedy's assassination in November 1963. Especially following U.S. failures in Vietnam, however, foreign policy plans for a progressive and democratic counterpoint to communism became the lost legacy of the New Frontier.

See also *Civil Rights Movement; Cold War; Great Society; Kennedy, John F.; Marches on Washington.*

DAVID BURNER, SUNY AT STONY BROOK

BIBLIOGRAPHY

Giglio, James N. *The Presidency of John F. Kennedy.* Lawrence: University Press of Kansas, 1991.

Parmet, Herbert S. *JFK: The Presidency of John F. Kennedy.* New York: Dial Press, 1983.

Unger, Irwin. *The Best of Intentions: The Triumphs and Failures of the Great Society under Kennedy, Johnson, and Nixon.* New York: Doubleday, 1996.

NEW NATIONALISM

New Nationalism was Theodore Roosevelt's name for his political platform in the presidential election of 1912. This platform promoted active government involvement as a means of making social justice more important than property rights.

As president from 1901 to 1909, Roosevelt was a bold champion of progressivism. This political movement arose in the late nineteenth century in response to the public's distaste for the growing influence of "Big Business." Progressivism sought to improve living conditions for the working class and to limit the upper class's political influence by making politics more egalitarian.

Roosevelt retired from politics in 1909, passing the leadership of the Progressive movement and the Republican Party to William Howard Taft, his loyal follower. But as president, Taft proved to be more conservative than progressive; his conservatism split the Republicans into two camps, thus limiting Taft's effectiveness. Appalled by this situation, Roosevelt returned to the political arena in 1910.

The occasion for Roosevelt's return was a political rally at Osawatomie, Kansas. Speaking before a mostly conservative audience, Roosevelt gave one of the most radical speeches of his career. He declared that the struggle for liberty always involves taking power away from a class of people who exercise it for their own selfish benefit and not for the service of their fellow humans. He suggested that, in the United States, such a struggle could best be won if a strong federal government were led by a president who clearly saw himself as a "steward of the public welfare." The time had come, he argued, to pay more attention to issues of social justice than to protect the property rights and personal profits of the upper class. He claimed that the community possessed the general right to regulate the use of personal property "to whatever degree the public welfare may require it."

Having established the theoretical groundwork of New Nationalism, Roosevelt then discussed how he would implement his agenda. The basic platform called for graduated taxes on income and inheritances, compensation to workers who were injured on the job, regulations to prevent employers from exploiting the labor of women and children, reduced tariffs on foreign manufactured goods so that American companies would be forced to lower prices, and greater government involvement in the regulation of big business.

Roosevelt failed to gain the Republican nomination for president in 1912, so he ran as the candidate of the Progressive or Bull Moose Party. Roosevelt and Taft split the Republican vote, and the election went to the Democratic candidate, Woodrow Wilson. Wilson implemented his own progressive agenda called New Freedom, and New Nationalism faded rapidly from the scene. However, virtually all of its platform was eventually passed into law, much of it during

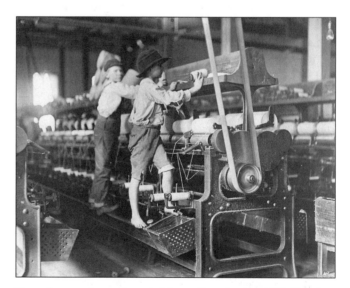

Young boys work on a loom in Macon, Georgia, circa 1910. Theodore Roosevelt championed federal regulation of child labor. Under pressure from Roosevelt progressives, President Woodrow Wilson would sign the Keating-Owen Act in 1916. *National Archives*

Wilson's administration. The Underwood-Simmons Tariff, which significantly reduced tariff rates, was passed by Congress in 1913; the Sixteenth Amendment, which legalized the income tax, was ratified in 1913; and the Keating-Owen Act, the first federal law regulating child labor, was passed in 1916. New Nationalism was important in another sense as well. It marked the first time in U.S. history that a president or presidential candidate gave a name to his proposed legislative agenda. In this sense, New Nationalism served as the precursor to Wilson's New Freedom, Franklin D. Roosevelt's New Deal, Harry S. Truman's Fair Deal, John F. Kennedy's New Frontier, and Lyndon Johnson's Great Society.

See also *New Freedom; Roosevelt, Theodore; Tariff History; Wilson, Woodrow.*

CHARLES CAREY, LYNCHBURG COLLEGE/
CENTRAL VIRGINIA COMMUNITY COLLEGE

BIBLIOGRAPHY

Brands, H. W. *T. R.: The Last Romantic.* New York: Basic Books, 1997.
Burton, David H. *Theodore Roosevelt, American Politician: An Assessment.* Madison, N.J.: Fairleigh Dickinson University Press, 1997.
Miller, Nathan. *Theodore Roosevelt: A Life.* New York: Morrow, 1992.

NEWSPAPERS AND POLITICAL PARTIES

The relationship between newspapers and political parties has evolved over time, with most historians identifying the early 1790s through the 1830s as the period when newspapers and political parties were most closely aligned. By 1840, when Democrat Martin Van Buren lost the presidency to Whig William Henry Harrison, the era of overt partisan support of and alignment with newspapers had peaked and was heading toward its nadir.

Important changes in the ways newspapers were produced, as well as changes in the potential news audience, hastened the decline of the party press and the rise of independent newspapers. Although still focused on delivering political news, the newspapers of the latter half of the nineteenth century and into the twentieth distanced themselves from open support of political parties, focusing instead on meeting the commercial demands of the consumer news audience.

NEWSPAPERS AT THE FOUNDING

Before the Revolution, American newspapers generally provided information for merchants and public notices, but they carried very little "news" as we think of it today. What news they did carry generally came from British newspapers and was outdated by the time a colonial newspaper printed it.

Newspapers were published by printers whose main revenue came from production of government documents, political pamphlets, popular literature, and religious materials.

The use of newspapers to spread political news increased during the Revolution, but most were still considered secondary outlets by comparison with the special newsletters and pamphlets distributed by political leaders. One famous exception was the *New York Weekly Journal,* whose publisher, John Peter Zenger, was arrested in 1734 by the colonial governor for publishing statements criticizing the governor's administration. Zenger was defended by Andrew Hamilton, whose arguments to the jury brought a swift acquittal and laid the grounds for the freedom of the press enjoyed today regarding public criticism of government officials. The Zenger case illustrated the tensions that resulted from the expanded use of newspapers as vehicles for critical discussion of public affairs, though the criticism paled in comparison with the overtly partisan attacks that were to come in the postcolonial period.

After the Revolutionary War, newspapers became the main source of government news, largely as a consequence of the bitter personal divisions among federal officials. Heading the competing factions, which evolved into the first organized political parties, were Alexander Hamilton, a proponent of a strong central government, and Thomas Jefferson, who favored balance between the national and state governments. Newspapers were formed, funded, and operated in the nation's capital and other eastern cities to promote the two factions, often in terms that were deeply personal and often filled with invective. The newspapers served to promote the positions of these leaders, provided a vehicle for their public statements, and defended them against attacks published in competing organs. The newspapers were viewed as mouthpieces of their sponsors.

BIRTH OF THE PARTISAN PRESS

The first overtly partisan newspaper was John Fenno's *Gazette of the United States,* a Federalist paper established in 1789. Other Federalist papers included Benjamin Russell's *Columbian Centinel* (1784), Noah Webster's *American Minerva* (1793), William Cobett's *Porcupine's Gazette* (1797), and William Coleman's *New York Evening Post* (1801). Opposing the Federalists were the Democratic (or Jeffersonian) Republicans, who had among their founders many of the original Anti-Federalists. The main Democratic-Republican papers were Benjamin Franklin Bache's *Aurora* (1790), Philip Freneau's *National Gazette* (1791), and Samuel Harrison Smith's *National Intelligencer* (1800).

As party organizations became more sophisticated, newspapers adapted their coverage to reflect the broader party coalitions, rather than the highly individualistic content of the earlier period. During the early decades of the nineteenth century, a number of party-sponsored or party-aligned newspapers were established in the western territories. The evolution of the party press was stimulated by Andrew Jackson's successful 1828 presidential campaign. Jackson used a network of Democratic newspapers founded and cultivated after his 1824 defeat to promote his campaign and the election of Democratic state and federal officials. This network of newly established newspapers in the western United States, along with older party papers in states such as New York, helped solidify support for his Democratic coalition. Among Jackson's staunchest allies were the *Argus of Western America,* published by Amos Kendall, Duff Green's *United States Telegraph,* and Francis P. Blair's *Washington Globe.* The Whigs, competing against Jacksonian Democrats, organized a network of their own presses, which included newspapers in the nation's capital, its biggest cities, and most of the sizable towns throughout the interior.

Both factions used ample space in their publications to discuss political news, promote the issues of their leaders, and bitterly attack their opponents. The antagonistic and personal nature of the attacks soured many historians on the nineteenth-century partisan press. Others, however, argue that the partisanship clarified newspapers' editorial positions and simplified decision making for the electorate. Where the former criticize the partisan press for its attacks and distortions, the latter wax nostalgic about its clearly articulated bias.

PARTISAN PAPERS AS NEWS SOURCES

Newspapers of the time were small operations with limited "news" gathering operations. Paid journalism was looked down upon as a profession, so most of the content was supplied in the form of editorials written by the editor/publisher or by the paper's political patrons, often under pseudonyms. Circulation was also small, with the largest papers boasting circulation of fewer than two thousand copies. Of the ninety-two U.S. newspapers published in 1790, only eight were dailies. Seventy others were published weekly, with the rest published less frequently or on unique timetables. Weekly publication was common in large part because more frequent publication was too costly. Most newspapers were published primarily for a sophisticated city audience.

The relationship between the early newspapers and political parties was based on economic self-interest as much as on firmly held political ideology. Government printing contracts provided the basis of the relationship between many newspaper printers and their patrons. Supporters of one party or the other depended on patronage contracts for their livelihood, and therefore had a keen and direct interest in ensuring that their patron won office and kept it.

EVOLUTION AND DECLINE

By the 1830s newspapers began to move away from a role strictly as partisan organs, though many maintained their allegiance to a single party. By 1840 technology had reduced the per-paper cost of printing newspapers in large quantities. These new, low-cost papers were dubbed "penny papers" because they cost only two cents, compared with the six-cent price of most early newspapers. Later, as more papers competed for a mass audience, their price was reduced still further to a penny, providing the name by which they are now commonly known. The penny papers were produced for the mass audience, particularly the immigrant classes that began to flood American cities in search of industrial jobs. Marketing to a mass audience meant avoiding overt partisan alliances that might cost newspapers readers and circulation. As a consequence, newspapers toned down their partisanship and supplanted it with "objective" reporting of the news of the day.

In addition, the process for contracting government printing changed. The increased size and sophistication of the national government made printing by patronage costly, inefficient, and prone to serious violations of secrecy. As a remedy, federal government printing contracts were gradually regulated and consolidated, leading eventually to establishment of the Government Printing Office in 1851. Of these two factors, the change in government printing was perhaps most significant because it severed the patronage link between electoral competition and newspapers.

In the years following the decline of the party press, newspapers continued to play a central role in politics and public affairs. Issue-based parties, such as the abolitionists before the Civil War and the Populists and the Progressives near the end of the nineteenth century, used newspapers to advance their positions, criticize their opponents, and mobilize the public agenda. *The Liberator,* published in Boston and edited by William Lloyd Garrison between 1831 and 1866, was perhaps the best known abolitionist paper of the time. Others, including Rev. Elijah Lovejoy's *St. Louis Observer,* renamed the *Alton Observer* after antiabolitionists chased Lovejoy across the Mississippi River into Illinois, gained notoriety from the suffering of their publishers for promoting their beliefs. Lovejoy eventually was murdered by antiabolitionists in Illinois.

The efforts of many smaller, issue-oriented papers often led to coverage of social-reform issues in the larger-circulation papers, such as Horace Greeley's *New York Tribune.* The *Tribune,* published under Greeley between 1841 and 1872, was a good example of a paper established to promote the views of the publisher. Unlike the party papers created after the Revolution, however, Greeley's paper was devoted not to promoting him but rather the interests and issues of his middle-class and working-class readers. Greeley served as the model for most

Horace Greeley, longtime publisher of the *New York Tribune,* set a course independent of the parties. *Library of Congress*

publishers who followed and similarly abandoned overt party advocacy for positions geared toward the commercial interests and ideological concerns of their readers.

The intense competition for the mass audience also elevated tabloid journalism to a new level, as exemplified by the "yellow journalism" of Joseph Pulitzer's *New York World* and William Randolph Hearst's *New York Journal.* Unlike the partisan press of the century's early decades, these papers took political views that served to promote the editors' opinions and that were controversial enough to sell newspapers. These papers also employed some of the best writers and artists of the day, in an effort to lure readers and advertisers. Competition was stiff, both from competing newspapers and from the exposé-minded serials such as *Harper's Weekly* and *Collier's.* In fact, it was the muckraking of magazine writers such as Sinclair Lewis and Ida Tarbell that propelled the Progressive era reforms, though newspapers also contributed with exposés of urban corruption and social problems.

PARTISANSHIP IN THE MODERN ERA

The decline of an overtly partisan press does not mean that the modern press is nonpartisan. Numerous studies have documented partisan biases among both newspaper owners and writers. Publishers and owners tend to be conservative, favoring the Republican Party. Notable examples include the *Chicago Tribune* under the McCormick family and the *Los Angeles Times* under the Otis family. (In 2000 the two papers came under common ownership.)

Reporters and editors, by contrast, tend to be slightly more liberal, favoring the Democratic Party agenda. For example, during the Watergate scandal that drove President Richard Nixon from office in 1974, Nixon complained that *Washington Post* editor Ben Bradlee was against him because of his liberal leanings and his friendships with prominent Democrats such as the Kennedys of Massachusetts.

Most newspapers today are considered nonpartisan largely because norms of professional journalism discourage displays of partisan bias outside of the editorial pages or signed columns of opinion. Editors require reporters to write balanced news stories that do not favor one candidate or party over another. Commercial pressures also encourage newspapers to sell across party lines. But some observers believe that journalists have gone too far in the opposite direction in their effort to avoid the appearance of favoring any particular ideology. Instead, they tend to criticize politicians of all stripes, leading many to question whether newspapers have come full circle from their days of overt political boosterism to a more cynical and pessimistic antipolitics position.

See also *Jackson, Andrew; Political Parties; Television and American Politics.*

BRIAN C. WHITE, UNIVERSITY OF ILLINOIS AT CHICAGO

BIBLIOGRAPHY

Schudson, Michael. *Discovering the News: A Social History of American Newspapers.* New York: Basic Books, 1978.

Sloan, W. David. "The Party Press, 1789–1833." In *The Media in America: A History.* 2d ed. Edited by W. David Sloan, James D. Startt, and James G. Stovall. Scottsdale: Arizona Publishing Horizons, 1993.

Smith, Culver H. *The Press, Politics, and Patronage: The American Government's Use of Newspapers, 1789–1875.* Athens: University of Georgia Press, 1977.

Streitmatter, Rodger. *Mightier than the Sword: How the News Media Have Shaped American History.* Boulder: Westview Press, 1997.

NIXON, RICHARD M.

Richard Milhous Nixon (1913–1994), president of the United States from 1969 to mid-1974, was one of the dominant—and most controversial—political figures of the late twentieth century. Entirely a self-made man, Nixon was deeply insecure, felt surrounded by enemies (especially in the liberal media), and was determined to build himself up by destroying them. With few close friends or advisers in or out of politics, Nixon was a conspicuous "loner" in American political history.

In 1942 Nixon was a lawyer for the Office of Price Administration (OPA), the vast New Deal program that regulated prices and rationed basic commodities during World War II. After serving in the U.S. Navy he entered an entirely unstructured California political environment—one where parties hardly existed in the 1940s and many voters were recent arrivals. As a result, Nixon, a Republican, never built a secure base in California (or anywhere else).

Nixon's first major breakthrough came in the U.S. House, to which he was elected in 1946. There his dogged investigation broke the impasse of the Alger Hiss spy case in 1948. At the hearings Hiss, who had been with President Franklin D. Roosevelt at the Yalta summit in 1945, denied allegations that he had ever been a communist. Nixon obtained copies of secret documents Hiss apparently had given to Whittaker Chambers, a one-time communist spy. The idea that Hiss could be a Soviet spy threatened to delegitimize the New Deal itself and made Nixon a hero to the late FDR's enemies. In reality, Nixon's moderate position on policy issues was closer to the Democratic Party center's position than to the GOP's. In 1952 Democrats sought to discredit Dwight D. Eisenhower's presidential candidacy by tarnishing his running mate, Nixon, with allegations that he accepted money and gifts, including his daughters' dog Checkers, from supporters. Nixon's televised defense of his actions and unapologetic determination to keep the dog became the "Checkers Speech," which turned the tables and persuaded Eisenhower to keep him on the ticket.

As vice president, Nixon traveled widely and gained a solid grounding in world affairs. With few formal duties, Nixon threw himself into state and local politics, making hundreds of speeches across the land. With Eisenhower uninvolved in party building, Nixon became the de facto national GOP leader, and his 1960 nomination for president was ensured. He lost an agonizingly close race to John F. Kennedy, conceding rather than challenge the vote count in Chicago, where vote fraud had been suspected. In 1962 Nixon was defeated again, this time for the governorship of California. Nixon became a New York City lawyer and built a network of associates who would eventually staff his administration. In 1964 Republican nominee Barry Goldwater's purge of the eastern liberals, followed by his massive loss to Lyndon B. Johnson, left the GOP leaderless; Nixon filled the void. With the Democratic Party bitterly split in 1968 over the Vietnam War and civil rights issues, Nixon won a tight three-way race against Democrat Hubert H. Humphrey and independent George C. Wallace. He entered the White House pledging to "bring us together again."

FOREIGN POLICY SUCCESSES AND FAILURES

As president, Nixon forged a remarkable partnership with his national security adviser and later secretary of state, Henry A. Kissinger. Although dissimilar in personality, the two men were committed to a realism that focused on American economic advantages and jettisoned moralism in foreign policy, seeking détente with the Soviet Union and confrontation with old allies that now had become economic adversaries. Everyone assumed, mistakenly, that Nixon's anticommunist reputation at home indicated a hardline cold warrior. But even as Eisenhower's vice president Nixon had been moving away from U.S. efforts to "contain" communism. In his 1959 "kitchen debate" with Soviet leader Nikita Khrushchev at a Moscow trade show, Nixon advocated more U.S.-Soviet competition in consumer goods and less in weapons systems. Nixon concluded that containment (which he saw as a policy of Harry S. Truman) had failed. As a realist he felt it was time to emphasize economic goals in foreign policy and to deemphasize expensive ideological or peripheral commitments.

By the mid-1960s the two largest communist powers, China and the Soviet Union, had become bitter enemies. Their armies sporadically threatened each other across a long border; the risk of war was serious. Both Moscow and Beijing realized it would be wise to deescalate tensions with the United States, but Lyndon Johnson ignored them both. Succeeding Johnson as president, Nixon sensed fresh opportunity and played the two communist giants against one another. In 1972 Nixon took a bold step and became the first U.S. president to visit communist China. The surprise trip in effect ended the cold war with China and ushered in an era of cautious friendship that was still unfolding three decades later.

The Soviets rushed to catch favor, and Nixon's summit meetings with Khrushchev's successor, Leonid I. Brezhnev, produced major arms agreements—especially a treaty banning antimissile defenses in space. (It was thought that the "balance of terror," with each side having thousands of nuclear missiles, guaranteed peace, and that a successful defense against missiles would dangerously destabilize this equilibrium.) Both Moscow and Beijing sharply reduced their military, economic, and diplomatic support for America's remaining enemy, communist North Vietnam.

In the 1968 election Nixon carefully avoided the issue of entanglement in Vietnam. (Humphrey ridiculed his silence by saying that Nixon was keeping "secret" his plans to end the war.) The United States was in Vietnam because of its commitment to the long-standing containment policy. Nixon's solution was "Vietnamization"—to turn the civil war over to the South Vietnamese government in Saigon, withdrawing all U.S. ground forces by 1971. Ignoring critics who said he was

President Richard M. Nixon greets Chinese Communist Party Chairman Mao Zedong in 1972. Nixon, long known for his anticommunism, reversed two decades of American policy toward China. *The White House*

prolonging the war, Nixon set his timetable by the rate at which he could obtain tacit approval from the Soviet Union, China, and South Vietnam. His policy succeeded in part. South Vietnam did take over the war, and elsewhere containment was replaced by the "Nixon Doctrine" that countries must defend themselves.

Meanwhile, segments of the antiwar forces on the home front were increasingly involved in violence, drugs, and a radicalism typified by collegiate protests that provoked a strong backlash in Nixon's favor. Opposition on college campuses reached a crescendo in May 1970 after six students were killed, four at Kent State University in Ohio and two at Jackson State College in Mississippi. The demonstrations had been touched off by the U.S. invasion of Cambodia to destroy sanctuaries of communist South Vietnamese Viet Cong guerrillas. In the wake of the campus deaths, student strikes shut down more than four hundred U.S. colleges; a few months later the campuses became quiet.

By February 1972, when Nixon met with Chinese premier Mao Zedong at Beijing, the guerrilla war in Vietnam was virtually over, with the Viet Cong essentially defeated. North Vietnam, however, disregarded the advice of its allies and launched its conventional forces in the Easter 1972 invasion of the South. Saigon fought back and, with strong American air support, routed the communists. Peace was at hand,

as Kissinger said, but first Saigon had to be reassured of continued U.S. support. An indication of this assurance came in the "Linebacker II" air campaign in December 1972, when for the first time in the war Hanoi and its port were attacked. Hanoi signed peace accords in Paris in January 1973 and released American prisoners.

The stepped-up U.S. support for South Vietnam proved to be short-lived. Nixon, having achieved what he called "peace with honor," immediately withdrew all U.S. air and naval combat forces and ended the draft; he continued heavy shipments of weapons into South Vietnam despite mounting demands from Congress that all aid be stopped.

DOMESTIC POLICIES

Nixon's domestic policies were as unpredictable as his foreign policies. His supporters and enemies always thought they knew where he stood and could foretell his actions, but they were wrong. They mistakenly assumed he opposed the New Deal's philosophy. In practice Nixon, like most eastern liberal Republicans in the tradition of Wendell Willkie, Thomas E. Dewey, and Nelson Rockefeller, supported the core of New Deal policies, while claiming they could do the job more efficiently.

Although Nixon dropped the less successful Great Society programs, he kept and expanded most of LBJ's new ventures. Welfare spending, aid to education, and support for the arts and humanities rose sharply, as did Social Security and Medicare payments. Poverty rates among the old fell by half. With the winding down of the cold war the defense budget was cut. The combination of prosperity, inflation, and progressive tax rates doubled federal revenues. There was little thought of tax cuts. Instead Nixon began sharing revenues with the states, in the form of direct grants. Nixon did not speak for the taxpayer and he ignored economists who called for deregulation. Environmentalism came of age around 1970, and the Nixon administration worked successfully with Congress to develop a suite of new environmental regulations and controls, including creation of the Environmental Protection Agency and passage of the Clean Water Act, which proved especially popular among educated voters.

Nixon campaigned against the Supreme Court in 1968, charging that under Chief Justice Earl Warren the Court was "seriously hampering the peace forces in our society and strengthening the criminal forces." He replaced Earl Warren, on Warren's retirement, with Warren Burger, who proved unable to reverse the Warren Court's liberalism. The Senate twice rejected conservative southerners; in 1971 Nixon did succeed with William H. Rehnquist of Arizona. Although at first he seemed far to the right, Rehnquist eventually became the dominant figure in the judiciary, and Nixon's most lasting legacy.

When an economic recession hit in 1971, Nixon declared himself a "Keynesian," in favor of using fiscal and monetary policy to stimulate the economy. He and Treasury Secretary John B. Connally of Texas, a former Democrat, designed a "New Economic Policy" that included a ninety-day wage and price freeze, an unlinking of the dollar to gold, devaluation of the dollar, a surtax on imports, and drastic measures to reduce the trade deficit. America's trading partners were aghast at what they considered brute force and inadequate consultation.

In 1973 the Organization of Petroleum Exporting Countries (OPEC) cut off oil shipments to the United States in retaliation for U.S. support of Israel in its war with Egypt. Oil prices rose sharply, just as the United States was changing from an exporter to an importer of the precious fluid. Inflation began to soar. Despite his steadily weakening political position, Nixon reacted to the energy-and-inflation crises with voluntary ("jawbone") regulations and controls, mandatory restrictions on heating and air conditioning, another devaluation of the dollar, another round of mandatory price controls, and the threat (never actually put in effect) of gasoline rationing. But unlike 1942, when Nixon helped enforce wartime price controls as an OPA lawyer, the U.S. economy was not thriving at all. When Nixon left office in 1974, the indicators were all headed downward, and the long-term prognosis was gloomy.

In race relations, Nixon had limited success in easing the black rage that erupted following the assassination of Martin Luther King Jr. in 1968. Under Johnson a series of civil rights bills had been passed, and many traditional forms of segregation, such as "whites only" sections in buses and restaurants, were ended. But tensions remained high between working-class whites and inner-city blacks. African Americans staged riots in more than two hundred cities; streets became unsafe, and whites fled inner-city schools and neighborhoods. Nixon gauged every policy by its political repercussions. He never expected more than a minuscule share of the African American vote, but it was important to retain the support of upper-middle-class suburban whites who favored integration as a long-term goal. At the same time he sought to win over the "silent majority" of working-class ethnics and white southerners who identified blacks with welfare and crime and who

strongly opposed giving them any special legal or political advantages or additional welfare payments. The dual system of schools was abolished in the South. Whites in numerous cities vehemently opposed forced busing of school children as ordered by federal judges. Nixon could do little to stop busing, except articulate his opposition. He promoted affirmative action quota plans in the construction trades, along with set-asides for minority contractors, designed in the long run to enlarge the African American middle class. As the Democratic Congress increased the overall level of welfare payments, the White House quietly went along. By 1973 the riots had burned out. Middle-class blacks, moreover, were starting to make dramatic progress in fields such as education, sports, entertainment, the military, and government service.

ASSESSMENT

The collapse of the New Deal voter coalition gave Nixon the opportunity to build what he called the "New Majority"—a conservative coalition that augmented the traditional upper-middle-class Republican base with formerly Democratic Catholics and southern whites. Seeing no further need for the GOP party apparatus, Nixon cut himself entirely loose from it for his 1972 reelection race. The coalition came together, and Nixon won a landslide against liberal Democrat George McGovern, who won only 17 of the 538 electoral votes. There were no coattails, however, as the Republicans remained a minority party in the electorate and in Congress. Nor was there a sense of identification with or loyalty to Nixonism. Instead Nixon had tapped a growing mood of malaise and alienation, not realizing that mood would soon turn against him.

The Watergate break-in was, in the words of a White House press aide, a "third-rate burglary" of the Democratic national headquarters. As such it was a risky move, one quite unnecessary to assist Nixon's reelection in 1972. But Nixon, always insecure, would do whatever it took to ensure victory and would cover up any resulting legal problems using the full powers of the presidency. Thread by thread for two years the whole Nixon cover-up unraveled. Every week in 1973–1974 came a new revelation or twist, as Nixon's stock sank. Congress, the courts, the special prosecutor, and the news media threw themselves into round after round of investigation. Each turned up fresh evidence of inconceivable crimes and bungled efforts to conceal them. Senate hearings disclosed the existence of a secret White House tape-recording system, which gave unprecedented access to Nixon's policy discussions. Nixon's top aides, H. R. Haldeman and John D. Ehrlichman, were forced to resign in April 1973; later they went to prison, as did several others, includ-

This subpoena was issued July 23, 1973, one week after former White House aide Alexander Butterfield revealed that a secret taping system had been installed in the Oval Office to preserve all presidential conversations. The subpoena ordered President Nixon or his representative to appear before the federal grand jury on July 26 and to bring taped conversations relevant to the investigation of the Watergate affair. *National Archives*

ing former attorney general John N. Mitchell. Nixon's denials grew less credible; his firing of Watergate special prosecutor Archibald Cox in October 1973 backfired. Coincidentally, the same month, Vice President Spiro Agnew, charged with taking bribes, resigned to avoid prosecution. Finally, the Supreme Court ordered the release of taped conversations that Nixon realized contained the "smoking gun"—explicit evidence that he had used federal power to try to cover up criminal activity. On August 9, 1974, a few days before the House could vote impeachment, Nixon became the first president to resign. One month later, on the eve of midterm elections, President Gerald R. Ford issued a pardon—saving Nixon from trial but devastating Ford and the Republican Party.

Nixon had remarkable skill in analyzing complex political situations, linking together all the main forces and anticipating with uncanny accuracy how all the major players would respond. His analytic skill substituted in large part for his unfitness for twisting arms like Lyndon Johnson or appealing directly to the populace like FDR or, later, Ronald Reagan. After his downfall Nixon wrote a series of penetrating books that helped restore his respectability. On the negative side was Nixon's unceasing fixation on his enemies, perceived and real. He was morbidly fascinated with their weaknesses and illicit secrets; always searching for another Alger Hiss, he sent

burglars to uncover more dirt—until the inept Watergate team was captured in 1972. His methods were a corruption of traditional republican values, and Nixon thereby generated deep and abiding dislike, not only from his enemies—he kept a written list—but also from observers who otherwise admired his skills. His epitaph may well be, "The smartest president, who did the dumbest things."

See also *Scandals and Corruption; Vietnam War; Watergate.*

RICHARD JENSEN,
RENSSELAER POLYTECHNIC INSTITUTE

BIBLIOGRAPHY

Aitken, Jonathan. *Nixon: A Life.* Washington, D.C.: Regnery Publishers, 1993.

Ambrose, Stephen E. *Nixon.* 3 vols. New York: Simon and Schuster, 1987–1991.

Bundy, William P. *A Tangled Web: The Making of Foreign Policy in the Nixon Presidency.* New York: Hill and Wang, 1998.

Congress and the Nation, 1968–1972. Washington, D.C.: Congressional Quarterly, 1973.

Nixon, Richard. *RN: The Memoirs of Richard Nixon.* New York: Grossett and Dunlap, 1978.

Schoenebaum, Eleanora W., ed. *Profiles of an Era: The Nixon/Ford Years.* New York: Harcourt Brace Jovanovich, 1979.

Small, Melvin. *The Presidency of Richard Nixon.* Lawrence: University Press of Kansas, 1999.

NORTHWEST ORDINANCE

Approved by the Continental Congress on July 13, 1787, the Northwest Ordinance outlined the rules for governing the area north of the Ohio River and established the process through which future states would enter the federal union.

In 1784 Thomas Jefferson had proposed a plan to govern the region, much of which his home state, Virginia, had ceded to the national government that same year. In Jefferson's plan, slavery was to be prohibited after 1800, and sixteen new states, equal in status to the original thirteen, were to be created out of the territory once their populations reached twenty thousand. Although Congress never enacted this plan, in May 1785 it adopted in revised form another land ordinance that Jefferson had proposed. This ordinance provided for surveying and distributing land into townships laid out in a grid pattern.

Settlement of the territory was slow, in part because of continued Indian fighting and the lack of any proposed government structure. Congress, desperate for money, finally passed the Northwest Ordinance in 1787 to provide the territory with a government and a system for settling the region, dealing with the Native Americans living there, and regularizing land sales. Most of the pressure for passage came from the Ohio Land Company, which was prepared to purchase five million acres in the region.

The ordinance outlined a three-stage process for statehood. Three to five states were to be created out of the territory, which was to be governed initially by a governor, secretary, and three judges, all appointed by Congress. After five thousand free adult males had settled in a territory, congressional rule would end and a transitional constitution and an elected bicameral legislature would govern the territory. Once a territory had a free population of sixty thousand, the inhabitants could write a constitution. After congressional approval the territory would achieve full statehood on equal terms with the original states. Other important clauses called for public support of education and provided for freedom of worship and the right to trial by jury. During the final reading of the ordinance, Congress added Article VI, which banned slavery in the territory but allowed masters from other places to recover fugitive slaves there.

The objective of the ordinance's draftees, led by Rep. Nathan Dane of Massachusetts, was to create a system that would encourage settlement and economic development to the west while ensuring that this development was integrated into the national economy. By providing political and legal stability under the direct control of the national government, Congress hoped to encourage settlement and sell land to raise money to run the national government. On October 5, 1787, Congress appointed Revolutionary War general Arthur St. Clair as the first governor of the Northwest Territory.

Considered one of the Confederation Congress's most important acts, the ordinance was largely successful in achieving its ends. In 1789 the new Congress, under the Constitution of 1787, reconfirmed the ordinance. Ambiguity within the document, however, contributed to boundary disputes and political controversies. Much of the ordinance's legacy revolved around the provision (Article VI) that banned slavery from the Northwest Territory. This clause had no enforcement provision, and it did not take into account the thousands of slaves already in the region. As late as the 1840s some slaves were found in the territory. Nor did Article VI expressly preclude the possibility that slavery could be legalized after statehood, something that the Illinois legislature seriously considered doing in 1823 and 1824. Nevertheless, in 1819 northern members of Congress used this provision to argue against admitting Missouri as a slave state, and in the antebellum period Article VI became an icon of the free-soil movement.

See also *Free Soil Party; Jefferson, Thomas; Slavery; Territorial Government and New State Formation*.

BRIAN D. SCHOEN, UNIVERSITY OF VIRGINIA

BIBLIOGRAPHY

Finkelman, Paul. *Slavery and the Founders: Race and Liberty in the Age of Jefferson.* Armonk, N.Y.: M.E. Sharpe, 1996.

Onuf, Peter S. *Statehood and Union: A History of the Northwest Ordinance.* Bloomington: Indiana University Press, 1987.

Williams, Frederick D., ed. *The Northwest Ordinance: Essays on Its Formulation, Provisions, and Legacy.* East Lansing: Michigan State University Press, 1989.

NULLIFICATION

Nullification is the prevention of enforcement of a federal statute or court decision by the government of a state within that state's territory on the basis of a judgment of unconstitutionality. The concept of nullification, also sometimes called "state interposition," arose naturally out of the idea that the federal government had limited powers—as is proved by the fact that in *The Federalist*, both Alexander Hamilton and James Madison asserted that state governments would retain sufficient power under the unamended constitution of 1787–1788 to prevent usurpations of the reserved rights of the states and the citizenry.

This idea received its first trial in 1798–1800, when Madison and Thomas Jefferson, as leaders of the Democratic-Republican Party, drafted the Virginia and Kentucky Resolutions. In these resolutions, the two states claimed the right or, in Madison's Virginia version, the *duty*, to "interpose" themselves between federal authorities and the affected citizens to prevent enforcement of statutes violative of certain political rights. This state power was the outgrowth, according to Jefferson's Kentucky Resolutions, of the fact that the states were the constituent elements of the American union and that it therefore was for them, not for the federal government (their creation), to decide disputes over the meaning of the charter that created and empowered that government. Virginia's and Kentucky's dispute with the federal government was resolved by the election of 1800, which elevated Jefferson to the presidency and made their position equally the position of the federal government.

The South Carolina nullification crisis of 1828–1833 also came to an end before the remedy contemplated by the antifederal side was fully implemented. In that case, Carolinian resentment of the federal tariffs of 1824 and 1828 provoked Vice President John C. Calhoun of South Carolina to spell out the recourse he thought a state might take consistently with the theory of the Virginia and Kentucky Resolutions. A state could, he held, call a convention of the sovereign people of the type that ratified the Constitution in the first place and have it declare the offending statute void in that state. If three-fourths of the states subsequently voted to adopt an amendment to make the nullified policy constitutional, it would be; otherwise, the sovereign state's interpretation of the Constitution that it had been a party to enacting was to be considered dispositive within that state.

President Jackson threatened the use of force to overcome the South Carolina convention's nullification of the tariffs, and nationalist senator Henry Clay took advantage of the standoff between the two antitariff factions (Jackson's Democrats and Vice President–cum–Senator Calhoun's nullifiers) to push adoption of a "compromise" tariff higher than that which the congressional majority might otherwise have favored. South Carolina declared victory. This sequence of events achieved what had been Calhoun's actual aim in writing his "South Carolina Exposition," which was to head off secession in South Carolina. Yet, it also permanently discredited nullification as an alternative to secession—one of the purposes for which it had been used both in 1798 and by Calhoun.

Opponents of the Fugitive Slave Law of 1850 resorted to nullification rhetoric from time to time, leading Chief Justice Roger B. Taney to denounce the doctrine in *Ableman v. Booth* (1859). However, the most famous reflorescence of the theory of nullification came in the wake of the Supreme Court's decision in the case of *Brown v. Board of Education* (1954). In a series of episodes, southern politicians desirous of giving the im-pression that they intended to resist federal integration efforts to the last pushed federal officials to the verge of violence (and sometimes, such as in the sequence of events surrounding the 1962 integration of the University of Mississippi, seemed to encourage mob violence). Arkansas governor Orval Faubus affected to ignore a federal court's integration order in 1957, thereby provoking President Dwight D. Eisenhower to federalize the Arkansas National Guard and use it to escort the first black students into Little Rock's Central High School. The Supreme Court, in the related case of *Cooper v. Aaron* (1958), staked a claim to ultimate authority to interpret the federal Constitution—thereby contradicting Jefferson, Madison, Calhoun, and Jackson. The end result, seemingly, was to sweep nullification into the dustbin of history.

See also *Calhoun, John C.; Civil Rights Movement; Fugitive Slave Laws; Sectionalism; States' Rights/Sovereignty; Tariff History.*

K. R. CONSTANTINE GUTZMAN, JOHN JAY COLLEGE, CUNY

BIBLIOGRAPHY

Ellis, Richard. *The Union at Risk: Jacksonian Democracy, States' Rights and the Nullification Crisis.* New York: Oxford University Press, 1987.

Freehling, William W. *Prelude to Civil War: The Nullification Controversy in South Carolina, 1816–1836.* New York: Harper and Row, 1966.

Gutzman, Kevin R. [Constantine]. "A Troublesome Legacy: James Madison and 'The Principles of '98,'" *Journal of the Early Republic* 15 (winter 1995), 569–589.

Lence, Ross M., ed. *Union and Liberty: The Political Philosophy of John C. Calhoun.* Indianapolis: Liberty Fund, 1992.

McCoy, Drew. *The Last of the Fathers: James Madison and the Republican Legacy* New York: Cambridge University Press, 1989.

OFFICE OF MANAGEMENT AND BUDGET

The primary mission of the Office of Management and Budget (OMB) is to help the president prepare the annual federal budget. OMB also assesses executive branch programs, policies, and procedures for their effectiveness and determines spending priorities among competing demands. It oversees administration reports, regulations, testimony, and draft legislation to check that they are consistent with and foster the president's policies.

Before passage of the Budget and Accounting Act of 1921, executive departments and federal agencies determined their own budget requests, which were gathered by the Treasury Department and then passed along—largely unexamined—to Congress. The 1921 act required that spending proposals be sent to the newly established Bureau of the Budget (BOB), within the Treasury Department. The bureau's central clearance function was to evaluate the appropriations requests and ensure that they adhered to the president's agenda; that is, that they fit within budgetary constraints and advanced the administration's legislative interests. BOB organized the funding requests into a unified annual budget that was presented to Congress. Budget Circular 49, issued in 1921, required that the president approve funding proposals before they were sent to Congress. In 1939 the bureau was transferred from the Treasury Department to the newly created Executive Office of the President. On July 1, 1970, the Bureau of the Budget was reconfigured as the Office of Management and Budget.

The budget bureau's duties expanded over time. In addition to examining funding requests, the bureau became responsible for assessing departmental legislative proposals that involved spending. It subsequently was entrusted to oversee all legislative proposals, executive orders, and proclamations. It was assigned the task of reviewing enrolled bills and advising the president on whether to sign or veto them. It also began to draft legislation, and bureau officials were called upon to appear before congressional committees to comment on pending bills. As federal programs grew more complex, the bureau became responsible for coordinating interagency activities and was expected to help improve the efficiency of government programs.

To a great extent, the role of the budget bureau and its credibility are determined by the president and the budget director. The president decides how politicized the position of budget director—and, by extension, the budget bureau—will be. The budget director offers the president a unique perspective, by serving as both a personal adviser to the president and the head of an institutional staff. The short-term interests of the president and the long-term interests of the presidency do not always coincide. For example, as President Richard M. Nixon became mired in the Watergate scandal, OMB essentially took over responsibility for the day-to-day management of the federal government. Political appointees displaced career officers in making domestic policy decisions. OMB was seen as doing the president's partisan bidding and, as a result, hurt its reputation. In 1974 Congress passed legislation requiring Senate confirmation of the budget director and the deputy director.

See also *Congressional Budget Office; Nixon, Richard M.; Watergate.*

COLLEEN MCGUINESS, INDEPENDENT AUTHOR

BIBLIOGRAPHY

Berman, Larry. *The Office of Management and Budget and the Presidency, 1921–1979.* Princeton, N.J.: Princeton University Press, 1979.

Congressional Quarterly's Guide to the Presidency, 2d ed., 496–501, 1112–1119. Washington, D.C.: Congressional Quarterly, 1996.

Mosher, Frederick C. *A Tale of Two Agencies: A Comparative Analysis of the General Accounting Office and the Office of Management and Budget.* Baton Rouge: Louisiana State University Press, 1984.

Office of Management and Budget Web site: *www.whitehouse.gov/OMB.*

P

PANIC OF 1819

A large balance of payments deficit, poor central bank leadership, and price inflation created a financial panic in 1819 that deepened into the nation's first major peacetime recession and laid the groundwork for the second party system.

Failure to recharter the Bank of the United States in 1811 and the fiscal emergency that emerged during the War of 1812 induced states to almost triple the number of banks by 1815. Shortly after British troops sacked Washington, D.C., in 1814, state banks outside of New England suspended specie payments, that is, they stopped exchanging gold and silver for their notes. In the absence of a strong central bank, regulatory authority, or specie convertibility, banks were free to expand the money supply, and they did so prodigiously. Despite their inconvertibility into specie, bank liabilities circulated as cash, displacing hard money from circulation.

The national government countered by chartering a new quasi-central bank, the second Bank of the United States (1816–1836). Unfortunately, its first president, William Jones, was not a banker. Instead of controlling state banks, he used the specie reserves of the Bank of the United States to restore the convertibility of their notes, which served only to fuel the monetary expansion. As the boom continued, imports outstripped exports, and specie flowed out to meet the balance of payments deficit. Dwindling specie stocks eventually undermined convertibility, causing specie to sell at a premium. In response, the Bank of the United States, under new president Langdon Cheves, began to contract the money supply quickly. The sudden loss of bank credit and an unfavorable exchange rate forced a number of important mercantile firms into insolvency. Panic ensued as people scrambled to turn debts receivable and tangible assets into specie, very little of which remained in circulation.

The Bank of the United States maintained a tight rein on bank liabilities. Prices plummeted, potential borrowers had difficulty finding lenders, and, predictably, aggregate output suffered. After several painful years the economy recovered on its own accord; the recession decreased merchandise imports, eventually inducing specie inflows.

The recession hurt almost everyone. Urban poor people were among the hardest hit. For example, the number of paupers and debtors in Manhattan increased significantly, and the number of debtors in prison jumped from 273 in 1818 to 382 in 1819 and continued steadily upward for at least the next two years. Similarly, the number of people in almshouses in New York City increased by 27 percent in 1820. Those individuals holding the notes of troubled banks suffered when the notes depreciated. Some corporate equity holders suffered when stock prices or dividends dropped. Finally, debtors obligated to repay a fixed sum of money found it more difficult to do so as their dollar incomes fell. Several states allowed debtors to delay repayment or prevented the sale of debtors' property at distressed prices. Such states merely succeeded in passing the pain of the panic on to creditors.

The panic of 1819 and the subsequent recession reignited the Jeffersonian antifinance sentiments that had subsided after 1800. The radical Jacksonian platform of 1828, which favored specie over bank notes, an independent treasury over a national bank, and a federal surplus over a national debt, can be traced to the financial difficulties of 1819 to 1821. The panic of 1819 encouraged moralizing about the importance of hard work and frugality and gave impetus to the nascent protective tariff movement.

See also *Bank War; Jackson, Andrew; Tariff History.*

ROBERT E. WRIGHT, UNIVERSITY OF VIRGINIA

BIBLIOGRAPHY

Blackson, Robert M. "Pennsylvania Banks and the Panic of 1819: A Reinterpretation." *Journal of the Early Republic* 9 (fall 1989): 335–358.

Perkins, Edwin J. *American Public Finance and Financial Services, 1700–1815.* Columbus: Ohio State University Press, 1994.

Remini, Robert. *Andrew Jackson and the Bank War: A Study in the Growth of Presidential Power.* New York: Norton, 1967.

Rothbard, Murray N. *The Panic of 1819: Reactions and Policies.* New York: Columbia University Press, 1962.

Smith, Walter B. *Economic Aspects of the Second Bank of the United States.* Cambridge: Harvard University Press, 1953.

PANIC OF 1837

The panic of 1837 precipitated a major economic depression nationwide. The panic had many causes, but shortsighted federal fiscal policy and weaknesses in the structure of the American banking system were major contributors. Politically, it plagued the administration of Martin Van Buren and contributed significantly to the 1840 election of the first Whig president, William Henry Harrison.

Ironically, the panic of 1837 resulted in large part because the federal government had gotten out of debt, the only time this has happened in U.S. history. Government land sales and tariff proceeds, both the results of an expanding economy, exceeded the cost of operating the government, so that in 1835 the federal treasury held a surplus. In 1836 Congress voted to disburse the surplus to the states as interest-free loans that were not expected to be repaid. The states spent these funds on a variety of transportation improvement projects, thus further stimulating the economy.

WEAK BANKING REGULATION

The problem arose when the federal government began to withdraw from the nation's banks the funds to be disbursed. At the time, the national banking system had virtually no federal supervision, since the Bank of the United States had lost its federal charter in 1836 after a four-year struggle to renew it. Although 80 percent privately owned, the Bank of the United States was the only legal repository for federal funds. Its unique position in this regard had allowed it to serve as an informal regulator of the national banking system by issuing securely backed bank notes. These notes were eagerly sought by knowledgeable investors, which forced other banks to offer the same level of security for their notes.

However, President Andrew Jackson attacked the bank because, he claimed, it was controlled by haughty aristocrats who were enriching themselves at the public's expense. Jackson wanted to spread federal money around to the various state-chartered banks, thus sharing the nation's wealth more evenly. But when Jackson ordered the withdrawal of federal deposits from the bank in 1832, he ran into a determined opponent in Nicholas Biddle, the bank's president.

Following Jackson's order, Biddle began tightening credit and calling in loans, partly to maintain the bank's reserves and partly to stimulate a recession, which he hoped to blame on Jackson. A recession did occur in 1833, but it was blamed on Biddle instead of Jackson. Jackson was able to discredit Biddle, which resulted in congressional revocation of the bank's charter when it came up for renewal in 1833.

No longer facing competition from the Bank of the United States, many banks began to loan out a far higher percentage of their assets. Most of these loans went to land speculators who purchased government land with the intention of reselling it at a profit. This situation left the banks with insufficient reserves to weather an emergency. Consequently, they were forced to call in many loans to meet the demands of the government withdrawals.

SPECIE CIRCULAR AND OTHER CAUSES

President Jackson made matters worse when he issued the Specie Circular (1836). This presidential order attempted to cool the economy by making it harder to speculate in land. Specifically, the circular demanded that land be paid for in specie—either gold or silver—rather than in paper money, most of which was printed by the banks themselves and was insufficiently guaranteed. Specie was in short supply, so the president's order greatly reduced people's ability to buy land. Many land speculators went bankrupt, which led to many bank failures. The circular also effectively reduced the value of paper money, which in turn drove up prices at a time when people could least afford to pay them.

The federal government's reaction exacerbated the panic. In the days before Keynesian economics (which would not be introduced until the Great Depression one hundred years later), little was known about the government's ability to end a recession via massive spending. Instead, government intervention in the economy was believed to be a bad thing. Consequently, the Van Buren administration took few steps to ease the situation. To make matters worse, the administration began borrowing money to pay its debts and insisted that taxes be paid in specie. Both measures further reduced the value of paper money and probably prolonged the depression.

Although the panic of 1837 resulted largely from financial and fiscal miscalculations, other causes bear mention. During the late 1830s western Europe experienced an economic recession of its own. This recession hit England hardest, prompting English investors to pull their investments out of American banks at a time when these banks could least afford to have deposits withdrawn. Also in the late 1830s, a series of American crop failures reduced the production of American farmers to a level so low that at one point the United States was forced to import significant quantities of foodstuffs. Paying to import food contributed further to the amount of money leaving the country, thus adding to the burden on an overworked banking system.

POLITICAL IMPLICATIONS OF THE PANIC

For five years—from 1837 to 1842—the panic held the United States in its grip. Politically, no one was affected more adversely than Martin Van Buren. The panic dominated political discussions across the country and undermined public confidence in Van Buren's ability to run the federal government. His fellow Democrats in Congress distanced themselves from his policies, which crippled his ability to push any legislation through Congress. In the 1840 election Van Buren was soundly defeated by Harrison, a famous general and Indian fighter who had practically no political experience.

The panic of 1837 was not the first major economic depression in U.S. history, nor would it be the last. It illustrates the fragility of the nineteenth-century American economy and the lack of knowledge among financial and government leaders about managing economic expansion.

See also *Bank War; Harrison, William Henry; Jackson, Andrew; Tariff History; Van Buren, Martin.*

CHARLES CAREY,
LYNCHBURG COLLEGE/CENTRAL VIRGINIA COMMUNITY COLLEGE

BIBLIOGRAPHY

Engerman, Stanley L., and Robert E. Gallman, eds. *The Cambridge Economic History of the United States.* New York: Cambridge University Press, 1996.

Feller, Daniel. *The Jacksonian Promise: America, 1815–1840.* Baltimore: Johns Hopkins University Press, 1995.

Poulson, Barry W. *Economic History of the United States.* New York: Macmillan, 1981.

PANIC OF 1857

The panic of 1857 is the American name for the global depression that followed the Crimean War. Although the panic was short-lived in the United States, it served to further exacerbate relations between the North and the South and so contributed in a small way to the outbreak of the Civil War.

Its immediate cause was the end of the Crimean War, a war fought from 1853 to 1856 in Crimea, a Russian-owned peninsula in the Black Sea, against Russia by Great Britain, France, Sardinia-Piedmont, and the Ottoman Empire. An allied blockade prevented the Russians from exporting Ukrainian wheat, so the European demand for American grain skyrocketed. This demand, coupled with an American economy that was expanding, fueled the development of more farmland in the West, which led to increased railroad construction and the manufacture of farm implements.

In an effort to profit from this economic expansion, banks made too many insufficiently secured loans and kept too low a percentage of deposits in reserve. When the Crimean War ended, the Russians resumed the shipment of wheat to western Europe at prices below the level at which American farmers could compete. The resultant loss of business spelled disaster for many farmers, railroad tycoons, and manufacturers who could no longer make payments on their loans.

The panic began in late 1857 when the Ohio Life Insurance Company of Cincinnati, which had loaned money heavily and recklessly, went bankrupt. The company's failure caused financiers throughout the East and Midwest, who sensed that the boom economy had gone bust, to panic. Suddenly, loans were next to impossible to obtain, which made it impossible for cash-strapped railroads and factories to continue operations. Hundreds of thousands of workers in the East and Midwest lost their jobs, and others were forced to take cuts in wages or hours.

The panic threatened to incite social unrest throughout the East and Midwest. Unemployed workers in several cities staged demonstrations demanding work and food, and an angry mob in New York City stormed the shops of several flour merchants and made off with their stocks. Another New York City mob, threatening to break into the subtreasury vault on Wall Street, had to be dispersed by the army. Fortunately, the financial crisis subsided relatively quickly. By early 1858 signs of recovery could be seen, and by mid-1859 practically all of the unemployed were working again.

While the East and Midwest were being ravaged by the panic, the South continued to enjoy economic prosperity. Land fever had long since abated in the South, which perhaps contributed to the greater stability and cautiousness of southern banks. Southerners touted their immunity to the panic as a sign that their agrarian way of life was superior to the northern industrialized lifestyle, and they claimed that southern slaves were happier and better fed than northern factory workers. Such claims only irritated northerners by making them even more uncomfortable with slavery, thus further poisoning relations between North and South.

CHARLES CAREY,
LYNCHBURG COLLEGE/CENTRAL VIRGINIA COMMUNITY COLLEGE

BIBLIOGRAPHY

Engerman, Stanley L., and Robert E. Gallman, eds. *The Cambridge Economic History of the United States.* New York: Cambridge University Press, 1996.

Poulson, Barry W. *Economic History of the United States.* New York: Macmillan, 1981.

Reisman, David A. *The Political Economy of James Buchanan.* College Station: Texas A & M University Press, 1990.

PANIC OF 1893

The panic of 1893 led to the second-worst economic depression in American history. Its immediate causes were the collapse of the stock market and uncertainties concerning the soundness of the nation's monetary standard. It lasted five years, during which thousands of businesses went bankrupt and one million people lost their jobs. The panic played a major role in the rise and fall of the Populist Party and the dominance of the Republican Party in national politics until the eve of World War I.

By 1893 the nation had stood on the brink of depression for six years. Low farm prices, depressed since 1887, severely limited the purchasing power of farmers. Railroads had once again expanded their lines beyond their ability to pay for operations from their revenues. Depression in Europe had forced European investors to withdraw funds from American enterprises, thus weakening U.S. stock exchanges. Moreover, investors were growing fearful that the government's reserves of gold, which backed federal paper money, were insufficient to guarantee the value of the dollar.

The panic began in earnest in March 1893 when the Philadelphia and Reading Railroad declared bankruptcy. It worsened in April when federal gold reserves dipped below $100 million, the amount that many believed was the minimum required to redeem the government's outstanding debt obligations. Widespread panic broke out in May when the National Cordage Company, which had threatened to corner the market on rope and related products, also declared bankruptcy.

Convinced that these three events signaled the beginning of a major economic decline, investors rushed to convert their paper holdings to gold, driving stock prices down. Many banks experienced a run on their reserves and were forced into bankruptcy. As stock prices fell and banks failed, many manufacturers and railroads were unable to raise the money they needed to survive tough economic times, and they too were forced into bankruptcy. By Christmas more than 150 railroads, 400 banks, and 8,000 other companies had gone out of business.

These business failures threw one million people out of work and resulted in an unemployment rate of 20 percent, the highest level in American history up to that time. The unemployed began demanding that the federal government act to reverse the economic decline. Jacob Coxey, an Ohio businessman, called for a massive federal public works program. To induce Congress to pass his proposal, he led a group of followers known as Coxey's Army on foot from Ohio to Washington, D.C., where he was largely ignored. Meanwhile, many labor unions went out on strike. The most serious strike, against the Pullman Palace Car Company in Chicago, was not settled until the federal army was called out to dispel the strikers.

Action to end the depression took two approaches. One was to raise the tariff on foreign manufactured goods, a move designed to protect domestic manufacturing from foreign competition and ease unemployment. The other was to reform the monetary standard by backing the nation's paper money and government securities with silver as well as gold. Miners and farmers mounted a major campaign to permit the minting of silver coins. Supporters of this "free silver" proposal hoped it would increase the amount of money in circulation, forcing down prices and making it easier to pay debts. "Free silver" became the central plank of the Populists, a party with a large following in the South and West; the party became a major force in the election of 1896. Despite an alliance between the Populists and the Democrats, however, the two parties were unable to keep the Republicans from capturing both the White House and Congress.

By 1898 the panic had ended. Crop failures in Europe sent the foreign demand for American foodstuffs skyrocketing. The Dingley Tariff of 1897 increased tariff rates and provided some relief for manufacturers and their employees. The discovery of gold in the Klondike in 1896 significantly increased

THE SACRILEGIOUS CANDIDATE.

No man who drags into the dust the most sacred symbols of the Christian world is fit to be president of the United States.

Although he was widely castigated for misappropriating religious imagery, William Jennings Bryan electrified the 1896 Democratic convention with his "Cross of Gold" speech. Bryan condemned opponents of the free coinage of silver: "You shall not press down upon the brow of labor this crown of thorns . . . you shall not crucify mankind upon a cross of gold." *Library of Congress*

the nation's gold supply, thus boosting investor confidence in the gold standard's ability to support the nation's monetary system.

The panic affected American politics in several ways. It helped transform the Populists from a regional to a national political party. It also contributed to their demise by thrusting them onto the national scene before they were ready to compete at this level. Public dissatisfaction with the severity and duration of the panic allowed the Republicans to gain control of the federal government in 1896 and retain it until the election of Woodrow Wilson sixteen years later.

See also *Civil Unrest and Rioting; Cleveland, Grover; Coxey's Army; Populist (People's) Party; Tariff History.*

CHARLES CAREY,
LYNCHBURG COLLEGE/CENTRAL VIRGINIA COMMUNITY COLLEGE

BIBLIOGRAPHY

Engerman, Stanley L., and Robert E. Gallman, eds. *The Cambridge Economic History of the United States.* New York: Cambridge University Press, 1996.

Poulson, Barry W. *Economic History of the United States.* New York: Macmillan, 1981.

Welch, Richard E. *The Presidencies of Grover Cleveland.* Lawrence: University Press of Kansas, 1988.

PEACE AND FREEDOM PARTY

The Peace and Freedom Party was formed in the 1960s when two political dynamics converged: opposition to the Vietnam War and increasing militancy in the civil rights movement. Demonstrations against the growing U.S. involvement in the war had increased in size, frequency, and intensity. On the civil rights front, devastating riots had convulsed the inner cities of several of the nation's largest cities. Militant black power advocates observed that a disproportionate number of black draftees were fighting and becoming casualties in Vietnam. Linking the two movements was, therefore, a feasible political arrangement.

The Peace and Freedom Party reached its highest level of popularity in 1968 when it nominated Eldridge Cleaver, the "minister of education" of the ultramilitant Black Panthers, as its presidential candidate. Jerry Rubin, a founder and leader of the Youth International Party, or "Yippies," was Cleaver's running mate. At the time, Cleaver was a convicted felon and Rubin was one of the "Chicago Seven" facing criminal charges for having disrupted the 1968 Democratic National Convention in that city. The party slate tallied almost 37,000 votes in the presidential election. By 1969 Cleaver had fled the country to avoid arrest. In 1972 Benjamin Spock, the famous pediatrician and antiwar activist, was the party's presidential standard bearer, winning fewer than 100,000 votes.

After these two presidential forays, and with the end of U.S. military involvement in Vietnam, the Peace and Freedom Party became an ideological battleground for militant Marxist-Leninists, Trotskyites, and other leftist militants. It remains so to this day. Centered in California, the party did so poorly in the 1998 elections that it lost its ballot status for the 2000 statewide elections.

See also *Black Panthers; Vietnam War.*

RON dePAOLO, INDEPENDENT AUTHOR

BIBLIOGRAPHY

Patterson, James T. *Grand Expectations: The United States, 1945–1974.* New York: Oxford University Press, 1996.

PERSIAN GULF WAR

Marking a peculiar moment in modern American history, the Persian Gulf War between Iraq and an American-led coalition of states in 1990–1991 began from ostensibly clear causes. By war's end, it had evolved into a complex political and military drama with lasting implications for both the United States and the Middle East. The war also came to represent a turning point in world politics—the final shot of a cold war gone lukewarm and the rebirth of American political and military hegemony.

The war began with Iraq's August 1990 invasion of Kuwait, a small, oil-rich Persian Gulf state carved out of the collapsing Ottoman Empire nearly a century before, although Kuwait had been an essentially autonomous sheikdom since 1756. Realpolitik considerations made the United States and Iraq uneasy allies during the 1980s. The United States, hoping to contain state-sponsored terrorism and Islamic fundamentalism in neighboring Iran, provided Iraqi president Saddam Hussein with information and economic aid. Occupied with events in Europe, the United States ignored numerous signs that the Iraqi government was creating a substantial military machine in the Gulf, although most Iraqi military hardware came through European sources, not, as was sometimes popularly believed, American ones. Iraq's invasion of Kuwait had many causes, chief among which were internal strife and a severe economic crisis wrought by its 1980–1988 war with Iran.

COALITION FORMATION AND THE OUTBREAK OF WAR

Within days of the invasion, U.S. president George Bush decided that the aggression could not stand and began to put together one of the most unlikely and shaky coalitions of the twentieth century; it included the Soviet Union, China, Saudi Arabia, NATO Europe, and much of the Arab Middle

East. The United States, backed by a mostly solid wall of United Nations support and decrees, placed intense political pressure on Iraq to withdraw from Kuwait, all the while preparing to defend Saudi Arabia, if it were attacked, and to overturn the invasion should the Iraqis refuse to comply with UN resolutions. Over the next six months, a massive concentration of American and allied forces arrived in the Gulf while Iraq continued to announce its "sovereign claims" to its new nineteenth province, Kuwait.

Critics of the Bush administration argued that the war was not about preserving Kuwaiti independence, but about preserving cheap and easy access to crude oil from the Gulf, a cornerstone of the economies of the United States, Europe, and East Asia. After its invasion of Kuwait, Iraq controlled 20 percent of the world's oil reserves; another 20 percent lay just across the frontier in Saudi Arabia. Oil considerations certainly played a significant role in every aspect of the conflict.

On January 17, 1991, with diplomatic solutions exhausted and the UN Security Council's deadline for an Iraqi withdrawal passed, Operation Desert Storm, the name for the offensive phase of the war, began, triggering one of the most massive aerial campaigns in history. Over the next five weeks, American and allied aircraft bombarded Iraqi troops, armor, and command-and-control, communications, and other sites that had political or military value. The extent to which the bombing campaign "won the war" and the role of laser-guided weapons have been bitterly debated. Attacks on Iraqi infrastructure probably did little to win the war, since they did not last long enough for serious shortages to develop, beyond those already being suffered before the war began because of embargoes implemented after the invasion of Kuwait. Air attacks on the Iraqi army, however, seem to have played an important role in undermining its will to resist. In any case, U.S. air power demonstrated decisively, often to the dismay of America's own NATO allies, that it and the threat of strategic bombing would be the cornerstones of the "new world order" and the bases of America's status as the lone remaining superpower.

The coalition was put to severe test when Iraq began to fire ground-to-ground SCUD missiles into the heart of Israel, hoping to provoke a military response that would shatter the coalition. Fearing just that, Washington convinced the Israelis to stand on the sidelines and not play into Saddam's hands. By war's end, allied aircraft had succeeded in isolating the troublesome mobile SCUD launchers to a relatively small area. The amount of resources dedicated to SCUD hunting was immense; some 40 percent of American sorties were devoted to this purpose, though the weapon proved no serious military threat. These decisions illustrate that the main strategic issues of this war were political and involved keeping the Arab-Western-Russian alliance together. Hunting and destroying the SCUD launchers was a major component of this strategy.

The ground attack began on February 24, and, by the time the cease-fire was declared on the morning of February 28, American and Allied divisions occupied all of Kuwait and much of southern Iraq up to a position just south of As Samawah on the Euphrates River. The centerpiece of the ground assault was a well-planned and masterfully executed "left hook," the large flanking assault that turned what was expected to be a fierce engagement into a rout that quickly led to the end of hostilities. Much controversy surrounded the decision to grant a cease-fire. Glad that the ground war had progressed as well as it had, and with such little loss of American life, the Bush administration was all too willing to call an end to the fighting, critics argued. Although the American 101st Airborne Division sat in the Euphrates Valley with nothing between it and Baghdad, Saddam was not removed from power and would remain a thorn in the American side for years to come. A good portion of the Iraqi military was allowed to escape, along with several elite Republican Guard elements. Dozens of attack helicopters escaped intact and were soon turned on rebellious Shi'ites and Kurds. Those same critics often ignore the sizable Iraqi force that remained north of the Euphrates, more than capable of putting down the Shi'ite and Kurdish rebellions. Perhaps additional deserved criticism can be found in the administration's failure to lend material support to the rebellions after having openly encouraged dissident Iraqi minorities to rise up against Saddam; the rebellions were quickly squashed.

The war was remarkable in that there were so few American casualties—148 killed in action and 458 wounded—especially given earlier estimates of the human toll expected in ousting Iraq from Kuwait. Yet, the mysterious "Gulf War syndrome," the term loosely applied to a series of problems including chronic fatigue, muscle pain, memory loss, sleep disorders, and more serious conditions, plagued many American troops after they returned from the Middle East. The causes of this condition, even its very existence, remain the subject of debate and conjecture, but explanations coalesce on exposure to chemical, biological, and nuclear materials.

AFTERMATH OF WAR

What appeared on the surface to be a clean military triumph quickly became tarnished by the complicated political situation that developed after the war. Within months after the conflict, both Bush and Prime Minister Margaret Thatcher of Britain were out of office, while Saddam Hussein's hold on office seemed as strong as ever.

Saddam's staying power was all the more galling to the United States given the Bush administration's decision before the war to cast Saddam as a middle eastern Adolf Hitler, one that was then allowed to remain in power after the end of the Gulf War. The early rhetoric might well have contributed to the disillusionment by many as to the causes, course, and consequences of the war. For his part, Saddam, emboldened by a lack of western resolve in making sure the terms of the cease-fire were carried out, continued to obstruct UN weapons inspectors sent to the region to ensure that Iraq was not a chemical, biological, or nuclear threat in the Middle East. Western economic sanctions, in particular, have proven to be of only limited effect in forcing compliance with UN resolutions. Saddam continues to challenge the American presence in the region, provoking conflicts in the northern and southern no-fly zones above Iraq.

U.S. Marines march in the victory parade in Washington, D.C., on June 8, 1991.   *R. Michael Jenkins, Congressional Quarterly*

As the Iraqi forces fell back, they conducted a scorched-earth policy and set hundreds of oil wells ablaze. Millions of barrels of oil were dumped into the Persian Gulf, producing an ecological disaster in addition to that unleashed in Iraq and Kuwait by the massive destruction of life and property. Ten years after the end of the war, concerns about chemical, biological, and nuclear capabilities in Iraq and other Middle East states remained. Iraq continued to be a major threat in state-sponsored terrorism, but the condition of the nation's conventional military was such that it could not seriously threaten neighboring states. In the decade after the war, the Iraqi economy struggled to cope with the massive destruction brought about by the war and external sanctions placed upon the nation for its refusal to comply with all UN resolutions. Despite shortages of food and medicine, popular support for Saddam remained strong.

Certainly some of the goodwill fostered by the allied coalition made the efforts to find a lasting peace between Israel and its neighbors more tenable in the decade that followed. Bush himself made good use of his new-found prestige to pressure Israel into negotiations, while regional economic crises, especially in regard to Jordan, led others to the table. Although Saddam remained in power and just weeks after the end of the war Americans had trouble explaining what all the fighting had accomplished, the political rhetoric in the Middle East during the 1990s was tempered by a tone of conciliation and efforts to address long-standing antagonisms.

Bush and many contemporary observers believed that the Gulf War finally purged the failure of Vietnam from the American psyche. American mistrust of, and lack of confidence in, its military forces, however, were replaced by a belief—potentially just as dangerous—in the overwhelming hegemony of American military force and technological ability. The military's effective information management during the Gulf War was in part to blame. Filling the insatiable appetite of the cable television networks for continuous information, the military offered video clips showing the surgical precision of smart weapons smashing through windows of apparently unoccupied buildings. This assault on the public perception led to the widespread belief that most, if not all, of the American assault used high-tech weaponry against Iraqi infrastructure. In reality, more than 90 percent of all bombs dropped were old-fashioned iron gravity bombs. The brutality of the battlefields largely escaped the American public. But the larger problem rested in American unwillingness to place troops in harm's way, even for the most just of causes, and the belief that "smart weapons" could protect national interests by themselves. The most curious by-product of the war seemed to be an increased willingness to use the American military machine in cases where diplomacy had been exhausted and U.S. goals were yet unrealized. The Gulf War also proved to be the last act of the cold war, marking as it did Soviet acquiescence to a major American military expedition into one of the world's most volatile and strategically valuable regions. When the fighting was over, the United States was left as the world's only superpower, yet one with no enemies left to fight.

See also *Bush, George.*

J. WAYNE JONES, UNIVERSITY OF ARKANSAS

BIBLIOGRAPHY

Atkinson, Rick. *Crusade.* Boston: Houghton Mifflin, 1993.
Freedman, Lawrence. *The Gulf Conflict, 1990–1991.* Princeton: Princeton University Press, 1993.
Gordon, Michael R. *The Generals' War.* Boston: Little, Brown, 1995.
Hallion, Richard. *Storm Over Iraq.* Washington, D.C.: Smithsonian Institution Press, 1993.
Hiro, Dilip. *Desert Shield to Desert Storm.* New York: Routledge, 1992.

PETITION CAMPAIGNS

Petitions are written, signed appeals to legislators requesting their support on issues of public policy. They have proved influential on many political controversies, ranging from slavery to women's suffrage.

The ability to petition the government for a redress of grievances is a basic constitutional guarantee protected by the First Amendment to the Constitution. Residents of colonial America had this right as subjects of Great Britain, a fact highlighted dramatically by the Declaration of Independence, which condemned the British government's disregard of colonial petitions. When the Bill of Rights was adopted, petitioning was already practiced in state legislatures. The petitioning clause of the First Amendment extended the same right to citizens of the United States. Although petitioning continued in state legislatures, the focus of many campaigns shifted to Congress as the responsibilities of the national government grew and Congress turned its attention to controversial policy issues.

Petitions were at first presented in the form of "prayers" that requested action or expressed opinions and were signed by one or more persons. During the late eighteenth and early nineteenth centuries, the typical petitions to Congress were individual claims for Revolutionary War pensions, demands for reparations, and even requests for jobs. Also common were those signed by multiple residents of a town requesting a post office, bridge, or lighthouse for their community. Churches and business groups circulated petitions among their members to express views on issues ranging from public morals to tariffs. As expressions of public pressure on government spending and public policy, petition campaigns were essentially an early form of what we today call "lobbying."

Petitions also provided a voice in legislatures for the otherwise disfranchised, since eligibility to vote has never been necessary to sign or submit a petition. Every year Congress received petitions from Native Americans, white women, residents of U.S. territories, and free African Americans. Women were especially active, in both collecting signatures and signing petitions themselves. Some scholars credit the skills women gained from organizing abolitionist petition campaigns as being instrumental to their later success in the women's suffrage movement.

As the postal service improved and access to newspapers and periodicals made political news more readily available, petition campaigns became better organized. Groups in different towns and states could more easily coordinate their petition activities. Consequently, the volume of petitions submitted to Congress increased dramatically during the early

Representatives of the Congressional Districts Modification League deliver to the steps of the U.S. Capitol petitions urging modification of the Volstead Act, which implemented enforcement of the Eighteenth (or Prohibition) Amendment. The petitions, delivered April 15, 1932, contain more than 5 million names.

nineteenth century. The more contentious questions produced hundreds of petitions, many signed by thousands of people. Congressional debate on issues such as the Alien and Sedition Acts of 1798, the establishment of the First and Second Bank of the United States in 1791 and 1816, and opposition to legislation passed in 1810 requiring Sunday mail delivery prompted a torrent of petitions on both sides.

The largest and most controversial petition campaigns resulted from the bitter division over slavery. Congress received thousands of petitions during debates on the prohibition of the slave trade, the Missouri Compromise of 1820, and the annexation of Texas in 1845. However, it was the more divisive question of whether slavery should be abolished altogether that made petition campaigns famous. Abolitionists deluged Congress with thousands of petitions, praying for the abolition of slavery. Southern representatives, furious that Congress's obligation to receive petitions forced discussion of the issue, succeeded in 1836 in adopting the so-called gag rule, which prohibited Congress from discussing or approving petitions about slavery. The rule was notorious because many people saw it as a restriction on free speech. Rep. John Quincy Adams, the former president, risked censure for challenging the gag rule's constitutionality by introducing abolitionists' petitions before Congress repealed the rule in 1844.

Fearful that future petition campaigns would again monopolize proceedings, the House adopted procedures that limited the time each week members could spend on petitions. As a result, petitioning became less effective as a method of forcing Congress to act, and the number of campaigns declined. But petitions did not disappear altogether. The temperance movement and suffragists organized petition campaigns that put pressure on state legislatures first to change state laws and eventually to ratify the Eighteenth (prohibition) and Nineteenth (women's suffrage) Amendments to the Constitution. Today, citizens continue to collect signatures and present petitions to their legislators as a means of demonstrating popular support for one or another policy.

See also *Gag Rule.*

LINDA KOWALCKY, NORTHEASTERN UNIVERSITY

BIBLIOGRAPHY

Bailey, Raymond C. *Popular Influence Upon Public Policy: Petitioning in Eighteenth-Century America.* Westport, Conn.: Greenwood Press, 1979.

Frederick, David C. "John Quincy Adams, Slavery, and the Disappearance of the Right of Petition." *Law and History Review* 9 (spring 1991): 113–155.

Higginson, Stephen A. "A Short History of the Right to Petition Government for the Redress of Grievances." *Yale Law Journal* 96 (1986): 142–166.

Miller, William Lee. *Arguing About Slavery.* New York: Knopf, 1996.

Venet, Wendy Hamand. *Neither Ballots Nor Bullets: Women Abolitionists and the Civil War.* Charlottesville: University Press of Virginia, 1991.

PIERCE, FRANKLIN

Born in Hillsborough, New Hampshire, on November 23, 1804, Franklin Pierce practiced law and served in the New Hampshire legislature, both houses of the U.S. Congress, and the U.S. Army in the Mexican-American War. Democrats, gratified by his support of the Compromise of 1850, nominated him as a compromise presidential candidate at their 1852 convention. In the general election, Pierce defeated the Whig candidate, Gen. Winfield Scott.

During his single term in the White House (1853–1857), Pierce made policies that favored slavery and the South and was generally considered a classic "doughface," a northern man with southern principles. States where slavery existed, he said, were entitled to "efficient remedies" to enforce the right to own slaves. He aggressively supported the enforcement of the Fugitive Slave Law of 1850 and also backed the opening of western territories to slavery in the Kansas-Nebraska Act (1854), even though it led to violent confrontations between proslavery and antislavery settlers in what was called "Bleeding Kansas." In this conflict he consistently sided with the proslavery settlers and ignored flagrant election fraud and violence by southerners in the territory.

Pierce approved the Ostend Manifesto, which declared that if Spain refused to sell Cuba, the United States could seize the island to curtail threats of a slave rebellion or general emancipation there. The ensuing uproar at home and abroad, however, forced Pierce to disclaim the document. In the 1856 election, the Democrats turned to James Buchanan. Pierce, when his term ended, went home to New Hampshire, but retirement proved just as troublesome. His criticism of President Abraham Lincoln during the Civil War left Pierce unpopular even in his home state. He died four years after the war ended, in 1869.

See also *Compromise of 1850; Mexican-American War.*

SABRA BISSETTE LEDENT, INDEPENDENT AUTHOR

BIBLIOGRAPHY

Bisson, Wilfred J. *Franklin Pierce: A Biography.* Westport: Greenwood Press, 1993.

Gara, Larry. *The Presidency of Franklin Pierce.* Lawrence: University Press of Kansas, 1991.

POLITICAL ACTION COMMITTEES

Political action committees, or PACs, have been part of the American political system since the 1940s, but only in the 1970s did they become a major factor in political campaigns. PACs are organizations that raise and distribute campaign contributions to candidates for the presidency, Congress, and other offices.

Political action committees fall into two main categories. Some are affiliated with specific economic interests such as businesses, professional associations, and labor unions. Others are independent organizations devoted to advancing the political beliefs of their members, usually a single issue such as reproductive rights or gun control.

As the giving arms of special interests, PACs serve as a megaphone for a group of individuals. Rather than one thousand people giving $5 apiece, a PAC can write a $5,000 check on behalf of all of those individuals. To qualify as a "multicandidate committee," its legal name, a PAC must raise money from at least fifty persons and contribute to at least five candidates. The maximum contribution is $5,000 per candidate per campaign, with the primary and general elections counted separately. A candidate can raise $100,000 from just ten PACs, each giving the maximum for the primary and general elections. Otherwise, it would take fifty persons giving the maximum $1,000 for the primary and $1,000 for the general election to reach that threshold. The PAC itself can accept no more than $5,000 from a particular individual for each campaign, and it must regularly report its contributions and expenditures to the Federal Election Commission.

Critics call PACs the "cash constituents of Congress," interests that may have no presence in a member's district but still can command the attention of the lawmaker or a top aide by virtue of their campaign contributions. Lawmakers and PAC directors admit that the contributions buy access. An industry's PAC donations tend to rise or fall depending on whether important issues are pending before Congress.

PACs date back to 1943 when the Congress of Industrial Organizations (CIO), banned from using union dues to aid favored candidates, set up a fund called the Political Action Committee to collect voluntary contributions from its members. The CIO later merged with the American Federation of Labor, and today the AFL-CIO's PAC is one of the largest in the country.

In 1971 Congress passed legislation codifying earlier bans on union and corporate contributions, allowing those groups instead to pay the costs of running PACs and soliciting the voluntary donations needed to fill the committee's coffers. As a result, the number of PACs skyrocketed, from 608 in 1974 to 4,268 in 1988. At the end of 1999, 3,835 PACs were registered with the Federal Election Commission.

Although PACs originally were considered a reform, some lawmakers trying to overhaul the campaign finance laws tried to ban PACs in 1996. Their colleagues, however, refused to go along. Led by Republican senator John McCain of Arizona and Democratic senator Russell Feingold of Wisconsin, the

reformers turned their attention away from PACs after the 1996 elections and instead launched an effort to ban "soft money," the unregulated contributions to political parties from corporations and unions which are banned from giving directly to campaigns.

Because incumbents usually win, PACs tend to favor incumbents over challengers—one reason it is difficult for insurgent candidates to raise enough money to compete. During the 1998 elections, PACs gave 78 percent of their money to incumbents. PACs play another important role in helping incumbents: Many give early in the election cycle, allowing a lawmaker to amass a large campaign bank account and dissuade potentially strong challengers from entering the race.

PACs usually direct their contributions to the lawmakers who oversee their interests. The Senate and House banking committees are considered plum fundraising assignments because they attract contributions from Wall Street and the financial community. Defense PACs tend to support members of the House and Senate panels that oversee the Pentagon budget. Lawmakers who switch committees find that their mix of PAC contributions changes to reflect their new assignments. Donations by advocacy groups such as the National Rifle Association tend to be more ideological in nature, favoring challengers who agree with them on the issues, rather than incumbents who disagree with them but are more likely to win in November.

Many members of Congress also have set up their own political action committees. These "leadership PACs" allow lawmakers to raise additional funds from special interests—money that is then used to help threatened incumbents and strong challengers win election. Later, lawmakers hoping to move up the leadership ladder can ask the colleagues they helped at election time to return the favor. Although most lawmakers who have leadership PACs use the money they raise to make contributions to other candidates, some use these accounts to defray expenses such as travel or attending the national political conventions.

See also *Campaign Finance; Interest Groups; Lobbyists; Political Contributions in the Late Nineteenth Century; Soft Money in Twentieth-Century Politics.*

JONATHAN D. SALANT, ASSOCIATED PRESS

BIBLIOGRAPHY

Biersack, Robert, Paul S. Herrnson, and Clyde Wilcox, eds. *Risky Business: PAC Decisionmaking in Congressional Elections.* Armonk, N.Y.: M. E. Sharpe, 1994.

Makinson, Larry. *The Price of Admission: Campaign Spending in the 1994 Elections.* Washington, D.C.: Center for Responsive Politics, 1995.

Salant, Jonathan D. "Introduction." In *Congressional Quarterly's Federal PACs Directory.* Washington, D.C.: Congressional Quarterly, 1998.

Sorauf, Frank J. *Inside Campaign Finance: Myths and Realities.* New Haven: Yale University Press, 1992.

POLITICAL CONTRIBUTIONS IN THE LATE NINETEENTH CENTURY

"Soft money" refers to contributions to political parties that are not limited in amount by federal campaign laws. Opponents of soft money maintain that these contributions threaten the principle of one person, one vote, whereas supporters argue that citizens have the right to financial participation in the electoral process. The term first came into common use in the 1980s, but the phenomenon of corporations making large contributions to political parties can be traced back at least a century. The issue of corporations and wealthy individuals financing elections intensified rapidly in the late 1800s and came to a head in the early 1900s.

The concentration of wealth and the influence of that concentration on the political process became major issues in the late nineteenth century. As America continued to industrialize, money from corporations, banks, railroads, and other businesses grew to large proportions by the end of the century. Amounts of $50,000 and more were donated to political parties. This phenomenon was addressed in the Progressive political movement, whose main theme was to rein in the power of big business in all aspects of American life.

During the successful presidential campaigns of William McKinley in 1896 and 1900, millions of dollars were raised from corporations by Mark Hanna, McKinley's leading fundraiser. Journalists, known at the time as "muckrakers," and members of the Progressive movement charged that large companies were buying favors and influence with their donations. When specific charges were leveled at Theodore Roosevelt in the 1904 presidential election by his opponent, Judge Alton Parker, the issue was forced to the spotlight, and in 1907 Congress acted by passing the Tillman Act. The law prohibited corporations and national banks from contributing to a federal campaign. Although the act still remains in effect, its power has been undermined by the expansion of soft (nonfederal) money, which national parties have attracted in increasing amounts in recent decades.

See also *Campaign Finance; Political Action Committees; Progressive Era.*

RICHARD J. CARROLL, INDEPENDENT SCHOLAR

BIBLIOGRAPHY

Corrado, Anthony, Thomas E. Mann, Daniel R. Ortiz, Trevor Potter, and Frank J. Sorauf. *Campaign Finance Reform: A Sourcebook.* Washington, D.C.: Brookings Institution, 1997.

POLITICAL PARTIES

Political parties are organizations that seek to gain control of government to further their social, economic, or ideological goals. The United States has usually had a two-party system, dominated since 1860 by the Democratic and Republican Parties. Yet more than eighty political parties have formed since the 1790s, and "third parties" have occasionally had a decisive impact on presidential elections. For example, in 1912 the "Bull Moose Party" of former president Theodore Roosevelt siphoned enough Republican votes from the incumbent, William Howard Taft, to enable the Democrat, Woodrow Wilson, to win the election.

The United States did not start out with a two-party system—or any parties at all. Initially there were no formal parties, and in the early 1820s the nation had in effect only one party. The Founders did not anticipate parties—which they derisively called factions—and this central aspect of American politics was unplanned and had no formal constitutional or legal status. Indeed, having seen the ill effects of overzealous parties in monarchical England and (beginning in 1789) revolutionary France, the Founders hoped to avoid similar pitfalls in the fledgling nation. Thus, in *Federalist 10* James Madison bragged that one of the Constitution's great virtues was that it would head off "the mischiefs of faction." In 1789 Thomas Jefferson declared: "If I could not go to heaven but with a party, I would not go there at all." Similarly, in his farewell address in 1796 George Washington warned that, in elective popular governments, the dangers of excess in the "spirit of party" demanded "a uniform vigilance to prevent its bursting into a flame."

By the time Washington issued his warning, he was the titular head of the Federalist Party, which faded after 1800 and, except for some local officeholders, was dead by 1821. Meanwhile, since 1794 Madison and Jefferson had been the leaders of another party, variously called the Democratic-Republicans, the Jeffersonian Democrats, and the Jeffersonian Republicans, but today understood as the kernel of what became the modern Democratic Party.

POLITICAL ISSUES AND THE EMERGENCE OF PARTIES

The debate over ratification of the Constitution led to the organization of factions but not parties. Future Democratic-Republicans and Federalists, like Madison and Alexander Hamilton, worked together for ratification, just as future Democratic-Republicans and Federalists, like James Monroe and Samuel Chase, worked against ratification of the Constitution.

Political parties emerged in part from differences over policy in President George Washington's cabinet. Left to right: President Washington, Secretary of War Henry Knox, Secretary of the Treasury Alexander Hamilton, Secretary of State Thomas Jefferson, and Attorney General Edmund Randolph. *Library of Congress*

Ratification brought about a new national government, where parties were unknown. Presidential electors unanimously elected Washington as the first president, and nearly half of them supported John Adams, who was easily elected vice president. Washington's cabinet included future leaders of the nation's first two parties: the future Federalist leader Alexander Hamilton and the future leader of the Democratic-Republicans, Thomas Jefferson.

By the end of Washington's administration two parties were fully engaged in politics. The parties differed over the nature of public policy and the interpretation of the Constitution. The Federalists, led by Hamilton, Adams, and John Jay, favored a national government vigorously involved in economic development. Key to the Federalist program was the establishment of a national bank, federal funding at face value of all state and national bonds issued during the Revolution, and a flexible interpretation of the Constitution. The Federalists also wanted to strengthen diplomatic and commercial ties with England.

Jefferson's followers, called Democratic-Republicans at this time, opposed funding the war debts at par because many of the original bond holders had sold their bonds at depreciated values to speculators. Their hostility to commerce and business also led them to oppose the establishment of a national bank. Unsuccessful on these issues, the Democratic-

Republicans were nonetheless able to thwart Hamilton's plan to use high tariffs to stimulate commerce and manufacturing in the new country. Jefferson and his followers wanted a strict interpretation of the Constitution, favored states' rights over national power, and in foreign policy supported France in its wars with England.

On issues involving race, slavery, and foreign policy, the parties also differed. The Federalists favored giving full diplomatic recognition to Haiti, a black republic in the Caribbean, and refused to seek the return of slaves who had escaped with the British at the end of the Revolution. Jefferson, by contrast, unsuccessfully demanded the return of the slaves but was successful as president in blocking any diplomatic ties to Haiti.

PRESIDENTS, PARTIES, AND POLICIES, 1800–1860

By the time of Jefferson's election in 1800, ending twelve years of Federalist control, the party concept was entrenched in U.S. politics. Despite his previous denunciation of parties, Jefferson justified his own party leadership as a necessary opposition to the "Monocrats of our country." Jefferson's election by the House, after a tie electoral vote between him and Aaron Burr, led to adoption of the Twelfth Amendment to the Constitution in 1804. That amendment, which required electors to vote separately for president and vice president, further buried the likelihood of "partyless" U.S. elections.

Federalists nearly won the presidency in 1800 and 1812, but the party quickly withered after the War of 1812, when many party leaders opposed the war and flirted with secession, most notably at the Hartford Convention of 1814–1815. Federalists made a brief comeback in 1819–1820 during the debates over allowing slavery in Missouri on its admission to the Union, but the party was effectively dead by the end of 1820, when James Monroe ran unopposed for reelection.

A system with only one party was less stable than a system with two or more parties. In 1824 four candidates competed for the presidency, with no one getting a majority of the popular or the electoral vote. The House of Representatives chose John Quincy Adams, who ran second in both categories. Andrew Jackson, who had led in popular and electoral votes, immediately began his campaign for the presidency, and he won in 1828. In 1832 the Anti-Masonic Party made its brief appearance, winning seven electoral votes, while Jackson was easily reelected. Jackson inherited the mantle of Jefferson and his party, while his political and personal opponents, such as Daniel Webster, Henry Clay, and John Quincy Adams, migrated in the 1830s to the newly formed Whig Party. In 1836 four Whigs, representing different regions of the country, competed for the presidency against Jackson's heir, Martin Van Buren.

The Whigs won the presidency in 1840 and 1848; Democrats won in 1836, 1844, 1852, and 1856. The Whigs favored a national bank, federal support for internal improvements, national bankruptcy laws, protective tariffs, and a relatively humane policy toward American Indians. The Democrats disagreed with all these positions. Whigs opposed territorial acquisition, especially by force, whereas Democrats annexed Texas and eventually pushed the United States into a war with Mexico to gain new territory in the Southwest, advocating that it was the "manifest destiny" of the United States to control the continent. The Jacksonian Democrats pushed for universal adult white male suffrage throughout the country, but at the same time worked to take the vote away from free blacks and to strengthen slavery at the national and local level. Jackson's presidency is most remembered for his veto of the rechartering of the Second Bank of the United States, his successful opposition to internal improvements, and his policy of Indian removal, which pushed almost all Native Americans in the East into the Indian Territory (present-day Oklahoma). On an important issue that seemed to transcend party politics, Jackson vigorously opposed extreme states' rights ideology when South Carolina attempted to nullify a federal tariff. However, following the nullification crisis, the Democrats became increasingly solicitous of states' rights and the southern demands for protections for slavery. Jackson and his fellow Democrats also accepted the South Carolinians' critique of the tariff, even as they rejected the Carolinians' response, nullification.

The nation had two major parties in the 1840s, but third parties influenced some elections. In 1844 the antislavery Liberty Party won enough votes in New York to cost the Whigs the state and the presidential election, assuming all the Liberty voters would have supported the Whigs. The Whig candidate, Henry Clay, opposed expansion and was more moderate on slavery than his opponent, but it seems unlikely that the committed abolitionists who voted for the Liberty Party would otherwise have voted for the slave-owning Clay as the lesser of two evils. In 1848, however, the Free Soil candidate, former president Martin Van Buren, won more than 290,000 votes, many of which would have otherwise gone to the Democratic candidate, Lewis Cass of Michigan. As a result, the Whig candidate, Gen. Zachary Taylor, won the election. Equally significant, Free Soilers won state and local

races, and in Ohio they held the balance of power in the state legislature and were able to elect an antislavery Democrat, Salmon P. Chase, to the U.S. Senate.

Yet the victorious Whigs of 1848 managed to carry only four states in 1852, and the party disappeared two years later. The 1856 election saw two new parties run candidates: the Know Nothing (American) Party and the Republican Party. The Know Nothing, or American, Party was a single-issue party, opposed to immigration in general and Catholic immigration in particular. The Know Nothings won a number of governorships and dominated a few state legislatures, including Massachusetts in this period. In 1856 the Speaker of the House of Representatives, Nathaniel Banks, was a Know Nothing.

The Republican Party adopted many Whig policies but opposed the extension of slavery into the western territories. Many Republican leaders were former Whigs, including Abraham Lincoln and his secretary of state, William H. Seward. Others came from the antislavery wing of the Democratic Party, among them Lincoln's vice president, Hannibal Hamlin, and secretary of the Treasury, Salmon P. Chase. By 1858 many Know Nothings had also joined this party. In 1856 the Republican candidate, John C. Frémont, and the Know Nothing candidate, Millard Fillmore, together won about 400,000 more popular votes than James Buchanan, but Buchanan had the plurality of popular votes and, more important, carried nineteen states to win the election. Buchanan was the first "sectional" president since 1824, as fourteen of the states he carried were in the South. This election underscored that the Democrats had become the party of slavery and the South.

The proslavery southerners who controlled the Democratic Party insisted on fidelity to their program to expand slavery into the territories. This arrangement unraveled in 1860, as the Democrats split into two parties—regular Democrats nominating Stephen A. Douglas of Illinois and southern Democrats nominating John C. Breckinridge of Kentucky. The Republican candidate, Abraham Lincoln, carried every northern state. Moderates in the North and the South supported the Constitutional Union Party, which hoped to hold the Union together by not discussing any of the key issues. The two Democratic parties and the Constitutional Unionists combined for more popular votes than Lincoln (who was not even on the ballot in many southern states), but Lincoln carried eighteen states and easily won a majority of the electoral college.

PARTIES IN U.S. POLITICS SINCE 1860

Lincoln's victory set the stage for Republican dominance in national politics for the next half-century. During this period the Republicans stood at various times for preservation of the

Union, homestead laws to facilitate western settlement, federal support for a transcontinental railroad, protective tariffs, abolition of slavery, guarantees of African Americans' civil rights, and the suppression of Mormon polygamists in the West. Democrats favored lower tariffs; opposed emancipation and civil rights; and championed white immigrants (but not immigrants from Asia), labor unions, and (at the end of the century) small farmers in the South and West. In international affairs, the late-nineteenth-century Republicans favored expansion, ultimately leading to war with Spain and the acquisition of an overseas empire, while Democrats opposed these trends, with Grover Cleveland (the only Democratic president in this period) refusing to annex Hawaii.

From 1868 to 1908 various third parties—including the Liberal Republican, Greenback, Prohibition, Equal Rights, Anti-Monopoly, Workers, Socialist Labor, Socialist, United Christian, and Populist—ran candidates. With the exception of the Populists in 1892, however, none ever won any electoral votes. Some of these parties did, however, elect candidates to state and local office and to Congress. James B. Weaver, for example, ran successfully for Congress on the Greenback ticket in 1878, 1884, and 1886; ran for president on the Greenback ticket in 1880; and ran for president on the Populist ticket in 1892.

In 1912 a third party determined the outcome of the presidential race. The Republicans split as former president Theodore Roosevelt tried, and failed, to gain renomination after a term out of the White House. Roosevelt thought that his successor, William Howard Taft, had abandoned the progressive goals of the party. Running on the Progressive ("Bull Moose") ticket, Roosevelt carried six states and won about half a million more popular votes than Taft. Together they outpolled Wilson, but Wilson carried forty states and won the election. The Socialist candidate, Eugene V. Debs, won nearly a million votes in the 1912 election, and, although he carried no states, Socialists won various local elections and sent some party members to Congress. Victor Berger of Milwaukee, for example, served in Congress as a Socialist from 1911 to 1913 and from 1923 to 1929. He was also elected in 1918, but in that year Congress refused to allow him to take his seat because of his opposition to World War I.

Between the 1910s and the 1940s, Democrats became increasingly internationalist, while Republicans opposed American entrance into the League of Nations after World War I and were isolationist in the 1930s as the world moved toward a second world war. Democratic support came from labor, white southerners, and most northern urban immigrant groups. By the 1930s, blacks began to leave the Republican Party, forced out by "lily white" Republicans in the South and welcomed into the emerging New Deal coalition. The Republicans by this time had become the party of conservative business interests, white Protestants (outside the South), small town and rural northerners, and owners of small businesses.

Various third parties ran presidential candidates in the 1920s and 1930s, but only Robert La Follette, running as the Progressive Party candidate in 1924, won any electoral votes. In 1948, though, southern "Dixiecrats," who abandoned the Democratic Party to protest President Harry S. Truman's support for civil rights and racial equality, took four Deep South states. Some other Democrats supported former vice president Henry A. Wallace, running on the Progressive ticket that year. Despite these defections, Truman won. At the state and local level, third parties were sometimes successful, and various candidates running on socialist, communist, or various other tickets sporadically held office. For example, Wisconsin elected Progressives Robert M. La Follette Jr. to the Senate in 1934 and 1940 and Merlin Hull to the House from 1934 to 1944. Benjamin J. Davis, running as a Communist, served on the New York City Council as the "Communist Councilman from Harlem," while Vito Marcantonio, who had served one term in Congress as a Republican (1935–1937), served six terms in Congress (1939–1951) running on the ticket of the American Labor Party, which had Communist Party support. Independents also had some success; Henry F. Reams of Ohio, for example, served two full terms in the House (1951–1955).

By the 1960s, Republicans and Democrats had swapped places on the issue of African Americans' civil rights since a hundred years earlier. In 1964 large numbers of white southerners left the Democratic Party over President Lyndon Johnson's support for civil rights. Since then the Democratic constituency has generally comprised urban, northern, and far western liberals; Catholics and Jews; African Americans, Hispanics, Asian-Americans, and ethnic minorities; blue-collar workers; and the underprivileged. Republicans are viewed as conservatives, southerners, white Protestants, and the affluent.

Third parties continued to run presidential candidates, and in some places candidates for Congress and state and local offices. In the 1960s John Lindsay, a former Republican congressman, was elected mayor of New York City on the Liberal Party line, and in 1970 James L. Buckley won a U.S. Senate seat from New York, running on the Conservative Party line. But third-party candidates have also been spoilers, as in 1980 when incumbent Republican senator Jacob Javits of New York lost his party's nomination and ran as a Liberal Party candidate, dividing the votes of moderates, liberals, and Democrats and thus allowing for the election of conservative Republican Alfonse D'Amato.

George C. Wallace, running in 1968 as the presidential candidate of the segregationist American Independent Party, captured five states in the South. Most of his supporters voted Republican in subsequent elections. In 1980 former U.S. representative John Anderson ran on the National Unity Party ticket and carried more than 5 million popular votes, but he did not affect the election of Ronald Reagan. In 1992 H. Ross Perot ran as an independent and won almost 20 million votes, and he may have cost the incumbent, George Herbert Walker Bush, a few states. Perot influenced policy in the 1990s by highlighting the importance of the national debt and thus nudging a change in policy that brought balanced budgets and a declining debt by the end of the decade. When he ran again in 1996, however, he had no effect on the election. In 1998 Jesse Ventura, a former professional wrestler running on Perot's Reform Party ticket, was elected governor of Minnesota. In 2000 Ralph Nader, running on the Green Party ticket, won enough votes in several states to give their electoral college votes to Gov. George W. Bush instead of Vice President Al Gore.

PARTY SYSTEMS

Historians and political scientists often use the concept "party systems" to refer to eras that more or less hang together in terms of major party alignment. The first, from 1789 to approximately 1824, marked the emergence of a two-party system and lasted from Washington's presidency through the end of the "Virginia Dynasty." The second, from 1828 through 1854, marked the years from Jackson's elections through the demise of the Whig Party. The third, from 1856 through 1896, marked the emergence of the Republican Party and its rise to dominance. The 1896 election marked a transition to a period that featured the Progressive era and persisted through World War I and the 1920s. The election of Franklin D. Roosevelt in 1932 marked another great electoral realignment, although the Democrats occasionally lost the presidency or one or both chambers of Congress in the years that followed.

In the sixty-eight-year period 1933 through 2001, Democrats held the White House forty years. The exceptions were the eight Eisenhower years (1953–1961), the eight Nixon-Ford years (1969–1977), and the twelve Reagan-Bush years (1981–1993). In Congress, Democratic dominance was even more striking. Democrats controlled the House for all but four years (1947–1949 and 1953–1955) from 1933 until the Republican takeover of both chambers in 1995. Democratic control of the Senate was less consistent, with four periods of Republican majorities totaling sixteen years between 1933 and 2001. During this period third-party candidates became increasingly less significant, although in 2000 one "socialist" and one "independent" served in the House.

INTERNAL PARTY POLITICS

Although all presidents since 1852 have been either Democrats or Republicans, their parties have sometimes borrowed ideas from third parties that quickly faded from the U.S. po-

litical scene. For example, the Democrats under Andrew Jackson in 1832 followed the example of the Anti-Masons in holding a national convention to nominate their presidential candidate. Previously, party caucuses in Congress, called King Caucus, chose their nominees in secret meetings. The 1824 election of John Quincy Adams, nominated by the Massachusetts legislature, spelled the end of King Caucus. The House decided the election when none of the four candidates, all Democratic-Republicans, failed to win the required electoral vote majority. The 1828 election, won by Jackson, marked a transition to the as-yet-unborn convention system.

National nominating conventions have remained a staple of the political party system, but they have been more show than substance in the age of primaries and television. With the presumptive nominee known well in advance, the convention nomination is a formality, although the convention still has the important duty of writing a party platform.

The Democratic convention of 1952, which chose Adlai Stevenson to oppose Republican Dwight D. Eisenhower, was the most recent to require more than one ballot to select a nominee. Multiple ballots were common earlier, particularly at Democratic conventions because of the party's rule requiring a two-thirds majority for nomination. Democrats dropped the rule, never used by Republicans, in 1936.

The primary system was a creation of the Progressive era of the early twentieth century. Progressive governor Robert M. La Follette of Wisconsin pushed through a state primary law in 1905, but few other states followed suit until after 1968. Primary elections and caucuses became the de facto presidential nominating mechanisms after the tumultuous 1968 Democratic convention, won by Hubert H. Humphrey without entering any primaries. As the Democrats strengthened their primary rules in the 1970s and 1980s, primaries proliferated in both parties, and they came earlier and earlier in the election year. In 1996 more than forty states held presidential primaries, most of them before April. In 2000 Al Gore and George W. Bush had locked up their nominations early in the primary season.

Federal and state campaign finance reforms enacted since the 1970s have both helped and hindered political parties. Beginning in 1976 presidential candidates became eligible for public financing of their campaigns, which reduced their reliance on money from party coffers. However, the legislation allowed "soft money," contributions given directly to the parties, ostensibly for party building but often diverted to indirect support for the party's candidate. The reform legislation also permitted interest groups and candidates to form political action committees (PACs) to raise and spend money for campaigns. This further reduced candidates' dependence on the political parties, with the result that more and more campaigns are candidate-centered rather than party-centered.

See also *African American Politics; Breckinridge Democrats; Campaign Finance; Dixiecrats (States' Rights Party); Federalists; Hartford Convention Resolutions; Landslide Elections; Political Action Committees; Progressive Era; Third Parties; Twelfth Amendment; Watershed Elections; individual parties by name.*

PAUL FINKELMAN, UNIVERSITY OF TULSA COLLEGE OF LAW,

AND JOHN MOORE, INDEPENDENT AUTHOR

BIBLIOGRAPHY

Cook, Rhodes. *Race for the Presidency: Winning the 2000 Nomination.* Washington, D.C.: CQ Press, 2000.

Gillespie, J. David. *Politics at the Periphery: Third Parties in Two-Party America.* Columbia: University of South Carolina Press, 1993.

Kruschke, Earl R. *Encyclopedia of Third Parties in the United States.* Santa Barbara, Calif.: ABC-CLIO, 1991.

Maisel, L. Sandy, ed. *Political Parties and Elections in the United States: An Encyclopedia.* 2 vols. New York: Garland Publishing, 1991.

Moore, John L. *Elections A to Z.* Washington, D.C.: Congressional Quarterly, 1999.

POLK, JAMES K.

James K. Polk was the eleventh president of the United States (1845–1849) and architect of the Mexican-American War and of the acquisition of the Far West.

The Democratic convention of 1844, stalemated between North and South, between egalitarian Jacksonians and states' rights Jacksonians, rejected ex-president Martin Van Buren and its other "big men," Lewis Cass and James Buchanan, in favor of an obscure candidate who might be entrusted with the party's compromise platform. This "dark horse"—the first in presidential politics—was James K. Polk.

Polk's attraction was that he was a loyal, young, vigorous Jacksonian who knew Capitol Hill well. He was forty-nine when inaugurated, younger than any previous president. Born in North Carolina (November 2, 1795) to parents who soon migrated to Tennessee, Polk had gone from the Nashville bar into politics as a friend of Andrew Jackson. Polk went from the state legislature to the House of Representatives, where he was Speaker (1835–1839). Polk returned to his home state for a term as governor, but he lost the office in the Whig resurgence of the early 1840s and was therefore available as standard-bearer in 1844.

Territorial expansion was in the air. Texas had revolted from Mexico, and many Americans, including the expansionist ex-Whig president, John Tyler, hankered to incorporate it. The Democratic platform of 1844 called for its annexation. Oregon Territory (comprising what is now British Columbia, Washington, Oregon, and Idaho) had been "jointly occupied" with Britain since 1818; to placate northerners, the platform called for the annexation of the whole, right up to

James K. Polk   *Library of Congress*

54°40'. Polk cast his eyes even further, toward California and the northern half of the Mexican republic.

Jackson, Van Buren, and Henry Clay, the Whig nominee in 1844, had all tried to keep Texas out of the Union, fearing the bubbling-over of sectional conflict if the United States expanded; and in the long term they were right. But Polk took his narrow victory in November 1844 as a mandate for fulfilling America's "manifest destiny" to expand to the Pacific, a grand aim. In terms of fulfilling ambitious expectations, perhaps no president has outstripped Polk.

The annexation of Texas in 1845 did not immediately lead to war, although Mexico refused to recognize American authority over Texas. The United States claimed that Texas extended to the Rio Grande, while Mexico argued that even if Texas was legitimately part of the United States, it extended only to the Nueces River, which was much further north. When Mexico refused to sell its northern territories to the United States, Polk sent troops under Gen. Zachary Taylor to the Rio Grande, which soon led to a skirmish just north of the river. Claiming American blood had been spilled on "American soil," Polk convinced Congress to declare war, and, before he left office, he presided over the annexation of what is now California, New Mexico, Arizona, and Utah. Meanwhile, Polk arranged with Britain to divide Oregon by continuing the existing frontier, the 49th parallel, to the Pacific.

In domestic affairs, too, Polk got what he wanted. The Walker tariff of 1846 made the United States almost a free-trade region, an implicit arrangement with Britain, which by repealing the Corn Laws was opening itself to American wheat. The independent treasury system was finally established; the Naval Academy at Annapolis and the Smithsonian Institution were created. Yet Polk's austere, bleak rectitude won him few friends; his presidential diary is remarkably despairing. His tenure saw partisan and sectional divisions reach a bitterness unmatched since the War of 1812, and he left the White House old and exhausted from overwork, going home to Nashville to die (June 15, 1849) within months.

See also *Mexican-American War; Sectionalism; Taylor, Zachary; Territorial Expansion.*

RICHARD MAJOR, INDEPENDENT SCHOLAR

BIBLIOGRAPHY

Farrell, John J., ed. *James K. Polk, 1795–1849: Chronology, Documents, Bibliographical Aids.* Dobbs Ferry, N.Y.: Oceana, 1970.

Haynes, Sam W. *James K. Polk and the Expansionist Impulse.* New York: Longman, 1957.

Polk, James K. *Diary of James K. Polk during his Presidency, 1845 to 1849,* 4 vols. Edited by M. M. Quaife. Chicago: A. C. McClurg, 1910.

Sellers, Charles G. *James K. Polk, Jacksonian, 1795–1843.* 3 vols. Princeton: Princeton University Press, 1957.

POLL TAX

Through much of U.S. history, the poll tax—a tax levied on a person without regard to property or income—was connected to the right to vote. From the 1870s to the 1960s, the poll tax symbolized an intent to disfranchise large numbers of people, particularly African Americans in the South.

The poll tax has a complex history. It was a significant source of public revenue in colonial America, but at that time it had no universal significance in sorting out voters from nonvoters. In antebellum America, payment of a poll tax sometimes provided an alternative means for would-be voters to qualify, if they could not satisfy a property requirement. After the Civil War, a resurgent poll tax took on its modern purpose and connotation. With the enfranchisement of women, they too became subject to any requirement that people pay a poll tax before being allowed to vote.

PRE–CIVIL WAR

One measure of the democratization of public life in the years after the American Revolution was the curtailment of the poll tax as a revenue measure. The preferred source of state and local revenue in the nineteenth century was the property tax. Although it was not progressive in the twentieth-century sense of applying higher percentages against higher amounts of income, it was nonetheless progressive in the sense that taxpayers paid in proportion to their wealth rather than at a flat rate per person.

The poll tax persisted in different guises. In some states in the early nineteenth century, potential voters could demonstrate their "stake in society" by satisfying a tax-paying requirement, even if they owned no taxable property and paid only a poll tax. The tax, while not negligible for people with only a small ability to pay, supplied a badge of citizenship. The rationale for payment of a poll tax typically linked it with access to public schools and the exercise of voting rights, a tidy trinity of considerations in pre–Civil War America.

White men paid a poll tax, sent their children to elementary schools supported in part by the tax, and exercised their citizenship by voting in elections. African Americans often encountered a very different situation. Georgia, for example, levied a much higher poll tax on free blacks—both men and women—than on white men and yet absolutely closed the schools and the franchise to black participation. Another kind of poll tax, imposed on whites for each slave they owned, was a kind of property tax—easily administered, limited to a specific amount, and levied without regard to value.

AFTER EMANCIPATION

Struggles over the poll tax reflected the political conflict in the post–Civil War South, as the poll tax veered in a new direction with the end of slavery. Even before the advent of black suffrage, states imposed postwar poll taxes on both races higher than the prewar rate on whites. In Georgia, for example, the twenty-five cent prewar poll tax on white men was hiked in 1866 to a dollar on each white or black man, with neither public schools nor voting rights as yet attached to the tax on freedmen. Only later did black men obtain the right to vote and the state establish schools for black children. When Republicans briefly came to power in Georgia during Reconstruction, they suspended operation of the poll tax law at election time. In 1877, after the Democrats retrieved power, Georgia made the poll tax cumulative, so that any backlog had to be paid off before a man's voting privileges were restored.

Virginia also revealed the general pattern of constitutional change and its correlation with political power. In 1876 Virginia made payment of the poll tax a prerequisite to voting, but a biracial insurgent group of reformers, known as the

Readjusters, overcame the tax barrier and, when they came to power for a time after 1879, broke the linkage to voting rights. In the 1902 state constitution Democrats restored the linkage and made the tax cumulative to three years. These steps fulfilled a two-fold purpose. They instituted a superficially nonracial means of disfranchising large numbers of black men without running afoul of the Fifteenth Amendment's rejection of race as a basis for exclusion. At the same time, they discouraged voting by people who were—as in the case of the Readjusters in Virginia and the Populists elsewhere—white, poor, and potential supporters of biracial challenges to elite Democratic control.

By 1904 every former Confederate state made payment of a poll tax a condition of voting rights. Texas relied heavily on the poll tax to reduce voting. Other southern states included it in a collection of requirements to reach that objective. Large numbers of whites, and larger numbers of blacks, were poor. A tax of a dollar or more, at a time when men spoke of their work and their income as "another day, another dollar," targeted a significant portion of their cash income. Delegates to Louisiana's constitutional convention in 1898, although determined to shut down black voting, differed over requiring a poll tax because they differed over whether to disfranchise a significant number of whites as well as blacks.

Scholars have debated the poll tax's effectiveness in reducing the southern electorate's size. However, there is no disagreement about the poll taxers' leading objectives and little doubt that the tax helped keep large numbers of poor people, especially black southerners, from participating in politics. Recognition of that reality propelled efforts by opponents to terminate the tax and by proponents to resist such change.

DISMANTLING THE POLL TAX

By the 1930s opponents of the poll tax launched efforts, at both the state and the national levels, to eliminate it as a screen to participation in elections. Within the South, opposition reflected a wish by many, both black and white, to end their political exclusion and powerlessness. Even some white leaders favored eliminating the poll tax as a requirement for voting. With little fanfare, North Carolina did so in 1920. With greater notice, Louisiana did the same in 1934. Florida followed suit in 1937, Georgia in 1945, South Carolina in 1951, and Tennessee in 1953, leaving only five former Confederate states—Alabama, Arkansas, Mississippi, Texas, and Virginia—with the tax. Strong efforts failed to end the tax in Texas and Virginia.

Action for repeal was initiated in part by political leaders and groups anticipating that their support would increase if the poll tax went away. The greatest opposition came from counties with large black populations, where whites' con-

cerns that poll tax abolition would mean increased black voting outweighed all other concerns. The gradual decline in black percentage in the population of every southern state reduced those concerns, and a variety of other restrictions on black voting reassured some whites that they could open the ballot to greater white participation without much of a rise in black participation.

At the national level, the campaign reflected a two-fold effort. Abolition of the poll tax would empower poor southerners in their state and local governments, and it would erode the power of southern elites in selecting members of both houses of Congress. For motivation, northerners needed to look no farther than the committee chairmen, who were elected for what amounted to life terms from single-party districts in the South that had small and virtually homogeneous white electorates. Their longevity brought them disproportionate power, as they chaired such committees as Appropriations and Rules and therefore controlled legislation, blocking progressive federal laws that large numbers of Americans wanted.

Efforts in Congress and the federal courts alike failed for many years. A unanimous Supreme Court upheld the constitutionality of the poll tax in a case from Georgia, *Breedlove v. Suttles* (1937), on the basis that the Constitution banned only race and gender as conditions for voting. Further efforts failed in two cases from Virginia, *Saunders v. Wilkins* (1946) and *Butler v. Thompson* (1951). Meanwhile, the same structure of power in Congress that motivated opponents of the poll tax to seek its prohibition prevented their success there. President Franklin D. Roosevelt came out against the poll tax in 1938; President Harry S. Truman did the same a decade later. A repeal measure was introduced in the House in 1939 and at every session thereafter. The House passed it in 1942, 1943, 1945, 1947, and 1949, but southern filibusters in the Senate killed it. Not until the 1960s did the campaign finally succeed, in both the Supreme Court and Congress.

The Twenty-fourth Amendment, approved in 1962 and ratified in 1964, banned the poll tax as a prerequisite to voting in federal elections but did not address the poll tax in state and local elections. Virginia attempted to supply a substitute for the poll tax in federal elections, but the Supreme Court rebuffed the effort in *Harman v. Forssenius* (1965). The five southern states that had not yet eliminated the poll tax had to determine whether and how to continue to impose the poll tax test in state elections while relinquishing it in federal elections. Arkansas changed its constitution to end the poll tax in state and local elections. Resistance to change persisted for a time in the four remaining states, but federal district court decisions in 1966 outlawed the poll tax requirement in Texas and Alabama, and a Supreme Court decision, *Harper v. Virginia*

Board of Elections (1966), outlawed the poll tax in state and local elections everywhere.

Stripped of its linkage to voting, the poll tax persisted into the twenty-first century in some states. New Hampshire continued to require evidence of payment of a "head tax" before people could renew their driver's licenses.

See also *Black Suffrage; Civil Rights Movement; Filibuster; Reconstruction; Suffrage.*

PETER WALLENSTEIN,
VIRGINIA POLYTECHNIC INSTITUTE AND STATE UNIVERSITY

BIBLIOGRAPHY

Kousser, J. Morgan. *The Shaping of Southern Politics: Suffrage Restriction and the Establishment of the One-Party South, 1880–1910.* New Haven: Yale University Press, 1974.

Lawson, Steven F. *Black Ballots: Voting Rights in the South, 1944–1969.* New York: Columbia University Press, 1976.

Ogden, Frederic D. *The Poll Tax in the South.* Tuscaloosa: University of Alabama Press, 1958.

Williamson, Chilton. *American Suffrage: From Property to Democracy, 1760–1860.* Princeton: Princeton University Press, 1960.

POLLING AND PUBLIC OPINION

Determining and measuring public opinion have been matters of concern for rulers, leaders, and governments for as long as publics have existed. Today, public opinion polls are so very much a part of our media content and political process that it is hard for us to realize that concepts such as "public," "opinion," and "measurement" had to be defined and methods devised to quantify them before scientific public opinion polling could be invented.

In 1888 James Bryce, a British lawyer, member of Parliament, and ambassador to the United States, wrote in his classic, *The American Commonwealth,* that whether a country was despotically governed or free, "both are generally ruled by opinion." Yet, he asked, how does one overcome the "mechanical difficulties" of ascertaining the will of citizens? One must "count votes" frequently, he felt, and that could be costly and inconvenient. Today, more than a hundred years later, "votes" are counted frequently and instantaneously. How is it being done?

Although public opinion polling is peculiarly American, it is based on concepts and theories that were developed in a number of mostly European countries. Gathering "passive data," such as demographics, goes back as far as written history. Governments needed the information to collect taxes and raise armies. Mercantile interests in the seventeenth and eighteenth centuries prompted the collection of population statistics in several European countries. Of special significance

for the development of public opinion polling was a study done by a Scottish landowner, Sir John Sinclair. He sent questionnaires to the Scottish clergy in the late 1780s asking about their parishes and parishioners. Britain's Parliament was so impressed by his report, *Statistical Account of Scotland (1791–1799),* that it ordered the first British census in 1801.

The American press also contributed to the development of polling. Newspapers and other businesses conducted straw polls in election years. The first such polls on record were in 1824. The *Harrisburg Pennsylvanian* and the *Raleigh Star* in North Carolina asked their readers how they planned to vote and based predictions on these straw votes. Circulations soared.

Polling theory was given its greatest boost in the mid–nineteenth century by a Belgian mathematician and social scientist. Adolphe Quetelet believed that the only way to turn social studies into a science was to define social concepts in replicable terms so that they could be measured or counted. In 1848 he also suggested that people had latent propensities or inclinations—we call them attitudes—that drove their visible propensities or behavior, including opinions. The first attitudinal survey or poll on record was done between 1907 and 1911 by a German labor leader, Adolf Levenstein, who sent eight thousand questionnaires to laborers asking about their aspirations; religious beliefs; political, cultural, and religious activities; work satisfaction; and drinking habits.

Several developments in survey research at the turn of the twentieth century advanced modern public opinion polling. Most important were the focus on the "popular will" as the "ultimate authority" in the American system, as Britain's Lord Bryce put it, and the theory, as Harvard president A. Lawrence Lowell wrote in his *Public Opinion and Popular Government,* that it was opinions held in common that created a community. Legislators sent out questionnaires to their constituents for their views on issues of the day. Thus, U.S. Rep. Ernest Lundeen of Minnesota in 1917 mailed fifty-four thousand letters to his constituents, asking "Shall the United States declare war?" He added: "I believe that the people should be consulted before Congress declares war."

One additional tool was needed to make polling a billion-dollar business, and that was sampling. In 1912 city leaders in Reading, England, wanted a study done of working-class conditions but lacked the necessary funds for a census. They asked a lecturer at the London School of Economics to do the study. Arthur Bowley had a degree in mathematics and an interest in economic and social issues. Papers on sampling had been presented at the International Statistical Institute conventions in Bern (1895) and Budapest (1901). He suggested a sample survey. He interviewed randomly but systematically selected citizens of Reading in working-class neighborhoods rather than all workers. Using statistical methods, he then projected his findings to the total population in three working-class neighborhoods.

By the turn of the twentieth century, all the necessary elements of a modern public opinion poll had emerged: (1) the concept of a public with opinions about common issues; (2) the theory that as visible characteristics, such as gender, age, or behavior, are distributed in a population, so are attitudes (invisible propensities); and (3) the idea that a small sample of randomly selected individuals drawn from a large population will faithfully mirror the distribution of the population's characteristics.

POLITICAL POLLING

In 1928 George Horace Gallup completed a Ph.D. in applied psychology at the State University of Iowa (renamed the University of Iowa in the late 1950s). His dissertation was titled "An Objective Method for Determining Reader-Interest in the Content of a Newspaper." Gallup taught journalism until 1932, when he conducted a public opinion poll that helped his mother-in-law, Ola Babcock Miller, run a successful campaign for lieutenant governor of Iowa. That year, he quit teaching and joined the advertising firm of Young and Rubicam as head of research.

Several American magazines had conducted election polls since the early 1900s, continuing after the elections by asking general political, economic, and social questions. Best known among these magazines was the *Literary Digest,* starting in 1916, although it had been collecting names and addresses since the 1890s. The *Farm Journal* had actually started polling on presidential elections in 1912.

The *Literary Digest* poll was amazingly accurate until its 1936 presidential predictions. In 1932, for example, its prediction was within 1.4 percent of the actual vote. But in 1936 it mailed out some 10 million ballots, based on names copied from telephone directories and car registrations, at a time when both telephones and cars were owned mostly by wealthier Americans who tended to vote Republican. Although about 2.3 million ballots were returned, they predicted an Alf Landon victory over Franklin D. Roosevelt by 54 to 41 percent. In the final count, Roosevelt received 60.8 percent of the votes. That put the *Literary Digest* poll out of business and gave prominence to three recently established "scientific" polling organizations. These were the American Institute of Public Opinion, founded by Gallup in 1935; Crossley Inc., founded by Archibald M. Crossley in 1936; and the Fortune Survey, headed by Elmo B. Roper Jr. for *Fortune* magazine, established in 1935. While Gallup, Crossley, and Roper were off by 6.8, 8.7, and 0.8 percent, respectively, they all correctly predicted a Roosevelt victory.

Between 1936 and 1948 the election forecasts of these "scientific pollsters" tended to be reasonably accurate. This was a period of experimentation in sampling, questionnaire construction, and interviewing techniques. Thus, Gallup soon found that he needed nowhere near the 125,000 interviews he had conducted for the 1936 presidential election poll.

However, the 1948 presidential election predictions were another setback for the polling pioneers. They forecast a victory for Thomas Dewey by 5 to 15 percentage points; Harry Truman won by 4.4 percentage points. Postmortems indicated they had stopped polling far too soon before election day, and that quota sampling, which involved determining the significant demographic characteristics of the population, figuring or estimating the proportion of each characteristic, and selecting interviewees in those proportions, violated the rule of randomness. Pollsters since then have attempted to avoid the mistakes of 1948, and the reliability of polling improved.

LATER DEVELOPMENTS IN POLLING

For serious political purposes, polling began to be useful in the late 1930s. President Roosevelt sought the advice of Princeton psychologist and survey research specialist Hadley Cantril. President Dwight D. Eisenhower, too, was intrigued by Cantril's insights. President Truman, on the other hand, was not a believer in polls, for understandable reasons.

Public opinion polls became an important campaign tool for John F. Kennedy, who commissioned pollster Louis Harris to conduct fifty surveys for his primary contests and another twenty-seven surveys following the Democratic convention. During his presidency, Kennedy requested some domestic polls and regularly asked Edward R. Murrow, then director of the U.S. Information Agency, for reports on foreign surveys conducted by the agency. President Lyndon B. Johnson, employing Oliver Quayle as his pollster, made even greater use of polls during his administration.

Richard Nixon used polls not only in his electoral campaigns but extensively in the governing process. Whereas Presidents Kennedy and Johnson frequently "piggybacked" questions on surveys done by various pollsters for the private sector, President Nixon wanted full control over his surveys and instructed his chief of staff, H. R. Haldeman, to keep tight control over the distribution of survey results. Similar controls were exercised by Richard Cheney, when he was President Gerald Ford's chief of staff. But beginning with President Jimmy Carter's administration, the distribution of survey findings in the White House appeared less constrained, both under Democrat and Republican presidents.

Probably the most important development in public opinion polling after 1948 was the shift, in the 1970s, from face-to-face interviews to telephone polling. With 92 to 96 per-

President Lyndon B. Johnson commissioned a number of private polls to measure the public response to his policies. Large boards bearing poll results sit in the White House. *Library of Congress*

cent of the population accessible by phone, it appeared safe to make that switch. Telephone interviewing brought with it random-digit dialing (RDD), which provides a much less biased sample. The sample is based on phone numbers picked with the help of a table of random numbers. It also led to the invention of computer-assisted telephone interviewing (CATI), in which interviewers enter responses directly into the computer databases, thus greatly reducing the time it takes to report the results. Starting with the 1980 elections, exit polling dramatically speeded up election day forecasting. Scientific samples of voters are interviewed as they leave polling stations, making it possible for networks to name the winner even before the polls close.

The mass media—newspapers, radio, and television—not only contributed to the development of opinion polls but used them to improve their news coverage and to increase their audiences. However, it would be wrong to assume that scientific sampling was the only kind of "polling" used by political analysts in the latter part of the twentieth century. Sampling enabled them to generalize about identifiable segments of the population—such as women, Republicans, Californians, or senior citizens. But many political reporters have used other statistics—some might call them databases—to arrive at very accurate predictions. In the 1940s and 1950s two political commentators became famous for their success in predicting the outcome of elections without doing any random-sample surveys. Louis H. Bean, an agricultural economist, made his predictions by studying past voting behavior.

Besides President Truman, Thomas Dewey's mother, and astrologer Marion Drew, Bean was the only political observer to predict Truman's triumph in 1948 (although he hedged three days before the election). He also correctly predicted other election outcomes, starting with Franklin Roosevelt's victory in 1936.

Another successful political reporter and analyst during the 1940s to 1960s was Samuel Lubell. He, too, studied past voting behavior, county by county, interviewing people in precincts where he perceived shifts in political opinion. He was an astute observer, focusing on the dynamics of changing beliefs and behavior and using his findings to make his successful predictions.

In the 2000 election campaign, some pollsters, including such veteran polling organizations as the Harris Poll, were abandoning telephones in favor of doing their surveys on the Internet. In response to the argument that only 48 percent of households are connected to the Internet, these pollsters say the Internet poll is just a new version of the mail survey. Harris has built a database of 5 million, which is reminiscent of the ill-fated *Literary Digest* poll. Harris's argument that limited household access can be handled through weighting is another way of reverting to quota sampling, the downfall of the 1948 polls.

Polling is one of the principal tools of the current trend toward continuous campaigning. Political consultants refer to it as the "permanent campaign." Presidential adviser Sidney Blumenthal says one reason presidents must rely on political consultants is the campaign-like environment in which modern presidents are forced to live. Every step is tested through opinion polls.

See also *Campaigning*.

L. JOHN MARTIN, UNIVERSITY OF MARYLAND

BIBLIOGRAPHY

Asher, Herbert. *Polling and the Public: What Every Citizen Should Know.* 5th ed. Washington, D.C.: CQ Press, 2001.

Herbst, Susan. *Numbered Voices: How Opinion Polling Has Shaped American Politics.* Chicago: University of Chicago Press, 1993.

Jacobs, Lawrence R., and Robert Y. Shapiro. "The Rise of Presidential Polling: The White House in Historical Perspective." *Public Opinion Quarterly* 59 (summer 1995): 163–195.

Martin, L. John, ed. "Polling and the Democratic Consensus." *Annals of the American Academy of Political and Social Science* 472 (March 1984).

Moore, David W. *The Super Pollsters: How They Measure and Manipulate Public Opinion.* New York: Four Walls Eight Windows, 1995.

POPULAR SOVEREIGNTY

Popular sovereignty, the principle that settlers in territories would decide whether to allow slavery, was one solution to the most divisive issue of the 1850s: the expansion of the institution. Rep. David Wilmot, D-Penn., proposed in 1846 a ban on slavery in any territory acquired during the Mexican-American War. Sen. Lewis Cass from Michigan, the Democratic nominee for president in 1848, supported popular sovereignty as an alternative that offered the political advantage of removing the contentious issue from Congress.

Stephen A. Douglas, chairman of the Senate Committee on Territories, drafted a bill delegating the power over domestic institutions—implying slavery—to territorial legislatures in New Mexico and Utah as part of the Compromise of 1850. He envisioned that the doctrine would unite Democrats against Whigs and ensure that citizens in the territories had the same right to self-government as those in states. Southerners believed that popular sovereignty guaranteed an equal opportunity to take slavery into a territory until settlers made a decision immediately before statehood, whereas northerners argued that the climate would ensure free soil. Douglas also believed that the doctrine should apply to the proposed Nebraska Territory, although the Missouri Compromise of 1820 had closed the area to slavery. The Kansas-Nebraska Act of 1854 created two territories, declared the Missouri Compromise void there, and left slavery's future to a vote of the territorial legislatures.

Northerners and southerners had accepted popular sovereignty as a compromise in 1850. Four years later, however, the possibility that slavery might spread to territory previously guaranteed free intensified sectional turmoil and cost the Democratic Party northern voters and congressional seats. Implementing popular sovereignty in Kansas precipitated the creation of the Republican Party, which opposed the expansion of slavery to any territory.

See also *Compromise of 1850; Free Soil Party; Kansas-Nebraska Act; Missouri Compromise.*

CAROL JACKSON ADAMS, SALT LAKE COMMUNITY COLLEGE

BIBLIOGRAPHY

Freehling, William W. *The Road to Disunion. Vol. 1. Secessionists at Bay, 1776–1854.* New York: Oxford University Press, 1990.
Holt, Michael F. *The Political Crisis of the 1850s.* New York: W. W. Norton, 1978.
Johannsen, Robert W. *The Frontier, the Union, and Stephen A. Douglas.* Urbana: University of Illinois Press, 1989.
Potter, David M. *The Impending Crisis, 1848–1861.* New York: Harper and Row, 1976.

POPULIST (PEOPLE'S) PARTY

The Populist (or People's) Party, a third party founded in May 1891 in Cincinnati, Ohio, grew out of a period of agrarian revolt and remained politically active until 1908.

Following the Civil War, farmers battled falling commodity prices, high railroad rates, and heavy mortgage debt. The Patrons of Husbandry (the Grange), organized in 1867 by Oliver Kelley, began as a group intent on improving educational and social opportunities for farm men and women but soon adopted economic and political initiatives such as the cooperative movement of the 1870s. The inability of the Grange to give farmers an effective political voice led many Grangers, in the 1880s, to join the Farmers' Alliance, a precursor to the Populist Party. More aggressive and politically oriented, the Farmers' Alliance considered all agricultural problems as economic and pursued remedies such as political education and cooperative marketing, particularly in the South, as a means to break the grip of the furnishing merchants, who extended credit through crop liens.

Women, while active members, held far fewer offices in the Farmers' Alliance than those in the Grange. Existing racial prejudices led to the separate creation of a Colored Farmers' National Alliance in 1888.

In June 1890 Kansas farmers founded the People's Party based on the Southern Alliance platform, which included government ownership of railroads, free and unlimited coinage of silver, and a subtreasury (a system by which farmers could turn over a staple crop to a government warehouse and receive a loan for 80 percent of its value at 2 percent interest per month). As a national third party in 1891, the Populists also sought a farmer-laborer political coalition that championed the belief, expressed by Minnesota Populist Ignatius Donnelly, that the "public good is paramount to private interests."

For a time, the party attempted to bridge the racial gulf and recruited black farmers as well as white. Populism in the South, however, became mired in the volatility of race, epitomized by Georgia's Tom Watson and South Carolina's Benjamin Tillman. Although not immune to the negative racial and ethnic overtones of the period, the Populist Party was nevertheless more concerned with achieving economic reforms, a humane industrial society, and a just polity than it was with attacking cultural issues. The party's greatest support came from white land-owning cotton farmers in the South and wheat farmers in the West.

The Populists rallied behind a policy of monetary inflation in the expectation that it would increase the amount of currency in circulation, boost commodity prices, and ease farm-

James B. Weaver   *Library of Congress*

BIBLIOGRAPHY

Argersinger, Peter H. *Populism, Its Rise and Fall.* Lawrence: University Press of Kansas, 1992.

Goodwyn, Lawrence. *The Populist Moment: A Short History of the Agrarian Revolt in America.* New York: Oxford University Press, 1978.

Hurt, R. Douglas. *American Agriculture: A Brief History.* Ames: Iowa State University Press, 1994.

McMath, Robert C., Jr. *American Populism: A Social History, 1877–1898.* New York: Hill and Wang, 1993.

Nugent, Walter T. K. *The Tolerant Populists: Kansas Populism and Nativism.* Chicago: University of Chicago Press, 1963.

Parsons, Stanley B. *The Populist Context: Rural Versus Urban Power on a Great Plains Frontier.* Westport: Greenwood Press, 1973.

Pollack, Norman. *The Just Polity: Populism, Law, and Human Welfare.* Urbana: University of Illinois Press, 1987.

PRESIDENCY

The American presidency, an invention of the Constitutional Convention of 1787, is different from any other national executive in history. The Framers designed the presidency as a one-person office, rejecting proposals for a committee-style plural executive. They stipulated that the president would be elected not by Congress, but by an electoral college representing the nation as a whole. To ensure that the president would be motivated to do the best possible job, the Framers placed no restriction on his eligibility for reelection. They fixed the president's term at four years, to be brought to an end prematurely only if Congress impeached and removed him on grounds of "Treason, Bribery, or other high Crimes and Misdemeanors." Finally, the framers assigned the presidency a share of virtually all of the national government's powers, but exclusive authority over almost none of them, except the power to pardon. Congress also was assigned a share of most of the government's powers. Thus, as James Sundquist has written, "The Constitution put two combatants in the ring and sounded the bell that sent them into endless battle."

THROUGH THE NINETEENTH CENTURY

Certainly, the presidency was not a very powerful combatant for most of its history. Although the Constitution had given the president several toeholds in the legislative process (including the veto, the obligation to report to Congress on the state of the Union, and the charge to "recommend to their Consideration such Measures as he shall judge necessary and expedient"), Congress initially dominated law making, disdaining any active presidential involvement. Until the 1830s, for example, the veto power was almost meaningless: presidents were enjoined by Congress to use it only if they believed a legislative act to be unconstitutional. Three of the

ers' indebtedness. In 1892, when the People's Party nominated James B. Weaver of Iowa as its presidential candidate, its demands included a graduated income tax, antitrust regulations, public ownership of railroads, and unlimited coinage of silver and gold at a ratio of sixteen to one. Democrat Grover Cleveland was elected to a second term, with Weaver carrying only four states in the West. In 1896 the Populists nominated William Jennings Bryan, a free-silver candidate from Nebraska who was also the Democratic nominee, but the Republicans won with William McKinley.

Having lost on the silver issue and having lost their identity through a "fusion" with the Democrats, the Populists declined in strength and influence, particularly as new discoveries of gold eased the monetary crisis and agricultural conditions improved. Although the People's Party receded, some of the reforms it had championed, including a graduated income tax, were instituted during the Progressive era. The Populists' main significance lay in their visionary use of politics to turn a spotlight on the conditions facing farm families and thereby seek more democratic reform measures.

See also *Currency and Money Supply; Democratic Party; McKinley, William; Panic of 1893; Progressive Era.*

GINETTE ALEY, IOWA STATE UNIVERSITY

first six presidents cast no vetoes at all. With a few exceptions, Congress was controlled by friends and allies of the president during this period, and the president usually supported most bills Congress passed.

Congress also limited the presidency's executive powers. The legislature not only defined the structure of the executive branch by statute, but also itemized every office in each of the departments and agencies it created and fixed the salary of every employee. The most important jobs required Senate confirmation, which meant presidents usually appointed men who had support in Congress. In this political environment, even cabinet members resisted the president's leadership when it conflicted with Congress's. Once, after President James Monroe (1817–1825) invoked his constitutional power to "require the opinion, in writing" of his department heads and asked cabinet members not to send messages to Congress before clearing them with him, he was told by one department head that the practice had existed "ever since the establishment of Government" and would continue.

Only in foreign affairs did the president's constitutionally enumerated powers seem to have any life during the early days of the Republic. The Senate ratified the Jay Treaty, despite its unpopularity, and supported the treaty to purchase Louisiana, as well as several dozen other treaties. It even agreed to certain unilateral presidential assertions of foreign policy, such as Thomas Jefferson's embargo and the Monroe Doctrine.

The reason for executive weakness can be found in the cultural and political environment of the late eighteenth and early nineteenth centuries. Americans wanted little from their national government. The inherent constitutional strengths of the presidency—namely, its ability to act with energy and dispatch and to claim the mandate of a national constituency when doing so—were largely irrelevant when the public had no desire for quick and decisive action by the federal government. Foreign affairs were the exception because the political environment surrounding that policy area was uniquely amenable to presidential power. The United States felt a real threat to its security from several European nations and thus a need to allow the president flexibility and license to act.

Could presidential leadership skill make a difference in such an environment? Only temporarily. George Washington's leadership (1789–1797) in most matters of government was accepted by Congress, but his personal stature as the hero of the Revolutionary War made him singular in that regard. Thomas Jefferson (1801–1809) was an adept leader. His skills, however, were exceptional in ways that affirmed the general rule of presidential weakness. To the extent that Jefferson led Congress, he did so with such sleight of hand as to persuade legislators that they were not being led at all. He had agents on Capitol Hill who advanced his proposals, but their success

sometimes depended on keeping their association with Jefferson confidential.

For the next president of strong will and ability, conditions were different. Andrew Jackson (1829–1837), like Jefferson, wanted to dominate the government, and changes in the political environment gave him advantages his predecessors had lacked. The popular base of American politics had broadened. By 1828 the suffrage belonged to virtually all white adult males, not just those who owned property. The growing population in the West gave Jackson, a military hero from Tennessee, powerful political support. The new voters still did not look to the federal government for much in the way of positive programs to better their lot, but they did begin turning to it for protection against eastern social and financial power.

Jackson rallied these new expectations in support of his efforts to revive some heretofore dormant constitutional powers of the presidency. In his first annual message to Congress, Jackson attacked the "corruption," "perversion," and "indifference" of an administrative system dominated by eastern elites, then declared his fabled system of rotation in office, known as the "spoils system." Jackson replaced more executive officers than had all of his predecessors combined.

Jackson also vetoed more bills than his six predecessors, often because he simply disapproved the bills' contents. Jackson's veto of the bill to recharter the Second Bank of the United States in 1832 offers the most dramatic example. "Though addressed to Congress," observes political scientist Wilfred Binkley, "the veto message was an appeal to the nation. . . . [T]he common man saw in it the apt expression of his own sentiments."

Presidents before Jackson had realized that the result of assertive behavior, such as the bank veto, would be congressional retaliation. The Senate did, in fact, pass a stinging resolution that censured Jackson. But because of changes in the political environment and Jackson's skill at capitalizing on them, the result of his action was far different from what it would have been in the past. The president and his partisans successfully pressured one state legislature after another to demand the resignation of senators who had voted for the censure resolution. (Until the Seventeenth Amendment was enacted in 1913, senators were elected by the state legislatures.) Not long after, in a historic mea culpa, the Senate, by then dominated by Jackson supporters, voted literally to "draw black lines round said resolves, and write across the face thereof in strong letters the following word: Expunged."

Indications of just how much Jackson had changed the presidency can be found in the fulminations of his opponents. "The American elective monarchy frightens me," wrote Chancellor James Kent to Justice Joseph Story. "A Briareus sits in the centre of our system," lamented Massachusetts senator Daniel Webster, "and with his hundred hands touches everything, controls everything." But the real test of the presidency's new power position came later, when John Tyler (1841–1845), a weak and unpopular president, exercised the same powers of veto, appointment, and removal and got away with it. If further indication of the enhanced importance of the presidency was needed, it came in 1860, when, in response to the election of a president who was regarded as hostile to slavery, seven southern states seceded.

Abraham Lincoln's (1861–1865) election did more than reflect presidential power; it also set in motion events that would enhance that power. In prosecuting the war, Lincoln exercised authority not specified in the Constitution. He suspended the writ of habeas corpus, declared martial law, increased the size of the army and navy beyond the levels authorized by Congress, spent money that Congress had not appropriated, and freed slaves by a unilateral proclamation of their emancipation. Congress, an essentially one-party Republican body after the Democratic South seceded, acquiesced in all of these decisions.

Lincoln's actions were especially surprising in light of his long affiliation with the Whig Party prior to becoming a Republican. Whigs, including Lincoln, were staunch supporters of congressional supremacy. Lincoln justified his extraordinary actions as president in a public letter to a Kentucky newspaper editor:

> Was it possible to lose the nation and yet preserve the Constitution? By general law, life and limb must be protected, yet often a limb must be amputated to save a life; but a life is never wisely given to protect a limb. I felt that measures otherwise unconstitutional might become lawful by becoming indispensable to the preservation of the Constitution through the preservation of the nation. Right or wrong, I assume this ground, and now avow it.

Lincoln's actions meant that a precedent (indeed, an expectation) had been set for prompt and strong presidential leadership in times of nation-threatening crises. But action brought reaction: a subsequent period of congressional ascendancy. Congress dominated the presidency through the rest of the nineteenth century, an era that was described in 1881 by government professor Woodrow Wilson as one of "congressional government." Congressional initiative prompted 78 percent of the major items of legislation that were enacted between 1870 and 1900, according to political scientist Lawrence Chamberlain; presidential initiative spawned only 8 percent.

TWENTIETH CENTURY

Even as Congress reigned, several developments in the late nineteenth century political environment were setting the stage for the next quantum leap in the powers of the presi-

dency. One such development was the rise of corporate power in a new national economy. The economic changes led to demands that the federal government create programs of welfare and regulation to protect workers and consumers from the negative side effects of a corporate economy. A second development was the glorification in business and in society generally of executive leadership. The success of entrepreneurs such as John D. Rockefeller, Andrew Carnegie, and Cornelius Vanderbilt seemed to demonstrate that all great things begin with executive power and initiative.

These developments helped pave the way for Theodore Roosevelt (1901–1909), the next strong-willed, politically skillful president, as did the fact that in 1901 both houses of Congress were controlled by the president's party, a rare occurrence in preceding decades. Roosevelt offered the most expansive theory of presidential power in ordinary times that had yet been expressed. He regarded the president as

> a steward of the people bound actively and affirmatively to do all he could for the people, and not to content himself with keeping his talents undamaged in a napkin. . . . My belief was that it was not only his right but his duty to do anything that the needs of the nation demanded unless such action was forbidden by the Constitution or by the law.

Roosevelt's bold actions matched his theory. He ordered the transformation of public lands into national forests, publicly attacked the trusts and intensified antitrust prosecution efforts, "took the [Panama] Canal Zone and let Congress debate," then ordered the naval fleet on an around-the-world sail and dared Congress not to appropriate the money to finance its return home. But TR's major innovation as president was to revive a long-dormant enumerated power of the presidency for which he said he had "specific authorization to do it" from the Constitution: the power to recommend legislation to Congress. The public quickly became accustomed to such presidential initiatives. Analyzing the unsuccessful presidency of Roosevelt's successor, William Howard Taft (1909–1913), a newspaper editor wrote that "failure to dominate Congress was Mr. Taft's chief shortcoming in the public mind."

Building on Roosevelt's precedent and the public's new expectations, and animated by a clear agenda of policy goals, Woodrow Wilson (1913–1921) was able to transform presidential involvement in the legislative process into presidential leadership. As a professor during his prepresidential career, Wilson had noted that although "the President is at liberty, both in law and conscience, to be as big a man as he can, . . . [he] has no means of compelling Congress except through public opinion." In 1913 Wilson took his New Freedom legislative platform directly to Capitol Hill, where he appeared on the floor of the House of Representatives—the first president since John Adams (1797–1801) to do so—to "give to the Congress information of the State of the Union" and to urge that his bills be enacted. Wilson's real audience for these speeches was the electorate, which, having chosen an overwhelmingly Democratic Congress in 1912, now was roused to encourage it to follow Wilson's lead. When the United States entered World War I in 1917, Congress passed the Overman Act, willingly granting the president the kind of emergency powers that Lincoln previously had to seize.

Wilson's success as "chief legislator" marked a milestone in the history of the presidency. After 125 years of American political history under the Constitution, every enumerated power of the office had been brought to life by some skilled and willful president and, because of changes in the political environment, had been accepted by Congress and the public. Practice at last conformed with theory.

Air Force One, the president's aircraft, flies over Mount Rushmore. The power and authority wielded today by the president owe much to earlier occupants of the office.   *The White House*

Making full use of the powers of his office, Franklin D. Roosevelt (1933–1945) mobilized public and congressional support to create a vast array of new federal social welfare programs, collectively known as the New Deal, that were aimed at combating the Great Depression. During his unprecedented third term, "Dr. New Deal" gave way to "Dr. Win the War," in the president's phrase. FDR died in 1945, just before World War II was concluded. War, like depression, heightened the power of the presidency in ways that in this case endured after the enemy surrendered. Roosevelt's successor, Harry S. Truman (1945–1953), served during the opening years of the cold war between the United States and its erstwhile ally, the Soviet Union.

The rivalry between the two superpowers dominated the postwar era, culminating in the early 1990s with the collapse and breakup of the Soviet empire. In the intervening decades, however, "shooting wars" in Korea and Vietnam were launched by Presidents Truman and Lyndon B. Johnson (1963–1969), respectively, each of them acting exclusively on presidential authority. Both wars were unpopular, leading the beleaguered presidents to decline to seek reelection. Johnson's fall from power was especially surprising. During the early years of his presidency, he had successfully emulated FDR as a legislative leader, pushing through Congress groundbreaking civil rights legislation and a major expansion of federal social welfare programs known as the Great Society.

The activism of the Roosevelt years and their aftermath spawned two innovations in the practice of presidential leadership. The first was the creation of a substantial White House staff. FDR believed that such a staff was necessary to advise and inform him on the vast and ever-expanding business of the federal government. Some subsequent presidents were less fortunate in their use of staff. Dwight D. Eisenhower (1953–1961), a generally successful president, suffered politically when his chief of staff, Sherman Adams, was discovered accepting gifts from influence-seekers. Richard Nixon (1969–1974) was forced to resign the presidency because of the misdeeds of the Watergate affair that he had committed in conjunction with members of his White House staff.

The other innovation associated with the Roosevelt years was the adroit presidential use of the new electronic mass media—radio and, in later years, television—to reach out to the American people in their homes. Roosevelt, who invented the "fireside chat," was a master of radio. John F. Kennedy (1961–1963) allowed television cameras to televise his news conferences live, presenting viewers with the image of a cool leader under pressure. Ronald Reagan (1981–1989), who had made his living for many years as a screen and television actor, was talented at delivering prime-time televised addresses to the nation from the Oval Office. Reagan, like Wilson, Franklin Roosevelt, and Lyndon Johnson before him, was able to persuade Congress to enact legislation that dramatically altered the role of the federal government in American society. Unlike them, however, he moved government in a conservative rather than a liberal direction. The centerpieces of his administration were large tax cuts and substantial reductions in federal social programs and economic regulation. Reagan's massive increases in defense spending strained the Soviet economy and hastened the American victory in the cold war.

Constitutionally, the presidency has not been substantially altered since 1787, with two important exceptions. The Twenty-second Amendment (1951) was adopted soon after Franklin Roosevelt died. Roosevelt's four elections had broken the long tradition of one- and two-term presidents. In a major departure from the Framers' desire that presidents always be eligible for reelection, the amendment imposed a two-term limit. The Twenty-fifth Amendment (1967) created a procedure for dealing with presidential disabilities, an increasingly serious problem in an age of nuclear weapons. It also provided that when the vice presidency became vacant, the president would appoint a new vice president with Congress's approval.

Even as the balance of power in the federal government has shifted over the years from Congress to the presidency, legislators have shown an occasional disposition to use their constitutional power of impeachment. During the period from 1789 to 1972, the House impeached only one president—Andrew Johnson (1865–1869)—and he was acquitted when the Senate fell one vote short of the two-thirds majority required for conviction. In 1974, with the Watergate-inspired impeachment process well under way, Nixon resigned in the face of certain removal. In 1998 the House impeached Bill Clinton (1993–2001) for perjury and obstruction of justice in connection with his affair with a White House intern. In early 1999 the Senate acquitted him on these charges.

See also *Constitution, U.S.; Constitutional Convention; Electoral College; Presidential Succession Amendments; Television and American Politics; Twelfth Amendment; individual presidents by name.*

MICHAEL NELSON, RHODES COLLEGE

BIBLIOGRAPHY

Binkley, Wilfred E. *President and Congress.* 3d ed. New York: Random House, 1962.

Genovese, Michael A. *The Power of the American Presidency, 1789–2000.* New York: Oxford University Press, 2000.

Milkis, Sidney M., and Michael Nelson. *The American Presidency: Origins and Development, 1776–1998.* 3d ed. Washington, D.C.: CQ Press, 1999.

Nelson, Michael, ed. *The Evolving Presidency: Addresses, Cases, Essays, Letters, Reports, Resolutions, Transcripts, and Other Landmark Documents, 1787–1998.* Washington, D.C.: CQ Press, 1999.

Riccards, Michael P. *The Ferocious Engine of Democracy: A History of the American Presidency.* 2 vols. Lanham, Md.: Madison Books, 1995.

Skowronek, Stephen. *The Politics Presidents Make: Leadership from John Adams to George Bush.* Cambridge: Harvard University Press, 1993.

Sundquist, James L. *The Decline and Resurgence of Congress.* Washington, D.C.: Brookings Institution, 1981.

PRESIDENTIAL ELECTIONS

Since George Washington took office in 1789 the United States has held a presidential election every four years, in years evenly divisible by four. Since 1804 the elections have been in November. Elections have come in the middle of depressions, wars, and even a civil war. Because of the electoral college, the voters never actually vote for a presidential candidate. Instead, they vote for "electors" who, since the 1840s, have been "pledged" to a particular candidate. The electors in each state meet in December to cast their ballots, and those ballots are passed on to the Senate, which opens and counts them in January. Aside from the elections of 1800, 1824, and 1876, the outcome of the electoral vote was always known well before the electoral ballots were counted in the Senate.

While a quadrennial affair, campaigning for the presidency has often begun years before an election. In 1796 John Adams and Thomas Jefferson competed for the office, with Adams the victor. Under the system in existence at the time (subsequently altered by the Twelfth Amendment to the Constitution) the runner-up, in this case Jefferson, became vice president. Almost immediately after the election of 1796, Jefferson began his next campaign for the presidency. Almost a year and a half before the election of 1800, the Federalist-dominated Congress passed the Sedition Act of 1798, which was designed to suppress criticism of Adams in the upcoming election. Indeed, the law was to expire on March 4, 1801, the day after the new president would take office. If Adams won, he would no longer need to suppress dissent; if Jefferson won (as in fact he did), he could not turn the law against the supporters of Adams.

Similarly, in 1825, shortly after the House of Representatives chose John Quincy Adams for president, the losing candidate, Andrew Jackson, began his quest to unseat Adams in 1828, which he did. William Jennings Bryan was the Democratic candidate for the presidency in 1896, 1900, and again in 1908, and in a sense was continuously campaigning for the office.

In the modern era, presidential bids tend to begin about two years before each election, as candidates create exploratory committees, raise funds, and prepare for the pri-

Although overshadowed by television advertising, campaign buttons remain a staple of presidential contests. *Courtesy of General Dynamics*

sat on his front porch, spoke to those who came to talk to him, but did little to campaign, leaving that to others. In the twentieth century, candidates have been active in their campaigns, crisscrossing the nation by train, boat, bus, and plane to bring their message to the voters.

From the beginning, presidential elections have involved songs, buttons, posters, memorabilia, and hoopla. In the late twentieth century, these aspects of elections were dwarfed by television advertising, professional pollsters, "spin doctors," and consultants, although these are in some sense only the modern version of professional political advisers that have been involved in presidential elections since the 1790s.

Usually, presidents have helped elect members of their own party to Congress, thus guaranteeing that in the first two years of an administration, a president has some chance of seeing his program enacted. Conversely, with a few exceptions (1934 and 1998, for example), a president's party loses ground in Congress in midterm elections.

Presidential elections have become, over the years, the barometer of American politics. This makes sense because the president is the only official elected, although indirectly, by all the voters in the nation. The president has come to embody the nation, and the presidential election is the focus of attention for most political historians and political scientists.

See also *Campaigning; Electoral College; Landslide Elections; Presidency; Presidential Succession Amendments; Twelfth Amendment; Watershed Elections.*

PAUL FINKELMAN,
UNIVERSITY OF TULSA COLLEGE OF LAW

maries. Caucuses, nonbinding "beauty contests," and primaries begin in the early winter of the presidential election year and continue through the spring until a few months before the summer nominating conventions. Since 1960, convention outcomes have never been in doubt; for both major parties the candidates have had the nomination in hand well before the convention. Thus, the conventions are an anticlimax that sometimes generate enthusiasm among the party faithful and sometimes lead to division and party disunity.

In the early years candidates did not campaign, but left the speech making to surrogates and supporters. Stephen A. Douglas was the first candidate to travel and speak in public after his nomination, in 1860. As late as 1896 William McKinley

PRESIDENTIAL SUCCESSION AMENDMENTS

The delegates to the Constitutional Convention were aware that merely to elect a president to a four-year term was no guarantee that the president would be willing, able, or deserving to fulfill the term. They provided for four circumstances in which a president might need to be chosen by succession rather than election: the president's resignation from office; the death of the president; the temporary or permanent inability of the president to fulfill the responsibilities of the office; and the impeachment and removal of a president by Congress for "Treason, Bribery, or other high Crimes and Misdemeanors." In any of these circumstances, the vice president was designated as the president's successor.

The Founders left several succession-related questions unanswered. To a greater or lesser extent, these question have since been addressed by laws and constitutional amendments.

The first unanswered question: In the event that the presidency became vacant, would the vice president serve the balance of the president's four-year term or would succession to the presidency be temporary, pending a special presidential election? The Framers seemed to intend the latter but did not make their intention plain in the Constitution itself. In early 1841, when William Henry Harrison became the first president to die in office, Vice President John Tyler asserted that he was the president and would remain so for the remaining forty-seven months of the term to which Harrison had been elected. Despite some grumbling in Congress, Tyler's *fait accompli* set the pattern for future vice-presidential successions to the presidency, which took place without controversy.

In 1967 the Twenty-fifth Amendment was adopted. Section 1 made the Tyler precedent a matter of constitutional law: "In case of the removal of the President from office or of his death or resignation, the Vice President shall become president."

The second unanswered question: Who would be the successor if the vice presidency were vacant at the time a vacancy occurred in the presidency? The Constitution instructed Congress to legislate for this eventuality, and it did so in 1792, 1886, and 1947. The 1792 succession act said that the president pro tempore of the Senate would be next in the line of succession, followed by the Speaker of the House of Representatives, but these individuals would hold office only until a special presidential election could be held. The 1886 act relocated the line of succession in the president's cabinet in the order the departments were created, beginning with the secretary of state. In 1947 Congress eliminated the special election provision and created the current line of succession after the vice president: Speaker of the House, president pro tempore of the Senate, secretary of state, and so on through the cabinet.

Neither President Gerald R. Ford (left) nor Vice President Nelson Rockefeller were ever elected to federal executive office. Both were appointed vice president under the Twenty-fifth Amendment. *Gerald R. Ford Library*

Section 2 of the Twenty-fifth Amendment did not affect the 1947 succession act, but it did reduce the likelihood that the vice presidency would ever be vacant for long. It provided that vacancies in the vice presidency would be filled by presidential nomination and "confirmation by a majority vote of both Houses of Congress." In 1973 Gerald Ford became the first appointed vice president, after Vice President Spiro T. Agnew resigned. When President Richard Nixon resigned the following year and Ford succeeded to the presidency, he nominated Nelson A. Rockefeller as vice president.

The third unanswered question: What would happen if a person whom the electoral college had chosen to be president died, withdrew, or was found to be constitutionally unqualified by reason of age, residency, or citizenship before being inaugurated? The Twentieth Amendment, which was ratified in 1933, dealt with this problem. Section 2 provided that the vice president-elect would become president under any of those circumstances. The amendment also called on Congress to pass a law covering situations in which the vice president-elect had also died, withdrawn, or been found unqualified before the inauguration. Congress has never acted on this provision of the Twentieth Amendment.

The fourth unanswered question: Who would determine if a president was disabled? "What is the extent of the term 'disability,'" delegate John Dickinson asked the convention, "& who is to be the judge of it?" No one answered his question until the Twenty-fifth Amendment was added to the Constitution in 1967. Although the amendment does not define the term *disability*, sections 3 and 4 establish procedures for dealing with situations of possible presidential disability.

Specifically, three situations are contemplated by the Twenty-fifth Amendment's disability provisions. In the first (so far the only one that has arisen since the amendment was enacted), the president acknowledges "that he is unable to discharge the powers and duties of his office" and writes a letter to that effect to the Speaker of the House and the president pro tempore of the Senate. The vice president then becomes acting president until the president "transmits to them [the two congressional leaders] a written declaration to the contrary." In 1985, at President Ronald Reagan's initiative, Vice President George Bush became acting president for eight hours while Reagan underwent surgery.

In the second situation, the president is disabled but, perhaps because he is unconscious, cannot write a letter that says so. Under the amendment, if the vice president and a majority of the heads of the departments agree that the president is disabled, the vice president becomes acting president—again until such time as the president informs the congressional leaders that the disability is ended.

In the third situation, the president believes that he is able but the vice president and a majority of the department heads disagree. The vice president would then become acting president, pending a final decision by Congress. Congress would have three weeks to determine whether the president was disabled. Two-thirds of both the House and the Senate would have to agree on the president's disability for the decision of the vice president and the department heads to be validated. Otherwise, the president would immediately resume the powers and duties of the office.

See also *Constitutional Amendments*.

MICHAEL NELSON, RHODES COLLEGE

BIBLIOGRAPHY

Berns, Walter, ed. *After the People Vote*. Washington, D.C.: American Enterprise Institute, 1992.

Feerick, John D. *The Twenty-fifth Amendment*. New York: Fordham University Press. 1992.

Silva, Ruth C. *Presidential Succession*. New York: Greenwood Press, 1968.

PRIVATE AND PUBLIC WELFARE, PRE–NEW DEAL

Prior to the New Deal programs of President Franklin D. Roosevelt, public welfare, especially federal welfare, was very limited. Until the establishment of the modern system of public social transfer payments, welfare, and safety nets, the United States dealt with poverty through a combination of private charity, based mainly on religion, and ad hoc local government programs.

In colonial America, paupers' needs were handled in town meetings or by parish churches. Some poor were indentured, and some were forced to work the farms in the community. Children of indentured poor were placed in homes at public expense. Before the American Revolution less than 1 percent of the American population received any outside assistance. By the end of the eighteenth century, dealing with the poor became more centralized, as control of aid moved from the town to the county government level. At the same time, almshouses became important in providing food and shelter to the poor.

EARLY ATTEMPTS AT FEDERAL WELFARE

Before the Civil War, the activities of Dorothea Dix, who championed the cause of the indigent in insane asylums, spurred an early initiative to mandate federal support for the poor. A breakthrough bill to provide federal support for the insane passed both houses of Congress, but President Franklin Pierce vetoed it. Pierce maintained that the Constitution did not contain any authority to make "the Federal Government the great almoner of public charity throughout the United States." Private charity continued to be the main source of welfare.

After the Civil War, families who had lost their main income provider were in particular need. At the same time the federal government began accumulating large budget surpluses, which persisted from 1866 until 1893. The government responded by authorizing increased benefits for Union veterans of the Civil War and their families. By 1890 veterans' benefits had risen to the point where they accounted for more than one-third of the federal budget. State and local governments also provided support to veterans, such as giving homes to disabled soldiers. To help African Americans make the transition from slavery to freedom, the Freedmen's Bureau was also established.

With industrialization and immigration came new demands for social welfare. Some Americans advocated social Darwinism, which applied Charles Darwin's theory of evolution to the laws of society. This view held that subsidizing the poor through welfare created more poor people, because the poor reproduced more rapidly than those in higher economic classes. This subsidy, the theory held, undermined society and would eventually destroy civilization. Rather, the poor must be subject to the harsh laws of nature and die out if need be.

Socialist and Christian forces approached public welfare differently. Socialists aimed their efforts at a fundamental restructuring of the economy to redistribute wealth and income in favor of the poor. Many Christians, until the twentieth century, regarded poverty as resulting from flaws in moral character, which if remedied would lead the way out of poverty. The purpose of relief was not only to provide material aid but also to transform paupers into self-supporting workers. This is one reason that churches played a large role in helping the poor before institutionalized welfare was established.

A number of voluntary private foundations, many of which are still active, came into being between the mid–nineteenth century and early twentieth century:

Young Men's Christian Association	1851
Young Women's Christian Association	1858
Salvation Army	1880
American Red Cross	1881
Volunteers of America	1896
Goodwill Industries	1902
Boy's Clubs of America	1907
Boy Scouts of America	1910
Catholic Charities	1910
Family Service Association of America	1911
Girl Scouts of America	1912

As poorhouses and workhouses disappeared in the 1890s, private charities were established in most major cities to provide food and lodging in return for work from the able-bodied poor. It was common to have wood yards next to homeless shelters to make work convenient. Female poor who were physically able would often work in a sewing room to make clothes for poor individuals who were not able-bodied.

The Progressive movement, which flourished from the early twentieth century until World War I, also sought to increase the living standard for the poor. Although the Progressive movement recorded most of its achievements in the form of regulation of big business, its members also believed that government should pursue the public good. Progressive measures were carried out to move toward an eight-hour workday, to restrict the trade of products of child labor, to improve working conditions for women, to improve agricultural credit facilities and education for farmers, and to establish a minimum wage for women.

GREAT DEPRESSION AND THE GROWTH OF FEDERAL WELFARE

The demands for welfare protection intensified with the Great Depression, which struck in September 1929, early in the administration of President Herbert Hoover. The demands for welfare soon overwhelmed the established private channels. Contrary to conventional belief, however, President Hoover did intervene as the depression deepened. Hoover first attempted to foster optimism and strengthen business in order to reemploy the 25 percent of the workforce that had lost jobs. In this regard, Hoover supported a number of measures to stimulate federal spending and government credit, including the establishment of the Federal Land Banks, the creation of the Agricultural Credit Banks and the Home Loan Banks, and the liberalization of the Federal Reserve Bank's lending authority by the Glass-Steagall Act of 1932.

Perhaps the most important initiative of the Hoover administration was the creation of the Reconstruction Finance Corporation, which assisted financial institutions in providing emergency aid for agriculture, commerce, industry, and other purposes. Hoover also recognized the need for immediate relief and increased appropriations for public works and secured passage of the Emergency Relief and Construction Act (ERCA) of 1932. The ERCA allowed the federal government to give state governments funds to use for relief of the unemployed.

Hoover, perhaps because of his experience in conducting the highly centralized food policy program under President Woodrow Wilson during World War I, was reluctant to go too far with federal intervention. Throughout his administration, he maintained his commitment to individualism and clung firmly to the belief that measures to revive the economy took precedence over transfer payments or using the federal government as the "employer of last resort." Late in his administration (August 1932), Hoover reiterated his principles for government aid: "It is not the function of the Government to relieve individuals of their responsibilities to their neighbors, or to relieve private institutions of their responsibilities to the public." He added, "It is vital that the programs of the Government shall not compete with or replace any of them but shall add to their initiative and their strength. . . . It is only by this release of initiative, this insistence on individual responsibility, that there accrue the great sums of individual accomplishment which carry this Nation forward."

When Franklin Roosevelt succeeded Herbert Hoover as president, his administration adopted the new demand-side economic policy advanced by British economist John Maynard Keynes. This theory recognized that increased welfare served a dual purpose: providing necessary relief to the poor and unemployed and stimulating the economy by putting much needed cash in the hands of consumers. Although Hoover and Roosevelt believed that balanced budgets were important to reestablishing business confidence, they both presided over large fiscal deficits. In the end the U.S. economy recovered somewhat during the 1930s, but, despite the many public programs during the depression, the nation did not completely emerge from depression until the advent of World War II.

See also *Freedmen's Bureau Acts; Hoover, Herbert C.; New Deal; Welfare State.*

RICHARD J. CARROLL, INDEPENDENT SCHOLAR

BIBLIOGRAPHY

Bremner, Robert H. *From the Depths: The Discovery of Poverty in the United States.* New York: New York University Press, 1967.

Higgs, Robert. *Crisis and Leviathan—Critical Episodes in the Growth of American Government.* New York: Oxford University Press, 1987.

Karger, Howard J., and David Stoesz. *American Social Welfare Policy—A Structural Approach.* New York: Longman, 1990.

National Center for Policy Analysis. *19th Century Charities.* NCPA Policy Brief. Washington, D.C.: National Center for Policy Analysis, 1997.

Skocpol, Theda. *Protecting Soldiers and Mothers: The Political Origins of Social Policy in the United States.* Cambridge: Harvard University Press, 1992.

Trattner, Walter I. *From Poor Law to Welfare State: A History of Social Welfare in America.* New York: Free Press, 1997.

PROGRESSIVE ERA

A series of political and social campaigns that affected all aspects of American society, the Progressive era (1890–1920) was a response to industrial growth and its problems at the end of the nineteenth century. This reform movement dominated much of American politics and produced changes in the way politics was conducted. The movement led to an expansion in the role of government at all levels.

In the wake of the economic depression of the 1890s and the political ferment associated with the Populist movement, concerned citizens sought to have government play a larger role in regulating the economy and society. Social workers in urban settlement houses, opponents of utilities and trolley companies, and middle-class residents fearful of the power of large corporations formed the nucleus of campaigns to lessen the power of political parties and enhance the role of government. Investigative journalists (known as "muckrakers" after 1906, when President Theodore Roosevelt compared them to the character in John Bunyan's *Pilgrim's Progress* who raked the muck from the floor) exposed business inequities and corrupt practices in city and state governments.

THE ORIGINS OF REFORM

In the cities, such movements led to the adoption of the commission form of government and later the city manager form as an alternative to ward-based urban machines. These shifts moved power from the lower classes to the middle class but also gave the cities more authority to oversee economic interests within their borders. As reformers sought to improve their cities, however, they often found themselves confronting institutional obstacles that limited their power. In many states,

city legislation was subject to control by the state legislature. Reformers agitated for "home rule" to give the cities greater autonomy. Some urban reformers such as Samuel L. "Golden Rule" Jones of Toledo, Ohio, and Tom Johnson of Cleveland, Ohio, gained national attention for their cities.

By the end of the 1890s the problem of reform on the state level was becoming more pressing in a number of states. In Wisconsin, Robert M. La Follette challenged the power of the Republican Party organization after he was elected governor in 1900. Albert B. Cummins in Iowa, Theodore Roosevelt in New York, John Lind in Minnesota, and other governors across the country at the beginning of the twentieth century argued for antitrust laws, for lowering the protective tariff, and for regulation of the railroads. To give more power to the average voter, the direct primary to choose candidates became popular as an alternative to the conventions where party leaders dominated. State railroad commissions were granted more power, and the regulatory reach of state governments expanded over working conditions, child labor, and social justice.

Progressives pursued two complementary themes in their campaigns. On the procedural level, they sought to make politics more open and accessible to voters. The primary was one such device. Others included the initiative to allow the electorate to propose laws, the referendum to give voters a chance to express their opinions on controversial issues, and the recall that would allow for elections to remove unpopular or corrupt officials. A deep suspicion of the political party animated these measures. The effort to make politics more nonpartisan was a key element in the progressive spirit. One important campaign that reflected the progressives' desire for more openness in government was the drive to achieve women's suffrage. Despite these goals, however, the period when progressivism was in the ascendancy saw a gradual decline in voter interest and participation in state and national elections.

The second strand of progressive thinking sought to take decisions out of the hands of politicians and the electoral process. It aimed to give greater control to experts and regulatory agencies. Many progressives believed that decisions about running a city, regulating a railroad, or setting a tax rate should not be left to the whims of electoral choices. Instead, they favored informed, unbiased experts serving on boards and commissions who would arrive at policy decisions in cool, rational ways. Railroad commissions, public utility commissions, and such entities as the Federal Reserve (1913) embodied this philosophy. In the proper hands, this approach to government had its advantages, but reformers failed to see that the appointment of individuals opposed to reform to a regulatory agency could defeat the purpose of the institution. Like many aspects of progressivism, reliance on experts proved to have unintended conservative and sometimes antidemocratic consequences.

Some progressive campaigns have not fared well among historians. The effort to achieve prohibition of alcohol, which attracted many reformers in the South and West between 1900 and 1920, branded the liquor industry as a special interest and a corrupting element in politics. The failure of the Prohibition experiment in the 1920s discredited what had been a genuine part of the Progressive era. Efforts to restrict immigration, another favorite of many reformers, came to be seen as prejudiced and narrow-minded. African Americans suffered through one of the most difficult periods of their postslavery history during the age of progressivism. Southern progressives considered segregation and black disfranchisement as positive reforms. The progressive president, Woodrow Wilson, ordered the segregation of all federal facilities.

Congress—Who's In It and Who Owns It
MARGUERITE YOUNG

Progressive-era reforms were multifaceted, aimed at a wide array of political, economic, and social ills at the local, state, and national levels. The influence of money on national politics was one of many important issues; John Pierpont Morgan was one of several wealthy bankers and industrialists to wield influence over politicians. *Library of Congress*

PROGRESSIVISM ON THE NATIONAL SCENE

The various currents of progressive change moved onto the national scene in 1901 when Theodore Roosevelt succeeded William McKinley as president. During his two terms in the White House, Roosevelt pushed for antitrust enforcement, regulation of railroads in the Hepburn Act of 1906, and other measures such as the Pure Food and Drug Act (1906) and the Meat Inspection Amendment (1906). He also campaigned for the conservation of natural resources. As his administration entered its final stages, Roosevelt became more innovative and advocated sweeping social justice measures including an inheritance tax, workmen's compensation laws, and a larger federal role in overseeing corporate behavior.

Roosevelt spoke for a public opinion that after 1905 witnessed evidence of corrupt business involvement in politics and became more committed to reform for several years. The Republicans had a progressive wing that was strongest in the Middle West. The Democrats under the leadership of William Jennings Bryan moved toward a more reformist posture. The presence of a strong Socialist Party, led by Eugene V. Debs, was a warning to many moderates of the more rad-

ical transformations that might take place if progressive changes did not occur.

When Roosevelt left office in 1909, he gave way to his former secretary of war William Howard Taft. More conservative than Roosevelt, Taft could not keep the Republican Party together, and the split between party regulars and progressives widened. By 1912 Taft and Roosevelt were no longer friendly. After a bitter battle for the party's nomination that saw Taft victorious, Roosevelt bolted and started his own Progressive Party. Meanwhile, the Democrats had selected a relative political newcomer in Woodrow Wilson, the governor of New Jersey. In the campaign, Roosevelt offered his vision of progressivism that he called "The New Nationalism." It looked to a strong national government and a program of social legislation. Wilson countered with "The New Freedom." He asserted that breaking up monopolies would represent more progressive action than Roosevelt's policy of regulation. A united Democratic Party carried Wilson to victory over Roosevelt, Taft, and Debs in 1912.

During his first term, Wilson achieved many progressive reforms. He persuaded Congress to lower the tariff, reform the antitrust laws through the Clayton Antitrust Act, and to set up the Federal Reserve System for a central bank. From 1914 to 1916, Wilson moved to the left and backed federal loans for farmers. He also supported child labor legislation and greater recognition of unions. The tide for progressive reform was beginning to run out, however. The Republicans reunited after their 1912 disaster and hoped to challenge the Democrats in 1916. The outbreak of World War I and the neutrality issues that it raised allowed Wilson to achieve a narrow reelection victory in 1916. The war then accelerated the adoption of women's suffrage and Prohibition.

THE END OF PROGRESSIVISM

By the time the war ended in 1918, the Republicans had regained control of Congress and were attacking the Democrats as proponents of higher taxes and an intrusive government. The sentiment for reform was ebbing as the country tired of crusades and agitation. The election of Warren G. Harding in a landslide in 1920 showed how far the United States had swung back to the right. After a generation of progressive change, the American people wanted a return to conservatism and older values.

Progressivism had made a difference, however. The federal government in 1920 had a far wider range of responsibilities than it faced in 1890. The political process had been made more open for women. The plight of working men and women was less dire than thirty years earlier. The power of the presidency had been strengthened under Roosevelt and Wilson. The operations of city and state government were more open and less corrupt in many parts of the nation. The progressives had not solved every problem that they faced, but they set the agenda of domestic politics for the remainder of the twentieth century. Few social movements in American history have done more to reshape the nature of the national life than had progressivism in the first two decades of the twentieth century.

See also *Antitrust; Initiative, Referendum, and Recall; New Freedom; New Nationalism; Panic of 1893; Private and Public Welfare, Pre–New Deal; Progressive Party (La Follette); Prohibition and Temperance; Roosevelt, Theodore; Wilson, Woodrow; Woman's Suffrage Movement.*

LEWIS L. GOULD, UNIVERSITY OF TEXAS AT AUSTIN

BIBLIOGRAPHY

Buenker, John D., and Edward R. Kantowicz, eds. *Historical Dictionary of the Progressive Era.* Westport, Conn.: Greenwood Press, 1988.

Diner, Stephen J. *A Very Different Age: Americans of the Progressive Era.* New York: Hill and Wang, 1998.

Gould, Lewis L. *Reform and Regulation: American Politics from Roosevelt to Wilson.* Prospect Heights, Ill.: Waveland Press, 1996.

Hofstadter, Richard. *The Age of Reform: From Bryan to F.D.R.* New York: Alfred A. Knopf, 1955.

Link, Arthur S., and Richard L. McCormick. *Progressivism.* Arlington Heights, Ill.: Harlan Davidson, 1983.

PROGRESSIVE LABOR PARTY

The Progressive Labor Party (PLP) emerged out of the Communist Party USA in the early 1960s. It was the first Maoist party in the United States, following the revolutionary philosophies of Joseph Stalin and Mao Zedong and adhering to Mao's dictum that "power emanates from the barrel of a gun." The PLP envisions Stalin's dictatorship as the ideal state and opposes democracy, elections, capitalism, religion, and freedom in any form.

The PLP took over the Students for a Democratic Society (SDS) in 1969, prompting the non–Progressive Labor people to walk out of SDS and leaving the organization as a shell of its former self. The SDS was an activist—its critics said radical—student organization that started in Michigan and drew many supporters on campuses nationwide, particularly during the Vietnam war years.

The PLP contends that experiments with socialism and communism failed in the former Soviet Union and in today's People's Republic of China, where, it says, capitalism has triumphed. The PLP's doctrine, proclaimed on its Web site, envisions the party leading an "armed struggle by masses of workers, soldiers, students and others, to destroy the dictatorship of the capitalist class and set up a dictatorship of the working class."

The PLP publishes a newspaper, *Challenge,* and a magazine, *Communist,* as well as leaflets on such topics as "The Imperialist War in the Mideast," "Smash Racist Police Terror," and "Fascism Grows in the Auto Industry." In strict adherence to its policy of "armed struggle," the party disavows electoral politics.

See also *Communist Party USA; Political Parties; Third Parties.*

RON dePAOLO, INDEPENDENT AUTHOR

PROGRESSIVE PARTY (H. WALLACE)

Henry A. Wallace, who had been Franklin D. Roosevelt's vice president from 1941 to 1945, differed with the tough policy of the Truman administration toward the Soviet Union during the early years of the cold war. President Harry S. Truman fired Wallace from his post as secretary of commerce in 1946 after Wallace criticized the administration's foreign policy. Wallace believed that the United States should not alienate the Soviet Union and that the best way to combat communism was through better living conditions for the world's population. An aggressive policy toward Moscow, Wallace warned, could lead to another world war. Partisans on the left created the Progressive Citizens of America, out of which emerged the Progressive Party in July 1948. To head its national ticket, the party's convention selected Wallace and then named Sen. Glen Taylor, an Idaho Democrat, as his running mate. The convention was seen as dominated by procommunist forces who framed a platform that was critical of Truman's foreign policy and was quiet on any indictment of the Soviet Union. The Communist Party threw its support behind Wallace's candidacy, and the Progressive Party that pushed the presidential candidacy of Wallace in 1948 became identified as a pro-Soviet political organization.

Wallace ran an aggressive campaign but had difficulty answering charges that his position and his candidacy encouraged the Soviets. Foreign policy events such as the pro-Soviet coup in Czechoslovakia (1948) and the Berlin blockade (1948–1949) undercut Wallace's claims that Moscow could be trusted to keep its commitments. Anticommunist members of the Democratic Party supported President Truman, and much of Wallace's early support melted away. Wallace received 1,157,000 popular votes (2.4 percent of the vote) and carried no states in the electoral contest. Wallace left politics for good after the election. Four years later the Progressive Party's ticket of Vincent Hallinan and Charlotte Bass captured only 140,000 votes, and the organization soon disappeared.

See also *Cold War; Democratic Party; Political Parties; Third Parties; Truman, Harry S.*

LEWIS L. GOULD, UNIVERSITY OF TEXAS AT AUSTIN

BIBLIOGRAPHY

Hamby, Alonzo. *Beyond the New Deal: Harry S. Truman and American Liberalism.* New York: Columbia University Press, 1973.

Markowitz, Norman. *The Rise and Fall of the People's Century: Henry A. Wallace and American Liberalism, 1941–1948.* New York: Free Press, 1973.

Patterson, James T. *Grand Expectations: The United States, 1945–1974.* New York: Oxford University Press, 1996.

PROGRESSIVE PARTY (LA FOLLETTE)

The Progressive Party in 1924 was the vehicle for the presidential ambitions of Sen. Robert M. La Follette Sr. of Wisconsin.

Robert M. La Follette Sr. (1855–1925) had long wanted to secure the Republican presidential nomination but had failed in 1908 and 1912 to gain any support outside the upper Middle West. During World War I, his antiwar senti-

ments caused his critics to label him as pro-German. In the period of postwar reaction, with the Republicans moving rightward, reformers associated with the progressive wing of the party created in 1922 the Conference for Progressive Political Action. In 1924, after Calvin Coolidge had been named the Republican presidential candidate and a conservative Democrat, John W. Davis, had been chosen to run against him, the CPPA rallied behind La Follette. He became the nominee of the new Progressive Party, with Burton K. Wheeler of Montana as his running mate.

In the election, La Follette was the Progressive Party. He made his usual vigorous canvass, and his speeches identified the threat of private monopoly power as the major social issue facing the nation. The Coolidge and Davis campaigns denounced La Follette as an advocate of radical economic and political change. The third-party candidate won 4.8 million votes, about one-sixth of the total, but carried only his home state of Wisconsin in the electoral count. La Follette died the following year. The Progressive Party of 1924, never much of a real organization, had already disappeared.

See also *Political Parties; Progressive Era; Third Parties.*

LEWIS L. GOULD, UNIVERSITY OF TEXAS AT AUSTIN

BIBLIOGRAPHY

Burner, David. "The Election of 1924." In *History of American Presidential Elections, 1789–1968.* 4 vols. Edited by Arthur M. Schlesinger Jr. and Fred I. Israel. New York: Chelsea House, 1971.

La Follette, Belle Case, and Fola La Follette. *Robert M. La Follette, June 14, 1855–June 18, 1925.* 2 vols. New York: Macmillan, 1953.

Weisberger, Bernard A. *The La Follettes of Wisconsin: Love and Politics in Progressive America.* Madison: University of Wisconsin Press, 1994.

PROHIBITION AND TEMPERANCE

Prohibition and temperance movements sought to legislate an end to consumption of intoxicating beverages. Colonial and early national Americans preferred alcohol to impure water or milk and more expensive coffee or tea. By 1825 those over fifteen years of age drank an average of seven gallons of pure alcohol per year, diluted in cider, beer, wine, and distilled liquor; white males typically consumed substantially more, women much less, and black slaves very little. Physicians, Protestant ministers, and temperance advocates concerned about damage to health, morals, and industrial production urged voluntary abstinence from drinking. After achieving remarkable success, the temperance movement sought legal banishment of liquor. During the 1850s a dozen states—led by Maine in 1851—adopted alcohol bans.

Agents of the Internal Revenue Service pose with a still that they confiscated in Washington, D.C., November 11, 1922. *Library of Congress*

After the Civil War, temperance crusaders created effective political pressure groups: the Prohibition Party in 1869, the Woman's Christian Temperance Union in 1874, and the Anti-Saloon League of America in 1895. Their campaigns won numerous statewide prohibition and local option laws, the latter giving individual communities the right to outlaw the sale of alcohol. In 1913 Congress banned shipment of liquor into any state that chose to bar it. Dissatisfied by uneven and sometimes short-lived state and local successes, goaded by rivalries between the Anti-Saloon League and competing temperance groups, and inspired by adoption of the first federal constitutional amendments in more than forty years (the income tax and direct Senate election amendments of 1913), reformers began calling for a total, permanent, nationwide solution to the liquor problem: a prohibition amendment to the Constitution.

National prohibition gathered support from evangelical Protestant denominations, feminists, nativists opposed to the recent flood of immigrants who drank, progressive social and political reformers, and industrial employers. Employing the unusual political tactic of pledging electoral support or pun-ishment solely on the basis of a candidate's stand on the single issue of alcohol, proponents of prohibition were able to get more and more supporters elected to Congress. U.S. entry into World War I against Germany added a final argument of patriotism, because the army needed the grain for bread and the troops needed to be sober to perform effectively. The Eighteenth (or Prohibition) Amendment was adopted with bipartisan backing in January 1919 and went into effect one year later; it operated with mixed success for fourteen years.

The Republicans, who were responsible for enforcement as the party in power throughout the 1920s, continued to defend Prohibition even as the Democrats' support was waning, especially in the urban North, as first Al Smith and later Franklin D. Roosevelt aligned with the repeal campaign. Differences regarding Prohibition were among the most clear-cut partisan divisions in the 1932 elections and helped account for the shift in the national political balance during the depths of the Great Depression. National Prohibition, widely viewed as a mistake, was repealed by the Twenty-first Amendment, approved by Congress in February 1933 and ratified in December 1933.

See also *Constitutional Amendments.*

DAVID E. KYVIG, NORTHERN ILLINOIS UNIVERSITY

BIBLIOGRAPHY

Blocker, Jack S. Jr. *American Temperance Movements: Cycles of Reform.* Boston: Twayne, 1989.

Hamm, Richard F. *Shaping the Eighteenth Amendment: Temperance Reform, Legal Culture, and the Polity, 1880–1920.* Chapel Hill: University of North Carolina Press, 1995.

Kyvig, David E. *Repealing National Prohibition.* Chicago: University of Chicago Press, 1979. Paperback edition, Kent, Ohio: Kent State University Press, 2000.

Murdock, Catherine Gilbert. *Domesticating Drink: Women, Men, and Alcohol in America, 1870–1940.* Baltimore: Johns Hopkins University Press, 1998.

RAINBOW COALITION

After thirteen years of leading Operation PUSH (People United to Save Humanity), a Chicago-based organization aimed at strengthening economic opportunity and educating black young people about drugs, pregnancy, and violence, Jesse Jackson organized a "rainbow coalition" of supporters for his national political campaigns.

Jackson joined the staff of Martin Luther King Jr.'s Southern Christian Leadership Conference (SCLC) in 1965. By 1967 Jackson was directing its Operation Breadbasket, which used the threat of economic boycotts to convince private businesses to end racial discrimination in employment and to award contracts to black businesses. Increasingly alienated from SCLC's leadership after King's assassination in 1968, Jackson left its staff in 1971 to organize Operation PUSH.

Modeled on Operation Breadbasket, Operation PUSH ostensibly was a multiracial coalition to mobilize the economic and political power of poor people. In fact, it was primarily a black vehicle to encourage white-owned firms to employ African Americans and to do business with black firms.

To support his campaign for the presidency in 1984, Jesse Jackson called on a "rainbow coalition" of racial and ethnic minorities, feminists, farmers and workers, and gays and lesbians. That year he won 19 percent of the 17 million votes cast in Democratic primaries, controlled the third largest number of delegates to the party's convention, and exercised considerable influence over the party platform. Four years later he called again for the support of the rainbow coalition, polled 30 percent of the 23 million votes cast in the Democratic primaries, and won the primaries in nine states.

In late 1988 Jackson became president of Rainbow Coalition, Inc., which formally promoted the progressive agenda he had championed in the 1984 and 1988 campaigns. In 1997 Operation PUSH merged with Rainbow Coalition, Inc., to become the Rainbow/PUSH Coalition. Based in Washington, D.C., at the end of the twentieth century the group claimed thirteen thousand members in all fifty states, pursued a progressive political agenda, and monitored the investment, hiring, and promotion practices of U.S. corporations.

See also *African American Politics*.

RALPH LUKER, VIRGINIA FOUNDATION FOR THE HUMANITIES

BIBLIOGRAPHY

Jackson, Jesse. *A Time to Speak: The Autobiography of Jesse Jackson*. New York: Simon and Schuster, 1988.

Luker, Ralph E. *Historical Dictionary of the Civil Rights Movement*. Lanham, Md.: Scarecrow Press, 1997.

Reed, Adolph, Jr. *The Jesse Jackson Phenomenon: Crisis of Purpose in African American Politics*. New Haven: Yale University Press, 1986.

REAGAN, RONALD

Born February 6, 1911, in Tampico, Illinois, Ronald Wilson Reagan was governor of California (1967–1975) and the fortieth president of the United States (1981–1989).

After graduating from Eureka College in 1932, Reagan became a play-by-play sports announcer on radio. Lured from radio to motion pictures, he made fifty-one films during an acting career than spanned more than two decades. His political career began with his service to the Screen Actor's Guild, first as an active member, and then as union president (1947–1952; 1959–1960).

Largely because of the impact of the postwar Red Scare on the film industry, during this period Reagan, originally a registered Democrat, evolved into a philosophical conservative and one of the nation's most recognizable voices in the anticommunist movement. By 1964 he was being touted for elective office. Although he was not a candidate that year, Reagan's speech in support of Republican presidential candidate Barry Goldwater was the most notable address of the campaign. Indeed, several scholars have dated the beginning of what would be called the New Conservative Movement from that speech, as Reagan supplanted Goldwater as the leading political figure representing conservative America.

ROAD TO THE WHITE HOUSE

Using the increased visibility gained from the Goldwater speech and the financial support it engendered as springboards, Reagan was elected governor of California in 1966 and served two terms. During that period, Reagan made his first serious run for the presidency; in 1968 he came to the Republican convention as a favorite son but was brushed aside by Richard M. Nixon's juggernaut. Eight years later, however, in the wake of Nixon's resignation and his pardon by President Gerald R. Ford, Reagan challenged Ford for the Republican nomination. Reagan's strengths were his outsider status and his calls for an end to détente and an increased military buildup, which played well in the South. However, Reagan was hampered by Ford's skillful use of the incumbency and his own poorly thought out fiscal package (Reagan argued that federal cutbacks could reduce the size of the federal deficit by some $90 billion—a plan that most observers noted would cause high unemployment). Reagan was defeated on the first ballot, 1,180 to 1,069, but his challenge cost Ford dearly, as did Reagan's refusal to campaign for the president that fall. Ford lost to Jimmy Carter, and virtually overnight Reagan became the frontrunner for the 1980 Republican nomination.

Throughout the 1980 campaign, Reagan was still hampered by his fiscal package, which was attacked by challenger George Bush—who would turn out to be Reagan's running mate—as "voodoo economics." But his message of contempt for what he viewed as American military weakness now found wide public acceptance because of the seemingly interminable crisis with Iran, where fifty-two hostages were being held captive by fundamentalist students in the American embassy in Tehran. Added to this was the advantage of running as a challenger during a period of high inflation and rising gasoline prices. Reagan capitalized on the economic situation by asking Americans this question during a debate with Carter: "Are you better off now than you were four years ago?" Reagan also seemed to be a calmer, more serene candidate than the nation had seen in 1976. Next to the often-harried Carter, Reagan was the epitome of self-confidence, as illustrated by his gentle riposte to Carter, also during a debate, and delivered with a smile: "There you go again." Reagan easily defeated Carter, garnering 50.7 percent of the popular vote to Carter's 41 percent and winning 489 electoral votes to Carter's 49. The rest of the vote went to third-party candidates, most notably Rep. John Anderson of Illinois.

Reagan's supporters felt that they were part of a true upheaval in American life and politics, that his eight-year tenure in office substantially reshaped America. In many ways, this assessment is defensible. In 1980 the American people elected an ideologue as their president. Reagan had preached a particular brand of conservatism with consistency since 1964, but it had taken hold of the Republican Party only after the Watergate scandal, which had cost President Nixon his job. Reagan's conservatism centered on three canons: reducing the tax burden on Americans, reversing the moral permissiveness that Reagan felt had been a legacy of the 1960s, and returning the post–Vietnam War United States to its rightful place as a world superpower.

IDEOLOGY AND PERSONALITY

Throughout his presidency, Reagan attacked each of these issues with gusto. Reagan earned the support of Middle America, as well as the support of a newly burgeoning fundamentalist Christian movement, with his clarion call for a return to the "traditional values" of the more placid pre–Vietnam period. His call ultimately resonated across class and party lines, and many scholars see the call for what Republicans would later call "family values" as the most enduring legacy of Reaganism. But Reagan also cut taxes as he promised. The Economic Recovery Tax Act of 1981 cut federal rates by 10 percent every year for three years. And Reagan's foreign policy was largely based upon his publicly stated belief that the Soviet Union was "the focus of evil in the modern world," which had to be checked by U.S. military force. The increase in military spending during his first term made it clear that Reagan meant what he said.

Reagan's appeal was more than policy-based. His charisma emboldened Americans in a way that no other president's had since John F. Kennedy. Indeed, the confident personality of the oldest elected president in American history (Reagan was seventy when he took office) hearkened directly back to Kennedy, the youngest chief executive. And it was not only middle-aged Americans who reacted with enthusiasm; Reagan energized young conservatives, who flocked to Washington to join in his "revolution." His appointment of Sandra Day O'Connor, the first woman to serve on the Supreme Court, and his nominations of Robert Bork—a social conservative who failed to gain Senate approval but whose nomination Reagan defended to the final vote—and Antonin Scalia—a conservative whose nomination met with more success—further endeared Reagan to young conservatives. Reagan's popularity was so widespread in 1984 that his reelection was never seriously in doubt. He defeated former vice president Walter Mondale with 59 percent of the popular vote and 525 electoral votes to Mondale's 13.

Taken at face value, the Reagan Revolution lived up to its name. However, there was a much less triumphant side to the Reagan years that emerged in his second term. Reagan's tax cuts had concealed the fact that the economy was becoming

President Ronald Reagan and his wife Nancy relax at Camp David, the presidential retreat in Maryland's Catoctin Mountains, located fifty miles northwest of Washington, D.C.   *Bill Fitzpatrick, The White House*

unstable; indeed, the cuts directly contributed to a national debt that tripled during Reagan's presidency to $2.7 trillion—by 1988 the payment on the interest alone was $140 billion a year. And although many upper-class Americans were enjoying even greater wealth as a result of Reagan's policies, the poor were getting progressively poorer. "Reaganomics" had been designed on the theory that tax cuts would put money into the economy that would "trickle down" to the less fortunate. By the time Reagan left office, the nation had worked its way—not entirely successfully—through a full-blown recession; the number of white Americans living below the poverty line had increased; and unemployment was rising. More important for some was Reagan's perceived lack of compassion for the plight of the poor; perhaps the low point was Reagan's comment that when considering a balanced meal for school lunches, ketchup should be considered a vegetable. For others, Reagan's lack of compassion for those outside his immediate station was best shown by his administration's refusal to commit either sizable monies or the president's "bully pulpit" to issuing warnings about the AIDS epidemic, which hit its apex during the Reagan years.

FOREIGN POLICY

Both liberals and conservatives criticized the administration's foreign policies. Liberals opposed the jingoist patriotism that Reagan's hard line toward the Soviet Union had helped en-

gender and were outspoken against the administration's excesses in Latin America. With the implicit approval of the president, White House staffers had sold arms to Iran, only recently an enemy of the United States. The goal of the sales—Iranian assistance to secure the release of American hostages in Lebanon—never materialized, and the excess profits from the sales were diverted, in direct contradiction of U.S. law, to the contras, a group of anti–Marxist rebels in Nicaragua. Reagan's consistent support of the contras as "freedom fighters" did little to change the public's view of the scandal.

Reagan also was criticized for his Soviet policy, which from the start had unnerved liberals, but which in his second term had become more flexible than doctrinaire conservatives were willing to accept. By 1987 Reagan had shifted from denunciations of the "evil empire" and had begun serious public talks with Mikhail Gorbachev, the new secretary general of the Communist Party. Despite rhetoric that forecast the end of communism within two years' time—in Berlin Reagan had demanded: "Mr. Gorbachev, tear down this wall"—in the short run Reagan's policies contributed to the legitimization of Gorbachev's attempts at reform and helped strengthen his hold on office. This was more than many conservatives could bear. Thanks to Reagan's continued popularity, they were loath to voice their criticisms while he was in office, but they refused to give to Reagan's successor the loyalty and support they had given to Reagan.

After the 1988 election of George Bush, Reagan retired to his California ranch. Six years later his family announced that he was suffering from Alzheimer's disease, and his public appearances came to an end. For many Americans, Ronald Reagan and his administration continued to represent the high point of American conservatism.

See also *Bush, George; Iran-Contra Scandal; Republican Party.*

JOHN ROBERT GREENE, CAZENOVIA COLLEGE

BIBLIOGRAPHY

Cannon, Lou. *President Reagan: The Role of a Lifetime.* New York: Simon and Schuster, 1991.

Pemberton, William E. *Exit with Honor: The Life and Presidency of Ronald Reagan.* Armonk, N.Y.: M.E. Sharpe, 1997.

Schaller, Michael. *Reckoning With Reagan: America and Its President in the 1980s.* New York: Oxford University Press, 1992.

REAPPORTIONMENT CASES

Reapportionment and redistricting are the two processes used to allocate seats in the U.S. House of Representatives among the fifty states and to draw the districts from which House members and state legislators are elected. The Constitution, as adopted in 1789, required a reapportionment of House seats every ten years but said nothing about redistricting. For most of the country's history, state legislatures had free rein to draw congressional and legislative districts as they saw fit.

By the early decades of the twentieth century, congressional and legislative districting in many states reflected substantial population inequities. With the population shift to the cities, rural districts came to be significantly smaller in population than urban districts, and rural voters were thereby overrepresented in state legislatures in comparison with people living in cities. Beginning in the 1960s, however, the U.S. Supreme Court forced legislatures to eliminate those population disparities. The "one-person, one-vote" requirement revolutionized American politics by bringing an end to rural domination of state legislatures and ensuring greater attention to the interests of urban and suburban residents.

Rural legislators and advocacy groups strongly opposed the Supreme Court's intervention at the time. Today, the one-person, one-vote principle is all but universally accepted. Its implementation, however, frequently puts the courts in the difficult position of superintending an inherently political process.

POLITICAL QUESTIONS

The Constitution specified the initial number of House seats to be allocated to each of the original thirteen states. Through the nineteenth century the size of the House was increased as new states were added and the populations of existing states grew. In 1911 Congress fixed the size of the House at 435 members. Unable to add new seats, Congress in the 1920s refused to pass a reapportionment law. In 1930, however, Congress complied with the constitutional command. Since then, House seats have been reallocated each decade.

Congress in the nineteenth century had passed laws requiring that House members be elected from single-member districts and that the districts be of approximately equal population. Congress dropped the equal-population requirement in 1929. Three years later the Supreme Court upheld a Mississippi scheme that failed to provide districts of equal population. One example of the resulting disparities came in Illinois, where the smallest House district in the 1940s had 800,000 fewer people than the largest.

Kenneth Colegrove, a Northwestern University political science professor, challenged the Illinois districting scheme as a violation of his rights under the Fourteenth Amendment's Equal Protection Clause. In a 4–3 decision, the Supreme Court in 1946 rejected the suit. Writing the main opinion in *Colegrove v. Green,* Justice Felix Frankfurter said the issue was "of a peculiarly political nature and therefore not meet for judicial determination." Dissenting justices argued that fed-

eral courts had the power to protect citizens' right to vote under the federal Constitution.

Many state constitutions included provisions requiring periodic legislative redistricting, but rural-dominated legislatures ignored the requirements with impunity. Over the next fifteen years federal and state courts alike relied on the *Colegrove* decision to throw out urban voters' efforts to challenge population inequities in either congressional or legislative districts.

"ONE PERSON, ONE VOTE"

The Supreme Court reversed itself in a 1962 decision, *Baker v. Carr,* that upheld federal courts' authority to entertain reapportionment and redistricting suits. Within the next two years the Court coined the now famous phrase "one person, one vote" and applied that standard as a matter of federal constitutional law not only to House districts but to state legislative districts as well.

In *Baker v. Carr* urban voters in Tennessee challenged a legislative districting scheme dating to 1901 that allowed one-third of the state's population to elect two-thirds of the members of the state legislature. State and federal courts rejected the suit, but the Supreme Court voted 6–2 to allow the claim. In a sparely worded opinion, Justice William J. Brennan Jr. said that the plaintiffs had made out a federal constitutional claim by alleging a "gross disproportion of representation." He rejected the *Colegrove* doctrine that the issue was a "political question" outside the federal courts' jurisdiction.

One year later the Court gave substance to its decision by striking down Georgia's so-called county unit primary system for electing state officials. The system weighted votes to give advantage to rural districts in statewide primary elections. By an 8–1 vote the Court in *Gray v. Sanders* held that the scheme violated the Equal Protection Clause. Political equality, Justice William O. Douglas wrote, "can mean only one thing—one person, one vote."

The Court completed the foundations of redistricting law in a pair of decisions in 1964. In the first of the rulings, *Wesberry v. Sanders,* the Court applied the "one-person, one-vote" principle to congressional districts. Four months later the Court held that the same requirement applied to both houses of bicameral state legislatures. "Legislators represent people, not trees or acres," Chief Justice Earl Warren wrote in *Reynolds v. Sims.* The Equal Protection Clause, he continued, "demands no less than substantially equal state legislative representation for all citizens."

The Court's rulings drew strong opposition from rural organizations and state legislators who faced a loss of power as a result. But the states failed to get Congress to approve legislation or a constitutional amendment to negate the decisions and fell just short of the number of states needed to force Congress to call a constitutional convention on the subject. For his part, Warren later described his opinion in *Reynolds v. Sims* as the most important of his career.

LONG-TERM IMPACT

In applying the one-person, one-vote standard, the Supreme Court has required strict mathematical equality for congressional districts but allowed some leeway for state legislative districts. In *Avery v. Midland County* (1968) it also extended the one-person, one-vote requirement to local legislative bodies. Two decades later the Court opened the door slightly to constitutional challenges to so-called political gerrymandering—the drawing of district lines to benefit one or the other political party. The ruling has proved to have little impact, however. Then in the 1990s the Court created greater political upheaval by ruling that white voters can raise equal protection challenges to the creation of "majority-minority" districts aimed at helping elect African Americans or Hispanics to Congress.

The insistence on relatively strict equality forced state legislators after each ten-year census to devote more attention to redrawing the maps for their own districts and for congressional districts. Redistricting schemes became more intricate, with districts crossing jurisdictional lines and sometimes zigzagging to pick up or skirt specific neighborhoods. The process—always political—became all the more susceptible to manipulation by the party that controlled the legislature.

A legal challenge to the historic practice of gerrymandering reached the Supreme Court in 1986 in a case brought by Indiana Democrats contesting a state legislative redistricting plan adopted by the Republican-controlled legislature. Echoing *Baker v. Carr,* the Court voted 6–3 in *Davis v. Bandemer* to allow such challenges in federal courts. But it went on to approve the challenged plan by a 7–2 vote and to set a relatively high hurdle for such challenges to succeed. Applying the test, lower federal courts generally rejected efforts to throw out redistricting plans on political grounds.

The reapportionment and redistricting cases had their greatest impact on state legislatures, where power shifted from rural areas to cities and suburbs. State legislatures, once widely viewed as moribund, became more active and more politically competitive. In Congress reapportionment meant that power shifted with the movement in population away from the industrial states of the Northeast and Midwest and to the states along the nation's southern tier from Florida to California—the so-called Sunbelt. The shift from traditionally Democratic states combined with Republican gains in the growing Sunbelt states to help the GOP capture control of the House of Representatives in 1994 for the first time in forty years.

See also *Apportionment; Census; Gerrymandering;* Shaw v. Reno, *Suffrage.*

KENNETH JOST, CONGRESSIONAL QUARTERLY

BIBLIOGRAPHY

Baker, Gordon E. *The Reapportionment Revolution: Representation, Political Power, and the Supreme Court.* New York: Random House, 1966.
Butler, David, and Bruce Cain. *Congressional Redistricting: Comparative and Theoretical Perspectives.* New York: Macmillan, 1992.
Cortner, Richard C. *The Apportionment Cases.* Knoxville: University of Tennessee Press, 1970.
Graham, Gene S. *One Man, One Vote: Baker v. Carr and the American Levellers.* Boston: Little, Brown, 1972.

RECONSTRUCTION

The era following the secession of eleven southern states in 1860–1861 and the Union victory in the Civil War in 1865 is known as Reconstruction, the period when those states were restored to full participation in the nation's politics and in some ways reconstructed. Reconstruction proper began in March 1867 when Congress enacted the first of several Reconstruction Acts.

BACKDROP

By some measures, Reconstruction began even as the war was being fought. From the beginning of the conflict, the United States of America had as its overriding aim restoring the seceded states to the Union. Restoration by itself, however, might be insufficient. As the war ground on, and emancipation was adopted by 1863 as a means to secure victory, northern policy makers came to see ever more clearly that the postwar world would have to be constructed along lines that, in some respects at least, contrasted sharply with prewar norms.

Slavery would be gone, whatever might replace it. Moreover, the death of slavery must be guaranteed, given the enormous political conflict that the institution had occasioned since the beginning of the Republic, especially in leading to the Civil War itself. Beyond that, the Republican Party wished to retain power, if possible, and to safeguard policies—enacted during the war—having to do with such matters as railroads, land, and banking. Republicans had no interest in committing political suicide by inviting back secessionist Democrats—who would surely seek to curtail their power and terminate their policies—unless guarantees were in place that would moderate the power of the Republicans' opposition, both in the South and in national politics.

In the waning months of the war, as a temporary war measure, Congress enacted a Freedmen's Bureau Act. A Siamese twin of the U.S. Army, the Freedmen's Bureau was designed to ease the dual transition from war to peace and from slavery to freedom by helping refugees and distributing emergency rations to people, both black and white. At the same time, the federal government took measures at some locations to distribute small parcels of land to former slaves on which they could farm. These actions did not address, however, the great questions of political restoration—who would control the South and who would control the nation. Nor did they do much to address the broader issues of what social system would replace slavery in the South.

ANDREW JOHNSON AND PRESIDENTIAL RESTORATION

The war largely ended in April 1865, soon after Abraham Lincoln began his second term as president. Days later, a Confederate sympathizer assassinated him. Andrew Johnson became president, and it fell to him, a former Democrat from Tennessee, to see the nation through the first postwar years. Congress would not reconvene until December that year, so the new president determined what the former Confederate states must do to take their places at the national political table.

Johnson established a provisional government in each of the eleven states, and he directed that the voters in each state elect delegates to a constitutional convention. Each convention had to rescind its state's ordinance of secession, accept the abolition of slavery, and pledge not to repay any public indebtedness their state had taken on to finance the war. Then elections could be held in which a regular government would be elected. With a new governor and legislature in place, state politics would return to normal. Moreover, the voters would elect representatives to Congress, and the legislatures would appoint U.S. senators. Restoration would have been accomplished. The Union would be restored—the central objective of the war—and all the states would once again be represented in Congress.

When Congress came back into session, the Republicans—who had a majority in each house—agreed that, while Johnson's plan provided a beginning, it did not go far enough. The Republican consensus would likely have imposed additional demands, even without events that reinforced their shared commitment to further change. Racial violence in places like Memphis and New Orleans, in which white and black Republicans were murdered by gangs of white perpetrators, demonstrated that the most loyal people in the South were vulnerable to continued violence. In that sense, it became clear that the war was not yet over. In addition, every southern state enacted Black Codes, new laws to recognize yet contain the new status that black residents had in the aftermath of slavery. Every one of those sets of laws offered

black residents more limited rights than their white neighbors enjoyed (freed people did not everywhere even have the right to buy and own land), so there was room for doubt that slavery had truly ended.

Moreover, the southern white electorates and state legislatures started sending former Confederate military and political leaders to Congress, hoping—in fact, expecting—that they would be permitted to take their seats there. Confederate vice president Alexander H. Stephens was one such, sent from Georgia to the U.S. Senate. Republican majorities in the two branches of Congress, determined to postpone seating any congressmen and senators from the states of the former Confederacy until a new federal policy had been worked up and put into place, established a joint Committee on Reconstruction to produce recommendations for such a policy.

THE REPUBLICAN PARTY AND CONGRESSIONAL RECONSTRUCTION: NATIONAL POLITICS AND POLICIES

In death as in life, southern slavery roiled national politics. Republicans cast about for a policy that would address the questions that emerged in the wake of the Union's victory and slavery's abolition, issues that, to them, made it clear that Johnson's policy of restoration would have to be improved upon. In the face of the Black Codes, Lyman Trumbull, chairman of the Senate Judiciary Committee, promised "to destroy all these discriminations." Perceiving that former slaves would count full value, rather than three-fifths, in future apportionments that determined power in the House of Representatives and the electoral college, U.S. Rep. Roscoe Conkling demanded to know: "Shall the death of slavery add two-fifths to the entire power which slavery had when slavery was living?"

The president and Congress collided in 1866. Congress passed a civil rights bill, declaring African Americans to be citizens and defining their core rights, and also a bill to extend the life and expand the powers of the Freedmen's Bureau. Johnson vetoed both bills, and Congress overrode both vetoes. Congress framed a Fourteenth Amendment, and Johnson publicly opposed it.

The Fourteenth Amendment embodied the congressional Republicans' program for Reconstruction. Section 1 would place in the Constitution the core of the Civil Rights Act of 1866, safe from subsequent congressional repeal or judicial invalidation. Section 2, which addressed the matter of abolition's impact on the meaning of the Three-fifths Clause, offered the former Confederate states a choice between granting black men the right to vote or giving up the congressional representation that reflected the presence of black citizens. Under section 2, white southerners could not continue to vote blacks' representation. Black southerners would vote their own representation, or nobody would.

In the 1866 congressional elections, Johnson stumped against Republican candidates. Republican victories demonstrated that, whatever might be said, then or later, about "Radical Republican" excesses, mainstream public opinion across the North insisted on the kinds of guarantees that the Fourteenth Amendment seemed to promise. With that mandate in hand, Congress acted. Before the new Congress could convene, the same Congress that had enacted the civil rights measure and the Freedmen's Bureau Act acted to secure ratification of the Fourteenth Amendment. Tennessee had ratified the amendment, but all ten other states of the former Confederacy rejected it. Unless at least some of those states ratified, the amendment could not obtain approval by three-fourths of the states, and the Republicans' program would fail.

Congressional Reconstruction, as enacted in March 1867 over Johnson's veto, terminated the civil governments of the ten former Confederate states that had rejected the Fourteenth Amendment. New elections had to be held in each of those states. Black men as well as white men would vote for delegates to new state constitutional conventions. These conventions would write constitutions that recognized the right of black men to vote. The new biracial electorate would then elect a new legislature, a new governor, and new members of Congress. The new legislature would have to ratify the Fourteenth Amendment before the senators it appointed, or the representatives who had just been elected, would be permitted to take their seats. When all those steps had been accomplished, then, and only then, would the ten states be restored.

Congress had occasion to consider additional legislation in the years ahead. The Fifteenth Amendment, banning race as the basis for denying anyone the vote, was ratified in 1870. When enormous political violence erupted against freedmen and other Republicans, especially political leaders, Congress passed the Ku Klux Klan Act in 1871. The Civil Rights Act of 1875 tried to curtail various dimensions of continuing racial discrimination. In the 1880s Congress considered but never passed a bill to provide federal funds for southern schools. In 1890 a Republican-controlled Congress proved unable to pass a Force Act that would have protected black southerners' right to vote as more and more restrictions were put in place by southern states, but it did pass a second Morrill Land-Grant Act that year that provided states with additional funds for their land-grant schools only if black citizens benefited from a portion of the money.

CONGRESSIONAL RECONSTRUCTION IN THE SOUTHERN STATES

Congressional Reconstruction had an immediate and dramatic impact in the politics of the ten recalcitrant southern states. Black men voted in all ten, and black delegates participated in framing new state constitutions. Black representa-

Sen. Hiram R. Revels of Mississippi   *Library of Congress*

tives were elected to the new state legislatures, and black officials filled many local offices.

The greatest changes took place in South Carolina, where the 1870 population was 59 percent African American, and in Mississippi, where it was 54 percent. In those two states, a majority of all residents before the Civil War had been slaves. With the death of slavery and the enfranchisement of black men, black political power in those states proved particularly startling. In South Carolina, of all the registered voters in 1867, 60 percent were black, and 70 of the 124 delegates (56 percent) to the constitutional convention elected that year were black. During Reconstruction, Mississippi sent two black men to the U.S. Senate, Hiram R. Revels, who completed a partial term (1870–1871) upon Mississippi's readmission, and Blanche K. Bruce, who served an entire term (1875–1881) in Jefferson Davis's old seat. Between the 1860s and the 1890s, at least one black U.S. representative was elected from each of the states of South Carolina, Mississippi, Georgia, Florida, Louisiana, Alabama, North Carolina, and Virginia—every former Confederate state but Texas, Tennessee, and Arkansas.

Given the revamped federal policies and the newly defined southern electorates, changes in public policy transformed every southern state during Reconstruction. Emancipation and presidential restoration had brought an end to laws against holding schools for black southerners but had done nothing to establish public schools that they might attend. Going beyond that point, every southern state during congressional Reconstruction enacted a law to provide for public schools, schools that were open to black students as well as white ones, although almost everywhere, from the beginning, on a segregated basis.

Black freedom and black suffrage affected higher education, too, as Mississippi in the 1870s and Virginia in the 1880s established public institutions of higher education for black students and brought other policy changes as well. By the 1880s, black southerners, like their white counterparts, attended special schools for blind and deaf students. As a consequence of Republican rule, in several states—Mississippi, South Carolina, Texas, Louisiana, and Alabama—legislatures passed laws or courts handed down decisions that, for a time, repealed or invalidated laws that had banned interracial marriage. In such states, the end of Republican power brought a resumption of such marriage laws. Affecting far more people, an erosion of black political power in every "reconstructed" state in the late–nineteenth century brought sharp reductions in state funding of black education.

Republicans controlled every one of the former Confederate states for at least a short while during the Reconstruction era. Already by the early 1870s, however, several Republican governments had fallen. In 1876 and 1877, those in Florida, South Carolina, and Louisiana also fell. The Compromise of 1877 made it clear that the federal government would not send troops to guarantee black suffrage, free elections, or the continued power of Republican state governments in the South. From that perspective, Reconstruction was over. Yet the rise to power by the "Readjusters" in Virginia a few years later demonstrated that black political power had not yet died and that biracial coalitions could still gain election.

RETROSPECTIVES AND LEGACIES

The general facts of Reconstruction—including its extraordinarily controversial, even violent, nature—have never been in dispute, though new research continues to bring new findings to light. Just as people at the time argued over what should be done, however, historians have differed over what should have been done. Before the 1960s, most white historians, whether northern or southern in origin, agreed that Reconstruction had gone too far, too fast, and had been an enormous mistake. The prevailing perspective then shifted, and many historians viewed the era as one in which the tragedy was that too little had been attempted and with too little commitment to seeing it through. The older perspective and the more recent one tended to share a sense that something had gone terribly wrong, but they differed profoundly as to what. Historians continued to differ among themselves over how best to understand the phenomenon, what options there had been, why developments unfolded the way they did, and what were the dominant motives behind the behavior of the proponents and opponents of congressional Reconstruction.

Reconstruction brought tremendous change in politics and policies, although much of that change proved temporary. A comparison of the First Amendment with the Fourteenth demonstrates the transformed relationships among individual liberty, state power, and federal authority that Reconstruction brought. Addressing concerns that the new federal government under the U.S. Constitution might have too much power, the First Amendment began with the phrase "Congress shall make no law . . ." By contrast, the Fourteenth Amendment, reflecting a recognition that the greatest threat to civil rights—particularly the liberties of black southerners—came from state governments, used the phrase "No state shall . . ." Under the new regime, federal power had the authority to limit state actions that undermined individual liberty.

Historians often say that Reconstruction ended in 1877. Yet popular discourse often dates twentieth-century political events such as a black candidate being elected to a state legislature or city council as the "first since Reconstruction" when the last previous example may have been in the 1880s or 1890s. Both perspectives have their place. The Republican-dominated governments of the states of the former Confederacy all fell to Democratic regimes by 1877. The Compromise of 1877, moreover, included a pledge that federal troops would end their presence in those states and any role in southern elections. Yet in some ways the political changes of the early postwar years persisted until late in the century. George H. White, an African American member of the U.S. House of Representatives elected from North Carolina, left office in 1901, and only then did Congress revert to all-white.

Regardless of when one dates the end of Reconstruction, black political power largely vanished from the "reconstructed" states, especially in the Deep South. The revolution went backward. Generations later, what is sometimes termed a "Second Reconstruction" emerged by the 1960s. Long after ratification in 1868, the Fourteenth Amendment proved the basis for bringing an end to segregation laws in the 1950s and 1960s. Federal troops sometimes played a role in the desegregation of a southern high school or university. The Voting Rights Act of 1965 was based on the Fifteenth Amendment, which had been ratified in 1870. Black voter registration in the 1960s returned black southerners to political participation, even political office, in every southern state.

In the twentieth century, moreover, the Fourteenth Amendment led to a "rights revolution" that related to all

Americans on a range of issues. The U.S. Supreme Court adopted an interpretation of the Fourteenth Amendment that it "incorporated" the Bill of Rights, so that liberties protected in the first eight amendments against congressional interference were to be guaranteed also against state interference. The politics and policies of Reconstruction laid the basis for enhanced federal power in many areas of American life.

See also *African American Politics; Bill of Rights; Black Suffrage; Civil Rights Act of 1866; Civil Rights Movement; Civil War; Compromise of 1877; Constitution, U.S.; Constitutional Amendments; Democratic Party; Freedmen's Bureau Acts; Grant, Ulysses S.; Johnson, Andrew; Morrill Land-Grant College Acts; Republican Party; Sectionalism; Slavery; Three-Fifths Clause.*

PETER WALLENSTEIN,
VIRGINIA POLYTECHNIC INSTITUTE AND STATE UNIVERSITY

BIBLIOGRAPHY

Benedict, Michael Les. *A Compromise of Principle: Congressional Republicans and Reconstruction, 1863–1869.* New York: Norton, 1974.

Bensel, Richard Franklin. *Yankee Leviathan: The Origins of Central State Authority in America, 1859–1877.* Cambridge: Cambridge University Press, 1990.

Foner, Eric. *Reconstruction: America's Unfinished Revolution, 1863–1877.* New York: Harper and Row, 1988.

Perman, Michael. *The Road to Redemption: Southern Politics, 1869–1879.* Chapel Hill: University of North Carolina Press, 1984.

Rable, George C. *But There Was No Peace: The Role of Violence in the Politics of Reconstruction.* Athens: University of Georgia Press, 1984.

RED SCARE

Following World War I, the United States embarked on a reckless campaign against an exaggerated threat of domestic radicalism. The armistice ending World War I on November 11, 1918, brought demobilization, political upheaval, and sharp economic dislocation to the United States. These factors, combined with fears fostered by the Bolshevik Revolution in Russia (1917), gave rise to the postwar Red Scare.

The nation's war effort had encouraged superpatriotism and xenophobia, both of which led to assaults on civil liberties. Wartime propaganda fostered contempt for German-Americans and dissenters of all stripes. New laws of questionable constitutional validity, notably the Espionage Act of 1917 and the Sedition Act of 1918, encouraged the assault on left-wing politics and civil liberties. At the same time, U.S. troops were posted in Siberian Russia as part of the allied military intervention in an ultimately futile struggle against the Bolsheviks.

Although wartime production had spurred economic growth, rampant inflation had eroded many of the gains made by American workers. Labor union membership had increased sharply during the war and included a 25 percent rise in American Federation of Labor membership between 1916 and 1919. Many newly organized workers were determined to challenge industry for collective bargaining rights.

The workers' demands, combined with the radicalism of a handful of intellectuals, prompted fears that the United States could be vulnerable to the threat of revolution then plaguing war-ravaged eastern and central Europe. A wave of strikes—3,600 involving some 4 million workers in 1919 alone—underscored the perceived threat. Particularly unsettling were a general strike in Seattle and an AFL-sanctioned police strike in Boston.

In Washington, D.C., A. Mitchell Palmer, an energetic former congressman from Pennsylvania who took over as U.S. attorney general in February 1919, worked closely with a young Department of Justice attorney, J. Edgar Hoover. Determined to destroy the perceived radical threat to the American way of life, Hoover and Palmer launched the postwar Red Scare.

Nativist and antiradical sentiments fostered the Red Scare despite the lack of any real threat to the United States. The radical movement was small, and some of its leaders, including the socialist Eugene Debs, had already been incarcerated during the war. In March 1919 the U.S. Supreme Court upheld Debs's conviction under the Espionage Act for a speech the fiery former railroad union leader had made denouncing American involvement in the Great War.

A series of bombing incidents in June, including an explosion outside Palmer's home in Washington, prompted the attorney general to act. Hoover began to compile dossiers not only on radicals but also on liberals, African American activists, and other dissenters. In all, Hoover amassed files on some 200,000 individuals and organizations. In January 1920 Palmer, using information compiled by Hoover, initiated the historic dragnet raids in which federal agents, aided by local police, burst into private homes and meeting halls to arrest alleged radicals and aliens. Some 6,000 persons were summarily arrested in the raids, their civil rights violated. Most, never formally charged, were released. About 550 were deported illegal aliens.

Palmer and Hoover had expected the preemptive raids to produce evidence of a communist plot and other radical conspiracies, but the Bolshevik threat in America was a chimera. Palmer, who had hoped the antiradical campaign would position him for a presidential bid, became discredited with the public. Newspapers and public officials who had initially applauded the raid against the radicals now acknowledged the massive violations of civil liberties.

The Red Scare abated in 1920, but its legacy continued. Strikes and bombings ended, leftist uprisings were put down in Europe, and the United States heeded Warren G. Harding's call for a return to "normalcy." However, nativism, xenophobia, and the scapegoating of immigrants, radicals, and racial minorities for social problems continued. The wrenching ordeal of Nicola Sacco and Bartolomeo Vanzetti, two Italian immigrants convicted and ultimately executed for murder, continued the legacy of the Red Scare. In April 1920 two men were shot in a robbery at a shoe factory in South Braintree, Massachusetts. Sacco and Vanzetti, both avowed anarchists, were arrested and charged with murder. The evidence against the two was circumstantial and manipulated by the police. The presiding judge failed to ensure a fair trial for the two men, having concluded himself that the "anarchist bastards" were guilty. The case became an international cause célèbre throughout the 1920s. Their appeals exhausted, Sacco and Vanzetti were executed on August 23, 1927.

Perhaps the most significant legacy of the Red Scare was the empowerment of J. Edgar Hoover, who remained fanatical on the subject of domestic radicalism. Hoover built the FBI into a powerful agency which, in addition to fighting crime, kept files on innocent civilians, harassing and spying on many of them. The Red Scare made a return appearance following World War II and the dawning of the cold war. Repression, intolerance of the left, and violations of civil rights—hallmarks of the first Red Scare—became institutionalized in American life.

See also *Labor Politics and Policies; McCarthyism; Nativism; World War I.*

WALTER HIXSON, UNIVERSITY OF AKRON

BIBLIOGRAPHY

Fariello, Griffin. *Red Scare: Memories of the American Inquisition: An Oral History.* New York: Norton, 1995.

Murray, Robert K. *Red Scare: A Study in National Hysteria, 1919–1920.* New York: McGraw-Hill, 1964.

Sabin, Arthur J. *Red Scare in Court: New York Versus the International Workers Order.* Philadelphia: University of Pennsylvania Press, 1993.

Young, William, and David E. Kaiser. *Postmortem: New Evidence in the Case of Sacco and Vanzetti.* Amherst: University of Massachusetts Press, 1995.

REFORM PARTY

H. Ross Perot, a computer billionaire from Texas, founded the Reform Party in 1995. Perot had campaigned as an independent in the 1992 presidential election, relying heavily on televised "infomercials" to advance a platform that castigated the federal government and promised to "fix the mess in Washington" and "clean out the barn." Early in the 1992 campaign, Perot ranked second in some national polls to President George Bush and seemed poised to win some southern and western states outright as economic troubles and subsequent anger toward the Bush administration grew. But as national interest in Perot's candidacy increased, so did media scrutiny, and Perot responded irritably; by autumn 1992, after several erratic episodes, he had slipped measurably in the polls.

Nevertheless, in November Perot and his "United We Stand" campaign managed to capture 18.9 percent of the popular vote but no electoral votes. It was the highest popular vote percent for a non–major party candidate since Theodore Roosevelt's 27.4 percent in 1912. The Texan's campaign, run by volunteers and without any formal party structure, drew on a well of discontent among voters; exit polls showed most Perot voters wanted "change" in Washington. Some analysts say the Perot candidacy cost Bush the election, but exit polls indicated that even if Perot had not been in the race, Democrat Clinton would have won.

Perot ran as the Reform Party's 1996 presidential nominee, but his heavy-handed maneuvering to gain the nomination angered many of his earlier supporters. Anger against government had lessened, and economic prosperity blunted his 1992 message. As a result, the 1996 Perot vote slipped to 8.4 percent of the total, less than half his 1992 tally.

In 1998 the Reform Party nominated candidates for various local elections and registered its first success at the polls with the election of former professional wrestler Jesse Ventura as governor of Minnesota. Ventura's victory set the stage for conflict between Perot and his followers. At the party's 1999 convention, Ventura's allies took control of the party. Ventura shortly thereafter quit to form the Independence Party. Conservative commentator Patrick Buchanan won the party's 2000 presidential nomination in a bitter intraparty struggle and fared poorly at the polls. Most observers saw the infighting as an inexorable sign that the Reform Party's time as a political force had come and gone.

See also *Third Parties.*

RON dePAOLO, INDEPENDENT AUTHOR

BIBLIOGRAPHY

Selecting the President from 1789 to 1996. Washington, D.C.: Congressional Quarterly, 1997.

REPRODUCTIVE RIGHTS

Reproductive rights can be defined as a woman's right to bodily integrity, including decisions about whether to become pregnant and whether to carry a pregnancy to term. Although reproductive rights include the use of birth control methods, frequently the term *reproductive rights* is considered synonymous with abortion.

The Constitution does not mention reproductive rights explicitly. Thus the law and social policy on this issue have evolved as an amalgam of common law history and tradition, complicated over time by the advent of new technologies and emerging concepts of constitutional interpretation.

GRADUAL AND PATCHWORK CRIMINALIZATION

Abortion was not illegal in the first days of the Republic but became so on a state-by-state basis during the late nineteenth century. This first pronounced wave of antiabortion activity occurred in conjunction with the rise of the American Medical Association (AMA), founded in 1847. Antiabortion rhetoric united the burgeoning medical community around the professionalization of the medical practitioner to the exclusion of the homeopathic caregivers and midwives. Most abortion techniques were utilized prior to the state of "quickening"—that is, when the first fetal movement could be felt in the beginning of the second trimester of pregnancy. But doctors argued that women were ignorant of the scientific facts of pregnancy and that the fetus was alive prior to the stage of quickening. This rallying cry had political dimensions in that it lent credibility to scientifically trained medical doctors, leading to licensing laws and exclusionary tactics that ultimately united the medical profession and excluded access to all but university-trained practitioners. White, middle-class women argued for first-trimester abortion, but the moral and scientific-technical rhetoric of the AMA won the day. States began responding to the AMA's calls for the criminalization of abortion, especially when untrained midwives were involved in the delivery of services.

The Supreme Court first addressed reproductive rights in *Buck v. Bell* (1927), a case involving compulsory sterilization of the mentally infirm. Justice Oliver Wendell Holmes asserted that the "principle that sustains compulsory vaccination is broad enough to cover cutting the Fallopian tubes. . . . Three generations of imbeciles is enough." This opinion emerged despite the fact that the litigant's family history showed no evidence of feeble-mindedness, only that Buck had borne a child at a young age. Today, Holmes's words seem quite harsh, but they represent a Victorian morality common at the time.

World events transformed the Supreme Court's view less than twenty years later when Germany's Adolf Hitler and his Nazi Party brought into stark relief the logical outcome of such eugenicist policies. In *Skinner v. Oklahoma* (1942), the Court affirmed the fundamental right to procreate and struck down the state statute that distinguished classes of convicts and slated some for compulsory sterilization. Although the Court did not explicitly overturn *Buck v. Bell,* this case was a testament to the changing political landscape. The divergent outcomes, when considered in the light of gender, however

(Skinner was male, Buck female), suggested that women still had a protracted struggle ahead to achieve equal rights under the law.

Much like midwives had worked in the early years of the nation to disseminate maternity care to all women regardless of economic means, a movement to broaden access to birth control took hold in New York, Massachusetts, and Connecticut in the 1920s and 1930s. Female activists such as Margaret Sanger (founder of Planned Parenthood) in New York and Katharine Houghton Hepburn (mother of actress Katharine Hepburn) in Connecticut worked to set up birth control clinics that would extend to working-class and poor women the services (birth control and contraception) readily available to the middle class. Some states reacted with legal restrictions against abortion; others passively allowed the practices of birth control and abortion to proceed. The U.S. Congress reacted by criminalizing abortion where providers were not medical doctors. Public opinion, however, quietly rallied around the right to contraception. Despite some animosity toward these developments from certain sectors (for example, the Catholic Church and religious fundamentalists), it was widely believed that contraception was acceptable to the vast majority of the public by the time *Griswold v. Connecticut* made it to the Supreme Court in 1965.

DECRIMINALIZATION

In 1961 Estelle Griswold opened a birth control clinic in New Haven, Connecticut, in violation of an 1879 state law prohibiting the use of contraceptives. She challenged the constitutionality of the statute, and in *Griswold v. Connecticut* the Court struck down the law and established a constitutionally protected right to privacy found within the "penumbras" of the Bill of Rights. The decision walked a fine line between constitutional interpretation and judge-made law. The Court extended the right of contraception only to married persons, but that right was extended to the unmarried in *Eisenstadt v. Baird* (1972). In their first explicit abortion decision, *Roe v. Wade* (1973), the justices created an elaborate methodology for determining the legality of abortion, based on trimesters of pregnancy. Although regarded by its detractors as a definite case of legislating from the bench, the trimester approach was not novel in practice.

In *Planned Parenthood of Southeastern Pennsylvania v. Casey* (1992), the Supreme Court allowed states to impose restrictions that made abortions more difficult to obtain, yet it also affirmed *Roe's* tripartite structure. In the 1992 ruling, Justice Harry Blackmun, the author of the *Roe v. Wade* decision, warned that he must soon leave the Court (he was eighty-three at the time) and conceded, "I fear for the darkness as four Justices anxiously await the single vote necessary to extinguish the light." That comment and other events catapulted abortion rights to center stage in the 1992 presidential election campaign. The Republican contender, President George Bush, vowed to overturn *Roe v. Wade* and allowed a plank in the Republican platform that made abortion illegal even in cases of rape, incest, and where the life of the mother was at stake. The Democratic contender, Bill Clinton, vowed to follow the opposite path. He would fight to maintain the rights embodied in the *Roe v. Wade* decision and would contest any encroachment of those rights. Given the number of aging justices on the Court and its composition, the future of abortion rights became a pivotal issue in the campaign, and Clinton's victory was widely attributed to the surge in support from women voters because of his prochoice stance.

The Republicans failed to gauge the significance of abortion rights in the presidential contest and repeated the same mistake in the 1996 campaign. Despite their losses, they have not modified the prolife plank of their platform and have allowed the issue of abortion rights to divide their ranks. The Court's composition remains in a delicate balance, ensuring that abortion will remain a central issue in presidential elections for years to come. In its 2000 decision on third-trimester abortion, *Stenberg v. Carhart,* the Court left *Roe* dangling by a thread, with five justices voting in the affirmative to protect the *Roe* decision and four in dissent. Future presidents may well have the power to alter that balance.

Abortion, then, remains controversial. States have intervened to outlaw third-trimester abortions and to institute waiting periods, and Congress has enacted legislation to disallow Medicaid coverage of abortions for indigent persons. Reproductive rights, women's rights, and the appropriate methodology for interpreting the Constitution remain interwoven in this political controversy.

DEBRA CLARK, VIRGINIA COMMONWEALTH UNIVERSITY

BIBLIOGRAPHY

Goldstein, Leslie. *The Constitutional Rights of Women: Cases in Law and Social Change.* Madison: University of Wisconsin Press, 1988.

Gordon, Linda. *Woman's Body, Woman's Right: Birth Control in America.* Revised and updated. New York: Penguin Books, 1990.

Luker, Kristin. *Abortion and the Politics of Motherhood.* Berkeley: University of California Press, 1984.

REPUBLICAN PARTY

The Republican Party, founded in 1854, dominated national politics from 1860 to the New Deal era and again from 1968 to the present. The party emerged in 1854–56 out of a political frenzy, in all northern states, revolving around the expansion of slavery into the western territories. The new party was so named because "republican-

ism" was the core value of American politics, and it seemed to be mortally threatened by the expanding "slave power." The enemy was not so much the institution of slavery nor the mistreatment of the slaves. Rather, it was the political-economic system that controlled the South, exerted disproportionate control over the national government, and threatened to seize power in the new territories.

ORIGINS THROUGH RECONSTRUCTION

The party came into being in reaction to federal legislation allowing the new settlers of Kansas Territory to decide for themselves whether to adopt slavery or to continue the Compromise of 1820, which explicitly forbade slavery there. The new party lost on this issue, but in addition to gaining most northern Whigs, it gained support from "Free Soil" northern Democrats who opposed the expansion of slavery. Only a handful of abolitionists joined. The Republicans adopted most of the modernization programs of the Whigs, favoring banks, tariffs, and internal improvements and adding, as well, a demand for a homestead law that would provide free farms to western settlers. In state after state, the Republicans outmaneuvered rival parties (the old Whigs, the prohibitionists, and the Know Nothings), absorbing most of their supporters without accepting their doctrines.

The 1856 campaign, with strong pietistic, Protestant overtones, was a crusade for "Free Soil, Free Labor, Free Men, and Frémont!" John C. Frémont was defeated by a sharp countercrusade that warned against fanaticism and the imminent risk of civil war. By the late 1850s the new party dominated every northern state. It controlled enough electoral votes to win, despite its almost complete lack of support below the Mason-Dixon line. Leaders like William H. Seward of New York and Salmon P. Chase of Ohio were passed over as presidential candidates in 1860 because they were too radical in their rhetoric and their states were safely in the Republican column. Abraham Lincoln was more moderate, and had more of an appeal in the closely divided western states of Illinois and Indiana. With only 40 percent of the popular vote, Lincoln swept the North and easily carried the electoral college. Interpreting the Republican victory as a signal of intense, permanent Yankee hostility, seven states of the Deep South seceded and formed their own country.

The Republicans had not expected secession and were baffled by it. The Lincoln administration, stiffened by the unionist pleas of conservative northern Democrats, rejected both the suggestion of abolitionists that the slaveholders be allowed to depart in peace and the insistence of Confederates that they had a right to revolution and self-governance.

Lincoln proved brilliantly successful in uniting all the factions of his party to fight for the Union. Most northern Democrats were likewise supportive until the fall of 1862, when

Lincoln added the abolition of slavery as a war goal. All the state Republican parties accepted the antislavery goal except Kentucky.

In Congress the party passed major legislation to promote rapid modernization, including measures for a national banking system, high tariffs, homestead laws, and aid to education and agriculture. How to deal with the ex-Confederates was a major issue; by 1864 radical Republicans controlled Congress and demanded more aggressive action against slavery and more vengeance toward the Confederates. Lincoln held them off, but just barely. His successor, Andrew Johnson, proved eager to reunite the nation, allowing the radicals to seize control of Congress, the party, and the army and nearly convict Johnson on a close impeachment vote.

Ulysses S. Grant was elected president in 1868 with strong support from radicals and the new Republican regimes in the South. He in turn vigorously supported radical reconstruction programs in the South, the Fourteenth Amendment, and equal civil and voting rights for the freedmen. Most of all, he was the hero of the war veterans, who marched to his tune. The party had become so large that factionalism was inevitable; it was hastened by Grant's tolerance of high levels of corruption. The Liberal Republicans split off in 1872 on the grounds that it was time to declare the war finished and bring the troops home.

LATE NINETEENTH CENTURY

The depression of 1873 energized the Democrats. They won control of the House and formed "Redeemer" coalitions that recaptured control of each southern state, often using threats and violence. The Compromise of 1877 resolved the disputed election of 1876 by giving the White House to the Republicans and all of the southern states to the Democrats. The GOP, as it was now nicknamed, split into "Stalwart" and "Half-Breed" factions. In 1884, "Mugwump" reformers split off and helped elect Democrat Grover Cleveland.

In the North the Republican Party proved most attractive to men with an ambitious vision of a richer, more modern, and more complex society and economy. The leading modernizers were well-educated men from business, finance, and the professions. Commercial farmers, skilled mechanics, and office clerks largely supported the GOP, while unskilled workers and traditional farmers were solidly Democratic. The moral dimension of the party attracted pietistic Protestants, especially Methodists, Congregationalists, Presbyterians, Scandinavian Lutherans, and Quakers. By contrast, the high church or "liturgical" denominations (Roman Catholics, Mormons, German Lutherans, and Episcopalians) were offended by Republican crusaders who wanted to impose their own moral standards, especially through prohibition and control over public schools.

Millions of immigrants entered the political system after 1850 and usually started voting only a few years after arrival. The Catholics (Irish, German, and Dutch) became Democrats, but the Republicans won majorities among the Protestant British, German, Dutch, and Scandinavian newcomers and among German Jews. After 1890 new, much poorer ethnic groups arrived in large numbers—especially Italians, Poles, and Yiddish-speaking Jews. For the most part they did not become politically active until the 1920s. After 1876 southern voting was quite distinct from the rest of America—with very few white Republicans, apart from pockets of GOP strength in the Appalachian and Ozark Mountain districts. The party remained popular among black southerners, even as disenfranchisement minimized their political role. (They were allowed to select delegates to the Republican national convention.)

In the 1888 election, for the first time since 1872, the Republicans gained control of the White House and both houses of Congress. New procedural rules in the House gave the Republican leaders (especially Speaker Thomas Reed) the ability to pass major legislation. New spending bills, such as one that provided generous pensions to Civil War veterans, coupled with the new McKinley tariff made the GOP the target of charges of "paternalism." Democrats ridiculed the "Billion Dollar Congress," to which Reed shot back, "It's a billion dollar country!"

At the grass roots, militant pietists overcame the advice of more tolerant professionals to endorse statewide prohibition. In the Midwest, reformers declared war on the large German community, trying to shut down their parochial schools as well as their saloons. The Republicans, relying too much on the old-stock coalition that had always dominated the party's voting base, were badly defeated in the 1890 off-year election and the 1892 presidential contest. Alarmed professionals thereupon reasserted control over the local organizations, leading to a sort of "bossism" that (after 1900) fueled the outrage of progressives. Meanwhile, a severe economic depression struck both rural and urban America in 1893—on Cleveland's watch. The depression, combined with violent nationwide coal and railway strikes and snarling factionalism inside the Democratic Party, led to a sweeping victory for the GOP in 1894.

The party seemed invincible in 1896, until the Democrats unexpectedly selected William Jennings Bryan as their presidential candidate. Bryan's hugely popular crusade against the gold, the financiers, the railroads, and the industrialists—indeed, against the cities—created a crisis for McKinley and his campaign manager, Mark Hanna. Because of civil service reforms, parties could no longer finance themselves internally. Hanna solved that problem by directly obtaining $3.5 million from large corporations threatened by Bryan. Over the next century, campaign finance would be hotly debated. McKinley promised prosperity for everyone and every group, with

Mining magnate and financier Mark Hanna (standing at the far right between President and Mrs. McKinley) raised millions of dollars for McKinley's 1896 and 1900 campaigns. *Library of Congress*

no governmental attacks on property or ethnic groups. The business community, factory workers, white-collar workers, and commercial farmers responded enthusiastically, becoming major components of the new Republican majority. As voter turnout soared to the 95 percent level throughout much of the North, Germans and other ethnic groups grew alarmed by Bryan's moralism and voted Republican.

EARLY TWENTIETH CENTURY

Rejuvenated by their triumphs in 1894 and 1896 and by the glamour of a highly popular short war in 1898, the GOP rolled to victory after victory. However, the party had again grown too large, and factionalism increasingly tore it apart. The break within the party came in 1912 over the issue of progressivism. President William Howard Taft favored conservative reform controlled by the courts; former president Theodore Roosevelt went to the grass roots, attacking Taft, bosses, courts, big business, and the "malefactors of great wealth." Defeated at the convention, Roosevelt bolted and formed a third party. The vast majority of progressive politicians refused to follow Roosevelt's rash action, for it allowed the conservatives to seize control of the GOP; they kept it for the next thirty years. Roosevelt's quixotic crusade also allowed Democrat Woodrow Wilson to gain the White House with only 40 percent of the vote. But after Wilson's fragile

coalition collapsed in 1920, the GOP won three consecutive presidential contests.

Herbert Hoover represented the quintessence of the modernizing engineer, bringing efficiency to government and the economy. His poor skills at negotiating with politicians hardly seemed to matter when the economy boomed and Democrats were in disarray. However, when the Depression hit, his political ineptitude compounded the party's weaknesses. For the next four decades, whenever Democrats were at a loss for words, they could always ridicule Hoover.

NEW DEAL AND DEMOCRATIC DOMINANCE

The Great Depression sidelined the GOP for decades. The old conservative formulas for prosperity had lost their magic. The Democrats, by contrast, built up majorities that depended on labor unions, big city machines, federal relief funds, and the mobilization of Catholics, Jews, and African Americans. However, middle-class hostility to new taxes, and fears about a repeat of the First World War, eventually led to a Republican rebound. Franklin Roosevelt's immense popularity gave him four consecutive victories, but by 1938 the GOP was doing quite well in off-year elections when FDR's magic was not at work.

In 1948 taxes were high, federal relief had ended, and big-city machines were collapsing, but union strength helped Harry S. Truman reassemble FDR's coalition for one last hurrah. The year 1948 proved to be the high-water mark of class polarization in American politics; afterward, the differences narrowed between the middle class and the working class.

The issues of Korea, communism, and corruption gave war hero Dwight D. Eisenhower a victory in 1952, along with narrow control of Congress. However, the GOP remained a minority party and was factionalized, with a northeastern liberal element basically favorable to the New Deal welfare state and the policy of containing communist expansion, versus midwestern conservatives who bitterly opposed New Deal taxes, regulation, labor unions, and internationalism. Both factions used the issue of anticommunism and attacked the Democrats for harboring spies and allowing communist gains in China and Korea. New York governors Thomas E. Dewey and Nelson Rockefeller led the liberal wing, while Sens. Robert Taft of Ohio and Barry Goldwater of Arizona spoke for the conservatives. Eisenhower represented internationalism in foreign policy, and he sidetracked the isolationism represented by Taft and Hoover.

Richard Nixon was aligned with the eastern liberal GOP; he lost in 1960 because the Democrats had a larger base of loyal supporters, especially among Catholics who turned out to support John F. Kennedy. The defeat of yet another candidate sponsored by the eastern "establishment" opened the way for Goldwater's 1964 crusade against the New Deal and Great Society. Goldwater permanently knocked out the eastern liberals, but in turn his crushing defeat retired many oldline conservatives. Goldwater in 1964 and independent George Wallace in 1968 ripped southern whites and many northern Catholics away from their Democratic roots, and at the same time the Democratic commitment to civil rights won over nine-tenths of all African American voters.

REPUBLICAN REVIVAL

Lyndon Johnson's Great Society collapsed in the mid-1960s in a frenzy of violence and protest over racial hatred, Vietnam, generational revolt, crime in the streets, burning inner cities, and runaway government. Nixon seized the moment. As president he largely ignored his party—his 1972 reelection campaign was practically nonpartisan. Even so, his self-destruction wreaked havoc in the 1974 election, setting the stage for the Carter interregnum.

Jimmy Carter's presidency crashed in 1980. Foreign affairs were unusually salient, as public opinion saw failure in policy toward the Soviet Union, Iran, and Mideast hostages. "Stagflation" in the economy meant a combination of high unemployment and high inflation. Most of all there was a sense of drift or, worse, of malaise. The country craved leadership. Ronald Reagan led a political revolution in 1980, capitalizing on grievances and mobilizing an entirely new voting bloc, the religious right. Southern Baptists and other fundamentalists and evangelicals had been voting Democratic since the New Deal, because of their low educational and economic status and their southern roots. Suddenly they began to react strongly against a perceived national tolerance of immorality (especially regarding abortion and homosexuality), rising crime, and America's apparent rejection of traditional family values. Reagan had vision and leadership qualities that workaholic policy gurus could never understand. Reagan oversaw a massive military buildup, the defeat of the antinuclear peace movement, and massive tax cuts.

By 1984 inflation had faded away, unemployment had eased, profits and fortunes were soaring, and Social Security had been reformed, and Reagan carried forty-nine states in winning reelection. Most astonishing of all was Reagan's revival of the cold war, followed closely by the total collapse of the Soviet empire. The best issue for the Democrats was the soaring national deficit—long a conservative theme—although their attacks doomed any hopes that they could ever return to the liberal tax-and-spend policies of yore. For the first time since 1932, the GOP pulled abreast of the Democrats in terms of party identification on the part of voters. A greater number of higher-income people were voting Republican, while the lower-income groups that had always been the mainstay of the Democratic Party increasingly lost interest and did not bother to vote. By the 1980s a gender gap was apparent, with men and housewives more Republican while single, divorced, and professional women tended to be Democratic. Thanks to the religious right, the GOP gained the votes of less-educated voters. Those gains were largely offset by the Democratic gains among holders of college and postgraduate degrees for the party's positions regarding multiculturalism and a tolerance of homosexuality and abortion.

George Bush rode to the White House on Reagan's popularity and could himself claim smashing victories in the cold war and the Persian Gulf War. The public was baffled that Bush—so knowledgeable and decisive on Kuwait and East Berlin—seemed unconcerned about taxes, deficits, and other domestic issues that bothered Americans far more. When independent Ross Perot polled an amazing 19 percent of the vote in 1992 by crusading against the deficit, Bush was doomed. However, the GOP roared back in 1994, gaining control of Congress for the first time since 1952 as well as control of governors' mansions in nearly all the major states. The rancorous leadership of Speaker Newt Gingrich soured politics in Washington; he was unable to deliver on most of his "Contract with America." Meanwhile, as a party the GOP for the first time had built a national infrastructure, based on its ability to raise hundreds of millions of dollars from political action committees and individual donors. While ideological Republicans in Congress failed in their efforts to remove President Bill Clinton by impeachment, the party did cooperate with the president to sharply reduce welfare spending and end the federal budget deficit. In 2000, Republican George W. Bush, the son of the former president, won a disputed election to recapture the White House for the party. Although a narrow victory, Bush's win reasserted the Republican dominance of presidential politics that had characterized most of the previous thirty years.

See also *Civil War; Free Soil Party; Immigration and Naturalization: Society and Politics; Kansas-Nebraska Act; Lincoln, Abraham; Popular Sovereignty; Reagan, Ronald; Roosevelt, Theodore; Third Parties; Whig Party.*

RICHARD JENSEN, RENSSELAER POLYTECHNIC INSTITUTE

BIBLIOGRAPHY

American National Biography. 24 vols. New York: Oxford University Press, 1999.

Foner, Eric. *Free Soil, Free Labor, Free Men: The Ideology of the Republican Party before the Civil War.* New York: Oxford University Press, 1970.

Gienapp, William E. *The Origins of the Republican Party, 1852–1856.* New York: Oxford University Press, 1987.

Jensen, Richard. *The Winning of the Midwest: Social and Political Conflict, 1888–1896.* Chicago: University of Chicago Press, 1971.

Lamis, Alexander P., ed. *Southern Politics in the 1990s.* Baton Rouge: Louisiana State University Press, 1999.

Mayer, George H. *The Republican Party, 1854–1966.* 2d ed. New York: Oxford University Press, 1967.

Rutland, Robert Allen. *The Republicans: From Lincoln to Bush.* Columbia: University of Missouri Press, 1996.

ROOSEVELT, FRANKLIN D.

Franklin Delano Roosevelt (FDR), born in Hyde Park, New York, on January 30, 1882, became the thirty-second president of the United States (1933–1945) and died at Warm Springs, Georgia, on April 12, 1945, while serving his fourth term as U.S. president. FDR left America with an almost larger-than-life legacy of political, social, and personal triumphs that set a new pace and altered the standards of performance for all future presidents.

FDR grew up as the privileged, well-educated son of a patrician family. In 1890 his father, James, hired Jeanne Sandoz, a French-speaking Swiss governess, to tutor the eight-year-old Franklin in language, physics, chemistry, and social responsibility according to the "social gospel." Arthur Dumper, a teacher from Cleveland, Ohio, replaced Ms. Sandoz at Hyde Park in 1893 and tutored the youngster in nature studies and formal subjects. At age fourteen FDR enrolled at the elite Groton School in Massachusetts, where he was trained in the classics and prepared for college coursework. At Groton FDR was an average student but excelled at team sports. As a member of one of New York's old-money families, FDR entered Harvard University in 1900 and earned average grades in a program filled with political science, history, and English courses. During his studies at Harvard the young FDR made a name for himself through his involvement in Harvard's student newspaper, the *Crimson.* After earning his bachelor's degree from Harvard, FDR began a law degree from Columbia University in 1905. He left law school and began his law career in 1907 after passing the New York State Bar. While still in law school, on March 17, 1905, FDR married his distant cousin, Anna Eleanor Roosevelt. Between 1906 and 1916 the couple had six children—one girl (Anna Eleanor) and five sons (Elliott; Franklin Junior, who died in infancy; Franklin Delano Jr.; James; and John).

EARLY POLITICAL CAREER AND PERSONAL SETBACKS

The young family man quickly climbed the New York political ladder. While practicing law, he won a seat in the state senate in 1910 as an anti-Tammany Democratic reformer and furthered his career by supporting Woodrow Wilson in the 1912 presidential election. FDR's continued political efforts resulted in his appointment as the assistant secretary of the navy (1913–1920) and his selection as the Democratic vice-presidential candidate on the ticket with James Cox in 1920.

During this time FDR sharpened his progressive reform ideologies, which he had patterned after those of his fourth cousin and political model, Teddy Roosevelt. Meanwhile FDR's wife, Eleanor, developed her own social and political niche relieving human suffering through work with the Red Cross.

Family crisis struck the Roosevelt home in 1918, when Eleanor discovered FDR's affair with her social secretary, Lucy Page Mercer. Despite her devastation by her husband's infidelity, Mrs. Roosevelt remained in the marriage, creating a companionate marriage in which she channeled her energies into social reform and political activism. Although punctuated by periods of separation, FDR's friendship with Mercer continued over the next twenty-five years. Mercer was with the president when he died.

On August 10, 1921, FDR suffered a crippling bout with poliomyelitis, a severe viral infection that left him paralyzed from the waist down. Despite seven years of treatment, FDR never walked again without leg braces, canes, or crutches. The medical setback did not slow his work with the Democratic Party and political climb to fame. While nominating Alfred E. Smith as the Democratic Party's presidential candidate in 1924 and 1928, FDR won the hearts of political observers by refusing to allow his polio to diminish his political career.

A four-time governor of New York, Smith persuaded FDR to run for governor. In the campaign, FDR perfected his self-assured and intuitive political style based on his personal charm and vitality. He won the governorship of New York in 1928 and 1930 and proved to doubters his physical stamina and political savvy.

As governor, FDR responded to the crash of 1929 and the onslaught of the Great Depression by shifting political power to the state's highest office and established a trend for a strong central leadership in the state's political system. Reform successes included farm assistance, highway construction, greater state responsibility for education costs, small farm tax relief, the 1930 Water Power Law (public power), defense of trade unions, and the Wicks Unemployment Act. Throughout his term as governor, FDR honed his ability to build political coalitions.

MOMENTOUS FIRST TERM

In 1932 FDR decisively defeated Republican presidential incumbent Herbert Hoover with 57 percent of the popular vote and 89 percent of the electoral vote. This big victory provided FDR the basis to implement a reform program he called the New Deal. FDR came to the White House well prepared for the office and with a spirit of reform and activism. More important, FDR instituted a process that used the basic premises of Populism and Progressivism and changed American politics for the rest of the century. He directed his staff to investigate new ideas, create new legislation, garner political support, and mobilize popular opinion. Using his great coalition-building skills, FDR shifted governmental policy to include federal acceptance of social responsibility for the American people (including the concepts of the welfare state or social safety net). FDR's administration won acceptance for the rise of an executive office capable of wielding both domestic and international power.

Under FDR America also began a move toward acceptance of collective bargaining for workers (the Wagner Act) and international support through aid to friendly nations (through aid to Great Britain in 1940). FDR's phenomenal success inspired historian William Leuchtenburg to develop a thesis that portrays FDR as a mythical president who cast a shadow over future presidents. FDR and his New Deal became the yardstick by which political analysts and historians measured future presidential success. Under the new relief, recovery, and reform programs the federal government became the means to democratize the political, economic, legal, and social aspects of American life and culture. The federal government increasingly entered into the everyday life of all Americans and simultaneously accepted leadership as a superpower in the international community.

As FDR took office in 1933 he assured troubled Americans that "the only thing we have to fear is fear itself." Joseph Zangara's failed assassination attempt on the president-elect on February 15, 1933 gave personal credibility to the new president's words. The incident left Chicago mayor Anton

Franklin D. Roosevelt   *Franklin D. Roosevelt Library*

Cermack wounded, and FDR's own courage earned the public's respect as he calmly attended to the wounded mayor.

On entering office FDR outlined his New Deal program and engaged Congress in a hundred days of fiscal and social reforms designed to provide relief, establish recovery programs for troubled sectors of the economy, and reform the past practices that created the Great Depression. FDR's ability to surround himself with skilled advisers and manage administrative problems created a model for future presidents and direction of public programs. Aided by his expanded cabinet and Brain Trust—which included advisers like Rexford Tugwell, Harold Ickes, and Harry Hopkins—FDR set out to establish a new federal policy capable of planning for the nation's future and saving American capitalism and democracy through public spending. New programs included banking reforms, the National Recovery Administration and the Public Works Administration designed to reorganize industry, the Agricultural Adjustment Act to rebuild agriculture, community planning, social relief in housing, employment programs, and family assistance. However, many of the initial New Deal policies and acts were limited by later Republican Congresses and Supreme Court decisions. In the first one hundred days of his administration FDR sent fifteen messages to Congress, delivered ten major addresses, guided fifteen pieces of legislation through Congress, launched his fireside chats, called numerous press conferences, and oversaw countless cabinet and advisory group meetings.

In 1935 FDR came under attack from both the right and the left of the political spectrum. Sen. Huey Long (D-La.) called on the nation to share the wealth. Father Charles Coughlin, a well-known radio priest, sought financial equity for the nation's retired and unemployed elderly. Dr. Francis Townsend, a labor activist, also sought aid for the elderly. Pressure from Long, Coughlin, Townsend, and others pushed FDR to adopt more liberal ideas and accept a larger role for the federal government in social reform. The New Deal moved to institutionalize a social safety net to protect citizens from the ravages of unregulated capitalism. In 1935 Congress approved the National Labor Relations Act (Wagner Act), the Work Progress Administration, and the Social Security Act. Working-class people responded to the new legislation and to the warm, human style of the president's radio "fireside chats." FDR's popularity helped sweep him to landslide reelection in 1936.

POLITICAL RESISTANCE AND EVOLVING COALITIONS

Resistance from more traditional conservatives, who feared governmental intrusion into personal life and control of the economy, slowed FDR's plans. Many southern Democrats joined with Republicans to resist expanded federal authority, the perceived decline of states' rights, legal recognition of organized labor, and expanded presidential power.

Between 1935 and 1937 the Supreme Court declared numerous New Deal measures to be unconstitutional. In response, FDR proposed increasing the size of the Supreme Court. The president hoped the new justices would give his programs constitutional support. However, FDR's Court-packing plan failed and the New Deal remained incomplete. By 1939 the conservative coalition controlled Congress.

FDR responded to the conservative congressional stalemate by forming his own coalition of farmers and southerners. By the 1944 election, however, FDR's coalition had grown to depend on urban blue-collar workers, organized labor, and the immigrant vote.

From the beginning of his presidency FDR embraced Jeffersonian agrarian principles and sought to bring relief and change to farmers. The president expressed his dedication to agriculture through his Agricultural Adjustment Act (1933), Commodity Credit Corporation (1933), Farm Credit Administration (1933), Tennessee Valley Authority (1933), Rural Electrification Administration (1935), Soil Conservation Service (1935), and Farm Security Act. Indeed, because of these programs farmers found themselves better off in 1936 than they had been in 1932. However, as the New Deal shifted the lion's share of its support to commercial agriculture, most farmers in the Middle West returned to the Republican Party. Consequently, FDR further expanded his political coalition in urban areas among common laborers and immigrants. By the 1940 election, the American Farm Bureau Federation leadership had concluded that the Roosevelt administration favored urban liberals.

After the 1940 election FDR depended less on the farmers and more on the urban and labor coalition. This shift provided FDR with the support necessary to continue to counter the conservative Congress. After the passage of the Wagner Act (1935) and the creation of the National Labor Relations Board (1935), union ranks grew fivefold, from less than 3 million members to 14 million. From this burgeoning organized power base FDR realigned American politics by giving the working class an institutional voice, which became the basis of the New Deal's welfare state policies. This urban, working-class, and immigrant coalition provided the Democratic Party with many of its voters for more than a half-century.

FDR'S INFLUENCE ON THE PRESIDENCY

In the end, World War II, not FDR's New Deal welfare state, repaired American capitalism and ended the catastrophic depression. The Roosevelt presidency proved to be an overwhelming success, and its legacy was the welfare state and an activist presidency. Just before the country's entrance into World War II, Congress moved to support FDR's interna-

tional measures and passed the Neutrality Act of 1939, removed arms embargoes, increased peacetime appropriations for arms sales, federalized the National Guard, and in 1941 adopted the Lend-Lease Act. Yet it was not until the American entrance into World War II (after Japan's December 7, 1941 attack on the American navy at Pearl Harbor) that the American workforce returned to work and the nation began to again produce and consume. FDR's unconditional surrender decree of January 24, 1944; Allied meetings in Casablanca, Cairo, Tehran, and Yalta; and the Bretton-Woods conferences provided the basis for the postwar world order. New presidential powers at home and in the world ushered in what has been called the American Century.

FDR extended the traditional two-term presidency, winning a third presidential term by defeating Wendell L. Willkie in 1940 and a fourth term by defeating Thomas E. Dewey in 1944. The president then faced a Congress that was supportive of war efforts and leery of presidential extensions of executive power through social programs. During the last re-election bid his health began to decline due to hypertension (stress from three terms in office), heart disease, and chronic bronchitis. The president died of a massive cerebral hemorrhage on April 12, 1945, three months after his fourth-term inauguration.

Perhaps one of the greatest legacies of FDR was his ability to courageously overcome a disability that made him more compassionate. FDR's presidential duties and responsibilities never were hampered by his handicap. Unwilling to give in to his physical limitations, FDR invented and commissioned many devices that allowed him greater access to everyday life. His example helped serve as the basis for modern legislation for equal access for the handicapped in public places.

Few presidents have made a more lasting change in executive-congressional relationships than did FDR during his twelve and one-quarter years as president. His active presidential style led him to initiate much legislation. FDR considered the executive branch to be more important than the other two branches of government and regarded Congress and the Supreme Court as obstructionist. In both domestic and international affairs FDR's presidency assumed tremendous powers, some of which future Congresses and conservative presidents have attempted to dismantle.

See also *Great Depression; Labor Politics and Policies; Landslide Elections; New Deal; Roosevelt, Theodore; Supreme Court; Taxation and Twentieth-Century Politics; Tennessee Valley Authority; Truman, Harry S.; Welfare State; World War II.*

VICTOR W. GERACI, CENTRAL CONNECTICUT STATE UNIVERSITY

BIBLIOGRAPHY

Leuchtenburg, William G. *In the Shadow of FDR: From Harry Truman to Bill Clinton.* 2d ed. Ithaca: Cornell University Press, 1993.

Zunz, Olivier. *Why the American Century.* Chicago: University of Chicago Press, 1998.

ROOSEVELT, THEODORE

Politician, soldier, writer, naturalist, reformer, and visionary, Theodore Roosevelt (president 1901–1909) served as a driving force behind the transformation of the United States into a twentieth-century great power. The nation honored his achievements by sculpting the popular "Teddy" on Mount Rushmore.

Born into an upper-class, wealthy family in New York City on October 27, 1858, Roosevelt graduated from Harvard University in 1880, with a book manuscript already in hand. Over the years, he would produce more than forty books on American history and life in the West. After several years in New York state politics, Roosevelt turned to national public service in 1889 when President Benjamin Harrison appointed him U.S. civil service commissioner. In that job and later as police commissioner of New York, Roosevelt waged a campaign against corruption and the spoils system.

In 1897 President William McKinley appointed Roosevelt assistant secretary of the navy, a post Roosevelt used to promote a mightier navy and to advocate war with Spain, which was busily quashing an independence movement in Cuba. In February 1898 he overstepped his authority by sending the Pacific Fleet to Hong Kong to prepare to defeat the Spanish fleet if war was declared. He was vindicated, however, when the American fleet defeated the Spanish in the Battle of Manila on May 1, 1898.

Soon after the United States declared war against Spain, Roosevelt resigned from the Navy Department so he could fight in Cuba. There, he led his cavalry regiment, known as the Rough Riders, in a famous charge up one of the San Juan Hills overlooking Santiago.

Roosevelt's exploits in Cuba made him a celebrity in the United States and gained him, in November 1898, the Republican nomination for governor of New York. He was narrowly elected. But the power brokers of his party, particularly New York Republican boss Thomas Platt, disliked his political independence and his refusal to promote the interests of big business. In 1900 they decided to get rid of him by kicking him upstairs—to the vice presidency.

At the national level, party leaders had mixed feelings about Roosevelt. While ever mindful of the votes his popularity would bring, they were appalled at the thought that the independent-minded New Yorker would be only a heartbeat away from the presidency. Mark Hanna, the Republican national chairman, may have been prescient when he warned his colleagues, "Don't any of you realize that there's only one life between this madman and the White House?"

On September 6, 1901, Roosevelt was hunting and fishing in the Adirondacks when he learned that President McKinley had been shot by an anarchist. Eight days later, McKinley died. At the age of forty-two, Roosevelt became the youngest person ever to serve as president.

During his two terms in office Roosevelt embodied the growing Progressive movement by acting decisively to end capitalist abuses and curb the rampant plundering of the nation's natural resources. In fact, no sooner did the Roosevelt administration move into the White House than it began to prepare an antitrust suit against Northern Securities Company, a giant railroad trust. In 1904 the Supreme Court ruled

Theodore Roosevelt (standing, center) poses with his unit atop the hill they captured in the battle of San Juan. *Library of Congress*

that the company should be dissolved. In 1902 Roosevelt responded to a coal strike in Pennsylvania by threatening to take over the mines unless the mine owners submitted to arbitration. When the mine owners relented, Roosevelt appointed a commission that gave the miners a 10 percent raise. Concerned about working conditions, Roosevelt successfully called in 1903 for the establishment of a Department of Commerce and Labor to stimulate industrial growth and improve conditions for the nation's workforce.

Abroad, the young president openly advocated territorial conquests by the United States. Some people even called him imperialistic. During his first term the nation acquired land to build the Panama Canal, but Colombia, which owned Panama, refused in August 1903 to approve a treaty giving the United States the rights to the land needed. Later that year, a determined Roosevelt supported a revolution in Panama that overthrew Colombian rule. When the new Panamanian government agreed to lease the zone to the United States, construction of the canal began.

In the 1904 presidential election, Roosevelt, running against New York judge Alton B. Parker, received over 56 percent of the popular vote and easily won in the electoral college, 336–140. By winning, he became the first president to win the White House in his own right after serving the unfinished term of his predecessor.

The second term found the Roosevelt administration promoting, as part of its "Square Deal," reform legislation, including the Pure Food and Drug Act, the Meat Inspection Act, and the Hepburn Act, which allowed the government to set railroad rates. An avid sportsman, Roosevelt continued to pursue conservation, a favorite cause. At his urging, Congress established the U.S. Forest Service in 1905, headed by conservationist Gifford Pinchot, and the government initiated thirty major federal irrigation projects, added 194 million acres to the national forest reserves, and doubled the number of national parks.

In foreign affairs Roosevelt continued to promote U.S. interests abroad, but his critics found him too aggressive. In late 1904 he issued the Roosevelt Corollary to the Monroe Doctrine, which declared that the United States would intervene in Latin American affairs to prevent European nations from intervening there. In 1905 the president mediated an agreement ending the Russo-Japanese War and received the Nobel Peace Prize for his efforts. In late 1907, in a blatant display of military power that was opposed by Congress, Roosevelt sent the U.S. naval fleet on a world cruise. The show of strength was intended to impress other nations, especially Japan, with U.S. willingness to "carry a big stick."

In the 1908 presidential election Roosevelt backed his friend and secretary of war William Howard Taft, but over the next two years the two became estranged. In 1912 Roosevelt decided to seek the Republican nomination for president. Although he won most of the primaries, the Republican National Convention in Chicago was controlled by supporters of President Taft, who received the nomination. Determined to challenge Taft, like-minded Republicans organized the Progressive Party and persuaded Roosevelt to run under its banner. The party was dubbed the "Bull Moose" Party because candidate Roosevelt pronounced himself "as fit as a bull moose."

On October 14, 1912, while campaigning in Milwaukee, Roosevelt was shot in the chest by an assailant, but he insisted on delivering his speech and later fully recovered (in fact, the draft of the speech he was holding took the brunt of the bullet and probably saved his life). When he resumed campaigning, the public showed that it was impressed with his heroics, but that did not mend the split among Republicans. Together, Roosevelt and Taft received over a million more popular votes than Democrat Woodrow Wilson, but, with his opposition divided, Wilson won the election.

The Progressives asked Roosevelt to run for president again in 1916, but he declined and supported Republican Charles Evans Hughes, who lost to President Wilson. When the United States entered World War I in 1917, Roosevelt went to the White House to request authority to raise a volunteer division to fight in the war, but Wilson turned him down. Roosevelt might have been his party's candidate for president in 1920 had he not died in his sleep on January 6, 1919.

See also *Anti-Trust Act; New Nationalism; Progressive Era; Spanish-American War; Square Deal; Third Parties.*

SABRA BISSETTE LEDENT, INDEPENDENT AUTHOR

BIBLIOGRAPHY

Beale, Howard K. *Theodore Roosevelt and the Rise of America to World Power.* Baltimore: Johns Hopkins University Press, 1956.

Blum, John Morton. *The Republican Roosevelt.* Cambridge: Harvard University Press, 1954.

Chessman, G. Wallace. *Theodore Roosevelt and the Politics of Power.* New York: HarperCollins, 1969.

Collin, Richard H. *Theodore Roosevelt, Culture, Diplomacy and Expansion: A New View of American Imperialism.* Baton Rouge: LSU Press, 1985.

Gould, Lewis L. *The Presidency of Theodore Roosevelt.* Lawrence: University Press of Kansas, 1990.

Miller, Nathan. *Theodore Roosevelt, a Life.* New York: Morrow, 1992.

S

SALLY HEMINGS AFFAIR

Enslaved Virginian Sally Hemings (1773–1835) is historically significant as a result of her complicated relationship with President Thomas Jefferson, who was not only her owner but also possibly her half brother-in-law and probably the father of her children. Since an 1802 newspaper report, authored by journalist James Thomson Callender, alleged that Jefferson fathered several children with a slave named Sally, various constituencies have used Hemings to advance a wide array of agendas.

Hemings, born into slavery in Cumberland County, Virginia, was the daughter of Elizabeth Hemings, a woman of mixed African and European descent who, according to the 1873 memoir of her grandson James Madison Hemings, served as the slave and mistress of white planter John Wayles. After Wayles's death in 1773, Jefferson inherited the Hemings family from his father-in-law through his wife, Martha Wayles Jefferson. Sally Hemings grew up at Jefferson's Albemarle County plantation, Monticello, where she worked as a house slave and, especially after Martha Jefferson's 1782 death, as a companion to Jefferson's youngest daughters. In this capacity, in 1787 Hemings traveled to Paris, where Jefferson had been serving as a diplomat since 1784. There, according to the accounts of Callender and Madison Hemings, the couple commenced a long-term sexual relationship. After Jefferson and his party returned to the United States in 1789, Hemings gave birth to at least six children: Harriet I (1795–1797), William Beverly (1798–?), an infant daughter who died in 1799, Harriet II (1801–?), James Madison (1805–1878), and Thomas Eston (1808–185?).

Callender's 1802 account of the Jefferson–Hemings relationship, which focused on race-mixing, failed to discredit the popular president because Callender, a one-time Jeffersonian Republican, lacked credibility among Federalists, who reprinted the story but rarely endorsed it. In addition, Jefferson's silence regarding Callender's charge deprived opponents of opportunities for further comment and earned the loyalty of southern planters, many of whom quietly engaged in sexual relationships with their slaves. Few people mentioned Callender's charges when Jefferson stood for reelection in 1804.

Even so, writers exploited the Jefferson–Hemings relationship after Jefferson's death in 1826. Although commentators at the time seem not to have noticed that the only slaves freed by his will were Madison and Eston Hemings—whose older siblings, William Beverly and Harriet II, had been allowed to leave Monticello in 1822—tales of the relationship continued. British travel writers of the mid–nineteenth century, for example, used the story to depict the hypocrisy of America's slave-holding democrats. The black abolitionist author William Wells Brown based his novel *Clotel* on the relationship. During the twentieth-century civil rights movement, Jefferson and Hemings were portrayed by some as interracial lovers; others focused on the inherent inequality of master–slave relationships. In 1998, according to some Republicans, the relationship was used to aid President Bill Clinton, who faced impeachment for covering up a sexual relationship with a White House intern. When, in the midst of the impeachment proceedings and on the eve of midterm congressional elections, scholars released a DNA study suggesting that Jefferson was the father of at least one of Hemings's children, some Republicans claimed that the move was timed to minimize Clinton's misdeeds, which gained the imprimatur of historical precedent.

See also *Clinton-Era Scandals; Jefferson, Thomas.*

ROBERT M. S. MCDONALD, UNITED STATES MILITARY ACADEMY

Gordon-Reed, Annette. *Thomas Jefferson and Sally Hemings: An American Controversy.* Charlottesville: University Press of Virginia, 1997.

Lewis, Jan Ellen, and Peter S. Onuf, eds. *Sally Hemings and Thomas Jefferson: History, Memory, and Civic Culture.* Charlottesville: University Press of Virginia, 1999.

McDonald, Robert M. S. "Race, Sex, & Reputation: Thomas Jefferson and the Sally Hemings Story." *Southern Cultures* 4 (summer 1998): 46–63.

Peterson, Merrill D. *The Jefferson Image in the American Mind.* New York: Oxford University Press, 1960.

SCANDALS AND CORRUPTION

American history is replete with political scandals and corruption. However, society's condemnation has not depended solely on the unethical or illegal nature of a deed. As important—and sometimes more important—was the public's perception of a particular action committed by a particular person at a particular time. The harshest judgments were saved for those officials who violated the public trust, using their privileged positions for personal or political gain.

The concepts of scandal and corruption in American history are often interchangeable, but not always. They come cloaked in various wrappings but almost always are about the twins of politics: money and power. Moreover, they do not stand isolated from national political, economic, and social development; rather, they are an integral part of that history and frequently, as scholars and commentators have noted, are the engines of political reform. At the national level, scandals have at times mirrored the natural tensions, based in the Constitution, between the branches of government, particularly Congress and the presidency.

Revolutionary changes in nineteenth-century America—rapid industrialization, commerce, westward expansion, the growth of political parties and mass politics, and significant immigration—provided wrongdoers with many opportunities. The century was noteworthy for widespread corruption and scandal at the state and local levels as well as the national level. The pattern can be traced to the 1820s and 1830s when national expansion demanded the involvement of government to acquire and distribute land and develop the economic infrastructure, particularly transportation. Andrew Jackson was elected president in 1828, an event historians usually identify as the beginning of mass political participation and political parties and the beginning of the end for the governing elite that founded the nation. In the ensuing decades, rapid economic advances and westward movement of white settlers gave rise to various scandals, including schemes to take land from Indians through fraud, bribery to get favorable treatment for railroad development, and rampant use of the spoils system in government to reward the party faithful. The latter led to development of the notorious state and local political machines whose bosses got rich through bribes, kickbacks, and graft.

Although President Ulysses S. Grant was considered honest, his administration (1869–1877) was one of the most scandal-ridden in U.S. history. His secretary of war, William W. Belknap, resigned in 1876 to avoid—unsuccessfully—impeachment by the House. He had been accused of accepting payments in return for making a military-related appointment involving a lucrative provisioning of soldiers at a western fort. Perhaps the worst scandal was Crédit Mobilier, which became public in 1872 and involved federal funding to finish the Union Pacific Railroad, part of the transcontinental railroad. The money, funneled through Crédit Mobilier of America, hugely enriched its owners, who—to avoid congressional investigations—bribed important members, often by giving them company stock. A serious if less notorious scandal in 1875 involved whiskey distillers across the country who bribed tax officials in exchange for a reduction in or elimination of federal excise taxes on their products. This scandal involved Grant's supervisor of internal revenue, who extorted more than $2.5 million from liquor distillers. A grand jury eventually returned indictments against more than two hundred distillers and government officials in the so-called Whiskey Ring.

As serious as these events were, perhaps even worse was the development of corrupt political machines at the state and local level, personified then and ever since by the Tammany machine in New York City and its leader, William "Boss" Tweed. The system created links between politicians, officeholders, party bosses, and business interests and—at the bottom level—rank-and-file party and government workers to cut deals, give profit and salary kickbacks, skim business revenues, and otherwise enrich those controlling the system. In turn, the machine produced the votes to elect the politicians who kept the system running. While big-city machine politics has had many defenders since this period, who often contrast the ineffectiveness of non–machine cities with governments run by bosses, the Tammany model was instrumental in stoking reform fires late in the nineteenth century.

EFFORTS AT REFORM

Out of the turmoil exemplified by the Grant administration and following the industrial development scandals and the machine politics of big cities came calls for reform of political and economic institutions. These developments set the stage for a remarkable period of political reform that began in the late nineteenth century and carried actively into the early days of the twentieth. The Progressive movement derived directly from the excesses of the post–Civil War age. Moreover, it became a model for reformers throughout the twentieth century who sought to hone down the rough and ragged edges of American politics into a system that restrained, if not blocked, the special privileges of wealth.

One of the earliest and best known reforms was the Pendleton Act in 1883, which established a federal civil service in which most government employees were isolated from political pressure and could not be forced to do political work. The Interstate Commerce Act, passed in 1887, sought to impose order, regulation, and fairness on railroad rates and shipping practices to balance power between shippers (particularly farmers) and railroad magnates. In the early days of the new century, Congress passed laws to regulate campaign contributions from corporations and the lobbying activities of powerful interests. Immigration restrictions were passed in an effort to restrict the power of big city bosses who had organized, aided, and protected the masses in return for their votes. Throughout the country, reformers got approval of initiative and recall laws, allowing voters to bypass legislatures they believed to be controlled by special interests and to remove corrupt officials from office. These and related reforms also pushed municipal government toward the concept of "professionalism." Cities were to be managed by experts (nominally subject to elected officials), special "nonpartisan" commissions, and independent special-function agencies, such as water, park, or transportation authorities (again, theoretically responsible to elected officials).

In 1914 the Federal Trade Commission was created as part of the effort to advance government oversight and regulation of commerce in the interests of consumers and smaller businesses against the power of large corporations. And in one of the most significant reforms of the era, the Constitution was amended in 1913 to provide for direct election of U.S. senators. Previously, senators were selected by state legislatures, which were often under the control of large corporations and wealthy special interests. This reform and the Pendleton Act were the bookends of a reform period that sought to remove political power from the vested interests in America and restore it to the citizens.

TWENTIETH-CENTURY SCANDALS

The success of these efforts, while undeniable, did not entirely stamp out special privilege or scandals and corruption in the twentieth century. By the 1920s Teapot Dome, one of the seamier scandals of the century, had erupted. This scandal occurred in the administration of President Warren G. Harding, who died before the worst of the events became public, saving his immediate reputation if not his historical place in the annals of the presidency. In 1921 Harding transferred control of oil reserves in Elk Hills and Buena Vista, California, and Teapot Dome, Wyoming, meant as a source of fuel for American warships, from the Navy Department to the Department of the Interior. Interior Secretary Albert B. Fall in 1922 leased Elk Hills and Teapot Dome to private oil companies. A Senate investigation in 1923 discovered that the secretary had accepted bribes from the oil companies. Fall became the first cabinet official convicted of a crime committed while in office. But unlike the scandals and corruption in the nineteenth century, this event did not lead to major political reform, although it did prompt passage of the Federal Corrupt Practices Act, which altered existing campaign financing law.

The Great Depression in the 1930s, world war and cold war in the 1940s, and the relative calm and prosperity of the 1950s pushed aside major scandals, even though the administrations of Harry S. Truman and Dwight D. Eisenhower were embarrassed by various incidents of improper and sometimes illegal conduct by people in official positions.

The scandals and corruption of the late twentieth century had a different flavor from those of earlier times, even as the events remained rooted in money and power—especially power. The four decades from 1960 on were characterized by efforts to control and direct money in politics, to vastly increase public disclosure about the activities of government and the source and use of money, and—on a darker side—the development of distrust in government and attack politics designed to cripple if not destroy political opposition. By century end, at the national level at least, the tone and practice of politics were more adversarial and confrontational than at any time since the Civil War period. Several important scandals were instrumental in leading the country to this point.

A relatively minor but important hint of things to come was an investigation into the activities of Robert G. (Bobby) Baker, secretary of the Senate majority led by Lyndon B. Johnson. As right-hand man to Johnson, Baker was in a position to use his position for personal gain. Court documents against Baker, who served a prison term, showed he combined law practice with influence peddling. The Senate probe in the mid-1960s concluded Baker was guilty of "gross improprieties" and recommended the Senate require full financial disclosures by senators and top employees of the Senate. This scandal is thought to be the impetus for broader financial disclosure throughout the federal government, a trend that was to accelerate in the following years. The Baker incident was reinforced in 1969 when a top aide to the House Speaker was charged and later convicted of misusing the Speaker's office to influence government decisions. The notoriety caused by these cases is credited with moving each chamber to create an ethics committee and establish codes of conduct.

Campaign financing was a principal arena of controversy, particularly from the 1970s onward, and was a part of the most infamous scandal of the century, Watergate, which forced the only presidential resignation in the nation's history. Campaign finance law dated from the early days of the century, when it became known that Theodore Roosevelt's 1904 presidential campaign was secretly funded by several corporations. Out of that came passage, in 1907, of the first federal campaign finance law, the Tillman Act, which made it unlawful for a corporation or a national bank to contribute to candidates for federal office. The Federal Corrupt Practices Act in 1910 established disclosure requirements for U.S. House candidates. A year later Congress extended the requirements to Senate candidates. In 1925 Congress passed a second Federal Corrupt Practices Act, which served as the basic campaign finance law until the early 1970s. The law modified existing—and created new—campaign financing disclosure requirements and prohibitions, but, as it turned out, it was riddled with loopholes. Nobody was ever prosecuted under the law, even though violations of its prohibitions were common knowledge. Further restrictions and disclosure requirements passed in 1971. That is where the law stood on the threshold of the Watergate scandal, which cost President Richard M. Nixon his job.

This complex scandal started with what one Republican called "a third rate burglary" at the Democratic National Headquarters at the Watergate hotel and apartment buildings in Washington, D.C., by persons associated with Nixon's Committee to Re-elect the President. Within weeks, the White House initiated efforts to cover up the connection between the break-in and his campaign. The cover-up continued and in time drew in congressional investigators, special prosecutors, the Supreme Court, and legions of investigative reporters in the press, making folk heroes of some senators and representatives, a judge, and several reporters. In the end,

Government evidence from the Watergate break-in, a "third rate" burglary that ended a presidency and reverberated through American politics and society for a generation. *National Archives*

the House Judiciary Committee determined that Nixon was deeply involved in the cover-up, despite his denials, and approved three articles of impeachment—for obstruction of justice, abuse of presidential power, and contempt of Congress. Facing certain conviction in the Senate, Nixon resigned on August 9, 1974.

The massive fallout from Watergate continued long after Nixon was gone. The executive branch abuses prompted Congress to reassert its power over the weakened presidency by, for example, approving the War Powers Resolution in 1973, which sought to curtail the president's war-making powers, and passing the Congressional Budget and Impoundment Control Act of 1974, which gave Congress more authority over the federal budget process.

Perhaps more important, the Watergate scandal, along with the public deception and presidential dissembling about the Vietnam War in the 1960s, demarcated a rising public disillusionment and suspicion of political institutions. Congress enacted various "sunshine" rules, intended to open its proceedings to the public; imposed new, stricter ethical standards on its members; and passed campaign finance reform legislation.

Although most members of both political parties agreed at the time that Nixon's conduct was indefensible and he had to go, the lingering bitterness of the events helped poison the Washington political atmosphere for years after. This was one reason for the rise of attack politics—often carried out in television spot ads—usually aimed at discrediting and frequently destroying an opponent's credentials.

Another of the signal repercussions of the Watergate period was the increasing reliance on special prosecutors—later called independent counsels—to investigate allegations of wrongdoing that in the past would have gone through established judicial channels such as the U.S. Justice Department. Such was the case in the investigation of the Iran-contra scandal of Ronald Reagan's administration, which came to light in November 1986. Iran-contra involved the secret sale of arms to Iran in the hopes of securing the release of Americans being held hostage in Lebanon and diversion of some of the profits from those sales to support the activities of the "contras," Nicaraguan rebels fighting the communist Sandinista government. Such support for the contras was a clear violation of U.S. law at the time. The independent counsel, Lawrence Walsh, did not issue his final report until 1994, five years after Reagan had left office. Republicans charged that the investigation was unnecessary, took too long, and was aimed at politically undercutting Ronald Reagan and his successor, George Bush.

In the decades following Watergate, members of Congress came under increasingly strict codes of conduct and were more closely scrutinized by the press, the public, and law enforcement. Ethics cases proliferated in a climate that found less tolerance for behavior that earlier had been overlooked. By the late 1980s, amid rising partisan rancor, Republicans began engaging in a new brand of attack politics—using charges of ethical misconduct as a political weapon.

After the Republicans became the majority party in both the House and Senate as a result of the 1994 elections, they opened numerous congressional investigations and called for the appointment of many independent counsels to look into alleged misdeeds by Democratic president Bill Clinton, his wife, and his administration. Among the matters raised were the Clintons' personal financial involvement in a 1970s failed Arkansas land deal known as Whitewater, the firing of White House travel office employees for alleged financial mismanagement, the requisition of FBI files on former Republican administration employees, and Democratic campaign financing practices.

Some observers saw this as a reprise of the Watergate and Iran-contra controversies, and even an opportunity to settle political scores. In time, court decisions involving complex legal charges and cases against Clinton led to investigations by Independent Counsel Kenneth W. Starr and a sensational report detailing an affair between Clinton and a young female White House intern. This in turn led to House approval of impeachment articles, largely along party lines, and a lopsided vote against conviction in the Senate. The House action came in December 1998, just a month after the GOP had suffered a stinging and humiliating defeat at the polls in off-year congressional elections: the party retained control of Congress, but just barely. Clinton's popularity suffered little. Many people drew a distinction between Clinton's official, public duties and his personal life and, while disapproving of his personal conduct, did not believe it warranted removal from office. Furthermore, most Americans overwhelmingly approved of the job he was doing as president.

Some observers believed that one effect of the House's somewhat casual use of the impeachment weapon, in circumstances that were far less compelling than existed with Nixon, lowered the bar and may have set a precedent for future politicians and Congresses to attack an opposition president with the most powerful weapon available. At the same time, optimists saw evidence in Washington of weariness with the years of take-no-prisoners warfare between the parties and hope, if slight and embryonic, that there would be a return in the new century to civility and cooperation in government.

See also *Clinton, Bill; Crédit Mobilier; Grant, Ulysses S.; Independent Counsel; Indian Policy; Iran-contra Scandal; Local Government; Nixon, Richard M.; Progressive Era, Reagan, Ronald; Teapot Dome; Watergate.*

DAVID R. TARR, CQ PRESS

BIBLIOGRAPHY

Conason, Joe, and Gene Lyons. *The Hunting of the President: The Ten-Year Campaign to Destroy Bill and Hillary Clinton.* New York: St. Martin's Press, 2000.

Congressional Quarterly's Guide to Congress. 5th ed. Washington, D.C.: CQ Press, 2000, 915–988.

Congressional Quarterly's Guide to the Presidency. 2d ed. Washington, D.C.: Congressional Quarterly, 1996.

Garment, Suzanne. *Scandal: The Crisis of Mistrust in American Politics.* New York: Times Books, 1991.

Van Tassel, Emily Field, and Paul Finkelman. *Impeachable Offenses: A Documentary History from 1787 to the Present.* Washington, D.C.: CQ Press, 1999.

Watergate: Chronology of a Crisis. Washington, D.C.: Congressional Quarterly, 1974.

SECESSION

The idea of secession is associated with the acts of eleven southern states in 1860–1861. Yet, despite the fact that the Confederate states were the only ones that undertook to secede from the American Union of 1788, secession as a constitutional option was not confined either to the South or to the middle of the nineteenth century. It had been seriously broached by opponents of ruling majorities from the time of the federal Constitution's adoption.

Americans also occasionally have discussed secession from their states. Thus, for example, Mayor Fernando Wood bandied the notion of New York City's secession from New York during the Civil War, and denizens of northern California bruited the idea of their region's leaving California late in the twentieth century. The only successful post-1788 intrastate secession movement led to the secession of West Virginia from Virginia.

PRE–CIVIL WAR NOTIONS

In the 1790s some southern Republicans feared that the domination of the federal government by New England Federalists would be permanent. When John Taylor of Caroline, a sometimes senator and Republican pamphleteer from Virginia, floated the idea of secession among leading Republicans in 1798, Vice President Thomas Jefferson responded that the proposal was premature. The urge to secede proved fleeting in Republican ranks, for the Republicans won the election of 1800. Soon, the New England Federalists—now in the minority—began to see merit in the idea of abandoning the Union. When President Jefferson purchased the enormous Louisiana Territory from France in 1803, some New Englanders believed that the incorporation of that expanse of land into the federal system would forever submerge New England in an essentially foreign America. So, they contemplated secession.

During the War of 1812, disaffection with Virginia's ascendancy in national politics and with the concomitant enactment of federal policies inconsistent with New England's economic interests reached a crescendo in the notorious Hartford Convention of 1814. Leading delegates, who included important politicians from southern New England, called for an ultimatum to President James Madison, followed by secession if necessary. Unfortunately for them and for the Federalist Party generally, news of the convention reached Washington almost at the same time as news of the Treaty of Ghent, ending the war. The result was the death of the Federalist Party in most of the country.

The most notable secessionist impulses in the decades after the War of 1812 arose among two groups with diametrically opposed programs: abolitionists and southern nationalists. One strain of abolitionist thought, commonly associated with William Lloyd Garrison and, for a time, Frederick Douglass, held the U.S. Constitution to be "a covenant with death" intrinsically defensive of slavery. Therefore, the Garrisonians advocated secession by the non–slaveholding states.

On the other hand, a substantial current in southern political thought held as early as the Missouri crises of 1819–1821 that the emerging northern majority eventually would move to abolish slavery. Some southerners therefore advocated establishment of an independent southern confederacy. In the years leading up to the nullification crisis of 1828–1833, as at other times, they were disappointed by what they took to be the obstructionist efforts of South Carolina's John C. Calhoun. Calhoun, whose name became a byword for southern extremism, actually often maneuvered within South Carolina to prevent secession.

SOUTHERN SECESSION

By the end of the 1850s, northern unwillingness to tolerate the South's demands for national legislation conducive to the extension of slavery, coupled with the breakdown of the second-party system, resulted in the splintering of the long-dominant Democratic Party into regional fragments. Meanwhile, the Democrats' opponents in the North coalesced into a new sectional party, the Republican Party, which won the presidential election of 1860. Citizens in the Deep South, convinced that they had entered into the Union with the tacit understanding that the federal government would always be administered by officials overtly or covertly friendly to slavery (such as the Jeffersonian Republicans and the Jacksonian Democrats), refused to accept any other kind of administration. They decided to secede even though the elections of 1860 had left Democrats in control of Congress and the federal courts.

President Abraham Lincoln insisted in the months between his election and his inauguration that he had no in-

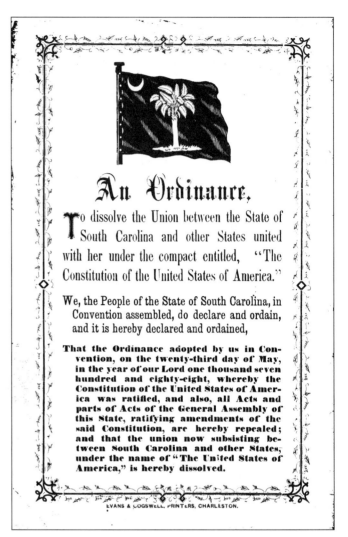

An Ordinance,

To dissolve the Union between the State of South Carolina and other States united with her under the compact entitled, "The Constitution of the United States of America."

We, the People of the State of South Carolina, in Convention assembled, do declare and ordain, and it is hereby declared and ordained,

That the Ordinance adopted by us in Convention, on the twenty-third day of May, in the year of our Lord one thousand seven hundred and eighty-eight, whereby the Constitution of the United States of America was ratified, and also, all Acts and parts of Acts of the General Assembly of this State, ratifying amendments of the said Constitution, are hereby repealed; and that the union now subsisting between South Carolina and other States, under the name of "The United States of America," is hereby dissolved.

EVANS & COGSWELL, PRINTERS, CHARLESTON.

On December 20, 1860, South Carolina became the first state to take itself out of the Union. The broadside reproduced above was printed shortly after the state convention voted for secession. *Library of Congress*

tention of moving against slavery in the states in which it already existed, but intended only to prevent its spread into new territories. His southern opponents, largely unconcerned with the feasibility of slave agriculture in Nevada or Arizona, knew that he had once told a northern audience that ending slavery's spread was a method of eventually ending slavery where it already existed. By the time Lincoln took office, seven Deep South states from Texas to South Carolina had seceded from the federal Union. When the major in command of the federal garrison in Charleston Harbor refused to evacuate his post, South Carolina's forces fired on Fort Sumter.

President Lincoln responded by calling for 75,000 troops. Virginia (which previously had voted not to secede), North Carolina, Arkansas, and Tennessee joined ranks with the first seven states to secede. Methods of secession varied from a simple legislative declaration of independence to an act of a sovereign convention to a popular referendum. Whatever the method, the southern states acted as if they were completely absolved of obligations to the federal Union.

Southern extremists long had feared that in case of confrontation with the North, the Upper South states would prove unreliable. They also calculated that a southern confederacy could win a war for independence only if Missouri, Delaware, Kentucky, and Maryland joined in secession. Their calculations proved correct.

The Confederate States of America failed to sustain their independence on the battlefield, but the effects of their attempt proved enormous. In plain politics, the program long favored by northern representatives in Congress was enacted *in toto* in the war years. High tariffs, the Homestead Act, land-grant colleges, the repeal of the Fugitive Slave Law, paper money, enormous gifts of federal lands to influential corporations, and many other procapital measures passed that never would have met with success in a Congress dominated by antebellum Democrats. In addition, the South's secession and the Union's victory in the ensuing Civil War allowed Congress and the executive branch to suppress the illegal African slave trade, to end slavery in federal jurisdictions, and eventually to propose, and then to secure, ratification of the Thirteenth, Fourteenth, and Fifteenth Amendments to the U.S. Constitution.

The Democratic Party had been the majority party in Congress since the election of Thomas Jefferson in 1800–1801, but decades of Republican dominance followed the war. The passage of the Thirteenth, Fourteenth, and Fifteenth Amendments, plus the association of states' rights with the defeated South, eventually led to a wholesale change in constitutional law. The idea of secession from the United States would no longer be viable, despite widespread American support for secessionist movements elsewhere in the world.

See also *Calhoun, John C.; Civil War; Constitution, Ratification; Constitution, U.S.; Democratic Party; Federalism; Federalists; Fugitive Slave Laws; Hartford Convention Resolutions; Kansas-Nebraska Act; Jefferson, Thomas; Lincoln, Abraham; Missouri Compromise; Nullification; Popular Sovereignty; Sectionalism; Senate Leadership, Early Period; Slavery; States' Rights; Tariff History; Territorial Expansion; Whig Party.*

K. R. CONSTANTINE GUTZMAN, JOHN JAY COLLEGE, CUNY

BIBLIOGRAPHY

Brandon, Mark E. *Free in the World: American Slavery and Constitutional Failure.* Princeton: Princeton University Press, 1998.

Banner, James M. *To the Hartford Convention: The Federalists and the Origins of Party Politics in Massachusetts, 1789–1815.* New York: Knopf, 1969.

Gordon, David, ed. *Secession, State, & Liberty.* New Brunswick, N.J.: Transaction, 1998.

Stephens, Alexander H. *A Constitutional View of the Late War Between the States.* 2 vols. Philadelphia: National Publishing Company, 1868, 1870.

SECTIONALISM

The advent of sectionalism antedated American independence. Its seeds were planted in the earliest decades of English settlement in North America. John Winthrop encouraged his auditors to think of their new England as the New Testament "city on a hill," and the notion that New England had a special mission colored that region's relations with all of the other colonies that sent delegates to the First Continental Congress in 1774. Contemporaneous observers commented on the clannish behavior and distinct manners of the northernmost soon-to-be rebels.

Delegates from the South, too, stood out from the rest in that first American deliberative body. Yet while the South Carolinians and Virginians were notable for their wealth, luxury, and special devotion to the institution of slavery (which still existed in all thirteen colonies), delegates from colonies south of Mason's and Dixon's line do not seem to have identified strongly enough with one another for their feeling to have qualified as "sectional." While New Englanders carried a strong devotion to their region's common history and culture, southern or Middle Atlantic delegates did not.

The American Revolution itself provoked strong sectional feelings in many Americans. As the main theater of war shifted from one area of the Atlantic seaboard to another, residents of the latest states to be attacked often blamed their suffering on the feebleness of other states' exertions. In addition, other contentious matters, such as the resolution of Virginia's enormous land claims in the Old Northwest, inflamed sectional resentments. Still, while New Englanders frequently understood themselves to share various interests with one another, the idea of a "South" organized around slavery progressed only fitfully. For example, the Northwest Ordinance of 1787 included a provision purporting to exclude slavery forever from the states to be carved out of that territory. Yet, William Grayson of Virginia, the acting president of the Confederation Congress when it adopted that ordinance, wrote home to Virginia *boasting* about his role in keeping slavery out of the Old Northwest: it was a real coup on his part, he reasoned, for it meant that no one in that region would ever be able to compete with Virginians in tobacco production. Tobacco, not slavery extension, seemed easily the more important interest to Grayson.

THE EARLY DAYS OF THE REPUBLIC

If the South had not yet coalesced by the end of the Confederation period, most historians agree that the Philadelphia Convention of 1787 prompted politicians from the two southernmost states to "calculate the value of the Union" insofar as slavery was concerned. John Rutledge, South Carolina's most important politician, responded to a proposal for taxing or banning slave imports by saying, "The true question at present is whether the Southern States shall or shall not be parties to the Union." In the end, South Carolina and Georgia secured a fugitive slave clause, a guarantee that slave imports would not be curtailed by federal action before 1808, and representation for three-fifths of their slaves in the new Congress and electoral college. What one day would be the "South" divided over the slavery importation provision, with George Mason of Virginia refusing to sign the Constitution in part because he opposed it and in part because he opposed the majority power to levy tariffs New England states had gained in return.

In the Philadelphia Convention, James Madison predicted that the most important division between the states would center on slavery. In saying this, though, Madison evidently intended at least in part to allay the fears of smaller states that population apportionment of both houses of Congress would mean their subordination to the larger ones. When the locus of discussion shifted to the ratification conventions of the individual states, though, talk of exploitative Yankees and slave-driving southerners arose in several different conventions. In addition, the Virginia Convention considered the meaning of ratification for the fledgling West, which, in the persons of delegates from the Kentucky district, had a powerful influence in that body. Kentucky delegates overwhelmingly opposed ratification, at least in part because of Congress's recent willingness to allow Spain to close the Mississippi to navigation.

Early in the history of the new government, Congress adopted a system of tariffs eerily similar to that which the Antifederalists had foreseen. Despite the fact that Virginians held the offices of president, secretary of state, and attorney general, disgruntled Virginians led the way in insisting that a northern majority in Congress intended to exploit them for its own financial gain. Largely as a result of this sectional feeling, former governor Patrick Henry, who had noted in the Richmond Convention that a broad reading of the "necessary and proper" and "general welfare" clauses might empower Congress to free the slaves, prompted the General Assembly to adopt a resolution insisting that Congress honor the promise of the Virginia Federalists that Congress would exercise only those powers it had been "expressly granted." Thus, 1790 saw the advent of the "Virginia Doctrine."

As the 1790s progressed, even Virginians who initially had borne large portions of the burden of creating the new federal government grew increasingly unhappy with its administration. The replacement of George Washington by John Adams as president and the outbreak of the quasi-war with France sparked, by decade's end, secessionist impulses among some southern political leaders. These impulses remained essentially localized in Virginia and its offspring, Kentucky, when James Madison and Vice President Thomas Jefferson penned their Virginia and Kentucky Resolutions in 1798. While Jefferson; John Taylor of Caroline, Virginia; and other Virginians occasionally spoke of "northern" and "southern" sides in national politics, other southern states conspicuously omitted endorsement of the "Principles of 1798" at that time.

Jefferson's election to the presidency spurred a recrudescence of religious chauvinism in New England, where influential ministers in Massachusetts, Connecticut, and other places lamented the advent of what they expected to be a forthrightly non-Christian administration. Just as Taylor and others had entered the 1790s intent on keeping the federal government on a short leash, so the New Englanders approached the Republican ascendancy in 1801 with great trepidation. Jefferson's purchase of the Louisiana Territory from France in 1803 and his later embargo of all international trade spurred antifederal, sectional feeling in New England. The former, some believed, would entail admission of so many new states into the federal Union that New England would forever be relegated to minority status; the latter, Jefferson's feeble response to Great Britain's superior naval power, threatened seafaring New England's economic ruin.

To the dismay of New Englanders, President James Madison opted in 1812 for a far different resolution of America's Napoleonic era foreign-policy problems: a declaration of war against Great Britain. New England, where pro–British sympathies long had marked the elite as substantially different from the one that ruled in Washington, soon came to be marked by even more widespread smuggling than had greeted the federal embargo and by growing secessionist sentiment. In 1814, at the Hartford Convention, several notable and many not-so-notable New Englanders went on the record in support of secession if Madison and his government did not give the Northeast its way.

With the war's end came a sudden end to sectional agitation. During the "Era of Good Feelings" that followed, Madison's successor and the third consecutive Virginian president, James Monroe, resolved to bring a permanent end to the old party divisions. Monroe intentionally neglected the Republican organization that had swept him and his predecessors to power, and the eight years of his administration saw the virtual disappearance of the Federalist Party.

The one exception to the trend, a major one, came in the Missouri crises of 1819–1821, when a New York Republican pressed the notion that Missouri should not be admitted to the Union until it adopted a constitutional ban on slavery. Ex-president Jefferson labeled this proposal "a firebell in the night," imagining that it tolled the death knell of the Union.

By the time Missouri's and Maine's admissions to the Union had been paired, keeping a kind of free state–slave state balance in the federal system, men in both sections had been driven to sectionalism with a force never present before. As Madison had observed in 1787, the line of demarcation was that between states heavily invested in slavery and those that were not. Secretary of State John Quincy Adams of Massachusetts noted in his diary that this issue had driven Secretary of War John C. Calhoun of South Carolina, whom Adams previously had judged the least partisan and least sectional of politicians, to promise Adams that the South never would compromise on slavery.

In his characteristically nonpartisan way, President Monroe signed the final bill resolving the Missouri imbroglio despite the fact that it cut deeply against his own section's interests. Back in Virginia, this act aroused bitterness and contempt even from those who were close to him. Yet Monroe, like Calhoun, thought the resolution worthwhile because it promised to put the issue of slavery's extension westward to rest. Both were mistaken.

TERRITORIAL EXPANSION RAISES SECTIONAL TENSIONS

America's acquisition of new lands to its west repeatedly prompted dust-ups over slavery in the antebellum period. From the 1820s on, the correspondence of men in the South is peppered with references to themselves as "slaveholders" and to the perceived hostility of nonsoutherners to their key domestic institution. Also in this period, Missouri Democrat Thomas Hart Benton, Kentucky Whig Henry Clay, and other statesmen from the western states attempted to ride "western" sentiment to greater influence in federal politics. However, the idea of a West never aroused the kind of passions that identification with New England or the South did. While Clay proved adept at extracting West-friendly legislation from Congress, he never won election to the presidency.

Calhoun, whose career in federal politics spanned four decades and whose early nationalism gave way to a twenty-six-year defense of the South against what he took to be the momentum of history, helped lay the groundwork for the eventual breakup of the Union by playing a key role in the annexation of Texas in 1845. Soon, though, Calhoun recognized the error of his ways, and he opposed the Mexican-American War that flowed from the Texas gambit. His reasoning was that the United States likely would crush Mexico, and then it would acquire a large section (if not all) of the defeated country's territory. Such an eventuality likely would lead to a situation in which the Missouri problem looked like only a trial run; in the end, disunion, civil war, or who knew what would result.

Calhoun was right. When he died in 1850, two years after the United States had taken half of Mexico's territory, the resulting slavery-related issues seemed intractable. Clay and Daniel Webster joined in pushing through the Compromise of 1850, whose chief components were a fugitive slave law devoid of even rudimentary procedural protections for purported slaves, for the South; and admission of California as a new free state, for the North. As Calhoun had predicted, Clay's and Webster's hopes for this legislation were frustrated in the years immediately following its passage. While new states in the West secured orderly admission to the Union, the Fugitive Slave Act of 1850 proved extremely unpopular, and almost unenforceable, in much of the North. As the 1850s went on, stories of free blacks kidnapped into slavery and other such harrowing tales grew common. Harriet Beecher Stowe's best-selling novel, *Uncle Tom's Cabin,* dramatically affected northern opinion. The book was banned throughout the South, where prominent intellectuals responded to it with great hostility. This increased the already great cultural divide between the two sections.

By the end of the 1850s the main Protestant organizations of the Union had split into northern and southern branches. The collapse of the Whig Party left the long-dominant Democratic Party without an established national opposition, but it, too, ran aground on the issue of slavery. In 1857 the confluence of the Supreme Court's decision in *Dred Scott v. Sandford,* the armed conflict in Kansas Territory over state constitutional arrangements regarding slavery, and the panic of 1857 left the impression that America was adrift in hostile seas. President James Buchanan, a traditional Democrat of the Thomas Jefferson/Andrew Jackson stamp, played a very complicated role in making the Court decision and the territorial problem redound to the great detriment of the Democrats, the only remaining Union-wide party.

In the 1858 Illinois campaign for the U.S. Senate, Sen. Stephen A. Douglas and former U.S. representative Abraham Lincoln debated the various problems related to slavery in the territories. Douglas argued for a "popular sovereignty" position, joining with the Supreme Court in insisting that the Missouri Compromise's exclusion of slavery from certain of the territories had been unconstitutional. Douglas would have left the matter to the territorial settlers themselves. Lincoln, on the other hand, leapt past the constitutional difficulty and lampooned Douglas as a man who did not care to address the moral issue of slavery extension. In a sense, Lincoln recapitulated the Puritan New England conception of America as an example to others. Most important, Lincoln exposed the divergence between Douglas's position and that of southern Democrats, who held that slavery could not be excluded from any territory prior to statehood. Douglas's attempted neutral-

The 1858 senatorial debates between Abraham Lincoln and Stephen Douglas, above, revealed fissures within the Democratic Party that could not be resolved before the election of 1860. *Library of Congress*

ity on the issue of slavery's extension westward foundered on southern Democrats' insistence that he effectively endorse their institution (as Chief Justice Taney had done).

When Douglas's position alienated southerners within his own party, the Democratic Party proved unable to agree on a common intersectional nominee in 1860. That year Lincoln, the second presidential nominee of the new Republican Party, achieved election on a platform that would cordon off slavery from the western territories. Although Lincoln was not abolitionist per se, proslavery southerners feared that Lincoln intended this platform as a way of eventually eliminating the institution throughout the Union.

SECESSION, WAR, AND RECONSTRUCTION

South Carolina, where sectionalism had waxed strong on several former occasions, precipitated the secession of the Deep South states. By the time of Lincoln's inauguration, the six Gulf states had followed the Palmetto State out of the federal Union of 1788. Among those states' explanations of their secession was the assertion that Lincoln had been elected on a purely sectional platform. Within months of

Lincoln's election, the events in Charleston Harbor culminating in the firing on Fort Sumter prompted Lincoln to call for seventy-five thousand recruits. At that, four Middle South states seceded.

When the Civil War ended in 1865, much of the South's economic infrastructure—its investments in slaves, factories, and railroads—had been destroyed. In the North, united into a cohesive political entity by the war, sectional feeling was tied closely to the determination that victory yield tangible results. For a generation and more, then, sectionalism moved from the defensive posture of a waning minority to a plank in the ideology of a ruling majority.

Southern sectionalism flourished in the wake of Confederate defeat. Well into the twentieth century, Confederate pensions, Confederate symbols, and Confederate tales remained powerful rallying points among a huge majority of white southerners. Notwithstanding the "lost cause" lore, however, exponents of the "New South Creed" wanted to integrate the southern economy into the national economy. The South's relative poverty and backwardness resulting from the war became a stereotype in the North and a vicious legacy in the South. However, northerners did not think in sectionalist terms: they were too concerned with national and international concerns to worry much about the South. After the Spanish-American War of 1898, northern opinion gradually welcomed the South back into the fold of "legitimate" American identity, and the South, as it desired, gained a free hand in the region's racial and economic matters.

SECTIONALISM'S LAST STAND

In the middle of the twentieth century, American involvement in World War II exposed a large number of black southerners to the world outside their small quarter, and they returned to America determined to demand a fairer legal and economic shake. The Supreme Court decision in *Brown v. Board of Education* (1954) focused the entire country's attention on the South's peculiar social arrangements. Confederate symbols, freighted with new meaning and new defiance, were taken up across the South in a last stand of southern sectionalism. In several postwar election cycles, "southern" candidates waged third-party presidential campaigns. In the end, though, as Calhoun had predicted in 1850, a northern majority in complete control of both Congress and the executive branch proved unwilling to treat with white southerners intent on resisting majority mores—in this case, equal legal treatment of slaves' descendants.

In the post–World War II era, a new West, well to the west of the Old Northwest, also seems to have acquired some distinguishing characteristics, a kind of political persona. Yet the massive immigration to the West of peoples alien to the conservative-to-libertarian ethic of Barry Goldwater and Ronald Reagan, plus the end of the cold war that long made conservatism a distinct American persuasion, may have nipped that development's tendency toward sectionalism in the bud.

With the passage and implementation of the great anti-segregation measures of the 1960s, sectionalism seems finally to have lost its place in the southern heart, as well. Sectionalism now seems to be merely vestigial. Modern means of communication and the post-1929 growth of the federal government seem to have cemented the old union of states together in ways not originally imagined.

See also *Compromise of 1850; Dixiecrats; Missouri Compromise; Nullification; Secession; States' Rights/Sovereignty.*

K. R. CONSTANTINE GUTZMAN, JOHN JAY COLLEGE, CUNY

BIBLIOGRAPHY

Banner, James M. *To the Hartford Convention.* New York: Knopf, 1970.

Cahodas, Nadine. *Strom Thurmond and the Politics of Southern Change.* New York: Simon and Schuster, 1993.

Carpenter, Jesse T. *The South as a Conscious Minority.* Columbia: University of South Carolina Press, 1990. Originally published 1930.

Freehling, William. *The Road to Disunion: Secessionists at Bay, 1776–1854.* New York: Oxford University Press, 1990.

Gutzman, Kevin R. [Constantine]. "Preserving the Patrimony: William Branch Giles and Virginia versus the Federal Tariff." *Virginia Magazine of History and Biography* 104 (1996): 341–372.

Gutzman, K. R. Constantine. "The Virginia and Kentucky Resolutions Reconsidered: 'An Appeal to the *Real Laws* of Our Country.'" *Journal of Southern History* 66 (August 2000): 473–496.

Holt, Michael F. *The Political Crisis of the 1850s.* New York: Oxford University Press, 1978.

SEDITION ACT OF 1798

The Alien and Sedition Acts is the name given to legislation against subversion enacted by the Federalist Party in 1798. The controversial laws were set in the context of embryonic political party development in the new country, with the Federalists—at that time led by the nation's second president, John Adams—set against the followers of Thomas Jefferson, who were to become known as Democratic-Republicans, or simply Jeffersonians. These two proto-parties disagreed on most fundamental aspects of the new nation's development, with the Democratic-Republicans opposing Federalist policies in international affairs as well as domestic matters. At this time, between the elections of 1796 and 1800, the United States also was caught up in European politics—in particular continuing war between England and France—and in the fear of conflict with France itself.

In spite of a French naval quasi-war against the Americans, Jefferson's Democratic-Republicans remained sympathetic of the French regime. Federalists also thought they saw disloyalty in an affinity of immigrants toward Jefferson's developing party. In response, Federalists pushed through Congress four bills in June and July 1798 to muzzle the opposition's leading politicians and journalists and to deal with other perceived dangers to their policies. The Alien Enemies Act gave the president power to deport suspect foreigners if war were declared; the Alien Act granted him similar powers in peacetime. The Naturalization Act extended from five to fourteen years the period foreigners had to reside before they could attain citizenship. Most controversial was the Act for the Punishment of Certain Crimes, usually called the Sedition Act. Only the latter two of these measures were actively enforced, and then rarely. A total of fifteen people were indicted for sedition, which was narrowly defined as "false, scandalous and malicious" statements about the government or its officials. Of those indicted, juries convicted and judges briefly jailed just ten, including four Democratic-Republican editors and a radical Vermont congressman repugnant to the Federalists. President Adams expelled two radical Irish journalists. Some hundreds of Frenchmen hurried back to Europe.

War with France never came. The Alien and Sedition Acts were to have expired automatically by 1801, and in fact the controversy ended when Jefferson was elected president in 1800, defeating Adams. From that point on, the Federalists faded from the scene and disappeared entirely by the 1820s. But the acts did give rise to important declarations of principle in what became known as the Kentucky and Virginia Resolutions. In those, Jefferson and future president James Madison denied that Congress had the authority to pass such measures under the Constitution, and they were therefore illegitimate. Madison argued they violated the First and Tenth Amendments in the Bill of Rights on freedom of speech and powers reserved to the states. The fight over these laws, and Madison's response in particular, thus became the first significant testing of constitutional boundaries on free speech, an unfettered press, and the rights of organized political opposition.

See also *Adams, John; Madison, James; States' Rights/Sovereignty.*

BIBLIOGRAPHY

Miller, John Chester. *Crisis in Freedom: The Alien and Sedition Acts.* Boston: Little, Brown, 1951.

Smith, James Morton. *Freedom's Fetters: The Alien and Sedition Laws and American Civil Liberties.* Ithaca: Cornell University Press, 1956.

Thompson, C. Bradley. *John Adams and the Spirit of Liberty.* Lawrence: University Press of Kansas, 1998.

Warfield, Ethelbert Dudley. *The Kentucky Resolutions of 1798: An Historical Study.* New York: Putnam's, 1887.

Hofstadter, Richard. *The Idea of a Party System: The Rise of Legitimate Opposition in the United States, 1780–1840.* Berkeley: University of California Press, 1969.

SEMINOLE WAR

The Seminole War (1835–1842), also known as the Second Seminole War, resulted from U.S. attempts to relocate Seminoles from Florida to the "Indian Territory" in Oklahoma.

Earlier, continuing conflicts between Florida territorial settlers and the Seminoles had been exacerbated because the Seminoles were providing refuge to escaped slaves. This led to the First Seminole War (1817–1818), fighting in Florida and southern Georgia, and Gen. Andrew Jackson's quick defeat of the Seminoles. By the 1820s most Seminoles lived on reservations in Florida, but constant hunger, despite federal aid, drove them off reservations in search of food. Mounting tensions prompted settlers to petition government officials for protection. As a result, the Legislative Council of Florida promulgated statutes permitting Florida whites who discovered Seminoles off reservations the right to capture them for presentation before a local judge for punishment. These measures only worsened tensions and increased interest in removal of the Indians.

President Andrew Jackson supported the removal of the Seminoles to make room for the expansion of white settlement and development in Florida. On May 28, 1830, the Indian Removal Act authorized the national government to facilitate this expulsion. Starvation among the Indians continued in 1831, and in 1832, under the pretext of relieving suffering and starvation, Jackson proposed that the Seminoles be absorbed into the Creek nation on lands west of the Mississippi River. This proposal was a major affront to the Seminoles, since the Creek tribe had been allied with whites against the Seminole. Under the terms of the Treaty of Payne's Landing (May 1832), Seminole chiefs were to inspect western lands and, if the chiefs approved, the Seminoles would be moved there over the following three years. However, several senior Seminole chiefs, including Micanopy, claimed that the treaty was a fraud.

Many Seminoles would not leave Florida out of fear that their own slaves would be stolen by the Creeks or that they would have to return escaped slaves who had sought refuge among the Seminole and were living as free people. By 1835 Seminole resistance to removal, led by the emerging leader Osceola, hinged upon this issue and hindered the efforts of influential Floridians determined to acquire Seminole slaves. In April 1835 talks broke down, and by December several skirmishes precipitated outright warfare, including the December 28 ambush and massacre by Osceola of Major Francis Dade and his command and the December 31 Battle of Withlacoochee.

The war had a significant impact on the settlement of Florida, focusing national attention on the territory and convincing the federal government to initiate improvement projects for defense purposes. During the 1830s more than 20,000 settlers poured into Florida, and by 1840 the territory had gained more than 850 miles of new wagon roads, 3,700 new feet of bridges, 50 new outposts, and regular steamer traffic. In 1842 Congress provided another incentive for settlement in Florida by enacting the Armed Occupation Bill, which provided settlers with 160-acre tracts of land that they were to settle, cultivate, and defend from Seminole attacks.

By the conclusion of the war, slavery and the territory became closely linked in national political debates. For years the Seminoles had harbored runaway slaves. In 1839 the Florida Territorial Legislature purchased thirty-three bloodhounds from Cuba for use by the U.S. Army in Florida. The bloodhounds were allegedly trained to track slaves rather than Seminoles, which caused a furor among abolitionists in Congress and across the nation. In 1840 abolitionists pressured the War Department to regulate the dogs' use, and Sen. James Buchanan, representing his Quaker constituents, and former president John Quincy Adams both introduced resolutions in Congress on the issue. In 1840 Democrats attributed Whig criticism about the war to abolitionist influence and efforts to prevent Florida from becoming a slave state. In 1841 abolitionist congressmen used debate on Florida to challenge the "gag rule" of 1836.

In 1842 the War Department declared the war ended, but no formal peace treaty was signed. Meanwhile, Congress continued debate on reducing the size of the U.S. military. Sectional divisions in Congress resulted in compromise legislation that regulated the military, reduced several army units, and rewarded navy wartime successes by expanding the service. The cost of the war was between $20 million and $40 million, with almost 2,000 Americans and countless Seminoles dead. By 1843 almost 4,000 Seminoles had been removed to Indian Territory. Continuing conflicts over land in Florida erupted in more fighting in the Third Seminole War (1855–1858), which further reduced the number of Seminoles in Florida to less than 200.

See also *Gag Rule; Indian Policy; Jackson, Andrew; Territorial Expansion.*

DONALD STELLUTO JR., CALIFORNIA STATE UNIVERSITY, FULLERTON

BIBLIOGRAPHY

Mahon, John K. *History of the Second Seminole War, 1835–1842.* Gainesville: University of Florida Press, 1967.

Walton, George. *Fearless and Free: The Seminole Indian War, 1835–1842.* Indianapolis: Bobbs-Merrill, 1977.

Weisman, Brent Richards. *Unconquered People: Florida's Seminole and Miccosukee Indians.* Gainesville: University Press of Florida, 1999.

Wright, J. Leitch. *Creeks and Seminoles: The Destruction and Regeneration of the Muscogulge People.* Lincoln: University of Nebraska Press, 1986.

SENATE LEADERSHIP: EARLY PERIOD

The U.S. Senate has traditionally been ruled from the floor instead of from the chair. Senate leadership resides with its members, not its presiding officer. The Constitution assigns the vice president of the United States to serve as president of the Senate, and senators elect a president pro tempore to preside in the vice president's absence. Except for the vice president's ability to break tie votes, a simple majority can overturn any ruling of the chair, causing presiding officers to act in a neutral manner at most times. This is in contrast with the House of Representatives, where the Speaker early evolved into a party leader.

During the Federalist era (1789–1801), the Senate set up a multitude of ad hoc committees to draft specific legislation. Those senators who served on a great number of committees developed expertise and personal leadership. When the Republicans took control in 1801, President Thomas Jefferson promoted his legislative programs through a few unofficial spokesmen and the party caucus in the Senate. Although the caucuses operated informally and exerted little party discipline, Federalist senators accused the Jeffersonian Republicans of trying to reconcile party differences in their caucuses before they debated the issues in public. In 1816 the Senate established standing committees, and committee chairmen achieved leadership as floor managers of legislation within their committees' jurisdictions. Other senators, for example, Henry Clay (Whig-Ky.), Daniel Webster (Whig-Mass.), and John C. Calhoun (Whig/D-S.C.) rose to personal leadership because of their debating skills, legislative talents, and regional identification. In fact, Clay persistently denied that he was the leader of the Whig Party in the Senate.

Proud of being a body of equals, the Senate during the nineteenth century operated without officially designated majority and minority leaders. In 1885 Woodrow Wilson (in *Congressional Government,* p. 213) asserted, "No one is *the* Senator. No one may speak for his party as for himself." Republicans, who held the majority almost continu-ously from the Civil War to the end of the century, began using the steering committee in their caucus to schedule legislation on the floor. Democrats adopted the same practice when they returned to the majority.

Although the chairs of the two party caucuses performed routine floor leadership chores, real power during the nineteenth century resided with the chairmen of the most powerful standing committees, particularly the Finance and Appropriations Committees. At the turn of the twentieth century, leadership was widely conceded to four influential senators: Nelson Aldrich (R-R.I.), chairman of the Finance Committee; William Allison (R-Iowa), chairman of the Appropriations Committee; John C. Spooner (R-Wis.); and Orville Platt (R-Conn.). The "Senate Four" could control the schedule and marshal a majority vote, which gave them power to block or defeat any measure that a president or the House of Representatives might support. Their resistance to reform during the Progressive era helped spark the movement for direct election of senators.

Early in the twentieth century, the caucus chairmen became the designated leaders in legislative battle. The parties by this time chose leaders for their skills as orators and debaters and expected them to manage their party's agenda on the Senate floor; they no longer simply elevated their senior members.

See also *Senate Leadership: Modern; Vice Presidency.*

DONALD A. RITCHIE, U.S. SENATE HISTORICAL OFFICE

The "Senate Four," who dominated the Senate at the turn of the twentieth century, relax at the home of Nelson W. Aldrich in Newport, Rhode Island, in 1903. *Senate Historical Office*

BIBLIOGRAPHY

Merrill, Horace Samuel, and Marion Galbraith Merrill. *The Republican Command, 1897–1913*. Lexington: University Press of Kentucky, 1971.

Rothman, David J. *Politics and Power: The United States Senate, 1869–1901*. Cambridge: Harvard University Press, 1966.

Swift, Elaine K. *The Making of an American Senate: Reconstitutive Change in Congress, 1787–1841*. Ann Arbor: University of Michigan Press, 1996.

Wilson, Woodrow. *Congressional Government: A Study in American Politics*. Boston: Houghton, Mifflin, 1885.

SENATE LEADERSHIP: MODERN

Members of each party conference in the Senate elect a leader and an assistant leader (also known as the whip) to represent their interests in Senate floor proceedings. The majority leader, usually in consultation with the minority leader, schedules Senate business and calls bills, nominations, and treaties from the calendar for debate and vote. The leaders plan legislative strategy, promote party unity, and consult with the president and with their counterparts in the House of Representatives.

These leadership positions are not mentioned in the Constitution, which simply designates the vice president to serve as president of the Senate and assigns the Senate to elect a president pro tempore. During the nineteenth century, Senate leadership resided with the chairmen of the party conferences and standing committees. In 1913, Democrats elected John Worth Kern of Indiana to chair their conference, and he assumed a range of floor duties that made him the first "majority leader." However, Democrats did not formally designate a floor leader until 1920, and Republicans not until 1925. Over time, both party leaders came to occupy the front-row desks on opposite sides of the center aisle in the Senate chamber. These prominent positions assisted the leaders in obtaining the preferential "right of first recognition," whereby the presiding officer always calls first on the majority leader, then on the minority leader, and then on the manager of the bill, before recognizing other senators. This right gives the leadership a greater degree of control over floor proceedings.

Unlike the House, where the Rules Committee votes for each bill a rule that sets the number of amendments that might be offered, allots specific time for debate, and determines when votes will be cast, Senate rules do not permit the majority leader to enforce such limitations on debate. Leaders instead offer unanimous consent agreements in an effort to set times and conditions for debating and voting. A single objection can halt such a request. Further complicating the leaders' task is the Senate's tradition of unlimited debate, also known as filibusters, through which a minority can delay the proceedings and prevent the majority from voting. Senate rules provide for a vote of cloture by three-fifths of the senators to cut off filibusters, and majority leaders frequently file cloture motions to determine the voting strength of a bill's opponents, to see how many vote against it.

Senate leaders have been compared to traffic police, keeping legislative business moving. The position requires them to accommodate the needs of one hundred senators, scheduling votes to fit members' travel plans and helping them receive desired committee assignments, office space, and other housekeeping favors to strengthen their loyalty to the leadership. The leaders conduct frequent head counts to anticipate the votes on pending bills, and the leaders inform each other of any "holds" that senators in their parties may have placed on legislation or nominations, indicating that unless their concerns were met they would object to a unanimous consent agreement. Lacking much ability to discipline independent-minded members, Senate Majority Leader Lyndon B. Johnson, D-Texas, observed that the chief power available to the leadership was the "power of persuasion."

See also *Cloture; Filibuster.*

DONALD A. RITCHIE, U.S. SENATE HISTORICAL OFFICE

BIBLIOGRAPHY

Baker, Richard A., and Roger O. Davidson, eds. *First among Equals: Outstanding Senate Leaders of the Twentieth Century*. Washington, D.C.: Congressional Quarterly, 1991.

Byrd, Robert C. "Party Floor Leaders." In *The Senate, 1789–1989: Addresses on the History of the United States Senate,* Vol. 2, 185–205. Washington, D.C.: U.S. Government Printing Office, 1991.

Kornacki, John J., ed. *Leading Congress: New Styles, New Strategies*. Washington, D.C.: Congressional Quarterly, 1990.

Sinclair, Barbara. *The Transformation of the U.S. Senate*. Baltimore: Johns Hopkins University Press, 1989.

Smith, Steven S. *Call to Order: Floor Politics in the House and Senate*. Washington, D.C.: Brookings Institution, 1989.

SENECA FALLS CONVENTION

Building on years of emerging ideas, the Seneca Falls Convention (1848) launched the organized women's movement in the United States. Elizabeth Cady Stanton lived near Seneca Falls, in upstate New York, and she, Lucretia Mott, and a few other women called a public meeting to be held there concerning women's rights.

Meeting on July 19–20, 1848, the group issued a "Declaration of Sentiments," largely drafted by Stanton and signed by sixty-eight women and thirty-two men. Modeled on the Declaration of Independence, it began by declaring: "We hold these truths to be self-evident: that all men and women are created equal." An indictment of the injustices that "man"

Elizabeth Cady Stanton, Susan B. Anthony, and Lucretia Mott are memorialized in this bust, which was dedicated in 1921 and resides in the Capitol. *Lisa Hartjens*

ticipation with man in the various trades, professions and commerce."

Two weeks later, a larger meeting convened in nearby Rochester. In the next few years conventions met in various northern states, including one in Salem, Ohio, in April 1850 and the first national women's rights convention, in Worcester, Massachusetts, in October 1850. Stanton and Mott continued, throughout their long lives, to press for women's rights, especially the vote.

Beginning in Wyoming, which adopted female suffrage in 1869 while still a territory and retained it when admitted as a state in 1890, a growing list of states adopted women's suffrage. In 1920 the Nineteenth Amendment to the Constitution extended women's voting rights to every state. Nonetheless, more than a century after the Seneca Falls Convention, many of the questions addressed in 1848 remained salient issues, and they spurred a new feminist movement that began in the 1960s. By that time the right to vote, the most controversial demand of 1848, had long since been achieved, yet many other aspirations remained unrealized. The Civil Rights Act of 1964 (Title VII on employment) and the Educational Amendments of 1972 (Title IX on education and athletics) built on the earlier victories. People still regard the Seneca Falls Convention as launching and symbolizing the quest for gender equality.

See also *Civil Rights Acts; Civil Rights Movement; Constitution, U.S.; Sex Discrimination in Employment: Title VII; Sex Discrimination in Higher Education: Title IX; Woman's Suffrage Movement.*

PETER WALLENSTEIN,
VIRGINIA POLYTECHNIC INSTITUTE AND STATE UNIVERSITY

had inflicted on "woman," the declaration spoke of women as "citizens of the United States" who had been "fraudulently deprived of their most sacred rights," starting with their "inalienable right to the elective franchise."

As a result of their political impotence, said the declaration, single women suffered taxation without representation, and married women were denied property rights and were left powerless in matters of divorce and child custody. Women were denied access to higher education and "profitable employments." Quite aside from unjust laws, in religion men monopolized the ministry, and in morals men imposed a double standard of behavior. Moreover, "man" had "endeavored . . . to destroy her confidence in her own powers, to lessen her self-respect, and to make her willing to lead a dependent and abject life." Unrepresented in legislatures, women would have to use their right of petition and freedom of speech to present their case for changes in the laws.

The convention issued a set of twelve "Resolutions," all of which obtained a unanimous vote except the one demanding voting rights for women. Two of them stated that laws placing women in "a position inferior to that of man" were "contrary to the great precept of Nature" and "of no force or authority." The final resolution declared "That the speedy success of our cause depends on the zealous and untiring efforts of men and women for the overthrow of the monopoly of the pulpit, and for the securing to women an equal par-

BIBLIOGRAPHY

Bernhard, Virginia, and Elizabeth Fox-Genovese, eds. *The Birth of American Feminism: The Seneca Falls Woman's Convention of 1848.* St. James, N.Y.: Brandywine Press, 1995.

DuBois, Ellen Carol. *Feminism and Suffrage: The Emergence of an Independent Women's Movement in America, 1848–1869.* Ithaca: Cornell University Press, 1978.

Griffith, Elisabeth. *In Her Own Right: The Life of Elizabeth Cady Stanton.* New York: Oxford University Press, 1994.

Isenberg, Nancy. *Sex and Citizenship in Antebellum America.* Chapel Hill: University of North Carolina Press, 1998.

Ward, Geoffrey C., ed. *Not for Ourselves Alone: The Story of Elizabeth Cady Stanton and Susan B. Anthony.* New York: Knopf, 1999.

SEX DISCRIMINATION IN EMPLOYMENT: TITLE VII

Title VII of the 1964 Civil Rights Act, which prohibited discrimination in employment on the basis of sex and created the Equal Employment Opportunity Commission (EEOC), was a landmark in the legislation of women's rights.

The civil rights movement of the late 1950s and early 1960s accomplished what abolitionists and other reformers had hoped to do for more than one hundred years and gave women perhaps the most important piece of legislation regarding equality: the Civil Rights Act of 1964. Title VII of that legislation prohibited discrimination by employers and labor unions based on not only race but also sex. It became unlawful for an employer to make employment decisions based on race, color, religion, national origin, or, notably, sex. Title VII also created the EEOC to deal with discrimination-related grievances.

Feminists had not actively sought Title VII. Instead they were trying to pass a constitutional amendment guaranteeing legal equality between men and women. When some feminists approached Rep. Howard Smith (D-Va.) for help on the equal rights amendment, he proposed to add sex to the list of protected classes in the civil rights legislation. Why Smith did this remains a mystery. Although he was against civil rights and hoped to see the bill defeated, he was a long-time ally of the National Woman's Party, which supported an equal rights amendment.

Smith's proposal created quite a controversy and delayed the passage of the 1964 act. Many liberals did not support the addition of sex to the legislation because they did not want to create further obstacles to obtaining equality for racial minorities. The Kennedy Commission on the Status of Women had also decided against treating racial and sex discrimination as equal issues. However, with the support of Sen. Margaret Chase Smith (R–Maine) and the administration of Lyndon B. Johnson, enough support was mustered to push the bill through Congress, and it passed in the summer of 1964.

The EEOC was ready for full operation by the summer of 1965. The commission had assumed that the majority of opposition to the amendment would revolve around race-related issues, but it was soon besieged with complaints from women claiming discrimination on the basis of sex. However, the only such complaints the commission chose to pursue were class actions. This unequal treatment spurred women into action. Because no public group was willing to lobby for women and apply pressure to the EEOC, a number of women organized to promote their own interests, forming the National Organization for Women (NOW), led by Betty Friedan. In 1966 NOW declared that the only way for women to achieve full equality was to "take action to bring American women in to full participation in the mainstream of American society now."

In 1972 and 1978 Title VII was amended to broaden the responsibilities of the EEOC. The EEOC was to concentrate on assisting similar state agencies, advising employers and labor unions, and exacting compliance by conciliation and legal action.

Title VII was one of the most important pieces of legislation in the twentieth century. With employers no longer allowed to discriminate on the basis of race and sex, many jobs were opened to racial minorities and women. Perhaps even more important, Title VII spurred feminists into collaborating for specific goals.

See also *Civil Rights Acts (Modern); Civil Rights Movement; Equal Rights Amendment; National Woman's Party.*

MICHELLE A. STRETCH, INDEPENDENT AUTHOR

BIBLIOGRAPHY

Babcock, Barbara Allen, Ann E. Freedman, Eleanor Holmes Norton, and Susan C. Ross. *Sex Discrimination and the Law: Causes and Remedies.* Boston: Little, Brown, 1975.

Fox-Genovese, Elizabeth. *Feminism Without Illusions: A Critique of Individualism.* Chapel Hill: University of North Carolina Press, 1991.

Kerber, Linda K., and Jane Sherron De Hart. *Women's America: Refocusing the Past.* 3d ed. New York: Oxford University Press, 1991.

Woloch, Nancy. *Women and the American Experience.* 2d ed. New York: McGraw-Hill, 1994.

SEX DISCRIMINATION IN HIGHER EDUCATION: TITLE IX

Title IX of the Education Amendments of 1972 was enacted to prohibit institutions that receive federal funding from practicing sex discrimination in academics and athletic programs. The passage of Title IX enabled a shift in societal attitudes and assumptions about what women can achieve if provided with the same opportunities as men. The legislation was modeled after Title VI of the Civil Rights Act of 1964 prohibiting discrimination based on race, color, and national origin. Supporting legislation included the Women's Educational Equity Act of 1974, Title IV of the Civil Rights of Act of 1964, and the 1976 amendments to the Vocational Education Act of 1963.

A basic premise of Title IX is that colleges must offer men and women equal opportunities to compete on sports teams, and the ratio of female to male athletes must be equivalent to the ratio of women to men in the undergraduate student body. In instances where the participation of women in sports differs from the proportion of women in the undergraduate student body, institutions must demonstrate their commitment to expanding opportunities to women or demonstrate that both sexes are equally accommodated. The U.S. Department of Education's Office of Civil Rights can recommend that federal funds be withheld from institutions that violate Title IX.

Title IX has been a powerful mechanism for improving educational and job-related opportunities for millions of women. It has also promoted their entry into sports activities. However, Title IX has not gone without criticism. In the area of athletics, for example, Title IX was not well received at first by many high school and collegiate athletic associations. Even today, many schools show ambivalence about their responsibility for increasing the availability of athletic programs for women. Opponents of Title IX argue that increasing athletic opportunities to young women reduces the numbers of scholarships, training facilities, and equipment available for young men. In response, some institutions have decided to eliminate sports programs for both sexes and concentrate instead on money-making sports such as football.

Some institutions have eliminated male sports teams in order to comply with Title IX regulations. As a result, some male athletes have filed lawsuits on the basis of reverse discrimination; however, the challenges have been rejected, leaving Title IX legislation intact. To some it appears that the federal government is limiting the control that institutions have over their sports programs. Those on the other side of the debate argue that young women should have the same opportunities as men to compete on sports teams with comparable athletic equipment and scholarships. Thus far, the athletic provisions of Title IX continue to have the support of the federal government and federal courts of appeal.

According to the U.S. Department of Education's National Center for Education Statistics, several indicators of progress in education are directly attributed to Title IX. One of the most noticeable is the steady increase in the number of women receiving college degrees. For example, the Digest of Education Statistics, 1999, states that between 1986–1987 and 1997, the number of bachelor's degrees awarded to men increased by 8 percent, while those awarded to women rose by 28 percent. The digest also reports that greater numbers of women are entering male-dominated fields such as science and technology. According to the digest, biological science degrees increased 49 percent between 1991–1992 and 1996–1997. During this period, the number of male graduates grew 42 percent, while the number of female graduates grew 56 percent.

Another noticeable effect of Title IX is the increasing number of women taking part in intercollegiate sports each year. The National Center for Education Statistics estimates that more than 100,000 women participate, representing a fourfold increase since 1971. In 1995 women comprised 37 percent of college student athletes, compared to just 15 percent in 1972.

Women also have made significant gains in employment. The earnings gap between men and women has closed considerably since the enactment of Title IX. Women who are college graduates exhibit the greatest gains in earnings. In addition, women have begun to enter occupations rarely held by women thirty years ago. Nonetheless, despite higher educational attainment among women, earnings disparities between men and women continue. For example, women earned only 76 percent of men's totals in 1998. Although women have begun to enter the higher-paying occupations, such as business, engineering, mathematics, and science, they remain concentrated in relatively low paying jobs. In addition, data show that women earn less in the same occupation than their male colleagues do. In spite of these shortcomings, Title IX has expanded employment opportunities available to women.

See also *Equal Rights Amendment; Higher Education Act; Sex Discrimination in Employment: Title VII.*

JACQUELINE SMITH-MASON,
STATE COUNCIL OF HIGHER EDUCATION FOR VIRGINIA

BIBLIOGRAPHY

Festle, Mary Jo. *Playing Nice: Politics and Apologies in Women's Sports.* New York: Columbia University Press, 1996.
United States Commission on Civil Rights. *More Hurdles to Clear: Women and Girls in Competitive Athletics.* Washington, D.C.: U.S. Commission on Civil Rights. Located at *http://www.usccr.gov/catalog/chpub.htm.*

SHAW V. RENO

*S*haw v. Reno (1993) was the first in a series of Supreme Court cases that limited the ability of states to consider race in drawing congressional or legislative districts. The closely divided decisions, all 5–4, barred so-called racial gerrymanders—irregularly shaped districts deliberately drawn to give racial or ethnic minorities a majority. Conservatives said the rulings would break down racial bloc voting, while traditional civil rights groups said they set back efforts to increase minority representation in Congress.

African Americans and Hispanics historically had been underrepresented in Congress in comparison to their overall percentage of the population. Even though barriers to minority group voting were eased in the 1960s, African American and Hispanic candidates were unable to compete effectively in districts with majority white populations. To try to correct the underrepresentation, civil rights groups—supported by the Justice Department—argued that states should create more "majority-minority" districts as part of the congressional redistricting after the 1990 census.

The Supreme Court previously had allowed some use of racial criteria in redistricting schemes. In *United Jewish Organizations of Williamsburgh, Inc. v. Carey* (1977) the Court rejected a challenge by a Hasidic Jewish community to a plan that divided its voting strength between two adjacent, predominantly black districts. The districting plans adopted in the 1990s drew more criticism, however, because some of the newly drawn districts zigzagged across many counties in order to pick up enough minority voters to constitute a majority of the population.

The districting plans helped elect a record number of African American and Hispanic members to Congress in 1992, but they also drew legal challenges in a number of states. In North Carolina white voters challenged the creation of a majority African American district that snaked more than 160 miles around the center of the state to include predominantly black neighborhoods in four metropolitan areas. The challengers contended the plan violated what they called their right to a "color-blind election." The state and the Justice Department defended the plan as necessary to comply with the federal Voting Rights Act, which they interpreted to require steps to increase minority voting strength.

The Supreme Court in *Shaw v. Reno* voted 5–4 to allow the white voters to proceed with their suit. For the majority, Justice Sandra Day O'Connor said that a "highly irregular" district could amount to "an effort to segregate voters by race" in violation of the Fourteenth Amendment's Equal Protection Clause. The ruling sent the case back to a three-judge federal court to see whether the state could produce sufficient justification to uphold the plan. Dissenting justices said the white voters had no basis for complaint.

In *Miller v. Johnson* (1995) the Court in another 5–4 ruling made it more difficult to create majority black districts by declaring that race ordinarily could not be "the predominant factor" in drawing district lines. The government, Justice Anthony M. Kennedy wrote, "may not separate its citizens into different voting districts on the basis of race." The ruling threw out a Georgia redistricting map that included a majority-minority district stretching from the Atlanta suburbs to the predominantly black neighborhoods of two cities, Augusta and Savannah.

In both cases the Court said states could justify racial redistricting schemes only by meeting the so-called strict scrutiny test. Under that standard, the government has to show that a racially motivated law has a compelling interest and is narrowly tailored to further that goal.

In a pair of rulings in 1996 the Court made clear that that standard would be hard to meet. In a Texas case, *Bush v. Vera*, the Court said that oddly shaped districts could not be justified on grounds of preserving incumbents' constituencies. On the same day the Court ruled in a follow-up to the North Carolina case, *Shaw v. Hunt*. A lower federal court had upheld the plan after getting the case back, but the Supreme Court threw it out. The justices rejected the states' effort to justify the irregular districts on grounds of eradicating past discrimination against racial minorities. The vote in each of the decisions was again 5–4.

Civil rights groups strongly criticized the line of decisions, but the criticisms were tempered by the election results in Georgia in November 1996. The two African Americans elected to Congress from newly drawn majority black districts won reelection even though their districts had been redrawn and no longer had a majority of black voters. Critics of racial redistricting said the results indicated that racial bloc voting was lessening.

See also Census; Reapportionment Cases; Suffrage.

KENNETH JOST, CONGRESSIONAL QUARTERLY

BIBLIOGRAPHY

Canon, David T. *Race, Redistricting, and Representation: The Unintended Consequences of Black Majority Districts.* Chicago: University of Chicago Press, 1999.

Grofman, Bernard, ed. *Race and Redistricting in the 1990s.* New York: Agathon Press, 1998.

Kousser, J. Morgan. *Colorblind Justice: Minority Voting Rights and the Undoing of the Second Reconstruction.* Chapel Hill: University of North Carolina Press, 1999.

Thernstrom, Abigail M. *Whose Votes Count? Affirmative Action and Minority Voting Rights.* Cambridge: Harvard University Press, 1997.

SHAYS'S REBELLION

Shays's Rebellion is the name given to agrarian unrest and armed insurrection in western Massachusetts in 1786 and 1787. The rebellion is named after Daniel Shays (c 1747–1825), who was widely perceived at the time as being the principal leader of the revolt. In actuality, the rebellion had many leaders, including Shays, and was loosely coordinated by local conventions and correspondence committees.

CAUSES OF THE REBELLION

The rebellion had numerous underlying causes, involving mainly economic adjustments in the aftermath of American independence. These adjustments included a transition from subsistence to commercial agriculture; a desire by the government of the Commonwealth of Massachusetts to fulfill the fiscal demands placed upon it by the government of the Confederation; a simultaneous desire by the government of Massachusetts to restore public credit by reintroducing sound currency; and an initial economic boom followed by a downturn in American overseas trade, which ultimately led to a chain of insolvencies and a wave of debt litigation throughout Massachusetts. While any one of these factors might have been sufficient to produce great hardship among the farmers of western Massachusetts, all of them, taken together, were sufficient to produce a mass fear of destitution, which led to unrest and, ultimately, to mob action.

In September 1785 Congress, attempting to restore the national credit, requisitioned an amount equal to a year's interest on the foreign and domestic debt of the United States. The Commonwealth of Massachusetts, in order to meet this requisition, levied a higher direct tax than had ever before been imposed in the state, through a then novel systematic valuation and taxation of land. At the same time, the Commonwealth, attempting to reduce its own debt and to restore public confidence in its creditworthiness, continued to pay its own obligations in full and did nothing to reduce local taxes in light of the national requisition. These taxes were all payable in specie, that is, gold or silver coins.

The increased government demand for specie came at a time of economic decline. An initial increase of trade with Great Britain, at the end of the Revolutionary War, had been followed by a downturn when the British government imposed regulations designed to remove the United States from the imperial economic system and to place American traders on the same footing as foreign, rather than colonial, merchants. British merchants, faced with the reduction in trade caused by these regulations, began to deny credit to American merchants and to demand repayment of credit already extended. This led to an export of specie from the United States at precisely the same time it was needed to meet the fiscal demands of the national and state governments.

The decline in trade and the demands placed upon American importers by their British creditors led to a chain reaction of debt collection and insolvencies throughout Massachusetts. Local merchants in western Massachusetts began to demand repayment from their rural customers. The farmers of the region, who were used to producing at a subsistence level and to settling debts with payments in kind or of labor, now found themselves faced with unusual financial burdens. The Commonwealth demanded higher taxes than had hitherto been seen, payable in hard currency. Private creditors demanded repayment, also in hard currency. While historians disagree on the extent of foreclosure, forced sale, loss of land, and imprisonment for debt, it is clear that an increase in debt litigation occurred in 1785 and 1786. This, coupled with widespread fear and uncertainty among farmers throughout New England, was sufficient to trigger general popular unrest.

COURSE OF THE REBELLION

Initially, protests were confined to a series of meetings and county conventions held throughout 1786. At these meetings a common program emerged. Conventions demanded that the legislature enact "tender" laws, allowing debtors to pay debts in kind. Other resolutions demanded the issuance of paper currency, a reduction of the tax burden, and an abolition or reform of the legal mechanisms to collect debt. While discontented farmers in other states were granted some relief, most notably in Rhode Island, the Massachusetts General Court, dominated by and sympathetic to Boston's mercantile interests, ignored all rural demands.

As a result, sporadic mob action began in August 1786 and continued throughout the fall. Mobs targeted local courts, the most readily available foci for discontent. On August 29, 1786, a large mob of farmers prevented the Court of Common Pleas in Northampton, Massachusetts, from meeting. Within two weeks, six other courts had been prevented from holding sessions. Disorder spread to every other New England state except Rhode Island by the end of the year. While other states took steps to conciliate the mob and to restore order, the government of Massachusetts initially failed to act, and instead it requested troops from the national government to help end the disturbances.

The Confederation, lacking funds, failed to raise troops. Boston merchants, by contrast, quickly raised funds sufficient to enlist and equip three thousand troops under the command of Benjamin Lincoln, a Revolutionary War hero. Gov. James Bowdoin II dispatched the force to restore order, open the courts, and arrest troublemakers. The Commonwealth troops moved initially to Worcester on January 19, 1787.

The appearance of an armed force incited intensified mob action. Committees planned concerted action against the Commonwealth government; the first of these was to be an assault upon the arsenal at Springfield, Massachusetts. The assault, on January 25, 1787, failed. The insurrectionary forces then withdrew toward Petersham to regroup, and they harassed merchants, lawyers, and local officials along the way. Lincoln, making an aggressive forced march through a snowstorm, was able to surprise and defeat the insurrectionary force of about two thousand farmers on the nights of February 3 and 4, 1787.

After the defeat at Petersham, the rebellion quickly collapsed. Encouraged by a liberal pardon, many farmers returned home. Others fled to neighboring states or to the open lands of the West. Shays, though eventually pardoned, chose to live the rest of his life in Vermont and New York.

Shays's Rebellion had three long-term consequences for American political history. The threat posed to civil order in Massachusetts and the failure of the Confederation to support Massachusetts in the defense of order focused attention on the need for a more powerful national government, capable of defending property rights and of maintaining order. Thus, the work of the Constitutional Convention and of subsequent efforts at ratification was somewhat eased. The response of the government of Massachusetts, and of the other New England state governments, in the face of threats from disgruntled citizens served to delegitimize violence and mob action as acceptable forms of opposition to authority. This change marked a break with colonial and revolutionary traditions. Finally, the program demanded by the Massachusetts farmers, of soft money and debtor relief, became central to the political ideology of the agrarian community in the United States.

See also *American Revolution; Civil Unrest and Rioting.*

JOSEPH ISENBERG, IOWA STATE UNIVERSITY, AMES

BIBLIOGRAPHY

Gross, Robert A., ed. *In Debt to Shays: The Bicentennial of an Agrarian Rebellion.* Charlottesville: University Press of Virginia, 1993.

Szatmary, David P. *Shays' Rebellion: The Making of an Agrarian Insurrection.* Amherst: University of Massachusetts Press, 1980.

SLAVERY

Slavery can be found in almost every culture and geographic location and in almost all periods from antiquity to the present. Even world condemnation and United Nations treaties have not completely eradicated slavery in the twenty-first century. Before the eighteenth century, however, few people anywhere questioned the legitimacy of slavery, although individual slaves surely objected to their own bondage and mistreatment. Because of its widespread acceptance, slavery was rarely a political issue. Slavery in the United States, however, was different from slavery in other places and times in many significant ways.

U.S. AND OTHER SLAVE SYSTEMS COMPARED

First, slavery in the United States was strictly tied to race. Racially based slavery was unknown outside of the New World, and even in other parts of the New World race was a more flexible category. Throughout the other New World slave cultures, people of mixed race were more likely to be free than not; in the United States, people of mixed African and European ancestry were more likely to be slaves than

free. *Black* and *slave* were almost synonymous from the late colonial period until the Civil War ended slavery in 1865.

Second, the new republican regime in the United States professed hostility to distinctions based on birth. There was an obvious tension between slavery and the fundamental credo set out in the Declaration of Independence (1776), that all people were "created equal" and entitled to the "unalienable Rights" of "Life, Liberty, and the Pursuit of Happiness." Unlike traditional cultures, in the United States freedom, liberty, and equality were the norm, and thus slavery presented a fundamental contradiction between the nation's political self-identity and its social reality.

Third, unlike in other New World societies, where slaves were more evenly distributed, those in the United States were concentrated in a particular section. By 1804 all of the northern states had either ended slavery outright or adopted gradual emancipation laws which were quickly reducing the slave population to insignificance while creating a society that was unequivocally free and fundamentally antislavery. The South was fully committed to slavery, which even before the American Revolution became its central social and economic institution.

Fourth, the United States contained a large and growing population that found slavery morally unacceptable. Rooted in pietistic and evangelical religious traditions and the libertarian political culture of the Revolution, these Americans were uncompromising and relentless in their opposition to slavery. Political pressure forced these people out of the South, and antislavery, like slavery, became sectionally located. Eventually, the opponents of slavery convinced many of their less pious or idealistic northern neighbors that slavery was morally wrong, corrupting, and dangerous to the nation's political culture, economic well being, and even its military security.

Fifth, unlike other New World slave cultures, the United States was a self-governing democracy. Southerners extolled the virtues of slavery and even argued that slavery made democracy flourish, but northerners saw slavery as inimical to the national democracy. One example illustrates this divide. Most political theorists agree that freedom of speech and the press are vital to a healthy democracy, because without these liberties the citizens are deprived of the opportunity to learn about and debate public issues. Early on, however, southerners rejected any debate over slavery, even though it was emerging as the most divisive social issue in the nation. Not only did southerners make it illegal to criticize slavery or advocate abolition within their region, but they tried to prevent northerners, and the U.S. Congress, from discussing or debating the issue.

Finally, the American constitutional system made it virtually impossible to end slavery through normal political means. The Constitution created a national government of limited powers. No one, either in 1787 when the Constitution was written or in 1861 when the Civil War began, believed that the U.S. Congress had the power to regulate the social and economic institutions within the states, including slavery. Nor could a constitutional amendment solve the problem, because the Constitution required that three-quarters of the states ratify any amendment. Even though the free states had an overwhelming majority of the population, they could not affect the change alone; as long as the slave states voted as a bloc, they could prevent the adoption of any antislavery constitutional amendment. Nor was it conceivable that the politics of the slave states would

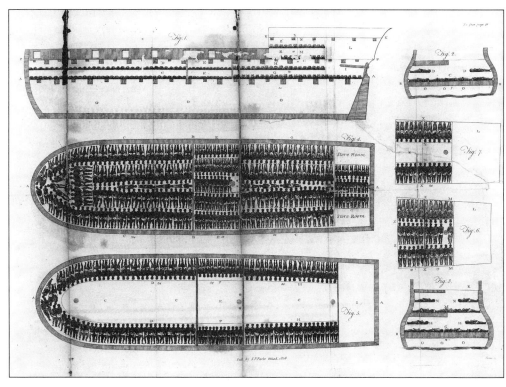

This engraving of a slave ship, created in 1802, illustrates the horrendous conditions under which slaves were transported to the New World. *Library of Congress*

change any time soon. The vast majority of southern whites did not own slaves, and had they voted against the system, change could have been possible. In the antebellum South, however, it was illegal to discuss or circulate antislavery arguments. The few southerners who spoke out against the institution were chased out of the region. Thus there was no opportunity to create an antislavery political constituency. The issue seemed unresolvable and remained a central issue in American politics from the Revolution to the Civil War.

THE POLITICS OF SLAVERY DURING THE REVOLUTION

During the American Revolution, delegates to the Continental Congress had to resolve whether blacks, including recently freed slaves, could serve in the army. In many cultures slaves had been used as soldiers, and even in colonial South Carolina slaves had fought in the militia during the Yamasee War (1715–1716). But in 1775 southerners objected to the service of free blacks in northern militias. Severe manpower needs, the valor of free blacks serving in northern militias, the persistence of free blacks demanding the right to serve, and the willingness of many northerners to free their slaves so they could fight in the war eventually led to black participation in the army. Gen. George Washington, who initially opposed black enlistments, changed his mind on this issue, but few other southerners did.

In the end, the Revolution completely undermined slavery in New England and Pennsylvania and crippled it in New York and New Jersey. The political climate of the revolutionary era led to gradual emancipation statutes or outright abolition in the North, along with the enfranchisement of free blacks in most of that region. Most southern states prohibited black enlistments, and few southern masters voluntarily freed their slaves during and immediately after the Revolution.

SLAVERY IN EARLY NATIONAL POLITICS

The Constitutional Convention accommodated slavery in a variety of ways, including counting slaves for representation, prohibiting Congress from interfering with the African slave trade before 1808, guaranteeing that the national government would suppress slave rebellions if necessary, and giving masters a right to claim their runaway slaves in any state. Many northern Antifederalists cited the first three of these provisions in their opposition to the Constitution.

Benjamin Franklin, in his role as president of the Pennsylvania Abolition Society, petitioned the First Congress to legislate against the African slave trade. This action led to an extraordinarily nasty attack on Franklin by southern congressmen. Less controversial was the readoption of the Northwest Ordinance, first passed by the Articles of Confederation Congress in 1787. This law banned slavery in the territory north of the Ohio River, but it provided no enforcement mechanism. The new Congress also organized the territories south of the Ohio, with an implicit understanding that slavery would be legal there. In 1791 a conflict between Virginia and Pennsylvania over the kidnapping of a free black and the extradition of the kidnappers led, in 1793, to the first fugitive slave law, which also set out the procedures for the return of fugitives from justice. Later in the decade southerners objected when free blacks in Pennsylvania petitioned Congress to prevent interstate kidnapping. In 1807, with little acrimony, Congress banned the African slave trade, starting on January 1, 1808. However, Congress provided virtually no funds to enforce the law, and until the administration of Abraham Lincoln took office in 1861 neither Congress nor the executive branch showed much interest in actually suppressing the trade.

MISSOURI COMPROMISE, THE GAG RULE, TEXAS ANNEXATION, AND THE RISE OF ANTISLAVERY POLITICS

In 1819 Missouri sought admission to the Union as a slave state, which led to a two-year congressional debate over slavery in the western territories. In the end Congress agreed, by a slim majority, to a compromise devised by Sen. Henry Clay of Kentucky. The Missouri Compromise allowed Missouri to enter the Union as a slave state but banned slavery in the rest of the western territories north and west of Missouri. The debate signaled the beginning of four decades of increasing political tensions over slavery. On the heels of the Missouri debate came the discovery of the Denmark Vesey conspiracy, a planned rebellion of slaves and free blacks in Charleston (1822); the emergence of militant opposition to slavery by free blacks and their northern white allies (1829–1831); and the Nat Turner Rebellion (1831), which left scores of whites and more than a hundred blacks dead in Virginia.

Led by William Lloyd Garrison, who began publishing his newspaper *The Liberator* in 1831, the new abolitionist movement demanded that southerners take immediate steps to begin to end slavery. Most abolitionists in the 1830s did not participate in traditional electoral politics. Rather, they flooded Congress with petitions on slavery, which led southern members of Congress to demand a "gag rule," preventing anyone from reading these petitions on the floor of Congress. From 1836 until 1844 the House maintained a gag rule, leading to vituperative debates on the power of Congress to reject, without a hearing, the petitions of citizens. Although they won a temporary victory in the House, in the end the supporters of slavery strengthened their opponents, who used the gag rule to make an important political point to the North: slavery threatened the liberty not only of blacks but of whites as well.

THE MEXICAN WAR, THE COMPROMISE OF 1850, AND THE CRISIS OF THE UNION

By the mid-1830s slavery had become the most dangerous element in American politics. Although they were proslavery expansionists, Presidents Andrew Jackson and Martin Van Buren refused to annex Texas because of the potential political fallout. Only as a lame duck did the slaveholding John Tyler dare attempt this. Texas annexation not only disrupted domestic politics but led to a war with Mexico, which in turn made slavery the central issue of American politics. Critics of the war saw it as proslavery aggression, designed to steal large portions of Mexico in order to provide new territory for slave settlement. Some of the shrewdest southern politicians, like John C. Calhoun, opposed the Mexican-American War because they correctly understood that it would reopen the issue of slavery in the territories, with potentially devastating results for the South.

This in fact happened. The war placed northern Democrats in a particularly difficult position. Their party supported the war, but if they did too, they might be accused of supporting the expansion of slavery into newly conquered territories. Rep. David Wilmot of Pennsylvania tried to finesse this issue by offering an amendment to an appropriations bill, known as the Wilmot Proviso, which would have banned slavery in any territories acquired from Mexico. Although the proviso passed the House, it failed in the Senate, and it paralyzed politics from 1847 until 1850 and drove a wedge between northern and southern Democrats that would ultimately destroy the party.

In 1840 and 1844 the Liberty Party had run ineffectual antislavery presidential campaigns. In 1848, however, disaffected northern Democrats, joined by most Liberty men, formed the Free Soil Party. Running on this ticket, former president Martin Van Buren won more than 290,000 popular votes and probably took enough votes away from the Democrat Lewis Cass to throw the election to the Whig candidate Gen. Zachary Taylor, a hero of the Mexican-American War. By the time Taylor took office, in March 1849, California was clamoring for admission to the Union as a free state, southern states were seriously discussing secession, and Texans were threatening to invade the New Mexico Territory over a boundary dispute. For the first seven months of 1850 Congress debated an omnibus bill, introduced by Sen. Henry Clay, that would bring California into the Union, create governments for the new territories, settle the Texas-New Mexico dispute, end the slave trade in Washington, D.C., and provide for a stronger fugitive slave law. The bill was designed to settle once again the issue of slavery in American politics. In July President Taylor died and was replaced by Millard Fillmore, a classic doughface—a northern man with southern principles. Fillmore was prepared to sign the bill, but when brought before Congress as a package, the compromise failed. Northerners voted against it because of the new fugitive slave law and southerners opposed it because of California statehood. A rising star in the Democratic Party, Stephen A. Douglas, then picked up the parts of the compromise and one-by-one guided them through Congress.

The Compromise of 1850 headed off secession in the short term but was ultimately doomed. The new fugitive slave act was a mockery of due process and justice, which led to resistance in the North. Southerners, meanwhile, were unhappy with California admission, which shifted the political balance in the Senate to the North. Northern resistance, in the form of state legislation and mobs rescuing fugitive slaves from federal marshals, further exacerbated sectional animosities. In 1854 Senator Douglas, anxious to see a transcontinental railroad, engineered the passage of the Kansas-Nebraska Act, which repealed the Missouri Compromise's ban on slavery in most of the territories west of the Mississippi. Under this new law the issue of slavery in the territories would be determined by a vote of the settlers under a theory known as "popular sovereignty."

Presidents Franklin Pierce (1853–1857) and James Buchanan (1857–1861) did everything in their power to make Kansas a slave state, including supporting fraudulent elections and harassing antislavery settlers while ignoring violence perpetrated by proslavery settlers. The result was a mini–Civil War in the territory known as "bleeding Kansas." In 1858 this policy collapsed when northern Democrats, now led by Douglas, refused to accept Kansas statehood under the proslavery Lecompton Constitution, written by the fraudulently elected convention that met in the town of Lecompton and ratified by a fraudulent election. The Douglas Democrats in the North, who would accept slavery in the territories only if it represented the will of the settlers, broke irrevocably from the southern Democrats and their doughface allies, led by Buchanan, who were prepared to force slavery on the territories at any cost.

In response to the Kansas-Nebraska Act, the Republican Party emerged. Made up of Free Soilers, Liberty Party men, and former Whigs, the party carried eleven northern states in the 1856 presidential election on a platform of prohibiting slavery in all the territories. In *Dred Scott v. Sandford* (1857) the Supreme Court ruled that any national ban on slavery in the territories was unconstitutional. This decision, aimed at the heart of the Republican platform, had no adverse effect on the party. The most succinct and persuasive critique of the decision came from an otherwise obscure Illinois lawyer,

Abraham Lincoln, who challenged Douglas for his U.S. Senate seat in 1858. Lincoln forced Douglas into a series of debates, and while not winning the election, he became, almost overnight, one of the nation's most prominent Republicans. In 1860 Lincoln gained the presidential nomination over better known candidates, such as Sens. William H. Seward of New York and Salmon P. Chase of Ohio. Lincoln ran on a platform of not touching slavery where it existed but also not allowing it to spread further west. He carried every northern state and handily won the election in a four-way race against Douglas running as a regular Democrat, Vice President John C. Breckinridge running as a southern Democrat, and Sen. John Bell of Tennessee running for the newly created Constitutional Union Party.

Facing a president dedicated to ending the spread of slavery, seven states passed ordinances of secession and formed the Confederate States of America. When Lincoln tried to send food and other supplies to a beleaguered fort in the harbor of Charleston, South Carolina, Confederate troops opened fire on the fort. Four more southern states left the Union as civil war began. From the beginning Lincoln claimed that the purpose of the war was to restore the Union, not to end slavery. As he later said in his second inaugural address, however, from the beginning "All knew" that slavery "was somehow the cause of the war." Certainly from the beginning southerners understood this. The Confederate vice president, Alexander Stephens, asserted that slavery was the "cornerstone of the Confederacy." By the end of the war slavery was destroyed, and in the war's aftermath the Constitution was amended to forever abolish bondage and to make citizens of former slaves and enfranchise them. The legacy of slavery would remain in American politics well into the twentieth century, in the form of segregation and disfranchisement. And even at the dawn of the twenty-first century debates over the nature of slavery and the racism it created remained part of American political culture.

See also *Breckinridge Democrats; Calhoun, John C.; Civil War; Compromise of 1850; Free Soil Party; Gag Rule; Kansas-Nebraska Act; Lincoln, Abraham; Mexican-American War; Northwest Ordinance; Republican Party; Secession; Sectionalism; Territorial Expansion; Whig Party.*

PAUL FINKELMAN, UNIVERSITY OF TULSA COLLEGE OF LAW

BIBLIOGRAPHY

Finkelman, Paul. *Dred Scott v. Sandford: A Brief History.* Boston: Bedford Books, 1997.
———. *Slavery and the Founders: Race and Liberty in the Age of Jefferson.* Armonk, N.Y.: M. E. Sharpe, 1996.
Potter, David. *The Impending Crisis, 1848–1861.* New York: Harper and Row, 1976.
Robinson, Donald. *Slavery in the Structure of American Politics, 1765–1820.* New York: Harcourt, Brace, Jovanovich, 1971.

SOCIAL SECURITY

The Social Security Act of 1935 was enacted in the depth of America's Great Depression as a cornerstone of President Franklin D. Roosevelt's New Deal. It was the foundation of what came to be known as the Second New Deal, an array of legislation enacted in 1935. Its immediate purpose was to create grants-in-aid to assist states in providing relief for the destitute aged. Its longer term purpose was to create a retirement pension system for older Americans and a national financing scheme for unemployment insurance.

GRANTS-IN-AID

The grants-in-aid for impoverished elders enjoyed wide popularity, since the plight of the old in the Depression was most alarming. States, squeezed by the fall in tax revenues from economic dislocations, were hard pressed to provide sufficient aid; private charities were devastated by declines in contributions, coupled with unprecedented demands for their services; and individual families were often in no position to aid elderly relations, given their own stressed economic circumstances.

Politically, these provisions were most palatable because grants-in-aid were not new, although they had not been employed for public assistance programs in the past. In addition to the aged needy, the grants-in-aid provided states with funds to be applied for dependent children, for the blind, for programs in public health, and for maternal and child welfare programs. The Townsend movement, which arose in California, had frightened the political establishment with its more overtly socialist aspects and its promise of a $200 per month pension for those at least sixty years of age. It was named after Francis Townsend, a physician who devised the concept and proselytized endlessly for its adoption. In addition, the aged poor were regarded with less disdain and prejudice than needy people of a younger age. Assistance to the aged was not believed to present the same dangers of demoralization and destruction of the work ethic, which was the common fear in dealing with the unemployed and the working poor.

UNEMPLOYMENT INSURANCE

The provisions for unemployment insurance were less well received. Only Wisconsin had an unemployment compensation system, which had been created in 1932 in the midst of the economic crisis. The unemployment provisions of the Social Security Act followed the basics of a plan originally put forward in 1934 in a bill cosponsored by Sen. Robert F. Wagner (D-N.Y.) and Rep. David J. Lewis (D-Md.). A federal payroll tax was imposed on all businesses, but in states that enacted unemployment compensation statutes, employers were allowed to deduct payments to the state unemployment system from federal tax owed.

Although unemployment compensation was new to the United States, it had been long established in most industrialized European nations (as had old-age pensions), where it had functioned moderately well. The Roosevelt plan had the advantage of leaving the administration of the new system essentially to the states. In addition, no state was compelled to establish the program, but the incentive to do so was almost irresistible because the taxation was carried out in any case and the full deductibility provision meant that there was virtually no cost to the participating state government. Without the federal payroll tax, however, a state that enacted the program would have found itself at a competitive disadvantage in commercial competition with other states that had not enacted it.

RETIREMENT PENSIONS

The heart of the Social Security Act was the provision for old-age retirement pensions, and this proved the most controversial as well. The ideas for the act had been developed by Arthur J. Altmeyer, the former secretary of Wisconsin's Industrial Commission, who would go on to serve as Social Security commissioner from 1937 to 1953, and Edwin E. Witte, the executive director of the Committee on Economic Security and a professor of economics at the University of Wisconsin. They looked at schemes that had been proposed back in the Progressive era by political thinkers and that had been established in Europe and in Wisconsin.

Social Security would guarantee a minimum standard of living to millions of elderly people and thus reduce poverty among a large segment of the American population. At the same time, it would encourage some persons to leave the active work force, thereby reducing unemployment and lifting wages for the workers who remained active. This combination of jobs, pensions, and retirement was expected to alleviate both poverty and unemployment. The program was designed to be self-financed rather than dependent on general revenues.

Employers and employees shared the costs. Half of the cost of the program's "premiums" were to come from a tax on workers' wages, collected by the employer; the other half was to come from a payroll tax on all businesses. The taxes went into effect January 1, 1937, with the first benefits scheduled for payment in 1942, although a revision of the act in 1939 moved the date up to 1940.

Many Republicans in both houses of Congress fought the provisions of the act, although many initial opponents voted for the final bill out of political necessity. Private insurance companies lobbied against the old-age pension provisions as unfair competition with their private plans. A proposed amendment to the plan that would exempt companies from paying the tax if they could demonstrate that they had an acceptable retirement system in place was defeated. A major political obstacle for Social Security was overcome when the U.S. Supreme Court in *Helvering v. Davis* (1937) upheld the constitutionality of the act.

EXPANSION AND ACCOMMODATION

Republican Party opposition to Social Security has faded over the decades since its adoption, with the unsuccessful 1964 presidential campaign of Sen. Barry Goldwater (R-Ariz.) standing as a notable exception. The Social Security Administration has proven a model of efficiency, with the lowest administrative costs of any large federal program. Over the years, Social Security coverage has been expanded significantly. Congress included farmers and the self-employed in 1950; provided disability benefits in 1956; added health insurance for the aged in 1965 (Medicare) and health care benefits for the disabled in 1972; and in 1972 voted a large increase in benefits and an automatic annual adjustment based on the inflation rate, as measured by the consumer price index. Finally, in 2000, an exceptionally tight labor market in a booming economy permitted Congress to eliminate provisions long a part of the law that placed limits on the amount of income Social Security recipients sixty-five years of age or older could earn without losing benefits.

In the closing decades of the twentieth century, concern grew about the long-term solvency of the system because of population trends, which included the looming retirement of millions of baby boomers, a declining proportion of contributors remaining in the workforce in relation to the number of beneficiaries, and the increasing longevity of senior citizens. Republicans generally promoted the idea of providing greater benefits in retirement by allowing a portion of a person's Social Security contribution to be set aside in private investment accounts linked to the stock market. Democrats insisted that any investment of Social Security to be made in the stock market or elsewhere should be made by the system as a whole, modeled on the state employee retirement funds.

See also *Great Depression; New Deal; Roosevelt, Franklin D.*

PATRICK M. O'NEIL, BROOME COMMUNITY COLLEGE,
STATE UNIVERSITY OF NEW YORK

BIBLIOGRAPHY

Derthick, Martha. *Policymaking for Social Security.* Washington, D.C.: Brookings Institution, 1979.

———. "Social Security Act." In *The Encyclopedia of the United States Congress,* ed. Donald C. Bacon, Roger H. Davidson, and Morton Keller. New York: Simon and Schuster, 1995.

Lubove, Roy M. *The Struggle for Social Security, 1900–1935.* Cambridge: Harvard University Press, 1968.

Schlesinger, Arthur M., Jr. *The Age of Roosevelt: The Coming of the New Deal.* Boston: Houghton Mifflin, 1959.

SOCIALIST PARTY

The inception of the Socialist Party marked a unique, brief era of leftist organizational unity. Founded in 1901 by New York attorney Morris Hillquit and railroad worker and labor leader Eugene Debs, the Socialist Party brought together the Social Democratic Party; Social Laborites; Christian Socialists; a wing of the Socialist Labor Party; and followers of Henry George, Edward Bellamy, and assorted populist sympathizers. Rapid growth and early success continued through the 1912 presidential election, when Debs earned 6 percent of the votes cast and some twelve hundred Socialist Party candidates won state and local elections, including seventy-nine mayoral races.

Despite the party's continued strong showing in the 1916 and 1920 elections, World War I took a toll on the Socialist Party. Although party members were already persecuted for their opposition to the war, the Sedition Act of 1918 resulted

Former American Railway Union president Eugene Debs was the Socialist candidate in five of the first six presidential elections of the twentieth century. Having been convicted of sedition in 1918 for an antiwar speech, Debs ran for the presidency in 1920 from the Atlanta federal penitentiary. *Tamiment Institute Library, New York University*

in additional arrests and prevented the Socialist Party from using the mail to communicate with branches beyond its East Coast and Midwest bases. While many, including Debs, were being sent to prison for either their pacifist views or Sedition Act violations, the 1917 Bolshevik Revolution in Russia led by Vladimir Lenin further hastened the party's demise.

By 1919, Leninist sympathizers threatened the Socialist Party leadership. A schism ensued, resulting in the expulsion of radical party elements and the invalidation of the national executive committee elections. Thereafter, the Socialist Party and the Communist Party became two distinct organizations with decidedly different agendas. By breaking with its labor roots, the Socialist Party lost its legitimacy as an agent of radical social action. Debs's death in 1926 signaled the end of the worker-oriented party and the start of a more urban-middle-class-centered party under Norman Thomas's leadership. The Socialist Party, which had 9,500 members in 1929, experienced a revival between 1929 and 1934: party membership increased during the Great Depression to almost 17,000 in 1932, when Thomas polled almost 900,000 votes in the presidential election, and to 20,000 in 1934.

Many new members were young militants who increasingly disagreed with the party's old guard. Until Hillquit died in 1933, the old guard held their own, but they lost their grip thereafter. At the 1934 party convention in Detroit, the young militant wing, joined by Thomas and the Milwaukee mayor, Daniel W. Hoan, passed a new Socialist Party declaration of principles that the old guard believed encouraged too forcefully the nonelectoral seizure of power and sympathized too greatly with Soviet Russia. The old guard formally broke away in 1936 and formed the Social Democratic Federation (SDF). Party membership fell to 12,000 in 1936 and shrank to 6,500 the following year. More important, Thomas garnered only 187,000 votes during the 1936 presidential election and less than 100,000 in 1940.

From 1933 to 1940 the Socialist Party experienced further internal strains by criticizing President Franklin D. Roosevelt and the New Deal. Party members viewed New Deal programs as more sympathetic to corporate interests than to organized labor's concerns. Remaining party members split over wartime policy, with Thomas leading a pacifist faction; and the party lost any influence it had as it was effectively coopted by Roosevelt. Only in the cities of Bridgeport, Connecticut, and Milwaukee, Wisconsin, did the old Socialist Party maintain a real presence. However, Thomas continued to run as the Socialist presidential candidate through the 1948 election.

In the post–World War II era, all radicalism was suspect. Although the Socialists made inroads into the Congress of Industrial Organizations and helped organize Detroit autoworkers and southern sharecroppers, the party disintegrated as an organization. The party continued to field a presidential candidate until the 1960 election, when it failed to run a candidate. Radicals shifted their emphasis from organized labor to civil rights and, later, worked against the war in Vietnam.

In the early 1960s the Democratic Socialist Organizing Committee (DSOC), the New American Movement (NAM), and the Students for a Democratic Society (SDS) became the main organizational vehicles for the New Left. The SDS faded after Martin Luther King's assassination in 1968 and the Paris Peace Accords in 1973. Meanwhile NAM devoted its energies to feminism, gay rights, and local community organizing into the early 1980s.

The DSOC continued to operate in the old socialist manner as the left wing of the New Deal coalition—not as a separate political party as much as a socialist force within the Democratic Party and the labor movement. The DSOC was successful in attracting activists such as machinist union leader William Winpisinger, feminist Gloria Steinem, and gay rights activist Harry Britt. Bernard Sanders, member of Congress from Vermont who was elected in 1991, was the first self-avowed socialist elected to Congress in decades and perhaps the best known since Victor Berger served in the House of Representatives during the 1920s.

NAM and DSOC completed a formal merger in 1983 and emerged as the Democratic Socialists of America (DSA). The DSA brought together for the first time since World War I the disparate segments of leftist opinion, including the SDF and former socialists and communists. Although the American left was in disarray in the late 1960s and the administrations of Richard M. Nixon, Ronald Reagan, George Bush, and Bill Clinton were by and large conservative, a kind of socialist revival occurred at the end of the twentieth century. Although membership remained low, Socialist Party influences such as government-supported health care, minimum wage, and human rights were more apparent in the national political debate than at any time since the 1960s. In addition, more than one socialist faction had fielded a candidate in every presidential election since 1976.

See also *Communist Party; Labor Politics and Policies; Red Scare; Third Parties.*

MARK J. CONNOLLY, DEVRY INSTITUTE OF TECHNOLOGY

BIBLIOGRAPHY

Kraditor, Aileen S. *The Radical Persuasion, 1890–1917: Aspects of the Intellectual History and Historiography of Three American Radical Organizations.* Baton Rouge: Louisiana State University Press, 1981.

Miller, Sally M. *Victor Berger and the Promise of Constructive Socialism, 1910–1920.* Westport, Conn.: Greenwood, 1973.

Warren, Frank A. *An Alternative Vision: The Socialist Party in the 1930s.* Bloomington: Indiana University Press, 1974.

SOFT MONEY AND TWENTIETH-CENTURY POLITICS

Soft money, the unlimited funds that can, under current election law, be donated to the political parties for what have been called "party-building activities," became a campaign issue in the 2000 presidential race.

The post–Watergate federal election laws of 1974, while restricting an individual's donation to a specific candidate to $1,000, allowed those same individuals, businesses, unions, and others to contribute unrestricted amounts to the parties for such ostensibly admirable activities as voter registration and get-out-the vote campaigns. It was not until 1988, however, that a torrent of soft money donations threatened to overwhelm the electoral process. In that year, fundraisers for Democrats and Republicans alike came up with the idea of asking wealthy contributors to make large donations to the parties; the parties, in turn, would use the monies collected to directly support their respective tickets, using the increasingly transparent justification that the direct mail and campaign commercials that were purchased with soft money merely informed voters on issues relevant to the campaign and did not benefit individual candidates. The advertisements, however, seemed to point out one candidate's failings or shortcomings and were initiated and paid for by groups friendly to the candidate's opponent.

In the 1996 election campaign, soft money contributions to both parties amounted to more than $262 million, with the Republicans holding a slight edge. It was estimated that the amount donated in 2000 would range as high as $500 million, as wealthy individuals, corporations, unions, and others with interest in influencing the nation's electoral choices (and subsequent legislative actions) pledged to donate at record paces. Both major parties decried the practice in public but pursued it aggressively in private. Both houses of Congress passed campaign reform bills in 1999, but Senate Republican filibusters prevented enactment.

See also *Campaign Finance; Political Action Committees.*

RON dePAOLO, INDEPENDENT AUTHOR

BIBLIOGRAPHY

Moore, John, ed. *Elections A to Z.* Washington, D.C.: CQ Press, 1999.
Selecting the President: From 1789 to 1996. Washington, D.C.: Congressional Quarterly, 1997.

SPANISH-AMERICAN WAR

The Spanish-American War (1898), between the United States and Spain, grew out of the Cuban independence movement. The war ended with the United States acquiring former Spanish territories in the Caribbean and the Pacific and marked the decline of Spain and the emergence of the United States to world power status.

The war was coined "a splendid little war" by U.S. Secretary of State John Hay days after the decisive U.S. victory in Santiago de Cuba. Because of the war's brevity and relatively little loss of American life, Hay's characterization was embraced by Americans and in the early historical record as well. The role of Cuban revolutionaries before and during the war was minimized, and the Filipino uprising that followed the war was viewed as the action of a misguided people rather than as a consequence of unwelcomed U.S. dominance.

SPANISH RULE IN CUBA

The sugar-rich island that lay ninety miles off U.S. shores in the Caribbean had long appealed to expansionists. Americans believed it was the U.S. mission to bring progress in the guise of democracy and free-market capitalism to lesser-developed societies. This belief in a "manifest destiny" propelled expansionists to seek an outlet beyond U.S. borders. Similarly, industrialists deemed new foreign markets as essential to the economic welfare of the country, while naval expansionists expounded on the benefits of global strategic ports. U.S. officials on several occasions had considered annexing Cuba or buying it outright from Spain, but domestic political concerns in the United States, complicated by slavery and race, always stopped any annexation. Ultimately, the United States conceded Spanish sovereignty and waited for an inevitably weakened Spain to relinquish its control over the island.

Cuban separatists had been in perpetual revolt since 1868, when the Ten Years' War (1868–1878) first pitted Cuban insurgents against Spanish imperialism. Led by Cuban intellectual José Martí in exile in the United States, a better-organized independence movement began in earnest in February 1895. The Cubans rebelled against Spanish maladministration and a host of social and economic ills. The revolutionary movement cut across class and racial lines. Guerrilla tactics proved successful until Spanish reinforcements arrived and Spanish general Valeriano Weyler y Nicolau, known as Butcher Weyler to Americans, implemented a reconcentration policy.

Weyler placed civilians in reconcentration camps and then instructed his troops to destroy anything of possible use to the rebels throughout the countryside, including crops and animals. Malnutrition and disease ravaged the camp populations, but that increased revolutionary fervor among the rebels. Weyler's policy also had a profound impact on public opinion in the United States.

The U.S. press correspondents who were sent to Cuba to cover the war frequently exaggerated events there, especially regarding Weyler's tactics. The *New York Journal* and the *New York World,* which were owned by newspaper moguls William Randolph Hearst and Joseph Pulitzer, respectively, were engaged in a fierce battle over readership. Competition increased as reporters from each paper wrote increasingly lurid and detailed accounts of Spanish atrocities against the helpless Cubans. These sensationalist techniques, which were dubbed "yellow journalism," inflamed U.S. public opinion against Spain and pressured the U.S. government to act.

Initially, President Grover Cleveland proclaimed U.S. neutrality when hostilities broke out. After William McKinley took office in March 1897, pressure from the public and Congress began to mount. McKinley offered to mediate between the two sides and urged the Spanish to discontinue their policy of reconcentration. The Spaniards recalled Weyler and offered the Cubans an autonomous government, but the insurgents rejected the proposal with the cry of "independence or death."

The Spaniards resented the United States for interfering and blamed U.S. support for rebel success. The United States deployed the battleship USS *Maine* to Havana harbor in January 1898 for the stated purpose of protecting U.S. citizens and their property from Spanish loyalists. Public outrage against Spain rose to a frenzy when on February 9 the *New York Journal* published a private letter from Spanish ambassador Enrique Dupuy de Lôme to a friend in Havana, criticizing President McKinley as a spineless politician. Front page headlines of the *Journal* read: "The Worst Insult to the United States in Its History."

WAR BREAKS OUT

Less than a week after the letter was made public, war fever climaxed when news hit that the battleship *Maine* had exploded in Havana harbor; 266 U.S. sailors were killed. Headlines screamed for war as the yellow press immediately blamed Spain for the explosion. "Remember the Maine!" became the nation's battle cry overnight.

President McKinley urged restraint until a cause of the explosion could be found. War fever continued to rise, however, as daily headlines called for war to free the Cuban people and to avenge the *Maine.* War seemed inevitable, despite the Naval Court of Inquiry's findings that a mine had caused the blast, but not enough evidence existed to allocate blame. The debate still continues over the cause of the explosion.

The wreck the USS *Maine* sits at the bottom of Havana Harbor. *National Archives*

Desperate to hold onto its empire and fearful of political backlash at home, the Spanish government was reluctant to comply with U.S. demands to implement an immediate armistice. After evacuating Americans from the island, McKinley bowed to public and political pressure and called for U.S. intervention in Cuba. Congress declared war on April 25. To emphasize that its motives were altruistic, Congress also adopted a resolution put forth by Sen. Henry M. Teller of Colorado. The Teller Resolution declared that the United States was taking up arms on behalf of Cuban independence and would not annex the island once Spain was defeated.

The war lasted four months and was fought in Cuba and the Philippines. The United States suffered more casualties from disease than it lost in battle. As the army organized and trained a battle-ready force to invade Cuba, Commodore George Dewey's squadron destroyed the small, decrepit Spanish force of wooden vessels in Manila Bay, Philippines. The battle, which took place on May 1, was over in a matter of hours, but he had to wait months for army troops to arrive. By August the U.S. flag flew over Manila.

The U.S. squadron in the Caribbean successfully blockaded the Spanish fleet in the port of Santiago de Cuba. Meanwhile, U.S. troops composed of regulars, national guard troops, and volunteer forces, including Theodore Roosevelt's Rough Riders, landed in Cuba. American and Cuban ground forces attacked and defeated the Spanish in Santiago, and the Spanish fleet was destroyed trying to escape to open seas. On July 22 peace negotiations opened, and an armistice was signed August 12, 1898.

On economic, legal, moral, and racial grounds, anti-imperialists within the United States opposed the annexation of the Philippines. After an intense debate within the U.S. Senate, however, expansionists won. By the Treaty of Paris, ratified in February 1899, the United States acquired Puerto Rico and Guam and agreed to pay Spain $20 million for the Philippines.

The Cuban people, whom the United States had pledged to help free in its declaration of war, gained their independence from Spain but came under American domination. The Teller Resolution thwarted outright U.S. annexation of the island, but the Platt Amendment (1902) limited Cuban sovereignty and stimulated a dependent relationship with the United States. The Platt Amendment, which was written into the Cuban Constitution, allowed the United States to intervene at its discretion if it feared that Cuba's political stability was threatened. It also required Cuba to designate land for a U.S. naval base at Guantanamo. Filipino insurgents, who had been fighting the Spaniards since 1896, similarly opposed U.S. dominance. The United States waged a four-year war against the Filipinos before the insurgents surrendered.

The U.S. victory over Spain brought the United States into the international arena as a world power. The flood of expansionist sentiment—so vital in its support of the war effort—waned after World War I. However, U.S. interference and intervention in Latin America and the Caribbean persisted until President Franklin D. Roosevelt proclaimed the Good Neighbor Policy in 1933.

See also *Manifest Destiny; McKinley, William; Roosevelt, Theodore; Territorial Expansion.*

APRIL L. BROWN, UNIVERSITY OF ARKANSAS

BIBLIOGRAPHY

Offner, John L. *An Unwanted War: The Diplomacy of the United States and Spain Over Cuba, 1895–1898.* Chapel Hill: University of North Carolina Press, 1992.

Pérez, Louis A., Jr. *The War of 1898: The United States and Cuba in History and Historiography.* Chapel Hill: University of North Carolina Press, 1998.

Trask, David F. *The War with Spain in 1898.* New York: Macmillan, 1981.

Traxel, David. *1898: The Birth of the American Century.* New York: Alfred Knopf, 1998.

SQUARE DEAL

President Theodore Roosevelt labeled his Progressivist administration (1901–1909) the "Square Deal"—the first administration to adopt a label. Roosevelt demonstrated that in politics, as in commercial ventures, a promotional slogan can be all-important. By calling his administration's programs the Square Deal, he gave them a pleasant and easily remembered tag. It paid off well in the 1904 elections when speeches, signs, and buttons could summon the idea of the administration's program with a two-word phrase. It is not surprising that President Franklin D.

Roosevelt, Theodore's cousin, would later call his reformist program the "New Deal."

One of Roosevelt's first Square Deal acts was to create the Department of Commerce and Labor (later divided), which was to assist commerce and help control both corporations and unions. The Justice Department also began suits against trusts that indulged in monopolistic practices. The most famous of the antitrust suits was against the Northern Securities Company, a railroad monopoly in the Northwest put together by J. P. Morgan, E. H. Harriman, and James J. Hill. Despite his image as a trust-buster, Roosevelt opposed concentration in commerce and industry only if a particular monopoly or oligopoly took advantage of its market share to damage consumer interests or to engage in unfair, anticompetitive trade practices.

Roosevelt personally mediated several serious strikes—especially the national coal strike of 1902. The Hepburn Act (1906) added considerable powers to the Interstate Commerce Commission (established 1887). In the area of product regulation, the Pure Food and Drug Act (1906) and the Meat Inspection Act (1906) were also passed.

Interestingly, there was little opposition to his drive for irrigation and reclamation projects in the western states, and in 1902 Congress enacted the Newlands Reclamation Act, which provided federal funding for projects such as dams, canals, and reservoirs—opening new lands for cultivation and supplying cheap electrical power for the West. Fear of splitting the Republican Party caused Roosevelt to avoid the issue of tariff reform altogether.

The Square Deal could also be felt in foreign policy. American naval forces were greatly increased, and the nation undertook the construction of the Panama Canal, which had enormous benefits for U.S. commerce and defense interests. U.S. diplomacy became increasingly forceful and more global, with Roosevelt personally mediating an end to the Russo-Japanese War, defending the Monroe Doctrine in the second Venezuelan crisis, and intervening in several Latin American crises to maintain stability, such as in Cuba and the Dominican Republic. As a result of the second Venezuelan crisis, Roosevelt proclaimed the Roosevelt Corollary to the Monroe Doctrine, which asserted that, as the defender of the Western Hemisphere, the United States had the right and the duty to mediate international disputes, keep order, and enforce international law in that region.

By his activism in setting up the Square Deal's domestic program, as well as pursuing its related military and foreign policy, Roosevelt returned the presidency to the prestige and power that it had enjoyed in the early republic and under Lincoln, setting the stage for the modern presidency.

See also *New Deal; Roosevelt, Theodore.*

PATRICK M. O'NEIL,
BROOME COMMUNITY COLLEGE, STATE UNIVERSITY OF NEW YORK

BIBLIOGRAPHY

Mowey, George E. *The Era of Theodore Roosevelt.* New York: Harper and Row, 1958.

Chessman, G. Wallace. *Theodore Roosevelt and the Politics of Power.* Boston: Little, Brown, 1969.

STATE APPORTIONMENT

For much of the United States's history, the Supreme Court took a laissez faire attitude toward state reapportionment, the process by which legislatures recraft the boundaries of their legislative districts to compensate for population shifts. The high panel long regarded reapportionment as a nonjusticiable political exercise best handled by individual states.

By the beginning of the 1960s, some state legislatures had not redrawn their legislative boundary lines in decades. Failure to adjust legislative boundaries for population shifts, coupled with the growth of the urban and suburban population and the decline of the rural population, spawned some stark discrepancies in political power. In California, for example, a state senate district in Los Angeles had about 6 million people, whereas a rural district had just fourteen thousand residents. Though the former district had 429 times more people than the latter district, both had an equal amount of power in the state senate.

The Court thrust itself headlong into state reapportionment with a spate of decisions in the 1960s. In 1962 the high panel ruled in *Baker v. Carr,* a reapportionment case from Tennessee, that citizens could challenge the constitutionality of state legislative reapportionment plans on the grounds of denial of equal protection of the laws under the Fourteenth Amendment.

In 1963 the Court, in *Gray v. Sanders,* struck down Georgia's system of voting in statewide and congressional primary elections. The Court said that the voting system deprived citizens of equal protection of the laws. In the February 1964 case of *Wesberry v. Sanders,* the Court declared that one person's vote in a congressional election should be worth as much as another's "as nearly as is practicable." The case was brought by voters in Georgia's Atlanta-based Fifth Congressional District, which had three times as many residents as the state's more rural Ninth District. In a June 1964 case, *Reynolds v. Sims,* the Court applied to state legislative line drawing the one-person, one-vote principle it had outlined in *Baker.* Chief Justice Earl Warren, writing for the Court in *Reynolds,* said that the Fourteenth Amendment's Equal Protection Clause "requires that the seats in both houses of a bicameral state legislature must be apportioned on a population basis."

The ramifications of those rulings reverberated in virtually every state legislature. In 1964 alone, about forty states were involved in court actions to create more equally populated districts. Critics argued that the *Reynolds* decision abrogated states' rights. The Court's decision was vehemently opposed by rural legislators, who long dominated the state legislatures and benefited politically from legislatures' failure to reapportion. Other detractors said that state referenda—not Supreme Court decisions—should determine how states reapportion their legislatures.

In Congress a coalition of Republicans and southern Democrats sought to nullify or restrict the Supreme Court decisions. Senate Minority Leader Everett Dirksen (R-Ill.) advocated a constitutional amendment permitting state legislatures to apportion one house on a basis other than population. Amendment supporters said states should be allowed to develop their own reapportionment plans. But liberals and civil rights advocates who opposed the amendment said that not using population as a basis for reapportionment could discriminate against black voters. In August 1965 and April 1966 Dirksen fell seven votes short of achieving the two-thirds majority required for approval of a constitutional amendment.

In the meantime, Dirksen helped lead a drive to encourage states to petition Congress for a constitutional convention to consider the issue of reapportionment. By March 1967, thirty-two states had passed such resolutions, two states short of the thirty-four required by the Constitution to call a convention. By the end of 1967 the once-heated debate on state reapportionment had significantly waned.

See also *Apportionment; Constitutional Amendments; Gerrymandering; Reapportionment Cases;* Shaw v. Reno.

GREGORY L. GIROUX, CONGRESSIONAL QUARTERLY

BIBLIOGRAPHY

Congressional Quarterly Weekly Report, February 5, 1965, 189–198; August 6, 1965, 1541–1542, 1569–1574; December 17, 1965, 2472–2473; April 15, 1966, 819–820; April 22, 1966, 827–828; March 24, 1967, 439–440.

Moore, John L., ed. *Congressional Quarterly's Guide to U.S. Elections.* 3d ed. Washington, D.C.: Congressional Quarterly, 1994.

STATE GOVERNMENT

States are an integral part of government in the United States. On the one hand, the states possess significant powers and a semisovereign status. On the other hand, they are bound together within a common political union that limits their authority. This duality complicates the evaluation of state governments but does not diminish their historical or contemporary significance. They have always been responsible for a large proportion of governance in the United States.

The Constitution granted Congress authority to admit new states, which increased from thirteen to thirty-four by the eve of the Civil War and to forty-eight by 1912, when all contiguous U.S. territory was brought into the Union. Alaska and Hawaii were admitted in 1959. Disputes over slavery complicated the admittance process until 1865, when the Thirteenth Amendment to the Constitution forbade slavery.

An important function of state officials was the creation of local governments, which were the civic workhorses during the nineteenth century. The towns, counties, and municipalities performed most public services before the Civil War. Later, as the tasks of government grew, state lawmakers assigned to the localities new civic responsibilities such as police protection, the operation of elementary and high schools, and the maintenance of parks. In the twentieth century states added special-purpose bodies (public authorities) to manage particular tasks such as turnpikes and drainage districts.

State governments have also played an important role in the recruitment of national officials. State legislatures chose U.S. senators until 1913 and also specify districts for representatives to the U.S. House of Representatives. Electors chosen in each state formally select the president of the United States. States with large blocs of electoral votes, such as Virginia (in the early days of the United States), New York, and California, serve as incubators of presidential candidates.

THE REVOLUTIONARY AND CONSTITUTIONAL ERAS

The American Revolution gave birth to the states, whose history originated during the nation's colonial period. Before the quarrel between Americans and Great Britain spiraled into military resistance in 1775, residents of the colonies formed temporary governments outside of royal control and sent delegates to the First Continental Congress. The Second Continental Congress recommended in 1776 that the people of the several "states" create new governments. Eleven of the original colonies responded by writing constitutions, while Connecticut and Rhode Island revised their existing colonial charters.

In their assertions that government was a voluntary compact among individuals, these original constitutions reflected the political ideology in the colonies at the time of the Revolution. The first constitutions placed disproportionate power in popularly elected legislatures, curtailed the powers of governors (Pennsylvania had none at all initially), and enumerated individual liberties in bills of rights. These documents and others adopted later, as well as numerous revisions to ex-

isting constitutions, reflected evolution in political attitudes. The first state constitutions were models for the Constitution of the United States.

State governments helped the patriots' cause by calling out their militias and contributing funds and goods to the war effort. Shortly after independence was secured in 1783 an economic depression swept the country, causing widespread personal indebtedness and acts of civil disobedience, such as Shays's Rebellion in 1786 and 1787. Many states adopted paper money laws and delayed tax collections to relieve the distress.

Nationalists condemned these actions and lamented the inability of the government under the Articles of Confederation to tame "the wicked projects" in the states, as James Madison phrased his criticism. In 1787 delegates to the Constitutional Convention in Philadelphia wrote a new Constitution that enhanced the authority of the central government and significantly curtailed the powers of states. The new framework created a federal system that allocated responsibilities between the states and the Union. The actions taken by the national government were the "supreme Law of the Land," while the states retained many powers. Yet the division of powers remained imprecise, laying the groundwork for constitutional disputes in the future.

THE EARLY REPUBLIC AND THE "MIDDLE PERIOD"

Despite a meager administrative capacity during the early republic (1789–1820s), state government played a vital role in the economy. Thinking at the time viewed state government as an inherent part of the community that officials were expected to nurture and protect. This outlook produced laws that granted special privileges to individual businesses and invested public funds in transportation projects. New York's Erie Canal, which opened in 1825, epitomized this type of state mercantilist promotion. The canal's success inspired imitations by other states such as Ohio, which developed an extensive system of canals, and Pennsylvania, which sponsored a main-line canal and rail link from Philadelphia to Pittsburgh.

The panic of 1837 and an ensuing depression undercut the enthusiasm for state internal improvements and caused some states to default on their transportation debts. The backlash to this misfortune produced a wave of constitutional revisions that restricted the ability of states to borrow money for public works projects.

In 1950 the economic historian Carter Goodrich called these restrictions on states a "revulsion against internal improvements" that produced a new policy era after 1837. During this "middle period" (1837–1877), reformers imposed numerous restrictions on state legislatures: meetings were shifted from an annual to a biennial basis and gubernatorial and judicial influence was enhanced.

By the 1830s the democratization of politics that had been occurring since 1800 had broadened into a general criticism of publicly bestowed privilege. Reflective of this development was the enactment of general laws that standardized the incorporation of businesses and banks. The states also experimented with regulation of business, public health, and morals. During the middle period, states provided free public education; benevolent institutions that housed the poor, orphaned, and infirm; and authorization for cities to create uniformed police.

The autonomy of the states grew during the middle decades of the nineteenth century. The courts contributed to this trend by articulating the doctrine of police powers, which established a firmer legal basis for state efforts to protect the health, safety, welfare, and morals of their citizens. The dominance of Jacksonian Democrats in Congress after 1838 contributed to a restriction of federal activities. Attacks on slavery prodded southerners to emphasize states' rights. The weakened bonds of the federal system became apparent in 1860 and 1861 when eleven southern states seceded from the Union and formed the Confederate States of America, events that triggered the Civil War.

The northern states played an important role in suppressing the rebellion. They administered the military draft; raised volunteer units; and levied taxes that helped to arm their troops, fund bounties for enlistees, and assist the families of combatants. After the war the defeated states of the Confederacy were controlled by coalitions of non–Confederates who instituted numerous reforms, such as the provision for public schools.

In 1867 Congress provided for the readmission of former Confederate states contingent on their adoption of acceptable constitutions and ratification of the Fourteenth Amendment (approved in 1868). This constitutional reform prohibited states from depriving individuals of fundamental liberties, including equal protection of the law. The Fifteenth Amendment (1870) prohibited state officials from denying the right to vote on account of race or former slave status. Southern states circumvented this restriction and disfranchised most African Americans by 1900.

THE GILDED AGE AND THE PROGRESSIVE ERA

The expansion of the West, industry, and population in the generations following the Civil War transformed the nation and posed new challenges for government. States responded to industrial change with a battery of statutes between the 1870s and the 1920s. The states adopted new regulations for business, especially railroads and utilities; enacted public health measures that improved drinking water and built sewer systems; and set standards for food, tenements, and factories. The states also assisted businesses, professions, and farmers; promoted transportation improvements such as good roads; and opened new resources to commercial development and recreational use. Southern states lagged the North in these actions but did use their authority to segregate and disfranchise African Americans. Before the 1930s no state did much to help the poor, the unemployed, or workers who wanted to bargain collectively or use strikes as a bargaining tool.

Reform blossomed during the Progressive era (1900–1916), when state governments enacted innovations in many policy areas. Reducing corruption in state and big-city governments was a top priority of political reformers. Although critics exaggerated the problem, the movement to eliminate graft and the influence of machine bosses produced a flurry of measures such as the secret ballot and primaries to select candidates. States also established greater control over their finances and administration, as well as over local governments. States restricted local borrowing and taxing in the aftermath of heavy local investment in public works after the Civil War.

After 1900 prosperity and new revenues underwrote greater direct state expenditures on public improvements. The adoption in the 1920s of gasoline taxes, which were earmarked for road building, illustrates this trend. Despite operating with part-time legislatures, fragmented administrative systems, and conservative courts that struck down restrictions on business and new taxes, state governments between the 1870s and the 1920s expanded the scope of regulations, developmental programs, and services.

THE STATES SINCE 1933

The states stumbled badly during the Great Depression of the 1930s, when the federal government took the lead in stimulating economic recovery and providing assistance for the unemployed. Some states followed Washington's lead by enacting "little New Deals" that imposed new regulations on business and imposed new taxes, frequently because of federal prodding or stipulations in national programs. Federal leadership in many domestic matters continued during the 1940s and 1950s and into the 1960s. During this New Deal–Great Society era of policy (1933–1972), Washington relied heavily on financial grants-in-aid to achieve policy objectives, such as providing welfare, interstate highways, and higher education.

By the 1970s the expansion of federal programs brought the states into a partnership with the national government in most areas of governance. This created numerous complaints that the states had become mere pawns of national officials. Yet the states had demonstrated independence after World

War II, as illustrated in the establishment of antidiscrimination programs in New York and Massachusetts before the federal government attacked racism. The states also reformed their governments by professionalizing their legislatures (approving better pay) and administrations and by adopting new taxes (additional sales and income taxes). Enhancing their fiscal capacity, the states surpassed local government as a revenue collector during this era.

The conservative tide that swept across the nation in the last quarter of the twentieth century contributed to a resurrection of the states. During the 1930s some political scientists had written off the states as anachronisms; later critics decried congressional preemptions and mandates as undercutting state initiative. The push to restrain federal influence began in the 1970s and flourished during Ronald Reagan's presidency (1981–1989).

The downsizing of the federal establishment shifted some responsibilities to the states. Following the 1977–1982 tax revolt that had stymied new taxation, many states raised additional monies to compensate for the loss of federal grants. States also took the initiative in areas such as protection of minority rights, the environment, and public health, where national politicians wavered. Symbolic of this new activism was the $206 billion settlement in 1998 of lawsuits against tobacco companies to recover Medicaid expenditures for health problems incurred by smoking. The states also got tougher on crime, which was reflected in the adoption of the three-strikes-and-you're-out laws, the restoration of capital punishment, and a boom in prison construction.

THE SIGNIFICANCE OF THE STATES

The significance of the states can be summarized by reference to two principles: that the states possess important powers and that their laws differ. Most other generalizations about state politics derive from these premises.

The states have exercised important powers since their creation. None has been more crucial than the power to tax, which is the essence of any viable government. In the nineteenth century, states supervised policy matters that rarely received congressional attention. Nearly all social policy—schools, family issues (for example, contraception), and the criminal justice process, including police—was virtually a state monopoly. The states promoted economic growth by incorporating businesses and sponsoring public works projects. Before 1887 the little regulation of commerce that existed was undertaken primarily by cities and states.

The states lost much of this exclusive control as the role of the national government expanded after 1887. The rise of cooperative federalism (between the 1930s and the 1970s approximately) blurred the distinction between separate state and national policy responsibilities. The states came to share many functions with Washington, often through federal grant programs such as interstate highways and in conjunction with national priorities such as environmental protection. Negotiations among state and national officials to implement national programs became standard. Nonetheless, the states retained important powers at the end of the twentieth century, and the federal courts reaffirmed the premise that states had semisovereign prerogatives.

The second principle, which is the diversity of state law, rests on the states' semisovereign powers. Because of this constitutional prerogative, differences among the states in statutes, programs, and court rulings are legal and occur frequently. New Hampshire sells packaged liquor through state-operated stores, for example, while neighboring Massachusetts permits private vendors to retail alcohol. Before 1865 both of these states had eliminated slavery, unlike the fifteen southern states that permitted it. Delaware was long famous for its permissive incorporation laws for business, and Nevada for easy divorces. These permutations in policy have been repeated continuously. The proliferation of divergent statutes during the Progressive era triggered a movement to adopt uniform state laws to forestall federal intervention. The effort won a few successes, yet legal diversity remains a fundamental characteristic of U.S. governance despite much federal standardization.

The diversity of state actions traces to several factors. The fifty states are distributed across a large continent that contains significant geographic, economic, cultural, and historical variations. These contrasting conditions have affected both elections and policy making among the states. The politics of urbanized states in the Northeast, for example, have tended to orient more closely around ethnic group differences and social welfare issues than have the politics in the Great Plains and Rocky Mountain states. Historically, political parties have exercised greater influence in some states, such as New York and Illinois, than in other states, such as California and Massachusetts. Southern states are historically distinct in this regard because the Democratic Party gained a monopoly in the region between the 1890s and the 1960s. Moreover, state legislative districts are much smaller than are constituencies for the U.S. House of Representatives and the Senate. As a result, candidates for state office face more homogeneous sets of voters than do politicians who run for Congress.

The existence of decentralized, semisovereign state authority has affected U.S. politics in various ways. One school of thought views the states as laboratories of democracy, in which the states' policy experiments serve as models for other states and the U.S. Congress. Congress has copied state laws on numerous occasions (for example, female suffrage). Other state innovations have spread across the nation, winning adoption in all or most the states; gasoline taxes are one example.

Others believe that federalism has constrained the states. A key premise of this view is that states compete against each other to attract and retain private businesses. To attract private enterprise, states are reluctant to regulate business, support unionization, or levy high taxes. This thinking has prompted some observers to predict that the welfare reform act of 1996 would cause a "race to the bottom," whereby each state would endeavor to spend less than its neighbors spend on the poor. The effect of returning welfare to state control is not clear, but history records that the states have copied and competed with one another.

See also *Federalism; Local Government; States' Rights/Sovereignty, Territorial Government and New State Formation.*

BALLARD C. CAMPBELL, NORTHEASTERN UNIVERSITY

BIBLIOGRAPHY

Brock, William R. *Investigation and Responsibility: Public Responsibility in the United States, 1865–1900.* New York: Cambridge University Press, 1984.

Graves, W. Brooke. *American State Government.* Boston: D.C. Heath, 1946.

Gray, Virginia, Russell L. Hanson, and Herbert Jacob. *Politics in the American States: A Comparative Analysis.* Washington, D.C. CQ Press, 1999.

Novak, William J. *The People's Welfare: Law and Regulation in Nineteenth-Century America.* Chapel Hill: University of North Carolina Press, 1996.

Patterson, James T. *The New Deal and the States: Federalism in Transition.* Princeton: Princeton University Press, 1969.

STATEHOOD

The United States is unique in that, instead of making newly acquired territory into one or more colonies, it usually offers that territory the opportunity to become a state in the Union. The statehood process was established by the Northwest Ordinance of 1787. Since then, thirty-one states have been admitted from territories. Although most transitions from territory to state were smooth, several were not, and one is still pending.

When the new nation was awarded the Northwest Territory by the Treaty of Paris in 1783, it acted to facilitate the entry of that territory into the Union on the same footing as the thirteen original states. In 1787 Congress passed the Northwest Ordinance, which outlined how the Northwest Territory could attain statehood and how it would be governed in the meantime. The territory would be broken up into three to five smaller territories. Until each territory had a population of five thousand, it would be administered by a governor and a council, both appointed by Congress. Once the number of residents exceeded five thousand, they could elect their own assembly with the power to pass laws, although the governor could veto them. Once the number of

residents exceeded sixty thousand, they could write a constitution and apply to Congress for statehood. If the application was approved by a majority in both houses, then the territory became a state. The Northwest Territory was eventually admitted to the Union as five states: Ohio (admitted in 1803), Indiana (1816), Illinois (1818), Michigan (1837), and Wisconsin (1848). This formula for statehood was also applied to territories created from the Old Southwest (Alabama and Mississippi), the Louisiana Purchase, Oregon Country, and the Mexican Cession.

A territory's constitution usually determined the success of its petition for statehood. The constitution was written by the territory's leading citizens, who generally used other state constitutions as models. Although most territorial constitutions differed little from model constitutions, they reflected the socioeconomic idiosyncrasies of time and place. For example, the Ohio constitution of 1803 did not limit state expenditures or state involvement in the economy, a feature it shared with the constitutions of the original thirteen states. By contrast, the Mississippi constitution of 1817 restricted the state's right to charter a bank, as this had become an issue during the intervening years.

SLAVERY AS AN ISSUE

Generally, the only provision in these constitutions that generated any significant debate in Congress was the territory's stance on slavery. Both North and South were intent on maintaining the balance between free states and slave states in the Senate so that neither side could outvote the other. The result was that states were admitted to the Union in pairs of one free and one slave; Indiana–Mississippi and Illinois–Alabama were the first two pairs. When Missouri applied for admission in 1819, there was no free territory seeking statehood. Not until Massachusetts agreed to allow its Maine district to enter the Union as a free state was Missouri permitted entry in 1821 as a slave state.

Five states were admitted between 1821 and 1848: three free (Michigan, Iowa, and Wisconsin) and two slave (Arkansas and Florida). In 1845 the Republic of Texas was brought into the Union as a slave state, thus preserving the balance between free and slave states. However, the admission of Texas, which was never a territory, stirred up a national debate, partly because it was still claimed by Mexico and partly because its constitution permitted slavery.

In 1850 California applied for admission as a free state. Since there was no slave territory seeking admission, southerners fought to keep California out of the Union. Only after much acrimonious debate and the promise of proslavery concessions such as a new, effective fugitive slave law did southern members of Congress permit the admission of California in 1850.

The slavery issue also held up the admission of Kansas to the Union. Throughout the 1850s Kansans were split between two rival "legislatures," one proslavery and one antislavery. In 1858 the proslavery legislature presented its constitution to Congress and asked that Kansas be admitted as a slave state. The debate was long and heated, and Kansas's petition was rejected. In January 1861, while many southern states were seceding from the Union, Kansas was admitted as a free state. Nevada, by contrast, was rushed into the Union in October 1864 so that it could help reelect Lincoln.

POST–CIVIL WAR ENTRANTS TO THE UNION

Although slavery ceased to be an issue after the Civil War, other issues peculiar to a certain territory sometimes delayed statehood. Utah Territory, which had been settled by Mormons in 1847 and achieved territorial status in 1850, saw its application for statehood rejected five times between 1856 and 1887. Congress objected primarily to the Mormon practice of polygamy, so in 1896 Mormon church leaders convinced Congress that Mormons now believed in "one man, one wife," and Utah was admitted as the forty-fifth state.

Arizona and New Mexico faced different problems in their quest for statehood. Although both had existed as separate territories since 1863, Congress refused to admit them to the Union for almost fifty years. One reason was that "Anglos" (white people of northern European ancestry) were significantly outnumbered by Hispanics and Indians in both territories. More important, both territories were dominated by Democrats at a time when Republicans controlled Congress, and the admission of the two territories probably would have increased the number of Democratic senators by four. Since they refused to be admitted as one state, Arizonans and New Mexicans had to wait until the Democrats gained control of Congress in 1912 before they could join the Union as separate states.

Hawaii, which was annexed in 1898, was not admitted to the Union until 1959, mostly because its residents were predominantly Asian. Had it not been for the influence of American sugar planters, Hawaii might have become a commonwealth like Puerto Rico. Acquired in 1898 via the Spanish-American War and given limited self-rule in 1917, Puerto Rico was granted commonwealth (that is, territorial) status in 1952. Although significant numbers of the island's predominantly Hispanic population favor either statehood or independence, Puerto Rico remains a U.S. colony.

See also *Compromise of 1850; Kansas-Nebraska Act; Missouri Compromise; Northwest Ordinance; Territorial Expansion; Territorial Government and New State Formation.*

CHARLES CAREY,
LYNCHBURG COLLEGE/CENTRAL VIRGINIA COMMUNITY COLLEGE

BIBLIOGRAPHY

Bell, Roger John. *Last among Equals: Hawaiian Statehood and American Politics.* Honolulu: University of Hawaii Press, 1984.
Thomas, Dana Lee. *The Story of American Statehood.* New York: W. Funk, 1961.
Verdoia, Ken, and Richard Firmage. *Utah: The Struggle for Statehood.* Salt Lake City: University of Utah Press, 1996.

STATES' RIGHTS/SOVEREIGNTY

The idea that the American states were sovereign was a fundamental concept of antebellum American political and constitutional history. Although the Civil War greatly reduced its influence, the idea that the American federal Union's constituent elements are the states has been reasserted periodically since 1865.

THE VIRGINIA TRADITION OF FEDERALISM

President Andrew Jackson referred to state sovereignty as the Virginia Doctrine, and the theoretical underpinnings of state-centered politics certainly were most fully worked out by prominent politicians from Virginia. Beginning with Richard Bland's proto-revolutionary pamphlets in the 1760s, Virginians had traced the Crown's assurances that their colony would always have various attributes of autonomy in an unbroken line back to the first decade of Virginia's settlement.

On June 29, 1776, Virginia's republican constitution became the first written, republican constitution adopted by a constituent people in the history of the world. Virginia's adoption of its constitution preceded the American Declaration of Independence by five days, and Virginia's delegates to the Continental Congress had no power to rescind Virginia's de facto declaration of independence. Of the thirteen colonies represented at the Continental Congress, Virginia was unique in having already adopted a permanent constitution that established its independence from the Crown.

The Declaration of Independence exhibited strong state-centered features. For example, when revising the declaration, Congress chose to retain Thomas Jefferson's statement that the colonies "are, and of right ought to be, free and independent states." The word *state,* first used in modern political science by Niccolò Machiavelli, had since the Florentine's day denoted a sovereign political unit.

As attorney general of Virginia from 1776 to 1786, Edmund Randolph was responsible for providing legal advice to members of Virginia's state government. In response to a Virginia governor's request for advice regarding another American state's request for extradition of a Virginian accused of having committed a felony in the other state, Randolph replied that Virginia's relationship to the other states was cer-

Edmund Randolph, a strong advocate of the federal Constitution, was instrumental in gaining its ratification in Virginia. However, his assurances that federal powers would be strictly limited proved unfounded. *Library of Congress*

tainly less close, as a matter of law, than the relationship between Great Britain and France.

In the Richmond Ratification Convention of 1788, Randolph served with James Madison, John Marshall, George Nicholas, and one other member on the all-Federalist committee charged with drafting an instrument of ratification of the U.S. Constitution. Randolph and George Nicholas reported the draft instrument of ratification to the floor, where they explained its import by saying that the new Congress would not have any powers that were not, in words Nicholas had borrowed from the Articles of Confederation, "expressly granted" to it. Virginia's "Republicans" (as those opposed to ratification called themselves) predicted that a new federal government would seek broader powers. But Randolph's and Nicholas's assurances concerning the limits on the proposed new government gained the five votes by which the closely divided Virginians ultimately ratified the constitution.

The new federal government was inaugurated in 1789 and soon adopted precisely the policies that the Republicans had predicted. Leading Virginia Federalists called leading Virginia Republicans prophets. Patrick Henry responded by twitting the Federalists—and by demonstrating that Randolph's and Nicholas's assurances would be remembered. In 1790 Henry sponsored a resolution against early Federalist legislation, taking care to quote (though without attribution) Nicholas's assertion that Congress had only those powers it had been "expressly granted."

By decade's end, after a string of electoral defeats and the apparent failure of their efforts to rouse their fellow Americans to oppose the Federalists' centralizing measures, Republicans—who had remained dominant in Virginia almost from the time of Henry's 1790 resolution—determined to elevate their states' rights principle to the status of a national platform. Sometime U.S. senators William Branch Giles, John Taylor, and Wilson Cary Nicholas pushed sets of similar resolutions, stating the Republicans' position, through the Kentucky and Virginia legislatures at the end of 1798. These Kentucky Resolutions (drafted by Thomas Jefferson) and Virginia Resolutions (the handiwork of James Madison) would, the Republicans hoped, serve both to rouse Americans across the federation against the administration of John Adams and to revive the Revolution's localist impulse.

The Kentucky and Virginia Resolutions propounded the traditional Virginia view of the origin of the federal Union of 1788, which they supported by reference to the Tenth Amendment to the U.S. Constitution. They claimed that each state had joined the Union as a state and concluded that it ultimately was for the states to declare what the Constitution meant. Madison's Virginia version even declared that, in such cases, the states were obliged to "interpose" themselves between the federal government and the citizens. The two states closed by calling on their sister states to join in this reading of history. The state legislatures north of Virginia attempted to refute the Virginia and Kentucky Resolutions, while those to its south maintained a stony silence.

Until 1800, then, it is appropriate to associate the doctrine of 1798 almost exclusively with Virginia. However, Thomas Jefferson's election to the presidency in 1800, along with the Republicans' victory in that year's congressional elections, made Virginians' view the federal government's view. Jefferson's platform, in fact, contemplated a radical reduction of the general government's activity and a profound shift in the locus of government activity back to the state governments.

Despite his localist commitments, Jefferson's Louisiana Purchase—the constitutionality of which he doubted—roused the ire of New Englanders, who were concerned lest their distinct regional culture be lost in a sea of new states. At the end of Jefferson's presidency, his foreign policy again sparked strong states' rights sentiments in seafaring New England when he proclaimed a seemingly unconstitutional embargo on imports and exports.

Madison followed Jefferson as president, and his second term ended in 1817 with a tip of the hat to states' rights. Madison vetoed the Bonus Bill, which had been whipped up in the House of Representatives partially in response to Madison's frequent calls for federally financed public works programs. The "Father of the Constitution" insisted that the power to build roads and various other transportation facilities had been left to the states, and he insisted, as he had in Congress throughout the 1790s, that the "necessary and proper" and "general welfare" clauses of the U.S. Constitution did not grant any substantive power to Congress.

Despite the Republicans' electoral victories, the Supreme Court remained a Federalist bastion. When Chief Justice John Marshall, the second significant Federalist from Virginia, handed down his opinions in *Martin v. Hunter's Lessee, Cohens v. Virginia,* and *McCulloch v. Maryland,* he provoked heated responses from Chief Judge Spencer Roane of the Virginia Court of Appeals. Roane's responses and the popularity of John Taylor of Caroline's polemical books proved that many leading Virginians remained convinced that the federal government threatened to absorb the states.

One of Taylor's earliest pamphlets, his 1795 screed against a federal excise on carriages, warned that the principle that legitimized the federal carriage tax also would support an excise on slave property. Thus, almost from the beginning, Jeffersonian Republicans' commitment to states' rights gained some of its motivation from their interest in slavery. This matter came sharply to the fore in the nullification crisis of 1828–1833.

Believing that federal tariffs bore especially hard on southerners and on slavery, a special South Carolina convention declared on November 24, 1832, that the tariffs to which South Carolina's leaders most forcefully objected would be void within the state. Following the prescription of Vice President John C. Calhoun, who claimed to be in the tradition of the Virginia and Kentucky Resolutions, South Carolina spoke through the same organ that had ratified the Constitution in the first place: a special convention of the sovereign people of South Carolina.

James Madison devoted much of the last eight years of his life to trying to distinguish his and other Republicans' behavior in the 1790s from that of the South Carolina nullifiers. Giles, the Virginia Senate sponsor of the Virginia Resolutions, was governor of Virginia from 1827 to 1830, and he disagreed sharply with Madison. Madison insisted that the recently deceased Jefferson would have sided with him, but Jefferson's namesake grandson produced the original draft of the Kentucky Resolutions, complete with the word "nullification"

(which Madison had denied Jefferson had ever used). Virginia's political establishment joined every other state's in disapproving of the particulars of Calhoun's position, but Virginia's politicians sympathized with South Carolina's antitariff, pro–states' rights stance more than did other states' leaders.

THE JACKSONIAN ERA THROUGH THE CIVIL WAR

President Andrew Jackson was a proponent of states' rights who rejected the theory of state sovereignty. Jackson pushed the South Carolinians to surrender their doctrine of nullification even as he faced a similar assertion of state authority from neighboring Georgia. While Jackson denied that South Carolina could nullify the tariff, he made no attempt to prevent Georgia from effectively nullifying a Supreme Court decision in favor of Indian land claims in Georgia. Georgia's actions, taken by that state's authorities in pursuit of what they understood to be a binding agreement regarding disposition of Indian land claims between the federal authorities and the state, led to virtual elimination of Cherokees from Georgia.

Ironically, between the end of the nullification crisis and 1861, Calhoun's theory would be turned against the social order it had been meant to support. The nationalization of slavery by Chief Justice Roger B. Taney's opinion in *Dred Scott v. Sandford* and renewed congressional support for a proslaveholder reading of the Constitution's fugitive slave clause seemingly made slavery a national right. Northern state legislatures and governors who opposed slavery turned, therefore, to states' rights in their opposition to proslavery federal policies. In the New York case of *Lemmon v. The People,* that state's highest court asserted that as a state, New York had power to prevent infringement of the principle of freedom within its own borders, apparently (at least as one dissenting judge saw it) despite whatever the federal Constitution or interstate comity might seem to require.

In the end, the antebellum disputes over slavery and the growth of anti–states' rights sentiment in the North combined to produce the Civil War of 1861–1865. Had President Abraham Lincoln accepted the Virginia Doctrine, he would have told the seceding states to depart in peace. Instead, by the war's end, the doctrine of state sovereignty had been temporarily expunged from American constitutionalism.

The seceded states undertook to create a new government rooted in what they believed to be the original American understanding (but which actually was the Virginia tradition) of federalism. The Constitution they adopted included significant clarifications of language from the original U.S. Constitution and a few state-centered changes. Among the latter was a provision making officers of the Confederate States of

America susceptible to impeachment by the legislatures in the states in which they served.

STATES' RIGHTS IN THE SECOND HALF OF THE TWENTIETH CENTURY

State sovereignty's next significant appearance in American political consciousness came in 1948, with the States' Rights Democratic presidential candidacy of South Carolina governor J. Strom Thurmond. In response to the inclusion of a strong civil rights plank in the 1948 Democratic Party platform, Thurmond and other leading southerners bolted from the regular party and pursued their own regional candidacy for president. They hoped to secure sufficient southern electoral votes to throw the election into the House of Representatives. Although Thurmond won four southern states' electoral votes, the Democratic Party's candidate won the election.

The Thurmond candidacy prefigured the day when, in opposition to the Supreme Court's 1954 decision in *Brown v. Board of Education of Topeka, Kansas,* southern politicians at large adopted a policy of *massive resistance* to what they characterized as unconstitutional infringement on their reserved right to make their own educational policy, and other, related racial policies.

Dusting off the Virginia and Kentucky Resolutions at the behest of Richmond newspaper editor James J. Kilpatrick, U.S. senator Harry F. Byrd of Virginia led a campaign to close down affected states' primary and secondary schools rather than comply with desegregation orders. This policy, based on the Tenth Amendment, struck most politicians and observers outside the South as not only wrongheaded, but anachronistic. Decades had passed since the Supreme Court had taken the old states' rights nostrums seriously. In the end, massive resistance proved a massive failure. In *Cooper v. Aaron* (1958), the U.S. Supreme Court laid claim to the final legal authority to expound the Constitution, directly rejecting massive resistance and the principles of 1798.

In the 1968 presidential campaign of Richard M. Nixon, when the Republican Party appealed for white southerners' votes, an important element of Nixon's strategy was a very public alliance with Senator Thurmond, who happily endorsed Nixon as a politician friendly to the states' rights tradition. This strategy proved successful, and President Nixon responded by nominating William H. Rehnquist to the Supreme Court. Justice Rehnquist put the old states' rights tradition at the center of his jurisprudence. Later Republican presidents, Ronald Reagan and George Bush, would elevate Rehnquist to chief justice of the United States and nominate Clarence Thomas (another states' rights–minded justice) to the Court. These appointments, coupled with these presidents' sporadic public endorsements of states' rights, helped return the states' rights tradition to the center of public debate. At the end of the twentieth century, though, localism was associated with opposition to Supreme Court decisions in the areas of abortion rights, integration of schools, and criminal procedure. Thus, the old Virginia Republican constitutionalism had been claimed by a different Republican Party based on different social and intellectual foundations.

See also: *Adams, John; American Revolution; Articles of Confederation;* Brown v. Board of Education; *Calhoun, John C.; Civil War; Constitution, Ratification; Constitution, U.S.; Declaration of Independence; Dixiecrats; Federalism; Federalists; Fugitive Slave Laws; Indian Policy; Jackson, Andrew; Jefferson, Thomas; Lincoln, Abraham; Madison, James; Newspapers and Political Parties; Nullification; Popular Sovereignty; Secession; Sectionalism; Slavery; State Government; Supreme Court; Tariff History; Territorial Expansion and New State Formation.*

K. R. CONSTANTINE GUTZMAN, JOHN JAY COLLEGE, CUNY

BIBLIOGRAPHY

Gunter, Gerald, ed. *John Marshall's Defense of* McCulloch v. Maryland. Stanford: Stanford University Press, 1969.

Gutzman, Kevin R. Constantine. "A Troublesome Legacy: James Madison and the 'Principles of '98'." *Journal of the Early Republic* 15 (winter 1995): 569–589.

———. "The Virginia and Kentucky Resolutions Reconsidered: 'An Appeal to the *Real Laws* of Our Country.'" *Journal of Southern History* 66 (August 2000): 473–496.

Taylor, John. *New Views of the Constitution.* 2d ed. Edited by James McClellan. Washington, D.C.: Regnery Publishing, 2000.

Van Schreeven, William J., and Robert L. Scribner, eds. *Revolutionary Virginia: The Road to Independence.* Charlottesville: University Press of Virginia, 1973.

SUFFRAGE

The right to vote is the hallmark—both symbolic and substantive—of a political democracy; much of U.S. history can be told in terms of the expansion or contraction of the electorate.

Not before the 1960s did the United States have an electorate that was defined in virtually identical terms in every state. Before the Civil War, states had complete autonomy in establishing conditions for the right to vote. Between 1867 and 1920, federal laws and constitutional amendments placed limits on that autonomy regarding race and gender. Further accomplishment of a national definition of voting rights, largely completed by 1972, went hand in hand with expansion of the electorate.

CORRELATES OF THE RIGHT TO VOTE

Citizenship and voting rights have been only loosely related in the nation's history. Before independence, various colonies curtailed the political rights of Jews, Catholics, or even dissenting Protestants. In the first half of the nineteenth century, citizenship often did not guarantee men the vote in the face of property-holding and racial requirements. Nowhere at the time of the Civil War did white women have the right to vote, though most were citizens. Immigrant men in the nineteenth century in some western states, among them Wisconsin and South Dakota, could vote if they had declared their intention to become citizens.

Various considerations governed the significance of the right to vote, no matter who had that right. What positions were filled through popular election, for example? And did all votes have about the same value, all voters the same power to elect officials? In Virginia before 1851, seats in the state legislature were the only state or local offices to be filled through popular election, and the apportionment scheme was such that the western half of the state, where a rapidly rising population would soon contain a majority of all white men, could never elect a majority of either house of the legislature even if voting restrictions were eliminated.

Similar questions arose in the twentieth century. The Seventeenth Amendment (1913) to the Constitution, for example, shifted the responsibility for selecting U.S. senators away from the state legislatures and to the voters. In the 1960s various decisions by the U.S. Supreme Court banned malapportionment in state legislatures and in congressional districts. Because the Court or Congress also threw out such barriers to voting as poll taxes and literacy tests at about the same time, the concept of "one person, one vote" applied to both the ability to vote and the value of that vote.

Other questions have emerged from time to time. Did voting rights carry with them the right to run for and hold public office? In 1869, during Reconstruction, a majority of white legislators in Georgia decided the answer to this question was no and expelled dozens of black Republican legislators so Democrats could take control. Could a woman be an attorney? The New Hampshire Supreme Court ruled in 1890 (*Ricker's Petition*) that, though a woman could not hold office in that state, she could qualify to practice as an attorney. Yet the New Hampshire attorney general ruled in 1910 that the same woman, Marilla Ricker, could not run for an office (the governorship) for which she could not vote.

TOWARD UNIVERSAL SUFFRAGE— FOR WHITE MEN

For many years under the U.S. Constitution, the right to vote was defined by the separate states, as it had been by the individual colonies. Dependent on the states to determine voting rights, the Constitution simply provided that each state's electorate for members of the U.S. House of Representatives would be the same as for the largest chamber of that state's legislature. The Virginia constitution of 1776, to take one example, did not specify the prerequisites for voting but simply

said that they would be the same as before; that is, substantial ownership of real estate would continue to be required.

Between the Revolution and the Civil War, state after state reduced the barriers to voting, at least for white men. Religious restrictions disappeared as the independent states wrote constitutions, as in New York and Maryland. The process of opening the political process to virtually all white men who were citizens continued through the era of "Jacksonian Democracy." Achieving universal white manhood suffrage was largely completed by 1851, when Virginia terminated any property-holding requirement.

By then, every state had adopted either "universal" suffrage or a taxpaying qualification that, in the absence of taxable property, could be fulfilled by paying a poll tax. States maintained varying residence requirements, however, often of a year in the state and perhaps a lesser period in the locality, consistent with the traditional idea of being able to demonstrate a stake in local society. Vermont distinguished between statewide elections, in which universal suffrage for men applied, and local elections, in which a taxpaying requirement long persisted.

By the Civil War, the most obvious remaining barriers to voting were gender, race, and citizenship. Nowhere could white women vote in state or federal elections, but a women's suffrage movement was under way. Some states had extended the right to vote to black men, but the pattern was by no means universal even in the North. Meanwhile, anti-immigrant groups sought to restrict the political rights of immigrants. For example, the American (Know Nothing) Party platform in the 1856 presidential election called for limiting the electorate to citizens and requiring twenty-one years of continuous residence in the United States before an immigrant could qualify for citizenship.

RACE, GENDER, SUFFRAGE, AND FEDERAL AUTHORITY

In the aftermath of the Civil War and the end of slavery in the South, the question of political rights for African Americans, particularly black southerners, came to the fore. It was hoped in the North that, if black men in the South could vote, they could look after their own interests and would not need federal authority monitoring postwar developments there. Regardless, if black southerners were going to be counted for purposes of determining the southern states' representation in the House of Representatives and the electoral college, then black men must be permitted to vote their own representation. Otherwise, the abolition of slavery, by inflating from three-fifths to full value the former slaves' worth in computing population for representation purposes, would give former rebels far more power in national life than had been the case before the Civil War brought emancipation. In the first postwar years, Congress had to decide how to proceed, whether to define the suffrage in terms of loyalty to the nation (regardless of race), let it be conditioned on being white (regardless of loyalty), leave the southern electorate defined in terms of race but restrict it in terms of loyalty, or ignore the issue and leave it up to the states.

After 1865, African Americans were all free, yet the pre–Civil War *Dred Scott* decision declared that they were not citizens, and they surely had no voting rights unless their states had made that determination. The Civil Rights Act of 1866 declared African Americans citizens. The Fourteenth Amendment, approved by Congress that year, included that act's declaration of black citizenship and spoke of "equal protection of the laws" and citizens' "privileges or immunities." As for voting rights, the Fourteenth Amendment proposed to leave the decision in the hands of a white political establishment in each southern state as to whether to enfranchise black men or accept reduced representation, but it demanded that states choose. Ten of the eleven former Confederate states rejected the amendment, however, so to obtain ratification, Congress voted in 1867 to require black enfranchisement in those ten states as a condition of readmission. In each of those states, black men as well as white men would vote in an election to choose delegates to a constitutional convention, and that convention had to establish black voting rights. Black men were therefore voting in most southern states even before the Fifteenth Amendment.

The Fifteenth Amendment, which was ratified in March 1870, declared that racial identity could not be used to exclude people from the right to vote. The amendment did not ban property tests or literacy requirements, and it did not say anything about holding public office. But it put the U.S. Constitution on record that race could no longer be the express basis for curtailing voting rights in any state in the nation.

Not for another fifty years would the Constitution say the same thing about gender. Indeed, many white women had hoped that their time for voting rights would also come in the 1860s. They were sorely disappointed. Their campaign continued on through the remainder of the nineteenth century and into the twentieth. Meanwhile, women did secure political rights in many states. Just as black men voted in some states long before 1870, white and black women voted in some states for years before 1920.

Some women tried to vote on the basis of the Fourteenth and Fifteenth Amendments. Susan B. Anthony, one of those who did, was arrested in 1872 for her attempt in New York and proceeded to give speeches like "Is It a Crime for a Citizen of the United States to Vote?" In a case from Missouri, *Minor v. Happersett* (1875), the Supreme Court ruled that, although women were indeed citizens, a citizen's Fourteenth Amendment "privileges" did not include voting. In short, the Reconstruction amendments did not confer voting rights on women. In 1878 an unsuccessful amendment was introduced in Congress that contained language identical to the Nineteenth Amendment, which brought women's suffrage when it was finally ratified in 1920.

Before 1920, nonetheless, various states extended voting rights to women. Some states—among them Colorado as well as North and South Dakota—permitted women to vote in elections concerning local schools. By 1896 four western states—Colorado, Idaho, Wyoming, and Utah—had granted women the right to vote in all elections. Two rival organizations merged in 1890 as the National American Woman Suffrage Association, which pushed the effort in additional states. Victories came slowly, but Washington came on board in 1910, California in 1911, and others soon followed, including New York in 1917.

Every victory at the local level produced another state whose members of Congress could generally be counted on to support the proposed national amendment. World War I brought more female suffrage states. It also occasioned recognition, even in nonsuffrage states, that women were making vital contributions to the war effort. The amendment gained the necessary two-thirds vote in the House of Representatives in January 1918 and in the Senate in June 1919. Ratification was secured in time for the presidential election in 1920.

The struggles to achieve voting rights, whether by race or gender, generated fierce controversy. Proponents argued for the importance of the right to protect oneself, assert one's interests, express one's citizenship. Particular attributes ascribed to people on the basis of race or gender shaped public debate on the issue of extending political rights. For example, proponents of female suffrage argued that women would purify politics. Their opponents, working from similar assumptions, argued instead that politics would sully women. The prospect of partisan advantage, and accompanying struggles over both abstract rights and material interests, inevitably shaped each fight. Political struggles over voting rights persisted long after 1920.

TOWARD A NATIONAL DEFINITION OF THE ELECTORATE

The Fifteenth Amendment prevented the states from using race as a barrier to voting a half-century before the Nineteenth Amendment prevented them from using gender. Yet black southerners' voting rights came under sustained assault in the late nineteenth century, at the same time that gender was in decline as a screen to voting in the North and West. Through much of the twentieth century, black men and black women challenged various impediments to their voting. One notable victory came with the Supreme Court's decision in *Smith v. Allwright* (1944), which invalidated racial restrictions against voting in so-called white Democratic primary elections.

The 1960s brought a transformation in the American political system with respect to both the ability to vote and the worth of a vote. Between 1962 and 1972, a combination of congressional legislation, constitutional amendment, and judicial interpretation went beyond the changes of the Fifteenth and Nineteenth Amendments in broadening voting rights.

The poll tax symbolized the various criteria, nominally nonracial, that had long been deployed in most southern states to curtail black voting. The Twenty-fourth Amendment, approved by Congress in 1962 and ratified in 1964, banned the requirement that prospective voters pay a poll tax as a condition of voting in presidential and congressional elections. In *Harper v. Virginia Board of Elections* (1966), the Supreme Court applied the ban to state and local elections as well.

The Voting Rights Act of 1965 curtailed various other obstacles to African Americans' voting. If local officials made it difficult to register, federal registrars might step in. Literacy tests could no longer be employed in states that had long prevented many black citizens from voting. The Fifteenth Amendment authorized Congress to enact measures to enforce voting rights, and the 1965 act was designed to enforce them. Subsequent amendments to the 1965 act extended the time of its application, and the area, and made the ban on literacy tests permanent.

What has been characterized as the "reapportionment revolution" came to American politics at about the same time as the Twenty-fourth Amendment and the Voting Rights Act. In *Baker v. Carr* (1962), the Supreme Court inaugurated a new epoch in American politics with respect to the relative numbers of voters in each legislative district. The Court applied that ruling in *Gray v. Sanders* (1963), in which Justice William O. Douglas insisted on the principle of "one person, one vote." *Reynolds v. Sims* (1964) declared that malapportioned state legislatures violated the Fourteenth Amendment's Equal Protection Clause, and *Wesberry v. Sanders* (1964) applied the principle to congressional districts. *Baker* led the way, but *Reynolds* (a case that, much like *Brown v. Board of Education* [1954], stands for a number of cases decided together) transformed state politics throughout the nation.

Beyond changes that had to do with race, literacy, wealth, and apportionment, the Twenty-sixth Amendment (ratified in 1971) established a national minimum voting age of eighteen in local, state, and federal elections. Until that time, few states permitted voting under the age of twenty-one, although the idea had surfaced in the context of World War II conscription, when the slogan "old enough to fight, old enough to vote" gained popularity and the state of Georgia adopted the change. The Vietnam War generated similar debate in the late 1960s, and Congress included the lower voting age in the Voting Rights Act Amendments of 1970. The Supreme Court, however, in *Oregon v. Mitchell* (1970), declared the voting-age provision beyond the authority of Congress insofar as it applied to state and local elections. The Twenty-sixth Amendment was swiftly approved and swiftly ratified.

To make it easier for a mobile population to qualify to vote, the 1970 Voting Rights Act permitted a maximum thirty-day residence requirement in presidential elections. In *Dunn v. Blumstein* (1972), the Supreme Court limited residence requirements in state elections to the same standard.

With expanded suffrage came expanded representation. Black representation in Congress reached a new high in the 103d Congress (1993–1995) at forty members, half of whom posed for the photograph above. *R. Michael Jenkins, Congressional Quarterly*

By the 1990s, moreover, "motor voter" legislation permitted a person to register while filing a state tax return or applying for a driver's license.

See also *Apportionment; Black Suffrage; Civil Rights Acts (Modern); Civil Rights Movement; Constitutional Amendments; Jacksonian Democracy; Know Nothing Party; Poll Tax; Seneca Falls Convention; Woman's Suffrage Movement.*

PETER WALLENSTEIN,
VIRGINIA POLYTECHNIC INSTITUTE AND STATE UNIVERSITY

BIBLIOGRAPHY

Claude, Richard. *The Supreme Court and the Electoral Process.* Baltimore: Johns Hopkins Press, 1970.

Gillette, William. *The Right to Vote: Politics and the Passage of the Fifteenth Amendment.* Baltimore: Johns Hopkins Press, 1965.

Porter, Kirk H. *A History of Suffrage in the United States.* Chicago: University of Chicago Press, 1918.

Scott, Anne F., and Andrew M. Scott. *One Half the People: The Fight for Woman Suffrage.* Philadelphia: Lippincott, 1975.

Williamson, Chilton. *American Suffrage: From Property to Democracy, 1760–1860.* Princeton: Princeton University Press, 1960.

SUPER MAJORITY

The federal government operates under rules that require the approval of more than a simple majority before various important actions can be taken.

Rather than require a simple majority for amendment, the Articles of Confederation required unanimous consent of the states. Therefore, two proposed amendments—to grant the central government the power to tax and the power to regulate interstate and international commerce—failed because one state objected. As a consequence, the Philadelphia Convention met in 1787, and the U.S. Constitution resulted.

Under the U.S. Constitution, most legislative action (passing a bill in either house; confirming a president's appointees in the Senate) requires only a simple majority. The Founders intended, however, that some actions be more difficult, and they established a higher threshold before those gained approval. A simple majority in the House can bring impeachment charges, but conviction in the Senate requires a two-thirds majority (Article I, sections 2–3); although Presidents Andrew Johnson and William Jefferson Clinton were each impeached, they escaped conviction and removal. A treaty binding the United States to an agreement with a foreign nation requires a two-thirds vote in the Senate (Article II, section 2); the failure of the United States to join the League of Nations in March 1920 is an example of a time when a simple majority could be obtained, but the required super majority could not. To become law over a president's veto, a bill requires a two-thirds majority in each house (Article I, section 7). Extreme discontent during the War of 1812 led to the Hartford Convention Resolutions, which called for an amendment that would have required a two-thirds vote in each house, rather than a simple majority, to declare war or admit new states.

To amend the Constitution requires a two-thirds vote in each house to propose the amendment and three-fourths of the states to ratify it (Article V). The 1787 convention also required, in effect, a two-thirds agreement among the states—nine of the thirteen states—before the proposed Constitution could go into operation (Article VII); laggard states like Rhode Island and North Carolina could not prevent ratification.

A super majority has appeared in another context, specified not in the Constitution but in the rules of procedure in Congress. In the Senate, a filibuster—endless speeches—can prevent action on a measure that a majority wants to pass, and twentieth-century civil rights bills often encountered this tactic from southern senators. To end a filibuster and force a floor vote requires a cloture vote by a super majority. From 1917 to 1975, cloture required approval of two-thirds of all senators present and voting, reduced in 1975 to 60 percent.

Although the concept of a super majority has been central to the operations of the federal government under the U.S. Constitution from the beginning, the term itself first gained widespread currency in the 1990s. In 1993 President Clinton nominated law professor Lani Guinier to serve as assistant U.S. attorney general in charge of civil rights enforcement. Republicans and conservative journalists generated a firestorm about her purportedly revolutionary ideas, and Clinton withdrew the nomination. Guinier had published law review articles in which the term "super majority" as well as the concept had been central to proposals designed to safeguard the electoral effectiveness of African Americans and other racial or ethnic minorities. Borrowing in part from experiments made under the Voting Rights Act of 1965, she was looking to modify electoral, not congressional, politics.

See also *Civil Rights Acts (Modern); Cloture; Constitution, U.S.; Constitutional Amendments; Filibuster; Hartford Convention Resolutions; Impeachment; Treaty Making.*

PETER WALLENSTEIN,
VIRGINIA POLYTECHNIC INSTITUTE AND STATE UNIVERSITY

BIBLIOGRAPHY

Guinier, Lani. *The Tyranny of the Majority: Fundamental Fairness in Representative Democracy.* New York: Free Press, 1994.

Tiefer, Charles. *Congressional Practice and Procedure: A Reference, Research, and Legislative Guide.* Westport, Conn.: Greenwood Press, 1989.

SUPREME COURT

The turn-of-the-century political commentator Mr. Dooley (a character created by Finley Peter Dunne) once commented that the Supreme Court follows the election returns, suggesting that the judicial branch of the government, although insulated from having to stand for office, nonetheless has a keen appreciation of political realities. This should not be surprising, since the judiciary is a branch of government, and government by its nature is political. The courts have the power of neither sword nor purse, and therefore have to rely on moral suasion if they hope to have the citizenry obey their decisions. Almost from the beginning of the Republic, courts have been keenly aware of this reality, and so they have played politics when necessary in order to preserve their status, or, in some instances, to further a specific political goal.

PRESERVING THE COURT'S STATUS AND FURTHERING POLITICAL GOALS

A good example of the first instance is the famous case of *Marbury v. Madison* (1803). William Marbury, one of the so-called midnight judges appointed by outgoing president John Adams, wanted his commission so that he might act as a justice of the peace in Washington. The outgoing secretary of state, John Marshall, had been unable to deliver all of the commissions before leaving office, and the new president, Thomas Jefferson, ordered Secretary of State James Madison not to deliver the remaining commissions. Marbury sued Madison and sought a writ of mandamus in the Supreme Court to force Madison to deliver.

Marshall, now chief justice, found himself in a quandary. If he ruled that Marbury should receive the commission, he knew that Jefferson and Madison would refuse to obey. If, on the other hand, he ruled against Marbury, it would appear that the Supreme Court lacked any power and had caved in to the executive. So Marshall crafted his now-famous opinion in which he held that Marbury did indeed have a right to the commission, chastised the Jefferson administration for not obeying the rule of law, but then held that the Supreme Court lacked the power to issue a writ of mandamus under original jurisdiction, since Congress had violated the Constitution by giving the Court that power in the Judiciary Act of 1789. In addition, Marshall laid claim for the Court to be the ultimate arbiter of the Constitution, thus making it a truly coequal branch of the government.

An example of the Court overtly trying to settle a political issue came in 1857 in *Dred Scott v. Sandford*. The Framers had recognized that without protection for slavery, southern

John Marshall   *Library of Congress*

states would not ratify the Constitution. Even though they never mentioned the word "slave," they wrote a number of provisions aimed at protecting the "peculiar institution." With the exceptions of the Missouri Compromise in 1820 and the abolitionist petition campaign of the 1830s, slavery had remained a relatively dormant issue until the war with Mexico. Slaveholders now demanded that they be allowed to take their "property" into the western territories and that the federal government should protect their passage and settlement. By the mid-1850s, slavery had become the dominant issue of American politics, and southern radicals began talking about secession if their demands were not met.

In 1857 the Court decided the case of a Missouri slave—Dred Scott—who claimed that when his former master had taken him into the free portion of the Louisiana Purchase he had become free. If ever a case called for judicial restraint, this one cried out for it. The tense national atmosphere precluded any definitive judgment of the Court from being accepted by a large part of the nation, yet many people hoped the Court could settle the issue of slavery in the territory once and for all.

The Court could easily have sidestepped the problem. A key constitutional question was whether a black had standing to sue in federal courts. A majority of the Court found that blacks—even if free—had no standing, and by proper jurisprudential process, this should have been the end of the matter because if a court lacks jurisdiction or if a party lacks standing, then the merits of the argument should not be reached.

But the southern majority on the Court, as well as the northern Democrats, wanted to settle the issue of slavery in the territories. Chief Justice Roger B. Taney went out of his way not only to answer the immediate questions, but to hold the Missouri Compromise unconstitutional and to claim that under the Constitution all of the southern demands for protection of slavery were warranted. Southern newspapers exploded in jubilation, and as one Georgia editor wrote, "The Southern opinion upon the subject of Southern slavery is now the supreme law of the land."

A majority of northerners opposed the *Dred Scott* decision, which set the stage for Lincoln's electoral victory in 1860 and the subsequent secession by the South. Even before Fort Sumter, however, northern politicians heaped scorn on the Court. So much calumny fell upon the Court that a later chief justice, Charles Evans Hughes, described the decision as a "self-inflicted wound." Taney almost destroyed by his clumsiness the moral authority that Marshall had carefully created through brilliant political strategy.

THE COURT AND INDIVIDUAL JUSTICES

Courts play politics in a variety of ways, as do individual justices. When Congress in 1894 attached an income tax rider to the Wilson-Gorman Tariff, backers fully believed that judicial precedent would uphold the levy. However, to conservative business leaders and their allies on the bench, the income tax appeared to be one more manifestation of the radicalism sweeping the country. Chief Justice Melville Fuller managed to get a 6–2 majority invalidating the main provisions of the tax as a direct but unapportioned tax on land, and therefore unconstitutional. But the Court split 4–4 on other questions, and this normally would have left the lower court decisions—in favor of the tax—undisturbed. But Fuller quickly granted the motion for a rehearing, and on the second vote managed to get a bare majority to strike down the other provisions as well. Justice Henry Brown—who could hardly be considered a liberal, much less a radical—noted that politics and not jurisprudence had determined the outcome. "The decision involves nothing less than a surrender of the taxing power to the moneyed class," he wrote in dissent. "Even the specter of socialism is conjured up to frighten

Congress from laying taxes upon the people in proportion to their ability to pay." The popular revulsion to the decision led eventually to the Sixteenth Amendment.

Merely supporting conservative measures or striking down liberal ones is not by itself a sign of political action. Political conservatives often hold a conservative jurisprudence, as political liberals hold a liberal jurisprudence. The decision in the income tax case, *Pollock v. Farmers' Loan & Trust Co.* (1895), went beyond a simple case of conservative jurists opposing the law on sound constitutional principles. Rather, Fuller and his cohorts had to ignore numerous precedents stretching back practically to the founding of the Republic and then twist the meaning of constitutional phrases to rationalize their opposition to a tax.

In one of the most famous incidents of alleged political action by the Court—the "switch in time that saved nine"—Justice Owen J. Roberts supposedly switched his vote in *West Coast Hotel v. Parrish* (1937) from opposition to minimum wage legislation to support; he is said to have chosen this course of action in order to thwart Franklin D. Roosevelt's Court-packing plan. We now know that this simplistic version of events is untrue; the vote on the case had been taken before the announcement of the president's plan and then delayed for internal administrative reasons. But if the Court as a body seemed to stand above the political struggle in the spring of 1937, individual justices—many of whom had had extensive political experience before going onto the bench—swung into action.

Harlan Fiske Stone told reporter Irving Brant what he thought of the plan, and Brant dutifully informed White House aides that not only Stone but all the members of the Court opposed the plan. Louis D. Brandeis, who had made it a rule not to talk to reporters after he became a justice in 1916, let it be known through a variety of sources that he abhorred the plan, and he arranged for Sen. Burton Wheeler to meet with Charles Evans Hughes. The chief justice then fashioned a letter to the Senate that took the president's supposed rationale—inefficiency and delay in the Court's work—and effectively rebutted it. Hughes then convinced Brandeis, representing the liberal wing of the Court, and Willis Van Devanter, a member of the conservative "Four Horsemen," to sign as well. Through the five months that Congress considered the bill, the Court never once made a formal institutional statement, yet most of its members lobbied quietly but effectively against the plan. After it finally went down to defeat, Robert H. Jackson, who had been one of the most effective defenders of the president's plan, told Roosevelt that Hughes's strategy during the fight had been "masterly. The old man put it over on you." The president did not deny it.

The Supreme Court justices in 1932, the year of Franklin D. Roosevelt's first election. Seated from left: Justices Louis D. Brandeis, Willis Van Devanter, Chief Justice Charles Evans Hughes, Justices James C. McReynolds, George Sutherland. Standing from left: Justices Owen J. Roberts, Pierce Butler, Harlan Fiske Stone, Benjamin N. Cardozo. By 1940 Roosevelt had replaced five of the nine justices: Brandeis, Van Devanter, Sutherland, Butler, and Cardozo. *Library of Congress*

NAVIGATING THROUGH POLITICAL DIFFICULTIES

The Court sometimes fashions its decisions in response to perceived political difficulties. Whether apocryphal or not, Andrew Jackson's comment on the Court's decision in the Cherokee cases—"John Marshall has made his decision, now let him enforce it"—is never out of mind for members of the Court. (In the Cherokee cases the Court sided with the Indian tribes against the state of Georgia.) The Court realizes that in order for some of its more controversial opinions to receive public acceptance, the decision must be framed in a politically acceptable manner. One can see this clearly in Earl Warren's masterful handling of the segregation case, *Brown v. Board of Education* (1954).

Apparently, a majority of the Court stood ready to strike down racial segregation in public schools after oral argument in the fall of 1953. But Warren believed that he had to have a unanimous Court, and he worked assiduously through the winter to bring every member of the bench onto the decision. The opinion itself did not address all of the issues of Jim Crow in the South, but spoke primarily to one group, namely, small schoolchildren and the effect racial discrimination had on them. The opinion did not lay out any remedies, but in-

vited the southern states and the federal government to return to the Court the following term to help fashion an appropriate remedy. In addition, Warren deliberately kept the opinion short and avoided legal jargon, so that newspapers could print the entire opinion on their front page and people could read it for themselves; he feared that a long opinion would be distorted by hostile writers and commentators on its way to the public.

The reaction in the South between May 1954 and the following fall were all Warren could have hoped for—moderate voices saying that the South could live with desegregation, that it was an inevitable development, and that the public should remain calm and use common sense. But in *Brown II,* the 1955 decision implementing the *Brown* decision, the Court made a major error in utilizing the phrase "all deliberate speed" to describe the pace at which it expected desegregation to proceed. While Warren and his colleagues no doubt wanted the process to move quickly, opponents latched onto the phrase to emphasize *deliberate,* and they adopted tactics that would yield snail-like progress for years to come.

Illustrations of these types of political involvement and calculation by the Court and its members abound. The notion that somehow the Court should be "pure" and "above" politics is simply naïve. Obviously, justices should not be involved in the overtly political actions of the executive or congressional branches, as Abe Fortas was during the administration of Lyndon B. Johnson or Felix Frankfurter with the administration of Franklin Roosevelt during World War II.

However, the judiciary is a branch of government, and as such it must be sensitive to political issues. Having the power neither of sword nor purse, it must rely on the public's confidence in it as an institution, a confidence that can be augmented by acute political perception or dissipated by inept blundering. For the most part, the truly effective chief justices, like John Marshall, William Howard Taft, Charles Evans Hughes, and Earl Warren, have also been seasoned politicians who well understood the processes of government and the opportunities as well as the limitations of their office. All presidents have appointed people who shared their political and jurisprudential views, but the Court's agenda often changes, and the justices have to face issues that were not on the president's list at the time of the appointment. This happened in the 1930s when Roosevelt appointed men sympathetic to New Deal economic measures, and within a very short time the Court's major issue was civil rights. In the 1980s presidents Ronald Reagan and George Bush, more than any of their predecessors, made ideological conformity a prerequisite for appointment, and the result is that the Court under William Rehnquist may well be the most conservative bench in the past century.

See also Brown v. Board of Education; *Civil Rights Movement; Fugitive Slave Laws; Judiciary Acts; New Deal.*

MELVIN I. UROFSKY, VIRGINIA COMMONWEALTH UNIVERSITY

BIBLIOGRAPHY

Dewey, Donald O. *Marshall versus Jefferson: The Political Background of Marbury v. Madison.* New York: Knopf, 1970.

Fehrenbacher, Don E. *The Dred Scott Case: Its Significance in American Law and Politics.* New York: Oxford, 1978.

Leuchtenburg, William E. *The Supreme Court Reborn: The Constitutional Revolution in the Age of Roosevelt.* New York: Oxford, 1995.

Stanley, Robert. *Dimensions of Law in the Service of Order: Origins of the Federal Income Tax, 1861–1913.* New York: Oxford, 1993.

Urofsky, Melvin I., and Paul Finkelman. *A March of Liberty.* Rev. ed. New York: Oxford, forthcoming.

Wiecek, William M. *Liberty under Law: The Supreme Court in American Life.* Baltimore: Johns Hopkins University Press, 1988.

TAFT, WILLIAM HOWARD

William Howard Taft, the twenty-seventh president of the United States (1909–1913), disliked politics and merely endured the presidency before taking the job he really wanted: chief justice of the United States.

Taft was born in Cincinnati, Ohio, on September 15, 1857. After graduating from Yale University and Cincinnati Law School, he practiced law before becoming a superior court judge. President Benjamin Harrison appointed him solicitor general in 1890, and in 1892 he returned to the bench as a circuit court judge.

An appointment in 1900 by President William McKinley sent Taft and his family abroad to the Philippines, where he served as governor for four years and encouraged limited self-government. While in the Philippines, a post he enjoyed, he twice refused coveted appointments to the U.S. Supreme Court because he did not want to abandon the Filipinos and his efforts to modernize the islands. When his good friend President Theodore Roosevelt appointed him secretary of war in 1904, Taft and his family returned to Washington.

As the 1908 presidential election approached, Roosevelt successfully threw his support behind the reluctant Taft for the Republican nomination. In the general election, Taft beat Democrat William Jennings Bryan handily.

Although wide of girth, Taft proved to be a political lightweight who was unable to continue the Progressive policies of his predecessor. For example, Taft called for lower tariffs, but the Payne-Aldrich Tariff Act, which he signed in 1909, fell far short of the Progressives' goals. As a result of this and other events, a rift began to develop between Taft and Roosevelt. The split was exacerbated by the Ballinger-Pinchot controversy over conservation policies in 1909. Richard Ballinger was secretary of the interior, and Gifford Pinchot was head of the Forestry Service in the Department of Agriculture and an outspoken conservationist who was instrumental in withdrawing substantial western land from the public domain under Roosevelt. Ballinger sought to reverse these withdrawals, acting under pressure of western senators and their constituents who wanted the land open for mining, lumber, and other exploitation. Pinchot vigorously attacked Ballinger on the latter's actions, leading Taft eventually to dismiss Pinchot from his government position. As the controversy lingered on, Roosevelt's popularity and Pinchot's highly visible connection to the growing conservation movement helped push the Republicans toward a split. More tension developed when Roosevelt and others alleged that Taft did not support reformers in the House who were trying to break the powerful grip of Speaker Joseph G. Cannon, a Republican from Illinois. Eventually, Roosevelt lost confidence in his friend and began to plot to retake the presidency.

Taft did not fall short on all fronts, however. For one thing, he excelled at trust-busting. His administration brought ninety antitrust suits in four years, compared with forty-four during Roosevelt's seven years in office. Taft also oversaw passage of two constitutional amendments: one calling for the popular election of senators, and the other a federal income tax.

In foreign affairs, Taft sought to use investments and trade to expand U.S. influence abroad, especially in Latin America—a policy later branded as "dollar diplomacy." Not averse to using force to maintain order and protect U.S. business interests in Latin America, he sent ships and troops to revolution-ridden Honduras in 1911 and to Nicaragua in 1910 and again in 1912 to protect American lives and property.

He was dogged, however, by several foreign policy defeats. In 1911 a trade reciprocity agreement he had negotiated to lower tariffs between the United States and Canada was rejected by the Canadian parliament. The same year the Senate attached crippling amendments to his treaty with Britain and France that would have established an arbitration process to settle international disputes between the signatories. Taft withdrew the treaty rather than sign it.

In 1912 the Republican Party nominated Taft for reelection, as his supporters controlled the Republican National Convention. Unhappy with this outcome, Roosevelt ran on a third-party ticket—the Progressive, or Bull Moose Party—

with the result that Roosevelt and Taft split the Republican vote, allowing Democrat Woodrow Wilson to capture the presidency.

When Taft's term expired, he taught law at Yale University but continued to yearn for an appointment to the Supreme Court. When Chief Justice Edward White died on May 19, 1921, President Warren G. Harding chose his friend and fellow Republican Taft to take his place. As chief justice, Taft was able to put into motion judicial reforms he had advocated while president. They led to passage of the Judiciary Act of 1925, which restricted the appellate jurisdiction of the Court, leaving it free to deal with statutory and constitutional questions. In judicial decisions, Taft's years on the Court were characterized by conservative rulings that generally reflected the interests of business and private groups. Taft resigned as chief justice on February 3, 1930, because of his weak heart. He died a few weeks later, on March 8, from heart failure.

See also *Progressive Era; Roosevelt, Theodore; Tariff History.*

SABRA BISSETTE LEDENT, INDEPENDENT AUTHOR

BIBLIOGRAPHY

Anderson, Donald F. *William Howard Taft: A Conservative's Conception of the Presidency.* Ithaca: Cornell University Press, 1973.

Anderson, Judith Icke. *William Howard Taft: An Intimate History.* New York: Norton, 1981.

Burton, David Henry. *The Learned Presidency: Theodore Roosevelt, William Howard Taft, Woodrow Wilson.* Rutherford, N.J.: Fairleigh Dickinson University Press, 1988.

Sen. Huey P. Long of Louisiana excoriates the New Deal in a national radio broadcast from Washington, D.C., on March 7, 1935. *Senate Historical Office*

TALK RADIO

Talk radio has existed since the birth of radio in the 1920s, when what was likely the first talk program, *Vox Populi,* or Voice of the People, first aired. From the early years through the 1960s and 1970s, few regular programs devoted strictly to political talk aired for national audiences, although talk programs existed on local stations, often sharing a frequency with popular entertainment programs and music.

During the early years of radio the format of talk radio was quite different from modern examples. Special public affairs broadcasts, speeches, or debates on significant policy issues comprised most programs. President Franklin D. Roosevelt's "fireside chats" are one notable example; radio speakers also frequently included Father Charles E. Coughlin, First Lady Eleanor Roosevelt, and Louisiana senator Huey P. Long. Debate programs included "Town Meeting on the Air."

In 1960 KABC in Los Angeles became the first major-market, all-talk station when it eliminated music programming entirely. One of the first big stars for KABC was Joe

Pyne, a host known for his contrarian political views, although he espoused no clear ideology. Pyne pioneered the confrontational style that is typical of modern talk shows. Callers were often treated brusquely, particularly if they disagreed with Pyne's views. The essence of the show was generating tension and confrontation. Pyne's program proved popular and spawned imitators around the nation, although primarily in local markets for local audiences.

EXPANSION OF PROGRAMMING

Two factors contributed to the meteoric rise of national talk radio in the late 1980s: technology and the deregulation of the telecommunications industry. The development of satellite technology during the early 1980s facilitated syndication of independent talk radio programs produced in local markets. Previously, only national networks could afford to produce national programs. With accessible satellite technology, local stations sampled from an array of programming much wider than previously possible and adopted programs tailored to the demographic characteristics of their local audiences.

This in turn attracted larger audiences and made talk radio more profitable, a particularly important feature given the decline of AM radio by the mid-1980s.

In addition, in an effort to assist deregulation of the telecommunications industry, the administration of Ronald Reagan stopped enforcing the "fairness doctrine." Under the fairness doctrine, broadcasters licensed by the Federal Communications Commission were required to provide political figures or groups criticized on air an opportunity to respond. Broadcasters risked stiff penalties, up to and including the loss of their licenses to broadcast, if they failed to provide for rebuttals. Rather than provide free air-time to political figures, radio stations either staged debates themselves or avoided political talk that was overtly critical. This was especially true of national networks. The end of the fairness doctrine allowed talk show hosts and their callers greater freedom to say what they liked without having to provide equal time to the other side. Deregulation encouraged a new degree of critical commentary and audience participation.

With these changes in the industry, new programs were launched that provided an outlet for opinions not heard in mainstream media, particularly political conservatives and those alienated by the modern welfare state. Far-right commentators like Chuck Hardin, whose "For the People" first aired in 1987, and more moderate conservatives such as Rush Limbaugh, who hit the airwaves with "The Rush Limbaugh Show" in 1988, acquired loyal audiences, largely consisting of "angry white males" looking for a place to vent their frustrations.

During the 1990s, with hosts like Limbaugh attracting huge audiences, other programs appealing to similar audiences were prepared for national network syndication. According to one survey, by 1996 there were 523 local political talk shows and 42 nationally syndicated political talk programs. Of these, the majority were hosted by white men, most of whom were conservative or libertarian in their views. Another popular program was "The Oliver North Show," which began airing in 1995. Oliver North, a central figure in the Iran-contra scandal during the Reagan administration, used his talk program to support a near-successful Senate bid in Virginia. Less overtly ideological programs included National Public Radio's "Talk of the Nation," which first aired in 1991.

TALK RADIO'S IMPACT ON POLITICS AND FUTURE

Talk radio's impact on politics is often linked to the rise of U.S. Rep. Newt Gingrich and other leaders of the so-called Republican Revolution, which resulted in Republicans winning the U.S. House and Senate in the 1994 elections. That new class of Republican House members made Limbaugh an honorary member of the caucus, symbolically rewarding him

for his role in their success. Talk radio also served as a vehicle in 1992 for Bill Clinton. Clinton used talk radio appearances in key primary states to build voter support when mainstream media largely ignored his candidacy. Later, during his presidency, talk radio cultivated public interest in personal scandals, such as Whitewater and the Monica Lewinsky affair, as well as policy blunders, including the federal raid on the Branch Davidian compound in Waco, Texas, and the unpopular effort to reform health care. During the 1990s talk radio was used to help build the Reform Party and continued to serve as a resource for candidates who ran at the fringes of their parties, particularly on the right side of the ideological spectrum.

At the start of the twenty-first century, talk radio's allure and significance have eroded somewhat. In part, talk radio has declined because it became more familiar and mainstream. In addition, Congress, which served as a convenient punching bag when controlled by the Democrats during the late 1980s and early 1990s, has been controlled by the Republicans since 1995. Finally, the Internet has become a mass media technology, providing average Americans with an interactive, real-time tool with which to acquire information and voice their views. Much like talk radio, the Internet has spawned unique personalities, the most notable of whom is perhaps Matt Drudge, creator of the *Drudge Report,* an on-line political tip sheet, gossip column, and opinion forum. By the end of 1998 both Limbaugh and Drudge had expanded their reach and become regular news analysts on television news shows, including NBC's venerable *Meet the Press.*

See also *Clinton, Bill; Newspapers and Political Parties; Reagan, Ronald; Roosevelt, Franklin D.; Television and American Politics.*

BRIAN C. WHITE, UNIVERSITY OF ILLINOIS AT CHICAGO

BIBLIOGRAPHY

Brewer, Annie M. *Talk Show Hosts on Radio.* 4th ed. Dearborn: Whiteford Press, 1996.
Hilliard, Robert L., and Michael C. Keith. *Waves of Rancor: Tuning in the Radical Right.* Armonk, N.Y.: M. E. Sharpe, 1999.
Kurtz, Howard. *Hot Air: All Talk, All the Time.* New York: Basic Books, 1997.
Laufer, Peter. *Inside Talk Radio.* New York: Birch Lane Press, 1995.

TARIFF HISTORY

There are two sides to the history of the tariff. On the one hand, the tariff was the major source of federal revenue from the 1790s to the eve of World War I, when it was finally surpassed by the income tax. So essential was this revenue source, and so easy was it to collect at the major ports, that all sides agreed that the nation should have a tariff for revenue purposes. In practice, the tariff was a tax of about 20 percent of the value of some imported goods. (Imports that were not taxed were "free.") On the other hand, despite this general agreement, the tariff and closely related issues such as import quotas and trade treaties have always generated enormous political stresses. At one point South Carolina threatened to break up the Union over the tariff issue.

EARLY TARIFFS

Congressional passage of the Tariff Act of 1789 was a key step toward breaking away from Britain and creating a unified, fully independent nation. The new Constitution allowed only the federal government to levy tariffs, so the old system of state rates disappeared. The new law taxed all imports at rates of 5 to 15 percent. These modest rates were designed primarily to generate revenue to service the national debt and meet the annual expenses of the federal government. Secretary of the Treasury Alexander Hamilton proposed a far-reaching scheme to use protective tariffs as a lever for rapid industrialization, but his proposals were ignored until 1816. Likewise, owners of the new small factories that were springing up in the Northeast to produce boots, hats, candles, nails, and other common items failed to obtain the higher tariffs that would have significantly protected them from more efficient British producers. A 10 percent discount on the tax was offered on goods imported in American ships, a device designed to help the carrying trade. Members of Congress proved keenly interested in supporting their local interests by suitable amendments to tweak the tariff schedules.

After the War of 1812, tariffs were raised sharply. Hatred of England was one reason, but the primary goal was protection of the manufacturing industries now growing rapidly in the Northeast. Every member of Congress was eager to "logroll" (trade votes for) a higher rate for his local industry. Massachusetts senator Daniel Webster, once a spokesperson for the Boston merchants who imported goods and wanted low tariffs, switched dramatically to represent the manufacturing interests. Rates were especially high for bolts of cloth and for bar iron, both of which Britain produced at low cost. The culmination was the 1828 "Tariff of Abominations," with duties averaging over 50 percent. South Carolinians reacted swiftly after concluding that under this tariff they would pay more for imports and sell less cotton abroad, so their economic interest was being injured. They attempted to "nullify" the federal tariff and spoke of secession from the Union. The compromise that ended the crisis included a lowering of the tariff.

Henry Clay and the Whigs, envisioning rapid modernization based on highly productive factories, sought a high tariff. Their main argument was that high tariffs were necessary to protect start-up factories, or "infant industries," which would at first be less efficient than European producers. Furthermore, American factory workers would be paid higher wages than their European competitors. These arguments proved highly persuasive in industrial districts. Those districts were not populous enough to outweigh rural America, however, so the Democrats controlled tariff policy. They sought minimal levels of a "tariff for revenue only" that would pay the cost of government but not show favoritism to one section or economic sector at the expense of another. As a result, rates fell steadily, bottoming out at 18 percent in 1861.

During the Civil War the federal government needed vast revenues. With the low-tariff southerners gone, the Republican-controlled Congress more than doubled the rates, which topped out at 49 percent in 1868. Advocates insisted that tariffs brought prosperity to the nation as a whole and injured no one. As the Northeast became more industrialized, some Democrats, especially Pennsylvanians, became tariff advocates. The Republican tariff advocates appealed to farmers with the theme that high-wage factory workers would pay premium prices for foodstuffs. This was the "home market" idea, but it had little relevance to the southern and western farmers who exported most of their cotton, tobacco, and wheat. In the late 1860s wool manufacturers based near Boston and Philadelphia formed the first national lobby and cut deals with wool-growing farmers in several states. They were faced with a challenge: fastidious wool producers in Britain and Australia were marketing a higher-quality fleece than the careless Americans. Moreover, British manufacturers enjoyed costs as low as those in the American mills. The result was a high tariff on imported wool that helped the farmers—a tariff American manufacturers had to pay—together with a high tariff on finished woolens and worsted goods.

Apart from wool and woolens, American industry and agriculture had become the most efficient in the world by the 1880s. They were not at risk from cheap imports. No other country had the industrial capacity, the high efficiency and low costs, or the complex distribution system needed to compete in the vast American market. Indeed, it was the British who watched in stunned horror as cheaper American products flooded their home islands. Wailed the *London Daily Mail* in 1900, "We have lost to the American manufacturer electrical machinery, locomotives, steel rails, sugar-producing and agricultural machinery, and latterly even stationary engines, the pride and backbone of the British engineering industry."

Nevertheless American manufacturers and workers demanded that the high tariff be maintained. The tariff itself represented a complex balance of forces. Railroads, for example, consumed vast quantities of steel. To the extent that tariffs raised steel prices, they felt injured. The Republicans became masters of negotiating exceedingly complex arrangements so that inside each of their congressional districts there were more satisfied "winners" than disgruntled "losers." The tariff after 1880 was an ideological relic with no economic rationale; it was a time bomb waiting to explode—and it repeatedly did explode.

Democratic president Grover Cleveland redefined the issue in 1887, with his stunning attack on the tariff as inherently corrupt, opposed to true republicanism, and inefficient to boot: "When we consider that the theory of our institutions guarantees to every citizen the full enjoyment of all the fruits of his industry and enterprise . . . it is plain that the exaction of more than [minimal taxes] is indefensible extortion and a culpable betrayal of American fairness and justice." The election of 1888 was fought primarily over the tariff issue, and Cleveland lost. Republican representative William McKinley argued, "Free foreign trade gives our money, our manufactures, and our markets to other nations to the injury of our labor, our tradespeople, and our farmers. Protection keeps money, markets, and manufactures at home for the benefit of our own people." Two years later, Democrats campaigned energetically against the high McKinley tariff of 1890 and scored sweeping gains in Congress; they restored Cleveland to the White House in 1892. The severe depression that started in 1893, however, undermined the Democratic Party. Cleveland insisted on a much lower tariff, but he was stymied by the fact that Democratic electoral successes had brought in Democratic members of Congress from industrial districts who were willing to raise rates to benefit their constituents. The Wilson-Gorman Tariff Act of 1894 did lower overall rates from 50 percent to 42 percent, but it contained so many concessions to protectionism that Cleveland refused to sign it.

In 1896 McKinley, now the Republican presidential candidate, campaigned heavily on the tariff as a positive solution to depression. Promising protection and prosperity to every economic sector, he won a smashing victory. The Republicans rammed the Dingley tariff through Congress in 1897, boosting rates back to the 50 percent level. Democrats protested that the high rates created "trusts" (monopolies) and led to higher consumer prices. In 1900 McKinley won reelection by an even larger majority and started talking about a post–tariff era of reciprocal trade agreements. Reciprocity, however, went nowhere; McKinley's vision was a half-century too early.

CONTINUED PARTISAN BICKERING AND WAR

The delicate balance flew apart on President William Howard Taft's watch. Taft, a Republican, campaigned in 1908 for tar-

iff "reform," which everyone assumed meant lower rates. The House lowered rates with the Payne bill, which it then sent to the Senate, where Nelson Aldrich of Rhode Island worked his sleight of hand. Whereas Aldrich was a New England businessman and a master of the complexities of the tariff, the midwestern Republican insurgents were rhetoricians and lawyers who distrusted the special interests and assumed the tariff was sheer robbery for the benefit of fat cats at the expense of the ordinary consumer. Aldrich, baiting the insurgents, lowered the protection on midwestern farm products, while raising rates favorable to his Northeast.

Meanwhile, Taft negotiated a reciprocity agreement with Canada that had the effect of sharply lowering tariffs. Democrats supported the plan, but midwestern Republicans bitterly opposed it. Barnstorming the country for his agreement, Taft undiplomatically pointed to the inevitable integration of the North American economy and suggested that Canada should come to a "parting of the ways" with Britain. Canada's Conservative Party now had an issue with which to regain power, and after a surge of proimperial anti–Americanism, the Conservatives won. Ottawa rejected reciprocity and turned its economy more toward London. In the end, then, the Payne-Aldrich tariff of 1909 changed little and had little economic impact one way or the other, but its political impact was enormous. The insurgents felt tricked and defeated and swore vengeance against Wall Street and its minions Taft and Aldrich. The insurgency led to a fatal split down the middle in 1912, which handed the Democrats the presidential election.

The winner, Woodrow Wilson, announced that a sharp reduction in tariff rates would be a major priority of his presidency. The 1913 Underwood-Simmons Tariff Act cut rates, but the outbreak of World War I in 1914 radically revised trade patterns and made tariffs much less important. When the Republicans regained power after the war, they restored the usual high rates. With the onset of the Great Depression in 1929, which was worldwide in scope, international trade shrank drastically. The crisis baffled the GOP, and it unwisely tried its magic one last time in the Hawley-Smoot Tariff Act of 1930. This time it backfired, as Britain, Germany, France, and other industrial countries retaliated with their own tariffs and special bilateral trade deals. American imports and exports went into a tailspin.

Upon taking office in 1933, Democrat Franklin D. Roosevelt and his New Dealers made promises about lowering tariffs on a reciprocal country-by-country basis (which they did), hoping such a step would expand foreign trade (which it did not). Frustrated, they gave much more attention to domestic remedies for the depression. By 1936 the tariff issue had faded from politics, and the revenue it raised was small. In World War II both tariffs and reciprocity were insignificant compared with trade channeled through the Lend-Lease arrangement approved by Congress in 1941 to provide goods and equipment to America's allies in the war.

POSTWAR CHANGES

After the war the United States promoted the General Agreement on Tariffs and Trade (GATT, 1947) to minimize tariffs and other restrictions and to liberalize trade among all capitalist countries. In 1995 GATT became the World Trade Organization (WTO). With the collapse of communism in the early 1990s, the WTO's open markets/low tariff ideology became dominant worldwide.

American industry and labor prospered after World War II, but hard times set in after 1970. For the first time there was stiff competition from low-cost producers around the globe. Many Rust Belt industries faded or collapsed, especially those manufacturing steel, television sets, shoes, toys, textiles, and clothing. Germany-based Volkswagen and Japan-based Honda threatened the giant U.S. automobile industry. In the late 1970s Detroit and the autoworkers union combined to fight for protection. They obtained not high tariffs, but import quotas. Quotas were two-country diplomatic agreements that had the same protective effect as high tariffs but did not invite retaliation from third countries. By limiting the number of Japanese automobiles that could be imported, for example, quotas forced consumers to buy American cars and allowed both the American and the Japanese car companies to raise prices and keep wages and profits high.

In the 1980s the GOP under Ronald Reagan and then George Bush abandoned the protective ideology and came out against quotas and in favor of the GATT/WTO policy of minimal economic barriers to global trade. The North American Free Trade Agreement (NAFTA) was the Bush plan to enlarge the scope of the market for American businesses to include Canada and Mexico. In 1993 President Bill Clinton, with strong Republican support, pushed NAFTA through Congress over the vehement objection of labor unions. Likewise in 2000 he worked with Republicans to give China entry to the WTO and most-favored-nation trading status (that is, low tariffs). NAFTA and WTO advocates promoted an optimistic vision of the future, with prosperity to be based on intellectual skills and managerial know-how more than on routine hand labor. They promised that free trade meant lower prices for consumers. However, it also meant lower wages and fewer jobs in older industries that could no longer compete. Labor unions were vocal in their opposition to liberalized trade, but their shrinking size and diminished political clout repeatedly left them on the losing side.

See also *Nullification*.

RICHARD JENSEN, RENSSELAER POLYTECHNIC INSTITUTE

BIBLIOGRAPHY

Eckes, Alfred. *Opening America's Market: U.S. Foreign Trade Policy since 1776.* Chapel Hill: University of North Carolina Press, 1995.

Taussig, F. W. *Some Aspects of the Tariff Question: An Examination of the Development of American Industries under Protection.* 1931. Reprint, New York: Greenwood Press, 1969.

Taussig, F. W. *The Tariff History of the United States.* 8th ed. New York: G. P. Putnam's, 1931.

Terrill, Tom E. *The Tariff, Politics, and American Foreign Policy, 1874–1901.* Westport, Conn.: Greenwood Press, 1973.

TAXATION AND TWENTIETH-CENTURY POLITICS

The power to tax is one of the most important economic powers of government. Taxation affects every individual and organization in the United States and is very important to the functioning of the economy as a whole. Parallel to the growth of federal, state, and local government over time, taxation has become an increasingly important economic and political issue. At the beginning of the twentieth century all taxes accounted for less than 7 percent of the gross domestic product (GDP). By the beginning of the twenty-first century taxes had grown to more than a third of the GDP.

As a political issue, taxation generally is of most use to officeholders who want to reduce tax levels. Some scholars, however, see debate over taxation as a handy surrogate for larger but more complex philosophical differences between those who believe in government and the government allocation of economic resources to what they consider public ends, and those who distrust government and believe these resources are better used when they are left in the hands of private citizens.

DIMENSIONS OF THE TAX SYSTEM

Tax policy has many dimensions and affects a broad range of economic decisions such as borrowing for education, purchasing a home, investing in the stock market, deciding whether and how to save, and making business investments. The tax system is composed of a set of tax rates—the percentage of income paid in taxes—that increase with higher-income levels (a system known as progressive taxation), as well as deductions, exemptions, and credits that lower the final tax bill.

The basic goal of tax policy is to generate the revenue needed to run the government, but taxes have other economic goals as well, including encouraging certain types of economic behavior by offering tax benefits. The tax system is also designed to redistribute income by providing programs to the lower-income classes through the progressive tax-rate structure and through certain types of cash payments, such as one called the earned-income credit that financially helps the lowest-income individuals even if they earn too little to pay taxes. With so many dimensions, the tax system has become increasingly complicated over time. For a number of years some political groups have lobbied for tax reform that usually entails tax simplification, or doing away with the myriad of tax brackets, rules, credits, and deductions.

EVOLUTION OF MODERN TAXATION

Americans' attitude toward taxation has always been strong. One of the first celebrated acts of the American Revolution was the dumping of crates of tea into Boston Harbor in opposition to a British tax on tea. Delegates to the Constitutional Convention in 1787, however, knew that effective government needed to be funded. The Constitution gave Congress the power to "collect Taxes, Duties, Imposts and Excises, to pay the Debts and provide for the common Defence and general Welfare of the United States." During the ensuing century, the federal government operated chiefly on the income from customs duties and excise taxes.

Tax policy expanded gradually as a political issue in step with the rise of taxes as a share of the economy. The first major milestone in the evolution of the tax system was the establishment of the federal income tax in 1913 under the Sixteenth Amendment to the U.S. Constitution. Prior to the income tax, about three-quarters of federal tax revenue came from sales taxes and customs duties. At the state level, most tax revenue was from property tax and sales taxes, and, at the local level, from property taxes. After the income tax amendment, most of the significant milestones came during the Great Depression of the 1930s and the decades that followed as the size and cost of government expanded enormously. Those milestones include:

Federal income tax (1913)
Social Security system and taxation (1935)
Federal withholding tax (1942)
Rewriting of the tax code (1954)
President John F. Kennedy's economic stimulation tax cut (1961)
Income tax bracket creep (1970s)
Economic Recovery Act of 1981
Tax Reform Act of 1986
President George Bush's "No new taxes" pledge (1988)
Omnibus Budget and Reconciliation Acts of 1990 and 1993
President Bill Clinton's tax increase (1993)

During the Great Depression in the 1930s not only were lessons learned regarding tax policy, but a major new tax was levied to fund the government-run pension plan known as Social Security. This law added a payroll tax, both for the employee and the employer, that was small at first but later grew to be a major factor in tax policy. The program was initially designed as a pay-as-you-go plan with annual tax receipts roughly equaling annual benefit payments. As a larger percentage of the population was covered under the program and demographics changed, the program became increasingly expensive. As a result, most Americans paid more in payroll taxes (dominated by Social Security and later Medicare) than in standard income taxes. Social Security, in becoming by far the largest government entitlement program, also became an important political issue.

This trend is also reflected in burden sharing for federal taxes. In the latter part of the twentieth century, the corporate share of total taxes paid declined from more than 20 percent to around 10 percent of total federal collections, while individuals' taxes remained at near 45 percent. There was a large increase in social insurance taxes (mainly for Social Security), which increased to nearly 35 percent of total taxes paid.

In the first half of the 1940s, World War II prompted important changes in the tax code. The major change was the institution of the withholding tax on pay checks, making employers the tax collector for the government. Withholding, too, became a political issue, with opponents of taxation and government activism regarding it as a hidden way to finance federal programs. These critics argued that withholding taxes desensitized citizens to the reality of paying tax because a wage earner, rather than actively writing a check to the government for the tax bill, passively pays taxes by accepting take-home pay as an after-tax residual. This change may have helped people accept the higher level of taxes that prevailed after World War II. (About half the costs of that war were financed by taxation, with the rest from government borrowing.)

Advocates of withholding always argued that it was the only way to operate a large and costly government, and the withholding controversy had all but disappeared by the end of the century. The massive rewriting of the entire tax code in 1954 created a tax system similar to the current system with personal and other deductions. Over time, the personal exemption has declined as a proportion of income, while other types of deductions have increased. Tax policy gained importance after World War II as a tool for economic stimulus. Previously, government spending was thought to be the one and only way to achieve fiscal stimulus. The use of tax policy as a way to accelerate growth (and perhaps to make recessions less frequent) was realized with the "Kennedy tax cut" of 1964, a plan originally put forward by President Kennedy before his death. Tax cuts were the perfect political tool because they simultaneously pleased constituencies and had benign economic effects.

During the 1960s inflation increased steadily to the point that President Lyndon Johnson and his economic team determined that tax increases were needed to curb it. Johnson's plan was a 10 percent tax surcharge, which also had the additional purpose of financing the Vietnam War. The measure failed, and inflation continued to climb in the 1970s, reaching peaks in 1974 and 1980.

In the 1970s, because income tax brackets were not indexed to inflation, taxpayers were pushed into higher and higher tax brackets even though their *real* incomes had not increased. This phenomenon, known as "bracket creep," resulted in increased tax revenue for the government without Congress having to vote for it. With the election of Ronald Reagan in 1980, tax policy changed significantly. First, Reagan pushed through Congress a 25 percent income tax cut to correct for most of the effects of bracket creep in the 1970s. Congressional indexing—at Reagan's prompting—of

President Ronald Reagan signs 1981 tax cut legislation. *Karl H. Schumacher, The White House*

income tax brackets to the rate of inflation in 1985 prevented the federal government from gaining additional revenues through inflation. Although the tax cuts resulted in strong national growth, a fiscal imbalance followed in which the federal debt increased from 33 percent of GDP to 56 percent during his administration. A significant buildup in defense expenditures by the Reagan administration also contributed to this debt increase.

An important piece of legislation, the Tax Reform Act of 1986, reduced the number of tax brackets for individuals from fifteen to two and eliminated many cherished tax breaks. Under the two-bracket system, married and single individuals were taxed at 15 percent up to a certain level of income and 28 percent thereafter. Among the significantly curtailed or eliminated tax deductions were those for interest on consumer loans, medical expenses, sales tax, political and charitable contributions, and unreimbursed business expenses. The 1986 law changed the tax code to reduce the attractiveness of tax shelters significantly by repealing the investment tax credit, scaling back the depreciation schedules of the 1981 tax legislation, and eliminating deduction for losses from tax shelters. Through these changes, the 1986 tax law is credited with significantly improving the efficiency of investment because more investment decisions would be based on their economic merits rather than their tax benefits. Elimination of deductions meant that the federal government pulled back from intervening in many consumption and investment decisions by the public and companies. However, in the years after 1986, the tax system's complexity gradually increased again. By the end of the 1990s there were five tax brackets, new deductions, and more forms required.

TAX REFORM PROPOSALS

The major proposals to reform the tax code generally attempt to simplify tax law and promote savings. Tax simplification usually means a reduction in power for the government because the tax code cannot be used as freely for constituent satisfaction; when deductions are minimized (in favor of lower overall rates), the tax code becomes less of a political tool. The impetus for tax reform tends to strengthen as the tax code becomes increasingly complex, as was the case during the 1990s. The concern over low savings rates also spurs some politicians to reform the tax system in favor of more incentives to encourage saving. Traditionally, Republicans favor lower, flatter taxes, while Democrats tend to favor more progressive and higher taxes. Democrats also tend to favor a greater number of specific interventions through the tax code in order to pursue social and other goals.

Major tax reform proposals include a flat tax (rather than a progressive or graduated tax), value-added tax (VAT), personal consumption tax, and national sales tax. Although the principle of tax reform has strong support, none of these proposals has gained sufficient votes for passage or even serious debate in Congress. The main argument against tax reform is the view that the current system reflects the government's priorities and that it should intervene in many areas to guide the economy to promote social goals. One of the most important practical obstacles to reform is rooted in the political fact that many special interests have deeply vested interests in the status quo and naturally resist change that could present an entirely new economic landscape, possibly to the detriment of their financial interests.

See also *Great Depression; Reagan, Ronald; World War II.*

RICHARD J. CARROLL, INDEPENDENT SCHOLAR

BIBLIOGRAPHY

Ando, Albert, Marshall E. Blume, and Irwin Friend. *The Structure and Reform of the U.S. Tax System.* Cambridge, Mass.: MIT Press, 1985.

Carroll, Richard J. *Desk Reference on the Economy: Over 600 Answers to Questions That Will Help You Understand News, Trends, and Issues.* Washington, D.C.: CQ Press, 2000.

General Accounting Office. *Tax Administration: Potential Impact of Alternative Taxes on Taxpayers and Administrators.* Washington, D.C.: Government Printing Office, 1998.

Hall, Arthur. "Compliance Costs of Alternative Tax Systems II—Special Brief." House Ways and Means Committee testimony. Washington, D.C.: Tax Foundation, 1996.

Jorgenson, Dale W. "The Agenda for U.S. Tax Reform." *Canadian Journal of Economics* (1996): 649–657.

"The Plethora of Consumption Tax Proposals: Putting Value Added Tax, Flat Tax, Retail Sales Tax and USA Tax into Perspective." *San Diego Law Review* (fall 1996): 1282–1327.

TAYLOR, ZACHARY

Born in Virginia on November 24, 1784, Zachary Taylor was a career soldier with no political experience before entering the White House. Indeed, he had never voted in a presidential election until he successfully ran for office in 1848. Taylor served in the army from 1807 until 1848. He was an enormously successful general during the Mexican-American War (1847–1848), winning important victories over much larger forces at Palo Alto, Rescara de Palma, Monterrey, and finally at Buena Vista, where he led six thousand soldiers, most of them inexperienced volunteers, to a decisive victory against twenty thousand seasoned troops under Gen. Santa Anna. In 1848, running as a Whig, Taylor followed in the image of Washington, Jackson, and Harrison, evolving from military hero to president.

His presidency was shaped by the crisis over slavery in the territories acquired from Mexico. Although a slaveholding sugar planter, Taylor was politically close to William H. Seward, the antislavery senator from New York. Taylor opposed the spread of slavery into the western territories, in part because he thought it impractical. He could never comprehend the proslavery arguments of men like John C. Calhoun, who wanted to force slavery into places, like New Mexico, where Taylor was certain it would be uneconomical. He was adamant about California entering the Union as a free state, because that was what the people there wanted. He also opposed attempts by Texas to expand into the New Mexico territory, and he threatened to use the army to stop Texas's encroachments. Consistent with Whig policy, he also opposed attempts to annex Cuba or interfere with the internal affairs of Latin American countries. He managed to avoid renewing the Seminole War and refused to use the army to remove peaceful Indians from their land in New Mexico.

The greatest issues of his presidency were slavery in the new territories and southern nationalist threats to leave the Union. He refused to tolerate the latter and, like Andrew Jackson, threatened to use the army to quell any southern resistance to federal law. For the first six months of 1850 Taylor watched Congress debate the measures that would become the Compromise of 1850. He supported popular sovereignty in the territories and was lukewarm on the idea of a new fugitive slave law. His main goal was to secure California's admission to the Union as a free state. He did not live to see this goal. On July 4, 1850, Taylor, who weighed over three hundred pounds, ate large quantities of fresh fruit and drank a great deal of milk while watching Independence Day parades. By the end of the day he was suffering from sunstroke and gastroenteritis. He might have recovered from both but could not recover from his medical treatment, which included calomel (which is made from mercury), opium, and induced bleeding. He died on July 9, 1850.

A war hero, patriotic nationalist, and southern slaveowner, Taylor had the right background to lead the nation through the crisis after the Mexican-American War. He was prepared to face down southern extremists while at the same time protect slavery where it existed. Had he lived, Taylor might have succeeded in reducing sectional tensions, in part by the sheer force of his will and prestige. His death left the nation in the hands of Millard Fillmore, a lilliputian president more concerned with winning the next election than with the large issues the nation faced.

See also *Mexican-American War; Territorial Expansion; Whig Party.*

PAUL FINKELMAN, UNIVERSITY OF TULSA COLLEGE OF LAW

BIBLIOGRAPHY

Hamilton, Holman. *Zachary Taylor: Soldier in the White House.* Indianapolis: Bobbs-Merrill, 1951.

———. *Zachary Taylor: Soldier of the Republic.* Indianapolis: Bobbs-Merrill, 1941.

Smith, Elbert B. *The Presidencies of Zachary Taylor and Millard Fillmore.* Lawrence: University Press of Kansas, 1988.

TEAPOT DOME AND OTHER HARDING ADMINISTRATION SCANDALS

Warren G. Harding, the twenty-ninth president of the United States, was selected as his party's candidate when the Republican convention in 1920 deadlocked and more prominent leaders failed to secure sufficient support. "This man," one Republican senator remarked, "is not a world beater, but the times do not require first raters." President Harding would confess to a friend, "I am not fit for this office and should never have been here."

The Teapot Dome scandal was one result of his administrative shortcomings. The people he put into office soon betrayed him. He told the well-known journalist William Allen White, "I have no trouble with my enemies . . . it is my friends that are giving me my trouble."

Many friends had followed the former senator from Ohio into the White House, where they were known as the "Ohio Gang." Several were responsible for a series of smaller scandals that ravaged the Harding administration before Teapot Dome. There was the activity at the "little green house on K Street," where cronies of Harding friend, Attorney General Harry Daugherty, sold pardons and paroles to prohibition law violators and income tax evaders. There was the Veterans Bureau scandal, whose director (a Harding friend not from Ohio) grafted or wasted more than $200 million in two years and was sent to a federal penitentiary. There was the problem in the Alien Property Custodian Office, whose director—another Harding Ohio pal—was sentenced to a term in prison for accepting bribes in a scandal that involved prominent politicians from New York and Connecticut and that ultimately led to Daugherty's resignation.

The greatest political scandal of the 1920s (which gave its name to all the others) was Teapot Dome. In Wyoming, a massive geologic formation known as Teapot Rock was located near an oil deposit set aside by the federal government in 1915. Oilmen connected the pool with the great sandstone formation and called the reserve Teapot Dome. Officially, it was known as U.S. Naval Oil Reserve Number Three. Together with two oil-rich tracts in California, it had been put under the care of the Department of the Navy to assure that the new fleet of oil-fueled American warships would have sufficient fuel to meet any emergency.

Secretary of the Interior Albert Fall, who had served in the Senate from 1912, where he was friendly with Senator Harding, until his appointment to the cabinet, was the major figure in this affair. Fall persuaded Secretary of the Navy Edwin

Who Says a Watched Pot Never Boils?

The Teapot Dome scandal would mar the reputation of President Warren G. Harding after his death. *Library of Congress*

Denby to transfer control of the naval oil reserves to the Department of the Interior in 1921. Secretary Fall then leased the reserves to two immensely wealthy and powerful oilmen: the entire area of Teapot Dome to Harry Sinclair's Mammoth Oil Company, and the California sites to Edward L. Doheny's Pan-American Oil Company.

Warren Harding died in August 1923 of a cerebral embolism after a long and enervating journey to Alaska, and the scandal that would destroy his reputation had not yet come to public attention. In fact, it took many months to unravel the full story of Teapot Dome. Several individuals played important roles in this process, including Harry A. Slattery, former secretary of the National Conservation Association and a self-appointed watchdog of public lands and resources; Robert La Follette of Wisconsin, the colorful leader of progressive Republicans and a bold and forceful spokesman for environmental concerns; and Sen. Thomas J. Walsh of Montana, whose reputation for integrity and fairness made him the unofficial leader of the congressional investigation of Teapot Dome conducted by the Senate Committee on Public Lands and Surveys.

In the end, the investigation revealed that the two oilmen had bribed Fall with more than $400,000 and a herd of cattle for his ranch in New Mexico. All three faced trial. Fall was sentenced to one year in prison and a massive fine. Suffering from chronic tuberculosis, he served nine months of his sentence before emerging a wasted (and bankrupt) figure.

Echoes of Teapot Dome resounded during the presidential election of 1924, but it was the opposition Democrats who were tarred by the politics of oil. President Calvin Coolidge, who stepped into the White House following Harding's death in August 1923, grasped the initiative in the scandal investigation, appointing his own special counsel to pursue the question and prosecute the cases in court. And while he was acting, a leading Democratic candidate for the presidency, former secretary of the Treasury William Gibbs McAdoo, was caught up in the backwash of the scandal. McAdoo had received a large yearly retainer from Edward Doheny, and after McAdoo left the cabinet, his firm had handled Doheny's tax cases before the Treasury Department. McAdoo was mercilessly ridiculed by hostile writers, and his presidential campaign foundered at the party convention, where enemies in the balconies shouted "Oil, Oil Oil" at him and his supporters.

Calvin Coolidge was an easy winner in the 1924 election, and concern with the Teapot Dome scandal quickly faded in the bright glow of the "Coolidge prosperity."

See also *Harding, Warren G.; Scandals and Corruption.*

DAVID H. BENNETT, SYRACUSE UNIVERSITY

BIBLIOGRAPHY

Bates, James Leonard. *Origins of Teapot Dome: Progressivism, Parties and Petroleum, 1909–1921.* Westport, Conn.: Greenwood Press, 1978.

Noggle, Burl. *Teapot Dome: Oil and Politics in the 1920s.* Westport, Conn: Greenwood Press, 1980.

Stratton, David A. *Tempest over Teapot Dome: The Story of Albert B. Fall.* Norman: University of Oklahoma Press, 1998.

TELEVISION AND AMERICAN POLITICS

Advances in technology have contributed greatly to changes in the conduct of politics. Examples include changes in printing technology that weakened the link between newspapers and parties, and the development of the Internet, which is providing individuals and groups with new ways to interact with each other and with the general public. Since the mid–twentieth century, the most important technological change affecting American politics has been television, a communication tool that can deliver politics and government to a mass audience in real time.

Television was developed in the 1920s and readied for a mass consumer audience by the early 1930s. Through the early 1940s, however, radio remained the electronic medium for politics and public affairs. During the Great Depression, President Franklin D. Roosevelt used his famous "fireside chats" to speak directly to the American people about the problems facing the nation and his administration's programs to address them. In times of crisis, presidents and other leaders would consistently turn to radio, then later to TV, to "go public" with their concerns.

During the 1930s radio was also used to broadcast news of the impending war in Europe. In particular, reports from William L. Shirer, Edward R. Murrow, and other CBS reporters alerted America to the growing tensions incited by Adolf Hitler's Nazi Germany. At home, anti-interventionist broadcasts, such as the often anti-Semitic speeches of Detroit's Father Charles E. Coughlin, the "fighting priest," stirred opposition to U.S. involvement in Europe's problems. As the war progressed, evocative and stirring reports of air attacks on civilian targets, including during the Battle of Britain in 1940, helped swing public opinion toward American intervention, which the Japanese attack on Pearl Harbor made inevitable. Although radio transformed news into a participatory exercise, TV enhanced the experience with visuals and graphics.

The federal government recognized the power of radio and television almost from the start. The Federal Communications Commission (FCC) was established in 1934 to regulate use of the airwaves along with interstate wire communications such as telephone and telegraph. The FCC's primary function is to license broadcasters, principally to avoid having two or more competing on the same frequency, but also to ensure that the airwaves are used responsibly. Although the First Amendment's free speech guarantees limit government control of the airwaves, two FCC rules significantly affect politics.

The "right of rebuttal" rule stipulates that any candidate or official attacked on the air be given an opportunity to rebut the charges. The "equal time" rule requires broadcasters to offer all candidates for the same elective office opportunities to buy air time. The main effect of these rules has been to limit owners' use of television (and radio) to promote pet candidates and to bash their opponents without giving them recourse. A third rule, no longer in effect, was the "fairness doctrine," which for thirty-eight years required broadcasters to provide air time for conflicting viewpoints on issues. Broadcasters complained that the rule infringed on their free speech rights, and to avoid violations they shied away from controversial programming. After President Ronald Reagan vetoed a congressional attempt to write the fairness doctrine into law, the FCC repealed it August 4, 1987.

At the onset, television's use in politics was limited by the high cost of owning a television set and by the limited number of broadcast stations across the country. The scarcity of metals during World War II also slowed the mass production of TV sets. Radio and print media remained the dominant means of mass communication through the mid-1950s. The first television news programs were in fact adapted by the networks out of their radio news departments and were staffed and anchored by radio and print journalists.

ADAPTING TO THE MEDIUM

By 1950 two national networks, CBS and NBC, were broadcasting nightly, fifteen-minute news programs, using the standard "talking-head" format. The newscasts covered political and other news from around the nation and the world. Newsreel companies provided most of the film footage. Unique and special events, such as the Senate investigations of organized crime (1950–1951), the national party conventions (every four years since 1952), and the McCarthy hearings on alleged communist influence in the U.S. Army (1954), were covered on live television as well as in the newscasts. These special programs allowed the American public to see politics and government in action, while also helping launch the careers of future leaders such as Richard Nixon and Robert F. Kennedy. In some cases, as with Wisconsin senator Joseph R. McCarthy, television helped shorten political careers.

Politicians in the 1950s recognized the power of television and tried to harness the technology in both politics and government. Each of the networks devoted near nonstop coverage to the 1952 Democratic and Republican nominating conventions, providing more than seventy hours of coverage per network. The TV coverage provided access to the public and established the conventions as arenas where unknown or semiobscure political figures could debut before a national audience. Illinois governor Adlai E. Stevenson, for example, became the 1952 Democratic nominee for president after a draft for him developed on the convention floor.

During the 1950s candidates also developed ads for television, although most advertising dollars continued to go to radio and print ads. The first national TV ads were used by Stevenson's Republican opponent, Dwight D. Eisenhower, in 1952. By the presidential election of 2000, more than two-thirds of an entire national campaign budget would be devoted to advertising, almost all of it on television. Over the years, politics has become more individualized, more candidate-centered, and less dependent on institutions such as parties. Today, much of the decline in the significance of parties can be directly attributed to the rise of television as a maker of political leaders.

Eisenhower was the first president to hire media advisers to help polish his television persona. He was also the first to hold regular news conferences filmed for television. Prior to his presidency, press conferences were granted to select print reporters generally favored by the president. Eisenhower opened press conferences to all news media, including radio and TV. Questions were allowed on any subject, giving the press a much greater role in shaping public perceptions of the president.

As with the conventions, the televised press conferences gave the American public greater access to politics than was available previously. With TV, they could watch the president take questions and respond, giving them an opportunity to assess the president's ability to "think on his feet." Since Eisenhower, televised press conferences have become a staple of presidential politics, though not all presidents fare so well with them as Eisenhower or his successor, John F. Kennedy, the first president to hold live-broadcast news conferences. Ronald Reagan, for instance, did poorly at press conferences, despite his training as an actor and his skilled delivery of prepared speeches. He often appeared confused by questions and uncertain in his responses. As a consequence, Reagan's advisers promoted carefully scripted public appearances to convey the Reagan message. By contrast, Bill Clinton, like Kennedy, excelled before the press. Both men had an unusually firm grasp of detailed policy questions and seemed comfortable making unscripted appearances on camera.

COMING OF AGE

In the 1960s television and politics synergized. The 1960 election is generally considered the one that marks the dawning of the television age in American politics. That year the famous Chicago debate between Vice President Richard Nixon and Senator Kennedy of Massachusetts was televised for a live national audience. The Nixon-Kennedy debates were notable because they demonstrated how a candidate's image and television poise could overcome perceived weaknesses in other areas.

Public opinion polls taken after the debate showed that TV viewers thought Kennedy came away the stronger candidate. By contrast, those who listened to the debate on radio thought Nixon and Kennedy were equal. Analysts suggest that Kennedy's youthful good looks and deep tan contrasted favorably with Nixon's sallow complexion and "five o'clock shadow." Nixon also sweated under the hot studio lights, making him seem shifty and uncomfortable with the questions. Kennedy appeared calm and collected. The debate introduced Kennedy to American voters and left them with a generally favorable impression.

Television brought into American living rooms many of the major social upheavals of the 1960s—the civil rights movement in the South and the images of fire hoses and dogs being used against marchers; the riots in major cities; and the

A family watches the September 28, 1960, debate between Sen. John F. Kennedy and Vice President Richard Nixon. The well spoken, photogenic Kennedy made good use of the medium. *National Archives*

war in Vietnam along with the protests the war generated. President Lyndon B. Johnson, who held the White House from 1963 to 1969, was so concerned about how television news discussed his stewardship of the government that he kept three TV sets in the Oval Office, where he regularly monitored the nightly newscasts. Johnson was not above calling the heads of the networks to chew them out when they ran news stories unfavorable to his administration. In 1968, after watching CBS News anchor Walter Cronkite suggest that the United States could not win in Vietnam, Johnson told aides privately that the war was lost. Johnson felt that if Cronkite came out against the war, so would the millions of viewers who trusted Cronkite's judgment. The example helps illustrate the growing importance that elected officials attached to television news.

In 1967 Congress amended the 1934 Communications Act to create the Corporation for Public Broadcasting, which supports nonprofit public radio and television broadcasting through federal grants. The corporation subsequently formed the Public Broadcasting Service to distribute national public television programs, including news and public affairs programs that emphasize coverage of politics and elections.

By 1970 and throughout the decade, television firmly established itself as the primary medium by which Americans learned about and followed politics and government. Millions of viewers tuned in to the daily live broadcasts of the Senate

Watergate hearings on the 1972 burglary of Democratic National Committee headquarters and the Nixon administration's subsequent attempts to cover up the crime. In August 1974 millions again watched as Nixon gave his farewell address after the scandal made him the first president to resign.

Later, the fall of Saigon and the evacuation of the U.S. embassy there in 1975 signaled the close of American involvement in Vietnam. By the end of the decade, television viewers would witness another embarrassment, the taking of American hostages in Tehran. For many, the images of Iranian students swarming over the embassy walls and later, the blindfolded hostages being led out, seared in the nation's consciousness a fear that the United States was no longer in control of its own destiny. ABC's *Nightline* news show was born during the Iran crisis under the title "America Held Hostage." Anchor Ted Koppel closed each program with the daily tally of how long the hostages had been held. The count reached 444 days when Iran released the hostages as President Reagan took office in 1981. The events of the 1970s and early 1980s demonstrated that television could serve those who held power, such as the American presidents, as well as those who sought power, such as the student revolutionary leaders in Tehran.

During the 1970s television news continued to expand outside the standard news format consisting of a talking head moderating and presenting the day's top stories. News magazine shows such as CBS's *Sixty Minutes* and ABC's *Twenty/Twenty* helped solidify the magazine format as a staple of news programming. These shows focused in greater depth on political issues and practiced a much more confrontational and independent news style than traditional news broadcasts. They took time to explore complex issues, much as newspapers do, while presenting stories with dramatic and visually gripping images. Magazine shows became among the most popular programs, with dozens of variations broadcast on network and cable television, both commercial and public.

GROWTH AND EXPANSION

In the 1980s a deregulated cable television industry expanded the public's opportunities to observe the government in action. In 1981 Ted Turner launched Cable News Network (CNN), providing round-the-clock coverage of news and world events. Although many initially dismissed the all-news format, CNN became a major medium in world and national politics.

In the late 1980s and early 1990s CNN helped bring viewers gavel-to-gavel coverage of the Iran-contra hearings and the Supreme Court nomination hearings of Judges Robert Bork and Clarence Thomas. The presence of cameras heightened the tension and drama of these events, adding to the hearings' divisive impact on the public and on the political parties. The Thomas hearings in particular attracted more than 90 percent of all households for at least part of the three days of coverage in October 1991, showing that public affairs issues could still hold people's attention despite increasing competition from entertainment-oriented programming.

During the Persian Gulf War following Iraq's invasion of Kuwait in 1991, CNN was the only western news organization broadcasting from inside Baghdad during the U.S.-led air strikes and Iraq's subsequent withdrawal. Consequently, American leaders relied heavily on CNN for information on the bombing campaign's impact. In other international crises, CNN has repeatedly been the only communication link between parties separated by distance, ideology, and circumstance.

The cable industry's C-SPAN (Cable-Satellite Public Affairs Network) was also launched during the early 1980s, providing Americans with gavel-to-gavel coverage of House and Senate floor proceedings. C-SPAN, although less pervasive than CNN, nonetheless contributed significantly to U.S. politics, again by bringing relatively unknown figures into large numbers of households.

The rise of Newt Gingrich and congressional conservatives during the late 1980s, for example, is often linked to C-SPAN's live broadcasts of House sessions. Gingrich was one of the first to take advantage of C-SPAN in bringing his criticism of Democrats to a wider audience. What the viewers did not realize, because the camera was closely focused on him standing in the well of the House, was that Gingrich usually was speaking to an empty chamber. The Democrats caught on quickly, however, and on occasion ordered the camera operators (who were House employees) to include the audience when showing members speaking. CNN and C-SPAN also provided extensive coverage of the Iran-contra hearings on use of illegal arms sales to Iran to bypass a congressional ban on military aid to antigovernment guerrillas in Nicaragua. The hearings undermined President Reagan's public standing near the end of his presidency.

In the 1990s television's role in American politics continued to expand. The growth of cable, public, and satellite television expanded significantly the number of hours of political news and talk available to viewers and politicians alike. Broadcasters, in an effort to stand out in the information glut, turned to "narrowcasting," or programming targeted to narrow, niche audiences, as a way to reach their target audience. Just as CNN introduced the twenty-four-hour news format

and C-SPAN a channel devoted to the legislative branch, Court-TV took cameras into courtrooms for a closer look at the judicial branch. MSNBC, a joint effort of Microsoft News and NBC, began offering a mostly news talk format. Dozens of other networks also found ways to try to capture the interests of niche news audiences around the nation and the world.

THE FUTURE

As the twenty-first century began, the increasing concentration of television and other media in the hands of a few giant media conglomerates was a major concern for political scientists and others interested in the future of American politics. Already most U.S. newspapers were owned and operated by a small number of companies. Many also owned television and radio outlets, as well as portions of Internet companies.

The concern among many observers was that with the concentration of news ownership comes a potential stifling of news diversity. At least one media conglomerate, the Tribune Company, owner of the *Chicago Tribune* and *Los Angeles Times,* as well as TV, Internet, and radio holdings, announced plans to have print journalists report stories on the electronic outlets and to have the so-called new media reporters also write for the newspapers. It was unclear how increased concentration of media ownership, on the one hand, and competition from the Internet, on the other hand, would affect television's future relationship with politics.

See also *Campaigning; Newspapers and Political Parties; Talk Radio; Scandals and Corruption.*

BRIAN C. WHITE, UNIVERSITY OF ILLINOIS AT CHICAGO

BIBLIOGRAPHY

Ansolabehere, Stephen, Roy Behr, and Shanto Iyengar. *The Media Game: American Politics in the Age of Television.* New York: Macmillan, 1993.

Davis, Richard, and Diana Owen. *New Media and American Politics.* New York: Oxford University Press, 1998.

Graber, Doris. *Mass Media and American Politics.* 6th ed. Washington, D.C.: CQ Press, 2000.

Hess, Stephen. *Live From Capitol Hill: Studies of Congress and the Media.* Washington, D.C.: Brookings Institution, 1991.

Lang, Kurt, and Gladys Engel Lang. *Politics and Television.* Chicago: Quadrangle Books, 1968.

West, Darrel M. *Air Wars: Television Advertising in Election Campaigns, 1952–1996.* 2d ed. Washington, D.C.: CQ Press, 1997.

TENNESSEE VALLEY AUTHORITY

On May 18, 1933, President Franklin D. Roosevelt signed into law the Tennessee Valley Authority (TVA) and reinvigorated the Progressive-era debate over public versus private stewardship of the nation's natural resources. In his proposal to Congress Roosevelt had warned, "Many hard lessons have taught us the human waste that results from lack of planning." Thus began a great political, social, and economic experiment in federal planning designed to harness the Tennessee River and supply rural and urban communities in seven states (Alabama, Georgia, Kentucky, Mississippi, North Carolina, Tennessee, and Virginia) with hydroelectric power. New Dealers hoped that the plan would help initiate a national power policy and in turn spawn seven "little TVAs" with local agencies capable of designing regional plans for flood control, production of hydroelectric power, and agricultural land-use schemes.

Public debate over strategies to tame the Tennessee River had entered public discourse by the late nineteenth century. Attempts to enhance navigation on the river and provide a national waterways policy included President Theodore Roosevelt's 1907 Inland Waterways Commission, the 1909 Conservation Congress, and the 1909 National Conservation Commission Report. President Woodrow Wilson extended the quest in 1916 with the National Defense Act, which culminated in the construction of the Wilson Dam and the $145 million Muscle Shoals power plant. Unable to dispose of the electricity generated from the plant, government officials began a campaign to find a means of distributing power resources to the local inhabitants. Over the next few years Sen. George Norris, a Nebraska Progressive Republican, proposed six public development bills to continue the federal venture into planning. Success was elusive as Presidents Calvin Coolidge and Herbert Hoover vetoed the bills in an effort to return resource development to the private sector.

When FDR took office in 1933 many Americans, devastated by the Great Depression, were in the mood for a radical departure into federal and regional resource planning. FDR decided that state boundaries should be overlooked for regional plans that promote the common good of the nation. With these ideas in mind Roosevelt established the TVA as a public corporation with three directors—Arthur E. Morgan (chairperson), H. A. Morgan, and David Lilienthal—and plans proceeded to produce and distribute electricity at a fair price.

Like many New Deal planning activities, the TVA faced numerous opponents and internal struggles. In 1934 the Alabama Power Company filed suit against the TVA on the constitutional grounds that the federal government could not usurp a state's control of its own lands. To make matters worse, by 1935 Arthur Morgan was fighting with Lilienthal over direction of the program. Despite setbacks and detractors, between 1933 and 1944 the program constructed nine main and numerous smaller dams and supplied the power for the manufacture of war munitions, fertilizer for farmers, and electricity for rural residents. At the end of World War II the TVA became solely a power-producing operation.

The TVA planted the seeds for modern-day political discourse on private versus public planning of national resources, extending to the national park system, environmental protection, federal oil reserves, soil management, and water rights.

See also *New Deal; Progressive Era; Roosevelt, Franklin D.*

VICTOR W. GERACI, CENTRAL CONNECTICUT STATE UNIVERSITY

BIBLIOGRAPHY

Grant, Nancy L. *TVA and Black Americans: Planning for the Status Quo.* Philadelphia: Temple University Press, 1990.

Hubbard, John Preston. *Origins of the TVA: The Muscle Shoals Controversy, 1920–1932.* New York: Norton, 1968.

McCraw, Thomas K. *Morgan vs. Lilienthal: The Feud within the TVA.* Chicago: Loyola University Press, 1970.

McDonald, Michael J., and John Muldowny. *TVA and the Dispossessed: The Resettlement of a Population in the Norris Dam Area.* Knoxville: University of Tennessee Press, 1982.

Talbert, Roy. *FDR's Utopian: Arthur Morgan of the TVA.* Jackson: University Press of Mississippi, 1987.

TERM LIMITS

Term limits have a long pedigree in American political history. The Articles of Confederation, which established annual terms for representatives to Congress, specified that nobody was eligible to serve more than three years out of any six years (Article V, section 2). Similarly, the Constitution of Virginia, adopted June 29, 1776, limited a governor to three successive annual terms and required the passage of four years from his last service to reeligibility. Term limits became a prominent part of national political debate in the 1990s, both as a partisan election device used mainly by Republicans against long-entrenched Democratic incumbents in Congress and as a more general complaint that often-reelected politicians had lost their connections with the voters.

EARLY HISTORY

In the Virginia Plan, proposed by Edmund Randolph at the Constitutional Convention, the president would be ineligible to serve a second term. In the debates of the convention various terms—from three years to seven years to a life term—were considered, along with proposals for and against reeligibility, until the four-year term with continual reeligibility was endorsed.

Term limits also were considered for members of both houses of Congress. For the House of Representatives, the Virginia Plan proposed ineligibility to serve again for a set number of years and popular recall while in office. In general, however, the Framers were opposed to term limits because of the demonstrated weakness of Congress under the Articles of Confederation and because of the "democratic licentiousness" witnessed in the proceedings of the state legislatures. During the debates on ratification of the Constitution, many Anti-Federalists expressed the need for term limitations, especially for the Senate. But James Madison objected because "[a] few of the members . . . will possess superior talent; will by frequent re-elections, become members of long standing; will be thoroughly masters of the public business."

President George Washington declined to stand for reelection to a third term, and John Adams was defeated in his bid for a second term. When the Vermont legislature urged Thomas Jefferson to seek a third term, he declined, citing Washington's precedent. Term limits continued to be a low-level issue thereafter. President Andrew Jackson suggested that a constitutional amendment be considered to allow only one four- or six-year term for a president. Overall, between 1789 and 1947, 270 proposals for term limits were introduced in Congress.

THE MODERN ERA

Franklin D. Roosevelt's election to four successive terms, starting in 1932, forced the issue of limits—at least for the president—to public debate. The Twenty-second Amendment was proposed in 1947, two years after Roosevelt's death, and ratified February 27, 1951. The amendment limits a president to two full terms. If the person has served more than two years of an unexpired term, he or she is eligible for one elected term. Since the amendment took effect, numerous calls have been made for repeal, including one by President Ronald Reagan, on grounds that the limitation seriously diminishes the effectiveness of a president's second term.

Although 141 proposals were introduced in Congress between 1789 and 1991 to limit term eligibility for members of Congress, it was a substantial congressional pay increase proposed in 1991 that reignited public interest in limitations. In addition to the pay increase controversy, there was a growing public sentiment—strongly encouraged by non-officeholders—that representatives and senators had become divorced from the sentiments of their constituents. In addition, defeating an incumbent, necessary for the proper functioning of democratic representation, was becoming increasingly difficult, at least in part because of name recognition, access to fund-raising opportunities, and the prerogatives of office, such as the franking (free mail) privilege.

In 1990 the group Americans To Limit Congressional Terms was formed to lobby for a constitutional amendment, and in 1994 the congressional Republicans' election platform, called the "Contract with America," called for congressional term limits. Neither the House nor Senate passed a constitutional amendment to accomplish this, however, and advocates of term limits shifted to lobbying state legislatures to restrict term length by law. But in 1995, by a 5–4 vote in *U.S. Term Limits, Inc. v. Thornton,* the Supreme Court ruled that it was not constitutionally permissible for states to limit the terms of their federal legislators. This decision was a fatal blow to efforts to limit congressional terms. However, opponents of term limits on state officeholders have failed to convince the federal judiciary that there is a federal issue involved, and many states and localities do limit the number of years elected officials can serve.

The *U.S. Term Limits* case arose out of an Arkansas law that prevented persons who had served three terms in the U.S. House of Representatives or two terms in the U.S. Senate from running again as an official candidate. Reelection by write-in ballot was not affected, apparently because of the relative difficulty of that method of election and in order that the amendment could be defended constitutionally as merely a state ballot matter, properly under state authority.

A number of constitutional amendments have been proposed to impose term limitations on congressional officeholders. None has received the required two-thirds vote in the House or Senate, although one imposing a twelve-year limit on service received a majority in the House in 1997. In light of these failures, term limit supporters turned to state legislatures to invoke an alternate—but never used—method of amending the Constitution. This procedure allows two-thirds of the states to call for a national constitutional convention. Also, some supporters have suggested a permissive amendment that would constitutionally empower each state to set such limits as they saw fit.

Some states have traditionally limited governors to a set number of terms or successive terms. Alabama's ban on governors succeeding themselves was effectively evaded by George C. Wallace, who was followed in office by his wife and then reelected in the next election. Some localities have established term limits, such as New York City, which now restricts its mayors to no more than two terms. But by far the most common restrictions passed in recent years have been upon the terms of state legislators. Between 1990 and 1995, eighteen states passed legislation placing term limits on state legislators.

The drive for term limits slowed after 1995, and several Republican members of Congress who were elected on a platform of supporting such legislation have repudiated their own pledges not to seek reelection after a few terms.

See also *Congress; Constitutional Amendments; State Government.*

PATRICK M. O'NEIL, BROOME COMMUNITY COLLEGE, STATE UNIVERSITY OF NEW YORK

BIBLIOGRAPHY

Farrand, Max, ed. *The Records of the Federal Convention of 1787.* 3 vols. New Haven: Yale University Press, 1966.

Hall, Kermit L. *"U.S. Term Limits v. Thornton."* In *The Oxford Guide to Supreme Court Cases,* ed. Kermit L. Hall. New York: Oxford University Press, 1999.

Hutson, James H., ed. *Supplement to Max Farrand's "The Records of the Federal Convention of 1787."* New Haven: Yale University Press, 1987.

Vile, John R. "Congressional Term Limits." In *Encyclopedia of Constitutional Amendments, Proposed Amendments, and Amending Issues, 1789–1995.* Santa Barbara, Calif.: ABC-CLIO, 1996.

———. "Twenty-Second Amendment." In *Encyclopedia of Constitutional Amendments, Proposed Amendments, and Amending Issues, 1789–1995.* Santa Barbara, Calif.: ABC-CLIO, 1996.

TERRITORIAL EXPANSION

Domestic politics—directly connected to matters of race, political power, and economic growth—went hand in hand with war, diplomacy, and the expansion of the United States from thirteen East Coast states to a continental nation with an overseas empire.

Between the ratification of the U.S. Constitution (1788) and the Spanish-American War (1898), territorial expansion went through three phases from the acquisition of foreign territory to the admission of new states. Through war and diplomacy, the United States extinguished the claims to territory by European nations and their successors—England, Spain, France, Russia, and Mexico. Through war and treaty making with Indian nations, the United States completed the process of securing title to territory. Through the delineation of territorial boundaries and the creation of territorial governments, the nation laid the groundwork for the eventual establishment of new states to be incorporated into the nation. Each phase brought political conflict, with some Americans opposing or seeking to redirect the process of expansion.

EXPANSION EAST OF THE MISSISSIPPI RIVER

Under the terms of the treaty that ended the American Revolution in 1783, Great Britain conceded the territorial claims of the original thirteen states, as they were eventually defined, and all the territory between those states and the Mississippi River. Britain did not immediately abandon physical possession of some of that territory north of the Ohio River, however, and Spain claimed territory south of the Tennessee River. Moreover, powerful Indian nations inhabited both the Old Northwest and the Old Southwest.

Subsequent negotiations clarified U.S. boundaries. In Pinckney's Treaty (1795), also called the Treaty of San Lorenzo, Spain agreed to relinquish claims to the land between the Tennessee River and the 31st parallel but retained Florida and a strip of land along the Gulf Coast. In Jay's Treaty (1794), Britain agreed to relinquish its forts along the Great Lakes. Into the 1790s U.S. soldiers suffered defeat at the hands of Indians who continued to block U.S. settlement in the northern Ohio Valley. Continued pressure on Indians by U.S. soldiers and settlers led to the admission of Ohio as a state in 1803. Through all these developments, people with an eye to migration west of the Appalachians were committed to the evacuation of Spain, England, and Native Americans from the West, as were those who had already made the move.

The Louisiana Purchase (1803) revealed some of the pressures for American territorial growth, and it also led to political conflict, with great opposition being voiced in New England both at the time regarding the acquisition and in later years regarding statehood and slavery. The main objective behind the U.S. acquisition of the Louisiana Territory—roughly defined as the western half of the Mississippi Valley—lay in the sense of urgency felt by settlers in the Ohio and Tennessee Valleys that they not be prevented from freely shipping goods via the Mississippi River to New Orleans and on to domestic and international markets by oceangoing ships. France sold its rights to all its holdings in the Mississippi Valley. The Mississippi was henceforth secure from European claims (although the British assault on New Orleans late in the War of 1812 demonstrated its vulnerability). The new trans-Mississippi West appeared an ideal place to which the United States could force the migration of Native Americans from east of the Mississippi River. Indian removal emerged as a major political issue through the 1830s. Northeastern critics were unable to turn back President Andrew Jackson's removal policy.

Quite aside from the question of Indian removal, westward expansion was not in favor everywhere in the nation. New Englanders made that perfectly clear in 1803 and again in the Hartford Convention Resolutions, approved late in the War of 1812 by delegates who protested what for their region was a disastrous war with England. The convention's demands included a constitutional amendment requiring a two-thirds vote in each house of Congress to admit a new state. The war ended at about the same time as the convention, however, so support for that proposal faded. The war proved disastrous for Native Americans who had sided with England in both the Old Northwest and the Old Southwest.

Through the 1820s and 1830s most Americans who migrated west were moving from the original thirteen states into the territory between those states and the Mississippi River. North of the Ohio River lay a cluster of new states in which slavery was banned. South of the Ohio River, slavery spread untrammeled. Acquiring new territory, each of the two systems—free labor and slave labor—had room to grow, at least for a time. Eventually, each would want far more territory.

Slavery and Indian removal were tied together in the South, as the War of 1812 and its aftermath demonstrated. Whites from Georgia characterized that war as "the war against the Creeks and the English." The Creeks were the major threat, until troops under the command of Gen. Andrew Jackson won the Battle of Horseshoe Bend (1814). After that, Indian removal proceeded apace, and a rich swath of territory opened up to cotton cultivation with slave labor. In the Adams-Onis Treaty of 1819 (also known as the Florida or Transcontinental Treaty), Spain conveyed all remaining claims in the Gulf Coast region to the United States and also relinquished all claims to the Pacific Coast north of California. Florida became American territory, at least as far as the Spanish were concerned. But the Seminole Indians maintained their own claims. The United States fought the Seminole War in the 1830s to wrest control of the region, relocate Seminoles, and terminate a sanctuary in which runaway slaves from Georgia had long found refuge.

EXPANSION WEST OF THE MISSISSIPPI RIVER

Territorial expansion continued to be inextricably entangled with Indian removal through the 1820s and 1830s, but slavery and the political and territorial expansion of the slave system were the central questions. For more than a year, beginning in 1819, Congress wrangled over the admission of Missouri, carved from the Louisiana Territory. Should it be admitted as a slave state, or should slavery be barred from future growth there? In the end, Missouri was admitted as a slave state, but so fierce was the debate over the issue that, seeking to prevent a recurrence, Congress split the remaining territory and decided in advance which portions were open to slavery.

In the 1840s Americans embraced the slogan "Manifest Destiny." James K. Polk and the Democratic Party ran a saber-rattling presidential campaign in 1844 with an expansionist theme punctuated with cries of "Fifty-Four Forty or Fight!" The battle cry focused on land in the Pacific Northwest, jointly claimed by the United States and Great Britain. The Democrats won, and the Polk administration reached an agreement with the British in 1846 to split the territory in dispute by extending the 49th parallel west to the Pacific (although western Democrats still wanted all of the Oregon country, not just the southern half). Instead of targeting the British, the warmongering was directed to the Southwest. In 1845 the United States annexed Texas, formerly a province of Mexico and more recently an independent republic, and admitted it as a state (although by joint resolution of Congress, rather than a treaty, because enough northerners continued to oppose admission of a slave state to prevent a two-thirds majority in the Senate). In a dispute over the southern boundary of Texas, the United States declared war on Mexico in 1846. Mexico lost the war and, with it, California and all the land between it and Texas. In an afterthought, related to the prospect of constructing a railroad to the Pacific, the Gadsden Purchase (1853) transferred from Mexico to the United States a chunk of land along the southwestern border between Texas and California.

Suddenly the United States fronted the Pacific Ocean as well as the Atlantic, and its northern and southern boundaries were defined with clarity from one coastline to the other. Then came the hard questions. Earlier, in 1836, northerners had opposed annexation of Texas because it would become a slave state. Viewing the war with Mexico as a slaveholders' conspiracy to extend their domain, northerners supported the Wilmot Proviso, a declaration that no territory acquired as a consequence of the war would ever be open to slavery. The North dominated the House of Representatives, where the proviso passed, but not the Senate, where it was rejected. Territorial expansion was inextricably connected to the issue of slavery's expansion, during and after the war with Mexico.

When California petitioned for statehood in 1850, it was admitted as a nonslave state, but the South extracted a stronger Fugitive Slave Act in return. In another part of the Compromise of 1850, Congress (which had banned the expansion of slavery into Oregon Territory in 1848) left the question open regarding Utah and New Mexico, the two huge territories it created from the rest of the Mexican cession. When the issue of slavery's territorial expansion flared again four years later, it focused on the old Louisiana Territory. The Kansas-Nebraska Act (1854) divided the remaining area (north of Indian Territory) into two territories, each open to slavery, in an express repeal of the Missouri Compromise's determination in 1820 that the region would be closed to slavery. From then through the rest of the decade—through "Bleeding Kansas," the rise of a new Republican Party, the *Scott v. Sandford* decision, and the presidential campaign of 1860—the issue of whether slavery would continue to expand into new territory was the most controversial and dangerous issue in U.S. politics. Only with Union victory in the Civil War, and the abolition of slavery itself, did the issue go away.

After the war was over, the West continued to move even farther west, and it continued to be the tail that wagged the dog in American national politics. Soldiers and officers who had only recently been fighting east of the Mississippi in the Civil War—among them George Armstrong Custer, Philip Sheridan, and William Tecumseh Sherman—were redeployed to fight Indians in territory west of the Mississippi River. Indian wars continued on the Great Plains through the 1880s. The sagas of Crazy Horse, Chief Joseph, Geronimo, and Sitting Bull ended in defeat and destruction. Protests from the East by no means sufficed to curtail the pressure in the West to eliminate Native Americans as a military force or even a

U.S. territorial acquisitions   *Library of Congress*

physical presence. A reservation policy emerged on a large scale in what became states that ranged from South Dakota to Arizona.

Partisan skirmishing continued to affect developments in the West. Concerns over how the voters in a territory would vote could either spur or retard statehood. Nevada was admitted during the Civil War to provide the Republicans three more votes in the electoral college in what was expected to be a close count in the 1864 election. Legislation in 1889 and 1890, when Republicans controlled Congress, brought a cluster of six western states into the Union. Arizona and New Mexico, the last of the contiguous forty-eight states, were admitted in 1912.

Political conflict and policy decisions were also tied to the distribution and use of land and the use of Treasury funds that resulted from land sales. One of the great questions of the 1830s resulted from a Treasury surplus, as money came into the federal coffers from the sale of public land east of the Mississippi. Three laws passed in 1862, during the Civil War, reflected the politics of territorial expansion in the West. The

Homestead Act supplied the basis for sales of 160-acre plots of land to settlers in the trans-Mississippi West. The Morrill Land-Grant College Act relied on federal land in the West to establish funds to support higher education in every state. The Transcontinental Railroad Act offered enormous tracts of land in return for the prospect that rail lines would foster settlement in the Great Plains and trade across the region. In the late nineteenth century, feuds between cattlemen and farmers—between people who wanted the open range for their vast herds and people who wanted to fence off their family farms—caused tensions, even violence, as did disputes over access to water. As with issues relating to slavery, a range of new questions, each of them demanding resolution, resulted from the nation's acquisition of new territory.

EXPANSION INTO ALASKA, THE CARIBBEAN, AND THE PACIFIC

In territorial expansion, domestic politics could govern what did and did not happen. In the years before the Civil War, proslavery southerners urged expansion into Cuba and

Nicaragua, lands that could bring more power in national politics to the proslavery side. Armed invasions of Central America and the Caribbean—private military actions called "filibustering" expeditions under leaders like William Walker and John A. Quitman—attempted to catalyze annexation. Both Democratic campaign platforms of 1860 spoke approvingly of acquiring Cuba. The Republicans rejected the idea, and nothing came of it.

Republicans nonetheless promoted expansion. In 1868, at Russia's initiative and with Secretary of State William H. Seward's enthusiastic support, the United States purchased Russia's claims in Alaska. In the 1890s Democratic president Grover Cleveland refused to approve annexation of the Hawaiian Islands, but, under Republican president William McKinley's administration and in the context of the Spanish-American War, Hawaii became American territory. Moreover, under one administration or another, from one decade to the next, the United States acquired other possessions in the Pacific and the Caribbean, among them Midway Island, American Samoa, and the Virgin Islands.

The war with Spain in 1898 inaugurated substantial American expansion beyond North America. Although the war began over affairs in Cuba, Spain's possessions also included Puerto Rico in the Caribbean and both Guam and the Philippines in the western Pacific. The United States did not annex Cuba, but it did acquire Puerto Rico and Guam. Moreover, it fought a war for several years to quell an independence movement in the Philippine Islands, which became a formal part of an overseas American empire until it gained political independence in 1946.

The war in the Philippines was no more universally supported than the War of 1812 or the war with Mexico had been. It attracted national debate, with various Republicans supporting the war effort and a host of people—among them Andrew Carnegie, Jane Addams, and William Jennings Bryan—on the other side. Republicans tended to be more attuned to matters of promoting trade and investment; Democrats were more troubled with the prospect of assimilating non-Caucasian peoples into the American polity.

By the end of the nineteenth century, the United States had expanded far beyond the boundaries of the original thirteen states and far beyond the confines of the territory to which Great Britain conceded any claim in 1783. Enormous numbers of casualties had resulted, on both sides, from warfare with Indians over control of western territory, from warfare between the Union and the Confederate states over slavery and its expansion into western territories, and from warfare to take control of overseas possessions. At every stage—extinguishing foreign title to land, struggling with natives, organizing territorial governments, and admitting new states—issues surrounding territorial expansion had been central to the history of American national politics.

EXPANSION IN THE TWENTIETH CENTURY

By the beginning of the twentieth century, the United States had secured all the territory that was eventually organized into the fifty states, and the thrust toward an overseas empire had largely ended. In the Caribbean, however, the nation acquired control of the Panama Canal Zone during Theodore Roosevelt's presidency and obtained the Virgin Islands from Denmark in 1917. Over great political opposition in 1978, during Jimmy Carter's presidency, the United States provided for a return of the Canal Zone to Panama in the year 2000. Even then it held on to a military base in southern Cuba, at Guantanamo Bay. In fact, during the cold war and beyond, into the twenty-first century, the United States maintained military bases around the world, including in Okinawa and Korea.

See also *Cold War; Compromise of 1850; Hartford Convention Resolutions; Indian Policy; Jackson, Andrew; Kansas-Nebraska Act; Manifest Destiny; Missouri Compromise; Mexican-American War; Morrill Land-Grant College Acts; Seminole War; Spanish-American War; Territorial Government and New State Formation; War of 1812.*

PETER WALLENSTEIN,
VIRGINIA POLYTECHNIC INSTITUTE AND STATE UNIVERSITY

BIBLIOGRAPHY

LaFeber, Walter. *The American Age: U.S. Foreign Policy at Home and Abroad, 1750 to the Present.* 2d ed. New York: Norton, 1994.

McDougall, Walter A. *Promised Land, Crusader State: The American Encounter with the World since 1776.* Boston: Houghton Mifflin, 1997.

Morison, Samuel Eliot, Frederick Merk, and Frank Freidel. *Dissent in Three American Wars* [the War of 1812, the war with Mexico, and the Spanish-American War]. Cambridge: Harvard University Press, 1970.

White, Richard. *"It's Your Misfortune and None of My Own": A New History of the American West.* Norman: University of Oklahoma Press, 1991.

TERRITORIAL GOVERNMENT AND NEW STATE FORMATION

Questions about the governing of territories that are owned by the United States and about the formation of states from such territories predate the federal government and persist to the present. Policies for territorial governance and new state formation initially took shape under the Confederation government of the mid-1780s. Ostensibly, this early blueprint guided territorial policy for more than a century. In fact, political (diplomatic, partisan, and sectional) and cultural (racial, ethnic, and religious) considerations eroded these policies from an early date. Beginning in the mid-1890s, the acquisition of a number of extracontinental territories that were not expected to become states finally led to the abandonment of almost any pretense of continuity in federal territorial policy from its origins in the 1780s.

THE EARLY BLUEPRINT

More than any other document, the Northwest Ordinance, which was adopted by the Confederation government in July 1787 and readopted by the federal government in August 1789, established the original framework of territorial government and state formation. The ordinance emerged from three years of debate that followed Virginia's cession of its claims to territory north and west of the Ohio River to the United States, on the condition that this territory would eventually be admitted into the Union as states. Three critical principles were accepted very quickly: the new states must be republican, must remain in the Union, and would be equal to the original states. However, important questions remained about the number of states, the government of the territories, and the process of becoming a state. The Northwest Ordinance answered these questions in ways that showed the impact of recent frontier movements—in western North Carolina, western Massachusetts, and Vermont—that seemed to demonstrate the separatist tendencies and democratic excesses of frontier settlers. It divided the region into a small number of states, reserved a large share of territorial governance for the central government, and set a high population threshold for statehood. Under the ordinance's three-stage process, each territory would first be governed by an appointed governor, secretary, and judges. Once its population included five thousand free, adult males, it could establish a bicameral legislature with a popularly elected lower house and send a nonvoting delegate to Congress. When its population reached sixty thousand free inhabitants, the territory would be admitted to the United States.

The underlying logic and basic structures developed for the Old Northwest were used for the Old Southwest and for most of the regions acquired by the Louisiana Purchase (1803), the Transcontinental Treaty (1819), and the Treaty of Guadalupe Hidalgo (1848). But practice often deviated from theory. Some states never passed through the territorial phase, either because they had been independent nations (Vermont and Texas), or because they were formed out of existing states (Kentucky, Maine, West Virginia).

Territories did not automatically become states as a function of population. Partisan or sectional calculations in Congress frequently delayed and occasionally accelerated admission to the Union. Cultural concerns also slowed the transition to statehood for various territories. The political power of Mormons in Utah and the demographic preponderance of Hispanics in New Mexico kept Congress from extending statehood long after those territories had reached the requisite populations. In other cases, the delays came from the territories themselves. Uncertain that the advantages of statehood outweighed the benefits of federal support, territorial voters defeated statehood referenda on a number of occasions (for example, Wisconsin, four times between 1840 and 1846; Colorado, 1864).

The basic source of the deviations from the policy established by the Northwest Ordinance can be found in the dual meaning of statehood—both self-governance and membership in the Union. Either a concern that the territory was not prepared for statehood or a fear that the Union was not prepared for a new state could produce delays. The former often arose from cultural differences between the territory and other states; the latter often derived from political, particularly sectional, issues.

INDIAN TERRITORY
AND NEW TERRITORIAL ACQUISITIONS

If the Old Northwest was the original, albeit imperfect, model for most nineteenth-century territories, Indian Territory served a similar function for most twentieth-century territories.

In 1834 Congress established Indian Territory as a new home for Indians who had been removed west of the Mississippi River. It was never expected to follow the developmental process laid out in the Northwest Ordinance and never replicated the political structures of the other territories. It was never treated as a single political entity. Instead, it was a region shared by a number of distinct tribal governments whose federally appointed Indian agents formed their most direct connection to the federal government. Destined for neither self-governance nor membership in the Union, Indian Territory long remained anomalous. However, at the end of the nineteenth century it provided a model—and was explicitly recognized as such—when Congress and the American people faced a decision about what to do with new extracontinental possessions that included Samoa, Hawaii, Guam, Puerto Rico, and the Philippines. Using the example of Indian Territory, and Indian reservations generally, turn-of-the-century imperialists could make a strong case that the American political system had long recognized that not all territories would become equal states and not all inhabitants would become full citizens. In a series of decisions known as the *Insular Cases* (1901–1904), the Supreme Court formally abandoned the view that territorial status guaranteed eventual statehood. Ironically, in the same period, the former Indian

Territory was admitted to the Union as the state of Oklahoma. Making Indian Territory into a state, however, had first required the dismantling of the tribal governments and the opening of the territory to non–Indian settlers.

By the end of the twentieth century, only two noncontiguous territories, Alaska and Hawaii, had become states. Two others were no longer American territories—the Philippines were granted independence in 1946 and the Canal Zone was restored to Panama in 1979. American Samoa, Guam, the Midway Islands, and the Virgin Islands remained "unincorporated territories," though both Guam and the Virgin Islands had populations far above the threshold for statehood. Puerto Rico, with a population around 4 million, remained a "commonwealth" with a locally elected government and a nonvoting representative in Congress.

See also *Immigration and Naturalization: Twentieth-Century Law and Policy; Northwest Ordinance; Territorial Expansion.*

JAMES E. LEWIS JR., INDEPENDENT SCHOLAR

BIBLIOGRAPHY

Eblen, Jack Ericson. *The First and Second United States Empires: Governors and Territorial Government, 1784–1912.* Pittsburgh: University of Pittsburgh Press, 1968.

Onuf, Peter S. *Statehood and Union: A History of the Northwest Ordinance.* Bloomington: Indiana University Press, 1987.

Pomeroy, Earl S. *The Territories and the United States: Studies in Colonial Administration.* Philadelphia: University of Pennsylvania Press, 1947.

THINK TANKS AND THE ACADEMIC POLICY COMMUNITY

A think tank is a not-for-profit research institute or other organization of scholars that looks for solutions to complex social, economic, or political problems. The academic policy community, also known as the policy elite, comprises the scholars who work for think tanks.

ACADEMIC POLICY COMMUNITY

Think tanks were made possible by the rise of the academic policy community. This community consists of professionally trained experts who spend their careers studying broad social and economic phenomena. Its importance began with the Progressive movement, which stressed the importance of social change driven and informed by the knowledge of experts. Early in the twentieth century American universities greatly expanded their graduate programs in the social sciences, and national organizations of social scientists were founded. The academic policy community received a major boost during World War I when President Woodrow Wilson,

a former college professor, recruited hundreds of experts to solve problems such as mobilization, propaganda, and the maintenance of world peace after the war. The community received another major boost between 1932 and 1945 when President Franklin D. Roosevelt recruited what he called the "Brains Trust" to help restore the national economy via the New Deal and then to help defeat the Germans and Japanese in World War II.

After World War II the community expanded as a succession of presidents called on it to deal with a wide range of domestic socioeconomic problems. Challenges included chronic poverty, urban blight, and the Soviet military threat during the cold war. After 1970 the academic policy community expanded once again when various political parties, constituencies, and candidates attempted to use scholarly expertise to help them win elections.

THINK TANKS

Think tanks originated in the United States in the early twentieth century as a way for members of the academic policy community to conduct independent research. The number of think tanks increased as the academic policy community expanded. By the late 1990s more than a thousand think tanks were in existence. Although Washington, D.C., was the center of the think tank "industry," think tanks could be found in virtually all parts of the country.

Much of the work of think tanks is done for the federal government, even though think tanks are privately owned. They receive their funding from contractual work, publication of their research findings, and contributions from foundations and wealthy individuals. Nonideological think tanks also receive major contributions from philanthropic groups such as the Ford Foundation and the Rockefeller Foundation. The more overtly political think tanks receive major funding from business corporations and partisan groups such as political action committees and ideologically based foundations.

Some of the most visible think tanks advocate either conservative or liberal views, while others adopt a more moderate ideological stance. Regardless of their political positions, think tanks play a significant role in the development of public policy because they provide government officials and political candidates with analyses and proposed solutions that have been researched and developed by some of the country's best minds.

MAJOR THINK TANKS

Think tanks vary tremendously in the size and scope of their interests and operations. Some think tanks employ hundreds of researchers and staffers and have multimillion-dollar budgets. Other think tanks employ a single researcher who operates on a shoestring budget. The following brief examination of ten major think tanks that were in operation in the 1990s reveals more about what think tanks do and how they have broadened their research interests and activities over the years.

The Russell Sage Foundation was founded in 1907, making it the first think tank and the model by which others would pattern themselves. The foundation was initially funded by Margaret Olivia Sage as a vehicle by which social workers could conduct research on public health and sanitation, children's issues, working conditions for women, and other issues of interest to Progressives. After World War II the foundation began to focus on basic social science research in order to improve social science methodology, enhance the techniques used to collect basic data, and advance social theory. Particular interests remain the social aspects of poverty and economic behavior.

The Brookings Institution was founded in 1916 as the Institute for Government Research, which espoused reform of the federal budget process and greater government efficiency. It was renamed in 1927 for Robert S. Brookings, a major benefactor, when it combined with two other research institutes to which he contributed. Since then the institute has focused on a broader study of economics, government, and foreign policy. Its research programs seek ways to foster economic growth and productivity, boost living standards, control the spread and use of nuclear weapons, and improve the selection of appointed and elected officials.

The Hoover Institution on War, Revolution, and Peace was founded in 1919 as the Hoover War Library on the campus of Stanford University. In 1960 the institution began expanding its operations to become a major policy research center. At one time, its research priority was international communism. Today it is more concerned with national security affairs and domestic policy studies. The Hoover Institution espouses a liberal view of government's role in the business world, tax policy, and welfare.

The American Enterprise Institute for Public Policy Research was founded in 1943 as the American Enterprise Association to conduct business research. Renamed in 1960 when it was reorganized as a center to investigate and promote conservative economic policies, the American Enterprise Institute seeks to give freer rein to private enterprise by reducing government intervention in business matters.

The RAND Corporation was founded in 1948 as an offshoot of a U.S. Air Force research and development project. In addition to conducting military research for the armed forces, the corporation conducts social research in a broad range of areas affecting domestic policy including aging, workers' health care benefits, vocational education, population research, health care financing, civil justice, education, employ-

ment, and drug policy. The RAND Corporation also operates a graduate school that offers a doctorate in public policy.

The Hudson Institute was founded in 1961 by several former associates of the RAND Corporation. This think tank perceives itself as "a lobby for the future" in that it attempts to foresee what will be needed in days to come and to promote solutions to those needs. The Hudson Institute's particular interests include energy, education, transportation, health, and global food supplies.

The Institute for Policy Studies was founded in 1963 by two scholars with leftist leanings. The institute was formed to counteract the influence of conservative think tanks on American foreign policy. Its primary purpose has been to increase citizen involvement in the making of public policy by educating the American public about various aspects of that policy. The institute's research activities focus on world economic integration, the state of democracy in the world, and how U.S. foreign policy should be reformulated following the end of the cold war.

The Urban Institute was founded in 1968 at the urging of the administration of President Lyndon B. Johnson, which sought solutions to the problems of urban decay as part of its War on Poverty. Since then the institute has branched out to assess the success of government projects that reach far beyond the nation's cities. The Urban Institute has worked to develop better techniques for evaluating government programs and measuring the productivity of the public sector. For example, it developed the Experimental Housing Allowance Program, a computer model for estimating housing trends and the effects of government policy changes on the housing market, and similar models for evaluating prospective changes to the Food Stamp and Medicare programs. Areas of research include the changing priorities of domestic policy, the development of workforce skills, and the inability of cities to offer greater chances of upward mobility to their residents.

The Heritage Foundation was founded in 1973 and quickly became one of the country's largest and most visible think tanks. It promotes conservative political ideology by influencing foreign policy and finding ways to stimulate economic growth throughout the Western Hemisphere. The foundation also seeks to inculcate a greater appreciation for conservative views among young people, thus creating a future generation of conservative leaders.

The Cato Institute was founded in 1977 by members of the Libertarian Party. It is primarily interested in influencing government policy as a means to increase individual liberty, limit government intervention in general, and promote international peace. The institute's long-term projects include researching alternatives to federal entitlement programs and ensuring that new developments in public policy are properly grounded in the underlying principles of the U.S. Constitution.

CHARLES CAREY, LYNCHBURG COLLEGE/
CENTRAL VIRGINIA COMMUNITY COLLEGE

BIBLIOGRAPHY

Dickson, Paul. *Think Tanks.* New York: Atheneum, 1971.

Orlans, Harold. *The Nonprofit Research Institute: Its Origins, Operation, Problems, and Prospects.* New York: McGraw-Hill, 1972.

Smith, James Allen. *The Idea Brokers.* New York: The Free Press, 1991.

THIRD PARTIES

Although the United States has always had a two-party system, third parties have frequently played a vital role in the political order. No third-party candidate has ever been elected to the presidency, but many have been elected to other federal, state, and local offices, and the votes third parties have garnered have often been a crucial factor in the outcome of elections. Moreover, the issues spotlighted by minor parties have often ended up being co-opted into the platforms of the major parties.

NINETEENTH-CENTURY THIRD PARTIES

As the original party system of Hamiltonian Federalists and Jeffersonian Democratic-Republicans broke down, and the National Republican Party developed and transformed itself into the Whig Party, there also arose the Anti-Masonic Party, which ran William Wirt for president in 1832, gaining almost 8 percent of the popular vote. Nonetheless, they achieved some state and local offices, particularly in New York State, where the party originated.

In 1844 the Liberty Party, which opposed slavery, won 2.3 percent of the popular vote, although it did not affect the outcome of the election. In 1848, however, the less radical Free Soil Party, which was dedicated to stopping the spread of slavery in the territories, played the role of spoiler. Running former president Martin Van Buren, the party won enough votes, mostly from Democrats, to enable the Whig candidate, Zachary Taylor, to defeat the Democrat, Lewis Cass. It ran John P. Hale for president in 1852, obtaining 5 percent of the popular vote. The demise of the Free Soil Party was caused primarily by the rise of the Republican Party, which took up its stance in opposition to slavery in the territories.

In the 1850s the American Party, otherwise known as the Know Nothing Party, reaped large votes in Pennsylvania and New York and even briefly gained control over the Massachusetts government. The party's main goals were excluding Catholics from public office, enacting restrictive immigration laws, and establishing literacy tests for voting.

Parties such as the Greenback Party (1876–1884) and the Prohibition Party, which started in 1869 and has continued ever since, never attracted many votes on the national level, but their success rested in convincing one of the major parties to take up their cause. Eventually the Republican Party embraced Prohibition, while the Democratic Party espoused the expansion of the money supply, albeit with the free coinage of silver rather than by printing greenbacks.

The Populist (or People's) Party, which represented the interests of farmers and labor, arose in the South and West in the 1880s. Because it spoke for a perennial debtor class, the party tended to favor the free coinage of silver and backed free trade and the regulation of the railroads. The Populist platform would eventually be adopted by the Democratic Party under its 1896 presidential candidate, William Jennings Bryan.

THIRD PARTIES IN THE TWENTIETH CENTURY

The Socialist Party came to prominence in the Progressive era, with members winning state and local offices and serving in Congress. In 1904 it ran Eugene V. Debs for president, winning 3 percent of the vote against the Republican incumbent Theodore Roosevelt and Alton B. Parker, the Democrat. Debs would run again in 1908, 1912, and 1920, and in this last election (campaigning from a federal penitentiary, where he was imprisoned for opposition to World War I), he tallied 915,490 votes (3.4 percent). Later, Norman Thomas would serve as the Socialist Party standard bearer in several elections, with his largest vote in 1932 when he won 884,649 votes (2.2 percent). Before World War I, socialist Victor Berger served as mayor of Milwaukee, and he served as a member of the House of Representatives from 1911 to 1913 and from 1923 to 1929.

Although they lack the long-term ideological impact of the third parties described above, some minor parties have served as vehicles for the candidacies of certain individuals. The Progressive (or Bull Moose) Party became a vehicle for Theodore Roosevelt's attempt to recapture the White House in 1912, running against Democrat Woodrow Wilson and Republican William Howard Taft. In that race, all three candidates were Progressives to an extent. When Taft's people prevented Roosevelt delegates from some states from being seated at the Republican convention, Roosevelt bolted the party and ran as a Progressive. The result was a split of the Republican vote and a victory for Wilson.

In 1924 the Progressive Party ran Robert M. La Follette for president, capturing 16.6 percent of the vote. In 1948, using the Progressive Party label, Henry A. Wallace, Franklin D. Roosevelt's former vice president and secretary of agriculture, scored 2.4 percent of the vote in a four-way race that saw Harry Truman reelected. Wallace ran to the left of Truman on both domestic and foreign affairs, where he pushed for greater cooperation with the Soviet Union. The 1948 election also saw the emergence of another third party, the States' Rights, or Dixiecrat, Party. The Dixiecrats ran J. Strom Thurmond, the governor of South Carolina, for president, opposing the Democratic Party's adoption of a civil rights plank in its 1948 platform. Thurmond won 2.4 percent of the vote.

In the close 1968 presidential race between Richard M. Nixon and Hubert H. Humphrey, George C. Wallace, the governor of Alabama, captured 13.5 percent of the popular vote and forty-six electoral votes. He ran on the American Independence ticket, pushing a conservative and somewhat racist agenda. In 1980 John B. Anderson ran on an independent line against Ronald Reagan and Jimmy Carter and received 6.6 percent of the popular vote but no electoral votes. In 1992 H. Ross Perot created the Reform Party and ran for president under its banner, receiving 18.9 percent of the vote but no electoral votes. This party has run candidates for state and local office across the country, and in 1998 Jesse Ventura was elected governor of Minnesota on the Reform Party line. In 2000 the Reform Party seemed destined for oblivion as it split down the middle over the contested nomination of Patrick J. Buchanan for president.

Today the Libertarian Party and the Green Party offer fairly consistent ideologies through their third-party movements. Because they are primarily ideologically based, however, they are the more likely to be absorbed eventually by a major party that has co-opted their ideas and raided their constituencies.

Finally, one must consider the regional and state-based third-party movements, although these are too numerous to consider in any detail. The Liberal, Conservative, and Right to Life Parties of New York State provide excellent examples of such movements. Each has had a significant influence on state politics, and the Conservative Party even elected James L. Buckley as U.S. senator in 1970. The Farmer Labor Party had similar success in the politics of Minnesota. Usually, however, such parties depend on the election law permitting cross-endorsements of candidates from the major parties.

See also individual parties by name.

PATRICK M. O'NEIL, BROOME COMMUNITY COLLEGE,
STATE UNIVERSITY OF NEW YORK

BIBLIOGRAPHY

Foner, Eric. *Free Soil, Free Labor, Free Men.* New York: Oxford University Press, 1970.

Goodwyn, Lawrence. *The Populist Moment.* New York: Oxford University Press, 1978.

Leonard, I. M., and R. D. Parmet. *American Nativism, 1830–1860.* Huntington, N.Y.: R. E. Krieger, 1979.

Livermore, Shaw. *The Twilight of Federalism.* Princeton: Princeton University Press, 1962.

Salvatore, Nick. *Eugene V. Debs: Citizen and Socialist.* Urbana: University of Illinois Press, 1982.

Timberlake, James T. *Prohibition and the Progressive Movement, 1900–1920.* Cambridge: Harvard University Press, 1963.

Vaughn, William Preston. *The Anti-Masonic Party in the United States, 1826–1843.* Lexington: University Press of Kentucky, 1983.

THREE-FIFTHS CLAUSE

The three-fifths clause, found in Article I, section 2, paragraph 3 of the U.S. Constitution, provided a mechanism for counting slaves in the allocation of representation in the House of Representatives. Under this clause the number of representatives each state would have in Congress would be determined by adding to "the whole Number of free Persons," including indentured servants and apprentices, but excluding tribal Indians, "three fifths of all other Persons." The "other Persons" were slaves. A common misunderstanding about the clause is that it is racist, in the sense that it declared black people to be three-fifths of a person. This was clearly not the case. The clause applied only to slaves, and free blacks, whether in the North or the South, were counted for representation as whole persons, just as whites were. Moreover, the fraction in no way governed African Americans' voting power, for slaves did not vote. The formula related to their owners' political power—to the relative value of a white vote, not of a black vote.

ORIGIN OF THE CLAUSE

The clause was part of a compromise at the Constitutional Convention. The northern states, including some that had significant numbers of slaves at this time, did not want slaves counted at all for purposes of representation. Their opposition was in part practical. If slaves were counted for representation, then the North would be at a political disadvantage, and Virginia would dominate the other states. In addition, the northerners thought it absurd to count slaves for representation. As Elbridge Gerry of Massachusetts noted: "The idea of property ought not to be the rule of representation. Blacks are property, and are used to the southward as horses and cattle to the northward; and why should their representation be increased to the southward on account of the number of slaves, than horses or oxen to the north?" Finally, there was an important moral component to the northern states' opposition. As Gouverneur Morris, who represented Pennsylvania at the convention, asserted:

> when fairly explained [it] comes to this: that the inhabitant of Georgia and South Carolina who goes to the Coast of Africa, and in defiance of the most sacred laws of humanity tears away his fellow creatures from their dearest connections and damns them to the most cruel bondages, shall have more votes in a Government instituted for protection

of the rights of mankind, than the Citizen of Pennsylvania or New Jersey who views with a laudable horror, so nefarious a practice.

Southern delegates, on the other hand, argued that slavery was a substantial economic interest, which significantly contributed to the nation's welfare and economy. Pierce Butler of South Carolina insisted

> that the labour of a slave in S. Carola. was as productive & valuable as that of a freeman in Massts., that as wealth was the great means of defence and utility to the Nation they were equally valuable to it with freemen; and that consequently an equal representation ought to be allowed for them in a Government which was instituted principally for the protection of property, and was itself to be supported by property.

The convention compromised and used the three-fifths ratio. (Members of the Congress under the Articles of Confederation had previously proposed the three-fifths ratio in a failed tax proposal.) The three-fifths formula reflected a compromise between a full count and none at all, and it also reflected a belief, probably accurate, that a slave annually produced about three-fifths as much wealth as a free person. Late in the convention the delegates also applied this ratio to "direct taxes," but this was merely a sop to the North, since no one at the Convention expected Congress to level substantial direct taxes.

Consequences of the Clause

The South gained a significant number of votes in the House because of the clause. Although after 1800 the growing northern population produced increasing power in Congress, in some close, crucial votes, the representatives created by counting slaves made the difference in Congress. The vote to admit Missouri as a slave state was razor thin; without the votes of members whose seats were based on counting slaves, it is unlikely this law would have passed, or passed in the manner it did. The same is true for the adoption of the Fugitive Slave Law of 1850. Equally important, in the antebellum period extra representatives allowed southerners to control the Democratic Party in the House, forcing northern Democrats to support the South on issues involving slavery, territorial expansion, and tariffs.

The clause also affected the election of the president, because a state's power in the electoral college was based on its representation in Congress. In the election of 1800 Thomas Jefferson, who owned about two hundred slaves, defeated John Adams, who had never owned a slave, by six votes in the electoral college. Most of Jefferson's strength came from the slave states, and had slaves not been counted for the electoral college, Adams would have won.

The three-fifths clause remained a sore point with northerners from the struggle over adoption of the Constitution until the beginning of the Civil War. A number of northern Antifederalists cited the clause as a key reason for opposing the Constitution. At the Hartford Convention (1814–1815), some New Englanders, upset by years of rule (which they saw as oppression) by Virginians, demanded a constitutional amendment to end the counting of slaves. Starting in the 1830s abolitionists cited the clause as one more reason for opposing slavery and even the Constitution itself.

The Civil War ended slavery, and that created an unexpected result. The three-fifths clause had applied only to slaves, not blacks. Thus, after the ratification of the Thirteenth Amendment all blacks were counted equally with whites for representation. This meant, ironically, that the former Confederate states would gain representation after losing the war. Republicans in Congress tried to compensate by including a clause in the Fourteenth Amendment that would reduce congressional representation for those states that denied the ballot to former slaves. Although adopted as section 2 of the Fourteenth Amendment, the clause was never applied to the southern states after they effectively disfranchised blacks in the late nineteenth century.

See also *Constitution, U.S.; Hartford Convention Resolutions; Reconstruction; Slavery.*

PAUL FINKELMAN, UNIVERSITY OF TULSA COLLEGE OF LAW

BIBLIOGRAPHY

Finkelman, Paul. *Slavery and the Founders: Race and Liberty in the Age of Jefferson.* Armonk, N.Y.: M.E. Sharpe, 1996.

Robinson, Donald. *Slavery in the Structure of American Politics, 1765–1820.* New York: Harcourt, Brace, Jovanovich, 1971.

TREATIES: COMMERCIAL

Early in American history, the government negotiated treaties to open trade and provide commercial opportunities. Even in 1776 the United States recognized the importance of commercial interaction among nations. Initially, the major goal of treaties signed with other powers was most-favored-nation status, meaning that if either nation allowed commercial benefits to one nation, then each signatory of the treaty would share in the same privileges. By the twentieth century, opportunities for American bankers and businesses abroad also became an important aspect of international relations. Present-day trade problems focus on breaking down barriers within the Western Hemisphere and on using the World Trade Organization (WTO) as the forum for negotiations.

EARLY TREATIES

The Second Continental Congress in 1776 drafted a "model treaty" that outlined the separation of political and economic goals and recognized the principle of "free ships, free goods" and freedom of the seas based on reciprocal commercial arrangements. During the American Revolutionary War, the United States negotiated an Alliance Treaty and the Treaty of Amity and Commerce, in which France recognized the United States. The latter treaty also endorsed neutral rights to trade with belligerents and the concept of a restricted list of contraband that did not include naval stores and foodstuffs. France recognized that if a ship flew a neutral flag, another nation could not confiscate its nonmilitary goods.

In the Pinckney Treaty with Spain, which the United States negotiated in the 1790s, the United States received free navigation of the Mississippi River and the renewable "right of deposit" at New Orleans for three years; it was also granted the right to store goods waiting for shipment. Spain approved the U.S. definition of neutral rights, set the boundary of Florida, and pledged not to foment Indian rebellion against either nation.

NINETEENTH-CENTURY TREATIES

Commercial relations improved with Britain following the Treaty of Ghent (1814), which ended the War of 1812, and the Convention of 1818. The latter granted the United States most-favored-nation status in India. Americans could also fish along Newfoundland and Labrador and around Magdalen Island, subject to certain restrictions. The Marcy-Elgin Treaty (1854) revisited these fishing limitations. The agreement was to be effective for ten years, after which each nation could abrogate with one-year notification. The treaty removed duties on several goods and allowed Americans to fish in areas that had been closed in 1818. In addition, Canadians gained fishing rights along the Atlantic coast above the 36th parallel. The United States gained navigation rights on the St. Lawrence River in exchange for British reciprocal rights to Lake Michigan. The Webster-Ashburton Treaty of 1842 addressed not only the northern boundary between Maine and Canada but also the African slave trade. The treaty established joint cruising squadrons along the African coast to suppress the trade, but the United States did not participate.

The United States also sought to open trade on the other side of the world. After the British won broader commercial rights in China by the Treaty of Nanking following the Opium War, the United States sought most-favored-nation status. The Treaty of Wangxia (1844) expanded U.S. trading privileges in China, established consular posts, and claimed extraterritoriality (the right of foreigners to trial in their own courts) in civil and criminal cases. The first Korean agreement with the West followed in 1882, granting most-favored-nation status to the United States in the Treaty of Peace, Amity, Commerce and Navigation. U.S. interest in Japan came later because the island remained closed to outside influence. But the Treaty of Wangxia enhanced Japan's importance as a natural port en route to China. The Treaty of Kanagawa (1854) awarded limited access by opening only two ports for coal and supplies and granted consular privileges for the United States in those ports. However, this treaty failed to guarantee coaling stations or extraterritorial rights.

The period from the American Civil War through 1930 witnessed high tariff rates to provide revenue and to satisfy protectionist sentiment. The Morrill Tariff Act of 1861 had raised the level to 47 percent, and it remained above 40 percent until World War I. Although these rates fell in the 1920s to below 20 percent, the administration of Herbert Hoover believed that higher tariffs would help faltering American industries. The Hawley-Smoot Tariff in 1930 raised the rate to almost 45 percent. European nations opposed the high tariffs at a time when they owed war debts to the United States.

TWENTIETH-CENTURY TREATIES

During the twentieth century, the goal of earning most-favored-nation status was replaced by promoting American businesses. In the early years of the century, commercial interests justified imperialism for many senators. The Great Depression prompted Americans to overlook the aggression of various nations in exchange for necessary trade. In the post–World War II period, cold war tensions between the United States and the Soviet Union preoccupied American foreign policy, affecting trade agreements.

The depression led to a change in trade policy. The Seventh International Conference of American States met in Montevideo, Uruguay, in December 1933 to promote trade throughout the Western Hemisphere. Secretary of State Cordell Hull moved toward establishing reciprocal trade agreements as desired by the nations in attendance. He argued that world trade would also promote peace at a time when aggression seemed on the horizon. Congress passed the Reciprocal Trade Agreements Act of June 1934, authorizing the president to lower tariffs on a reciprocal basis up to 50 percent through bilateral executive agreements based on the most-favored-nation principle. This act guaranteed each nation the lowest tariff rate awarded to any other party. Although these agreements lowered duties and encouraged international trade, they did not ensure world peace.

In July 1944, forty-four nations attended the UN Monetary and Financial Conference at Bretton Woods, a resort in New Hampshire. They established the International Bank for Reconstruction and Development, or World Bank, and composed the Articles of Agreement for an International Monetary Fund (IMF). The primary goals were to reestablish financial stability and multilateral trade in the postwar world and to avoid problems of postwar reconstruction. The United States provided most of the financing.

The United States and twenty-two other nations established the General Agreement on Tariffs and Trade (GATT) in 1948. If two countries reached trade agreements, these agreements would automatically be extended to the other signatories based on the most-favored-nation principle. The United States hoped to use the agreement to expand capitalism at the expense of totalitarianism. Eight bargaining rounds from 1947 to 1993 produced various tariff reductions. The United States lowered its average tariff from the 60-percent level before the Trade Agreements Program began in 1934 to about 4 percent. By the mid-1980s GATT needed to expand its regulations to cover trade in services, protection of intellectual property, and requirements placed by governments on foreign investors. The Uruguay Round was the longest and most comprehensive round of negotiations; 88 of the 117 participants were developing countries. This agreement went into effect on January 1, 1995, and established the WTO, which succeeded what had been GATT. Another goal of this round was to decrease exempted sectors such as textiles, agriculture, and services. Multilateral trade negotiations included the topics of trade-related investment measures and trade-related intellectual property rights. The United States has reserved unilateral action in matters not covered by the Uruguay Round.

Canada, Mexico, and the United States signed the North American Free Trade Agreement (NAFTA) in October 1992. The U.S. Senate approved it in an attempt to build greater commercial ties in North America. Proponents claimed the agreement would increase trade throughout the Americas, but critics asserted that the agreement would move jobs to Mexico because of the vast differences in wages and labor market regulations between Mexico and the United States or Canada. Environmental problems also raised concerns, as Mexico is more lax in its enforcement of standards.

In recent years, critics of the IMF and the World Bank also have focused on the impact on emerging nations of funding and the requirements to receive such aid. The organizations have funded projects in underdeveloped nations that may endanger the environment. Critics also argue that the IMF's programs of reform and loan conditionality are too severe and may plunge the economies of emerging countries into hardship. There is a question about whether the funding actually helps nations, as more than half of those who received IMF money for a thirty-year period until the mid-1990s were not improved in per capita wealth, and a third were actually poorer. The Structural Adjustment Programs, a package

The North American Free Trade Agreement was highly controversial. President Bill Clinton worked hard to rally support, both in Congress and around the nation, for its passage. *R. Michael Jenkins, Congressional Quarterly*

of reforms imposed on nations receiving funds, often decrease a country's sovereignty because the governments will not receive money if they refuse any of the stipulations. These programs demand balanced budgets, and because typically the nations do not slash their military budgets, the cuts come in social and educational programs. Further, the countries must sell off state-owned enterprises, thereby opening themselves to foreign investment, again endangering sovereignty by losing control over assets.

Protests erupted during the WTO ministerial conference held in Seattle, Washington, from November 30 through December 3, 1999. The activists charged the WTO with considering the needs of multinational corporations at the expense of environmental safeguards and workers' rights. The conference ended without launching a new round of global trade talks. Similarly, the following April, thousands protested in Washington, D.C., during annual meetings of the World Bank and IMF.

Expanding world trade to include economies in Asia, Latin America, and the former Soviet empire will bring new consumers to the marketplace but will also create new producers working at lower wage rates. Future trade negotiations will focus on labor practices, environmental concerns, and the growing number of multinational corporations. In addition, regional trade pacts such as NAFTA and the European Union may take precedence over multilateral trade arrangements. Lastly, the trade deficit will remain an ongoing concern for the United States.

See also *Tariff History*.

CAROL JACKSON ADAMS, SALT LAKE COMMUNITY COLLEGE

BIBLIOGRAPHY

Bognanno, Mario F., and Kathryn J. Ready, eds. *The North American Free Trade Agreement: Labor, Industry, and Government Perspectives*. Westport, Conn.: Quorum Books, 1993.

Jones, Howard. *Quest for Security: A History of U.S. Foreign Relations*. 2 vols. New York: McGraw-Hill, 1996.

Kirshner, Orin, ed. *The Bretton Woods–GATT System: Retrospect and Prospect after Fifty Years*. Armonk, N.Y.: M. E. Sharpe, 1996.

Sander, Harald, and András Inotai, eds. *World Trade after the Uruguay Round: Prospects and Policy Options for the Twenty-First Century*. New York: Routledge, 1996.

TREATIES: PEACE, ARMAMENT, AND DEFENSE

From the treaty ending the American Revolution through present-day negotiations over arms control, the United States has sought peace through different means. Treaties ending wars have guaranteed the acquisition of territory, commercial supremacy, and the U.S. position as a world power. During the latter half of the twentieth century, disarmament preoccupied negotiations to prevent a nuclear war between superpowers involved in a cold war that had the potential to destroy both nations.

ESTABLISHING AND VALIDATING AMERICAN INDEPENDENCE

John Jay, John Adams, and Benjamin Franklin negotiated the Treaty of Paris of 1783 that ended the American Revolution. Britain recognized the independence of the United States, with a northern boundary following the St. Lawrence River to the Great Lakes, to the northwest point of the Lake of the Woods and west to the Mississippi River. Spain received the Floridas to the 31st parallel, the southern boundary of the new nation. The British promised to withdraw all forces "with all convenient speed." Both nations would have access to the Mississippi River, and Americans gained the "liberty" to fish in waters off Newfoundland and Canada. The United States agreed to recommend to the states the return of property of "real" British subjects and to noninterference with British businesses' collection of debts from Americans. Most Loyalists had been born in America, however, and did not qualify to regain property, nor did the Articles of Confederation, the government in effect, have the power over states to enforce these provisions. Unresolved issues between Britain and the United States led to Jay's Treaty, the Treaty of Amity, Commerce, and Navigation (1794). British soldiers had remained in northwest fur posts long after the Treaty of Paris. In one provision, Britain agreed to evacuate these posts by June 1, 1796.

The United States and Britain fought once more in the War of 1812, in what Americans considered a second war for independence. The war was primarily over neutral rights, as Britain harassed American shipping during the Napoleonic Wars to prevent trade with France. In addition, the United States accused Britain of impressing American sailors, or removing them from merchant vessels and forcing them into service in the British navy. Negotiations began in earnest in Ghent, Belgium, in August 1814. The talks did not focus on the causes of the war, for the European War had ended. Henry Clay, John Quincy Adams, Albert Gallatin, and James Bayard represented the United States in its negotiations with Lord Gambier, Henry Goulburn, and William Adams for the British. The renunciation of impressment, acquisition of Canada, definition of neutral rights in favor of the United States, return of slaves taken by the British, and payment for confiscated property had constituted original American demands but disappeared completely. The only requirement became status quo antebellum, or a return to the situation before the war. Neither side wished to continue fighting. Britain was exhausted from the war in Europe; the United States feared a struggle with an enemy that could now focus all its attention on defeating America. The treaty, signed on December 24, 1814, ignored impressment and the other causes of the war. Although the war ended in a stalemate, the treaty did validate American independence and ushered in a period of Anglo-American rapprochement and trade.

TERRITORIAL EXPANSION

The United States fought Mexico from 1846 to 1848, ostensibly to settle a boundary dispute between the newest American state, Texas, and Mexico, but in reality also to acquire California and its ports. In the Treaty of Guadalupe Hidalgo of February 2, 1848, the United States acquired the Mexican Cession, comprising present-day New Mexico, Arizona, Utah, Nevada, and the all-important California. (Mexico had recognized the annexation of Texas in 1845 and accepted the Rio Grande as the boundary.) The United States paid Mexico $15 million and assumed $3.25 million in damage claims made by American citizens. The war had become unpopular at home with antislavery northerners who viewed it as a means to expand slavery. There were also southern extremists who supported the All-Mexico Movement or the acquisition of much more territory. President James K. Polk sent the treaty to the Senate with only a mild recommendation. The territorial dispute even threatened the treaty in the Senate, as senators could not agree how much, if any, land should be kept. Nonetheless, they approved the treaty, which went into effect on July 4, 1848.

Northerners and southerners joined militarily, for the first time after the Civil War, in the Spanish-American War of 1898. President William McKinley realized that the Philippines were of strategic and commercial importance to trade with Asia, particularly with China. He also questioned the suitability of the Filipino population for self-government. In the Treaty of Paris of 1898, Spain assumed Cuba's debt, and the United States offered $20 million to Spain for it to relinquish any claims on the island. The United States did not annex Cuba, for Sen. Henry Teller of Colorado had added to the resolution to use force against Spain an amendment that the United States would not annex the island. The amendment omitted any reference to other Spanish islands, and the United States did acquire the Philippines, Guam, Puerto Rico, and other Spanish possessions in the West Indies.

A bitter debate over the treaty centered on imperialism. Opponents believed that owning the Philippines against the will of the native population violated U.S. principles. Those who supported imperialism emphasized the importance of trade and strategic benefits to the U.S. Navy. Some imperialists highlighted the spreading of American civilization to the "inferior" people of the Philippines as a humanitarian goal. The Senate approved the Treaty of Paris on February 6, 1899, by only one vote over the required

two-thirds majority. A few days before this, Emilio Aguinaldo started a rebellion against U.S. occupation of the Philippines that lasted until July 1902.

WORLD WAR I AND ITS AFTERMATH

President Woodrow Wilson believed that he could mediate an end to the Great War that began in Europe in August 1914. As the war continued and appeared to threaten neutral rights, the United States entered the conflict against Germany and Austria-Hungary in 1917 in an effort to "make the world safe for democracy" by "fighting the war to end all wars." In January 1918 the president announced his Fourteen Points, including a general disarmament after the war. He believed that the arms race between Germany and Britain had precipitated the war and that disarmament would prevent future conflicts. Wilson's list of war aims did not become the basis for peace that he had hoped it would.

The "Big Four"—French premier Georges Clemenceau, British prime minister David Lloyd George, Italian prime minister Vittorio Orlando, and Wilson—wrote the Treaty of Versailles in 1919. The president wanted to include the provision to establish a league of nations as a worldwide peace-

President Woodrow Wilson made a successful European tour to promote his postwar foreign policy agenda. The agenda proved to be more popular in Europe than in the United States, where his efforts to gain Senate approval of the Treaty of Versailles failed. *National Archives*

keeping organization, whereas the other leaders wanted the treaty first and an organization later. To ensure the league's inclusion, Wilson compromised on territorial changes demanded by his European counterparts. The treaty, in Article 231, blamed Germany for the damages and losses caused by the war. The punishment included the forfeiture of 6 million people to other nations, or one-tenth of its total population, and one-eighth of its territory. Germany lost its colonies, most of its merchant vessels, its industrial and agricultural resources, and its deposits of coal in Saar and iron ore in Lorraine. The newly created "Polish Corridor" separated East Prussia from the rest of Germany. Important for the future was Japan's acquisition of Germany's islands in the northern Pacific: the Marshalls, Carolines, and Marianas. Japan also won Germany's economic rights in Shandong in exchange for the return of the Shantung Peninsula to China, reserving only the economic privileges that Germany had held.

Opponents of the League of Nations in the U.S. Senate feared that Article 10 of the covenant, which established the principle of collective security and joint action by league members to protect against external aggression, would cost the United States sovereignty over its own foreign affairs. The treaty became a political struggle between the Democratic president, who refused to accept any changes, and the Republican-controlled Senate. Many Republicans were willing to accept the league but only with reservations. Wilson prevented a compromise, and the Senate defeated the treaty for the final time on March 19, 1920. In July of the following year, the United States concluded the Treaty of Berlin with Germany, accepting all provisions of the Versailles peace treaty except membership in the League of Nations.

In the aftermath of World War I, nations began questioning war and the arms race. The United States had refused to join the League of Nations and the World Court, yet it did support the goal of world peace. It sent observers to the league meetings in Geneva and participated in its talks on social work, drug control, the white slave trade, and arms control. Washington's primary focus became disarmament conferences. Naval construction worried the new Republican administration of Warren G. Harding. The cost could have forced a continuation of high wartime tax rates. The United States boasted an Atlantic and a Pacific fleet that could rival Britain's and ranked as the second-most-powerful nation in naval strength. Japan was expanding its naval power and ranked third in strength; it did not trust France, Britain, or the United States, believing they had designs in East Asia. Japan resented the failure of western powers to adopt a statement supporting racial equality at the Versailles Peace Conference.

These circumstances led to the Washington Naval Conference of November 1921. The United States believed that it had to check Japan's ambitions in China and the South Pacific to preserve its control over the Philippines, Guam, and Samoa. Secretary of State Charles Evans Hughes shocked the conference by proposing a ten-year moratorium on the construction of ships of more than 10,000 tons fitted with a minimum of eight-inch guns and the scrapping of vessels to meet specific arms limitations. The Five-Power Agreement outlined the relative naval strength of the United States, Great Britain, Japan, France, and Italy for disarmament as 5:5:3: 1.67:1.67. This ratio of maximum tonnage for battleship and battle cruisers assigned the number one as the equivalent of about 100,000 tons. It also called for a ten-year moratorium on building capital ships. The Nine-Power Treaty signed by the United States, Britain, Japan, and France plus Belgium, China, Italy, the Netherlands, and Portugal guaranteed the territorial integrity of China, conditional on its having an effective and stable government, but omitted any means of enforcement. The Four-Power Treaty among the United States, Britain, Japan, and France respected the holdings in the Pacific favoring the Japanese.

The London Treaty of 1930 extended the ratio system to include cruisers, destroyers, and submarines, but only the United States, Britain, and Japan signed. France and Italy refused to do so because France would not accept parity with Italy or the numbers that Britain and the United States proposed. The United States gained equality with Britain, even if that meant an increase in American armament. The powers extended the moratorium for five additional years, but growing tensions in East Asia and Europe hampered future attempts at disarmament. The World Disarmament Conference in Geneva in 1932 failed to accomplish any limitations, as did the London Conference of 1935. Japan refused to accept less than parity with Britain and the United States in tonnage for all warships and walked out of the conference.

THE END OF DISARMAMENT AND NEUTRALITY

Once World War II began, emphasis shifted in Washington from disarmament to provision of war materiel to defeat the Axis powers of Germany, Italy, and Japan. Although the United States professed neutrality, President Franklin D. Roosevelt sought avenues to make the nation an arsenal for democracy. After France accepted collaboration with Nazi Germany to prevent the loss of all its territory, Great Britain stood as the sole power fighting Adolf Hitler's forces. Roosevelt warned the American people that the nation must either help Britain as the German air assault escalated or fight Hitler on U.S. soil. The president traded fifty overaged destroyers for ninety-nine-year leases on eight British bases in the western hemisphere. He concluded the deal in early September 1940 as an executive agreement to avoid the necessity of obtaining Senate approval for a treaty.

The administration further aided Britain by lending war supplies to use against Germany, thus replacing the "cash and carry" terms required by the Neutrality Act of 1939. The Lend-Lease Act, signed in March 1941, allowed the United States to sell, lend, or lease any supplies to any nation whose defense the president considered vital to America's own defense. The assumption was that Britain would return or replace the supplies at the end of the war. When Hitler attacked the Soviet Union the following June, the United States extended Lend-Lease to that nation as well. The destroyers-for-bases deal and Lend-Lease effectively ended neutrality as U.S. policy.

The roots of the cold war can be found in World War II. The partners in the Grand Alliance—Great Britain, the Soviet Union, and the United States—worked together to defeat a common enemy. Without that purpose, however, the alliance would disintegrate over ideological differences. By the time the Big Three—British prime minister Winston Churchill, Soviet premier Joseph Stalin, and U.S. president Roosevelt—met at Yalta on the Black Sea in February 1945 to plan for the postwar world, Europe was dividing into two camps. The leaders agreed to partition Germany into four temporary occupation zones, including a small portion for France. They postponed a final decision on reparations but agreed that an Allied commission would eventually meet and use $20 billion as a starting figure for discussion, with half allotted to the Soviet Union. The future of Poland consumed much of the talks, thus predicting postwar tension over the type of government eastern European nations would adopt. The leaders agreed to a coalition government for Poland that included noncommunist Poles, a tenuous arrangement at best. All three signed the Declaration on Liberated Europe, pledging to hold free and unsupervised elections in areas under their control as soon as possible. Satisfying Roosevelt's primary goal, the Soviet leader promised to enter the war against Japan two-to-three months after the defeat of Germany in exchange for Outer Mongolia, the Kurile Islands, the southern half of Sakhalin Island, and the opportunity to reestablish political and economic control of Manchuria. As the cold war became a reality, many Americans considered the Yalta agreements as unnecessary concessions to Stalin in Eastern Europe, forgetting that the Soviet military occupied much of the region by the time of the conference.

In August 1941 Roosevelt and Churchill had discussed war aims, although the United States was not yet a belliger-

The "Big Three"—British prime minister Winston Churchill, President Franklin D. Roosevelt, and Soviet premier Joseph Stalin—confer in Yalta. *Library of Congress*

ent, and the establishment of a permanent international body to maintain general security following the end of the war. Talks over the organization of such a body took place among the Big Three powers at Dumbarton Oaks in Georgetown. They ended, however, without settling major questions such as the representation of Soviet republics and voting rights in the UN Security Council. Roosevelt hoped at Yalta to resolve these issues. The Big Three agreed to require unanimity of the five permanent members of the Security Council on all but procedural matters and to grant veto power to any of the five in all decisions. The UN Charter was signed in San Francisco on June 25, 1945.

When Roosevelt died on April 12, 1945, Harry S. Truman assumed the presidency, and his role as one of the Big Three emerged at the Potsdam Conference outside Berlin in July. Clement Atlee replaced the ousted Churchill; thus Stalin was the only Grand Alliance leader still in power as the men discussed plans for postwar Germany and for ending the war with Japan. During the conference, the president learned that the Manhattan Project had produced a successful atomic explosion, and he informed his counterparts. Truman doubted the future of cooperation with the Soviet Union and worried because the Soviet military controlled Eastern Europe with the support of local communists. The coalition government in Poland had already failed, and a communist one had taken its place. The new Big Three finalized the Yalta accord, dividing Germany into four occupation zones, and decided that each power would exact reparations only from its zone until an undetermined date. They also created a future council of foreign ministers of the four powers to address unsettled matters.

To end the war in the Far East, Britain, China, and the United States in the Potsdam Declaration demanded Japan's unconditional surrender and warned of destruction if it did not comply. When the government in Tokyo did not surrender, the United States faced the decision to launch an invasion of the Japanese islands or to use the new atomic weapon. On August 6, 1945, the United States dropped the first atomic bomb on Hiroshima, a center for war production. Truman expected an immediate surrender, and when Japan did not act, he ordered a second bomb dropped on Nagasaki. Stalin's invasion of Manchuria, held by the Japanese, honored his promise at Yalta but may have influenced Truman's decision. The longer the war continued, the greater the possibility of postwar Soviet involvement in the Far East. Atomic warfare and the origins of the cold war were thereby linked. Nonetheless, Truman always maintained that his primary goal was to save American lives by quickly bringing an end to the war. Japan accepted the terms of the Potsdam Declaration on August 10 without accepting any of the demands as to the emperor's future. The Allies did allow Emperor Hirohito to retain his throne with little power. Formal surrender took place on September 2, 1945.

COLD WAR AND MUTUAL DEFENSE

Following the defeat of the Axis powers, the cold war replaced conventional wars as the dominant American concern. The new enemy was the Soviet Union, and the arms race preoccupied both sides. President Dwight D. Eisenhower's Open Skies proposal in 1955 suggested a reduction in risk of surprise attacks through the exchange of military information and broad verification reconnaissance flights and ground inspections. The Soviets rejected this suggestion. The Cuban missile crisis in October 1962 made the possibility of nuclear war all too real. The two superpowers subsequently negotiated the Nuclear Test Ban Treaty in 1963, which banned tests in the atmosphere, in outer space, and under water. The treaty did not ban testing underground because of opposition to on-site inspection, but it did provide for verification without direct inspection by using seismic and other instruments deployed outside of national borders. The United States wanted direct inspection of each country's facilities; however, the Soviets viewed inspection as a type of espionage. Either side could abrogate the treaty with a year's notice. Although it was the first arms limitation agreement between the United States and the Soviet Union, the race continued. In 1969, 182 nations signed the Nuclear Non-Proliferation Treaty and pledged not to develop nuclear weapons, leaving only five nations as officially nuclear states.

Amid the cold war and its arms race, the United States signed several treaties for mutual defense. On April 4, 1949, twelve nations established a defense organization for Europe, the North Atlantic Treaty Organization (NATO), which included the United States, Britain, Canada, France, Italy, Belgium, Luxembourg, Norway, Denmark, Iceland, Portugal, and the Netherlands. Greece, Turkey, and West Germany joined by the mid–1950s. Although concerned over permanent involvement in Europe, the Senate approved U.S. membership. Representatives of the United States attended a conference in Rio de Janeiro that established collective security for the hemisphere through the Inter-American Treaty for Mutual Assistance (the Rio Pact). During the Korean War, the United States sought an alliance in East Asia and signed the Tripartite Security Treaty (ANZUS) with Australia and New Zealand. As the United States feared Soviet influence in the Middle East, the Eisenhower administration attempted to build a defense system. In 1959 the president negotiated separate agreements with Turkey, Iran, and Pakistan and promised military assistance to those nations if attacked. The Central Treaty Organization (CENTO) emerged with Turkey, Britain, Iran, and Pakistan as members. Also under Eisenhower, the United States sought to aid the noncommunists in the southern part of Vietnam. The United States established the Southeast Asia Treaty Organization (SEATO) to protect South Vietnam, Laos, and Cambodia from communism. The organization went into effect in 1955, and the United States used it to justify its involvement in the region.

Mutual defense did not prevent the use of U.S. armed forces to implement the policy of containing the spread of communism. When North Korean troops invaded South Korea, the Truman administration proposed a UN resolution condemning the action and deployed American combat troops. Sixteen members of the United Nations participated against North Korea and eventually the People's Republic of China. The fighting continued although armistice discussions began in July 1951. The talks stalled over repatriation of prisoners. The communists demanded the return of all prisoners, but the United Nations refused to repatriate those who did not want to return to their homeland. Talks resumed in July 1953 in Panmunjom. The agreement established a neutral commission to handle repatriation. The line dividing the two Koreas was approximately the 38th parallel (the boundary before the war), protected by a demilitarized zone.

VIETNAM

The United States viewed Southeast Asia as another region endangered by communism, against the backdrop of the cold war with the Soviet Union and the People's Republic of China. Successive administrations backed a South Vietnamese government that increasingly lost the support of its own population. President Lyndon Johnson escalated America's involvement by sending combat troops despite waning domestic support. Peace talks began in Paris in May 1968, but there was little progress by the time of Richard Nixon's inauguration in January 1969. The administration opened secret peace talks between Secretary of State Henry Kissinger and North Vietnam's negotiator Le Duc Tho, offering to withdraw and tacitly acknowledging communist control over much of South Vietnam. North Vietnam wanted the United States out completely, so the war continued. By October 1972 it appeared that peace was imminent. However, South Vietnamese leader Nguyen Van Thieu opposed American withdrawal and the presence of North Vietnamese forces in his country; the agreement seemed doomed. Nixon won reelection in 1972 and ordered the bombing of Hanoi and Haiphong in North Vietnam in late December.

The United States and North Vietnam reopened the talks, and negotiators signed a cease-fire agreement on January 27, 1973. The terms included American withdrawal of troops from South Vietnam and the return of all American POWs within sixty days; implementation of an election through a National Council of Reconciliation and Concord; enforcement of treaty provisions through an international commission; conduct of an international conference on Vietnam; and authorization for the United States to replace South Vietnam's damaged military equipment. Unofficially, the United States also agreed to furnish North Vietnam $4.75 billion for reconstruction and threatened to withdraw aid from Thieu's government to force his acquiescence. Nonetheless, Nixon secretly promised to provide military aid to Thieu if North Vietnam violated the cease-fire agreement. The terms left North Vietnamese troops in the south and Hanoi still determined to unite the country. In April 1975 North Vietnamese troops invaded South Vietnam and captured the capital of Saigon.

DÉTENTE AND STRATEGIC ARMS LIMITATION

As détente began easing tensions between the superpowers, disarmament would benefit both sides. The United States had not wanted to produce anti–ballistic missile systems (ABMs) because of cost and doubts over effectiveness. The Soviet Union spent twice as much of its gross national product as the United States on arms, but after the ABM treaty could spend more on consumer goods. In the early 1970s, the Soviet economy needed grain and technological assistance. The Soviet Union signed nonaggression agreements over West Germany and its borders, easing tensions with the United States. During his unprecedented visit to Moscow in May 1972, President Nixon and Leonid Brezhnev signed an agreement based on two years of strategic arms limitations talks. SALT I included the Treaty of Anti–Ballistic Missile Systems and the Interim Agreement on Limitation of Strategic Offensive Arms. Based on the concept of mutual assured destruction (MAD)—recognizing that major cities on both sides would be vulnerable—the concept held that neither power would begin a war. Under the first agreement, each side would be permitted one ABM system that could intercept and neutralize approaching warheads. The second agreement set an upper limit on the number of offensive missiles for the Soviet Union and the United States. SALT I set the number of intercontinental ballistic missiles (ICBMs) but omitted any reference to multiple independently targeted reentry vehicles (MIRVs), an area in which the United States had supremacy over the USSR. The U.S. advantage grew to 2 to 1 by the time the SALT I agreements expired in 1977. In reality, SALT I encouraged the arms race in the new technology while restricting merely older models.

Negotiations lasted seven years until the signing of SALT II in 1979. The maximum number of long-range missiles and bombers that each side would be permitted would be lowered to 2,250 by 1981. The agreement limited MIRVed ballistic missiles to 1,200, established maximum warhead figures for other launchers, established verification procedures, and guaranteed that future talks would attempt to reduce nuclear stockpiles. SALT II did not restrict cruise missiles capable of striking the Soviet Union carrying a single warhead, Pershing II ballistic missiles guided by radar and capable of accurately hitting targets more than 1,000 miles away, or the Trident-II sea-launched ballistic missile (SLBM) that could carry fourteen warheads. Each side agreed to stop construction on new fixed ICBMs and not to relocate its current fixed ICBMs, not to convert light ICBMs into heavy ones, and not to increase the destructive power of warheads. The treaty did not address Soviet development of its Backfire supersonic bomber or the SS-20 intermediate-range nuclear missile, which could carry three warheads. The treaty was set to expire in 1985.

Whereas the Senate welcomed SALT I, there was mixed reaction and more mistrust over SALT II. A national debate ensued, and many people questioned the maximum limits and the trustworthiness of the Soviet Union. During the debate, President Jimmy Carter discovered the existence of a Soviet brigade of 2,500 troops in Cuba and announced a suspension of discussion of ratification until the withdrawal of the soldiers. The Soviets in turn accused the president of publicizing the confrontation to enhance his own reelection chances. Hearings of the Foreign Relations Committee were postponed despite the accuracy of Soviet claims that the troops had been in Cuba for years. Carter ultimately accepted their presence but withdrew the treaty from the Senate in January 1980, as its defeat appeared inevitable.

Carter's successor, Ronald Reagan, postponed SALT talks as he proposed changes in the U.S. strategic plan. The new

president supported a single-warhead missile to be distributed throughout the Untied States to lower its vulnerability to attack. He ordered one hundred B-1 bombers, although experts believed the plane to be too expensive and less effective than the projected Stealth bomber that could better evade radar detection. He also pushed for production of cruise missiles amid warnings that their ability to avoid verification would escalate the arms race because the Soviets would develop them as well. Reagan criticized the 1970s policy of arms control as endangering national security and believed that the Soviets had nuclear superiority. He proposed a program that could increase the arms race while attempting to hurt the Soviet economy.

FROM ARMS LIMITATION TO ARMS REDUCTION

In the mid-1980s there were signs that renewed tensions between the United States and the Soviet Union were relaxing once again. President Ronald Reagan met with Mikhail Gorbachev several times and discussed arms control and disarmament. In December 1987 they signed the Intermediate-Range Nuclear Forces Treaty (INF), which eliminated a class of weapons for the first time rather than merely limiting further growth. It disbanded the U.S. and Soviet INF missiles in Europe and authorized on-site inspections. The Senate ratified the treaty overwhelmingly, and the treaty went into effect in June 1988.

The strategic arms reduction talks (START) replaced SALT and yielded an agreement in July 1991. The two superpowers were to reduce nuclear warheads from a level of 11,000 or 12,000 to 6,000 on a maximum of 1,600 strategic arms carriers. The Soviet Union's disintegration in December 1991 resulted in Belarus, Ukraine, and Kazakhstan becoming nuclear powers and possessing almost one-third of weapons that had previously been Soviet. In the Lisbon agreement of March 1972, these states agreed to destroy or move to Russia all nuclear weapons in their possession.

The United States and Russia signed the START II treaty to reduce the maximum nuclear weapons within ten years and to prohibit MIRVed warheads on land-based missiles. The Russians promised to reduce by the end of the century the number of warheads from 10,909 to 3,000, and the United States reduced its warheads from 9,862 to 3,500. Problems erupted when in late 1992 unrest in Russia threatened the treaty's implementation. The Russian economy faced problems that hampered relations with the United States. The disintegration of the Soviet state weakened many Americans' resolve about the need for disarmament. By 1998 the United States had ratified the treaty, but Russia had not.

The U.N. General Assembly adopted the Comprehensive Test Ban Treaty (CTBT) in 1996, and 154 countries signed it. The Republican-controlled U.S. Senate voted against it in October 1999 because of problems with verification and the capability of dealing with violations. The United States is the only nuclear power to reject the CTBT. The treaty banned all nuclear weapons testing by the signatories. President Bill Clinton had proposed computer simulations of nuclear testing to replace real testing.

After the end of the cold war, the United States decreased its defense budget but remains the largest spender on arms. Russia's economic crises led to a decline in defense spending and a halt in production of new weapons systems. The idea of arms limitation has been to prevent an increase in the number of weapons that countries possess, whereas arms reduction is decreasing the number and types of weapons of each country. Nonproliferation is preventing countries without certain types of weapons from getting them. Despite the history of negotiations, proliferation may prove to be the hardest to control, as countries outside prior multilateral agreements obtain nuclear capabilities.

See also *American Revolution; Cold War; Indian Policy; Korean War; Mexican-American War; Spanish-American War; Treaty Making; Vietnam War; War of 1812; World War I; World War II.*

CAROL JACKSON ADAMS, SALT LAKE COMMUNITY COLLEGE

BIBLIOGRAPHY

Ambrosius, Lloyd E. *Woodrow Wilson and the American Diplomatic Tradition: The Treaty Fight in Perspective.* New York: Cambridge University Press, 1987.

Horsman, Reginald. *The Diplomacy of the New Republic, 1776–1815.* Arlington Heights, Ill.: H. Davidson, 1985.

Jones, Howard. *Quest for Security: A History of U.S. Foreign Relations.* 2 vols. New York: McGraw-Hill, 1996.

Kaufman, Robert Gordon. *Arms Control during the Pre-nuclear Era: The United States and Naval Limitation Between the Two World Wars.* New York: Columbia University Press, 1990.

Lundestad, Geir. *East, West, North, South: Major Developments in International Politics Since 1945.* New York: Oxford University Press, 1999.

Schulzinger, Robert. *American Diplomacy in the Twentieth Century.* New York: Oxford University Press, 1994.

Varg, Paul A. *United States Foreign Relations 1820–1860.* East Lansing: Michigan State University Press, 1979.

TREATY MAKING

Article II, section 2, of the U.S. Constitution gives the president the power to make treaties with the advice and consent of two-thirds of the senators present. The treaty-making process includes three stages. The president, or the president's representative, negotiates a treaty with one or more nations. The president must send the treaty to the Senate for approval, rejection, amendment, or added reservations. Finally, to complete the ratification process and place the treaty into effect, the president must accept the document as approved by the Senate. The Senate has voted down about twenty treaties, or approximately 1 percent, and has accepted about 15 percent after changes.

The Senate does not formally advise on treaties before or during negotiations. The Founders expected the president to consult with the Senate during the treaty-making process rather than merely presenting to it the final document. President George Washington attempted to accomplish such a joint presidential-senatorial action in writing the Indian Treaty in 1789. He went to the chamber personally to learn senators' opinions, expecting their immediate consent. The body delayed, however, angering Washington. Since then, presidents have consulted with the Senate only in writing. Nonetheless, senators have informally advised presidents in order to ward off potential problems during the ratification process.

FAILED TREATIES

At the end of World War I, President Woodrow Wilson, a Democrat, was fervent in his desire to include the League of Nations, a worldwide peacekeeping organization, in the text of the Treaty of Versailles. The Senate was concerned with Article 10 of the league covenant, which established the principle of collective security so that league members would protect each other against external aggression. The status of the League of Nations was so tightly woven within the Treaty of Versailles that a defeat of the league would guarantee a refusal of the treaty itself. The Senate had never refused to approve a peace treaty, and Wilson believed that it would not do so this time.

The Republican Party controlled the Senate by a mere two votes. The chairman of the Foreign Relations Committee, Henry Cabot Lodge, opposed the league but recommended amendments and reservations. He required the United States to have the right to withdraw from the League of Nations without conditions. According to his reservations, the nation would not accept any obligations of collective security without congressional approval.

Wilson rejected any changes in the treaty, forbade the Senate Democrats to compromise, and toured the country, urging the population to demand Senate ratification of the treaty. Physical exhaustion overcame the president, and he suffered a massive stroke upon his return to Washington. His illness did not diminish his resolve to keep the treaty with the league intact.

Democrats united against any amendments to the treaty; and Republicans would not approve it without amendments. Therefore, both parties joined forces to defeat it. In 1920, during the last debate on the treaty, twenty-one Democrats broke ranks with the president and even supported the latest version with reservations; however, it failed. The United States concluded the Treaty of Berlin with Germany in July 1921, tying the United States to all parts of the Treaty of Versailles except the League of Nations. As a consequence of this treaty fight, presidents began to advise the Senate during the negotiations process of crucial treaties.

The SALT II treaty marked another failure in the process of Senate approval of a treaty, due to conditions imposed by the Senate, concerns raised by the American public, and problems raised by Soviet military actions. The Strategic Arms Limitation Talks II negotiations began in 1972 and lasted for seven years. The agreement set the limit on the number of strategic delivery vehicles for each side at 2,400 long-range missiles and bombers. The level was to be reduced to 2,250 by 1981. It further limited the number of ballistic missiles with multiple independently targetable reentry vehicles (MIRVs), set maximum warhead numbers, and established procedures for verification. The Foreign Relations Committee reported the treaty by a vote of nine to six but added twenty-three conditions. Nineteen senators urged President Jimmy Carter in 1979 to postpone the vote. In the aftermath of the Soviet invasion of Afghanistan in December, the president asked the Senate to delay the vote.

American sentiment over ratification was divided. Many believed that the limits were too high, and others did not trust the Soviet government or the concept of verification. Carter supported the treaty because it would slow down Soviet arms production while allowing the United States fewer restrictions. The discovery of Soviet combat troops in Cuba further intensified anti-Soviet sentiment. In January 1980 Carter withdrew the treaty from the Senate.

SUCCESSFUL TREATY MAKING

After the Panamanian revolution in 1903, the United States concluded a treaty with the new Republic of Panama. The United States gained control of a ten-mile wide strip of Panama and the future canal's operation. American domination resulted in Panamanian resentment until riots broke out in the early 1960s. Treaty renegotiations lasted from 1964 until the signing in 1977. The Panama Canal Treaty abolished the Canal Zone but granted the United States the right to operate the canal with Panamanian participation until the end of 1999. Following that date, the United States transferred administration of the canal to Panama. The Neutrality Treaty stipulated that the region of the canal would be permanently neutral.

President Carter involved the Senate even before the treaties were signed. Debate lasted thirty-eight days, second in length only to the deliberations over the Treaty of Versailles. Senators discussed eighty-eight changes and added more than twenty reservations, understandings, and conditions. Forty-two senators traveled to Panama, some of whom actually ne-

The battleship USS *New Jersey* traverses the Panama Canal. President Jimmy Carter returned the Canal Zone to Panamanian sovereignty through a highly controversial treaty. *U.S. Navy*

gotiated with the leadership there after the conclusion of the treaty. Ratification became the focal point of public opinion surveys in the United States, and concern over national security convinced many Americans to oppose it. After months, the Senate approved the Neutrality Treaty and the Canal Treaty in April 1978, both with only one vote over the required two-thirds.

TREATY TERMINATION

The Constitution does not address the procedure for terminating a treaty, but the following question has arisen: Must the Senate vote to end a treaty because it approved the treaty in the first place? Presidents historically have exercised sole power over the termination process. When Congress was out of session in December 1978, President Carter terminated a treaty with the Republic of China (Taiwan) prior to full recognition of the People's Republic of China. Sen. Barry Goldwater, R-Ariz., and twenty other members of Congress filed a suit in federal court to prevent this termination as unconstitutional because two-thirds of the Senate had not approved it. The district court ruled in Goldwater's favor, but the court of appeals reversed the ruling. The U.S. Supreme Court dismissed the case as a matter for the political branches to settle. The justices disagreed over their reasoning but left the termination in effect and presidential prerogative over the process in place.

Treaty making exemplifies Senate and presidential cooperation. The president has the responsibility for execution and the primary role in interpretation and also enforces treaty obligations. Foreign governments turn to the president when there is an issue of U.S. compliance. The president also decides the proper response if there is a breach by the other party. Although the House of Representatives does not have a constitutional role in the treaty-making process, it does have a role in appropriations to implement any treaty arrangements. In the final analysis, the power belongs to the president, who must gain the support of two-thirds of the Senate, even if the process involves partisan politics or supporting favorite projects to earn a positive vote.

Partisan politics and personalities can threaten the treaty-making process. In April 2000 Senate Foreign Relations chairman Jesse Helms (R-N.C.) confronted Democratic president Bill Clinton over amending the 1972 Anti–Ballistic Missile Treaty. The lame-duck administration's goal to negotiate changes to allow deployment of a limited national missile-defense system faced a Republican-controlled Congress. Tests of the new system failed; thus the issue remained unresolved during the presidential campaign of 2000.

See also *Treaties: Commercial; Treaties: Peace, Armament, and Defense.*

CAROL JACKSON ADAMS, SALT LAKE COMMUNITY COLLEGE

BIBLIOGRAPHY

Adler, David Gray, and Larry N. George, eds. *The Constitution and the Conduct of American Foreign Policy.* Lawrence: University Press of Kansas, 1996.

Ambrosius, Lloyd E. *Woodrow Wilson and the American Diplomatic Tradition.* New York: Cambridge University Press, 1987.

Glennon, Michael J. *Constitutional Diplomacy.* Princeton: Princeton University Press, 1990.

Henkin, Louis. *Foreign Affairs and the United States Constitution.* New York: Clarendon Press, 1996.

TRUMAN, HARRY S.

Harry S. Truman, the thirty-third president of the United States, came into office at a crucial time, near the end of World War II, and in the postwar years advocated forward-looking domestic policies and brought the country into participation in world affairs. An "accidental president," assuming office upon the death of Franklin D. Roosevelt, he served almost two full terms, from April 12, 1945, to January 20, 1953.

At the time of his presidency his countrymen did not always appreciate him. When Truman became president his

Harry S. Truman takes the presidential oath of office as his wife Bess and daughter Margaret look on. *Harry S. Truman Library*

popularity rating in opinion polls was high, an extraordinary 87 percent. Approval declined during the immediate postwar era, a function of reconversion from a wartime to peacetime economy, with demands by both labor and industry for repeal of wartime controls. Truman's popularity rebounded during his successful campaign for election as president in his own right in 1948, drifted down again after outbreak of the Korean War in 1950, and reached a nadir in 1951 when a Gallup poll placed his approval rating at 23 percent—one percentage point below the rating President Richard M. Nixon would receive in 1974 on the eve of his resignation.

Through ups and downs Truman doughtily continued to seek his domestic and foreign goals. A seasoned leader, proud of the word *politician,* which he considered a designation as worthy as that of teacher, physician, or clergy, Truman believed that if he did his best, history would vindicate him. In the initial years of his presidency he wrote his brother Vivian that, as he put it, he was doing the best he could, and if people did not like it they could "go to hell."

History has come to his support. Born in 1884, he died in 1972; at the time of his death he perhaps did not sense that already his reputation was rising from its low estate during the Korean War. In the years that followed, his reputation as president has reached a category usually described as "near great"—eighth or ninth in the pantheon of presidents. A C-SPAN survey of fifty-eight presidential experts, released in February

2000, rated him fifth, after Abraham Lincoln, George Washington, and Theodore and Franklin D. Roosevelt.

Before becoming president, Truman served twenty years in local and national offices—ten as a county commissioner of Jackson County, Missouri, which includes Kansas City; ten in the U.S. Senate (1935–1945). With his considerable experience in domestic politics and his understanding of the importance of programs that were of practical value and attractive to constituents, one might have thought that his domestic program as president would have proved more successful. In September 1945 he sent to Congress a seventeen-thousand-word message asking for a resurrection of New Deal programs and policy: a federal guarantee of full employment, fair employment practices, unemployment compensation, a housing program, and development of natural resources. Congress ignored the proposals, and voters had tired of proposals for reform—Roosevelt's program had virtually ended with the coming of World War II.

PUSHING FOR A "FAIR DEAL"

In 1946 and 1947 Truman did little to advance his domestic program, turning instead to foreign policy proposals, and in 1948 he was preoccupied by the presidential election. After election he returned in 1949 to domestic policy in a program that opened with the words: "Every segment of our population and every individual has the right to expect from our government a fair deal." He sought again to extend the New Deal, with federal control of prices, credit, commodities, exports, wages, and rents. Truman asked for a broadening of civil rights laws, low-cost housing, and a seventy-five-cent minimum wage. He sought the repeal of the Taft-Hartley Act (1947), which had restricted unions. His Fair Deal proposed wider coverage of Social Security laws and sought compulsory health insurance (the president wrote a friend asking what the world was coming to when hospital rooms cost sixty dollars a day). The Fair Deal measures for the most part failed, to be taken up by later presidential administrations. In the instance of health insurance the American Medical Association accused Truman of sponsoring "socialized medicine," and health care became the province of private insurance.

Truman sought to reorganize the farm program of the Roosevelt administration through a plan named for Secretary of Agriculture Charles F. Brannan. It sought to protect smaller farmers against large, through allotting a maximum number of "units" of production. Republican opponents criticized the proposal's subsidy payments and continued New Deal regulations that disguised payments as being for conservation and price supports.

The Fair Deal triumphed in one aspect—the espousal of civil rights for black Americans. The president appointed a committee that in 1947 brought in a proposal entitled "To Secure These Rights." Defeated in the Republican-controlled Eightieth Congress of 1947–1949, the proposal received hearty support from the president through executive acts, forbidding discrimination in federal contracts, and, just before and then during the Korean War, integrating the armed services. It has often been pointed out that when Truman was a youth and even during his senatorial days he displayed intolerance, sometimes using racist language. But he also had a life-long hostility to the Ku Klux Klan in Missouri. He confronted the problem of gross injustice when he was president and took forthright measures against it. He felt so strongly on the subject that he was willing to chance a break in the Democratic Party in 1948, when southerners formed the States' Rights Democrats, known as Dixiecrats, in response to the adoption of a civil rights plank in the Democrats' 1948 platform. The party saw another break as supporters of Henry A. Wallace, Franklin Roosevelt's former vice president, entered the fray under the Progressive Party label. Truman won election with 49.5 percent of the popular vote.

The Truman administration was accused of infringing civil liberties with its loyalty program, established by executive act in 1947, in which it screened 4 million government employees. Dismissals were minuscule—378 in all (0.022 percent). The president undertook the program with reluctance, virtually forced into it by Congress. It nonetheless constituted a blot, one might say, on his administration. It grew out of the period that later came to be characterized by the term *McCarthyism,* named after Sen. Joseph McCarthy (R–Wis.), and reflected the fear of communist infiltration of the government that grew as tension with the Soviet Union increased following World War II. McCarthy, and many others who shared his views, became an anticommunist crusader, often adopting tactics of suspicion, questionable information, intimidation, and other techniques that violated Americans' civil liberties and ruined many careers in the process.

Truman was criticized for making poor appointments, and there were allegations of corruption among appointees and employees of the Bureau of Internal Revenue (BIR) and the Reconstruction Finance Corporation (RFC). He placed BIR collectorships under civil service, and Congress terminated the RFC in 1953. Truman believed in the need for party loyalty, which meant that appointees should be loyal to him, and he should protect them until any alleged transgressions were proved. For this reason he tended to protect appointees to a point where they became liabilities.

BRINGING EFFICIENCY TO BUREAUCRACY

The Truman administration never received credit for the largely successful effort to bring efficiency to the huge federal bureaucracy, which numbered 2.6 million when inherited from the Roosevelt administration. His predecessor had not been a good administrator, and Truman brought the sprawling bureaucracy under control. He gave supervision mostly to members of his cabinet. Truman's cabinet meetings were serious affairs, with the president asking advice from all attendees, listening to problems, and reserving decision for himself. He welcomed the organizational abilities of former president Herbert Hoover, who did yeoman work in this regard. Roosevelt had ignored Hoover, but Truman put him to work.

The president enlarged the numbers of his White House assistants, increased the White House staff, and added to the executive office staff, the latter including the Bureau of the Budget. Congress in 1946, not trusting the new president of whom it was said had failed as a haberdasher years before because of his inability to measure money, insisted upon the Council of Economic Advisers, and Truman welcomed their help. In 1947–1949 Truman reorganized the military into a single cabinet position, that of the Department of Defense; reduced service secretaries to subcabinet status; and added a secretary for the new subcabinet Department of the Air Force. Creation of a Central Intelligence Agency came in 1947, and with onset of the Korean War the president began giving it attention. The National Security Council, organized in 1947, similarly gained importance during the war when the president began attending its meetings. Truman refused to appoint a chief of staff, abhorring the notion of an individual standing between him and his principal administrative officers. His successor, Dwight D. Eisenhower, was the first president to designate such an intermediary, an arrangement he had known when in the military.

MAKING THE HARD FOREIGN POLICY DECISIONS

It was in foreign policy that the Truman administration proved remarkably successful and made its reputation. The president's initial decision on foreign policy was really a military decision that was to have international repercussions over the years. This was his decision to employ nuclear weapons against Japan in the bombings of Hiroshima on August 6, 1945, and Nagasaki on August 9—a decision that both Truman and the majority of Americans at the time believed ended the war in the Pacific on August 14. In subsequent years none of Truman's decisions proved as controversial. The president believed that the alternative to what Secretary of War Henry L. Stimson described as a massive shock to the military leaders of Japan was "an Okinawa from one end of Japan to the other," a massively costly invasion that would have made the death toll of American troops in the Okinawa invasion during the first months of 1945—thirteen thousand dead—seem small. The president's advisers, civil and military, recommended use of all available force to forestall the invasion scheduled for November 1, 1945, and possible continuation of the war against Japan into 1946 and beyond. No one will ever be able to be sure that Truman took the right course, allowing use of the weapons that became available to the military after explosion of a test device on July 16, 1945.

After the end of the Pacific war the question of postwar policy quickly began to hinge upon policy toward the Soviet Union, and the result was the cold war, a phrase popularized by newspaper columnist Walter Lippmann. During the European war's last months, acrimony developed over the surrender of German troops in Italy, about which Russia was not consulted, and the Soviets were criticized for exploiting Germany during occupation of that zone. The Soviets took offense at the U.S.-dominated occupation of Japan, despite the fact that they entered the war in the Pacific only six days before its end. Truman sought to allay Russian sensitivities by journeying to a suburb of Berlin, Potsdam, for a conference in July–August 1945. Thereafter he moved slowly against Soviet acts of increasing hostility, and it was only a decision by the British government early in 1947 that moved Truman to his first large countermeasure. When he learned that the British government no longer could afford to support the friendly governments in Greece and Turkey, he asked Congress on March 12, 1947, for $400 million for the two countries, with an accompanying explanation that took the name of the Truman Doctrine.

Truman's foreign policy developed with, first, a declaration of principle, the Truman Doctrine, followed by economic support for Western Europe, including Britain, in the Marshall Plan, which was announced in June 1947. Before it ended in 1950, the Marshall Plan cost $13 billion. Truman's foreign policy culminated in 1949 with the formation of the North Atlantic Treaty Organization, which was galvanized into an important military organization by General Eisenhower during the Korean War. In the course of these measures, the Soviet Union attempted to expel its former allies from the city of Berlin by starving and perhaps freezing out its German residents through a blockade of the western sectors, allowing only access by air. The airlift of 1948–1949 managed to supply the city with food and coal.

The Korean War proved the most difficult foreign policy decision of Truman's presidency. In retrospect, with knowledge derived years later that the North Korean attack on South Korea was not only sanctioned but encouraged by the Soviets, it is clear that intervention was necessary to reestablish a power balance in East Asia, thereby protecting Japan. Truman acted accordingly. However, he failed to ask Congress for a declaration of war in June 1950, skirting the war-making powers assigned by the Constitution to Congress by describing the Korean situation as a "police action." He did not ask for rationing and price controls to protect U.S. citizens against the inflation that took place in the war's first months. He allowed the invasion of North Korea in late 1950 that brought Chinese intervention, and he lingered over relieving Gen. Douglas MacArthur for insubordination until April 1951. He seized the country's steel mills during a strike resulting from an acrid contention between the mills' owners and union leaders, at a time when there was talk of shortages for the troops in Korea. He justified seizure under his powers as president, and the Supreme Court reversed his action and declared it unconstitutional, administering a stinging rebuke to a sitting president. As the conflict wore on,

A mushroom cloud arises from Nagasaki, Japan, site of the second of two atomic attacks. When he succeeded to office after President Franklin D. Roosevelt's death, Truman was unaware of the research under way on the atomic bomb. The momentous decisions of whether and how to use it fell to Truman. *Library of Congress*

turning into stalemate and becoming increasingly unpopular, Truman's popularity fell, and when he left office in January 1953 it stood at 31 percent. The Eisenhower administration's ending of the war in an uneasy armistice in June 1953 proved a popular move and another rebuke to Truman's policy of prosecuting the war.

A special achievement of the Truman administration, not often heralded at the time nor celebrated later, was its nuclear policy. Despite first use of nuclear weapons, their production in the postwar years was at the outset very slow. In fact, early in 1947 it was questioned whether the American arsenal possessed more than a single workable weapon, this because of the transfer of the weapons program from military control to that of the civilian-led Atomic Energy Commission. After production increased there was another problem, whether the air force's strategic air command could actually deliver on Soviet targets what weapons the United States then had. With resolution of that concern by the time of the Korean War, pressure again arose to use nuclear weapons. During Truman's administration the control of such weapons was under the president, he affirmed, and no one else. He pursued a very conservative, indeed prohibitory, policy regarding their use.

THE FINAL EVALUATION

It is hard to measure the presidency of Harry S. Truman, an "accidental president" who became the chief executive in a dangerous time. This first postwar president oversaw an unsuccessful domestic program and an immensely successful foreign policy. It is necessary to relate what students of the presidency sometimes forget, that in the American political system the president presides and is not the leader of everything. Truman took advice and acted usually after consensus, although he did not hesitate to lead, as at the beginning of the change in foreign policy during 1947–1949 and the Korean War. He failed in most of his domestic proposals, leaving their fulfillment to his successors. But he also bequeathed a government mechanism that functioned superbly, and he offered an example of willingness to work for the country's well-being even if those efforts did not result in momentary popularity.

See also *Eisenhower, Dwight D.; Fair Deal; Korean War; New Deal; Roosevelt, Franklin D.; War Powers; World War II.*

ROBERT H. FERRELL, INDIANA UNIVERSITY

BIBLIOGRAPHY

Donovan, Robert J. *Conflict and Crisis: The Presidency of Harry S. Truman, 1945–1948.* New York: Norton, 1977.
———. *Tumultuous Years, 1949–1953.* New York: Norton, 1982.
Ferrell, Robert H. *Harry S. Truman: A Life.* Columbia: University of Missouri Press, 1994.
Hamby, Alonzo L. *Man of the People: A Life of Harry S. Truman.* New York: Oxford University Press, 1995.
McCullough, David. *Truman.* New York: Simon and Schuster, 1992.
Truman, Margaret. *Harry S. Truman.* New York: Morrow, 1973.

TWELFTH AMENDMENT

The Twelfth Amendment, which altered the procedures for selection of president and vice president, was proposed in 1803 and ratified June 15, 1804. The amendment became necessary because, with the rise of national political parties, the election of two chief executive officers from rival political parties would likely create an unfortunate friction within the executive branch. The original procedures for the selection of the president were deemed inadequate because the outcome could be the election of a president from one party and a vice president from another, as was the case in 1796 when John Adams (Federalist) was elected president and Thomas Jefferson (Democratic-Republican) was elected vice president.

As originally specified in Article II of the Constitution, electors were to cast two votes, with the person receiving a majority of the electors' votes elected president and the person receiving the second highest number elected vice president. If two persons received an equal number of votes (if constituting a majority), then the House of Representatives would decide between those two candidates. If no candidate received a majority of the votes, the House would choose the president from the five candidates receiving the highest total votes. The person receiving the second highest total was to be vice president; in case of a tie, the Senate would choose the vice president from among the tied candidates.

The major change embodied in the Twelfth Amendment was the provision that electors were to cast separate ballots for president and vice president, with the stipulation that no person constitutionally ineligible to the office of president could become vice president. If no person received a majority of electoral votes, the president would be chosen by the House, as before, but from the top three candidates, with each state delegation having one vote. The Senate would select the vice president from the top two candidates if no candidate received a majority of the electoral votes. In addition, the amendment specified that if the House failed to select a president by the following March 4, then the vice president would become president. The amendment kept the electoral college, continued to allow states to choose the method for the selection of their electors, and continued to require that electors cast one of their two ballots for a candidate not from their own state.

Another major incentive for the adoption of the Twelfth Amendment was the chaotic situation that developed in the election of 1800. The Jeffersonians won the majority of electors in the presidential election and had planned to have one of their electors abstain from voting for Aaron Burr, their vice presidential candidate, so that Jefferson would be elected president and Burr vice president. The plan miscarried, however, and the two candidates each received seventy-three votes, resulting in the election being thrown into the House of Representatives, where Jefferson was selected president.

The Twentieth Amendment (1933) brought additional changes to government structure by changing the beginning date of presidential terms from March 4 to January 20 at noon. The amendment also provided that when a president failed to qualify for the office (for example, by not yet having received a majority vote in the House), then the vice president would serve as acting president until the president had been qualified.

The courts have heard a limited number of cases brought under the Twelfth Amendment. The U.S. Supreme Court decided in *MacPherson v. Blacker* (1892) that electors could be selected at large or by district, as specified in state legislation. In *Ray v. Blair* (1952) the Court upheld the practice of parties running slates of electors pledged to vote for the candidate of the party. Finally, in *Buckley v. Valeo* (1976), wherein a number of restrictions on campaign contributions were struck down on First Amendment grounds, the Court required that members of the Federal Election Commission be nominated by the president and confirmed by the Senate.

See also *Constitutional Amendments; Electoral College; Presidency.*

PATRICK M. O'NEIL, BROOME COMMUNITY COLLEGE, STATE UNIVERSITY OF NEW YORK

BIBLIOGRAPHY

Ceaser, James W. *Presidential Selection: Theory and Development.* Princeton: Princeton University Press, 1979.

Elliott, Ward E. Y. *The Rise of Guardian Democracy: The Supreme Court's Role in Voting Rights Disputes, 1845–1969.* Cambridge: Harvard University Press, 1975.

———. "Electoral College." In *Encyclopedia of the American Constitution,* ed. Leonard W. Levy, Kenneth L. Karst, and Dennis J. Mahoney. New York: Macmillan, 1986.

Gottlieb, Stephen E. "Twelfth Amendment." In *The Oxford Companion to the Supreme Court,* ed. Kermit L. Hall. New York: Oxford University Press, 1992.

Kuroda, Tadahisa. *The Origins of the Twelfth Amendment: The Electoral College in the Early Republic, 1787–1804.* Westport, Conn.: Greenwood Press, 1994.

Mahoney, Dennis J. "Twelfth Amendment." In *Encyclopedia of the American Constitution,* ed. Leonard W. Levy, Kenneth L. Karst, and Dennis J. Mahoney. New York: Macmillan, 1986.

Pierce, Neal R. *The People's President: The Electoral College in American History and the Direct-Vote Alternative.* New York: Simon and Schuster, 1968.

TYLER, JOHN

Born in Charles City County, Virginia, on March 29, 1790, John Tyler became America's first "accidental president" at the death of President William Henry Harrison. Tyler was a conservative, states' rights Democrat whose personal animosity to Andrew Jackson led him into the Whig Party, where he helped balance the ticket with westerner William Henry Harrison. Tyler had little in common with the Whigs, and when Harrison died, the Whigs found their great victory of 1840 had dissolved. Tyler opposed Whig policies on banking and tariffs, and after he vetoed key bills of the Whig program, five of his six Whig cabinet members resigned. In his four years in office Tyler had twenty-two different men in the six cabinet positions. He also appointed six of his relatives to various political positions. Meanwhile, Whig members in Congress constantly attacked him, and at one point they passed resolutions of censure. Tyler's only successes were in foreign relations, and they were mostly due to his secretary of state, Daniel Webster, who negotiated a number of important treaties, including the Webster-Ashburton Treaty with Great Britain. Tyler also initiated the annexation of Texas, which would lead to a war with Mexico after he left office.

Tyler's wife died while he was in office, a first, as was his marriage, in 1844, to a woman thirty years his junior. In general Tyler's presidency was an abysmal failure. He left office with little political support and returned to Virginia, where he practiced law. In 1861 he served in the Provisional Congress of the Confederate States of America, thus becoming the only former president to serve an enemy government.

PAUL FINKELMAN, UNIVERSITY OF TULSA COLLEGE OF LAW

BIBLIOGRAPHY

Peterson, Norma Lois. *The Presidencies of William Henry Harrison and John Tyler.* Lawrence: University Press of Kansas, 1989.

VAN BUREN, MARTIN

Martin Van Buren, the eighth president of the United States (1837–1841), assumed the presidency with the approval of his predecessor, Andrew Jackson, but Jackson's legacy proved dangerous—the conditions that led to the massive fiscal crisis known as the panic of 1837.

Born on December 5, 1782, in Kinderhook, New York, Van Buren became one of the most powerful Democratic politicians in New York, relying on his "Albany Regency," a political machine that controlled state politics through patronage, party newspapers, and a tightly run Democratic caucus in the state legislature.

In 1821 the legislature elected Van Buren to the U.S. Senate. In Washington Van Buren's political career became interwoven with that of Jackson, the Carolina woodsman and military hero. The two men became close political allies, although they were quite different. According to Rep. Davy Crockett, who found Van Buren to be a "dandy," "Van Buren is as opposite to General Jackson as dung is to a diamond." In 1828 Van Buren resigned from the Senate to run for New York governor so he could help Jackson in his presidential bid. After Jackson won the presidency he named Van Buren, by then one of his closest political advisers, secretary of state. When Jackson ran for reelection in 1832 Van Buren replaced John C. Calhoun as Jackson's running mate, and the ticket won easily.

In 1836, benefiting from Democratic recognition that he was Jackson's protégé, Van Buren ran for president on the Democratic ticket and defeated William Henry Harrison, the closest of several Whig opponents. At his inauguration, Van Buren vowed to continue Jackson's policies and help farmers, laborers, and small businessmen. The nineteenth-century economy of "boom and bust" interfered, however, and a severe depression began two months after he took office. Banks closed, businesses failed, and unemployment soared. Hoping to help the economy, Van Buren established a ten-hour day

Martin Van Buren *Library of Congress*

for federal workers and tried to make cheap land available to farmers, but conservative Democrats and Whigs in Congress blocked his efforts. When he followed the conventional economic wisdom of the period by cutting government expenditures, the depression worsened. In a related development, Van Buren continued Jackson's policy of opposing a national bank, but he did propose an independent federal treasury system, which was enacted by Congress in 1840.

During his presidency, conflicts on both the southern and northern U.S. borders tested Van Buren's diplomatic prowess. He opposed the annexation of Texas, thereby preventing the addition of another slave state to the Union and avoiding war with Mexico. But his opposition damaged his relationship with his mentor, Jackson. On the northern border the effort of some U.S. citizens to help Canada overthrow British rule drew a presidential proclamation of neutrality in the conflict. When the governor of Maine prepared to call up militia to fight Canada over a border dispute, the president stepped in and negotiated an agreement with the British ambassador to the United States.

In 1840 Van Buren's vulnerability on the economic crisis left him unsuccessful in his bid for reelection against Harrison. Van Buren even failed to win his home state of New York. He tried again in 1844 to secure his party's nomination but was defeated by dark-horse candidate James K. Polk, who advocated annexation of Texas. In 1848 Van Buren adopted the banner of the antislavery Free Soil Party, but his candidacy split the Democratic vote, allowing Whig Zachary Taylor to win.

Van Buren then left politics, toured Europe (the first former president to do so), and wrote a political discourse on the origin and course of U.S. political parties. He died in 1862.

See also *Free Soil Party; Jackson, Andrew; Panic of 1837; Whig Party.*

SABRA BISSETTE LEDENT, INDEPENDENT AUTHOR

BIBLIOGRAPHY

Cole, Donald B. *Martin Van Buren and the American Political System.* Princeton: Princeton University Press, 1984.

Curtis, James C. *The Fox at Bay: Martin Van Buren and the Presidency, 1837–1841.* Lexington: University Press of Kentucky, 1970.

Wilson, Major. *The Presidency of Martin Van Buren.* Lawrence: University Press of Kansas, 1984.

VETO POWER

The Constitution grants the president of the United States the power to block the enactment of bills already passed by Congress. The power of the veto is one of the few express powers granted to the president in the Constitution that directly involves the president in the legislative process. A successful veto—one that is not overridden by Congress—blocks enactment of legislation passed by the two houses of Congress. If, during congressional consideration of a bill, the president threatens a veto, that threat can also shape the content of a bill.

ORIGINS OF THE VETO

Dissatisfied with the Articles of Confederation, which provided a Congress but no federal executive or federal judiciary, the Constitutional Convention that met in 1787 created an independent executive with a limited veto power. A few people, such as Alexander Hamilton and James Wilson, argued at the convention that the president should have an absolute veto (not subject to override), but most rejected the proposal as too close to the baneful absolute veto of British monarchs and colonial governors.

According to Article I, section 7 of the Constitution, the president has four choices when presented with a bill passed by both houses of Congress: (1) sign the bill into law within ten days (not counting Sundays); (2) do nothing, in which case the bill automatically becomes law without presidential signature after ten days; (3) exercise the regular, or return, veto and send the bill, along "with his Objections," to the house from which it originated; or (4) withhold signature at times of congressional adjournment, when the bill's return is impossible, in which case the president kills the bill by pocket veto. The regular, or return, veto may be overridden by a two-thirds vote of both houses of Congress to enact the bill into law. Because no return is possible after a pocket veto, the bill dies.

The Constitution's drafters believed it was important to give Congress the option for review, and possible override, of presidential vetoes. The pocket veto was included to prevent Congress from passing a bill the president disapproved and quickly adjourning to avoid a veto. Without Congress in session, the president could not veto the bill because no one would receive the returned bill. Federal court cases have clarified that the override votes need be only two-thirds of a quorum, not of the entire membership of Congress (*Missouri Pacific Railway Co. v. Kansas* [1919]); that Congress may designate agents to receive vetoed bills when Congress is not in session, just as the president may designate agents to receive bills passed by Congress when the president is out of the country (*Wright v. United States* [1938]); and that a pocket veto is justified only when Congress has adjourned sine die at the end of a two-year Congress (*Kennedy v. Sampson* [1974]).

Although the veto is considered a negative power today, the Founders envisioned the veto as a constructive, positive device—it was often called the "revisionary power"—that would allow for a final round of debate and consideration for controversial or suspect legislation. Although some scholars in the twentieth century claimed that the veto was designed to be used rarely or only for constitutionally suspect legislation, no such legal restriction applies to its use by presidents.

HISTORICAL USE OF THE VETO

Early presidents used the veto power cautiously. From President George Washington's two terms to the end of President Andrew Johnson's term in 1869, only eighty-eight bills were vetoed. From 1869 until 2000, more than twenty-four hundred bills were vetoed. Even when used rarely, the veto provoked fierce outcry from Congress in the first half of the nineteenth century. An angry Congress sharply criticized President Andrew Jackson for his twelve vetoes, including his 1832 veto of a bank bill that proved to be the pivotal issue in that year's presidential election. Of all the presidents, John Tyler faced the greatest veto-related difficulties, as the controversy surrounding his ten vetoes was a key factor in the attempt to impeach him in 1843; two of the charges of impeachment centered on his alleged improper use of the veto power. Tyler was also the first president to use the pocket veto.

President Andrew Johnson's twenty-nine vetoes set a record at a time when the Republican-controlled reconstructionist Congress was eager to challenge Johnson's power. Of his twenty-one regular vetoes, fifteen were overridden, some within minutes of their return to Congress. Johnson's vetoes helped fan anti-Johnson sentiment, but no charge of veto misuse was leveled against him when he was impeached. Although President Franklin D. Roosevelt holds the record for the most vetoes, 635, in his four terms, President Grover Cleveland ranks first on the basis of the number of vetoes per year, averaging 73.

The veto power is effective: approximately 7 percent of all regular presidential vetoes have been overridden. Although modern presidents exercise much more power over the legislative process than they did in the nineteenth century, the veto continues to be a vital presidential tool. Presidents Gerald R. Ford, Ronald Reagan, George Bush, and Bill Clinton (after the Republicans won control of Congress in 1994) made extensive and effective use of vetoes and threats of vetoes to shape the flow and content of legislation.

The president does not have the power to veto specific items in a bill, a power possessed by most state governors. A brief experiment in 1997 with a limited item veto, called "enhanced rescission," ended when the Supreme Court in *Clinton v. City of New York* (1998) declared even a limited item veto unconstitutional, arguing that an item veto could be granted only by constitutional amendment.

See also *Presidency.*

ROBERT J. SPITZER, STATE UNIVERSITY OF NEW YORK, CORTLAND

BIBLIOGRAPHY

Jackson, Carlton. *Presidential Vetoes, 1792–1945.* Athens: University of Georgia Press, 1967.

Spitzer, Robert J. *The Presidential Veto: Touchstone of the American Presidency.* Albany: SUNY Press, 1988.

U.S. Senate Library. *Presidential Vetoes, 1789–1996.* Washington, D.C.: Government Printing Office, 1997.

Watson, Richard A. *Presidential Vetoes and Public Policy.* Lawrence: University Press of Kansas, 1993.

Zinn, Charles J. *The Veto Power of the President.* Washington, D.C.: U.S. Government Printing Office, 1951.

VICE PRESIDENCY

The Founders of the Republic created the vice presidency to solve the problem of how to elect a president. The electoral college was an elegant way to make sure that neither Congress nor the state legislatures would make this important decision, thus keeping the executive branch independent of both. However, using an electoral college raised another problem: What if the electors from each state voted for their "favorite sons," that is, for candidates from their home states? If that were to happen, no candidate would receive a majority of the votes and the House of Representatives would make the decision, thus nullifying the usefulness of the electoral college.

The solution was for each elector to cast two votes. Although one vote could be cast for a favorite son, the other vote had to be cast for someone from another state. The Founders believed that, in most cases, this second vote would be cast for the person most qualified to be elected president.

However, this solution created another problem: What should be done with the person receiving the second highest number of votes? Because that person would possess considerable political talent and be held in high regard by the nation's political elite, the Founders decided to make the runner-up the vice president, or president-in-waiting.

While standing ready to substitute for the president of the United States whenever necessary, the vice president would serve as the presiding officer of the Senate and thus become familiar with the affairs of the federal government.

EVOLVING PERCEPTIONS OF THE OFFICE

At first the vice presidency was seen as a stepping-stone to the presidency. John Adams, the first vice president, was elected president in 1796, and Thomas Jefferson, the second vice president, was elected president in 1800. However, the election of 1800 exposed a serious flaw in the electoral college system. Both Jefferson and Aaron Burr received the same number of votes, and the election was thrown into the House, where it was decided only after many rancorous partisan debates.

The solution to this problem was the Twelfth Amendment to the U.S. Constitution, which was ratified in 1804. Instead of voting for the two people most qualified to be president and making the number-two vote-getter vice president, electors now were required to cast one vote for president and the other for vice president. A person now could be elected vice president without receiving any votes for president.

By divorcing the two elections, the Twelfth Amendment may have diminished the vice presidency's prestige. In the nearly two centuries that followed the elections of Adams and Jefferson, only two other sitting vice presidents—Martin Van Buren and George Bush—have been elected president. A former vice president, Richard M. Nixon, was elected president eight years after he left the vice presidency. Four other vice presidents—Theodore Roosevelt, Calvin Coolidge, Harry S. Truman, and Lyndon B. Johnson—became president following the death of the previous president. All four subsequently were elected to serve full terms as president. Generally, however, since 1804 vice presidents have declined in prominence—and some say in quality—largely because they have been elected for reasons other than their possession of presidential abilities.

The rise of partisan politics in the early nineteenth century meant that party interests increasingly determined who became vice president. Political parties nominated vice presidential candidates from different regions and different wings of their parties than their presidential nominees in order to appeal to voters across the country. For example, in 1860 Abraham Lincoln, a westerner and former Whig, ran with Hannibal Hamlin, a former Democrat from Maine. One century later, John F. Kennedy of Massachusetts picked Lyndon Johnson of Texas to be his vice-presidential running mate, and in 1968 Richard M. Nixon of California had Spiro Agnew of Maryland as his. Many vice-presidential nominees have been chosen from large states in the hope that the candidates would help capture those states' electoral votes. Other vice-presidential nominees were chosen to appease a party faction that was otherwise cool to the presidential nominee, or to reward party loyalists who helped the presidential nominee win the nomination. In some cases, the selection or retention of a running mate has harmed the party ticket. The 1992 candidacy of incumbent president George Bush clearly was harmed by the retention of his vice president, Dan Quayle, who during his four years as vice president displayed little competence for high political office.

Once elected, the vice president's main job is to take the president's place in case the president can no longer serve. However, the Constitution did not make explicit how the president's fitness for office was to be determined. At least three times in the twentieth century, during the administrations of Woodrow Wilson, Franklin D. Roosevelt, and Dwight D. Eisenhower, the president's poor health seemed to keep him from discharging his duties. However, the vice president was never called upon to assume those duties, even temporarily.

DUTIES OF OFFICE

The Twenty-fifth Amendment, ratified in 1967, clarified some of the ambiguities concerning the vice president's duties. The amendment outlines the procedure by which a vice president may assume an ailing president's duties without actually be-

coming the president. The amendment also permits the appointment of a vice president, with the consent of Congress, whenever that office becomes vacant. Previously, the vice presidency remained vacant until the next national election. The Twenty-fifth Amendment virtually eliminates the likelihood that any government official below vice president will ever become president as a result of the president's death.

For most of the nineteenth and twentieth centuries, the vice presidency was afforded little respect. Daniel Webster once declined a vice-presidential nomination on the grounds that he did not want to be buried until he was dead. John Nance Garner, Franklin Roosevelt's first-term vice president, suggested that a vice president was about as valuable as "a bucket of warm spit." Since 1960, however, the office has become more important in American politics. The president's increased vulnerability to assassination and the vice president's increased involvement in national affairs have both contributed to this trend.

Between 1960 and 2000, four of nine vice presidents—Lyndon Johnson, Nixon, Gerald Ford, and George Bush—became president. Three others—Hubert Humphrey, Walter Mondale, and Albert Gore—received their party's nomination for president. One sitting vice president, Nixon, received his party's nomination in 1960, lost the election, but ran again and won in a later (1968) election.

Vice presidents still run various political errands for the president. However, since 1977, when President Jimmy Carter made Vice President Walter Mondale a major figure in his administration, the second-in-command has increasingly become an important adviser to the president in a manner not seen since the early days of the Republic.

CHARLES CAREY, LYNCHBURG COLLEGE/
CENTRAL VIRGINIA COMMUNITY COLLEGE

BIBLIOGRAPHY

Walch, Timothy, ed. *At the President's Side: The Vice Presidency in the Twentieth Century.* Columbia: University of Missouri Press, 1997.

Waldrup, Carole Chandler. *The Vice Presidents: Biographies of the 45 Men Who Have Held the Second Highest Office in the United States.* Jefferson, N.C.: McFarland, 1996.

Witcover, Jules. *Crapshoot: Rolling the Dice on the Vice Presidency.* New York: Crown Publishers, 1992.

VIETNAM WAR

The Vietnam War was a military conflict fought in Southeast Asia from 1954 to 1975. The war stemmed from the Indochinese War (1946–1954) between Vietnamese nationalists and the French, who attempted to reclaim colonial territory lost during World War II. Fearful that South Vietnam would fall to communism and cause a domino effect throughout Southeast Asia, the United States joined the war with the South Vietnamese army against the army of North Vietnam and the National Liberation Front, a communist-led, guerrilla force in South Vietnam.

Initially, U.S. involvement was limited, but as the war dragged on each administration escalated U.S. involvement on the basis of its belief in a "light at the end of the tunnel." War weariness at home contributed to the withdrawal of U.S. troops after 1971, and a cease-fire was called in 1973. South Vietnam fell to communist forces after the United States officially withdrew in 1975.

BACKGROUND TO U.S. MILITARY INTERVENTION

Since 1882 France had governed Indochina, which was composed of Vietnam, Laos, and Cambodia. Japanese troops seized control of the region in 1941 after France fell to Nazi Germany during World War II. Vietnamese nationalists, who established the League for the Independence of Vietnam (the Viet Minh), rose up against Japanese colonialism. The United States denounced the Japanese invasion and formed an alliance with Ho Chi Minh, the communist leader of the Viet Minh, against the Japanese.

The Japanese surrendered on September 2, 1945, and Ho declared Vietnam's independence, naming the fledgling state the Democratic Republic of Vietnam. The French refused to recognize Vietnamese sovereignty, however, and pressured the United States to support their reclamation of the territory. Fearful that communism might gain a foothold in France as it had in Eastern Europe, U.S. policy makers decided it was critical to support its European ally. The United States denounced Ho for his communist ideology despite intelligence reports that the Viet Minh leader was not a puppet of the Soviet Union and likely would be a strong ally in the region.

Initial French victories were offset as anticolonialist sentiment intensified throughout Vietnam. Ho Chi Minh and the Viet Minh drew tens of thousands of supporters who resented foreign domination. In May 1954 the Viet Minh resoundingly defeated the French at Dien Bien Phu in northwestern Vietnam. At the peace conference held in Geneva, Switzerland, from May 8 to July 21, 1954, the war-weary French agreed to withdraw from Vietnam. Representatives from France, Great Britain, the Soviet Union, China, Vietnam, Cambodia, Laos, and the United States attended the conference. The Geneva Accords divided Vietnam at the 17th parallel and created a demilitarized zone. Ho Chi Minh and the Viet Minh forces controlled the North, while Bao Dai, whom the French had installed as leader, remained in power in the South. The United States refused to sign the accords because of the stipulation

that elections be held in 1956. U.S. policy makers feared that communism would gain legitimate control in Vietnam through the elections and would spread to nearby nations.

In violation of the Geneva Accords but with U.S. approval, Ngo Dinh Diem, who had served in the French-controlled government before World War II, held separate elections in the South in October 1955. That Diem won the election by an overwhelming majority was no surprise, and reports claimed the election had been rigged. The United States recognized the independent nation of South Vietnam, which Diem named the Republic of Vietnam.

The United States sent monetary aid and advisers to assist the Diem regime. A devout Catholic who had been educated by the French in an overwhelmingly Buddhist nation, Diem increasingly relied on his fellow Catholics and his family to rule the country. Diem ordered the Army of the Republic of Vietnam (ARVN) to return land to landowners who had been forced by the Viet Minh to give up their land to the peasants. Diem used his brother, Nhu, who was head of the secret police, to persecute and suppress opponents of the regime.

Members of the Viet Minh, who had returned to their ancestral homes in the South in 1954 to await elections, had begun to attract new recruits from among the oppressed. Diem labeled the southern units of the Viet Minh as Viet Cong, a Vietnamese derivative of "commie," or communist. South Vietnamese communists formed the National Liberation Front (NLF) in 1959 and began training guerrilla forces called the People's Liberation Armed Forces. The NLF also welcomed members of the militant Viet Cong to its ranks.

As opposition to Diem mounted, the United States stepped up its efforts to aid his government. President John F. Kennedy increased the number of U.S. advisers in South Vietnam exponentially and ordered in U.S. Army Special Forces units to train the ARVN in counterinsurgency tactics because the NLF was soundly defeating its enemy in the field despite the ARVN's superior training and weaponry. Kennedy hoped the introduction of the Special Forces would help win over the "hearts and minds" of the population and demoralize the NLF. To deprive the NLF of food and jungle cover, U.S. helicopters sprayed defoliants such as Agent Orange.

The Diem regime implemented what was called the strategic hamlet program to separate the villagers from the guerrillas. With Diem's brother Nhu in charge, the ARVN forcibly removed civilians from their ancestral lands to the fortified hamlets. Efforts by Diem and the United States proved counterproductive, however, as more villagers flocked to the NLF's guerrilla units to fight against oppression.

The Kennedy administration blamed Diem and Nhu's repressive tactics for NLF gains and for the much publicized suicides by Buddhist monks, who set themselves on fire in the streets of Saigon in protest of the regime. When a group of ARVN generals plotted the overthrow of Diem, Washington looked the other way. A coup d'état took place on November 1, 1963, and one day later Diem and Nhu were murdered. The overthrow of Diem did not stabilize the South Vietnamese government, however. For eighteen months after Diem's overthrow, several governments rose and fell in Saigon.

KENNEDY'S LITTLE WAR BECOMES JOHNSON'S BIG WAR

In the United States, leadership changed hands after President Kennedy was assassinated on November 22, 1963. Lyndon B. Johnson took over the presidency and inherited the Vietnam situation. Johnson, like his predecessors, wanted to support and maintain an independent, noncommunist South Vietnam. Johnson was also keenly aware of the probable political fallout within the United States if South Vietnam fell to communism as China had in 1949. U.S. credibility with other nations was also on the line. Therefore, any action that might be construed as being "soft on communism" was not an option.

Johnson continued his predecessors' policies of economic aid and advisers, and he expanded the U.S. role by authorizing top-secret, covert attacks against North Vietnamese territory and along the Ho Chi Minh trail, a network of roads in Laos and Cambodia used by the North Vietnamese and the NLF to transport supplies to the South. Johnson also authorized the U.S. Navy to conduct surveillance missions along North Vietnam's coast.

On August 2, 1964, a North Vietnamese gunboat torpedoed the USS *Maddox,* a U.S. destroyer on patrol in North Vietnamese territorial waters in the Gulf of Tonkin. Johnson then ordered the *Maddox* to return to the area along with the USS *C. Turner Joy.* On August 4 the *Maddox* and the *Turner Joy* fired upon North Vietnamese gunboats after the *Turner Joy* reported it had been attacked. Johnson used the incident as an excuse to engage North Vietnam directly, although subsequent investigations raised suspicions about whether the second attack had in fact taken place. It was later learned that the *Maddox* had been on an intelligence-gathering mission within waters claimed by North Vietnam. Congress overwhelmingly passed the Gulf of Tonkin Resolution, which gave the president the authority to protect U.S. forces against armed attack by any means necessary.

Johnson's top advisers, including Secretary of Defense Robert S. McNamara and Assistant to the President for National Security Affairs McGeorge Bundy, were convinced that an intensive bombing campaign against the North would demoralize the enemy and raise morale in the South. Johnson initially refused to escalate the war effort, but on February 28, 1965, after two successful North Vietnamese and Viet Cong attacks against U.S. air bases at Pleiku and Qui Nhon in the first weeks of 1965, Johnson ordered full-scale aerial attacks. Two weeks later Johnson sent in two U.S. Marine Corps battalions to protect the airfield from which the bombing attacks were being launched. Gen. William Westmoreland convinced Johnson that the troops should be used in search-and-destroy missions to wear down the enemy. Three months after the Gulf of Tonkin incident, 25,000 U.S. military personnel were in Vietnam. By July 1965, 75,000 military men and women were in Vietnam, and by November that number had more than doubled.

The North Vietnamese responded to U.S. escalation by funneling northern troops and supplies into South Vietnam via the Ho Chi Minh trail. The North Vietnamese and South Vietnamese guerrillas, who were poorly armed compared with U.S. troops, avoided open contact. Instead, they made use of underground bunkers and tunnels and used hit-and-run tactics to demoralize U.S. forces.

As the war intensified in 1965, the continuous U.S. bombing and defoliation caused a massive refugee problem. Approximately 4 million men, women, and children fled from the countryside to cities and towns in order to survive. Malnutrition and disease were rampant. The U.S. objective of winning the "hearts and minds" of the people was failing.

WAR AND ANTIWAR

Antiwar sentiment was on the rise in the United States as well. The first student demonstrations against the war took place in the spring of 1965, and in January and February of 1966, Senate Foreign Relations Committee chairman J. William Fulbright (D-Ark.) held six televised hearings about the war, which helped turn popular sentiment against U.S. involvement in Vietnam. Secretary of State Dean Rusk defended the administration's stance on the war as necessary to fulfill the U.S. commitment to protect the South from outside communist aggression.

By 1967 the war had spawned a bitter debate within the United States between the "hawks," cold war warriors who supported the war, and the "doves," those who opposed U.S. involvement. The administration received reports from the Central Intelligence Agency (CIA) and the Department of Defense that U.S. bombing had not significantly affected North Vietnam's capacity or will to fight. The bombing was ineffective because North Vietnam had little industrial capacity to destroy and received much of its weaponry and supplies from China and the Soviet Union. If anything, the bombing was strengthening the North's resolve against what it perceived to be the actions of an imperialist, occupying force in the South.

While the U.S. military called for more troops to add to the 436,000 already in Vietnam in May 1967, the CIA reported that victory was virtually unattainable unless the United States was willing to invade North Vietnam or launch a nuclear attack. Johnson was in the quagmire of a war he could neither win nor end without severe political repercussions at home and abroad.

In January 1968 North Vietnam and the NLF mounted an all-out offensive aimed at inflicting heavy casualties on both U.S. and ARVN forces. The Tet Offensive (named after the Vietnamese New Year celebration) was initially successful as NLF forces simultaneously attacked every major city in the South. For approximately eight hours the NLF even controlled the U.S. embassy in Saigon—a location that had been deemed invulnerable. The offensive lasted until the autumn of 1968, but the NLF suffered heavy casualties. Statistically, the United States and the South Vietnamese were the clear victors, but the brilliantly conceived attack demonstrated the enemy's resolve and proved that no area was safe.

General Westmoreland wanted to capitalize on the enemy's weakened state and asked Johnson for more troops. The American public and President Johnson had reached their breaking point, however. Despite promises of seeing a "light at the end of the tunnel," most Americans knew the war could not be won.

Daily television reports brought the cruelty of war to U.S. living rooms each night. Students burned their draft cards, fled to Canada, or professed religious awakenings that prevented them from taking up arms. Civil rights organizations denounced conscription as racist because the poor and minorities made up the bulk of the U.S. fighting force, and the wealthy or well-connected stayed home.

Antiwar sentiment was growing among soldiers' ranks as well. Americans commonly referred to all Vietnamese as "gooks," whether ally or enemy. This general dehumanization of the Vietnamese people along with the combat troops' task of ferreting out Viet Cong from an often-hostile population led to atrocities. The massacre of five hundred villagers—mostly women and children—in March 1968 at My Lai was just one startling example. The irony of destroying villages in an attempt to save them was not lost on the U.S. troops. "Fragging" incidents, when soldiers attacked their own, often less experienced, officers, had become frequent. There were no front lines in Vietnam. U.S. combat troops

Anti-Vietnam War protesters brand Lyndon B. Johnson a war criminal.   *Library of Congress*

were under constant threat of attack, whether on patrol or at a base. Many soldiers used illicit drugs to escape the horrors of war.

NIXON'S WAR

As antiwar sentiment climaxed in 1968 and the successes of Johnson's Great Society were overshadowed by the war, Johnson announced he would not seek reelection in November of that year. Two antiwar candidates—Robert F. Kennedy and Eugene McCarthy—vied with Vice President Hubert H. Humphrey for the Democratic presidential nomination, which Humphrey received. Promising "peace with honor," the Republican nominee, Richard M. Nixon, was elected president by a slim margin. Like his predecessors, Nixon was unwilling to lose Vietnam to communism, and he announced a plan he called Vietnamization. Johnson had already called a halt to attacks on the North, and Nixon expanded the policy by withdrawing U.S. troops. The war was to be turned over to the South Vietnamese.

While Nixon gradually pulled ground troops out of Vietnam, he expanded the air war. In March 1969, to weaken the communist infiltration networks into South Vietnam, Nixon ordered the secret bombing of Cambodia. One month later

Nixon publicly ordered an invasion of Cambodia, a campaign that had disastrous consequences. The destructive bombings left hundreds of thousands of Cambodians homeless, and the invasion force turned many Cambodians toward the communist opposition group, the Khmer Rouge. A similar ARVN invasion force supported by U.S. air power entered Laos, met great resistance, and contributed to the rise of the Pathet Lao, another communist organization.

In the United States, Nixon's announcement of the Cambodian invasion rekindled antiwar demonstrations and violence across the nation. At Kent State University in Ohio, four students were killed after National Guard troops opened fire on a mass of protesters. Matters worsened for the Nixon administration in the spring of 1972 when the North Vietnamese launched the Easter offensive, sending more than thirty thousand troops across the demilitarized zone between the North and the South. Nixon responded by renewing bombing raids over the North—the first since 1969.

THE WAR ENDS BUT LEAVES A LEGACY

A renewed sense of urgency to end the war accompanied Secretary of State Henry Kissinger to the peace talks in Paris. The publication of the Pentagon Papers, a complete history of U.S. involvement in Vietnam, by the *New York Times* in June 1971 highlighted a pattern of government deception of the American public. Congress clamored to cut off funding for the war, and public opinion polls conducted in 1972 in the United States showed that 65 percent of respondents believed U.S. fighting in Vietnam was "morally wrong."

On January 27, 1973, peace accords were signed. The United States promised to remove its troops from South Vietnam in return for the release of all U.S. prisoners of war. All foreign military operations in Cambodia and Laos were to end, and a cease-fire between North Vietnam and South Vietnam was to be implemented. On March 29, 1973, the last U.S. combat troops withdrew from Vietnam. In 1975 North Vietnamese troops launched a final offensive. Within weeks, on April 30, 1975, Saigon fell to communist forces, who renamed the capital Ho Chi Minh City. The U.S. objective of protecting South Vietnam from communism had failed, and more than fifty-eight thousand Americans had died in the conflict.

The war left a lasting legacy in the United States. After 1975, when U.S. troops were sent overseas, Congress and the public demanded clear objectives and a definite time frame for withdrawal. When the dominoes failed to fall in Southeast Asia despite the communization of Laos and Cambodia, policy makers began rethinking cold war frameworks. The Vietnam experience shook the very foundations of U.S. identity. No longer would Americans view their nation as invincible.

See also *Civil Unrest and Rioting; Cold War; Great Society; Johnson, Lyndon B.; Kennedy, John F.; New Frontier; Nixon, Richard M.; War Powers.*

APRIL L. BROWN, UNIVERSITY OF ARKANSAS

BIBLIOGRAPHY

Berman, Larry. *Planning a Tragedy: The Americanization of the War in Vietnam.* New York: Norton, 1982.

Hunt, Michael H. *Lyndon Johnson's War: America's Cold War Crusade in Vietnam, 1945–1968.* New York: Hill and Wang, 1996.

Kaiser, David E. *American Tragedy: Kennedy, Johnson, and the Origins of the Vietnam War.* Cambridge: Belknap Press of Harvard University Press, 2000.

Karnow, Stanley. *Vietnam: A History.* New York: Viking, 1983.

O'Nan, Stewart, ed. *The Vietnam Reader: The Definitive Collection of American Fiction and Nonfiction on the War.* New York: Anchor Books, 1998.

WAR OF 1812

In retrospect, the Anglo-American War of 1812 was one of the most avoidable, most divisive, and most inconclusive wars fought by the United States. When it began, neither the American public, nor Congress, nor the administration of James Madison seemed fully convinced that war was necessary; if they had known that Great Britain had just removed one of the main points of contention, the war would certainly have been delayed and possibly avoided entirely. The ambivalence with which the nation declared war almost ensured that the war effort would suffer from inadequate preparation and internal dissent. Under these conditions, the United States was perhaps fortunate that the war ended with the restoration of the status quo antebellum in December 1814.

CAUSES OF THE WAR

The causes of the war have been much debated by historians. Some have stressed a concern for American commerce, while others have emphasized a desire for territorial expansion, directed, in particular, toward British Canada and Spanish Florida. Some have highlighted the defense of national honor, while others have seen the war as an effort to strengthen the Republican Party and thus republican government. Ultimately, the Anglo-American war must be viewed in the context of the European war that had raged intermittently for two decades and reached a new intensity after 1803.

The Anglo-French war had produced the British orders-in-council and French decrees that constrained American trade; had sparked the Spanish turmoil that made expansion into Florida possible; had prompted the British impressment of American seamen that affronted national honor; and had attached an international dimension to the party divisions between Federalists and Republicans. These explanations of the origins of the war are mutually reinforcing rather than mutually exclusive. Though reluctant to declare war against Great Britain, President Madison, Secretary of State James Monroe, other cabinet members, and the Republican leaders in Congress apparently concluded that the United States would not survive without a stronger effort to assert its independence, protect its trade, and redeem its republican government. In the summer of 1811 Madison decided to move toward war, urging Congress in that direction in his annual message that November. On June 1, 1812, he formally requested a declaration of war, which passed the House of Representatives (79–49) and the Senate (19–13) by June 18.

The War of 1812 represented a change in the administration's tactics more than in its basic strategy. Madison had long viewed as a source of strength the roles of Americans as producers of foods and raw materials for British markets, especially in the West Indies, and as consumers of the output of British factories. War would allow him to increase the pressure on the British economy, forcing the British cabinet to rescind its restrictions on trade and end the practice of impressment of sailors. The administration hoped to use the nation's small army and navy to make effective its real strength—its links to the British economy. Its war plans called for seizing Canada in order to deprive the British of both Canadian and American goods and markets; ending all American trade with the British by redefining it as trading with the enemy; and commissioning privateers to prey on British shipping.

COURSE AND OUTCOME OF THE WAR

But the war itself became a tremendous embarrassment for the young nation. The federal government failed to raise enough money; to recruit and train enough men; to feed, clothe, and arm its troops; and to pick competent officers. The army was riddled with problems that resulted in frequent disasters, including the surrender of Detroit in the war. The war effort also suffered because the people refused to enlist in the army or abandon a profitable trade with the enemy. In Federalist New England, the states added to these problems by passing laws that hindered recruitment and refusing to call out their militias for federal service. Federalist opponents of the war encouraged popular protests and voted against war measures in Congress. In the fall of 1812 this strong antiwar sentiment nearly cost Madison his reelection in the closest presidential contest of the Republican era. Just as the administration began to take charge in the spring of 1814, the nature of the war changed dramatically as peace in Europe freed thousands of British troops for American service. For the United States the war shifted from an offensive one aimed at invading Canada to a defensive one geared toward protecting American cities. This change became obvious in August 1814, when a British force captured Washington, D.C., and burned the public buildings.

As the capital smoldered, American negotiators—including John Quincy Adams, Henry Clay, and Albert Gallatin—began talks with their British counterparts in Ghent, Belgium. Nearly every post from the United States pointed to the deterioration of the American position as Congress and the states made clear that they did not trust the administration to conduct the war. Still, the American negotiators managed to block every British demand. On December 24, 1814, the two sides agreed to a treaty that ended the war but said nothing about the issues that had produced it. Two weeks later, before news of the treaty came, the United States won its greatest victory in the Battle of New Orleans.

The War of 1812 ultimately had relatively little impact on Anglo-American relations; its greater significance can be found within the United States and in its relations to other North American powers. American gains came at the expense not of the British, but of the Spanish and the Indians. During the war the United States occupied Spanish West Florida and acquired over 22 million acres of land in Alabama and Georgia from the Creeks. Many other tribes emerged from the war badly weakened and largely abandoned by the British, leading to further land cessions. Internally, a surge of popular nationalism followed upon the realization that the United States not only had not lost the war, but had even scored some impressive victories on land and sea. If most policy makers did not share this new confidence, the war did inspire them to adopt measures to prepare the nation for future wars. Over the next two years the administration and Congress cooperated in expanding the peacetime army and navy and undertaking frontier and coastal defenses. Their broad view of preparedness also encompassed a new national bank that would stabilize the currency and loan money to the government. The new view also called for a protective tariff to support domestic manufacturers of war materiel. Ultimately, the War of 1812 helped transform the Republican approach to federal power.

See also *Hartford Convention Resolutions; Madison, James; Territorial Expansion; Treaties: Peace, Armament, and Defense; Treaty Making.*

JAMES E. LEWIS JR., INDEPENDENT SCHOLAR

BIBLIOGRAPHY

Brown, Roger H. *The Republic in Peril: 1812.* New York: Columbia University Press, 1964.

Hickey, Donald R. *The War of 1812: A Forgotten Conflict.* Urbana: University of Illinois Press, 1989.

Horsman, Reginald. *The Causes of the War of 1812.* Philadelphia: University of Pennsylvania Press, 1962.

Perkins, Bradford. *Prologue to War: England and the United States, 1805–1812.* Berkeley: University of California Press, 1961.

Stagg, J. C. A. *Mr. Madison's War: Politics, Diplomacy, and Warfare in the Early American Republic, 1783–1830.* Princeton: Princeton University Press, 1983.

WAR POWERS

The U.S. Constitution divides war-making powers between the legislative and executive branches. Congress has the power to declare war, raise and support the military, and levy and collect taxes for defense. As commander in chief, the president supervises the use of troops, but only Congress can provide funding for them.

In 1964 Congress passed the Gulf of Tonkin Resolution, the closest it came to declaring war in Vietnam, expanding the president's role in committing military forces. As support for the conflict waned, Congress adopted the War Powers Resolution in 1973, reasserting its check on presidential action. The resolution stated that its goal was not to alter the constitutional authority of Congress or the president.

WAR POWERS AND THE VIETNAM WAR

On August 4, 1964, two U.S. destroyers reported an attack by torpedo boats while cruising the Gulf of Tonkin off the coast of North Vietnam. The United States launched air strikes the next day in response to the unsubstantiated attack. On August 7 Congress passed the Gulf of Tonkin Resolution, giving President Lyndon B. Johnson authority to take all measures necessary to protect U.S. armed forces. It empowered the president to assist any member of the Southeast Asia Treaty Organization that asked for aid to defend its freedom (the treaty did not obligate the United States to do so). Only two senators voted against the resolution; most members believed the administration's denial of any American provocation despite earlier raids by U.S. ships along the North Vietnamese coast. Johnson used the resolution first to diffuse the war as an issue in the upcoming election of 1964 and then to justify deployment of air and ground forces the following year.

Richard Nixon, elected president in 1968, publicly adopted a policy of "Vietnamization" that gradually turned the fighting over to the South Vietnamese, but he secretly broadened the war with the April 1970 invasion of Cambodia. In January 1971 Congress enacted the Cooper-Church Amendment, barring the use of ground forces in Cambodia and Laos in the future and, in essence, repealing the Tonkin resolution. Sen. Jacob Javits, a moderate Republican from

New York who had supported the American presence in Vietnam in the past, proposed legislation to limit the war powers of the president in the future. The Senate began moving in the direction of the legislation, but the House of Representatives did not.

Events in late 1972, such as the massive Christmas bombings of North Vietnam, increased Congress's distrust over the handling of the conflict by Johnson and Nixon. After the withdrawal of U.S. combat troops from South Vietnam at the end of March 1973, Congress debated an end to funding for military operations in Southeast Asia. Bombing raids against communist positions in Cambodia after the peace agreement also contributed to growing disillusionment. Congress further believed that its role in foreign policy, as related to the use of armed forces, had diminished through the war.

After months of debate, Congress adopted the War Powers Resolution of 1973, requiring the president to consult with the legislative branch before introducing forces into hostilities or situations where involvement in hostilities appears imminent. Without a declaration of war, the president must report to Congress within forty-eight hours after the deployment of troops. Without approval, withdrawal of the troops must occur within sixty days unless Congress declares war or enacts authorization, extends the sixty-day period, or fails to meet because of an attack upon the United States. If the president decides that force is needed to protect and remove American troops, the deadline can be extended thirty days.

Nixon vetoed the bill because he considered the law impractical and dangerous. He claimed that the resolution would hurt the nation's capability to act during crises and its credibility in the eyes of both allies and adversaries. The Watergate investigation affected the final outcome of the resolution. On October 20, 1973, Nixon accepted the resignations of two attorneys general, removed the special prosecutor investigating Watergate, and abolished that office. The public considered the events of that evening, known as the "Saturday Night Massacre," a constitutional crisis. Previously, Congress did not have the votes to override the veto. As a result of Nixon's actions, on November 7, 1973, the House voted 284–135—only four votes over the required two-thirds majority—to do so. Polling showed that 80 percent of the public approved.

SUBSEQUENT CONTROVERSIES

Gerald R. Ford was the first president to act under the War Powers Resolution. In 1975 he asked Congress to clarify the restrictions within nine days to enable him to evacuate American citizens and foreign nationals from Southeast Asia. When Congress debated the issue for weeks, he acted without approval. Ford also used forces to rescue the American crew of the *Mayaguez,* a U.S. merchant ship seized by Cambodian patrol boats. The president informed Congress, but many members doubted that his actions sufficiently fulfilled the requirement for consultation.

Later administrations complained about the constitutionality of the resolution and complied with its requirements only as they saw fit. The globalization of the U.S. economy increased American interests so that a president can interpret an attack on other nations as endangering national security. Moreover, the advent of nuclear warfare requires a president to respond more quickly than the Framers of the Constitution could have envisioned. The assumption exists that the president has the authority to order retaliation against a nuclear attack without prior consultation with Congress. Ronald Reagan claimed that one thousand Americans on Grenada, part of the British commonwealth, were in danger when he sent a military force to the island in October 1983 without consulting either the British government or the U.S. Congress. George Bush did not consult Congress before the 1989 invasion of Panama, but neither house challenged the action, a popular move to remove an unpopular dictator. In January 1991 the UN Security Council approved a resolution that set a deadline for withdrawal of Iraqi troops from Kuwait and authorized the use of force. Consequently, Bush argued that he did not have to consult Congress, and both houses approved the use of armed forces in relation to the UN vote.

Presidents have also tested the definition of compliance with the resolution. The president must consult with Congress in every possible case but also has discretion as to the type and timing of the required consultation. If the president delays the report to Congress, the timing of congressional control is similarly delayed. In addition, Congress has been hesitant to restrict the use of forces once deployed, particularly if the move was popular. Proposed amendments have addressed these weaknesses, but Congress has not passed any of them. The exercise of war powers will remain a point of tension between the branches based on the level of confrontation and the role of partisan politics during any crisis requiring military action.

See also *Persian Gulf War; Presidency; Vietnam War.*

CAROL JACKSON ADAMS, SALT LAKE COMMUNITY COLLEGE

BIBLIOGRAPHY

Fisher, Louis. *Constitutional Conflicts between Congress and the President.* Princeton: Princeton University Press, 1985.

Glennon, Michael J. *Constitutional Diplomacy.* Princeton: Princeton University Press, 1990.

Henkin, Louis. *Foreign Affairs and the United States Constitution.* Oxford: Clarendon Press, 1996.

WASHINGTON, GEORGE

George Washington was not only the first president of the United States (1789–1797), but also the only one to be elected two times by a unanimous vote of the electoral college. This singular distinction reveals a great deal about Washington's unsurpassed popularity and his unique place in American political history. At the same time, Washington's presidency marked a period of extreme uncertainty, conflict, and controversy for the young nation. As president, Washington was both a builder of consensus and a fomenter of dissension. A balanced assessment cannot ignore either aspect of this legacy.

EARLY CAREER

The future president was born into the home of a moderately successful planter in Westmoreland County, Virginia, on February 22, 1732. When George was eleven years old, his father died, leaving him in the care of his mother, Mary Ball Washington, and under the tutelage of his half-brother Lawrence, an officer in the British navy. Unlike many of his political counterparts, Washington received little formal education. Although he learned to read, write, and do mathematics, he did not attend college. His professional training was as a land surveyor. He traveled abroad only once, on a journey to the West Indies with his ailing brother.

Washington's earliest ambitions were for a military career in the British army. As a young man, he served as a volunteer in the French and Indian War, attaining the rank of colonel. His performance gained him a reputation for courage, coolness under fire, and leadership ability. Despite these achievements, British officials rebuffed Washington's repeated efforts to secure a regular commission in the army. This experience left him with a deep and abiding resentment of Britain. After the successful British assault on the French Fort Duquesne in 1758, Washington resigned from the army and married Martha Custis, a wealthy widow with two children. Mount Vernon, the plantation he inherited from his brother, became the focus of his activities.

Yet the wider world continually beckoned. As a member of the Virginia House of Burgesses, Washington was forced to respond to Britain's policy toward the colonies. By the late 1760s and 1770s he, like other elite Virginians, became increasingly convinced that England was engaged in a comprehensive conspiracy to deprive the colonists of their liberties. At the First Continental Congress, in Philadelphia, Washington served as a representative from Virginia. In 1775 he appeared at the Second Continental Congress dressed in his military uniform. By this time the colonists had concluded that they must defend their rights through force of arms. Washington was selected as commander in chief of the newly formed Continental Army, an appointment that acknowledged his military achievements and boosted support for the war in the South, where patriotic sentiment was more tenuous than in the North.

More than anything else, Washington's leadership during the American Revolution paved the way for his future election as president. As commander in chief, Washington displayed an instinctive grasp for the nuances of power. He served his country with honor, courage, and skill. Although not a brilliant strategist, Gen. Washington possessed other qualities that helped ensure American victory. Realizing his own limitations, he sought help from the Prussian general Baron von Steuben to discipline the Americans into a respectable fighting force. Learning from his early military defeats, he realized that his most important task was to keep the army in the field rather than to win conventional battles. His troops won enough key contests to keep the British off balance and exhaust their will to fight. He constantly pressured a recalcitrant Congress to give him more men, money, and supplies. Always aware of larger principles, Washington accepted the proposition that in a republic military power should be subordinate to civilian authority. He restrained his own pursuit of power and imposed restraint on those around him. He merged his personal destiny with that of his country.

These actions made Washington enormously popular. Americans transferred their loyalty from George III to George Washington. In a fractious nation of states, Washington emerged as the single common symbol that people throughout the union shared. He was their uncrowned king. After securing independence, Washington shocked the world by voluntarily resigning his commission. Promising never again to return to public life, he planned to live out his days as a private citizen. Ironically, this action heightened rather than diminished his reputation.

FIRST PRESIDENT, FIRST TERM

In the years immediately following the revolution, the United States experienced internal upheavals that jeopardized American liberties as surely as Britain had. The weakness of government under the Articles of Confederation, combined with the overweening power of the state governments, led to internal insurrections, economic instability, and a crisis of confidence in the central government. Something had to be done to preserve the union. Delegates gathered in Philadelphia in 1787 to address these problems. Although initially hesitant, Washington agreed to attend the Philadelphia convention. As president of the meeting, Washington spoke rarely and made only a few substantive contributions to the deliberations. Nonetheless, his presence added prestige and legitimacy to its endeavors. Even more important, the Framers of the Constitution crafted its provisions believing that Washington would be the first occupant of the executive office.

After the convention ended, Washington did not speak publicly in favor of ratification of the Constitution. Fearing even the appearance of impropriety, he believed that his statements might be misconstrued as an effort to win the presidency. Instead, Washington voiced his approval of the proposed system in letters to friends and colleagues. After the requisite number of states had ratified the Constitution, the first federal elections were held. Washington emerged as the unanimous choice of the electoral college. Yet the general himself did not know whether he should accept the position. Tormented by self-doubt and fearing accusations of hypocrisy if he came out of retirement, Washington had to be persuaded that he was the only person who could lead the nation through the difficult and delicate process of putting the new government into operation. With some reluctance, he acceded to the popular will. On April 30, 1789, in the national capital at New York City, Washington was inaugurated the first president of the United States.

As president, Washington knew that his actions would be both symbol and precedent. They would help set the tone and style of the new government. His goal was to instill respect for the executive office without replicating the excesses of Old World monarchies. Although John Adams proposed to address him as, "His Highness, the President of the United States of America and Protector of their Liberties," he accepted Congress's more prosaic designation as "Mr. President." He furnished the president's house handsomely but not opulently. He held weekly levees that anyone could attend. He refused to accept private invitations. He carried himself in a manner that inspired admiration, bordering on adulation, among many Americans. He was, according to Adams, one of the "best Actor[s] of the Presidency we have ever had."

One of Washington's most important challenges during his first term was to establish the powers and prerogatives of the executive. Although the Constitution made no explicit provision for a board of advisers, Washington took it upon himself to appoint a cabinet, which included Henry Knox as secretary of war, Edmund Randolph as attorney general, Thomas Jefferson as secretary of state, and Alexander Hamilton as secretary of the Treasury. With a genius for delegating authority, Washington frequently sought his cabinet's advice and accepted their recommendations. In many ways, Washington saw himself as an impartial mediator who sorted out conflicting ideas and made the best decision for the entire nation.

Washington was also conscious of the need to define the executive's relationship with Congress. He proceeded cautiously in interpreting the Senate's constitutional power to

George Washington   *Library of Congress*

give "advice and consent" on treaties. In 1789 he appeared in person to discuss with the Senate the terms of a treaty being negotiated with the Southern Indians. This fiasco produced neither advice nor consent. Over the years, Washington developed another method of consultation. He met informally with various members of Congress and conferred on particular provisions through letters and correspondence. Formal consent was sought only after a treaty had been finalized.

Washington also devised other principles for dealing with the legislative branch. Although he possessed veto power over laws passed by Congress, he refrained from using the sanction except in extreme cases. Acceding to Congress's role as representatives of the people, he rejected bills not if he disagreed with their substance, but only if he believed they violated the Constitution. He exercised the veto only twice, once in 1792 and once in 1796.

SECOND TERM

Despite his successes, Washington did not seek reelection in 1792. He felt weary and exhausted and wanted nothing more than to return to his home at Mount Vernon. Once again, however, his friends and advisers appealed to him to stand for office for the sake of the nation. Once again he won election, running unopposed. Yet Washington's second term witnessed growing internal conflict within his Cabinet and expanding controversy in the country at large. Issues and problems that had festered during the previous term came to a head, permanently altering the nation's political landscape.

Washington believed himself to be a president above party. Like many others of the founding generation, he considered parties as factions, insidious groups of individuals seeking to promote their own interests at the expense of the common good. Washington wanted to govern through consensus. Yet disagreements had surfaced almost from the beginning of Washington's first term. By the early 1790s Hamilton and his supporters in Congress had become the advocates of an aggressive fiscal policy. They wanted to expand the federal government's role in the economy and create a Bank of the United States, pay off state Revolutionary War debts, and stimulate the development of American industries. If the words of the Constitution did not provide explicit support for their plans, they invoked its spirit to justify their claims. Some prominent patriots disagreed. Jefferson and Madison envisioned a country populated by industrious small farmers. They and their supporters opposed what they saw as the national government's encroachments on state power—policies that they said violated the Constitution. At first, neither group identified itself as a party. Over time, however, like-minded men consistently gravitated toward one position or the other. Voting blocs formed in Congress; differences became entrenched. The Federalist and Democratic-Republican parties were born.

Washington's foreign policy caused particular divisiveness. The Republicans supported the French Revolution because they saw the French as kindred spirits; the Federalists, fearing anarchy, opposed it. The war between Britain and France created other problems, especially on the high seas. Claiming that American ships carried contraband, both France and England seized American ships, confiscated American goods, and sometimes impressed American sailors into service in their navies. Washington advocated a policy of neutrality. He wanted the United States to remain free from the manipulation and threats of European powers. Although both parties claimed to support a neutral position, neither did in practice. The Federalists, seeking commercial advantages, wanted closer ties with England. The Republicans, stressing ideological kinship, desired to come to the aid of France.

In his first term Washington appeared to remain above party. He attempted to reconcile differences and mediate between warring factions. By his second term, however, it was increasingly obvious—to everyone but Washington—that the president more often than not favored Hamilton and the

Federalists. After Jefferson's resignation at the end of 1793, Washington filled his cabinet with Federalist sympathizers. In the same year he supported the recall of the renegade French diplomat, Edmond Charles Genêt. In 1794, exercising his prerogative as commander in chief, Washington called out the army to put down violence in western Pennsylvania, provoked by opponents of the excise tax on whiskey. The army met no opposition because, according to the Republicans, there had been no rebellion. The Federalists, they said, merely wanted to intimidate the civilian population with a show of force. At the same time, Washington publicly condemned the debating clubs sponsored by the Democratic-Republicans as "self-created societies" and urged that they disband. In 1795 he backed a controversial treaty negotiated by John Jay with the British. Under its terms, Americans won some minor trade concessions and a promise to vacate the forts in the western territory. In return, the United States acquiesced to Britain's definition of neutral rights, a move that in effect betrayed the French. These actions led Republicans to conclude that Washington was not above party considerations.

Such controversies saddened the president. When the time came for the next general election, Washington chose not to run. Washington's two-term precedent remained in effect until Franklin D. Roosevelt broke it in 1940.

Washington accomplished much during his presidency: he set the new government on a firm course, created an environment of economic prosperity, and united the country into a coherent whole. Yet Washington himself harbored doubts about his achievements. Among other things, he worried about the contradiction between slavery for black people and freedom for whites. Although he freed his own slaves in his will, he never spoke out publicly against the institution and feared that a conflict over slavery might rend the union. He also worried about Europe. He knew that there were many unresolved issues with England and France. In his farewell address he urged his fellow Americans to avoid entangling alliances so that the country could develop its potential unmolested by outsiders. Most of all, he lamented the spirit of partisanship. He hoped that Americans could move beyond their passions to see their common interests. The union must be preserved.

LATER YEARS

After his retirement, Washington appeared only once more in the public spotlight. In anticipation of a foreign invasion, President John Adams appointed him commander in chief of the armed services during the Quasi-War with France. He died just a year later, on December 14, 1799. In death, Washington achieved one of his most elusive goals: to reunite the country. Americans of both parties celebrated his contributions, praised his example, and mourned his passing. These commemorations reflect the irony of the first president's legacy. To his surprise and perhaps dismay, Washington created a system of government that was strong enough to withstand the party conflict he so despised.

See also *American Revolution; Constitution, Ratification; Constitution, U.S.; Federalists; Political Parties; Treaties: Peace, Armament, and Defense; Treaty Making; Whiskey Rebellion.*

ROSEMARIE ZAGARRI, GEORGE MASON UNIVERSITY

BIBLIOGRAPHY

Cunliffe, Marcus. *George Washington: Man and Monument.* New York: New American Library, 1958.

Elkins, Stanley, and Eric McKitrick. *The Age of Federalism: The Early American Republic, 1788–1800.* New York: Oxford University Press, 1993.

Flexner, James Thomas. *Washington: The Indispensable Man.* New York: New American Library, 1969.

Freeman, Douglas Southall. *George Washington: A Biography,* 7 vols. New York: Charles Scribner's Sons, 1948–1957.

Phelps, Glenn A. *George Washington and American Constitutionalism.* Lawrence: University Press of Kansas, 1993.

WATERGATE

"Watergate" is shorthand for a complicated network of scandals that engulfed President Richard M. Nixon's administration from 1972 until his resignation, unique in American history, in August 1974.

The election of 1972 was a predictable one. In November, as expected, Nixon won reelection by a landslide over the liberal, anti–Vietnam War candidate, Democrat George McGovern. Nixon then achieved some of his greatest foreign and domestic policy successes, including the process of beginning to disentangle America from Vietnam. But all the while a "cancer" was consuming his presidency, and eighteen months into his second term Nixon resigned to avoid his almost certain impeachment, conviction, and removal from office.

THE BURGLARY AND ITS INVESTIGATION

The immediate origin of this calamity was a surprising event—what Nixon's own press secretary called a "third-rate" burglary. In June 1972 four Cuban émigrés and James W. McCord Jr., security director of CREEP, the Committee for the Reelection of the President, were caught bugging telephones at the Democratic National Committee headquarters in the Watergate, a fashionable Washington, D.C., hotel–apartment complex. G. Gordon Liddy and E. Howard Hunt, who directed the burglary, were arrested elsewhere.

The White House denied any involvement in the break-in, and the affair, such as it was, had dropped from sight by Nixon's reelection in November. But in early 1973 two young investigative reporters from the *Washington Post,* Bob Woodward and Carl Bernstein (the latter, as it happens, a registered Republican), began to dig deeper into the origins and aftermath of the Watergate burglary, and Democratic members of Congress awoke to the political possibilities of a Republican scandal of major importance.

Later it was revealed that the Watergate break-in and its subsequent cover-up were merely the tip of the iceberg of the abuses of power. Among other disclosures were the Nixon administration's "enemies list"—men and women targeted for harassment through tax audits, prosecution, and other government actions; administration-arranged wiretaps of government and newspaper employees to prevent leaks of confidential material to the press; and the creation of a special unit within the White House, the "Plumbers," also assigned to plugging leaks of information. In January 1973, among whispers of hush money, Hunt and some of the burglars pled guilty. McCord and Liddy, who decided to stand trial, were convicted in the D.C. court of Judge John J. Sirica, who was to play a key role throughout the Watergate investigation.

Alarmed by events, the Senate established in February 1973 the Select Committee on Presidential Campaign Activities, chaired by Democrat Samuel J. Ervin of North Carolina. On April 30 Nixon announced on television that he had just, after all, discovered White House involvement in a cover-up. He then jettisoned aides H. R. Haldeman, John Ehrlichman, and John W. Dean III and Attorney General Richard G. Kleindienst. At the insistence of his new attorney general, Elliot Richardson, he appointed Archibald Cox to the position of special prosecutor to investigate the affair. In the televised Senate Watergate hearings that began in May, Dean charged that Nixon himself had been actively involved in the cover-up. Former White House aide Alexander P. Butterfield also revealed that Nixon had since 1971 secretly tape-recorded his Oval Office conversations.

In October 1973 Nixon was forced by Judge Sirica, who was upheld by a U.S. appeals court, to surrender White House tapes to the special prosecutor. When Cox refused the president's compromise—transcripts of certain tapes in return for Cox's promise not to subpoena others—Nixon decided to fire him for exceeding his authority. In a series of events known as the "Saturday Night Massacre," Attorney General Richardson and his deputy resigned rather than obey Nixon's orders to fire Cox, and the job of firing Cox fell to the third-ranking member of the Justice Department, Robert H. Bork. About the same time, other half-related abuses of power began to emerge. For example, in 1971 the "Plumbers" unit had ransacked the offices of the psychiatrist of antiwar activist and former government employee Daniel Ellsberg, seeking damaging information. Ellsberg had leaked a Pentagon-commissioned history of the Vietnam War (known informally as the Pentagon Papers), which revealed a pattern of government deception about escalation of the war. It was later revealed that Gordon Liddy also undertook various "dirty tricks" to discredit the Democrats during the 1972 election campaign. One victim was Maine senator Edmund Muskie, because he appeared to be a stronger contender than Democrat George McGovern. Meanwhile, in October 1973 Vice President Spiro T. Agnew was indicted for tax evasion and corruption. By a plea bargain he resigned, pled guilty to the least of the charges, and avoided jail.

In late July 1974 the House Judiciary Committee approved three articles of impeachment charging the president

Richard Nixon bids farewell to President Gerald R. Ford on August 9, 1974, the day of his resignation from the presidency. *Nixon Project, National Archives*

with obstruction of justice, abuse of executive authority, and contempt of Congress. The Supreme Court sustained the subpoena of Cox's successor, Leon Jaworski, for more transcripts over Nixon's assertion of executive privilege. On August 5 Nixon released these new conversations, which showed that he had indeed known about and authorized the Watergate cover-up—paying hush money, thwarting the FBI—soon after the burglary. The tapes also revealed disturbing presidential behavior—antisemitism, racism, and paranoia, laced with bitter profanity. Republican support in Congress evaporated; impeachment was certain; and conviction in the Senate was almost certain. On August 9, 1974, after an unrepentant farewell address to the people, Nixon resigned.

THE LEGACY

Watergate was not, as is now sometimes suggested, a fraud or a spasm of hysteria comparable to the Red Scare of 1919 or McCarthyism, whipped up by liberal journalists who found the electoral verdict of 1972 intolerable. The scandal was about scandalous behavior, and Nixon's resignation was commensurate. And what has been Watergate's legacy?

The most tangible immediate result was damage to the standing of Nixon's Republican Party. The midterm elections of 1974 brought a big majority of angry, reforming Democrats to Congress, and it was largely the legacy of Watergate that allowed the moderate Democrat Jimmy Carter to edge out Nixon's conservative successor, Gerald R. Ford (who had meanwhile pardoned Nixon). The scandal thus interrupted the conservative trend of the presidency throughout the last third of the twentieth century.

Watergate and the Vietnam debacle, together with other foreign policy crises (Afghanistan, Iran), oil shocks, and high inflation, unemployment, and interest rates led to weary disillusion in the 1970s. In the 1980s, America, weary of weariness, elected Republican Ronald Reagan to exorcise the "Vietnam syndrome" in foreign affairs—and, as it turned out, the Watergate syndrome as well. Far more significant than Watergate's partisan impact was a shift in the constitutional balance. Nixon's near-impeachment had something of the same effect as the impeachment of Andrew Johnson in 1868: strengthening Congress at the expense of the presidency. It also unleashed calls for campaign reform, calls that continued but remained largely unfulfilled.

See also *Independent Counsel; Nixon, Richard M.*

RICHARD MAJOR, INDEPENDENT SCHOLAR

BIBLIOGRAPHY

Bernstein, Carl, and Bob Woodward. *All the President's Men.* New York: Simon and Schuster, 1974.

Dean, John W., III. *Blind Ambition: The White House Years.* New York: Simon and Schuster, 1976.

Gold, Gerald, ed. *The White House Transcripts: Submission of Recorded Presidential Conversations to the Committee on the Judiciary of the House of the Representatives by President Richard Nixon*. New York: New York Times, 1973.

Haldeman, H. R. *The Ends of Power*. London: Sidgwick and Jackson, 1978.

Nixon, Richard M. *RN: The Memoirs of Richard Nixon*. New York: Grosset and Dunlap, 1978.

WATERSHED ELECTIONS

Five presidential contests stand out as "watershed elections," or crucial turning points in American political history. They are the elections of 1800, 1828, 1860, 1896, and 1932. Each led to a long-lasting shift in party power and a fundamental change in national policy. Each also led to the election of a president generally considered to be "great" or "near great," including two of the nation's three greatest presidents: Abraham Lincoln and Franklin D. Roosevelt.

In 1800 Thomas Jefferson defeated the incumbent John Adams for the presidency. This was the first time in the history of the modern world that an incumbent national executive was "overthrown" by a peaceful revolution at the ballot box. Jefferson's ascension to office confirmed the success of the American political system created by the Constitution of 1787. The election also signaled the emergence of the most important nonconstitutional aspect of American politics, the political party. Finally, the election set the stage for twenty-eight years of domination of American politics by the Democratic-Republican Party, as Jefferson's followers called themselves.

With the effective demise of the Federalist Party as a national force by 1816, the Democratic-Republican Party of Thomas Jefferson evolved into an amorphous organization that incorporated virtually all political viewpoints. The inherent instability of a one-party system became apparent in 1824 when four candidates competed for the presidency, with no one getting a majority of the popular or electoral vote. Andrew Jackson led in both categories, but the House of Representatives chose John Quincy Adams, the heir apparent to President James Monroe. In 1828 Jackson and Adams squared off directly, leading to a huge victory for Jackson and the emergence of a new Democratic Party. The nationalist wing of the old Democratic-Republican Party—led by men like Henry Clay, Daniel Webster, and John Quincy Adams—eventually coalesced into a new party, the Whigs. Jackson's victory set the stage for his party to dominate American politics until 1860. The party abandoned the nationalism of Madison and Monroe, with Jackson vetoing a recharter of the Bank of the United States, ending federal support for internal improvements, and deferring to state demands for the removal of Indians in the east. Jackson also in-

stituted an aggressively proslavery domestic policy, using the Fugitive Slave Law of 1793 as a litmus test for judicial appointments, while creating an aggressive foreign policy that led, after his presidency, to the annexation of Texas and war with Mexico.

By the 1850s the sectional pressures caused by slavery undermined the Jacksonian coalition. The Democratic Party's repeal of the ban on slavery in the trans-Mississippi West to force slavery into Kansas led to a huge northern backlash and the creation of a new party, the Republicans. In 1860 Lincoln carried every non–slave state, and with it the election. By the time of his inauguration seven slave states had seceded from the Union, and four years of horribly costly and bloody civil war followed, ending with the elimination of slavery in the United States, a reunification of the states, and the assassination of Lincoln shortly after he began his second term in office. Lincoln's party dominated politics for the next two decades, controlling the White House, one or both houses of Congress, and the courts. The party favored high tariffs, federal support for railroads, federal protections for the recently emancipated slaves, and suppression of Mormons in the West.

Democrats made a comeback in 1884, taking the White House for the first time since Lincoln's election, and they recaptured it in 1892, along with both houses of Congress. In 1896 the Democrats nominated the radical midwestern populist William Jennings Bryan. The Democrats offered a sharp contrast to the Republicans, demanding lower tariffs, railroad regulations, banking reform, and inflationary policies based on increased production of silver and higher farm prices. The Republicans responded with a highly organized, well financed national campaign that raised $4 million and sent out more than 250,000 pieces of literature. The campaign appealed to traditional Republicans, new captains of industry, and, most important, to urban workers and some new immigrants, who were convinced that Bryan's agrarian populism was not in their best interest. Bryan carried twenty-two states to McKinley's twenty-three, but the Republican had a decisive majority in both the electoral and popular vote and was the first president since Ulysses S. Grant to win more than 50 percent of the popular vote. He was also the first president since Grant to win more than 60 percent of the electoral vote. McKinley's election set the stage for Republican dominance of Congress and the presidency for sixteen years, and then for another twelve after Woodrow Wilson's two terms.

The collapse of the American economy following the stock market crash of 1929 set the stage for the most successful political realignment in American history. In 1932, running against Herbert Hoover's failure to come to terms with the Great Depression on either a policy or a psychological level, Franklin D. Roosevelt carried forty-two states, with

472 electoral votes to Hoover's 59. In the 1934 off-year elections, the Democrats increased their majority in the House and Senate, setting the stage for a massive landslide victory in 1936, with FDR carrying forty-six of forty-eight states and 61 percent of the popular vote. The FDR victory in 1932 led to Democratic domination of Congress for most of the next sixty years, as well as Democratic control of the White House for twenty-eight of the next thirty-six years. The "Roosevelt coalition" of urban workers, midwestern and southern farmers, Catholics, Jews, eastern and southern European immigrants and their children, Asian-Americans, southern whites, northern blacks, and intellectuals seemed invincible until the Vietnam War and the demise of Jim Crow in the South tore it apart in the late 1960s.

From 1968 to the end of the century the parties were more evenly divided. Five Republican presidential victories were balanced by three Democratic victories. Although Congress remained in Democratic control for much of this period, Republicans regained the House in the mid-1990s, even while a Democrat sat in the White House. Should Republicans gain control of the White House in 2000 and hold it for a few terms, it will be possible to see the election of Richard M. Nixon in 1968, or Ronald Reagan in 1980, as watersheds which altered the trajectory of politics. On the other hand, if Democrats regain control of Congress and keep the White House in the first part of the twenty-first century, scholars may look back on Bill Clinton's 1992 victory as a watershed that defeated a sitting president and paved the way for a new Democratic coalition of industrial workers, blacks, Hispanics, Jews, Asian-Americans, new economy "techies," and women of all ethnic backgrounds.

See also *Clinton, Bill; Democratic Party; Jackson, Andrew; Jefferson, Thomas; Landslide Elections; Lincoln, Abraham; Republican Party; Roosevelt, Franklin D.; Slavery; Tariff History.*

PAUL FINKELMAN, UNIVERSITY OF TULSA COLLEGE OF LAW

BIBLIOGRAPHY

Burnham, Walter Dean. *Critical Elections and the Mainsprings of American Politics.* New York: Norton, 1970.

Chambers, William Nisbet, and Walter Dean Burnham, eds. *The American Party System: Stages of Political Development.* New York: Oxford University Press, 1975.

Kleppner, Paul, et al. *The Evolution of American Political Systems.* Westport, Conn.: Greenwood Press, 1981.

WELFARE STATE

The term *welfare state* typically refers to a capitalist economy that has a well-developed, central government–administered system for providing social services. These social services include old-age benefits, disability insurance, unemployment compensation, support for dependent children and surviving spouses, income supplements for the poor—both in cash and in kind—and health care for the poor and elderly. The goals of the welfare state are not limited to meeting short-term basic needs, but also seek long-term improvements in the standard of living in the poorer segments of society. The modern welfare state did not emerge in the United States until the New Deal programs of President Franklin D. Roosevelt were put into place. Prior to that, the federal government had a very small role in providing welfare, which was mainly carried out by private-sector charity.

The term *welfare state* has the connotation of dependency, yet it characterizes all modern economies. The level and manner of welfare delivery are contentious in the political arena. Some politicians argue that, if overly generous, welfare programs act as a disincentive for people to work and make economic contributions to society. For evidence they point to the dependence of successive generations on government welfare. Politicians who support greater welfare argue that social payments for nutrition, education, and basic needs often save money in the long run by increasing the likelihood of economic contributions from welfare recipients in the future. Head Start and children's nutrition programs, it is asserted, improve individuals' capacity to be productive and lower the potential for juvenile delinquency and crime.

The major programs comprising the U.S. welfare system, in order of level of government expenditures, include: Social Security (Old Age, Survivors and Disability Insurance), Medicare, Medicaid, Food and Nutrition Assistance, Supplemental Income, Earned Income Tax Credit, Unemployment Compensation, and Temporary Assistance to Needy Families. Individual states also fund programs, in particular, Medicaid. Over time, human resources programs have taken an increasing share of the gross domestic product and the federal budget, increasing from 2.5 percent and 9.9 percent respectively in 1946 to 11.6 percent and 62.2 percent respectively in 1999.

The principal components of the welfare state required major legislative efforts. Many efforts failed. Passage of Roosevelt's programs, which constituted a large portion of the welfare state, was facilitated by huge Democratic majorities in both houses of Congress. Passage of the social programs of President Lyndon Johnson was also aided by large Democratic majorities in Congress. Medicare passed in 1965 but was carried by generous increases in Social Security benefits that were tied to the Medicare legislation. In health care, desired improvements, such as retaining health coverage after job loss and increased coverage of the population, have progressed. Not so successful were the Fair Deal and New Frontier initiatives of Presidents Harry S. Truman and John F. Kennedy. Truman's Fair Deal, for example, proposed federal funding for education, federal health care and insurance, and unemployment insurance benefits. Many of Kennedy's initiatives were successfully taken up by his successor, President Johnson.

The main legislation of the 1990s affecting the welfare state was the Welfare Reform Act of 1996, which placed time and eligibility limits on the receipt of income supplements. The health sector, however, received the most attention in the political arena in the 1990s and beyond. Early in his administration, President Bill Clinton attempted to expand both health care coverage and the government's role in the sector with the Health Security Act of 1993. The proposal incorporated principles of publicly funded health systems of other welfare state economies, including Canada, such as universality, portability, and accessibility, but stopped short of the more radical "single payer" approach. The proposed act bogged down mainly over the issue of central government control of the health care system, and it did not pass.

The successes and failures of the welfare state are difficult to separate from the advances of the general economy. In the latter part of the twentieth century, indicators of progress that the welfare state seeks to address—such as literacy, child mortality, years of education, and life expectancy—all showed progress across the population. At the same time, there was rapid economic progress, which is usually correlated with these improvements. Although the population as a whole was becoming better off, the percentage of the population below the poverty line had not declined since the early 1970s. Thus, even though there was substantial progress in most social indicators, the income distribution goals of the welfare state do not appear to have been realized.

See also *Fair Deal; G.I. Bill; New Deal; Private and Public Welfare, Pre–New Deal.*

RICHARD J. CARROLL, INDEPENDENT SCHOLAR

BIBLIOGRAPHY

Carroll, Richard J. *Desk Reference on the Economy: Over 600 Answers to Questions That Will Help You Understand News, Issues, and Trends.* Washington, D.C.: CQ Press, 2000.

Karger, Howard J., and David Stoesz. *American Social Welfare Policy—A Structural Approach.* White Plains: Longman, 1990.

U.S. Office of Management and Budget. *Historical Tables: Budget of the United States Government—Fiscal Year 2001.* Washington, D.C.: U.S. Government Printing Office, 2000.

WHIG PARTY

Whigs were nineteenth-century modernizers who saw President Andrew Jackson (1829–1837) as a dangerous man with a reactionary opposition to the forces of social, economic, and moral change. As Jackson purged his opponents, vetoed internal improvements, and killed the Bank of the United States, alarmed local elites fought back.

The Whigs, led by Henry Clay, celebrated Clay's vision of the "American System." They demanded government support for a more modern, market-oriented economy, in which skill, expertise, and bank credit would count for more than physical strength or land ownership. They also sought to promote industrialization through high tariffs, a business-oriented money supply based on a national bank, and a vigorous program of government-funded "internal improvements," especially expansion of the road and canal systems. To modernize the inner American, the Whigs helped create public schools, private colleges, charities, and cultural institutions.

The Democrats, by contrast, harkened to the Jeffersonian ideal of an equalitarian agricultural society, insisting that traditional farm life bred republican simplicity, whereas modernization threatened to create a politically powerful caste of rich aristocrats who might subvert democracy. In general, the Democrats enacted their policies at the national level; the Whigs succeeded in passing modernization projects in most states.

Although the Whigs won votes in every socioeconomic class, including the poorest, they appealed especially to more

Henry Clay *Library of Congress*

prosperous Americans. The Democrats likewise won support up and down the scale, but they often sharpened their appeals to the lower half by ridiculing the aristocratic pretensions of the Whigs. Most bankers, storekeepers, factory owners, master mechanics, clerks, and professionals favored the Whigs. Moreover, commercially oriented farmers in the North voted Whig, as did most large-scale planters in the South.

In general, the commercial and manufacturing towns and cities were heavily Whig, save for Democratic wards filled with recent Irish Catholic and German immigrants. Waves of Protestant religious revivals in the 1830s injected a moralistic element into the Whig ranks. Nonreligious individuals who found themselves the targets of moral reform, such as calls for prohibition, denounced the Whigs as Puritans and sought refuge in the Democratic Party. Rejecting the automatic party loyalty that was the hallmark of the tight Democratic Party organization, the Whigs suffered from factionalism. Yet the party's superb network of newspapers provided an internal information system.

Whigs clashed with Democrats throughout what historians term the "Second American Party System." When they controlled the Senate, Whigs passed a censure motion in 1834 denouncing Jackson's arrogant assumption of executive power in the face of the true will of the people as represented by Congress. Backing Henry Clay in 1832 and a medley of candidates in 1836, the opposition finally coalesced in 1840 behind a popular general, William Henry Harrison, and proved that the national Whig Party could win. Moreover, in the 1840s Whigs won 49 percent of gubernatorial elections, with strong bases in the manufacturing Northeast and in the border states. Yet the party revealed limited staying power. Whigs were ready to enact their programs in 1841, but Harrison died and was succeeded by John Tyler, an old-line Democrat who never believed in Whiggery and was, in fact, disowned by the party while he was president. Factionalism ruined the party's program and helped defeat Henry Clay, the Whig presidential candidate, in 1844. In 1848 opportunity beckoned as the Democrats split. By ignoring Clay and nominating a famous war hero, Gen. Zachary Taylor, the Whigs papered over their deepening splits on slavery, and they won. The trend, however, was for the Democratic vote to grow faster and for the Whigs to lose more and more marginal states and districts. After the close 1844 contest, the Democratic advantage widened and the Whigs could win the White House only if the Democrats split.

The Whigs were unable to deal with the slavery issue after 1850. Almost all of their southern leaders owned slaves. The northeastern Whigs, led by Daniel Webster, represented businessmen who loved the national flag and a national market but cared little about slavery one way or another. Many Whig voters in the North, however, felt slavery was incompatible with a free labor–free market economy, and no one discovered a compromise that would keep the party united. Furthermore, the burgeoning economy made full-time careers in business or law much more attractive than politics for ambitious young Whigs. For example, the party leader in Illinois, Abraham Lincoln, simply abandoned politics for several years after 1849. When new issues of nativism, prohibition, and antislavery burst on the scene in the mid-1850s, no one looked to the fast-disintegrating Whig Party for answers. In the North most ex-Whigs joined the new Republican Party, and in the South they flocked to a new, short-lived "American" (Know Nothing) Party. During the Lincoln administration (1861–1865), ex-Whigs enacted much of the "American System"; in the long run, America adopted Whiggish economic policies coupled with a Democratic strong presidency.

See also *Harrison, William Henry; Jackson, Andrew; Know Nothing Party; Republican Party; Taylor, Zachary; Tyler, John.*

RICHARD JENSEN, RENSSELAER POLYTECHNIC INSTITUTE

BIBLIOGRAPHY

Holt, Michael F. *The Rise and Fall of the American Whig Party: Jacksonian Politics and the Onset of the Civil War.* New York: Oxford University Press, 1999.
Remini, Robert V. *Henry Clay: Statesman for the Union.* New York: Norton, 1991.
Van Deusen, Glyndon. "The Whig Party." In *History of U.S. Political Parties,* Vol. 1, edited by Arthur M. Schlesinger Jr., 331–363. New York: Chelsea House, 1973.

WHISKEY REBELLION

Backcountry Pennsylvania farmers instigated a large-scale resistance movement, known as the Whiskey Rebellion, to protest a federal excise tax on domestically produced whiskey. In March 1791, in an attempt to increase national revenue, Congress, despite substantial opposition, passed Secretary of the Treasury Alexander Hamilton's plan for an excise tax equivalent to one-fourth of whiskey's retail value. Western farmers, accustomed to selling distilled alcohol to eastern markets, drew on principles and tactics employed by American revolutionaries against British taxation and fervently opposed the tax. The farmers also resented the enforcement, which required offenders to travel to distant federal courts in eastern Pennsylvania rather than appear before the more sympathetic and convenient western state courts.

Despite a reduction of the excise in 1792 and a resolution to allow prosecution in state courts, resistance turned violent in July and August 1794. Insurgents responded to a court summons of sixty delinquent taxpayers by attacking government officials, seizing Pittsburgh, proclaiming Pennsylvania's six western counties an independent country, and making overtures to British and Spanish officials. Fearing further western unrest or even secession—at a time when Britain and Spain were thought to be threatening American control of interior lands—and wanting to protect Congress's constitutional authority to tax, Hamilton and other nationalist forces condemned the rebellion as lawless and urged an immediate and strong response.

After hesitant attempts at negotiation failed, President George Washington mustered nearly thirteen thousand militiamen from surrounding states and marched them west under his own command. Opposition dissipated, and although approximately 150 suspects were seized, only a handful served prison terms.

The Whiskey Rebellion symbolized the ambiguous meaning of the Revolution and the uncertainty of federalism's future, illustrating the strength of sectional tension. Washington's response also sent a forceful message that the government's laws were to be challenged only through legal channels, not by force.

See also *American Revolution; Constitution, U.S.; Washington, George.*

BRIAN D. SCHOEN, UNIVERSITY OF VIRGINIA

BIBLIOGRAPHY

Baldwin, Leland D. *Whiskey Rebels: The Story of a Frontier Uprising.* Pittsburgh: University of Pittsburgh Press, 1939.

Boyd, Stephen R., ed. *The Whiskey Rebellion: Past and Present Perspectives.* Westport, Conn.: Greenwood Press, 1985.

Slaughter, Thomas P. *The Whiskey Rebellion: Frontier Epilogue to the American Revolution.* New York: Oxford University Press, 1986.

WILSON, WOODROW

Woodrow Wilson (1856–1924) served two terms as the twenty-eighth president of the United States (1913–1921). Wilson was born in Virginia and grew up in the South before attending Princeton University, from which he graduated in 1879. He studied law briefly at the University of Virginia, tried his hand at lawyering in Georgia, and then studied constitutional and political history at Johns Hopkins University, where he earned a Ph.D. in 1886. After teaching at Bryn Mawr College in Pennsylvania and Middlebury College in Connecticut (he had been unhappy at Bryn Mawr, a women's college, because he wished to train men for national leadership), he returned to Princeton, where he taught jurisprudence and political economy beginning in 1890 and served as university president from 1902 until 1910. Then he entered elective politics.

In 1910, Wilson, running as a Democrat, was elected governor of New Jersey. He quickly gained a reputation as a pro-

gressive governor by securing legislation that regulated public utilities, established workmen's compensation, and improved women's working conditions. At the Democratic Party's 1912 presidential convention, after no candidate secured the two-thirds majority necessary for nomination, other candidates' supporters shifted to Wilson, and he was nominated.

In the general election, a Republican split between incumbent William Howard Taft and former president Theodore Roosevelt permitted Wilson to win. His campaign called for the New Freedom, a collection of ideas that would attempt to use federal law to shape the economy in ways more efficient and more democratic. Traditional Democratic positions included a call for a lower tariff on imported goods. Adopted in part from the Populist Party of the 1890s were ideas concerning the regulation of banking, currency, and large corporations.

FIRST TERM—PROGRESSIVE LEGISLATION

Although Wilson's first book, *Congressional Government* (1885), had stressed the power of the legislative branch in American national politics, he had observed Roosevelt's strong executive leadership, had reconceived the role of the president in *Con-*

Woodrow Wilson   *Library of Congress*

stitutional Government in the United States (1908), and could now put into practice the ideas about which he had long written and taught. Reviving a practice that had been dropped after the presidencies of George Washington and John Adams, he delivered messages orally to Congress rather than sending written versions. In addition, as the first president to hold frequent press conferences, he attempted to shape public opinion in support of his legislative agenda.

During his first year in the White House, Wilson signed the Underwood Tariff Act (1913), which reduced tariffs and replaced the lost federal revenue with an income tax, and the Federal Reserve Act (1913), which created a new Federal Reserve System to regulate the nation's money supply. The Federal Trade Commission Act (1914) and the Clayton Antitrust Act (1914) soon followed.

Although he had long thought primarily in terms of domestic politics, Wilson encountered challenges that led him to exert similar leadership in foreign affairs. Seeking to impose American control of political and economic developments in the Caribbean, he sent U.S. troops to both halves of the island of Hispaniola: Haiti in 1915 and the Dominican Republic in 1916. He also sent U.S. troops into Mexico in 1914 and again in 1916, and he intervened elsewhere as well.

SECOND TERM—WORLD WAR I

When the Great War broke out in Europe in 1914, Wilson called for American neutrality and tried to keep from having to send U.S. troops there. His efforts proved largely successful through the election of 1916, which he won by a narrow margin in the electoral college, 277 to 254, largely because he could argue that he had kept the nation out of the war and that a victory by the Republicans, who appeared to side with the Allies, might lead to American involvement. He had hardly begun his second term, however, when Germany adopted a policy of unrestricted submarine warfare, something Wilson had strenuously opposed. The president could no longer keep the nation out of the war and at the same time, as he saw it, protect U.S. trading rights and interests. Congress declared war.

American entry into the war led to a spate of additional laws, programs, and offices. The Railroad Administration and the National War Labor Board helped the federal government manage a wartime economy. Under the Selective Service Act (1917), men were drafted into the American Expeditionary Force to fight in Europe. Under the Lever Act (1917), Wilson established the Food Administration, which Herbert Hoover directed. Wilson also established the Committee on Public Information under George Creel to broadcast propaganda and manage the national dialogue on the war. Congress passed the Espionage Act (1917) and a Sedition Act (1918), laws that the Wilson administration used to crush antiwar ac-

tivity and jail dissenters like his Socialist Party opponent in the 1912 election, Eugene Debs.

U.S. soldiers arrived late in the war but turned the tide in favor of England and France and against Germany, and the war ended in November 1918. President Wilson played a major role at the 1919 peace conference in France, where he called for a League of Nations to lower the likelihood of future wars on such a devastating scale. Back home later that year, he pushed strenuously for Senate ratification of the peace treaty, including U.S. membership in the League of Nations.

Although a majority of senators supported the treaty, Wilson could not obtain a two-thirds majority for the treaty as it stood, and he refused to make concessions that would have secured ratification. Wilson went on a tour of the country to mobilize support, but his health broke, and he suffered a massive stroke. He considered running for a third term in 1920, with the presidential election a referendum on the League of Nations, but such was not to be. His health was so bad that, for many months, he hardly ran the White House. And the Republican candidate, Warren G. Harding, swept to victory in 1920 with a cry for a return to "normalcy."

WILSON'S LEGACY

Wilson pushed progressive legislation that had widespread support during the Progressive era. The legislation of the New Freedom established a framework that persisted into the next century in significant ways, most notably the Federal Reserve System. The New Deal response to the Great Depression later built on—and went way beyond—policy innovations of the Wilson years. Wilson embodied the active presidency of the twentieth century, although his failure on the treaty demonstrated that even activist presidents would ultimately be tethered by the extent of their political savvy and by congressional priorities and public opinion.

Wilson's presidency left an ambiguous legacy. In foreign affairs, his call for a League of Nations succeeded a generation later, in the sense that the victorious Allies in World War II established the United Nations. The quest for free trade, or at least lower tariff barriers, anticipated a national catchword of the 1980s and 1990s. Wilson's innovation in according recognition only to national governments of which he approved— denying recognition of a new leader of Mexico after a bloody coup there in 1913; rejecting the Bolshevik Revolution in Russia in 1917—raised new questions regarding the conduct of foreign relations. Should the United States accept as fact the developments within other countries, the traditional practice, or should it intervene? Wilson's frequent meddling in the Caribbean stood in contrast to what would later be known as the "Good Neighbor Policy." His willingness to intervene between 1918 and 1920 in the Russian Civil War marked the United States as an early enemy of the Soviet Union.

In a variety of areas of society and domestic politics, the Wilson years left a legacy that large numbers of Americans, then and later, had ample reason to reject. The repression of the war years, followed by the Red Scare of 1919, found an ugly echo in the McCarthyism of the years following World War II. Wilson had long rejected the idea of women's suffrage, and he stoutly resisted the innovation during his first term, although he changed course during the war. Wilson introduced racial segregation into the operations of the federal government in ways that went substantially beyond prevailing practice at the time he entered the White House. The Wilson administration proved hostile to the civil rights of African Americans from day one, and it proved hostile to the civil liberties of dissenters during and after World War I. Yet, in a significant gesture toward political inclusion, in 1916 Wilson appointed Louis D. Brandeis the first Jew on the Supreme Court.

See also *African American Politics; Federal Reserve System; Labor Politics and Policy; New Deal; New Freedom; Populist Party; Progressive Era; Red Scare; Roosevelt, Theodore; Socialist Party; Tariff History; Treaty Making; Woman's Suffrage Movement; World War I.*

PETER WALLENSTEIN,
VIRGINIA POLYTECHNIC INSTITUTE AND STATE UNIVERSITY

BIBLIOGRAPHY

Clements, Kendrick A. *The Presidency of Woodrow Wilson.* Lawrence: University Press of Kansas, 1992.

Cooper, John Milton, Jr. *The Warrior and the Priest: Woodrow Wilson and Theodore Roosevelt.* Cambridge: Belknap Press of Harvard University Press, 1983.

Link, Arthur S. *Woodrow Wilson and the Progressive Era, 1910–1917.* New York: Harper, 1954.

WOMAN'S SUFFRAGE MOVEMENT

The American woman's suffrage movement grew out of an expansive struggle for women's rights that quickly focused its efforts on gaining women the right to vote. This movement lasted for over seventy years and attracted an impressive array of feminist thinkers and organizers, including Elizabeth Cady Stanton, Susan B. Anthony, Carrie Chapman Catt, and Alice Paul. By the time women won the right to vote in 1920, the movement had grown from a small contingent of largely white, middle-class female reformers to a mass movement that encompassed a diversity of members and tactics. Although the Nineteenth Amendment did not lead to the radical social transformation that many predicted, women's struggle for the vote led to the development of an independent women's movement and helped move women into the formerly all-male political sphere.

ORIGINS OF THE SUFFRAGE MOVEMENT

The woman's suffrage movement officially began on July 19, 1848, in Seneca Falls, New York. Its early activists traced their roots to the antislavery movement, where white female abolitionists, working for the independence and equality of enslaved blacks, became painfully aware of their own second-class status. In the summer of 1848, five of these women, including Lucretia Mott, a well-known Quaker activist, and Elizabeth Cady Stanton, the wife of a prominent abolitionist leader, called a meeting to address their concerns. To the surprise of many, more than three hundred women and men attended the gathering and participated in two days of speeches and discussion. Stanton's Declaration of Sentiments, modeled after the Declaration of Independence, called for an end to women's social, economic, and political dependence on men. This was a far-reaching program. The goals of female property rights, increased educational opportunities for women, and an end to the moral double standard shared the stage with demands for the rights of full citizenship and suffrage. The only resolution that did not gain unanimous support was the one that called on women "to secure to themselves the sacred right to the elective franchise." Nevertheless, it was this demand that soon moved to the forefront of the nineteenth-century woman's movement.

Of the many women who devoted their time and energy to the cause, few could match the power or influence of Stanton and Anthony. Stanton was the movement's most outstanding philosopher. Saddled at home with a growing family and the never-ending responsibilities of housework, she still found time to write treatises and exhortations and to map out the strategy of this nascent political movement. Anthony, a Quaker activist from Rochester, New York, soon joined Stanton in the struggle. As a single, educated woman, Anthony had the time and the skills to do the practical organizing work that Stanton could not. Theirs was an incomparable match: Stanton articulated the ideology of the movement while Anthony put ideas into action. Both believed that gaining the vote was the only way women could guarantee their social and economic freedom, and they placed suffrage at the center of their political concerns. The deep bonds between the two women aided their efforts in what became, for each, a lifelong struggle.

POSTWAR DIVISION

The Civil War and the emancipation of the slaves raised the hopes of many involved in the struggle for women's rights. If slaves could gain their freedom, activists reasoned, then certainly it was possible for women to gain the right to vote. Their success seemed even more likely once African American citizenship and voting rights emerged as defining political issues during the Reconstruction years. The passage of constitutional amendments guaranteeing blacks these rights became a central focus for those women and men who had been involved in the antislavery cause. Democracy appeared to be expanding its inclusiveness, and Stanton and Anthony believed that it could expand to include women as well.

Stanton and Anthony saw black male suffrage and women's suffrage as linked political goals, but they found themselves a distinct minority among those fighting for black civil rights. Most former abolitionists who supported the idea of women's rights insisted that "this is the Negro's hour" and put women's demands on hold. Stanton and Anthony, on the other hand, refused to let go of what had become an all-consuming goal. Their single-minded commitment to women's equality, however, came at the expense of a similar commitment to equality for black women and men. Both women opposed the passage of the Fourteenth Amendment, which for the first time in the Constitution specified citizenship rights on the basis of sex. Having lost their original allies, they willingly collaborated with anyone who supported women's right to vote, even if that meant working with those who opposed black civil rights. Ultimately, the woman's suffrage movement split. Stanton and Anthony forged ahead, leaving their former allies behind.

The 1870s and 1880s were thus a time of conflict within the woman's suffrage movement. Those who fully supported the Fourteenth and Fifteenth Amendments, which granted blacks their basic citizenship and political rights, gathered together in what became the American Woman's Suffrage Association (AWSA). Stanton, Anthony, and their followers meanwhile formed the rival National Woman Suffrage Association (NWSA). While the AWSA worked to gain women the right to vote on a state-by-state basis, the NWSA continued to focus on the federal Constitution as a means for expanding women's political rights. In 1878 a sympathetic senator introduced what became known as the "Anthony Amendment," guaranteeing women the right to vote. Although its original wording remained intact, it took forty years for the amendment to pass.

THE MOVEMENT'S FINAL PHASE

The fight for women's suffrage entered its final, successful phase in 1890, when the AWSA and NWSA joined forces as the National American Woman Suffrage Association (NAWSA). Animosities that had once divided the movement no longer seemed relevant. Stanton, and then Anthony, led the organization during its early years, but it took a new generation of female leaders, infused with the spirit of Progressive reform, to revitalize and transform what had become an aging and elite suffrage movement.

Harriot Stanton Blatch, Elizabeth Cady Stanton's daughter, epitomized the way in which activists passed the torch from one generation to the next. Blatch joined the New York suffrage movement in 1894 and in the early 1900s assumed a leading role. Although in many ways her mother's daughter, Blatch brought a new sensibility and a new constituency to the suffrage cause. Blatch emphasized the importance of women's work to society at large and linked economic independence to the larger issue of women's emancipation and equal rights. More concretely, she worked to create alliances between the traditionally elite suffrage activists and organizations of working-class women. While such cross-class alliances were not without tension, they infused the movement with a militancy of action that brought it much needed publicity and new recruits. By the early 1910s, open-air meetings and outdoor parades had become hallmarks of Blatch's innovative organizing style, and they helped turn the suffrage campaign into a mass movement.

Carrie Chapman Catt, using a different set of tactics, similarly transformed the suffrage movement into a potent political force. A protégé of Susan B. Anthony, Catt succeeded Anthony as president of NAWSA in 1900. Catt was a skilled political leader, renowned for her ability to organize and carry out difficult campaigns. She left NAWSA after her husband's death in 1904 but returned to the presidency in 1915. While Catt did not embrace the militancy espoused by Blatch, she did believe in the power of mass political mobilization. In 1916 Catt launched her "Winning Plan," designed to revive the organization and achieve passage of a federal suffrage amendment. Catt rallied state associations to a program that combined grassroots organizing with a highly disciplined Capitol Hill lobbying effort. She ran the organization like a general would run an army, and with great success. Under her guidance, NAWSA grew and the federal suffrage amendment gained increasing congressional support.

Despite Catt's call for a unity of purpose, the suffrage movement was anything but unified during its final years. African American women enthusiastically worked for the right to vote, believing that political equality between the sexes would raise the status of the men and women of their race. The suffrage movement, however, did not greet these activists with open arms. Both NAWSA and the more militant National Woman's Party promoted a strategy of political expediency, in which they distanced themselves from the activism of black women as they worked to win white southern support. Some white suffragists went so far as to argue that giving white women the vote would help ensure white supremacy. Others simply refused to consider racial injustice as part of their work for equal rights. Echoing the dynamics of the Reconstruction years, race continued to divide women's struggle for the vote.

Political differences divided the movement as well. In 1917 a group of women committed to more militant action

Suffragists picket the White House during the administration of Woodrow Wilson. *Library of Congress*

broke off from NAWSA to form the National Woman's Party (NWP). The NWP was led by Alice Paul, a young Quaker who had been radicalized by her experiences with the radical British suffragettes. Passionately committed to the cause of women's rights, Paul initiated a controversial policy of attacking the "party in power," and she began conducting daily pickets against President Woodrow Wilson at the White House's front gate. Catt had no tolerance for Paul's tactics; she believed that they undermined NAWSA's careful efforts to win the favor of national political leaders. In Catt's opinion, the NWP's work was divisive and counterproductive.

The differences between these two wings of the suffrage movement increased after April 1917, when the United States entered World War I. Catt believed women could best advance the suffrage cause by acting as patriotic citizens, and she counseled women to devote their energy to supporting the war effort. Paul and the NWP, however, continued their White House protests. As the war progressed, the country's declining tolerance for political dissent made such demonstrations extremely unpopular. Paul and her picketers, carrying banners that called the president "Kaiser Wilson," were attacked by crowds and arrested by police. The jailed suffragists, white and mostly middle class, insisted on being treated as political prisoners and, when they were not, began a hunger strike in protest. Prison officials responded with beatings and force-feedings, but to no avail. Instead, the sacrifices of these well-connected militant protesters made suffrage a newsworthy item, even in the midst of war.

On January 9, 1918, President Wilson announced his support for the suffrage amendment. The following day, it passed in the House with the exact two-thirds majority needed. The NWP credited this victory to the public pressure sparked by their protests, but Catt's lobbying efforts undoubtedly played a critical role. Suffragists were elated, even though their work was not yet over. Another year and a half passed before the "Anthony Amendment" successfully made it through the U.S. Senate in June 1919. Fourteen months later, in August 1920, Tennessee became the final state necessary to ratify the Nineteenth Amendment. The struggle begun more than seventy years before had finally achieved its end.

The woman's movement, having won its primary battle, went on to pursue other goals. Catt steered former NAWSA members into the nonpartisan League of Women Voters. Continuing Stanton and Anthony's quest for women's equality, Paul and the National Woman's Party began to work for an Equal Rights Amendment. Contrary to the hopes of many suffragists and the fears of their opponents, women never voted as a single political bloc. Women's political involvement endured, but the organized women's movement ceased to exist.

See also *Black Suffrage; Equal Rights Amendment; National Woman's Party; Seneca Falls Convention; Suffrage; Wilson, Woodrow.*

MARIAN MOLLIN,
VIRGINIA POLYTECHNIC INSTITUTE AND STATE UNIVERSITY

BIBLIOGRAPHY

Cott, Nancy. *The Grounding of Modern Feminism.* New Haven: Yale University Press, 1987.

DuBois, Ellen Carol. *Feminism and Suffrage: The Emergence of an Independent Women's Movement in America, 1848–1969.* Ithaca: Cornell University Press, 1978.

———. *Woman Suffrage and Women's Rights.* New York: New York University Press, 1998.

Flexner, Eleanor. *Century of Struggle: The Woman's Rights Movement in the United States.* Cambridge: The Belknap Press of Harvard University Press, 1959.

Terborg-Penn, Rosalyn. *African American Women in the Struggle for the Vote, 1850–1920.* Bloomington: Indiana University Press, 1998.

WORLD WAR I

The United States was enveloped in the First World War, the "Great War," in the spring of 1917, after three years of attempting to stay neutral. Victory was rapid and not, for America, expensive in terms of lives. However, the peace was lost and the triumph thrown away so that in 1939 war was renewed in Europe and in 1941 America was again involved.

ORIGINS

There were no European-wide wars (and therefore, in the age of European world empire, no worldwide wars) between 1815 and 1914, and it was generally thought, certainly in America, that the epoch of great wars had passed. In fact, tension began to rise after 1890, in part because of the political and military ambitions of a Germany which was now much the richest and strongest nation on the Continent. In late July 1914 a Balkan crisis finally triggered the universal explosion of Europe, with the German, Austro-Hungarian, and Ottoman Empires pitted against Russia, France, and Britain in a ferocious conflict which, in the West, soon froze into horrific trench warfare.

The American people and the progressive Democratic administration of Woodrow Wilson were equally astonished and, at first, equally adamant that America's tradition of isolation from European squabbles must be maintained. Wilson's Proclamation of Neutrality of August 4, 1914, was generally accepted as viable, as right, and even as inevitable policy. Wilson urged Americans to be neutral in their thoughts—despite his own anglophilia and despite the atrocities Germans were said to be committing, especially in Belgium.

AMERICAN NEUTRALITY

America was an Atlantic nation, and as Americans had discovered in 1798, when sucked into a naval war with France, and again in the 1860s, when the federal blockade of the South almost caused war with England and France, any big Atlantic war tends to entangle both ocean shores. The British Royal Navy soon established mastery of all surface seas, cutting Germany and its allies off from trade with the rest of the world, and in particular with America; the Germans tried in turn to starve Britain with a "U-boat" (submarine) fleet, sinking not only Allied but also neutral shipping, and not just warships but also merchantmen. In May 1915 a British passenger liner, the *Lusitania*, was torpedoed on her way from New York to Liverpool, and Wilson was moved to such strong protest that William Jennings Bryan, his pacifist secretary of state, resigned, sure it would cause war. The Germans backed down and suspended submarine warfare. Wilson was narrowly reelected in November 1916 as "The Man Who Kept Us Out of the War," and he began to try to mediate a negotiated peace.

At the beginning of 1917, however, the Germans decided to risk a resumption of unrestricted submarine warfare, since they felt poised to crush Russia, knock out France, and starve Britain into surrender before American troops could tip the balance. Wilson broke off relations. Alfred Zimmermann, the German under foreign secretary, proposed to Mexico that

Mexico should reconquer the territory lost to the United States in 1848 with German aid; the British intercepted the famous "Zimmermann telegram" and passed it to the Americans. U-boats continued to destroy Allied and neutral vessels, including three U.S. merchant ships in March 1917. On April 2, 1917, Wilson asked Congress to declare war on Germany; he proclaimed it an ideological crusade to make the world "safe for democracy." Congress and most of the people overwhelmingly followed his lead.

AMERICA AS A BELLIGERENT

Wilson's administration waged the eighteen-month war energetically. The economy was essentially nationalized, with Herbert Hoover in charge of agriculture as food administrator, and Bernard Baruch as head of the War Industries Board. Larger taxes were imposed, rationing introduced, labor relations settled by decree, and severe Espionage and Sedition Acts passed (hundreds, mainly leftists, including the socialist leader Eugene Debs, were imprisoned for opposing the war effort).

Some million men had been dispatched to Europe by September 1918, by which time the Germans realized that they had miscalculated and lost the war. Their gamble had been

A U.S. Marine receives first aid in the trenches in the Toulon Sector of France, March 22, 1918. Fresh U.S. troops turned the tide against the Central Powers. *National Archives*

slightly off. Russia was indeed eliminated, and the Western Front very nearly broken in spring 1918. But with American naval support, the U-boats had been cleared from the Atlantic, and so Britain survived. Now it was too late: the German army in France was facing seemingly unlimited American reinforcements, who had already helped save Paris at the Second Battle of the Marne (July), and at the battle of the Argonne in October flung back the last of the German offensive. The Germans, still uninvaded, hoped to cut their losses; they contacted Wilson and offered to surrender on the basis of his famous Fourteen Points. He agreed, insisting that they first overthrow their kaiser and military government, which they did, and fall back to the Rhine. On these terms an armistice was signed on November 11, 1918.

THE WILSONIAN PEACE MADE AND REJECTED

What sort of world was to emerge from the "war to end war"? Wilson had been thinking profoundly and had issued an idealistic program, the Fourteen Points, which envisaged a peace without financial or territorial penalty for the losers, a new Europe based on the principle of "national self-determination," total freedom of the seas in peace and war, and an international body, the League of Nations, to replace the "international anarchy" of the last four years. In early 1919 Wilson sailed for the Paris peace conference—the first serving president to leave America—and thorough defeat.

The British and French wanted Germany punished and weakened; they had promised themselves and their allies a carving up of the Ottoman Empire and the German colonies. They would not tolerate any prohibition on wartime blockades, and they largely got their way. Wilson got his League of Nations written into the peace treaties, and the Versailles settlement was signed in June 1919. However, he then faced final defeat at home, for the Republicans had regained Congress the previous November, and their isolationist minority was intent on keeping America out of Wilson's league. Wilson would not compromise, and in February 1920 the Senate definitively rejected the Treaty of Versailles. A purely formal peace was agreed between the United States and Germany and signed only in 1921, after Wilson left office. By then the age of American isolationism was already under way.

RICHARD MAJOR, INDEPENDENT SCHOLAR

BIBLIOGRAPHY

Cashman, Sean Dennis. *America in the Age of the Titans: The Progressive Era and World War I.* New York: New York University Press, 1988.

Cooper, John Milton Jr., ed. *Causes and Consequences of World War I.* New York: Quadrangle Books, 1972.

Schaffer, Ronald. *The United States in World War I: A Selected Bibliography.* Santa Barbara: Clio Books, 1978.

WORLD WAR II: DOMESTIC POLITICS

World War II profoundly affected political, economic, and social developments within the United States. Even before entering the war against Germany and Japan, Americans felt the effects of the war, as burgeoning production for export created jobs and ended the Great Depression. Economic revival did not shake Americans from their political isolationism, however. Even the fall of France in June 1940 was not enough to rouse popular support for U.S. military intervention; but, in December 1941, after the surprise Japanese attack on Pearl Harbor, Hawaii, the United States declared war. For nearly four years, Americans produced enormous quantities of weapons and supplied millions of military personnel as war raged in both Europe and the Pacific. In the meantime, the nation crafted policies to win the war, and social change at home kept pace with the nation's involvement overseas.

THE INTERWAR PERIOD AND ISOLATIONISM IN THE UNITED STATES

Although the United States had been on the victorious side in World War I, many Americans felt disappointed and disillusioned. President Woodrow Wilson had called the conflict the "war to end all wars" and the "war to make the world safe for democracy," but wars did not end, and democracies were not safe. The United States never joined the League of Nations; instead it pulled back from much involvement in world affairs.

As Italy's fascist leader, Benito Mussolini, ordered an attack on Ethiopia (1935) and as Germany's Adolf Hitler began rearmament (1933), introduced compulsory military service (1935), and reoccupied the Rhineland (1936)—all in violation of the Treaty of Versailles that ended World War I—the United States did nothing. Having read books like H. C. Engelbracht's *Merchants of Death* (1934) and Walter Millis's *The Road to War* (1935), many Americans believed that thousands of U.S. soldiers had died on the battlefields of World War I to line the pockets of greedy arms manufacturers looking for big profits. This feeling gained political legitimacy between 1934 and 1936 as the Senate Munitions Investigating Committee, headed by Gerald Nye, held public hearings that stressed the clandestine activities of arms manufacturers who supposedly forced America into World War I. Moreover, Dalton Trumbo's profoundly antiwar novel, *Johnny Got His Gun* (1939), set in World War I, challenged the idea of entering another war.

As tensions flared in Europe during the mid-1930s, Americans sought to disentangle themselves from foreign wars entirely. After Italy invaded Ethiopia, Congress passed the Neutrality Act of 1935, which authorized the president to prohibit all arms shipments to nations at war and forbade U.S. citizens from traveling on vessels of belligerent nations except at their own risk. In 1936 the Neutrality Act was broadened, and loans and credits to belligerent nations were forbidden. After the Spanish Civil War began in 1937, Congress moved to prohibit participation in civil wars (the previous legislation dealt only with wars between nations). The Neutrality Act of 1937 further authorized the president to embargo all trade with nations at war, and it made travel by Americans on belligerent vessels illegal.

Many historians have argued that U.S. isolationism aided the fascist powers in Italy, Germany, and Spain. Falling back on the neutrality acts, the United States denied Ethiopia arms to fight against Mussolini's Italian assault; even a simple oil embargo might have halted that attack. Also, during the Spanish Civil War, the United States watched while Gen. Francisco Franco—aided by Mussolini and Hitler—took power from the recognized republican government in Spain. The most damning defeat for neutrality legislation and the appeasement policy came after the Munich conference in 1938, at which the British prime minister, Neville Chamberlain, offered Hitler the Sudetenland of Czechoslovakia with the hope of satisfying German expansionism. In response to this agreement, Roosevelt sent Chamberlain the two-word cable, "Good Man." When Hitler took the rest of Czechoslovakia in 1939, the failure of appeasement became obvious.

ROOSEVELT, THE EARLY WAR, AND THE ELECTION OF 1940

Despite his letter to Chamberlain after the Munich conference, Roosevelt was not an isolationist. In a famous Chicago speech in October 1937, the president argued that the international quarantine of aggressor nations was the only way to preserve peace in the era ahead. When war between the Anglo-French alliance and Germany began in September 1939, Roosevelt spoke to the nation in a fireside chat: "This nation will remain a neutral nation, but I cannot ask that every American remain neutral in thought as well." Although under the Neutrality Act of 1937 he briefly prohibited the export of arms and munitions to all the belligerents, the president called a special session of Congress to repeal the arms embargo because it was hurting England and France. As a result, the Neutrality Act of 1939 allowed for the export of arms and munitions, but only on a cash-and-carry basis. The democracies, although at war, could buy goods from America, but they would have to pay in cash and transport the goods themselves.

This belated support was not enough to save most of Europe from the Nazi onslaught. Hitler's forces quickly overran Denmark and Norway (April 1940), the Netherlands and Belgium (May 1940), and then France (June 1940). Following the shocking fall of France, Hitler launched a summer air raid over the British Isles to soften resistance to a cross-channel invasion. The Royal Air Force's defense of the British homeland made a German invasion impossible. As radio broadcasts from London brought the Battle of Britain into millions of U.S. homes, Congress appropriated $9.25 billion between July and September to foster preparedness and instituted the first peacetime draft in U.S. history in September 1940, calling up 1.2 million troops and 800,000 reserves. By executive order, the president transferred fifty out-of-date destroyers to the British navy in exchange for the right to ninety-nine-year leases on naval and air bases all over the world.

In the midst of this foreign crisis, Roosevelt was running for a controversial third term as president. Although he had said he would not seek the Democratic nomination in 1940, he allowed that he would accept it if drafted; and he was nominated. Roosevelt's Democratic platform supported the New Deal domestic agenda, national and hemispheric defense, and all possible aid to Britain short of war. The Republican nominee, Wendell Willkie, attacked the New Deal and said he would not allow American boys to fight someone else's war. Willkie called the destroyers-for-bases deal the "most arbitrary and dictatorial action ever taken by any president in the history of the United States." Many Republicans saw the deal, like Roosevelt's Court-packing plan of 1937, as a perfect example of Roosevelt's rule by fiat. Yet Roosevelt won in 1940, and in 1944 he won a fourth term.

LEND-LEASE, ATLANTIC CHARTER, AND PEARL HARBOR

In January 1941 President Roosevelt, in his State of the Union address, proclaimed his hope for "a world founded upon four essential human freedoms"—freedom of speech, freedom of worship, freedom from want, and freedom from fear. Britain, meanwhile, in dire need of financial and military support, could no longer afford to buy military supplies under cash and carry.

The Roosevelt administration again stepped forward, offering lend-lease aid to Britain. With this package, the United States, while remaining out of the war, would send massive supplies of free arms and munitions to states at war with Germany. At the end of the war, debts were to be settled by returning the used supplies or their equivalents to the United States. The idea was hotly debated in Congress and throughout the nation. Isolationists said the United States would be forced to enter the war to protect its investment, and Republicans argued that used supplies were like used pieces of chewing gum that no one wanted back. However, lend-lease passed on March 11, 1941.

The isolationists who opposed lend-lease proved to be correct about the program's danger. As U.S. convoys escorted or carried supplies to Britain, German submarines began sinking U.S. vessels on the high seas. In May 1941 President Roosevelt declared an "unlimited national emergency" to combat the German aggression. In June 1941, when Hitler violated the 1939 Soviet-German nonaggression pact and invaded the Soviet Union, the United States immediately extended to Russia a $1 billion aid package that grew to $11 billion by war's end.

In the summer of 1941 Roosevelt secretly met with British prime minister Winston Churchill on warships off the Newfoundland coast. On August 14 the two leaders issued a press release that became known as the Atlantic Charter. Although it called for the "final destruction of Nazi tyranny," the charter centered on the "common principles" for which the two countries were fighting. These eight idealistic goals included the self-determination of all peoples, equal access to raw materials, economic international cooperation, freedom of the seas, and a new organization for collective security.

Although Germany continued to sink U.S. ships in the fall of 1941, the United States did not join the war until December 1941, after the Japanese launched an attack against the U.S. Pacific Fleet at Pearl Harbor, Hawaii. U.S.-Japan relations had been deteriorating for a number of years as Japan sought to extend its sphere of influence in East Asia, especially in China, French Indochina, and the Dutch East Indies. The attack on Pearl Harbor was a calculated attempt by the Japanese to prevent the United States from resisting Japanese expansion, but its most immediate effect was to end isolationism in America.

One day after the attack, Congress (with only one dissenting vote) declared war on Japan. When Japan's allies—Italy and Germany—declared war on the United States on December 11, the United States entered the war against those nations as well. Without the unity that Pearl Harbor gave the American people, substantial opposition to U.S. involvement might have continued, as it had during World War I.

AMERICA'S DOMESTIC WAR EFFORT

The nation's participation in a two-front global war led to tremendous change at home. Congress passed two war powers acts: the first, in December 1941, authorized the president to reorganize federal agencies for the war effort, and the second, in March 1942, sanctioned government allotment of materials and facilities needed for defense. The selective service had already drafted more than one million men, and fourteen million more were called up during the war years.

Backing these men in arms was the strongest industrial force on the planet. As in World War I, in January 1942 the federal government created the War Production Board, which oversaw the conversion of domestic manufacturing to wartime production. Two American business leaders—Donald Nelson from Sears and Charles E. Wilson from General Electric—headed the organization. By halting the manufacture of nonessential items like passenger cars and allocating scarce resources, especially steel, rubber, and oil, the board orchestrated the production of 40 billion bullets, 300,000 aircraft, 76,000 ships, 86,000 tanks, and 2.6 million machine guns. To pay for this war production, Congress passed the Revenue Act of 1942, which brought in billions of dollars in increased revenue that paid off much of the cost of the war even as it was being waged. At the same time, Americans were encouraged to buy war bonds, and their purchases totaled about $150 billion.

As men left for the war and industry grew, the government encouraged women to enter the work force. They did so in unprecedented numbers. Taking jobs outside the home were more than 6 million women; over half had never worked for wages before. Many of their jobs were traditionally men's jobs—toolmaker, machinist, blacksmith, railroad worker, and aircraft specialist—that required skilled labor and paid high wages. When the war ended, however, women were encouraged to leave the workforce to make way for their returning husbands and sons.

Women at work as riveters at the Lockheed Aircraft Corp. plant in Burbank, California. The war opened many opportunities for women and minorities. *National Archives*

Shortly after the attack on Pearl Harbor, President Franklin D. Roosevelt began issuing executive orders that placed restrictions on Japanese Americans living on the West Coast. Eventually, more than 110,000 Japanese Americans—including native-born U.S. citizens—were removed to internment camps. *Farm Security Administration—Office of War Information Photograph Collection, Library of Congress*

Race relations became a national issue, especially as African Americans entered the armed services and wartime production. African Americans made dramatic—although temporary—gains during the war as 1.6 million black southerners left for jobs in the North and the West. In 1941, before the nation declared war, A. Philip Randolph, an African American leader who headed the Brotherhood of Sleeping Car Porters, threatened President Roosevelt with a mass march on Washington if African Americans were not given equal opportunities in the armed forces and war jobs. Roosevelt responded with an executive order forbidding discrimination in defense industries, and he also established the Fair Employment Practices Commission to oversee compliance with the order.

With far less dissent than during World War I, Americans improved their civil liberties record, with the enormous exception of the intense hatred and bigotry that Japanese Americans suffered during the war. Although more than 100,000 U.S. citizens of Japanese descent were removed from their homes and businesses in the West Coast states and placed in so-called war relocation camps, many men left the camps to join the nation's military effort in Europe, where they were decorated for their heroic efforts.

THE WAR COMES TO AN END

As the fighting in Europe became more intense in 1943, President Roosevelt and Prime Minister Churchill met at Casablanca (January 14–24, 1943), in French Morocco. They declared that the war would be fought until the "uncondi-

tional surrender" of each enemy had been secured. Joseph Stalin, the leader of the Soviet Union, was included in the next major Allied meeting, at Tehran (November 28–December 1, 1943). There the Big Three reached agreement on broad plans for the defeat of Germany. An Anglo-U.S. force would attack Germany in western Europe while the Soviets would move in from the east. The Allies also laid plans for the United Nations, an international organization (modeled in part on the League of Nations) to keep the peace after the war. The Anglo-U.S. D-Day invasion of Normandy followed six months later, in June 1944, and the Soviets continued their move from the east.

As the battle for Germany reached its climax in late 1944 and early 1945, the Big Three met again at Yalta (February 4–11, 1945). With victory over Germany near, Stalin agreed that Poland, Bulgaria, and Romania should have free elections and be independent states—a promise he soon broke. In addition, Stalin agreed to enter the war against Japan within three months of war's end in Europe. In return, Roosevelt promised Stalin the southern half of Sakhalin Island and Japan's Kurile Islands as well. The Soviet Union was also granted joint control over the railroads in Manchuria and received special privileges in the two key seaports of that area, Dairen and Port Arthur. The war in Europe ended on May 8, 1945; the next month, Germany was divided into four occupational zones: American, British, French, and Soviet.

Following President Roosevelt's death on April 12, 1945, Vice President Harry S. Truman became president. Some people, then and later, wondered: Had Roosevelt been too sick to negotiate successfully at the Yalta conference; had he given too much to the Soviets in the Far East; was unconditional surrender a realistic objective over Japan; and could Truman carry on with an administration he knew almost nothing about? Yet Truman quickly established himself as his own man, removing officials he could not work with. And when the experimental atomic bomb was ready, he ordered it dropped on Hiroshima (August 6) and Nagasaki (August 9) to bring the war against Japan to an end. Japan's surrender came on August 14, 1945.

CONCLUSION

World War II transformed America's role in the world. The nation emerged as one of only two superpowers and had the world's strongest economy, with a gross national product that continued to grow rapidly, from $200 billion in 1945 to $600 billion in 1960. The United States ended World War II with a monopoly on atomic weaponry, but soon a long and fearful cold war threatened U.S. security, affected every nation, and profoundly shaped the domestic politics and policies of the United States for a generation and more.

Many soldiers and their families—whether of European, African, Asian, or Native American ancestry—had come to think of service in the armed forces as a citizen-soldier's duty for the nation's cause. After the war ended, soldiers benefited from provisions of the G.I. Bill (1944), which helped veterans attend college, obtain professional training, start businesses, buy homes, and in all those ways pursue their own deferred dreams, even as they contributed to such postwar phenomena as a baby boom, sustained economic growth, the development of suburbia, the civil rights movement, and a legacy as the "Greatest Generation."

See also *Civil Rights Movement; Cold War; G.I. Bill; Roosevelt, Franklin D.; Truman, Harry S.; World War I; World War II: Foreign and Military Policy.*

JEFFREY LITTLEJOHN, UNIVERSITY OF ARKANSAS

BIBLIOGRAPHY

Blum, John Morton. *V Was for Victory: Politics and American Culture during World War II.* New York: Harcourt Brace Jovanovich, 1976.

Dallek, Robert. *Franklin D. Roosevelt and American Foreign Policy, 1932–1945.* New York: Oxford University Press, 1979.

Hartmann, Susan M. *The Home Front and Beyond: American Women in the 1940s.* Boston: Twayne Publishers, 1982.

Irons, Peter. *Justice at War.* New York: Oxford University Press, 1983.

Keegan, John. *The Second World War.* New York: Viking, 1990.

MacDonald, Charles B. *The Mighty Endeavor: American Armed Forces in the European Theater in World War II.* New York: Oxford University Press, 1969.

Wynn, Neil. *The Afro-American and the Second World War.* New York: Holmes and Meier Publishers, 1976.

WORLD WAR II: FOREIGN AND MILITARY POLICY

World War II (1939–1945)—the second global military conflict of the twentieth century—saw even more death and destruction than the horrific First World War (1914–1918). Although repeated attempts were made during the 1920s and 1930s to strengthen the Treaty of Versailles, which ended World War I, depression infected the global economy, and militaristic nationalist regimes rose up in countries dissatisfied with the postwar settlement. Peace, therefore, became hard to preserve. The intermittent local conflicts of the 1930s finally gave way to world war in September 1939 as an expansionist Germany under Adolf Hitler invaded Poland, leading England and France to declare

war on Germany. Soon, almost every country in Europe and Asia had chosen a side: the "Allies," led by England, France, and Russia, faced the "Axis," led by Germany, Italy, and Japan.

America remained neutral at first, but after the fall of France in 1940 the country began actively supporting England with money, military supplies, and strategic intelligence. After the Japanese surprise attack at Pearl Harbor, Hawaii, on December 7, 1941, the United States joined the Allied war effort as a combatant. All the cultural, economic, and industrial resources of the country were harnessed to support the 15 million servicemen called up for the war. In the end, six years of intense fighting brought the downfall of Hitler and the Nazis in Germany, the defeat of the Japanese in Asia, and America's emergence as one of only two postwar superpowers.

THE TREATY OF VERSAILLES AND THE RISE OF TOTALITARIANISM

The roots of World War II lay in German, Italian, and Japanese resentment of the Treaty of Versailles. As the principal loser of World War I, Germany was excluded from treaty negotiations and was forced to accept a $33 billion reparations debt, the eradication of its armed forces, and the guilt for the entire war. Italy—which had shifted from the German to the Allied side during the war—felt it had made great sacrifices during the conflict and was not satisfied with its small territorial gains. Japan, like Italy, felt that because it had fought heroically and received little, it deserved China and hegemony in East Asia.

In all three of these countries—Germany, Italy, and Japan—militaristic, totalitarian regimes came to power during the interwar period. With his fascist mixture of nationalism and militarism, Benito Mussolini gained control of Italy between 1922 and 1925. In Germany, Adolf Hitler headed the National Socialist (Nazi) Party, which used Jews, Gypsies, and other groups as scapegoats for the postwar problems the Weimar Republic faced. Promising to overturn the Treaty of Versailles and return Germany to greatness, Hitler became German chancellor in 1933 and was soon running the country as a fascist dictator. Japan had a long history of militarism, and by 1936 an increasingly militant and racist government was directing the foreign policy of the nation.

AGGRESSION AND APPEASEMENT, 1933–1939

The rise of Mussolini, Hitler, and the militarists in Japan led to fighting even before World War II. In Italy, Mussolini used his power to initiate a military campaign against Ethiopia in North Africa (1936). In Germany, Hitler began rearmament (1933), introduced compulsory military service for able-bodied men (1935), and reoccupied the demilitarized Rhineland (1936)—all in violation of the Treaty of Versailles. Hitler and Mussolini joined in a military alliance in 1936 called the

Rome-Berlin Axis and then gave support to Gen. Francisco Franco, the leader of the fascist forces that overthrew the legal government of Spain during the Spanish Civil War (1936–1939). In the Sino-Japanese War (1937–1939), the Japanese invaded China and sought to take gains beyond Manchuria (renamed Manchuko in 1931) in East Asia. Then, in 1940, Japan entered the German-Italian alliance, creating the Rome-Berlin-Tokyo Axis.

These early developments did not lead England, France, or the United States to move for war against the Axis powers. In fact, disillusionment with World War I had led the U.S. Congress to pass a series of Neutrality Acts (1935, 1936, and 1937), which declared that Americans could neither travel in a war zone nor sell, transport, or loan munitions or money to a belligerent. Even after Hitler occupied Austria in March 1938, claiming it as a province of greater Germany, there was no call for war. However, when he began demanding the Sudetenland of Czechoslovakia, the British initially stepped up to meet the German threat. At the Munich Conference (September 1938), Prime Minister Neville Chamberlain agreed to allow Hitler the Sudetenland, if he would cease further German expansion in Europe. When Hitler agreed, Chamberlain returned home, claiming to have secured "peace in our time." However, when Hitler took the rest of Czechoslovakia in March 1939, the weakness of appeasement became obvious: all the Western democracies had done was give Hitler more time to build his war machine.

THE EARLY WAR, AUGUST 1939–NOVEMBER 1941

In August 1939 things took a turn for the worse for the western democracies, as Germany and the Union of Soviet Socialist Republics (USSR) signed a nonaggression treaty, known as the Hitler-Stalin Pact, pledging not to fight each other. With this insurance against Soviet retaliation, Hitler invaded Russia's neighbor, Poland, on September 1, 1939. Britain and France, honoring their commitments to defend Polish sovereignty, declared war on Germany on September 3, and World War II began. Although the United States was neutral in theory, America had always supported France and England, as it became more and more obvious that Hitler was bent on world domination. Congress passed a revised Neutrality Act in 1939, declaring that the democracies of the West could buy goods from America—despite being at war—as long as they paid cash and carried the supplies on their own ships. However, this support was not enough to halt Hitler's war machine, which overran Denmark and Norway (April 1940), the Netherlands and Belgium (May 1940), and then France (June 1940).

In August 1940 Hitler initiated an air campaign over Britain to break the islands' resistance to a cross-channel land-ing. In the resulting Battle of Britain, the new prime minister of England—Winston Churchill—and the British Royal Air Force proved tenacious in their defense of the British Isles. No German invasion would be possible. Air raids over Britain brought a quick response from the United States. At President Franklin D. Roosevelt's request, Congress appropriated $37 billion for military preparedness; created the first peacetime draft, calling up 1.2 million troops and 800,000 reserves; and approved Lend-Lease aid to countries fighting Germany, by which other countries might "borrow" military and other essential supplies.

After failure over England, Hitler turned his attention to the Eastern Front. In June 1941 he invaded the USSR and the Balkans to get Russian oil and to remove all continental impediments to his rule. Britain offered Stalin an alliance, and the United States extended Lend-Lease aid to the USSR, giving the country more than $11 billion during the war. The Russians were able to hold Moscow in November 1941 in part because German troops were not outfitted for the winter. The war on the Eastern Front went on, but developments in the Pacific overshadowed it in December 1941.

AMERICA JOINS THE WAR

With Russian defeat seemingly near in November 1941, Japan sought to obtain its oil and other natural resources in Southeast Asia. The United States had prohibited the export of steel, scrap iron, and aviation fuel to Japan and had frozen its assets after Japan had seized both halves of Indochina (Northern, 1940; Southern, 1941). To capitalize on the Russian situation and to move further into Southeast Asia, Japan would be forced to confront the United States. Japan hoped that a surprise attack could disable the U.S. Pacific Fleet at Pearl Harbor, Hawaii. On December 7, 1941, Japanese carrier-based planes attacked the fleet, killing 2,400 American servicemen, wounding 1,178, and destroying eight battleships and thirteen other vessels. The next day, the United States declared war on Japan. Then, on December 11, Germany and Italy declared war on the United States.

At the same time as the assault on Pearl Harbor, the Japanese launched attacks on Guam, Wake Island, the Philippines (American possessions), and British Hong Kong and Malaya. Quick victories gave Japan great strategic power in the South Pacific. However, the United States had broken the Japanese communication code even before Pearl Harbor, and when another surprise attack was aimed at Midway Island, the U.S. Pacific Fleet was ready and waiting. On June 4, 1941, four Japanese aircraft carriers—the most important naval vessels in the war—were sunk. Midway Island was held by the United States, and the Pacific Fleet began its move toward the Japanese home islands.

The battleships USS *West Virginia* and USS *Tennessee* burn following the Japanese attack on Pearl Harbor. The surprise attack greatly reduced isolationist sentiment in the United States.   *National Archives*

WAR IN EUROPE, 1942–1945

Although aggression in the Pacific drew America into the war, Roosevelt had agreed with Churchill in August 1941 to make the defeat of Hitler America's top priority. On January 1, 1942, this agreement was reaffirmed, and the United States, Britain, the USSR, and twenty-three other nations signed the Declaration of the United Nations in which they pledged to fight against the Axis powers until they were all defeated. However, the burden of fighting Hitler rested on the USSR for most of 1942. As the Germans drove into the Caucasus, the Russians held in the north at Stalingrad, where, suffering enormous casualties, they turned the Germans back by January 1943. British and American forces initiated a move against Hitler in North Africa during the fall of 1942.

Roosevelt and Churchill met at the Casablanca Conference in French Morocco on January 14–24, 1943, to discuss the development of a second front in Europe against Hitler. American military leaders wanted to assemble an army in Britain and cross the English Channel, but British leaders, including Churchill, believed an Italian and Balkan invasion would be best. Roosevelt finally sided with Churchill. In addition, Roosevelt and Churchill declared that nothing but "unconditional surrender" would be acceptable from the Axis powers.

The Anglo-American invasion of Italy began on July 10, 1943. As Allied forces moved up the peninsula, Italian leaders stripped Mussolini of his powers (July 25) and signed a separate armistice between the Allies and Italy on September 3, 1943. By the time Roosevelt and Churchill met their eastern ally Joseph Stalin at the Tehran Conference (November 28–December 1, 1943), they had decided to launch Operation Overlord, a cross-channel invasion of the continent. Anglo-American forces would attack Germany from the west, while the Soviets would move in from the east. In return, Stalin promised to enter the war against Japan in the Pacific. All three agreed that after the war a new international organization—the United Nations—would be needed to promote peace and international justice.

On June 6, 1944, the Anglo-American D-Day invasion was set in motion. Allied forces concentrated in southern England invaded a sixty-mile line along the coast of Normandy. Gen. Dwight D. Eisenhower oversaw the entire invasion, which utilized 176,000 troops, 600 warships, 4,000 smaller craft, and 11,000 planes in the largest amphibious assault in world history. By July 2 more than 1 million troops had been landed at Normandy, and on September 11 France was liberated from German control. As American and British forces pushed on Germany from the west, the USSR launched its offensive in late June. During the fall and winter of 1944–1945, the Germans launched counter-offensives in both the east and west. However, Allied forces held at the Battle of the Bulge in December 1944.

By February 1945 victory over Germany was imminent. Roosevelt, Churchill, and Stalin met at Yalta, in the Crimea, to discuss the end of the war in Europe and the fight in the Pacific. Stalin agreed to enter the war against Japan within three months after the close of the European war. In return, Roosevelt and Churchill made territorial concessions to Stalin in East Asia. The war ended in Europe on May 8, 1945, and Germany was divided into four occupation zones on June 5, 1945.

THE PACIFIC FRONT AND THE THREE SHOCKS THAT ENDED THE WAR

War in the Pacific dragged on until mid–August 1945. After the Battle of Midway (June 1942), the United States adopted a Pacific strategy called "island hopping," by which the most heavily fortified enemy islands were bypassed as forces captured smaller islands, set up air bases, and then sought to destroy the neighboring fortified islands through air campaigns. The Marianas were the first major prize of the U.S. strategy, in July and August 1944. From this island chain, U.S. B-29 Superfortress bombers carried out constant raids on the Japanese home islands. The capture of Iwo Jima and fire raids on Tokyo in March 1945 brought the end of the war near. With the end near, President Roosevelt—elected to an unprecedented fourth term in 1944—died on April 12, 1945.

Roosevelt's successor, Harry S. Truman, was faced with bringing the war to an end. He met with Stalin and British leaders at the Potsdam Conference in July 1945, where the Allies issued an unwavering ultimatum to the people of Japan: surrender or be destroyed. Truman had not known of plans for America's new weapon, the atomic bomb, before he became president. It was successfully tested on July 16, 1945, at Alamogordo, New Mexico, and when the weapon became available, Truman decided to use it. On August 6, 1945, the first atomic bomb was dropped on Hiroshima, Japan, killing 180,000 people. On August 8, Stalin joined the American effort against Japan as he had promised at Yalta. Then on August 9 the United States dropped a second atomic bomb, on Nagasaki; 80,000 people died. The next day, Japan sued for peace, asking that Emperor Hirohito be allowed to retain his ancestral throne. On August 14 the Allies accepted this condition, and the war ended.

The greatest shock that Americans faced at the war's end was not Roosevelt's death, nor even the atomic bomb. It was the ghastly death and work camps of the Nazi Holocaust, in which more than six million Jews, tens of thousands of Romani, and hundreds of thousands of others had been systematically exterminated by ordinary Germans. The Holocaust introduced an even deeper questioning of human nature than did the war. What now was possible? The atomic bomb and human evil together could and might destroy the world.

CONCLUSION

In the end, World War II brought the defeat of Germany and Japan and America's emergence as one of only two postwar superpowers with the USSR. Fifteen million American men and women had been mobilized for war, more than six million women had entered jobs outside the home, and the U.S. government had spent over $340 billion to win the war. The armed forces lost 292,131 men and women to battle deaths and 115,187 to other related causes. This loss was minimal compared with the civilian and military casualties of other countries: 20 million Russian, 13 million Chinese, 7 million German, and 2 million Japanese.

The most dramatic consequence of World War II was the division of Europe and Asia between the two postwar superpowers. The territories that Anglo-American forces had moved through to defeat Germany and Japan were liberated at the close of the war. However, the land on which the Russian army sat came under the power of Joseph Stalin and the communists in Russia. This outcome set the stage for the cold war between the United States and the USSR from 1945 to 1989.

See also *Cold War; Eisenhower, Dwight D.; Roosevelt, Franklin D.; Treaties: Peace, Armament, and Defense.*

JEFFREY LITTLEJOHN, UNIVERSITY OF ARKANSAS

BIBLIOGRAPHY

Dower, John W. *War Without Mercy.* New York: Pantheon Books, 1986.

Keegan, John. *The Second World War.* New York: Viking, 1990.

Willmott, H. P. *The Great Crusade: A New Complete History of the Second World War.* New York: Free Press, 1990.

Wright, G. *The Ordeal of Total War, 1939–45.* New York: Harper and Row, 1968.

APPENDIX: ACRONYMS AND ABBREVIATIONS

A

AAA—Agricultural Adjustment Administration, created in 1933 to help stabilize farm prices during the Great Depression. Part of President Franklin D. Roosevelt's "First New Deal." The Supreme Court declared it unconstitutional in 1936, but Congress recreated it in 1938, and the Court later upheld its constitutionality. It was merged with the Agriculture Department in 1942.

AAA—American Automobile Association, first organized in 1902, is the nation's largest organization of motorists, with branches throughout the United States and more than 20 million members.

AAAS—American Academy of Arts and Sciences, organized by John Adams and chartered by the state of Massachusetts in 1780 "to cultivate every art and science which may tend to advance the interest, honor, dignity, and happiness of a free, independent, and virtuous people." The AAAS remains an important component of American scholarly life through its research centers and its publication, *Daedalus*.

AAAS—American Association for the Advancement of Science, founded in 1840 but did not hold its first meeting until 1848. Devoted to "the advancement of science" in the nation, it is a major force in American scientific development and has worked closely with the national government as well as with scientists throughout the nation.

AALS—American Association of Law Schools, umbrella organization that includes most accredited American law schools, founded in 1900.

AASS—American Antislavery Society, founded by William Lloyd Garrison in 1833.

AAUP—American Association of University Professors, the largest professional organization of college and university professors. It sometimes functions as a union where college faculty are unionized.

ABA—American Bar Association, organized in 1878, is the largest organization of lawyers in the nation. Sets standards for legal education and provides services to lawyers and nonlawyers.

ABC Countries—Argentina, Brazil, and Chile, the most economically important nations in Latin America. Term originated with the ABC Conference in Niagara Falls, N.Y., in 1914 to help prevent war between the United States and Mexico.

ABC—Alcoholic Beverage Commission, term used in many states for the agency that regulates liquor, beer, wine, and other alcoholic beverages.

ACLS—American Council of Learned Societies, an umbrella organization of academic and scholarly societies that are not connected to the hard sciences.

ACLU—American Civil Liberties Union, founded in 1920 to protect the liberties of all Americans against encroachment by government. Well known for bringing cases to the courts on various issues concerning freedom of religion, speech, press, and association and the rights of the accused.

ACS—American Colonization Society, formed in 1817 to encourage free blacks to return to Africa and used by some masters as a vehicle for freeing their slaves. Most free blacks saw it as an attack on their right to remain in the land of their birth, the United States.

AEC—Atomic Energy Commission, established in 1945 to regulate atomic power and atomic weapons research in the United States. Replaced in 1975 by the Energy Research and Development Association and the more important Nuclear Regulatory Commission.

AEF—American Expeditionary Forces, term used for U.S. military forces sent to Europe in World War I. Also used for U.S. troops sent to specific regions during the war, such as the AEF in Italy and the AEF in Russia.

AFL—American Federation of Labor, organized in 1886 under its great leader Samuel Gompers; umbrella organization of skilled trade unions, merged with the Congress of Industrial Organizations (CIO) in 1955.

AFL-CIO—Nation's largest labor organization, created by the merger of the American Federation of Labor (AFL) and the Congress of Industrial Organizations (CIO) in 1955.

AFSCME—American Federation of State, County, and Municipal Employees, the nation's largest union of government workers, established in 1936 but greatly expanded since the 1960s.

AFT—American Federation of Teachers, largest teachers union in the nation, founded in 1916.

AHA—American Historical Association, founded in 1884, the main professional association for historians in all fields in the United States.

ALA—American Library Association, the primary organization of professional librarians in the United States, founded in 1876.

AMA—American Medical Association, established in 1847, the main professional organization for American physicians.

AME Church—African Methodist Episcopal Church, founded by Rev. Richard Allen of Philadelphia in 1816, the oldest national black church organization in the United States.

AMEX—American Stock Exchange, until the 1990s the second largest stock exchange in the United States.

ANZUS—A security alliance formed for the Pacific in 1951 by Australia, New Zealand, and the United States.

AP—Associated Press, cooperative news gathering organization founded in 1848.

APA—American Protective Association, formed in 1887 to lobby against foreign, especially Catholic, immigration. Had a million members by 1896 but ceased operations in 1911.

APSA—American Political Science Association, founded in 1903, the main professional organization of political scientists.

ARU—American Railway Union, organized in 1893 by labor leader Eugene V. Debs to bring all railroad workers into one great union. The union collapsed in 1894 in the wake of the Pullman strike.

ASPCA—American Society for the Prevention of Cruelty to Animals, founded in 1866 to prevent cruel treatment of animals.

AT&T—American Telephone and Telegraph, the largest telephone company in the United States, controlling most of the local and long-distance business in the nation, at the time of its breakup in 1982. At one time it had more stockholders than any other company in the country.

B

BIA—Bureau of Indian Affairs, an executive branch office created in the War Department in 1824 as the Office of Indian Affairs, which was transferred to the Department of Interior (initially called the Home Department) when that cabinet-level department was established in 1849.

B & O—Baltimore and Ohio, first railroad in the United States, established in Baltimore, ran first train in 1830.

BSA—Boy Scouts of America, an organization of clubs for boys and young men founded in 1910 and given a federal charter in 1916.

C

C & O—Chesapeake and Ohio, a company founded in 1824 to build a canal from Washington, D.C., to the Ohio River, some 360 miles away. Only 186 miles, to western Maryland, were completed. Although operated as late as 1924, its economic viability was undermined early on by railroads.

CAB—Civil Aeronautics Board, established in 1938 under the Civil Aeronautics Administration to regulate air safety for private and commercial planes.

CAP—Community Action Programs, created as part of President Lyndon Johnson's War on Poverty to fund local, community-based antipoverty organizations. Abolished under President Ronald Reagan in 1981.

CBO—Congressional Budget Office, a bipartisan office established by Congress in 1974 to provide the House and Senate with information about the federal budget that is independent of the executive branch.

CCC—Civilian Conservation Corps, established in 1933 as part of New Deal programs to employ young men to work on reforestation, land reclamation, and programs to stop soil erosion. Abolished in 1942.

CEA—Council of Economic Advisers, created by the Employment Act of 1946 to give the president economic advice.

CENTO—A defense alliance established in 1959 by Britain, Iran, Pakistan, Turkey, and the United States. It collapsed by the late 1970s as the interests of these countries diverged.

CIA—Central Intelligence Agency, established in 1947 to oversee intelligence gathering, including spying, for the United States. Evolved from Office of Strategic Services (OSS), the World War II–era spy organization.

CIO—Congress of Industrial Organizations, umbrella organization of industrial unions, originated in the 1930s and merged with the AFL in 1955.

CORE—Congress of Racial Equality, founded in 1942 as an interracial organization to oppose segregation through nonviolent action. Successful in the early 1960s at using sit-ins and freedom rides to integrate restaurants, lunch counters, and buses in the South. Became increasingly black nationalist in the late 1960s, purged most whites from its membership, and lost most of its influence and importance.

CPI—Consumer Price Index, a measure of the cost of living, based on the cost of a "market basket" of goods and services, including food, rent, fuel, and clothing.

CPPA—Conference for Progressive Political Action, umbrella organization supporting the Progressive Party presidential candidacy of Robert M. La Follette Sr. in 1924.

CPUSA—Communist Party of the United States, established in 1919.

CNO—Chief of naval operations, position established by the U.S. Navy in 1915 to advise the secretary of the navy.

CQ—Congressional Quarterly, privately held publishing company that specializes in reference materials on government and publishes *CQ Weekly,* the leading "insider" magazine for Washington, D.C., political professionals.

CREEP—Committee to Re-elect the President, an organization formed to reelect President Richard M. Nixon in 1972 and implicated in efforts to bug Democratic campaign offices in the Watergate office complex and then cover up that criminal enterprise.

CRS—Congressional Research Service, an arm of the Library of Congress. Created by Congress as the Legislative Reference Service in 1914 to provide research to members of the House and Senate.

CSA—Confederate States of America, formed in 1861 by seven southern states seeking to leave the United States, later joined by four others. Ceased to exist after defeat of Confederate armies in 1865.

D

DAB—*Dictionary of American Biography,* first published between 1928 and 1936 and subsequently supplemented, long the most important source of biographical information for historical figures and still today a leading source.

DAR—Daughters of the American Revolution, organized in 1890 and closed to all but female descendants of men who fought for the patriot cause in the American Revolution.

DEA—Drug Enforcement Agency, executive branch agency formed to enforce antidrug laws nationwide, functions as a police force for drug crimes.

DJIA—Dow Jones Industrial Average, average value of thirty major stocks, often used as a proxy for the rise or fall of the stock market.

DOD—Department of Defense, created in 1949 to consolidate the authority of the secretary of defense over the secretaries of the individual military services.

DOJ—Department of Justice, cabinet-level agency created in 1870, headed by the attorney general, is the main law enforcement agency of the United States. The office of attorney general had been established by the First Congress in 1789.

DOT—Department of Transportation, cabinet-level agency established in 1966.

DSC—Distinguished Service Cross, the second-highest military honor that a member of the U.S. Army can win, after the Congressional Medal of Honor. Established in 1918 and followed by the Navy Cross in 1919 and the Air Force Cross in 1960.

E

ERA—Equal Rights Amendment, approved by Congress and sent to the states in 1972 for ratification, would have prohibited denial of equality based on sex. Amendment died in 1982 while still three states short of the three-quarters of the states needed for ratification.

F

FAA—Federal Aviation Agency, established in 1958 to regulate air traffic and commercial airlines and inspect airplanes in the United States. Renamed the Federal Aviation Administration in 1966.

FBI—Federal Bureau of Investigation, the investigative arm of the Department of Justice, established in 1935 but grew out of the Bureau of Investigation, created by the attorney general in 1908. J. Edgar Hoover became head of the Bureau of Investigation in 1924 and remained its dominant figure until his death in 1972.

FCC—Federal Communications Commission, independent commission in the executive branch established in 1934 to regulate radio, television, and telecommunication industries. Its predecessor was the Federal Radio Commission, established in 1927.

FDA—Food and Drug Administration, established in 1933 to regulate the quality of foods and drugs sold in the nation.

FDIC—Federal Deposit Insurance Corporation, established in 1933 by Congress to insure accounts in banks and to help regulate and examine banks for financial soundness. All banks affiliated with the Federal Reserve System must belong to the FDIC as well.

FDR—Franklin Delano Roosevelt, president of the United States from 1933 until his death in April 1945 and principal architect of the New Deal programs designed to lift the United States out of the Great Depression.

FECA—Federal Election Campaign Act, passed in 1972 and revised since, regulates spending, donations, and campaign financing in elections for federal office (president and Congress).

FEPC—Fair Employment Practices Commission, established by executive order in 1941 to monitor race discrimination in federal hiring, and after 1943 also oversaw nondiscrimination clauses in all federal military contracts. Disbanded after World War II when Congress refused to make the commission permanent.

FERA—Federal Emergency Relief Administration, founded in 1933 to provide emergency relief, with money from Congress being distributed through the states.

FERC—Federal Energy Regulatory Commission, established in 1977 to replace the Federal Power Commission. Oversees and regulates gas and electrical transmissions and has certain powers over rates, safety, and other matters involving these energy sources.

FFA—Future Farmers of America, national organization to promote farming among young people, founded in 1928.

FHA—Federal Housing Administration, created under the National Housing Act of 1934 to provide loans for homeowners.

Remains one of the longest lasting and most popular accomplishments of the New Deal, still in existence, administered by the Department of Housing and Urban Development.

FLP—Farmer-Labor Party, a third party in Minnesota that successfully ran candidates from 1918 until 1944, when it merged with the Democratic Party.

Four-H Clubs—Founded in 1902, a national organization of clubs for children that encourages interest in agriculture. "4-H" stands for "head, heart, hands, and health." Under the Smith-Lever Act of 1914 Congress provides federal support to 4-H clubs, through the Department of Agriculture.

FSLIC—Federal Savings and Loan Insurance Corporation, established in 1934 to protect deposits of individuals in federally insured savings and loan companies and to guarantee mortgages issued by these banks.

FTC—Federal Trade Commission, independent agency established by Congress in 1914 to investigate unfair trade practices and police fraudulent advertising, and later to regulate television and radio advertising.

G

GAO—General Accounting Office, established in 1921 as part of the Budget and Accounting Act of 1921, is the main accounting agency for the federal government.

GAR—Grand Army of the Republic, organized in 1866 by Civil War veterans of the U.S. Army. A powerful political organization through the end of the nineteenth century, as every elected president but one (Grover Cleveland) was a former U.S. Army Civil War officer. It had more than 400,000 members by 1890 but declined in importance after 1912, as veterans died. It continues to exist through membership of descendants of the original GAR members and other interested people.

GATT—General Agreement on Tariffs and Trade, signed in 1947 but grew out of the Trade Agreements Act of 1934; GATT sets the standards for reciprocal trade agreements between nations with the general goal of reducing tariffs and trade barriers.

GE—General Electric, major manufacturer of electric equipment, one of the oldest large companies in the United States.

G.I.—"Government Issue," term for clothing and other equipment issued to U.S. military personnel in World War II; became slang for any soldier.

G.I. Bill—Officially the Servicemen's Readjustment Act of 1944, passed by Congress to provide educational and other benefits for military veterans after World War II. One of the most important and far-reaching social welfare programs of the century; provided funds for millions of veterans to attend college.

GM—General Motors, largest manufacturer of automobiles in the United States and the world and one of the largest corporations in the United States.

GOP—Grand Old Party, nickname for the Republican Party.

GPO—Government Printing Office, established in 1860 as an agency of Congress, oversees all federal printing and prints most federal documents and other publications.

GSA—General Services Administration, executive branch agency, established in 1949, responsible for all federal property.

GSA—Girl Scouts of America, founded by Juliette Low in 1912 and chartered by Congress in 1950, an organization of clubs for girls and young women.

H

HEW—Health, Education and Welfare, a cabinet-level department established in 1953 under President Dwight D. Eisenhower's Reorganization Plan No. 1 to replace the Federal Security Agency. Reorganized in 1979 as HHS, with its education mission transferred to a new cabinet-level Department of Education.

HHS—Health and Human Services, a cabinet-level department created in 1979 from the Department of Health, Education, and Welfare.

HOLC—Home Owners Loan Corporation, founded by Congress in 1933 for a three-year period to lend money to homeowners during the Great Depression.

HUAC—House Un-American Activities Committee, a committee of the House of Representatives founded in 1938 to investigate alleged subversives, communists, radicals, and right- and left-wing extremists. Noted for its heavy-handed tactics and sometimes its character assassinations of social reformers not connected to any subversive organization. Renamed the Internal Security Committee in 1969 and abolished in 1975.

HUD—Housing and Urban Development, cabinet-level department established in 1965 to oversee urban and housing policy.

I

IBM—International Business Machines, one of the largest corporations in the United States and one of the first to exploit the emerging computer industry, creating the "standard" for personal computers (PCs) in the 1980s with the IBM-PC.

ICBM—Intercontinental ballistic missile, a long-range missile that leaves Earth's atmosphere and reenters thousands of miles away.

ICC—Interstate Commerce Commission, the nation's first independent regulatory commission, established in 1887 under the Interstate Commerce Act. Came to regulate railroads and road traffic, including freight charges by shipping companies and railroads, as well as highway safety standards for interstate truckers. Abolished by 1995 legislation and its responsibilities trans-

INDEX

elections of 1856, 33, 219, 291
presidency, 146, 389
slavery, 96, 356–357
as vice president, 146
Firearms Owners' Protection Act
(1986), 166
Fisher, Frederick G., Jr., 249
Fiske, Robert B., Jr., 83, 85
Fitzgerald, John F. "Honey Fitz," 216
Florida
homesteading, 149
Jackson, Andrew, and, 201
poll tax, 296
racial issues, 5, 321
Reconstruction, 321
Republican Party, 322
secession, 77
Seminole War, 346
Spain and, 397, 407
statehood and slavery, 368
War of 1812, 432
Florida A&M University, 255
Florida Treaty (1819), 398
Fonda, Jane, 238, 246
Food Administration, 444
Forbes, Steve, 44
Ford, Gerald R.
Bush, George, and, 35
cabinet, president's, 41
campaign finance, 46
Douglas, William O., and, 184–185
early political career, 146
elections of 1976, 51, 125
Nixon, Richard M., and, 51, 125,
274, 316
presidency, 146–147, 426
public opinion polls, 298
Reagan, Ronald W., 316
vetoes, 425
as vice president, 307
War Powers Resolution and,
433
World War II, 146
Ford (Gerald) administration, 147
Ford, Henry, 15
Ford Motor Company, 73
Force Acts (1870, 1871, 1890), 160,
321
Ford, Betty, 138
Forest Service, U.S., 334
Fortas, Abe, 379
Fort Atkinson, 189
Fort Finney, 188
Fort Laramie, 189
Fort McIntosh, 188
Fort Stanwix, 188
Fort Sumter (SC), 76, 77, 232, 340,
344, 357
Fortune magazine, 298
Fortune Survey, 298
Foster, Vincent, 85
Foster, Z. William, 95
Fourteen Points. *See* Wilson,
Woodrow

France. *See also* World War I; World
War II
American Revolution, 12–13, 20,
119
anticommunists, 87
Crimean War, 281
Embargo Act, 136
French Revolution, 206, 436
Indochina and, 89, 426, 427
Logan, George, and, 237
nuclear power, 90
Québec and, 9, 12
trade, 385, 397, 407
United Kingdom and, 241,
345
United States and, 1–2, 203
Franco-American Treaty of Alliance,
60
Franco, Francisco, 450, 454
Frank, Barney, 246
Frankfurter, Felix, 318, 379
Franklin, Benjamin, 13, 19, 119, 183,
355, 409
Frasier, Leroy Benjamin, 68
Freedmen's Bureau Acts (1865,
1866), 148–150, 209, 308,
319–320
Freedom Riders, 70, 73
Freemasons, 13
Free-soil movement, 275
Free Soil Party
elections of 1848, 291, 404,
424
Liberty Party and, 230, 356
overview, 147–148
Republican Party and, 76, 326,
357
Free speech movement, 74
Frelinghuysen, Frederick T., 62
Frémont, John C., 33, 135, 232, 291,
326
Freneau, Philip, 268
French and Indian War, 434
French Revolution (1789), 177, 206,
436
Frick, Henry Clay, 72–73
Friedan, Betty, 246, 350
Fuchs, Klaus, 248
Fugitive Slave Laws (1793, 1850)
1793, 142, 150, 439
1850, 33, 76, 96, 97, 150–151,
276, 287, 343, 356–357, 368,
406
elections of 1860, 30
Fillmore, Millard, and, 146
historical background, 341–342
repeal of, 341
Fulbright, J. William, 92, 428
Full Employment and Balanced
Growth Act (1978), 141
Fuller, Melville, 378
Fullilove v. Klutznick (1980), 5
Fundamentalist Christian movement,
316, 325, 329

G

Gadsden Purchase (1853), 398
Gage, Thomas, 11, 12
Gallagher, Cornelius, 219
Gallatin, Albert, 207, 409, 432
Gallup, George Horace, 298
Gardner, Henry J., 218
Garfield, James A., 19, 116, 153–154
Garner, John Nance, 210, 426
Garner, Margaret, 151
Garrison, William Lloyd, 269, 340,
356
Gary (IN), 73
Gates, Bill, 15
GATT. *See* General Agreement on
Tariffs and Trade
Gay and lesbian issues. *See*
Homosexual issues
Gazette of the United States, 268
General Agreement on Tariffs and
Trade, 130, 386, 408
General Federation of Women's
Clubs, 137
*General Theory of Employment, Interest,
and Money* (Keynes), 162
Genet, Edmond Charles, 436
Geneva Accords (1954), 427
George I, 9
George II, 9
George III, 9–10, 12, 13, 119, 120,
205, 434
George, David Lloyd, 410
George, Henry, 359
Georgia
American Revolution, 13
apportionment and districting,
17, 155, 156, 352, 364
Civil War, 159
Constitutional Convention, 105
election of officials, 318, 321
Native Americans, 189
secession, 77
Seminole War, 346
slavery, 342
states' rights and sovereignty, 371
Tennessee Valley Authority, 395
voting, 28, 165, 295, 296, 375
War of 1812, 432
Germain, George, 12
Germany. *See also* Berlin blockade;
Berlin Wall
division of, 412–413
emigrants from, 177–178, 179,
180
tariffs, 385
World War I, 444
World War II, 391, 411, 420
Germany, East, 87, 88, 90, 217, 317,
452, 455
Germany, West, 87, 90, 217, 414, 452,
455
Geronimo, 398
Gerry, Elbridge, 2, 24, 114, 154, 405

Gerrymandering, 154–156, 319,
351–352
Gibbons v. Ogden (1824), 142
G.I. Bill (1944), 156–157, 172, 453
G.I. Bill of Rights (1966), 140, 211
Gideon v. Wainwright (1963), 25
Gilded Age, 157–159, 366
Gilded Age, The: A Tale of Today (Twain
and Warner), 158
Giles, William Branch, 184, 370, 371
Gingrich, Newt, 82, 84, 176, 329,
383, 394
Glass-Steagall Act (1932), 309
Glass-Steagall Act (1933), 141, 261
Goldwater, Barry
Civil Rights Act of 1964, 125
conservatism, 211
elections of 1964, 29, 66, 104,
125, 164, 173, 211
Reagan, Ronald, and, 315
Republican Party and, 328
Social Security, 359
Taiwan treaty, 417
Gompers, Samuel, 225
GOP (Grand Old Party). *See*
Republican Party
Good Neighbor Policy (1933), 363
Goodrich, Carter, 365
Gorbachev, Mikhail, 36–37, 91, 92,
317, 415
Gore, Albert
campaign finance reform, 44
debates, 50
elections of 2000, 126, 227, 293,
426
National Partnership for
Reinventing Government,
83
as vice president, 81, 125
Goulburn, Henry, 409
Government, federal. *See also*
Federalism; Welfare
affirmative action, 3–4, 5
Constitution, 240
domestic affairs, 265, 267
downsizing, 367
education policy, 172
financial disclosure, 337
gun policy, 166
highways, 196
history of, 365
immigration, 182
independent counsel/special
prosecutor, 338, 339
interstate highway system, 197
iron triangles, 195
labor issues, 224, 225
loyalty program, 419
merit system, 19
money supply, 117
newspapers and, 268, 269
nullification, 275–276
Reconstruction, 322
regulation, 124, 261